HEATH Literature for Composition

Alice S. Landy

Robert F. Sommer
University of Missouri — Kansas City

D. C. Heath and Company
Lexington, Massachusetts · *Toronto*

Acquisitions Editor: Paul A. Smith
Developmental Editor: H. Holton Johnson
Production Editor: Anne Rebecca Starr
Production Coordinator: Lisa Arcese
Text Permissions Editor: Margaret Roll
Cover: *July Hay* by Thomas Hart Benton, the Metropolitan Museum of Art.
George A. Hearn Fund, 1943. (43.159.1)

Published simultaneously in Canada.

Printed in the United States of America.

International Standard Book Number: 0-669-20884-1

Library of Congress Catalog Card Number: 89-84719

10 9 8 7 6 5 4 3 2 1

Credits

PREFACE

The *Heath Literature for Composition* is intended to fulfill a specific need in second-semester freshman composition or introductory literature courses. Recent trends in the teaching of writing have led to an emphasis on the writing process—a laudable effort, for students are writing more and better papers in introductory courses. Teaching writing as a process has enabled students to approach writing tasks with less anxiety and to view writing as a form of problem-solving. These introductory college courses now include in-class writing, peer group discussion, and a variety of other methods that transform a writing class into a place for doing rather than simply listening.

Traditionally, freshman and sophomore English courses have provided an introduction to various techniques for reading and understanding literature. The *Heath Literature for Composition,* adapted from *The Heath Introduction to Literature,* brings together new methods in teaching writing and traditional approaches to literature. This new text includes a strong literary component with an emphasis upon developing student writing skills.

One important section, Reading and Writing About Literature, takes students through the stages of the writing process from prewriting to proofreading within a literary context. This section demonstrates how to use writing as a way of learning about literature; it emphasizes connections between writing and the discovery of ideas; it provides guidance on how to use writing to solve literary problems, how to keep a journal, how to write for a particular audience, and how to develop a paper through successive drafts.

The *Heath Literature for Composition* is a four-genre textbook encompassing essays, short stories, poetry, and drama. The section on nonfiction includes a variety of classic essays set within a discussion that is aimed at both generating writing about them as literature and at demonstrating how closely allied these essays are to the kind of writing students do in academic settings. This section covers the history and idea of the essay as a genre, featuring essays by Montaigne and Bacon, and offering selections by some of the great nonfiction stylists, including Virginia Woolf, Ralph Waldo Emerson, Mark Twain, and T. S. Eliot. A student essay about AIDS, a current topic of concern, appears as a model for students who are challenged by the nature of writing essays.

Throughout the text, I have emphasized broad representation in literary selections. Thus the fiction section includes a story by Ursula K. Le Guin, and the story selected for the introductory chapters on the writing process is by Mary Wilkins Freeman. The text also includes numerous works by minority authors, including pieces by Alice Walker and Gwendolyn Brooks, as well as a broad offering from the traditional literary canon. In fact, while my primary effort has been to guide students as they write about literature, teachers who wish to move about the text and focus only on selected works can do so easily. The text has the flexibility to provide as much or as little support as a teacher may wish to suit his or her classroom style.

I have prepared the *Heath Literature for Composition* with sensitivity to the divergent nature of teaching writing and literature, a vocation that has undergone considerable change during the past decade. New methods in writing instruction have greatly enhanced freshman composition courses throughout the country, and new ideas about the literary canon have influenced the syllabi in many courses. I have developed this textbook to respond to the needs created by recent trends, yet with care to avoid trendiness for its own sake. As Thoreau declared in *Walden*, "A written word is the choicest of relics." And I have tried to respect the life of those relics and the efforts of those who study them.

Acknowledgments

I once thought—perhaps as a victim of romantic myth—that writing was a solitary activity. While few would argue that solitude is at once a necessary, a welcome, and a despised element of writing, little is written that reaches a larger audience without the efforts of many. Several instructors in the composition program at the University of Missouri, Kansas City, aided me by providing samples of student work and insights into their methods for teaching writing. These include Mickey Dyer, Joan Gilson, Judy Kelly, and Terri McFerrin-Smith. I also received generous help in developing the new literary selections for this textbook from Professor David Weinglass, University of Missouri, Kansas City, and Professor George J. Sommer, Marist College. I would also like to thank my colleagues who reviewed the manuscript in this and earlier versions: Ethel Bonds, Virginia Western Community College; Robert Burke, Joliet Junior College; Kitti Carriker, Notre Dame College; Brian Cleary, Henry Ford Community College; John Driscoll, Phoenix College; Allan Duane, Ulster County Community College; Ruben Friedman, Hofstra University; James F. Gordon, Jr., Mississippi Delta Community College; Maria Hamann, Louisiana Technical University; Jeff Jeske, University of California, Los Angeles; Vernon Miles, University of Arkansas; Margaret Shepherd, Surry Community College; Rebecca Shuttleworth, Mississippi Delta Community College; Margaret Sullivan, University of California, Los Angeles; Jean Williams, Southwest Mississippi Community College. At D. C. Heath, I would like to thank Karen M. Wise for her lively copyediting, Anne Starr, who oversaw the production of this text, and Paul A. Smith, whose many gifts as an editor include a rare combination of practicality and sensitivity. Finally, the support and enthusiasm of my wife Heather, who must endure the solitary part of the writing enterprise and reinforce my own sense of the vitality of this kind of work. To her I owe more thanks than these lines can carry.

Robert F. Sommer

CONTENTS

AN ANTHOLOGY OF POEMS   575

READING AND WRITING ABOUT DRAMA

READING AND WRITING
ABOUT LITERATURE

1 Reading and Writing for Ideas

Reading and writing are closely related activities. Writing will help you to learn more about what you have read, and wide reading will increase your ability to write well. We have therefore chosen to treat these activities in relation to one another, rather than as separate skills or disciplines. In order to get started right away, we'd like you to read the following story by Mary E. Wilkins Freeman, "A Far-Away Melody." But you don't have to wait to start writing. Take up a pen or pencil and jot some notes in the margins of the text or in a notebook. Look for elements of the story that are striking to you. One way to be an active reader is to have a pen in your hand.

MARY E. WILKINS FREEMAN (1852–1930)

A Far-Away Melody

The clothes-line was wound securely around the trunks of four gnarled, crooked old apple-trees, which stood promiscuously about the yard back of the cottage. It was tree-blossoming time, but these were too aged and sapless to blossom freely, and there was only a white bough here and there shaking itself triumphantly from among the rest, which had only their new green leaves. There was a branch occasionally which had not even these, but pierced the tender green and the flossy white in hard, gray nakedness. All over the yard, the grass was young and green and short, and had not yet gotten any feathery heads. Once in a while there was a dandelion set closely down among it.

The cottage was low, of a dark-red color, with white facings around the windows, which had no blinds, only green paper curtains.

The back door was in the centre of the house, and opened directly into the green yard, with hardly a pretence of a step, only a flat, oval stone before it.

Through this door, stepping cautiously on the stone, came presently two tall, lank women in chocolate-colored calico gowns, with a basket of clothes between them. They set the basket underneath the line on the grass, with a little clothes-pin bag beside it, and then proceeded methodically to hang out the clothes. Everything of a kind went together, and the best things on the outside line, which could be seen from the street in front of the cottage.

The two women were curiously alike. They were about the same height, and moved in the same way. Even their faces were so similar in feature and expression that it might have been a difficult matter to distinguish between them. All the difference, and that would have been scarcely apparent to an ordinary observer, was a difference of degree, if it might be so expressed. In one face the features were both bolder and sharper in outline, the eyes were a trifle larger and brighter, and the whole expression more animated and decided than in the other.

One woman's scanty drab hair was a shade darker than the other's, and the negative fairness of complexion, which generally accompanies drab hair, was in one relieved by a slight tinge of warm red on the cheeks.

This slightly intensified woman had been commonly considered the more attractive of the two, although in reality there was very little to choose between the personal appearance of these twin sisters, Priscilla and Mary Brown. They moved about the clothes-line, pinning the sweet white linen on securely, their thick, white-stockinged ankles showing beneath their limp calicoes as they stepped, and their large feet in cloth slippers flattening down the short, green grass. Their sleeves were rolled up, displaying their long, thin, muscular arms, which were sharply pointed at the elbows.

They were homely women; they were fifty and over now, but they never could have been pretty in their teens, their features were too irredeemably irregular for that. No youthful freshness of complexion or expression could have possibly done away with the impression that they gave. Their plainness had probably only been enhanced by the contrast, and these women, to people generally, seemed better-looking than when they were young. There was an honesty and patience in both faces that showed all the plainer for their homeliness.

One, the sister with the darker hair, moved a little quicker than the other, and lifted the wet clothes from the basket to the line more frequently. She was the first to speak, too, after they had been hanging out the clothes for some little time in silence. She stopped as she did so, with a wet pillow-case in her hand, and looked up reflectively at the flowering apple-boughs overhead, and the blue sky showing between, while the sweet spring wind ruffled her scanty hair a little.

"I wonder, Mary," said she, "if it would seem so very queer to die a mornin' like this, say. Don't you believe there's apple branches a-hangin' over them walls made out of precious stones, like these, only there ain't any dead limbs among 'em, an' they're all covered thick with flowers? An' I wonder if it would seem such an awful change to go from this air into the air of the New Jerusalem." Just then a robin hidden somewhere in the trees began to sing. "I s'pose," she went on, "that there's angels instead of robins, though, and they don't roost up in trees to sing, but stand on the ground, with lilies growin' round their feet, maybe, up to their knees, or on the gold stones in the street, an' play on their harps to go with the singin'."

The other sister gave a scared, awed look at her. "Lor, don't talk that way, sister," said she. "What has got into you lately? You make me crawl all over, talkin' so much about dyin'. You feel well, don't you?"

"Lor, yes," replied the other, laughing, and picking up a clothes-pin for her pillow-case; "I feel well enough, an' I don't know what has got me to talkin' so much about dyin' lately, or thinkin' about it. I guess it's the spring weather. P'r'aps flowers growin' make anybody think of wings sproutin' kinder naterally. I won't talk so much about it if it bothers you, an' I don't know but it's sorter nateral it should. Did you get the potatoes before we came out, sister?"—with an awkward and kindly effort to change the subject.

"No," replied the other, stooping over the clothes-basket. There was such a film of tears in her dull blue eyes that she could not distinguish one article from another.

"Well, I guess you had better go in an' get 'em, then; they ain't worth anything, this time of year, unless they soak a while, an' I'll finish hangin' out the clothes while you do it."

"Well, p'r'aps I'd better," the other woman replied, straightening herself up from the clothes-basket. Then she went into the house without another word; but down in the damp cellar, a minute later, she sobbed over the potato barrel as if her heart would break. Her sister's remarks had filled her with a vague apprehension and grief which she could not throw off. And there was something a little singular about it. Both these women had always been of a deeply religious cast of mind. They had studied the Bible faithfully, if not understandingly, and their religion had strongly tinctured their daily life. They knew almost as much about the Old Testament prophets as they did about their neighbors; and that was saying a good deal of two single women in a New England country town. Still this religious element in their natures could hardly have been termed spirituality. It deviated from that as much as anything of religion—which is in one way spirituality itself—could.

Both sisters were eminently practical in all affairs of life, down to their very dreams, and Priscilla especially so. She had dealt in religion with the bare facts of sin and repentance, future punishment and reward. She had dwelt very little, probably, upon the poetic splendors of the Eternal City, and talked about them still less. Indeed, she had always been reticent about her religious convictions, and had said very little about them even to her sister.

The two women, with God in their thoughts every moment, seldom had spoken his name to each other. For Priscilla to talk in the strain that she had to-day, and for a week or two previous, off and on, was, from its extreme deviation from her usual custom, certainly startling.

Poor Mary, sobbing over the potato barrel, thought it was a sign of approaching death. She had a few superstitious-like grafts upon her practical, commonplace character.

She wiped her eyes finally, and went up-stairs with her tin basin of potatoes, which were carefully washed and put to soak by the time her sister came in with the empty basket.

At twelve exactly the two sat down to dinner in the clean kitchen, which was one of the two rooms the cottage boasted. The narrow entry ran from the front door to the back. On one side was the kitchen and living-room; on the other, the room where the sisters slept. There were two small unfinished lofts overhead, reached by a step-ladder through a little scuttle in the entry ceiling: and that was all. The sisters had earned the cottage and paid for it years before, by working as tailoresses. They had, besides, quite a snug little sum in the bank, which they had saved out of their hard earnings. There was no need for Priscilla and Mary to work so hard, people said; but work hard they did, and work hard they would as long as they lived. The mere habit of work had become as necessary to them as breathing.

Just as soon as they had finished their meal and cleared away the dishes, they put on some clean starched purple prints, which were their afternoon dresses, and seated themselves with their work at the two front windows; the house faced southwest, so the sunlight streamed through both. It was a very warm day for the season, and the windows were open. Close to them in the yard outside stood great clumps of lilac bushes. They grew on the other side of the front door too; a little later the low cottage would look half-buried in them. The shadows of their leaves made a dancing net-work over the freshly washed yellow floor.

The two sisters sat there and sewed on some coarse vests all the afternoon. Neither made a remark often. The room, with its glossy little cooking-stove, its eight-day clock on the mantel, its chintz-cushioned rocking-chairs, and the dancing shadows of the lilac leaves on its yellow floor, looked pleasant and peaceful.

Just before six o'clock a neighbor dropped in with her cream pitcher to borrow some milk for tea, and she sat down for a minute's chat after she had got it filled. They had been talking a few moments on neighborhood topics, when all of a sudden Priscilla let her work fall and raised her hand. "Hush!" whispered she.

The other two stopped talking, and listened, staring at her wonderingly, but they could hear nothing.

"What is it, Miss Priscilla?" asked the neighbor, with round blue eyes. She was a pretty young thing, who had not been married long.

"Hush! Don't speak. Don't you hear that beautiful music?" Her ear was inclined towards the open window, her hand still raised warningly, and her eyes fixed on the opposite wall beyond them.

Mary turned visibly paler than her usual dull paleness, and shuddered. "I don't hear any music," she said. "Do you, Miss Moore?"

"No-o," replied the caller, her simple little face beginning to put on a scared look, from a vague sense of a mystery she could not fathom.

Mary Brown rose and went to the door, and looked eagerly up and down the street. "There ain't no organ-man in sight anywhere," said she, returning, "an' I can't hear any music, an' Miss Moore can't, an' we're both sharp enough o' hearin'. You're jest imaginin' it, sister."

"I never imagined anything in my life," returned the other, "an' it ain't likely I'm goin' to begin now. It's the beautifulest music. It comes from over the orchard there. Can't you hear it? But it seems to me it's growin' a little fainter like now. I guess it's movin' off, perhaps."

Mary Brown set her lips hard. The grief and anxiety she had felt lately turned suddenly to unreasoning anger against the cause of it; through her very love she fired with quick wrath at the beloved object. Still she did not say much, only, "I guess it must be movin' off," with a laugh, which had an unpleasant ring in it.

After the neighbor had gone, however, she said more, standing before her sister with her arms folded squarely across her bosom. "Now, Priscilla Brown," she exclaimed, "I think it's about time to put a stop to this. I've heard about enough of it. What do you s'pose Miss Moore thought of you? Next thing it'll be all over town that you're gettin' spiritual notions. To-day it's music that nobody else can hear, an' yesterday you smelled roses, and there ain't one in blossom this time o' year, and all the time you're talkin' about dyin'. For my part, I don't see why you ain't as likely to live as I am. You're uncommon hearty on vittles. You ate a pretty good dinner to-day for a dyin' person."

"I didn't say I was goin' to die," replied Priscilla, meekly: the two sisters seemed suddenly to have changed natures. "An' I'll try not to talk so, if it plagues you. I told you I wouldn't this mornin', but the music kinder took me by surprise like, an' I thought maybe you an' Miss Moore could hear it. I can jest hear it a little bit now, like the dyin' away of a bell."

"There you go agin!" cried the other, sharply. "Do, for mercy's sake, stop, Priscilla. There ain't no music."

"Well, I won't talk any more about it," she answered, patiently; and she rose and began setting the table for tea, while Mary sat down and resumed her sewing, drawing the thread through the cloth with quick, uneven jerks.

That night the pretty girl neighbor was aroused from her first sleep by a distressed voice at her bedroom window, crying, "Miss Moore! Miss Moore!"

She spoke to her husband, who opened the window. "What's wanted?" he asked, peering out into the darkness.

"Priscilla's sick," moaned the distressed voice; "awful sick. She's fainted, an' I can't bring her to. Go for the doctor—quick! quick! *quick!*" The voice ended in a shriek on the last word, and the speaker turned and ran back to the cottage, where, on the bed, lay a pale, gaunt woman, who had not stirred since she left it. Immovable through all her sister's agony, she lay there, her features shaping themselves out more and more from the shadows, the bedclothes that covered her limbs taking on an awful rigidity.

"She must have died in her sleep," the doctor said, when he came, "without a struggle."

When Mary Brown really understood that her sister was dead, she left her to the kindly ministrations of the good women who are always ready at such times in a country place, and went and sat by the kitchen window in the chair which her sister had occupied that afternoon.

There the women found her when the last offices had been done for the dead.

"Come home with me to-night," one said; "Miss Green will stay with *her*," with a turn of her head towards the opposite room, and an emphasis on the pronoun which distinguished it at once from one applied to a living person.

"No," said Mary Brown; "I'm a-goin' to set here an' listen." She had the window wide open, leaning her head out into the chilly night air.

The women looked at each other; one tapped her head, another nodded hers. "Poor thing!" said a third.

"You see," went on Mary Brown, still speaking with her head leaned out of the window, "I was cross with her this afternoon because she talked about hearin' music. I was cross, an' spoke up sharp to her, because I loved her, but I don't think she knew. I didn't want to think she was goin' to die, but she was. An' she heard the music. It was true. An' now I'm a-goin' to set here an' listen till I hear it too, an' then I'll know she 'ain't laid up what I said agin me, an' that I'm a-goin' to die too."

They found it impossible to reason with her; there she sat till morning, with a pitying woman beside her, listening all in vain for unearthly melody.

Next day they sent for a widowed niece of the sisters, who came at once, bringing her little boy with her. She was a kindly young woman, and took up her abode in the little cottage, and did the best she could for her poor aunt, who, it soon became evident, would never be quite herself again. There she would sit at the kitchen window and listen day after day. She took a great fancy to her niece's little boy, and used often to hold him in her lap as she sat there. Once in a while she would ask him if he heard any music. "An innocent little thing like him might hear quicker than a hard, unbelievin' old woman like me," she told his mother once.

She lived so for nearly a year after her sister died. It was evident that she failed gradually and surely, though there was no apparent disease. It seemed to trouble her exceedingly that she never heard the music she listened for. She had an idea that she could not die unless she did, and her whole soul seemed filled with longing to join her beloved twin sister, and be assured of her forgiveness. This sister-love was all she had ever felt, besides her love of God, in any strong degree; all the passion of devotion of which this homely, commonplace woman was capable was centered in that, and the unsatisfied strength of it was killing her. The weaker she grew, the more earnestly she listened. She was too feeble to sit up, but she would not consent to lie in bed, and made them bolster her up with pillows in a rocking-chair by the window. At last she died, in the spring, a week or two before her sister had the preceding year. The season was a little more advanced this year, and the apple-trees were blossomed out further than they were then. She died about ten o'clock in the morning. The day before, her niece had been called into the room by a shrill cry of rapture from her: "I've heard it! I've heard it!" she cried. "A faint sound o' music, like the dyin' away of a bell."

Now that you've read the story we can discuss some strategies for learning more about it through writing. Our primary method for writing about literature will be through what has become known as the *writing process*. This phrase has been used in many ways, but it essentially means that we will place emphasis not only on the finished product—for example, an essay or research paper that you may write for this course—but also on the various techniques that writers use to get ideas and develop them. Usually the writing process includes these five activities: **prewriting, drafting, revising, editing,** and **publishing.** However, the writing process as a whole does not mean that these activities necessarily proceed in a straight line; in fact, there's much overlap. For example, even as you're editing a final draft, you may get an idea for a new paragraph or section and decide to draft it on the spot.

The word **publishing** may also surprise you. We think of **publishing** as any sort of writing that is in its final state, ready for a reader. Thus the essay you finally submit to your instructor or student group (if your class works in groups) is a form of publication. On pages 98–101, we've included a student paper that actually *was* published in a collection of student essays from a writing course like yours to show you that aiming high for your writing may lead to publication in printed form. (We also think it's a first-rate essay.)

Writing about literature is different from many other types of writing because the focus of your writing and thinking is a written text. This means, for one thing, that you are using language while you write about an object that exists only through language. Sometimes this problem confuses and inhibits beginning writers. You may wonder how anything you have to say can do justice to a poem by Wordsworth or a story by Hawthorne. Or perhaps the language of the poetry and prose you read is so removed from your own language that you feel that writing like that is unnatural to you. There may seem to be little common ground between the authors you read and what you may want to say about their work. Writing process methods are largely intended to help break down those inhibitions.

Writing about literature enables you to become part of the larger community in which that literature exists. Even within your classroom, the things that are said and written about the literature you read and discuss will make the entire class what one literary critic calls an "interpretive community." Much of what we have to say is intended to help you increase the quality of your participation in that community.

Invention and Prewriting

You have read a story and now may be faced with questions like these: "What do I write about it?" "What do I have to say?" "The story seems complete as it is, so what more is needed?" Although there's nothing wrong with reading a story simply for pleasure and then going on to something else without looking back, there is a larger world of enjoyment and understanding that you'll miss if you do that. It is there that learning takes place and a whole variety of language and thinking skills can be developed. For the moment we are concerned with how you can use writing to answer the three questions at the beginning of this paragraph. Put aside any idea of writing to be graded, as you might for an essay exam or a paper. Just write to get ideas. Think of writing as a tool for understanding and exploration, a sort of technology of the mind. Writing is not just a way of saying something but a way of finding out what you may want to say, a method for allowing thoughts, ideas, responses, and reactions to emerge. Many of these don't even exist until you write, and this means that writing is a kind of exploration.

Writing that you do to get ideas and develop them is called *prewriting.* Prewriting is a way of thinking with a pen, of finding out what ideas you may have, what evidence you may need, and what sort of organization and tone and style may be most appropriate to your writing task. Classical authors placed much emphasis on the process of developing ideas for speeches or written tracts, an activity they referred to as *inventio,* or invention. The quality of your finished essay will depend heavily on the effort put into prewriting and invention.

Freewriting

One writer calls freewriting "the easiest way to get words on paper." Here's how freewriting works. Take an empty page and begin writing without stopping for ten or fifteen minutes. You must use a set amount of time (it may lengthen as you get used to writing more) and you must not stop writing for any reason until the time is up. Don't stop to think, don't stop to check the spelling of any word, and don't stop to rewrite any sentence. Just keep on going.

Before you look at the sample in Figure 1, do a freewriting about this question: Are Mary and Priscilla superstitious, religious, or deluded?

Reading Journals

A reading journal allows you to combine a variety of written responses to literature, from simply copying out authors' names, titles of works, and characters' names to giving you a place to do freewriting about literature. Keep your reading journal separate from your class notes and plan to make an entry whenever you read. After a reading assignment commit yourself to ten minutes of writing in your journal. If you do that much regularly, the odds are very good that you'll soon be writing for fifteen or even twenty minutes.

How do you use such a journal? What goes in it? There really are no limits, and the journal will offer you the most flexibility if you don't concern yourself with correctness and neatness as much as honesty and thoroughness. Unlike notebooks for your class notes in economics, psychology, or even literature, the reading journal combines personal responses, exploratory writings (such as freewriting), and some factual information, copied out to help in retention. Here are some suggestions.

1. *Enter all of your freewritings into a reading journal.*
2. *In your own words, write descriptions of the major characters in a story or play.*
3. *Write a plot summary.*

Mary and Priscilla – deluded, super-stitious, or religious?! I don't know! I guess religious. They were very religious in the story. They both knew about the Bible. But maybe Mary took it as superstitious when Priscilla said she heard the music. That's true! Mary Freeman even said that Mary was somewhat superstitious. Of course, to me they both seemed a little crazy, maybe from living to-gether for so long and probably never going anywhere but that little town they live in. I can't imagine what it would be like to live in such a place. You'd hear music in your mind because that's the only music you'd ever hear. Imagine if you never heard Bruce Springsteen or any music but the church organ!!

Figure 1   Sample Freewriting

4. *Write a fictional dialogue between characters from two separate works.*

5. *Write a fictional dialogue between two authors.*

6. *Narrate a personal experience you have had that compares to a situation described in the work you have just read.* Describe how your experience helps you to understand the poem, story, play, or essay.

7. *Copy out some key lines, images, sections.* This may seem like a "rote" activity, but for several centuries students, writers, and even general readers kept "commonplace books." These were similar to reading journals but consisted almost entirely of passages copied by readers in order to learn

better, and even to memorize, what an author had to say. The selection of items to include in a commonplace book, sometimes thematically arranged and sometimes arbitrary, was entirely unique to every writer of a commonplace book. Thus commonplace books often assume a very individual quality. In addition, copying helps the writer to memorize passages and provides much easier and better organized access to key sections of literary works than flipping the pages of a textbook like this one in search of highlighted passages or cursory marginal comments.

8. *Keep "hard" information in your reading journal.* Record information that may be helpful for exams; for example, authors' names (spelled correctly!) and titles of works (quotation marks for stories, poems, and essays; underlining for novels, plays, and books), characters (also spelled correctly), key images and scenes, any references or allusions that may help you to recall a particular poem or story. (Note: Although we have deemphasized spelling and other mechanical matters in the section on prewriting, we mention them here because one of the purposes of writing out "hard" information is to learn it. Writing out names and titles now will help you to recall them correctly when you later have to use them on a quiz or exam.)

Suggestions for a Reading Journal Entry on "A Far-Away Melody"

Write out the title and the characters' names at the top of a blank page in your journal. Now write brief descriptions of Mary and Priscilla, their physical characteristics, personal traits, clothing, and so forth. Write objectively, as though they were missing persons you had to describe to the police, and write in your own words. On the next page of your journal do one of these: write a dialogue you have made up between the two sisters during a typical dinner; from the actual text, copy out examples of their dialogue that show their regional accents; or describe someone you know (a relative, acquaintance, neighbor) who is similar in some way to these sisters.

Writing to Solve Literary Problems

Whether you keep a journal or just use some scratch paper that may or may not be saved, do your thinking about literary problems with a pen or pencil in hand. Below are some questions to ask yourself that may help distinguish one problem from another. That is always the first task you face. If you're confused about a literary work, you need to decide on what confuses you. Try to look at separate elements of the work. Don't worry about the "whole" work; it's still intact. You haven't ripped it apart or dissected it, as is sometimes thought. You are simply locating yourself on a very intricate map that many travelers follow in different directions.

1. *What does the title of the work mean?* Are there references to the title within the text? Are there images used that are related to it? Do a ten-minute freewriting about the title.

2. *Are there words or phrases in the text that you don't understand?* If so, copy them into your reading journal, leaving lots of space between each. Now circle them, draw some lines outward, and jot in some possible meanings. (See the section on "clusters" on pages 16–19 in the next chapter.) The dictionary may seem an obvious place to turn, and for words you don't recognize, it should be the first place. But what if the word isn't there, or the definition doesn't help you to understand the sentence? Perhaps you need to know more about the history of a word, in which case the place to turn is the *Oxford English Dictionary.* You'll probably need to make a trip to the library to consult the *OED,* as it is known, so prepare a list of words you'd like to investigate. You'll find examples of how a word was used by many authors, sometimes across the centuries. Don't underestimate your author; he or she may have been fully aware of how a word was used two centuries ago when deciding to include it in a poem or story.

3. *What about the overall language of the text?* Language, of course, is at the heart of what literature is, so in a sense you are looking past the obvious if you look for "meanings" and "ideas" that are separate from the language in which they appear. How would you describe the tone or atmosphere set by an author's style? Take a sentence or phrase or set of lines and look closely at them. Describe how their arrangement, word choice, or any other notable characteristics set a tone or style that in some way contributes to the total effect of the literary work.

4. *In one or two sentences write out what you believe to be the central problem faced by a character, even a minor one.* Now do a freewriting about the ways in which that problem or dilemma might have been resolved differently from the resolution in the text.

Using Personal Observations and Experiences to Respond to Literature

You may think of your personal experiences and ideas—the ones you have and live with, the ones that make you the unique person you are—as entirely distinct from the reading you do for this course and the discussions you have in the classroom about your reading. Nothing could be further from the truth. In fact, one of the reasons that literature remains such an important part of our shared cultural experience is for the very reason that it addresses the identities we have in our nonacademic worlds. Some literature may seem remote because of unfamiliar ideas or language usage to which you are not accustomed, but that's just a matter of acquaintance, like entering a room full of people you don't know. The ice needs to be broken and common interests established, then a wholesome and enriching conversation may follow. Your experiences and observations are not only the best place to start as you read and look for topics to write about, but they're the *only* place to start, for what else have you but what you think and what you've done?

Suggestions for Reading Journal Entries That Include Personal Experience

1. Through sibling relationships, marriage, or sometimes just friendship, two people sometimes find their lives so interwoven that they nearly think alike, as Mary and Priscilla did. Describe your personal experience of such a relationship. Perhaps you have been able to observe two people very closely, or perhaps you have had such a relationship with a sibling or a friend. As you write look for the ways in which your knowledge of that relationship helps you to understand the story and the ways in which the story has helped you to better understand the relationship.

2. Mary and Priscilla seem very much to be products of the small town in which they live. Describe a community you know well, whether it is a small town you have lived in (or still live in) or a neighborhood within a larger city. Describe some of the ways in which living in that community has affected how people think and live. Look for ways in which this description helps you to understand the kind of characters Mary E. Wilkins Freeman created.

3. Freeman describes her characters as "homely," and the story seems to center around very routine activities like hanging out the laundry and soaking the potatoes. Pick a person (or group of people) you know whose life would seemingly have little interest for a story and write a description of the person and some activities he or she pursues during an average day. Follow this writing with a few paragraphs on why Freeman may have decided to focus on seemingly unimportant people doing apparently uninteresting things.

2 Developing and Organizing Ideas for Writing

In the previous chapter we explored some ways to use writing as part of the thinking process—in a sense to write without thinking about it and even to think without thinking about it. This is not literally true, of course. What you have actually found are some ways to generate ideas in writing without as much anxiety and intimidation as we often associate with the act of writing. In the process, too, you are probably seeing how writing enhances thinking and the discovery of ideas. No doubt many of the things you have written have led to thoughts you never would have had without writing.

In this chapter we will consider some ways to develop and organize your thinking and writing to lead you toward writing for a reader, or published writing. Don't forget that there's no quick path or surefire formula that will always work for every situation. Our goal here is simply to expand the repertoire of strategies you have available to you.

More Prewriting for Ideas: Using Clusters and Lists

Sometimes an idea appears in very rough form, useless in its present state, perhaps not even recognizable as an idea. Such is the case, for example, for much of the freewriting that you may do. Here are two ways to chip at a rock and see if anything worth mining is underneath. If not, don't be disappointed. Like the goldminers of the early west, you have to be determined. Pick up another rock and try again. Some of those miners struck it rich, but many others found that gold came in different forms than they expected, as they discovered many other opportunities in the new land to which the promise of gold had brought them.

1. *Use a cluster to explore an idea.* Here's a way to be sloppy and graphic, to give your thoughts a tangible and visual form on paper. Turn your notebook sideways, just to get away from the rigid lines, or better yet, use a large unlined sheet from an artist's notebook. Put your topic at the center of the page in a circle or box and let some related thoughts spiral outward. Notice in the example in Figure 2 how one thought or detail generates others. Clusters are a form of verbal and visual free association. They are very helpful both for discovering how ideas are related and for generating the details and the appropriate questions to help you develop further ideas.

2. *Create a series of lists to develop your ideas.* Writing lists is something we do a lot in American society—grocery lists, laundry lists, things-to-do lists—so you probably have some practice at writing lists. When you write a things-to-do list, you are not merely trying to remember all that you have to do. You are doing something creative by deciding, choosing, and even thinking up tasks. That same energy can help you in writing about literature.

Let's say you are getting ready to write a description that compares Mary and Priscilla in " A Far-Away Melody." Instead of just plunging in, use a list to decide what you'd like to say. Figure 3 shows an example.

A list such as this one does more than simply catalogue the features of the women; it organizes those features. First it finds the common ground between them, and then it establishes the differences. Such a list may be a helpful study reference or a way to prepare for a writing task. Just writing a list helps you to refine details you probably recognized while you were reading.

What can you do with these writings? Their main function is to generate ideas, which may come in several shapes.

1. *Use a cluster or list to help refine a topic.* At the very edge of a cluster may be a topic or idea that has the potential to generate an interesting paper. To pursue that idea, start another cluster, now using the idea you've discovered as the starting point. You are creating a second-generation cluster, now working outward again to see how your idea develops.

2. *Take one of your ideas and put it into one or two clear sentences.* Using complete sentences helps you to find out whether the thought is complete, whether it holds up when it is expressed in clear language, or whether its logic may be faulty. Don't give up after one try. Fill up a couple of pages with such sentences.

3. *Use your cluster or list to determine where you may need more information.* For example, the queries on the sample cluster show places where the writer knew information could be found but wasn't completely certain of that

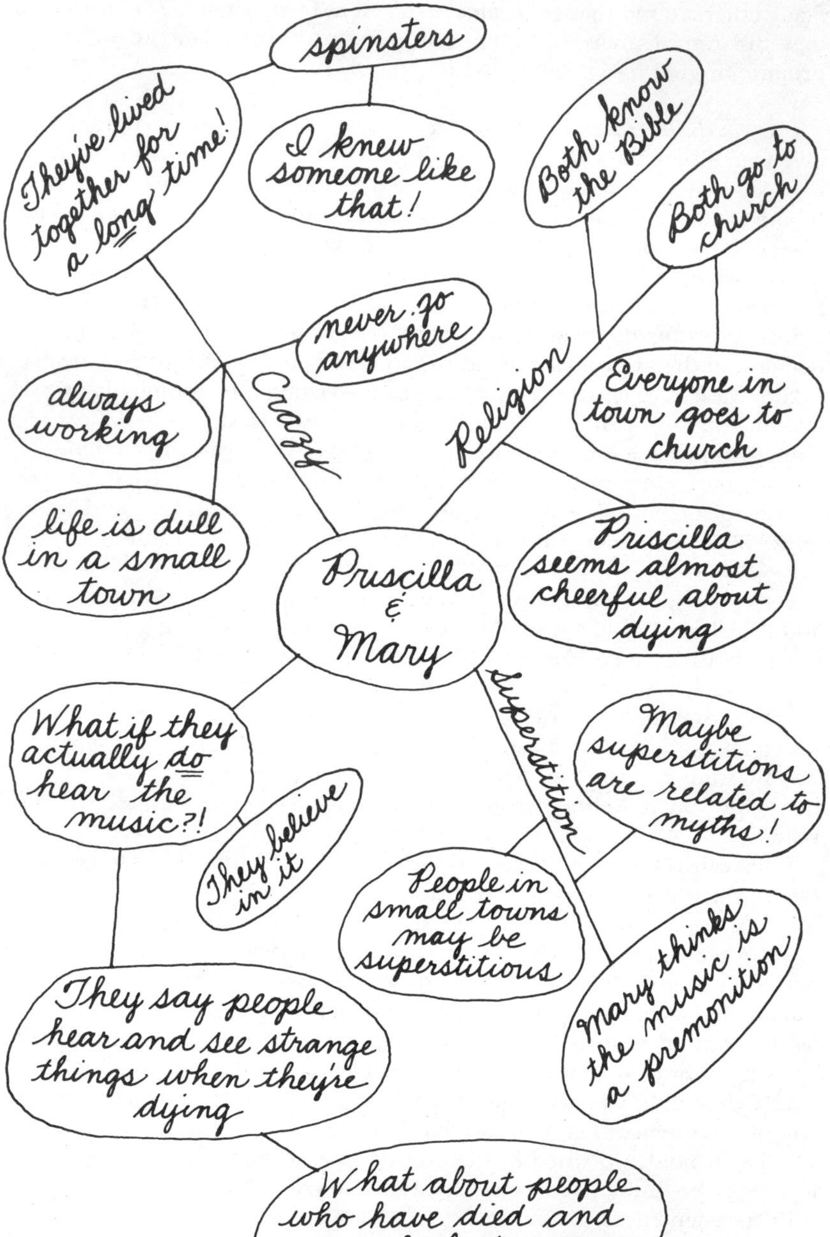

Figure 2 A Cluster Based on "A Far-Away Melody"

Mary   Priscilla

"curiously alike"
tall
lanky
calico gowns
homely
over 50 years old
"honesty and patience"

                              darker hair
                              warm red cheeks
                              quicker movements
frightened   slightly more attractive
superstitious   reflective
doesn't hear music   talks of dying
hears music later   hears music first

**Figure 3   A List of Ideas for Writing About
"A Far-Away Melody"**

information. Perhaps a quotation or incident in the story or historical fact needs to be verified in order to support an argument the writer may want to make.

4. *Transfer the ideas you may have onto another sheet of paper, now cataloguing or listing them in order to clarify the logical relationships.* Your first cluster or list may be quite random; it may also circle back over information and ideas. The initial attempt may be something like hacking at thick foliage with a machete. Now you'll want to organize the area you've cleared and begin to build upon it.

Clarifying Your Reasons for Writing: Thesis

Some of the writing strategies we have suggested thus far are simply ways to help you learn more about literature by using writing. However, it is quite likely that you will be called upon to do some formal writing, such as essays and papers. To be successful at this sort of writing it is important to be able to focus your thinking and write with a purpose. The point of focus for a paper is called a *thesis*. You may have heard this word many times before in high school and college English courses, but what does it literally mean? The word *thesis* comes from a Greek verb *tithenai*, which means "to put"—an odd root for a word that gets so much attention by composition teachers! The idea of "putting" is related to a long tradition of argumentation, in which speakers would "put forth" a point and then support it by offering all of their evidence, usually based on complex rules of logic. Whether you are writing a critical essay about a work of literature or a feature story for the *New York Times Magazine,* there must be a reason for writing: some single idea or argument or purpose that you wish to convey to the reader.

Writers have many tactics for presenting the thesis. Some state it very obviously, while others leave it implicit. Whichever way you handle it, you still have to decide clearly on what your purpose is for writing. As a writer you assume an obligation to make your purpose clear to a reader. Most academic writing, whether about literature or any other subject, tries to let the reader know at or near the beginning of the essay what the writer's purpose or thesis is. Let's assume that your best bet for the moment is to follow that general tactic. As your writing experience progresses you may want to try other tactics—and you may do so with considerable success.

How do you find your thesis? So far, having followed the suggestions from this chapter and the one that precedes it, you may have accumulated some freewritings, journal entries, clusters, and a variety of details, all of which seem to have equal value. No one thing seems more important than another. Abundance is a happy problem for you to have as a writer; it allows you to make choices, evaluate ideas, and try out different strategies. First, you need to limit your options. You can't say all there is to say about a literary work or author; no one can. All you have is your perspective, your individual viewpoint. Let's say you've narrowed your interest in the Freeman story, "A Far-Away Melody," to one of these topics:

religion
small-town life
the power of the imagination

Try using a cluster or freewriting on one of the topics to see where it leads, what ideas and details emerge, and how your understanding of the topic changes as you explore it in writing.

Now, take some blank paper and try writing your thesis—or if you prefer, call it your purpose or message or point—in *one sentence*. Don't cheat on this:

Make sure to use a subject and a verb. Don't rely on just a phrase. Writing in a sentence helps you to flesh out the essence of the idea. It shows you whether your idea will stand up under the test of being converted into language. Write a page full of such sentences. Figure 4 shows an example.

Next, decide upon which statement is closest to what you want. The sentences are still rough, perhaps vague, but you have something with which to work. Take another sheet of paper and copy the statement you have chosen at the top of the page. Now begin again. Some possible developments are seen in Figure 5.

Don't stop here. If necessary, try another round and then put your paper aside for a few hours and come back to it. See how your choice holds up now. Is it clear to you? Here's a key question: Is it an idea that *you* believe in strongly enough to pursue? Maybe you're still not sure. Run it past a fellow student from your class: Is it clear to him or her? You might even try buttonholing the teacher. What does he or she think? Most teachers are happy to review work at this stage. You might only need a couple of minutes in the hallway with your teacher to glance at the sentence and discuss it, and this may save you hours of futile labor.

When you have settled on a thesis statement (though you should still keep yourself open to modifying and revising it), the next step is to develop it. Sometimes students think of this as a "filling in" process. In some ways this is true, though it may be more helpful to think of it as a filling *out* process, an expansion or exploration that helps you to find all of the possibilities your ideas or thesis has to offer. Now everything you do is directed toward or centered around that central idea. Nothing will go into your essay except that which enhances your idea, and nothing should be left out that will help to support and illustrate that idea.

Writing a Zero Draft

A zero draft precedes a first draft. Here's how you write a zero draft. Put aside all of your notes, journal entries, clusters, and even the textbook itself. Most of all put aside your thesis statement pages. Get everything out of sight—and thus out of mind. Now sit down with some blank paper (or a new file on your screen, if you're using a computer) *and write your paper.*

This may sound like an odd thing to do without your notes and so forth, but you can fill in quotations or check out factual items later. In fact, there'll be a lot of that kind of work to do after you've finished the zero draft. The only object at this point is to allow the logic of your thinking to develop a very rough prose draft of the paper you want to write. What you will get is more likely to be faithful to your own ideas and words than if you allowed all of the notes and quotations to interrupt the flow of your thinking as it evolves through the process of writing.

Figure 6 is a sample zero draft based on some of the ideas we have developed so far.

Small-town Life

Small-town life made Priscilla and Mary think they heard things.

No wonder they heard things.

You're in trouble if you don't do as everyone else does in a small town.

Priscilla and Mary seemed to be products of a small town (but no one else heard the music!?).

Religion is very strong in a small town.

Small-town life is so dull that you start hearing things.

Maybe living in a small town kept them from getting their lives cluttered up with unimportant matters — like fashion and social life. (!!??)

Figure 4   Sample Thesis Statements

Mary and Priscilla were products of a small town.

In a small town you ...?

~~*A small town has many advantages and disadvantages.*~~

A small town can be very religious.

As products of a small town, Mary and Priscilla led simple, religious lives.

Figure 5   Developing a Thesis Statement

What to Do with a Zero Draft

Don't be unsettled by sentences that seem vague or ideas that take unintended leaps in logic. The zero draft is meant to help you find those weaknesses; it is also a way to give you something to work with. The zero draft is not writing for a reader; it is writing that helps you begin to turn your ideas into prose. It does neither more nor less than giving you something with which you can work: actual words on paper.

1. *Write an outline based on your zero draft.* The outline has often been considered something that precedes the writing of an essay, but in practice many writers work in reverse. Now that the internal logic of ideas and language skills have been given a chance to work in the act of writing, it is easier to see how they fit together. The outline is part of that assembly process. Ideas and details that didn't even exist until the zero draft was written can now be reassembled and enhanced through an outline. In a sense, writing an outline now is like drawing a map of the forest or jungle through which you've just hacked your way for the first time.

2. *Use scissors and paste.* If you have trouble getting organized, cutting your paper up into pieces and rearranging them may help you to see things differently. Much rewriting will follow, of course, but this is a graphic and

As products of a small town, Mary and Priscilla led simple, religious lives. They lived together in a tidy home, and even when they were hanging out the laundry, religion was part of their conversation.

Maybe it's not surprising that one day Priscilla spoke up to say that she heard music that might have been from heaven. Whether religious or not, Mary took it as an omen that her sister would die. Even as the music continued, Mary remained unconvinced that it was genuine.

Yet Priscilla claimed that she didn't imagine things and she continued to hear it until she soon died. With little exposure to any life beyond her town and her church it wouldn't be surprising if she actually _did_ hear the music. After all, her religious faith was an important part of her life. Indeed, Mary mourned for a year after her sister's death, until she too was "called home."

Overall, the story shows the power of religion and the strength of sisterly love.

Figure 6   Example of a Zero Draft

tangible way of handling (literally) organizational problems. If you are using a computer, you will find that "cutting and pasting" blocks of text is very easy to do indeed.

3. *Write notes in the margins and in between lines.* Make a mess of your zero draft. Don't be tentative with it; mark it up! The point of writing it is simply to get some words on paper. Now is the time to make that writing begin to work for you.

4. *Check your notes and text for the accuracy of any statements or references you made in the zero draft.* While writing the draft you worked without notes or text. Now go back to make sure that you were right about what you have said. Often you will find not only that your memory served you well, but that other items and quotations that didn't come to mind will further bear out ideas you may have begun to develop in a zero draft.

5. *Look for opportunities to revise statements that may seem general or vague.* The zero draft is a chance to clear out the rubbish. *All* writers face this gruesome task, not only students. One writer keeps a thirteen-gallon drum next to his desk; another calls the garbage pail "a writer's best friend." While we are not advocating tossing away the entire draft, there are certainly statements that you may write that are simply too vague or general to be included, or that have strayed from the topic. Learning how to find what's useful in your work and leave aside the rest is one of the most important skills a writer can develop. Your zero draft may have many good ideas or only one or none at all; in any case it is a success, for the good ideas can be developed and those that are questionable needn't take any more of your time. If you find that you need to write another zero draft, take a break and then plunge right in.

6. *Look for opportunities to develop ideas.* This is one of the ways that writing a zero draft can best serve you. An idea that supports one paragraph may lead to enough detail and support for two or three more paragraphs, if you give it a chance to grow. This is not merely a question of adding on more details, but rather of looking more closely at the idea. Just as you see only the color and general pattern of flowers in a garden from a distance but notice the wonderful intricacy of individual flowers and petals when you take time to observe up close, ideas can be even more revealing when they are examined; their intricacy and refinement and potential only become available to someone who takes the time to look closely and from many angles.

Maintaining Focus in Your Paper

The most important thing your paper should accomplish is to maintain a clear focus on the central idea or thesis that you want to convey to the reader. That's why it is so important to invest time and energy, as we did earlier, in settling on a thesis that you believe to be worth developing. In your revision of the zero draft be sure that everything you say goes toward this end. Everything should in some way enhance, develop, explore, and enlighten your central idea. Look at the zero draft to see if you went off on a tangent. (Maybe the tangent will become your central idea!) Ask yourself if the zero draft clearly states and develops the idea that you want to convey.

Writing the First Draft

When you've done the follow-up we suggested above on your zero draft, you'll be ready to write the first draft. This draft will look quite different from the zero draft, perhaps almost completely so. Your thesis or central idea may have been completely reworked; new ideas, information, and organizational patterns may be incorporated. Any quotations you want to include should be cited in full; any statements that needed to be checked for accuracy should by now be clarified. In all, the effort to go from the zero draft to the first draft may be considerable, but it's true, too, that you should be gaining confidence in the value of what you have to say. Remember also that the writing process is not necessarily a linear, step-by-step activity. Perhaps you'll need to use freewriting or clusters to develop a new idea that occurs even as you're writing the first draft. Though you're getting closer to work that a reader will see, you still have the luxury of developing new points and trying out new ideas.

Audience: Who Will Read What You Write?

This is probably one of the most difficult problems that student writers face. The obvious answer is that the teacher will read what you write, and for much of your formal writing this is probably true, but in some ways it makes your challenge as a writer all the more difficult. How can you say something of interest when the teacher seems to know so much more about the subject matter? How much should you include and how much should you leave out?

At this point you have a more difficult problem than most professional writers, who give a lot of thought to their readership as they make decisions about what to include and leave out, what style and vocabulary is most appropriate, what words may require definitions, and which ideas are likely to be challenged by a particular audience. Few writers expect to please every human being who may happen to pick up their work. Chapters such as this one in this textbook, for example, are clearly directed to a specific population of student readers. Much thought and effort by ourselves and our editors have gone into making things clear and accessible for this group. Others who read this book may or may not find sections like this of interest. That's okay because our main concern has been to address students in introductory literature courses. This is but one of many examples of how audience considerations play a part in writing.

How can you resolve the various dilemmas you face in deciding to whom you should direct your writing?

1. *When you write, use your own words.* Your instructor doesn't expect you to sound like anyone but yourself. In fact, the more faithful you are to what *you* think and what *you* want to say, the more likely you are to meet with success. Therefore, don't feel that you have to sound like a literary critic whose essay you may have just read, and don't use any language or words that you don't fully understand.

2. *Envision one of your friends or colleagues from class reading your paper.* What would he or she like to know about the work you are discussing? Would your central idea be clear to him or her? The odds are very high that if such a reader would honestly remain interested in what you have to say, your instructor will too. But the key word is *honestly.* If such a reader didn't have to read your paper, would he or she continue to read? If your instructor consents, you may want to form a small group to exchange work. In this way you can get feedback from different readers with different interests. Such groups can be very helpful, but they do require some planning and ground rules. Be sure to discuss any such plans with your instructor.

3. *How much is too much?* Many students worry about saying too much because they figure the teacher already knows it. This is not always true, however. Your reading and discussion of a literary work may be more recent and closer than the teacher's. As a reader, he or she may need some background information. Although it's safe to assume that your teacher has read the literary work, it is good policy as a writer to assume that the reader is not as close to the work as you are after many days or weeks of reading, notetaking, prewriting, and thinking about it. You may find it helpful to imagine a friend or class acquaintance reading the paper. He or she may have read the literary work too, but perhaps not as closely as you did in order to write your paper. What would such a reader need to know?

4. *Finally, keeping your audience interested (even if you're not sure who your audience may be) has a lot to do with whether you think what you have to say is worth saying.* If you work in groups within your class or even give a draft to a friend to read before you type it up, you may want to pick up all the signals you can, whether expressed overtly or subtly. Do such readers think your idea is clear, valuable, interesting? Have you actually developed a clear purpose for your paper, or does it merely give coverage to a topic without expressing an idea or direction?

Effective Openings

An effective opening very quickly gets your reader's attention and holds it. There are, of course, many ways to get someone's attention. If you scream "Fire!" in a crowded theater (whether it's real or not), you will get everyone's attention, but this may also be the last word you have before chaos ensues. So as you consider effective openings, you need to think about how you want to focus the reader's attention. Keep in mind that a reader, whether one of your classmates or your teacher, has taken your paper in hand with an interest in reading a work about literature. Part of your battle has been won. You only need to go the next step by ensuring the reader that what you have to say has interest and is worth the investment of time he or she has already committed to it.

Some writers need to spend a lot of time refining the opening of a paper, whether it's one paragraph or many, before they can go on to the rest; others don't even write the opening until they've completed the paper. You have written a thesis statement and a zero draft, so you have done the most difficult part. It may, however, be useful to devote some writing time to refining your introductory section.

Effective Closings

Bringing your paper to an effective close has less to do with arriving somewhere than with assuring the reader of completeness. In this sense, an effective closing is largely dependent upon how much effort you've put into the paper as a whole. Many of the faulty closings we've seen in student work are not due to how a paper ends so much as its incompleteness. In this sense, the work you do on developing substantive ideas and writing and revising your drafts will naturally lead to effective closure.

Here are a few hints.

1. *Avoid abrupt endings.* Your paper shouldn't end with the last item or topic you discuss. It needs to bring the overview of the whole paper into a meaningful perspective for the reader.

2. *Suggest to the reader where the argument may next lead.* You can't begin another paper with the possibilities you may discover (though this is sometimes how writers find the material for a series of essays or a book), but you should suggest to your reader some implications and consequences of the ideas you have discussed. You may additionally have ideas, which necessarily remain suggestions, about what sort of thinking or research might follow on the paper you are bringing to a close.

3. *Restate the argument and the basic evidence of your paper.* Do this in different words than you used in the paper, and do so for the purpose of illustrating how you've come to the conclusions you've reached, not merely as a means of summary. In short papers (say, under ten pages), summarizing the paper in the last paragraph can appear superfluous and even patronizing.

4. *A closing may sometimes be an occasion to make statements that are slightly more personal and less formal than the rest of the paper.* You might suggest, for example, after showing how Freeman uses the small town setting effectively in her story, in what ways the story has altered your own attitudes toward small town life.

Titles

Titles are a neglected art, but they can not only enliven your experience in writing a paper, they can also help you to understand the paper.

Here's a title for a paper about Mary E. Wilkins Freeman's "A Far-Away Melody": "Mary E. Wilkins Freeman's 'A Far-Away Melody'." Your reader's heart will sink before he or she even starts to read the paper. The message of such a title is clear: "I couldn't think of anything to call this paper since I don't really have anything to say about the story." If you have done all of the work we have suggested thus far, nothing could be further from the truth. You have developed a central idea and many details and ideas. Your paper has grown with each successive draft. Your title should do justice to the value of your paper.

Here are a couple of thoughts on titles.

1. *Use the title to make your topic clear to the reader.* As a reader, you appreciate such clarity, for example, when you're in the library trying to decide whether a book or journal article will help you in your research. Put yourself in such a position when you decide on a title. "Small Town Life in Mary E. Wilkins Freeman's 'A Far-Away Melody' " leaves no doubt about your topic or about the work you are discussing.

2. *Use a striking quotation from the work(s) you are writing about.* One way to do this is to cite the quotation and then follow it with a colon that introduces a title that clarifies your paper topic. For example, "'A faint sound o' music': Musical Images in Mary E. Wilkins Freeman's 'A Far-Away Melody'."

3. *Try out several titles.* Put your paper aside and on a blank sheet jot as many possibilities as may come to mind. Just as you did with earlier drafts, set the sheet aside and see how some of the titles strike you after a few hours or a day has passed.

4. *Think about titles as part of the writing process.* Don't leave it until the end because a working title may help you to keep the focus of your paper clear. Many authors entitle their work while it is in progress, and change the title along the way. The title is part of the paper, not an appendage. As much as it may help the reader to know what you're writing about, it may help you to understand your own work even as you do it.

3 *Revising and Editing*

Effective Revision

The word *revision* contains its own definition: *re-vision*. Consider how a vacation site or monument differs in the way you may see it upon returning after a year or more. While it may have changed little, if at all, your distance from it, in both time and space, may have altered the way you see it. Effective writing depends upon your ability to gain a measure of distance from your work.

Revision, then, means more than editing, which we'll discuss shortly. In revising a paper, you are looking at large issues: How does the paper hold together? Is the thesis clear? Does the argument move fluidly from one idea to another? *Instead of trying to imagine how someone else will read a paper written by you, imagine how you would read the paper if someone else had written it.* Now that your paper is in a draft that has benefited from all of the effort at developing a thesis, organizing ideas, writing a zero draft and then a first draft—in other words, now that you are getting closer to a product that is intended to be seen by a reader—you need to step back and look at your work as a reader would. Putting the paper aside for a day or so may help considerably. The paper needs to simmer, and you may need some distance from it.

Refocusing a Paper: The Second Draft

Revision may involve significant changes in the paper, but not necessarily starting over from scratch. The following paragraph illustrates a first draft introductory paragraph.

```
 Mary E. W. Freeman's "A Far-Away Melody"
shows how religious belief is deeply in-
grained in the lives of small-town people.
Mary and Priscilla are two "plain folks." They
are twin sisters. They have lived together for
many years and know each other well. After all
that time Priscilla hears music that her sis-
ter does not hear, and Priscilla thus realizes
that she will soon die.
```

Simply revising sentences—say, for example, the three that follow the opening sentence, which are somewhat choppy—wouldn't address the real problem, namely, that after a strong thesis statement in the first sentence the paragraph loses sight of the central idea and devolves into plot summary. Revising the paragraph for a second draft may lead to substantive changes.

```
 Mary E. W. Freeman's "A Far-Away Melody"
shows how religious belief is deeply in-        effective transition
grained in the lives of small-town people. Two  to keep on topic
such people are Mary and Priscilla Brown, twin  emphasis on
sisters and people of strong religious con-     original topic:
victions. "[T]heir religion," Freeman writes,   religious belief
"had strongly tinctured their daily life."      support for
Religion had a place in their daily chores and  statement and
finally in the way they died.                   a fluid transi-
                                                tion to the
                                                analysis of how
                                                religion was
                                                ingrained in
                                                their lives
```

Now the paragraph has a point of transition from which to begin exploring the evidence and the truth of the statement made in the first sentence.

Organization

Revision may involve organizational changes. If you've ever worked on a school newspaper or yearbook, you know that organization can be a messy and physical activity. You sometimes take cuttings of writing and move them around; you scribble a possible headline with a magic marker to see how it looks at the top of a column; you scrawl a note on a blank sheet of paper to say what will go in that space and then insert the sheet into the sheaf you may be compiling. Even as we revised the manuscript for this book we did plenty of that kind of work.

The two principles that govern most organizational activity are *logic* and *emphasis*: Are the ideas and information placed in a logical order? Do they receive the appropriate emphasis? In writing about literature these questions are often answered in the following ways.

Logic

1. *Your essay may follow the chronological or narrative order of the work you are discussing.* The second draft of the paper based on the introductory paragraph above, for example, may lead into a discussion that starts with how religion emerges in the conversation of Mary and Priscilla while they hang out the laundry at the outset of the story and then continues through the drama of their respective deaths. If you follow the events of the story in order, be careful not to substitute a paraphrase of the story for your analysis of the argument you are making.

2. *Your argument may have a logic of its own, which has little to do with the narrative flow of the literary work.* This may be especially true, for example, when you discuss more than one work of literature or more than one author. If you wish to show that Mary E. Wilkins Freeman and Shirley Jackson (author of "The Lottery" on pages 120–129) have different ideas about small town life, you would have to consider how you want to contrast their ideas. Your essay might then discuss their respective views of individual people, the collective behavior of many people, and the distinctive ways in which religion manifests itself. Thus your analysis would *classify* ideas and details for discussion. Another form of logic is *cause and effect*. In this case, you might examine how religious faith causes Mary and Priscilla to hear music that others can't hear. Analytical methods such as these would not lend themselves easily to following the narrative of the story. Rather, they require you to reassemble the details and evidence to support the particular argument and methodology you wish to follow.

3. *Organize your descriptive writing so that it is consistent.* Description may go from near to far, top to bottom, left to right, or the reverse of all of these. It may also be dominated by a single impression or series of impressions, say, how a person's attitude dominates his or her physical characteristics or how the mood of the viewer affects the things or scene he or she is describing. There is no single mode of description that is better than another. Rather, the method you choose must be appropriate to what you are saying. The important thing is not to jump around without any logic.

In revising your paper for the second draft, you may discover descriptive passages that have organizational problems like the following one. Happily, they are not difficult to set right.

```
    Mary and Priscilla are alike in many ways.
They dress similarly and look very much alike,
Priscilla being slightly prettier and quicker
than her sister. It is Priscilla who first
hears the calling of the music.
    Mary, on the other hand, is more supersti-
tious than Priscilla, and she is easily upset
by Priscilla's talk about death and mysteri-
ous music.
```

The logic of this description is based upon a comparison of the two sisters; therefore, the writer should describe one woman and then the other before moving on with her analysis of the story.

```
    Mary and Priscilla are alike in many ways.
They dress similarly and look very much alike,
Priscilla being slightly prettier and quicker
than her sister. Mary, on the other hand, is
more superstitious than Priscilla, and she is
easily upset by Priscilla's talk about death
and mysterious music.
    It is Priscilla who first hears the calling
of the music.
```

Emphasis

Supporting evidence for an argument may be arranged according to its value. As you consider organizational patterns for your paper and reconsider them as part of the revision process, ask yourself whether some ideas and details carry more weight than others. You can rearrange your evidence based on patterns that go *from the least important to the most important,* or the reverse. You may also consider how the nature of your argument lends itself to other forms of emphasis. For example, your argument may have *negative and positive* sides: the pros and cons of small town life. In writing such an essay, you may want to leave your reader with a positive feeling, and therefore you will cover the cons first and then move to the pros. Another pattern of organization is *the universal and the specific,* which may be covered in either order, depending on its appropriateness to your argument. Going from the specific to the universal, for instance, you might argue that Freeman's story exemplifies small town life in general. So you'd first describe the elements of the story that have to do with small-town life and then show how they apply to the larger concept of "the small town."

In general, you need to consider which pattern is best suited to the thesis you are developing and then revise accordingly. Often, an essay will find its own shape, like water taking the shape of its container, and the revision process thus becomes an opportunity to step back and analyze the suitability of that shape, and perhaps to refine it.

Transitions

Even when you have your ideas developed in a clear organizational pattern, your writing may have a stilted feeling because you need to create effective transitions between sentences and paragraphs. Here's an example.

```
Priscilla speaks cheerfully of death and the
afterlife while she hangs out the wash with
her sister. Her words frighten Mary, who takes
them as a premonition.
```

The logical connection between the two sentences is already there, but it needs to be highlighted.

```
Priscilla speaks cheerfully of death and the
afterlife while she hangs out the wash with
her sister. However, her words frighten Mary,
who takes them as a premonition.
```

The logic is based on a contrast in attitudes.

transition word highlights the contrast

Here's a list of words and phrases to use for different kinds of transitions.

To show examples or to specify: for example, for instance, specifically, namely, as an illustration, in particular

To show cause and effect: as a result, therefore, accordingly, thus, because, for, so

To introduce an opposite view: but, however, although, on the contrary, on the other hand, in contrast, still, yet, nevertheless

To concede to the opposing view: still, granted, certainly, naturally, of course, it is true

To show contrast or comparison: similarly, likewise, yet, still, nevertheless, even, whereas

To add evidence or emphasis: moreover, furthermore, too, also, besides, in addition

To conclude: finally, in conclusion, clearly, to sum up, altogether, to conclude

Effective Editing

In many ways editing and revision overlap. However, the distinction we are making here between revision and editing has to do with how broad a view one takes of the rewriting process. While revision is very broad in its scope, emphasizing unity and organization, editing is more localized, addressing ways to improve a manuscript through sentence structure, word choice, usage, and so forth. Proofreading, which we will shortly discuss, takes the most limited view of rewriting, in which the writer concentrates on typography and other minutiae. All are important, and writers often do several activities simultaneously. Yet, to learn more about how writers work, it is helpful to talk about these activities separately. A diagram of the pattern we've followed would look like this:

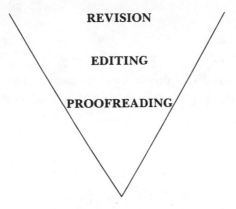

Clearly, the point when one activity shifts to another is not rigidly marked. Each activity is defined better by your intent as a writer than by the process itself, and it may not be necessary at all times to think about whether you are doing one or another. If, when you read a completed draft, for example, you believe that the overall message of your paper—your thesis or argument—is not clear, your effort to sharpen that message throughout may involve all of these activities in one way or another, and you don't have to trouble yourself about which you are doing.

Editing for Tone and Style

There are many things you can do to enliven your writing and add clarity to it. As you reread a draft look for some of these elements of style.

Coherence.   Does each sentence lead clearly to the next? Sometimes you need only add a transition word or phrase to make the coherence in your ideas evident. Sometimes, however, in the act of composition, two ideas emerge at the same time, and you don't notice until much later that one has been left hanging while you jumped to another.

Freeman focuses on the routine, even unimpor- *An important statement which may require de-velopment at a later point. Here, it inter-rupts the development of the idea in the first sentence.*
tant, activities in the lives of her charac-
ters. <u>Religion plays an important part too.</u> We
see Mary and Priscilla hanging out their laundry and preparing for dinner.

Sentence combining.   A series of sentences that use the same syntactical structure (for example, two or three simple sentences in a row) or repeat a word may be combined into a single sentence.

Priscilla heard the music that signaled her
death. Mary did not hear the music until much
later.

combine to:

Priscilla heard the music that signaled her
death, but Mary did not hear it until much
later.

Here's another example.

Priscilla heard the music.
Priscilla soon died.

combine to:

Priscilla heard the music and soon died.

Wordiness.   Review your paper for words and phrases that are wasteful or sound inflated. Sometimes these are just stock phrases that come into use and prevent us from really thinking about what we're saying. Everyone uses some, especially in speech, but in writing you have a chance to clear away the deadwood with careful editing. Here are a few examples.

Wordy	Concise
at this point in time at this particular time	now
have the ability to have the capacity for be in a position to	can

in the not too distant future
on the occasion when   } soon, when
during the period when

on account of
due to the fact that
for the reason that
that is why   } because, why, for
the reason why
because of the fact that
for the purpose of
inasmuch as

Wordiness may also result from careless repetition.

Freeman's central characters are <u>unattractive</u>
<u>in appearance</u> yet their quiet sisterly love is
shown in the way they <u>cooperate together</u>.

Edit to: *unattractive, cooperate*. Another cause of wordiness is overuse of the passive voice.

Mary and Priscilla <u>were shown</u> (understood subject:
by Freeman) to be hardworking and religious
women.

The passive voice combines a form of the verb *to be* (in this case, *were*) with a past participle (*shown*). It also moves the subject of the sentence to the object position, and in the sentence above allows the writer to conceal it. Sometimes this structure is useful when the subject is unknown. A journalist, for example, may turn in a story with the following sentence.

A murder <u>was committed.</u>

The journalist doesn't know who committed the murder and would prefer to avoid a sentence like the following, which does use the active voice.

A murderer committed a murder.

Thus passive sentences may be helpful to shift the emphasis of a sentence to what is known or what is important. Often, however, they weaken sentences or conceal information that a writer may not have firmly in hand. Consider how the following sentence uses the passive voice.

It <u>was thought</u> that hearing voices and music
meant you were crazy or had been called to
heaven.

Here the writer is trying to hold up a weak idea by using the passive construction: Who thought such things? Where has the writer found this information? The writer seems to have made a generalization based on the limited experience of reading a single short story.

Using the passive voice is not wrong or right; it has a place on certain occasions and can add sentence variety to your writing. Review your paper to find any such constructions and see how changing them to the active voice will affect their meaning and the tone and style of the paragraphs in which they appear.

Another way to pare the wordiness out of your writing is to look for statements that are vague, obvious, or clichéd.

> Vague: Freeman's story offers the reader many opportunities for interpretation.
>
> Obvious: Mary and Priscilla have many likenesses and differences.
>
> Clichéd: Mary and Priscilla are tried and true.

Here's a slightly more extended example of clichés at work.

```
Freeman's story holds more than meets the eye.
It all boils down to a moving experience for
two poor but honest sisters who slowly but
surely find the right track and discover some-
thing that is worth its weight in gold. The
story simply hits the nail on the head.
```

As all of the examples of wordiness show, the reader, whether your roommate or your instructor, is seldom fooled by language that is empty. As you write an early draft there's nothing wrong with using such words and phrases—in fact, stopping to linger over every word may impede a more valuable creative activity—but when you revise and edit, a large part of your job is to find them and change or eliminate them.

Usage

A word or phrase may be appropriate for one context and inappropriate for another. A paper that begins, " 'A Far-Away Melody' is totally awesome!" may not convince your instructor, or even your classmates, as well as it would your immediate group of friends. Usage, then, has a lot to do with your audience and your relationship to it. Words and phrases that are very informal—including *slang* and *colloquialisms*—are not out of place simply because they're "not formal enough" for a paper about literature, but rather because they may unduly restrict your audience.

Standard English is the language that the greatest possible majority of readers will accept as correct or appropriate. In other words, Standard English will allow you to reach a large audience that may include people whose expectations, educational backgrounds, and familiarity with the material you may not be able to anticipate. Standard English is the language in which most business and legal matters are conducted; it is the language used for the exchange of knowledge through academic writing; and it is the language in which nearly all broadcasters and journalists deliver news and other information to us each day. We would prefer not to have the anchorperson on a network news show have a strong accent from Maine or Alabama, because if we're not from the Northeast or the South we may feel excluded.

In writing papers about literature, you may be tempted to err on the opposite side of using nonstandard words and phrases by writing in language that is too formal or that includes words you're not accustomed to using. However, an extreme use of formality will have the effect of distancing you from your audience rather than including the broadest possible audience. In no case should you use language that is unfamiliar to you. If you're not comfortable using a word or phrase when you speak, then it's a good idea to avoid it in writing. When you're in doubt about a word's usage, check the dictionary. Nonstandard forms are marked as *colloquial, slang,* and *dialect.* If a word is not so designated, it is *standard.*

Editing Words and Sentences

Verbs.   One of the surest ways to add life to your writing is to find worn-out verbs and replace them with livelier ones. Here are some examples to circle in your paper.

be (in all tenses)	have	take place
do	go	happen
make	occur	

How can the substitution of one verb for another change a sentence? Let's take an example.

```
Priscilla is the first to hear the music. The
same thing happens later to Mary.
```

Change to:

```
Priscilla first hears the music, and Mary
later discovers it.
```

Notice how the substitution of new verbs leads to a restructuring and tightening of the whole idea, originally expressed in two somewhat dull sentences and now stated in one livelier sentence.

Verb Tenses.   Tense sometimes presents difficulty to inexperienced writers, which is compounded by problems associated with writing about literature. Note that the examples above are written in the present tense. Yet the same paper might include the following sentence: "Mary E. Wilkins Freeman *wrote* this and many other stories as a result of her experience living in northern Vermont." The difference between this and the sentences above is that Mary E. Wilkins Freeman *was* an actual living person; the sentence, then, makes a historical statement. On the other hand, Mary and Priscilla Brown are still very much with us as characters in a story we read and reread, even though they represent people who might have lived a hundred years ago. Generally, when you write about literature you should do so in the present tense (sometimes known as the "timeless present" when used for this purpose) and when you write about historical incidents (for example, the life of the writer) you should use the past tense.

Of course, such a rule of thumb may lead to confusion. You don't want your reader to be hopping in and out of the past, never knowing quite where he or she is. Examine your work for consistency and clarity in this respect. Pick out a couple of sentences randomly, decide what tense you've used, and then ask yourself if it is appropriate for your purpose. Here's an example that shows the end of one paragraph and the transition to another.

Freeman <u>included</u> this story in a collection
entitled <u>A Humble Romance</u>, which <u>portrayed</u>   All sentences in
similar instances of small town life in New   the past tense
for discussion
England. Freeman, of course, <u>lived</u> only a por-   of the writer's
tion of her life in Vermont, subsequently set-   life.
tling in New Jersey, where she <u>continued</u> to
write about her experiences in Vermont.
                                                    Use of past
Mary and Priscilla <u>exemplify</u> what Freeman   tense in
clause to help
<u>knew</u> of small town life. They <u>are</u> hardworking,   with transi-
tion
religious, stubborn, and even a bit cheap.
Priscilla <u>may be</u> the more romantic of the two,   Present
tense used to
but neither <u>has</u> a vivid imagination, as   discuss characters
in the story.
Priscilla somewhat defensively <u>insists</u> at one
point, "I never imagined anything in my life
. . . an' it ain't likely I'm goin' to begin
now."

Spelling and Punctuation.   Putting aside these matters until late in your revising and editing process allows you to concentrate creative energy on developing and organizing worthwhile ideas without the hinderance of wondering how to spell a word or punctuate a sentence. Yet the paper is not complete until even the apparently superficial matters receive attention. Although the labor is of a different kind—and therefore worth doing separately—it is important to the success of your work. At the very least, editing carefully for mechanics and punctuation shows that you have put care into your work, but it may also clarify ambiguities that result from carelessness. Certainly, if you've labored to write something that you believe to be worth saying, you don't want your reader distracted by matters that are relatively easy to resolve on the scale of what makes writing so hard.

Spelling is perhaps one of the most prominent of such matters. Spelling is largely a matter of social custom. It's possible to communicate effectively without spelling well, but you wouldn't expect a potential employer to call you for an interview if your application letter was full of misspelled words. If spelling presents special problems to you, it may be advisable to get a dictionary of commonly misspelled words. Certainly, no one should write without having a standard dictionary (for example, *Webster's New World Dictionary* or the *American Heritage Dictionary*) within reach. Mark the dictionary up when you check words, or keep a list of words you check over the course of a year. You may be able to spot some problem words as you write, just by virtue of the doubt that enters your mind as you put the word on paper. Don't stop to check a word if it will interrupt the flow of thought. Just circle it and then go back later to look up all the words you've circled. If you're still in doubt about possible misspellings on your paper, ask a friend to read it and circle all the words he or she is not sure of when reading your paper. Your friend doesn't have to know how to spell the words and shouldn't correct them for you. (What if your friend is wrong?) But if another reader has a doubt when seeing the word, it may be misspelled. The key to correct spelling is not knowing how to spell every word but simply developing a strategy to find problem words.

Punctuation also seems to present unnecessary complications to inexperienced writers. In lieu of a set of rules, which any good handbook provides, it may be worth suggesting here that as you edit your work you should circle items or occasions for punctuation that are not one hundred percent clear to you and then consider why you've used the punctuation mark you have.

Some other special cases that may apply to literary writing include:

1. *Titles.*
   Poems, short stories, essays: quotation marks; e.g., "A Far-Away Melody," "My Papa's Waltz," "On Marriage"
   Novels, plays, epic poems: underline; e.g., <u>For Whom the Bell Tolls</u>, <u>Hamlet</u>, <u>Paradise Lost</u>
   (Note: Don't put the title of your own paper in quotation marks and don't use capitalization except to begin the title and at the beginning of all words except prepositions, conjunctions, and articles.)

Proofreader's Checklist

Spelling   Circle all words in question; get a friend to circle words; keep a list of problem words.

Punctuation   Select random instances of comma usage and ask if that is the correct mark; ask whether the comma is being used to hold two main clauses together; semicolon may be needed between two main clauses when the second is introduced by *however, nevertheless, moreover, therefore, then, also, besides.*

Fragment   (an incomplete sentence, sometimes used for emphasis) Read aloud to determine if sentences sound complete; check to see that each sentence has a verb.

Modifiers   Ask whether they are near the words and phrases they are supposed to modify; rewrite sentences to avoid problems with misplaced modifiers.

Quotations   Ask whether they fit comfortably into the text; use quotations to support points you are making, not the reverse.

Titles of literary works   Check to make sure they are correctly cited.

Author's name   Make sure it is spelled correctly.

Words used clearly   Avoid any words or phrases that you wouldn't be comfortable using in conversation.

---

2. *Quotation marks* present particular problems when writing about literature. Use quotation marks when you cite work within a paragraph but not if you set it off in a block quotation. In writing about "A Far-Away Melody" you may have to use a quote within a quote: "She spoke to her husband, who opened the window. 'What's wanted?' he asked, peering out into the darkness." In this instance the double marks go outside the entire passage, and the single marks enclose the question asked by the character. Also, commas and periods usually fall within the quotation, as in the example above. When punctuation falls outside of a quotation, it is usually for the purpose of including the quotation in a larger sentence: I had no idea he'd say, "What's wanted?"!

3. *Colon.* Used to introduce a quotation either within the text (see the preceding paragraph) or when set off in a block.

4. *Apostrophes.* Sometimes, as Mary Freeman does, they are used to enhance dialect speech. Apostrophes are more commonly used for possession and contractions. Check over any apostrophes you have used for correct-

ness. Look at some random plurals and ask yourself if an apostrophe may be needed (e.g., the horses mane—the horse's mane? or the horses' manes?).

Proofreading

At this stage, read your paper closely for typographical errors, spelling errors you may yet have missed, and other minutiae that may spoil the effect of an otherwise thorough effort. You should proofread carefully before the final typing and then once more afterwards.

Some writers will read their work backwards, one word or one sentence at a time in order to check for spelling and usage without having the flow of thought obstruct their ability to examine the paper. Use a half sheet of blank paper to block off sections of the text and then read closely (forward or backwards) for correctness and clarity. You may also consider forming a small group or simply exchanging papers with a friend just to have someone objective aid in the proofreading stage. If you do this, the decision to make a change and the changes themselves are up to the individual writers, but as most professionals readily acknowledge, it's simply not possible for the writer to find every error in his or her own work.

READING AND WRITING
ABOUT NONFICTION

1 What Is Nonfiction?

Of the four genres of literature discussed in this book, nonfiction is perhaps the broadest and the one that varies most in shape and purpose. Nonfiction includes journalism, business writing, letters, legal documents, and essays. The term *nonfiction* (with its *non-* prefix) seems to be a catchall for the many forms of writing that fall outside of the genres we associate with "imaginative" or "creative" writing. Nonfiction includes writing that is intended to accomplish things in the social, business, and legal worlds; its references are usually to people, places, and things that actually exist; its purposes may include informing, persuading, and recording. Nonfiction may entertain us, but it is most often connected with the worlds of work, of social and political issues, and of cultural and personal life.

Definitions of nonfiction may create more problems than they solve. In response to the distinctions made above, Edmund Wilson once asserted that "all writing is creative." Conversely, we can find many instances of fiction, drama, and poetry that are written to inform or persuade. Yet the purpose of defining nonfiction as a genre that informs and persuades is to describe distinctions we already recognize, not to create a category into which the literature must fit. The differences between a poem in a literary magazine and a chapter from a medical textbook are evident to us before we decide on the definition of *poem* or *essay*. (As a writing exercise you might try listing some of these differences in your reading journal.)

Interestingly, the problem of separating nonfiction from other types of writing is a modern one, perhaps not unrelated to the ever-increasing tendency of contemporary society toward specialization and categorization. *The Song of Roland,* for instance, is an epic poem from the middle ages that is based on historical events in the ninth century in Spain. Like much ancient and medieval poetry, it performed the dual functions of recording history and entertaining its listeners. (It was traditionally recited aloud from memory rather than read silently by individuals.) The *jongleur* (the singer who recited the poem) and his audience did not distinguish between history and poetry or between information and inspiration. This example suggests that when we read and write we have certain expectations or assumptions for what that writing should accomplish, and these have much to do with our cultural and social place in history. Definitions such as nonfiction and fiction are not written on stone tablets for all time. Rather, we are continually revising and altering them as we read and write.

The Essay

Unless you plan to take a fine arts major in creative writing, nearly all of the writing you will do in college is nonfiction. Your writing may take the form of lab reports, case studies, term papers, essay exams, journals, and so forth. The essay is the basis for term papers and other informative or expository writing that you do. Although you may have already gained a long acquaintance with this form, both as something you write and as something you read, do you know what it is? As with other forms of writing (such as sonnets, short stories, and epic poems), there is both a history and a purpose associated with the essay. The word *essay* comes from the French word *essai,* which means "trial, attempt, endeavor, experiment, or testing." It was first attached to a collection of short writings by Michel de Montaigne in 1580, which he entitled *Essais.* Montaigne's essays were meditative and personal; they were often based upon personal experience, which he sifted and examined in search of universal truths.

Read the following essay by Montaigne and then do a freewriting in your journal on the subject of idleness.

MICHEL DE MONTAIGNE (1533–1592)

Of Idleness

As we see ground that lies fallow, if it is rich and fertile, abound with innumerable sorts of wild and useless plants; and that, to make it perform its true office, we must cultivate and sow it with certain seeds for our service; and as we see that women do entirely of themselves bring forth formless masses and lumps of flesh, but that to produce a natural and perfect generation they must be husbanded with another kind of seed; even so it is with minds, if they are not applied to some certain study that may check and restrain them, they will cast themselves in disorder hither and thither in the vague fields of the imagination.

> As in a brazen bowl the water's shimmering light
> Reflects the radiant sun or Luna's glowing disk,
> And dances round on every side, and then aloft
> Springs up, and o'er the high and panelled ceiling strikes.[1]

There is no folly nor idle fancy that they do not bring forth in this agitation:

> They form their idle fancies like
> A sick man's dreams.[2]

The mind that has no established aim loses itself; for as the saying goes, to be everywhere is to be nowhere.

> He who dwells everywhere, Maximus, dwells nowhere.[3]

When I lately retired to my own house, determined as far as possible to concern myself with nothing else than spending in privacy and repose the little remainder of time I have to live, I fancied I could not more oblige my mind than to permit it a full leisure to entertain itself and come to rest in itself, which I hoped it might now the more easily do, having with time become more settled and mature; but I find,

> Idleness produces ever-changing thoughts.[4]

that, quite the contrary, like a runaway horse it gives itself a hundred times more trouble than it used to take for others, and creates me so many

---

[1] Virgil (70–19 B.C.), *The Aeneid*, Bk. 8, 1. 22.
[2] Horace (65–8 B.C.), *Ars Poetica*, 1. 7.
[3] Martial (40?–104? A.D.), *Epigrams*, VII, no. 73.
[4] Lucan (39–65 A.D.), *The Civil War*, Vol. 4, 1. 704.

chimeras and fantastic monsters, one upon another, without order or design, that, the better at leisure to contemplate their strangeness and absurdity. I have begun to record them, hoping in time to make it ashamed of them.

Montaigne's word *essai* came into English usage as a literary term when Francis Bacon published his own *Essays* in 1597. Bacon's collection was a group of ten short pieces, and like Montaigne's, they were personal and meditative. They examined experience in search of truth. Both writers understood that the essay was an unfinished type of writing—unfinished in the sense of being inconclusive. For Bacon and Montaigne, essays literally were "attempts." Like Montaigne's, the essays of Bacon evolve from his explorations of a single theme or topic. But they are known best for the pithiness of expression, exemplified in the often-quoted first sentence of the essay below.

FRANCIS BACON (1561–1626)

Of Revenge

Revenge is a kind of wild justice, which, the more man's nature runs to, the more ought law to weed it out; for as for the first wrong, it doth but offend the law, but the revenge of that wrong putteth the law out of office. Certainly, in taking revenge a man is but even with his enemy, but in passing it over he is superior, for it is a prince's part to pardon. And Solomon, I am sure, saith: "It is the glory of a man to pass by an offence." That which is past is gone and irrevocable, and wise men have enough to do with things present and to come; therefore they do but trifle with themselves that labor in past matters. There is no man doth a wrong for the wrong's sake, but thereby to purchase himself profit, or pleasure, or honor, or the like. Therefore, why should I be angry with a man for loving himself better than me? And if any man should do wrong merely out of ill nature, why, yet it is but like the thorn or briar, which prick and scratch because they can do no other. The most tolerable sort of revenge is for those wrongs which there is no law to remedy; but then let a man take heed the revenge be such as there is no law to punish, else a man's enemy is still beforehand, and it is two for one. Some, when they take revenge, are desirous the party should know whence it cometh. This is the more generous, for the delight seemeth to be, not so much in doing the hurt as in making the party repent; but base and crafty cowards are like the arrow that flieth in the dark. Cosmos, Duke of Florence, had a desperate saying against perfidious or neglecting friends, as if those wrongs were unpardonable. "You shall read," saith he, "that we are commanded to forgive our enemies, but you never read that we are commanded to forgive our friends." But yet the spirit of Job was in a better tune. "Shall we," saith he, "take good at God's hands, and not be content to take evil also?" And so of friends, in a proportion. This is certain, that a man that studieth revenge keeps his own wounds green, which otherwise would heal and do well. Public revenges are for the most part, fortunate; as that for the death of Caesar, for the death of Pertinax, for the death of Henry the Third of France, and many more. But in private revenges it is not so; nay, rather, vindictive persons live the life of witches, who, as they are mischievous, so end they unfortunate.

As both of these readings show, an essay may start in one place and end up somewhere altogether different. For example, by the end of his essay Montaigne seems to have acknowledged that the horrifying image of "formless masses and lumps of flesh" in the first sentence may be one of the "many chimeras and fantastic monsters" that he needs to purge from his imagination through writing. This essay also helps explain what an essay is, as

Montaigne understood it, and he thus uses it as a prefatory essay for those that follow. Essays as they were first written did not have the formality and even the predictability that have come to be associated with them. (Many contemporary writers, such as E. B. White, Joan Didion, and Tom Wolfe, have maintained the unpredictability, informality, and personal qualities of the essay with considerable success.) Montaigne and Bacon wrote for small audiences about personal subjects, even though their works were ultimately published for larger audiences than originally imagined.

Your essays and term papers have a more public and impersonal intent. They are often modeled on forms that are practiced in the disciplines you are studying in college. Yet the necessary formality of some of the finished work you must do for college courses should not prevent you from experimenting, as Bacon and Montaigne did. In fact, such "attempts" or "trials" are excellent practice in writing and thinking skills.

Below is a partial list of topics on which these men wrote essays. Pick one and write an essay in your journal on it. Use freewriting techniques to keep your pen going. In another day or so, come back to this list and pick another for a similar writing.

Topics for Essays

education	marriage	riches
friendship	envy	beauty
health	love	deformity
reputation	solitude	gardens
truth	books	repentance
death	cruelty	coaches
religion	superstition	conversation
adversity	travel	vanity
parents and children	cunning	experience

Roxanne Ervin, a freshman at the University of Missouri at Kansas City, wrote the following pages in response to such an exercise. The first passage (Figure 7) is from an in-class freewriting that she did in less than twenty minutes. She later revised the passage twice prior to typing it. We've included one of those revised drafts (Figure 8) plus her final version (Figure 9).

Friendship. There are many types of friendship. Friendships can develop in the classroom, your neighborhood, and in the family. You don't always have to be friends with your parents or your sisters and brothers. I think these friendships develop later in life when you start to become an indivrdual and less dependent on your parents. I think that is when the transition of parents' role as a person who rears and guides us into a person who we look to as a companion — they become human beings instead of indispensible godlike figures in our minds. I do not believe friendships can hold the same power in caring and sharing. I am not saying all friendships will come to an end, but they do have a tendency to be stronger in different periods of our lives. I had a best friend in high school. We did everything together. We agreed on a lot of things, but more importantly than that we accepted one another for what each individual was. We knew each other so well — you could even say at times we knew what each other was thinking. I guess

Figure 7   Sample Journal Entry

you could say an outside force was the end of our friendship — someone who I could not compete with and would not want to. Barb married who was at the time a wonderful loving man. We all became good friends only to find he did not value our friendship as we did (including Barb and I). Tom took his friendship — including his friendship with his wife Barb — and abused it in the worst way. I don't want to go into the details but Tom paid a high price for his "mistake": all of his friendship.

Figure 7   (Continued)

True friendship is a gift. It reaches beyond a mutual interest; it involves trust, patience, understanding, and ~~an~~ *a* ~~interest~~ ~~involve-ment in~~ *reaching out by* both individuals to develop a relationship. ~~of friendship.~~ Friends share their dreams, secrets, and objectives *and clothes.* They ~~in~~ *have* time for one another. Friends are unselfish about their wants and think of the other person. A friend ~~will~~ *would* stand ~~beside my~~ ~~with~~ *up for* you ~~who~~ when noone else would. A friend would never laugh when everyone else would be laughing at you. A friend would have the Kleenex to wipe away your tears. ~~and give~~ *A friend* is your foundation when you feel you are wandering aimlessly. A friend offers you a smile and a hug and knows when it's needed most. A friend ~~also knows when to be silent~~ *knows how to be understanding,* even if it means their silence. A friend understands your reasons, whether they are right or wrong in societies view. A friend will overlook your faults and accept you ~~as the person~~ *for who* you are. A friend is honest and recognizes the importance of their honesty. *True* ∧ Friendship never gives up but remains forever in your heart and mind.

Figure 8   Sample Revised Draft

True friendship is a gift. It reaches beyond a mutual interest; it involves trust, patience, understanding, and a reaching out by both individuals to develop a friendship.

Friends share their dreams, secrets, and objectives. They have time for one another. Friends are unselfish about their wants and think of the other person first. They stand up for one another when no one else will. Friends never laugh when everyone else is laughing at you. A friend would have the Kleenex to wipe away your tears. Friendship offers the foundation when you feel you are wandering aimlessly. A friend offers you a smile and a hug when it's needed most and knows how to be understanding—even if it means their silence. A friend understands your reasons even when society objects. This is the hardest at times to do because you may not always agree with your friend's reasoning.

Friendship is based on honesty and recognizes the significance of it in a relationship. True friendship never gives up, but remains forever deep in our hearts and souls.

Figure 9   Sample Final Version

2 Understanding Occasion: Reading and Responding

Bacon's and Montaigne's essays—and those you may have written in your journal—are personal in the sense that there is no immediate public need or occasion for them. They are written to fulfill individual curiosity, not for any other specific occasion. Many types of essays are written to fulfill external requirements. Political speeches, for example, are prepared for rallies or debates; book reviews in magazines and newspapers are written on the occasion of a book's publication; opinion and editorial essays respond to particular, often urgent, social or political issues. Academic writing, too, falls into the category of writing that has an occasion. A scientist makes a discovery in a laboratory and writes a journal article to publicize these findings; an educator develops an effective method for teaching a foreign language and writes a book about it; a literary scholar discovers a theme or motif in *Hamlet* that others had not previously seen and writes an essay to present at a professional conference. In many ways, the occasions for essay writing that you do in your studies are similar to such occasions for professional writing.

The essay by Virginia Woolf, "How Should One Read a Book?" was first prepared as a lecture that she gave at a girls' school on January 30, 1926. It was later revised for inclusion in a collection of essays, *The Common Reader: Second Series* (1932). As you read it consider, first, how the essay would affect you if you were a member of the audience when she read her lecture, and second, what qualities the essay has that make it worth reading and responding to even after more than sixty years have passed.

VIRGINIA WOOLF (1882–1941)

How Should One Read a Book?

In the first place, I want to emphasise the note of interrogation at the end of my title. Even if I could answer the question for myself, the answer would apply only to me and not to you. The only advice, indeed, that one person can give another about reading is to take no advice, to follow your own instincts, to use your own reason, to come to your own conclusions. If this is agreed between us, then I feel at liberty to put forward a few ideas and suggestions because you will not allow them to fetter that independence which is the most important quality that a reader can possess. After all, what laws can be laid down about books? The battle of Waterloo[1] was certainly fought on a certain day; but is *Hamlet* a better play than *Lear*? Nobody can say. Each must decide that question for himself. To admit authorities, however heavily furred and gowned, into our libraries and let them tell us how to read, what to read, what value to place upon what we read, is to destroy the spirit of freedom which is the breath of those sanctuaries. Everywhere else we may be bound by laws and conventions—there we have none.

But to enjoy freedom, if the platitude is pardonable, we have of course to control ourselves. We must not squander our powers, helplessly and ignorantly, squirting half the house in order to water a single rose-bush; we must train them, exactly and powerfully, here on the very spot. This, it may be, is one of the first difficulties that faces us in a library. What is "the very spot"? There may well seem to be nothing but a conglomeration and huddle of confusion. Poems and novels, histories and memoirs, dictionaries and blue-books, books written in all languages by men and women of all tempers, races, and ages jostle each other on the shelf. And outside the donkey brays, the women gossip at the pump, the colts gallop across the fields. Where are we to begin? How are we to bring order into this multitudinous chaos and so get the deepest and widest pleasure from what we read?

It is simple enough to say that since books have classes—fiction, biography, poetry—we should separate them and take from each what it is right that each should give us. Yet few people ask from books what books can give us. Most commonly we come to books with blurred and divided minds, asking of fiction that it shall be true, of poetry that it shall be false, of biography that it shall be flattering, of history that it shall enforce our own prejudices. If we could banish all such preconceptions when we read, that would be an admirable beginning. Do not dictate to your author; try to become him. Be his fellow-worker and accomplice. If you hang back, and reserve and criticise at first, you are preventing yourself from getting the fullest possible value from what you read. But if you open your mind as

---

[1] The town in Belgium where Napolean Bonaparte suffered his final defeat in 1815.

widely as possible, then signs and hints of almost imperceptible fineness, from the twist and turn of the first sentences, will bring you into the presence of a human being unlike any other. Steep yourself in this, acquaint yourself with this, and soon you will find that your author is giving you, or attempting to give you, something far more definite. The thirty-two chapters of a novel—if we consider how to read a novel first—are an attempt to make something as formed and controlled as a building: but words are more impalpable than bricks; reading is a longer and more complicated process than seeing. Perhaps the quickest way to understand the elements of what a novelist is doing is not to read, but to write; to make your own experiment with the dangers and difficulties of words. Recall, then, some event that has left a distinct impression on you—how at the corner of the street, perhaps, you passed two people talking. A tree shook; an electric light danced; the tone of the talk was comic, but also tragic; a whole vision, an entire conception, seemed contained in that moment.

But when you attempt to reconstruct it in words, you will find that it breaks into a thousand conflicting impressions. Some must be subdued; others emphasised; in the process you will lose, probably, all grasp upon the emotion itself. Then turn from your blurred and littered pages to the opening pages of some great novelist—Defoe, Jane Austen, Hardy.[2] Now you will be better able to appreciate their mastery. It is not merely that we are in the presence of a different person—Defoe, Jane Austen, or Thomas Hardy—but that we are living in a different world. Here, in *Robinson Crusoe*, we are trudging a plain highroad; one thing happens after another; the fact and the order of the fact is enough. But if the open air and adventure mean everything to Defoe they mean nothing to Jane Austen. Hers is the drawing-room, and people talking, and by the many mirrors of their talk revealing their characters. And if, when we have accustomed ourselves to the drawing-room and its reflections, we turn to Hardy, we are once more spun round. The moors are round us and the stars are above our heads. The other side of the mind is now exposed—the dark side that comes uppermost in solitude, not the light side that shows in company. Our relations are not towards people, but towards Nature and destiny. Yet different as these worlds are, each is consistent with itself. The maker of each is careful to observe the laws of his own perspective, and however great a strain they may put upon us they will never confuse us, as lesser writers so frequently do, by introducing two different kinds of reality into the same book. Thus to go from one great novelist to another—from Jane Austen to Hardy, from Peacock to Trollope, from Scott to Meredith[3]—is to be wrenched and up-

---

[2] Daniel Defoe (1660?–1731), author of *Robinson Crusoe* (1719); Jane Austen (1775–1817), author of *Emma* (1816); Thomas Hardy, (1840–1928), author of *Return of the Native* (1878).

[3] Thomas Love Peacock (1785–1866), English poet and novelist; Anthony Trollope (1815–82), English novelist and travel writer; Sir Walter Scott (1771–1832), Scottish novelist and poet; George Meredith (1828–1909), English poet and novelist, known as a member of the pre-Raphaelites.

rooted; to be thrown this way and then that. To read a novel is a difficult and complex art. You must be capable not only of great fineness of perception, but of great boldness of imagination if you are going to make use of all that the novelist—the great artist—gives you.

But a glance at the heterogeneous company on the shelf will show you that writers are very seldom "great artists"; far more often a book makes no claim to be a work of art at all. These biographies and autobiographies, for example, lives of great men, of men long dead and forgotten, that stand cheek by jowl with the novels and poems, are we to refuse to read them because they are not "art"? Or shall we read them, but read them in a different way, with a different aim? Shall we read them in the first place to satisfy that curiosity which possesses us sometimes when in the evening we linger in front of a house where the lights are lit and the blinds not yet drawn, and each floor of the house shows us a different section of human life in being? Then we are consumed with curiosity about the lives of these people—the servants gossiping, the gentlemen dining, the girl dressing for a party, the old woman at the window with her knitting. Who are they, what are they, what are their names, their occupations, their thoughts, and adventures?

Biographies and memoirs answer such questions, light up innumerable such houses; they show us people going about their daily affairs, toiling, failing, succeeding, eating, hating, loving, until they die. And sometimes as we watch, the house fades and the iron railings vanish and we are out at sea; we are hunting, sailing, fighting; we are among savages and soldiers; we are taking part in great campaigns. Or if we like to stay here in England, in London, still the scene changes; the street narrows; the house becomes small, cramped, diamond-paned, and malodorous. We see a poet, Donne,[4] driven from such a house because the walls were so thin that when the children cried their voices cut through them. We can follow him, through the paths that lie in the pages of books, to Twickenham; to Lady Bedford's[5] Park, a famous meeting-ground for nobles and poets; and then turn our steps to Wilton, the great house under the downs, and hear Sidney[6] read the *Arcadia* to his sister; and ramble among the very marshes and see the very herons that figure in that famous romance; and then again travel north with that other Lady Pembroke, Anne Clifford,[7] to her wild moors, or plunge into the city and control our merriment at the sight of Gabriel Harvey[8] in his black velvet suit arguing about poetry with Spenser. Nothing is more fascinating than to grope and stumble in the alternate darkness and splendour of Elizabethan London. But there is no staying there. The Temples and the

---

[4] John Donne (1571 or -72–1631), English poet.
[5] Lady Lucy Bedford, patroness of John Donne.
[6] Sir Philip Sidney (1554–86), English poet.
[7] Lady Anne Clifford (1590–1676), diarist.
[8] Gabriel Harvey (1545?–1630), English satirist and poet, best remembered for condemning Spenser's *The Faerie Queene*.

Swifts, the Harleys and the St. Johns beckon us on; hour upon hour can be spent disentangling their quarrels and deciphering their characters; and when we tire of them we can stroll on, past a lady in black wearing diamonds, to Samuel Johnson and Goldsmith and Garrick: or cross the channel, if we like, and meet Voltaire and Diderot, Madame du Deffand; and so back to England and Twickenham—how certain places repeat themselves and certain names!—where Lady Bedford had her Park once and Pope lived later, to Walpole's[9] home at Strawberry Hill. But Walpole introduces us to such a swarm of new acquaintances, there are so many houses to visit and bells to ring that we may well hesitate for a moment, on the Miss Berrys'[10] doorstep, for example, when behold, up comes Thackeray; he is the friend of the woman whom Walpole loved; so that merely by going from friend to friend, from garden to garden, from house to house, we have passed from one end of English literature to another and wake to find ourselves here again in the present, if we can so differentiate this moment from all that have gone before. This, then, is one of the ways in which we can read these lives and letters; we can make them light up the many windows of the past; we can watch the famous dead in their familiar habits and fancy sometimes that we are very close and can surprise their secrets, and sometimes we may pull out a play or a poem that they have written and see whether it reads differently in the presence of the author. But this again rouses other questions. How far, we must ask ourselves, is a book influenced by its writer's life—how far is it safe to let the man interpret the writer? How far shall we resist or give way to the sympathies and antipathies that the man himself rouses in us—so sensitive are words, so receptive of the character of the author? These are questions that press upon us when we read lives and letters, and we must answer them for ourselves, for nothing can be more fatal than to be guided by the preferences of others in a matter so personal.

But also we can read such books with another aim, not to throw light on literature, not to become familiar with famous people, but to refresh and exercise our own creative powers. Is there not an open window on the right hand of the bookcase? How delightful to stop reading and look out! How

---

[9] Sir William Temple (1628–99), political essayist; Jonathan Swift (1667–1745), author of *Gulliver's Travels* and many political writings; Lady Brilliana Harley (1600?–43), author of a volume of letters; Henry St. John Bolingbroke (1678–1751), writer of political and philosophical tracts; Samuel Johnson (1709–84), literary critic and lexicographer, immortalized in Boswell's *Life of Johnson*; Oliver Goldsmith (1730?–74), playwright; David Garrick (1717–79), actor and playwright; Voltaire is the pseudonym for François Marie Arouet (1694–1778), French philosopher and author of *Candide* (1759); Denis Diderot (1713–84), French philosopher, dramatist, critic; Madame du Deffand, Marie de Vichy-Chamrond (1697–1789), hosted a famous literary *salon* attended by Montesquieu; Alexander Pope (1688–1744), English poet, known for his translations of Homer and his great mock epics, including *The Rape of the Lock* (1714) and *The Dunciad* (1728–43); Horace Walpole (1717–97), fourth earl of Oxford, author of *The Castle of Otranto* (1764).

[10] The Misses Berry, characters in the novel *Judith Paris* (pub. 1931), by Sir Hugh (Seymour) Walpole (1884–1941).

stimulating the scene is, in its unconsciousness, its irrelevance, its perpetual movement—the colts galloping round the field, the woman filling her pail at the well, the donkey throwing back his head and emitting his long, acrid moan. The greater part of any library is nothing but the record of such fleeting moments in the lives of men, women, and donkeys. Every literature, as it grows old, has its rubbish-heap, its record of vanished moments and forgotten lives told in faltering and feeble accents that have perished. But if you give yourself up to the delight of rubbish-reading you will be surprised, indeed you will be overcome, by the relics of human life that have been cast out to moulder. It may be one letter—but what a vision it gives! It may be a few sentences—but what vistas they suggest! Sometimes a whole story will come together with such beautiful humour and pathos and completeness that it seems as if a great novelist had been at work, yet it is only an old actor, Tate Wilkinson,[11] remembering the strange story of Captain Jones; it is only a young subaltern serving under Arthur Wellesley[12] and falling in love with a pretty girl at Lisbon; it is only Maria Allen[13] letting fall her sewing in the empty drawing-room and sighing how she wishes she had taken Dr. Burney's good advice and had never eloped with her Rishy. None of this has any value; it is negligible in the extreme; yet how absorbing it is now and again to go through the rubbish-heaps and find rings and scissors and broken noses buried in the huge past and try to piece them together while the colt gallops round the field, the woman fills her pail at the well, and the donkey brays.

But we tire of rubbish-reading in the long run. We tire of searching for what is needed to complete the half-truth which is all that the Wilkinsons, the Bunburys,[14] and the Maria Allens are able to offer us. They had not the artist's power of mastering and eliminating; they could not tell the whole truth even about their own lives; they have disfigured the story that might have been so shapely. Facts are all that they can offer us, and facts are a very inferior form of fiction. Thus the desire grows upon us to have done with half-statements and approximations; to cease from searching out the minute shades of human character, to enjoy the greater abstractness, the purer truth of fiction. Thus we create the mood, intense and generalised, unaware of detail, but stressed by some regular, recurrent beat, whose natural expression is poetry; and that is the time to read poetry when we are almost able to write it.

> Western wind, when wilt thou blow?
> The small rain down can rain.
>
> Christ, if my love were in my arms,
> And I in my bed again![15]

---

[11] Tate Wilkinson (1739–1803), English actor and author of *Memoirs of His Own Life* (1790).

[12] Arthur Wellesley (Wellington), author of *Letters of the Duke of Wellington to Miss J. [sic], 1834–1851 . . . with Extracts from the Diary of the Latter* (1924).

[13] Maria Allen, step-sister of Frances Burney.

[14] *Memoir and Literary Remains of Lt.-Gen. Sir Henry Edward Bunbury (1778–1860)* (1868) and *Life, Letters and Journals of Sir Charles J. F. Bunbury, Bart* (1894).

[15] Anonymous 16th-century lyric, see p. 471.

The impact of poetry is so hard and direct that for the moment there is no other sensation except that of the poem itself. What profound depths we visit then—how sudden and complete is our immersion! There is nothing here to catch hold of; nothing to stay us in our flight. The illusion of fiction is gradual; its effects are prepared; but who when they read these four lines stops to ask who wrote them, or conjures up the thought of Donne's house or Sidney's secretary; or enmeshes them in the intricacy of the past and the succession of generations? The poet is always our contemporary. Our being for the moment is centered and constricted, as in any violent shock of personal emotion. Afterwards, it is true, the sensation begins to spread in wider rings through our minds; remoter senses are reached; these begin to sound and to comment and we are aware of echoes and reflections. The intensity of poetry covers an immense range of emotion. We have only to compare the force and directness of

> I shall fall like a tree, and find my grave,
> Only remembering that I grieve,[16]

with the wavering modulation of

> Minutes are numbered by the fall of sands,
> As by an hour glass; the span of time
> Doth waste us to our graves, and we look on it;
> An age of pleasure, revelled out, comes home
> At last, and ends in sorrow; but the life,
> Weary of riot, numbers every sand,
> Wailing in sighs, until the last drop down,
> So to conclude calamity in rest,[17]

or place the meditative calm of

> whether we be young or old,
> Our destiny, our being's heart and home,
> Is with infinitude, and only there;
> With hope it is, hope that can never die,
> Effort, and expectation, and desire,
> And something evermore about to be,[18]

beside the complete and inexhaustible loveliness of

> The moving Moon went up the sky,
> And no where did abide:
> Softly she was going up,
> And a star or two beside—[19]

---

[16] Francis Beaumont (1584–1616) and John Fletcher (1579–1625), *The Maid's Tragedy* (1619), IV, i, 214–15.
[17] John Ford (1586?–1639?), *The Lover's Melancholy* (1629), IV, iii, 57–64.
[18] William Wordsworth (1770–1850), *The Prelude*, VI, 603–8.
[19] Samuel Taylor Coleridge (1772–1834), "The Rime of the Ancient Mariner," part IV.

or the splendid fantasy of

> And the woodland haunter
> Shall not cease to saunter
>   When, far down some glade,
> Of the great world's burning,
> One soft flame upturning
> Seems, to his discerning,
>   Crocus in the shade.[20]

to bethink us of the varied art of the poet; his power to make us at once actors and spectators; his power to run his hand into character as if it were a glove, and be Falstaff or Lear; his power to condense, to widen, to state, once and for ever.

"We have only to compare"—with those words the cat is out of the bag, and the true complexity of reading is admitted. The first process, to receive impressions with the utmost understanding, is only half the process of reading; it must be completed, if we are to get the whole pleasure from a book, by another. We must pass judgment upon these multitudinous impressions; we must make of these fleeting shapes one that is hard and lasting. But not directly. Wait for the dust of reading to settle; for the conflict and the questioning to die down; walk, talk, pull the dead petals from a rose, or fall asleep. Then suddenly without our willing it, for it is thus that Nature undertakes these transitions, the book will return, but differently. It will float to the top of the mind as a whole. And the book as a whole is different from the book received currently in separate phrases. Details now fit themselves into their places. We see the shape from start to finish; it is a barn, a pig-sty, or a cathedral. Now then we can compare book with book as we compare building with building. But this act of comparison means that our attitude has changed; we are no longer the friends of the writer, but his judges; and just as we cannot be too sympathetic as friends, so as judges we cannot be too severe. Are they not criminals, books that have wasted our time and sympathy; are they not the most insidious enemies of society, corrupters, defilers, the writers of false books, faked books, books that fill the air with decay and disease? Let us then be severe in our judgments; let us compare each book with the greatest of its kind. There they hang in the mind the shapes of the books we have read solidified by the judgments we have passed on them—*Robinson Crusoe, Emma, The Return of the Native.* Compare the novels with these—even the latest and least of novels has a right to be judged with the best. And so with poetry—when the intoxication of rhythm has died down and the splendour of words has faded a visionary shape will return to us and this must be compared with *Lear*, with *Phèdre*,[21] with *The Prelude*; or if not with these, with whatever is the best or seems to us

---

[20] Ebenezer Jones (1820–60), "When the World is Burning" (1860), II, 21–27.
[21] Jean Racine (1639–99), *Phèdre* (1677).

to be the best in its own kind. And we may be sure that the newness of new poetry and fiction is its most superficial quality and that we have only to alter slightly, not to recast, the standards by which we have judged the old.

It would be foolish, then, to pretend that the second part of reading, to judge, to compare, is as simple as the first—to open the mind wide to the fast flocking of innumerable impressions. To continue reading without the book before you, to hold one shadow-shape against another, to have read widely enough and with enough understanding to make such comparisons alive and illuminating—that is difficult; it is still more difficult to press further and to say, "Not only is the book of this sort, but it is of this value; here it fails; here it succeeds; this is bad; that is good." To carry out this part of a reader's duty needs such imagination, insight, and learning that it is hard to conceive any one mind sufficiently endowed; impossible for the most self-confident to find more than the seeds of such powers in himself. Would it not be wiser, then, to remit this part of reading and to allow the critics, the gowned and furred authorities of the library, to decide the question of the book's absolute value for us? Yet how impossible! We may stress the value of sympathy; we may try to sink our own identity as we read. But we know that we cannot sympathise wholly or immerse ourselves wholly; there is always a demon in us who whispers, "I hate, I love," and we cannot silence him. Indeed, it is precisely because we hate and we love that our relation with the poets and novelists is so intimate that we find the presence of another person intolerable. And even if the results are abhorrent and our judgments are wrong, still our taste, the nerve of sensation that sends shocks through us, is our chief illuminant; we learn through feeling; we cannot suppress our own idiosyncrasy without impoverishing it. But as time goes on perhaps we can train our taste; perhaps we can make it submit to some control. When it has fed greedily and lavishly upon books of all sorts— poetry, fiction, history, biography—and has stopped reading and looked for long spaces upon the variety, the incongruity of the living world, we shall find that it is changing a little; it is not so greedy, it is more reflective. It will begin to bring us not merely judgments on particular books, but it will tell us that there is a quality common to certain books. Listen, it will say, what shall we call *this*? And it will read us perhaps *Lear* and then perhaps the *Agamemnon*[22] in order to bring out that common quality. Thus, with our taste to guide us, we shall venture beyond the particular book in search of qualities that group books together; we shall give them names and thus frame a rule that brings order into our perceptions. We shall gain a further and a rarer pleasure from that discrimination. But as a rule only lives when it is perpetually broken by contact with the books themselves—nothing is easier and more stultifying than to make rules which exist out of touch with facts, in a vacuum—now at last, in order to steady ourselves in this difficult attempt, it

---

[22] Aeschylus (525–456 B.C.), *Agamemnon.*

may be well to turn to the very rare writers who are able to enlighten us upon literature as an art. Coleridge and Dryden[23] and Johnson, in their considered criticism, the poets and novelists themselves in their unconsidered sayings, are often surprisingly relevant; they light up and solidify the vague ideas that have been tumbling in the misty depths of our minds. But they are only able to help us if we come to them laden with questions and suggestions won honestly in the course of our own reading. They can do nothing for us if we herd ourselves under their authority and lie down like sheep in the shade of a hedge. We can only understand their ruling when it comes in conflict with our own and vanquishes it.

If this is so, if to read a book as it should be read calls for the rarest qualities of imagination, insight, and judgment, you may perhaps conclude that literature is a very complex art and that it is unlikely that we shall be able, even after a lifetime of reading, to make any valuable contribution to its criticism. We must remain readers; we shall not put on the further glory that belongs to those rare beings who are also critics. But still we have our responsibilities as readers and even our importance. The standards we raise and the judgments we pass steal into the air and become part of the atmosphere which writers breathe as they work. An influence is created which tells upon them even if it never finds its way into print. And that influence, if it were well instructed, vigorous and individual and sincere, might be of great value now when criticism is necessarily in abeyance; when books pass in review like the procession of animals in a shooting-gallery, and the critic has only one second in which to load and aim and shoot and may well be pardoned if he mistakes rabbits for tigers, eagles for barndoor fowls, or misses altogether and wastes his shot upon some peaceful cow grazing in a further field. If behind the erratic gunfire of the press the author felt that there was another kind of criticism, the opinion of people reading for the love of reading, slowly and unprofessionally, and judging with great sympathy and yet with great severity, might this not improve the quality of his work? And if by our means books were to become stronger, richer, and more varied, that would be an end worth reaching.

Yet who reads to bring about an end however desirable? Are there not some pursuits that we practise because they are good in themselves, and some pleasures that are final? And is not this among them? I have sometimes dreamt, at least, that when the Day of Judgment dawns and the great conquerors and lawyers and statesmen come to receive their rewards—their crowns, their laurels, their names carved indelibly upon imperishable marble—the Almighty will turn to Peter and will say, not without a certain envy when He sees us coming with our books under our arms, "Look, these need no reward. We have nothing to give them here. They have loved reading."

---

[23] John Dryden (1631–1700), English poet, critic, and dramatist.

QUESTIONS FOR THINKING AND WRITING

1. Virginia Woolf's writing is often quotable. Find three or four sentences or passages that are striking and copy them into your reading journal. Now select one of them and write a brief analysis of why the sentence or passage is memorable.

2. Woolf writes of "rubbish reading." List some contemporary examples of such reading and write a few paragraphs on why you selected these examples. (Note: To expand on this writing suggestion, you may wish to include examples from movies, television, and music.)

3. Woolf seems to feel that responding to reading is part of the process of reading. It even completes the act of reading. How does her essay exemplify this idea? Do a freewriting in which you respond to her essay.

4. In an essay of five to seven pages, analyze Woolf's essay for the characteristics that suggest its occasion. Consider how language, ideas, and examples reveal that the author had a particular audience and occasion in mind when she wrote the essay. You may wish to consider, too, how the essay would need to be updated or changed if it were written for a contemporary audience, such as you and your fellow students.

Like Woolf's essay, Ralph Waldo Emerson's "The American Scholar" was composed for an audience of students and teachers. Emerson delivered a longer version of this essay as the annual Phi Beta Kappa address at Harvard College on August 31, 1837, the beginning of the academic year.

RALPH WALDO EMERSON (1803–1882)

The American Scholar

Mr. President and Gentlemen:

I greet you on the recommencement of our literary year. Our anniversary is one of hope, and, perhaps, not enough of labor. We do not meet for games of strength or skill, for the recitation of histories, tragedies, and odes, like the ancient Greeks; for parliaments of love and poesy, like the Troubadours; nor for the advancement of science, like our contemporaries in the British and European capitals. Thus far, our holiday has been simply a friendly sign of the survival of the love of letters amongst a people too busy to give to letters any more. As such it is precious as the sign of an indestructible instinct. Perhaps the time is already come when it ought to be, and will be, something else; when the sluggard intellect of this continent will look from under its iron lids and fill the postponed expectation of the world with something better than the exertions of mechanical skill. Our day of dependence, our long apprenticeship to the learning of other lands, draws to a close. The millions that around us are rushing into life, cannot always be fed on the sere remains of foreign harvests. Events, actions arise, that must be sung, that will sing themselves. Who can doubt that poetry will revive and lead in a new age, as the star in the constellation Harp, which now flames in our zenith, astronomers announce, shall one day be the polestar for a thousand years?

In this hope I accept the topic which not only usage but the nature of our association seem to prescribe to this day,—the American Scholar. Year by year we come up hither to read one more chapter of his biography. Let us inquire what light new days and events have thrown on this character and his hopes.

It is one of those fables which out of an unknown antiquity convey an unlooked-for wisdom, that the gods, in the beginning, divided Man into men, that he might be more helpful to himself; just as the hand was divided into fingers, the better to answer its end.

The old fable covers a doctrine ever new and sublime; that there is One Man,—present to all particular men only partially, or through one faculty; and that you must take the whole society to find the whole man. Man is not a farmer, or a professor, or an engineer, but he is all. Man is priest, and scholar, and statesman, and producer, and soldier. In the *divided* or social state these functions are parcelled out to individuals, each of whom aims to do his stint of the joint work, whilst each other performs his. The fable implies that the individual, to possess himself, must sometimes return from his own labor to embrace all the other laborers. But, unfortunately, this original unit, this fountain of power, has been so distributed to multitudes, has been so minutely subdivided and peddled out, that it is spilled into drops, and cannot be gathered. The state of society is one in which the members have suffered amputation from the trunk, and strut about so many walking monsters,—a good finger, a neck, a stomach, an elbow, but never a man.

Man is thus metamorphosed into a thing, into many things. The planter, who is Man sent out into the field to gather food, is seldom cheered by any idea of the true dignity of his ministry. He sees his bushel and his cart, and nothing beyond, and sinks into the farmer, instead of Man on the farm. The tradesman scarcely ever gives an ideal worth to his work, but is ridden by the routine of his craft, and the soul is subject to dollars. The priest becomes a form; the attorney a statute-book; the mechanic a machine; the sailor a rope of the ship.

In this distribution of functions the scholar is the delegated intellect. In the right state he is *Man Thinking.* In the degenerate state, when the victim of society, he tends to become a mere thinker, or still worse, the parrot of other men's thinking.

In this view of him, as Man Thinking, the theory of his office is contained. Him Nature solicits with all her placid, all her monitory pictures; him the past instructs; him the future invites. Is not indeed every man a student, and do not all things exist for the student's behoof? And, finally, is not the true scholar the only true master? But the old oracle said, "All things have two handles: beware of the wrong one." In life, too often, the scholar errs with mankind and forfeits his privilege. Let us see him in his school, and consider him in reference to the main influences he receives.

I. The first in time and the first in importance of the influences upon the mind is that of nature. Every day, the sun; and, after sunset, Night and her stars. Ever the winds blow; ever the grass grows. Every day, men and women, conversing—beholding and beholden. The scholar is he of all men whom this spectacle most engages. He must settle its value in his mind. What is nature to him? There is never a beginning, there is never an end, to the inexplicable continuity of this web of God, but always circular power return-ing into itself. Therein it resembles his own spirit, whose beginning, whose ending, he never can find,—so entire, so boundless. Far too as her splendors shine, system on system shooting like rays, upward, downward, without center, without circumference,—in the mass and in the particle, Nature hastens to render account of herself to the mind. Classification begins. To the young mind every thing is individual, stands by itself. By and by, it finds how to join two things and see in them one nature; then three; then three thousand; and so, tyrannized over by its own unifying instinct, it goes on tying things together, diminishing anomalies, discovering roots running under ground whereby contrary and remote things cohere and flower out from one stem. It presently learns that since the dawn of history there has been a constant accumulation and classifying of facts. But what is classifica-tion but the perceiving that these objects are not chaotic, and are not foreign, but have a law which is also a law of the human mind? The astronomer discovers that geometry, a pure abstraction of the human mind, is the measure of planetary motion. The chemist finds proportions and intelligible method throughout matter; and science is nothing but the finding of analogy, identity, in the most remote parts. The ambitious soul sits down before each refractory fact; one after another reduces all strange constitutions, all new powers, to their class and their law, and goes on forever to animate the last fiber of organization, the outskirts of nature, by insight.

Thus to him, to this schoolboy under the bending dome of day, is suggested that he and it proceed from one root; one is leaf and one is flower; relation, sympathy, stirring in every vein. And what is that root? Is not that the soul of his soul? A thought too bold; a dream too wild. Yet when this spiritual light shall have revealed the law of more earthly natures,—when he has learned to worship the soul, and to see that the natural philosophy that now is, is only the first gropings of its gigantic hand, he shall look forward to an ever expanding knowledge as to a becoming creator. He shall see that nature is the opposite of the soul, answering to it part for part. One is seal and one is print. Its beauty is the beauty of his own mind. Its laws are the laws of his own mind. Nature then becomes to him the measure of his attainments. So much of nature as he is ignorant of, so much of his own mind does he not yet possess. And, in fine, the ancient precept, "Know thyself," and the modern precept, "Study nature," become at last one maxim.

II. The next great influence into the spirit of the scholar is the mind of the Past,—in whatever form, whether of literature, of art, of institutions, that mind is inscribed. Books are the best type of the influence of the past, and perhaps we shall get at the truth,—learn the amount of this influence more conveniently,—by considering their value alone.

The theory of books is noble. The scholar of the first age received into him the world around; brooded thereon; gave it the new arrangement of his own mind, and uttered it again. It came into him life; it went out from him truth. It came to him short-lived actions; it went out from him immortal thoughts. It came to him business; it went from him poetry. It was dead fact; now, it is quick[1] thought. It can stand, and it can go. It now endures, it now flies, it now inspires. Precisely in proportion to the depth of mind from which it issued, so high does it soar, so long does it sing.

Or, I might say, it depends on how far the process had gone, of transmuting life into truth. In proportion to the completeness of the distillation, so will the purity and imperishableness of the product be. But none is quite perfect. As no air-pump can by any means make a perfect vacuum, so neither can any artist entirely exclude the conventional, the local, the perishable from his book, or write a book of pure thought, that shall be as efficient, in all respects, to a remote posterity, as to contemporaries, or rather to the

---

[1] living

second age. Each age, it is found, must write its own books; or rather, each generation for the next succeeding. The books of an older period will not fit this.

Yet hence arises a grave mischief. The sacredness which attaches to the act of creation, the act of thought, is transferred to the record. The poet chanting was felt to be a divine man: henceforth the chant is divine also. The writer was a just and wise spirit: henceforward it is settled the book is perfect; as love of the hero corrupts into worship of his statue. Instantly the book becomes noxious: the guide is a tyrant. The sluggish and perverted mind of the multitude, slow to open to the incursions of Reason, having once so opened, having once received this book, stands upon it, and makes an outcry if it is disparaged. Colleges are built on it. Books are written on it by thinkers, not by Man Thinking; by men of talent, that is, who start wrong, who set out from accepted dogmas, not from their own sight of principles. Meek young men grow up in libraries, believing it their duty to accept the views which Cicero, which Locke, which Bacon, have given; forgetful that Cicero, Locke, and Bacon were only young men in libraries when they wrote these books.

Hence, instead of Man Thinking, we have the bookworm. Hence the book-learned class, who value books, as such; not as related to nature and the human constitution, but as making a sort of Third Estate[2] with the world and the soul. Hence the restorers of readings, the emendators, the bibliomaniacs of all degrees.

Books are the best of things, well used; abused, among the worst. What is the right use? What is the one end which all means go to effect? They are for nothing but to inspire. I had better never see a book than to be warped by its attraction clean out of my own orbit, and made a satellite instead of a system. The one thing in the world, of value, is the active soul. This every man is entitled to; this every man contains within him, although in almost all men obstructed and as yet unborn. The soul active sees absolute truth and utters truth, or creates. In this action it is genius; not the privilege of here and there a favorite, but the sound estate of every man. In its essence it is progressive. The book, the college, the school of art, the institution of any kind, stop with some past utterance of genius. This is good, say they,—let us hold by this. They pin me down. They look backward and not forward. But genius looks forward: the eyes of man are set in his forehead, not in his hindhead: man hopes: genius creates. Whatever talents may be, if the man create not, the pure efflux of the Deity is not his;—cinders and smoke there may be, but not yet flame. There are creative manners, there are creative actions, and creative words; manners, actions, words, that is, indicative of no custom or authority, but springing spontaneous from the mind's own sense of good and fair. . . .

---

[2] one of three divisions in the medieval parliament, including the nobility, the clergy, and the commons

Of course there is a portion of reading quite indispensable to a wise man. History and exact science he must learn by laborious reading. Colleges, in like manner, have their indispensable office,—to teach elements. But they can only highly serve us when they aim not to drill, but to create; when they gather from far every ray of various genius to their hospitable halls, and by the concentrated fires, set the hearts of their youth on flame. Thought and knowledge are natures in which apparatus and pretension avail nothing. Gowns and pecuniary foundations, though of towns of gold, can never countervail the least sentence or syllable of wit. Forget this, and our American colleges will recede in their public importance, whilst they grow richer every year.

III. There goes in the world a notion that the scholar should be a recluse, a valetudinarian,—as unfit for any handiwork or public labor as a penknife for an axe. The so-called "practical men" sneer at speculative men, as if, because they speculate or *see*, they could do nothing. I have heard it said that the clergy,—who are always, more universally than any other class, the scholars of their day,—are addressed as women; that the rough, spontaneous conversation of men they do not hear, but only a mincing and diluted speech. They are often virtually disfranchised; and indeed there are advocates for their celibacy. As far as this is true of the studious classes, it is not just and wise. Action is with the scholar subordinate, but it is essential. Without it he is not yet man. Without it thought can never ripen into truth. Whilst the world hangs before the eye as a cloud of beauty, we cannot even see its beauty. Inaction is cowardice, but there can be no scholar without the heroic mind. The preamble of thought, the transition through which it passes from the unconscious to the conscious, is action. Only so much do I know, as I have lived. Instantly we know whose words are loaded with life, and whose not.

The world,—this shadow of the soul, or *other me*,—lies wide around. Its attractions are the keys which unlock my thoughts and make me acquainted with myself. I run eagerly into this resounding tumult. I grasp the hands of those next me, and take my place in the ring to suffer and to work, taught by an instinct that so shall the dumb abyss be vocal with speech. I pierce its order; I dissipate its fear; I dispose of it within the circuit of my expanding life. So much only of life as I know by experience, so much of the wilderness have I vanquished and planted, or so far have I extended my being, my dominion. I do not see how any man can afford, for the sake of his nerves and his nap, to spare any action in which he can partake. It is pearls and rubies to his discourse. Drudgery, calamity, exasperation, want, are instructors in eloquence and wisdom. The true scholar grudges every opportunity of action past by, as a loss of power. It is the raw material out of which the intellect molds her splended products. A strange process too, this by which experience is converted into thought, as a mulberry leaf is converted into satin. The manufacture goes forward at all hours.

The actions and events of our childhood and youth are now matters of calmest observation. They lie like fair pictures in the air. Not so with our recent actions,—with the business which we now have in hand. On this we are quite unable to speculate. Our affections as yet circulate through it. We no more feel or know it than we feel the feet, or the hand, or the brain of our body. The new deed is yet a part of life,—remains for a time immersed in our unconscious life. In some contemplative hour it detaches itself from the life like a ripe fruit, to become a thought of the mind. Instantly it is raised, transfigured; the corruptible has put on incorruption. Henceforth it is an object of beauty, however base its origin and neighborhood. Observe too the impossibility of antedating this act. In its grub state, it cannot fly, it cannot shine, it is a dull grub. But suddenly, without observation, the self-same thing unfurls beautiful wings, and is an angel of wisdom. So is there no fact, no event, in our private history, which shall not, sooner or later, lose its adhesive, inert form, and astonish us by soaring from our body into the empyrean.[3] Cradle and infancy, school and playground, the fear of boys, and dogs, and ferules, the love of little maids and berries, and many another fact that once filled the whole sky, are gone already; friend and relative, profession and party, town and country, nation and world, must also soar and sing.

Of course, he who has put forth his total strength in fit actions has the richest return of wisdom. I will not shut myself out of this globe of action, and transplant an oak into a flower-pot, there to hunger and pine; nor trust the revenue of some single faculty, and exhaust one vein of thought, much like those Savoyards,[4] who, getting their livelihood by carving shepherds, shepherdesses, and smoking Dutchmen, for all Europe, went out one day to the mountain to find stock, and discovered that they had whittled up the last of their pine trees. Authors we have, in numbers, who have written out their vein, and who, moved by a commendable prudence, sail for Greece or Palestine, follow the trapper into the prairie, or ramble round Algiers, to replenish their merchantable stock.

If it were only for a vocabulary, the scholar would be covetous of action. Life is our dictionary. Years are well spent in country labors; in town; in the insight into trades and manufactures; in frank intercourse with many men and women; in science; in art; to the one end of mastering in all their facts a language by which to illustrate and embody our perceptions. I learn immediately from any speaker how much he has already lived, through the poverty or the splendor of his speech. Life lies behind us as the quarry from whence we get tiles and copestones for the masonry of today. This is the way to learn grammar. Colleges and books only copy the language which the field and the work-yard made.

But the final value of action, like that of books, and better than books, is that it is a resource. That great principle of Undulation in nature, that shows

---

[3] in the medieval cosmos, the highest part of the heavens, the sphere of light, true paradise
[4] people from Savoy in eastern France

itself in the inspiring and expiring of the breath; in desire and satiety; in the ebb and flow of the sea; in day and night; in heat and cold; and, as yet more deeply ingrained in every atom and every fluid, is known to us under the name of Polarity,—these "fits of easy transmission and reflection," as Newton called them, are the law of nature because they are the law of spirit.

The mind now thinks, now acts, and each fit reproduces the other. When the artist has exhausted his materials, when the fancy no longer paints, when thoughts are no longer apprehended and books are a weariness,—he has always the resource *to live.* Character is higher than intellect. Thinking is the function. Living is the functionary. The stream retreats to its source. A great soul will be strong to live, as well as strong to think. Does he lack organ or medium to impart his truths? He can still fall back on this elemental force of living them. This is a total act. Thinking is a partial act. Let the grandeur of justice shine in his affairs. Let the beauty of affection cheer his lowly roof. Those "far from fame," who dwell and act with him, will feel the force of his constitution in the doings and passages of the day better than it can be measured by any public and designed display. Time shall teach him that the scholar loses no hour which the man lives. Herein he unfolds the sacred germ of his instinct, screened from influence. What is lost in seemliness is gained in strength. Not out of those on whom systems of education have exhausted their culture, comes the helpful giant to destroy the old or to build the new, but out of unhandselled savage nature; out of terrible Druids[5] and Berserkers[6] come at last Alfred and Shakespeare.

I hear therefore with joy whatever is beginning to be said of the dignity and necessity of labor to every citizen. There is virtue yet in the hoe and the spade, for learned as well as for unlearned hands. And labor is everywhere welcome; always we are invited to work; only be this limitation observed, that a man shall not for the sake of wider activity sacrifice any opinion to the popular judgments and modes of action.

I have now spoken of the education of the scholar by nature, by books, and by action. It remains to say somewhat of his duties.

They are such as become Man Thinking. They may all be comprised in self-trust. The office of the scholar is to cheer, to raise, and to guide men by showing them facts amidst appearances. He plies the slow, unhonored, and unpaid task of observation. Flamsteed and Herschel,[7] in their glazed observatories, may catalogue the stars with the praise of all men, and the results being splendid and useful, honor is sure. But he, in his private observatory, cataloguing obscure and nebulous stars of the human mind, which as yet no man has thought of as such,—watching days and months sometimes for a

---

[5] priests of an ancient tribe in England
[6] Berserker was a Scandinavian warrior who fought without armor. Thus Berserkers refers to those who fight wildly and fiercely.
[7] John Flamsteed (1646–1719) and Sir William Herschel (1738–1822), astronomers.

few facts; correcting still his old records;—must relinquish display and immediate fame. In the long period of his preparation he must betray often an ignorance and shiftlessness in popular arts, incurring the disdain of the able who shoulder him aside. Long he must stammer in his speech; often forego the living for the dead. Worse yet, he must accept—how often!—poverty and solitude. For the ease and pleasure of treading the old road, accepting the fashions, the education, the religion of society, he takes the cross of making his own, and, of course, the self-accusation, the faint heart, the frequent uncertainty and loss of time, which are the nettles and tangling vines in the way of the self-relying and self-directed; and the state of virtual hostility in which he seems to stand to society, and especially to educated society. For all this loss and scorn, what offset? He is to find consolation in exercising the highest functions of human nature. He is one who raises himself from private considerations and breathes and lives on public and illustrious thoughts. He is the world's eye. He is the world's heart. He is to resist the vulgar prosperity that retrogrades ever to barbarism, by preserving and communicating heroic sentiments, noble biographies, melodious verse, and the conclusions of history. Whatsoever oracles the human heart, in all emergencies, in all solemn hours, has uttered as its commentary on the world of actions,—these he shall receive and impart. And whatsoever new verdict Reason from her inviolable seat pronounces on the passing men and events of today,—this he shall hear and promulgate.

These being his functions, it becomes him to feel all confidence in himself, and to defer never to the popular cry. He and he only knows the world. The world of any moment is the merest appearance. Some great decorum, some fetish of a government, some ephemeral trade, or war, or man, is cried up by half mankind and cried down by the other half, as if all depended on this particular up or down. The odds are that the whole question is not worth the poorest thought which the scholar has lost in listening to the controversy. Let him not quit his belief that a popgun is a popgun, though the ancient and honorable of the earth affirm it to be the crack of doom. In silence, in steadiness, in severe abstraction, let him hold by himself; add observation to observation, patient of neglect, patient of reproach, and bide his own time,—happy enough if he can satisfy himself alone that this day he has seen something truly. Success treads on every right step. For the instinct is sure, that prompts him to tell his brother what he thinks. He then learns that in going down into the secrets of his own mind he has descended into the secrets of all minds. He learns that he who has mastered any law in his private thoughts, is master to that extent of all men whose language he speaks, and of all into whose language his own can be translated. The poet, in utter solitude remembering his spontaneous thoughts and recording them, is found to have recorded that which men in crowded cities find true for them also. The orator distrusts at first the fitness of his frank confessions, his want of knowledge of the persons he addresses, until he finds that he is the complement of his hearers;—that they drink his words because he fulfils for them their own nature; the deeper he dives into his privatest, secretest presentiment, to his wonder he finds this is the most acceptable, most public, and universally true. The people delight in it; the better part of every man feels, This is my music; this is myself. . . .

But I have dwelt perhaps tediously upon this abstraction of the Scholar. I ought not to delay longer to add what I have to say of nearer reference to the time and to this country.

Historically, there is thought to be a difference in the ideas which predominate over successive epochs, and there are data for marking the genius of the Classic, of the Romantic, and now of the Reflective or Philosophical age. With the views I have intimated of the oneness or the identity of the mind through all individuals, I do not much dwell on these differences. In fact, I believe each individual passes through all three. The boy is a Greek; the youth, romantic; the adult, reflective. I deny not, however, that a revolution in the leading idea may be distinctly enough traced.

Our age is bewailed as the age of Introversion. Must that needs be evil? We, it seems, are critical; we are embarrassed with second thoughts; we cannot enjoy any thing for hankering to know whereof the pleasure consists; we are lined with eyes; we see with our feet; the time is infected with Hamlet's unhappiness,—

"Sicklied o'er with the pale cast of thought."[8]

It is so bad then? Sight is the last thing to be pitied. Would we be blind? Do we fear lest we should outsee nature and God, and drink truth dry? I look upon the discontent of the literary class as a mere announcement of the fact that they find themselves not in the state of mind of their fathers, and regret the coming state as untried; as a boy dreads the water before he has learned that he can swim. If there is any period one would desire to be born in, is it not the age of Revolution; when the old and the new stand side by side and admit of being compared; when the energies of all men are searched by fear and by hope; when the historic glories of the old can be compensated by the rich possibilities of the new era? This time, like all times, is a very good one, if we but know what to do with it.

I read with some joy of the auspicious signs of the coming days, as they glimmer already through poetry and art, through philosophy and science, through church and state.

One of these signs is the fact that the same movement which effected the elevation of what was called the lowest class in the state, assumed in literature a very marked and as benign an aspect. Instead of the sublime and beautiful, the near, the low, the common, was explored and poetized. That which had been negligently trodden under foot by those who were harnessing and provisioning themselves for long journeys into far countries, is

---

[8] William Shakespeare (1564–1616), *Hamlet,* III, i, 10, see p. 721.

suddenly found to be richer than all foreign parts. The literature of the poor, the feelings of the child, the philosophy of the street, the meaning of household life, are the topics of the time. It is a great stride. It is a sign—is it not?—of new vigor when the extremities are made active, when currents of warm life run into the hands and the feet. I ask not for the great, the remote, the romantic; what is doing in Italy or Arabia; what is Greek art, or Provençal minstrelsy; I embrace the common, I explore and sit at the feet of the familiar, the low. Give me insight into today, and you may have the antique and future worlds. What would we really know the meaning of? The meal in the firkin;[9] the milk in the pan; the ballad in the street; the news of the boat; the glance of the eye; the form and the gait of the body;—show me the ultimate reason of these matters; show me the sublime presence of the highest spiritual cause lurking, as always it does lurk, in these suburbs and extremities of nature; let me see every trifle bristling with the polarity that ranges it instantly on an eternal law; and the shop, the plough, and the ledger referred to the like cause by which light undulates and poets sing;— and the world lies no longer a dull miscellany and lumber-room, but has form and order; there is no trifle, there is no puzzle, but one design unites and animates the farthest pinnacle and the lowest trench. . . .

Another sign of our times, also marked by an analogous political movement, is the new importance given to the single person. Every thing that tends to insulate the individual,—to surround him with barriers of natural respect, so that each man shall feel the world is his, and man shall treat with man as a sovereign state with a sovereign state,—tends to true union as well as greatness. "I learned," said the melancholy Pestalozzi,[10] "that no man in God's wide earth is either willing or able to help any other man." Help must come from the bosom alone. The scholar is that man who must take up into himself all the ability of the time, all the contributions of the past, all the hopes of the future. He must be a university of knowledges. If there be one lesson more than another which should pierce his ear, it is, The world is nothing, the man is all; in yourself is the law of all nature, and you know not yet how a globule of sap ascends; in yourself slumbers the whole of Reason; it is for you to know all; it is for you to dare all. Mr. President and Gentlemen, this confidence in the unsearched might of man belongs, by all motives, by all prophecy, by all preparation, to the American Scholar. We have listened too long to the courtly muses of Europe. The spirit of the American freeman is already suspected to be timid, imitative, tame. Public and private avarice make the air we breathe thick and fat. The scholar is decent, indolent, complaisant. See already the tragic consequence. The mind of this country, taught to aim at low objects, eats upon itself. There is no work for any but the decorous and the complaisant. Young men of the fairest prom-

---

[9] a small wooden vessel or bowl
[10] Johann Heinrich Pestalozzi (1746–1827), educator who influenced such contemporaries of Emerson as Bronson Alcott and Elizabeth Peabody.

ise, who begin life upon our shores, inflated by the mountain winds, shined upon by all the stars of God, find the earth below not in unison with these, but are hindered from action by the disgust which the principles on which business is managed inspire, and turn drudges, or die of disgust, some of them suicides. What is the remedy? They did not yet see, and thousands of young men as hopeful now crowding to the barriers for the career do not yet see, that if the single man plant himself indomitably on his instincts, and there abide, the huge world will come round to him. Patience,—patience; with the shades of all the good and great for company; and for solace the perspective of your own infinite life; and for work the study and the communication of principles, the making those instincts prevalent, the conversion of the world. Is it not the chief disgrace in the world, not to be a unit;—not to be reckoned one character;—not to yield that peculiar fruit which each man was created to bear, but to be reckoned in the gross, in the hundred, or the thousand, of the party, the section, to which we belong; and our opinion predicted geographically, as the north, or the south? Not so, brothers and friends—please God, ours shall not be so. We will walk on our own feet; we will work with our own hands; we will speak our own minds. The study of letters shall be no longer a name for pity, for doubt, and for sensual indulgence. The dread of man and the love of man shall be a wall of defence and a wreath of joy around all. A nation of men will for the first time exist, because each believes himself inspired by the Divine Soul which also inspires all men.

QUESTIONS FOR THINKING AND WRITING

1. In your reading journal, write an extended outline of Emerson's "American Scholar" in which you summarize the main idea and each of the major sections of the essay. Your outline is "extended" in the sense that it should include brief paraphrases for each section and may also include quotations from the text.

2. Write a journal entry for one or more of the following concepts discussed by Emerson: nature, action, the past, the duties of the scholar, books. Describe your understanding of what Emerson is saying and then respond to that idea.

3. In an essay of five or more pages, write an "American Scholar" for today. You might pretend that you have been selected to address your freshman class at the outset of the academic year. What would you want to tell your fellow students about the meaning of their educational enterprise? As you develop your ideas, try to weed out clichés that you may have heard in some graduation speeches. Using your own language, try to develop one or more of the concerns that Emerson raises, such as the meaning of the past and the place of the scholar (including poets and artists) in society. Find examples from your own experience to include in your essay.

3

Understanding Purpose: Reading and Responding

Although an essay may leave the reader with a multitude of details and impressions, to be successful it must be more than the sum of its parts. Writers often turn to the essay form because they have a clear purpose for writing: an idea they wish to convey to the reader. The shape the essay then takes—its tone and its various rhetorical techniques—all evolve from the effort to deliver that single idea. The essay may call attention to a problem or issue; it may attempt to influence the reader's thinking about that problem or issue; it may even ask for a response or an action on the part of the reader.

The three essays in this chapter are examples of writing that has a purpose. The first two essays deal with literary issues; the third confronts a social problem of considerable immediacy. In all three instances, the ideas developed by the authors have implications that go beyond their avowed purpose for writing. Mark Twain's "Fenimore Cooper's Literary Offenses" uses humor to address a literary issue that Twain believed to have serious consequences. The morality of realism, as Twain had developed it in *Adventures of Huckleberry Finn* and other works, depended on the ability of an individual to see things for what they were. Cooper's romanticizing of Indians is comparable to the romantic images of the "happy and contented" slaves that the character of Jim belies in *Huckleberry Finn*. T. S. Eliot's "Tradition and the Individual Talent" is a landmark in twentieth-century criticism, an essay to which readers who agree or disagree must in some way respond. Finally, we have included an essay written by Pervez Huda, a sophomore in the undergraduate medical program at the University of Missouri at Kansas City. "A Call for Compassion" exhibits a purpose that is evident in its title. It demonstrates how a writer's purpose can become a reader's occasion. It is also a fine example of how a project for a college composition course can lead to meaningful experiences and writing.

Fenimore Cooper's Literary Offenses

> The Pathfinder *and* The Deerslayer *stand at the head of Cooper's novels as artistic creations. There are others of his works which contain parts as perfect as are to be found in these, and scenes even more thrilling. Not one can be compared with either of them as a finished whole.*
>
> *The defects in both of these tales are comparatively slight. They were pure works of art.*
> Prof. Lounsbury[1]
>
> *The five tales reveal an extraordinary fullness of invention. . . . One of the very greatest characters in fiction, Natty Bumppo. . . .*
> *The craft of the woodsman, the tricks of the trapper, all the delicate art of the forest, were familiar to Cooper from his youth up.*
> Prof. Brander Matthews[2]
>
> *Cooper is the greatest artist in the domain of romantic fiction yet produced by America.*
> Wilkie Collins[3]

It seems to me that it was far from right for the Professor of English Literature in Yale, the Professor of English Literature in Columbia, and Wilkie Collins to deliver opinions on Cooper's literature without having read some of it. It would have been much more decorous to keep silent and let persons talk who have read Cooper.

Cooper's art has some defects. In one place in *Deerslayer,* and in the restricted space of two-thirds of a page, Cooper has scored 114 offenses against literary art out of a possible 115. It breaks the record.

There are nineteen rules governing literary art in the domain of romantic fiction—some say twenty-two. In *Deerslayer* Cooper violated eighteen of them. These eighteen require:

1. That a tale shall accomplish something and arrive somewhere. But the *Deerslayer* tale accomplishes nothing and arrives in the air.
2. They require that the episodes of a tale shall be necessary parts of the tale, and shall help to develop it. But as the *Deerslayer* tale is not a tale, and accomplishes nothing and arrives nowhere, the episodes have no rightful place in the work, since there was nothing for them to develop.

---

[1] Thomas R. Lounsbury (1838–1915), professor of English literature at Yale who wrote *The Life of James Fenimore Cooper* (1882).
[2] Brander Matthews (1852–1929), novelist, critic, playwright, later a professor of literature at Columbia University.
[3] Wilkie Collins (1824–89), English novelist.

3. They require that the personages in a tale shall be alive, except in the case of corpses, and that always the reader shall be able to tell the corpses from the others. But this detail has often been overlooked in the *Deerslayer* tale.

4. They require that the personages in a tale, both dead and alive, shall exhibit a sufficient excuse for being there. But this detail also has been overlooked in the *Deerslayer* tale.

5. They require that when the personages of a tale deal in conversation, the talk shall sound like human talk, and be talk such as human beings would be likely to talk in the given circumstances, and have a discoverable meaning, also a discoverable purpose, and a show of relevancy, and remain in the neighborhood of the subject in hand, and be interesting to the reader, and help out the tale, and stop when the people cannot think of anything more to say. But this requirement has been ignored from the beginning of the *Deerslayer* tale to the end of it.

6. They require that when the author describes the character of a personage in his tale, the conduct and conversation of that personage shall justify said description. But this law gets little or no attention in the *Deerslayer* tale, as Natty Bumppo's case will amply prove.

7. They require that when a personage talks like an illustrated, gilt-edged, tree-calf, hand-tooled, seven-dollar Friendship's Offering in the beginning of a paragraph, he shall not talk like a negro minstrel in the end of it. But this rule is flung down and danced upon in the *Deerslayer* tale.

8. They require that crass stupidities shall not be played upon the reader as "the craft of the woodsman, the delicate art of the forest," by either the author or the people in the tale. But this rule is persistently violated in the *Deerslayer* tale.

9. They require that the personages of a tale shall confine themselves to possibilities and let miracles alone; or, if they venture a miracle, the author must so plausibly set it forth as to make it look possible and reasonable. But these rules are not respected in the *Deerslayer* tale.

10. They require that the author shall make the reader feel a deep interest in the personages of his tale and in their fate; and that he shall make the reader love the good people in the tale and hate the bad ones. But the reader of the *Deerslayer* tale dislikes the good people in it, is indifferent to the others, and wishes they would all get drowned together.

11. They require that the characters in a tale shall be so clearly defined that the reader can tell beforehand what each will do in a given emergency. But in the *Deerslayer* tale this rule is vacated.

In addition to these large rules there are some little ones. These require that the author shall

12. *Say* what he is proposing to say, not merely come near it.

13. Use the right word, not its second cousin.

14. Eschew surplusage.

15. Not omit necessary details.
16. Avoid slovenliness of form.
17. Use good grammar.
18. Employ a simple and straightforward style.

Even these seven are coldly and persistently violated in the *Deerslayer* tale.

Cooper's gift in the way of invention was not a rich endowment; but such as it was he liked to work it, he was pleased with the effects, and indeed he did some quite sweet things with it. In his little box of stage-properties he kept six or eight cunning devices, tricks, artifices for his savages and woodsmen to deceive and circumvent each other with, and he was never so happy as when he was working these innocent things and seeing them go. A favorite one was to make a moccasined person tread in the tracks of the moccasined enemy, and thus hide his own trail. Cooper wore out barrels and barrels of moccasins in working that trick. Another stage-property that he pulled out of his box pretty frequently was his broken twig. He prized his broken twig above all the rest of his effects, and worked it the hardest. It is a restful chapter in any book of his when somebody doesn't step on a dry twig and alarm all the reds and whites for two hundred yards around. Every time a Cooper person is in peril, and absolute silence is worth four dollars a minute, he is sure to step on a dry twig. There may be a hundred handier things to step on, but that wouldn't satisfy Cooper. Cooper requires him to turn out and find a dry twig; and if he can't do it, go and borrow one. In fact, the Leatherstocking Series ought to have been called the Broken Twig Series.

I am sorry there is not room to put in a few dozen instances of the delicate art of the forest, as practised by Natty Bumppo and some of the other Cooperian experts. Perhaps we may venture two or three samples. Cooper was a sailor—a naval officer; yet he gravely tells us how a vessel, driving toward a lee shore in a gale, is steered for a particular spot by her skipper because he knows of an *undertow* there which will hold her back against the gale and save her. For just pure woodcraft, or sailorcraft, or whatever it is, isn't that neat? For several years Cooper was daily in the society of artillery, and he ought to have noticed that when a cannon-ball strikes the ground it either buries itself or skips a hundred feet or so; skips again a hundred feet or so—and so on, till finally it gets tired and rolls. Now in one place he loses some "females"—as he always calls women—in the edge of a wood near a plain at night in a fog, on purpose to give Bumppo a chance to show off the delicate art of the forest before the reader. These mislaid people are hunting for a fort. They hear a cannon-blast, and a cannon-ball presently comes rolling into the wood and stops at their feet. To the females this suggests nothing. The case is very different with the admirable Bumppo. I wish I may never know peace again if he doesn't strike out promptly and *follow the track* of that cannon-ball across the plain through the dense fog and find the fort. Isn't it a daisy? If Cooper had any real knowledge of Nature's ways of doing things, he had a most delicate art in concealing the fact. For instance: one of his acute Indian experts, Chingachgook (pronounced Chicago, I think), has lost the trail of a person he is tracking through the forest. Apparently that trail is hopelessly lost. Neither you nor I could ever have guessed out the way to find it. It was very different with Chicago. Chicago was not stumped for long. He turned a running stream out of its course, and there, in the slush in its old bed, were that person's moccasin tracks. The current did not wash them away, as it would have done in all other like cases—no, even the eternal laws of Nature have to vacate when Cooper wants to put up a delicate job of woodcraft on the reader.

We must be a little wary when Brander Matthews tells us that Cooper's books "reveal an extraordinary fullness of invention." As a rule, I am quite willing to accept Brander Matthews's literary judgments and applaud his lucid and graceful phrasing of them; but that particular statement needs to be taken with a few tons of salt. Bless your heart, Cooper hadn't any more invention than a horse; and I don't mean a high-class horse, either; I mean a clothes-horse. It would be very difficult to find a really clever "situation" in Cooper's books, and still more difficult to find one of any kind which he has failed to render absurd by his handling of it. Look at the episodes of "the caves"; and at the celebrated scuffle between Maqua and those others on the table-land a few days later; and at Hurry Harry's queer water-transit from the castle to the ark; and at Deerslayer's half-hour with his first corpse; and at the quarrel between Hurry Harry and Deerslayer later; and at—but choose for yourself; you can't go amiss.

If Cooper had been an observer his inventive faculty would have worked better; not more interestingly, but more rationally, more plausibly. Cooper's proudest creations in the way of "situations" suffer noticeably from the absence of the observer's protecting gift. Cooper's eye was splendidly inaccurate. Cooper seldom saw anything correctly. He saw nearly all things as through a glass eye, darkly. Of course a man who cannot see the commonest little every-day matters accurately is working at a disadvantage when he is constructing a "situation." In the *Deerslayer* tale Cooper has a stream which is fifty feet wide where it flows out of a lake; it presently narrows to twenty as it meanders along for no given reason, and yet when a stream acts like that it ought to be required to explain itself. Fourteen pages later the width of the brook's outlet from the lake has suddenly shrunk thirty feet, and become "the narrowest part of the stream." This shrinkage is not accounted for. The stream has bends in it, a sure indication that it has alluvial banks and cuts them; yet these bends are only thirty and fifty feet long. If Cooper had been a nice and punctilious observer he would have noticed that the bends were oftener nine hundred feet long than short of it.

Cooper made the exit of that stream fifty feet wide, in the first place, for no particular reason; in the second place, he narrowed it to less than twenty to accommodate some Indians. He bends a "sapling" to the form of an arch over this narrow passage, and conceals six Indians in its foliage. They are "laying" for a settler's scow or ark which is coming up the stream on its way to the lake; it is being hauled against the stiff current by a rope whose stationary end is anchored in the lake; its rate of progress cannot be more than a mile an hour. Cooper describes the ark, but pretty obscurely. In the matter of dimensions "it was little more than a modern canal-boat." Let us guess, then, that it was about one hundred and forty feet long. It was of "greater breadth than common." Let us guess, then, that it was about sixteen feet wide. This leviathan had been prowling down bends which were but a third as long as itself, and scraping between banks where it had only two feet of space to spare on each side. We cannot too much admire this miracle. A low-roofed log dwelling occupies "two-thirds of the ark's length"—a dwelling ninety feet long and sixteen feet wide, let us say—a kind of vestibule train. The dwelling has two rooms—each forty-five feet long and sixteen feet wide, let us guess. One of them is the bedroom of the Hutter girls, Judith and Hetty; the other is the parlor in the daytime, at night it is papa's bedchamber. The ark is arriving at the stream's exit now, whose width has been reduced to less than twenty feet to accommodate the Indians—say to eighteen. There is a foot to spare on each side of the boat. Did the Indians notice that there was going to be a tight squeeze there? Did they notice that they could make money by climbing down out of that arched sapling and just stepping aboard when the ark scraped by? No, other Indians would have noticed these things, but Cooper's Indians never notice anything. Cooper thinks they are marvelous creatures for noticing, but he was almost always in error about his Indians. There was seldom a sane one among them.

The ark is one hundred and forty feet long; the dwelling is ninety feet long. The idea of the Indians is to drop softly and secretly from the arched sapling to the dwelling as the ark creeps along under it at the rate of a mile an hour, and butcher the family. It will take the ark a minute and a half to pass under. It will take the ninety-foot dwelling a minute to pass under. Now, then, what did the six Indians do? It would take you thirty years to guess, and even then you would have to give it up, I believe. Therefore, I will tell you what the Indians did. Their chief, a person of quite extraordinary intellect for a Cooper Indian, warily watched the canal-boat as it squeezed along under him, and when he had got his calculations fined down to exactly the right shade, as he judged, he let go and dropped. And *missed the house!* That is actually what he did. He missed the house, and landed in the stern of the scow. It was not much of a fall, yet it knocked him silly. He lay there unconscious. If the house had been ninety-seven feet long he would have made the trip. The fault was Cooper's, not his. The error lay in the construction of the house. Cooper was no architect.

There still remained in the roost five Indians. The boat has passed under and is now out of their reach. Let me explain what the five did—you would not be able to reason it out for yourself. No. 1 jumped for the boat, but fell in the water astern of it. Then No. 2 jumped for the boat, but fell in the water still farther astern of it. Then No. 3 jumped for the boat, and fell a good way astern of it. Then No. 4 jumped for the boat, and fell in the water *away* astern. Then even No. 5 made a jump for the boat—for he was a Cooper Indian. In the matter of intellect, the difference between a Cooper Indian and the Indian that stands in front of the cigar-shop is not spacious. The scow episode is really a sublime burst of invention; but it does not thrill, because the inaccuracy of the details throws a sort of air of fictitiousness and general improbability over it. This comes of Cooper's inadequacy as an observer.

The reader will find some examples of Cooper's high talent for inaccurate observation in the account of the shooting-match in *The Pathfinder.*

A common wrought nail was driven lightly into the target, its head having been first touched with paint.

The color of the paint is not stated—an important omission, but Cooper deals freely in important omissions. No, after all, it was not an important omission; for this nail-head is *a hundred yards from* the marksmen, and could not be seen by them at that distance, no matter what its color might be. How far can the best eyes see a common house-fly? A hundred yards? It is quite impossible. Very well; eyes that cannot see a house-fly that is a hundred yards away cannot see an ordinary nail-head at that distance, for the size of the two objects is the same. It takes a keen eye to see a fly or a nail-head at fifty yards—one hundred and fifty feet. Can the reader do it?

The nail was lightly driven, its head painted, and game called. Then the Cooper miracles began. The bullet of the first marksman chipped an edge of the nail-head; the next man's bullet drove the nail a little way into the target—and removed all the paint. Haven't the miracles gone far enough now? Not to suit Cooper; for the purpose of this whole scheme is to show off his prodigy, Deerslayer-Hawkeye-Long-Rifle-Leatherstocking-Pathfinder-Bumppo before the ladies.

"Be all ready to clench it, boys!" cried out Pathfinder, stepping into his friend's tracks the instant they were vacant. "Never mind a new nail; I can see that, though the paint is gone, and what I can see I can hit at a hundred yards, though it were only a mosquito's eye. Be ready to clench!"

The rifle cracked, the bullet sped its way, and the head of the nail was buried in the wood, covered by the piece of flattened lead.

There, you see, is a man who could hunt flies with a rifle, and command a ducal salary in a Wild West show to-day if we had him back with us.

The recorded feat is certainly surprising just as it stands; but it is not surprising enough for Cooper. Cooper adds a touch. He has made Pathfinder do this miracle with another man's rifle; and not only that, but Pathfinder did not have even the advantage of loading it himself. He had everything against him, and yet he made that impossible shot; and not only made it, but did it with absolute confidence, saying, "Be ready to clench." Now a person like that would have undertaken that same feat with a brick-bat, and with Cooper to help he would have achieved it, too.

Pathfinder showed off handsomely that day before the ladies. His very first feat was a thing which no Wild West show can touch. He was standing with the group of marksmen, observing—a hundred yards from the target, mind; one Jasper raised his rifle and drove the center of the bull's-eye. Then the Quartermaster fired. The target exhibited no result this time. There was a laugh. "It's a dead miss," said Major Lundie. Pathfinder waited an impressive moment or two; then said, in that calm, indifferent, know-it-all way of his, "No, Major, he has covered Jasper's bullet, as will be seen if any one will take the trouble to examine the target."

Wasn't it remarkable! How *could* he see that little pellet fly through the air and enter that distant bullet-hole? Yet that is what he did; for nothing is impossible to a Cooper person. Did any of those people have any deep-seated doubts about this thing? No; for that would imply sanity, and these were all Cooper people.

> The respect for Pathfinder's skill and for his *quickness and accuracy of sight* [the italics are mine] was so profound and general, that the instant he made this declaration the spectators began to distrust their own opinions, and a dozen rushed to the target in order to ascertain the fact. There, sure enough, it was found that the Quartermaster's bullet had gone through the hole made by Jasper's, and that, too, so accurately as to require a minute examination to be certain of the circumstance, which, however, was soon clearly established by discovering one bullet over the other in the stump against which the target was placed.

They made a "minute" examination; but never mind, how could they know that there were two bullets in that hole without digging the latest one out? For neither probe nor eyesight could prove the presence of any more than one bullet. Did they dig? No; as we shall see. It is the Pathfinder's turn now; he steps out before the ladies, takes aim, and fires.

But, alas! here is a disappointment; an incredible, an unimaginable disappointment—for the target's aspect is unchanged; there is nothing there but that same old bullet-hole!

> "If one dared to hint at such a thing," cried Major Duncan, "I should say that the Pathfinder has also missed the target!"

As nobody had missed it yet, the "also" was not necessary; but never mind about that, for the Pathfinder is going to speak.

> "No, no Major," said he, confidently, "that *would* be a risky declaration. I didn't load the piece, and can't say what was in it; but if it was lead, you will find the bullet driving down those of the Quartermaster and Jasper, else is not my name Pathfinder."

A shout from the target announced the truth of this assertion.

Is the miracle sufficient as it stands? Not for Cooper. The Pathfinder speaks again, as he "now slowly advances toward the stage occupied by the females":

> "That's not all, boys, that's not all; if you find the target touched at all, I'll own to a miss. The Quartermaster cut the wood, but you'll find no wood cut by that last messenger."

The miracle is at last complete. He knew—doubtless *saw*—at the distance of a hundred yards—that his bullet had passed into the hole *without fraying the edges.* There were now three bullets in that one hole—three bullets embedded processionally in the body of the stump back of the target. Everybody knew this—somehow or other—and yet nobody had dug any of them out to make sure. Cooper is not a close observer, but he is interesting. He is certainly always that, no matter what happens. And he is more interesting when he is not noticing what he is about than when he is. This is a considerable merit.

The conversations in the Cooper books have a curious sound in our modern ears. To believe that such talk really ever came out of people's mouths would be to believe that there was a time when time was of no value to a person who thought he had something to say; when it was the custom to spread a two-minute remark out to ten; when a man's mouth was a rolling-mill, and busied itself all day long in turning four-foot pigs of thought into thirty-foot bars of conversational railroad iron by attenuation; when subjects were seldom faithfully stuck to, but the talk wandered all around and arrived nowhere; when conversations consisted mainly of irrelevancies, with here and there a relevancy, a relevancy with an embarrassed look, as not being able to explain how it got there.

Cooper was certainly not a master in the construction of dialogue. Inaccurate observation defeated him here as it defeated him in so many other enterprises of his. He even failed to notice that the man who talks corrupt English six days in the week must and will talk it on the seventh, and can't help himself. In the *Deerslayer* story he lets Deerslayer talk the showiest kind of book-talk sometimes, and at other times the basest of base dialects. For instance, when some one asks him if he has a sweetheart, and if so, where she abides, this is his majestic answer:

> "She's in the forest—hanging from the boughs of the trees, in a soft rain— in the dew on the open grass—the clouds that float about in the blue heavens—the birds that sing in the woods—the sweet springs where I slake my thirst—and in all the other glorious gifts that come from God's Providence!"

And he preceded that, a little before, with this:

> "It consarns me as all things that touches a fri'nd consarns a fri'nd."

And this is another of his remarks:

> "If I was Injin born, now, I might tell of this, or carry in the scalp and boast

of the expl'ite afore the whole tribe; or if my inimy had only been a bear"—
[and so on].

We cannot imagine such a thing as a veteran Scotch Commander-in-Chief
comporting himself in the field like a windy melodramatic actor, but Cooper
could. On one occasion Alice and Cora were being chased by the French
through a fog in the neighborhood of their father's fort:

> *"Point de quartier aux coquins!"*[4] cried an eager pursuer, who seemed to direct
> the operations of the enemy.
> "Stand firm and be ready, my gallant sixtieths!" suddenly exclaimed a
> voice above them; "wait to see the enemy; fire low, and sweep the glacis."
> "Father! father" exclaimed a piercing cry from out the mist; "it is I! Alice!
> thy own Elsie! spare, O! save your daughters!"
> "Hold!" shouted the former speaker, in the awful tones of parental agony,
> the sound reaching even to the woods, and rolling back in solemn echo.
> "'Tis she! God has restored me my children! Throw open the sally-port; to
> the field, sixtieths, to the field! pull not a trigger, lest ye kill my lambs! Drive
> off these dogs of France with your steel!"

Cooper's word-sense was singularly dull. When a person has a poor ear
for music he will flat and sharp right along without knowing it. He keeps
near the tune, but it is *not* the tune. When a person has a poor ear for words,
the result is a literary flatting and sharping; you perceive what he is intending to say, but you also perceive that he doesn't say it. This is Cooper. He was
not a word-musician. His ear was satisfied with the *approximate* word. I will
furnish some circumstantial evidence in support of this charge. My instances
are gathered from half a dozen pages of the tale called *Deerslayer*. He uses
"verbal" for "oral"; "precision" for "facility"; "phenomena" for "marvels";
"necessary" for "predetermined"; "unsophisticated" for "primitive"; "preparation" for "expectancy"; "rebuked" for "subdued"; "dependent on" for
"resulting from"; "fact" for "condition"; "fact" for "conjecture"; "precau-
tion" for "caution"; "explain" for "determine"; "mortified" for "disappointed"; "meretricious" for "factitious"; "materially" for "considerably";
"decreasing" for "deepening"; "increasing" for "disappearing"; "embedded" for "inclosed"; "treacherous" for "hostile"; "stood" for "stooped";
"softened" for "replaced"; "rejoined" for "remarked"; "situation" for "condition"; "different" for "differing"; "insensible" for "unsentient"; "brevity"
for "celerity"; "distrusted" for "suspicious"; "mental imbecility" for "imbecility"; "eyes" for "sight"; "counteracting" for "opposing"; "funeral obsequies"
for "obsequies."

There have been daring people in the world who claimed that Cooper
could write English, but they are all dead now—all dead but Lounsbury. I
don't remember that Lounsbury makes the claim in so many words, still he
makes it, for he says that *Deerslayer* is a "pure work of art." Pure, in that

---

[4] No mercy for the knaves!

connection, means faultless—faultless in all details—and language is a detail. If Mr. Lounsbury had only compared Cooper's English with the English which he writes himself—but it is plain that he didn't; and so it is likely that he imagines until this day that Cooper's is as clean and compact as his own. Now I feel sure, deep down in my heart, that Cooper wrote about the poorest English that exists in our language, and that the English of *Deerslayer* is the very worst that even Cooper ever wrote.

I may be mistaken, but it does seem to me that *Deerslayer* is not a work of art in any sense; it does seem to me that it is destitute of every detail that goes to the making of a work of art; in truth, it seems to me that *Deerslayer* is just simply a literary *delirium tremens*.

A work of art? It has no invention; it has no order, system, sequence, or result; it has no life-likeness, no thrill, no stir, no seeming of reality; its characters are confusedly drawn, and by their acts and words they prove that they are not the sort of people the author claims that they are; its humor is pathetic; its pathos is funny; its conversations are—oh! indescribable; its love-scenes odious; its English a crime against the language.

Counting these out, what is left is Art. I think we must all admit that.

QUESTIONS FOR THINKING AND WRITING

1. Mark Twain cites three "experts" at the beginning of his essay. He then implies that they haven't read any of Cooper's work. Is this literally true? In a paragraph or two, describe the effect of this ploy. Is it successful? How do you know if you can believe Twain about whether the "experts" have read Cooper's novels.
2. While Twain speaks only of Cooper's work, it may be possible to apply what he says to other literature, and even to films and television programs. Select a book or movie or program and write an essay about its "literary offenses." Begin with a freewriting to sound out your topic and then follow the guidelines in the first section of this text to develop an essay of five to seven pages.
3. If Cooper's faults, according to Twain, could be summed up in one or two sentences, what would they be? Use your journal to develop and refine those sentences. Then write a few paragraphs that analyze their implications for nonliterary issues.

T. S. ELIOT (1888–1965)

Tradition and the Individual Talent

I

In English writing we seldom speak of tradition, though we occasionally apply its name in deploring its absence. We cannot refer to 'the tradition' or to 'a tradition'; at most, we employ the adjective in saying that the poetry of So-and-so is 'traditional' or even 'too traditional'. Seldom, perhaps, does the word appear except in a phrase of censure. If otherwise, it is vaguely approbative, with the implication, as to the work approved, of some pleasing archaeological reconstruction. You can hardly make the word agreeable to English ears without this comfortable reference to the reassuring science of archaeology.

Certainly the word is not likely to appear in our appreciations of living or dead writers. Every nation, every race, has not only its own creative, but its own critical turn of mind; and is even more oblivious of the shortcomings and limitations of its critical habits than of those of its creative genius. We know, or think we know, from the enormous mass of critical writing that has appeared in the French language the critical method or habit of the French; we only conclude (we are such unconscious people) that the French are 'more critical' than we, and sometimes even plume ourselves a little with the fact, as if the French were the less spontaneous. Perhaps they are; but we might remind ourselves that criticism is as inevitable as breathing, and that we should be none the worse for articulating what passes in our minds when we read a book and feel an emotion about it, for criticizing our own minds in their work of criticism. One of the facts that might come to light in this process is our tendency to insist, when we praise a poet, upon those aspects of his work in which he least resembles anyone else. In these aspects or parts of his work we pretend to find what is individual, what is the peculiar essence of the man. We dwell with satisfaction upon the poet's difference from his predecessors, especially his immediate predecessors; we endeavour to find something that can be isolated in order to be enjoyed. Whereas if we approach a poet without this prejudice we shall often find that not only the best, but the most individual parts of his work may be those in which the dead poets, his ancestors, assert their immortality most vigorously. And I do not mean the impressionable period of adolescence, but the period of full maturity.

Yet if the only form of tradition, of handing down, consisted in following the ways of the immediate generation before us in a blind or timid adherence to its successes, 'tradition' should positively be discouraged. We have seen many such simple currents soon lost in the sand; and novelty is better than repetition. Tradition is a matter of much wider significance. It cannot be inherited, and if you want it you must obtain it by great labour. It involves, in the first place, the historical sense, which we may call nearly indispensable to anyone who would continue to be a poet beyond his twenty-fifth year; and the historical sense involves a perception, not only of the pastness of the past, but of its presence; the historical sense compels a man to write not merely with his own generation in his bones, but with a feeling that the whole of the literature of Europe from Homer and within it the whole of the literature of his own country has a simultaneous existence and composes a simultaneous order. This historical sense, which is a sense of the timeless as well as of the temporal and of the timeless and of the temporal together, is what makes a writer traditional. And it is at the same time what makes a writer most acutely conscious of his place in time, of his own con-temporaneity.

No poet, no artist of any art, has his complete meaning alone. His sig-nificance, his appreciation is the appreciation of his relation to the dead poets and artists. You cannot value him alone; you must set him, for contrast and comparison, among the dead. I mean this as a principle of aesthetic, not merely historical, criticism. The necessity that he shall conform, that he shall cohere, is not onesided; what happens when a new work of art is created is something that happens simultaneously to all the works of art which pre-ceded it. The existing monuments form an ideal order among themselves, which is modified by the introduction of the new (the really new) work of art among them. The existing order is complete before the new work arrives; for order to persist after the supervention of novelty, the *whole* existing order must be, if ever so slightly, altered; and so the relations, proportions, values of each work of art toward the whole are readjusted; and this is conformity between the old and the new. Whoever has approved this idea of order, of the form of European, of English literature will not find it prepos-terous that the past should be altered by the present as much as the present is directed by the past. And the poet who is aware of this will be aware of great difficulties and responsibilities.

In a peculiar sense he will be aware also that he must inevitably be judged by the standards of the past. I say judged, not amputated, by them; not judged to be as good as, or worse or better than, the dead; and certainly not judged by the canons of dead critics. It is a judgment, a comparison, in which two things are measured by each other. To conform merely would be for the new work not really to conform at all; it would not be new, and would therefore not be a work of art. And we do not quite say that the new is more valuable because it fits in; but its fitting in is a test of its value—a test, it is true, which can only be slowly and cautiously applied, for we are none of us infallible judges of conformity. We say: it appears to conform, and is perhaps individual, or it appears individual, and may conform; but we are hardly likely to find that it is one and not the other.

To proceed to a more intelligible exposition of the relation of the poet to the past: he can neither take the past as a lump, an indiscriminate bolus, nor can he form himself wholly on one or two private admirations, nor can he form himself wholly upon one preferred period. The first course is inadmissible, the second is an important experience of youth, and the third is a pleasant and highly desirable supplement. The poet must be very conscious of the main current, which does not at all flow invariably through the most distinguished reputations. He must be quite aware of the obvious fact that art never improves, but that the material of art is never quite the same. He must be aware that the mind of Europe—the mind of his own country—a mind which he learns in time to be much more important than his own private mind—is a mind which changes, and that this change is a development which abandons nothing *en route,* which does not superannuate either Shakespeare, or Homer, or the rock drawing of the Magdalenian draughtsmen.[1] That this development, refinement perhaps, complication certainly, is not, from the point of view of the artist, any improvement. Perhaps not even an improvement from the point of view of the psychologist or not to the extent which we imagine; perhaps only in the end based upon a complication in economics and machinery. But the difference between the present and the past is that the conscious present is an awareness of the past in a way and to an extent which the past's awareness of itself cannot show.

Someone said: 'The dead writers are remote from us because we *know* so much more than they did'. Precisely, and they are that which we know.

I am alive to a usual objection to what is clearly part of my programme for the *métier* of poetry. The objection is that the doctrine requires a ridiculous amount of erudition (pedantry), a claim which can be rejected by appeal to the lives of poets in any pantheon. It will even be affirmed that much learning deadens or perverts poetic sensibility. While, however, we persist in believing that a poet ought to know as much as will not encroach upon his necessary receptivity and necessary laziness, it is not desirable to confine knowledge to whatever can be put into a useful shape for examinations, drawing-rooms, or the still more pretentious modes of publicity. Some can absorb knowledge, the more tardy must sweat for it. Shakespeare acquired more essential history from Plutarch than most men could from the whole British Museum. What is to be insisted upon is that the poet must develop or procure the consciousness of the past and that he should continue to develop this consciousness throughout his career.

What happens is a continual surrender of himself as he is at the moment to something which is more valuable. The progress of an artist is a continual self-sacrifice, a continual extinction of personality.

---

[1] refers to cave drawings from the Paleolithic period found in La Madeleine, France

There remains to define this process of depersonalization and its relation to the sense of tradition. It is in this depersonalization that art may be said to approach the condition of science. I therefore invite you to consider, as a suggestive analogy, the action which takes place when a bit of finely filiated platinum is introduced into a chamber containing oxygen and sulphur dioxide.

II

Honest criticism and sensitive appreciation is directed not upon the poet but upon the poetry. If we attend to the confused cries of the newspaper critics and the *susurrus*[2] of popular repetition that follows, we shall hear the names of poets in great numbers; if we seek not Blue-book knowledge but the enjoyment of poetry, and ask for a poem, we shall seldom find it. I have tried to point out the importance of the relation of the poem to other poems by other authors, and suggested the conception of poetry as a living whole of all the poetry that has ever been written. The other aspect of this Impersonal theory of poetry is the relation of the poem to its author. And I hinted, by an analogy, that the mind of the mature poet differs from that of the immature one not precisely in any valuation of 'personality', not being necessarily more interesting, or having 'more to say', but rather by being a more finely perfected medium in which special, or very varied, feelings are at liberty to enter into new combinations.

The analogy was that of the catalyst. When the two gases previously mentioned are mixed in the presence of a filament of platinum, they form sulphurous acid. This combination takes place only if the platinum is present; nevertheless the newly formed acid contains no trace of platinum, and the platinum itself is apparently unaffected: has remained inert, neutral, and unchanged. The mind of the poet is the shred of platinum. It may partly or exclusively operate upon the experience of the man himself; but, the more perfect the artist, the more completely separate in him will be the man who suffers and the mind which creates; the more perfectly will the mind digest and transmute the passions which are its material.

The experience, you will notice, the elements which enter the presence of the transforming catalyst, are of two kinds: emotions and feelings. The effect of a work of art upon the person who enjoys it is an experience different in kind from any experience not of art. It may be formed out of one emotion, or may be a combination of several; and various feelings, inhering for the writer in particular words or phrases or images, may be added to compose the final result. Or great poetry may be made without the direct use of any emotion whatever: composed out of feelings solely. Canto

---

[2] muttering, whispering

XV of the *Inferno* (Brunetto Latini[3]) is a working up of the emotion evident in the situation; but the effect, though single as that of any work of art, is obtained by considerable complexity of detail. The last quatrain gives an image, a feeling attaching to an image, which 'came', which did not develop simply out of what precedes, but which was probably in suspension in the poet's mind until the proper combination arrived for it to add itself to. The poet's mind is in fact a receptacle for seizing and storing up numberless feelings, phrases, images, which remain there until all the particles which can unite to form a new compound are present together.

If you compare several representative passages of the greatest poetry you see how great is the variety of types of combination, and also how completely any semi-ethical criterion of 'sublimity' misses the mark. For it is not the 'greatness', the intensity, of the emotions, the components, but the intensity of the artistic process, the pressure, so to speak, under which the fusion takes place, that counts. The episode of Paolo and Francesca[4] employs a definite emotion, but the intensity of the poetry is something quite different from whatever intensity in the supposed experience it may give the impression of. It is no more intense, furthermore, than Canto XXVI, the voyage of Ulysses, which has not the direct dependence upon an emotion. Great variety is possible in the process of transmutation of emotion: the murder of Agamemnon, or the agony of Othello, gives an artistic effect apparently closer to a possible original than the scenes from Dante. In the *Agamemnon*, the artistic emotion approximates to the emotion of an actual spectator; in *Othello* to the emotion of the protagonist himself. But the difference between art and the event is always absolute; the combination which is the murder of Agamemnon is probably as complex as that which is the voyage of Ulysses. In either case there has been a fusion of elements. The ode of Keats[5] contains a number of feelings which have nothing particular to do with the nightingale, but which the nightingale, partly perhaps because of its attractive name, and partly because of its reputation, served to bring together.

The point of view which I am struggling to attack is perhaps related to the metaphysical theory of the substantial unity of the soul: for my meaning is, that the poet has, not a 'personality' to express, but a particular medium, which is only a medium and not a personality, in which impressions and experiences combine in peculiar and unexpected ways. Impressions and experiences which are important for the man may take no place in the poetry, and those which become important in the poetry may play quite a negligible part in the man, the personality.

---

[3] Brunetto Latini is someone Dante knew personally.

[4] Francesca describes how she and her brother-in-law, Paolo, fell in love and were stabbed to death by her husband.

[5] John Keats (1795–1821), "Ode to a Nightingale," see pp. 535–538.

I will quote a passage which is unfamiliar enough to be regarded with fresh attention in the light—or darkness—of these observations:

> And now methinks I could e'en chide myself
> For doating on her beauty, though her death
> Shall be revenged after no common action.
> Does the silkworm expend her yellow labours
> For thee? For thee does she undo herself?
> Are lordships sold to maintain ladyships
> For the poor benefit of a bewildering minute?
> Why does yon fellow falsify highways,
> And put his life between the judge's lips,
> To refine such a thing—keeps horse and men
> To beat their valours for her? . . .[6]

In this passage (as is evident if it is taken in its context) there is a combination of positive and negative emotions: an intensely strong attraction toward beauty and an equally intense fascination by the ugliness which is contrasted with it and which destroys it. This balance of contrasted emotion is in the dramatic situation to which the speech is pertinent, but that situation alone is inadequate to it. This is, so to speak, the structural emotion, provided by the drama. But the whole effect, the dominant tone, is due to the fact that a number of floating feelings, having an affinity to this emotion by no means superficially evident, having combined with it to give us a new art emotion.

It is not in his personal emotions, the emotions provoked by particular events in his life, that the poet is in any way remarkable or interesting. His particular emotions may be simple, or crude, or flat. The emotion in his poetry will be a very complex thing, but not with the complexity of the emotions of people who have very complex or unusual emotions in life. One error, in fact, of eccentricity in poetry is to seek for new human emotions to express; and in this search for novelty in the wrong place it discovers the perverse. The business of the poet is not to find new emotions, but to use the ordinary ones and, in working them up into poetry, to express feelings which are not in actual emotions at all. And emotions which he has never experienced will serve his turn as well as those familiar to him. Consequently, we must believe that 'emotion recollected in tranquillity'[7] is an inexact formula. For it is neither emotion, nor recollection, nor without distortion of meaning, tranquillity. It is a concentration, and a new thing resulting from the concentration, of a very great number of experiences which to the practical and active person would not seem to be experiences at all; it is a concentration which does not happen consciously or of deliberation. These experiences are not 'recollected', and they finally unite in an atmosphere which is 'tranquil' only in that it is a passive attending upon the

---

[6] Cyril Tourneur (1575?–1626), *The Revenger's Tragedy* (1607), III, v.
[7] William Wordsworth (1770–1850), from the preface to the second edition of *Lyrical Ballads*.

event. Of course this is not quite the whole story. There is a great deal, in the writing of poetry, which must be conscious and deliberate. In fact, the bad poet is usually unconscious where he ought to be conscious, and conscious where he ought to be unconscious. Both errors tend to make him 'personal'. Poetry is not a turning loose of emotion, but an escape from emotion; it is not the expression of personality, but an escape from personality. But, of course, only those who have personality and emotions know what it means to want to escape from these things.

III

ὁ δὲ νοῦς ἴσως θειότερόν τι καὶ ἀπαθές ἐστιν.[8]

This essay proposes to halt at the frontiers of metaphysics or mysticism, and confine itself to such practical conclusions as can be applied by the responsible person interested in poetry. To divert interest from the poet to the poetry is a laudable aim: for it would conduce to a juster estimation of actual poetry, good and bad. There are many people who appreciate the expression of sincere emotion in verse, and there is a smaller number of people who can appreciate technical excellence. But very few know when there is an expression of *significant* emotion, emotion which has its life in the poem and not in the history of the poet. The emotion of art is impersonal. And the poet cannot reach this impersonality without surrendering himself wholly to the work to be done. And he is not likely to know what is to be done unless he lives in what is not merely the present, but the present moment of the past, unless he is conscious, not of what is dead, but of what is already living.

QUESTIONS FOR THINKING AND WRITING

1. T. S. Eliot says that "criticism is as inevitable as breathing." Copy this passage into your reading journal and write a brief description of what you understand him to mean. (Note: If you have also read the essays by Virginia Woolf and Mark Twain, you may want to consider how they help explain this quotation.)

2. In one paragraph, summarize Eliot's essay, citing his main point and the two or three most important ideas he develops to support it. When you have a draft of this summary, revise it for accuracy. Is your summary faithful to the ideas of the author? Now do a freewriting in which you respond to Eliot's essay. Do you agree or disagree? What evidence can you produce to support whichever stance you take?

3. "Poetry is not a turning loose of emotion," Eliot says near the end of his essay, "but an escape from emotion." Use this quotation as the point of departure for an essay of your own about poetry. You may support or dispute it. Select several readings from the poetry section of this text to help you develop your essay.

---

[8] From Aristotle's (384–322 B.C.) *De Anima*, Bk. I, Ch. 4: "Doubtless the mind is something more divine and less subject to passion."

PERVEZ HUDA (1967–)

A Call for Compassion

He has been diagnosed as having AIDS [Acquired Immune Deficiency Syndrome]. He appears listless and totally disinterested. He refuses to talk to anyone. When spoken to, he can barely turn his head because of his loss of strength and motor coordination. His body is so emaciated that it appears as if his skin were being forcibly stretched over his bones. There are lesions throughout his body, and the overall deformations make him look almost as if he were a wax figure. He has severe headaches, and the body aches are so intense that pain killers must be administered regularly. The degenerative nature of the disease has now reached the later stages in which it affects the brain, causing him to show signs of dementia. His family came in once, but after hearing the diagnosis, they became extremely indifferent toward him, merely telephoning now and then. He once thought he had many close friends but somehow they hadn't bothered to come by to see him either. He is receiving the best medical care available, yet he is treated as if he were a leper, an outcast; even hospital staff members sometimes appear apathetic toward his plight. In the months to come, he is going to die an extremely painful death, and yet he feels that no one will even take note of his absence.

I can see how natural this reaction is simply because most of us fear AIDS. We start creating our own misconceptions about the disease by simply basing our actions on what we hear from other people. I did this myself, but as a medical student, I felt an obligation to think through my reactions when one day a fellow medical student was telling me about his experience treating an AIDS patient:

> This guy came in. He couldn't speak any English. All he could do was speak Spanish. I tried asking him what was wrong. All he could do was make these weird gestures. Finally he pointed to one of the male orderlies and made kissing gestures toward him. I started yelling, "Oh my God, we've got a homo on the ward with AIDS."

I made a stupid smile, but somehow the med student's attempt to make the situation funny bothered me. I hoped to God that his attitude had been greatly exaggerated.

As medical students and future physicians, we must remain unbiased toward our patients. My feelings should not get in the way of administering the best possible treatment program for a particular patient. I knew little if anything at all about AIDS patients or their disease. If placed in the same room with an AIDS patient, I probably would have been more concerned with my chances of getting the disease than I would with the patient's problems. So the first question I wanted to answer when I decided on this assignment was what are the various ways one can contract the disease?

I soon found out that the AIDS virus is an extremely difficult virus to contract. It is not an airborne transmitted disease; therefore, talking to an AIDS patient does not place anyone in any danger of getting the disease. According to the latest report on AIDS from C. Everett Koop, United States Surgeon General, hugging, shaking hands, crying, social kissing, coughing, or sneezing do not transmit the AIDS virus. AIDS cannot be contracted from swimming in hot tubs or pools or from eating in a restaurant where one of the restaurant workers carries the virus. The disease cannot be contracted through bed linens, towels, straws, cups, dishes, or other utensils. The virus cannot be transmitted from contact with doorknobs, telephones, toilets, household furniture, or office machinery, or from body massages, masturbation, or nonsexual body contact with a carrier. The disease is a sexually transmitted blood-borne disease.

Putting the fears of the meaning of the disease behind me, I tried to get an interview with an AIDS patient to find out more about both the victims and the disease; how having AIDS differs from other diseases which also have grim prognoses. This interview turned out to be much easier to think about having than to actually complete.

I contacted my Year II adviser, plus several doctors I knew to be affiliated with UMKC [the University of Missouri at Kansas City], and I tried calling free health clinics, but each call produced the same response. One health clinic volunteer asked, "What do you mean you want to know what it's like having AIDS? I'll tell you what it's like; they're dying, that's what. They don't want to talk to anyone. They just want to be left alone."

I thought there just had to be someone out there who wanted his story to be told, but clearance and access to these patients was like trying to break into Fort Knox. I got close to dropping the whole idea, thinking maybe I really wasn't qualified enough to deal with such controversial subject matter. (On top of this, many of my friends started giving me funny looks.) Finally, I settled for an interview with someone who dealt with AIDS patients on a regular basis.

I ended up interviewing Virginia Allen, head of the Good Samaritan Project in Kansas City. She has gained national recognition as one of the sole authorities in AIDS counseling. She has had numerous interviews for television and newspapers throughout the country. She later told me that one of the reasons she agreed to our interview was that she had once been a student at UMKC.

The Good Samaritan Project is unique because it is one of very few organizations in the United States that deals solely with the problem of AIDS patients. The project covers all aspects of the disease: the medical and social issues, grieving, in-home health care, and the many other problems which are peculiar to AIDS victims. The project is vital to those who have the disease, because most patients are unable to accept the diagnosis with the strength needed to cope with their condition. And they have received very little understanding from either the medical profession or the general public. According to Ms. Allen, although most hospitals have shown a dramatic improvement in the care of AIDS patients, many are still not able to fulfill their patients' emotional needs. There was one instance recorded of an individual who was told of his positive reaction to the AIDS test through a telephone call placed by the hospital to him. The hospital did not bother telling him where to seek help, or what measures he might take. He was simply at the other end of the line, knowing that he was to die soon. (Morin 1288)

I think the most important thing I got from my interview with Ms. Allen was depth; the AIDS patients actually came across to me in a way that no textbook or newsletter possibly could. Along with receiving factual information from my interview, for the first time, I was able to think of myself in the position of the AIDS patient and realize how helpless these patients must really feel. According to Ms. Allen:

> I think the most memorable lesson I have learned is that it is impossible to love too much, to give too much, because it all comes back, a hundredfold. I was with my first AIDS victim, a woman who had been raped. She was exactly my age. I was with her when she died and I could look at her and see myself. All I could think of was that it could have been I in her place. I watched her as she was slowly losing control, losing her independence, losing her strength, and saying goodbye to everyone she had known and loved.

AIDS patients are exceptionally fragile. Social support, as that offered by The Good Samaritan Project, is essential if patients are to cope with having the disease. The loss of job, family, and social position are psychologically devastating. The social isolation that follows an AIDS patient is unique, since with most diseases, one usually finds support in numerous forms. Not so with AIDS. This isolation frequently leads patients to have feelings of guilt for having contracted the disease. The fact that everyone has deserted them reinforces these attitudes. (Heillard and Tross, 762)

Many hold the idea that people with AIDS deserve their plight because of their promiscuous lifestyles. It is well known that the initial onset of AIDS appeared in an extremely stigmatized section of society, the homosexuals. Homosexuals account for nearly ninety percent of all AIDS cases reported now, but by the year 1991, an estimated five million Americans may be carrying the AIDS virus, and a great number of these carriers will not be homosexuals. (Morganthau 30)

According to the latest report in *Newsweek*:

> There is no doubt that AIDS will pose profound questions to American society, and it will surely test the nation's reserves of compassion and common sense. It is already forcing millions of people to reconsider their sexual behavior and may well bring the sexual revolution of the sixties and seventies to an abrupt close. AIDS is raising a host of difficult legal issues about discrimination, and it may yet erupt in national politics. (Morganthau 31)

In the years to come, AIDS will affect all aspects of American life. To call it the "gay plague" is ridiculous, because it threatens millions of sexually active Americans regardless of age, gender, race, or sexual preference, and since most of us do not intend to live celibate lives and the idea of quarantine for AIDS victims appears inhumane, all of us will be affected as the number of people infected increases. It has become extremely important for us to be educated about the disease's transmission; otherwise we will continue with our misconceived notions, as well as with our neglect of AIDS victims. There is already a move for an increase in sex education in schools, and education serves as the best preventive measure against the disease's spread. I hope we will give the care, understanding, and compassion which AIDS patients deserve.

Works Cited

Allen, Virginia. Personal interview. 25 Oct. 1986.

Anonymous health care worker. Personal interview. Oct. 1986.

Anonymous medical student. Personal interview. Nov. 1986.

Cassens, Brett J. "Social Consequences of the Acquired Immunodeficiency Syndrome." *Annals of Internal Medicine* 103 (1985): 768–71.

Heillard, Jamie C., and Susan Tross. "The Psychosocial and Neuropsychiatric Sequelae of the Acquired Immunodeficiency Syndrome and Related Disorders." *Annals of Internal Medicine* 103 (1985): 760–64.

Koop, C. Everett. "A Most Explicit Report." *Time* 24 Nov. 1986: 76.

Morganthau, Tom. "Future Shock." *Newsweek* 24 Nov. 1986: 30–39.

Morin, Stephan F. "Aids in One City—An Interview with Marvyn Silverman, Director of Health, San Francisco." *American Psychologist* 39 (1984): 1294–96.

Wasylenko, Mark A., University of Missouri at Kansas City medical student. Personal interview. Oct. 1986.

QUESTIONS FOR THINKING AND WRITING

1. Pervez Huda's essay is based upon a blend of personal experience and formal research. In fact, the essay is finally successful because the distinction between experience and research dissolves. Write two or three paragraphs analyzing how this dissolution takes place. Cite instances from the essay that show the personal involvement of the author and the reliability of his information working side by side.

2. As much as Huda's essay is informative, it also seems to be a personal odyssey or revelation by the writer. In your journal write some ideas for essay topics that may lead you on a similar odyssey. Select one topic for a fifteen-minute freewriting. Do a second freewriting to analyze what you observe about yourself and your relationship to the topic in your first freewriting.

3. Huda's occasion for writing was to fulfill a writing assignment in a second-semester composition class, yet his purpose for writing ultimately became more profound, more urgent than that. Dig out an old essay you wrote for a high school or college course and reread it. Write an analysis in your journal of how the assignment fulfilled similar ends for you (or if it didn't, why). Consider how you might have expanded the paper to make it readable for a large audience, or how you might have tackled the writing task differently in order to become more involved with the topic.

READING AND WRITING
ABOUT SHORT FICTION

1 Reading and Writing About Short Fiction

Literary forms, like other historical trends, have their time, and the short story is thought by many to have come into its own during the past hundred and fifty years. In fact, Edgar Allan Poe (1809–1849), who was one of the most adept writers of short stories, also wrote a lasting commentary on the nature of the form when he reviewed a collection of stories by Nathaniel Hawthorne (1804–1864) entitled *Twice-Told Tales.* Poe emphasized the compression of the form and the effort of the writer to develop a single effect. There is no waste in a successful short story, no tangents or idle thoughts. Much has been written about the form since Poe first analyzed it, and many variations have been devised, but the essentials that he outlined remain valid.

One of Poe's convictions about the short story was that it should be readable in about an hour. This amount of time, Poe argued, allows the writer to maintain complete control of the reader's attention. (Unlike the novel form, the short story does not subject the reader to distractions that arise between reading sessions.) This means that as we study how different writers have developed the form, we may read stories more than once without exhaustive effort. We suggest that you take pleasure in your first reading of each story just as you would watch a movie or play. Stories are entertaining, so be entertained! Then come back to each story and reread for understanding and for writing.

Writing about literature is a way of understanding it and sharing that understanding. Poe might never have given us his famous definition of the short story if he did not have Hawthorne's new collection of stories before him to stimulate his thinking about the form of the short story. The suggestions below are intended to help you think and write as part of your reading.

Writing for Discovery and Understanding

Use your reading journal to explore and understand the craft of the short story.

1. *Describe the structure of the story.* A successful story will usually work around a single idea or *motif* that holds it together. For one story, the motif may be that of a survivor retelling the story of a catastophe he experienced; for another, a series of letters or diary entries; and for another the incidents of many years compressed into a single telling. As you read, ask yourself what holds the story together. What technique(s) has the author used to create the story?

2. *Describe the central conflict of the story.* From the earliest days of storytelling, when ancient tribes retold their hunting tales as the fire burned, narratives have dealt with conflict: man against himself, man against other men, man against nature, man against the gods. Poe's idea of a "single *effect*" largely has to do with the idea that one conflict will dominate a story, though sometimes other lesser conflicts may contribute to it. Write an entry in your reading journal in which you describe the conflict in the story you've just read. Who is against whom or what? Is the conflict resolved? What does it mean? What issues complicate things and prevent the characters from resolving their differences?

3. *Describe one or more of the characters in the story.* We have already seen how this is done in the chapter on Mary Freeman's "A Far-Away Melody." To amplify how you can learn about characters by writing about them, we suggest the following: a) Rewrite the story from a different character's perspective. For example, if the story is told by one character who describes others, pick one of the others and write the story as he or she would tell it. b) Write hypothetical dialogues between characters. For example, place two characters (from the same story or from different stories) in a situation that does not occur in the story and then create a dialogue that they might have in that situation. c) Write a description of one character by another.

4. *Characterize the atmosphere or setting of the story.* Both the emotional and physical environments are central to the craft of the short story, for the writer has but little time to create them and they must be effective and complete. Write a list of adjectives to describe the atmosphere. In your own words, write a single paragraph that describes the setting—its physical characteristics, its geography, the place or places where the story happens. Even if drawing isn't your strong point, it may be helpful to sketch one of the settings as you imagine it in your journal. Review the story and write a list of

items—words, phrases, objects mentioned—that make the story believable, tangible.

5. *Consider the connections among two or more stories.* There are many ways to do this, and in the next four chapters we suggest a few. Here are some general hints: Writers may use the same technique—narration, dialogue, surprise endings—in a variety of ways. Think about methods to compare technique. Settings may also recur among stories; for example, life in a small town is the subject of stories by Mary Freeman, I. L. Peretz, and Shirley Jackson. Look for similarities among characters. When you've read several stories, you can write a list of "hopes and aspirations" and then describe what each character from a series of stories seems to want from life. Creating such a list will enable you to discover connections that may not be readily obvious.

FICTION AS NARRATIVE

 The Art of Narration:
Giving Meaning to Action

There are two elements that are essential to a work of literature: someone to speak, and someone to listen. In the short story that follows, Saki's "The Story-Teller," the plot is shaped by two stories that are narrated *within* Saki's larger story by a woman and a man who have met by chance on a train. As a prologue to our study of fiction, let us look then at this very short story that swiftly, skillfully, and humorously examines speakers and listeners and the ways in which they relate to each other. Note the comparative absence of physical action in Saki's tale—it is dialogue that dominates "The Story-Teller."

SAKI (H. H. MUNRO)   (1870–1916)

The Story-Teller

It was a hot afternoon, and the railway carriage was correspondingly sultry, and the next stop was at Templecombe, nearly an hour ahead. The occupants of the carriage were a small girl, and a smaller girl, and a small boy. An aunt belonging to the children occupied one corner seat, and the further corner seat on the opposite side was occupied by a bachelor who was a stranger to their party, but the small girls and the small boy emphatically occupied the compartment. Both the aunt and the children were conversational in a limited, persistent way, reminding one of the attentions of a housefly that refused to be discouraged. Most of the aunt's remarks seemed to begin with "Don't," and nearly all of the children's remarks began with "Why?" The bachelor said nothing out loud.

"Don't, Cyril, don't," exclaimed the aunt, as the small boy began smacking the cushions of the seat, producing a cloud of dust at each blow.

"Come and look out of the window," she added.

The child moved reluctantly to the window. "Why are those sheep being driven out of that field?" he asked.

"I expect they are being driven to another field where there is more grass," said the aunt weakly.

"But there is lots of grass in that field," protested the boy; "there's nothing else but grass there. Aunt, there's lots of grass in that field."

"Perhaps the grass in the other field is better," suggested the aunt fatuously.

"Why is it better?" came the swift, inevitable question.

"Oh, look at those cows!" exclaimed the aunt. Nearly every field along the line had contained cows or bullocks, but she spoke as though she were drawing attention to a rarity.

"Why is the grass in the other field better?" persisted Cyril.

The frown on the bachelor's face was deepening to a scowl. He was a hard, unsympathetic man, the aunt decided in her mind. She was utterly unable to come to any satisfactory decision about the grass in the other field.

The smaller girl created a diversion by beginning to recite "On

109

the Road to Mandalay." She only knew the first line, but she put her limited knowledge to the fullest possible use. She repeated the line over and over again in a dreamy but resolute and very audible voice; it seemed to the bachelor as though some one had had a bet with her that she could not repeat the line aloud two thousand times without stopping. Whoever it was who had made the wager was likely to lose his bet.

"Come over here and listen to a story," said the aunt, when the bachelor had looked twice at her and once at the communication cord.

The children moved listlessly towards the aunt's end of the carriage. Evidently her reputation as a story-teller did not rank high in their estimation.

In a low, confidential voice, interrupted at frequent intervals by loud, petulant questions from her listeners, she began an unenterprising and deplorably uninteresting story about a little girl who was good, and made friends with every one on account of her goodness, and was finally saved from a mad bull by a number of rescuers who admired her moral character.

"Wouldn't they have saved her if she hadn't been good?" demanded the bigger of the small girls. It was exactly the question that the bachelor had wanted to ask.

"Well, yes," admitted the aunt lamely, "but I don't think they would have run quite so fast to her help if they had not liked her so much."

"It's the stupidest story I've ever heard," said the bigger of the small girls, with immense conviction.

"I didn't listen after the first bit, it was so stupid," said Cyril.

The smaller girl made no actual comment on the story, but she had long ago recommenced a murmured repetition of her favourite line.

"You don't seem to be a success as a story-teller," said the bachelor suddenly from his corner.

The aunt bristled in instant defence of this unexpected attack.

"It's a very difficult thing to tell stories that children can both understand and appreciate," she said stiffly.

"I don't agree with you," said the bachelor.

"Perhaps *you* would like to tell them a story," was the aunt's retort.

"Tell us a story," demanded the bigger of the small girls.

"Once upon a time," began the bachelor, "there was a little girl called Bertha, who was extraordinarily good."

The children's momentarily-aroused interest began at once to flicker; all stories seemed dreadfully alike, no matter who told them.

"She did all that she was told, she was always truthful, she kept her clothes clean, ate milk puddings as though they were jam tarts, learned her lessons perfectly, and was polite in her manners."

"Was she pretty?" asked the bigger of the small girls.

"Not as pretty as any of you," said the bachelor, "but she was horribly good."

There was a wave of reaction in favour of the story; the word *horrible* in connection with goodness was a novelty that commended itself. It seemed to introduce a ring of truth that was absent from the aunt's tales of infant life.

"She was so good," continued the bachelor, "that she won several medals for goodness, which she always wore, pinned on to her dress. There was a medal for obedience, another medal for punctuality, and a third for good behaviour. They were large metal medals and they clicked against one another as she walked. No other child in the town where she lived had as many as three medals, so everybody knew that she must be an extra good child."

"Horribly good," quoted Cyril.

"Everybody talked about her goodness, and the Prince of the country got to hear about it, and he said that as she was so very good she might be allowed once a week to walk in his park, which was just outside the town. It was a beautiful park, and no children were ever allowed in it, so it was a great honour for Bertha to be allowed to go there."

"Were there any sheep in the park?" demanded Cyril.

"No," said the bachelor, "there were no sheep."

"Why weren't there any sheep?" came the inevitable question arising out of that answer.

The aunt permitted herself a smile, which might almost have been described as a grin.

"There were no sheep in the park," said the bachelor, "because the Prince's mother had once had a dream that her son would either be killed by a sheep or else by a clock falling on him. For that reason the Prince never kept a sheep in his park or a clock in his palace."

The aunt suppressed a gasp of admiration.

"Was the Prince killed by a sheep or by a clock?" asked Cyril.

"He is still alive so we can't tell whether the dream will come true," said the bachelor unconcernedly; "anyway, there were no sheep in the park, but there were lots of little pigs running all over the place."

"What colour were they?"

"Black with white faces, white with black spots, black all over, grey with white patches, and some were white all over."

The story-teller paused to let a full idea of the park's treasures sink into the children's imaginations; then he resumed:

"Bertha was rather sorry to find that there were no flowers in the park. She had promised her aunts, with tears in her eyes, that she would not pick any of the kind Prince's flowers, and she had meant to keep her promise, so of course it made her feel silly to find that there were no flowers to pick."

"Why weren't there any flowers?"

"Because the pigs had eaten them all," said the bachelor promptly. "The gardeners had told the Prince that you couldn't have pigs and flowers, so he decided to have pigs and no flowers."

There was a murmur of approval at the excellence of the Prince's decision; so many people would have decided the other way.

"There were lots of other delightful things in the park. There were ponds with gold and blue and green fish in them, and trees with beautiful parrots that said clever things at a moment's notice, and humming birds that hummed all the popular tunes of the day. Bertha walked up and down and enjoyed herself immensely, and thought to herself: 'If I were not so extraordinarily good I should not have been allowed to come into this beautiful park and enjoy all that there is to be seen in it,' and her three medals clinked against one another as she walked and helped to remind her how very good she really was. Just then an enormous wolf came prowling into the park to see if it could catch a fat little pig for its supper."

"What colour was it?" asked the children, amid an immediate quickening of interest.

"Mud-colour all over, with a black tongue and pale grey eyes that gleamed with unspeakable ferocity. The first thing that it saw in the park was Bertha; her pinafore was so spotlessly white and clean that it could be seen from a great distance. Bertha saw the wolf and saw that it was stealing towards her, and she began to wish that she had never been allowed to come into the park. She ran as hard as she could, and the wolf came after her with huge leaps and bounds. She managed to reach a shrubbery of myrtle bushes and she hid herself in one of the thickets of the bushes. The wolf came sniffing among the branches, its black tongue lolling out of its mouth and its pale grey eyes glaring with rage. Bertha was terribly frightened, and thought to herself: 'If I had not been so extraordinarily good I should have been safe in the town at this moment.' However, the scent of the myrtle was so strong that the wolf could not sniff out where Bertha was hiding, and the bushes were so thick that he might have hunted about in them for a long time without catching sight of her, so he thought he might as well go off and catch a little pig instead. Bertha was trembling very much at having the wolf prowling and sniffing so near her, and as she trembled the medal for obedience clinked against the medals for good conduct and punctuality. The wolf was just moving away when he heard the sound of the medals clinking and stopped to listen; they clinked again in a bush quite near him. He dashed into the bush, his pale grey eyes gleaming with ferocity and triumph, and dragged Bertha out and devoured her to the last morsel. All that were left of her were her shoes, bits of clothing, and the three medals for goodness."

"Were any of the little pigs killed?"

"No, they all escaped."

"The story began badly," said the smaller of the small girls, "but it had a beautiful ending."

"It is the most beautiful story that I ever heard," said the bigger of the small girls, with immense decision.

"It is the *only* beautiful story I have ever heard," said Cyril.

A dissentient opinion came from the aunt.

"A most improper story to tell to young children! You have undermined the effect of years of careful teaching."

"At any rate," said the bachelor, collecting his belongings preparatory to leaving the carriage, "I kept them quiet for ten minutes, which was more than you were able to do."

"Unhappy woman!" he observed to himself as he walked down the platform of Templecombe station; "for the next six months or so those children will assail her in public with demands for an improper story!"

QUESTIONS FOR THINKING AND WRITING

1. How do the tales of the two storytellers differ? What motives are behind each tale? How do the motives differ from each other?
2. Although Saki calls this story "The Story-Teller," *two* people within it tell stories. Which of the two do you think is the storyteller of the title? Why do you think so?
3. Saki's story, like the bachelor's, is meant to amuse its audience. Do you think that, like the aunt, Saki also hopes to teach his readers something? If you do, what do you think this something might be?
4. We all tell stories among our family and friends. In your reading journal, write a story that you have either told or heard recently. As ideas and details come to you, allow yourself to elaborate on them as you may not have when the story was spoken.

As Saki's tale suggests, fiction is the art of the storyteller. Not only are writers of fiction storytellers themselves, but within every story they create a new storyteller, the narrator of the tale. It is the narrator's voice we hear speaking as we read a novel or short story. The narrator introduces the tale to us, keeps us amused during its telling, and dismisses us at its end. The narrator describes scenes and characters, relates events, sets the tone of the tale, and supplies whatever meanings or explanations the author sees fit to provide.

Reader and story are thus brought together by the narrator. For this reason, the study of fiction usually begins with a study of types of narrators and narrations. Let us now look at a very brief story, a modern tale that, strongly reminiscent of folk tales, suggests some of the oldest traditions of storytelling. Notice the simplicity of the action and the sharp contrasts drawn among the few characters. Listen to the voice of the storyteller as he builds his tale.

I. L. PERETZ (1851–1915)

If Not Higher

Early every Friday morning, at the time of the Penitential Prayers, the Rabbi of Nemirov would vanish.

He was nowhere to be seen—neither in the synagogue nor in the two Houses of Study nor at a *minyan*. And he was certainly not at home. His door stood open; whoever wished could go in and out; no one would steal from the rabbi. But not a living creature was within.

Where could the rabbi be? Where should he be? In heaven, no doubt. A rabbi has plenty of business to take care of just before the Days of Awe. Jews, God bless them, need livelihood, peace, health, and good matches. They want to be pious and good, but our sins are so great, and Satan of the thousand eyes watches the whole earth from one end to the other. What he sees he reports; he denounces, informs. Who can help us if not the rabbi!

That's what the people thought.

But once a Litvak came, and he laughed. You know the Litvaks. They think little of the Holy Books but stuff themselves with Talmud and law. So this Litvak points to a passage in the *Gemarah* —it sticks in your eyes—where it is written that even Moses, our Teacher, did not ascend to heaven during his lifetime but remained suspended two and a half feet below. Go argue with a Litvak!

So where can the rabbi be?

"That's not my business," said the Litvak, shrugging. Yet all the while—what a Litvak can do!—he is scheming to find out.

That same night, right after the evening prayers, the Litvak steals into the rabbi's room, slides under the rabbi's bed, and waits. He'll watch all night and discover where the rabbi vanishes and what he does during the Pentitential Prayers.

Someone else might have got drowsy and fallen asleep, but a Litvak is never at a loss; he recites a whole tractate of the Talmud by heart.

At dawn he hears the call to prayers.

The rabbi has already been awake for a long time. The Litvak has heard him groaning for a whole hour.

Whoever has heard the Rabbi of Nemirov groan knows how much

sorrow for all Israel, how much suffering, lies in each groan. A man's heart might break, hearing it. But a Litvak is made of iron; he listens and remains where he is. The rabbi, long life to him, lies on the bed, and the Litvak under the bed.

Then the Litvak hears the beds in the house begin to creak; he hears people jumping out of their beds, mumbling a few Jewish words, pouring water on their fingernails, banging doors. Everyone has left. It is again quiet and dark; a bit of light from the moon shines through the shutters.

(Afterward the Litvak admitted that when he found himself alone with the rabbi a great fear took hold of him. Goose pimples spread across his skin, and the roots of his earlocks pricked him like needles. A trifle: to be alone with the rabbi at the time of the Penitential Prayers! But a Litvak is stubborn. So he quivered like a fish in water and remained where he was.)

Finally the rabbi, long life to him, arises. First he does what befits a Jew. Then he goes to the clothes closet and takes out a bundle of peasant clothes: linen trousers, high boots, a coat, a big felt hat, and a long wide leather belt studded with brass nails. The rabbi gets dressed. From his coat pocket dangles the end of a heavy peasant rope.

The rabbi goes out, and the Litvak follows him.

On the way the rabbi stops in the kitchen, bends down, takes an ax from under the bed, puts it in his belt, and leaves the house. The Litvak trembles but continues to follow.

The hushed dread of the Days of Awe hangs over the dark streets. Every once in a while a cry rises from some *minyan* reciting the Penitential Prayers, or from a sickbed. The rabbi hugs the sides of the streets, keeping to the shade of the houses. He glides from house to house, and the Litvak after him. The Litvak hears the sound of his heartbeats mingling with the sound of the rabbi's heavy steps. But he keeps on going and follows the rabbi to the outskirts of the town.

A small wood stands behind the town.

The rabbi, long life to him, enters the wood. He takes thirty or forty steps and stops by a small tree. The Litvak, overcome with amazement, watches the rabbi take the ax out of his belt and strike the tree. He hears the tree creak and fall. The rabbi chops the tree into logs and the logs into sticks. Then he makes a bundle of the wood and ties it with the rope in his pocket. He puts the bundle of wood on his back, shoves the ax back into his belt, and returns to the town.

He stops at a back street beside a small broken-down shack and knocks at the window.

"Who is there?" asks a frightened voice. The Litvak recognizes it as the voice of a sick Jewish woman.

"I," answers the rabbi in the accent of a peasant.

"Who is I?"

Again the rabbi answers in Russian. "Vassil."

"Who is Vassil, and what do you want?"

"I have wood to sell, very cheap." And, not waiting for the woman's reply, he goes into the house.

The Litvak steals in after him. In the gray light of early morning he sees a poor room with broken, miserable furnishings. A sick woman, wrapped in rags, lies on the bed. She complains bitterly, "Buy? How can I buy? Where will a poor widow get money?"

"I'll lend it to you," answers the supposed Vassil. "It's only six cents."

"And how will I ever pay you back?" said the poor woman, groaning.

"Foolish one," says the rabbi reproachfully. "See, you are a poor sick Jew, and I am ready to trust you with a little wood. I am sure you'll pay. While you, you have such a great and mighty God and you don't trust him for six cents."

"And who will kindle the fire?" said the widow. "Have I the strength to get up? My son is at work."

"I'll kindle the fire," answers the rabbi.

As the rabbi put the wood into the oven he recited, in a groan, the first portion of the Penitential Prayers.

As he kindled the fire and the wood burned brightly, he recited, a bit more joyously, the second portion of the Penitential Prayers. When the fire was set he recited the third portion, and then he shut the stove.

The Litvak who saw all this became a disciple of the rabbi.

And ever after, when another disciple tells how the Rabbi of Nemirov ascends to heaven at the time of the Penitential Prayers, the Litvak does not laugh. He only adds quietly, "If not higher."

"Early every Friday morning . . . the Rabbi of Nemirov would vanish." The statement is blunt and surprising. Rabbis do not usually vanish. We read on, expecting some explanation for the rabbi's behavior. But we find only more mystery. First the narrator tells us where the rabbi isn't. Then he tells us where the townspeople think he is; then he introduces the Litvak who argues that the rabbi can't be there, either. "So where can the rabbi be?" By the time the Litvak sets out to discover the answer, we may be pardoned for being curious ourselves. The narrator has certainly done his best to catch our interest and make us curious.

We notice, meanwhile, that the narrator is not unbiased. Although he takes no direct part in the tale, he does identify himself somewhat with the townspeople, slipping from the statement that "*they* want to be pious and good" to the recognition that *"our* sins are so great. . . . Who can help us if not the rabbi!" He pulls back in the next sentence: "That's what the people thought"; but the identification remains in our minds.

That "our" and "us", in fact, might almost include us, the readers. Certainly the narrator treats us as people who share with him knowledge of rabbis and religious matters and Litvaks—especially Litvaks. "You know the Litvaks . . . . Go argue with a Litvak!" The Litvak has an important role in the story. In contrast to the townspeople, who are ready to spread and believe miraculous rumors, the Litvak is a sceptic. He is a well-read man, so studied in law and religious books that he can keep himself awake all night by reciting Biblical commentaries; but he is a sceptic, nonetheless. It is precisely because he is sceptical, however, that the Litvak becomes curious enough to find out the real answer to the mystery; and it is he who has the final word at the end of the tale.

The Litvak is almost a type or symbol of the person with more knowledge than faith. The narrator, in fact, insists on seeing him as a type— "the Litvak" rather than a man with a name. At the same time, his prejudice characterizes the narrator. We feel that he'd like to see the Litvak shown up, the rabbi and townsfolk triumphant; we feel he himself has a stake in the outcome of the tale.

As the tale continues, the suspense builds. The narrator helps it along by his talk of "groaning" and "hushed dread," his relation of how even the Litvak suffers "goose pimples" and "a great fear," how he "trembles" and quivers "like a fish in water."

Finally, the mystery is revealed. Now, for the first time, we hear voices other than the narrator's. We hear the rabbi (the only words we do hear from him) and the sick woman (the only characterization we have of her; and it's enough). We see what the Litvak sees, hear what he hears; and we are not told what to think about any of it. The narrator, who heretofore has been generous with his comments, is now letting actions and characters speak for themselves.

Even the conclusion is restrained. We learn that "the Litvak who saw all this became a disciple of the rabbi," and we learn his new attitude toward the tale that the rabbi ascends to heaven on Fridays. Note that this is the Litvak's attitude; it is he, not the narrator, who says, "If not higher," and so makes the final judgment on the rabbi's actions. Note, too, that we are told nothing else of how the Litvak's life may have changed. What does becoming the rabbi's disciple mean for him? That we must figure out for ourselves.

The tale is rich in interpretive value. There is no need for the narrator to characterize the rabbi's actions; we can all supply our own view of their significance. Similarly, we can all tell what the Litvak means by his comment, "If not higher," though we might each phrase the meaning somewhat differently. At the start of the story, the Litvak was looking for something. At the end, he has found it, and we feel the value to him of the discovery. Yet even this is lightly handled, in keeping with the slightly humorous tone of the story. The narrator continues to focus on his one question, "Where does the rabbi go early Friday mornings?" It is the solution of that mystery, the resolution of that conflict between Litvak and the townspeople, that he presents as the "quietly" triumphant ending of his story. Anything else we choose to read into it is our own affair.

"If Not Higher," then, is a tale (almost a "tall tale") told by a narrator who takes no direct part in the action, but who has some concern that the story come out well. His voice is a speaking voice, sometimes humorous, sometimes emphatic, sometimes exasperated. Clearly, this is a practiced speaker, a man who enjoys telling stories. We sense his enjoyment in every line of the tale.

In contrast, look at this next story. It too is told by a narrator who remains outside the action; it too is a tale that lends itself to symbolic interpretation. But notice the differences in tone and technique. What attitudes does this narrator convey? How far does she go in interpreting actions and characters for us?

SHIRLEY JACKSON (1919–1965)

The Lottery

The morning of June 27th was clear and sunny, with the fresh warmth of a full-summer day; the flowers were blossoming profusely and the grass was richly green. The people of the village began to gather in the square, between the post office and the bank, around ten o'clock; in some towns there were so many people that the lottery took two days and had to be started on June 26th, but in this village, where there were only about three hundred people, the whole lottery took less than two hours, so it could begin at ten o'clock in the morning and still be through in time to allow the villagers to get home for noon dinner.

The children assembled first, of course. School was recently over for the summer, and the feeling of liberty sat uneasily on most of them; they tended to gather together quietly for a while before they broke into boisterous play, and their talk was still of the classroom and the teacher, of books and reprimands. Bobby Martin had already stuffed his pockets full of stones, and the other boys soon followed his example, selecting the smoothest and roundest stones; Bobby and Harry Jones and Dickie Delacroix—the villagers pronounced this name "Dellacroy"—eventually made a great pile of stones in one corner of the square and guarded it against the raids of the other boys. The girls stood aside, talking among themselves, looking over their shoulders at the boys, and the very small children rolled in the dust or clung to the hands of their older brothers or sisters.

Soon the men began to gather, surveying their own children, speaking of planting and rain, tractors and taxes. They stood together, away from the pile of stones in the corner, and their jokes were quiet and they smiled rather than laughed. The women, wearing faded house dresses and sweaters, came shortly after their menfolk. They greeted one another and exchanged bits of gossip as they went to join their husbands. Soon the women, standing by their husbands, began to call to their children, and the children came reluctantly, having to be called four or five times. Bobby Martin ducked under his mother's grasping hand and ran, laughing, back to the pile of stones. His father spoke up sharply, and Bobby came quickly and took his place between his father and his oldest brother.

The lottery was conducted—as were the square dances, the teenage club, the Halloween program—by Mr. Summers, who had time and energy to devote to civic activities. He was a round-faced, jovial man and he ran the coal business, and people were sorry for him, because he had no children and his wife was a scold. When he arrived in the square, carrying the black wooden box, there was a murmur of conversation among the villagers, and he waved and called, "Little late today, folks." The postmaster, Mr. Graves, followed him, carrying a three-legged stool, and the stool was put in the center of the square and Mr. Summers set the black box down on it. The villagers kept their distance, leaving a space between themselves and the stool, and when Mr. Summers said, "Some of you fellows want to give me a hand?" there was a hesitation before two men, Mr. Martin and his oldest son, Baxter, came forward to hold the box steady on the stool while Mr. Summers stirred up the papers inside it.

The original paraphernalia for the lottery had been lost long ago, and the black box now resting on the stool had been put into use even before Old Man Warner, the oldest man in town, was born. Mr. Summers spoke frequently to the villagers about making a new box, but no one liked to upset even as much tradition as was represented by the black box. There was a story that the present box had been made with some pieces of the box that had preceded it, the one that had been constructed when the first people settled down to make a village here. Every year, after the lottery, Mr. Summers began talking again about a new box, but every year the subject was allowed to fade off without anything's being done. The black box grew shabbier each year; by now it was no longer completely black but splintered badly along one side to show the original wood color, and in some places faded or stained.

Mr. Martin and his oldest son, Baxter, held the black box securely on the stool until Mr. Summers had stirred the papers thoroughly with his hand. Because so much of the ritual had been forgotten or discarded, Mr. Summers had been successful in having slips of paper substituted for the chips of wood that had been used for generations. Chips of wood, Mr. Summers had argued, had been all very well when the village was tiny, but now that the population was more than three hundred and likely to keep on growing, it was necessary to use something that would fit more easily into the black box. The night before the lottery, Mr. Summers and Mr. Graves made up the slips of paper and put them in the box, and it was then taken to the safe of Mr. Summers' coal company and locked up until Mr. Summers was ready to take it to the square next morning. The rest of the year, the box was put away, sometimes one place, sometimes another; it had spent one year in Mr. Graves's barn and another year underfoot in the post office, and sometimes it was set on a shelf in the Martin grocery and left there.

There was a great deal of fussing to be done before Mr. Summers declared the lottery open. There were the lists to make up—of heads of families, heads of households in each family, members of each household in each family. There was the proper swearing-in of Mr. Summers by the postmaster, as the official of the lottery; at one time, some people remembered, there had been a recital of some sort, performed by the official of the lottery, a perfunctory, tuneless chant that had been rattled off duly each year; some people believed that the official of the lottery used to stand just so when he said or sang it, others believed that he was supposed to walk among the people, but years and years ago this part of the ritual had been allowed to lapse. There had been, also, a ritual salute, which the official of the lottery had had to use in addressing each person who came up to draw from the box, but this also had changed with time, until now it was felt necessary only for the official to speak to each person approaching. Mr. Summers was very good at all this; in his clean white shirt and blue jeans, with one hand resting carelessly on the black box. he seemed very proper and important as he talked interminably to Mr. Graves and the Martins.

Just as Mr. Summers finally left off talking and turned to the assembled villagers, Mrs. Hutchinson came hurriedly along the path to the square, her sweater thrown over her shoulders, and slid into place in the back of the crowd. "Clean forgot what day it was," she said to Mrs. Delacroix, who stood next to her, and they both laughed softly. "Thought my old man was out back stacking wood," Mrs. Hutchinson went on, "and then I looked out the window and the kids were gone, and then I remembered it was the twenty-seventh and came a-running." She dried her hands on her apron, and Mrs. Delacroix said, "You're in time, though. They're still talking away up there."

Mrs. Hutchinson craned her neck to see through the crowd and found her husband and children standing near the front. She tapped Mrs. Delacroix on the arm as a farewell and began to make her way through the crowd. The people separated good-humoredly to let her through; two or three people said, in voices just loud enough to be heard across the crowd, "Here comes your Missus, Hutchinson," and "Bill, she made it after all." Mrs. Hutchinson reached her husband, and Mr. Summers, who had been waiting, said cheerfully, "Thought we were going to have to get on without you, Tessie." Mrs. Hutchinson said, grinning, "Wouldn't have me leave m'dishes in the sink, now, would you, Joe?" and soft laughter ran through the crowd as the people stirred back into position after Mrs. Hutchinson's arrival.

"Well, now," Mr. Summers said soberly, "guess we better get started, get this over with, so's we can go back to work. Anybody ain't here?"

"Dunbar," several people said. "Dunbar, Dunbar."

Mr. Summers consulted his list. "Clyde Dunbar," he said. "That's right. He's broke his leg, hasn't he? Who's drawing for him?"

"Me, I guess," a woman said, and Mr. Summers turned to look at her. "Wife draws for her husband," Mrs. Summers said. "Don't you have a grown boy to do it for you, Janey?" Although Mr. Summers and everyone else in the village knew the answer perfectly well, it was the business of the official of the lottery to ask such questions formally. Mr. Summers waited with an expression of polite interest while Mrs. Dunbar answered.

"Horace's not but sixteen yet," Mrs. Dunbar said regretfully. "Guess I gotta fill in for the old man this year."

"Right," Mr. Summers said. He made a note on the list he was holding. Then he asked, "Watson boy drawing this year?"

A tall boy in the crowd raised his hand. "Here," he said. "I'm drawing for m'mother and me." He blinked his eyes nervously and ducked his head as several voices in the crowd said things like "Good fellow, Jack," and "Glad to see your mother's got a man to do it."

"Well," Mr. Summers said, "guess that's everyone. Old Man Warner make it?"

"Here," a voice said, and Mr. Summers nodded.

A sudden hush fell on the crowd as Mr. Summers cleared his throat and looked at the list. "All ready?" he called. "Now, I'll read the names—heads of families first—and the men come up and take a paper out of the box. Keep the paper folded in your hand without looking at it until everyone has had a turn. Everything clear?"

The people had done it so many times that they only half listened to the directions; most of them were quiet, wetting their lips, not looking around. Then Mr. Summers raised one hand high and said, "Adams." A man disengaged himself from the crowd and came forward. "Hi, Steve," Mr. Summers said, and Mr. Adams said, "Hi, Joe." They grinned at one another humorlessly and nervously. Then Mr. Adams reached into the black box and took out a folded paper. He held it firmly by one corner as he turned and went hastily back to his place in the crowd, where he stood a little apart from his family, not looking down at his hand.

"Allen," Mr. Summers said. "Anderson . . . Bentham."

"Seems like there's no time at all between lotteries any more," Mrs. Delacroix said to Mrs. Graves in the back row. "Seems like we got through with the last one only last week."

"Time sure goes fast," Mrs. Graves said.

"Clark . . . Delacroix."

"There goes my old man," Mrs. Delacroix said. She held her breath while her husband went forward.

"Dunbar," Mr. Summers said, and Mrs. Dunbar went steadily to the box while one of the women said, "Go on, Janey," and another said, "There she goes."

"We're next," Mrs. Graves said. She watched while Mr. Graves came around from the side of the box, greeted Mr. Summers gravely, and selected a slip of paper from the box. By now, all through the crowd there were men holding the small folded papers in their large hands, turning them over and over nervously. Mrs. Dunbar and her two sons stood together, Mrs. Dunbar holding the slip of paper.

"Harburt . . . Hutchinson."

"Get up there, Bill," Mrs. Hutchinson said, and the people near her laughed.

"Jones."

"They do say," Mr. Adams said to Old Man Warner, who stood next to him, "that over in the north village they're talking of giving up the lottery."

Old Man Warner snorted. "Pack of crazy fools," he said. "Listening to the young folks, nothing's good enough for *them*. Next thing you know, they'll be wanting to go back to living in caves, nobody work any more, live *that* way for a while. Used to be a saying about 'Lottery in June, corn be heavy soon.' First thing you know, we'd all be eating stewed chickweed and acorns. There's *always* been a lottery," he added petulantly. "Bad enough to see young Joe Summers up there joking with everybody."

"Some places have already quit lotteries," Mrs. Adams said.

"Nothing but trouble in *that*," Old Man Warner said stoutly. "Pack of young fools."

"Martin." And Bobby Martin watched his father go forward. "Overdyke . . . Percy."

"I wish they'd hurry," Mrs. Dunbar said to her older son. "I wish they'd hurry."

"They're almost through," her son said.

"You get ready to run tell Dad," Mrs. Dunbar said.

Mr. Summers called his own name and then stepped forward precisely and selected a slip from the box. Then he called, "Warner."

"Seventy-seventh year I been in the lottery," Old Man Warner said as he went through the crowd. "Seventy-seventh time."

"Watson." The tall boy came awkwardly through the crowd. Someone said, "Don't be nervous, Jack," and Mr. Summers said, "Take your time, son."

"Zanini."

After that, there was a long pause, a breathless pause, until Mr. Summers, holding his slip of paper in the air, said, "All right, fellows." For a minute, no one moved, and then all the slips of paper were opened. Suddenly, all the women began to speak at once, saying, "Who is it?" "Who's got it?" "Is it the Dunbars?" "Is it the Watsons?" Then the voices began to say, "It's Hutchinson. It's Bill," "Bill Hutchinson's got it."

"Go tell your father," Mrs. Dunbar said to her older son.

People began to look around to see the Hutchinsons. Bill Hutchinson was standing quiet, staring down at the paper in his hand.

Suddenly, Tessie Hutchinson shouted to Mr. Summers, "You didn't give him time enough to take any paper he wanted. I saw you. It wasn't fair."

"Be a good sport, Tessie," Mrs. Delacroix called, and Mrs. Graves said, "All of us took the same chance."

"Shut up, Tessie," Bill Hutchinson said.

"Well, everyone," Mr. Summers said, "that was done pretty fast, and now we've got to be hurrying a little more to get done in time." He consulted his next list. "Bill," he said, "you draw for the Hutchinson family. You got any other households in the Hutchinsons?"

"There's Don and Eva," Mrs. Hutchinson yelled. "Make *them* take their chance!"

"Daughters draw with their husbands' families, Tessie," Mr. Summers said gently. "You know that as well as anyone else."

"It wasn't *fair*," Tessie said.

"I guess not, Joe," Bill Hutchinson said regretfully. "My daughter draws with her husband's family, that's only fair. And I've got no other family except the kids."

"Then, as far as drawing for families is concerned, it's you," Mr. Summers said in explanation, "and as far as drawing for households is concerned, that's you, too. Right?"

"Right," Bill Hutchinson said.

"How many kids, Bill?" Mr. Summers asked formally.

"Three," Bill Hutchinson said. "There's Bill, Jr., and Nancy, and little Dave. And Tessie and me."

"All right, then," Mr. Summers said. "Harry, you got their tickets back?"

Mr. Graves nodded and held up the slips of paper. "Put them in the box, then," Mr. Summers directed. "Take Bill's and put it in."

"I think we ought to start over," Mrs. Hutchinson said, as quietly as she could. "I tell you it wasn't *fair*. You didn't give him time enough to choose. *Every*body saw that."

Mr. Graves had selected the five slips and put them in the box, and he dropped all the papers but those onto the ground, where the breeze caught them and lifted them off.

"Listen, everybody," Mrs. Hutchinson was saying to the people around her.

"Ready, Bill?" Mr. Summers asked, and Bill Hutchinson, with one quick glance around at his wife and children, nodded.

"Remember," Mr. Summers said, "take the slips and keep them folded until each person has taken one. Harry, you help little Dave." Mr. Graves took the hand of the little boy, who came willingly with him up to the box. "Take a paper out of the box, Davy," Mr. Summers said. Davy put his hand into the box and laughed. "Take just *one* paper," Mr. Summers said. "Harry, you hold it for him." Mr. Graves took the child's hand and removed the folded paper from the tight fist and held it while little Dave stood next to him and looked up at him wonderingly.

"Nancy next," Mr. Summers said. Nancy was twelve, and her school friends breathed heavily as she went forward, switching her skirt, and took a slip daintily from the box. "Bill, Jr.," Mr. Summers said, and Billy, his face red and his feet over-large, nearly knocked the box over as he got a paper out. "Tessie," Mr. Summers said. She hesitated for a minute, looking around defiantly, and then set her lips and went up to the box. She snatched a paper out and held it behind her.

"Bill," Mr. Summers said, and Bill Hutchinson reached into the box and felt around, bringing his hand out at last with the slip of paper in it.

The crowd was quiet. A girl whispered, "I hope it's not Nancy," and the sound of the whisper reached the edges of the crowd.

"It's not the way it used to be," Old Man Warner said clearly. "People ain't the way they used to be."

"All right," Mr. Summers said. "Open the papers. Harry, you open little Dave's."

Mr. Graves opened the slip of paper and there was a general sigh through the crowd as he held it up and everyone could see that it was blank. Nancy and Bill, Jr., opened theirs at the same time, and both beamed and laughed, turning around to the crowd and holding their slips of paper above their heads.

"Tessie," Mr. Summers said. There was a pause, and then Mr. Summers looked at Bill Hutchinson, and Bill unfolded his paper and showed it. It was blank.

"It's Tessie," Mr. Summers said, and his voice was hushed. "Show us her paper, Bill."

Bill Hutchinson went over to his wife and forced the slip of paper out of her hand. It had a black spot on it, the black spot Mr. Summers had made the night before with the heavy pencil in the coal-company office. Bill Hutchinson held it up, and there was a stir in the crowd.

"All right, folks," Mr. Summers said. "Let's finish quickly."

Although the villagers had forgotten the ritual and lost the original black box, they still remembered to use stones. The pile of stones the boys had made earlier was ready; there were stones on the ground with the blowing scraps of paper that had come out of the box. Mrs. Delacroix selected a stone so large she had to pick it up with both hands and turned to Mrs. Dunbar. "Come on," she said. "Hurry up."

Mrs. Dunbar had small stones in both hands, and she said, gasping for breath, "I can't run at all. You'll have to go ahead and I'll catch up with you."

The children had stones already, and someone gave little Davy Hutchinson a few pebbles.

Tessie Hutchinson was in the center of a cleared space by now, and she held her hands out desperately as the villagers moved in on her. "It isn't fair," she said. A stone hit her on the side of the head.

Old Man Warner was saying, "Come on, come on, everyone." Steve Adams was in the front of the crowd of villagers, with Mrs. Graves beside him.

"It isn't fair, it isn't right," Mrs. Hutchinson screamed, and then they were upon her.

"If Not Higher" concentrates on action: the rabbi's mysterious Friday morning activities, the Litvak's detective work. Characterization is less important. The rabbi, the Litvak, and the sick woman are types rather than fully characterized individuals; and, except for the Litvak's conversion (about which we are told very little) they do not change or develop during the story.

"The Lottery," too, centers on action and mystery almost to the exclusion of individual characterization. Of all the townspeople, Old Man Warner alone stands out as a distinguishable figure. Even he is a type: the "Old Man," fiercely proud of his past, dismissing as "young fools" all those who would change things. The rest are simply members of a small farming community, so like each other that one description often serves for all. Thus, "the children came reluctantly, having to be called four or five times," and "the people . . . only half listened to the directions; most of them were quiet, wetting their lips, not looking around." These descriptions, moreover, center on observable facts: the number of times the children have to be called, the posture and nervous motions of the villagers. We were given some inside knowledge of the Litvak's sensations, being told that "a great fear took hold of him," that he "hears the sound of his heartbeats mingling with the sound of the rabbi's heavy steps." We are told almost nothing about the villagers' thoughts and emotions that any reporter at the scene of the lottery could not have told us.

The narrator can tell us facts about the lottery, however, that only a very well informed reporter could supply. She can inform us that "the original paraphernalia for the lottery had been lost long ago," that the current black box (which "had been put into use even before Old Man Warner, the oldest man in the town, was born") is still used because "no one liked to upset even as much tradition as was represented by the black box." She knows what parts of the ritual have been lost and what parts are imperfectly remembered; and from time to time, she doles out some bit of this information as background to the unfolding ritual.

Does the narrator also know why the lottery was originally instituted, or what this group of villagers, who have lost so much of its history, think it accomplishes? If she does, she doesn't tell us. The narrator of "If Not Higher" made a great mystery of the rabbi's whereabouts by insisting that they were a great mystery and by depicting all the townspeople as being in a state of wonder and suspense. The narrator of "The Lottery" creates suspense by describing in a calm, matter-of-fact way the matter-of-fact behavior of a group of undemonstrative people. The people are engaged in some poorly defined event that seems to represent a mildly exciting once-a-year break in their normal routine. Therefore, our suspense comes largely from the fact that we feel ourselves to be the only people who don't know what's going on. (Until Tessie Hutchinson first cries "It wasn't fair," for instance, we don't even know whether the "winner" of this lottery is lucky or unlucky.) And so we keep waiting for the explanation, which never comes.

We are given some clues as to what's going on; but the author slips them in so quietly that we may not realize that they are clues until we read the story a second time. The "pile of stones," for instance, is introduced as though it were merely part of the children's "boisterous play": "Bobby and Harry Jones and Dickie Delacroix . . . eventually made a great pile of stones in one corner of the square and guarded it against the raids of the other boys." Not until the very end of the story do we find out the significance of those stones: "Although the villagers had forgotten the ritual and lost the original black box, they still remembered to use stones." But we still are not told what meaning—if any—the townsfolk find in their use.

We are not even told directly that Tessie is killed. We have to fill in that fact for ourselves, an act of participation that for some readers adds a last gruesome twist to the end of the story. Tessie's protests have warned us that the lottery ends badly for the chosen one. But many readers still have trouble at first realizing just how badly it does end, especially since the narrator's calm, reportorial voice never changes its tone, reporting as objectively as ever the women's conversation and the fact that "someone gave little Davy Hutchinson a few pebbles." The almost casual acceptance by villagers and narrator alike of the stoning to death of a woman by her neighbors and family throws the full burden of reaction on us, while the "just plain folks" characterization of the villagers forces us to interpret the action in the broadest possible terms, asking not only, "Can these villagers really be doing this?" but also "Do people really act this way?"

All the unanswered questions rise at this point. Why are these people doing this thing? How do they justify it to themselves? All the action in "If Not Higher" was slightly unrealistic (one man hiding under a bed, another disguising himself), so the not-quite-realistic ending came as no shock. But the style of "The Lottery" has been unrelentingly realistic throughout, and its ending is a deliberate shock. All along we've been feeling, "Yes, a group of neighbors would behave as this group behaves. What a careful observer this writer is; what a fine eye for details of behavior she has." Now we want to say, "No; she's mistaken; they wouldn't do that." But the acceptance we've given the story so far, linked with our own knowledge of the ways people do behave toward each other, makes our rebellion all but impossible. We can dismiss the actual details; ritual stonings rarely occur in the twentieth century. But we cannot dismiss the symbolic import of the action, nor escape the grim vision of human nature that "The Lottery" 's action and narrator thrust upon us. Good humor and neighborliness are part of that vision; but what else is there? How would you personally interpret "The Lottery?"

QUESTIONS FOR THINKING AND WRITING

When we study literature, we first look at each story as an entity in itself, existing on its own terms. We enter the world of the story and speak of its characters and narrator as though they were living people. Eventually, however, we begin to wonder about the writers of the stories. Why did they choose to create these characters, to have them perform these actions, to tell their tales from this particular point of view?

We can never know exactly what writers had in mind when they were writing their stories. The process of writing is too complex, with too much of it hidden even from the writers themselves, to allow any sure or simple answers to that question. But we should examine our own ideas on the subject—our sense of what the writers seem to consider important and what values or feelings of ours they seem to be invoking; for our impression of the writers' values and intentions plays an important part in our response to their work.

If we look back at "The Lottery" and "If Not Higher," for instance, we notice that these stories project nearly opposite views of their characters. To define the contrast, we can ask such questions as, "What things seem most important to the characters in each story? What mood are we in at the end of the story?" Judging from this opposition, we can then ask what aspects of human life each author seems to consider important. We can ask, "To what feelings of mine does each story appeal? To what values?" And we can then try to decide whether our own values and feelings, and our sense of the authors', are as sharply opposed as our sense of the characters' values, or whether our interpretations of the authors' views and of the appeals their tales make to us do in fact share some common elements.

Draw a straight line down the middle of a fresh page in your reading journal. At the top of each column write the titles of the preceding two stories. Now chart out the values of the people in each village by writing brief descriptions of such characteristics as neighborliness, cooperation, atmosphere, and religious attitudes. You may wish to refine this list and then use it as the basis for an essay about these two stories.

3 The Omniscient Narrator

"If Not Higher" and "The Lottery" are tales related by omniscient narrators. As the term implies, these narrators "know all" about the characters and events of which they tell. Somewhat distanced by their greater knowledge from action and actors alike, omniscient narrators project an air of authority over their material.

Their relation to the readers is a more variable matter. Peretz's narrator treats us familiarly, sharing occasional asides with us ("You know the Litvaks") or letting us into his characters' secrets. Jackson's narrator keeps us at the same distance that she keeps her material. (This type of narrator, who takes no sides, makes no interpretations, and lets us watch only the characters' public actions, rather than letting us into their private thoughts and feelings, is sometimes called an **objective narrator,** with the term **omniscient narrator** being reserved for those who do relate their characters' thoughts or interpret their actions for us.)

We begin this chapter with another told by an omniscient narrator. Read it through and read the questions that follow it. Then read it again with the questions in mind, seeing how the narrators' voices help shape your view of the story's action and characters.

NATHANIEL HAWTHORNE (1804–1864)

Young Goodman Brown

Young Goodman Brown came forth at sunset, into the street of Salem village, but put his head back, after crossing the threshold, to exchange a parting kiss with his young wife. And Faith, as the wife was aptly named, thrust her own pretty head into the street, letting the wind play with the pink ribbons of her cap, while she called to Goodman Brown.

"Dearest heart," whispered she, softly and rather sadly, when her lips were close to his ear, "prithee, put off your journey until sunrise, and sleep in your own bed to-night. A lone woman is troubled with such dreams and such thoughts, that she's afeard of herself, sometimes. Pray, tarry with me this night, dear husband, of all nights in the year!"

"My love and my Faith," replied young Goodman Brown, "of all nights in the year, this one night must I tarry away from thee. My journey, as thou callest it, forth and back again, must needs be done 'twixt now and sunrise. What, my sweet, pretty wife, dost thou doubt me already, and we but three months married!"

"Then God bless you!" said Faith with the pink ribbons, "and may you find all well, when you come back."

"Amen!" cried Goodman Brown. "Say thy prayers, dear Faith, and go to bed at dusk, and no harm will come to thee."

So they parted; and the young man pursued his way, until, being about to turn the corner by the meeting-house, he looked back and saw the head of Faith still peeping after him, with a melancholy air, in spite of her pink ribbons.

"Poor little Faith!" thought he, for his heart smote him. "What a wretch am I, to leave her on such an errand! She talks of dreams, too. Methought, as she spoke, there was trouble in her face, as if a dream had warned her what work is to be done to-night. But no, no! 't would kill her to think it. Well; she's a blessed angel on earth; and after this one night, I'll cling to her skirts and follow her to Heaven."

With this excellent resolve for the future, Goodman Brown felt himself justified in making more haste on his present evil purpose. He had taken a dreary road, darkened by all the gloomiest trees of the forest, which barely stood aside to let the narrow path creep through, and closed immediately behind. It was all as lonely as could be; and there is this peculiarity in such a solitude, that the traveller knows not who may be concealed by the innumerable trunks and the thick boughs overhead; so that, with lonely footsteps, he may yet be passing through an unseen multitude.

"There may be a devilish Indian behind every tree," said Goodman Brown to himself; and he glanced fearfully behind him, as he added, "What if the devil himself should be at my very elbow!"

His head being turned back, he passed a crook of the road, and looking forward again, beheld the figure of a man, in grave and decent attire, seated at the foot of an old tree. He arose at Goodman Brown's approach, and walked onward, side by side with him.

"You are late, Goodman Brown," said he. "The clock of the Old South was striking, as I came through Boston; and that is full fifteen minutes agone."

"Faith kept me back awhile," replied the young man, with a tremor in his voice, caused by the sudden appearance of his companion, though not wholly unexpected.

It was now deep dusk in the forest, and deepest in that part of it where these two were journeying. As nearly as could be discerned, the second traveller was about fifty years old, apparently in the same rank of life as Goodman Brown, and bearing a considerable resemblance to him, though perhaps more in expression than features. Still, they might have been taken for father and son. And yet, though the elder person was as simply clad as the younger, and as simple in manner too, he had an indescribable air of one who knew the world, and would not have felt abashed at the governor's dinner-table, or in King William's court, were it possible that his affairs should call him thither. But the only thing about him that could be fixed upon as remarkable, was his staff, which bore the likeness of a great black snake, so curiously wrought, that it might almost be seen to twist and wriggle itself like a living serpent. This, of course, must have been an ocular deception, assisted by the uncertain light.

"Come, Goodman Brown!" cried his fellow-traveller, "this is a dull pace for the beginning of a journey. Take my staff, if you are so soon weary."

"Friend," said the other, exchanging his slow pace for a full stop, "having kept covenant by meeting thee here, it is my purpose now to return whence I came. I have scruples, touching the matter thou wot'st of."

"Sayest thou so?" replied he of the serpent, smiling apart. "Let us walk on, nevertheless, reasoning as we go, and if I convince thee not, thou shalt turn back. We are but a little way in the forest, yet."

"Too far, too far!" exclaimed the goodman, unconsciously resuming his walk. "My father never went into the woods on such an errand, nor his father before him. We have been a race of honest men and good Christians, since the days of the martyrs. And shall I be the first of the name of Brown that ever took this path and kept—"

"Such company, thou wouldst say," observed the elder person, interrupting his pause. "Well said, Goodman Brown! I have been as well acquainted with your family as with ever a one among the Puritans; and that's no trifle to say. I helped your grandfather, the constable, when he lashed the Quaker woman so smartly through the streets of Salem. And it was I that brought your father a pitch-pine knot, kindled at my own hearth, to set fire to an Indian village, in King Philip's war. They were my good friends, both; and many a pleasant walk have we had along this path, and returned merrily after midnight. I would fain be friends with you, for their sake."

"If it be as thou sayest," replied Goodman Brown, "I marvel they never spoke of these matters. Or, verily, I marvel not, seeing that the least rumor of the sort would have driven them from New England. We are a people of prayer, and good works to boot, and abide no such wickedness."

"Wickedness or not," said the traveller with twisted staff, "I have a very general acquaintance here in New England. The deacons of many a church have drunk the communion wine with me; the selectmen, of divers towns, make me their chairman; and a majority of the Great and General Court are firm supporters of my interest. The governor and I, too—but these are state secrets."

"Can this be so!" cried Goodman Brown, with a stare of amazement at his undisturbed companion. "Howbeit, I have nothing to do with the governor and council; they have their own ways, and are no rule for a simple husbandman like me. But, were I to go on with thee, how should I meet the eye of that good old man, our minister, at Salem village? Oh, his voice would make me tremble, both Sabbath-day and lecture-day!"

Thus far, the elder traveller had listened with due gravity, but now burst into a fit of irrepressible mirth, shaking himself so violently, that his snakelike staff actually seemed to wriggle in sympathy.

"Ha! ha! ha!" shouted he, again and again; then composing himself, "Well, go on, Goodman Brown, go on; but, prithee, don't kill me with laughing!"

"Well, then, to end the matter at once," said Goodman Brown, considerably nettled, "there is my wife, Faith. It would break her dear little heart; and I'd rather break my own!"

"Nay, if that be the case," answered the other, "e'en go thy ways, Goodman Brown. I would not, for twenty old women like the one hobbling before us, that Faith should come to any harm."

As he spoke, he pointed his staff at a female figure on the path, in whom Goodman Brown recognized a very pious and exemplary dame, who had taught him his catechism in youth, and was still his moral and spiritual adviser, jointly with the minister and Deacon Gookin.

"A marvel, truly, that Goody Cloyse should be so far in the

wilderness, at nightfall!" said he. "But, with your leave, friend, I shall take a cut through the woods, until we have left this Christian woman behind. Being a stranger to you, she might ask whom I was consorting with, and whither I was going."

"Be it so," said his fellow-traveller. "Betake you to the woods, and let me keep the path."

Accordingly, the young man turned aside, but took care to watch his companion, who advanced softly along the road, until he had come within a staff's length of the old dame. She, meanwhile, was making the best of her way, with singular speed for so aged a woman, and mumbling some indistinct words, a prayer, doubtless, as she went. The traveller put forth his staff, and touched her withered neck with what seemed the serpent's tail.

"The devil!" screamed the pious old lady.

"Then Goody Cloyse knows her old friend?" observed the traveller, confronting her, and leaning on his writhing stick.

"Ah, forsooth, and is it your worship, indeed?" cried the good dame. "Yea, truly is it, and in the very image of my old gossip, Goodman Brown, the grandfather of the silly fellow that now is. But, would your worship believe it? my broomstick hath strangely disappeared, stolen, as I suspect, by that unhanged witch, Goody Cory, and that, too, when I was all anointed with the juice of smallage and cinque-foil and wolf's-bane—"

"Mingled with fine wheat and the fat of a new-born babe," said the shape of old Goodman Brown.

"Ah, your worship knows the recipe," cried the old lady, cackling aloud. "So, as I was saying, being all ready for the meeting, and no horse to ride on, I made up my mind to foot it; for they tell me there is a nice young man to be taken into communion to-night. But now your good worship will lend me your arm, and we shall be there in a twinkling."

"That can hardly be," answered her friend. "I may not spare you my arm, Goody Cloyse, but here is my staff, if you will."

So saying, he threw it down at her feet, where, perhaps, it assumed life, being one of the rods which its owner had formerly lent to the Egyptian Magi. Of this fact, however, Goodman Brown could not take cognizance. He had cast up his eyes in astonishment, and looking down again, beheld neither Goody Cloyse nor the serpentine staff, but his fellow-traveller alone, who waited for him as calmly as if nothing had happened.

"That old woman taught me my catechism!" said the young man; and there was a world of meaning in this simple comment.

They continued to walk onward, while the elder traveller exhorted his companion to make good speed and persevere in the path, discoursing so aptly, that his arguments seemed rather to spring up in the bosom of his auditor, than to be suggested by himself. As they went he plucked a branch of maple, to serve for a walking-stick, and began to strip it of the twigs and little boughs, which were wet with evening dew. The moment his fingers touched them, they became strangely withered and dried up, as with a week's sunshine. Thus the pair proceeded, at a good free pace, until suddenly, in a gloomy hollow of the road, Goodman Brown sat himself down on the stump of a tree, and refused to go any farther.

"Friend," said he, stubbornly, "my mind is made up. Not another step will I budge on this errand. What if a wretched old woman do choose to go to the devil, when I thought she was going to Heaven! Is that any reason why I should quit my dear Faith, and go after her?"

"You will think better of this by and by," said his acquaintance, composedly. "Sit here and rest yourself awhile; and when you feel like moving again, there is my staff to help you along."

Without more words, he threw his companion the maple stick, and was as speedily out of sight as if he had vanished into the deepening gloom. The young man sat a few moments by the roadside, applauding himself greatly, and thinking with how clear a conscience he should meet the minister, in his morning walk, nor shrink from the eye of good old Deacon Gookin. And what calm sleep would be his, that very night, which was to have been spent so wickedly, but purely and sweetly now, in the arms of Faith! Amidst these pleasant and praiseworthy meditations, Goodman Brown heard the tramp of horses along the road, and deemed it advisable to conceal himself within the verge of the forest, conscious of the guilty purpose that had brought him thither, though now so happily turned from it.

On came the hoof-tramps and the voices of the riders, two grave old voices, conversing soberly as they drew near. These mingled sounds appeared to pass along the road, within a few yards of the young man's hiding-place; but owing, doubtless, to the depth of the gloom, at that particular spot, neither the travellers nor their steeds were visible. Though their figures brushed the small boughs by the wayside, it could not be seen that they intercepted, even for a moment, the faint gleam from the strip of bright sky, athwart which they must have passed. Goodman Brown alternately crouched and stood on tiptoe, pulling aside the branches, and thrusting forth his head as far as he durst, without discerning so much as a shadow. It vexed him the more, because he could have sworn, were such a thing possible, that he recognized the voices of the minister and Deacon Gookin, jogging along quietly, as they were wont to do, when bound to some ordination or ecclesiastical council. While yet within hearing, one of the riders stopped to pluck a switch.

"Of the two, reverend Sir," said the voice like the deacon's, "I had rather miss an ordination dinner than to-night's meeting. They tell me that some of our community are to be here from Falmouth and beyond, and others from Connecticut and Rhode Island; besides several of the Indian powwows, who, after their fashion, know almost as much deviltry as the best of us. Moreover, there is a goodly young woman to be taken into communion."

"Mighty well, Deacon Gookin!" replied the solemn old tones of the minister. "Spur up, or we shall be late. Nothing can be done, you know, until I get on the ground."

The hoofs clattered again, and the voices, talking so strangely in the empty air, passed on through the forest, where no church had ever been gathered, nor solitary Christian prayed. Whither, then, could these holy men be journeying, so deep into the heathen wilderness? Young Goodman Brown caught hold of a tree, for support, being ready to sink down on the ground, faint and over-burthened with the heavy sickness of his heart. He looked up to the sky, doubting whether there really was a Heaven above him. Yet, there was the blue arch, and the stars brightening in it.

"With Heaven above, and Faith below, I will yet stand firm against the devil!" cried Goodman Brown.

While he still gazed upward, into the deep arch of the firmament, and had lifted his hands to pray, a cloud, though no wind was stirring, hurried across the zenith, and hid the brightening stars. The blue sky was still visible, except directly overhead, where this black mass of cloud was sweeping swiftly northward. Aloft in the air, as if from the depths of the cloud, came a confused and doubtful sound of voices. Once, the listener fancied that he could distinguish the accents of town's-people of his own, men and women, both pious and ungodly, many of whom he had met at the communion-table, and had seen others rioting at the tavern. The next moment, so indistinct were the sounds, he doubted whether he had heard aught but the murmur of the old forest, whispering without a wind. Then came a stronger swell of those familiar tones, heard daily in the sunshine, at Salem village, but never, until now, from a cloud at night. There was one voice, of a young woman, uttering lamentations, yet with an uncertain sorrow, and entreating for some favor, which, perhaps, it would grieve her to obtain. And all the unseen multitude, both saints and sinners, seemed to encourage her onward.

"Faith!" shouted Goodman Brown, in a voice of agony and desperation; and the echoes of the forest mocked him, crying—"Faith! Faith!" as if bewildered wretches were seeking her, all through the wilderness.

The cry of grief, rage, and terror was yet piercing the night, when the unhappy husband held his breath for a response. There was a scream, drowned immediately in a louder murmur of voices fading into far-off laughter, as the dark cloud swept away, leaving the clear and silent sky above Goodman Brown. But something fluttered lightly down through the air, and caught on the branch of a tree. The young man seized it and beheld a pink ribbon.

"My Faith is gone!" cried he, after one stupefied moment. "There is no good on earth, and sin is but a name. Come, devil! for to thee is this world given."

And maddened with despair, so that he laughed loud and long, did Goodman Brown grasp his staff and set forth again, at such a rate, that he seemed to fly along the forest path, rather than to walk or run. The road grew wilder and drearier, and more faintly traced, and vanished at length, leaving him in the heart of the dark wilderness, still rushing onward, with the instinct that guides mortal man to evil. The whole forest was peopled with frightful sounds; the creaking of the trees, the howling of wild beasts, and the yell of Indians; while, sometimes, the wind tolled like a distant church bell, and sometimes gave a broad roar around the traveller, as if all Nature were laughing him to scorn. But he was himself the chief horror of the scene, and shrank not from its other horrors.

"Ha! ha! ha!" roared Goodman Brown, when the wind laughed at him. "Let us hear which will laugh loudest! Think not to frighten me with your deviltry! Come witch, come wizard, come Indian powwow, come devil himself! and here comes Goodman Brown. You may as well fear him as he fear you!"

In truth, all through the haunted forest, there could be nothing more frightful than the figure of Goodman Brown. On he flew, among the black pines, brandishing his staff with frenzied gestures, now giving vent to an inspiration of horrid blasphemy, and now shouting forth such laughter, as set all the echoes of the forest laughing like demons around him. The fiend in his own shape is less hideous, than when he rages in the breast of man. Thus sped the demoniac on his course, until, quivering among the trees, he saw a red light before him, as when the felled trunks and branches of a clearing have been set on fire, and throw up their lurid blaze against the sky, at the hour of midnight. He paused, in a lull of the tempest that had driven him onward, and heard the swell of what seemed a hymn, rolling solemnly from a distance, with the weight of many voices. He knew the tune. It was a familiar one in the choir of the village meeting-house. The verse died heavily away, and was lengthened by a chorus, not of human voices, but of all the sounds of the benighted wilderness, pealing in awful harmony together. Goodman Brown cried out; and his cry was lost to his own ear, by its unison with the cry of the desert.

In the interval of silence, he stole forward, until the light glared full upon his eyes. At one extremity of an open space, hemmed in by the dark wall of the forest, arose a rock, bearing some rude, natural resemblance either to an altar or a pulpit, and surrounded by four blazing pines, their tops aflame, their stems untouched, like candles at an evening meeting. The mass of foliage, that had overgrown the summit of the rock, was all on fire, blazing high into the night, and fitfully illuminating the whole field. Each pendent twig and leafy festoon was in a blaze. As the red light arose and fell, a numerous congregation alternately shone forth, then disappeared in shadow, and again grew, as it were, out of the darkness, peopling the heart of the solitary woods at once.

"A grave and dark-clad company!" quoth Goodman Brown.

In truth, they were such. Among them, quivering to-and-fro, between gloom and splendor, appeared faces that would be seen, next day, at the council-board of the province, and others which, Sabbath after Sabbath, looked devoutly heavenward, and benignantly over the crowded pews, from the holiest pulpits in the land. Some affirm that the lady of the governor was there. At least, there were high dames well known to her, and wives of honored husbands, and widows a great multitude, and ancient maidens, all of excellent repute, and fair young girls, who trembled lest their mothers should espy them. Either the sudden gleams of light, flashing over the obscure field, bedazzled Goodman Brown, or he recognized a score of the church members of Salem village, famous for their especial sanctity. Good old Deacon Gookin had arrived, and waited at the skirts of that venerable saint, his reverend pastor. But, irreverently consorting with these grave, reputable, and pious people, these elders of the church, these chaste dames and dewy virgins, there were men of dissolute lives and women of spotted fame, wretches given over to all mean and filthy vice, and suspected even of horrid crimes. It was strange to see, that the good shrank not from the wicked, nor were the sinners abashed by the saints. Scattered, also, among their pale-faced enemies, were the Indian priests, or powwows, who had often scared their native forest with more hideous incantations than any known to English witchcraft.

"But, where is Faith?" thought Goodman Brown; and, as hope came into his heart, he trembled.

Another verse of the hymn arose, a slow and mournful strain, such as the pious love, but joined to words which expressed all that our nature can conceive of sin, and darkly hinted at far more. Unfathomable to mere mortals is the lore of fiends. Verse after verse was sung, and still the chorus of the desert swelled between, like the deepest tone of a mighty organ. And, with the final peal of that dreadful anthem, there came a sound, as if the roaring wind, the rushing streams, the howling beasts, and every other voice of the unconverted wilderness were mingling and according with the voice of guilty man, in homage to the prince of all. The four blazing pines threw up a loftier flame, and obscurely discovered shapes and visages of horror on the smoke-wreaths, above the impious assembly. At the same moment, the fire on the rock shot redly forth, and formed a glowing arch above its base, where now appeared a figure. With reverence be it spoken, the apparition bore no slight similitude, both in garb and manner, to some grave divine of the New England churches.

"Bring forth the converts!" cried a voice, that echoed through the field and rolled into the forest.

At the word, Goodman Brown stepped forth from the shadow of the trees, and approached the congregation, with whom he felt a loathful brotherhood, by the sympathy of all that was wicked in his heart. He could have well-nigh sworn, that the shape of his own dead father beckoned him to advance, looking downward from a smoke-wreath, while a woman, with dim features of despair, threw out her hand to warn him back. Was it his mother? But he had no power to retreat one step, nor to resist, even in thought, when the minister and good old Deacon Gookin seized his arms, and led him to the blazing rock. Thither came also the slender form of a veiled female, led between Goody Cloyse, that pious teacher of the catechism, and Martha Carrier, who had received the devil's promise to be queen of hell. A rampant hag was she! And there stood the proselytes, beneath the canopy of fire.

"Welcome, my children," said the dark figure, "to the communion of your race! Ye have found, thus young, your nature and your destiny. My children, look behind you!"

They turned; and flashing forth, as it were, in a sheet of flame, the fiend-worshippers were seen; the smile of welcome gleamed darkly on every visage.

"There," resumed the sable form, "are all whom ye have reverenced from youth. Ye deemed them holier than yourselves, and shrank from your own sin, contrasting it with their lives of righteousness and prayerful aspirations heavenward. Yet, here are they all, in my worshipping assembly! This night it shall be granted you to know their secret deeds; how hoary-bearded elders of the church have whispered wanton words to the young maids of their households; how many a woman, eager for widow's weeds, has given her husband a drink at bedtime, and let him sleep his last sleep in her bosom; how beardless youths have made haste to inherit their father's wealth; and how fair damsels—blush not, sweet ones!—have dug little graves in the garden, and bidden me, the sole guest, to an infant's funeral. By the sympathy of your human hearts for sin, ye shall scent out all the places—whether in church, bed-chamber, street, field, or forest—where crime has been committed, and shall exult to behold the whole earth one stain of guilt, one mighty blood-spot. Far more than this! It shall be yours to penetrate, in every bosom, the deep mystery of sin, the fountain of all wicked arts, and which inexhaustibly supplies more evil impulses than human power—than my power, at its utmost!—can make manifest in deeds. And now, my children, look upon each other."

They did so; and, by the blaze of the hell-kindled torches, the wretched man beheld his Faith, and the wife her husband, trembling before that unhallowed altar.

"Lo! there ye stand, my children," said the figure, in a deep and solemn tone, almost sad, with its despairing awfulness, as if his once angelic nature could yet mourn for our miserable race. "Depending upon one another's hearts, ye had still hoped that virtue were not all a dream! Now are ye undeceived!—Evil is the nature of mankind. Evil must be your only happiness. Welcome, again, my children, to the communion of your race!"

"Welcome!" repeated the fiend-worshippers, in one cry of despair and triumph.

And there they stood, the only pair, as it seemed, who were yet hesitating on the verge of wickedness, in this dark world. A basin was hollowed, naturally, in the rock. Did it contain water, reddened by the lurid light? or was it blood? or, perchance, a liquid flame? Herein did the Shape of Evil dip his hand, and prepare to lay the mark of baptism upon their foreheads, that they might be partakers of the mystery of sin, more conscious of the secret guilt of others, both in deed and thought, than they could now be of their own. The husband cast one look at his pale wife, and Faith at him. What polluted wretches would the next glance show them to each other, shuddering alike at what they disclosed and what they saw!

"Faith! Faith!" cried the husband. "Look up to Heaven, and resist the Wicked One!"

Whether Faith obeyed, he knew not. Hardly had he spoken, when he found himself amid calm night and solitude, listening to a roar of the wind, which died heavily away through the forest. He staggered against the rock, and felt it chill and damp, while a hanging twig, that had been all on fire, besprinkled his cheek with the coldest dew.

The next morning, young Goodman Brown came slowly into the street of Salem village staring around him like a bewildered man. The good old minister was taking a walk along the grave-yard, to get an appetite for breakfast and meditate his sermon, and bestowed a blessing, as he passed, on Goodman Brown. He shrank from the venerable saint, as if to avoid an anathema. Old Deacon Gookin was at domestic worship, and the holy words of his prayer were heard through the open window. "What God doth the wizard pray to?" quoth Goodman Brown. Goody Cloyse, that excellent old Christian, stood in the early sunshine, at her own lattice, catechising a little girl, who had brought her a pint of morning's milk. Goodman Brown snatched away the child, as from the grasp of the fiend himself. Turning the corner by the meeting-house, he spied the head of Faith, with the pink ribbons, gazing anxiously forth, and bursting into such joy at sight of him that she skipt along the street, and almost kissed her husband before the whole village. But Goodman Brown looked sternly and sadly into her face, and passed on without a greeting.

Had Goodman Brown fallen asleep in the forest, and only dreamed a wild dream of a witch-meeting?

Be it so, if you will. But, alas! it was a dream of evil omen for young Goodman Brown. A stern, a sad, a darkly meditative, a distrustful, if not a desperate man did he become, from the night of that fearful dream. On the Sabbath day, when the congregation were singing a holy psalm, he could not listen, because an anthem of sin rushed loudly upon his ear, and drowned all the blessed strain. When the minister spoke from the pulpit, with power and fervid eloquence, and with his hand on the open Bible, of the sacred truths of our religion, and of saint-like lives and triumphant deaths, and of future bliss or misery unutterable, then did Goodman Brown turn pale, dreading lest the roof should thunder down upon the gray blasphemer and his hearers. Often, awaking suddenly at midnight, he shrank from the bosom of Faith, and at morning or eventide, when the family knelt down at prayer, he scowled, and muttered to himself, and gazed sternly at his wife, and turned away. And when he had lived long, and was borne to his grave, a hoary corpse, followed by Faith, an aged woman, and children and grandchildren, a goodly procession, besides neighbors not a few, they carved no hopeful verse upon his tombstone; for his dying hour was gloom.

QUESTIONS FOR THINKING AND WRITING

1. Though the main action of "Young Goodman Brown" takes place in the woods outside Salem, the story begins and ends inside Salem village. What is gained by organizing the story in this way?

2. In the opening scene, we might particularly notice the introduction of Goodman Brown's wife, Faith. Why does the narrator say she is "aptly named"? How do Faith's talk of her "fears" and Brown's emphasis on the newness of their marriage set the stage for the story that follows?

3. How does the narrator's description of the forest and of Brown's thoughts (pp. 131–132) establish the atmosphere of the story? How would you describe the atmosphere thus created?

4. On pp. 132–136, what sort of argument is going on within young Goodman Brown, or between him and his companion? What people does he encounter

during this time? What significance do these people have for him? What do you notice about the order in which he meets them?

5. On p. 137, the narrator remarks that "the fiend in his own shape is less hideous, than when he rages in the breast of man." Why does he place such a comment at this point in the story? What development of action or characterization does it emphasize?

6. In the scene on pp. 139–140, with what is the fiend tempting Faith and Goodman Brown? What sort of faith is he trying to get them to renounce? With what would he replace it?

7. On p. 141, the narrator enters the story again to raise (and dismiss) the question of whether Brown's experience had been real or only a dream. Why should he raise the question if he does not intend to answer it? What is your reaction to the passage? (Had the notion that Brown's adventures might be a dream already entered your mind? If it had, what clues had put it there?)

8. Another way to read the story, already hinted at by the narrator in the opening scene, is as an **allegory**, a tale that has not only a literal but also a metaphorical meaning. The central figure in an allegory most often represents any or every person, while the action usually presents a struggle between good and evil forces anxious to save or damn the central character. Since the battleground for this struggle is the mind or soul of the disputed character, this type of allegory is called a **psychomachia**, or soul-battle. How would you interpret "Young Goodman Brown" as allegory? If it is a battle, who has won?

9. Is there one reading of the story—either as the tale of an actual happening, as a tale of a dream, or as an allegory—that seems most satisfactory to you? (If so, what reading is it, and why? If not, what is there in the story that keeps you from deciding?) How does the narrator seem to regard the story? How do his attempts to interpret it and the choice of interpretations he forces on you affect your response to the tale?

A Student Paper on "Young Goodman Brown"

On the pages that follow we have reproduced the prewriting and revisions of a paper that Sheila Montgomery wrote for Joan Gilson's Advanced Expository Writing class at the University of Missouri at Kansas City. Interestingly, Ms. Gilson's assignment was very general. The students had read five short stories, including "Young Goodman Brown," and were asked to write a brief observation about one of the stories in their journal. Then they did a freewriting on that observation. Sheila's journal entry is shown in Figure 10.

Young Goodman Brown

Goodman Brown is a man who
* has the flaw of curiosity. We see a
man who prides himself in his puri-
* tan ethics; rigid traditional values
that give himself and his community
substance, meaning. His wife, Faith,
personifies the devout goodly wife. The
portrait of innocence, pink ribbons
flowing from her cap. Totally trusting
in her husband's judgment. Childlike—
hence possibly the curiosity that leads
Goodman to find and experience evil.
That blind innocence that allows
him to stumble unexperienced into a
world of darkness. But to discover
your fellow alderman in the middle
of all this madness is another thing
entirely. Goodman Brown allows
himself to be led into the forest
with what we presume is an older,
wiser gentleman. But where did
Goodman Brown meet such a fel-
* low? And how did this mentor of
sorts convince Goodman to leave behind his puritan ethics and search
for that which would normally be

Figure 10   Sheila's Journal Entry

shunned? That is not spelled out for us by Hawthorne. That is the subliminal forces at work in the morality of Goodman Brown. The darkness, the voices, laughter. Recognition of familiarity in these voices. Does Goodman know these people? He does. His feeling of disbelief as he watches a pagan ceremony with Satan himself conducting the service from a fiery altar where the glow from the fire casts an evil red spell over everything. *But Goodman resists, as he thinks he sees his wife Faith resist. Again a reference to the pink ribbons (a combination of red and white, evil and innocence).

Then it's over. Goodman wakes up (in the forest?). His life in the puritan community still existing as it was when he left it. The elderly women (Goodie something) still teaching the scripture to the children — but weren't they at the Satanic ritual the night before? The alderman still preaching and spouting the word of God, the same ones he again saw the night before.

Figure 10 (Continued)

His banal innocence turns into heavy distrust of all those around him—his wife, the fellow Puritans—he doesn't know who to believe—and it transforms him from an <u>optimistically devout</u> to an <u>unhappy disbelieving</u> old man.

Figure 10   (Continued)

One week later, Sheila submitted a first draft of an essay based on her journal entry.

The Usage of Imagery and Symbolism in "Young Goodman Brown"

Just as plot, theme, ~~theme~~ and character are important to the making of quality fiction, so ~~in some cases, is the usage~~ too can be the use of symbolism and imagery. One particular story that embodies a significant amount of both is Nathaniel Hawthorne's "Young Goodman Brown," an allegory ~~involving~~ comprised of Puritan ethics jux- ✱ taposed with revelations of evil.

The story's protagonist is named Goodman Brown. A young, devout Puritan, ~~who~~ Goodman leaves his pretty young wife Faith to go on a search for evil. Hawthorne does not tell us the exact circumstances as to why Goodman Brown consents to delve into the forest with an elusive older "father figure" in search of sin. One gets the feeling, however, that <u>it's Good-</u> ✱ <u>man's curiosity at play and not an act of</u> <u>moralism.</u>

The symbolism comes into effect with Good—
man's wife, Faith. The portrait of innocence,
Faith seems the model Puritan wife. Yet what
continues to reappear throughout the story
concerning Faith is the pink ribbons that are
fastened to her cap. One first assumes this
pink to be symbolic of sweet innocence found
in a small child. Pink, however, derives from
the primary colors red and white. Hence Faith   ✳
comes to symbolize intrinsic evil hidden in
the folds of pure goodness. The hedonism that
lies in the hearts of all mankind, needing
✳ merely to be prodded by [curiosity] in order   frag.
that it might win us over.

Also in Faith we find a reference to Goodman
Brown's own faith in goodness. "My love and my
Faith . . . of all nights in the year, this
one night must I tarry away from thee." Here
Goodman is saying more than a mere goodbye to
his wife. [His absence also refers to his own
spiritual faith in order that he may search
for evil.] Goodman makes these references
again and again throughout the story. In
speaking of his wife we hear such things as
"Faith kept me back awhile" or "My Faith is
gone!" All of these loose statements so
skillfully placed in the story by Hawthorne
symbolize Goodman's own faith. His problems
stem much deeper than what the literal dialogue suggests.

As Goodman walks into the forest to meet his
mysterious friend with whom he is going on his
mission, Hawthorne begins to set an eerie
stage with wonderful Gothic imagery. "He had

taken a dreary road, darkened by all the gloomiest trees of the forest, which barely stood aside to let the narrow path creep through, and closed immediately behind." In using such language Hawthorne becomes the ✳ perfect storyteller, giving us mental pictures of dark windy nights where sin and perversion run rampant. We also get the feeling that Goodman may not be coming back from his quest; the forest having now taken on a life of its own. And when Goodman begins to hear familiar voices of those in his parish in the "heathen wilderness," he begins to question his own beliefs in spirituality. As these details unfold we the audience certainly share Goodman's anxieties. It is here that Hawthorne tells us that Goodman "looked up at the sky, doubting whether there really was a heaven above him. Yet there was the blue arch, and the stars brightening in it." This symbolism of truth to Goodman allows him to continue his journey, having received inspiration from the "blue arch" in the sky. For the reader, however, it only adds to the excitement, knowing that Goodman's vision of truth may very well be shattered as he journeys through the darkness.

The most powerful imagery is displayed for us when Goodman actually comes upon the satanic ritual taking place in the heart of the forest. He comes upon a stone altar, much resembling a crude, barbaric form of a pulpit in a church. Great blazing torches of pine act as the ceremonial candles, again giving a life-

like quality to the surrounding wilderness.
"Each pend$\overset{a}{\wedge}$nt twig and leafy festoon was in a
blaze." Here the images and symbols involved
with fire combine to create an unmistakable
aura of evil, the image reminding us of the
fires of Hell; the symbolism of red coinciding
with evil and perversion. Here too we find
reddened water resting in a basin carved in
the rock. (One also can think of a sacrificial *good* *connection*
rock as in Abraham and Isaac.) Hawthorne gives
us several possibilities as to what the liquid
could be. Such guidance almost isn't necessary, however, as we can well imagine in our
own mind's eye what it is. I'm willing to bet
that none of us would say JELL-O.

Ms. Gilson and Sheila's classmates commented on her first draft. A week
later Sheila submitted the following revision. All of the markings on it are
hers.

        The Usage of Imagery and Symbolism
            in "Young Goodman Brown"

                                    essential
     Just as plot, theme, and character are ~~im-~~
components which work to create a living, breathing story,
~~portant to the making of quality fiction~~, so
to can be the use of symbolism and imagery.
One particular story that embodies a significant amount of both is Nathaniel Hawthorne's
"Young Goodman Brown," an allegory comprised of Puritan ethics juxtaposed with revelations of evil.
     The story's protagonist is named Goodman
Brown. A young, devout Puritan, Goodman
leaves his pretty young wife Faith to go on a
search for evil. Hawthorne does not tell us
the exact circumstances as to why Goodman

Brown consents to delve into the forest with
an elusive older "father figure" in search
of sin. One gets the feeling, however, that
it's Goodman's curiosity at play and not an
act of moralism.

The symbolism comes into effect with Goodman's wife, Faith. The portrait of innocence,
Faith seems the model Puritan wife. Yet what
continues to reappear throughout the story no symbolism
concerning Faith is not her persona but the
pink ribbons that are fastened to her cap. One
first assumes this pink to be symbolic of
sweet innocence found in a small child. Pink,
however, derives from red and white. The
archetype of red is associated with blood,
sacrifice, or violent passion. White, on the
other hand, signifies purity and innocence.
(Although on the negative end of the spectrum,
white has been associated with the super- frag.
natural.) Hence Faith comes to symbolize intrinsic evil hidden in the folds of pure
goodness--the hedonism that lies in the
hearts of all mankind, needing merely to be
prodded by curiosity in order that it might
win us over.

Also in Faith we find a reference to Goodman
Brown's own faith in goodness. "My love and
my Faith . . . of all nights in the year, this
one night must I tarry away from thee." Here
Goodman is saying more than a mere goodbye to
his wife. His absence also refers to his own
spiritual faith in order that he may search
for evil. Goodman makes these references
again and again throughout the story. In

~~speaking of his wife we hear such things as "Faith kept me back awhile," or "My Faith is gone!" All of these loose statements so skillfully placed in the story by Hawthorne symbolize Goodman's own faith. His problems stem much deeper than what the literal dialogue suggests.~~ colloquial

As Goodman walks into the forest to meet his mysterious friend with whom he is going on his mission, Hawthorne begins to set an eerie stage with wonderful Gothic imagery. "He had taken a dreary road, darkened by all the gloomiest trees of the forest, which barely   Breakup stood aside to let the narrow path creep   expound through, and closed immediately behind." In using such language Hawthorne becomes the perfect storyteller, giving us mental pictures of dark windy nights where sin and perversion run rampant. We also get the feeling
                    come
that Goodman may not ~~be coming~~ back from his quest⊙ the forest having now taken on a life of its own. And when Goodman begins to hear familiar voices of those in his parish in the "heathen wilderness," he begins to question his own beliefs in spirituality. As these details unfold we the audience certainly share Goodman's anxieties. It is here that Hawthorne tells us that Goodman "looked up at the sky, doubting whether there really was a   page # ? heaven above him. Yet there was the blue arch, and the stars brightening in it." ~~The color blue is a common motif ususually associated   no symbolism with spiritual truth and security. Hawthorne places great emphasis on this idea~~. "The blue

sky was still visible, except directly overhead, where this black mass of cloud was
sweeping swiftly northward." Here Goodman
has a visual revelation of the forces of good
and evil naturally occuring in the night
sky. ~~The black signifying chaos and the un-~~) *Does this*
~~known; the blue, spiritual truth and secu-~~) *work?*
~~rity.~~ Furthermore, Hawthorne once again gives
animate qualities to inanimate objects:
"While he still gazed upward into the deep
arch of the firmament and had lifted his hands
to pray, a cloud, though no wind was stirring,
hurried across the zenith and hid the brightening stars." But it isn't until Goodman actually begins distinguishing familiar voices in
the foreboding forest that he becomes painfully aware of the situation, and when a pink
ribbon blows onto the branch of a nearby tree,
Goodman looses all reason. Goodman then, let-
ting out a strange, guttaral laugh, as if he   *aural imagery*
too has become a part of the hysteria, begins
to run blindly into the heart of the obscure
wilderness. The excitement begins to mount,
however, when Hawthorne once again fills the
ungodly forest with Gothic imagery that gives
life to the wind and the trees and sets an   *before he runs*
eerie, churchlike tone to the ghoulish sur-   *thru the*
roundings. "The whole forest was peopled with   *forest*
frightful sounds—the creaking of the trees,
the howling of wild beasts, and yells of
Indians; while sometimes the wind tolled like
a distant church bell, and sometimes gave a   *good*
broad roar around the traveller, as if all Nature were laughing him to scorn. ~~But he was~~

~~himself the chief horror of the scene, and~~
~~shrank not from its other horrors."~~

The most powerful imagery is displayed for
us when Goodman actually comes upon the satanic ritual taking place in the depth of the
forest. He comes upon a stone altar, much resembling a crude, barbaric form of a pulpit in
a church. (~~One~~ We're also ~~is~~ reminded of a sacrificial rock, much like that in the story of
Abraham and Isaac.) Great blazing torches of
pine act as the ceremonial candles, again giving a lifelike quality to the surrounding
wilderness. "Each pendant twig and leafy
festoon was in a blaze." Here the images and
symbols involved with fire combine to create
an unmistakable aura of evil. The image reminding us of the fires of Hell; the symbolism
of red coinciding with evil and perversion.
Here too we find reddened water resting in a
basin carved in the rock. Hawthorne gives us
several possibilities as to what the liquid
could be. Such guidance almost isn't necessary, however, as we can well imagine in our
own mind's eye just what it is. *— overstatement*

With the (superb) usage of Gothic imagery and
the emphasis placed on various symbols, Nathaniel Hawthorne's "Young Goodman Brown" becomes much more than an excellent choice for a
Halloween tale. Perhaps if this story were
narrated by a well-seasoned storyteller over
a campfire, ~~one~~ we would get a taste of just how *Stupid!*
essential imagery and symbolism can be to
a good tale. (Such stories were always at-

tempted at Girl Scout camp, but luckily enough
no Hawthornes existed in troop #417.) In
reading a story such as "Young Goodman Brown"
then, ~~one~~ **we** merely needs to let the imagination
play, and a whole sphere of sights and sounds
come rushing in <u>to thrill our senses and raise</u>
<u>our appreciation for good literature.</u> **works**

The paper was still not done. It went through a third and fourth draft, and many of the changes and comments were as radical as those we have already seen. Finally, Sheila submitted the following paper to Ms. Gilson.

The Usage of Imagery and Symbolism
in "Young Goodman Brown"

It would be impossible to tell a tale in which
there were no characters or conflict. These
elements must be present for the story to exist at all. Writers who have mastered the basic elements go on to use more complicated
tools to produce fiction that arouses our
senses and elicits emotion. One such tool is
imagery--the use of words and phrases that
create a mental picture or mood. An audience
may not be aware of the effort to create imagery. We discover that we are seeing and hearing and feeling things without realizing that
the author has helped us do so. We may simply
read and enjoy with uninhibited pleasure,
concentrating not on the parts, but on the sum
of the whole experience. It may not occur to
us that the author is using a literary device.
Thus it may happen that many people, if we
were to ask them **the meaning of imagery,** ~~what the definition of imag-~~

~~ory was,~~ would not be able to give an adequate literary definition. Yet ask them after reading Nathaniel Hawthorne's "Young Goodman Brown" what the forest looked like, or better yet, how it felt to be in the forest with Goodman, and many may surprise us with insightful, detailed observations. In this respect, the effects of imagery transcend and heighten our awareness.

Hawthorne's "Young Goodman Brown," an allegory comprised of Puritan ethics juxtaposed with revelations of evil, includes a significant amount of imagery. Filled with words and phrases that awaken our senses, Hawthorne's imagery takes us on a visual and aural excursion. The difference, after experiencing a story such as this, is like listening to a high fidelity stereo system when we're used to the squeak of a transistor radio. We can savor the rich, full detail. Yet what seems to trigger our gut reactions more than the sensory elements of sight and sound is the dream-like qualities of Hawthorne's imagery. It's as if Hawthorne slightly adjusts the fine tuning on our picture. We listen and watch with Goodman; we share in his confusion as he flounders in the sights and sounds of an uncooperative environment. He journeys into the forest with an elusive elderly man at dusk. As he descends deeper in the woods his vision begins to fail, or so we think. What Goodman sees now may become entirely different from what we would see. Hawthorne allows us to determine whether

Goodman's sensibility is threatened or not. Here Hawthorne states, "It was now deep dusk in the forest, and deepest in that part of it where these two were journeying." Goodman notes the appearance of his companion in the darkness of the forest, and discovers the elder traveler ". . . bearing a considerable resemblance to him, though perhaps more in expression than features." That Goodman senses the traveler's resemblance to himself seems plausible in the darkness of the wilderness. Many of us have had the experience of straining our eyes in the dark to make out features. To say with certainty that we know exactly what that object looked like would be impossible. Hawthorne continues, however, by writing, "Still they might have been taken for father and son." Now we can almost feel Goodman's shift in rationale with every line Hawthorne writes. In this manner the story seems to lure us into a vast gray area of uncertainty, much like what Goodman himself experiences. Henceforth, Goodman's ambiguity becomes ours. It is from such cloudy imagery that we can choose to doubt or believe what Goodman experiences. We share his experience, subconsciously participating in a rational assessment of what we see and hear in the forest.

Another possible reason that Hawthorne's imagery transcends our realm of certainty may be the lifelike quality he attributes to inanimate objects. Goodman encounters trees

". . . which barely stood aside to let the
narrow path creep through, and closed immediately behind." The familiar voices he
hears become mixed with ". . . the murmur of
the old forest, whispering without a wind."
With each subsequent step Goodman takes into
the forest, the imagery becomes more alive.
The result is a forest that plays a major role
in Hawthorne's cast of characters. This living, breathing, unspoken character proves to
be a driving force behind Goodman's confusion. We also get the feeling that Goodman may
not be coming back from his quest, because the
forest has taken on a life of its own. When
Goodman loses his power to reason and runs
blindly into the depth of the wilderness,
Hawthorne again gives life to the wind and the
trees. "The whole forest was peopled with
frightful sounds—the creaking of the trees,
the howling of wild beasts, and the yells of
Indians."

The most powerful imagery is displayed for
us when Goodman actually comes upon the satanic ritual taking place in the depth of the
forest. He ~~comes upon~~ a *sees* *large* stone altar, much resembling a crude, barbaric form of a pulpit in
a church. (This may also remind us of a sacrificial rock, much like that in the story of
Abraham and Isaac.) Great blazing torches of
pine act as the ceremonial candles, again giving a lifelike quality to the surrounding
wilderness. "Each pendant twig and leafy festoon was in a blaze." Here the image of fire

succeeds in creating an unmistakable aura of
evil. Goodman then sees the faces of all those
whom he admired and respected. Again Hawthorne plays on Goodman's inability to see
clearly in the forest, and presents the possibility that Goodman may be blinded by the
brightness of the fire. Our confusion matches
with Goodman's. We're not sure what to believe, yet the fascination with a barbaric
ritual in the height of the Puritan era seems
to supersede any concern for Goodman's fate.
And the sights and sounds are there to thrill
our senses, and raise our appreciation for
good literature.

STEPHEN CRANE (1871–1900)

The Open Boat

A Tale intended to be after the fact. Being the Experience of Four Men from the Sunk Steamer "Commodore"

I

None of them knew the color of the sky. Their eyes glanced level, and were fastened upon the waves that swept toward them. These waves were of the hue of slate, save for the tops, which were of foaming white, and all of the men knew the colors of the sea. The horizon narrowed and widened, and dipped and rose, and at all times its edge was jagged with waves that seemed thrust up in points like rocks.

Many a man ought to have a bath-tub larger than the boat which here rode upon the sea. These waves were most wrongfully and barbarously abrupt and tall, and each froth-top was a problem in small boat navigation.

The cook squatted in the bottom and looked with both eyes at the six inches of gunwale which separated him from the ocean. His sleeves were rolled over his fat forearms, and the two flaps of his unbuttoned vest dangled as he bent to bail out the boat. Often he said: "Gawd! That was a narrow clip." As he remarked it he invariably gazed eastward over the broken sea.

The oiler, steering with one of the two oars in the boat, sometimes raised himself suddenly to keep clear of water that swirled in over the stern. It was a thin little oar and it seemed often ready to snap.

The correspondent, pulling at the other oar, watched the waves and wondered why he was there.

The injured captain, lying in the bow, was at this time buried in that profound dejection and indifference which comes, temporarily at least, to even the bravest and most enduring when, willy nilly, the firm fails, the army loses, the ship goes down. The mind of the master of a vessel is rooted deep in the timbers of her, though he command for a day or a decade, and this captain had on him the stern impression of a scene in the grays of dawn of seven turned faces, and later a stump of a top-mast with a white ball on it that slashed to and fro at the waves, went low and lower, and down. Thereafter there was something strange in his voice. Although steady, it was deep with mourning, and of a quality beyond oration or tears.

"Keep 'er a little more south, Billie," said he.

" 'A little more south,' sir," said the oiler in the stern.

A seat in this boat was not unlike a seat upon a bucking broncho, and, by the same token, a broncho is not much smaller. The craft pranced and reared, and plunged like an animal. As each wave came, and she rose for it, she seemed like a horse making at a fence outrageously high. The manner of her scramble over these walls of water is a mystic thing, and, moreover, at the top of them were ordinarily these problems in white water, the foam racing down from the summit of each wave, requiring a new leap, and a leap from the air. Then, after scornfully bumping a crest, she would slide, and race, and splash down a long incline, and arrive bobbing and nodding in front of the next menace.

A singular disadvantage of the sea lies in the fact that after successfully surmounting one wave you discover that there is another behind it just as important and just as nervously anxious to do something effective in the way of swamping boats. In a ten-foot dingey one can get an idea of the resources of the sea in the line of waves that is not probable to the average experience which is never at sea in a dingey. As each slaty wall of water approached, it shut all else from the view of the men in the boat, and it was not difficult to imagine that this particular wave was the final outburst of the ocean, the last effort of the grim water. There was a terrible grace in the move of the waves, and they came in silence, save for the snarling of the crests.

In the wan light, the faces of the men must have been gray. Their eyes must have glinted in strange ways as they gazed steadily astern. Viewed from a balcony, the whole thing would doubtless have been weirdly picturesque. But the men in the boat had no time to see it, and if they had had leisure there were other things to occupy their minds. The sun swung steadily up the sky, and they knew it was broad day because the color of the sea changed from slate to emerald-green, streaked with amber lights, and the foam was like tumbling snow. The process of the breaking day was unknown to them. They were aware only of this effect upon the color of the waves that rolled toward them.

In disjointed sentences the cook and the correspondent argued as to the difference between a life-saving station and a house of refuge. The cook had said: "There's a house of refuge just north of the Mosquito Inlet Light, and as soon as they see us, they'll come off in their boat and pick us up."

"As soon as who see us?" said the correspondent.

"The crew," said the cook.

"Houses of refuge don't have crews," said the correspondent. "As I understand them, they are only places where clothes and grub are stored for the benefit of shipwrecked people. They don't carry crews."

"Oh, yes, they do," said the cook.

"No, they don't," said the correspondent.

"Well, we're not there yet, anyhow," said the oiler, in the stern.

"Well," said the cook, "perhaps it's not a house of refuge that I'm thinking of as being near Mosquito Inlet Light. Perhaps it's a life-saving station."

"We're not there yet," said the oiler, in the stern.

II

As the boat bounced from the top of each wave, the wind tore through the hair of the hatless men, and as the craft plopped her stern down again the spray slashed past them. The crest of each of these waves was a hill, from the top of which the men surveyed, for a moment, a broad tumultuous expanse, shining and wind-riven. It was probably splendid. It was probably glorious, this play of the free sea, wild with lights of emerald and white and amber.

"Bully good thing it's an on-shore wind," said the cook. "If not, where would we be? Wouldn't have a show."

"That's right," said the correspondent.

The busy oiler nodded his assent.

Then the captain, in the bow, chuckled in a way that expressed humor, contempt, tragedy, all in one. "Do you think we've got much of a show now, boys?" said he.

Whereupon the three were silent, save for a trifle of hemming and hawing. To express any particular optimism at this time they felt to be childish and stupid, but they all doubtless possessed this sense of the situation in their mind. A young man thinks doggedly at such times. On the other hand, the ethics of their condition was decidedly against any open suggestion of hopelessness. So they were silent.

"Oh, well," said the captain, soothing his children, "we'll get ashore all right."

But there was that in his tone which made them think, so the oiler quoth: "Yes! If this wind holds!"

The cook was bailing: "Yes! If we don't catch hell in the surf."

Canton flannel gulls flew near and far. Sometimes they sat down on the sea, near patches of brown seaweed that rolled over the waves with a movement like carpets on a line in a gale. The birds sat comfortably in groups, and they were envied by some in the dingey, for the wrath of the sea was no more to them than it was to a covey of prairie chickens a thousand miles inland. Often they came very close and stared at the men with black bead-like eyes. At these times they were uncanny and sinister in their unblinking scrutiny, and the men hooted angrily at them, telling them to be gone. One came, and evidently decided to alight on the top of the captain's head. The bird flew parallel to the boat and did not circle, but made short sidelong jumps in the air in chicken-fashion. His black eyes were wistfully fixed upon the captain's head. "Ugly brute," said the oiler to the bird. "You look as if you were made with a jack-knife." The cook and the correspondent swore darkly at the creature. The captain naturally wished to knock it away with the end of the heavy painter; but he did not dare do it, because anything resembling an emphatic gesture would have capsized this freighted boat, and so with his open hand, the captain gently and carefully waved the gull away. After it had been discouraged from the pursuit the captain breathed easier on account of his hair, and others breathed easier because the bird struck their minds at this time as being somehow gruesome and ominous.

In the meantime the oiler and the correspondent rowed. And also they rowed.

They sat together in the same seat, and each rowed an oar. Then the oiler took both oars; then the correspondent took both oars; then the oiler; then the correspondent. They rowed and they rowed. The very ticklish part of the business was when the time came for the reclining one in the stern to take his turn at the oars. By the very last star of truth, it is easier to steal eggs from under a hen than it was to change seats in the dingey. First the man in the stern slid his hand along the thwart and moved with care, as if he were of Sèvres. Then the man in the rowing seat slid his hand along the other thwart. It was all done with the most extraordinary care. As the two sidled past each other, the whole party kept watchful eyes on the coming wave, and the captain cried: "Look out now! Steady there!"

The brown mats of seaweed that appeared from time to time were like islands, bits of earth. They were travelling, apparently, neither one way nor the other. They were, to all intents, stationary. They informed the men in the boat that it was making progress slowly toward the land.

The captain, rearing cautiously in the bow, after the dingey soared on a great swell, said that he had seen the lighthouse at Mosquito Inlet. Presently the cook remarked that he had seen it. The correspondent was at the oars then, and for some reason he too wished to look at the lighthouse, but his back was toward the far shore and the waves were important, and for some time he could not seize an opportunity to turn his head. But at last there came a wave more gentle than the others, and when at the crest of it he swiftly scoured the western horizon.

"See it?" said the captain.

"No," said the correspondent slowly. "I didn't see anything."

"Look again," said the captain. He pointed. "It's exactly in that direction."

At the top of another wave, the correspondent did as he was bid, and this time his eyes chanced on a small still thing on the edge of the swaying horizon. It was precisely like the point of a pin. It took an anxious eye to find a lighthouse so tiny.

"Think we'll make it, captain?"

"If this wind holds and the boat don't swamp, we can't do much else," said the captain.

The little boat, lifted by each towering sea, and splashed viciously by the crests, made progress that in the absence of seaweed was not apparent to those in her. She seemed just a wee thing wallowing, miraculously top up, at the mercy of five oceans. Occasionally, a great spread of water, like white flames, swarmed into her.

"Bail her, cook," said the captain serenely.

"All right, captain," said the cheerful cook.

III

It would be difficult to describe the subtle brotherhood of men that was here established on the seas. No one said that it was so. No one mentioned it. But it dwelt in the boat, and each man felt it warm him. They were a captain, an oiler, a cook, and a correspondent, and they were friends, friends in a more curiously iron-bound degree than may be common. The hurt captain, lying against the water-jar in the bow, spoke always in a low voice and calmly, but he could never command a more ready and swiftly obedient crew than the motley three of the dingey. It was more than a mere recognition of what was best for the common safety. There was surely in it a quality that was personal and heartfelt. And after this devotion to the commander of the boat there was this comradeship that the correspondent, for instance, who had been taught to be cynical of men, knew even at the time was the best experience of his life. But no one said that it was so. No one mentioned it.

"I wish we had a sail," remarked the captain. "We might try my overcoat on the end of an oar and give you two boys a chance to rest." So the cook and the correspondent held the mast and spread wide the overcoat. The oiler steered, and the little boat made good way with her new rig. Sometimes the oiler had to scull sharply to keep a sea from breaking into the boat, but otherwise sailing was a success.

Meanwhile the lighthouse had been growing slowly larger. It had now almost assumed color, and appeared like a little gray shadow on the sky. The man at the oars could not be prevented from turning his head rather often to try for a glimpse of this little gray shadow.

At last, from the top of each wave the men in the tossing boat could see land. Even as the lighthouse was an upright shadow on the sky, this land seemed but a long black shadow on the sea. It certainly was thinner than paper. "We must be about opposite New Smyrna," said the cook, who had coasted this shore often in schooners. "Captain, by the way, I believe they abandoned that life-saving station there about a year ago."

"Did they?" said the captain.

The wind slowly died away. The cook and the correspondent were not now obliged to slave in order to hold high the oar. But the waves continued their old impetuous swooping at the dingey, and the little craft, no longer under way, struggled woundily over them. The oiler or the correspondent took the oars again.

Shipwrecks are apropos of nothing. If men could only train for them and have them occur when the men had reached pink condition, there would be less drowning at sea. Of the four in the dingey none had slept any time worth mentioning for two days and two nights previous to embarking in the dingey, and in the excitement of clambering about the deck of a foundering ship they had also forgotten to eat heartily.

For these reasons, and for others, neither the oiler nor the correspondent was fond of rowing at this time. The correspondent wondered ingenuously how in the name of all that was sane could there be people who thought it amusing to row a boat. It was not an amusement; it was a diabolical punishment, and even a genius of mental aberrations could never conclude that it was anything but a horror to the muscles and a crime against the back. He mentioned to the boat in general how the amusement of rowing struck him, and the weary-faced oiler smiled in full sympathy. Previously to the foundering, by the way, the oiler had worked double-watch in the engine-room of the ship.

"Take her easy, now, boys," said the captain. "Don't spend yourselves. If we have to run a surf you'll need all your strength, because we'll sure have to swim for it. Take your time."

Slowly the land arose from the sea. From a black line it became a line of black and a line of white, trees and sand. Finally, the captain said that he could make out a house on the shore. "That's the house of refuge, sure," said the cook. "They'll see us before long, and come out after us."

The distant lighthouse reared high. "The keeper ought to be able to make us out now, if he's looking through a glass," said the captain. "He'll notify the life-saving people."

"None of those other boats could have got ashore to give word of the wreck," said the oiler, in a low voice. "Else the life-boat would be out hunting us."

Slowly and beautifully the land loomed out of the sea. The wind came again. It had veered from the north-east to the south-east. Finally, a new sound struck the ears of the men in the boat. It was the low thunder of the surf on the shore. "We'll never be able to make the lighthouse now," said the captain. "Swing her head a little more north, Billie."

" 'A little more north,' sir," said the oiler.

Whereupon the little boat turned her nose once more down the wind, and all but the oarsman watched the shore grow. Under the influence of this expansion doubt and direful apprehension was leaving the minds of the men. The management of the boat was still most absorbing, but it could not prevent a quiet cheerfulness. In an hour, perhaps, they would be ashore.

Their backbones had become thoroughly used to balancing in the boat, and they now rode this wild colt of a dingey like circus men. The correspondent thought that he had been drenched to the skin, but happening to feel in the top pocket of his coat, he found therein eight cigars. Four of them were soaked with sea-water; four were perfectly scatheless. After a search, somebody produced three dry matches, and thereupon the four waifs rode in their little boat, and with an assurance of an impending rescue shining in their eyes, puffed at the big cigars and judged well and ill of all men. Everybody took a drink of water.

IV

"Cook," remarked the captain, "there don't seem to be any signs of life about your house of refuge."

"No," replied the cook. "Funny they don't see us!"

A broad stretch of lowly coast lay before the eyes of the men. It was of low dunes topped with dark vegetation. The roar of the surf was plain, and sometimes they could see the white lip of a wave as it spun up the beach. A tiny house was blocked out black upon the sky. Southward, the slim lighthouse lifted its little gray length.

Tide, wind, and waves were swinging the dingey northward. "Funny they don't see us," said the men.

The surf's roar was here dulled, but its tone was, nevertheless, thunderous and mighty. As the boat swam over the great rollers, the men sat listening to this roar. "We'll swamp sure," said everybody.

It is fair to say here that there was not a life-saving station within twenty miles in either direction, but the men did not know this fact, and in consequence they made dark and opprobrious remarks concerning the eyesight of the nation's life-savers. Four scowling men sat in the dingey and surpassed records in the invention of epithets.

"Funny they don't see us."

The light-heartedness of a former time had completely faded. To their sharpened minds it was easy to conjure pictures of all kinds of incompetency and blindness and, indeed, cowardice. There was the shore of the populous land, and it was bitter and bitter to them that from it came no sign.

"Well," said the captain, ultimately, "I suppose we'll have to make a try for ourselves. If we stay out here too long, we'll none of us have strength left to swim after the boat swamps."

And so the oiler, who was at the oars, turned the boat straight for the shore. There was a sudden tightening of muscles. There was some thinking.

"If we don't all get ashore—" said the captain. "If we don't all get ashore, I suppose you fellows know where to send news of my finish?"

They then briefly exchanged some addresses and admonitions. As for the reflections of the men, there was a great deal of rage in them. Perchance they might be formulated thus: "If I am going to be drowned—if I am going to be drowned—if I am going to be drowned, why, in the name of the seven mad gods who rule the sea, was I allowed to come thus far and contemplate sand and trees? Was I brought here merely to have my nose dragged away as I was about to nibble the sacred cheese of life? It is preposterous. If this old ninny-woman, Fate, cannot do better than this, she should be deprived of the management of men's fortunes. She is an old hen who knows not her intention. If she has decided to drown me, why did she not do it in the beginning and save me all this trouble? The whole affair is absurd. . . . But no, she cannot mean to drown me. She dare not drown me. She cannot drown me. Not after all this work." Afterward the man might have had an impulse to shake his fist at the clouds: "Just you drown me, now, and then hear what I call you!"

The billows that came at this time were more formidable. They seemed always just about to break and roll over the little boat in a turmoil of foam. There was a preparatory and long growl in the speech of them. No mind unused to the sea would have concluded that the dingey could ascend these sheer heights in time. The shore was still afar. The oiler was a wily surfman. "Boys," he said swiftly, "she won't live three minutes more, and we're too far out to swim. Shall I take her to sea again, captain?"

"Yes! Go ahead!" said the captain.

This oiler, by a series of quick miracles, and fast and steady oarsmanship, turned the boat in the middle of the surf and took her safely to sea again.

There was a considerable silence as the boat bumped over the furrowed sea to deeper water. Then somebody in gloom spoke. "Well, anyhow, they must have seen us from the shore by now."

The gulls went in slanting flight up the wind toward the gray desolate east. A squall, marked by dingy clouds, and clouds brick-red, like smoke from a burning building, appeared from the south-east.

"What do you think of those life-saving people? Ain't they peaches?"

"Funny they haven't seen us."

"Maybe they think we're out here for sport! Maybe they think we're fishin'. Maybe they think we're damned fools."

It was a long afternoon. A changed tide tried to force them southward, but wind and wave said northward. Far ahead, where coastline, sea, and sky formed their mighty angle, there were little dots which seemed to indicate a city on the shore.

"St. Augustine?"

The captain shook his head. "Too near Mosquito Inlet."

And the oiler rowed, and then the correspondent rowed. Then the oiler rowed. It was a weary business. The human back can become the seat of more aches and pains than are registered in books for the composite anatomy of a regiment. It is a limited area, but it can become the theater of innumerable muscular conflicts, tangles, wrenches, knots, and other comforts.

"Did you ever like to row, Billie?" asked the correspondent.

"No," said the oiler. "Hang it!"

When one exchanged the rowing-seat for a place in the bottom of the boat, he suffered a bodily depression that caused him to be careless of everything save an obligation to wiggle one finger. There was cold sea-water swashing to and fro in the boat, and he lay in it. His head, pillowed on a thwart, was within an inch of the swirl of a wave crest, and sometimes a particularly obstreperous sea came inboard and drenched him once more. But these matters did not annoy him. It is almost certain that if the boat had capsized he would have tumbled comfortably out upon the ocean as if he felt sure that it was a great soft mattress.

"Look! There's a man on the shore!"

"Where?"

"There! See 'im? See 'im?"

"Yes, sure! He's walking along."

"Now he's stopped. Look! He's facing us!"

"He's waving at us!"

"So he is! By thunder!"

"Ah, now we're all right! Now we're all right! There'll be a boat out here for us in half an hour."

"He's going on. He's running. He's going up to that house there."

The remote beach seemed lower than the sea, and it required a searching glance to discern the little black figure. The captain saw a floating stick and they rowed to it. A bath-towel was by some weird chance in the boat, and tying this on the stick, the captain waved it. The oarsman did not dare turn his head, so he was obliged to ask questions.

"What's he doing now?"

"He's standing still again. He's looking. I think. . . . There he goes again. Toward the house. . . . Now he's stopped again."

"Is he waving at us?"

"No, not now! he was, though."

"Look! There comes another man!"

"He's running."

"Look at him go, would you."

"Why, he's on a bicycle. Now he's met the other man. They're both waving at us. Look!"

"There comes something up the beach."

"What the devil is that thing?"

"Why, it looks like a boat."

"Why, certainly it's a boat."

"No, it's on wheels."

"Yes, so it is. Well, that must be the life-boat. They drag them along shore on a wagon."

"That's the life-boat, sure."

"No, by—, it's—it's an omnibus."

"I tell you it's a life-boat."

"It is not! It's an omnibus. I can see it plain. See? One of these big hotel omnibuses."

"By thunder, you're right. It's an omnibus, sure as fate. What do you suppose they are doing with an omnibus? Maybe they are going around collecting the life-crew, hey?"

"That's it, likely. Look! There's a fellow waving a little black flag. He's standing on the steps of the omnibus. There come those other two fellows. Now they're all talking together. Look at the fellow with the flag. Maybe he ain't waving it."

"That ain't a flag, is it? That's his coat. Why, certainly, that's his coat."

"So it is. It's his coat. He's taken it off and is waving it around his head. But would you look at him swing it."

"Oh, say, there isn't any life-saving station there. That's just a winter resort hotel omnibus that has brought over some of the boarders to see us drown."

"What's that idiot with the coat mean? What's he signaling, anyhow?"

"It looks as if he were trying to tell us to go north. There must be a life-saving station up there."

"No! He thinks we're fishing. Just giving us a merry hand. See? Ah, there, Willie."

"Well, I wish I could make something out of those signals. What do you suppose he means?"

"He don't mean anything. He's just playing."

"Well, if he'd just signal us to try the surf again, or to go to sea and wait, or go north, or go south, or go to hell—there would be some reason in it. But look at him. He just stands there and keeps his coat revolving like a wheel. The ass!"

"There come more people."

"Now there's quite a mob. Look! Isn't that a boat."

"Where? Oh, I see where you mean. No, that's no boat."

"That fellow is still waving his coat."

"He must think we like to see him do that. Why don't he quit it? It don't mean anything."

"I don't know. I think he is trying to make us go north. It must be that there's a life-saving station there somewhere."

"Say, he ain't tired yet. Look at 'im wave."

"Wonder how long he can keep that up. He's been revolving his coat ever since he caught sight of us. He's an idiot. Why aren't they getting men to bring a boat out? A fishing boat—one of those big yawls—could come out here all right. Why don't he do something?"

"Oh, it's all right, now."

"They'll have a boat out here for us in less than no time, now that they've seen us."

A faint yellow tone came into the sky over the low land. The shadows on the sea slowly deepened. The wind bore coldness with it, and the men began to shiver.

"Holy smoke!" said one, allowing his voice to express his impious mood, "if we keep on monkeying out here! If we've got to flounder out here all night!"

"Oh, we'll never have to stay here all night! Don't you worry. They've seen us now, and it won't be long before they'll come chasing out after us."

The shore grew dusky. The man waving a coat blended gradually into this gloom, and it swallowed in the same manner the omnibus and the group of people. The spray, when it dashed uproariously over the side, made the voyagers shrink and swear like men who were being branded.

"I'd like to catch the chump who waved the coat. I feel like soaking him one, just for luck."

"Why? What did he do?"

"Oh, nothing, but then he seemed so damned cheerful."

In the meantime the oiler rowed, and then the correspondent rowed, and then the oiler rowed. Gray-faced and bowed forward, they mechanically, turn by turn, plied the leaden oars. The form of the lighthouse had vanished from the southern horizon, but finally a pale star appeared, just lifting from the sea. The streaked saffron in the west passed before the all-merging darkness, and the sea to the

east was black. The land had vanished, and was expressed only by
the low and drear thunder of the surf.

"If I am going to be drowned—if I am going to be drowned—if I
am going to be drowned, why, in the name of the seven mad gods
who rule the sea, was I allowed to come thus far and contemplate
sand and trees? Was I brought here merely to have my nose dragged
away as I was about to nibble the sacred cheese of life?"

The patient captain, drooped over the water-jar, was sometimes
obliged to speak to the oarsman.

"Keep her head up! Keep her head up!"

" 'Keep her head up,' sir." The voices were weary and low.

This was surely a quiet evening. All save the oarsman lay heavily
and listlessly in the boat's bottom. As for him, his eyes were just
capable of noting the tall black waves that swept forward in a most
sinister silence, save for an occasional subdued growl of a crest.

The cook's head was on a thwart, and he looked without interest at
the water under his nose. He was deep in other scenes. Finally he
spoke. "Billie," he murmured, dreamfully, "what kind of pie do you
like best?"

V

"Pie," said the oiler and the correspondent, agitatedly. "Don't talk
about those things, blast you!"

"Well," said the cook, "I was just thinking about ham sandwiches,
and—"

A night on the sea in an open boat is a long night. As darkness
settled finally, the shine of the light, lifting from the sea in the south,
changed to full gold. On the northern horizon a new light appeared,
a small bluish gleam on the edge of the waters. These two lights were
the furniture of the world. Otherwise there was nothing but waves.

Two men huddled in the stern, and distances were so magnificent
in the dingey that the rower was enabled to keep his feet partly
warmed by thrusting them under his companions. Their legs indeed
extended far under the rowing-seat until they touched the feet of the
captain forward. Sometimes, despite the efforts of the tired oarsman,
a wave came piling into the boat, an icy wave of the night, and the
chilling water soaked them anew. They would twist their bodies for a
moment and groan, and sleep the dead sleep once more, while the
water in the boat gurgled about them as the craft rocked.

The plan of the oiler and the correspondent was for one to row
until he lost the ability, and then arouse the other from his sea-water
couch in the bottom of the boat.

The oiler plied the oars until his head drooped forward, and the overpowering sleep blinded him. And he rowed yet afterward. Then he touched a man in the bottom of the boat, and called his name. "Will you spell me for a little while?" he said, meekly.

"Sure, Billie," said the correspondent, awakening and dragging himself to a sitting position. They exchanged places carefully, and the oiler, cuddling down in the sea-water at the cook's side, seemed to go to sleep instantly.

The particular violence of the sea had ceased. The waves came without snarling. The obligation of the man at the oars was to keep the boat headed so that the tilt of the rollers would not capsize her, and to preserve her from filling when the crests rushed past. The black waves were silent and hard to be seen in the darkness. Often one was almost upon the boat before the oarsman was aware.

In a low voice the correspondent addressed the captain. He was not sure that the captain was awake, although this iron man seemed to be always awake. "Captain, shall I keep her making for that light north, sir?"

The same steady voice answered him. "Yes. Keep it about two points off the port bow."

The cook had tied a life-belt around himself in order to get even the warmth which this clumsy cork contrivance could donate, and he seemed almost stove-like when a rower, whose teeth invariably chattered wildly as soon as he ceased his labor, dropped down to sleep.

The correspondent, as he rowed, looked down at the two men sleeping underfoot. The cook's arm was around the oiler's shoulders, and, with their fragmentary clothing and haggard faces, they were the babes of the sea, a grotesque rendering of the old babes in the wood.

Later he must have grown stupid at his work, for suddenly there was a growling of water, and a crest came with a roar and a swash into the boat, and it was a wonder that it did not set the cook afloat in his life-belt. The cook continued to sleep, but the oiler sat up, blinking his eyes and shaking with the new cold.

"Oh, I'm awful sorry, Billie," said the correspondent, contritely.

"That's all right, old boy," said the oiler, and lay down again and was asleep.

Presently it seemed that even the captain dozed, and the correspondent thought that he was the one man afloat on all the oceans. The wind had a voice as it came over the waves, and it was sadder than the end.

There was a long, loud swishing astern of the boat, and a gleaming trail of phosphorescence, like blue flame, was furrowed on the black waters. It might have been made by a monstrous knife.

Then there came a stillness, while the correspondent breathed with the open mouth and looked at the sea.

Suddenly there was another swish and another long flash of bluish light, and this time it was alongside the boat, and might almost have been reached with an oar. The correspondent saw an enormous fin speed like a shadow through the water, hurling the crystalline spray and leaving the long glowing trail.

The correspondent looked over his shoulder at the captain. His face was hidden, and he seemed to be asleep. He looked at the babes of the sea. They certainly were asleep. So, being bereft of sympathy, he leaned a little way to one side and swore softly into the sea.

But the thing did not then leave the vicinity of the boat. Ahead or astern, on one side or the other, at intervals long or short, fled the long sparkling streak, and there was to be heard the whiroo of the dark fin. The speed and power of the thing was greatly to be admired. It cut the water like a gigantic and keen projectile.

The presence of this biding thing did not affect the man with the same horror that it would if he had been a picnicker. He simply looked at the sea dully and swore in an undertone.

Nevertheless, it is true that he did not wish to be alone. He wished one of his companions to awaken by chance and keep him company with it. But the captain hung motionless over the water-jar, and the oiler and the cook in the bottom of the boat were plunged in slumber.

VI

"If I am going to be drowned—if I am going to be drowned—if I am going to be drowned, why, in the name of the seven mad gods who rule the sea, was I allowed to come thus far and contemplate sand and trees?"

During this dismal night, it may be remarked that a man would conclude that it was really the intention of the seven mad gods to drown him, despite the abominable injustice of it. For it was certainly an abominable injustice to drown a man who had worked so hard, so hard. The man felt it would be a crime most unnatural. Other people had drowned at sea since galleys swarmed with painted sails, but still—

When it occurs to a man that nature does not regard him as important, and that she feels she would not maim the universe by disposing of him, he at first wishes to throw bricks at the temple, and he hates deeply the fact that there are no bricks and no temples. Any visible expression of nature would surely be pelleted with his jeers.

Then, if there be no tangible thing to hoot he feels, perhaps, the desire to confront a personification and indulge in pleas, bowed to one knee, and with hands supplicant, saying: "Yes, but I love myself."

A high cold star on a winter's night is the word he feels that she says to him. Thereafter he knows the pathos of his situation.

The men in the dingey had not discussed these matters, but each had, no doubt, reflected upon them in silence and according to his mind. There was seldom any expression upon their faces save the general one of complete weariness. Speech was devoted to the business of the boat.

To chime the notes of his emotion, a verse mysteriously entered the correspondent's head. He had even forgotten that he had forgotten this verse, but it suddenly was in his mind.

> "A soldier of the Legion lay dying in Algiers,
> There was lack of woman's nursing, there was dearth of woman's tears;
> But a comrade stood beside him, and he took that comrade's hand,
> And he said: 'I shall never see my own, my native land.' "

In his childhood, the correspondent had been made acquainted with the fact that a soldier of the Legion lay dying in Algiers, but he had never regarded the fact as important. Myriads of his schoolfellows had informed him of the soldier's plight, but the dinning had naturally ended by making him perfectly indifferent. He had never considered it his affair that a soldier of the Legion lay dying in Algiers, nor had it appeared to him as a matter for sorrow. It was less to him than the breaking of a pencil's point.

Now, however, it quaintly came to him as a human, living thing. It was no longer merely a picture of a few throes in the breast of a poet, meanwhile drinking tea and warming his feet at the grate; it was an actuality—stern, mournful, and fine.

The correspondent plainly saw the soldier. He lay on the sand with his feet out straight and still. While his pale left hand was upon his chest in an attempt to thwart the going of his life, the blood came between his fingers. In the far Algerian distance, a city of low square forms was set against a sky that was faint with the last sunset hues. The correspondent, plying the oars and dreaming of the slow and slower movements of the lips of the soldier, was moved by a profound and perfectly impersonal comprehension. He was sorry for the soldier of the Legion who lay dying in Algiers.

The thing which had followed the boat and waited had evidently grown bored at the delay. There was no longer to be heard the slash of the cut water, and there was no longer the flame of the long trail. The light in the north still glimmered, but it was apparently no nearer to the boat. Sometimes the boom of the surf rang in the correspondent's ears, and he turned the craft seaward then and rowed harder. Southward, someone had evidently built a watch-fire on the beach. It was too low and too far to be seen, but it made a shimmering, roseate reflection upon the bluff back of it, and this could be discerned from the boat. The wind came stronger, and sometimes a wave suddenly raged out like a mountain-cat, and there was to be seen the sheen and sparkle of a broken crest.

The captain, in the bow, moved on his water-jar and sat erect. "Pretty long night," he observed to the correspondent. He looked at the shore. "Those life-saving people take their time."

"Did you see that shark playing around?"

"Yes, I saw him. He was a big fellow, all right."

"Wish I had known you were awake."

Later the correspondent spoke into the bottom of the boat.

"Billie!" There was a slow and gradual disentanglement. "Billie, will you spell me?"

"Sure," said the oiler.

As soon as the correspondent touched the cold comfortable sea-water in the bottom of the boat, and had huddled close to the cook's life-belt he was deep in sleep, despite the fact that his teeth played all the popular airs. This sleep was so good to him that it was but a moment before he heard a voice call his name in a tone that demonstrated the last stages of exhaustion. "Will you spell me?"

"Sure, Billie."

The light in the north had mysteriously vanished, but the correspondent took his course from the wide-awake captain.

Later in the night they took the boat farther out to sea, and the captain directed the cook to take one oar at the stern and keep the boat facing the seas. He was to call out if he should hear the thunder of the surf. This plan enabled the oiler and the correspondent to get respite together. "We'll give those boys a chance to get into shape again," said the captain. They curled down and, after a few preliminary chatterings and trembles, slept once more the dead sleep. Neither knew they had bequeathed to the cook the company of another shark, or perhaps the same shark.

As the boat caroused on the waves, spray occasionally bumped over the side and gave them a fresh soaking, but this had no power to break their repose. The ominous slash of the wind and the water affected them as it would have affected mummies.

"Boys," said the cook, with the notes of every reluctance in his voice, "she's drifted in pretty close. I guess one of you had better take her to sea again." The correspondent, aroused, heard the crash of the toppled crests.

As he was rowing, the captain gave him some whiskey-and-water, and this steadied the chills out of him. "If I ever get ashore and anybody shows me even a photograph of an oar—"

At last there was a short conversation.

"Billie . . . Billie, will you spell me?"

"Sure," said the oiler.

VII

When the correspondent again opened his eyes, the sea and the sky were each of the gray hue of the dawning. Later, carmine and gold was painted upon the waters. The morning appeared finally, in its splendor, with a sky of pure blue, and the sunlight flamed on the tips of the waves.

On the distant dunes were set many little black cottages, and a tall white windmill reared above them. No man, nor dog, nor bicycle appeared on the beach. The cottages might have formed a deserted village.

The voyagers scanned the shore. A conference was held in the boat. "Well," said the captain, "if no help is coming, we might better try a run through the surf right away. If we stay out here much longer we will be too weak to do anything for ourselves at all." The others silently acquiesced in this reasoning. The boat was headed for the beach. The correspondent wondered if none ever ascended the tall wind-tower, and if then they never looked seaward. This tower was a giant, standing with its back to the plight of the ants. It represented in a degree, to the correspondent, the serenity of nature amid the struggles of the individual—nature in the wind, and nature in the vision of men. She did not seem cruel to him then, nor beneficent, nor treacherous, nor wise. But she was indifferent, flatly indifferent. It is, perhaps, plausible that a man in this situation, impressed with the unconcern of the universe, should see the innumerable flaws of his life, and have them taste wickedly in his mind and wish for another chance. A distinction between right and wrong seems absurdly clear to him, then, in this new ignorance of the grave-edge, and he understands that if he were given another opportunity he would mend his conduct and his words, and be better and brighter during an introduction or at a tea.

"Now, boys," said the captain, "she is going to swamp sure. All we can do is to work her in as far as possible, and then when she swamps, pile out and scramble for the beach. Keep cool now, and don't jump until she swamps sure."

The oiler took the oars. Over his shoulders he scanned the surf. "Captain," he said, "I think I'd better bring her about, and keep her head-on to the seas and back her in."

"All right, Billie," said the captain. "Back her in." The oiler swung the boat then and, seated in the stern, the cook and the correspondent were obliged to look over their shoulders to contemplate the lonely and indifferent shore.

The monstrous in-shore rollers heaved the boat high until the men were again enabled to see the white sheets of water scudding up the slanted beach. "We won't get in very close," said the captain. Each time a man could wrest his attention from the rollers, he turned his glance toward the shore, and in the expression of the eyes during this contemplation there was a singular quality. The correspondent, observing the others, knew that they were not afraid, but the full meaning of their glances was shrouded.

As for himself, he was too tired to grapple fundamentally with the fact. He tried to coerce his mind into thinking of it, but the mind was dominated at this time by the muscles, and the muscles said they did not care. It merely occurred to him that if he should drown it would be a shame.

There were no hurried words, no pallor, no plain agitation. The men simply looked at the shore. "Now, remember to get well clear of the boat when you jump," said the captain.

Seaward the crest of a roller suddenly fell with a thunderous crash, and the long white comber came roaring down upon the boat.

"Steady now," said the captain. The men were silent. They turned their eyes from the shore to the comber and waited. The boat slid up the incline, leaped at the furious top, bounced over it, and swung down the long back of the waves. Some water had been shipped and the cook bailed it out.

But the next crest crashed also. The tumbling, boiling flood of white water caught the boat and whirled it almost perpendicular. Water swarmed in from all sides. The correspondent had his hands on the gunwale at this time, and when the water entered at that place he swiftly withdrew his fingers, as if he objected to wetting them.

The little boat, drunken with this weight of water, reeled and snuggled deeper into the sea.

"Bail her out, cook! Bail her out," said the captain.

"All right, captain," said the cook.

"Now, boys, the next one will do for us, sure," said the oiler. "Mind to jump clear of the boat."

The third wave moved forward, huge, furious, implacable. It fairly swallowed the dingey, and almost simultaneously the men tumbled into the sea. A piece of life-belt had lain in the bottom of the boat, and as the correspondent went overboard he held this to his chest with his left hand.

The January water was icy, and he reflected immediately that it was colder than he had expected to find it off the coast of Florida.

This appeared to his dazed mind as a fact important enough to be noted at the time. The coldness of the water was sad; it was tragic. This fact was somehow so mixed and confused with his opinion of his own situation that it seemed almost a proper reason for tears. The water was cold.

When he came to the surface he was conscious of little but the noisy water. Afterward he saw his companions in the sea. The oiler was ahead in the race. He was swimming strongly and rapidly. Off to the correspondent's left, the cook's great white and corked back bulged out of the water, and in the rear the captain was hanging with his one good hand to the keel of the overturned dingey.

There is a certain immovable quality to a shore, and the correspondent wondered at it amid the confusion of the sea.

It seemed also very attractive, but the correspondent knew that it was a long journey, and he paddled leisurely. The piece of life-preserver lay under him, and sometimes he whirled down the incline of a wave as if he were on a hand-sled.

But finally he arrived at a place in the sea where travel was beset with difficulty. He did not pause swimming to inquire what manner of current had caught him, but there his progress ceased. The shore was set before him like a bit of scenery on a stage, and he looked at it and understood with his eyes each detail of it.

As the cook passed, much farther to the left, the captain was calling to him, "Turn over on your back, cook! Turn over on your back and use the oar."

"All right, sir." The cook turned on his back, and, paddling with an oar, went ahead as if he were a canoe.

Presently the boat also passed to the left of the correspondent with the captain clinging with one hand to the keel. He would have appeared like a man raising himself to look over a board fence, if it were not for the extraordinary gymnastics of the boat. The correspondent marvelled that the captain could still hold to it.

They passed on, nearer to shore—the oiler, the cook, the captain—and following them went the water-jar, bouncing gaily over the seas.

The correspondent remained in the grip of this strange new enemy—a current. The shore, with its white slope of sand and its green bluff, topped with little silent cottages, was spread like a picture before him. It was very near to him then, but he was impressed as one who in a gallery looks at a scene from Brittany or Algiers.

He thought: "I am going to drown? Can it be possible? Can it be possible? Can it be possible?" Perhaps an individual must consider his own death to be the final phenomenon of nature.

But later a wave perhaps whirled him out of this small deadly current, for he found suddenly that he could again make progress toward the shore. Later still, he was aware that the captain, clinging with one hand to the keel of the dingey, had his face turned away from the shore and toward him, and was calling his name. "Come to the boat! Come to the boat!"

In his struggle to reach the captain and the boat, he reflected that when one gets properly wearied, drowning must really be a comfortable arrangement, a cessation of hostilities accompanied by a large degree of relief, and he was glad of it, for the main thing in his mind for some moments had been horror of the temporary agony. He did not wish to be hurt.

Presently he saw a man running along the shore. He was undressing with most remarkable speed. Coat, trousers, shirt, everything flew magically off him.

"Come to the boat," called the captain.

"All right, captain." As the correspondent paddled, he saw the captain let himself down to bottom and leave the boat. Then the correspondent performed his one little marvel of the voyage. A large wave caught him and flung him with ease and supreme speed completely over the boat and far beyond it. It struck him even then as an event in gymnastics, and a true miracle of the sea. An overturned boat in the surf is not a plaything to a swimming man.

The correspondent arrived in water that reached only to his waist, but his condition did not enable him to stand for more than a moment. Each wave knocked him into a heap, and the under-tow pulled at him.

Then he saw the man who had been running and undressing, and undressing and running, come bounding into the water. He dragged ashore the cook, and then waded toward the captain, but the captain waved him away, and sent him to the correspondent. He was naked, naked as a tree in winter, but a halo was about his head, and he shone like a saint. He gave a strong pull, and a long drag, and a bully heave at the correspondent's hand. The correspondent, schooled in the minor formulae, said: "Thanks, old man." But suddenly the man cried: "What's that?" He pointed a swift finger. The correspondent said: "Go."

In the shallows, face downward, lay the oiler. His forehead touched sand that was periodically, between each wave, clear of the sea.

The correspondent did not know all that transpired afterward. When he achieved safe ground he fell, striking the sand with each particular part of his body. It was as if he had dropped from a roof, but the thud was grateful to him.

It seems that instantly the beach was populated with men, with blankets, clothes, and flasks, and women with coffee-pots and all the remedies sacred to their minds. The welcome of the land to the men from the sea was warm and generous, but a still and dripping shape was carried slowly up the beach, and the land's welcome for it could only be the different and sinister hospitality of the grave.

When it came night, the white waves paced to and fro in the moonlight, and the wind brought the sound of the great sea's voice to the men on shore, and they felt that they could then be interpreters.

The Structure of a Story

The ordering of incidents within a story may be spoken of as its **structure**. Traditionally, a story's structure has been said to consist of four basic parts:

1. **The exposition.** The beginning of the story, which introduces the reader to the tale's setting (time and place) and to some or all of its characters.
2. **The conflict.** Every story centers on a conflict of some sort: one person, or group of people, against another; people against nature; an individual against some rule or custom of society. Generally the conflict increases in tension or in complexity until it reaches a climax.
3. **The climax.** The point of greatest tension, at which the turning-point or breaking-point is reached.
4. **The denouement** or **resolution.** The ending, which brings the tale to a close, picking up the pieces of the action and reordering the lives left disordered by the conflict and its climax.

Of these four parts, only numbers two and three, the conflict and the climax, are essential. You don't have to begin with an exposition; your first sentence can show your characters already embroiled in their conflict. You don't have to end with a resolution; you can stop your tale short at its climactic moment, as Shirley Jackson does in "The Lottery." But you must have some sort of conflict in your action; and it must rise to some peak of intensity somewhere between the middle and end of your story.

To familiarize yourself with the notion of structure, analyze the structures of "Young Goodman Brown" and "The Open Boat." Do all four parts appear in these stories? What parts of each story would you assign to each section?

We round out our selection of stories told by omniscient narrators with "A Worn Path," which follows. Although this story focuses on a single figure, it is told by an **objective narrator.** The last two stories gained much of their impact by studying their characters as they tried to find some meaning or place some interpretation on the world around them and the events in which they were caught up. In contrast, this tale gains much of its effectiveness from its protagonist's willingness to accept things as they are, and from the steadfastness with which she declares herself to be a natural part of the universe in which she lives.

EUDORA WELTY (1909–   )

A Worn Path

It was December—a bright frozen day in the early morning. Far out in the country there was an old Negro woman with her head tied in a red rag, coming along a path through the pinewoods. Her name was Phoenix Jackson. She was very old and small and she walked slowly in the dark pine shadows, moving a little from side to side in her steps, with the balanced heaviness and lightness of a pendulum in a grandfather clock. She carried a thin, small cane made from an umbrella, and with this she kept tapping the frozen earth in front of her. This made a grave and persistent noise in the still air, that seemed meditative like the chirping of a solitary little bird.

She wore a dark striped dress reaching down to her shoetops, and an equally long apron of bleached sugar sacks, with a full pocket; all neat and tidy, but every time she took a step she might have fallen over her shoe-laces, which dragged from her unlaced shoes. She looked straight ahead. Her eyes were blue with age. Her skin had a pattern all its own of numberless branching wrinkles and as though a whole little tree stood in the middle of her forehead, but a golden color ran underneath, and the two knobs of her cheeks were illuminated by a yellow burning under the dark. Under the red rag her hair came down on her neck in the frailest of ringlets, still black, and with an odor like copper.

Now and then there was a quivering in the thicket. Old Phoenix said, "Out of my way, all you foxes, owls, beetles, jack rabbits, coons, and wild animals! . . . Keep out from under these feet, little bob-whites. . . . Keep the big wild hogs out of my path. Don't let none of those come running my direction. I got a long way." Under her small black-freckled hand her cane, limber as a buggy whip, would switch at the brush as if to rouse up any hiding things.

On she went. The woods were deep and still. The sun made the pine needles almost too bright to look at, up where the wind rocked. The cones dropped as light as feathers. Down in the hollow was the mourning dove—it was not too late for him.

The path ran up a hill. "Seems like there is chains about my feet, time I get this far," she said, in the voice of argument old people keep to use with themselves. "Something always take a hold on his hill—pleads I should stay."

After she got to the top she turned and gave a full, severe look behind her where she had come. "Up through pines," she said at length. "Now down through oaks."

Her eyes opened their widest and she started down gently. But before she got to the bottom of the hill a bush caught her dress.

Her fingers were busy and intent, but her skirts were full and long, so that before she could pull them free in one place they were caught in another. It was not possible to allow the dress to tear. "I in the thorny bush," she said. "Thorns, you doing your appointed work. Never want to let folks pass—no sir. Old eyes thought you was a pretty little green bush."

Finally, trembling all over, she stood free, and after a moment dared to stoop for her cane.

"Sun so high!" she cried, leaning back and looking, while the thick tears went over her eyes. "The time getting all gone here."

At the foot of this hill was a place where a log was laid across the creek.

"Now comes the trial," said Phoenix.

Putting her right foot out, she mounted the log and shut her eyes. Lifting her skirt, levelling her cane fiercely before her, like a festival figure in some parade, she began to march across. Then she opened her eyes and she was safe on the other side.

"I wasn't as old as I thought," she said.

But she sat down to rest. She spread her skirts on the bank around her and folded her hands over her knees. Up above her was a tree in a pearly cloud of mistletoe. She did not dare to close her eyes, and when a little boy brought her a little plate with a slice of marble-cake on it she spoke to him. "That would be acceptable," she said. But when she went to take it there was just her own hand in the air.

So she left that tree, and had to go through a barbed-wire fence. There she had to creep and crawl, spreading her knees and stretching her fingers like a baby trying to climb the steps. But she talked loudly to herself: she could not let her dress be torn now, so late in the day, and she could not pay for having her arm or her leg sawed off if she got caught fast where she was.

At last she was safe through the fence and risen up out in the clearing. Big dead trees, like black men with one arm, were standing in the purple stalks of the withered cotton field. There sat a buzzard.

"Who you watching?"

In the burrow she made her way along.

"Glad this not the season for bulls," she said, looking sideways, "and the good Lord made his snakes to curl up and sleep in the winter. A pleasure I don't see no two-headed snake coming around that tree, where it come once. It took a while to get by him, back in the summer."

She passed through the old cotton and went into a field of dead corn. It whispered and shook, and was taller than her head. "Through the maze now," she said, for there was no path.

Then there was something tall, black, and skinny there, moving before her.

At first she took it for a man. It could have been a man dancing in the field. But she stood still and listened, and it did not make a sound. It was as silent as a ghost.

"Ghost," she said sharply, "who be you the ghost of? For I have heard of nary death close by."

But there was no answer, only the ragged dancing in the wind.

She shut her eyes, reached out her hand, and touched a sleeve. She found a coat and inside that an emptiness, cold as ice.

"You scarecrow," she said. Her face lighted. "I ought to be shut up for good," she said with laughter. "My senses is gone. I too old. I the oldest people I ever know. Dance, old scarecrow," she said, "while I dancing with you."

She kicked her foot over the furrow, and with mouth drawn down shook her head once or twice in a little strutting way. Some husks blew down and whirled in streamers about her skirts.

Then she went on, parting her way from side to side with the cane, through the whispering field. At last she came to the end, to a wagon track, where the silver grass blew between the red ruts. The quail were walking around like pullets, seeming all dainty and unseen.

"Walk pretty," she said. "This the easy place. This the easy going."

She followed the track, swaying through the quiet bare fields, through the little strings of trees silver in their dead leaves, past cabins silver from weather, with the doors and windows boarded shut, all like old women under a spell sitting there. "I walking in their sleep," she said, nodding her head vigorously.

In a ravine she went where a spring was silently flowing through a hollow log. Old Phoenix bent and drank. "Sweetgum makes the water sweet," she said, and drank more. "Nobody knows who made this well, for it was here when I was born."

The track crossed a swampy part where the moss hung as white as lace from every limb. "Sleep on, alligators, and blow your bubbles." Then the track went into the road.

Deep, deep the road went down between the high green-colored banks. Overhead the live-oaks met, and it was as dark as a cave.

A black dog with a lolling tongue came up out of the weeds by the ditch. She was meditating, and not ready, and when he came at her she only hit him a little with her cane. Over she went in the ditch, like a little puff of milk-weed.

Down there, her senses drifted away. A dream visited her, and she reached her hand up, but nothing reached down and gave her a pull.

So she lay there and presently went to talking. "Old woman," she said to herself, "that black dog came up out of the weeds to stall you off, and now there he sitting on his fine tail, smiling at you."

A white man finally came along and found her—a hunter, a young man, with his dog on a chain.

"Well, Granny!" he laughed. "What are you doing there?"

"Lying on my back like a June-bug waiting to be turned over, mister," she said, reaching up her hand.

He lifted her up, gave her a swing in the air, and set her down, "Anything broken, Granny?"

"No sir, them old dead weeds is springy enough," said Phoenix, when she had got her breath. "I thank you for your trouble."

"Where do you live, Granny?" he asked, while the two dogs were growling at each other.

"Away back yonder, sir, behind the ridge. You can't even see it from here."

"On your way home?"

"No, sir, I going to town."

"Why, that's too far! That's as far as I walk when I come out myself, and I get something for my trouble." He patted the stuffed bag he carried, and there hung down a little closed claw. It was one of the bobwhites, with its beak hooked bitterly to show it was dead. "Now you go on home, Granny!"

"I bound to go to town, mister," said Phoenix. "The time come around."

He gave another laugh, filling the whole landscape. "I know you colored people! Wouldn't miss going to town to see Santa Claus!"

But something held Old Phoenix very still. The deep lines in her face went into a fierce and different radiation. Without warning she had seen with her own eyes a flashing nickel fall out of the man's pocket on to the ground.

"How old are you, Granny?" he was saying.

"There is no telling, mister," she said, "no telling."

Then she gave a little cry and clapped her hands, and said, "Git on away from here, dog! Look at that dog!" She laughed as if in admiration. "He ain't scared of nobody. He a big black dog." She whispered, "Sick him!"

"Watch me get rid of that cur," said the man. "Sick him, Pete! Sick him!"

Phoenix heard the dogs fighting and heard the man running and throwing sticks. She even heard a gunshot. But she was slowly bending forward by that time, further and further forward, the lids stretched down over her eyes, as if she were doing this in her sleep. Her chin was lowered almost to her knees. The yellow palm of her hand came out from the fold of her apron. Her fingers slid down and along the ground under the piece of money with the grace and care they would have in lifting an egg from under a sitting hen. Then she slowly straightened up, she stood erect, and the nickel was in her apron pocket. A bird flew by. Her lips moved. "God watching me the whole time. I come to stealing."

The man came back, and his own dog panted about them. "Well, I scared him off that time," he said, and then he laughed and lifted his gun and pointed it at Phoenix.

She stood straight and faced him.

"Doesn't the gun scare you?" he said, still pointing it.

"No, sir, I seen plenty go off closer by, in my day, and for less than what I done," she said, holding utterly still.

He smiled, and shouldered the gun. "Well, Granny," he said, "you must be a hundred years old and scared of nothing. I'd give you a dime if I had any money with me. But you take my advice and stay home, and nothing will happen to you."

"I bound to go on my way, mister," said Phoenix. She inclined her head in the red rag. Then they went in different directions, but she could hear the gun shooting again and again over the hill.

She walked on. The shadows hung from the oak trees to the road like curtains. Then she smelled wood-smoke, and smelled the river, and she saw a steeple and the cabins on their steep steps. Dozens of little black children whirled around her. There ahead was Natchez shining. Bells were ringing. She walked on.

In the paved city it was Christmas time. There were red and green electric lights strung and crisscrossed everywhere, and all turned on in the daytime. Old Phoenix would have been lost if she had not distrusted her eyesight and depended on her feet to know where to take her.

She paused quietly on the sidewalk, where people were passing by. A lady came along in the crowd, carrying an armful of red-, green-, and silver-wrapped presents; she gave off perfume like the red roses in hot summer, and Phoenix stopped her.

"Please, missy, will you lace up my shoe?" She held up her foot.

"What do you want, Grandma?"

"See my shoe," said Phoenix. "Do all right for out in the country, but wouldn't look right to go in a big building."

"Stand still then, Grandma," said the lady. She put her packages down carefully on the sidewalk beside her and laced and tied both shoes tightly.

"Can't lace 'em with a cane," said Phoenix. "Thank you, missy. I doesn't mind asking a nice lady to tie up my shoe when I gets out on the street."

Moving slowly and from side to side, she went into the stone building and into a tower of steps, where she walked up and around and around until her feet knew to stop.

She entered a door, and there she saw nailed up on the wall the document that had been stamped with the gold seal and framed in the gold frame which matched the dream that was hung up in her head.

"Here I be," she said. There was a fixed and ceremonial stiffness over her body.

"A charity case, I suppose," said an attendant who sat at the desk before her.

But Phoenix only looked above her head. There was sweat on her face; the wrinkles shone like a bright net.

"Speak up, Grandma," the woman said. "What's your name? We must have your history, you know. Have you been here before? What seems to be the trouble with you?"

Old Phoenix only gave a twitch to her face as if a fly were bothering her.

"Are you deaf?" cried the attendant.

But then the nurse came in.

"Oh, that's just old Aunt Phoenix," she said. "She doesn't come for herself—she has a little grandson. She makes these trips just as regular as clockwork. She lives away back off the Old Natchez Trace." She bent down. "Well, Aunt Phoenix, why don't you just take a seat? We won't keep you standing after your long trip." She pointed.

The old woman sat down, bolt upright in the chair.

"Now, how is the boy?" asked the nurse.

Old Phoenix did not speak.

"I said, how is the boy?"

But Phoenix only waited and stared straight ahead, her face very solemn and withdrawn into rigidity.

"Is his throat any better?" asked the nurse. "Aunt Phoenix, don't you hear me? Is your grandson's throat any better since the last time you came for the medicine?"

With her hand on her knees, the old woman waited, silent, erect and motionless, just as if she were in armor.

"You mustn't take up our time this way, Aunt Phoenix," the nurse said. "Tell us quickly about your grandson, and get it over. He isn't dead, is he?"

At last there came a flicker and then a flame of comprehension across her face, and she spoke.

"My grandson. It was my memory had left me. There I sat and forgot why I made my long trip."

"Forgot?" The nurse frowned. "After you came so far?"

Then Phoenix was like an old woman begging a dignified forgiveness for waking up frightened in the night. "I never did go to school

—I was too old at the Surrender," she said in a soft voice. "I'm an old woman without an education. It was my memory fail me. My little grandson, he is just the same, and I forgot it in the coming."

"Throat never heals, does it?" said the nurse, speaking in a loud, sure voice to Old Phoenix. By now she had a card with something written on it, a little list. "Yes. Swallowed lye. When was it—January —two—three years ago—"

Phoenix spoke unasked now. "No, missy, he not dead, he just the same. Every little while his throat begin to close up again, and he not able to swallow. He not get his breath. He not able to help himself. So the time come around, and I go on another trip for the soothing-medicine."

"All right. The doctor said as long as you came to get it you could have it," said the nurse. "But it's an obstinate case."

"My little grandson, he sit up there in the house all wrapped up, waiting by himself," Phoenix went on. "We is the only two left in the world. He suffer and it don't seem to put him back at all. He got a sweet look. He going to last. He wear a little patch quilt and peep out, holding his mouth open like a little bird. I remembers so plain now. I not going to forget him again, no, the whole enduring time. I could tell him from all the others in creation."

"All right." The nurse was trying to hush her now. She brought her a bottle of medicine. "Charity," she said, making a check mark in a book.

Old Phoenix held the bottle close to her eyes and then carefully put it into her pocket.

"I thank you," she said.

"It's Christmas time, Grandma," said the attendant. "Could I give you a few pennies out of my purse?"

"Five pennies is a nickel," said Phoenix stiffly.

"Here's a nickel," said the attendant.

Phoenix rose carefully and held out her hand. She received the nickel and then fished the other nickel out of her pocket and laid it beside the new one. She stared at her palm closely, with her head on one side.

Then she gave a tap with her cane on the floor.

"This is what come to me to do," she said. "I going to the store and buy my child a little windmill they sells, made out of paper. He going to find it hard to believe there such a thing in the world. I'll march myself back where he waiting, holding it straight up in this hand."

She lifted her free hand, gave a little nod, turned round, and walked out of the doctor's office. Then her slow step began on the stairs, going down.

QUESTIONS FOR THINKING AND WRITING

1. How much of the story takes place with Granny Phoenix as its only character? What happens in this first part of the tale? What effect does it have on you, the reader?
2. Describe Granny's first meeting with another person. What new information do we learn from it?
3. The story's climax comes at the point of the scene in the clinic. Here we finally learn why Granny has made her long journey. What is your reaction to this scene? How have the story and its narrator brought you to feel as you do?

4 *The First-Person Narrator*

Omniscient narrators stand somewhat apart from their stories. Having no role in the action themselves, they can interpret its events and characters impartially. Thus, the narrator of "The Open Boat" speaks for all his tale's characters when he opens the story by declaring that "none of them knew the color of the sky" and closes it with, "they felt that they could then be interpreters." Even when an omniscient narrator shows us most of the story through one central character's eyes, as does the narrator of "Young Goodman Brown," he can still give us glimpses into minds and actions that the character cannot see, as when Hawthorne's narrator tells us that Brown's townsmen "carved no hopeful verse upon his tombstone." Moreover, he can still interpret the events he relates from his own point of view, even when his view of the matter conflicts with his central character's: "Had Goodman Brown fallen asleep in the forest . . . ?"

First-person narrators, on the other hand, are participants in their own stories. They are telling us of something that happened to them, and are telling their tale from their own point of view. They cannot see into the minds of the other characters; indeed, they may hardly understand their own actions. In contrast to the total knowledge of the omniscient narrator, the first-person narrator's powers of interpretation may be slight indeed.

As the narrator's knowledge shrinks, the readers' role expands. If we cannot trust the narrator as an omniscient, final authority, then our own wisdom and judgment must come into play. We must weigh the narrator's perceptions against our own and so create our own understanding of the actions and characters within the story.

Often, therefore, first-person narratives are rich in **irony,** with the narrators describing what they think they see and the readers interpreting the descriptions to discover what "really" happened. In these stories the relationship between reader and narrator is completely reversed. Now we are the wise ones, the ones with the fullest perception of what's going on. If we could only speak to these narrators, as they seem to be speaking to us, how much we could tell them!

In other stories, however, first-person narrators retain the full authority of the storyteller. Indeed, if the tales they tell are set far enough in their pasts, the narrators may view themselves as nearly omniscient. They know what they were thinking and feeling when the events took place, so they can take us into their major character's mind; they know how events turned out, so they feel that they can interpret the patterns within them. Moreover, they may feel that they have grown considerably wiser since the time of the actions they are relating and can therefore combine past feelings and present understanding to interpret events and emotions as no one else could.

In either case, and in less extreme cases as well, we often feel closer to first-person narrators than we feel either to omniscient narrators or to the characters they describe. The limitations of human knowledge and insight within which the first-person narrators work, the blend of attempted objectivity and personal involvement their voices convey, and their apparent openness in telling their own stories appeal to our sympathy and our sense of fellowship. In telling us, as they often do, of their dreams and desires, first-person narrators speak eloquently of human aspirations; in confessing (consciously or unconsciously) their shortcomings, they speak no less eloquently of human limitations.

The narrators of "Bartleby the Scrivener" and "The Secret Sharer" are storytellers in the grand tradition. Don't plan to read these stories in haste. Their narrators set a leisurely pace for tales that are rich in detail and in reflection; and they will not be hurried. Melville's narrator, in particular, is conscientious both in telling his story as fully as he can and in admitting the limits of his knowledge; while Conrad's tale echoes the pace and rhythms of the spoken word.

"The Yellow Wall-Paper" and "Really, *Doesn't* Crime Pay?" represent a second tradition in first-person narrative: the creation of a tale in the shape of a journal or diary. Unlike the first two stories, which claim clear descent from the oral tradition of tale-telling, these latter two stories come from a purely written tradition. You must have journals—and hence writing—

way of life is the best. Hence, though I belong to a profession proverbially energetic and nervous, even to turbulence, at times, yet nothing of that sort have I ever suffered to invade my peace. I am one of
those unambitious lawyers who never addresses a jury, or in any way
draws down public applause; but, in the cool tranquillity of a snug
retreat, do a snug business among rich men's bonds, and mortgages,
and title-deeds. All who know me, consider me an eminently *safe*
man. The late John Jacob Astor,[1] a personage little given to poetic
enthusiasm, had no hesitation in pronouncing my first grand point to
be prudence; my next, method. I do not speak it in vanity, but
simply record the fact, that I was not unemployed in my profession
by the late John Jacob Astor, a name which, I admit, I love to
repeat; for it hath a rounded and orbicular sound to it, and rings
like unto bullion. I will freely add, that I was not insensible to the
late John Jacob Astor's good opinion.

Some time prior to the period at which this little history begins, my
avocations had been largely increased. The good old office, now
extinct in the State of New York, of a Master in Chancery, had been
conferred upon me. It was not a very arduous office, but very pleasantly remunerative. I seldom lose my temper; much more seldom
indulge in dangerous indignation at wrongs and outrages; but, I
must be permitted to be rash here, and declare, that I consider the
sudden and violent abrogation of the office of Master in Chancery, by
the new Constitution, as a —— premature act; inasmuch as I had
counted upon a life-lease of the profits, whereas I only received those
of a few short years. But this is by the way.

My chambers were up stairs, at No. — Wall Street. At one end,
they looked upon the white wall of the interior of a spacious sky-light
shaft, penetrating the building from top to bottom.

This view might have been considered rather tame than otherwise,
deficient in what landscape painters call "life." But, if so, the view
from the other end of my chambers offered, at least, a contrast, if
nothing more. In that direction, my windows commanded an unob-
structed view of a lofty brick wall, black by age and everlasting
shade; which wall required no spy-glass to bring out its lurking
beauties, but, for the benefit of all near-sighted spectators, was
pushed up to within ten feet of my window panes. Owing to the great
height of the surrounding buildings, and my chambers being on the
second floor, the interval between this wall and mine not a little
resembled a huge square cistern.

At the period just preceding the advent of Bartleby, I had two
persons as copyists in my employment, and a promising lad as an

---

[1] *John Jacob Astor* (1763–1848), an American fur trader and financier.

office-boy. First, Turkey; second, Nippers; third, Ginger Nut. These may seem names, the like of which are not usually found in the Directory. In truth, they were nicknames, mutually conferred upon each other by my three clerks, and were deemed expressive of their respective persons or characters. Turkey was a short, pursy Englishman, of about my own age—that is, somewhere not far from sixty. In the morning, one might say, his face was of a fine florid hue, but after twelve o'clock, meridian—his dinner hour—it blazed like a grate full of Christmas coals; and continued blazing—but, as it were, with a gradual wane—till six o'clock, P.M., or thereabouts; after which, I saw no more of the proprietor of the face, which, gaining its meridian with the sun, seemed to set with it, to rise, culminate, and decline the following day, with the like regularity and undiminished glory. There are many singular coincidences I have known in the course of my life, not the least among which was the fact, that, exactly when Turkey displayed his fullest beams from his red and radiant countenance, just then, too, at that critical moment, began the daily period when I considered his business capacities as seriously disturbed for the remainder of the twenty-four hours. Not that he was absolutely idle, or averse to business, then; far from it. The difficulty was, he was apt to be altogether too energetic. There was a strange, inflamed, flurried, flighty recklessness of activity about him. He would be incautious in dipping his pen into his inkstand. All his blots upon my documents were dropped there after twelve o'clock, meridian. Indeed, not only would he be reckless, and sadly given to making blots in the afternoon, but, some days, he went further, and was rather noisy. At such times, too, his face flamed with augmented blazonry, as if cannel coal had been heaped on anthracite. He made an unpleasant racket with his chair; spilled his sand-box; in mending his pens, impatiently split them all to pieces, and threw them on the floor in a sudden passion; stood up, and leaned over his table, boxing his papers about in a most indecorous manner, very sad to behold in an elderly man like him. Nevertheless, as he was in many ways a most valuable person to me, and all the time before twelve o'clock, meridian, was the quickest, steadiest creature, too, accomplishing a great deal of work in a style not easily to be matched—for these reasons, I was willing to overlook his eccentricities, though, indeed, occasionally, I remonstrated with him. I did this very gently, however, because, though the civilest, nay, the blandest and most reverential of men in the morning, yet, in the afternoon, he was disposed, upon provocation, to be slightly rash with his tongue—in fact, insolent. Now, valuing his morning services as I did, and resolved not to lose them—yet, at the same time, made uncomfortable by his inflamed ways after twelve o'clock—and being a man of peace, unwilling by my admonitions to call forth unseemly retorts from him, I took upon me, one Saturday noon (he was always worse on Saturdays) to hint to him, very kindly, that, perhaps, now that he was growing old, it might be well to abridge his labors; in short, he need not come to my chambers after twelve o'clock, but, dinner over, had best go home to his lodgings, and rest himself till tea-time. But no; he insisted upon his afternoon devotions. His countenance became intolerably fervid, as he oratorically assured me—gesticulating with a long ruler at the other end of the room—that if his services in the morning were useful, how indispensable, then, in the afternoon?

"With submission, sir," said Turkey, on this occasion, "I consider myself your right-hand man. In the morning I but marshal and deploy my columns; but in the afternoon I put myself at their head, and gallantly charge the foe, thus"—and he made a violent thrust with the ruler.

"But the blots, Turkey," intimated I.

"True; but, with submission, sir, behold these hairs! I am getting old. Surely, sir, a blot or two of a warm afternoon is not to be severely urged against gray hairs. Old age—even if it blot the page— is honorable. With submission, sir, we *both* are getting old."

This appeal to my fellow-feeling was hardly to be resisted. At all events, I saw that go he would not. So, I made up my mind to let him stay, resolving, nevertheless, to see to it that, during the afternoon, he had to do with my less important papers.

Nippers, the second on my list, was a whiskered, sallow, and, upon the whole, rather piratical-looking young man, of about five and twenty. I always deemed him the victim of two evil powers—ambition and indigestion. The ambition was evinced by a certain impatience of the duties of a mere copyist, an unwarrantable usurpation of strictly professional affairs, such as the original drawing up of legal documents. The indigestion seemed betokened in an occasional nervous testiness and grinning irritability, causing the teeth to audibly grind together over mistakes committed in copying; unnecessary maledictions, hissed, rather than spoken, in the heat of business; and especially by a continual discontent with the height of the table where he worked. Though of a very ingenious mechanical turn, Nippers could never get this table to suit him. He put chips under it, blocks of various sorts, bits of pasteboard, and at last went so far as to attempt an exquisite adjustment, by final pieces of folded blotting-paper. But no invention would answer. If, for the sake of easing his back, he brought the table lid at a sharp angle well up towards his chin, and wrote there like a man using the steep roof of a Dutch house for his desk, then he declared that it stopped the circulation in his arms. If now he lowered the table to his waistbands, and stooped over it in writing, then there was a sore aching in his back. In short, the truth of the matter was, Nippers knew not what he wanted. Or, if he wanted anything, it was to be rid of a scrivener's table altogether. Among the manifestations of his diseased ambition was a fondness he had for receiving visits from certain ambiguous-looking fellows in seedy coats, whom he called his clients. Indeed, I was aware that not only was he, at times, considerable of a ward-politician, but he occasionally did a little business at the Justices' courts, and was not unknown on the steps of the Tombs. I have good reason to believe, however, that one individual who called upon him at my chambers, and who, with a grand air, he insisted was his client, was no other than a dun, and the alleged title-deed, a bill. But, with all his failings, and the annoyances he caused me, Nippers, like his compatriot Turkey, was a very useful man to me; wrote a neat, swift hand; and, when he chose, was not deficient in a gentlemanly sort of deportment. Added to this, he always dressed in a gentlemanly sort of way; and so, incidentally, reflected credit upon my chambers. Whereas, with respect to Turkey, I had much ado to keep him from being a reproach to me. His clothes were apt to look oily, and smell of eating-houses. He wore his pantaloons very loose and baggy in summer. His coats were execrable; his hat not to be handled. But while the hat was a thing of indifference to me, inasmuch as his natural civility and deference, as a dependent Englishman, always led him to doff it the moment he entered the room, yet his coat was another matter. Concerning his coats, I reasoned with him; but with no effect. The truth was, I suppose, that a man with so small an income could not afford to sport such a lustrous face and a lustrous coat at one and the same time. As Nippers once observed, Turkey's money went chiefly for red ink. One winter day, I presented Turkey with a highly respectable-looking coat of my own—a padded gray coat, of a most comfortable warmth, and which buttoned straight up from the knee to the neck. I thought Turkey would appreciate the favor, and abate his rashness and obstreperousness of afternoons. But no; I verily believe that buttoning himself up in so downy and blanket-like a coat had a pernicious effect upon him—upon the same principle that too much oats are bad for horses. In fact, precisely as a rash, restive horse is said to feel his oats, so Turkey felt his coat. It made him insolent. He was a man whom prosperity harmed.

Though, concerning the self-indulgent habits of Turkey, I had my own private surmises, yet, touching Nippers, I was well persuaded that, whatever might be his faults in other respects, he was, at least, a temperate young man. But, indeed, nature herself seemed to have been his vintner, and, at his birth, charged him so thoroughly with an irritable, brandy-like disposition, that all subsequent potations were needless. When I consider how, amid the stillness of my chambers, Nippers would sometimes impatiently rise from his seat, and stooping over his table, spread his arms wide apart, seize the whole desk, and move it, and jerk it, with a grim, grinding motion on the floor, as if the table were a perverse voluntary agent, intent on thwarting and vexing him, I plainly perceive that, for Nippers, brandy-and-water were altogether superfluous.

It was fortunate for me that, owing to its peculiar cause—indigestion—the iritability and consequent nervousness of Nippers were mainly observable in the morning, while in the afternoon he was comparatively mild. So that, Turkey's paroxysms only coming on about twelve o'clock, I never had to do with their eccentricities at one time. Their fits relieved each other, like guards. When Nippers' was on, Turkey's was off; and *vice versa*. This was a good natural arrangement, under the circumstances.

Ginger Nut, the third on my list, was a lad, some twelve years old. His father was a car-man, ambitious of seeing his son on the bench instead of a cart, before he died. So he sent him to my office, as student at law, errand-boy, cleaner and sweeper, at the rate of one dollar a week. He had a little desk to himself, but he did not use it much. Upon inspection, the drawer exhibited a great array of the shells of various sorts of nuts. Indeed, to this quick-witted youth, the whole noble science of the law was contained in a nut-shell. Not the least among the employments of Ginger Nut, as well as one which he discharged with the most alacrity, was his duty as cake and apple purveyor for Turkey and Nippers. Copying law-papers being proverbially a dry, husky sort of business, my two scriveners were fain to moisten their mouths very often with Spitzenbergs, to be had at the numerous stalls nigh the Custom House and Post Office. Also, they sent Ginger Nut very frequently for that peculiar cake—small, flat, round, and very spicy—after which he had been named by them. Of a cold morning, when business was but dull, Turkey would gobble up scores of these cakes, as if they were mere wafers—indeed, they sell them at the rate of six or eight for a penny—the scrape of his pen blending with the crunching of the crisp particles in his mouth. Of all the fiery afternoon blunders and flurried rashnesses of Turkey, was his once moistening a ginger-cake between his lips, and clapping it on to a mortgage, for a seal. I came within an ace of dismissing him then. But he mollified me by making an oriental bow, and saying—

"With submission, sir, it was generous of me to find you in stationery on my own account."

Now my original business—that of a conveyancer and title hunter, and drawer-up of recondite documents of all sorts—was considerably increased by receiving the master's office. There was now great work for scriveners. Not only must I push the clerks already with me, but I must have additional help.

In answer to my advertisement, a motionless young man one morning stood upon my office threshold, the door being open, for it was summer. I can see that figure now—pallidly neat, pitiably respectable, incurably forlorn! It was Bartleby.

After a few words touching his qualifications, I engaged him, glad to have among my corps of copyists a man of so singularly sedate an aspect, which I thought might operate beneficially upon the flighty temper of Turkey, and the fiery one of Nippers.

I should have stated before that ground glass folding-doors divided my premises into two parts, one of which was occupied by my scriveners, the other by myself. According to my humor, I threw open these doors, or closed them. I resolved to assign Bartleby a corner by the folding-doors, but on my side of them, so as to have this quiet man within easy call, in case any trifling thing was to be done. I placed his desk close up to a small side-window in that part of the room, a window which originally had afforded a lateral view of certain grimy backyards and bricks, but which, owing to subsequent erections, commanded at present no view at all, though it gave some light. Within three feet of the panes was a wall, and the light came down from far above, between two lofty buildings, as from a very small opening in a dome. Still further to a satisfactory arrangement, I procured a high green folding screen, which might entirely isolate Bartleby from my sight, though not remove him from my voice. And thus, in a manner, privacy and society were conjoined.

At first, Bartleby did an extraordinary quantity of writing. As if long famishing for something to copy, he seemed to gorge himself on my documents. There was no pause for digestion. He ran a day and night line, copying by sun-light and by candle-light. I should have been quite delighted with his application, had he been cheerfully industrious. But he wrote on silently, palely, mechanically.

It is, of course, an indispensable part of a scrivener's business to verify the accuracy of his copy, word by word. Where there are two or more scriveners in an office, they assist each other in this examination, one reading from the copy, the other holding the original. It is a very dull, wearisome, and lethargic affair. I can readily imagine that, to some sanguine temperaments, it would be altogether intolerable. For example, I cannot credit that the mettlesome poet, Byron, would have contentedly sat down with Bartleby to examine a law document of, say five hundred pages, closely written in a crimpy hand.

Now and then, in the haste of business, it had been my habit to assist in comparing some brief document myself, calling Turkey or Nippers for this purpose. One object I had, in placing Bartleby so handy to me behind the screen, was, to avail myself of his services on such trivial occasions. It was on the third day, I think, of his being with me, and before any necessity had arisen for having his own writing examined, that, being much hurried to complete a small affair I had in hand, I abruptly called to Bartleby. In my haste and natural expectancy of instant compliance, I sat with my head bent over the original on my desk, and my right hand sideways, and somewhat nervously extended with the copy, so that, immediately upon emerging from his retreat, Bartleby might snatch it and proceed to business without the least delay.

In this very attitude did I sit when I called to him, rapidly stating what it was I wanted him to do—namely, to examine a small paper with me. Imagine my surprise, nay, my consternation, when, without moving from his privacy, Bartleby, in a singularly mild, firm voice, replied, "I would prefer not to."

I sat awhile in perfect silence, rallying my stunned faculties. Immediately it occurred to me that my ears had deceived me, or Bartleby had entirely misunderstood my meaning. I repeated my request in the clearest tone I could assume; but in quite as clear a one came the previous reply, "I would prefer not to."

"Prefer not to," echoed I, rising in high excitement, and crossing the room with a stride. "What do you mean? Are you moon-struck? I want you to help me compare this sheet here—take it," and I thrust it towards him.

"I would prefer not to," said he.

I looked at him steadfastly. His face was leanly composed; his gray eye dimly calm. Not a wrinkle of agitation rippled him. Had there been the least uneasiness, anger, impatience or impertinence in his manner; in other words, had there been any thing ordinarily human about him, doubtless I should have violently dismissed him from the premises. But as it was, I should have as soon thought of turning my pale plaster-of-paris bust of Cicero out of doors. I stood gazing at him awhile, as he went on with his own writing, and then reseated myself at my desk. This is very strange, thought I. What had one best do? But my business hurried me. I concluded to forget the matter for the present, reserving it for my future leisure. So calling Nippers from the other room, the paper was speedily examined.

A few days after this, Bartleby concluded four lengthy documents, being quadruplicates of a week's testimony taken before me in my High Court of Chancery. It became necessary to examine them. It was an important suit, and great accuracy was imperative. Having all things arranged, I called Turkey, Nippers, and Ginger Nut, from the next room, meaning to place the four copies in the hands of my four clerks, while I should read from the original. Accordingly, Turkey, Nippers, and Ginger Nut had taken their seats in a row, each with his document in his hand, when I called to Bartleby to join this interesting group.

"Bartleby! quick, I am waiting."

I heard a slow scrape of his chair legs on the uncarpeted floor, and soon he appeared standing at the entrance of his hermitage.

"What is wanted?" said he, mildly.

"The copies, the copies," said I, hurriedly. "We are going to examine them. There"—and I held towards him the fourth quadruplicate.

"I would prefer not to," he said, and gently disappeared behind the screen.

For a few moments I was turned into a pillar of salt, standing at the head of my seated column of clerks. Recovering myself, I advanced towards the screen, and demanded the reason for such extraordinary conduct.

"*Why* do you refuse?"

"I would prefer not to."

With any other man I should have flown outright into a dreadful passion, scorned all further words, and thrust him ignominiously from my presence. But there was something about Bartleby that not only strangely disarmed me, but, in a wonderful manner, touched and disconcerted me. I began to reason with him.

"These are your own copies we are about to examine. It is labor saving to you, because one examination will answer for your four papers. It is common usage. Every copyist is bound to help examine his copy. Is it not so? Will you not speak? Answer!"

"I prefer not to," he replied in a flutelike tone. It seemed to me that, while I had been addressing him, he carefully revolved every statement that I made; fully comprehended the meaning; could not gainsay the irresistible conclusion; but, at the same time, some paramount consideration prevailed with him to reply as he did.

"You are decided, then, not to comply with my request—a request made according to common usage and common sense?"

He briefly gave me to understand, that on that point my judgment was sound. Yes: his decision was irreversible.

It is not seldom the case that, when a man is browbeaten in some unprecedented and violently unreasonable way, he begins to stagger in his own plainest faith. He begins, as it were, vaguely to surmise that, wonderful as it may be, all the justice and all the reason is on the other side. Accordingly, if any disinterested persons are present, he turns to them for some reinforcement of his own faltering mind.

"Turkey," said I, "what do you think of this? Am I not right?"

"With submission, sir," said Turkey, in his blandest tone, "I think that you are."

"Nippers," said I, "what do *you* think of it?"

"I think I should kick him out of the office."

(The reader, of nice perceptions, will here perceive that, it being morning, Turkey's answer is couched in polite and tranquil terms, but Nippers' replies in ill-tempered ones. Or, to repeat a previous sentence, Nippers' ugly mood was on duty, and Turkey's off.)

"Ginger Nut," said I, willing to enlist the smallest suffrage in my behalf, "what do *you* think of it?"

"I think, sir, he's a little *luny*," replied Ginger Nut, with a grin.

"You hear what they say," said I, turning towards the screen, "come forth and do your duty."

But he vouchsafed no reply. I pondered a moment in sore perplexity. But once more business hurried me. I determined again to postpone the consideration of this dilemma to my future leisure. With a little trouble we made out to examine the papers without Bartleby, though at every page or two Turkey deferentially dropped his opinion, that this proceeding was quite out of the common; while Nippers, twitching in his chair with a dyspeptic nervousness, ground out, between his set teeth, occasional hissing maledictions against the stubborn oaf behind the screen. And for his (Nippers') part, this was the first and the last time he would do another man's business without pay.

Meanwhile Bartleby sat in his hermitage, oblivious to everything but his own peculiar business there.

Some days passed, the scrivener being employed upon another lengthy work. His late remarkable conduct led me to regard his ways narrowly. I observed that he never went to dinner; indeed, that he never went anywhere. As yet I had never, of my personal knowledge, known him to be outside of my office. He was a perpetual sentry in the corner. At about eleven o'clock though, in the morning, I noticed that Ginger Nut would advance toward the opening in Bartleby's screen, as if silently beckoned thither by a gesture invisible to me where I sat. The boy would then leave the office, jingling a few pence, and reappear with a handful of ginger-nuts, which he delivered in the hermitage, receiving two of the cakes for his trouble.

He lives, then, on ginger-nuts, thought I; never eats a dinner, properly speaking; he must be a vegetarian, then; but no; he never eats even vegetables, he eats nothing but ginger-nuts. My mind then ran on in reveries concerning the probable effects upon the human constitution of living entirely on ginger-nuts. Ginger-nuts are so called, because they contain ginger as one of their peculiar constituents, and the final flavoring one. Now, what was ginger? A hot, spicy thing. Was Bartleby hot and spicy? Not at all. Ginger, then, had no effect upon Bartleby. Probably he preferred it should have none.

Nothing so aggravates an earnest person as a passive resistance. If the individual so resisted be of a not inhumane temper, and the resisting one perfectly harmless in his passivity, then, in the better moods of the former, he will endeavor charitably to construe to his imagination what proves impossible to be solved by his judgment. Even so, for the most part, I regarded Bartleby and his ways. Poor fellow! thought I, he means no mischief; it is plain he intends no insolence; his aspect sufficiently evinces that his eccentricities are involuntary. He is useful to me. I can get along with him. If I turn him away, the chances are he will fall in with some less-indulgent employer, and then he will be rudely treated, and perhaps driven forth miserably to starve. Yes. Here I can cheaply purchase a delicious self-approval. To befriend Bartleby; to humor him in his strange willfulness, will cost me little or nothing, while I lay up in my soul what will eventually prove a sweet morsel for my conscience. But this mood was not invariable with me. The passiveness of Bartleby sometimes irritated me. I felt strangely goaded on to encounter him in new opposition—to elicit some angry spark from him answerable to my own. But, indeed, I might as well have essayed to strike fire with my knuckles against a bit of Windsor soap. But one afternoon the evil impulse in me mastered me, and the following little scene ensued:

"Bartleby," said I, "when those papers are all copied, I will compare them with you."

"I would prefer not to."

"How? Surely you do not mean to persist in that mulish vagary?" No answer.

I threw open the folding-doors near by, and, turning upon Turkey and Nippers, exclaimed:

"Bartleby a second time says, he won't examine his papers. What do you think of it, Turkey?"

It was afternoon, be it remembered. Turkey sat glowing like a brass boiler; his bald head steaming; his hands reeling among his blotted papers.

"Think of it?" roared Turkey; "I think I'll just step behind his screen, and black his eyes for him!"

So saying, Turkey rose to his feet and threw his arms into a pugilistic position. He was hurrying away to make good his promise, when I detained him, alarmed at the effect of incautiously rousing Turkey's combativeness after dinner.

"Sit down, Turkey," said I, "and hear what Nippers has to say. What do you think of it, Nippers? Would I not be justified in immediately dismissing Bartleby?"

"Excuse me, that is for you to decide, sir. I think his conduct quite unusual, and, indeed, unjust, as regards Turkey and myself. But it may only be a passing whim."

"Ah," exclaimed I, "you have strangely changed your mind, then —you speak very gently of him now."

"All beer," cried Turkey; "gentleness is effects of beer—Nippers and I dined together to-day. You see how gentle *I* am, sir. Shall I go and black his eyes?"

"You refer to Bartleby, I suppose. No, not to-day, Turkey," I replied; "pray, put up your fists."

I closed the doors, and again advanced towards Bartleby. I felt additional incentives tempting me to my fate. I burned to be rebelled against again. I remember that Bartleby never left the office.

"Bartleby," said I, "Ginger Nut is away; just step around to the Post Office, won't you? (it was but a three minutes' walk), and see if there is anything for me."

"I would prefer not to."

"You *will* not?"

"I *prefer* not."

I staggered to my desk, and sat there in a deep study. My blind inveteracy returned. Was there any other thing in which I could procure myself to be ignominiously repulsed by this lean, penniless wight?—my hired clerk? What added thing is there, prefectly reasonable, that he will be sure to refuse to do?

"Bartleby!"

No answer.

"Bartleby," in a louder tone.

No answer.

"Bartleby," I roared.

Like a very ghost, agreeably to the laws of magical invocation, at the third summons, he appeared at the entrance of his hermitage.

"Go to the next room, and tell Nippers to come to me."

"I prefer not to," he respectfully and slowly said, and mildly disappeared.

"Very good, Bartleby," said I, in a quiet sort of serenely-severe self-possessed tone, intimating the unalterable purpose of some terrible retribution very close at hand. But upon the whole, as it was drawing towards my dinner-hour, I thought it best to put on my hat and walk home for the day, suffering much from perplexity and distress of mind.

Shall I acknowledge it? The conclusion of this whole business was, that it soon became a fixed fact of my chambers, that a pale young scrivener, by the name of Bartleby, had a desk there; that he copied for me at the usual rate of four cents a folio (one hundred words); but he was permanently exempt from examining the work done by him, that duty being transferred to Turkey and Nippers, out of compliment, doubtless, to their superior acuteness; moreover, said Bartleby was never, on any account, to be dispatched on the most trivial errand of any sort; and that even if entreated to take upon him such a matter, it was generally understood that he would "prefer not to"—in other words, that he would refuse point-blank.

As days passed on, I became considerably reconciled to Bartleby. His steadiness, his freedom from all dissipation, his incessant industry (except when he chose to throw himself into a standing revery behind his screen), his great stillness, his unalterableness of demeanor under all circumstances, made him a valuable acquisition. One prime thing was this—*he was always there*—first in the morning, continually through the day, and the last at night. I had a singular confidence in his honesty. I felt my most precious papers perfectly safe in his hands. Sometimes, to be sure, I could not, for the very soul of me, avoid falling into sudden spasmodic passions with him. For it was exceeding difficult to bear in mind all the time those strange peculiarities, privileges, and unheard of exemptions, forming the tacit stipulations on Bartleby's part under which he remained in my office. Now and then, in the eagerness of dispatching pressing business, I would inadvertently summon Bartleby, in a short, rapid tone, to put his finger, say, on the incipient tie of a bit of red tape with which I was about compressing some papers. Of course, from behind the screen the usual answer, "I prefer not to," was sure to come; and then, how could a human creature, with the common infirmities of our nature, refrain from bitterly exclaiming upon such perverseness—such unreasonableness. However, every added repulse of this sort which I received only tended to lessen the probability of my repeating the inadvertence.

Here it must be said, that according to the custom of most legal gentlemen occupying chambers in densely-populated law buildings, there were several keys to my door. One was kept by a woman residing in the attic, which person weekly scrubbed and daily swept and dusted my apartments. Another was kept by Turkey for convenience sake. The third I sometimes carried in my own pocket. The fourth I knew not who had.

Now, one Sunday morning I happened to go to Trinity Church, to hear a celebrated preacher, and finding myself rather early on the ground I thought I would walk around to my chambers for a while. Luckily I had my key with me; but upon applying it to the lock, I found it resisted by something inserted from the inside. Quite surprised, I called out; when to my consternation a key was turned from within; and thrusting his lean visage at me, and holding the door ajar, the apparition of Bartleby appeared, in his shirt sleeves, and otherwise in a strangely tattered deshabille, saying quietly that he was sorry, but he was deeply engaged just then, and—preferred not admitting me at present. In a brief word or two, he moreover added, that perhaps I had better walk around the block two or three times, and by that time he would probably have concluded his affairs.

Now, the utterly unsurmised appearance of Bartleby, tenanting my law-chambers of a Sunday morning, with his cadaverously gentlemanly *nonchalance,* yet withal firm and self-possessed, had such a strange effect upon me, that incontinently I slunk away from my own door, and did as desired. But not without sundry twinges of impotent rebellion against the mild effrontery of this unaccountable scrivener. Indeed, it was his wonderful mildness chiefly, which not only disarmed me, but unmanned me as it were. For I consider that one, for the time, is somehow unmanned when he tranquilly permits his hired clerk to dictate to him, and order him away from his own premises. Furthermore, I was full of uneasiness as to what Bartleby could possibly be doing in my office in his shirt sleeves, and in an otherwise dismantled condition of a Sunday morning. Was anything amiss going on? Nay, that was out of the question. It was not to be thought of for a moment that Bartleby was an immoral person. But what could he be doing there?—copying? Nay again, whatever might be his eccentricities, Bartleby was an eminently decorous person. He would be the last man to sit down to his desk in any state approaching to nudity. Besides, it was Sunday; and there was something about Bartleby that forbade the supposition that he would by any secular occupation violate the proprieties of the day.

Nevertheless, my mind was not pacified; and full of a restless curiosity, at last I returned to the door. Without hindrance I inserted my key, opened it, and entered. Bartleby was not to be seen. I looked round anxiously, peeped behind his screen; but it was very plain that he was gone. Upon more closely examining the place, I surmised that for an indefinite period Bartleby must have ate, dressed, and slept in my office, and that, too, without plate, mirror, or bed. The cushioned seat of a rickety old sofa in one corner bore the faint impression of a lean, reclining form. Rolled away under his desk, I found a blanket; under the empty grate, a blacking box and brush; on a chair, a tin basin, with soap and a ragged towel; in a newspaper a few crumbs of ginger-nuts and a morsel of cheese. Yes, thought I, it is evident enough that Bartleby has been making his home here, keeping bachelor's hall all by himself. Immediately then the thought came sweeping across me, what miserable friendlessness and loneliness are here revealed! His poverty is great; but his solitude, how horrible! Think of it. Of a Sunday, Wall Street is deserted as Petra;[2] and every night of every day it is an emptiness. This building, too, which of week-days hums with industry and life, at nightfall echoes with sheer vacancy, and all through Sunday is forlorn. And here Bartleby makes his home; sole spectator of a solitude which he has seen all populous —a sort of innocent and transformed Marius brooding among the ruins of Carthage!

For the first time in my life a feeling of over-powering stinging

---

[2] *Petra,* ancient city in Syria.

melancholy seized me. Before, I had never experienced aught but a not unpleasing sadness. The bond of a common humanity now drew me irresistibly to gloom. A fraternal melancholy! For both I and Bartleby were sons of Adam. I remembered the bright silks and sparkling faces I had seen that day, in gala trim, swan-like sailing down the Mississippi of Broadway; and I contrasted them with the pallid copyist, and thought to myself, Ah, happiness courts the light, so we deem the world is gay; but misery hides aloof, so we deem that misery there is none. These sad fancyings—chimeras, doubtless, of a sick and silly brain—led on to other and more special thoughts, concerning the eccentricities of Bartleby. Presentiments of strange discoveries hovered round me. The scrivener's pale form appeared to me laid out, among uncaring strangers, in its shivering winding sheet.

Suddenly I was attracted by Bartleby's closed desk, the key in open sight left in the lock.

I mean no mischief, seek the gratification of no heartless curiosity, thought I; besides, the desk is mine, and its contents, too, so I will make bold to look within. Everything was methodically arranged, the papers smoothly placed. The pigeon holes were deep, and removing the files of documents, I groped into their recesses. Presently I felt something there, and dragged it out. It was an old bandanna hand-kerchief, heavy and knotted. I opened it, and saw it was a saving's bank.

I now recalled all the quiet mysteries which I had noted in the man. I remembered that he never spoke but to answer; that, though at intervals he had considerable time to himself, yet I had never seen him reading—no, not even a newspaper; that for long periods he would stand looking out, at his pale window behind the screen, upon the dead brick wall; I was quite sure he never visited any refectory or eating house; while his pale face clearly indicated that he never drank beer like Turkey, or tea and coffee even, like other men; that he never went anywhere in particular that I could learn; never went out for a walk, unless, indeed, that was the case at present; that he had declined telling who he was, or whence he came, or whether he had any relatives in the world; that though so thin and pale, he never complained of ill health. And more than all, I remembered a certain unconscious air of pallid—how shall I call it?—of pallid haughtiness, say, or rather an austere reserve about him, which had positively awed me into my tame compliance with his eccentricities, when I had feared to ask him to do the slightest incidental thing for me, even though I might know, from his long-continued motionless-ness, that behind his screen he must be standing in one of those dead-wall reveries of his.

Revolving all these things, and coupling them with the recently discovered fact, that he made my office his constant abiding place and home, and not forgetful of his morbid moodiness; revolving all these things, a prudential feeling began to steal over me. My first emotions had been those of pure melancholy and sincerest pity; but just in proportion as the forlornness of Bartleby grew and grew to my imagination, did that same melancholy merge into fear, that pity into repulsion. So true it is, and so terrible, too, that up to a certain point the thought or sight of misery enlists our best affections; but, in certain special cases, beyond that point it does not. They err who would assert that invariably this is owing to the inherent selfishness of the human heart. It rather proceeds from a certain hopelessness of remedying excessive and organic ill. To a sensitive being, pity is not seldom pain. And when at last it is perceived that such pity cannot lead to effectual succor, common sense bids the soul be rid of it. What I saw that morning persuaded me that the scrivener was the victim of inate and incurable disorder. I might give alms to his body; but his body did not pain him; it was his soul that suffered, and his soul I could not reach.

I did not accomplish the purpose of going to Trinity Church that morning. Somehow, the things I had seen disqualified me for the time from church-going. I walked homeward, thinking what I would do with Bartleby. Finally, I resolved upon this—I would put certain calm questions to him the next morning, touching his history, etc., and if he declined to answer them openly and unreservedly (and I supposed he would prefer not), then to give him a twenty dollar bill over and above whatever I might owe him, and tell him his services were no longer required; but that if in any other way I could assist him, I would be happy to do so, especially if he desired to return to his native place, wherever that might be, I would willingly help to defray the expenses. Moreover, if, after reaching home, he found himself at any time in want of aid, a letter from him would be sure of a reply.

The next morning came.

"Bartleby," said I, gently calling to him behind his screen.

No reply.

"Bartleby," said I, in a still gentler tone, "come here; I am not going to ask you to do anything you would prefer not to do—I simply wish to speak to you."

Upon this he noiselessly slid into view.

"Will you tell me, Bartleby, where you were born?"

"I would prefer not to."

"Will you tell me *anything* about yourself?"

"I would prefer not to."

"But what reasonable objection can you have to speak to me? I feel friendly towards you."

He did not look at me while I spoke, but kept his glance fixed upon my bust of Cicero, which, as I then sat, was directly behind me, some six inches above my head.

"What is your answer, Bartleby," said I, after waiting a considerable time for a reply, during which his countenance remained immovable, only there was the faintest conceivable tremor of the white attenuated mouth.

"At present I prefer to give no answer," he said, and retired into his hermitage.

It was rather weak in me I confess, but his manner, on this occasion, nettled me. Not only did there seem to lurk in it a certain calm disdain, but his perverseness seemed ungrateful, considering the undeniable good usage and indulgence he had received from me.

Again I sat ruminating what I should do. Mortified as I was at his behavior, and resolved as I had been to dismiss him when I entered my office, nevertheless I strangely felt something superstitious knocking at my heart, and forbidding me to carry out my purpose, and denouncing me for a villain if I dared to breathe one bitter word against this forlornest of mankind. At last, familiarly drawing my chair behind his screen, I sat down and said: "Bartleby, never mind, then, about revealing your history; but let me entreat you, as a friend, to comply as far as may be with the usages of this office. Say now, you will help to examine papers to-morrow or next day: in short, say now, that in a day or two you will begin to be a little reasonable:—say so, Bartleby."

"At present I would prefer not to be a little reasonable," was his mildly cadaverous reply.

Just then the folding-doors opened, and Nippers approached. He seemed suffering from an unusually bad night's rest, induced by severer indigestion than common. He overheard those final words of Bartleby.

"*Prefer not,* eh?" gritted Nippers—"I'd *prefer* him, if I were you, sir," addressing me—"I'd *prefer* him; I'd give him preferences, the stubborn mule! What is it, sir, pray, that he *prefers* not to do now?"

Bartleby moved not a limb.

"Mr. Nippers," said I, "I'd prefer that you would withdraw for the present."

Somehow, of late, I had got into the way of involuntarily using this word "prefer" upon all sorts of not exactly suitable occasions. And I trembled to think that my contact with the scrivener had already and seriously affected me in a mental way. And what further and deeper aberration might it not yet produce? This apprehension had not been without efficacy in determining me to summary measures.

As Nippers, looking very sour and sulky, was departing, Turkey blandly and deferentially approached.

"With submission, sir," said he, "yesterday I was thinking abut Bartleby here, and I think that if he would but prefer to take a quart of good ale every day, it would do much towards mending him, and enabling him to assist in examining his papers."

"So you have got the word, too," said I, slightly excited.

"With submission, what word, sir," asked Turkey, respectfully crowding himself into the contracted space behind the screen, and by so doing, making me jostle the scrivener. "What word, sir?"

"I would prefer to be left alone here," said Bartleby, as if offended at being mobbed in his privacy.

"*That's* the word, Turkey," said I—"*that's* it."

"Oh, *prefer?* oh yes—queer word. I never use it myself. But, sir, as I was saying, if he would but prefer—"

"Turkey," interrupted I, "you will please withdraw."

"Oh, certainly, sir, if you prefer that I should."

As he opened the folding-door to retire, Nippers at his desk caught a glimpse of me, and asked whether I would prefer to have a certain paper copied on blue paper or white. He did not in the least roguishly accent the word prefer. It was plain that it involuntarily rolled from his tongue. I thought to myself, surely I must get rid of a demented man, who already has in some degree turned the tongues, if not the heads of myself and clerks. But I thought it prudent not to break the dismission at once.

The next day I noticed that Bartleby did nothing but stand at his window in his dead-wall revery. Upon asking him why he did not write, he said that he had decided upon doing no more writing.

"Why, how now? what next?" exclaimed I, "do no more writing?"

"No more."

"And what is the reason?"

"Do you not see the reason for yourself," he indifferently replied.

I looked steadfastly at thim, and perceived that his eyes looked dull and glazed. Instantly it occurred to me, that his unexampled diligence in copying by his dim window for the first few weeks of his stay with me might have temporarily impaired his vision.

I was touched. I said something in condolence with him. I hinted that of course he did wisely in abstaining from writing for a while; and urged him to embrace that opportunity of taking wholesome exercise in the open air. This, however, he did not do. A few days after this, my other clerks being absent, and being in a great hurry to dispatch certain letters by the mail, I thought that, having nothing else earthly to do, Bartleby would surely be less inflexible than usual, and carry these letters to the post-office. But he blankly declined. So, much to my inconvenience, I went myself.

Still added days went by. Whether Bartleby's eyes improved or not, I could not say. To all appearance, I thought they did. But when I asked him if they did, he vouchsafed no answer. At all events, he would do no copying. At last, in reply to my urgings, he informed me that he had permanently given up copying.

"What!" exclaimed I; "suppose your eyes should get entirely well—better than ever before—would you not copy then?"

"I have given up copying," he answered, and slid aside.

He remained as ever, a fixture in my chamber. Nay—if that were possible—he became still more of a fixture than before. What was to be done? He would do nothing in the office; why should he stay there? In plain fact, he had now become a millstone to me, not only useless as a necklace, but afflictive to bear. Yet I was sorry for him. I speak less than truth when I say that, on his own account, he occasioned me uneasiness. If he would but have named a single relative or friend, I would instantly have written, and urged their taking the poor fellow away to some convenient retreat. But he seemed alone, absolutely alone in the universe. A bit of wreck in the mid Atlantic. At length, necessities connected with my business tyrannized over all other considerations. Decently as I could, I told Bartleby that in six days time he must unconditionally leave the office. I warned him to take measures, in the interval, for procuring some other abode. I offered to assist him in this endeavor, if he himself would but take the first step towards a removal. "And when you finally quit me, Bartleby," added I, "I shall see that you go not away entirely unprovided. Six days from this hour, remember."

At the expiration of that period, I peeped behind the screen, and lo! Bartleby was there.

I buttoned up my coat, balanced myself; advanced slowly towards him, touched his shoulder, and said, "The time has come; you must quit this place; I am sorry for you; here is money; but you must go."

"I would prefer not," he replied, with his back still towards me.

"You *must*."

He remained silent.

Now I had an unbounded confidence in this man's common honesty. He had frequently restored to me sixpences and shillings carelessly dropped upon the floor, for I am apt to be very reckless in such shirt-button affairs. The proceeding, then, which followed will not be deemed extraordinary.

"Bartleby," said I, "I owe you twelve dollars on account; here are thirty-two; the odd twenty are yours—Will you take it?" and I handed the bills towards him.

But he made no motion.

"I will leave them here, then," putting them under a weight on the table. Then taking my hat and cane and going to the door, I tranquilly turned and added—"After you have removed your things from these offices, Bartleby, you will of course lock the door—since every one is now gone for the day but you—and if you please, slip your key underneath the mat, so that I may have it in the morning. I shall not see you again; so good-by to you. If, hereafter, in your new place of abode, I can be of any service to you, do not fail to advise me by letter. Good-by, Bartleby, and fare you well."

But he answered not a word; like the last column of some ruined temple, he remained standing mute and solitary in the middle of the otherwise deserted room.

As I walked home in a pensive mood, my vanity got the better of my pity. I could not but highly plume myself on my masterly management in getting rid of Bartleby. Masterly I call it, and such it must appear to any dispassionate thinker. The beauty of my procedure seemed to consist in its perfect quietness. There was no vulgar bullying, no bravado of any sort, no choleric hectoring, and striding to and fro across the apartment, jerking out vehement commands for Bartleby to bundle himself off with his beggarly traps. Nothing of the kind. Without loudly bidding Bartleby depart—as an inferior genius might have done—I *assumed* the ground that depart he must; and upon that assumption built all I had to say. The more I thought over my procedure, the more I was charmed with it. Nevertheless, next morning, upon awakening, I had my doubts—I had somehow slept off the fumes of vanity. One of the coolest and wisest hours a man has, is just after he awakes in the morning. My procedure seemed as sagacious as ever—but only in theory. How it would prove in practice—there was the rub. It was truly a beautiful thought to have assumed Bartleby's departure; but, after all, that assumption was simply my own, and none of Bartleby's. The great point was, not whether I had assumed that he would quit me, but whether he would prefer so to do. He was more a man of preferences than assumptions.

After breakfast, I walked down town, arguing the probabilities *pro* and *con*. One moment I thought it would prove a miserable failure, and Bartleby would be found all alive at my office as usual; the next moment it seemed certain that I should find his chair empty. And so I kept veering about. At the corner of Broadway and Canal Street, I saw quite an excited group of people standing in earnest conversation.

"I'll take odds he doesn't," said a voice as I passed.

"Doesn't go?—done!" said I, "put up your money."

I was instinctively putting my hand in my pocket to produce my own, when I remembered that this was an election day. The words I had overheard bore no reference to Bartleby, but to the success or nonsuccess of some candidate for the mayoralty. In my intent frame of mind, I had, as it were, imagined that all Broadway shared in my excitement, and were debating the same question with me. I passed on, very thankful that the uproar of the street screened my momentary absent-mindedness.

As I had intended, I was earlier than usual at my office door. I stood listening for a moment. All was still. He must be gone. I tried the knob. The door was locked. Yes, my procedure had worked to a charm; he indeed must be vanished. Yet a certain melancholy mixed with this: I was almost sorry for my brilliant success. I was fumbling under the door mat for the key, which Bartleby was to have left there for me, when accidentally my knee knocked against a panel, producing a summoning sound, and in response a voice came to me from within—"Not yet; I am occupied."

It was Bartleby.

I was thunderstruck. For an instant I stood like the man who, pipe in mouth, was killed one cloudless afternoon long ago in Virginia, by summer lightning; at his own warm open window he was killed, and remained leaning out there upon the dreamy afternoon, till some one touched him, when he fell.

"Not gone!" I murmured at last. But again obeying that wondrous ascendancy which the inscrutable scrivener had over me, and from which ascendancy, for all my chafing, I could not completely escape, I slowly went down stairs and out into the street, and while walking round the block, considered what I should next do in this unheard-of perplexity. Turn the man out by an actual thrusting I could not; to drive him away by calling him hard names would not do; calling in the police was an unpleasant idea; and yet, permit him to enjoy his cadaverous triumph over me—this, too, I could not think of. What was to be done? or, if nothing could be done, was there anything further that I could *assume* in the matter? Yes, as before I had prospectively assumed that Bartleby would depart, so now I might retrospectively assume that departed he was. In the legitimate carrying out of this assumption, I might enter my office in a great hurry, and pretending not to see Bartleby at all, walk straight against him as if he were air. Such a proceeding would in a singular degree have the appearance of a home-thrust. It was hardly possible that Bartleby could withstand such an application of the doctrine of assumptions. But upon second thoughts the success of the plan seemed rather dubious. I resolved to argue the matter over with him again.

"Bartleby," said I, entering the office, with a quietly severe expression, "I am seriously displeased. I am pained, Bartleby. I had thought better of you. I had imagined you of such a gentlemanly organization, that in any delicate dilemma a slight hint would suffice—in short, an assumption. But it appears I am deceived. Why," I added, unaffectedly starting, "you have not even touched that money yet," pointing to it, just where I had left it the evening previous.

He answered nothing.

"Will you, or will you not, quit me?" I now demanded in a sudden passion, advancing close to him.

"I would prefer *not* to quit you," he replied, gently emphasizing the *not*.

"What earthly right have you to stay here? Do you pay any rent? Do you pay my taxes? Or is this property yours?"

He answered nothing.

"Are you ready to go on and write now? Are your eyes recovered? Could you copy a small paper for me this morning? or help examine a few lines? or step round to the post-office? In a word, will you do anything at all, to give a coloring to your refusal to depart the premises?"

He silently retired into his hermitage.

I was now in such a state of nervous resentment that I thought it but prudent to check myself at present from further demonstrations. Bartleby and I were alone. I remembered the tragedy of the unfortunate Adams and the still more unfortunate Colt in the solitary office of the latter; and how poor Colt, being dreadfully incensed by Adams, and imprudently permitting himself to get wildly excited, was at unawares hurried into his fatal act—an act which certainly no man could possibly deplore more than the actor himself. Often it had occurred to me in my ponderings upon the subject, that had that altercation taken place in the public street, or at a private residence, it would not have terminated as it did. It was the circumstance of being alone in a solitary office, up stairs, of a building entirely unhallowed by humanizing domestic associations—an uncarpeted office, doubtless, of a dusty, haggard sort of appearance—this it must have been, which greatly helped to enhance the irritable desperation of the hapless Colt.[3]

But when this old Adam of resentment rose in me and tempted me concerning Bartleby, I grappled him and threw him. How? Why, simply by recalling the divine injunction: "A new commandment give I unto you, that ye love one another." Yes, this it was that saved me. Aside from higher considerations, charity often operates as a vastly wise and prudent principle—a great safeguard to its possessor. Men have committed murder for jealousy's sake, and anger's sake, and hatred's sake, and selfishness' sake, and spiritual pride's sake; but no man, that ever I heard of, ever committed a diabolical murder for

---

[3] *Adams* . . . *Colt*, a widely publicized murder-case in which John C. Colt killed Samuel Adams, in New York City, in January, 1842.

sweet charity's sake. Mere self-interest, then, if no better motive can be enlisted, should, especially with high-tempered men, prompt all beings to charity and philanthropy. At any rate, upon the occasion in question, I strove to drown my exasperated feelings towards the scrivener by benevolently construing his conduct. Poor fellow, poor fellow! thought I, he don't mean anything; and besides, he has seen hard times, and ought to be indulged.

I endeavored, also, immediately to occupy myself, and at the same time to comfort my despondency. I tried to fancy, that in the course of the morning, at such time as might prove agreeable to him, Bartleby, of his own free accord, would emerge from his hermitage and take up some decided line of march in the direction of the door. But no. Half-past twelve o'clock came; Turkey began to glow in the face, overturn his inkstand, and become generally obstreperous; Nippers abated down into quietude and courtesy; Ginger Nut munched his noon apple; and Bartleby remained standing at his window in one of his profoundest dead-wall reveries. Will it be credited? Ought I to acknowledge it? That afternoon I left the office without saying one further word to him.

Some days now passed, during which, at leisure intervals I looked a little into "Edwards on the Will," and "Priestly on Necessity." Under the circumstances, those books induced a salutary feeling. Gradually I slid into the persuasion that these troubles of mine, touching the scrivener, had been all predestinated from eternity, and Bartleby was billeted upon me for some mysterious purpose of an allwise Providence, which it was not for a mere mortal like me to fathom. Yes, Bartleby, stay there behind your screen, thought I; I shall persecute you no more; you are harmless and noiseless as any of these old chairs; in short, I never feel so private as when I know you are here. At last I see it, I feel it; I penetrate to the predestinated purpose of my life. I am content. Others may have loftier parts to enact; but my mission in this world, Bartleby, is to furnish you with office-room for such period as you may see fit to remain.

I believe that this wise and blessed frame of mind would have continued with me, had it not been for the unsolicited and uncharitable remarks obtruded upon me by my professional friends who visited the rooms. But thus it often is, that the constant friction of illiberal minds wears out at last the best resolves of the more generous. Though to be sure, when I reflected upon it, it was not strange that people entering my office should be struck by the peculiar aspect of the unaccountable Bartleby, and so be tempted to throw out some sinister observations concerning him. Sometimes an attorney, having business with me, and calling at my office, and finding no one but the scrivener there, would undertake to obtain some sort of precise information from him touching my whereabouts;

but without heeding his idle talk, Bartleby would remain standing immovable in the middle of the room. So after contemplating him in that position for a time, the attorney would depart, no wiser than he came.

Also, when a reference was going on, and the room full of lawyers and witnesses, and business driving fast, some deeply-occupied legal gentleman present, seeing Bartleby wholly unemployed, would request him to run round to his (the legal gentleman's) office and fetch some papers for him. Thereupon, Bartleby would tranquilly decline, and yet remain idle as before. Then the lawyer would give a great stare, and turn to me. And what could I say? At last I was made aware that all through the circle of my professional acquaintance, a whisper of wonder was running round, having reference to the strange creature I kept at my office. This worried me very much. And as the idea came upon me of his possibly turning out a long-lived man, and keep occupying my chambers, and denying my authority; and perplexing my visitors; and scandalizing my professional reputation; and casting a general gloom over the premises; keeping soul and body together to the last upon his savings (for doubtless he spent but half a dime a day), and in the end perhaps outlive me, and claim possession of my office by right of his perpetual occupancy: as all these dark anticipations crowded upon me more and more, and my friends continually intruded their relentless remarks upon the apparition in my room; a great change was wrought in me. I resolved to gather all my faculties together, and forever rid me of this intolerable incubus.

Ere revolving any complicated project, however, adapted to this end, I first simply suggested to Bartleby the propriety of his permanent departure. In a calm and serious tone, I commended the idea to his careful and mature consideration. But, having taken three days to meditate upon it, he apprised me, that his original determination remained the same; in short, that he still preferred to abide with me.

What shall I do? I now said to myself, buttoning up my coat to the last button. What shall I do? what ought I to do? what does conscience say I *should* do with this man, or, rather, ghost. Rid myself of him, I must; go, he shall. But how? You will not thrust him, the poor, pale, passive mortal—you will not thrust such a helpless creature out of your door? you will not dishonor yourself by such cruelty? No, I will not, I cannot do that. Rather would I let him live and die here, and then mason up his remains in the wall. What, then, will you do? For all your coaxing, he will not budge. Bribes he leaves under your own paper-weight on your table; in short, it is quite plain that he prefers to cling to you.

Then something severe, something unusual must be done. What! surely you will not have him collared by a constable, and commit his innocent pallor to the common jail? And upon what ground could you procure such a thing to be done?—a vagrant, is he? What! he a vagrant, a wanderer, who refuses to budge? It is because he will *not* be a vagrant, then, that you seek to count him *as* a vagrant. That is too absurd. No visible means of support: there I have him. Wrong again: for indubitably he *does* support himself, and that is the only unanswerable proof that any man can show of his possessing the means so to do. No more, then. Since he will not quit me, I must quit him. I will change my offices; I will move elsewhere, and give him fair notice, that if I find him on my new premises I will then proceed against him as a common trespasser.

Acting accordingly, next day I thus addressed him: "I find these chambers too far from the City Hall; the air is unwholesome. In a word, I propose to remove my offices next week, and shall no longer require your services. I tell you this now, in order that you may seek another place."

He made no reply, and nothing more was said.

On the appointed day I engaged carts and men, proceeded to my chambers, and, having but little furniture, everything was removed in a few hours. Throughout, the scrivener remained standing behind the screen, which I directed to be removed the last thing. It was withdrawn; and, being folded up like a huge folio, left him the motionless occupant of a naked room. I stood in the entry watching him a moment, while something from within me upbraided me.

I re-entered, with my hand in my pocket—and—and my heart in my mouth.

"Good-by, Bartleby; I am going—good-by, and God some way bless you; and take that," slipping something in his hand. But it dropped upon the floor, and then—strange to say—I tore myself from him whom I had so longed to be rid of.

Established in my new quarters, for a day or two I kept the door locked, and started at every footfall in the passages. When I returned to my rooms, after any little absence, I would pause at the threshold for an instant, and attentively listen, ere applying my key. But these fears were needless. Bartleby never came nigh me.

I thought all was going well, when a perturbed-looking stranger visited me, inquiring whether I was the person who had recently occupied rooms at No. — Wall Street.

Full of forebodings, I replied that I was.

"Then, sir," said the stranger, who proved a lawyer, "you are responsible for the man you left there. He refuses to do any copying; he refuses to do anything; he says he prefers not to; and he refuses to quit the premises."

"I am very sorry, sir," said I, with assumed tranquillity, but an inward tremor, "but, really, the man you allude to is nothing to me—he is no relation or apprentice of mine, that you should hold me responsible for him."

"In mercy's name, who is he?"

"I certainly cannot inform you. I know nothing about him. Formerly I employed him as a copyist; but he has done nothing for me now for some time past."

"I shall settle him, then—good morning, sir."

Several days passed, and I heard nothing more; and, though I often felt a charitable prompting to call at the place and see poor Bartleby, yet a certain squeamishness, of I know not what, withheld me.

All is over with him, by this time, thought I, at last, when, through another week, no further intelligence reached me. But, coming to my room the day after, I found several persons waiting at my door in a high state of nervous excitement.

"That's the man—here he comes," cried the foremost one, whom I recognized as the lawyer who had previously called upon me alone.

"You must take him away, sir, at once," cried a portly person among them, advancing upon me, and whom I knew to be the landlord of No. — Wall Street. "These gentlemen, my tenants, cannot stand it any longer; Mr. B——," pointing to the lawyer, "has turned him out of his room, and he now persists in haunting the building generally, sitting upon the banisters of the stairs by day, and sleeping in the entry by night. Everybody is concerned; clients are leaving the offices; some fears are entertained of a mob; something you must do, and that without delay."

Aghast at this torrent, I fell back before it, and would fain have locked myself in my new quarters. In vain I persisted that Bartleby was nothing to me—no more than to any one else. In vain—I was the last person known to have anything to do with him, and they held me to the terrible account. Fearful, then, of being exposed in the papers (as one person present obscurely threatened), I considered the matter, and, at length, said, that if the lawyer would give me a confidential interview with the scrivener, in his (the lawyer's) own room, I would, that afternoon, strive my best to rid them of the nuisance they complained of.

Going up stairs to my old haunt, there was Bartleby silently sitting upon the banister at the landing.

"What are you doing here, Bartleby?" said I.

"Sitting upon the banister," he mildly replied.

I motioned him into the lawyer's room, who then left us.

"Bartleby," said I, "are you aware that you are the cause of great tribulation to me, by persisting in occupying entry after being dismissed from the office?"

No answer.

"Now one of two things must take place. Either you must do something, or something must be done to you. Now what sort of business would you like to engage in? Would you like to re-engage in copying for some one?"

"No; I would prefer not to make any change."

"Would you like a clerkship in a dry-goods store?"

"There is too much confinement about that. No, I would not like a clerkship; but I am not particular."

"Too much confinement," I cried, "why you keep yourself confined all the time!"

"I would prefer not to take a clerkship," he rejoined, as if to settle that little item at once.

"How would a bar-tender's business suit you? There is no trying of the eye-sight in that."

"I would not like it at all; though, as I said before, I am not particular."

His unwonted wordiness inspirited me. I returned to the charge.

"Well, then, would you like to travel through the country collecting bills for the merchants? That would improve your health."

"No, I would prefer to be doing something else."

"How, then, would going as a companion to Europe, to entertain some young gentleman with your conversation—how would that suit you?"

"Not at all. It does not strike me that there is anything definite about that. I like to be stationary. But I am not particular."

"Stationary you shall be, then," I cried, now losing all patience, and, for the first time in all my exasperating connection with him, fairly flying into a passion. "If you do not go away from these premises before night, I shall feel bound—indeed, I *am* bound—to—to—to quit the premises myself!" I rather absurdly concluded, knowing not with what possible threat to try to frighten his immobility into compliance. Despairing of all further efforts, I was precipitately leaving him, when a final thought occurred to me—one which had not been wholly unindulged before.

"Bartleby," said I, in the kindest tone I could assume under such exciting circumstances, "will you go home with me now—not to my office, but my dwelling—and remain there till we can conclude upon some convenient arrangement for you at our leisure? Come, let us start now, right away."

"No: at present I would prefer not to make any change at all."

I answered nothing; but, effectually dodging every one by the suddenness and rapidity of my flight, rushed from the building, ran up Wall Street towards Broadway, and, jumping into the first omnibus, was soon removed from pursuit. As soon as tranquillity returned, I distinctly perceived that I had now done all that I possibly could, both in respect to the demands of the landlord and his tenants, and with regard to my own desire and sense of duty, to benefit Bartleby, and shield him from rude persecution. I now strove to be entirely care-free and quiescent; and my conscience justified me in the attempt; though, indeed, it was not so successful as I could have wished. So fearful was I of being again hunted out by the incensed landlord and his exasperated tenants, that, surrendering my business to Nippers, for a few days, I drove about the upper part of the town and through the suburbs, in my rockaway; crossed over to Jersey City and Hoboken, and paid fugitive visits to Manhattanville and Astoria. In fact, I almost lived in my rockaway for the time.

When again I entered my office, lo, a note from the landlord lay upon the desk. I opened it with trembling hands. It informed me that the writer had sent to the police, and had Bartleby removed to the Tombs as a vagrant. Moreover, since I knew more about him than any one else, he wished me to appear at that place, and make a suitable statement of the facts. These tidings had a conflicting effect upon me. At first I was indignant; but, at last, almost approved. The landlord's energetic, summary disposition, had led him to adopt a procedure which I do not think I would have decided upon myself; and yet, as a last resort, under such peculiar circumstances, it seemed the only plan.

As I afterwards learned, the poor scrivener, when told that he must be conducted to the Tombs, offered not the slightest obstacle, but, in his pale, unmoving way, silently acquiesced.

Some of the compassionate and curious bystanders joined the party; and headed by one of the constables arm in arm with Bartleby, the silent procession filed its way through all the noise, and heat, and joy of the roaring thoroughfares at noon.

The same day I received the note, I went to the Tombs, or, to speak more properly, the Halls of Justice. Seeking the right officer, I stated the purpose of my call, and was informed that the individual I described was, indeed, within. I then assured the functionary that Bartleby was a perfectly honest man, and greatly to be compassionated, however unaccountably eccentric. I narrated all I knew, and closed by suggesting the idea of letting him remain in as indulgent confinement as possible, till something less harsh might be done— though, indeed, I hardly knew what. At all events, if nothing else could be decided upon, the almshouse must receive him. I then begged to have an interview.

Being under no disgraceful charge, and quite serene and harmless in all his ways, they had permitted him freely to wander about the prison, and, especially, in the inclosed grass-platted yards thereof. And so I found him there, standing all alone in the quietest of the yards, his face towards a high wall, while all around, from the narrow slits of the jail windows, I thought I saw peering out upon him the eyes of murderers and thieves.

"Bartleby!"

"I know you," he said without looking round—"and I want nothing to say to you."

"It was not I that brought you here, Bartleby," said I, keenly pained at his implied suspicion. "And to you, this should not be so vile a place. Nothing reproachful attaches to you by being here. And see, it is not so sad a place as one might think. Look, there is the sky, and here is the grass."

"I know where I am," he replied, but would say nothing more, and so I left him.

As I entered the corridor again, a broad meat-like man, in an apron, accosted me, and, jerking his thumb over his shoulder, said—"Is that your friend?"

"Yes."

"Does he want to starve? If he does, let him live on the prison fare, that's all."

"Who are you?" asked I, not knowing what to make of such an unofficially speaking person in such a place.

"I am the grub-man. Such gentlemen as have friends here, hire me to provide them with something good to eat."

"Is this so?" said I, turning to the turnkey.

He said it was.

"Well, then," said I, slipping some silver into the grub-man's hands (for so they called him), "I want you to give particular attention to my friend there; let him have the best dinner you can get. And you must be as polite to him as possible."

"Introduce me, will you?" said the grub-man, looking at me with an expression which seemed to say he was all impatience for an opportunity to give a specimen of his breeding.

Thinking it would prove of benefit to the scrivener, I acquiesced; and, asking the grub-man his name, went up with him to Bartleby.

"Bartleby, this is a friend; you will find him very useful to you."

"Your sarvant, sir, your sarvant," said the grub-man, making a low salutation behind his apron. "Hope you find it pleasant here, sir; nice grounds—cool apartments—hope you'll stay with us sometime—try to make it agreeable. What will you have for dinner to-day?"

"I prefer not to dine to-day," said Bartleby, turning away. "It would disagree with me; I am unused to dinners." So saying, he slowly moved to the other side of the inclosure, and took up a position fronting the dead-wall.

"How's this?" said the grub-man, addressing me with a stare of astonishment, "He's odd, ain't he?"

"I think he is a little deranged," said I, sadly.

"Deranged? deranged is it? Well, now, upon my word, I thought that friend of yourn was a gentleman forger; they are always pale and genteel-like, them forgers. I can't help pity 'em—can't help it, sir. Did you know Monroe Edwards?" he added, touchingly, and paused. Then, laying his hand piteously on my shoulder, sighed, "he died of consumption at Sing-Sing. So you weren't acquainted with Monroe?"

"No, I was never socially acquainted with any forgers. But I cannot stop longer. Look to my friend yonder. You will not lose by it. I will see you again."

Some few days after this, I again obtained admission to the Tombs, and went through the corridors in quest of Bartleby; but without finding him.

"I saw him coming from his cell not long ago," said a turnkey, "may be he's gone to loiter in the yards."

So I went in that direction.

"Are you looking for the silent man?" said another turnkey, passing me. "Yonder he lies—sleeping in the yard there. 'Tis not twenty minutes since I saw him lie down."

The yard was entirely quiet. It was not accessible to the common prisoners. The surrounding walls, of amazing thickness, kept off all sounds behind them. The Egyptian character of the masonry weighed upon me with its gloom. But a soft imprisoned turf grew under foot. The heart of the eternal pyramids, it seemed, wherein, by some strange magic, through the clefts, grass-seed, dropped by birds, had sprung.

Strangely huddled at the base of the wall, his knees drawn up, and lying on his side, his head touching the cold stones, I saw the wasted Bartleby. But nothing stirred. I paused; then went close up to him; stooped over, and saw that his dim eyes were open; otherwise he seemed profoundly sleeping. Something prompted me to touch him. I felt his hand, when a tingling shiver ran up my arm and down my spine to my feet.

The round face of the grub-man peered upon me now. "His dinner is ready. Won't he dine to-day, either? Or does he live without dining?"

"Lives without dining," said I, and closed the eyes.

"Eh!—He's asleep, ain't he?"

"With kings and counselors," murmured I.

There would seem little need for proceeding further in this history. Imagination will readily supply the meagre recital of poor Bartleby's interment. But, ere parting with the reader, let me say, that if this little narrative has sufficiently interested him, to awaken

curiosity as to who Bartleby was, and what manner of life he led
prior to the present narrator's making his acquaintance, I can only
reply, that in such curiosity I fully share, but am wholly unable to
gratify it. Yet here I hardly know whether I should divulge one little
item of rumor, which came to my ear a few months after the scrivener's decease. Upon what basis it rested, I could never ascertain;
and hence, how true it is I cannot now tell. But, inasmuch as this
vague report has not been without a certain suggestive interest to me,
however sad, it may prove the same with some others; and so I will
briefly mention it. The report was this: that Bartleby had been a
subordinate clerk in the Dead Letter Office at Washington, from
which he had been suddenly removed by a change in the administration. When I think over this rumor, hardly can I express the emotions which seize me. Dead letters! does it not sound like dead men?
Conceive a man by nature and misfortune prone to a pallid hopelessness, can any business seem more fitted to heighten it than that of
continually handling these dead letters, and assorting them for the
flames? For by the cartload they are annually burned. Sometimes from
out the folded paper the pale clerk takes a ring—the finger it was
meant for, perhaps, moulders in the grave; a bank-note sent in
swiftest charity—he whom it would relieve, nor eats nor hungers any
more; pardon for those who died despairing; hope for those who died
unhoping; good tidings for those who died stifled by unrelieved
calamities. On errands of life, these letters speed to death.

Ah, Bartleby! Ah, humanity!

QUESTIONS FOR THINKING AND WRITING

1. The narrator of "Bartleby the Scrivener" begins his narration with the word
   I and ends it with the word *humanity*. We may wonder, therefore, if the
   events that form the conflict and climax of the story have altered the narrator's vision to allow his attention to shift from himself to others. If so, how
   did this happen? The following questions may help you develop your answer.
2. We note that the narrator begins his tale by introducing himself. Why does
   he do so? What does he reveal as his goals? What things does he seem to
   value most highly?
3. We might ask what tone of voice the narrator is using in this early part of
   the story. (Paragraph five may be especially helpful here.)
4. We then look at his introduction of his office and of his first staff member,
   Turkey. How does the lawyer/narrator act toward Turkey? What reasons
   does he give for acting as he does? Do his actions seem to match his reasons?
   What impression of the lawyer's character do we receive?
5. We then look at his introductions of Nippers and Ginger Nut, and end our
   study of the tale's introductory section by asking how the narrator's characterization of his three employees, and our impression of his interactions

with them, prepare the way for the introduction of Bartleby and for the narrator's response to him and to his behavior.

6. Having seen how the narrator prepares the way for the introduction of his main character, we now look at the first episodes involving that character (pp. 197–202). How well does Bartleby fit into our picture of the office? What does this do for our sense of him and of his relationship with his employer?

7. We next ask, what is the turning-point of the story? How does it change the narrator's view of Bartleby? What emotions does it raise in him? What action does it prompt him to take? What are the results of that action?

8. We then examine the story's progress from this turning-point to Bartleby's death. We ask ourselves, what changes are taking place in the tone of the narrative? the actions? the characterizations? We examine our reactions to these changes and developments. Have we been prepared for them? Can we accept them, or do we find them out of character or hard to believe? How do we react to Bartleby's death? Has the death been made to seem inevitable? Does it seem appropriate that the narrator be the one to discover it? How do we feel now about the narrator's relation to Bartleby?

9. At this point, too, we might notice the use of walls to set scenes throughout the story. This will let us glance at the whole story once more and will give us a good key for discussing some of the shifts in tone and atmosphere that occur as the story progresses. It will also let us sum up some of our impressions of Bartleby, since he is the character most closely associated with these walls. What is the effect on us of the combination of walls and Bartleby?

10. Similarly, we might look at mentions of money throughout the story. What character is most closely associated with them? What characterization do we draw from this association?

11. We must look as well at the after-note that ends the story, and ask what it adds to our sense of Bartleby, the narrator, and the story.

12. And then we must sum up our thoughts for ourselves. Has the narrator changed during the story? And, if he has, what do we make of the change?

13. Another way to approach the story would be to look at the effects of keeping Bartleby so sketchily characterized. We might ask how essential this pared-down characterization is to the story; how the narrator's sense of his own lack of knowledge about Bartleby affects him; and how it affects our feelings toward Bartleby, toward the narrator, and toward the relationship that develops between the two men. We might also ask whether the characterization given Bartleby suggests any symbolic values for Bartleby, the narrator, or their relationship; or whether you feel the story is better dealt with as a realistic tale.

JOSEPH CONRAD   (1857–1924)

The Secret Sharer

On my right hand there were lines of fishing stakes resembling a
mysterious system of half-submerged bamboo fences, incomprehensible in its division of the domain of tropical fishes, and crazy of
aspect as if abandoned forever by some nomad tribe of fishermen
now gone to the other end of the ocean; for there was no sign of
human habitation as far as the eye could reach. To the left a group
of barren islets, suggesting ruins of stone walls, towers, and block-
houses, had its foundations set in a blue sea that itself looked solid,
so still and stable did it lie below my feet; even the track of light
from the westering sun shone smoothly, without that animated glitter
which tells of an imperceptible ripple. And when I turned my head
to take a parting glance at the tug which had just left us anchored
outside the bar, I saw the straight line of the flat shore joined to
the stable sea, edge to edge, with a perfect and unmarked closeness,
in one leveled floor half brown, half blue under the enormous dome
of the sky. Corresponding in their significance to the islets of the sea,
two small clumps of trees, one on each side of the only fault in the
impeccable joint, marked the mouth of the river Meinam we had
just left on the first preparatory stage of our homeward journey;
and, far back on the inland level, a larger and loftier mass, the grove
surrounding the great Paknam pagoda, was the only thing on which
the eye could rest from the vain task of exploring the monotonous
sweep of the horizon. Here and there gleams as of a few scattered
pieces of silver marked the windings of the great river; and on the
nearest of them, just within the bar, the tug steaming right into the
land became lost to my sight, hull and funnel and masts, as though
the impassive earth had swallowed her up without an effort, without
a tremor. My eye followed the light cloud of her smoke, now here,
now there, above the plain, according to the devious curves of the
stream, but always fainter and farther away, till I lost it at last behind the miter-shaped hill of the great pagoda. And then I was left
alone with my ship, anchored at the head of the Gulf of Siam.

She floated at the starting point of a long journey, very still in an
immense stillness, the shadows of her spars flung far to the eastward
by the setting sun. At that moment I was alone on her decks. There
was not a sound in her—and around us nothing moved, nothing
lived, not a canoe on the water, not a bird in the air, not a cloud
in the sky. In this breathless pause at the threshold of a long passage

we seemed to be measuring our fitness for a long and arduous enterprise, the appointed task of both our existences to be carried out, far from all human eyes, with only sky and sea for spectators and for judges.

There must have been some glare in the air to interfere with one's sight, because it was only just before the sun left us that my roaming eyes made out beyond the highest ridge of the principal islet of the group something which did away with the solemnity of perfect solitude. The tide of darkness flowed on swiftly; and with tropical suddenness a swarm of stars came out above the shadowy earth, while I lingered yet, my hand resting lightly on my ship's rail as if on the shoulder of a trusted friend. But, with all that multitude of celestial bodies staring down at one, the comfort of quiet communion with her was gone for good. And there were also disturbing sounds by this time—voices, footsteps forward; the steward flitted along the main deck, a busily ministering spirit; a hand bell tinkled urgently under the poop deck. . . .

I found my two officers waiting for me near the supper table, in the lighted cuddy. We sat down at once, and as I helped the chief mate, I said:

"Are you aware that there is a ship anchored inside the islands? I saw her mastheads above the ridge as the sun went down."

He raised sharply his simple face, overcharged by a terrible growth of whisker, and emitted his usual ejaculations: "Bless my soul, sir! You don't say so!"

My second mate was a round-cheeked, silent young man, grave beyond his years, I thought; but as our eyes happened to meet I detected a slight quiver on his lips. I looked down at once. It was not my part to encourage sneering on board my ship. It must be said, too, that I knew very little of my officers. In consequence of certain events of no particular significance, except to myself, I had been appointed to the command only a fortnight before. Neither did I know much of the hands forward. All these people had been together for eighteen months or so, and my position was that of the only stranger on board. I mention this because it has some bearing on what is to follow. But what I felt most was my being a stranger to the ship; and if all the truth must be told, I was somewhat of a stranger to myself. The youngest man on board (barring the second mate), and untried as yet by a position of the fullest responsibility, I was willing to take the adequacy of the others for granted. They had simply to be equal to their tasks; but I wondered how far I should turn out faithful to that ideal conception of one's own personality every man sets up for himself secretly.

Meantime the chief mate, with an almost visible effect of collaboration on the part of his round eyes and frightful whiskers, was trying to evolve a theory of the anchored ship. His dominant trait was to take all things into earnest consideration. He was of a painstaking turn of mind. As he used to say, he "liked to account to himself" for practically everything that came in his way, down to a miserable scorpion he had found in his cabin a week before. The why and the wherefore of that scorpion—how it got on board and came to select his room rather than the pantry (which was a dark place and more what a scorpion would be partial to), and how on earth it managed to drown itself in the inkwell of his writing desk— had exercised him infinitely. The ship within the islands was much more easily accounted for; and just as we were about to rise from the table he made his pronouncement. She was, he doubted not, a ship from home lately arrived. Probably she drew too much water to cross the bar except at the top of spring tides. Therefore she went into that natural harbor to wait for a few days in preference to remaining in an open roadstead.

"That's so," confirmed the second mate, suddenly, in his slightly hoarse voice. "She draws over twenty feet. She's the Liverpool ship *Sephora* with a cargo of coal. Hundred and twenty-three days from Cardiff."

We looked at him in surprise.

"The tugboat skipper told me when he came on board for your letters, sir," explained the young man. "He expects to take her up the river the day after tomorrow."

After thus overwhelming us with the extent of his information he slipped out of the cabin. The mate observed regretfully that he "could not account for that young fellow's whims." What prevented him telling us all about it at once, he wanted to know.

I detained him as he was making a move. For the last two days the crew had had plenty of hard work, and the night before they had very little sleep. I felt painfully that I—a stranger—was doing something unusual when I directed him to let all hands turn in without setting an anchor watch. I proposed to keep on deck myself till one o'clock or thereabouts. I would get the second mate to relieve me at that hour.

"He will turn out the cook and the steward at four," I concluded, "and then give you a call. Of course at the slightest sign of any sort of wind we'll have the hands up and make a start at once."

He concealed his astonishment. "Very well, sir." Outside the cuddy he put his head in the second mate's door to inform him of my unheard-of caprice to take a five hours' anchor watch on myself. I heard the other raise his voice incredulously: "What? The captain himself?" Then a few more murmurs, a door closed, then another. A few moments later I went on deck.

My strangeness, which had made me sleepless, had prompted that unconventional arrangement, as if I had expected in those solitary hours of the night to get on terms with the ship of which I knew nothing, manned by men of whom I knew very little more. Fast alongside a wharf, littered like any ship in port with a tangle of unrelated things, invaded by unrelated shore people, I had hardly seen her yet properly. Now, as she lay cleared for sea, the stretch of her main deck seemed to me very fine under the stars. Very fine, very roomy for her size, and very inviting. I descended the poop and paced the waist, my mind picturing to myself the coming passage through the Malay Archipelago, down the Indian Ocean, and up the Atlantic. All its phases were familiar enough to me, every characteristic, all the alternatives which were likely to face me on the high seas—everything! . . . except the novel responsibility of command. But I took heart from the reasonable thought that the ship was like other ships, the men like other men, and that the sea was not likely to keep any special surprises expressly for my discomfiture.

Arrived at that comforting conclusion, I bethought myself of a cigar and went below to get it. All was still down there. Everybody at the after end of the ship was sleeping profoundly. I came out again on the quarter-deck, agreeably at ease in my sleeping suit on that warm breathless night, barefooted, a glowing cigar in my teeth, and, going forward, I was met by the profound silence of the fore end of the ship. Only as I passed the door of the forecastle I heard a deep, quiet, trustful sigh of some sleeper inside. And suddenly I rejoiced in the great security of the sea as compared with the unrest of the land, in my choice of that untempted life presenting no disquieting problems, invested with an elementary moral beauty by the absolute straight-forwardness of its appeal and by the singleness of its purpose.

The reading light in the fore-rigging burned with a clear, untroubled, as if symbolic, flame, confident and bright in the mysterious shades of the night. Passing on my way aft along the other side of the ship, I observed that the rope side-ladder, put over, no doubt, for the master of the tug when he came to fetch away our letters, had not been hauled in as it should have been. I became annoyed at this, for exactitude in small matters is the very soul of discipline. Then I reflected that I had myself peremptorily dismissed my officers from duty, and by my own act had prevented the anchor watch being formally set and things properly attended to. I asked myself whether it was wise ever to interfere with the established routine of duties even from the kindest of motives. My action might have made me appear eccentric. Goodness only knew how that absurdly whiskered mate would "account" for my conduct, and what the whole ship thought of that informality of their new captain. I was vexed with myself.

Not from compunction certainly, but, as it were mechanically, I proceeded to get the ladder in myself. Now a side ladder of that sort is a light affair and comes in easily, yet my vigorous tug, which should have brought it flying on board, merely recoiled upon my body in a totally unexpected jerk. What the devil . . . I was so astounded by the immovableness of that ladder that I remained stock-still, trying to account for it to myself like that imbecile mate of mine. In the end, of course, I put my head over the rail.

The side of the ship made an opaque belt of shadow on the darkling glassy shimmer of the sea. But I saw at once something elongated and pale floating very close to the ladder. Before I could form a guess a faint flash of phosphorescent light, which seemed to issue suddenly from the naked body of a man, flickered in the sleeping water with the elusive, silent play of summer lightning in a night sky. With a gasp I saw revealed to my stare a pair of feet, the long legs, a broad livid back immersed right up to the neck in a greenish cadaverous glow. One hand awash, clutched the bottom rung of the ladder. He was complete but for the head. A headless corpse! The cigar dropped out of my gaping mouth with a tiny plop and a short hiss quite audible in the absolute stillness of all things under heaven. At that I suppose he raised up his face, a dimly pale oval in the shadow of the ship's side. But even then I could only barely make out down there the shape of his blackhaired head. However, it was enough for the horrid, frost-bound sensation which had gripped me about the chest to pass off. The moment of vain exclamations was past, too. I only climbed on the spare spar and leaned over the rail as far as I could, to bring my eyes nearer to that mystery floating alongside.

As he hung by the ladder, like a resting swimmer, the sea lightning played about his limbs at every stir; and he appeared in it ghastly, silvery, fishlike. He remained as mute as a fish, too. He made no motion to get out of the water, either. It was inconceivable that he should not attempt to come on board, and strangely troubling to suspect that perhaps he did not want to. And my first words were prompted by just that troubled incertitude.

"What's the matter?" I asked in my ordinary tone; speaking down to the face upturned exactly under mine.

"Cramp," it answered, no louder. Then slightly anxious, "I say, no need to call anyone."

"I was not going to," I said.

"Are you alone on deck?"

"Yes."

I had somehow the impression that he was on the point of letting go the ladder to swim away beyond my ken—mysterious as he came. But, for the moment, this being appearing as if he had risen from the bottom of the sea (it was certainly the nearest land to the ship) wanted only to know the time. I told him. And he, down there, tentatively:

"I suppose your captain's turned in?"

"I am sure he isn't," I said.

He seemed to struggle with himself, for I heard something like the low, bitter murmur of doubt. "What's the good?" His next words came out with a hesitating effort.

"Look here, my man. Could you call him out quietly?"

I thought the time had come to declare myself.

"*I* am the captain."

I heard a "By Jove!" whispered at the level of the water. The phosphorescence flashed in the swirl of the water all about his limbs, his other hand seized the ladder.

"My name's Leggatt."

The voice was calm and resolute. A good voice. The self-possession of that man had somehow induced a corresponding state in myself. It was very quietly that I remarked:

"You must be a good swimmer."

"Yes. I've been in the water practically since nine o'clock. The question for me now is whether I am to let go this ladder and go on swimming till I sink from exhaustion, or—to come on board here."

I felt this was no mere formula of desperate speech, but a real alternative in the view of a strong soul. I should have gathered from this that he was young; indeed, it is only the young who are ever confronted by such clear issues. But at the time it was pure intuition on my part. A mysterious communication was established already between us two—in the face of that silent, darkened tropical sea. I was young, too; young enough to make no comment. The man in the water began suddenly to climb up the ladder, and I hastened away from the rail to fetch some clothes.

Before entering the cabin I stood still, listening in the lobby at the foot of the stairs. A faint snore came through the closed door of the chief mate's room. The second mate's door was on the hook, but the darkness in there was absolutely soundless. He, too, was young and could sleep like a stone. Remained the steward, but he was not likely to wake up before he was called. I got a sleeping suit out of my room and, coming back on deck, saw the naked man from the sea sitting on the main hatch, glimmering white in the darkness, his elbows on his knees and his head in his hands. In a moment he had concealed his damp body in a sleeping suit of the same gray-stripe pattern as the one I was wearing and followed me like my double on the poop. Together we moved right aft, barefooted, silent.

"What is it?" I asked in a deadened voice, taking the lighted lamp out of the binnacle, and raising it to his face.

"An ugly business."

He had rather regular features; a good mouth; light eyes under somewhat heavy, dark eyebrows; a smooth, square forehead; no growth on his cheeks; a small, brown mustache, and a well-shaped, round chin. His expression was concentrated, meditative, under the inspecting light of the lamp I held up to his face; such as a man thinking hard in solitude might wear. My sleeping suit was just right for his size. A well-knit young fellow of twenty-five at most. He caught his lower lip with the edge of white, even teeth.

"Yes," I said, replacing the lamp in the binnacle. The warm, heavy tropical night closed upon his head again.

"There's a ship over there," he murmured.

"Yes, I know. The *Sephora*. Did you know of us?"

"Hadn't the slightest idea. I am the mate of her—" He paused and corrected himself. "I should say I *was*."

"Aha! Something wrong?"

"Yes. Very wrong indeed. I've killed a man."

"What do you mean? Just now?"

"No, on the passage. Weeks ago. Thirty-nine south. When I say a man—"

"Fit of temper," I suggested, confidently.

The shadowy, dark head, like mine, seemed to nod imperceptibly above the ghostly gray of my sleeping suit. It was, in the night, as though I had been faced by my own reflection in the depths of a somber and immense mirror.

"A pretty thing to have to own up to for a *Conway* boy," murmured my double, distinctly.

"You're a *Conway* boy?"

"I am," he said, as if startled. Then slowly . . . "Perhaps you too—"

It was so; but being a couple of years older I had left before he joined. After a quick interchange of dates a silence fell; and I thought suddenly of my absurd mate with his terrific whiskers and the "Bless my soul—you don't say so" type of intellect. My double gave me an inkling of his thoughts by saying:

"My father's a parson in Norfolk. Do you see me before a judge and jury on that charge? For myself I can't see the necessity. There are fellows that an angel from heaven— And I am not that. He was one of those creatures that are just simmering all the time with a silly sort of wickedness. Miserable devils that have no business to live at all. He wouldn't do his duty and wouldn't let anybody else do theirs. But what's the good of talking! You know well enough the sort of ill-conditioned snarling cur—"

He appealed to me as if our experiences had been as identical as our clothes. And I knew well enough the pestiferous anger of such a character where there are no means of legal repression. And I knew well enough also that my double there was no homicidal ruffian. I did not think of asking him for details, and he told me the story roughly in brusque, disconnected sentences. I needed no more. I saw it all going on as though I were myself inside that other sleeping suit.

"It happened while we were setting a reefed foresail, at dusk. Reefed foresail! You understand the sort of weather. The only sail we had left to keep the ship running; so you may guess what it had been like for days. Anxious sort of job, that. He gave me some of his cursed insolence at the sheet. I tell you I was overdone with this terrific weather that seemed to have no end to it. Terrific, I tell you—and a deep ship. I believe the fellow himself was half crazed with funk. It was no time for gentlemanly reproof, so I turned round and felled him like an ox. He up and at me. We closed just as an awful sea made for the ship. All hands saw it coming and took to the rigging, but I had him by the throat, and went on shaking him like a rat, the men above us yelling, 'Look out! look out!' Then a crash as if the sky had fallen on my head. They say that for over ten minutes hardly anything was to be seen of the ship—just the three masts and a bit of the forecastle head and of the poop all awash driving along in a smother of foam. It was a miracle that they found us, jammed together behind the forebits. It's clear that I meant business, because I was holding him by the throat still when they picked us up. He was black in the face. It was too much for them. It seems they rushed us aft together, gripped as we were, screaming 'Murder!' like a lot of lunatics, and broke into the cuddy. And the ship running for her life, touch and go all the time, any minute her last in a sea fit to turn your hair gray only a-looking at it. I understand that the skipper, too, started raving like the rest of them. The man had been deprived of sleep for more than a week, and to have this sprung on him at the height of a furious gale nearly drove him out of his mind. I wonder they didn't fling me overboard after getting the carcass of their precious shipmate out of my fingers. They had rather a job to separate us, I've been told. A sufficiently fierce story to make an old judge and a respectable jury sit up a bit. The first thing I heard when I came to myself was the maddening howling of that endless gale, and on that the voice of the old man. He was hanging on to my bunk, staring into my face out of his sou'wester.

" 'Mr. Leggatt, you have killed a man. You can act no longer as chief mate of this ship.' "

His care to subdue his voice made it sound monotonous. He rested a hand on the end of the skylight to steady himself with, and all that time did not stir a limb, so far as I could see. "Nice little tale for a quiet tea party," he concluded in the same tone.

One of my hands, too, rested on the end of the skylight; neither did I stir a limb, so far as I knew. We stood less than a foot from each other. It occurred to me that if old "Bless my soul—you don't say so" were to put his head up the companion and catch sight of us, he would think he was seeing double, or imagine himself come upon a scene of weird witchcraft; the strange captain having a quiet confabulation by the wheel with his own gray ghost. I became very much concerned to prevent anything of the sort. I heard the other's soothing undertone.

"My father's a parson in Norfolk," it said. Evidently he had forgotten he had told me this important factor before. Truly a nice little tale.

"You had better slip down into my stateroom now," I said, moving off stealthily. My double followed my movements; our bare feet made no sound; I let him in, closed the door with care, and, after giving a call to the second mate, returned on deck for my relief.

"Not much sign of any wind yet," I remarked when he approached.

"No, sir. Not much," he assented, sleepily, in his hoarse voice, with just enough deference, no more, and barely suppressing a yawn.

"Well, that's all you have to look out for. You have got your orders."

"Yes, sir."

I paced a turn or two on the poop and saw him take up his position face forward with his elbow in the ratlines of the mizen-rigging before I went below. The mate's faint snoring was still going on peacefully. The cuddy lamp was burning over the table on which stood a vase with flowers, a polite attention from the ships' provision merchant—the last flowers we should see for the next three months at the very least. Two bunches of bananas hung from the beam symmetrically, one on each side of the rudder casing. Everything was as before in the ship—except that two of her captain's sleeping suits were simultaneously in use, one motionless in the cuddy, the other keeping very still in the captain's stateroom.

It must be explained here that my cabin had the form of the capital letter L, the door being within the angle and opening into the short part of the letter. A couch was to the left, the bed-place to the right; my writing desk and the chronometers' table faced the door. But anyone opening it, unless he stepped right inside, had no view of what I call the long (or vertical) part of the letter. It contained some lockers surmounted by a book case; and a few clothes, a thick jacket or two, caps, oilskin coat, and such like, hung on hooks. There was at the bottom of that part a door opening into my bathroom, which could be entered also directly from the saloon. But that way was never used.

The mysterious arrival had discovered the advantage of this particular shape. Entering my room, lighted strongly by a big bulkhead lamp swung on gimbals above my writing desk, I did not see him anywhere till he stepped out quietly from behind the coats hung in the recessed part.

"I heard somebody moving about, and went in there at once," he whispered.

I, too, spoke under my breath.

"Nobody is likely to come in here without knocking and getting permission."

He nodded. His face was thin and the sunburn faded, as though he had been ill. And no wonder. He had been, I heard presently, kept under arrest in his cabin for nearly seven weeks. But there was nothing sickly in his eyes or in his expression. He was not a bit like me, really; yet, as we stood leaning over my bed-place, whispering side by side, with our dark heads together and our backs to the door, anybody bold enough to open it stealthily would have been treated to the uncanny sight of a double captain busy talking in whispers with his other self.

"But all this doesn't tell how you came to hang on to our side ladder," I inquired, in the hardly audible murmurs we used, after he had told me something more of the proceedings on board the *Sephora* once the bad weather was over.

"When we sighted Java Head I had had time to think all those matters out several times over. I had six weeks of doing nothing else, and with only an hour or so every evening for a tramp on the quarter-deck."

He whispered, his arms folded on the side of my bed-place, staring through the open port. And I could imagine perfectly the manner of this thinking out—a stubborn if not a steadfast operation; something of which I should have been perfectly incapable.

"I reckoned it would be dark before we closed with the land," he continued, so low that I had to strain my hearing, near as we were to each other, shoulder touching shoulder almost. "So I asked to speak to the old man. He always seemed very sick when he came to see me— as if he could not look me in the face. You know, that foresail saved the ship. She was too deep to have run long under bare poles. And it was I that managed to set it for him. Anyway, he came. When I had him in my cabin—he stood by the door looking at me as if I had the halter around my neck already—I asked him right away to leave my cabin door unlocked at night while the ship was going through Sunda Straits. There would be the Java coast within two or three miles, off Angier Point. I wanted nothing more. I've had a prize for swimming my second year in the *Conway*."

"I can believe it," I breathed out.

"God only knows why they locked me in every night. To see some of their faces you'd have thought they were afraid I'd go about at night strangling people. Am I a murdering brute? Do I look it? By Jove! if I had been he wouldn't have trusted himself like that in my room. You'll say I might have chucked him aside and bolted out, there and then—it was dark already. Well, no. And for the same reason I wouldn't think of trying to smash the door. There would have been a rush to stop me at the noise, and I did not mean to get into a confounded scrimmage. Somebody else might have got killed—for I would not have broken out only to get chucked back, and I did not want any more of that work. He refused, looking more sick than ever. He was afraid of the men, and also of that old second mate of his who had been sailing with him for years—a gray-headed old humbug; and his steward, too, had been with him devil knows how long—seventeen years or more—a dogmatic sort of loafer who hated me like poison, just because I was the chief mate. No chief mate ever made more than one voyage in the *Sephora*, you know. Those two old chaps ran the ship. Devil only knows what the skipper wasn't afraid of (all his nerve went to pieces altogether in that hellish spell of bad weather we had)—of what the law would do to him—of his wife, perhaps. Oh, yes! she's on board. Though I don't think she would have meddled. She would have been only too glad to have me out of the ship in any way. The 'brand of Cain' business, don't you see. That's all right. I was ready enough to go off wandering on the face of the earth—and that was price enough to pay for an Abel of that sort. Anyhow, he wouldn't listen to me. 'This thing must take its course. I represent the law here.' He was shaking like a leaf. 'So you won't?' 'No!' 'Then I hope you will be able to sleep on that,' I said, and turned my back on him. 'I wonder that *you* can,' cries he, and locks the door.

"Well, after that, I couldn't. Not very well. That was three weeks ago. We have had a slow passage through the Java Sea; drifted about Carimata for ten days. When we anchored here they thought, I suppose, it was all right. The nearest land (and that's five miles) is the ship's destination; the consul would soon set about catching me; and there would have been no object in bolting to these islets there. I don't suppose there's a drop of water on them. I don't know how it was, but tonight that steward, after bringing me my supper, went out to let me eat it, and left the door unlocked. And I ate it—all there was, too. After I had finished I strolled out on the quarter-deck. I don't know that I meant to do anything. A breath of fresh air was all I wanted, I believe. Then a sudden temptation came over me.

I kicked off my slippers and was in the water before I had made up my mind fairly. Somebody heard the splash and they raised an awful hullabaloo. 'He's gone! Lower the boats! He's committed suicide! No, he's swimming.' Certainly I was swimming. It's not so easy for a swimmer like me to commit suicide by drowning. I landed on the nearest islet before the boat left the ship's side. I heard them pulling about in the dark, hailing, and so on, but after a bit they gave up. Everything quieted down and the anchorage became as still as death. I sat down on a stone and began to think. I felt certain they would start searching for me at daylight. There was no place to hide on those stony things—and if there had been, what would have been the good? But now I was clear of that ship, I was not going back. So after a while I took off all my clothes, tied them up in a bundle with a stone inside, and dropped them in the deep water on the outer side of that islet. That was suicide enough for me. Let them think what they liked, but I didn't mean to drown myself. I meant to swim till I sank—but that's not the same thing. I struck out for another of these little islands, and it was from that one that I first saw your riding light. Something to swim for. I went on easily, and on the way I came upon a flat rock a foot or two above water. In the daytime, I dare say, you might make it out with a glass from your poop. I scrambled up on it and rested myself for a bit. Then I made another start. That last spell must have been over a mile."

His whisper was getting fainter and fainter, and all the time he stared straight out through the porthole, in which there was not even a star to be seen. I had not interrupted him. There was something that made comment impossible in his narrative, or perhaps in himself; a sort of feeling, a quality, which I can't find a name for. And when he ceased, all I found was a futile whisper: "So you swam for our light?"

"Yes—straight for it. It was something to swim for. I couldn't see any stars low down because the coast was in the way, and I couldn't see the land, either. The water was like glass. One might have been swimming in a confounded thousand-feet deep cistern with no place for scrambling out anywhere; but what I didn't like was the notion of swimming round and round like a crazed bullock before I gave out; and as I didn't mean to go back . . . No. Do you see me being hauled back, stark naked, off one of these little islands by the scruff of the neck and fighting like a wild beast? Somebody would have got killed for certain, and I did not want any of that. So I went on. Then your ladder—"

"Why didn't you hail the ship?" I asked, a little louder.

He touched my shoulder lightly. Lazy footsteps came right over our heads and stopped. The second mate had crossed from the other side of the poop and might have been hanging over the rail, for all we knew.

"He couldn't hear us talking—could he?" My double breathed into my ear, anxiously.

His anxiety was an answer, a sufficient answer, to the question I had put to him. An answer containing all the difficulty of that situation. I closed the porthole quietly, to make sure. A louder word might have been overheard.

"Who's that?" he whispered then.

"My second mate. But I don't know much more of the fellow than you do."

And I told him a little about myself. I had been appointed to take charge while I least expected anything of the sort, not quite a fortnight ago. I didn't know either the ship or the people. Hadn't had the time in port to look about me or size anybody up. And as to the crew, all they knew was that I was appointed to take the ship home. For the rest, I was almost as much of a stranger on board as himself, I said. And at the moment I felt it most acutely. I felt that it would take very little to make me a suspect person in the eyes of the ship's company.

He had turned about meantime; and we, the two strangers in the ship, faced each other in identical attitudes.

"Your ladder—" he murmured, after a silence. "Who'd have thought of finding a ladder hanging over at night in a ship anchored out here! I felt just then a very unpleasant faintness. After the life I've been leading for nine weeks, anybody would have got out of condition. I wasn't capable of swimming round as far as your rudder chains. And, lo and behold! there was a ladder to get hold of. After I gripped it I said to myself, 'What's the good?' When I saw a man's head looking over I thought I would swim away presently and leave him shouting—in whatever language it was. I didn't mind being looked at. I—I liked it. And then you speaking to me so quietly—as if you had expected me—made me hold on a little longer. It had been a confounded lonely time—I don't mean while swimming. I was glad to talk a little to somebody that didn't belong to the *Sephora*. As to asking for the captain, that was a mere impulse. It could have been no use, with all the ship knowing about me and the other people pretty certain to be round here in the morning. I don't know—I wanted to be seen, to talk with somebody, before I went on. I don't know what I would have said. . . . 'Fine night, isn't it?' or something of the sort."

"Do you think they will be round here presently?" I asked with some incredulity.

"Quite likely," he said faintly.

He looked extremely haggard all of a sudden. His head rolled on his shoulders.

"H'm. We shall see then. Meantime get into that bed," I whispered. "Want help? There."

It was a rather high bed-place with a set of drawers underneath. This amazing swimmer really needed the lift I gave him by seizing his leg. He tumbled in, rolled over on his back, and flung one arm across his eyes. And then, with his face nearly hidden, he must have looked exactly as I used to look in that bed. I gazed upon my other self for a while before drawing across carefully the two green serge curtains which ran on a brass rod. I thought for a moment of pinning them together for greater safety, but I sat down on the couch, and once there I felt unwilling to rise and hunt for a pin. I would do it in a moment. I was extremely tired, in a peculiarly intimate way, by the strain of stealthiness, by the effort of whispering and the general secrecy of this excitement. It was three o'clock by now and I had been on my feet since nine, but I was not sleepy; I could not have gone to sleep. I sat there, fagged out, looking at the curtains, trying to clear my mind of the confused sensation of being in two places at once, and greatly bothered by an exasperating knocking in my head. It was a relief to discover suddenly that it was not in my head at all, but on the outside of the door. Before I could collect myself the words "Come in" were out of my mouth, and the steward entered with a tray, bringing in my morning coffee. I had slept, after all, and I was so frightened that I shouted, "This way! I am here, steward," as though he had been miles away. He put down the tray on the table next the couch and only then said, very quietly, "I can see you are here, sir." I felt him give me a keen look, but I dared not meet his eyes just then. He must have wondered why I had drawn the curtains of my bed before going to sleep on the couch. He went out, hooking the door open as usual.

I heard the crew washing decks above me. I knew I would have been told at once if there had been any wind. Calm, I thought, and I was doubly vexed. Indeed, I felt dual more than ever. The steward reappeared suddenly in the doorway. I jumped up from the couch so quickly that he gave a start.

"What do you want here?"

"Close your port, sir—they are washing decks."

"It is closed," I said, reddening.

"Very well, sir." But he did not move from the doorway and returned my stare in an extraordinary, equivocal manner for a time. Then his eyes wavered, all his expression changed, and in a voice unusually gentle, almost coaxingly:

"May I come in to take the empty cup away, sir?"

"Of course!" I turned my back on him while he popped in and

out. Then I unhooked and closed the door and even pushed the bolt. This sort of thing could not go on very long. The cabin was as hot as an oven, too. I took a peep at my double, and discovered that he had not moved, his arm was still over his eyes; but his chest heaved; his hair was wet; his chin glistened with perspiration. I reached over him and opened the port.

"I must show myself on deck," I reflected.

Of course, theoretically, I could do what I liked, with no one to say nay to me within the whole circle of the horizon; but to lock my cabin door and take the key away I did not dare. Directly I put my head out of the companion I saw the group of my two officers, the second mate barefooted, the chief mate in long india-rubber boots, near the break of the poop, and the steward halfway down the poop ladder talking to them eagerly. He happened to catch sight of me and dived, the second ran down on the main deck shouting some order or other, and the chief mate came to meet me, touching his cap.

There was a sort of curiosity in his eye that I did not like. I don't know whether the steward had told them that I was "queer" only, or downright drunk, but I know the man meant to have a good look at me. I watched him coming with a smile which, as he got into point-blank range, took effect and froze on his very whiskers. I did not give him time to open his lips.

"Square the yards by lifts and braces before the hands go to breakfast."

It was the first particular order I had given on board that ship; and I stayed on deck to see it executed, too. I had felt the need of asserting myself without loss of time. That sneering young cub got taken down a peg or two on that occasion, and I also seized the opportunity of having a good look at the face of every foremast man as they filed past me to go to the after braces. At breakfast time, eating nothing myself, I presided with such frigid dignity that the two mates were only too glad to escape from the cabin as soon as decency permitted and all the time the dual working of my mind distracted me almost to the point of insanity. I was constantly watching myself, my secret self, as dependent on my actions as my own personality, sleeping in that bed, behind that door which faced me as I sat at the head of the table. It was very much like being mad, only it was worse because one was aware of it.

I had to shake him for a solid minute, but when at last he opened his eyes it was in the full possession of his senses, with an inquiring look.

"All's well so far," I whispered. "Now you must vanish into the bathroom."

He did so, as noiseless as a ghost, and I then rang for the steward, and facing him boldly, directed him to tidy up my stateroom while

I was having my bath—"and be quick about it." As my tone admitted of no excuses, he said, "Yes, sir," and ran off to fetch his dustpan and brushes. I took a bath and did most of my dressing, splashing, and whistling softly for the steward's edification, while the secret sharer of my life stood drawn up bolt upright in that little space, his face looking very sunken in daylight, his eyelids lowered under the stern, dark line of his eyebrows drawn together by a slight frown.

When I left him there to go back to my room the steward was finishing dusting. I sent for the mate and engaged him in some insignificant conversation. It was, as it were, trifling with the terrific character of his whiskers; but my object was to give him an opportunity for a good look at my cabin. And then I could at last shut, with a clear conscience, the door of my stateroom and get my double back into the recessed part. There was nothing else for it. He had to sit still on a small folding stool, half smothered by the heavy coats hanging there. We listened to the steward going into the bathroom out of the saloon, filling the water bottles there, scrubbing the bath, setting things to rights, whisk, bang, clatter—out again into the saloon—turn the key—click. Such was my scheme for keeping my second self invisible. Nothing better could be contrived under the circumstances. And there we sat; I at my writing desk ready to appear busy with some papers, he behind me, out of sight of the door. It would not have been prudent to talk in daytime; and I could not have stood the excitement of that queer sense of whispering to myself. Now and then, glancing over my shoulder, I saw him far back there, sitting rigidly on the low stool, his bare feet close together, his arms folded, his head hanging on his breast—and perfectly still. Anybody would have taken him for me.

I was fascinated by it myself. Every moment I had to glance over my shoulder. I was looking at him when a voice outside the door said:

"Beg pardon, sir."

"Well!" . . . I kept my eyes on him, and so, when the voice outside the door announced, "There's a ship's boat coming our way, sir," I saw him give a start—the first movement he had made for hours. But he did not raise his bowed head.

"All right. Get the ladder over."

I hesitated. Should I whisper something to him? But what? His immobility seemed to have been never disturbed. What could I tell him he did not know already? . . . Finally I went on deck.

II

The skipper of the *Sephora* had a thin red whisker all round his face, and the sort of complexion that goes with hair of that color;

also the particular, rather smeary shade of blue in the eyes. He was not exactly a showy figure; his shoulders were high, his stature but middling—one leg slightly more bandy than the other. He shook hands, looking vaguely around. A spiritless tenacity was his main characteristic, I judged. I behaved with a politeness which seemed to disconcert him. Perhaps he was shy. He mumbled to me as if he were ashamed of what he was saying; gave his name (it was something like Archbold—but at this distance of years I hardly am sure), his ship's name, and a few other particulars of that sort, in the manner of a criminal making a reluctant and doleful confession. He had had terrible weather on the passage out—terrible—terrible—wife aboard, too.

By this time we were seated in the cabin and the steward brought in a tray with a bottle and glasses. "Thanks! No." Never took liquor. Would have some water, though. He drank two tumblerfuls. Terrible thirsty work. Ever since daylight had been exploring the islands round his ship.

"What was that for—fun?" I asked, with an appearance of polite interest.

"No!" He sighed. "Painful duty."

As he persisted in his mumbling and I wanted my double to hear every word, I hit upon the notion of informing him that I regretted to say I was hard of hearing.

"Such a young man, too!" he nodded, keeping his smeary blue, unintelligent eyes fastened upon me. What was the cause of it—some disease? he inquired, without the least sympathy and as if he thought that, if so, I'd got no more than I deserved.

"Yes; disease," I admitted in a cheerful tone which seemed to shock him. But my point was gained, because he had to raise his voice to give me his tale. It is not worth while to record that version. It was just over two months since all this had happened, and he had thought so much about it that he seemed completely muddled as to its bearings, but still immensely impressed.

"What would you think of such a thing happening on board your own ship? I've had the *Sephora* for these fifteen years. I am a well-known shipmaster."

He was densely distressed—and perhaps I should have sympathized with him if I had been able to detach my mental vision from the unsuspected sharer of my cabin as though he were my second self. There he was on the other side of the bulkhead, four or five feet from us, no more, as we sat in the saloon. I looked politely at Captain Archbold (if that was his name), but it was the other I saw, in a gray sleeping suit, seated on a low stool, his bare feet close together, his arms folded, and every word said between us falling into the ears of his dark head bowed on his chest.

"I have been at sea now, man and boy, for seven-and-thirty years, and I've never heard of such a thing happening in an English ship. And that it should be my ship. Wife on board, too."

I was hardly listening to him.

"Don't you think," I said, "that the heavy sea which, you told me, came aboard just then might have killed the man? I have seen the sheer weight of a sea kill a man very neatly, by simply breaking his neck."

"Good God!" he uttered, impressively, fixing his smeary blue eyes on me. "The sea! No man killed by the sea ever looked like that." He seemed positively scandalized at my suggestion. And as I gazed at him, certainly not prepared for anything original on his part, he advanced his head close to mine and thrust his tongue out at me so suddenly that I couldn't help starting back.

After scoring over my calmness in this graphic way he nodded wisely. If I had seen the sight, he assured me, I would never forget it as long as I lived. The weather was too bad to give the corpse a proper sea burial. So next day at dawn they took it up on the poop, covering its face with a bit of bunting; he read a short prayer, and then, just as it was, in its oilskins and long boots, they launched it amongst those mountainous seas that seemed ready every moment to swallow up the ship herself and the terrified lives on board of her.

"That reefed foresail saved you," I threw in.

"Under God—it did," he exclaimed fervently. "It was by a special mercy, I firmly believe, that it stood some of those hurricane squalls."

"It was the setting of that sail which—" I began.

"God's own hand in it," he interrupted me. "Nothing less could have done it. I don't mind telling you that I hardly dared give the order. It seemed impossible that we could touch anything without losing it, and then our last hope would have been gone."

The terror of that gale was on him yet. I let him go on for a bit, then said, casually—as if returning to a minor subject:

"You were very anxious to give up your mate to the shore people, I believe?"

He was. To the law. His obscure tenacity on that point had in it something incomprehensible and a little awful; something, as it were, mystical, quite apart from his anxiety that he should not be suspected of "countenancing any doings of that sort." Seven-and-thirty virtuous years at sea, of which over twenty of immaculate command, and the last fifteen in the *Sephora* seemed to have laid him under some pitiless obligation.

"And you know," he went on, groping shamefacedly amongst his feelings, "I did not engage that young fellow. His people had some interest with my owners. I was in a way forced to take him on. He looked very smart, very gentlemanly, and all that. But do you know—

I never liked him, somehow. I am a plain man. You see, he wasn't exactly the sort for the chief mate of a ship like the *Sephora*."

I had become so connected in thoughts and impressions with the secret sharer of my cabin that I felt as if I, personally, were being given to understand that I, too, was not the sort that would have done for the chief mate of a ship like the *Sephora*. I had no doubt of it in my mind.

"Not at all the style of man. You understand," he insisted, super-fluously, looking hard at me.

I smiled urbanely. He seemed at a loss for a while.

"I suppose I must report a suicide."

"Beg pardon?"

"Sui-cide! That's what I'll have to write to my owners directly I get in."

"Unless you manage to recover him before tomorrow," I assented, dispassionately . . . "I mean, alive."

He mumbled something which I really did not catch, and I turned my ear to him in a puzzled manner. He fairly bawled:

"The land—I say, the mainland is at least seven miles off my anchorage."

"About that."

My lack of excitement, of curiosity, of surprise, of any sort of pro-nounced interest, began to arouse his distrust. But except for the felicitous pretense of deafness I had not tried to pretend anything. I had felt utterly incapable of playing the part of ignorance prop-erly, and therefore was afraid to try. It is also certain that he had brought some ready-made suspicions with him, and that he viewed my politeness as a strange and unnatural phenomenon. And yet how else could I have received him? Not heartily! That was impossible for psychological reasons, which, I need not state here. My only object was to keep off his inquiries. Surlily? Yes, but surliness might have provoked a point-blank question. From its novelty to him and from its nature, punctilious courtesy was the manner best calculated to restrain the man. But there was the danger of his breaking through my defense bluntly. I could not, I think, have met him by a direct lie, also for psychological (not moral) reasons. If he had only known how afraid I was of his putting my feeling of identity with the other to the test! But, strangely enough—(I thought of it only after-ward)—I believe that he was not a little disconcerted by the reverse side of that weird situation, by something in me that reminded him of the man he was seeking—suggested a mysterious similitude to the young fellow he had distrusted and disliked from the first.

However that might have been, the silence was not very prolonged. He took another oblique step.

"I reckon I had no more than a two-mile pull to your ship. Not a bit more."

"And quite enough, too, in this awful heat," I said.

Another pause full of mistrust followed. Necessity, they say, is mother of invention, but fear, too, is not barren of ingenious suggestions. And I was afraid he would ask me pointblank for news of my other self.

"Nice little saloon, isn't it?" I remarked, as if noticing for the first time the way his eyes roamed from one closed door to the other. "And very well fitted out, too. Here, for instance," I continued, reaching over the back of my seat negligently and flinging the door open, "is my bathroom."

He made an eager movement, but hardly gave it a glance. I got up, shut the door of the bathroom, and invited him to have a look round, as if I were very proud of my accommodation. He had to rise and be shown round, but he went through the business without any raptures whatever.

"And now we'll have a look at my stateroom," I declared, in a voice as loud as I dared to make it, crossing the cabin to the starboard side with purposely heavy steps.

He followed me in and gazed around. My intelligent double had vanished. I played my part.

"Very convenient—isn't it?"

"Very nice. Very com . . ." He didn't finish, and went out brusquely as if to escape from some unrighteous wiles of mine. But it was not to be. I had been too frightened not to feel vengeful; I felt I had him on the run, and I meant to keep him on the run. My polite insistence must have had something menacing in it, because he gave in suddenly. And I did not let him off a single item; mate's room, pantry, storerooms, the very sail locker which was also under the poop—he had to look into them all. When at last I showed him out on the quarter-deck he drew a long, spiritless sigh, and mumbled dismally that he must really be going back to his ship now. I desired my mate, who had joined us, to see to the captain's boat.

The man of whiskers gave a blast on the whistle which he used to wear hanging round his neck, and yelled, "*Sephora* away!" My double down there in my cabin must have heard, and certainly could not feel more relieved than I. Four fellows came running out from somewhere forward and went over the side, while my own men, appearing on deck too, lined the rail. I escorted my visitor to the gangway ceremoniously, and nearly overdid it. He was a tenacious beast. On the very ladder he lingered, and in that unique, guiltily conscientious manner of sticking to the point:

"I say . . . you . . . you don't think that—"

I covered his voice loudly:

"Certainly not . . . I am delighted. Good-by."

I had an idea of what he meant to say, and just saved myself by the privilege of defective hearing. He was too shaken generally to insist, but my mate, close witness of that parting, looked mystified and his face took on a thoughtful cast. As I did not want to appear as if I wished to avoid all communication with my officers, he had the opportunity to address me.

"Seems a very nice man. His boat's crew told our chaps a very extraordinary story, if what I am told by the steward is true. I suppose you had it from the captain, sir?"

"Yes. I had a story from the captain."

"A very horrible affair—isn't it, sir?"

"It is."

"Beats all these tales we hear about murders in Yankee ships."

"I don't think it beats them. I don't think it resembles them in the least."

"Bless my soul—you don't say so! But of course I've no acquaintance whatever with American ships, not I, so I couldn't go against your knowledge. It's horrible enough for me . . . But the queerest part is that those fellows seemed to have some idea the man was hidden aboard here. They had really. Did you ever hear of such a thing?"

"Preposterous—isn't it?"

We were walking to and fro athwart the quarterdeck. No one of the crew forward could be seen (the day was Sunday), and the mate pursued:

"There was some little dispute about it. Our chaps took offense. 'As if we would harbor a thing like that,' they said. 'Wouldn't you like to look for him in our coal hole?' Quite a tiff. But they made it up in the end. I suppose he did drown himself. Don't you, sir?"

"I don't suppose anything."

"You have no doubt in the matter, sir?"

"None whatever."

I left him suddenly. I felt I was producing a bad impression, but with my double down there it was most trying to be on deck. And it was almost as trying to be below. Altogether a nerve-trying situation. But on the whole I felt less torn in two when I was with him. There was no one in the whole ship whom I dared take into my confidence. Since the hands had got to know his story, it would have been impossible to pass him off for anyone else, and an accidental discovery was to be dreaded now more than ever. . . .

The steward being engaged in laying the table for dinner, we could talk only with our eyes when I first went down. Later in the afternoon we had a cautious try at whispering. The Sunday quietness of the ship was against us; the elements, the men were against us—everything was against us in our secret partnership; time itself— for this could not go on forever. The very trust in Providence was, I suppose, denied to his guilt. Shall I confess that this thought cast me down very much? And as to the chapter of accidents which counts for so much in the book of success, I could only hope that it was closed. For what favorable accident could be expected?

"Did you hear everything?" were my first words as soon as we took up our position side by side, leaning over my bed-place.

He had. And the proof of it was his earnest whisper, "The man told you he hardly dared to give the order."

I understood the reference to be to that saving foresail.

"I assure you he never gave the order. He may think he did, but he never gave it. He stood there with me on the break of the poop after the maintopsail blew away, and whimpered about our last hope —positively whimpered about it and nothing else—and the night coming on! To hear one's skipper go on like that in such weather was enough to drive any fellow out of his mind. It worked me up into a sort of desperation. I just took it into my own hands and went away from him, boiling, and—But what's the use telling you? *You* know! . . . Do you think that if I had not been pretty fierce with them I should have got the men to do anything? Not it! The bosun perhaps? Perhaps! It wasn't a heavy sea—it was a sea gone mad! I suppose the end of the world will be something like that; and a man may have the heart to see it coming once and be done with it—but to have to face it day after day—I don't blame anybody. I was precious little better than the rest. Only—I was an officer of that old coal-wagon, anyhow—"

"I quite understand," I conveyed that sincere assurance into his ear. He was out of breath with whispering; I could hear him pant slightly. It was all very simple. The same strung-up force which had given twenty-four men a chance, at least, for their lives, had, in a sort of recoil, crushed an unworthy mutinous existence.

But I had no leisure to weigh the merits of the matter—footsteps in the saloon, a heavy knock. "There's enough wind to get under way with, sir." Here was the call of a new claim upon my thoughts and even upon my feelings.

"Turn the hands up," I cried through the door. "I'll be on deck directly."

I was going out to make the acquaintance of my ship. Before I left the cabin our eyes met—the eyes of the only two strangers on board. I pointed to the recessed part where the little campstool awaited him and laid my finger on my lips. He made a gesture—somewhat vague—a little mysterious, accompanied by a faint smile, as if of regret.

This is not the place to enlarge upon the sensations of a man who feels for the first time a ship move under his feet to his own independent word. In my case they were not unalloyed. I was not wholly alone with my command; for there was that stranger in my cabin. Or rather, I was not completely and wholly with her. Part of me was absent. That mental feeling of being in two places at once affected me physically as if the mood of secrecy had penetrated my very soul. Before an hour had elapsed since the ship had begun to move, having occasion to ask the mate (he stood by my side) to take a compass bearing of the Pagoda, I caught myself reaching up to his ear in whispers. I say I caught myself, but enough had escaped to startle the man. I can't describe it otherwise than by saying that he shied. A grave, preoccupied manner, as though he were in possession of some perplexing intelligence, did not leave him henceforth. A little later I moved away from the rail to look at the compass with such a stealthy gait that the helmsman noticed it—and I could not help noticing the unusual roundness of his eyes. These are trifling instances, though it's to no commander's advantage to be suspected of ludicrous eccentricities. But I was also more seriously affected. There are to a seaman certain words, gestures, that should in given conditions come as naturally, as instinctively as the winking of a menaced eye. A certain order should spring on to his lips without thinking; a certain sign should get itself made, so to speak, without reflection. But all unconscious alertness had abandoned me. I had to make an effort of will to recall myself back (from the cabin) to the conditions of the moment. I felt that I was appearing an irresolute commander to those people who were watching me more or less critically.

And, besides, there were the scares. On the second day out, for instance, coming off the deck in the afternoon (I had straw slippers on my bare feet) I stopped at the open pantry door and spoke to the steward. He was doing something there with his back to me. At the sound of my voice he nearly jumped out of his skin, as the saying is, and incidentally broke a cup.

"What on earth's the matter with you?" I asked, astonished.

He was extremely confused. "Beg pardon, sir. I made sure you were in your cabin."

"You see I wasn't."

"No, sir. I could have sworn I had heard you moving in there not a moment ago. It's most extraordinary . . . very sorry, sir."

I passed on with an inward shudder. I was so identified with my secret double that I did not even mention that fact in those scanty, fearful whispers we exchanged. I suppose he had made some slight noise of some kind or other. It would have been miraculous if he hadn't at one time or another. And yet, haggard as he appeared, he looked always perfectly self-controlled, more than calm—almost invulnerable. On my suggestion he remained almost entirely in the bathroom, which, upon the whole, was the safest place. There could be really no shadow of an excuse for anyone ever wanting to go in there, once the steward had done with it. It was a very tiny place. Sometimes he reclined on the floor, his legs bent, his head sustained on one elbow. At others I would find him on the campstool, sitting in his gray sleeping suit and with his cropped dark hair like a patient, unmoved convict. At night I would smuggle him into my bed-place, and we would whisper together, with the regular footfalls of the officer of the watch passing and repassing over our heads. It was an infinitely miserable time. It was lucky that some tins of fine preserves were stowed in a locker in my stateroom; hard bread I could always get hold of; and so he lived on stewed chicken, paté de foie gras, asparagus, cooked oysters, sardines—on all sorts of abominable sham delicacies out of tins. My early morning coffee he always drank; and it was all I dared do for him in that respect.

Every day there was the horrible maneuvering to go through so that my room and then the bathroom should be done in the usual way. I came to hate the sight of the steward, to abhor the voice of that harmless man. I felt that it was he who would bring on the disaster of discovery. It hung like a sword over our heads.

The fourth day out, I think (we were then working down the east side of the Gulf of Siam, tack for tack, in light winds and smooth water)—the fourth day, I say, of this miserable juggling with the unavoidable, as we sat at our evening meal, that man, whose slightest movement I dreaded, after putting down the dishes ran upon deck busily. This could not be dangerous. Presently he came down again; and then it appeared that he had remembered a coat of mine which I had thrown over a rail to dry after having been wetted in a shower which had passed over the ship in the afternoon. Sitting stolidly at the head of the table I became terrified at the sight of the garment on his arm. Of course he made for my door. There was no time to lose.

"Steward," I thundered. My nerves were so shaken that I could not govern my voice and conceal my agitation. This was the sort of thing that made my terrifically whiskered mate tap his forehead with his forefinger. I had detected him using that gesture while talking on deck with a confidential air to the carpenter. It was too far to hear a word, but I had no doubt that this pantomime could only refer to the strange new captain.

"Yes, sir," the pale-faced steward turned resignedly to me. It was this maddening course of being shouted at, checked without rhyme or reason, arbitrarily chased out of my cabin, suddenly called into it, sent flying out of his pantry on incomprehensible errands, that accounted for the growing wretchedness of his expression.

"Where are you going with that coat?"

"To your room, sir."

"Is there another shower coming?"

"I'm sure I don't know, sir. Shall I go up again and see, sir?"

"No! never mind."

My object was attained, as of course my other self in there would have heard everything that passed. During this interlude my two officers never raised their eyes off their respective plates; but the lip of that confounded cub, the second mate, quivered visibly.

I expected the steward to hook my coat on and come out at once. He was very slow about it; but I dominated my nervousness sufficiently not to shout after him. Suddenly I became aware (it could be heard plainly enough) that the fellow for some reason or other was opening the door of the bathroom. It was the end. The place was literally not big enough to swing a cat in. My voice died in my throat and I went stony all over. I expected to hear a yell of surprise and terror, and made a movement, but had not the strength to get on my legs. Everything remained still. Had my second self taken the poor wretch by the throat? I don't know what I would have done next moment if I had not seen the steward come out of my room, close the door, and then stand quietly by the sideboard.

Saved, I thought. But no! Lost! Gone! He was gone!

I laid my knife and fork down and leaned back in my chair. My head swam. After a while, when sufficiently recovered to speak in a steady voice, I instructed my mate to put the ship round at eight o'clock himself.

"I won't come on deck," I went on. "I think I'll turn in, and unless the wind shifts I don't want to be disturbed before midnight. I feel a bit seedy."

"You did look middling bad a little while ago," the chief mate remarked without showing any great concern.

They both went out, and I stared at the steward clearing the table. There was nothing to be read on that wretched man's face. But why did he avoid my eyes I asked myself. Then I thought I should like to hear the sound of his voice.

"Steward!"

"Sir!" Startled as usual.

"Where did you hang up that coat?"

"In the bathroom, sir." The usual anxious tone. "It's not quite dry yet, sir."

For some time longer I sat in the cuddy. Had my double vanished as he had come? But of his coming there was an explanation, whereas his disappearance would be inexplicable . . . I went slowly into my dark room, shut the door, lighted the lamp, and for a time dared not turn round. When at last I did I saw him standing bolt upright in the narrow recessed part. It would not be true to say I had a shock, but an irresistible doubt of his bodily existence flitted through my mind. Can it be, I asked myself, that he is not visible to other eyes than mine? It was like being haunted. Motionless, with a grave face, he raised his hands slightly at me in a gesture which meant clearly, "Heavens! what a narrow escape!" Narrow indeed. I think I had come creeping quietly as near insanity as any man who has not actually gone over the border. That gesture restrained me, so to speak.

The mate with the terrific whiskers was now putting the ship on the other tack. In the moment of profound silence which follows upon the hands going to their stations I heard on the poop his raised voice: "Hard alee!" and the distant shout of the order repeated on the main-deck. The sails, in that breeze, made but a faint fluttering noise. It ceased. The ship was coming round slowly; I held my breath in the renewed stillness of expectation; one wouldn't have thought that there was a single living soul on her decks. A sudden brisk shout, "Mainsail haul!" broke the spell, and in the noisy cries and rush overhead of the men running away with the main brace we two, down in my cabin, came together in our usual position by the bed-place.

He did not wait for my question. "I heard him fumbling here and just managed to squat myself down in the bath," he whispered to me. "The fellow only opened the door and put his arm in to hang the coat up. All the same—"

"I never thought of that," I whispered back, even more appalled than before at the closeness of the shave, and marvelling at that something unyielding in his character which was carrying him through so finely. There was no agitation in his whisper. Whoever was being driven distracted, it was not he. He was sane. And the proof of his sanity was continued when he took up the whispering again.

"It would never do for me to come to life again."

It was something that a ghost might have said. But what he was alluding to was his old captain's reluctant admission of the theory of suicide. It would obviously serve his turn—if I had understood at all the view which seemed to govern the unalterable purpose of his action.

"You must maroon me as soon as ever you can get amongst these islands off the Cambodje shore," he went on.

"Maroon you! We are not living in a boy's adventure tale," I protested. His scornful whispering took me up.

"We aren't indeed! There's nothing of a boy's tale in this. But there's nothing else for it. I want no more. You don't suppose I am afraid of what can be done to me? Prison or gallows or whatever they may please. But you don't see me coming back to explain such things to an old fellow in a wig and twelve respectable tradesmen, do you? What can they know whether I am guilty or not—or of *what* I am guilty, either? That's my affair. What does the Bible say? 'Driven off the face of the earth.' Very well. I am off the face of the earth now. As I came at night so I shall go."

"Impossible!" I murmured. "You can't."

"Can't? . . . Not naked like a soul on the Day of Judgment. I shall freeze on to this sleeping suit. The Last Day is not yet—and . . . you have understood thoroughly. Didn't you?"

I felt suddenly ashamed of myself. I may say truly that I understood—and my hesitation in letting that man swim away from my ship's side had been a mere sham sentiment, a sort of cowardice.

"It can't be done now till next night," I breathed out. "The ship is on the offshore tack and the wind may fail us."

"As long as I know that you understand," he whispered. "But of course you do. It's a great satisfaction to have got somebody to understand. You seem to have been there on purpose." And in the same whisper, as if we two whenever we talked had to say things to each other which were not fit for the world to hear, he added, "It's very wonderful."

We remained side by side talking in our secret way—but sometimes silent or just exchanging a whispered word or two at long intervals. And as usual he stared through the port. A breath of wind came now and again into our faces. The ship might have been moored in dock, so gently and on an even keel she slipped through the water, that did not murmur even at our passage, shadowy and silent like a phantom sea.

At midnight I went on deck, and to my mate's great surprise put the ship round on the other tack. His terrible whiskers flitted round me in silent criticism. I certainly should not have done it if it had been only a question of getting out of that sleepy gulf as quickly as possible. I believe he told the second mate, who relieved him, that it was a great want of judgment. The other only yawned. That intolerable cub shuffled about so sleepily and lolled against the rails in such a slack, improper fashion that I came down on him sharply.

"Aren't you properly awake yet?"

"Yes, sir! I am awake."

"Well, then, be good enough to hold yourself as if you were. And keep a lookout. If there's any current we'll be closing with some islands before daylight."

The east side of the gulf is fringed with islands, some solitary, others in groups. On the blue background of the high coast they seem to float on silvery patches of calm water, arid and gray, or dark green and rounded like clumps of evergreen bushes, with the larger ones, a mile or two long, showing the outlines of ridges, ribs of gray rock under the dark mantle of matted leafage. Unknown to trade, to travel, almost to geography, the manner of life they harbor is an unsolved secret. There must be villages—settlements of fishermen at least—on the largest of them, and some communication with the world is probably kept up by native craft. But all that forenoon, as we headed for them, fanned along by the faintest of breezes, I saw no sign of man or canoe in the field of the telescope I kept on pointing at the scattered group.

At noon I gave no orders for a change of course, and the mate's whiskers became much concerned and seemed to be offering themselves unduly to my notice. At last I said:

"I am going to stand right in. Quite in—as far as I can take her."

The stare of extreme surprise imparted an air of ferocity also to his eyes, and he looked truly terrific for a moment.

"We're not doing well in the middle of the gulf," I continued, casually. "I am going to look for the land breezes tonight."

"Bless my soul! Do you mean, sir, in the dark amongst the lot of all them islands and reefs and shoals?"

"Well—if there are any regular land breezes at all on this coast one must get close inshore to find them, mustn't one?"

"Bless my soul!" he exclaimed again under his breath. All that afternoon he wore a dreamy, contemplative appearance which in him was a mark of perplexity. After dinner I went into my stateroom as if I meant to take some rest. There we two bent our dark heads over a half-unrolled chart lying on my bed.

"There," I said. "It's got to be Koh-ring. I've been looking at it ever since sunrise. It has got two hills and a low point. It must be inhabited. And on the coast opposite there is what looks like the mouth of a biggish river—with some town, no doubt, not far up. It's the best chance for you that I can see."

"Anything. Koh-ring let it be."

He looked thoughtfully at the chart as if surveying chances and distances from a lofty height—and following with his eyes his own figure wandering on the blank land of Cochin-China, and then passing off that piece of paper clean out of sight into uncharted regions. And it was as if the ship had two captains to plan her course for her. I had been so worried and restless running up and down that I had not had the patience to dress that day. I had remained in my sleeping suit, with straw slippers and a soft floppy hat. The closeness of the heat in the gulf had been most oppressive, and the crew were used to see me wandering in that airy attire.

"She will clear the south point as she heads now," I whispered into his ear. "Goodness only knows when, though, but certainly after dark. I'll edge her in to half a mile, as far as I may be able to judge in the dark—"

"Be careful," he murmured, warningly—and I realized suddenly that all my future, the only future for which I was fit, would perhaps go irretrievably to pieces in any mishap to my first command.

I could not stop a moment longer in the room. I motioned him to get out of sight and made my way on the poop. That unplayful cub had the watch. I walked up and down for a while thinking things out, then beckoned him over.

"Send a couple of hands to open the two quarter-deck ports," I said, mildly.

He actually had the impudence, or else so forgot himself in his wonder at such an incomprehensible order, as to repeat:

"Open the quarter-deck ports! What for, sir?"

"The only reason you need concern yourself about is because I tell you to do so. Have them open wide and fastened properly."

He reddened and went off, but I believe made some jeering remark to the carpenter as to the sensible practice of ventilating a ship's quarter-deck. I know he popped into the mate's cabin to impart the fact to him because the whiskers came on deck, as it were by chance, and stole glances at me from below—for signs of lunacy or drunkenness, I suppose.

A little before supper, feeling more restless than ever, I rejoined, for a moment, my second self. And to find him sitting so quietly was surprising, like something against nature, inhuman.

I developed my plan in a hurried whisper.

"I shall stand in as close as I dare and then put her round. I shall presently find means to smuggle you out of here into the sail locker, which communicates with the lobby. But there is an opening, a sort of square for hauling the sails out which gives straight on the quarter-deck and which is never closed in fine weather, so as to give air to the sails. When the ship's way is deadened in stays and all the hands are aft at the main braces you shall have a clear road to slip out and get overboard through the open quarter-deck port. I've had them both fastened up. Use a rope's end to lower yourself into the water so as to avoid a splash—you know. It could be heard and cause some beastly complication."

He kept silent for a while, then whispered, "I understand."

"I won't be there to see you go," I began with an effort. "The rest . . . I only hope I have understood, too."

"You have. From first to last," and for the first time there seemed to be a faltering, something strained in his whisper. He caught hold of my arm, but the ringing of the supper bell made me start. He didn't, though; he only released his grip.

After supper I didn't come below again till well past eight o'clock. The faint, steady breeze was loaded with dew; and the wet, darkened sails held all there was of propelling power in it. The night, clear and starry, sparkled darkly, and the opaque, lightless patches shifting slowly against the low stars were the drifting islets. On the port bow there was a big one more distant and shadowily imposing by the great space of sky it eclipsed.

On opening the door I had a back view of my very own self looking at a chart. He had come out of the recess and was standing near the table.

"Quite dark enough," I whispered.

He stepped back and leaned against my bed with a level, quiet glance. I sat on the couch. We had nothing to say to each other. Over our heads the officer of the watch moved here and there. Then I heard him move quickly. I knew what that meant. He was making for the companion; and presently his voice was outside my door.

"We are drawing in pretty fast, sir. Lands look rather close."

"Very well," I answered. "I am coming on deck directly."

I waited till he was gone out of the cuddy, then rose. My double moved too. The time had come to exchange our last whispers, for neither of us was ever to hear each other's natural voice.

"Look here!" I opened a drawer and took out three sovereigns. "Take this, anyhow. I've got six and I'd give you the lot, only I must keep a little money to buy some fruit and vegetables for the crew from native boats as we go through Sunda Straits."

He shook his head.

"Take it," I urged him, whispering desperately. "No one can tell what—"

He smiled and slapped meaningly the only pocket of the sleeping jacket. It was not safe, certainly. But I produced a large old silk handkerchief of mine, and tying the three pieces of gold in a corner, pressed it on him. He was touched, I suppose, because he took it at last and tied it quickly round his waist under the jacket, on his bare skin.

Our eyes met; several seconds elapsed, till, our glances still mingled, I extended my hand and turned the lamp out. Then I passed through the cuddy, leaving the door of my room wide open . . . "Steward!"

He was still lingering in the pantry in the greatness of his zeal, giving a rub-up to a plated cruet stand the last thing before going to bed. Being careful not to wake up the mate, whose room was opposite, I spoke in an undertone.

He looked round anxiously. "Sir!"

"Can you get me a little hot water from the galley?"

"I am afraid, sir, the galley fire's been out for some time now."

"Go and see."

He fled up the stairs.

"Now," I whispered, loudly, into the saloon—too loudly, perhaps, but I was afraid I couldn't make a sound. He was by my side in an instant—the double captain slipped past the stairs—through the tiny dark passage . . . a sliding door. We were in the sail locker, scrambling on our knees over the sails. A sudden thought struck me. I saw myself wandering barefooted, bareheaded, the sun beating on my dark poll. I snatched off my floppy hat and tried hurriedly in the dark to ram it on my other self. He dodged and fended off silently. I wonder what he thought had come to me before he understood and suddenly desisted. Our hands met gropingly, lingered united in a steady, motionless clasp for a second . . . No word was breathed by either of us when they separated.

I was standing quietly by the pantry door when the steward returned.

"Sorry, sir. Kettle barely warm. Shall I light the spirit lamp?"

"Never mind."

I came out on deck slowly. It was now a matter of conscience to shave the land as close as possible—for now he must go overboard whenever the ship was put in stays. Must! There could be no going back for him. After a moment I walked over to leeward and my heart flew into my mouth at the nearness of the land on the bow. Under any other circumstances I would not have held on a minute longer. The second mate had followed me anxiously.

I looked on till I felt I could command my voice.

"She will weather," I said then in a quiet tone.

"Are you going to try that, sir?" he stammered out incredulously. I took no notice of him and raised my tone just enough to be heard by the helmsman.

"Keep her good full."

"Good full, sir."

The wind fanned my cheek, the sails slept, the world was silent. The strain of watching the dark loom of the land grow bigger and denser was too much for me. I had shut my eyes—because the ship must go closer. She must! The stillness was intolerable. Were we standing still?

When I opened my eyes the second view started my heart with a thump. The black southern hill of Koh-ring seemed to hang right over the ship like a towering fragment of the everlasting night. On that enormous mass of blackness there was not a gleam to be seen, not a sound to be heard. It was gliding irresistibly toward us and yet seemed already within reach of the hand. I saw the vague figures of the watch grouped in the waist, gazing in awed silence.

"Are you going on, sir?" inquired an unsteady voice at my elbow.

I ignored it. I had to go on.

"Keep her full. Don't check her way. That won't do now," I said warningly.

"I can't see the sails very well," the helmsman answered me, in strange, quavering tones.

Was she close enough? Already she was, I won't say in the shadow of the land, but in the very blackness of it, already swallowed up as it were, gone too close to be recalled, gone from me altogether.

"Give the mate a call," I said to the young man who stood at my elbow as still as death. "And turn all hands up."

My tone had a borrowed loudness reverberated from the height of the land. Several voices cried out together: "We are all on deck, sir."

Then stillness again, with the great shadow gliding closer, towering higher, without a light, without a sound. Such a hush had fallen on the ship that she might have been a bark of the dead floating in slowly under the very gate of Erebus.

"My God! Where are we?"

It was the mate moaning at my elbow. He was thunderstruck, and as it were deprived of the moral support of his whiskers. He clapped his hands and absolutely cried out, "Lost!"

"Be quiet," I said sternly.

He lowered his tone, but I saw the shadowy gesture of his despair. "What are we doing here?"

"Looking for the land wind."

He made as if to tear his hair, and addressed me recklessly.

"She will never get out. You have done it, sir. I knew it'd end in something like this. She will never weather, and you are too close now to stay. She'll drift ashore before she's round. O my God!"

I caught his arm as he was raising it to batter his poor devoted head, and shook it violently.

"She's ashore already," he wailed, trying to tear himself away.

"Is she? . . . Keep good full there!"

"Good full, sir," cried the helmsman in a frightened, thin, child-like voice.

I hadn't let go the mate's arm and went on shaking it. "Ready about, do you hear? You go forward"—shake—"and stop there"—shake—"and hold your noise"—shake—"and see these head sheets properly overhauled"—shake, shake—shake.

And all the time I dared not look toward the land lest my heart should fail me. I released my grip at last and he ran forward as if fleeing for dear life.

I wondered what my double there in the sail locker thought of this commotion. He was able to hear everything—and perhaps he was able to understand why, on my conscience, it had to be thus close—no less. My first order, "Hard alee!" re-echoed ominously under the towering shadow of Koh-ring as if I had shouted in a mountain gorge. And then I watched the land intently. In that smooth water and light wind it was impossible to feel the ship coming-to. No! I could not feel her. And my second self was making now ready to slip out and lower himself overboard. Perhaps he was gone already . . . ?

The great black mass brooding over our very mastheads began to pivot away from the ship's side silently. And now I forgot the secret stranger ready to depart, and remembered only that I was a total stranger to the ship. I did not know her. Would she do it? How was she to be handled?

I swung the mainyard and waited helplessly. She was perhaps stopped, and her very fate hung in the balance, with the black mass of Koh-ring like the gate of the everlasting night towering over her taffrail. What would she do now? Had she way on her yet? I stepped to the side swiftly, and on the shadowy water I could see nothing except a faint phosphorescent flash revealing the glassy smoothness of the sleeping surface. It was impossible to tell—and I had not learned yet the feel of my ship. Was she moving? What I needed was something easily seen, a piece of paper, which I could throw overboard and watch. I had nothing on me. To run down for it I didn't dare. There was no time. All at once my strained, yearning stare distinguished a white object floating within a yard of the ship's side. White on the black water. A phosphorescent flash passed under it. What was that thing? . . . I recognized my own floppy hat. It must have fallen off his head . . . and he didn't bother. Now I had what I wanted—the saving mark for my eyes. But I hardly thought of my other self, now gone from the ship, to be hidden forever from all friendly faces, to be a fugitive and a vagabond on the earth, with no brand of the curse on his sane forehead to stay a slaying hand . . . too proud to explain.

And I watched the hat—the expression of my sudden pity for his mere flesh. It had been meant to save his homeless head from the dangers of the sun. And now—behold—it was saving the ship, by serving me for a mark to help out the ignorance of my strangeness. Ha! It was drifting forward, warning me just in time that the ship had gathered sternway.

"Shift the helm," I said in a low voice to the seaman standing still like a statue.

The man's eyes glistened wildly in the binnacle light as he jumped round to the other side and spun round the wheel.

I walked to the break of the poop. On the overshadowed deck all hands stood by the forebraces waiting for my order. The stars ahead seemed to be gliding from right to left. And all was so still in the world that I heard the quiet remark "She's round," passed in a tone of intense relief between two seamen.

"Let go and haul."

The foreyards ran round with a great noise, amidst cheery cries. And now the frightful whiskers made themselves heard giving various orders. Already the ship was drawing ahead. And I was alone with her. Nothing! no one in the world should stand now between us, throwing a shadow on the way of silent knowledge and mute affection, the perfect communion of a seaman with his first command.

Walking to the taffrail, I was in time to make out, on the very edge of a darkness thrown by a towering black mass like the very gateway of Erebus—yes, I was in time to catch an evanescent glimpse of my white hat left behind to mark the spot where the secret sharer of my cabin and of my thoughts, as though he were my second self, had lowered himself into the water to take his punishment: a free man, a proud swimmer striking out for a new destiny.

QUESTIONS FOR THINKING AND WRITING

"The Secret Sharer" is a complex tale. It can be approached and interpreted in many ways. After the first question, therefore, this set of questions is not sequential. Rather, the questions represent some of the different approaches an essay might take. We suggest, therefore, that you first consider each question to see where an essay based on it might lead and what sort of comments on the story it might provide; and then choose one question (from questions 2 through 4) to write on at length.

1. The responsibility held by the captain of a sailing vessel plays an important part in this story. What are the captain's responsibilities? What authority does he have? (Answer from your own knowledge and from what Conrad's narrator tells you.)
2. What happens to our (and, presumably, the narrator's) normal moral values in this story? Are they adhered to? Discarded? Replaced (and, if so, replaced by what other values)? (Remember to quote specific passages from the story to substantiate your answer.)
3. One frequently useful method for approaching a story is to consider how the author balances his characters. In this story, for instance, one can see the "secret sharer" as a man balanced between the two captains: the one captain representing the "law," the other representing what? (Notice that this second captain finds himself occasionally threatened by a "sentimental pity . . . a sort of cowardice." How does this affect the balance between the two men?)

4. If one concentrates on the hero, one can see him as a man caught between his duty to the ship on the one hand, and his response to the "secret sharer" and his predicament on the other hand. How does he work out his dilemma? Is he ever in danger? If so, of what sort? How successful do you think he is in the end?

5. How would you compare the narrative style of "The Secret Sharer" with that of "The Open Boat"? Which do you prefer? Why?

CHARLOTTE PERKINS GILMAN (1860–1935)

The Yellow Wall-Paper

It is very seldom that mere ordinary people like John and myself secure ancestral halls for the summer.

A colonial mansion, a hereditary estate, I would say a haunted house, and reach the height of romantic felicity—but that would be asking too much of fate!

Still I will proudly declare that there is something queer about it.

Else, why should it be let so cheaply? And why have stood so long untenanted?

John laughs at me, of course, but one expects that in marriage.

John is practical in the extreme. He has no patience with faith, an intense horror of superstition, and he scoffs openly at any talk of things not to be felt and seen and put down in figures.

John is a physician, and *perhaps*—(I would not say it to a living soul, of course, but this is dead paper and a great relief to my mind)—*perhaps* that is one reason I do not get well faster.

You see he does not believe I am sick!

And what can one do?

If a physician of high standing, and one's own husband, assures friends and relatives that there is really nothing the matter with one but temporary nervous depression—a slight hysterical tendency—what is one to do?

My brother is also a physician, and also of high standing, and he says the same thing.

So I take phosphates or phosphites—whichever it is, and tonics, and journeys, and air, and exercise, and am absolutely forbidden to "work" until I am well again.

Personally, I disagree with their ideas.

Personally, I believe that congenial work, with excitement and change, would do me good.

But what is one to do?

I did write for a while in spite of them; but it *does* exhaust me a good deal—having to be so sly about it, or else meet with heavy opposition.

I sometimes fancy that in my condition if I had less opposition and more society and stimulus—but John says the very worst thing I can do is to think about my condition, and I confess it always makes me feel bad.

So I will let it alone and talk about the house.

The most beautiful place! It is quite alone, standing well back from the road, quite three miles from the village. It makes me think of English places that you read about, for there are hedges and walls and gates that lock, and lots of separate little houses for the gardeners and people.

There is a *delicious* garden! I never saw such a garden—large and shady, full of box-bordered paths, and lined with long grape-covered arbors with seats under them.

There were greenhouses, too, but they are all broken now.

There was some legal trouble, I believe, something about the heirs and coheirs; anyhow, the place has been empty for years.

That spoils my ghostliness, I am afraid, but I don't care—there is something strange about the house—I can feel it.

I even said so to John one moonlight evening, but he said what I felt was a *draught,* and shut the window.

I get unreasonably angry with John sometimes. I'm sure I never used to be so sensitive. I think it is due to this nervous condition.

But John says if I feel so, I shall neglect proper self-control; so I take pains to control myself—before him, at least, and that makes me very tired.

I don't like our room a bit. I wanted one downstairs that opened on the piazza and had roses all over the window, and such pretty old-fashioned chintz hangings! but John would not hear of it.

He said there was only one window and not room for two beds, and no near room for him if he took another.

He is very careful and loving, and hardly lets me stir without special direction.

I have a schedule prescription for each hour in the day; he takes all care from me, and so I feel basely ungrateful not to value it more.

He said we came here solely on my account, that I was to have perfect rest and all the air I could get. "Your exercise depends on your strength, my dear," said he, "and your food somewhat on your appetite; but air you can absorb all the time." So we took the nursery at the top of the house.

It is a big, airy room, the whole floor nearly, with windows that look all ways, and air and sunshine galore. It was nursery first and then playroom and gymnasium, I should judge; for the windows are barred for little children, and there are rings and things in the walls.

The paint and paper look as if a boys' school had used it. It is stripped off—the paper—in great patches all around the head of my bed, about as far as I can reach, and in a great place on the other side of the room low down. I never saw a worse paper in my life.

One of those sprawling flamboyant patterns committing every artistic sin.

It is dull enough to confuse the eye in following, pronounced enough to constantly irritate and provoke study, and when you follow the lame uncertain curves for a little distance they suddenly commit suicide— plunge off at outrageous angles, destroy themselves in unheard of contradictions.

The color is repellent, almost revolting; a smouldering unclean yellow, strangely faded by the slow-turning sunlight.

It is a dull yet lurid orange in some places, a sickly sulphur tint in others.

No wonder the children hated it! I should hate it myself if I had to live in this room long.

There comes John, and I must put this away,—he hates to have me write a word.

We have been here two weeks, and I haven't felt like writing before, since that first day.

I am sitting by the window now, up in this atrocious nursery, and there is nothing to hinder my writing as much as I please, save lack of strength.

John is away all day, and even some nights when his cases are serious.

I am glad my case is not serious!

But these nervous troubles are dreadfully depressing.

John does not know how much I really suffer. He knows there is no *reason* to suffer, and that satisfies him.

Of course it is only nervousness. It does weigh on me so not to do my duty in any way!

I meant to be such a help to John, such a real rest and comfort, and here I am a comparative burden already!

Nobody would believe what an effort it is to do what little I am able,— to dress and entertain, and order things.

It is fortunate Mary is so good with the baby. Such a dear baby!

And yet I *cannot* be with him, it makes me so nervous.

I suppose John never was nervous in his life. He laughs at me so about this wall-paper!

At first he meant to repaper the room, but afterwards he said that I was letting it get the better of me, and that nothing was worse for a nervous patient than to give way to such fancies.

He said that after the wall-paper was changed it would be the heavy bedstead, and then the barred windows, and then that gate at the head of the stairs, and so on.

"You know the place is doing you good," he said, "and really, dear, I don't care to renovate the house just for a three months' rental."

"Then do let us go downstairs," I said, "there are such pretty rooms there."

Then he took me in his arms and called me a blessed little goose, and said he would go down to the cellar, if I wished, and have it whitewashed into the bargain.

But he is right enough about the beds and windows and things.

It is an airy and comfortable room as any one need wish, and, of course, I would not be so silly as to make him uncomfortable just for a whim.

I'm really getting quite fond of the big room, all but that horrid paper.

Out of one window I can see the garden, those mysterious deep-shaded arbors, the riotous old-fashioned flowers, and bushes and gnarly trees.

Out of another I get a lovely view of the bay and a little private wharf belonging to the estate. There is a beautiful shaded lane that runs down there from the house. I always fancy I see people walking in these numerous paths and arbors, but John has cautioned me not to give way to fancy in the least. He says that with my imaginative power and habit of story-making, a nervous weakness like mine is sure to lead to all manner of excited fancies, and that I ought to use my will and good sense to check the tendency. So I try.

I think sometimes that if I were only well enough to write a little it would relieve the press of ideas and rest me.

But I find I get pretty tired when I try.

It is so discouraging not to have any advice and companionship about my work. When I get really well, John says we will ask Cousin Henry and Julia down for a long visit; but he says he would as soon put fireworks in my pillow-case as to let me have those stimulating people about now.

I wish I could get well faster.

But I must not think about that. This paper looks to me as if it *knew* what a vicious influence it had!

There is a recurrent spot where the pattern lolls like a broken neck and two bulbous eyes stare at you upside down.

I get positively angry with the impertinence of it and the everlastingness. Up and down and sideways they crawl, and those absurd, unblinking eyes are everywhere. There is one place where two breadths didn't match, and the eyes go all up and down the line, one a little higher than the other.

I never saw so much expression in an inanimate thing before, and we all know how much expression they have! I used to lie awake as a child and get more entertainment and terror out of blank walls and plain furniture than most children could find in a toy-store.

I remember what a kindly wink the knobs of our big, old bureau used to have, and there was one chair that always seemed like a strong friend.

I used to feel that if any of the other things looked too fierce I could always hop into that chair and be safe.

The furniture in this room is no worse than inharmonious, however, for we had to bring it all from downstairs. I suppose when this was used as a playroom they had to take the nursery things out, and no wonder! I never saw such ravages as the children have made here.

The wall-paper, as I said before, is torn off in spots, and it sticketh closer than a brother—they must have had perseverance as well as hatred.

Then the floor is scratched and gouged and splintered, the plaster itself is dug out here and there, and this great heavy bed which is all we found in the room, looks as if it had been through the wars.

But I don't mind it a bit— only the paper.

There comes John's sister. Such a dear girl as she is, and so careful of me! I must not let her find me writing.

She is a perfect and enthusiastic housekeeper, and hopes for no better profession. I verily believe she thinks it is the writing which made me sick!

But I can write when she is out, and see her a long way off from these windows.

There is one that commands the road, a lovely shaded winding road, and one that just looks off over the country. A lovely country, too, full of great elms and velvet meadows.

This wall-paper has a kind of sub-pattern in a different shade, a particularly irritating one, for you can only see it in certain lights, and not clearly then.

But in the places where it isn't faded and where the sun is just so—I can see a strange, provoking, formless sort of figure, that seems to skulk about behind that silly and conspicuous front design.

There's sister on the stairs!

Well, the Fourth of July is over! The people are all gone and I am tired out. John thought it might do me good to see a little company, so we just had mother and Nellie and the children down for a week.

Of course I didn't do a thing. Jennie sees to everything now.

But it tired me all the same.

John says if I don't pick up faster he shall send me to Weir Mitchell in the fall.

But I don't want to go there at all. I had a friend who was in his hands once, and she says he is just like John and my brother, only more so!

Besides, it is such an undertaking to go so far.

I don't feel as if it was worth while to turn my hand over for anything, and I'm getting dreadfully fretful and querulous.

I cry at nothing, and cry most of the time.

Of course I don't when John is here, or anybody else, but when I am alone.

And I am alone a good deal just now. John is kept in town very often by serious cases, and Jennie is good and lets me alone when I want her to.

So I walk a little in the garden or down that lovely lane, sit on the porch under the roses, and lie down up here a good deal.

I'm getting really fond of the room in spite of the wall-paper. Perhaps *because* of the wall-paper.

It dwells in my mind so!

I lie here on this great immovable bed—it is nailed down, I believe—and follow that pattern about by the hour. It is as good as gymnastics, I assure you. I start, we'll say, at the bottom, down in the corner over there where it has not been touched, and I determine for the thousandth time that I *will* follow that pointless pattern to some sort of a conclusion.

I know a little of the principle of design, and I know this thing was not arranged on any laws of radiation, or alternation, or repetition, or symmetry, or anything else that I ever heard of.

It is repeated, of course, by the breadths, but not otherwise.

Looked at in one way each breadth stands alone, the bloated curves and flourishes—a kind of "debased Romanesque" with *delirium tremens*—go waddling up and down in isolated columns of fatuity.

But, on the other hand, they connect diagonally, and the sprawling outlines run off in great slanting waves of optic horror, like a lot of wallowing seaweeds in full chase.

The whole thing goes horizontally, too, at least it seems so, and I exhaust myself in trying to distinguish the order of its going in that direction.

They have used a horizontal breadth for a frieze, and that adds wonderfully to the confusion.

There is one end of the room where it is almost intact, and there, when the crosslights fade and the low sun shines directly upon it, I can almost fancy radiation after all,—the interminable grotesques seem to form around a common centre and rush off in headlong plunges of equal distraction.

It makes me tired to follow it. I will take a nap I guess.

I don't know why I should write this.

I don't want to.

I don't feel able.

And I know John would think it absurd. But I *must* say what I feel and think in some way—it is such a relief!

But the effort is getting to be greater than the relief.

Half the time now I am awfully lazy, and lie down ever so much.

John says I mustn't lose my strength, and has me take cod liver oil and lots of tonics and things, to say nothing of ale and wine and rare meat.

Dear John! He loves me very dearly, and hates to have me sick. I tried to have a real earnest reasonable talk with him the other day, and tell him how I wish he would let me go and make a visit to Cousin Henry and Julia.

But he said I wasn't able to go, nor able to stand it after I got there; and I did not make out a very good case for myself, for I was crying before I had finished.

It is getting to be a great effort for me to think straight. Just this nervous weakness I suppose.

And dear John gathered me up in his arms, and just carried me upstairs and laid me on the bed, and sat by me and read to me till it tired my head.

He said I was his darling and his comfort and all he had, and that I must take care of myself for his sake, and keep well.

He says no one but myself can help me out of it, that I must use my will and self-control and not let any silly fancies run away with me.

There's one comfort, the baby is well and happy, and does not have to occupy this nursery with the horrid wall-paper.

If we had not used it, that blessed child would have! What a fortunate escape! Why, I wouldn't have a child of mine, an impressionable little thing, live in such a room for worlds.

I never thought of it before, but it is lucky that John kept me here after all, I can stand it so much easier than a baby, you see.

Of course I never mention it to them any more—I am too wise,—but I keep watch of it all the same.

There are things in that paper that nobody knows but me, or ever will.

Behind that outside pattern the dim shapes get clearer every day.

It is always the same shape, only very numerous.

And it is like a woman stooping down and creeping about behind that pattern. I don't like it a bit. I wonder—I begin to think—I wish John would take me away from here!

It is so hard to talk with John about my case, because he is so wise, and because he loves me so.

But I tried it last night.

It was moonlight. The moon shines in all around just as the sun does.

I hate to see it sometimes, it creeps so slowly, and always comes in by one window or another.

John was asleep and I hated to waken him, so I kept still and watched the moonlight on that undulating wall-paper till I felt creepy.

The faint figure behind seemed to shake the pattern, just as if she wanted to get out.

I got up softly and went to feel and see if the paper *did* move, and when I came back John was awake.

"What is it, little girl?" he said. "Don't go walking about like that— you'll get cold."

I thought it was a good time to talk, so I told him that I really was not gaining here, and that I wished he would take me away.

"Why darling!" said he, "our lease will be up in three weeks, and I can't see how to leave before.

"The repairs are not done at home, and I cannot possibly leave town just now. Of course if you were in any danger, I could and would, but you really are better, dear, whether you can see it or not. I am a doctor, dear, and I know. You are gaining flesh and color, your appetite is better, I feel really much easier about you."

"I don't weigh a bit more," said I, "nor as much; and my appetite may be better in the evening when you are here, but it is worse in the morning when you are away!"

"Bless her little heart!" said he with a big hug, "she shall be as sick as she pleases! But now let's improve the shining hours by going to sleep, and talk about it in the morning!"

"And you won't go away?" I asked gloomily.

"Why, how can I, dear? It is only three weeks more and then we will take a nice little trip of a few days while Jennie is getting the house ready. Really dear you are better!"

"Better in body perhaps—" I began, and stopped short, for he sat up straight and looked at me with such a stern, reproachful look that I could not say another word.

"My darling," said he, "I beg of you, for my sake and for our child's sake, as well as for your own, that you will never for one instant let that idea enter your mind! There is nothing so dangerous, so fascinating, to a temperament like yours. It is a false and foolish fancy. Can you not trust me as a physician when I tell you so?"

So of course I said no more on that score, and we went to sleep before long. He thought I was asleep first, but I wasn't, and lay there for hours trying to decide whether that front pattern and the back pattern really did move together or separately.

On a pattern like this, by daylight, there is a lack of sequence, a defiance of law, that is a constant irritant to a normal mind.

The color is hideous enough, and unreliable enough, and infuriating enough, but the pattern is torturing.

You think you have mastered it, but just as you get well underway in following, it turns a back-somersault and there you are. It slaps you in the face, knocks you down, and tramples upon you. It is like a bad dream.

The outside pattern is a florid arabesque, reminding one of a fungus. If you can imagine a toadstool in joints, an interminable string of toadstools, budding and sprouting in endless convolutions—why, that is something like it.

That is, sometimes!

There is one marked peculiarity about this paper, a thing nobody seems to notice but myself, and that is that it changes as the light changes.

When the sun shoots in through the east window—I always watch for that first long, straight ray—it changes so quickly that I never can quite believe it.

That is why I watch it always.

By moonlight—the moon shines in all night when there is a moon—I wouldn't know it was the same paper.

At night in any kind of light, in twilight, candle light, lamplight, and worst of all by moonlight, it becomes bars! The outside pattern I mean, and the woman behind it is as plain as can be.

I didn't realize for a long time what the thing was that showed behind, that dim sub-pattern, but now I am quite sure it is a woman.

By daylight she is subdued, quiet. I fancy it is the pattern that keeps her so still. It is so puzzling. It keeps me quiet by the hour.

I lie down ever so much now. John says it is good for me, and to sleep all I can.

Indeed he started the habit by making me lie down for an hour after each meal.

It is a very bad habit I am convinced, for you see I don't sleep.

And that cultivates deceit, for I don't tell them I'm awake—O no!

The fact is I am getting a little afraid of John.

He seems very queer sometimes, and even Jennie has an inexplicable look.

It strikes me occasionally, just as a scientific hypothesis,—that perhaps it is the paper!

I have watched John when he did not know I was looking, and come into the room suddenly on the most innocent excuses, and I've caught him several times *looking at the paper!* And Jennie too. I caught Jennie with her hand on it once.

She didn't know I was in the room, and when I asked her in a quiet, a very quiet voice, with the most restrained manner possible, what she was doing with the paper—she turned around as if she had been caught stealing, and looked quite angry—asked me why I should frighten her so!

Then she said that the paper stained everything it touched, that she had found yellow smooches on all my clothes and John's, and she wished we would be more careful!

Did not that sound innocent? But I know she was studying that pattern, and I am determined that nobody shall find it out but myself!

Life is very much more exciting now than it used to be. You see I have something more to expect, to look forward to, to watch. I really do eat better, and am more quiet than I was.

John is so pleased to see me improve! He laughed a little the other day, and said I seemed to be flourishing in spite of my wall-paper.

I turned it off with a laugh. I had no intention of telling him it was *because* of the wall-paper—he would make fun of me. He might even want to take me away.

I don't want to leave now until I have found it out. There is a week more, and I think that will be enough.

I'm feeling ever so much better! I don't sleep much at night, for it is so interesting to watch developments; but I sleep a good deal in the day-time.

In the daytime it is tiresome and perplexing.

There are always new shoots on the fungus, and new shades of yellow all over it. I cannot keep count of them, though I have tried conscientiously.

It is the strangest yellow, that wall-paper! It makes me think of all the yellow things I ever saw—not beautiful ones like buttercups, but old foul, bad yellow things.

But there is something else about that paper—the smell! I noticed it the moment we came into the room, but with so much air and sun it was not bad. Now we have had a week of fog and rain, and whether the windows are open or not, the smell is here.

It creeps all over the house.

I find it hovering in the dining-room, skulking in the parlor, hiding in the hall, lying in wait for me on the stairs.

It gets into my hair.

Even when I go to ride, if I turn my head suddenly and surprise it—there is that smell!

Such a peculiar odor, too! I have spent hours in trying to analyze it, to find what it smelled like.

It is not bad—at first, and very gentle, but quite the subtlest, most enduring odor I ever met.

In this damp weather it is awful, I wake up in the night and find it hanging over me.

It used to disturb me at first. I thought seriously of burning the house—to reach the smell.

But now I am used to it. The only thing I can think of that it is like is the *color* of the paper! A yellow smell.

There is a very funny mark on this wall, low down, near the mopboard. A streak that runs round the room. It goes behind every piece of furniture, except the bed, a long, straight, even *smooch*, as if it had been rubbed over and over.

I wonder how it was done and who did it, and what they did it for. Round and round and round—round and round and round—it makes me dizzy!

I really have discovered something at last.

Through watching so much at night, when it changes so, I have finally found out.

The front pattern *does* move—and no wonder! The woman behind shakes it!

Sometimes I think there are a great many women behind, and sometimes only one, and she crawls around fast, and her crawling shakes it all over.

Then in the very bright spots she keeps still, and in the very shady spots she just takes hold of the bars and shakes them hard.

And she is all the time trying to climb through. But nobody could climb through that pattern—it strangles so; I think that is why it has so many heads.

They get through, and then the pattern strangles them off and turns them upside down, and makes their eyes white!

If those heads were covered or taken off it would not be half so bad.

I think that woman gets out in the daytime!

And I'll tell you why—privately—I've seen her!

I can see her out of every one of my windows!

It is the same woman, I know, for she is always creeping, and most women do not creep by daylight.

I see her on that long road under the trees, creeping along, and when a carriage comes she hides under the blackberry vines.

I don't blame her a bit. It must be very humiliating to be caught creeping by daylight!

I always lock the door when I creep by daylight. I can't do it at night, for I know John would suspect something at once.

And John is so queer now, that I don't want to irritate him. I wish he would take another room! Besides, I don't want anybody to get that woman out at night but myself.

I often wonder if I could see her out of all the windows at once.

But, turn as fast as I can, I can only see out of one at one time.

And though I always see her, she *may* be able to creep faster than I can turn!

I have watched her sometimes away off in the open country, creeping as fast as a cloud shadow in a high wind.

If only that top pattern could be gotten off from the under one! I mean to try it, little by little.

I have found out another funny thing, but I shan't tell it this time! It does not do to trust people too much.

There are only two more days to get this paper off, and I believe John is beginning to notice. I don't like the look in his eyes.

And I heard him ask Jennie a lot of professional questions about me. She had a very good report to give.

She said I slept a good deal in the daytime.

John knows I don't sleep very well at night, for all I'm so quiet!

He asked me all sorts of questions, too, and pretended to be very loving and kind.

As if I couldn't see through him!

Still, I don't wonder he acts so, sleeping under this paper for three months.

It only interests me, but I feel sure John and Jennie are secretly affected by it.

Hurrah! This is the last day, but it is enough. John is to stay in town over night, and won't be out until this evening.

Jennie wanted to sleep with me—the sly thing! but I told her I should undoubtedly rest better for a night all alone.

That was clever, for really I wasn't alone a bit! As soon as it was moonlight and that poor thing began to crawl and shake the pattern, I got up and ran to help her.

I pulled and she shook, I shook and she pulled, and before morning we had peeled off yards of that paper.

A strip about as high as my head and half around the room.

And then when the sun came and that awful pattern began to laugh at me, I declared I would finish it to-day!

We go away to-morrow, and they are moving all my furniture down again to leave things as they were before.

Jennie looked at the wall in amazement, but I told her merrily that I did it out of pure spite at the vicious thing.

She laughed and said she wouldn't mind doing it herself, but I must not get tired.

How she betrayed herself that time!

But I am here, and no person touches this paper but me,—not *alive!*

She tried to get me out of the room—it was too patent! But I said it was so quiet and empty and clean now that I believed I would lie down again and sleep all I could; and not to wake me even for dinner—I would call when I woke.

So now she is gone, and the servants are gone, and the things are gone, and there is nothing left but that great bedstead nailed down, with the canvas mattress we found on it.

We shall sleep downstairs to-night, and take the boat home to-morrow.

I quite enjoy the room, now it is bare again.

How those children did tear about here!

This bedstead is fairly gnawed!

But I must get to work.

I have locked the door and thrown the key down into the front path.

I don't want to go out, and I don't want to have anybody come in, till John comes.

I want to astonish him.

I've got a rope up here that even Jennie did not find. If that woman does get out, and tries to get away, I can tie her!

But I forgot I could not reach far without anything to stand on!

This bed will *not* move!

I tried to lift and push it until I was lame, and then I got so angry I bit off a little piece at one corner—but it hurt my teeth.

Then I peeled off all the paper I could reach standing on the floor. It sticks horribly and the pattern just enjoys it! All those strangled heads and bulbous eyes and waddling fungus growths just shriek with derision!

I am getting angry enough to do something desperate. To jump out of the window would be admirable exercise, but the bars are too strong even to try.

Besides I wouldn't do it. Of course not. I know well enough that a step like that is improper and might be misconstrued.

I don't like to *look* out of the windows even—there are so many of those creeping women, and they creep so fast.

I wonder if they all come out of that wall-paper as I did?

But I am securely fastened now by my well-hidden rope—you don't get *me* out in the road there!

I suppose I shall have to get back behind the pattern when it comes night, and that is hard!

It is so pleasant to be out in this great room and creep around as I please!

I don't want to go outside. I won't, even if Jennie asks me to.

For outside you have to creep on the ground, and everything is green instead of yellow.

But here I can creep smoothly on the floor, and my shoulder just fits in that long smooch around the wall, so I cannot lose my way.

Why there's John at the door!

It is no use, young man, you can't open it!

How he does call and pound!

Now he's crying for an axe.

It would be a shame to break down that beautiful door!

"John dear!" said I in the gentlest voice, "the key is down by the front steps, under a plantain leaf!"

That silenced him for a few moments.

Then he said—very quietly indeed, "Open the door, my darling!"

"I can't," said I. "The key is down by the front door under a plantain leaf!"

And then I said it again, several times, very gently and slowly, and said it so often that he had to go and see, and he got it of course, and came in. He stopped short by the door.

"What is the matter?" he cried. "For God's sake, what are you doing!"

I kept on creeping just the same, but I looked at him over my shoulder.

"I've got out at last," said I, "in spite of you and Jennie. And I've pulled off most of the paper, so you can't put me back!"

Now why should that man have fainted? But he did, and right across my path by the wall, so that I had to creep over him every time!

QUESTIONS FOR THINKING AND WRITING

1. Obviously, the yellow wall-paper is the central image in the story. One way to analyze the story, therefore, would be to trace the narrator's impressions of the wall-paper throughout the tale. We might ask how large a part the paper plays in her narration of each episode; how her description of the paper itself changes from scene to scene; how she describes the effect the paper has on her; and how those descriptions change. We might also ask how we respond to each change, each new description. How do we use the changing descriptions to interpret the narrator's state of mind? What feelings toward her do we have, and how do they change (or develop) as the story progresses?

2. For a brief paper, you might concentrate on the wall-paper as part of the tale's setting. Notice how the surroundings narrow for the narrator, from her description of the house and its grounds on the first day to her description of her path around the room on the final day. How has this narrowing been accomplished? What does it symbolize?

3. Another approach might be to ask why the wall-paper is in the narrator's room at all? What does her explanation of its presence tell you about her marriage—about her feelings about herself and her husband, and about his feelings about himself and her? How is this theme developed throughout the story? How does it end? (Make sure you take note of the tone of the story's final sentence!)

4. "The Yellow Wall-Paper" is certainly a tale that demands much participation from its readers. The narrator and her husband disagree about her needs and her health; and we feel ourselves called on to decide who is right. The wife also describes herself in solitude (particularly with reference to the wall-paper); and again we must decide how far to believe what she says, or how to reinterpret it. You might write a paper, therefore, discussing the narrative style of the tale, explaining where your sympathies lie at various points and describing the means by which the narrative shifts you from being a listener in the first scene (which is a fairly straightforward description) to being the only person who really understands what is going on in the final scene, the one who could answer the narrator's final question.

5. Unlike the central character of "Young Goodman Brown," who seems to have withdrawn from his fellow humans at least partly of his own volition, the narrators of "Bartleby the Scrivener" and "The Yellow Wall-Paper" want to communicate with other people, but are prevented from doing so. What would you say is blocking communication for them? Who or what is to be blamed for the miseries all three characters endure?

ALICE WALKER (1944–)

Really, Doesn't *Crime Pay?*

(Myrna)
<small>SEPTEMBER,</small> 1961

page 118

I sit here by the window in a house with a thirty-year mortgage, writing in this notebook, looking down at my Helena Rubenstein hands . . . and why not? Since I am not a serious writer my nails need not be bitten off, my cuticles need not have jagged edges. I can indulge myself—my hands—in Herbessence nail-soak, polish, lotions, and creams. The result is a truly beautiful pair of hands: sweet-smelling, small, and soft. . . .

I lift them from the page where I have written the line "Really, *Doesn't Crime Pay?*" and send them seeking up my shirt front (it is a white and frilly shirt) and smoothly up the column of my throat, where gardenia scent floats beneath my hairline. If I should spread my arms and legs or whirl, just for an instant, the sweet smell of my body would be more than I could bear. But I fit into my new surroundings perfectly; like a jar of cold cream melting on a mirrored vanity shelf.

page 119

"I have a surprise for you," Ruel said, the first time he brought me here. And you know how sick he makes me now when he grins.

"What is it?" I asked, not caring in the least.

And that is how we drove up to the house. Four bedrooms and two toilets and a half.

"Isn't it a beauty?" he said, not touching me, but urging me out of the car with the phony enthusiasm of his voice.

"Yes," I said. It is "a beauty." Like new Southern houses everywhere. The bricks resemble cubes of raw meat; the roof presses down, a field hat made of iron. The windows are narrow, beady eyes; the aluminum glints. The yard is a long undressed wound, the few trees as bereft of foliage as hairpins stuck in a mud cake.

"Yes," I say, "it sure is a beauty." He beams, in his chill and reassured way. I am startled that he doesn't still wear some kind of military uniform. But no. He came home from Korea a hero, and a glutton for sweet smells.

"Here we can forget the past," he says.

page 120

We have moved in and bought new furniture. The place reeks of newness, the green walls turn me bilious. He stands behind me, his hands touching the edges of my hair. I pick up my hairbrush and brush his hands away. I have sweetened my body to such an extent that even he (especially he) may no longer touch it.

I do not want to forget the past; but I say "Yes," like a parrot. "We can forget the past here."

The past of course is Mordecai Rich, the man who, Ruel claims, caused my breakdown. The past is the night I tried to murder Ruel with one of his chain saws.

MAY, 1958

page 2

Mordecai Rich

Mordecai does not believe Ruel Johnson is my husband. *"That* old man," he says, in a mocking, cruel way.

"Ruel is not old," I say. "Looking old is just his way." Just as, I thought, looking young is your way, although you're probably not much younger than Ruel.

Maybe it is just that Mordecai is a vagabond, scribbling down impressions of the South, from no solid place, going to none . . . and Ruel has never left Hancock County, except once, when he gallantly went off to war. He claims travel broadened him, especially his two months of European leave. He married me because although my skin is brown he thinks I look like a Frenchwoman. Sometimes he tells me I look Oriental: Korean or Japanese. I console myself with this thought: My family tends to darken and darken as we get older. One day he may wake up in bed with a complete stranger.

"He works in the store," I say. "He also raises a hundred acres of peanuts." Which is surely success.

"That many," muses Mordecai.

It is not pride that makes me tell him what my husband does, is. It is a way I can tell him about myself.

page 4

Today Mordecai is back. He tells a funny/sad story about a man in town who could not move his wife. "He huffed and puffed," laughed Mordecai, "to no avail." Then one night as he was sneaking up to her bedroom he heard joyous cries. Rushing in he found his wife in the arms of another woman! The wife calmly dressed and began to pack her bags. The husband begged and pleaded. "Anything you want," he promised. "What *do* you want?" he pleaded. The wife began to chuckle and, laughing, left the house with her friend.

Now the husband gets drunk every day and wants an ordinance passed. He cannot say what the ordinance will be against, but that is what he buttonholes people to say: "I want a goddam ordinance passed!" People who know the story make jokes about him. They pity him and give him enough money to keep him drunk.

page 5

I think Mordecai Rich has about as much heart as a dirt-eating toad. Even when he makes me laugh I know that nobody ought to look on other people's confusion with that cold an eye.

"But that's what I am," he says, flipping through the pages of his scribble pad. "A cold eye. An eye looking for Beauty. An eye looking for Truth."

"Why don't you look for other things?" I want to know. "Like neither Truth nor Beauty, but places in people's lives where things have just slipped a good bit off the track."

"That's too vague," said Mordecai, frowning.

"So is Truth," I said. "Not to mention Beauty."

page 10

Ruel wants to know why "the skinny black tramp"—as he calls Mordecai—keeps hanging around. I made the mistake of telling him Mordecai is thinking of using our house as the setting for one of his Southern country stories.

"Mordecai is from the North," I said. "He never saw a wooden house with a toilet in the yard."

"Well maybe he better go back where he from," said Ruel, "and shit the way he's used to."

It's Ruel's pride that is hurt. He's ashamed of this house that seems perfectly adequate to me. One day we'll have a new house, he says, of brick, with a Japanese bath. How should I know why?

page 11

When I told Mordecai what Ruel said he smiled in that snake-eyed way he has and said, "Do *you* mind me hanging around?"

I didn't know what to say. I stammered something. Not because of his question but because he put his hand point-blank on my left nipple. He settled his other hand deep in my hair.

"I am married more thoroughly than a young boy like you could guess," I told him. But I don't expect that to stop him. Especially since the day he found out I wanted to be a writer myself.

It happened this way: I was writing in the grape arbor, on the ledge by the creek that is hidden from the house by trees. He was right in front of me before I could put my notebook away. He snatched it from me and began to read. What is worse, he read aloud. I was embarrassed to death.

"No wife of mine is going to embarrass me with a lot of foolish, vulgar stuff," Mordecai read. (This is Ruel's opinion of my writing.) *Every time he tells me how peculiar I am for wanting to write stories he brings up having a baby or going shopping, as if these things are the same. Just something to occupy my time.*

"If you have time on your hands," he said today, "why don't you go shopping in that new store in town."

I went. I bought six kinds of face cream, two eyebrow pencils, five nightgowns and a longhaired wig. Two contour sticks and a pot of gloss for my lips.

And all the while I was grieving over my last story. Outlined—which is as far as I take stories now—but dead in embryo. My hand stilled by cowardice, my heart the heart of a slave.

page 14

Of course Mordecai wanted to see the story. What did I have to lose?

"Flip over a few pages," I said. "It is the very skeleton of a story, but one that maybe someday I will write."

"The One-Legged Woman," Mordecai began to read aloud, then continued silently.

> The characters are poor dairy farmers. One morning the husband is too hung over to do the milking. His wife does it and when she has finished the cows are frightened by thunder and stampede, trampling her. She is also hooked severely in one leg. Her husband is asleep and does not hear her cry out. Finally she drags herself home and wakes him up. He washes her wounds and begs her to forgive him. He does not go for a doctor because he is afraid the doctor will accuse him of being lazy and a drunk, undeserving of his good wife. He wants the doctor to respect him. The wife, understanding, goes along with this.
>
> However, gangrene sets in and the doctor comes. He lectures the husband and amputates the leg of the wife. The wife lives and tries to forgive her husband for his weakness.

While she is ill the husband tries to show he loves her, but cannot look at the missing leg. When she is well he finds he can no longer make love to her. The wife, sensing his revulsion, understands her sacrifice was for nothing. She drags herself to the barn and hangs herself.

The husband, ashamed that anyone should know he was married to a one-legged woman, buries her himself and later tells everyone that she is visiting her mother.

While Mordecai was reading the story I looked out over the fields. If he says one good thing about what I've written, I promised myself, I will go to bed with him. (How else could I repay him? All I owned in any supply were my jars of cold cream!) As if he read my mind he sank down on the seat beside me and looked at me strangely.

"*You* think about things like this?" he asked.

He took me in his arms, right there in the grape arbor. "You sure do have a lot of heavy, sexy hair," he said, placing me gently on the ground. After that, a miracle happened. Under Mordecai's fingers my body opened like a flower and carefully bloomed. And it was strange as well as wonderful. For I don't think love had anything to do with this at all.

page 17

After that, Mordecai praised me for my intelligence, my sensitivity, the depth of the work he had seen—and naturally I showed him every-thing I had: old journals from high school, notebooks I kept hidden under tarpaulin in the barn, stories written on paper bags, on table napkins, even on shelf paper from over the sink. I am amazed—even more amazed than Mordecai—by the amount of stuff I have written. It is over twenty years' worth, and would fill, easily, a small shed.

"You must give these to me," Mordecai said finally, holding three notebooks he selected from the rather messy pile. "I will see if some-thing can't be done with them. You could be another Zora Hurston—" he smiled—"another Simone de Beauvoir!"

Of course I am flattered. "Take it! Take it!" I cry. Already I see myself as he sees me. A famous authoress, miles away from Ruel, miles away from anybody. I am dressed in dungarees, my hands are a mess. I smell of sweat. I glow with happiness.

"How could such pretty brown fingers write such ugly, deep stuff?" Mordecai asks, kissing them.

page 20

For a week we deny each other nothing. If Ruel knows (how could he not know? His sheets are never fresh), he says nothing. I realize now that he never considered Mordecai a threat. Because Mordecai seems to

have nothing to offer but his skinny self and his funny talk. I gloat over
this knowledge. Now Ruel will find that I am not a womb without a brain
that can be bought with Japanese bathtubs and shopping sprees. The
moment of my deliverance is at hand!

page 24

Mordecai did not come today. I sit in the arbor writing down those
words and my throat begins to close up. I am nearly strangled by my
fear.

page 56

I have not noticed anything for weeks. Not Ruel, not the house.
Everything whispers to me that Mordecai has forgotten me. Yesterday
Ruel told me not to go into town and I said I wouldn't, for I have been
hunting Mordecai up and down the streets. People look at me strangely,
their glances slide off me in a peculiar way. It is as if they see something
on my face that embarrasses them. Does everyone know about Mordecai
and me? Does good loving show so soon? . . . But it is not soon. He has
been gone already longer than I have known him.

page 61

Ruel tells me I act like my mind's asleep. It is asleep, of course.
Nothing will wake it but a letter from Mordecai telling me to pack my
bags and fly to New York.

page 65

If I could have read Mordecai's scribble pad I would know exactly
what he thought of me. But now I realize he never once offered to show
it to me, though he had a chance to read every serious thought I ever
had. I'm afraid to know what he thought. I feel crippled, deformed. But
if he ever wrote it down, that would make it true.

page 66

Today Ruel brought me in from the grape arbor, out of the rain. I
didn't know it was raining. "Old folks like us might catch rheumatism if
we don't be careful," he joked. I don't know what he means. I am thirty-
two. He is forty. I never felt old before this month.

page 79

Ruel came up to bed last night and actually cried in my arms! He would give anything for a child, he says.

"Do you think we could have one?" he said.

"Sure," I said. "Why not?"

He began to kiss me and carry on about my goodness. I began to laugh. He became very angry, but finished what he started. He really does intend to have a child.

page 80

I must really think of something better to do than kill myself.

page 81

Ruel wants me to see a doctor about speeding up conception of the child.

"Will you go, honey?" he asks, like a beggar.

"Sure," I say. "Why not?"

page 82

Today at the doctor's office the magazine I was reading fell open at a story about a one-legged woman. They had a picture of her, drawn by someone who painted the cows orange and green, and painted the woman white, like a white cracker, with little slit-blue eyes. Not black and heavy like she was in the story I had in mind. But it is still my story, filled out and switched about as things are. The author is said to be Mordecai Rich. They show a little picture of him on a back page. He looks severe and has grown a beard. And underneath his picture there is that same statement he made to me about going around looking for Truth.

They say his next book will be called "The Black Woman's Resistance to Creativity in the Arts."

page 86

Last night while Ruel snored on his side of the bed I washed the prints of his hands off my body. Then I plugged in one of his chain saws and tried to slice off his head. This failed because of the noise. Ruel woke up right in the nick of time.

page 95

The days pass in a haze that is not unpleasant. The doctors and nurses do not take me seriously. They fill me full of drugs and never even bother to lock the door. When I think of Ruel I think of the song the British sing: "Ruel Britannia"! I can even whistle it, or drum it with my fingers.

SEPTEMBER, 1961

page 218

People tell my husband all the time that I do not look crazy. I have been out for almost a year and he is beginning to believe them. Nights, he climbs on me with his slobber and his hope, cursing Mordecai Rich for messing up his life. I wonder if he feels our wills clashing in the dark. Sometimes I see the sparks fly inside my head. It is amazing how normal everything is.

page 223

The house still does not awaken to the pitter-patter of sweet little feet, because I religiously use the Pill. It is the only spot of humor in my entire day, when I am gulping that little yellow tablet and washing it down with soda pop or tea. Ruel spends long hours at the store and in the peanut field. He comes in sweaty, dirty, tired, and I wait for him smelling of Arpège, My Sin, Wind Song, and Jungle Gardenia. The women of the community feel sorry for him, to be married to such a fluff of nothing.

I wait, beautiful and perfect in every limb, cooking supper as if my life depended on it. Lying unresisting on his bed like a drowned body washed to shore. But he is not happy. For he knows now that I intend to do nothing but say yes until he is completely exhausted.

I go to the new shopping mall twice a day now; once in the morning and once in the afternoon, or at night. I buy hats I would not dream of wearing, or even owning. Dresses that are already on their way to Goodwill. Shoes that will go to mold and mildew in the cellar. And I keep the bottles of perfume, the skin softeners, the pots of gloss and eye shadow. I amuse myself painting my own face.

When he is quite, quite tired of me I will tell him how long I've relied on the security of the Pill. When I am quite, quite tired of the sweet, sweet smell of my body and the softness of these Helena Rubenstein hands I will leave him and this house. Leave them forever without once looking back.

280   *Really,* Doesn't *Crime Pay?*

QUESTIONS FOR THINKING AND WRITING

1. "Sweet smells" are an important motif in "Really, *Doesn't* Crime Pay?". Discuss the use of this motif. What do the smells mean to each of the characters who care about them? With what are they associated?
2. "Really, *Doesn't* Crime Pay?" is a tale built, in part, on the so-called "eternal triangle" (in this case, one woman and two men). What is it within each participant's personality that creates the dynamics of this particular triangle? How does each one interpret the part that the relationships play in the story's plot?
3. Within "Really, *Doesn't* Crime Pay?" is a second story, "The One-Legged Woman." How does this second story figure in the plot? What does it mean to the narrator? What does it tell us about her? How does she resemble and differ from her one-legged heroine?
4. Compare the organization of "The Yellow Wall-Paper" and "Really, *Doesn't* Crime Pay?" Note that each has one feature that distinguishes the story from a genuine day-by-day journal. How do these features add to the stories' impact?
5. How would you characterize the narrators of these two tales? How do they resemble each other? How do they differ?
6. The narrator's relationship with her husband is crucial in these two tales. Discuss the similarities and differences in the relationships and in the way the narrators discuss them and react to them.
7. In each story, one external feature of the narrator's world takes on undue prominence: the wallpaper in the first tale, cosmetics in the second. Discuss how the differing treatment of these motifs in the two tales reflects the different narrative styles.
8. What does each story suggest about the future for its narrator? What might you predict for each?

CHARACTER STUDY AND SOCIAL COMMENT

5 *Looking Inward and Outward*

Fiction is the most flexible of literary forms. A story can focus on two or three characters, as "If Not Higher" and "Bartleby the Scrivener" do; or it may include an entire community in its cast of characters, as do "The Lottery" and "Young Goodman Brown." It may keep us distanced from its characters, as "The Lottery" does, or it may take us into their minds, as do "The Secret Sharer" and "Young Goodman Brown."

A story may focus exclusively on the events of a few hours, as "The Open Boat" does; it may suggest the years of history that lie behind the few hours it covers, as "The Lottery" does; or its action may cover the events of many years. Fiction writers may place their narrators inside the tale or outside it; they may choose to let all the tale's characters speak freely, or they may allow us to hear only the narrator's voice. They may restrict their narrators to reporting things heard or seen, or they may let them comment, interpret, or moralize freely. In choice of characters, action, and stance, the freedom that fiction gives its writers is immense.

Fiction also offers its writers the full range from realism to fantasy in which to place their stories. "The Open Boat," with its seemingly objective stance and its careful reporting of a common type of event, is an example of realism. "Young Goodman Brown," with its action poised between dream and waking and its use of supernatural characters, is an example of fantasy. These styles, realism and fantasy, may be seen as the two ends of a scale, with other, less extreme styles falling between them. Where on the scale would you place "The Lottery"? "The Secret Sharer"? "If Not Higher"? "Bartleby the Scrivener"?

Fiction, then, is an art form of great flexibility. Largely because of this flexibility, works of fiction have the power to look in two directions at once. They can look into their characters, revealing their minds and feelings to us, exploring their personalities. And they can look out at the society to which the characters belong. Looking inward, they seem to ask, "What sort of people are these?" Looking outward, they seem to ask, "What has made them that way?"

Writers of fiction have long felt that their form's unique ability to deal with the common reality of everyday life made it an ideal vehicle for examining the interaction of individuals with their society. We find that concern reflected in nearly all forms of fiction, from old and traditional tales such as "Bartleby the Scrivener" to some of the most experimental contemporary works. Many Americans in the latter half of the twentieth century are deeply concerned with questions of society's influence and power over the individual and of the individual's own power to shape his or her own personality and future. Contemporary fiction reflects these concerns.

The stories that follow are all works that engage our concern for some central character or characters, while forcing upon us some realization of or comment on the society in which these characters live. In these stories, as in others we have read, the physical settings often become metaphors for the social settings. The influence of society, and the characters' reactions to it, thus form an important part of each tale.

As you read these stories, therefore, it will be helpful to keep notes in your reading journal on the physical and social settings, and how these settings are used to define the characters' actions and personalities. Keep notes, too, on the narrators' voices. Describe what tones you hear in these stories and what attitudes they convey. How do the narrators blend their stories' dual focus on individual and society into a concern for the fulfillment or happiness of their central characters? What moods do they leave you in at the stories' ends? How do they get you there?

WILLIAM FAULKNER (1897–1962)

A Rose for Emily

I

When Miss Emily Grierson died, our whole town went to her funeral: the men through a sort of respectful affection for a fallen monument, the women mostly out of curiosity to see the inside of her house, which no one save an old man-servant—a combined gardener and cook—had seen in at least ten years.

It was a big, squarish frame house that had once been white, decorated with cupolas and spires, and scrolled balconies in the heavily lightsome style of the seventies, set on what had once been our most select street. But garages and cotton gins had encroached and obliterated even the august names of that neighborhood; only Miss Emily's house was left, lifting its stubborn and coquettish decay above the cotton wagons and the gasoline pumps—an eyesore among eyesores. And now Miss Emily had gone to join the representatives of those august names where they lay in the cedar-bemused cemetery among the ranked and anonymous graves of Union and Confederate soldiers who fell at the battle of Jefferson.

Alive, Miss Emily had been a tradition, a duty, and a care; a sort of hereditary obligation upon the town, dating from that day in 1894 when Colonel Sartoris, the mayor—he who fathered the edict that no Negro woman should appear on the street without an apron—remitted her taxes, the dispensation dating from the death of her father on into perpetuity. Not that Miss Emily would have accepted charity. Colonel Sartoris invented an involved tale to the effect that Miss Emily's father had loaned money to the town, which the town, as a matter of business, preferred this way of repaying. Only a man of Colonel Sartoris' generation and thought could have invented it, and only a woman could have believed it.

When the next generation, with its more modern ideas, became mayors and aldermen, this arrangement created some little dissatis-faction. On the first of the year they mailed her a tax notice. February came, and there was no reply. They wrote her a formal letter, asking her to call at the sheriff's office at her convenience. A week later the mayor wrote her himself, offering to call or to send his car for her, and received in reply a note on paper of an archaic shape, in a thin, flowing calligraphy in faded ink, to the effect that she no longer went out at all. The tax notice was also enclosed, without comment.

They called a special meeting of the Board of Aldermen. A deputation waited upon her, knocked at the door through which no visitor had passed since she ceased giving china-painting lessons eight or ten years earlier. They were admitted by the old Negro into a dim hall from which a stairway mounted into still more shadow. It smelled of dust and disuse—a close, dank smell. The Negro led them into the parlor. It was furnished in heavy, leather-covered furniture. When the Negro opened the blinds of one window, they could see that the leather was cracked; and when they sat down, a faint dust rose sluggishly about their thighs, spinning with slow motes in the single sun-ray. On a tarnished gilt easel before the fireplace stood a crayon portrait of Miss Emily's father.

They rose when she entered—a small, fat woman in black, with a thin gold chain descending to her waist and vanishing into her belt, leaning on an ebony cane with a tarnished gold head. Her skeleton was small and spare; perhaps that was why what would have been merely plumpness in another was obesity in her. She looked bloated, like a body long submerged in motionless water, and of that pallid hue. Her eyes, lost in the fatty ridges of her face, looked like two small pieces of coal pressed into a lump of dough as they moved from one face to another while the visitors stated their errand.

She did not ask them to sit. She just stood in the door and listened quietly until the spokesman came to a stumbling halt. Then they could hear the invisible watch ticking at the end of the gold chain.

Her voice was dry and cold. "I have no taxes in Jefferson. Colonel Sartoris explained it to me. Perhaps one of you can gain access to the city records and satisfy yourselves."

"But we have. We are the city authorities, Miss Emily. Didn't you get a notice from the sheriff, signed by him?"

"I received a paper, yes," Miss Emily said. "Perhaps he considers himself the sheriff . . . I have no taxes in Jefferson."

"But there is nothing on the books to show that, you see. We must go by the—"

"See Colonel Sartoris. I have no taxes in Jefferson."

"But Miss Emily—"

"See Colonel Sartoris." (Colonel Sartoris had been dead almost ten years.) "I have no taxes in Jefferson. Tobe!" The Negro appeared. "Show these gentlemen out."

II

So she vanquished them, horse and foot, just as she had vanquished their fathers thirty years before about the smell. That was two years after her father's death and a short time after her sweetheart—the one we believed would marry her—had deserted her. After her father's death she went out very little; after her sweetheart went away, people hardly saw her at all. A few of the ladies had the temerity to call, but were not received, and the only sign of life about the place was the Negro man—a young man then—going in and out with a market basket.

"Just as if a man—any man—could keep a kitchen properly," the ladies said; so they were not surprised when the smell developed. It was another link between the gross, teeming world and the high and mighty Griersons.

A neighbor, a woman, complained to the mayor, Judge Stevens, eighty years old.

"But what will you have me do about it, madam?" he said.

"Why, send her word to stop it," the woman said. "Isn't there a law?"

"I'm sure that won't be necessary," Judge Stevens said. "It's probably just a snake or a rat that nigger of hers killed in the yard. I'll speak to him about it."

The next day he received two more complaints, one from a man who came in diffident deprecation. "We really must do something about it, Judge. I'd be the last one in the world to bother Miss Emily, but we've got to do something." That night the Board of Aldermen met—three graybeards and one younger man, a member of the rising generation.

"It's simple enough," he said. "Send her word to have her place cleaned up. Give her a certain time do it in, and if she don't . . ."

"Dammit, sir," Judge Stevens said, "will you accuse a lady to her face of smelling bad?"

So the next night, after midnight, four men crossed Miss Emily's lawn and slunk about the house like burglars, sniffing along the base of the brickwork and at the cellar openings while one of them performed a regular sowing motion with his hand out of a sack slung from his shoulder. They broke open the cellar door and sprinkled lime there, and in all the outbuildings. As they recrossed the lawn, a window that had been dark was lighted and Miss Emily sat in it, the light behind her, and her upright torso motionless as that of an idol. They crept quietly across the lawn and into the shadow of the locusts that lined the street. After a week or two the smell went away.

That was when people had begun to feel really sorry for her. People in our town, remembering how old lady Wyatt, her great-aunt, had gone completely crazy at last, believed that the Griersons held themselves a little too high for what they really were. None of the young men were quite good enough for Miss Emily and such. We had long thought of them as a tableau, Miss Emily a slender figure in white in the background, her father a spraddled silhouette in the foregound, his back to her and clutching a horsewhip, the two of them framed by the backflung front door. When she got to be thirty and was still single, we were not pleased exactly, but vindicated; even with insanity in the family she wouldn't have turned down all of her chances if they had really materialized.

When her father died, it got about that the house was all that was left to her; and in a way, people were glad. At last they could pity Miss Emily. Being left alone, and a pauper, she had become humanized. Now she too would know the old thrill and the old despair of a penny more or less.

The day after his death all the ladies prepared to call at the house and offer condolence and aid, as is our custom. Miss Emily met them at the door, dressed as usual and with no trace of grief on her face. She told them that her father was not dead. She did that for three days, with the ministers calling on her, and the doctors, trying to persuade her to let them dispose of the body. Just as they were about to resort to law and force, she broke down, and they buried her father quickly.

We did not say she was crazy then. We believed she had to do that. We remembered all the young men her father had driven away, and we knew that with nothing left, she would have to cling to that which had robbed her, as people will.

III

She was sick for a long time. When we saw her again, her hair was cut short, making her look like a girl, with a vague resemblance to those angels in colored church windows—sort of tragic and serene.

The town had just let the contracts for paving the sidewalks, and in the summer after her father's death they began the work. The construction company came with niggers and mules and machinery, and a foreman named Homer Barron, a Yankee—a big, dark, ready man, with a big voice and eyes lighter than his face. The little boys would follow in groups to hear him cuss the niggers, and the niggers singing in time to the rise and fall of picks. Pretty soon he knew everybody in town. Whenever you heard a lot of laughing anywhere about the square, Homer Barron would be in the center of the group.

Presently we began to see him and Miss Emily on Sunday afternoons driving in the yellow-wheeled buggy and the matched team of bays from the livery stable.

At first we were glad that Miss Emily would have an interest, because the ladies all said, "Of course a Grierson would not think seriously of a Northerner, a day laborer." But there were still others, older people, who said that even grief could not cause a real lady to forget *noblesse oblige*—without calling it *noblesse oblige*. They just said, "Poor Emily. Her kinsfolk should come to her." She had some kin in Alabama; but years ago her father had fallen out with them over the estate of old Lady Wyatt, the crazy woman, and there was no communication between the two families. They had not even been represented at the funeral.

And as soon as the old people said, "Poor Emily," the whispering began. "Do you suppose it's really so?" they said to one another. "Of course it is. What else could . . . ." This behind their hands; rustling of craned silk and satin behind jalousies closed upon the sun of Sunday afternoon as the thin, swift clop-clop-clop of the matched team passed: "Poor Emily."

She carried her head high enough—even when we believed that she was fallen. It was as if she demanded more than ever the recognition of her dignity as the last Grierson; as if it had wanted that touch of earthiness to reaffirm her imperviousness. Like when she bought the rat poison, the arsenic. That was over a year after they had begun to say "Poor Emily," and while the two female cousins were visiting her.

"I want some poison," she said to the druggist. She was over thirty then, still a slight woman, though thinner than usual, with cold, haughty black eyes in a face the flesh of which was strained across the temples and about the eye-sockets as you imagine a lighthouse-keeper's face ought to look. "I want some poison," she said.

"Yes, Miss Emily. What kind? For rats and such? I'd recom—"

"I want the best you have. I don't care what kind."

The druggist named several. "They'll kill anything up to an elephant. But what you want is—"

"Arsenic," Miss Emily said. "Is that a good one?"

"Is . . . arsenic? Yes, ma'am. But what you want—"

"I want arsenic."

The druggist looked down at her. She looked back at him, erect, her face like a strained flag. "Why, of course," the druggist said. "If that's what you want. But the law requires you to tell what you are going to use it for."

Miss Emily just stared at him, her head tilted back in order to look him eye for eye, until he looked away and went and got the arsenic and wrapped it up. The Negro delivery boy brought her the package; the druggist didn't come back. When she opened the package at home there was written on the box, under the skull and bones: "For rats."

IV

So the next day we all said, "She will kill herself"; and we said it would be the best thing. When she had first begun to be seen with Homer Barron, we had said, "She will marry him." Then we said, "She will persuade him yet," because Homer himself had remarked— he liked men, and it was known that he drank with the younger men in the Elks' Club—that he was not a marrying man. Later we said, "Poor Emily" behind the jalousies as they passed on Sunday afternoon in the glittering buggy, Miss Emily with her head high and Homer Barron with his hat cocked and cigar in his teeth, reins and whip in a yellow glove.

Then some of the ladies began to say that it was a disgrace to the town and a bad example to the young people. The men did not want to interfere, but at last the ladies forced the Baptist minister— Miss Emily's people were Episcopal—to call upon her. He would never divulge what happened during that interview, but he refused to go back again. The next Sunday they again drove about the streets, and the following day the minister's wife wrote to Miss Emily's relations in Alabama.

So she had blood-kin under her roof again and we sat back to watch developments. At first nothing happened. Then we were sure that they were to be married. We learned that Miss Emily had been to the jeweler's and ordered a man's toilet set in silver, with the letters H. B. on each piece. Two days later we learned that she had bought a complete outfit of men's clothing, including a nightshirt, and we said, "They are married." We were really glad. We were glad because the two female cousins were even more Grierson than Miss Emily had ever been.

So we were not surprised when Homer Barron—the streets had been finished some time since—was gone. We were a little disappointed that there was not a public blowing-off, but we believed that he had gone on to prepare for Miss Emily's coming, or to give her a chance to get rid of the cousins. (By that time it was a cabal, and we were all Miss Emily's allies to help circumvent the cousins.) Sure enough, after another week they departed. And, as we had expected all along, within three days Homer Barron was back in town. A neighbor saw the Negro man admit him at the kitchen door at dusk one evening.

And that was the last we saw of Homer Barron. And of Miss Emily for some time. The Negro man went in and out with the market basket, but the front door remained closed. Now and then we would see her at a window for a moment, as the men did that night when they sprinkled the lime, but for almost six months she did not appear on the streets. Then we knew that this was to be expected too; as if that quality of her father which had thwarted her woman's life so many times had been too virulent and too furious to die.

When we next saw Miss Emily, she had grown fat and her hair was turning gray. During the next few years it grew grayer and grayer until it attained an even pepper-and-salt iron-gray, when it ceased turning. Up to the day of her death at seventy-four it was still that vigorous iron-gray, like the hair of an active man.

From that time on her front door remained closed, save for a period of six or seven years, when she was about forty, during which she gave lessons in china-painting. She fitted up a studio in one of the downstairs rooms, where the daughters and granddaughters of Colonel Sartoris' contemporaries were sent to her with the same regularity and in the same spirit that they were sent to church on Sunday with a twenty-five-cent piece for the collection plate. Meanwhile her taxes had been remitted.

Then the newer generation became the backbone and the spirit of the town, and the painting pupils grew up and fell away and did not send their children to her with boxes of color and tedious brushes and pictures cut from the ladies' magazines. The front door closed upon the last one and remained closed for good. When the town got free postal delivery, Miss Emily alone refused to let them fasten the metal numbers above her door and attach a mailbox to it. She would not listen to them.

Daily, monthly, yearly we watched the Negro grow grayer and more stooped, going in and out with the market basket. Each December we sent her a tax notice, which would be returned by the post office a week later, unclaimed. Now and then we would see her in one of the downstairs windows—she had evidently shut up the top floor of the house—like the carven torso of an idol in a niche, looking or not looking at us, we could never tell which. Thus she passed from generation to generation—dear, inescapable, impervious, tranquil, and perverse.

And so she died. Fell ill in the house filled with dust and shadows, with only a doddering Negro man to wait on her. We did not even know she was sick; we had long since given up trying to get any information from the Negro. He talked to no one, probably not even to her, for his voice had grown harsh and rusty, as if from disuse.

She died in one of the downstairs rooms, in a heavy walnut bed with a curtain, her gray head propped on a pillow yellow and moldy with age and lack of sunlight.

V

The Negro met the first of the ladies at the front door and let them in, with their hushed, sibilant voices and their quick, curious glances, and then he disappeared. He walked right through the house and out the back and was not seen again.

The two female cousins came at once. They held the funeral on the second day, with the town coming to look at Miss Emily beneath a mass of bought flowers, with the crayon face of her father musing profoundly above the bier and the ladies sibilant and macabre; and the very old men—some in their brushed Confederate uniforms—on the porch and the lawn, talking of Miss Emily as if she had been a contemporary of theirs, believing that they had danced with her and courted her perhaps, confusing time with its mathematical progression, as the old do, to whom all the past is not a diminishing road but, instead, a huge meadow which no winter ever quite touches, divided from them now by the narrow bottle-neck of the most recent decade of years.

Already we knew that there was one room in that region above stairs which no one had seen in forty years, and which would have to be forced. They waited until Miss Emily was decently in the ground before they opened it.

The violence of breaking down the door seemed to fill this room with pervading dust. A thin, acrid pall of the tomb seemed to lie everywhere upon this room decked and furnished as for a bridal: upon the valance curtains of faded rose color, upon the rose-shaded lights, upon the dressing table, upon the delicate array of crystal and the man's toilet things backed with tarnished silver, silver so tarnished that the monogram was obscured. Among them lay a collar and tie, as if they had just been removed, which, lifted, left upon the surface a pale crescent in the dust. Upon a chair hung the suit, carefully folded; beneath it the two mute shoes and the discarded socks.

The man himself lay in the bed.

For a long while we just stood there, looking down at the profound and fleshless grin. The body had apparently once lain in the attitude of an embrace, but now the long sleep that outlasts love, that conquers even the grimace of love, had cuckolded him. What was left of him, rotted beneath what was left of the nightshirt, had become inextricable from the bed in which he lay; and upon him and upon the pillow beside him lay that even coating of the patient and biding dust.

Then we noticed that in the second pillow was the indentation of a head. One of us lifted something from it, and leaning forward, that faint and invisible dust dry and acrid in the nostrils, we saw a long strand of iron-gray hair.

QUESTIONS FOR THINKING AND WRITING

1. Part of the effectiveness of "A Rose for Emily" comes from its surprise ending. How effective do you find the ending? Why?
2. How do the narrator and the townsfolk view the young Miss Emily? How does Miss Emily change with time? How does the town? How does the narrator's view of Miss Emily change? How does yours?
3. Miss Emily doesn't really get to tell her own side of the story, but suppose she had left a diary. Write a series of diary entries in her voice that describe the events recounted in the story. Feel free to elaborate on them and to make up new facts and incidents to help explain statements that "you" might make.
4. Time seems to change things. Write a series of passages on how the town, its people, and Miss Emily change during the story. Finally, write an entry on how your own attitude changes during the story.

JAMES BALDWIN (1924–   )

Sonny's Blues

I read about it in the paper, in the subway, on my way to work. I read it, and I couldn't believe it, and I read it again. Then perhaps I just stared at it, at the newsprint spelling out his name, spelling out the story. I stared at it in the swinging lights of the subway car, and in the faces and bodies of the people, and in my own face, trapped in the darkness which roared outside.

It was not to be believed and I kept telling myself that as I walked from the subway station to the high school. And at the same time I couldn't doubt it. I was scared, scared for Sonny. He became real to me again. A great block of ice got settled in my belly and kept melting there slowly all day long, while I taught my classes algebra. It was a special kind of ice. It kept melting, sending trickles of ice water all up and down my veins, but it never got less. Sometimes it hardened and seemed to expand until I felt my guts were going to come spilling out or that I was going to choke or scream. This would always be at a moment when I was remembering some specific thing Sonny had once said or done.

When he was about as old as the boys in my classes his face had been bright and open, there was a lot of copper in it; and he'd had wonderfully direct brown eyes, and great gentleness and privacy. I wondered what he looked like now. He had been picked up, the evening before, in a raid on an apartment downtown, for peddling and using heroin.

I couldn't believe it: but what I mean by that is that I couldn't find any room for it anywhere inside me. I had kept it outside me for a long time. I hadn't wanted to know. I had had suspicions, but I didn't name them, I kept putting them away. I told myself that Sonny was wild, but he wasn't crazy. And he'd always been a good boy, he hadn't ever turned hard or evil or disrespectful, the way kids can, so quick, so quick, especially in Harlem. I didn't want to believe that I'd ever see my brother going down, coming to nothing, all that light in his face gone out, in the condition I'd already seen so many others. Yet it had happened and here I was, talking about algebra to a lot of boys who might, every one of them for all I knew, be popping off needles every time they went to the head. Maybe it did more for them than algebra could.

I was sure that the first time Sonny had ever had horse, he couldn't have been much older than these boys were now. These boys, now, were living as we'd been living then, they were growing up with a rush and their heads bumped abruptly against the low ceiling of their actual possibilities. They were filled with rage. All they really knew were two darknesses, the darkness of their lives, which was now closing in on them, and the darkness of the movies, which had blinded them to that other darkness, and in which they now, vindictively, dreamed, at once more together than they were at any other time, and more alone.

When the last bell rang, the last class ended, I let out my breath. It seemed I'd been holding it for all that time. My clothes were wet—I may have looked as though I'd been sitting in a steam bath, all dressed up, all afternoon. I sat alone in the classroom a long time. I listened to the boys outside, downstairs, shouting and cursing and laughing. Their laughter struck me for perhaps the first time. It was not the joyous laughter which—God knows why—one associates with children. It was mocking and insular, its intent was to denigrate. It was disenchanted, and in this, also, lay the authority of their curses. Perhaps I was listening to them because I was thinking about my brother and in them I heard my brother. And myself.

One boy was whistling a tune, at once very complicated and very simple, it seemed to be pouring out of him as though he were a bird, and it sounded very cool and moving through all that harsh, bright air, only just holding its own through all those other sounds.

I stood up and walked over to the window and looked down into the courtyard. It was the beginning of the spring and the sap was rising in the boys. A teacher passed through them every now and again, quickly, as though he or she couldn't wait to get out of that courtyard, to get those boys out of their sight and off their minds. I started collecting my stuff. I thought I'd better get home and talk to Isabel.

The courtyard was almost deserted by the time I got downstairs. I saw this boy standing in the shadow of a doorway, looking just like Sonny. I almost called his name. Then I saw that it wasn't Sonny, but somebody we used to know, a boy from around our block. He'd been Sonny's friend. He'd never been mine, having been too young for me, and, anyway, I'd never liked him. And now, even though he was a grown-up man, he still hung around that block, still spent hours on the street corner, was always high and raggy. I used to run into him from time to time and he'd often work around to asking me for a quarter or fifty cents. He always had some real good excuse, too, and I always gave it to him, I don't know why.

But now, abruptly, I hated him. I couldn't stand the way he looked at me, partly like a dog, partly like a cunning child. I wanted to ask him what the hell he was doing in the school courtyard.

He sort of shuffled over to me, and he said, "I see you got the papers. So you already know about it."

"You mean about Sonny? Yes, I already know about it. How come they didn't get you?"

He grinned. It made him repulsive and it also brought to mind what he'd looked like as a kid. "I wasn't there. I stay away from them people."

"Good for you." I offered him a cigarette and I watched him through the smoke. "You come all the way down here just to tell me about Sonny?"

"That's right." He was sort of shaking his head and his eyes looked strange, as though they were about to cross. The bright sun deadened his damp dark brown skin and it made his eyes look yellow and showed up the dirt in his conked hair. He smelled funky. I moved a little away from him and I said, "Well, thanks. But I already know about it and I got to get home."

"I'll walk you a little ways," he said. We started walking. There were a couple of kids still loitering in the courtyard and one of them said good night to me and looked strangely at the boy beside me.

"What're you going to do?" he asked me. "I mean, about Sonny?"

"Look. I haven't seen Sonny for over a year, I'm not sure I'm going to do anything. Anyway, what the hell *can* I do?"

"That's right," he said quickly, "ain't nothing you can do. Can't much help old Sonny no more, I guess."

It was what I was thinking and so it seemed to me he had no right to say it.

"I'm surprised at Sonny, though," he went on—he had a funny way of talking, he looked straight ahead as though he were talking to himself—"I thought Sonny was a smart boy, I thought he was too smart to get hung."

"I guess he thought so too," I said sharply, "and that's how he got hung. And how about you? You're pretty goddamn smart, I bet."

Then he looked directly at me, just for a minute. "I ain't smart," he said. "If I was smart, I'd have reached for a pistol a long time ago."

"Look. Don't tell *me* your sad story, if it was up to me, I'd give you one." Then I felt guilty—guilty, probably, for never having supposed that the poor bastard *had* a story of his own, much less a sad one, and I asked, quickly, "What's going to happen to him now?"

He didn't answer this. He was off by himself some place. "Funny thing," he said, and from his tone we might have been discussing the quickest way to get to Brooklyn, "when I saw the papers this morning, the first thing I asked myself was if I had anything to do with it. I felt sort of responsible."

I began to listen more carefully. The subway station was on the corner, just before us, and I stopped. He stopped, too. We were in front of a bar and he ducked slightly, peering in, but whoever he was looking for didn't seem to be there. The juke box was blasting away with something black and bouncy and I half watched the barmaid as she danced her way from the juke box to her place behind the bar. And I watched her face as she laughingly responded to something someone said to her, still keeping time to the music. When she smiled one saw the little girl, one sensed the doomed, still-struggling woman beneath the battered face of the semi-whore.

"I never *give* Sonny nothing," the boy said finally, "but a long time ago I come to school high and Sonny asked me how it felt." He paused, I couldn't bear to watch him, I watched the barmaid, and I listened to the music which seemed to be causing the pavement to shake. "I told him it felt great." The music stopped, the barmaid paused and watched the juke box until the music began again. "It did."

All this was carrying me some place I didn't want to go. I certainly didn't want to know how it felt. It filled everything, the people, the houses, the music, the dark, quicksilver barmaid, with menace; and this menace was their reality.

"What's going to happen to him now?" I asked again.

"They'll send him away some place and they'll try to cure him." He shook his head. "Maybe he'll even think he's kicked the habit. Then they'll let him loose"—he gestured, throwing his cigarette into the gutter. "That's all."

"What do you mean, that's *all*?"

But I knew what he meant.

"I *mean*, that's all." He turned his head and looked at me, pulling down the corners of his mouth. "Don't you know what I mean?" he asked softly.

"How the hell *would* I know what you mean?" I almost whispered it, I don't know why.

"That's right," he said to the air, "how would *he* know what I mean?" He turned toward me again, patient and calm, and yet I somehow felt him shaking, shaking as though he were going to fall apart. I felt that ice in my guts again, the dread I'd felt all afternoon; and again I watched the barmaid, moving about the bar, washing glasses, and singing. "Listen. They'll let him out and then it'll just start all over again. That's what I mean."

"You mean—they'll let him out. And then he'll just start working his way back in again. You mean he'll never kick the habit. Is that what you mean?"

"That's right," he said, cheerfully. "*You* see what I mean."

"Tell me," I said at last, "why does he want to die? He must want to die, he's killing himself, why does he want to die?"

He looked at me in surprise. He licked his lips. "He don't want to die. He wants to live. Don't nobody want to die, ever."

Then I wanted to ask him—too many things. He could not have answered, or if he had, I could not have borne the answers. I started walking. "Well, I guess it's none of my business."

"It's going to be rough on old Sonny," he said. We reached the subway station. "This is your station?" he asked. I nodded. I took one step down. "Damn!" he said, suddenly. I looked up at him. He grinned again. "Damn if I didn't leave all my money home. You ain't got a dollar on you, have you? Just for a couple of days, is all."

All at once something inside gave and threatened to come pouring out of me. I didn't hate him any more. I felt that in another moment I'd start crying like a child.

"Sure," I said. "Don't sweat." I looked in my wallet and didn't have a dollar, I only had a five. "Here," I said. "That hold you?"

He didn't look at it—he didn't want to look at it. A terrible, closed look came over his face, as though he were keeping the number on the bill a secret from him and me. "Thanks," he said, and now he was dying to see me go. "Don't worry about Sonny. Maybe I'll write him or something."

"Sure," I said. "You do that. So long."

"Be seeing you," he said. I went on down the steps.

And I didn't write Sonny or send him anything for a long time. When I finally did, it was just after my little girl died, he wrote me back a letter which made me feel like a bastard.

Here's what he said:

DEAR BROTHER,

You don't know how much I needed to hear from you. I wanted to write you many a time but I dug how much I must have hurt you and so I didn't write. But now I feel like a man who's been trying to climb up out of some deep, real deep and funky hole and just saw the sun up there, outside. I got to get outside.

I can't tell you much about how I got here. I mean I don't know how to tell you. I guess I was afraid of something or I was trying to escape from something and you know I have never been very strong in the head (smile). I'm glad Mama and Daddy are dead and can't see what's happened to their son and I swear if I'd known what I was doing I would never have hurt you so, you and a lot of other fine people who were nice to me and who believed in me.

I don't want you to think it had anything to do with me being a musician. It's more than that. Or maybe less than that. I can't get anything straight in my head down here and I try not to think about what's going to happen to me when I get outside again. Sometime I think I'm going to flip and *never* get outside and sometime I think I'll come straight back. I tell you one thing, though, I'd rather blow my brains out than go through this again. But that's what they all say, so they tell me. If I tell you when I'm coming to New York and if you could meet me, I sure would appreciate it. Give my love to Isabel and the kids and I was sorry to hear about little Gracie. I wish I could be like Mama and say the Lord's will be done, but I don't know it seems to me that trouble is the one thing that never does get stopped and I don't know what good it does to blame it on the Lord. But maybe it does some good if you believe it.

Your brother,

SONNY

Then I kept in constant touch with him and I sent him whatever I could and I went to meet him when he came back to New York. When I saw him many things I thought I had forgotten came flooding back to me. This was because I had begun, finally, to wonder about Sonny, about the life that Sonny lived inside. This life, whatever it was, had made him older and thinner and it had deepened the distant stillness in which he had always moved. He looked very unlike my baby brother. Yet, when he smiled, when we shook hands, the baby brother I'd never known looked out from the depths of his private life, like an animal waiting to be coaxed into the light.

"How you been keeping?" he asked me.

"All right. And you?"

"Just fine." He was smiling all over his face. "It's good to see you again."

"It's good to see you."

The seven years' difference in our ages lay between us like a chasm: I wondered if these years would ever operate between us as a bridge. I was remembering, and it made it hard to catch my breath, that I had been there when he was born; and I had heard the first words he had ever spoken. When he started to walk, he walked from our mother straight to me. I caught him just before he fell when he took the first steps he ever took in this world.

"How's Isabel?"

"Just fine. She's dying to see you."

"And the boys?"

"They're fine, too. They're anxious to see their uncle."

"Oh, come on. You know they don't remember me."

"Are you kidding? Of course they remember you."

He grinned again. We got into a taxi. We had a lot to say to each other, far too much to know how to begin.

As the taxi began to move, I asked, "You still want to go to India?"

He laughed. "You still remember that. Hell, no. This place is Indian enough for me."

"It used to belong to them," I said.

And he laughed again. "They damn sure knew what they were doing when they got rid of it."

Years ago, when he was around fourteen, he'd been all hipped on the idea of going to India. He read books about people sitting on rocks, naked, in all kinds of weather, but mostly bad, naturally, and walking barefoot through hot coals and arriving at wisdom. I used to say that it sounded to me as though they were getting away from wisdom as fast as they could. I think he sort of looked down on me for that.

"Do you mind," he asked, "if we have the driver drive alongside the park? On the west side—I haven't seen the city in so long."

"Of course not," I said. I was afraid that I might sound as though I were humoring him, but I hoped he wouldn't take it that way.

So we drove along, between the green of the park and the stony, lifeless elegance of hotels and apartment buildings, toward the vivid, killing streets of our childhood. These streets hadn't changed, though housing projects jutted up out of them now like rocks in the middle of a boiling sea. Most of the houses in which we had grown up had vanished, as had the stores from which we had stolen, the basements in which we had first tried sex, the rooftops from which we had hurled tin cans and bricks. But houses exactly like the houses of our past yet dominated the landscape, boys exactly like the boys we once had been found themselves smothering in these houses, came down into the streets for light and air and found themselves encircled by disaster. Some escaped the trap, most didn't. Those who got out always left something of themselves behind, as some animals amputate a leg and leave it in the trap. It might be said, perhaps, that I had escaped, after all, I was a school teacher; or that Sonny had, he hadn't lived in Harlem for years. Yet, as the cab moved uptown through streets which seemed, with a rush, to darken with dark people, and as I covertly studied Sonny's face, it came to me that what we both were seeking through our separate cab windows was that part of ourselves which had been left behind. It's always at the hour of trouble and confrontation that the missing member aches.

We hit 110th Street and started rolling up Lenox Avenue. And I'd known this avenue all my life, but it seemed to me again, as it had seemed on the day I'd first heard about Sonny's trouble, filled with a hidden menace which was its very breath of life.

"We almost there," said Sonny.

"Almost." We were both too nervous to say anything more.

We live in a housing project. It hasn't been up long. A few days after it was up it seemed uninhabitably new, now, of course, it's already run-down. It looks like a parody of the good, clean, faceless life—God knows the people who live in it do their best to make it a parody. The beat-looking grass lying around isn't enough to make their lives green, the hedges will never hold out the streets, and they know it. The big windows fool no one, they aren't big enough to make space out of no space. They don't bother with the windows, they watch the TV screen instead. The playground is most popular with the children who don't play at jacks, or skip rope, or roller skate, or swing, and they can be found in it after dark. We moved in partly because it's not too far from where I teach, and partly for the kids; but it's really just like the houses in which Sonny and I grew up. The same things happen, they'll have the same things to remember. The moment Sonny and I started into the house I had the feeling that I was simply bringing him back into the danger he had almost died trying to escape.

Sonny has never been talkative. So I don't know why I was sure he'd be dying to talk to me when supper was over the first night. Everything went fine, the oldest boy remembered him, and the youngest boy liked him, and Sonny had remembered to bring something for each of them; and Isabel, who is really much nicer than I am, more open and giving, had gone to a lot of trouble about dinner and was genuinely glad to see him. And she's always been able to tease Sonny in a way that I haven't. It was nice to see her face so vivid again and to hear her laugh and watch her make Sonny laugh. She wasn't, or, anyway, she didn't seem to be, at all uneasy or embarrassed. She chatted as though there were no subject which had to be avoided and she got Sonny past his first, faint stiffness. And thank God she was there, for I was filled with that icy dread again. Everything I did seemed awkward to me, and everything I said sounded freighted with hidden meaning. I was trying to remember everything I'd heard about dope addiction and I couldn't help watching Sonny for signs. I wasn't doing it out of malice. I was trying to find out something about my brother. I was dying to hear him tell me he was safe.

"Safe!" my father grunted, whenever Mama suggested trying to move to a neighborhood which might be safer for children. "Safe, hell! Ain't no place safe for kids, nor nobody."

He always went on like this, but he wasn't, ever, really as bad as he sounded, not even on weekends, when he got drunk. As a matter of fact, he was always on the lookout for "something a little better," but he died before he found it. He died suddenly, during a drunken weekend in the middle of the war, when Sonny was fifteen. He and Sonny hadn't ever got on too well. And this was partly because Sonny was the apple of his father's eye. It was because he loved Sonny so much and was frightened for him, that he was always fighting with him. It doesn't do any good to fight with Sonny. Sonny just moves back, inside himself, where he can't be reached. But the principal reason that they never hit it off is that they were so much alike. Daddy was big and rough and loud-talking, just the opposite of Sonny, but they both had—that same privacy.

Mama tried to tell me something about this, just after Daddy died. I was home on leave from the army.

This was the last time I ever saw my mother alive. Just the same, this picture gets all mixed up in my mind with pictures I had of her when she was younger. The way I always see her is the way she used to be on a Sunday afternoon, say, when the old folks were talking after the big Sunday dinner. I always see her wearing pale blue. She'd be sitting on the sofa. And my father would be sitting in the easy chair, not far from her. And the living room would be full of church folks and relatives. There they sit, in chairs all around the living room, and the night is creeping up outside, but nobody knows it yet. You can see the darkness growing against the window-panes and you hear the street noises every now and again, or maybe the jangling beat of a tambourine from one of the churches close by, but it's real quiet in the room. For a moment nobody's talking, but every face looks darkening, like the sky outside. And my mother rocks a little from the waist, and my father's eyes are closed. Everyone is looking at something a child can't see. For a minute they've forgotten the children. Maybe a kid is lying on the rug half asleep. Maybe somebody's got a kid on his lap and is absent-mindedly stroking the kid's head. Maybe there's a kid, quiet and big-eyed, curled up in a big chair in the corner. The silence, the darkness coming, and the darkness in the faces frightens the child obscurely. He hopes that the hand which strokes his forehead will never stop—will never die. He hopes that there will never come a time when the old folks won't be sitting around the living room, talking about where they've come from, and what they've seen, and what's happened to them and their kinfolk.

But something deep and watchful in the child knows that this is bound to end, is already ending. In a moment someone will get up and turn on the light. Then the old folks will remember the children and they won't talk any more that day. And when light fills the room, the child is filled with darkness. He knows that every time this happens he's moved just a little closer to that darkness outside. The darkness outside is what the old folks have been talking about. It's what they've come from. It's what they endure. The child knows that they won't talk any more because if he knows too much about what's happened to *them,* he'll know too much too soon, about what's going to happen to *him.*

The last time I talked to my mother, I remember I was restless. I wanted to get out and see Isabel. We weren't married then and we had a lot to straighten out between us.

There Mama sat, in black, by the window. She was humming an old church song, *Lord, you brought me from a long ways off.* Sonny was out somewhere. Mama kept watching the streets.

"I don't know," she said, "if I'll ever see you again, after you go off from here. But I hope you'll remember the things I tried to teach you."

"Don't talk like that," I said, and smiled. "You'll be here a long time yet."

She smiled, too, but she said nothing. She was quiet for a long time. And I said, "Mama, don't you worry about nothing. I'll be writing all the time, and you be getting the checks. . . ."

"I want to talk to you about your brother," she said, suddenly. "If anything happens to me he ain't going to have nobody to look out for him."

"Mama," I said, "ain't nothing going to happen to you *or* Sonny. Sonny's all right. He's a good boy and he's got good sense."

"It ain't a question of his being a good boy," Mama said, "nor of his having good sense. It ain't only the bad ones, nor yet the dumb ones that gets sucked under." She stopped, looking at me. "Your Daddy once had a brother," she said, and she smiled in a way that made me feel she was in pain. "You didn't never know that, did you?"

"No," I said, "I never knew that," and I watched her face.

"Oh, yes," she said, "your Daddy had a brother." She looked out of the window again. "I know you never saw your Daddy cry. But *I* did—many a time, through all these years."

I asked her, "What happened to his brother? How come nobody's ever talked about him?"

This was the first time I ever saw my mother look old.

"His brother got killed," she said, "when he was just a little younger than you are now. I knew him. He was a fine boy. He was maybe a little full of the devil, but he didn't mean nobody no harm."

Then she stopped and the room was silent, exactly as it had sometimes been on those Sunday afternoons. Mama kept looking out into the streets.

"He used to have a job in the mill," she said, "and, like all young folks, he just liked to perform on Saturday nights. Saturday nights, him and your father would drift around to different places, go to dances and things like that, or just sit around with people they knew, and your father's brother would sing, he had a fine voice, and play along with himself on his guitar. Well, this particular Saturday night, him and your father was coming home from some place, and they were both a little drunk and there was a moon that night, it was bright like day. Your father's brother was feeling kind of good, and he was whistling to himself, and he had his guitar slung over his shoulder. They was coming down a hill and beneath them was a road that turned off from the highway. Well, your father's brother, being always kind of frisky, decided to run down this hill, and he did, with that guitar banging and clanging behind him, and he ran across the road, and he was making water behind a tree. And your father was sort of amused at him and he was still coming down the hill, kind of slow. Then he heard a car motor and that same minute his brother stepped from behind the tree, into the road, in the moon-light. And he started to cross the road. And your father started to run down the hill, he says he don't know why. This car was full of white men. They was all drunk, and when they seen your father's brother they let out a great whoop and holler and they aimed the car straight at him. They was having fun, they just wanted to scare him, the way they do sometimes, you know. But they was drunk. And I guess the boy, being drunk, too, and scared, kind of lost his head. By the time he jumped it was too late. Your father says he heard his brother scream when the car rolled over him, and he heard the wood of that guitar when it give, and he heard them strings go flying, and he heard them white men shouting, and the car kept on a-going and it ain't stopped till this day. And, time your father got down the hill, his brother weren't nothing but blood and pulp."

Tears were gleaming on my mother's face. There wasn't anything I could say.

"He never mentioned it," she said, "because I never let him mention it before you children. Your Daddy was like a crazy man that night and for many a night thereafter. He says he never in his life seen anything as dark as that road after the lights of that car had gone away. Weren't nothing, weren't nobody on that road, just your Daddy and his brother and that busted guitar. Oh, yes. Your Daddy never did really get right again. Till the day he died he weren't sure but that every white man he saw was the man that killed his brother."

She stopped and took out her handkerchief and dried her eyes and looked at me.

"I ain't telling you all this," she said, "to make you scared or bitter or to make you hate nobody. I'm telling you this because you got a brother. And the world ain't changed."

I guess I didn't want to believe this. I guess she saw this in my face. She turned away from me, toward the window again, searching those streets.

"But I praise my Redeemer," she said at last, "that He called your Daddy home before me. I ain't saying it to throw no flowers at myself, but, I declare, it keeps me from feeling too cast down to know I helped your father get safely through this world. Your father always acted like he was the roughest, strongest man on earth. And everybody took him to be like that. But if he hadn't had *me* there—to see his tears!"

She was crying again. Still, I couldn't move. I said, "Lord, Lord, Mama, I didn't know it was like that."

"Oh, honey," she said, "there's a lot that you don't know. But you are going to find it out." She stood up from the window and came over to me. "You got to hold on to your brother," she said, "and don't let him fall, no matter what it looks like is happening to him and no matter how evil you gets with him. You going to be evil with him many a time. But don't you forget what I told you, you hear?"

"I won't forget," I said. "Don't you worry, I won't forget. I won't let nothing happen to Sonny."

My mother smiled as though she were amused at something she saw in my face. Then, "You may not be able to stop nothing from happening. But you got to let him know you's *there.*"

Two days later I was married, and then I was gone. And I had a lot of things on my mind and I pretty well forgot my promise to Mama until I got shipped home on a special furlough for her funeral.

And, after the funeral, with just Sonny and me alone in the empty kitchen, I tried to find out something about him.

"What do you want to do?" I asked him.

"I'm going to be a musician," he said.

For he had graduated, in the time I had been away, from dancing to the juke box to finding out who was playing what, and what they were doing with it, and he had bought himself a set of drums.

"You mean, you want to be a drummer?" I somehow had the feeling that being a drummer might be all right for other people but not for my brother Sonny.

"I don't think," he said, looking at me very gravely, "that I'll ever be a good drummer. But I think I can play a piano."

I frowned. I'd never played the role of the older brother quite so seriously before, had scarcely ever, in fact, *asked* Sonny a damn thing. I sensed myself in the presence of something I didn't really know how to handle, didn't understand. So I made my frown a little deeper as I asked: "What kind of musician do you want to be?"

He grinned. "How many kinds do you think there are?"

"Be *serious*," I said.

He laughed, throwing his head back, and then looked at me. "I *am* serious."

"Well, then, for Christ's sake, stop kidding around and answer a serious question. I mean, do you want to be a concert pianist, you want to play classical music and all that, or—or what?" Long before I finished he was laughing again. "For Christ's *sake*, Sonny!"

He sobered, but with difficulty. "I'm sorry. But you sound so— *scared!*" and he was off again.

"Well, you may think it's funny now, baby, but it's not going to be so funny when you have to make your living at it, let me tell you *that.*" I was furious because I knew he was laughing at me and I didn't know why.

"No," he said, very sober now, and afraid, perhaps, that he'd hurt me, "I don't want to be a classical pianist. That isn't what interests me. I mean"—he paused, looking hard at me, as though his eyes would help me to understand, and then gestured helplessly, as though perhaps his hand would help—"I mean, I'll have a lot of studying to do, and I'll have to study *everything*, but I mean, I want to play *with*—jazz musicians." He stopped. "I want to play jazz," he said.

Well, the word had never before sounded as heavy, as real, as it sounded that afternoon in Sonny's mouth. I just looked at him and I was probably frowning a real frown by this time. I simply couldn't see why on earth he'd want to spend his time hanging around night clubs, clowning around on bandstands, while people pushed each other around a dance floor. It seemed—beneath him, somehow. I had never thought about it before, had never been forced to, but I suppose I had always put jazz musicians in a class with what Daddy called "good-time people."

"Are you *serious?*"

"Hell, *yes*, I'm serious."

He looked more helpless than ever, and annoyed, and deeply hurt.

I suggested, helpfully: "You mean—like Louis Armstrong?"

His face closed as though I'd struck him. "No. I'm not talking about none of that old-time, down home crap."

"Well, look, Sonny, I'm sorry, don't get mad. I just don't altogether get it, that's all. Name somebody—you know, a jazz musician you admire."

"Bird."

"Who?"

"Bird! Charlie Parker! Don't they teach you nothing in the goddamn army?"

I lit a cigarette. I was surprised and then a little amused to discover that I was trembling. "I've been out of touch," I said, "You'll have to be patient with me. Now. Who's this Parker character?"

"He's just one of the greatest jazz musicians alive," said Sonny, sullenly, his hands in his pockets, his back to me. "Maybe *the* greatest," he added, bitterly, "that's probably why *you* never heard of him."

"All right," I said, "I'm ignorant. I'm sorry. I'll go out and buy all the cat's records right away, all right?"

"It don't," said Sonny, with dignity, "make any difference to me. I don't care what you listen to. Don't do me no favors."

I was beginning to realize that I'd never seen him so upset before. With another part of my mind I was thinking that this would probably turn out to be one of those things kids go through and that I shouldn't make it seem important by pushing it too hard. Still, I didn't think it would do any harm to ask: "Doesn't all this take a lot of time? Can you make a living at it?"

He turned back to me and half leaned, half sat, on the kitchen table. "Everything takes time," he said, "and—well, yes, sure, I can make a living at it. But what I don't seem to be able to make you understand is that it's the only thing I want to do."

"Well Sonny," I said, gently, "you know people can't always do exactly what they *want* to do—"

"*No*, I don't know that," said Sonny, surprising me. "I think people *ought* to do what they want to do, what else are they alive for?"

"You getting to be a big boy," I said desperately, "it's time you started thinking about your future."

"I'm thinking about my future," said Sonny, grimly. "I think about it all the time."

I gave up. I decided, if he didn't change his mind, that we could always talk about it later. "In the meantime," I said, "you got to finish school." We had already decided that he'd have to move in with Isabel and her folks. I knew this wasn't the ideal arrangement because Isabel's folks are inclined to be dicty and they hadn't especially wanted Isabel to marry me. But I didn't know what else to do. "And we have to get you fixed up at Isabel's."

There was a long silence. He moved from the kitchen table to the window. "That's a terrible idea. You know it yourself."

"Do you have a *better* idea?"

He just walked up and down the kitchen for a minute. He was as tall as I was. He had started to shave. I suddenly had the feeling that I didn't know him at all.

He stopped at the kitchen table and picked up my cigarettes. Looking at me with a kind of mocking, amused defiance, he put one between his lips. "You mind?"

"You smoking already?"

He lit the cigarette and nodded, watching me through the smoke. "I just wanted to see if I'd have the courage to smoke in front of you." He grinned and blew a great cloud of smoke to the ceiling. "It was easy." He looked at my face. "Come on, now. I bet you was smoking at my age, tell the truth."

I didn't say anything but the truth was on my face, and he laughed. But now there was something very strained in his laugh. "Sure. And I bet that ain't all you was doing."

He was frightening me a little. "Cut the crap," I said. "We already decided that you was going to go and live at Isabel's. Now what's got into you all of a sudden?"

"*You* decided it," he pointed out. "*I* didn't decide nothing." He stopped in front of me, leaning against the stove, arms loosely folded. "Look, brother. I don't want to stay in Harlem no more, I really don't." He was very earnest. He looked at me, then over toward the kitchen window. There was something in his eyes I'd never seen before, some thoughtfulness, some worry all his own. He rubbed the muscle of one arm. "It's time I was getting out of here."

"Where do you want to *go,* Sonny?"

"I want to join the army. Or the navy, I don't care. If I say I'm old enough they'll believe me."

Then I got mad. It was because I was so scared. "You must be crazy. You goddamn fool, what the hell do you want to go and join the *army* for?"

"I just told you. To get out of Harlem."

"Sonny, you haven't even finished *school.* And if you really want to be a musician, how do you expect to study if you're in the *army?*"

He looked at me, trapped, and in anguish. "There's ways. I might be able to work out some kind of deal. Anyway, I'll have the G.I. Bill when I come out."

"*If* you come out." We stared at each other. "Sonny, please. Be reasonable. I know the setup is far from perfect. But we got to do the best we can."

"I ain't learning nothing in school," he said. "Even when I go." He turned away from me and opened the window and threw his cigarette out into the narrow alley. I watched his back. "At least, I ain't learning nothing you'd want me to learn." He slammed the window so hard I thought the glass would fly out, and turned back to me. "And I'm sick of the stink of these garbage cans!"

"Sonny," I said, "I know how you feel. But if you don't finish school now, you're going to be sorry later that you didn't." I grabbed him by the shoulders. "And you only got another year. It ain't so bad. And I'll come back and I swear I'll help you do *whatever* you want to do. Just try to put up with it till I come back. Will you please do that? For me?"

He didn't answer and he wouldn't look at me.

"Sonny. You hear me?"

He pulled away. "I hear you. But you never hear anything *I* say."

I didn't know what to say to that. He looked out of the window and then back at me. "OK," he said, and sighed. "I'll try."

Then I said, trying to cheer him up a little, "They got a piano at Isabel's. You can practice on it."

And as a matter of fact, it did cheer him up for a minute. "That's right," he said to himself. "I forgot that." His face relaxed a little. But the worry, the thoughtfulness, played on it still, the way shadows play on a face which is staring into the fire.

But I thought I'd never hear the end of that piano. At first, Isabel would write me, saying how nice it was that Sonny was so serious about his music and how, as soon as he came in from school, or wherever he had been when he was supposed to be at school, he went straight to that piano and stayed there until suppertime. And, after supper, he went back to that piano and stayed there until everybody went to bed. He was at the piano all day Saturday and all day Sunday. Then he bought a record player and started playing records. He'd play one record over and over again, all day long sometimes, and he'd improvise along with it on the piano. Or he'd play one section of the record, one chord, one change, one progression, then he'd do it on the piano. Then back to the record. Then back to the piano.

Well, I really don't know how they stood it. Isabel finally confessed that it wasn't like living with a person at all, it was like living with sound. And the sound didn't make any sense to her, didn't make any sense to any of them—naturally. They began, in a way, to be afflicted by this presence that was living in their home. It was as though Sonny were some sort of god, or monster. He moved in an atmosphere which wasn't like theirs at all. They fed him and he ate, he washed himself, he walked in and out of their door; he certainly wasn't nasty or unpleasant or rude, Sonny isn't any of those things; but it was as though he were all wrapped up in some cloud, some fire, some vision all his own; and there wasn't any way to reach him.

At the same time, he wasn't really a man yet, he was still a child, and they had to watch out for him in all kinds of ways. They certainly couldn't throw him out. Neither did they dare to make a great scene about that piano because even they dimly sensed, as I sensed, from so many thousands of miles away, that Sonny was at that piano playing for his life.

But he hadn't been going to school. One day a letter came from the school board and Isabel's mother got it—there had, apparently, been other letters but Sonny had torn them up. This day, when Sonny came in, Isabel's mother showed him the letter and asked where he'd been spending his time. And she finally got it out of him that he'd been down in Greenwich Village, with musicians and other characters, in a white girl's apartment. And this scared her and she started to scream at him and what came up, once she began—though she denies it to this day—was what sacrifices they were making to give Sonny a decent home and how little he appreciated it.

Sonny didn't play the piano that day. By evening, Isabel's mother had calmed down but then there was the old man to deal with, and Isabel herself. Isabel says she did her best to be calm but she broke down and started crying. She says she just watched Sonny's face. She could tell, by watching him, what was happening with him. And what was happening was that they penetrated his cloud, they had reached him. Even if their fingers had been a thousand times more gentle than human fingers ever are, he could hardly help feeling that they had stripped him naked and were spitting on that nakedness. For he also had to see that his presence, that music, which was life or death to him, had been torture for them and that they had endured it, not at all for his sake, but only for mine. And Sonny couldn't take that. He can take it a little better today than he could then but he's still not very good at it and, frankly, I don't know anybody who is.

The silence of the next few days must have been louder than the sound of all the music ever played since time began. One morning, before she went to work, Isabel was in his room for something and she suddenly realized that all of his records were gone. And she knew for certain that he was gone. And he was. He went as far as the navy would carry him. He finally sent me a postcard from some place in Greece and that was the first I knew that Sonny was still alive. I didn't see him any more until we were both back in New York and the war had long been over.

He was a man by then, of course, but I wasn't willing to see it. He came by the house from time to time, but we fought almost every time we met. I didn't like the way he carried himself, loose and dreamlike all the time, and I didn't like his friends, and his music seemed to be merely an excuse for the life he led. It sounded just that weird and disordered.

Then we had a fight, a pretty awful fight, and I didn't see him for months. By and by I looked him up, where he was living, in a furnished room in the Village, and I tried to make it up. But there were lots of other people in the room and Sonny just lay on his bed, and he wouldn't come downstairs with me, and he treated these other people as though they were his family and I weren't. So I got mad and then he got mad, and then I told him that he might just as well be dead as live the way he was living. Then he stood up and he told me not to worry about him any more in life, that he *was* dead as far as I was concerned. Then he pushed me to the door and the other people looked on as though nothing were happening, and he slammed the door behind me. I stood in the hallway, staring at the door. I heard somebody laugh in the room and then the tears came to my eyes. I started down the steps, whistling to keep from crying, I kept whistling to myself, *You going to need me, baby, one of these cold, rainy days.*

I read about Sonny's trouble in the spring. Little Grace died in the fall. She was a beautiful little girl. But she only lived a little over two years. She died of polio and she suffered. She had a slight fever for a couple of days, but it didn't seem like anything and we just kept her in bed. And we would certainly have called the doctor, but the fever dropped, she seemed to be all right. So we thought it had just been a cold. Then, one day, she was up, playing, Isabel was in the kitchen fixing lunch for the two boys when they'd come in from school, and she heard Grace fall down in the living room. When you have a lot of children you don't always start running when one of them falls, unless they start screaming or something. And, this time, Grace was quiet. Yet, Isabel says that when she heard that *thump* and then that silence, something happened in her to make her afraid. And she ran to the living room and there was little Grace on the floor, all twisted up and the reason she hadn't screamed was that she couldn't get her breath. And when she did scream, it was the worst sound, Isabel says, that she'd ever heard in all her life, and she still hears it sometimes in her dreams. Isabel will sometimes wake me up with a low, moaning, strangled sound and I have to be quick to awaken her and hold her to me and where Isabel is weeping against me seems a mortal wound.

I think I may have written Sonny the very day that little Grace was buried. I was sitting in the living room in the dark, by myself, and I suddenly thought of Sonny. My trouble made his real.

One Saturday afternoon, when Sonny had been living with us, or, anyway, been in our house, for nearly two weeks, I found myself wandering aimlessly about the living room, drinking from a can of beer, and trying to work up the courage to search Sonny's room. He was out, he was usually out whenever I was home, and Isabel had taken the children to see their grandparents. Suddenly I was standing still in front of the living room window, watching Seventh Avenue. The idea of searching Sonny's room made me still. I scarcely dared to admit to myself what I'd be searching for. I didn't know what I'd do if I found it. Or if I didn't.

On the sidewalk across from me, near the entrance to a barbecue joint, some people were holding an old-fashioned revival meeting. The barbecue cook, wearing a dirty white apron, his conked hair reddish and metallic in the pale sun, and a cigarette between his lips, stood in the doorway, watching them. Kids and older people paused in their errands and stood there, along with some older men and a couple of very tough-looking women who watched everything that happened on the avenue, as though they owned it, or were maybe owned by it. Well, they were watching this, too. The revival was being carried on by three sisters in black, and a brother. All they had were their voices and their Bibles and a tambourine. The brother was testifying and while he testified two of the sisters stood together, seeming to say, Amen, and the third sister walked around with the tambourine outstretched and a couple of people dropped coins into it. Then the brother's testimony ended and the sister who had been taking up the collection dumped the coins into her palm and transferred them to the pocket of her long black robe. Then she raised both hands, striking the tambourine against the air, and then against one hand, and she started to sing. And the two other sisters and the brother joined in.

It was strange, suddenly, to watch, though I had been seeing these street meetings all my life. So, of course, had everybody else down there. Yet, they paused and watched and listened and I stood still at the window. *"Tis the old ship of Zion,"* they sang, and the sister with the tambourine kept a steady, jangling beat, *"It has rescued many a thousand!"* Not a soul under the sound of their voices was hearing this song for the first time, not one of them had been rescued. Nor had they seen much in the way of rescue work being done around them. Neither did they especially believe in the holiness of the three sisters and the brother, they knew too much about them, knew where they lived, and how. The woman with the tambourine, whose voice dominated the air, whose face was bright with joy, was divided by very little from the woman who stood watching her, a cigarette between her heavy, chapped lips, her hair a cuckoo's nest, her face scarred and swollen from many beatings, and her black eyes glittering like coal. Perhaps they both knew this, which was why, when, as rarely, they addressed each other, they addressed each other as Sister. As the singing filled the air the watching, listening faces underwent a change, the eyes focusing on something within; the music seemed to soothe a poison out of them; and time seemed, nearly, to fall away from the sullen, belligerent, battered faces, as though they were fleeing back to their first condition, while dreaming of their last. The barbecue cook half shook his head and smiled, and dropped his cigarette and disappeared into his joint. A man fumbled in his pockets for change and stood holding it in his hand impatiently, as though he had just remembered a pressing appointment further up the avenue. He looked furious. Then I saw Sonny, standing on the edge of the crowd. He was carrying a wide, flat notebook with a green cover, and it made him look, from where I was standing, almost like a schoolboy. The coppery sun brought out the copper in his skin, he was very faintly smiling, standing very still. Then the singing stopped, the tambourine turned into a collection plate again. The furious man dropped in his coins and vanished, so did a couple of the women, and Sonny dropped some change in the plate, looking directly at the woman with a little smile. He started across the avenue, toward the house. He has a slow, loping walk, something like the way Harlem hipsters walk, only he's imposed on this his own halfbeat. I had never really noticed it before.

I stayed at the window, both relieved and apprehensive. As Sonny disappeared from my sight, they began singing again. And they were still singing when his key turned in the lock.

"IIey," he said.

"Hey, yourself. You want some beer?"

"No. Well, maybe." But he came up to the window and stood beside me, looking out. "What a warm voice," he said.

They were singing *If I could only hear my mother pray again!*

"Yes," I said, "and she can sure beat that tambourine."

"But what a terrible song," he said, and laughed. He dropped his notebook on the sofa and disappeared into the kitchen. "Where's Isabel and the kids?"

"I think they went to see their grandparents. You hungry?"

"No." He came back into the living room with his can of beer. "You want to come some place with me tonight?"

I sensed, I don't know how, that I couldn't possibly say No. "Sure. Where?"

He sat down on the sofa and picked up his notebook and started leafing through it. "I'm going to sit in with some fellows in a joint in the Village."

"You mean, you're going to play, tonight?"

"That's right." He took a swallow of his beer and moved back to the window. He gave me a sidelong look. "If you can stand it."

"I'll try," I said.

He smiled to himself and we both watched as the meeting across the way broke up. The three sisters and the brother, heads bowed, were singing *God be with you till we meet again*. The faces around them were very quiet. Then the song ended. The small crowd dispersed. We watched the three women and the lone man walk slowly up the avenue.

"When she was singing before," said Sonny, abruptly, "her voice reminded me for a minute of what heroin feels like sometimes—when it's in your veins. It makes you feel sort of warm and cool at the same time. And distant. And—and sure." He sipped his beer, very deliberately not looking at me. I watched his face. "It makes you feel—in control. Sometimes you've got to have that feeling."

"Do you?" I sat down slowly in the easy chair.

"Sometimes." He went to the sofa and picked up his notebook again. "Some people do."

"In order," I asked, "to play?" And my voice was very ugly, full of contempt and anger.

"Well"—he looked at me with great, troubled eyes, as though, in fact, he hoped his eyes would tell me things he could never otherwise say—"they *think* so. And *if* they think so—!"

"And what do *you* think?" I asked.

He sat on the sofa and put his can of beer on the floor. "I don't know," he said, and I couldn't be sure if he were answering my question or pursuing his thoughts. His face didn't tell me. "It's not so much to *play*. It's to *stand* it, to be able to make it at all. On any level." He frowned and smiled: "In order to keep from shaking to pieces."

"But these friends of yours," I said, "they seem to shake themselves to pieces pretty goddamn fast."

"Maybe." He played with the notebook. And something told me that I should curb my tongue, that Sonny was doing his best to talk, that I should listen. "But of course you only know the ones that've gone to pieces. Some don't—or at least they haven't *yet* and that's just about all *any* of us can say." He paused. "And then there are some who just live, really, in hell, and they know it and they see what's happening and they go right on. I don't know." He sighed, dropped the notebook, folded his arms. "Some guys, you can tell from the way they play, they on something *all* the time. And you can see that, well, it makes something real for them. But of course," he picked up his beer from the floor and sipped it and put the can down again, "they *want* to, too, you've got to see that. Even some of them that say they don't—*some,* not all."

"And what about you?" I asked—I couldn't help it. "What about you? Do *you* want to?"

He stood up and walked to the window and remained silent for a long time. Then he sighed. "Me," he said. Then: "While I was downstairs before, on my way here, listening to that woman sing, it struck me all of a sudden how much suffering she must have had to go through—to sing like that. It's *repulsive* to think you have to suffer that much."

I said: "But there's no way not to suffer—is there, Sonny?"

"I believe not," he said, and smiled, "but that's never stopped anyone from trying." He looked at me. "Has it?" I realized, with this mocking look, that there stood between us, forever, beyond the power of time or forgiveness, the fact that I had held silence—so long!—when he had needed human speech to help him. He turned back to the window. "No, there's no way not to suffer. But you try all kinds of ways to keep from drowning in it, to keep on top of it, and to make it seem—well, like *you*. Like you did something, all right, and now you're suffering for it. You know?" I said nothing. "Well you know," he said, impatiently, "why *do* people suffer? Maybe it's better to do something to give it a reason, *any* reason."

"But we just agreed," I said, "that there's no way not to suffer. Isn't it better, then, just to—take it?"

"But nobody just takes it," Sonny cried, "that's what I'm telling you! *Everybody* tries not to. You're just hung up on the *way* some people try—it's not *your* way!"

The hair on my face began to itch, my face felt wet. "That's not true," I said, "that's not true. I don't give a damn what other people do, I don't even care how they suffer. I just care how *you* suffer." And he looked at me. "Please believe me," I said, "I don't want to see you—die—trying not to suffer."

"I won't," he said, flatly, "die trying not to suffer. At least, not any faster than anybody else."

"But there's no need," I said, trying to laugh, "is there? in killing yourself."

I wanted to say more, but I couldn't. I wanted to talk about will power and how life could be—well, beautiful. I wanted to say that it was all within; but was it? or, rather, wasn't that exactly the trouble? And I wanted to promise that I would never fail him again. But it would all have sounded—empty words and lies.

So I made the promise to myself and prayed that I would keep it.

"It's terrible sometimes, inside," he said, "that's what's the trouble. You walk these streets, black and funky and cold, and there's not really a living ass to talk to, and there's nothing shaking, and there's no way of getting it out—that storm inside. You can't talk it and you can't make love with it, and when you finally try to get with it and play it, you realize *nobody's* listening. So *you've* got to listen. You got to find a way to listen."

And then he walked away from the window and sat on the sofa again, as though all the wind had suddenly been knocked out of him.

"Sometimes you'll do *anything* to play, even cut your mother's throat." He laughed and looked at me. "Or your brother's." Then he sobered. "Or your own." Then: "Don't worry. I'm all right now and I think I'll *be* all right. But I can't forget—where I've been. I don't mean just the physical place I've been, I mean where I've *been*. And *what* I've been."

"What have you been, Sonny?" I asked.

He smiled—but sat sideways on the sofa, his elbow resting on the back, his fingers playing with his mouth and chin, not looking at me. "I've been something I didn't recognize, didn't know I could be. Didn't know anybody could be." He stopped, looking inward, looking helplessly young, looking old. "I'm not talking about it now because I feel *guilty* or anything like that—maybe it would be better if I did, I don't know. Anyway, I can't really talk about it. Not to you, not to anybody," and now he turned and faced me. "Sometimes, you know, and it was actually when I was most *out* of the world, I felt that I was in it, and that I was *with* it, really, and I could play or I didn't really have to *play*, it just came out of me, it was there. And I don't know how I played, thinking about it now, but I know I did awful things, those times, sometimes, to people. Or it wasn't that I *did* anything to them—it was that they weren't real." He picked up the beer can; it was empty; he rolled it between his palms: "And other times—well, I needed a fix, I needed to find a place to lean, I needed to clear a space to *listen*—and I couldn't find it, and I—went crazy, I did terrible things to *me*, I was terrible *for* me." He began pressing the beer can between his hands, I watched the metal begin to give. It glittered, as he played with it, like a knife, and I was afraid he would cut himself, but I said nothing. "Oh well. I can never tell you. I was all by myself at the bottom of something, stinking and sweating and crying and shaking, and I smelled it, you know? *my* stink, and I thought I'd die if I couldn't get away from it and yet, all the same, I knew that everything I was doing was just locking me in with it. And I didn't know," he paused, still flattening the beer can, "I didn't know, I still *don't* know, something kept telling me that maybe it was good to smell your own stink, but I didn't think that *that* was what I'd been trying to do—and—who can stand it?" and he abruptly dropped the ruined beer can, looking at me with a small, still smile, and then rose, walking to the window as though it were the lodestone rock. I watched his face, he watched the avenue. "I couldn't tell you when Mama died—but the reason I wanted to leave Harlem so bad was to get away from drugs. And then, when I ran away, that's what I was running from—really. When I came back, nothing had changed, *I* hadn't changed, I was just—older." And he stopped, drumming with his fingers on the windowpane. The sun had vanished, soon darkness would fall. I watched his face. "It can come again," he said, almost as though speaking to himself. Then he turned to me. "It can come again," he repeated. "I just want you to know that."

"All right," I said, at last. "So it can come again. All right."

He smiled, but the smile was sorrowful. "I had to try to tell you," he said.

"Yes," I said. "I understand that."

"You're my brother," he said, looking straight at me, and not smiling at all.

"Yes," I repeated, "yes. I understand that."

He turned back to the window, looking out. "All that hatred down there," he said, "all that hatred and misery and love. It's a wonder it doesn't blow the avenue apart."

We went to the only night club on a short, dark street, downtown. We squeezed through the narrow, chattering, jam-packed bar to the entrance of the big room, where the bandstand was. And we stood there for a moment, for the lights were very dim in this room and we couldn't see. Then, "Hello, boy," said a voice and an enormous black man, much older than Sonny or myself, erupted out of all that atmospheric lighting and put an arm around Sonny's shoulder. "I been sitting right here," he said, "waiting for you."

He had a big voice, too, and heads in the darkness turned toward us.

Sonny grinned and pulled a little away, and said, "Creole, this is my brother. I told you about him."

Creole shook my hand. "I'm glad to meet you, son," he said, and it was clear that he was glad to meet me *there*, for Sonny's sake. And he smiled, "You got a real musician in *your* family," and he took his arm from Sonny's shoulder and slapped him, lightly, affectionately, with the back of his hand.

"Well. Now I've heard it all," said a voice behind us. This was another musician, and a friend of Sonny's, a coal-black, cheerful-looking man, built close to the ground. He immediately began confiding to me, at the top of his lungs, the most terrible things about Sonny, his teeth gleaming like a lighthouse and his laugh coming up out of him like the beginning of an earthquake. And it turned out that everyone at the bar knew Sonny, or almost everyone; some were musicians, working there, or nearby, or not working, some were simply hangers-on, and some were there to hear Sonny play. I was introduced to all of them and they were all very polite to me. Yet, it was clear that, for them, I was only Sonny's brother. Here, I was in Sonny's world. Or, rather: his kingdom. Here, it was not even a question that his veins bore royal blood.

They were going to play soon and Creole installed me, by myself, at a table in a dark corner. Then I watched them, Creole, and the little black man, and Sonny, and the others, while they horsed around, standing just below the bandstand. The light from the bandstand spilled just a little short of them and, watching them laughing and gesturing and moving about, I had the feeling that they, nevertheless, were being most careful not to step into that circle of light too suddenly: that if they moved into the light too suddenly, without thinking, they would perish in flame. Then, while I watched, one of them, the small, black man, moved into the light and crossed the bandstand and started fooling around with his drums. Then— being funny and being, also, extremely ceremonious—Creole took Sonny by the arm and led him to the piano. A woman's voice called Sonny's name and a few hands started clapping. And Sonny, also being funny and being ceremonious, and so touched, I think, that he could have cried, but neither hiding it nor showing it, riding it like a man, grinned, and put both hands to his heart and bowed from the waist.

Creole then went to the bass fiddle and a lean, very bright-skinned brown man jumped up on the bandstand and picked up his horn. So there they were, and the atmosphere on the bandstand and in the room began to change and tighten. Someone stepped up to the microphone and announced them. Then there were all kinds of murmurs. Some people at the bar shushed others. The waitress ran around, frantically getting in the last orders, guys and chicks got closer to each other, and the lights on the bandstand, on the quartet, turned to a kind of indigo. Then they all looked different there. Creole looked about him for the last time, as though he were making certain that all his chickens were in the coop, and then he—jumped and struck the fiddle. And there they were.

All I know about music is that not many people ever really hear it. And even then, on the rare occasions when something opens within, and the music enters, what we mainly hear, or hear corroborated, are personal private, vanishing evocations. But the man who creates the music is hearing something else, is dealing with the roar rising from the void and imposing order on it as it hits the air. What is evoked in him, then, is of another order, more terrible because it has no words, and triumphant, too, for that same reason. And his triumph, when he triumphs, is ours. I just watched Sonny's face. His face was troubled, he was working hard, but he wasn't with it. And I had the feeling that, in a way, everyone on the bandstand was waiting for him, both waiting for him and pushing him along. But as I began to watch Creole, I realized that it was Creole who held them all back. He had them on a short rein. Up there, keeping the beat with his whole body, wailing on the fiddle, with his eyes half closed, he was listening to everything, but he was listening to Sonny. He was having a dialogue with Sonny. He wanted Sonny to leave the shore line and strike out for the deep water. He was Sonny's witness that deep water and drowning were not the same thing—he had been there, and he knew. And he wanted Sonny to know. He was waiting for Sonny to do the things on the keys which would let Creole know that Sonny was in the water.

And, while Creole listened, Sonny moved, deep within, exactly like someone in torment. I had never before thought of how awful the relationship must be between the musician and his instrument. He has to fill it, this instrument, with the breath of life, his own. He has to make it do what he wants it to do. And a piano is just a piano. It's made out of so much wood and wires and little hammers and big ones, and ivory. While there's only so much you can do with it, the only way to find this out is to try and make it do everything.

And Sonny hadn't been near a piano for over a year. And he wasn't on much better terms with his life, not the life that stretched before him now. He and the piano stammered, started one way, got scared, stopped; started another way, panicked, marked time, started again; then seemed to have found a direction, panicked again, got stuck. And the face I saw on Sonny I'd never seen before. Everything had been burned out of it, and, at the same time, things usually hidden were being burned in, by the fire and fury of the battle which was occurring in him up there.

Yet, watching Creole's face as they neared the end of the first set, I had the feeling that something had happened, something I hadn't heard. Then they finished, there was scattered applause, and then, without an instant's warning, Creole started into something else, it was almost sardonic, it was *Am I Blue*. And, as though he commanded, Sonny began to play. Something began to happen. And Creole let out the reins. The dry, low, black man said something awful on the drums, Creole answered, and the drums talked back. Then the horn insisted, sweet and high, slightly detached perhaps, and Creole listened, commenting now and then, dry, and driving, beautiful and calm and old. Then they all came together again, and Sonny was part of the family again. I could tell this from his face. He seemed to have found, right there beneath his fingers, a damn brand-new piano. It seemed that he couldn't get over it. Then, for awhile, just being happy with Sonny, they seemed to be agreeing with him that brand-new pianos certainly were a gas.

Then Creole stepped forward to remind them that what they were playing was the blues. He hit something in all of them, he hit something in me, myself, and the music tightened and deepened, apprehension began to beat the air. Creole began to tell us what the blues were all about. They were not about anything very new. He and his boys up there were keeping it new, at the risk of ruin, destruction, madness, and death, in order to find new ways to make us listen. For, while the tale of how we suffer, and how we are delighted, and how we may triumph is never new, it always must be heard. There isn't any other tale to tell, it's the only light we've got in all this darkness.

And this tale, according to that face, that body, those strong hands on those strings, has another aspect in every country, and a new depth in every generation. Listen, Creole seemed to be saying, listen. Now these are Sonny's blues. He made the little black man on the drums know it, and the bright, brown man on the horn. Creole wasn't trying any longer to get Sonny in the water. He was wishing him Godspeed. Then he stepped back, very slowly, filling the air with the immense suggestion that Sonny speak for himself.

Then they all gathered around Sonny and Sonny played. Every now and again one of them seemed to say, Amen. Sonny's fingers filled the air with life, his life. But that life contained so many others. And Sonny went all the way back, he really began with the spare, flat statement of the opening phrase of the song. Then he began to make it his. It was very beautiful because it wasn't hurried and it was no longer a lament. I seemed to hear with what burning he had made it his, with what burning we had yet to make it ours, how we could cease lamenting. Freedom lurked around us and I understood, at last, that he could help us to be free if we would listen, that he would never be free until we did. Yet, there was no battle in his face now. I heard what he had gone through, and would continue to go through until he came to rest in earth. He had made it his: that long line, of which we knew only Mama and Daddy. And he was giving it back, as everything must be given back, so that, passing through death, it can live forever. I saw my mother's face again, and felt, for the first time, how the stones of the road she had walked on must have bruised her feet. I saw the moonlit road where my father's brother died. And it brought something else back to me, and carried me past it, I saw my little girl again and felt Isabel's tears again, and I felt my own tears begin to rise. And I was yet aware that this was only a moment, that the world waited outside, as hungry as a tiger, and that trouble stretched above us, longer than the sky.

Then it was over. Creole and Sonny let out their breath, both soaking wet, and grinning. There was a lot of applause and some of it was real. In the dark, the girl came by and I asked her to take drinks to the bandstand. There was a long pause, while they talked up there in the indigo light and after awhile I saw the girl put a Scotch and milk on top of the piano for Sonny. He didn't seem to notice it, but just before they started playing again, he sipped from it and looked toward me, and nodded. Then he put it back on top of the piano. For me, then, as they began to play again, it glowed and shook above my brother's head like the very cup of trembling.

QUESTIONS FOR THINKING AND WRITING

1. Explore the use of music as a metaphor in "Sonny's Blues." How many types of music do you find in the story? What meanings does the narrator give them?

2. The narrator says that he and Sonny, riding through the streets of New York, "both were seeking through our separate cab windows . . . that part of ourselves which had been left behind. It's always at the hour of trouble and confrontation that the missing member aches." What has been amputated? For each of these characters, write a stream-of-consciousness monologue in which you describe or narrate what they are seeing and thinking as they look out their separate windows.

3. "He wanted Sonny to leave the shore line and strike out for the deep water. He was Sonny's witness that deep water and drowning were not the same thing—he had been there, and he knew." Discuss this metaphor. Notice the word *witness*. It could come from legal terminology, but in this story it has a different connotation. Discuss.

AN ANTHOLOGY OF SHORT STORIES

EDGAR ALLAN POE (1809–1849)

The Purloined Letter

Nil sapientae odiosius acumine nimio.
                           —Seneca[1]

At Paris, just after dark one gusty evening in the autumn of 18—, I was enjoying the twofold luxury of meditation and a meerschaum, in company with my friend C. Auguste Dupin, in his little back library, or book-closet, *au troisième, No. 33, Rue Donôt, Faubourg St. Germain.*[2] For one hour at least we had maintained a profound silence; while each, to any casual observer, might have seemed intently and exclusively occupied with the curling eddies of smoke that oppressed the atmosphere of the chamber. For myself, however, I was mentally discussing certain topics which had formed matter for conversation between us at an earlier period of the evening; I mean the affair of the Rue Morgue, and the mystery attending the murder of Marie Rogêt.[3] I looked upon it, therefore, as something of a coincidence, when the door of our apartment was thrown open and admitted our old acquaintance, Monsieur G——, the Prefect of the Parisian police.

We gave him a hearty welcome; for there was nearly half as much of the entertaining as of the contemptible about the man, and we had not seen him for several years. We had been sitting in the dark, and Dupin now arose for the purpose of lighting a lamp, but sat down again, without doing so, upon G.'s saying that he had called to consult us, or rather to ask the opinion of my friend, about some official business which had occasioned a great deal of trouble.

"If it is any point requiring reflection," observed Dupin, as he forbore to enkindle the wick, "we shall examine it to better purpose in the dark."

"That is another of your odd notions," said the Prefect, who had a fashion of calling every thing "odd" that was beyond his comprehension, and thus lived amid an absolute legion of "oddities."

---

[1] "Nothing is more distasteful to good sense than too much cunning"; Lucius Annaeus Seneca (4 B.C.–65 A.D.), Roman poet and philosopher.

[2] Fashionable quarter of Paris. The "troisième" is literally the third floor, but is equivalent to the fourth floor in North America.

[3] "The Mystery of Marie Rogêt" and "The Murders in the Rue Morgue" are titles of earlier Dupin tales by Poe.

"Very true," said Dupin, as he supplied his visitor with a pipe, and rolled towards him a comfortable chair.

"And what is the difficulty now?" I asked. "Nothing more in the assassination way, I hope?"

"Oh no; nothing of that nature. The fact is, the business is *very* simple indeed, and I make no doubt that we can manage it sufficiently well ourselves; but then I thought Dupin would like to hear the details of it, because it is so excessively *odd*."

"Simple and odd," said Dupin.

"Why, yes; and not exactly that either. The fact is, we have all been a good deal puzzled because the affair *is* so simple, and yet baffles us altogether."

"Perhaps it is the very simplicity of the thing which puts you at fault," said my friend.

"What nonsense you *do* talk!" replied the Prefect, laughing heartily.

"Perhaps the mystery is a little *too* plain," said Dupin.

"Oh, good heavens! who ever heard of such an idea?"

"A little *too* self-evident."

"Ha! ha! ha!—ha! ha! ha!—ho! ho! ho!"—roared our visitor, profoundly amused, "oh, Dupin, you will be the death of me yet!"

"And what, after all, *is* the matter on hand?" I asked.

"Why, I will tell you," replied the Prefect, as he gave a long, steady, and contemplative puff, and settled himself in his chair. "I will tell you in a few words; but, before I begin, let me caution you that this is an affair demanding the greatest secrecy, and that I should most probably lose the position I now hold, were it known that I confided it to any one."

"Proceed," said I.

"Or not," said Dupin.

"Well, then; I have received personal information, from a very high quarter, that a certain document of the last importance has been purloined from the royal apartments. The individual who purloined it is known; this beyond a doubt; he was seen to take it. It is known, also, that it still remains in his possession."

"How is this known?" asked Dupin.

"It is clearly inferred," replied the Prefect, "from the nature of the document, and from the non-appearance of certain results which would at once arise from its passing *out* of the robber's possession;—that is to say, from his employing it as he must design in the end to employ it."

"Be a little more explicit," I said.

"Well, I may venture so far as to say that the paper gives its holder a certain power in a certain quarter where such power is immensely valuable." The Prefect was fond of the cant of diplomacy.

"Still I do not quite understand," said Dupin.

"No? Well; the disclosure of the document to a third person, who shall be nameless, would bring in question the honour of a personage of most exalted station; and this fact gives the holder of the document an ascendancy over the illustrious personage whose honour and peace are so jeopardized."

"But this ascendancy," I interposed, "would depend upon the robber's knowledge of the loser's knowledge of the robber. Who would dare—"

"The thief," said G., "is the Minister D——, who dares all things, those unbecoming as well as those becoming a man. The method of the theft was not less ingenious than bold. The document in question—a letter, to be frank—had been received by the personage robbed while alone in the royal *boudoir*. During its perusal she was suddenly interrupted by the entrance of the other exalted personage from whom especially it was her wish to conceal it. After a hurried and vain endeavour to thrust it in a drawer, she was forced to place it, open it was, upon a table. The address, however, was uppermost, and, the contents thus unexposed, the letter escaped notice. At this juncture enters the Minister D——. His lynx eye immediately perceives the paper, recognizes the handwriting of the address, observes the confusion of the personage addressed, and fathoms her secret. After some business transactions, hurried through in his ordinary manner, he produces a letter somewhat similar to the one in question, opens it, pretends to read it, and then places it in close juxtaposition to the other. Again he converses, for some fifteen minutes, upon the public affairs. At length, in taking leave, he takes also from the table the letter to which he had no claim. Its rightful owner saw, but, of course, dared not call attention to the act, in the presence of the third personage who stood at her elbow. The minister decamped; leaving his own letter—one of no importance—upon the table."

"Here, then," said Dupin to me, "you have precisely what you demand to make the ascendancy complete—the robber's knowledge of the loser's knowledge of the robber."

"Yes," replied the Prefect; "and the power thus attained has, for some months past, been wielded, for political purposes, to a very dangerous extent. The personage robbed is more thoroughly convinced, every day, of the necessity of reclaiming her letter. But this, of course, cannot be done openly. In fine, driven to despair, she has committed the matter to me."

"Than whom," said Dupin, amid a perfect whirlwind of smoke, "no more sagacious agent could, I suppose, be desired, or even imagined."

"You flatter me," replied the Prefect; "but it is possible that some such opinion may have been entertained."

"It is clear," said I, "as you observe, that the letter is still in the possession of the minister; since it is this possession, and not any employment of the letter, which bestows the power. With the employment the power departs."

"True," said G.; "and upon this conviction I proceeded. My first care was to make thorough search of the minister's hotel;[4] and here my chief embarrassment lay in the necessity of searching without his knowledge. Beyond all things, I have been warned of the danger which would result from giving him reason to suspect our design."

"But," said I, "you are quite *au fait*[5] in these investigations. The Parisian police have done this thing often before."

"O yes; and for this reason I did not despair. The habits of the minister gave me, too, a great advantage. He is frequently absent from home all night. His servants are by no means numerous. They sleep at a distance from their master's apartment, and being chiefly Neapolitans, are readily made drunk. I have keys, as you know, with which I can open any chamber or cabinet in Paris. For three months a night has not passed, during the greater part of which I have not been engaged, personally, in ransacking the D———— Hôtel. My honour is interested, and, to mention a great secret, the reward is enormous. So I did not abandon the search until I had become fully satisfied that the thief is a more astute man than myself. I fancy that I have investigated every nook and corner of the premises in which it is possible that the paper can be concealed."

"But is it not possible," I suggested, "that although the letter may be in the possession of the minister, as it unquestionably is, he may have concealed it elsewhere than upon his own premises?"

"This is barely possible," said Dupin. "The present peculiar condition of affairs at court, and especially of those intrigues in which D———— is known to be involved, would render the instant availability of the document—its susceptibility of being produced at a moment's notice—a point of nearly equal importance with its possession."

"Its susceptibility of being produced?" said I.

"That is to say, of being *destroyed*," said Dupin.

"True," I observed; "the paper is clearly then upon the premises. As for its being upon the person of the minister, we may consider that as out of the question."

"Entirely," said the Prefect. "He had been twice waylaid, as if by footpads, and his person rigorously searched under my own inspection."

"You might have spared yourself this trouble," said Dupin. "D————, I presume, is not altogether a fool, and, if not, must have anticipated these waylayings, as a matter of course."

"Not *altogether* a fool," said G., "but then he is a poet, which I take to be only one remove from a fool."

---

[4] *hotel,* town house.

[5] *au fait,* adept.

"True," said Dupin, after a long and thoughtful whiff from his meerschaum, "although I have been guilty of certain doggerel myself."

"Suppose you detail," said I, "the particulars of your search."

"Why the fact is, we took our time, and we searched *every where*. I have had long experience in these affairs. I took the entire building, room by room; devoting the nights of a whole week to each. We examined, first, the furniture of each apartment. We opened every possible drawer; and I presume you know that, to a properly trained police agent, such a thing as a *secret* drawer is impossible. Any man is a dolt who permits a 'secret' drawer to escape him in a search of this kind. The thing is *so* plain. There is a certain amount of bulk—of space—to be accounted for in every cabinet. Then we have accurate rules.[6] The fiftieth part of a line could not escape us. After the cabinets we took the chairs. The cushions we probed with the fine long needles you have seen me employ. From the tables we removed the tops."

"Why so?"

"Sometimes the top of a table, or other similarly arranged piece of furniture, is removed by the person wishing to conceal an article; then the leg is excavated, the article deposited within the cavity, and the top replaced. The bottoms and tops of bedposts are employed in the same way."

"But could not the cavity be detected by sounding?" I asked.

"By no means, if, when the article is deposited, a sufficient wadding of cotton be placed around it. Besides, in our case, we were obliged to proceed without noise."

"But you could not have removed—you could not have taken to pieces *all* articles of furniture in which it would have been possible to make a deposit in the manner you mention. A letter may be compressed into a thin spiral roll, not differing much in shape or bulk from a large knitting-needle, and in this form it might be inserted into the rung of a chair, for example. You did not take to pieces all the chairs?"

"Certainly not; but we did better—we examined the rungs of every chair in the hotel, and indeed the jointings of every description of furniture, by the aid of a most powerful microscope.[7] Had there been any traces of recent disturbance we should not have failed to detect it instantly. A single grain of gimlet-dust, for example, would have been as obvious as an apple. Any disorder in the glueing—any unusual gaping in the joints—would have sufficed to insure detection."

"I presume you looked to the mirrors, between the boards and the plates, and you probed the beds and the bed-clothes, as well as the curtains and carpets."

---

[6] *rules*, rulers.
[7] *microscope*, magnifying glass.

"That of course; and when we had absolutely completed every particle of the furniture in this way, then we examined the house itself. We divided its entire surface into compartments, which we numbered, so that none might be missed; then we scrutinized each individual square inch throughout the premises, including the two houses immediately adjoining, with the microscope as before."

"The two houses adjoining!" I exclaimed; "you must have had a great deal of trouble."

"We had; but the reward offered is prodigious."

"You include the *grounds* about the houses?"

"All the grounds are paved with brick. They gave us comparatively little trouble. We examined the moss between the bricks, and found it undisturbed."

"You looked among D———'s papers, of course, and into the books of the library?"

"Certainly; we opened every package and parcel; we not only opened every book, but we turned over every leaf in each volume, not contenting ourselves with a mere shake, according to the fashion of some of our police officers. We also measured the thickness of every book-*cover*, with the most accurate admeasurement, and applied to each the most jealous scrutiny of the microscope. Had any of the bindings been recently meddled with, it would have been utterly impossible that the fact should have escaped observation. Some five or six volumes, just from the hands of the binder, we carefully probed, longitudinally, with the needles."

"You explored the floors beneath the carpets?"

"Beyond doubt. We removed every carpet, and examined the boards with the microscope."

"And the paper on the walls?"

"Yes."

"You looked into the cellars?"

"We did."

"Then," I said, "you have been making a miscalculation, and the letter is *not* upon the premises as you suppose."

"I fear you are right there," said the Prefect. "And now, Dupin, what would you advise me to do?"

"To make a thorough re-search of the premises."

"That is absolutely needless," replied G———. "I am not more sure that I breathe than I am that the letter is not at the Hôtel."

"I have no better advice to give you," said Dupin. "You have, of course, an accurate description of the letter?"

"Oh, yes!"—And here the Prefect, producing a memorandum-book, proceeded to read aloud a minute account of the internal, and especially of the external, appearance of the missing document. Soon after finishing the perusal of this description, he took his departure, more entirely depressed in spirits than I had ever known the good gentleman before.

In about a month afterward he paid us another visit, and found us occupied very nearly as before. He took a pipe and a chair and entered into some ordinary conversation. At length I said;—

"Well, but G———, what of the purloined letter? I presume you have at last made up your mind that there is no such thing as overreaching the Minister?"

"Confound him, say I—yes; I made the re-examination, however, as Dupin suggested—but it was all labour lost, as I knew it would be."

"How much was the reward offered, did you say?" asked Dupin.

"Why, a very great deal—a *very* liberal reward—I don't like to say how much, precisely; but one thing I *will* say, that I wouldn't mind giving my individual check for fifty thousand francs to any one who could obtain me that letter. The fact is, it is becoming of more and more importance every day; and the reward has been lately doubled. If it were trebled, however, I could do no more than I have done."

"Why, yes," said Dupin, drawlingly, between the whiffs of his meerschaum, "I really—think, G———, you have not exerted yourself—to the utmost in this matter. You might—do a little more, I think, eh?"

"How?—in what way?"

"Why—puff, puff,—you might—puff, puff—employ counsel in the matter, eh?—puff, puff, puff. Do you remember the story they tell of Abernethy?"

"No; hang Abernethy!"

"To be sure! hang him and welcome. But, once upon a time, a certain rich miser conceived the design of spunging upon this Abernethy for a medical opinion. Getting up, for this purpose, an ordinary conversation in a private company, he insinuated his case to the physician, as that of an imaginary individual.

" 'We will suppose,' said the miser, 'that his symptoms are such and such; now, doctor, what would *you* have directed him to take?'"

" 'Take!' said Abernethy, 'why, take *advice,* to be sure.' "

"But," said the Prefect, a little discomposed, "I am *perfectly* willing to take advice, and to pay for it. I would *really* give fifty thousand francs to any one who would aid me in the matter."

"In that case," replied Dupin, opening a drawer, and producing a check-book, "you may as well fill me up a check for the amount you mentioned. When you have signed it, I will hand you the letter."

I was astounded. The Prefect appeared absolutely thunderstricken. For some minutes he remained speechless and motionless, looking incredulously at my friend with open mouth, and eyes that seemed starting from their sockets; then, apparently recovering himself in some measure, he seized a pen, and after several pauses and vacant stares, finally filled up and signed a check for fifty thousand francs, and handed it across the table to Dupin. The latter examined it carefully and deposited it in his pocket-book; then, unlocking an *escritoire*,[8] took thence a letter and gave it to the Prefect. This functionary grasped it in a perfect agony of joy, opened it with a trembling hand, cast a rapid glance at its contents, and then, scrambling and struggling to the door, rushed at length unceremoniously from the room and from the house, without having uttered a syllable since Dupin had requested him to fill up the check.

When he had gone, my friend entered into some explanations.

"The Parisian police," he said, "are exceedingly able in their way. They are persevering, ingenious, cunning, and thoroughly versed in the knowledge which their duties seem chiefly to demand. Thus, when G—— detailed to us his mode of searching the premises at the Hôtel D——, I felt entire confidence in his having made a satisfactory investigation—so far as his labours extended."

"So far as his labours extended?" said I.

"Yes," said Dupin. "The measures adopted were not only the best of their kind, but carried out to absolute perfection. Had the letter been deposited within the range of their search, these fellows would, beyond a question, have found it."

I merely laughed—but he seemed quite serious in all that he said.

"The measures, then," he continued, "were good in their kind, and well executed; their defect lay in their being inapplicable to the case, and to the man. A certain set of highly ingenious resources are, with the Prefect, a sort of Procrustean bed,[9] to which he forcibly adapts his designs. But he perpetually errs by being too deep or too shallow, for the matter in hand; and many a schoolboy is a better reasoner than he. I knew one about eight years of age, whose success at guessing in the game of 'even and odd' attracted universal admiration. This game is simple, and is played with marbles. One player holds in his hand a number of these toys, and demands of another whether that number is even or odd. If the guess is right, the guesser wins one; if wrong, he loses one. The boy to whom I allude won all the marbles of the school. Of course he had some principle of guessing; and this lay in mere observation and admeasurement of the astuteness of his opponents. For example, an arrant simpleton is his opponent, and, holding up his closed hand, asks: 'Are they even or odd?' Our schoolboy replies, 'Odd,' and loses; but upon the second trial he wins, for he then says to himself, 'The simpleton had them even upon the first trial, and his amount of

---

[8] *escritoire,* a writing table.
[9] In Greek mythology the giant Procrustes tied travelers to an iron bed and made them fit it by either stretching or amputating their limbs.

cunning is just sufficient to make him have them odd upon the second; I will therefore guess odd;'—he guesses odd, and wins. Now, with a simpleton a degree above the first, he would have reasoned thus: 'This fellow finds that in the first instance I guessed odd, and, in the second, he will propose to himself upon the first impulse, a simple variation from even to odd, as did the first simpleton; but then a second thought will suggest that this is too simple a variation, and finally he will decide upon putting it even as before. I will therefore guess even';—he guesses even, and wins. Now this mode of reasoning in the schoolboy, whom his fellows termed 'lucky,'—what, in its last analysis, is it?"

"It is merely," I said, "an identification of the reasoner's intellect with that of his opponent."

"It is," said Dupin; "and, upon inquiring of the boy by what means he effected the *thorough* identification in which his success consisted, I received answer as follows: 'When I wish to find out how wise, or how stupid, or how good, or how wicked is any one, or what are his thoughts at the moment, I fashion the expression on my face, as accurately as possible, in accordance with the expression of his, and then wait to see what thoughts or sentiments arise in my mind or heart, as if to match or correspond with the expression.' This response of the schoolboy lies at the bottom of all the spurious profundity which has been attributed to Rochefoucault, to La Bougive, to Machiavelli, and to Campanella."[10]

"And the identification," I said, "of the reasoner's intellect with that of his opponent, depends, if I understand you aright, upon the accuracy with which the opponent's intellect is admeasured."

"For its practical value it depends upon this," replied Dupin; "and the Prefect and his cohort fail so frequently, first, by default of this identification, and secondly, by ill-admeasurement, or rather through non-admeasurement, of the intellect with which they are engaged. They consider only their *own* ideas of ingenuity; and, in searching for anything hidden, advert only to the modes in which *they* would have hidden it. They are right in this much—that their own ingenuity is a faithful representative of that of *the mass;* but when the cunning of the individual felon is diverse in character from their own, the felon foils them, of course. This always happens when it is above their own, and very usually when it is below. They have no variation of principle in their investigations; at best, when urged by some unusual emergency—by some extraordinary reward—they extend or exaggerate their old modes of *practice,* without touching their principles. What, for example, in this case of D———, has been done to vary the principle of action? What is all this

---

[10] François, Duc de la Rochefoucauld (1613–1680), French moralist and courtier; La Bougive is probably Jean de la Bruyere (1645–1696); Niccolò Machiavelli (1469–1527), Italian statesman and writer; Tommaso Campanella (1568–1639), Italian philosopher and Dominican monk.

boring, and probing, and sounding, and scrutinizing with the microscope, and dividing the surface of the building into registered square
inches—what is it all but an exaggeration *of the application* of one principle or set of principles of search, which are based upon the one set of
notions regarding human ingenuity, to which the Prefect, in the long
routine of his duty, has been accustomed? Do you not see he has taken it
for granted that *all* men proceed to conceal a letter,—not exactly in a
gimlet-hole bored in a chair-leg—but, at least, in *some* out-of-the-way
hole or corner suggested by the same tenor or thought which would
urge a man to secrete a letter in a gimlet-hole bored in a chair-leg? And
do you not see also, that such *recherchés*[11] nooks for concealment are
adapted only for ordinary occasions, and would be adopted only by
ordinary intellects; for, in all cases of concealment, a disposal of the
article concealed—a disposal of it in this *recherché* manner—is, in the
very first instance, presumable and presumed; and thus its discovery
depends, not at all upon the acumen, but altogether upon the mere
care, patience, and determination of the seekers; and where the case is
of importance—or, what amounts to the same thing in the political eyes,
when the reward is of magnitude,—the qualities in question have *never*
been known to fail. You will now understand what I meant in suggesting
that, had the purloined letter been hidden anywhere within the limits of
the Prefect's examination—in other words, had the principle of its concealment been comprehended within the principles of the Prefect—its
discovery would have been a matter altogether beyond question. This
functionary, however, has been thoroughly mystified; and the remote
source of his defeat lies in the supposition that the Minister is a fool,
because he has acquired renown as a poet. All fools are poets; this the
Prefect *feels;* and he is merely guilty of a *non distributio medii*[12] in thence
inferring that all poets are fools.

"But is this really the poet?" I asked. "There are two brothers, I know;
and both have attained reputation in letters. The Minister I believe has
written learnedly on the Differential Calculus. He is a mathematician,
and no poet."

"You are mistaken; I know him well: he is both. As poet *and* mathematician, he would reason well; as mere mathematician, he could not
have reasoned at all, and thus would have been at the mercy of the
Prefect."

"You surprise me," I said, "by these opinions, which have been con-
tradicted by the voice of the world. You do not mean to set at naught the
well-digested idea of centuries. The mathematical reason has long been
regarded as *the* reason *par excellence.*"

---

[11] *recherchés,* excessively cunning.
[12] *non distributio medii,* the undistributed middle, an error in logic.

" '*Il y a à parier,*' " replied Dupin, quoting from Chamfort, " '*que toute idée publique, toute convention reçue, est une sottise, car elle a convenu au plus grand nombre.*'[13] The mathematicians, I grant you, have done their best to promulgate the popular error to which you allude, and which is none the less an error for its promulgation as truth. With an art worthy a better cause, for example, they have insinuated the term 'analysis' into application to algebra. The French are the originators of this particular deception; but if a term is of any importance—if words derive any value from applicability—then 'analysis' conveys 'algebra' about as much as, in Latin, '*ambitus*' implies 'ambition,' '*religio*' 'religion,' or '*homines honesti,*' a set of *honourable* men."

"You have a quarrel on hand, I see," said I, "with some of the algebraists of Paris; but proceed."

"I dispute the availability, and thus the value, of that reason which is cultivated in any especial form other than the abstractly logical. I dispute, in particular, the reason educed by mathematical study. The mathematics are the science of form and quantity; mathematical reasoning is merely logic applied to observation upon form and quantity. The great error lies in supposing that even the truths of what is called *pure* algebra, are abstract or general truths. And this error is so egregious that I am confounded at the universality with which it has been received. Mathematical axioms are *not* axioms of general truth. What is true of *relation*—of form and quantity—is often grossly false in regard to morals, for example. In this latter science it is very usually *un*true that the aggregated parts are equal to the whole. In chemistry also the axiom fails. In the consideration of motive it fails; for two motives, each of a given value, have not, necessarily, a value when united, equal to the sum of their values apart. There are numerous other mathematical truths which are only truths within the limits of *relation*. But the mathematician argues from his *finite truths*, through habit, as if they were of an absolutely general applicability—as the world indeed imagines them to be. Bryant, in his very learned 'Mythology,'[14] mentions an analogous source of error, when he says that 'although the Pagan fables are not believed, yet we forget ourselves continually, and make inferences from them as existing realities.' With the algebraists, however, how are Pagans themselves, the 'Pagan fables' *are* believed, and the inferences are made, not so much through lapse of memory as through an unaccountable addling of the brains. In short, I never yet encountered the mere mathematician who could be trusted out of equal roots, or one who did not clandes-

---

[13] "The odds are that every popular idea, every accepted convention is nonsense, because it has suited itself to the majority"; from *Maximes et Pensées* by Sébastian Chamfort (1741–1794).

[14] *A New System, or an Analysis of Antient Mythology*, by Jacob Bryant (1715–1804), an English scholar.

tinely hold it as a point of his faith that $x^2 + px$ was absolutely and unconditionally equal to q. Say to one of these gentlemen, by way of experiment, if you please, that you believe occasions may occur where $x^2 + px$ is *not* altogether equal to q, and having made him understand what you mean, get out of his reach as speedily as convenient, for, beyond doubt, he will endeavour to knock you down.

"I mean to say," continued Dupin, while I merely laughed at his last observations, "that if the Minister had been no more than a mathematician, the Prefect would have been under no necessity of giving me this check. I knew him, however, as both mathematician and poet, and my measures were adapted to his capacity, with reference to the circumstances by which he was surrounded. I knew him as a courtier, too, and as a bold *intriguant*.[15] Such a man, I considered, could not fail to be aware of the ordinary political modes of action. He could not have failed to anticipate—and events have proved that he did not fail to anticipate—the waylayings to which he was subjected. He must have foreseen, I reflected, the secret investigations of his premises. His frequent absences from home at night, which were hailed by the Prefect as certain aids to his success, I regarded only as *ruses*, to afford opportunity for thorough search to the police, and thus the sooner to impress them with the conviction to which G———, in fact, did finally arrive—the conviction that the letter was not upon the premises. I felt, also, that the whole train of thought, which I was at some pains in detailing to you just now, concerning the invariable principle of political action in searches for articles concealed—I felt that this whole train of thought would necessarily pass through the mind of the Minister. It would imperatively lead him to despise all the ordinary *nooks* of concealment. *He* could not, I reflected, be so weak as not to see that the most intricate and remote recess of his hotel would be as open as his commonest closets to the eyes, to the probes, to the gimlets, and to the microscopes of the Prefect. I saw, in fine, that he would be driven, as a matter of course, to simplicity, if not deliberately induced to it as a matter of choice. You will remember, perhaps, how desperately the Prefect laughed when I suggested, upon our first interview, that it was just possible this mystery troubled him so much on account of its being so *very* self-evident."

"Yes," said I, "I remember his merriment well. I really thought he would have fallen into convulsions."

"The material world," continued Dupin, "abounds with very strict analogies to the immaterial; and thus some color of truth has been given to the rhetorical dogma, that metaphor, or simile, may be made to strengthen an argument as well as to embellish a description. The principle of the *vis inertiae*,[16] for example, seems to be identical in physics

---

[15] *intriguant*, intriguer.
[16] *vis inertiae*, the power of inertia.

and metaphysics. It is not more true in the former, that a large body is with more difficulty set in motion than a smaller one, and that its subsequent *momentum* is commensurate with this difficulty, than it is, in the latter, that intellects of the vaster capacity, while more forcible, more constant, and more eventful in their movements than those of inferior grade, are yet the less readily moved, and more embarrassed and full of hesitation in the first few steps of their progress. Again: have you ever noticed which of the street signs, over the shop doors, are the most attractive of attention?"

"I have never given the matter a thought," I said.

"There is a game of puzzles," he resumed, "which is played upon a map. One party playing requires another to find a given word—the name of town, river, state, or empire—any word, in short, upon the motley and perplexed surface of the chart. A novice in the game generally seeks to embarrass his opponents by giving them the most minutely lettered names; but the adept selects such words as stretch, in large characters, from one end of the chart to the other. These, like the over-largely lettered signs and placards of the street, escape observation by the dint of being excessively obvious; and here the physical oversight is precisely analogous with the moral inapprehension by which the intellect suffers to pass unnoticed those considerations which are too obtrusively and too palpably self-evident. But this is a point, it appears, somewhat above or beneath the understanding of the Prefect. He never once thought it probable, or possible, that the Minister had deposited the letter immediately beneath the nose of the whole world, by way of best preventing any portion of that world from perceiving it.

"But the more I reflected upon the daring, dashing, and discriminating ingenuity of D———; upon the fact that the document must always have been *at hand,* if he intended to use it to good purpose; and upon the decisive evidence, obtained by the Prefect, that it was not hidden within the limits of that dignitary's ordinary search—the more satisfied I became that, to conceal this letter, The Minister had resorted to the comprehensive and sagacious expedient of not attempting to conceal it at all.

"Full of these ideas, I prepared myself with a pair of green spectacles, and called one fine morning, quite by accident, at the Ministerial hotel. I found D——— at home, yawning, lounging, and dawdling, as usual, and pretending to be in the last extremity of *ennui.* He is, perhaps, the most really energetic human being now alive—but that is only when nobody sees him.

"To be even with him, I complained of my weak eyes, and lamented the necessity of the spectacles, under cover of which I cautiously and thoroughly surveyed the whole apartment, while seemingly intent only upon the conversation of my host.

"I paid especial attention to a large writing-table near which he sat, and upon which lay confusedly, some miscellaneous letters and other papers, with one or two musical instruments and a few books. Here, however, after a long and very deliberate scrutiny, I saw nothing to excite particular suspicion.

"At length my eyes, in going the circuit of the room, fell upon a trumpery filigree card-rack of pasteboard, that hung dangling by a dirty blue ribbon, from a little brass knob just beneath the middle of the mantel-piece. In this rack, which had three or four compartments, were five or six visiting cards and a solitary letter. This last was much soiled and crumpled. It was torn nearly in two, across the middle—as if a design, in the first instance, to tear it entirely up as worthless, had been altered, or stayed, in the second. It had a large black seal, bearing the D——— cipher *very* conspicuously, and was addressed, in a diminutive female hand, to D———, the minister, himself. It was thrust carelessly, and even, as it seemed, contemptuously, into one of the upper divisions of the rack.

"No sooner had I glanced at this letter than I concluded it to be that of which I was in search. To be sure, it was, to all appearance, radically different from the one of which the Prefect had read us so minute a description. Here the seal was large and black, with the D——— cipher; there it was small and red, with the ducal arms of the S——— family. Here, the address, to the Minister, was diminutive and feminine; there the superscription, to a certain royal personage, was markedly bold and decided; the size alone formed a point of correspondence. But, then, the *radicalness* of these differences, which was excessive; the dirt; the soiled and torn condition of the paper, so inconsistent with the *true* methodical habits of D———, and so suggestive of a design to delude the beholder into an idea of the worthlessness of the document; these things, together with the hyperobtrusive situation of this document, full in the view of every visitor, and thus exactly in accordance with the conclusions to which I had previously arrived; these things, I say, were strongly corroborative of suspicion, in one who came with the intention to suspect.

"I protracted my visit as long as possible, and, while I maintained a most animated discussion with the Minister, upon a topic which I knew well had never failed to interest and excite him, I kept my attention really riveted upon the letter. In this examination, I committed to memory its external appearance and arrangement in the rack; and also fell, at length, upon a discovery which set at rest whatever trivial doubt I might have entertained. In scrutinizing the edges of the paper, I observed them to be more *chafed* than seemed necessary. They presented the *broken* appearance which is manifested when a stiff paper, having been once folded and pressed with a folder, is refolded in a reversed direction, in the same creases or edges which had formed the original fold. This discovery was sufficient. It was clear to me that the letter had been turned, as a glove, inside out, re-directed, and re-sealed. I bade the Minister good morning, and took my departure at once, leaving a gold snuff-box upon the table.

"The next morning I called for the snuff-box, when we resumed, quite eagerly, the conversation of the preceding day. While thus engaged, however, a loud report, as if of a pistol, was heard immediately beneath the windows of the hotel, and was succeeded by a series of fearful screams, and the shoutings of a mob. D——— rushed to a casement, threw it open, and looked out. In the meantime I stepped to the card-rack, took the letter, put it in my pocket, and replaced it by a *facsimile*, (so far as regards externals) which I had carefully prepared at my lodgings; imitating the D——— cipher, very readily, by means of a seal formed of bread.

"The disturbance in the street had been occasioned by the frantic behaviour of a man with a musket. He had fired it among a crowd of women and children. It proved, however, to have been without ball, and the fellow was suffered to go his way as a lunatic or a drunkard. When he had gone, D——— came from the window, whither I had followed him immediately upon securing the object in view. Soon afterward I bade him farewell. The pretended lunatic was a man in my own pay."

"But what purpose had you," I asked, "in replacing the letter by a *facsimile*? Would it not have been better, at the first visit, to have seized it openly, and departed?"

"D———," replied Dupin, "is a desperate man, and a man of nerve. His hotel, too, is not without attendants devoted to his interests. Had I made the wild attempt you suggest, I might never have left the Ministerial presence alive. The good people of Paris might have heard of me no more. But I had an object apart from these considerations. You know my political prepossessions. In this matter, I act as a partisan of the lady concerned. For eighteen months the Minister has had her in his power. She has now him in hers; since, being unaware that the letter is not in his possession, he will proceed with his exactions as if it was. Thus will he inevitably commit himself, at once, to his political destruction. His downfall, too, will not be more precipitate than awkward. It is all very well to talk about the *facilis descensus Averni;*[17] but in all kinds of climbing, as Catalani[18] said of singing, it is far more easy to get up than to come down. In the present instance I have no sympathy—at least no pity—for him who descends. He is that *monstrum horrendum,*[19] an unprincipled man of genius. I confess, however, that I should like very

---

[17] "Easy is the descent into hell . . . but to recall thy steps and issue to upper air, this is the task, this the burden"; *Aeneid* 6.126, by Virgil (70–19 B.C.), Roman poet.

[18] Angelica Catalani (1780–1844), Italian singer.

[19] The description of Polyphemus the Cyclops after his one eye had been put out by Ulysses; *Aeneid* 3.658.

well to know the precise character of his thoughts, when, being defied
by her whom the Prefect terms 'a certain personage,' he is reduced to
opening the letter which I left for him in the card-rack."

"How? did you put any thing particular in it?"

"Why—it did not seem altogether right to leave the interior blank—
that would have been insulting. D———, at Vienna once, did me an evil
turn, which I told him, quite good-humouredly, that I should remember. So, as I knew he would feel some curiosity in regard to the identity
of the person who had outwitted him, I thought it a pity not to give him
a clue. He is well acquainted with my MS., and I just copied into the
middle of the blank sheet the words—

> ———*Un dessein si funeste,*
> *S'il n'est digne d'Atrée, est digne*
> *de Thyeste.*

They are to be found in Crébillon's 'Atrée.' "[20]

---

[20] "So baneful a plot, if not worthy of Atreus, is worthy of Thyestes"; from *Atrée et Thyeste* by
Prosper Jolyot de Crébillon (1674–1762).

ANTON CHEKHOV (1860–1904)

Gooseberries

The sky had been covered with rain-clouds ever since the early morning, it was a still day, cool and dull, one of those misty days when the clouds have long been lowering overhead and you keep thinking it is just going to rain, and the rain holds off. Ivan Ivanich, the veterinary surgeon, and Burkin, the high-school teacher, had walked till they were tired, and the way over the fields seemed endless to them. Far ahead they could just make out the windmill of the village of Mironositskoye, and what looked like a range of low hills at the right extending well beyond the village, and they both knew that this range was really the bank of the river, and that further on were meadows, green willow-trees, country-estates; if they were on top of these hills, they knew they would see the same boundless fields and telegraph-posts, and the train, like a crawling caterpillar in the distance, while in fine weather even the town would be visible. On this still day, when the whole of nature seemed kindly and pensive, Ivan Ivanich and Burkin felt a surge of love for this plain, and thought how vast and beautiful their country was.

"The last time we stayed in Elder Prokofy's hut," said Burkin, "you said you had a story to tell me."

"Yes. I wanted to tell you the story of my brother."

Ivan Ivanich took a deep breath and lighted his pipe as a preliminary to his narrative, but just then the rain came. Five minutes later it was coming down in torrents and nobody could say when it would stop. Ivan Ivanich and Burkin stood still, lost in thought. The dogs, already soaked, stood with drooping tails, gazing at them wistfully.

"We must try and find shelter," said Burkin. "Let's go to Alekhin's. It's quite near."

"Come on, then."

They turned aside and walked straight across the newly reaped field, veering to the right till they came to a road. Very soon poplars, an orchard, and the red roofs of barns came into sight. The surface of a river gleamed, and they had a view of an extensive reach of water, a windmill and a whitewashed bathing-shed. This was Sofyino, where Alekhin lived.

The mill was working, and the noise made by its sails drowned the sound of the rain; the whole dam trembled. Horses, soaking wet, were standing near some carts, their heads drooping, and people were moving about with sacks over their heads and shoulders. It was wet, muddy, bleak, and the water looked cold and sinister. Ivan Ivanich and Burkin were already experiencing the misery of dampness, dirt, physical discomfort, their boots were caked with mud, and when, having passed the mill-dam, they took the upward path to the landowner's barns, they fell silent, as if vexed with one another.

The sound of winnowing[1] came from one of the barns; the door was open, and clouds of dust issued from it. Standing in the doorway was Alekhin himself, a stout man of some forty years, with longish hair, looking more like a professor or an artist than a landed proprietor. He was wearing a white shirt, greatly in need of washing, belted with a piece of string, and long drawers with no trousers over them. His boots, too, were caked with mud and straw. His eyes and nose were ringed with dust. He recognized Ivan Ivanich and Burkin, and seemed glad to see them.

"Go up to the house, gentlemen," he said, smiling. "I'll be with you in a minute."

It was a large two-storey house. Alekhin occupied the ground floor, two rooms with vaulted ceilings and tiny windows, where the stewards had lived formerly. They were poorly furnished, and smelled of rye-bread, cheap vodka, and harness. He hardly ever went into the upstairs rooms, excepting when he had guests. Ivan Ivanich and Burkin were met by a maid-servant, a young woman of such beauty that they stood still involuntarily and exchanged glances.

"You have no idea how glad I am to see you here, dear friends," said Alekhin, overtaking them in the hall. "It's quite a surprise! Pelageya," he said, turning to the maid, "find the gentlemen a change of clothes. And I might as well change, myself. But I must have a wash first, for I don't believe I've had a bath since the spring. Wouldn't you like to go and have a bathe while they get things ready here?"

The beauteous Pelageya, looking very soft and delicate, brought them towels and soap, and Alekhin and his guests set off for the bathing-house.

"Yes, it's a long time since I had a wash," he said, taking off his clothes. "As you see I have a nice bathing-place, my father had it built, but somehow I never seem to get time to wash."

He sat on the step, soaping his long locks and his neck, and all round him the water was brown.

---

[1] *winnowing*, the separation of the chaff, or husks, from grain.

"Yes, you certainly..." remarked Ivan Ivanich, with a significant glance at his host's head.

"It's a long time since I had a wash..." repeated Alekhin, somewhat abashed, and he soaped himself again, and now the water was dark-blue, like ink.

Ivan Ivanich emerged from the shed, splashed noisily into the water, and began swimming beneath the rain, spreading his arms wide, making waves all round him, and the white water-lilies rocked on the waves he made. He swam into the very middle of the river and then dived, a moment later came up at another place and swam further, diving constantly, and trying to touch the bottom. "Ah, my God," he kept exclaiming in his enjoyment. "Ah, my God...." He swam up to the mill, had a little talk with some peasants there and turned back, but when he got to the middle of the river, he floated, holding his face up to the rain. Burkin and Alekhin were dressed and ready to go, but he went on swimming and diving.

"God! God!" he kept exclaiming. "Dear God!"

"Come out!" Burkin shouted to him.

They went back to the house. And only after the lamp was lit in the great drawing-room on the upper floor, and Burkin and Ivan Ivanich, in silk dressing-gowns and warm slippers, were seated in arm-chairs, while Alekhin, washed and combed, paced the room in his new frock-coat, enjoying the warmth, the cleanliness, his dry clothes and comfortable slippers, while the fair Pelageya, smiling benevolently, stepped noiselessly over the carpet with her tray of tea and preserves, did Ivan Ivanich embark upon his yarn, the ancient dames, young ladies, and military gentlemen looking down at them severely from the gilded frames, as if they, too, were listening.

"There were two of us brothers," he began. "Ivan Ivanich (me), and my brother Nikolai Ivanich, two years younger than myself. I went in for learning and became a veterinary surgeon, but Nikolai started working in a government office when he was only nineteen. Our father, Chimsha-Himalaisky, was educated in a school for the sons of private soldiers, but was later promoted to officer's rank, and was made a hereditary nobleman and given a small estate. After his death the estate had to be sold for debts, but at least our childhood was passed in the freedom of the country-side, where we roamed the fields and the woods like peasant children, taking the horses to graze, peeling bark from the trunks of lime-trees, fishing, and all that sort of thing. And anyone who has once in his life fished for perch, or watched the thrushes fly south in the autumn, rising high over the village on clear, cool days, is spoilt for town life, and will long for the country-side for the rest of his days. My brother pined in his government office. The years passed and he sat in the same place every day, writing out the same documents and thinking all the time of the same thing—how to get back to the country. And these longings of his gradually turned into a definite desire, into a dream of purchasing a little estate somewhere on the bank of a river or the shore of a lake.

"He was a meek, good-natured chap, I was fond of him, but could feel no sympathy with the desire to lock oneself up for life in an estate of one's own. They say man only needs six feet of earth. But it is a corpse, and not man, which needs these six feet. And now people are actually saying that it is a good sign for our intellectuals to yearn for the land and try to obtain country-dwellings. And yet these estates are nothing but those same six feet of earth. To escape from the town, from the struggle, from the noise of life, to escape and hide one's head on a country-estate, is not life, but egoism, idleness, it is a sort of renunciation, but renunciation without faith. It is not six feet of earth, not a country-estate, that man needs, but the whole globe, the whole of nature, room to display his qualities and the individual characteristics of his soul.

"My brother Nikolai sat at his office-desk, dreaming of eating soup made from his own cabbages, which would spread a delicious smell all over his own yard, of eating out of doors, on the green grass, of sleeping in the sun, sitting for hours on a bench outside his gate, and gazing at the fields and woods. Books on agriculture, and all those hints printed on calendars were his delight, his favourite spiritual nourishment. He was fond of reading newspapers, too, but all he read in them was advertisements of the sale of so many acres of arable and meadowland, with residence attached, a river, an orchard, a mill, and ponds fed by springs. His head was full of visions of garden paths, flowers, fruit, nesting-boxes, carp-ponds, and all that sort of thing. These visions differed according to the advertisements he came across, but for some reason gooseberry bushes invariably figured in them. He could not picture to himself a single estate or picturesque nook that did not have gooseberry bushes in it.

" 'Country life has its conveniences,' he would say. 'You sit on the verandah, drinking tea, with your own ducks floating on the pond, and everything smells so nice, and . . . and the gooseberries ripen on the bushes.'

"He drew up plans for his estate, and every plan showed the same features: a) the main residence, b) the servant's wing, c) the kitchen-garden, d) gooseberry bushes. He lived thriftily, never ate or drank his fill, dressed anyhow, like a beggar, and saved up all his money in the bank. He became terribly stingy. I could hardly bear to look at him, and whenever I gave him a little money, or sent him a present on some holiday, he put that away, too. Once a man gets an idea into his head, there's no doing anything with him.

"The years passed, he was sent to another gubernia,[2] he was over forty, and was still reading advertisements in the papers, and saving up. At last I heard he had married. All for the same purpose, to buy himself an estate with gooseberry bushes on it, he married an ugly elderly widow, for whom he had not the slightest affection, just because she had some money. After his marriage he went on living as thriftily as ever, half-starving his wife, and putting her money in his own bank account. Her first husband had been a postmaster, and she was used to pies and cordials, but with her second husband she did not even get enough black bread to eat. She began to languish under such a regime, and three years later yielded up her soul to God. Of course my brother did not for a moment consider himself guilty of her death. Money, like vodka, makes a man eccentric. There was a merchant in our town who asked for a plate of honey on his deathbed and ate up all his bank-notes and lottery tickets with the honey, so that no one else should get it. And one day when I was examining a consignment of cattle at a railway station, a drover fell under the engine and his leg was severed from his body. We carried him all bloody into the waiting-room, a terrible sight, and he did nothing but beg us to look for his leg, worrying all the time—there were twenty rubles in the boot, and he was afraid they would be lost."

"You're losing the thread," put in Burkin.

Ivan Ivanich paused for a moment, and went on: "After his wife's death my brother began to look about for an estate. You can search for five years, of course, and in the end make a mistake and buy something quite different from what you dreamed of. My brother Nikolai bought three hundred acres, complete with gentleman's house, servants' quarters, and a park, as well as a mortgage to be paid through an agent, but there were neither an orchard, gooseberry bushes, nor a pond with ducks on it. There was a river, but it was as dark as coffee, owing to the fact that there was a brick-works on one side of the estate, and bone-kilns on the other. Nothing daunted, however, my brother Nikolai Ivanich ordered two dozen gooseberry bushes and settled down as a landed proprietor.

"Last year I paid him a visit. I thought I would go and see how he was getting on there. In his letters my brother gave his address as Chumbaroklova Pustosh or Himalaiskoye. I arrived at Himalaiskoye in the afternoon. It was very hot. Everywhere were ditches, fences, hedges, rows of fir-trees, and it was hard to drive into the yard and find a place to leave one's carriage. As I went a fat ginger-coloured

---

2 *gubernia,* a province.

dog, remarkably like a pig, came out to meet me. It looked as if it would have barked if it were not so lazy. The cook, who was also fat and like a pig, came out of the kitchen, barefoot, and said her master was having his after-dinner rest. I made my way to my brother's room, and found him sitting up in bed, his knees covered by a blanket. He had aged, and grown stout and flabby. His cheeks, nose and lips protruded—I almost expected him to grunt into the blanket.

"We embraced and wept—tears of joy, mingled with melancholy— because we had once been young and were now both grey-haired and approaching the grave. He put on his clothes and went out to show me over his estate.

" 'Well, how are you getting on here?' I asked.

" 'All right, thanks be, I'm enjoying myself.' "

"He was no longer the poor, timid clerk, but a true proprietor, a gentleman. He had settled down, and was entering with zest into country life. He ate a lot, washed in the bath-house, and put on flesh. He had already got into litigation with the village commune, the brick-works and the bone-kilns, and took offence if the peasants failed to call him 'Your Honour.' He went in for religion in a solid, gentlemanly way, and there was nothing casual about his pretentious good works. And what were these good works? He treated all the diseases of the peasants with bicarbonate of soda and castor-oil, and had a special thanksgiving service held on his name-day, after which he provided half a pail of vodka, supposing that this was the right thing to do. Oh, those terrible half pails! Today the fat landlord hauls the peasants before the Zemstvo representative[3] for letting their sheep graze on his land, tomorrow, on the day of rejoicing, he treats them to half a pail of vodka, and they drink and sing and shout hurrah, prostrating themselves before him when they are drunk. Any improvement in his conditions, anything like satiety or idleness, de- velops the most insolent complacency in a Russian. Nikolai Ivanich, who had been afraid of having an opinion of his own when he was in the government service, was now continually coming out with axioms, in the most ministerial manner: 'Education is essential, but the people are not ready for it yet,' 'corporal punishment is an evil, but in certain cases it is beneficial and indispensable.'

" 'I know the people and I know how to treat them,' he said. 'The people love me. I only have to lift my little finger, and the people will do whatever I want.'

"And all this, mark you, with a wise, indulgent smile. Over and

---

[3] *Zemstvo representative,* a law-enforcing official of the Zemstvo, the elective council responsible for the local administration of a province.

over again he repeated: 'We the gentry,' or 'speaking as a gentleman,' and seemed to have quite forgotten that our grandfather was a peasant, and our father a common soldier. Our very surname—Chimsha-Himalaisky—in reality so absurd, now seemed to him a resounding, distinguished, and euphonious name.

"But it is of myself, and not of him, that I wish to speak. I should like to describe to you the change which came over me in those few hours I spent on my brother's estate. As we were drinking tea in the evening, the cook brought us a full plate of gooseberries. These were not gooseberries bought for money, they came from his own garden, and were the first fruits of the bushes he had planted. Nikolai Ivanich broke into a laugh and gazed at the gooseberries, in tearful silence for at least five minutes. Speechless with emotion, he popped a single gooseberry into his mouth, darted at me the triumphant glance of a child who has at last gained possession of a longed-for toy, and said:

" 'Delicious!'

"And he ate them greedily, repeating over and over again:

" 'Simply delicious! You try them.' "

"They were hard and sour, but, as Pushkin says: 'The lie which elates us is dearer than a thousand sober truths.' I saw before me a really happy man, one whose dearest wish had come true, who had achieved his aim in life, got what he wanted, and was content with his lot and with himself. There had always been a tinge of melancholy in my conception of human happiness, and now, confronted by a happy man, I was overcome by a feeling of sadness bordering on desperation. This feeling grew strongest of all in the night. A bed was made up for me in the room next to my brother's bedroom, and I could hear him moving about restlessly, every now and then getting up to take a gooseberry from a plate. How many happy, satisfied people there are, after all, I said to myself! What an overwhelming force! Just consider this life—the insolence and idleness of the strong, the ignorance and bestiality of the weak, all around intolerable poverty, cramped dwellings, degeneracy, drunkenness, hypocrisy, lying. . . . And yet peace and order apparently prevail in all those homes and in the streets. Of the fifty thousand inhabitants of a town, not one will be found to cry out, to proclaim his indignation aloud. We see those who go to the market to buy food, who eat in the day-time and sleep at night, who prattle away, marry, grow old, carry their dead to the cemeteries. But we neither hear nor see those who suffer, and the terrible things in life are played out behind the scenes. All is calm and quiet, only statistics, which are dumb, protest: so many have gone mad, so many barrels of drink have been consumed, so many children died of malnutrition. . . . And apparently this is as it should be. Apparently those who are happy can only enjoy themselves because the unhappy bear their burdens in silence, and but for this silence happiness would be impossible. It is a kind of universal hypnosis. There ought to be a man with a hammer behind the door of every happy man, to remind him by his constant knocks that there are unhappy people, and that happy as he himself may be, life will sooner or later show him its claws, catastrophe will overtake him—sickness, poverty, loss—and nobody will see it, just as he now neither sees nor hears the misfortunes of others. But there is no man with a hammer, the happy man goes on living and the petty vicissitudes of life touch him lightly, like the wind in an aspen-tree, and all is well.

"That night I understood that I, too, was happy and content," continued Ivan Ivanich, getting up. "I, too, while out hunting, or at the dinner table, have held forth on the right way to live, to worship, to manage the people. I, too, have declared that without knowledge there can be no light, that education is essential, but that bare literacy is sufficient for the common people. Freedom is a blessing, I have said, one can't get on without it, any more than without air, but we must wait. Yes, that is what I said, and now I ask: In the name of what must we wait?" Here Ivan Ivanich looked angrily at Burkin. "In the name of what must we wait, I ask you. What is there to be considered? Don't be in such a hurry, they tell me, every idea materializes gradually, in its own time. But who are they who say this? What is the proof that it is just? You refer to the natural order of things, to the logic of facts, but according to what order, what logic do I, a living, thinking individual, stand on the edge of a ditch and wait for it to be gradually filled up, or choked with silt, when I might leap across it or build a bridge over it? And again, in the name of what must we wait? Wait, when we have not the strength to live, though live we must and to live we desire!

"I left my brother early the next morning, and ever since I have found town life intolerable. The peace and order weigh on my spirits, and I am afraid to look into windows, because there is now no sadder spectacle for me than a happy family seated around the tea-table. I am old and unfit for the struggle, I am even incapable of feeling hatred. I can only suffer inwardly, and give way to irritation and annoyance, at night my head burns from the rush of thoughts, and I am unable to sleep. . . . Oh, if only I were young!"

Ivan Ivanich began pacing backwards and forwards, repeating:

"If only I were young still!"

Suddenly he went up to Alekhin and began pressing first one of his hands, and then the other.

"Pavel Konstantinich," he said in imploring accents. "Don't *you* fall into apathy, don't *you* let your conscience be lulled to sleep! While you are still young, strong, active, do not be weary of well-doing. There is no such thing as happiness, nor ought there to be, but if there is any sense or purpose in life, this sense and purpose are to be found not in our own happiness, but in something greater and more rational. Do good!"

Ivan Ivanich said all this with a piteous, imploring smile, as if he were asking for something for himself.

Then they all three sat in their armchairs a long way apart from one another, and said nothing. Ivan Ivanich's story satisfied neither Burkin or Alekhin. It was not interesting to listen to the story of a poor clerk who ate gooseberries, when from the walls generals and fine ladies, who seemed to come to life in the dark, were looking down from their gilded frames. It would have been much more interesting to hear about elegant people, lovely women. And the fact that they were sitting in a drawing-room in which everything—the swathed chandeliers, the arm-chairs, the carpet on the floor, proved that the people now looking out of the frames had once moved about here, sat in the chairs, drunk tea, where the fair Pelageya was now going noiselessly to and fro, was better than any story.

Alekhin was desperately sleepy. He had got up early, at three o'clock in the morning, to go about his work on the estate, and could now hardly keep his eyes open. But he would not go to bed, for fear one of his guests would relate something interesting after he was gone. He could not be sure whether what Ivan Ivanich had just told them was wise or just, but his visitors talked of other things besides grain, hay, or tar, of things which had no direct bearing on his daily life, and he liked this, and wanted them to go on. . . .

"Well, time to go to bed," said Burkin, getting up. "Allow me to wish you a good night."

Alekhin said good night and went downstairs to his own room, the visitors remaining on the upper floor. They were allotted a big room for the night, in which were two ancient bedsteads of carved wood, and an ivory crucifix in one corner. There was a pleasant smell of freshly laundered sheets from the wide, cool beds which the fair Pelageya made up for them.

Ivan Ivanich undressed in silence and lay down.

"Lord have mercy on us, sinners," he said, and covered his head with the sheet.

There was a strong smell of stale tobacco from his pipe, which he put on the table, and Burkin lay awake a long time, wondering where the stifling smell came from.

The rain tapped on the window-panes all night.

JAMES JOYCE (1882–1941)

Araby

North Richmond Street, being blind, was a quiet street except at the hour when the Christian Brothers' School set the boys free. An uninhabited house of two stories stood at the blind end, detached from its neighbours in a square ground. The other houses of the street, conscious of decent lives within them, gazed at one another with brown imperturbable faces.

The former tenant of our house, a priest, had died in the back drawing-room. Air, musty from having been long enclosed, hung in all the rooms, and the waste room behind the kitchen was littered with old useless papers. Among these I found a few paper-covered books, the pages of which were curled and damp: *The Abbot,* by Walter Scott, *The Devout Communicant,* and *The Memoirs of Vidocq.* I liked the last best because its leaves were yellow. The wild garden behind the house contained a central apple tree and a few straggling bushes under one of which I found the late tenant's rusty bicycle pump. He had been a very charitable priest; in his will he had left all his money to institutions and the furniture of his house to his sister.

When the short days of winter came dusk fell before we had well eaten our dinners. When we met in the street the houses had grown sombre. The space of sky above us was the colour of ever-changing violet and towards it the lamps of the street lifted their feeble lanterns. The cold air stung us and we played till our bodies glowed. Our shouts echoed in the silent street. The career of our play brought us through the dark muddy lanes behind the houses where we ran the gauntlet of the rough tribes from the cottages, to the back doors of the dark dripping gardens where odours arose from the ash-pits, to the dark odorous stables where a coachman smoothed and combed the horse or shook music from the buckled harness. When we returned to the street, light from the kitchen windows had filled the areas. If my uncle was seen turning the corner we hid in the shadow until we had seen him safely housed. Or if Mangan's sister came out on the doorstep to call her brother in to his tea we watched her from our shadow peer up and down the street. We waited to see whether she would remain or go in and, if she remained, we left our shadow and walked up to Mangan's steps resignedly. She was waiting for us, her figure defined by the light from the half-opened door. Her brother always teased her before he obeyed and I stood by the railings looking at her. Her dress swung as she moved her body and the soft rope of her hair tossed from side to side.

Every morning I lay on the floor in the front parlour watching her door. The blind was pulled down to within an inch of the sash so that I could not be seen. When she came out on the doorstep my heart leaped. I ran to the hall, seized my books and followed her. I kept her brown figure always in my eye and, when we came near the point at which our ways diverged, I quickened my pace and passed her. This happened morning after morning. I had never spoken to her, except for a few casual words, and yet her name was like a summons to all my foolish blood.

Her image accompanied me even in places the most hostile to romance. On Saturday evenings when my aunt went marketing I had to go to carry some of the parcels. We walked through the flaring streets, jostled by drunken men and bargaining women, amid the curses of labourers, the shrill litanies of shop-boys who stood on guard by the barrels of pigs' cheeks, the nasal chanting of street-singers, who sang a *come-all-you* about O'Donovan Rossa, or a ballad about the troubles in our native land. These noises converged in a single sensation of life for me: I imagined that I bore my chalice safely through a throng of foes. Her name sprang to my lips at moments in strange prayers and praises which I myself did not understand. My eyes were often full of tears (I could not tell why) and at times a flood from my heart seemed to pour itself out into my bosom. I thought little of the future. I did not know whether I would ever speak to her or not or, if I spoke to her, how I could tell her of my confused adoration. But my body was like a harp and her words and gestures were like fingers running upon the wires.

One evening I went into the back drawing-room in which the priest had died. It was a dark rainy evening and there was no sound in the house. Through one of the broken panes I heard the rain impinge upon the earth, the fine incessant needles of water playing in the sodden beds. Some distant lamp or lighted window gleamed below me. I was thankful that I could see so little. All my senses seemed to desire to veil themselves and, feeling that I was about to slip from them, I pressed the palms of my hands together until they trembled, murmuring: *"O love! O love!"* many times.

At last she spoke to me. When she addressed the first words to me I was so confused that I did not know what to answer. She asked me was I going to *Araby*. I forgot whether I answered yes or no. It would be a splendid bazaar, she said she would love to go.

"And why can't you?" I asked.

While she spoke she turned a silver bracelet round and round her wrist. She could not go, she said, because there would be a retreat that week in her convent. Her brother and two other boys were fighting for their caps and I was alone at the railings. She held one of the spikes, bowing her head towards me. The light from the lamp opposite our door caught the white curve of her neck, lit up her hair that rested there and, falling, lit up the hand upon the railing. It fell over one side of her dress and caught the white border of a petticoat, just visible as she stood at ease.

"It's well for you," she said.

"If I go," I said, "I will bring you something."

What innumerable follies laid waste my waking and sleeping thoughts after the evening! I wished to annihilate the tedious intervening days. I chafed against the work of school. At night in my bedroom and by day in the classroom her image came between me and the page I strove to read. The syllables of the word *Araby* were called to me through the silence in which my soul luxuriated and cast an Eastern enchantment over me. I asked for leave to go to the bazaar on Saturday night. My aunt was surprised and hoped it was not some Freemason affair. I answered few questions in class. I watched my master's face pass from amiability to sternness; he hoped I was not beginning to idle, I could not call my wandering thoughts together. I had hardly any patience with the serious work of life which, now that it stood between me and my desire, seemed to me child's play, ugly monotonous child's play.

On Saturday morning I reminded my uncle that I wished to go to the bazaar in the evening. He was fussing at the hall-stand, looking for the hat brush, and answered me curtly:

"Yes, boy, I know."

As he was in the hall I could not go into the front parlour and lie at the window. I left the house in bad humour and walked slowly towards the school. The air was pitilessly raw and already my heart misgave me.

When I came home to dinner my uncle had not yet been home. Still it was early. I sat staring at the clock for some time and, when its ticking began to irritate me, I left the room. I mounted the staircase and gained the upper part of the house. The high cold empty gloomy rooms liberated me and I went from room to room singing. From the front window I saw my companions playing below in the street. Their cries reached me weakened and indistinct and, leaning my forehead against the cool glass, I looked over at the dark house where she lived. I may have stood there for an hour, seeing nothing but the brown-clad figure cast by my imagination, touched discreetly by the lamplight at the curved neck, at the hand upon the railings and at the border below the dress.

When I came downstairs again I found Mrs. Mercer sitting at the fire. She was an old garrulous woman, a pawnbroker's widow, who collected used stamps for some pious purpose. I had to endure the gossip of the tea-table. The meal was prolonged beyond an hour and still my uncle did not come. Mrs. Mercer stood up to go: she was sorry she couldn't wait any longer, but it was after eight o'clock and she did not like to be out late, as the night air was bad for her. When she had gone I began to walk up and down the room, clenching my fists. My aunt said:

"I'm afraid you may put off your bazaar for this night of Our Lord."

At nine o'clock I heard my uncle's latchkey in the hall-door. I heard him talking to himself and heard the hall-stand rocking when it had received the weight of his overcoat. I could interpret these signs. When he was midway through his dinner I asked him to give me the money to go to the bazaar. He had forgotten.

"The people are in bed and after their first sleep now," he said.

I did not smile. My aunt said to him energetically:

"Can't you give him the money and let him go? You've kept him late enough as it is."

My uncle said he was very sorry he had forgotten. He said he believed in the old saying: "All work and no play makes Jack a dull boy." He asked me where I was going and, when I had told him a second time, he asked me did I know *The Arab's Farewell to his Steed*. When I left the kitchen he was about to recite the opening lines of the piece to my aunt.

I held a florin tightly in my hand as I strode down Buckingham Street towards the station. The sight of the streets thronged with buyers and glaring with gas recalled to me the purpose of my journey. I took my seat in a third-class carriage of a deserted train. After an intolerable delay the train moved out of the station slowly. It crept onward among ruinous houses and over the twinkling river. At Westland Row Station a crowd of people pressed to the carriage doors; but the porters moved them back, saying that it was a special train for the bazaar. I remained alone in the bare carriage. In a few minutes the train drew up beside an improvised wooden platform. I passed out on the road and saw by the lighted dial of a clock that it was ten minutes to ten. In front of me was a large building which displayed the magical name.

I could not find any sixpenny entrance and, fearing that the bazaar would be closed, I passed in quickly through a turnstile, handing a shilling to a weary-looking man. I found myself in a big hall girdled at half its height by a gallery. Nearly all the stalls were closed and the greater part of the hall was in darkness. I recognized a silence like that which pervades a church after a service. I walked into the center of the bazaar timidly. A few people were gathered about the stalls which were still open. Before a curtain, over which the words *Café Chantant* were written in coloured lamps, two men were counting money on a salver. I listened to the fall of the coins.

Remembering with difficulty why I had come I went over to one of the stalls and examined porcelain vases and flowered tea-sets. At the door of the stall a young lady was talking and laughing with two young gentlemen. I remarked their English accents and listened vaguely to their conversation.

"O, I never said such a thing!"

"O, but you did!"

"O, but I didn't!"

"Didn't she say that?"

"Yes. I heard her."

"O, there's a . . . fib!"

Observing me, the young lady came over and asked me did I wish to buy anything. The tone of her voice was not encouraging; she seemed to have spoken to me out of a sense of duty. I looked humbly at the great jars that stood like eastern guards at either side of the dark entrance to the stall and murmured:

"No, thank you."

The young lady changed the position of one of the vases and went back to the two young men. They began to talk of the same subject. Once or twice the young lady glanced at me over her shoulder.

I lingered before her stall, though I knew my stay was useless, to make my interest in her wares seem the more real. Then I turned away slowly and walked down the middle of the bazaar. I allowed the two pennies to fall against the sixpence in my pocket. I heard a voice call from one end of the gallery that the light was out. The upper part of the hall was now completely dark.

Gazing up into the darkness I saw myself as a creature driven and derided by vanity; and my eyes burned with anguish and anger.

The Bucket-Rider

Coal all spent; the bucket empty, the shovel useless; the stove breathing out cold; the room freezing; the leaves outside the window rigid, covered with rime; the sky a silver shield against anyone who looks for help from it. I must have coal; I cannot freeze to death; behind me is the pitiless stove, before me the pitiless sky, so I must ride out between them and on my journey seek aid from the coal-dealer. But he has already grown deaf to ordinary appeals; I must prove irrefutably to him that I have not a single grain of coal left, and that he means to me the very sun in the firmament. I must approach like a beggar who, with the death-rattle already in his throat, insists on dying on the doorstep, and to whom the grand people's cook accordingly decides to give the dregs of the coffee-pot; just so must the coal-dealer, filled with rage, but acknowledging the command, "Thou shalt not kill," fling a shovelful of coal into my bucket.

My mode of arrival must decide the matter; so I ride off on the bucket. Seated on the bucket, my hands on the handle, the simplest kind of bridle, I propel myself with difficulty down the stairs; but once down below my bucket ascends, superbly, superbly; camels humbly squatting on the ground do not rise with more dignity, shaking themselves under the sticks of their drivers. Through the hard frozen streets we go at a regular canter; often I am upraised as high as the first story of a house; never do I sink as low as the house doors. And at last I float at an extraordinary height above the vaulted cellar of the dealer, whom I see far below crouching over his table, where he is writing; he has opened the door to let out the excessive heat.

"Coal-dealer!" I cry in a voice burned hollow by the frost and muffled in the cloud made by my breath, "please, coal-dealer, give me a little coal. My bucket is so light that I can ride on it. Be kind. When I can I'll pay you."

The dealer puts his hand to his ear. "Do I hear rightly?" He throws the question over his shoulder to his wife. "Do I hear rightly? A customer."

"I hear nothing," says his wife, breathing in and out peacefully while she knits on, her back pleasantly warmed by the heat.

"Oh, yes, you must hear," I cry. "It's me; an old customer; faithful and true; only without means at the moment."

"Wife," says the dealer, "it's some one, it must be; my ears can't have deceived me so much as that; it must be an old, a very old customer, that can move me so deeply."

"What ails you, man?" says his wife, ceasing from her work for a moment and pressing her knitting to her bosom. "It's nobody, the street is empty, all our customers are provided for; we could close down the shop for several days and take a rest."

"But I'm sitting up here on the bucket," I cry, and unfeeling frozen tears dim my eyes, "please look up here, just once; you'll see me directly; I beg you, just a shovelful; and if you give me more it'll make me so happy that I won't know what to do. All the other customers are provided for. Oh, if I could only hear the coal clattering into the bucket!"

"I'm coming," says the coal-dealer, and on his short legs he makes to climb the steps of the cellar, but his wife is already beside him, holds him back by the arm and says: "You stay here; seeing you persist in your fancies I'll go myself. Think of the bad fit of coughing you had during the night. But for a piece of business, even if it's one you've only fancied in your head, you're prepared to forget your wife and child and sacrifice your lungs. I'll go."

"Then be sure to tell him all the kinds of coal we have in stock; I'll shout out the prices after you."

"Right," says his wife, climbing up to the street. Naturally she sees me at once. "Frau Coal-dealer," I cry, "my humblest greetings; just one shovelful of coal; here in my bucket; I'll carry it home myself. One shovelful of the worst you have. I'll pay you in full for it, of course, but not just now, not just now." What a knell-like sound the words "not just now" have, and how bewilderingly they mingle with the evening chimes that fall from the church steeple nearby!

"Well, what does he want?" shouts the dealer. "Nothing," his wife shouts back, "there's nothing here; I see nothing, I hear nothing; only six striking, and now we must shut up the shop. The cold is terrible; tomorrow we'll likely have lots to do again."

She sees nothing and hears nothing; but all the same she loosens her apron-strings and waves her apron to waft me away. She succeeds, unluckily. My bucket has all the virtues of a good steed except powers of resistance, which it has not; it is too light; a woman's apron can make it fly through the air.

"You bad woman!" I shout back, while she, turning into the shop, half-contemptuous, half-reassured, flourishes her fist in the air. "You bad woman! I begged you for a shovelful of the worst coal and you would not give me it." And with that I ascend into the regions of the ice mountains and am lost forever.

D. H. LAWRENCE (1885–1930)

The Rocking-Horse Winner

There was a woman who was beautiful, who started with all the advantages, yet she had no luck. She married for love, and the love turned to dust. She had bonny children, yet she felt they had been thrust upon her, and she could not love them. They looked at her coldly, as if they were finding fault with her. And hurriedly she felt she must cover up some fault in herself. Yet what it was that she must cover up she never knew. Nevertheless, when her children were present, she always felt the centre of her heart go hard. This troubled her, and in her manner she was all the more gentle and anxious for her children, as if she loved them very much. Only she herself knew that at the centre of her heart was a hard little place that could not feel love, no, not for anybody. Everybody else said of her: "She is such a good mother. She adores her children." Only she herself, and her children themselves, knew it was not so. They read it in each other's eyes.

There were a boy and two little girls. They lived in a pleasant house, with a garden, and they had discreet servants, and felt themselves superior to anyone in the neighbourhood.

Although they lived in style, they felt always an anxiety in the house. There was never enough money. The mother had a small income, and the father had a small income, but not nearly enough for the social position which they had to keep up. The father went into town to some office. But though he had good prospects, these prospects never materialized. There was always the grinding sense of the shortage of money, though the style was always kept up.

At last the mother said: "I will see if I can't make something." But she did not know where to begin. She racked her brains, and tried this thing and the other, but could not find anything successful. The failure made deep lines come into her face. Her children were growing up, they would have to go to school. There must be more money, there must be more money. The father, who was always very handsome and expensive in his tastes, seemed as if he never would be able to do anything worth doing. And the mother, who had a great belief in herself, did not succeed any better, and her tastes were just as expensive.

And so the house came to be haunted by the unspoken phrase: There must be more money! There must be more money! The children could hear it all the time, though nobody said it aloud. They heard it at Christmas, when the expensive and splendid toys filled the nursery. Behind the shining modern rocking horse, behind the smart doll's-house, a voice would start whispering: "There must be more money! There must be more money!" And the children would stop playing, to listen for a moment. They would look into each other's eyes, to see if they had all heard. And each one saw in the eyes of the other two that they too had heard. "There must be more money! There must be more money!"

It came whispering from the springs of the still-swaying rocking horse, and even the horse, bending his wooden, champing head, heard it. The big doll, sitting so pink and smirking in her new pram, could hear it quite plainly, and seemed to be smirking all the more self-consciously because of it. The foolish puppy, too, that took the place of the Teddy bear, he was looking so extraordinarily foolish for no other reason but that he heard the secret whisper all over the house: "There must be more money!"

Yet nobody ever said it aloud. The whisper was everywhere, and therefore no one spoke it. Just as no one ever says: "We are breathing!" in spite of the fact that breath is coming and going all the time.

"Mother," said the boy Paul one day, "why don't we keep a car of our own? Why do we always use uncle's, or else a taxi?"

"Because we're the poor members of the family," said the mother.

"But why are we, mother?"

"Well—I suppose," she said slowly and bitterly, "it's because your father has no luck."

The boy was silent for some time.

"Is luck money, mother?" he asked, rather timidly.

"No, Paul. Not quite. It's what causes you to have money."

"Oh!" said Paul vaguely. "I thought when Uncle Oscar said filthy lucker, it meant money."

"Filthy lucre does mean money," said the mother. "But it's lucre, not luck."

"Oh!" said the boy. "Then what is luck, mother?"

"It's what causes you to have money. If you're lucky you have money. That's why it's better to be born lucky than rich. If you're rich, you may lose your money. But if you're lucky, you will always get more money."

"Oh! Will you? And is father not lucky?"

"Very unlucky, I should say," she said bitterly.

The boy watched her with unsure eyes.

"Why?" he asked.

"I don't know. Nobody ever knows why one person is lucky and another unlucky."

"Don't they? Nobody at all? Does nobody know?"

"Perhaps God. But He never tells."

"He ought to, then. And aren't you lucky either, mother?"

"I can't be, if I married an unlucky husband."

"But by yourself, aren't you?"

"I used to think I was, before I married. Now I think I am very unlucky indeed."

"Why?"

"Well—never mind! Perhaps I'm not really," she said.

The child looked at her, to see if she meant it. But he saw, by the lines of her mouth, that she was only trying to hide something from him.

"Well, anyhow," he said stoutly, "I'm a lucky person."

"Why?" said his mother, with a sudden laugh.

He stared at her. He didn't even know why he had said it.

"God told me," he asserted, brazening it out.

"I hope He did, dear!" she said, again with a laugh, but rather bitter.

"He did, mother!"

"Excellent!" said the mother, using one of her husband's exclamations.

The boy saw she did not believe him; or, rather, that she paid no attention to his assertion. This angered him somewhat, and made him want to compel her attention.

He went off by himself, vaguely, in a childish way, seeking for the clue to "luck." Absorbed, taking no heed of other people, he went about with a sort of stealth, seeking inwardly for luck. He wanted luck, he wanted it, he wanted it. When the two girls were playing dolls in the nursery, he would sit on his big rocking horse, charging madly into space, with a frenzy that made the little girls peer at him uneasily. Wildly the horse careered, the waving dark hair of the boy tossed, his eyes had a strange glare in them. The little girls dared not speak to him.

When he had ridden to the end of his mad little journey, he climbed down and stood in front of his rocking horse, staring fixedly into its lowered face. Its red mouth was slightly open, its big eye was wide and glassy-bright.

"Now!" he would silently command the snorting steed. "Now, take me to where there is luck! Now take me!"

And he would slash the horse on the neck with the little whip he had asked Uncle Oscar for. He knew the horse could take him to where there was luck, if only he forced it. So he would mount again, and start on his furious ride, hoping at last to get there. He knew he could get there.

"You'll break your horse, Paul!" said the nurse.

"He's always riding like that! I wish he'd leave off!" said his elder sister Joan.

But he only glared down on them in silence. Nurse gave him up.

She could make nothing of him. Anyhow he was growing beyond her.

One day his mother and his Uncle Oscar came in when he was on one of his furious rides. He did not speak to them.

"Hallo, you young jockey! Riding a winner?" said his uncle.

"Aren't you growing too big for a rocking horse? You're not a very little boy any longer, you know," said his mother.

But Paul only gave a blue glare from his big, rather close-set eyes. He would speak to nobody when he was in full tilt. His mother watched him with an anxious expression on her face.

At last he suddenly stopped forcing his horse into the mechanical gallop, and slid down.

"Well, I got there!" he announced fiercely, his blue eyes still flaring, and his sturdy long legs straddling apart.

"Where did you get to?" asked his mother.

"Where I wanted to go," he flared back at her.

"That's right, son!" said Uncle Oscar. "Don't you stop till you get there. What's the horse's name?"

"He doesn't have a name," said the boy.

"Gets on without all right?" asked the uncle.

"Well, he has different names. He was called Sansovino last week."

"Sansovino, eh? Won the Ascot. How did you know his name?"

"He always talks about horse races with Bassett," said Joan.

The uncle was delighted to find that his small nephew was posted with all the racing news. Bassett, the young gardener, who had been wounded in the left foot in the war and had got his present job through Oscar Cresswell, whose batman he had been, was a perfect blade of the "turf." He lived in the racing events, and the small boy lived with him.

Oscar Cresswell got it all from Bassett.

"Master Paul comes and asks me, so I can't do more than tell him, sir," said Bassett, his face terribly serious, as if he were speaking of religious matters.

"And does he ever put anything on a horse he fancies?"

"Well—I don't want to give him away—he's a young sport, a fine sport, sir. Would you mind asking him yourself? He sort of takes a pleasure in it, and perhaps he'd feel I was giving him away, sir, if you don't mind."

Bassett was serious as a church.

The uncle went back to his nephew, and took him off for a ride in the car.

"Say, Paul, old man, do you ever put anything on a horse?" the uncle asked.

The boy watched the handsome man closely.

"Why, do you think I oughtn't to?" he parried.

"Not a bit of it! I thought perhaps you might give me a tip for the Lincoln."

The car sped on into the country, going down to Uncle Oscar's place in Hampshire.

"Honour bright?" said the nephew.

"Honour bright, son!" said the uncle.

"Well, then, Daffodil."

"Daffodil! I doubt it, sonny. What about Mirza?"

"I only know the winner," said the boy. "That's Daffodil."

"Daffodil, eh?"

There was a pause. Daffodil was an obscure horse comparatively.

"Uncle!"

"Yes, son?"

"You won't let it go any further, will you? I promised Bassett."

"Bassett be damned, old man! What's he got to do with it?"

"We're partners. We've been partners from the first. Uncle, he lent me my first five shillings, which I lost. I promised him, honour bright, it was only between me and him; only you gave me that ten-shilling note I started winning with, so I thought you were lucky. You won't let it go any further, will you?"

The boy gazed at his uncle from those big, hot, blue eyes, set rather close together. The uncle stirred and laughed uneasily.

"Right you are, son! I'll keep your tip private. Daffodil, eh? How much are you putting on him?"

"All except twenty pounds," said the boy. "I keep that in reserve."

The uncle thought it a good joke.

"You keep twenty pounds in reserve, do you, you young romancer? What are you betting, then?"

"I'm betting three hundred," said the boy gravely. "But it's between you and me, Uncle Oscar! Honour bright?"

The uncle burst into a roar of laughter.

"It's between you and me all right, you young Nat Gould," he said, laughing. "But where's your three hundred?"

"Bassett keeps it for me. We're partners."

"You are, are you! And what is Bassett putting on Daffodil?"

"He won't go quite as high as I do, I expect. Perhaps he'll go a hundred and fifty."

"What, pennies?" laughed the uncle.

"Pounds," said the child, with a surprised look at his uncle. "Bassett keeps a bigger reserve than I do."

Between wonder and amusement Uncle Oscar was silent. He pursued the matter no further, but he determined to take his nephew with him to the Lincoln races.

"Now, son," he said, "I'm putting twenty on Mirza, and I'll put five for you on any horse you fancy. What's your pick?"

"Daffodil, uncle."

"No, not the fiver on Daffodil!"

"I should if it was my own fiver," said the child.

"Good! Good! Right you are! A fiver for me and a fiver for you on Daffodil."

The child had never been to a race meeting before, and his eyes were blue fire. He pursed his mouth tight, and watched. A Frenchman just in front had put his money on Lancelot. Wild with excitement, he flayed his arms up and down, yelling "Lancelot! Lancelot!" in his French accent.

Daffodil came in first, Lancelot second, Mirza third. The child, flushed and with eyes blazing, was curiously serene. His uncle brought him four five-pound notes, four to one.

"What am I to do with these?" he cried, waving them before the boy's eyes.

"I suppose we'll talk to Bassett," said the boy. "I expect I have fifteen hundred now; and twenty in reserve; and this twenty."

His uncle studied him for some moments.

"Look here, son!" he said. "You're not serious about Bassett and that fifteen hundred, are you?"

"Yes, I am. But it's between you and me, uncle. Honour bright!"

"Honour bright all right, son! But I must talk to Bassett."

"If you'd like to be a partner, uncle, with Bassett and me, we could all be partners. Only, you'd have to promise, honour bright, uncle, not to let it go beyond us three. Bassett and I are lucky, and you must be lucky, because it was your ten shillings I started winning with . . ."

Uncle Oscar took both Bassett and Paul into Richmond Park for an afternoon, and there they talked.

"It's like this, you see, sir," Bassett said. "Master Paul would get me talking about racing events, spinning yarns, you know, sir. And he was always keen on knowing if I'd made or if I'd lost. It's about a year since, now, that I put five shillings on Blush of Dawn for him—and we lost. Then the luck turned, with that ten shillings he had from you, that we put on Singhalese. And since that time, it's been pretty steady, all things considering. What do you say, Master Paul?"

"We're all right when we're sure," said Paul. "It's when we're not quite sure that we go down."

"Oh, but we're careful then," said Bassett.

"But when are you sure?" smiled Uncle Oscar.

"It's Master Paul, sir," said Bassett, in a secret, religious voice. "It's as if he had it from heaven. Like Daffodil, now, for the Lincoln. That was as sure as eggs."

"Did you put anything on Daffodil?" asked Oscar Cresswell.

"Yes, sir, I made my bit."

"And my nephew?"

Bassett was obstinately silent, looking at Paul.

"I made twelve hundred, didn't I, Bassett? I told uncle I was putting three hundred on Daffodil."

"That's right," said Bassett, nodding.

"But where's the money?" asked the uncle.

"I keep it safe locked up, sir. Master Paul he can have it any minute he likes to ask for it."

"What, fifteen hundred pounds?"

"And twenty! and forty, that is, with the twenty he made on the course."

"It's amazing!" said the uncle.

"If Master Paul offers you to be partners, sir, I would, if I were you; if you'll excuse me," said Bassett.

Oscar Cresswell thought about it.

"I'll see the money," he said.

They drove home again, and sure enough, Bassett came round to the garden-house with fifteen hundred pounds in notes. The twenty pounds reserve was left with Joe Glee, in the Turf Commission deposit.

"You see, it's all right, uncle, when I'm sure! Then we go strong, for all we're worth. Don't we, Bassett?"

"We do that, Master Paul."

"And when are you sure?" said the uncle, laughing.

"Oh, well, sometimes I'm absolutely sure, like about Daffodil," said the boy; "and sometimes I have an idea; and sometimes I haven't even an idea, have I, Bassett? Then we're careful, because we mostly go down."

"You do, do you! And when you're sure, like about Daffodil, what makes you sure, sonny?"

"Oh, well, I don't know," said the boy uneasily. "I'm sure, you know, uncle; that's all."

"It's as if he had it from heaven, sir," Bassett reiterated.

"I should say so!" said the uncle.

But he became a partner. And when the Leger was coming on, Paul was "sure" about Lively Spark, which was a quite inconsiderable horse. The boy insisted on putting a thousand on the horse, Bassett went for five hundred, and Oscar Cresswell two hundred. Lively Spark came in first, and the betting had been ten to one against him. Paul had made ten thousand.

"You see," he said, "I was absolutely sure of him."

Even Oscar Cresswell had cleared two thousand.

"Look here, son," he said, "this sort of thing makes me nervous."

"It needn't, uncle! Perhaps I shan't be sure again for a long time."

"But what are you going to do with your money?" asked the uncle.

"Of course," said the boy, "I started it for mother. She said she had no luck, because father is unlucky, so I thought if I was lucky, it might stop whispering."

"What might stop whispering?"

"Our house. I hate our house for whispering."

"What does it whisper?"

"Why—why"—the boy fidgeted—"why, I don't know. But it's always short of money, you know, uncle."

"I know it, son, I know it."

"You know people send mother writs, don't you, uncle?"

"I'm afraid I do," said the uncle.

"And then the house whispers, like people laughing at you behind your back. It's awful, that is! I thought if I was lucky . . ."

"You might stop it," added the uncle.

The boy watched him with big blue eyes that had an uncanny cold fire in them, and he said never a word.

"Well, then!" said the uncle. "What are we doing?"

"I shouldn't like mother to know I was lucky," said the boy.

"Why not, son?"

"She'd stop me."

"I don't think she would."

"Oh!"—and the boy writhed in an odd way—"I don't want her to know, uncle."

"All right, son! We'll manage it without her knowing."

They managed it very easily. Paul, at the other's suggestion, handed over five thousand pounds to his uncle, who deposited it with the family lawyer, who was then to inform Paul's mother that a relative had put five thousand pounds into his hands, which sum was to be paid out a thousand pounds at a time, on the mother's birthday, for the next five years.

"So she'll have a birthday present of a thousand pounds for five successive years," said Uncle Oscar. "I hope it won't make it all the harder for her later."

Paul's mother had her birthday in November. The house had been "whispering" worse than ever lately, and, even in spite of his luck, Paul could not bear up against it. He was very anxious to see the effect of the birthday letter, telling his mother about the thousand pounds.

When there were no visitors, Paul now took his meals with his parents, as he was beyond the nursery control. His mother went into town nearly every day. She had discovered that she had an odd knack of sketching furs and dress materials, so she worked secretly in the studio of a friend who was the chief "artist" for the leading drapers. She drew the figures of ladies in furs and ladies in silk and sequins for the newspaper advertisements. This young woman artist earned several thousand pounds a year, but Paul's mother only made several hundreds, and she was again dissatisfied. She so wanted to be first in something, and she did not suceed, even in making sketches for drapery advertisements.

She was down to breakfast on the morning of her birthday. Paul watched her face as she read her letters. He knew the lawyer's letter. As his mother read it, her face hardened and became more expressionless. Then a cold, determined look came on her mouth. She hid the letter under the pile of others, and said not a word about it.

"Didn't you have anything nice in the post for your birthday, mother?" said Paul.

"Quite moderately nice," she said, her voice cold and absent.

She went away to town without saying more.

But in the afternoon Uncle Oscar appeared. He said Paul's mother had had a long interview with the lawyer, asking if the whole five thousand could be advanced at once, as she was in debt.

"What do you think, uncle?" said the boy.

"I leave it to you, son."

"Oh, let her have it, then! We can get some more with the other," said the boy.

"A bird in the hand is worth two in the bush, laddie!" said Uncle Oscar.

"But I'm sure to know for the Grand National; or the Lincolnshire; or else the Derby. I'm sure to know for one of them," said Paul.

So Uncle Oscar signed the agreement, and Paul's mother touched the whole five thousand. Then something very curious happened. The voices in the house suddenly went mad, like a chorus of frogs on a spring evening. There were certain new furnishings, and Paul had a tutor. He was really going to Eton, his father's school, in the following autumn. There were flowers in the winter, and a blossoming of the luxury Paul's mother had been used to. And yet the voices in the house, behind the sprays of mimosa and almond blossom, and from under the piles of iridescent cushions, simply trilled and screamed in a sort of ecstasy: "There must be more money! Oh-h-h, there must be more money. Oh, now, now-w! Now-w-w—there must be more money—more than ever! More than ever!"

It frightened Paul terribly. He studied away at his Latin and Greek with his tutors. But his intense hours were spent with Bassett. The Grand National had gone by: he had not "known," and had lost a hundred pounds. Summer was at hand. He was in agony for the Lincoln. But even for the Lincoln he didn't "know" and he lost fifty pounds. He became wild-eyed and strange, as if something were going to explode in him.

"Let it alone, son! Don't you bother about it!" urged Uncle Oscar. But it was as if the boy couldn't really hear what his uncle was saying.

"I've got to know for the Derby! I've got to know for the Derby!" the child reiterated, his big blue eyes blazing with a sort of madness.

His mother noticed how overwrought he was.

"You'd better go to the seaside. Wouldn't you like to go now to the seaside, instead of waiting? I think you'd better," she said, looking down at him anxiously, her heart curiously heavy because of him.

But the child lifted his uncanny blue eyes.

"I couldn't possibly go before the Derby, mother!" he said. "I couldn't possibly!"

"Why not?" she said, her voice becoming heavy when she was opposed. "Why not? You can still go from the seaside to see the Derby with your Uncle Oscar, if that's what you wish. No need for you to wait here. Besides, I think you care too much about these races. It's a bad sign. My family has been a gambling family, and you won't know till you grow up how much damage it has done. But it has done damage. I shall have to send Bassett away, and ask Uncle Oscar not to talk racing to you, unless you promise to be reasonable about it; go away to the seaside and forget it. You're all nerves!"

"I'll do what you like, mother, so long as you don't send me away till after the Derby," the boy said.

"Send you away from where? Just from this house?"

"Yes," he said, gazing at her.

"Why, you curious child, what makes you care about this house so much, suddenly? I never knew you loved it."

He gazed at her without speaking. He had a secret within a secret, something he had not divulged, even to Bassett or to his Uncle Oscar.

But his mother, after standing undecided and a little bit sullen for some moments, said:

"Very well, then! Don't go to the seaside till after the Derby, if you don't wish it. But promise me you won't let your nerves go to pieces. Promise you won't think so much about horse racing and events, as you call them!"

"Oh, no," said the boy casually. "I won't think much about them, mother. You needn't worry. I wouldn't worry, mother, if I were you."

"If you were me and I were you," said his mother, "I wonder what we should do!"

"But you know you needn't worry, mother, don't you?" the boy repeated.

"I should be awfully glad to know it," she said wearily.

"Oh, well, you can, you know. I mean, you ought to know you needn't worry," he insisted.

"Ought I? Then I'll see about it," she said.

Paul's secret of secrets was his wooden horse, that which had no name. Since he was emancipated from a nurse and a nursery-governess, he had had his rocking horse removed to his own bedroom at the top of the house.

"Surely, you're too big for a rocking horse!" his mother had remonstrated.

"Well, you see, mother, till I can have a real horse, I like to have some sort of animal about," had been his quaint answer.

"Do you feel he keeps you company?" she laughed.

"Oh, yes! He's very good, he always keeps me company, when I'm there," said Paul.

So the horse, rather shabby, stood in an arrested prance in the boy's bedroom.

The Derby was drawing near, and the boy grew more and more tense. He hardly heard what was spoken to him, he was very frail, and his eyes were really uncanny. His mother had sudden seizures of uneasiness about him. Sometimes, for half-an-hour, she would feel a sudden anxiety about him that was almost anguish. She wanted to rush to him at once, and know he was safe.

Two nights before the Derby, she was at a big party in town, when one of her rushes of anxiety about her boy, her first-born, gripped her heart till she could hardly speak. She fought with the feeling, might and main, for she believed in common sense. But it was too strong. She had to leave the dance and go downstairs to telephone to the country. The children's nursery-governess was terribly surprised and startled at being rung up in the night.

"Are the children all right, Miss Wilmot?"

"Oh, yes, they are quite all right."

"Master Paul? Is he all right?"

"He went to bed as right as a trivet. Shall I run up and look at him?"

"No," said Paul's mother reluctantly. "No! Don't trouble. It's all right. Don't sit up. We shall be home fairly soon." She did not want her son's privacy intruded upon.

"Very good," said the governess.

It was about one o'clock when Paul's mother and father drove up to their house. All was still. Paul's mother went to her room and slipped off her white fur coat. She had told her maid not to wait up for her. She heard her husband downstairs, mixing a whisky-and-soda.

And then, because of the strange anxiety at her heart, she stole upstairs to her son's room. Noiselessly she went along the upper corridor. Was there a faint noise? What was it?

She stood, with arrested muscles, outside his door, listening. There was a strange, heavy, and yet not loud noise. Her heart stood still. It was a soundless noise, yet rushing and powerful. Something huge, in violent, hushed motion. What was it? What in God's name was it? She ought to know. She felt that she knew the noise. She knew what it was.

Yet she could not place it. She couldn't say what it was. And on and on it went, like a madness.

Softly, frozen with anxiety and fear, she turned the door handle.

The room was dark. Yet in the space near the window, she heard and saw something plunging to and fro. She gazed in fear and amazement.

Then suddenly she switched on the light, and saw her son, in his green pyjamas, madly surging on the rocking horse. The blaze of light suddenly lit him up, as he urged the wooden horse, and lit her up, as she stood, blonde, in her dress of pale green and crystal, in the doorway.

"Paul!" she cried. "Whatever are you doing?"

"It's Malabar!" he screamed, in a powerful, strange voice. "It's Malabar."

His eyes blazed at her for one strange and senseless second, as he ceased urging his wooden horse. Then he fell with a crash to the ground, and she, all her tormented motherhood flooding upon her, rushed to gather him up.

But he was unconscious, and unconscious he remained, with some brain-fever. He talked and tossed, and his mother sat stonily by his side.

"Malabar! It's Malabar! Bassett, Bassett, I know it! It's Malabar!"

So the child cried, trying to get up and urge the rocking horse that gave him his inspiration.

"What does he mean by Malabar?" asked the heart-frozen mother.

"I don't know," said the father stonily.

"What does he mean by Malabar?" she asked her brother Oscar.

"It's one of the horses running for the Derby," was the answer.

And, in spite of himself, Oscar Cresswell spoke to Bassett, and himself put a thousand on Malabar: at fourteen to one.

The third day of the illness was critical: they were waiting for a change. The boy, with his rather long, curly hair, was tossing ceaselessly on the pillow. He neither slept nor regained consciousness, and his eyes were like blue stones. His mother sat, feeling her heart had gone, turned actually into a stone.

In the evening, Oscar Cresswell did not come, but Bassett sent a message, saying could he come up for one moment, just one moment? Paul's mother was very angry at the intrusion, but on second thought she agreed. The boy was the same. Perhaps Bassett might bring him to consciousness.

The gardener, a shortish fellow with a little brown moustache, and sharp little brown eyes, tiptoed into the room, touched his imaginary cap to Paul's mother, and stole to the bedside, staring with glittering, smallish eyes, at the tossing, dying child.

"Master Paul!" he whispered. "Master Paul! Malabar come in first all right, a clean win. I did as you told me. You've made over seventy thousand pounds, you have; you've got over eighty thousand. Malabar came in all right, Master Paul."

"Malabar! Malabar! Did I say Malabar, mother? Did I say Malabar? Do you think I'm lucky, mother? I knew Malabar, didn't I? Over eighty thousand pounds! I call that lucky, don't you, mother? Over eighty thousand pounds! I knew, didn't I know I knew? Malabar came in all right. If I ride my horse till I'm sure, then I tell you, Bassett, you can go as high as you like. Did you go for all you were worth, Bassett?"

"I went a thousand on it, Master Paul."

"I never told you, mother, that if I can ride my horse, and get there, then I'm absolutely sure—oh, absolutely! Mother, did I ever tell you? I'm lucky."

"No, you never did," said the mother.

But the boy died in the night.

And even as he lay dead, his mother heard her brother's voice saying to her: "My God, Hester, you're eighty-odd thousand to the good and a poor devil of a son to the bad. But, poor devil, poor devil, he's best gone out of a life where he rides his rocking horse to find a winner."

RING LARDNER   (1885–1933)

Haircut

I got another barber that comes over from Carterville and helps me out Saturdays, but the rest of the time I can get along all right alone. You can see for yourself that this ain't no New York City and besides that, the most of the boys works all day and don't have no leisure to drop in here and get themselves prettied up.

You're a newcomer, ain't you? I thought I hadn't seen you round before. I hope you like it good enough to stay. As I say, we ain't no New York City or Chicago, but we have pretty good times. Not as good, though, since Jim Kendall got killed. When he was alive, him and Hod Meyers used to keep this town in an uproar. I bet they was more laughin' done here than any town its size in America.

Jim was comical, and Hod was pretty near a match for him. Since Jim's gone, Hod tries to hold his end up just the same as ever, but it's tough goin' when you ain't got nobody to kind of work with.

They used to be plenty fun in here Saturdays. This place is jam-packed Saturdays, from four o'clock on. Jim and Hod would show up right after their supper, round six o'clock. Jim would set himself down in that big chair, nearest the blue spittoon. Whoever had been settin' in that chair, why they'd get up when Jim come in and give it to him.

You'd of thought it was a reserved seat like they have sometimes in a theayter. Hod would generally always stand or walk up and down, or some Saturdays, of course, he'd be settin' in this chair part of the time, gettin' a haircut.

Well, Jim would set there a w'ile without openin' his mouth only to spit, and then finally he'd say to me, "Whitey,"—my right name, that is, my right first name, is Dick, but everybody round here calls me Whitey—Jim would say, "Whitey, your nose looks like a rosebud tonight. You must of been drinkin' some of your aw de cologne."

So I'd say, "No, Jim, but you look like you'd been drinkin' somethin' of that kind or somethin' worse."

Jim would have to laugh at that, but then he'd speak up and say, "No, I ain't had nothin' to drink, but that ain't sayin' I wouldn't like somethin'. I wouldn't even mind if it was wood alcohol."

Then Hod Meyers would say, "Neither would your wife." That would set everybody to laughin' because Jim and his wife wasn't on very good terms. She'd of divorced him only they wasn't no chance to get alimony and she didn't have no way to take care of herself and the kids. She couldn't never understand Jim. He *was* kind of rough, but a good fella at heart.

Him and Hod had all kinds of sport with Milt Sheppard. I don't suppose you've seen Milt. Well, he's got an Adam's apple that looks more like a mushmelon.[1] So I'd be shavin' Milt and when I'd start to shave down here on his neck, Hod would holler, "Hey, Whitey, wait a minute! Before you cut into it, let's make up a pool and see who can guess closest to the number of seeds."

And Jim would say, "If Milt hadn't of been so hoggish, he'd of ordered a half a cantaloupe instead of a whole one and it might not of stuck in his throat."

All the boys would roar at this and Milt himself would force a smile, though the joke was on him. Jim certainly was a card!

There's his shavin' mug, settin' on the shelf, right next to Charley Vail's. "Charles M. Vail." That's the druggist. He comes in regular for his shave, three times a week. And Jim's is the cup next to Charley's. "James H. Kendall." Jim won't need no shavin' mug no more, but I'll leave it there just the same for old time's sake. Jim certainly was a character!

Years ago, Jim used to travel for a canned goods concern over in Carterville. They sold canned goods. Jim had the whole northern half of the State and was on the road five days out of every week. He'd drop in here Saturdays and tell his experiences for that week. It was rich.

I guess he paid more attention to playin' jokes than makin' sales. Finally the concern let him out and he come right home here and told everybody he'd been fired instead of sayin' he'd resigned like most fellas would of.

It was a Saturday and the shop was full and Jim got up out of that chair and says, "Gentlemen, I got an important announcement to make. I been fired from my job."

Well, they asked him if he was in earnest and he said he was and nobody could think of nothin' to say till Jim finally broke the ice himself. He says, "I been sellin' canned goods and now I'm canned goods myself."

You see, the concern he'd been workin' for was a factory that made canned goods. Over in Carterville. And now Jim said he was canned himself. He was certainly a card!

Jim had a great trick that he used to play w'ile he was travelin'. For instance, he'd be ridin' on a train and they'd come to some little

---

[1] that is, a muskmelon.

town like, well, like, we'll say, like Benton. Jim would look out the train window and read the signs on the stores.

For instance, they'd be a sign, "Henry Smith, Dry Goods." Well, Jim would write down the name and the name of the town and when he got to wherever he was goin' he'd mail back a postal card to Henry Smith at Benton and not sign no name to it, but he'd write on the card, well, somethin' like "Ask your wife about that book agent that spent the afternoon last week," or "Ask your Missus who kept her from gettin' lonesome the last time you was in Carterville." And he'd sign the card, "A Friend."

Of course, he never knew what really come of none of these jokes, but he could picture what *probably* happened and that was enough.

Jim didn't work very steady after he lost his position with the Carterville people. What he did earn, doin' odd jobs round town, why he spent pretty near all of it on gin and his family might of starved if the stores hadn't of carried them along. Jim's wife tried her hand at dressmakin', but they ain't nobody goin' to get rich makin' dresses in this town.

As I say, she'd of divorced Jim, only she seen that she couldn't support herself and the kids and she was always hopin' that some day Jim would cut out his habits and give her more than two or three dollars a week.

They was a time when she would go to whoever he was workin' for and ask them to give her his wages, but after she done this once or twice, he beat her to it by borrowin' most of his pay in advance. He told it all round town, how he had outfoxed his Missus. He certainly was a caution!

But he wasn't satisfied with just outwittin' her. He was sore the way she had acted, tryin' to grab off his pay. And he made up his mind he'd get even. Well, he waited till Evans's Circus was advertised to come to town. Then he told his wife and two kiddies that he was goin' to take them to the circus. The day of the circus, he told them he would get the tickets and meet them outside the entrance to the tent.

Well, he didn't have no intentions of bein' there or buyin' tickets or nothin'. He got full of gin and laid round Wright's poolroom all day. His wife and the kids waited and waited and of course he didn't show up. His wife didn't have a dime with her, or nowhere else, I guess. So she finally had to tell the kids it was all off and they cried like they wasn't never goin' to stop.

Well, it seems, w'ile they was cryin', Doc Stair came along and he asked what was the matter, but Mrs. Kendall was stubborn and wouldn't tell him, but the kids told him and he insisted on takin' them and their mother in the show. Jim found this out afterwards and it was one reason why he had it in for Doc Stair.

Doc Stair come here about a year and a half ago. He's a mighty handsome young fella and his clothes always look like he has them made to order. He goes to Detroit two or three times a year and w'ile he's there he must have a tailor take his measure and then make him a suit to order. They cost pretty near twice as much, but they fit a whole lot better than if you just bought them in a store.

For a w'ile everybody was wonderin' why a young doctor like Doc Stair should come to a town like this where we already got old Doc Gamble and Doc Foote that's both been here for years and all the practice in town was always divided between the two of them.

Then they was a story got round that Doc Stair's gal had throwed him over, a gal up in the Northern Peninsula somewheres, and the reason he come here was to hide himself away and forget it. He said himself that he thought they wasn't nothin' like general practice in a place like ours to fit a man to be a good all round doctor. And that's why he'd came.

Anyways, it wasn't long before he was makin' enough to live on, though they tell me that he never dunned nobody for what they owed him, and the folks here certainly has got the owin' habit, even in my business. If I had all that was comin' to me for just shaves alone, I could go to Carterville and put up at the Mercer for a week and see a different picture every night. For instance, they's old George Purdy—but I guess I shouldn't ought to be gossipin'.

Well, last year, our coroner died, died of the flu. Ken Beatty, that was his name. He was the coroner. So they had to choose another man to be coroner in his place and they picked Doc Stair. He laughed at first and said he didn't want it, but they made him take it. It ain't no job that anybody would fight for and what a man makes out of it in a year would just about buy seeds for their garden. Doc's the kind, though, that can't say no to nothin' if you keep at him long enough.

But I was goin' to tell you about a poor boy we got here in town—Paul Dickson. He fell out of a tree when he was about ten years old. Lit on his head and it done somethin' to him and he ain't never been right. No harm in him, but just silly. Jim Kendall used to call him cuckoo; that's a name Jim had for anybody that was off their head, only he called people's head their bean. That was another of his gags, callin' head bean and callin' crazy people cuckoo. Only poor Paul ain't crazy, but just silly.

You can imagine that Jim used to have all kinds of fun with Paul. He'd send him to the White Front Garage for a left-handed monkey wrench. Of course they ain't no such a thing as a left-handed monkey wrench.

And once we had a kind of a fair here and they was a baseball game between the fats and the leans and before the game started

Jim called Paul over and sent him way down to Schrader's hardware store to get a key for the pitcher's box.

They wasn't nothin' in the way of gags that Jim couldn't think up, when he put his mind to it.

Poor Paul was always kind of suspicious of people, maybe on account of how Jim had kept foolin' him. Paul wouldn't have much to do with anybody only his own mother and Doc Stair and a girl here in town named Julie Gregg. That is, she ain't a girl no more, but pretty near thirty or over.

When Doc first come to town, Paul seemed to feel like here was a real friend and he hung around Doc's office most of the w'ile; the only time he wasn't there was when he'd go home to eat or sleep or when he seen Julie Gregg doin' her shoppin'.

When he looked out Doc's window and seen her, he'd run downstairs and join her and tag along with her to the different stores. The poor boy was crazy about Julie and she always treated him mighty nice and made him feel like he was welcome, though of course it wasn't nothin' but pity on her side.

Doc done all he could to improve Paul's mind and he told me once that he really thought the boy was gettin' better, that they was times when he was as bright and sensible as anybody else.

But I was goin' to tell you about Julie Gregg. Old Man Gregg was in the lumber business, but got to drinkin' and lost the most of his money and when he died, he didn't leave nothin' but the house and just enough insurance for the girl to skimp along on.

Her mother was a kind of a half invalid and didn't hardly ever leave the house. Julie wanted to sell the place and move somewheres else after the old man died, but the mother said she was born here and would die here. It was tough on Julie, as the young people round this town—well, she's too good for them.

She's been away to school and Chicago and New York and different places and they ain't no subject she can't talk on, where you take the rest of the young folks here and you mention anything to them outside of Gloria Swanson or Tommy Meighan and they think you're delirious. Did you see Gloria in Wages of Virtue? You missed somethin'!

Well, Doc Stair hadn't been here more than a week when he come in one day to get shaved and I recognized who he was as he had been pointed out to me, so I told him about my old lady. She's been ailin' for a couple of years and either Doc Gamble or Doc Foote, neither one, seemed to be helpin' her. So he said he would come out and see her, but if she was able to get out herself, it would be better to bring her to his office where he could make a completer examination.

So I took her to his office and w'ile I was waitin' for her in the reception room, in come Julie Gregg. When somebody comes in Doc Stair's office, they's a bell that rings in his inside office so as he can tell they's somebody to see him.

So he left my old lady inside and come out to the front office and that's the first time him and Julie met and I guess it was what they call love at first sight. But it wasn't fifty-fifty. This young fella was the slickest lookin' fella she'd ever seen in this town and she went wild over him. To him she was just a young lady that wanted to see the doctor.

She'd came on about the same business I had. Her mother had been doctorin' for years with Doc Gamble and Doc Foote and without no results. So she'd heard they was a new doc in town and decided to give him a try. He promised to call and see her mother that same day.

I said a minute ago that it was love at first sight on her part. I'm not only judgin' by how she acted afterwards but how she looked at him that first day in his office. I ain't no mind reader, but it was wrote all over her face that she was gone.

Now Jim Kendall, besides bein' a jokesmith and a pretty good drinker, well, Jim was quite a lady-killer. I guess he run pretty wild durin' the time he was on the road for them Carterville people, and besides that, he'd had a couple little affairs of the heart right here in town. As I say, his wife would of divorced him, only she couldn't.

But Jim was like the majority of men, and women, too, I guess. He wanted what he couldn't get. He wanted Julie Gregg and worked his head off tryin' to land her. Only he'd of said bean instead of head.

Well, Jim's habits and his jokes didn't appeal to Julie and of course he was a married man, so he didn't have no more chance than, well, than a rabbit. That's an expression of Jim's himself. When somebody didn't have no chance to get elected or somethin', Jim would always say they didn't have no more chance than a rabbit.

He didn't make no bones about how he felt. Right in here, more than once, in front of the whole crowd, he said he was stuck on Julie and anybody that could get her for him was welcome to his house and his wife and kids included. But she wouldn't have nothin' to do with him; wouldn't even speak to him on the street. He finally seen he wasn't gettin' nowheres with his usual line so he decided to try the rough stuff. He went right up to her house one evenin' and when she opened the door he forced his way in and grabbed her But she broke loose and before he could stop her, she run in the next room and locked the door and phoned to Joe Barnes. Joe's the marshal. Jim could hear who she was phonin' to and he beat it before Joe got there.

Joe was an old friend of Julie's pa. Joe went to Jim the next day and told him what would happen if he ever done it again.

I don't know how the news of this little affair leaked out. Chances is that Joe Barnes told his wife and she told somebody else's wife and they told their husband. Anyways, it did leak out and Hod Meyers had the nerve to kid Jim about it, right here in this shop. Jim didn't deny nothin' and kind of laughed it off and said for us all to wait; that lots of people had tried to make a monkey out of him, but he always got even.

Meanw'ile everybody in town was wise to Julie's bein' wild mad over the Doc. I don't suppose she had any idear how her face changed when him and her was together; of course she couldn't of, or she'd of kept away from him. And she didn't know that we was all noticin' how many times she made excuses to go up to his office or pass it on the other side of the street and look up in his window to see if he was there. I felt sorry for her and so did most other people.

Hod Meyers kept rubbin' it into Jim about how the Doc had cut him out. Jim didn't pay no attention to the kiddin' and you could see he was plannin' one of his jokes.

One trick Jim had was the knack of changin' his voice. He could make you think he was a girl talkin' and he could mimic any man's voice. To show you how good he was along this line, I'll tell you the joke he played on me once.

You know, in most towns of any size, when a man is dead and needs a shave, why the barber that shaves him soaks him five dollars for the job; that is, he don't soak *him,* but whoever ordered the shave. I just charge three dollars because personally I don't mind much shavin' a dead person. They lay a whole lot stiller than live customers. The only thing is that you don't feel like talkin' to them and you get kind of lonesome.

Well, about the coldest day we ever had here, two years ago last winter, the phone rung at the house w'ile I was home to dinner and I answered the phone and it was a woman's voice and she said she was Mrs. John Scott and her husband was dead and would I come out and shave him.

Old John had always been a good customer of mine. But they live seven miles out in the country, on the Streeter road. Still I didn't see how I could say no.

So I said I would be there, but would have to come in a jitney[2]

---

2 *jitney,* an automobile or a small bus that transports passengers along a set route for a small fare.

and it might cost three or four dollars besides the price of the shave. So she, or the voice, it said that was all right, so I got Frank Abbott to drive me out to the place and when I got there, who should open the door but old John himself! He wasn't no more dead than, well, than a rabbit.

It didn't take no private detective to figure out who had played me this little joke. Nobody could of thought it up but Jim Kendall. He certainly was a card!

I tell you this incident just to show you how he could disguise his voice and make you believe it was somebody else talkin'. I'd of swore it was Mrs. Scott had called me. Anyways, some woman.

Well, Jim waited till he had Doc Stair's voice down pat; then he went after revenge.

He called Julie up on a night when he knew Doc was over in Carterville. She never questioned but what it was Doc's voice. Jim said he must see her that night; he couldn't wait no longer to tell her somethin'. She was all excited and told him to come to the house. But he said he was expectin' an important long distance call and wouldn't she please forget her manners for once and come to his office. He said they couldn't nothin' hurt her and nobody would see her and he just *must* talk to her a little w'ile. Well, poor Julie fell for it.

Doc always keeps a night light in his office, so it looked to Julie like they was somebody there.

Meanw'ile Jim Kendall had went to Wright's poolroom, where they was a whole gang amusin' themselves. The most of them had drank plenty of gin, and they was a rough bunch even when sober. They was always strong for Jim's jokes and when he told them to come with him and see some fun they give up their card games and pool games and followed along.

Doc's office is on the second floor. Right outside his door they's a flight of stairs leadin' to the floor above. Jim and his gang hid in the dark behind these stairs.

Well, Julie come up to Doc's door and rung the bell and they was nothin' doin'. She rung it again and rung it seven or eight times. Then she tried the door and found it locked. Then Jim made some kind of a noise and she heard it and waited a minute, and then she says, "Is that you, Ralph?" Ralph is Doc's first name.

They was no answer and it must of came to her all of a sudden that she'd been bunked. She pretty near fell downstairs and the whole gang after her. They chased her all the way home, hollerin', "Is that you, Ralph?" and "Oh, Ralphie, dear, is that you?" Jim says he couldn't holler it himself, as he was laughin' too hard.

Poor Julie! She didn't show up here on Main Street for a long, long time afterward.

And of course Jim and his gang told everybody in town, everybody but Doc Stair. They was scared to tell him, and he might of never knowed only for Paul Dickson. The poor cuckoo, as Jim called him, he was here in the shop one night when Jim was still gloatin' yet over what he'd done to Julie. And Paul took in as much of it as he could understand and he run to Doc with the story.

It's a cinch Doc went up in the air and swore he'd make Jim suffer. But it was a kind of a delicate thing, because if it got out that he had beat Jim up, Julie was bound to hear of it and then she'd know that Doc knew and of course knowin' that he knew would make it worse for her than ever. He was goin' to do somethin', but it took a lot of figurin'.

Well, it was a couple days later when Jim was here in the shop again, and so was the cuckoo. Jim was goin' duck-shootin' the next day and had came in lookin' for Hod Meyers to go with him. I happened to know that Hod had went over to Carterville and wouldn't be home till the end of the week. So Jim said he hated to go alone and he guessed he would call it off. Then poor Paul spoke up and said if Jim would take him he would go along. Jim thought a w'ile and then he said, well, he guessed a half-wit was better than nothin'.

I suppose he was plottin' to get Paul out in the boat and play some joke on him, like pushin' him in the water. Anyways, he said Paul could go. He asked him had he ever shot a duck and Paul said no, he'd never even had a gun in his hands. So Jim said he could set in the boat and watch him and if he behaved himself, he might lend him his gun for a couple of shots. They made a date to meet in the mornin' and that's the last I seen of Jim alive.

Next mornin', I hadn't been open more than ten minutes when Doc Stair come in. He looked kind of nervous. He asked me had I seen Paul Dickson. I said no, but I knew where he was, out duck-shootin' with Jim Kendall. So Doc says that's what he had heard, and he couldn't understand it because Paul had told him he wouldn't never have no more to do with Jim as long as he lived.

He said Paul had told him about the joke Jim had played on Julie. He said Paul had asked him what he thought of the joke and the Doc had told him that anybody that would do a thing like that ought not to be let live.

I said it had been a kind of a raw thing, but Jim just couldn't resist no kind of a joke, no matter how raw. I said I thought he was all right at heart, but just bubblin' over with mischief. Doc turned and walked out.

At noon he got a phone call from old John Scott. The lake where Jim and Paul had went shootin' is on John's place. Paul had come runnin' up to the house a few minutes before and said they'd been an accident. Jim had shot a few ducks and then give the gun to Paul and told him to try his luck. Paul hadn't never handled a gun and he was nervous. He was shakin' so hard that he couldn't control the gun. He let fire and Jim sunk back in the boat, dead.

Doc Stair, bein' the coroner, jumped in Frank Abbott's flivver[3] and rushed out to Scott's farm. Paul and old John was down on the shore of the lake. Paul had rowed the boat to shore, but they'd left the body in it, waitin' for Doc to come.

Doc examined the body and said they might as well fetch it back to town. They was no use leavin' it there or callin' a jury, as it was a plain case of accidental shootin'.

Personally I wouldn't never leave a person shoot a gun in the same boat I was in unless I was sure they knew somethin' about guns. Jim was a sucker to leave a new beginner have his gun, let alone a half-wit. It probably served Jim right, what he got. But still we miss him round here. He certainly was a card!

Comb it wet or dry?

---

3 *flivver*, a small, cheap automobile—especially an old one.

SHERWOOD ANDERSON (1876–1941)

I'm a Fool

It was a hard jolt for me, one of the most bitterest I ever had to face. And it all came about through my own foolishness, too. Even yet sometimes, when I think of it, I want to cry or swear or kick myself. Perhaps, even now, after all this time, there will be a kind of satisfaction in making myself look cheap by telling of it.

It began at three o'clock one October afternoon as I sat in the grand stand at the fall trotting and pacing meet at Sandusky, Ohio.

To tell the truth, I felt a little foolish that I should be sitting in the grand stand at all. During the summer before I had left my home town with Harry Whitehead and, with a nigger named Burt, had taken a job as swipe with one of the two horses Harry was campaigning through the fall race meets that year. Mother cried and my sister Mildred, who wanted to get a job as a schoolteacher in our town that fall, stormed and scolded about the house all during the week before I left. They both thought it something disgraceful that one of our family should take a place as a swipe with race horses. I've an idea Mildred thought my taking the place would stand in the way of her getting the job she'd been working so long for.

But after all I had to work, and there was no other work to be got. A big lumbering fellow of nineteen couldn't just hang around the house and I had got too big to mow people's lawns and sell newspapers. Little chaps who could get next to people's sympathies by their sizes were always getting jobs away from me. There was one fellow who kept saying to everyone who wanted a lawn mowed or a cistern cleaned that he was saving money to work his way through college, and I used to lay awake nights thinking up ways to injure him without being found out. I kept thinking of wagons running over him and bricks falling on his head as he walked along the street. But never mind him.

I got the place with Harry and I liked Burt fine. We got along splendid together. He was a big nigger with a lazy sprawling body and soft, kind eyes, and when it came to a fight he could hit like Jack Johnson. He had Bucephalus, a big black pacing stallion that could do 2.09 or 2.10 if he had to, and I had a little gelding named

Doctor Fritz that never lost a race all fall when Harry wanted him to win.

We set out from home late in July, in a box car with the two horses and after that, until late November, we kept moving along to the race meets and the fairs. It was a peachy time for me, I'll say that. Sometimes now I think that boys who are raised regular in houses, and never have a fine nigger like Burt for best friend, and go to high schools and college, and never steal anything, or get drunk a little, or learn to swear from fellows who know how, or come walking up in front of a grand stand in their shirt sleeves and with dirty horsy pants on when the races are going on and the grand stand is full of people all dressed up—What's the use of talking about it? Such fellows don't know nothing at all. They've never had no opportunity.

But I did. Burt taught me how to rub down a horse and put the bandages on after a race and steam a horse out and a lot of valuable things for any man to know. He could wrap a bandage on a horse's leg so smooth that if it had been the same color you would think it was his skin, and I guess he'd have been a big driver, too, and got to the top like Murphy and Walter Cox and the others if he hadn't been black.

Gee whizz! it was fun. You got to a county-seat town, maybe say on a Saturday or Sunday, and the fair began the next Tuesday and lasted until Friday afternoon. Doctor Fritz would be, say, in the 2.25 trot on Tuesday afternoon and on Thursday afternoon Bucephalus would knock 'em cold in the "free-for-all" pace. It left you a lot of time to hang around and listen to horse talk, and see Burt knock some yap cold that got too gay, and you'd find out about horses and men and pick up a lot of stuff you could use all the rest of your life, if you had some sense and salted down what you heard and felt and saw.

And then at the end of the week when the race meet was over, and Harry had run home to tend up to his livery-stable business, you and Burt hitched the two horses to carts and drove slow and steady across country, to the place for the next meeting, so as to not overheat the horses, etc., etc., you know.

Gee whizz! Gosh amighty! the nice hickory-nut and beechnut and oaks and other kinds of trees along the roads, all brown and red, and the good smells, and Burt singing a song called "Deep River," and the country girls at the windows of houses and everything. You can stick your colleges up your nose for all me. I guess I know where I got my education.

Why, one of those little burgs of towns you came to on the way, say now on a Saturday afternoon, and Burt says, "Let's lay up here." And you did.

And you took the horses to a livery stable and fed them, and you got your good clothes out of a box and put them on.

And the town was full of farmers gaping, because they could see you were racehorse people, and the kids maybe never see a nigger before and was afraid and run away when the two of us walked down their main street.

And that was before prohibition and all that foolishness, and so you went into a saloon, the two of you, and all the yaps come and stood around, and there was always some one pretended he was horsy and knew things and spoke up and began asking questions, and all you did was to lie and lie all you could about what horses you had, and I said I owned them, and then some fellow said, "Will you have a drink of whisky?" and Burt knocked his eye out the way he could say, offhand like, "Oh, well, all right, I'm agreeable to a little nip. I'll split a quart with you." Gee whizz!

But that isn't what I want to tell my story about. We got home late in November and I promised mother I'd quit the race horses for good. There's a lot of things you've got to promise a mother because she don't know any better.

And so, there not being any work in our town any more than when I left there to go to the races, I went off to Sandusky and got a pretty good place taking care of horses for a man who owned a teaming and delivery and storage and coal and real-estate business there. It was a pretty good place with good eats, and a day off each week, and sleeping on a cot in a big barn, and mostly just shoveling in hay and oats to a lot of big good-enough skates of horses that couldn't have trotted a race with a toad. I wasn't dissatisfied and I could send money home.

And then, as I started to tell you, the fall races come to Sandusky and I got the day off and I went. I left the job at noon and had on my good clothes and my new brown derby hat I'd bought the Saturday before, and a stand-up collar.

First of all I went downtown and walked about with the dudes. I've always thought to myself, "Put up a good front," and so I did it. I had forty dollars in my pockets and so I went into the West House, a big hotel, and walked up to the cigar stand. "Give me three twenty-five cent cigars," I said. There was a lot of horsemen and strangers and dressed-up people from other towns standing around in the lobby and in the bar, and I mingled amongst them. In the bar there was a fellow with a cane and a Windsor tie on, that it made me sick to look at him. I like a man to be a man and dressed up, but not to go put on that kind of airs. So I pushed him aside, kind of rough, and had me a drink of whisky. And then he looked at me, as though he thought maybe he'd get gay, but he changed his mind and didn't say anything. And then I had another drink of whisky, just to show him something, and went out and had a hack out to the races, all to myself, and when I got there I bought myself the best seat I could get up in the grand stand, but didn't go in for any of these boxes. That's putting on too many airs.

And so there I was, sitting up in the grand stand as gay as you please and looking down on the swipes coming out with their horses, and with their dirty horsy pants on and the horseblankets swung over their shoulders, same as I had been doing all the year before. I liked one thing about the same as the other, sitting up there and feeling grand and being down there and looking up at the yaps and feeling grander and more important, too.

One thing's about as good as another, if you take it just right. I've often said that.

Well, right in front of me, in the grand stand that day, there was a fellow with a couple of girls and they was about my age. The young fellow was a nice guy, all right. He was the kind maybe that goes to college and then comes to be a lawyer or maybe a newspaper editor or something like that, but he wasn't stuck on himself. There are some of that kind are all right and he was one of the ones.

He had his sister with him and another girl and the sister looked around over his shoulder, accidental at first, not intending to start anything—she wasn't that kind—and her eyes and mine happened to meet.

You know how it is. Gee, she was a peach! She had on a soft dress, kind of a blue stuff and it looked carelessly made, but was well sewed and made and everything. I knew that much. I blushed when she looked right at me and so did she. She was the nicest girl I've ever seen in my life. She wasn't stuck on herself and she could talk proper grammar without being like a schoolteacher or something like that. What I mean is, she was O.K. I think maybe her father was well-to-do, but not rich to make her chesty because she was his daughter, as some are. Maybe he owned a drug store or a dry-goods store in their home town, or something like that. She never told me and I never asked.

My own people are all O.K. too, when you come to that. My grandfather was Welsh and over in the old country, in Wales he was— But never mind that.

The first heat of the first race come off and the young fellow setting there with the two girls left them and went down to make a bet. I knew what he was up to, but he didn't talk big and noisy and let everyone around know he was a sport, as some do. He wasn't that kind. Well, he come back and I heard him tell the two girls what horse he'd bet on, and when the heat trotted they all half got to their feet and acted in the excited, sweaty way people do when they've got money down on a race, and the horse they bet on is up there pretty close at the end, and they think maybe he'll come on with a rush, but he never does because he hasn't got the old juice in him, come right down to it.

And then, pretty soon, the horses came out for the 2.18 pace and there was a horse in it I knew. He was a horse Bob French had in his string but Bob didn't own him. He was a horse owned by a Mr. Mathers down at Marietta, Ohio.

This Mr. Mathers had a lot of money and owned some coal mines or something and he had a swell place out in the country, and he was stuck on race horses, but was a Presbyterian or something, and I think more than likely his wife was one, too, maybe a stiffer one than himself. So he never raced his horses hisself, and the story round the Ohio race tracks was that when one of his horses got ready to go to the races he turned him over to Bob French and pretended to his wife he was sold.

So Bob had the horses and he did pretty much as he pleased and you can't blame Bob, at least, I never did. Sometimes he was out to win and sometimes he wasn't. I never cared much about that when I was swiping a horse. What I did want to know was that my horse had the speed and could go out in front, if you wanted him to.

And, as I'm telling you, there was Bob in this race with one of Mr. Mathers' horses, was named "About Ben Ahem" or something like that, and was fast as a streak. He was a gelding and had a mark of 2.21, but could step in .08 or .09.

Because when Burt and I were out, as I've told you, the year before, there was a nigger Burt knew, worked for Mr. Mathers and we went out there one day when we didn't have no race on at the Marietta Fair and our boss Harry was gone home.

And so everyone was gone to the fair but just this one nigger and he took us all through Mr. Mathers' swell house and he and Burt tapped a bottle of wine Mr. Mathers had hid in his bedroom, back in a closet, without his wife knowing, and he showed us this Ahem horse. Burt was always stuck on being a driver but didn't have much chance to get to the top, being a nigger, and he and the other nigger gulped the whole bottle of wine and Burt got a little lit up.

So the nigger let Burt take this About Ben Ahem and step him a mile in a track Mr. Mathers had all to himself, right there on the farm. And Mr. Mathers had one child, a daughter, kinda sick and not very good looking, and she came home and we had to hustle to get About Ben Ahem stuck back in the barn.

I'm only telling you to get everything straight. At Sandusky, that afternoon I was at the fair, this young fellow with the two girls was fussed, being with the girls and losing his bet. You know how a fellow is that way. One of them was his girl and the other his sister. I had figured that out.

"Gee whizz," I says to myself, "I'm going to give him the dope."

He was mighty nice when I touched him on the shoulder. He and the girls were nice to me right from the start and clear to the end. I'm not blaming them.

And so he leaned back and I give him the dope on About Ben Ahem. "Don't bet a cent on this first heat because he'll go like an oxen hitched to a plow, but when the first heat is over go right down and lay on your pile." That's what I told him.

Well, I never saw a fellow treat any one sweller. There was a fat man sitting beside the little girl, that had looked at me twice by this time, and I at her, and both blushing, and what did he do but have the nerve to turn and ask the fat man to get up and change places with me so I could set with his crowd.

Gee whizz, craps amighty. There I was. What a chump I was to go and get gay up there in the West House bar, and just because that dude was standing there with a cane and that kind of a necktie on, to go and get all balled up and drink that whisky, just to show off.

Of course she would know, me setting right beside her and letting her smell of my breath. I could have kicked myself right down out of that grand stand and all around that race track and made a faster record than most of the skates of horses they had there that year.

Because that girl wasn't any mutt of a girl. What wouldn't I have give right then for a stick of chewing gum to chew, or a lozenger, or some licorice, or most anything. I was glad I had those twenty-five cent cigars in my pocket and right away I give that fellow one and lit one myself. Then that fat man got up and we changed places and there I was, plunked right down beside her.

They introduced themselves and the fellow's best girl, he had with him, was named Miss Elinor Woodbury, and her father was a manufacturer of barrels from a place called Tiffin, Ohio. And the fellow himself was named Wilbur Wessen and his sister was Miss Lucy Wessen.

I suppose it was their having such swell names that got me off my trolley. A fellow, just because he has been a swipe with a race horse, and works taking care of horses for a man in the teaming, delivery, and storage business isn't any better or worse than any one else. I've often thought that, and said it too.

But you know how a fellow is. There's something in that kind of nice clothes, and the kind of nice eyes she had, and the way she had looked at me, awhile before, over her brother's shoulder, and me looking back at her, and both of us blushing.

I couldn't show her up for a boob, could I?

I made a fool of myself, that's what I did. I said my name was Walter Mathers from Marietta, Ohio, and then I told all three of them the smashingest lie you ever heard. What I said was that my father owned the horse About Ben Ahem and that he had let him out to this Bob French for racing purposes, because our family was proud and had never gone into racing that way, in our own name, I mean, and Miss Lucy Wessen's eyes were shining, and I went the whole hog.

I told about our place down at Marietta, and about the big stables and the grand brick house we had on a hill, up above the Ohio River, but I knew enough not to do it in no bragging way. What I did was to start things and then let them drag the rest out of me. I acted just as reluctant to tell as I could. Our family hasn't got any barrel factory, and since I've known us, we've always been pretty poor, but not asking anything of any one at that, and my grandfather, over in Wales—but never mind that.

We set there talking like we had known each other for years and years, and I went and told them that my father had been expecting maybe this Bob French wasn't on the square, and had sent me up to Sandusky on the sly to find out what I could.

And I bluffed it through I had found out all about the 2.18 pace, in which About Ben Ahem was to start.

I said he would lose the first heat by pacing like a lame cow and then he would come back and skin 'em alive after that. And to back up what I said I took thirty dollars out of my pocket and handed it to Mr. Wilbur Wessen and asked him, would he mind, after the first heat, to go down and place it on About Ben Ahem for whatever odds he could get. What I said was that I didn't want Bob French to see me and none of the swipes.

Sure enough the first heat come off and About Ben Ahem went off his stride, up the back stretch, and looked like a wooden horse or a sick one, and come in to be last. Then this Wilbur Wessen went down to the betting place under the grand stand and there I was with the two girls, and when that Miss Woodbury was looking the other way once, Lucy Wessen kinda, with her shoulder you know, kinda touched me. Not just tucking down, I don't mean. You know how a woman can do. They get close, but not getting gay either. You know what they do. Gee whizz.

And then they give me a jolt. What they had done, when I didn't know, was to get together, and they had decided Wilbur Wessen would bet fifty dollars, and the two girls had gone and put in ten dollars each, of their own money, too. I was sick then, but I was sicker later.

About the gelding, About Ben Ahem, and their winning their money, I wasn't worried a lot about that. It came out O.K. Ahem stepped the next three heats like a bushel of spoiled eggs going to market before they could be found out, and Wilbur Wessen had got nine to two for the money. There was something else eating at me.

Because Wilbur come back, after he had bet the money, and after that he spent most of his time talking to that Miss Woodbury, and Lucy Wessen and I was left alone together like on a desert island. Gee, if I'd only been on the square or if there had been any way of getting myself on the square. There ain't any Walter Mathers, like I said to her and them, and there hasn't ever been one, but if there was, I bet I'd go to Marietta, Ohio, and shoot him tomorrow.

There I was, big boob that I am. Pretty soon the race was over, and Wilbur had gone down and collected our money, and we had a hack downtown, and he stood us a swell supper at the West House, and a bottle of champagne beside.

And I was with the girl and she wasn't saying much, and I wasn't saying much either. One thing I know. She wasn't stuck on me because of the lie about my father being rich and all that. There's a way you know . . . Craps amighty. There's a kind of girl you see just once in your life, and if you don't get busy and make hay, then you're gone for good and all, and might as well go jump off a bridge. They give you a look from inside of them somewhere, and it ain't no vamping, and what it means is—you want that girl to be your wife, and you want nice things around her like flowers and swell clothes, and you want her to have the kids you're going to have, and you want good music played and no ragtime. Gee whizz.

There's a place over near Sandusky, across a kind of bay, and it's called Cedar Point. And after we had supper we went over to it in a launch, all by ourselves. Wilbur and Miss Lucy and that Miss Woodbury had to catch a ten o'clock train back to Tiffin, Ohio, because, when you're out with girls like that you can't get careless and miss any trains and stay out all night, like you can with some kinds of Janes.

And Wilbur blowed himself to the launch and it cost him fifteen cold plunks, but I wouldn't never have knew if I hadn't listened. He wasn't no tin horn kind of a sport.

Over at the Cedar Point place, we didn't stay around where there was a gang of common kind of cattle at all.

There was big dance halls and dining places for yaps, and there was a beach you could walk along and get where it was dark, and we went there.

She didn't talk hardly at all and neither did I, and I was thinking how glad I was my mother was all right, and always made us kids learn to eat with a fork at the table, and not swill soup, and not be noisy and rough like a gang you see around a race track that way.

Then Wilbur and his girl went away up the beach and Lucy and I sat down in a dark place, where there was some roots of old trees the water had washed up, and after that the time, till we had to go back in the launch and they had to catch their trains, wasn't nothing at all. It went like winking your eye.

Here's how it was. The place we were setting in was dark, like I said, and there was the roots from that old stump sticking up like arms, and there was a watery smell, and the night was like—as if you could put your hand out and feel it—so warm and soft and dark and sweet like an orange.

I most cried and I most swore and I most jumped up and danced, I was so mad and happy and sad.

When Wilbur come back from being alone with his girl, and she saw him coming, Lucy she says, "We got to go to the train now," and she was most crying too, but she never knew nothing I knew, and she couldn't be so all busted up. And then, before Wilbur and Miss Woodbury got up to where we was, she put her face up and kissed me quick and put her head up against me and she was all quivering and—Gee whizz.

Sometimes I hope I have cancer and die. I guess you know what I mean. We went in the launch across the bay to the train like that, and it was dark, too. She whispered and said it was like she and I could get out of the boat and walk on water, and it sounded foolish, but I knew what she meant.

And then quick we were right at the depot, and there was a big gang of yaps, the kind that goes to the fairs, and crowded and milling around like cattle, and how could I tell her? "It won't be long because you'll write and I'll write to you." That's all she said.

I got a chance like a hay barn afire. A swell chance I got.

And maybe she would write me, down at Marietta that way, and the letter would come back, and stamped on the front of it by the U.S.A. "there ain't any such guy," or something like that, whatever they stamp on a letter that way.

And me trying to pass myself off for a big-bug and a swell—to her, as decent a little body as God ever made. Craps amighty—swell chance I got!

And then the train come in, and she got on it, and Wilbur Wessen, he come and shook hands with me, and that Miss Woodbury was nice too and bowed to me, and I at her, and the train went and I busted out and cried like a kid.

Gee, I could have run after the train and made Dan Patch look like a freight train after a wreck but, socks amighty, what was the use? Did you ever see such a fool?

I'll bet you what—if I had an arm broke right now or a train had run over my foot—I wouldn't go to no doctor at all. I'd go set down and let her hurt and hurt—that's what I'd do.

I'll bet you what—if I hadn't a drunk that booze I'd never been such a boob as to go tell such a lie—that couldn't never be made straight to a lady like her.

I wish I had that fellow right here that had on a Windsor tie and carried a cane. I'd smash him for fair. Gosh darn his eyes. He's a big fool—that's what he is.

And if I'm not another you just go find me one and I'll quit working and be a bum and give him my job. I don't care nothing for working, and earning money, and saving it for no such boob as myself.

JAMES THURBER (1894–1961)

The Secret Life of Walter Mitty

"We're going through!" The Commander's voice was like thin ice breaking. He wore his full-dress uniform, with the heavily braided white cap pulled down rakishly over one cold gray eye. "We can't make it, sir. It's spoiling for a hurricane, if you ask me." "I'm not asking you, Lieutenant Berg," said the Commander. "Throw on the power lights! Rev her up to 8,500! We're going through!" The pounding of the cylinders increased: ta-pocketa-pocketa-pocketa-*pocketa-pocketa.* The Commander stared at the ice forming on the pilot window. He walked over and twisted a row of complicated dials. "Switch on No. 8 auxiliary!" he shouted. "Switch on No. 8 auxiliary!" repeated Lieutenant Berg. "Full strength in No. 3 turret!" shouted the Commander. "Full strength in No. 3 turret!" The crew, bending to their various tasks in the huge, hurtling eight-engined Navy hydroplane, looked at each other and grinned. "The Old Man'll get us through," they said to one another. "The Old Man ain't afraid of Hell!" . . .

"Not so fast! You're driving too fast!" said Mrs. Mitty. "What are you driving so fast for?"

"Hmm?" said Walter Mitty. He looked at his wife, in the seat beside him, with shocked astonishment. She seemed grossly unfamiliar, like a strange woman who had yelled at him in a crowd. "You were up to fifty-five," she said. "You know I don't like to go more than forty. You were up to fifty-five." Walter Mitty drove on toward Waterbury in silence, the roaring of the SN202 through the worst storm in twenty years of Navy flying fading in the remote, intimate airways of his mind. "You're tensed up again," said Mrs. Mitty. "It's one of your days. I wish you'd let Dr. Renshaw look you over."

Walter Mitty stopped the car in front of the building where his wife went to have her hair done. "Remember to get those overshoes while I'm having my hair done," she said. "I don't need overshoes," said Mitty. She put her mirror back into her bag. "We've been all through that," she said, getting out of the car. "You're not a young man any longer." He raced the engine a little. "Why don't you wear your gloves? Have you lost your gloves?" Walter Mitty reached in a pocket and brought out the gloves. He put them on, but after she had turned and gone into the building and he had driven on to a red light, he took them off again. "Pick it up, brother!" snapped a cop as the light changed, and Mitty hastily pulled on his gloves and lurched ahead. He drove around the streets aimlessly for a time, and then he drove past the hospital on his way to the parking lot.

. . . "It's the millionaire banker, Wellington McMillan," said the pretty nurse. "Yes?" said Walter Mitty, removing his gloves slowly. "Who has the case?" "Dr. Renshaw and Dr. Benbow, but there are two specialists here, Dr. Remington from New York and Dr. Pritchard-Mitford from London. He flew over." A door opened down a long, cool corridor and Dr. Renshaw came out. He looked distraught and haggard. "Hello, Mitty," he said. "We're having the devil's own time with McMillan, the millionaire banker and close personal friend of Roosevelt. Obstreosis of the ductal tract. Tertiary.[1] Wish you'd take a look at him." "Glad to," said Mitty.

In the operating room there were whispered introductions: "Dr. Remington, Dr. Mitty, Dr. Pritchard-Mitford, Dr. Mitty." "I've read your book on streptothricosis," said Pritchard-Mitford, shaking hands. "A brilliant performance, sir." "Thank you," said Walter Mitty. "Didn't know you were in the States, Mitty," grumbled Remington. "Coals to Newcastle, bringing Mitford and me up here for a tertiary." "You are very kind," said Mitty. A huge, complicated machine, connected to the operating table, with many tubes and wires, began at this moment to go pocketa-pocketa-pocketa. "The new anesthetizer is giving way!" shouted an interne. "There is no one in the East who knows how to fix it!" "Quiet, man!" said Mitty, in a low, cool voice. He sprang to the machine, which was now going pocketa-pocketa-queep-pocketa-queep. He began fingering delicately a row of glistening dials. "Give me a fountain pen!" he snapped. Someone handed him a fountain pen. He pulled a faulty piston out of the machine and inserted the pen in its place. "That will hold for ten minutes," he said. "Get on with the operation." A nurse hurried over and whispered to Renshaw, and Mitty saw the man turn pale. "Coreopsis[2] has set in," said Renshaw nervously. "If you would take over, Mitty?" Mitty looked at him and at the craven figure of Benbow, who drank, and at the grave, uncertain faces of the two great specialists. "If you wish," he said. They slipped a white gown on him; he adjusted a mask and drew on thin gloves; nurses handed him shining . .

"Back it up, Mac! Look out for that Buick!" Walter Mitty jammed on the brakes. "Wrong lane, Mac," said the parking-lot attendant, looking at Mitty closely. "Gee. Yeh," muttered Mitty. He began cautiously to back out of the lane marked "Exit Only." "Leave her sit there," said the attendant. "I'll put her away." Mitty got out of the car. "Hey, better leave the key." "Oh," said Mitty, handing the man the ignition key. The attendant vaulted into the car, backed it up with insolent skill, and put it where it belonged.

---

[1] *tertiary,* at the third—advanced—stage of the disease. "Obstreosis" and "streptothricosis" (below) are nonsense words for imaginary diseases.
[2] *coreopsis,* a genus of herb, not a medical condition.

They're so damn cocky, thought Walter Mitty, walking along Main Street; they think they know everything. Once he had tried to take his chains off, outside New Milford, and he had got them wound around the axles. A man had had to come out in a wrecking car and unwind them, a young, grinning garageman. Since then Mrs. Mitty always made him drive to the garage to have the chains taken off. The next time, he thought, I'll wear my right arm in a sling; they won't grin at me then. I'll have my right arm in a sling and they'll see I couldn't possibly take the chains off myself. He kicked at the slush on the sidewalk. "Overshoes," he said to himself, and he began looking for a shoe store.

When he came out into the street again, with the overshoes in a box under his arm, Walter Mitty began to wonder what the other thing was his wife had told him to get. She had told him, twice, before they set out from their house for Waterbury. In a way he hated these weekly trips to town—he was always getting something wrong. Kleenex, he thought, Squibb's, razor blades? No. Toothpaste, toothbrush, bicarbonate, carborundum, initiative and referendum? He gave it up. But she would remember it. "Where's the what's-its-name?" she would ask. "Don't tell me you forgot the what's-its-name." A newsboy went by shouting something about the Waterbury trial.

. . . "Perhaps this will refresh your memory." The District Attorney suddenly thrust a heavy automatic at the quiet figure on the witness stand. "Have you ever seen this before?" Walter Mitty took the gun and examined it expertly. "This is my Webley-Vickers 50.80," he said calmly. An excited buzz ran around the courtroom. The Judge rapped for order. "You are a crack shot with any sort of firearms, I believe?" said the District Attorney, insinuatingly. "Objection!" shouted Mitty's attorney. "We have shown that the defendant could not have fired the shot. We have shown that he wore his right arm in a sling on the night of the fourteenth of July." Walter Mitty raised his hand briefly and the bickering attorneys were stilled. "With any known make of gun," he said evenly, "I could have killed Gregory Fitzhurst at three hundred feet *with my left hand*." Pandemonium broke loose in the courtroom. A woman's scream rose above the bedlam and suddenly a lovely, dark-haired girl was in Walter Mitty's arms. The District Attorney struck at her savagely. Without rising from his chair, Mitty let the man have it on the point of the chin. "You miserable cur!" . . .

"Puppy biscuit," said Walter Mitty. He stopped walking and the buildings of Waterbury rose up out of the misty courtroom and surrounded him again. A woman who was passing laughed. "He said 'Puppy biscuit,' " she said to her companion. "That man said 'Puppy biscuit' to himself." Walter Mitty hurried on. He went into an A. & P., not the first one he came to but a smaller one farther up the street. "I want some biscuit for small, young dogs," he said to the clerk. "Any special brand, sir?" The greatest pistol shot in the world thought a moment. "It says 'Puppies Bark for It' on the box," said Walter Mitty.

His wife would be through at the hairdresser's in fifteen minutes, Mitty saw in looking at his watch, unless they had trouble drying it; sometimes they had trouble drying it. She didn't like to get to the hotel first; she would want him to be there waiting for her as usual. He found a big leather chair in the lobby, facing a window, and he put the over-shoes and the puppy biscuit on the floor beside it. He picked up an old copy of *Liberty*[3] and sank down into the chair. "Can Germany Conquer the World Through the Air?" Walter Mitty looked at the pictures of bombing planes and of ruined streets.

. . . "The cannonading has got the wind up in young Raleigh, sir," said the sergeant. Captain Mitty looked up at him through touseled hair. "Get him to bed," he said wearily. "With the others. I'll fly alone." "But you can't, sir," said the sergeant anxiously. "It takes two men to handle that bomber and the Archies[4] are pounding hell out of the air. Von Richtman's circus[5] is between here and Saulier." "Somebody's got to get that ammunition dump," said Mitty. "I'm going over. Spot of brandy?" He poured a drink for the sergeant and one for himself. War thundered and whined around the dugout[6] and battered at the door. There was a rending of wood and splinters flew through the room. "A bit of a near thing," said Captain Mitty carelessly. "The box barrage[7] is closing in," said the sergeant. "We only live once, Sergeant," said Mitty, with his faint, fleeting smile. "Or do we?" He poured another brandy and tossed it off. "I never see a man could hold his brandy like you, sir," said the sergeant. "Begging your pardon, sir." Captain Mitty stood up and strapped on his huge Webley-Vickers automatic. "It's forty kilometers through hell, sir," said the sergeant. Mitty finished one last brandy. "After all," he said softly, "what isn't?" The pounding of the cannon increased; there was the rat-tat-tatting of machine guns, and from somewhere came the menacing pocketa-pocketa-pocketa of the new flame-throwers. Walter Mitty walked to the door of the dugout humming "Auprès de Ma Blonde."[8] He turned and waved to the sergeant. "Cheerio!" he said. . . .

Something struck his shoulder. "I've been looking all over this hotel for you," said Mrs. Mitty. "Why do you have to hide in this old chair? How did you expect me to find you?" "Things close in," said Walter Mitty vaguely. "What?" Mrs. Mitty said. "Did you get the what's-its-name? The puppy biscuit? What's in that box?" "Overshoes," said Mitty.

---

[3] *Liberty*, popular weekly magazine (1924–1951).
[4] *Archies*, slang for antiaircraft guns.
[5] In World War I the battle groups of fighter squadrons were known as "flying circuses"; the group commanded by Baron Manfred von Richthofen (1892–1918) was the most deadly German flying circus.
[6] *dugout*, sheltered area dug out of the side of a trench.
[7] *box barrage*, an artillery barrage from all four sides.
[8] "Close to My Blonde," French song popular during World War I.

"Couldn't you have put them on in the store?" "I was thinking," said Walter Mitty. "Does it ever occur to you that I am sometimes thinking?" She looked at him. "I'm going to take your temperature when I get you home," she said.

They went out through the revolving doors that made a faintly derisive whistling sound when you pushed them. It was two blocks to the parking lot. At the drugstore on the corner she said, "Wait here for me. I forgot something. I won't be a minute." She was more than a minute. Walter Mitty lighted a cigarette. It began to rain, rain with sleet in it. He stood up against a wall of the drugstore, smoking. . . . He put his shoulders back and his heels together. "To hell with the handkerchief," said Walter Mitty scornfully. He took one last drag on his cigarette and snapped it away. Then, with that faint, fleeting smile playing about his lips, he faced the firing squad; erect and motionless, proud and disdainful, Walter Mitty the Undefeated, inscrutable to the last.

JORGE LUIS BORGES (1899–   )

The South

The man who landed in Buenos Aires in 1871 bore the name of Johannes Dahlmann and he was a minister in the Evangelical Church. In 1939, one of his grandchildren, Juan Dahlmann, was secretary of a municipal library on Calle Córdoba, and he considered himself profoundly Argentinian. His maternal grandfather had been that Francisco Flores, of the Second Line-Infantry Division, who had died on the frontier of Buenos Aires, run through with a lance by Indians from Catriel; in the discord inherent between his two lines of descent, Juan Dahlmann (perhaps driven to it by his Germanic blood) chose the line represented by his romantic ancestor, his ancestor of the romantic death. An old sword, a leather frame containing the daguerreotype of a blank-faced man with a beard, the dash and grace of certain music, the familiar strophes of *Martin Fierro,* the passing years, boredom and solitude, all went to foster this voluntary, but never ostentatious nationalism. At the cost of numerous small privations, Dahlmann had managed to save the empty shell of a ranch in the South which had belonged to the Flores family; he continually recalled the image of the balsamic eucalyptus trees and the great rose-colored house which had once been crimson. His duties, perhaps even indolence, kept him in the city. Summer after summer he contented himself with the abstract idea of possession and with the certitude that his ranch was waiting for him on a precise site in the middle of the plain. Late in February, 1939, something happened to him.

Blind to all fault, destiny can be ruthless at one's slightest distraction. Dahlmann had succeeded in acquiring, on that very afternoon, an imperfect copy of Weil's edition of *The Thousand and One Nights.* Avid to examine this find, he did not wait for the elevator but hurried up the stairs. In the obscurity, something brushed by his forehead: a bat, a bird? On the face of the woman who opened the door to him he saw horror engraved, and the hand he wiped across his face came away red with blood. The edge of a recently painted door which someone had forgotten to close had caused this wound. Dahlmann was able to fall asleep, but from the moment he awoke at dawn the savor of all things was atrociously poignant. Fever wasted

him and the pictures in *The Thousand and One Nights* served to
illustrate nightmares. Friends and relatives paid him visits and, with
exaggerated smiles, assured him that they thought he looked fine.
Dahlmann listened to them with a kind of feeble stupor and he
marveled at their not knowing that he was in hell. A week, eight days
passed, and they were like eight centuries. One afternoon, the usual
doctor appeared, accompanied by a new doctor, and they carried him
off to a sanitarium on the Calle Ecuador, for it was necessary to X-
ray him. Dahlmann, in the hackney coach which bore them away,
thought that he would, at last, be able to sleep in a room different
from his own. He felt happy and communicative. When he arrived at
his destination, they undressed him, shaved his head, bound him
with metal fastenings to a stretcher; they shone bright lights on him
until he was blind and dizzy, auscultated him, and a masked man
stuck a needle into his arm. He awoke with a feeling of nausea,
covered with a bandage, in a cell with something of a well about it;
in the days and nights which followed the operation he came to
realize that he had merely been, up until then, in a suburb of hell.
Ice in his mouth did not leave the least trace of freshness. During
these days Dahlmann hated himself in minute detail: he hated his
identity, his bodily necessities, his humiliation, the beard which
bristled upon his face. He stoically endured the curative measures,
which were painful, but when the surgeon told him he had been on
the point of death from septicemia, Dahlmann dissolved in tears of
self-pity for his fate. Physical wretchedness and the incessant anticipation of horrible nights had not allowed him time to think of
anything so abstract as death. On another day, the surgeon told him
he was healing and that, very soon, he would be able to go to his
ranch for convalescence. Incredibly enough, the promised day
arrived.

Reality favors symmetries and slight anachronisms: Dahlmann had
arrived at the sanitarium in a hackney coach and now a hackney
coach was to take him to the Constitución station. The first fresh
tang of autumn, after the summer's oppressiveness, seemed like a
symbol in nature of his rescue and release from fever and death.
The city, at seven in the morning, had not lost that air of an old
house lent it by the night; the streets seemed like long vestibules, the
plazas were like patios. Dahlmann recognized the city with joy on the
edge of vertigo: a second before his eyes registered the phenomena
themselves, he recalled the corners, the billboards, the modest variety
of Buenos Aires. In the yellow light of the new day, all things
returned to him.

Every Argentine knows that the South begins at the other side of
Rivadavia. Dahlmann was in the habit of saying that this was no
mere convention, that whoever crosses this street enters a more

ancient and sterner world. From inside the carriage he sought out, among the new buildings, the iron grill window, the brass knocker, the arched door, the entrance way, the intimate patio.

At the railroad station he noted that he still had thirty minutes. He quickly recalled that in a café on the Calle Brazil (a few dozen feet from Yrigoyen's house) there was an enormous cat which allowed itself to be caressed as if it were a disdainful divinity. He entered the café. There was the cat, asleep. He ordered a cup of coffee, slowly stirred the sugar, sipped it (this pleasure had been denied him in the clinic), and thought, as he smoothed the cat's black coat, that this contact was an illusion and that the two beings, man and cat, were as good as separated by a glass, for man lives in time, in succession, while the magical animal lives in the present, in the eternity of the instant.

Along the next to the last platform the train lay waiting. Dahlmann walked through the coaches until he found one almost empty. He arranged his baggage in the network rack. When the train started off, he took down his valise and extracted, after some hesitation, the first volume of *The Thousand and One Nights*. To travel with this book, which was so much a part of the history of his ill-fortune, was a kind of affirmation that his ill-fortune had been annulled; it was a joyous and secret defiance of the frustrated forces of evil.

Along both sides of the train the city dissipated into suburbs; this sight, and then a view of the gardens and villas, delayed the beginning of his reading. The truth was that Dahlmann read very little. The magnetized mountain and the genie who swore to kill his benefactor are—who would deny it?—marvelous, but not so much more than the morning itself and the mere fact of being. The joy of life distracted him from paying attention to Scheherezade and her superfluous miracles. Dahlmann closed his book and allowed himself to live.

Lunch—the bouillon served in shining metal bowls, as in the remote summers of childhood—was one more peaceful and rewarding delight.

Tomorrow I'll wake up at the ranch, he thought, and it was as if he was two men at a time: the man who traveled through the autumn day and across the geography of the fatherland, and the other one, locked up in a sanitarium and subject to methodical servitude. He saw unplastered brick houses, long and angled, time-lessly watching the trains go by; he saw horsemen along the dirt roads; he saw gullies and lagoons and ranches; he saw great luminous clouds that resembled marble; and all these things were accidental, casual, like dreams of the plain. He also thought he recognized trees and crop fields; but he would not have been able to name them, for his actual knowledge of the countryside was quite inferior to his nostalgic and literary knowledge.

From time to time he slept, and his dreams were animated by the impetus of the train. The intolerable white sun of high noon had already become the yellow sun which precedes nightfall, and it would not be long before it would turn red. The railroad car was now also different; it was not the same as the one which had quit the station siding at Constitución; the plain and the hours had transfigured it. Outside, the moving shadow of the railroad car stretched toward the horizon. The elemental earth was not perturbed either by settlements or other signs of humanity. The country was vast but at the same time intimate and, in some measure, secret. The limitless country sometimes contained only a solitary bull. The solitude was perfect, perhaps hostile, and it might have occurred to Dahlmann that he was traveling into the past and not merely south. He was distracted from these considerations by the railroad inspector who, on reading his ticket, advised him that the train would not let him off at the regular station but at another: an earlier stop, one scarcely known to Dahlmann. (The man added an explanation which Dahlmann did not attempt to understand, and which he hardly heard, for the mechanism of events did not concern him.)

The train laboriously ground to a halt, practically in the middle of the plain. The station lay on the other side of the tracks; it was not much more than a siding and a shed. There was no means of conveyance to be seen, but the station chief supposed that the traveler might secure a vehicle from a general store and inn to be found some ten or twelve blocks away.

Dahlmann accepted the walk as a small adventure. The sun had already disappeared from view, but a final splendor exalted the vivid and silent plain, before the night erased its color. Less to avoid fatigue than to draw out his enjoyment of these sights, Dahlmann walked slowly, breathing in the odor of clover with sumptuous joy.

The general store at one time had been painted a deep scarlet, but the years had tempered this violent color for its own good. Something in its poor architecture recalled a steel engraving, perhaps one from an old edition of *Paul et Virginie*. A number of horses were hitched up to the paling. Once inside, Dahlmann thought he recognized the shopkeeper. Then he realized that he had been deceived by the man's resemblance to one of the male nurses in the sanitarium. When the shopkeeper heard Dahlmann's request, he said he would have the shay made up. In order to add one more event to that day and to kill time, Dahlmann decided to eat at the general store.

Some country louts, to whom Dahlmann did not at first pay any attention, were eating and drinking at one of the tables. On the floor, and hanging on to the bar, squatted an old man, immobile as an object. His years had reduced and polished him as water does a stone or the generations of men do a sentence. He was dark, dried up, diminutive, and seemed outside time, situated in eternity. Dahlmann noted with satisfaction the kerchief, the thick poncho, the long *chiripá*, and the colt boots, and told himself, as he recalled futile discussions with people from the Northern counties or from the province of Entre Rios, that gauchos like this no longer existed outside the South.

Dahlmann sat down next to the window. The darkness began overcoming the plain, but the odor and sound of the earth penetrated the iron bars of the window. The shop owner brought him sardines, followed by some roast meat. Dahlmann washed the meal down with several glasses of red wine. Idling, he relished the tart savor of the wine, and let his gaze, now grown somewhat drowsy, wander over the shop. A kerosene lamp hung from a beam. There were three customers at the other table: two of them appeared to be farm workers; the third man, whose features hinted at Chinese blood, was drinking with his hat on. Of a sudden, Dahlmann felt something brush lightly against his face. Next to the heavy glass of turbid wine, upon one of the stripes in the table cloth, lay a spit ball of breadcrumb. That was all: but someone had thrown it there.

The men at the other table seemed totally cut off from him. Perplexed, Dahlmann decided that nothing had happened, and he opened the volume of *The Thousand and One Nights,* by way of suppressing reality. After a few moments another little ball landed on his table, and now the *peones* laughed outright. Dahlmann said to himself that he was not frightened, but he reasoned that it would be a major blunder if he, a convalescent, were to allow himself to be dragged by strangers into some chaotic quarrel. He determined to leave, and had already gotten to his feet when the owner came up and exhorted him in an alarmed voice:

"*Señor* Dahlmann, don't pay any attention to those lads; they're half high."

Dahlmann was not surprised to learn that the other man, now, knew his name. But he felt that these conciliatory words served only to aggravate the situation. Previous to this moment, the *peones'* provocation was directed against an unknown face, against no one in particular, almost against no one at all. Now it was an attack against him, against his name, and his neighbors knew it. Dahlmann pushed the owner aside, confronted the *peones,* and demanded to know what they wanted of him.

The tough with a Chinese look staggered heavily to his feet. Almost in Juan Dahlmann's face he shouted insults, as if he had been a long way off. His game was to exaggerate his drunkenness, and this extravagance constituted a ferocious mockery. Between curses and obscenities, he threw a long knife into the air, followed it with his eyes, caught and juggled it, and challenged Dahlmann to a knife fight. The owner objected in a tremulous voice, pointing out that Dahlmann was unarmed. At this point, something unforeseeable occurred.

From a corner of the room, the old ecstatic gaucho—in whom Dahlmann saw a summary and cipher of the South (his South) — threw him a naked dagger, which landed at his feet. It was as if the South had resolved that Dahlmann should accept the duel. Dahlmann bent over to pick up the dagger, and felt two things. The first, that this almost instinctive act bound him to fight. The second, that the weapon, in his torpid hand, was no defense at all, but would merely serve to justify his murder. He had once played with a poniard, like all men, but his idea of fencing and knife-play did not go further than the notion that all strokes should be directed upwards, with the cutting edge held inwards. *They would not have allowed such things to happen to me in the sanitarium,* he thought.

"Let's get on our way," said the other man.

They went out and if Dahlmann was without hope, he was also without fear. As he crossed the threshold, he felt that to die in a knife fight, under the open sky, and going forward to the attack, would have been a liberation, a joy, and a festive occasion, on the first night in the sanitarium, when they stuck him with the needle. He felt that if he had been able to choose, then, or to dream his death, this would have been the death he would have chosen or dreamt.

Firmly clutching his knife, which he perhaps would not know how to wield, Dahlmann went out into the plain.

FLANNERY O'CONNOR (1925–1964)

A Good Man Is Hard to Find

The grandmother didn't want to go to Florida. She wanted to visit some of her connections in east Tennessee and she was seizing at every chance to change Bailey's mind. Bailey was the son she lived with, her only boy. He was sitting on the edge of his chair at the table, bent over the orange sports section of the *Journal*. "Now look here, Bailey," she said, "see here, read this," and she stood with one hand on her thin hip and the other rattling the newspaper at his bald head. "Here this fellow that calls himself The Misfit is aloose from the Federal Pen and headed toward Florida and you read here what it says he did to these people. Just you read it. I wouldn't take my children in any direction with a criminal like that aloose in it. I couldn't answer to my conscience if I did."

Bailey didn't look up from his reading so she wheeled around then and faced the children's mother, a young woman in slacks, whose face was as broad and innocent as a cabbage and was tied round with a green head-kerchief that had two points on the top like rabbit's ears. She was sitting on the sofa, feeding the baby his apricots out of a jar. "The children have been to Florida before," the old lady said. "You all ought to take them somewhere else for a change so they would see different parts of the world and be broad. They never have been to east Tennessee."

The children's mother didn't seem to hear her but the eight-year-old boy, John Wesley, a stocky child with glasses, said, "If you don't want to go to Florida, why dontcha stay at home?" He and the little girl, June Star, were reading the funny papers on the floor.

"She wouldn't stay at home to be queen for a day," June Star said without raising her yellow head.

"Yes and what would you do if this fellow, The Misfit, caught you?" the grandmother asked.

"I'd smack his face," John Wesley said.

"She wouldn't stay at home for a million bucks," June Star said. "Afraid she'd miss something. She has to go everywhere we go."

"All right, Miss," the grandmother said. "Just remember that the next time you want me to curl your hair."

June Star said her hair was naturally curly.

The next morning the grandmother was the first one in the car, ready to go. She had her big black valise that looked like the head of a hippopotamus in one corner, and underneath it she was hiding a basket with Pitty Sing, the cat, in it. She didn't intend for the cat to be left alone in the house for three days because he would miss her too much and she was afraid he might brush against one of the gas burners and accidentally asphyxiate himself. Her son, Bailey, didn't like to arrive at a motel with a cat.

She sat in the middle of the back seat with John Wesley and June Star on either side of her. Bailey and the children's mother and the baby sat in the front and they left Atlanta at eight forty-five with the mileage on the car at 55890. The grandmother wrote this down because she thought it would be interesting to say how many miles they had been when they got back. It took them twenty minutes to reach the outskirts of the city.

The old lady settled herself comfortably, removing her white cotton gloves and putting them up with her purse on the shelf in front of the back window. The children's mother still had on slacks and still had her head tied up in a green kerchief, but the grandmother had on a navy blue straw sailor hat with a bunch of white violets on the brim and a navy blue dress with a small white dot in the print. Her collar and cuffs were white organdy trimmed with lace and at her neckline she had pinned a purple spray of cloth violets containing a sachet. In case of an accident, anyone seeing her dead on the highway would know at once that she was a lady.

She said she thought it was going to be a good day for driving, neither too hot nor too cold, and she cautioned Bailey that the speed limit was fifty-five miles an hour and that the patrolmen hid themselves behind billboards and small clumps of trees and sped out after you before you had a chance to slow down. She pointed out interesting details of the scenery: Stone Mountain; the blue granite that in some places came up to both sides of the highway; the brilliant red clay banks slightly streaked with purple; and the various crops that made rows of green lace-work on the ground. The trees were full of silver-white sunlight and the meanest of them sparkled. The children were reading comic magazines and their mother had gone back to sleep.

"Let's go through Georgia fast so we won't have to look at it much," John Wesley said.

"If I were a little boy," said the grandmother, "I wouldn't talk about my native state that way. Tennessee has the mountains and Georgia has the hills."

"Tennessee is just a hillbilly dumping ground," John Wesley said, "and Georgia is a lousy state too."

"You said it," June Star said.

"In my time," said the grandmother, folding her thin veined fingers, "children were more respectful of their native states and their parents and everything else. People did right then. Oh look at the cute little pickaninny!" she said and pointed to a Negro child standing in the door of a shack. "Wouldn't that make a picture, now?" she asked and they all turned and looked at the little Negro out of the back window. He waved.

"He didn't have any britches on," June said.

"He probably didn't have any," the grandmother explained. "Little niggers in the country don't have things like we do. If I could paint, I'd paint that picture," she said.

The children exchanged comic books.

The grandmother offered to hold the baby and the children's mother passed him over the front seat to her. She set him on her knee and bounced him and told him about the things they were passing. She rolled her eyes and screwed up her mouth and stuck her leathery thin face into his smooth bland one. Occasionally he gave her a faraway smile. They passed a large cotton field with five or six graves fenced in the middle of it, like a small island. "Look at the grave-yard!" the grandmother said, pointing it out. "That was the old family burying ground. That belonged to the plantation."

"Where's the plantation?" John Wesley asked.

"Gone With the Wind," said the grandmother. "Ha. Ha."

When the children finished all the comic books they had brought, they opened the lunch and ate it. The grandmother ate a peanut butter sandwich and an olive and would not let the children throw the box and the paper napkins out the window. When there was nothing else to do they played a game by choosing a cloud and making the other two guess what shape it suggested. John Wesley took one the shape of a cow and June Star guessed a cow and John Wesley said, no, an automobile, and June Star said he didn't play fair, and they began to slap each other over the grandmother.

The grandmother said she would tell them a story if they would keep quiet. When she told a story, she rolled her eyes and waved her head and was very dramatic. She said once when she was a maiden lady she had been courted by a Mr. Edgar Atkins Teagarden from Jasper, Georgia. She said he was a very good-looking man and a gentleman and that he brought her a watermelon every Saturday afternoon with his initials cut in it, E. A. T. Well, one Saturday, she said, Mr. Teagarden brought the watermelon and there was nobody at home and he left it on the front porch and returned in his buggy to Jasper, but she never got the watermelon, she said, because a nigger boy ate it when he saw the initials, E. A. T.! This story tickled John Wesley's funny bone and he giggled and giggled but June Star didn't think it was any good. She said she wouldn't marry a man that just brought her a watermelon on Saturday. The grandmother said she would have done well to marry Mr. Teagarden because he was a gentleman and had bought Coca-Cola stock when it first came out and that he had died only a few years ago, a very wealthy man.

They stopped at The Tower for barbecued sandwiches. The Tower was a part stucco and part wood filling station and dance hall set in a clearing outside of Timothy. A fat man named Red Sammy Butts ran it and there were signs stuck here and there on the building and for miles up and down the highway saying, TRY RED SAMMY'S FAMOUS BARBECUE. NONE LIKE FAMOUS RED SAMMY'S! RED SAM! THE FAT BOY WITH THE HAPPY LAUGH. A VETERAN! SAMMY'S YOUR MAN!

Red Sammy was lying on the bare ground outside The Tower with his head under a truck while a gray monkey about a foot high, chained to a small chinaberry tree, chattered nearby. The monkey sprang back into the tree and got on the highest limb as soon as he saw the children jump out of the car and run toward him.

Inside, The Tower was a long dark room with a counter at one end and tables at the other and dancing space in the middle. They all sat down at a broad table next to the nickelodeon and Red Sam's wife, a tall burnt-brown woman with hair and eyes lighter than her skin, came and took their order. The children's mother put a dime in the machine and played "The Tennessee Waltz," and the grandmother said that tune always made her want to dance. She asked Bailey if he would like to dance but he only glared at her. He didn't have a naturally sunny disposition like she did and trips made him nervous. The grandmother's brown eyes were very bright. She swayed her head from side to side and pretended she was dancing in her chair. June Star said play something she could tap to so the children's mother put in another dime and played a fast number and June Star stepped out onto the dance floor and did her tap routine.

"Ain't she cute?" Red Sam's wife said, leaning over the counter. "Would you like to come be my little girl?"

"No I certainly wouldn't," June Star said. "I wouldn't live in a broken-down place like this for a million bucks!" and she ran back to the table.

"Ain't she cute?" the woman repeated, stretching her mouth politely.

"Aren't you ashamed?" hissed the grandmother.

Red Sam came in and told his wife to quit lounging on the counter and hurry with these people's order. His khaki trousers reached just to his hip bones and his stomach hung over them like a sack of meal swaying under his shirt. He came over and sat down at a table nearby and let out a combination sigh and yodel. "You can't win," he said. "You can't win," and he wiped his sweating red face off with a gray handkerchief. "These days you don't know who to trust," he said. "Ain't that the truth?"

"People are certainly not nice like they used to be," said the grandmother.

"Two fellers come in here last week," Red Sammy said, "driving a Chrysler. It was a old beat-up car but it was a good one and these boys looked all right to me. Said they worked at the mill and you know I let them fellers charge the gas they bought? Now why did I do that?"

"Because you're a good man!" the grandmother said at once.

"Yes'm, I suppose so," Red Sam said as if he were struck with the answer.

His wife brought the orders, carrying the five plates all at once without a tray, two in each hand and one balanced on her arm. "It isn't a soul in this green world of God's that you can trust," she said. "And I don't count anybody out of that, not nobody," she repeated, looking at Red Sammy.

"Did you read about that criminal, The Misfit, that's escaped?" asked the grandmother.

"I wouldn't be a bit surprised if he didn't attact this place right here," said the woman. "If he hears about it being here, I wouldn't be none surprised to see him. If he hears it's two cent in the cash register, I wouldn't be a tall surprised if he . . ."

"That'll do," Red Sam said. "Go bring these people their Co'Colas," and the woman went off to get the rest of the order.

"A good man is hard to find," Red Sammy said. "Everything is getting terrible. I remember the day you could go off and leave your screen door unlatched. Not no more."

He and the grandmother discussed better times. The old lady said that in her opinion Europe was entirely to blame for the way things were now. She said the way Europe acted you would think we were made of money and Red Sam said it was no use talking about it, she was exactly right. The children ran outside into the white sunlight and looked at the monkey in the lacy chinaberry tree. He was busy catching fleas on himself and biting each one carefully between his teeth as if it were a delicacy.

They drove off again into the hot afternoon. The grandmother took cat naps and woke up every few minutes with her own snoring. Outside of Toombsboro she woke up and recalled an old plantation that she had visited in this neighborhood once when she was a young lady. She said the house had six white columns across the front and that there was an avenue of oaks leading up to it and two little wooden trellis arbors on either side in front where you sat down with your suitor after a stroll in the garden. She recalled exactly which road to turn off to get to it. She knew that Bailey would not be willing to lose any time looking at an old house, but the more she talked about it, the more she wanted to see it once again and find out if the little twin arbors were still standing. "There was a secret panel in this house," she said craftily, not telling the truth but wishing that she were, "and the story went that all the family silver was hidden in it when Sherman came through but it was never found . . ."

"Hey!" John Wesley said. "Let's go see it! We'll find it! We'll poke all the woodwork and find it! Who lives there? Where do you turn off at? Hey Pop, can't we turn off there?"

"We never have seen a house with a secret panel!" June Star shrieked. "Let's go to the house with the secret panel! Hey, Pop, can't we go see the house with the secret panel!"

"It's not far from here, I know," the grandmother said. "It wouldn't take over twenty minutes."

Bailey was looking straight ahead. His jaw was as rigid as a horseshoe. "No," he said.

The children began to yell and scream that they wanted to see the house with the secret panel. John Wesley kicked the back of the front seat and June Star hung over her mother's shoulder and whined desperately into her ear that they never had any fun even on their vacation, and that they could never do what THEY wanted to do. The baby began to scream and John Wesley kicked the back of the seat so hard that his father could feel the blows in his kidney.

"All right!" he shouted, and drew the car to a stop at the side of the road. "Will you all shut up? Will you all just shut up for one second? If you don't shut up, we won't go anywhere."

"It would be very educational for them," the grandmother murmured.

"All right," Bailey said, "but get this: this is the only time we're going to stop for anything like this. This is the one and only time."

"The dirt road that you have to turn down is about a mile back," the grandmother directed. "I marked it when we passed."

"A dirt road," Bailey groaned.

After they had turned around and were headed toward the dirt road, the grandmother recalled other points about the house, the beautiful glass over the front doorway and the candle-lamp in the hall. John Wesley said that the secret panel was probably in the fireplace.

"You can't go inside this house," Bailey said. "You don't know who lives there."

"While you all talk to the people in front, I'll run around behind and get in a window," John Wesley suggested.

"We'll all stay in the car," his mother said.

They turned onto the dirt road and the car raced roughly along in a swirl of pink dust. The grandmother recalled the times when there were no paved roads and thirty miles was a day's journey. The dirt road was hilly and there were sudden washes in it and sharp curves on dangerous embankments. All at once they would be on a hill, looking down over the blue tops of trees for miles around, then the next minute, they would be in a red depression with the dust-coated trees looking down on them.

"This place had better turn up in a minute," Bailey said, "or I'm going to turn around."

The road looked as if no one had traveled on it in months.

"It's not much farther," the grandmother said and just as she said it, a horrible thought came to her. The thought was so embarrassing that she turned red in the face and her eyes dilated and her feet jumped up, upsetting her valise in the corner. The instant the valise moved, the newspaper top she had over the basket under it rose with a snarl and Pitty Sing, the cat, sprang onto Bailey's shoulder.

The children were thrown to the floor and their mother, clutching the baby, was thrown out the door onto the ground, the old lady was thrown into the front seat. The car turned over once and landed right-side-up in a gulch on the side of the road. Bailey remained in the driver's seat with the cat—gray-striped with a broad white face and an orange nose—clinging to his neck like a caterpillar.

As soon as the children saw they could move their arms and legs, they scrambled out of the car, shouting. "We've had an ACCIDENT!" The grandmother was curled up under the dashboard, hoping she was injured so that Bailey's wrath would not come down on her all at once. The horrible thought she had had before the accident was that the house she had remembered so vividly was not in Georgia but in Tennessee.

Bailey removed the cat from his neck with both hands and flung it out the window against the side of a pine tree. Then he got out of the car and started looking for the children's mother. She was sitting against the side of the red gutted ditch, holding the screaming baby, but she only had a cut down her face and a broken shoulder. "We've had an ACCIDENT!" the children screamed in a frenzy of delight.

"But nobody's killed," June Star said with disappointment as the grandmother limped out of the car, her hat still pinned to her head but the broken front brim standing up at a jaunty angle and the violet spray hanging off the side. They all sat down in the ditch, except the children, to recover from the shock. They were all shaking.

"Maybe a car will come along," said the children's mother hoarsely.

"I believe I have injured an organ," said the grandmother, pressing her side, but no one answered her. Bailey's teeth were clattering.

He had on a yellow sport shirt with bright blue parrots designed in it and his face was as yellow as the shirt. The grandmother decided that she would not mention that the house was in Tennessee.

The road was about ten feet above and they could see only the tops of the trees on the other side of it. Behind the ditch they were sitting in there were more woods, tall and dark and deep. In a few minutes they saw a car some distance away on top of a hill, coming slowly as if the occupants were watching them. The grandmother stood up and waved both arms dramatically to attract their attention. The car continued to come on slowly, disappeared around a bend and appeared again, moving even slower, on top of the hill they had gone over. It was a big black battered hearse-like automobile. There were three men in it.

It came to a stop just over them and for some minutes, the driver looked down with a steady expressionless gaze to where they were sitting, and didn't speak. Then he turned his head and muttered something to the other two and they got out. One was a fat boy in black trousers and a red sweat shirt with a silver stallion embossed on the front of it. He moved around on the right side of them and stood staring, his mouth partly open in a kind of loose grin. The other had on khaki pants and a blue striped coat and a gray hat pulled down very low, hiding most of his face. He came around slowly on the left side. Neither spoke.

The driver got out of the car and stood by the side of it, looking down at them. He was an older man than the other two. His hair was just beginning to gray and he wore silver-rimmed spectacles that gave him a scholarly look. He had a long creased face and didn't have on any shirt or undershirt. He had on blue jeans that were too tight for him and was holding a black hat and a gun. The two boys also had guns.

"We've had an ACCIDENT!" the children screamed.

The grandmother had the peculiar feeling that the bespectacled man was someone she knew. His face was as familiar to her as if she had known him all her life but she could not recall who he was. He moved away from the car and began to come down the embankment, placing his feet carefully so that he wouldn't slip. He had on tan and white shoes and no socks, and his ankles were red and thin. "Good afternoon," he said. "I see you all had you a little spill."

"We turned over twice!" said the grandmother.

"Oncet," he corrected. "We seen it happen. Try their car and see will it run, Hiram," he said quietly to the boy with the gray hat.

"What you got that gun for?" John Wesley asked. "Whatcha gonna do with that gun?"

"Lady," the man said to the children's mother, "would you mind calling them children to sit down by you? Children make me nervous. I want all you all to sit down right together there where you're at."

"What are you telling us what to do for?" June Star asked.

Behind them the line of woods gaped like a dark open mouth. "Come here," said their mother.

"Look here now," Bailey began suddenly, "we're in a predicament! We're in . . ."

The grandmother shrieked. She scrambled to her feet and stood staring. "You're The Misfit!" she said. "I recognized you at once."

"Yes'm," the man said, smiling slightly as if he were pleased in spite of himself to be known, "but it would have been better for all of you, lady, if you hadn't of reckernized me."

Bailey turned his head sharply and said something to his mother that shocked even the children. The old lady began to cry and The Misfit reddened.

"Lady," he said, "don't you get upset. Sometimes a man says things he don't mean. I don't reckon he meant to talk to you thataway."

"You wouldn't shoot a lady, would you?" the grandmother said and removed a clean handkerchief from her cuff and began to slap at her eyes with it.

The Misfit pointed the toe of his shoe into the ground and made a little hole and then covered it up again. "I would hate to have to," he said.

"Listen," the grandmother almost screamed, "I know you're a good man. You don't look a bit like you have common blood. I know you must come from nice people!"

"Yes mam," he said, "finest people in the world." When he smiled he showed a row of strong white teeth. "God never made a finer woman than my mother and my daddy's heart was pure gold," he said. The boy with the red sweat shirt had come around behind them and was standing with his gun at his hip. The Misfit squatted down on the ground. "Watch them children, Bobby Lee," he said. "You know they make me nervous." He looked at the six of them huddled together in front of him and he seemed to be embarrassed as if he couldn't think of anything to say. "Ain't a cloud in the sky," he remarked, looking up at it. "Don't see no sun but don't see no cloud neither."

"Yes, it's a beautiful day," said the grandmother. "Listen," she said, "you shouldn't call yourself The Misfit because I know you're a good man at heart. I can just look at you and tell."

"Hush!" Bailey yelled. "Hush! Everybody shut up and let me handle this!" He was squatting in the position of a runner about to sprint forward but he didn't move.

"I pre-chate that, lady," The Misfit said and drew a little circle in the ground with the butt of his gun.

"It'll take a half a hour to fix this here car," Hiram called, looking over the raised hood of it.

"Well, first you and Bobby Lee get him and that little boy to step over yonder with you," The Misfit said, pointing to Bailey and John Wesley. "The boys want to ask you something," he said to Bailey. "Would you mind stepping back in them woods there with them?"

"Listen," Bailey began, "we're in a terrible predicament. Nobody realizes what this is," and his voice cracked. His eyes were as blue and intense as the parrots in his shirt and he remained perfectly still.

The grandmother reached up to adjust her hat brim as if she were going to the woods with him but it came off in her hand. She stood staring at it and after a second she let it fall on the ground. Hiram pulled Bailey up by the arm as if he were assisting an old man. John Wesley caught hold of his father's hand and Bobby Lee followed. They went off toward the woods and just as they reached the dark edge, Bailey turned and supporting himself against a gray naked pine trunk, he shouted, "I'll be back in a minute, Mamma, wait on me!"

"Come back this instant!" his mother shrilled but they all disappeared into the woods.

"Bailey Boy!" the grandmother called in a tragic voice but she found she was looking at The Misfit squatting on the ground in front of her. "I just know you're a good man," she said desperately. "You're not a bit common!"

"Nome, I ain't a good man," The Misfit said after a second as if he had considered her statement carefully, "but I ain't the worst in the world neither. My daddy said I was different breed of dog from my brothers and sisters. 'You know,' Daddy said, 'it's some that can live their whole life out without asking about it and it's others has to know why it is, and this boy is one of the latters. He's going to be into everything!'" He put on his black hat and looked up suddenly and then away deep into the woods as if he were embarrassed again. "I'm sorry I don't have on a shirt before you ladies," he said, hunching his shoulders slightly. "We buried our clothes that we had on when we escaped and we're just making do until we can get better. We borrowed these from some folks we met," he explained.

"That's perfectly all right," the grandmother said. "Maybe Bailey has an extra shirt in his suitcase."

"I'll look and see terrectly," The Misfit said.

"Where are they taking him?" the children's mother screamed.

"Daddy was a card himself," the Misfit said. "You couldn't put anything over on him. He never got in trouble with the Authorities though. Just had the knack of handling them."

"You could be honest too if you'd only try," said the grandmother. "Think how wonderful it would be to settle down and live a comfortable life and not have to think about somebody chasing you all the time."

The Misfit kept scratching in the ground with the butt of his gun as if he were thinking about it. "Yes'm, somebody is always after you," he murmured.

The grandmother noticed how thin his shoulder blades were just behind his hat because she was standing up looking down on him. "Do you ever pray?" she asked.

He shook his head. All she saw was the black hat wiggle between his shoulder blades. "Nome," he said.

There was a pistol shot from the woods, followed closely by another. Then silence. The old lady's head jerked around. She could hear the wind move through the tree tops like a long satisfied insuck of breath. "Bailey Boy!" she called.

"I was a gospel singer for a while," The Misfit said. "I been most everything. Been in the arm service, both land and sea, at home and abroad, been twict married, been an undertaker, been with the railroads, plowed Mother Earth, been in a tornado, seen a man burnt alive oncet," and he looked up at the children's mother and the little girl who were sitting close together, their faces white and their eyes glassy; "I even seen a woman flogged," he said.

"Pray, pray," the grandmother began, "pray, pray . . ."

"I never was a bad boy that I remember of," The Misfit said in an almost dreamy voice, "but somewheres along the line I done something wrong and got sent to the penitentiary. I was buried alive," and he looked up and held her attention to him by a steady stare.

"That's when you should have started to pray," she said. "What did you do to get sent to the penitentiary that first time?"

"Turn to the right, it was a wall," The Misfit said, looking up again at the cloudless sky. "Turn to the left, it was a wall. Look up it was a ceiling, look down it was a floor. I forgot what I done, lady. I set there and set there, trying to remember what it was I done and I ain't recalled it to this day. Oncet in a while, I would think it was coming to me, but it never come."

"Maybe they put you in by mistake," the old lady said vaguely.

"Nome," he said. "It wasn't no mistake. They had the papers on me."

"You must have stolen something," she said.

The Misfit sneered slightly. "Nobody had nothing I wanted," he said. "It was a head-doctor at the penitentiary said what I had done was kill my daddy but I know that for a lie. My daddy died in nineteen ought nineteen of the epidemic flu and I never had a thing to do with it. He was buried in the Mount Hopewell Baptist churchyard and you can go there and see for yourself."

"If you would pray," the old lady said, "Jesus would help you."

"That's right," The Misfit said.

"Well then, why don't you pray?" she asked trembling with delight suddenly.

"I don't want no hep," he said. "I'm doing all right by myself."

Bobby Lee and Hiram came ambling back from the woods. Bobby Lee was dragging a yellow shirt with bright blue parrots in it.

"Throw me that shirt, Bobby Lee," The Misfit said. The shirt came flying at him and landed on his shoulder and he put it on. The grandmother couldn't name what the shirt reminded her of. "No, lady," The Misfit said while he was buttoning it up. "I found out the crime don't matter. You can do one thing or you can do another, kill a man or take a tire off his car, because sooner or later you're going to forget what it was you done and just be punished for it."

The children's mother had begun to make heaving noises as if she couldn't get her breath. "Lady," he asked, "would you and that little girl like to step off yonder with Bobby Lee and Hiram and join your husband?"

"Yes, thank you," the mother said faintly. Her left arm dangled helplessly and she was holding the baby, who had gone to sleep, in the other. "Hep that lady up, Hiram," The Misfit said as she struggled to climb out of the ditch, "and Bobby Lee, you hold onto that little girl's hand."

"I don't want to hold hands with him," June Star said. "He reminds me of a pig."

The fat boy blushed and laughed and caught her by the arm and pulled her off into the woods after Hiram and her mother.

Alone with The Misfit, the grandmother found that she had lost her voice. There was not a cloud in the sky nor any sun. There was nothing around her but woods. She wanted to tell him that he must pray. She opened and closed her mouth several times before anything came out. Finally she found herself saying, "Jesus, Jesus," meaning Jesus will help you, but the way she was saying it, it sounded as if she might be cursing.

"Yes'm," The Misfit said as if he agreed. "Jesus thown everything off balance. It was the same case with Him as with me except He hadn't committed any crime and they could prove I had committed one because they had the papers on me. Of course," he said, "they never shown me any papers. That's why I sign myself now. I said long ago, you get you a signature and sign everything you do and keep a copy of it. Then you'll know what you done and you can hold up the crime to the punishment and see do they match and in the end you'll have something to prove you ain't been treated right. I call myself The Misfit," he said, "because I can't make what all I done wrong fit what all I gone through in punishment."

There was a piercing scream from the woods, followed closely by a pistol report. "Does it seem right to you, lady, that one is punished a heap and another ain't punished at all?"

"Jesus!" the old lady cried. "You've got good blood! I know you wouldn't shoot a lady! I know you come from nice people! Pray! Jesus, you ought not to shoot a lady. I'll give you all the money I've got!"

"Lady," The Misfit said, looking beyond her far into the woods, "there never was a body that give the undertaker a tip."

There were two more pistol reports and the grandmother raised her head like a parched old turkey hen crying for water and called, "Bailey Boy, Bailey Boy!" as if her heart would break.

"Jesus was the only One that ever raised the dead," The Misfit continued, "and He shouldn't have done it. He thown everything off balance. If He did what He said, then it's nothing for you to do but thow away everything and follow Him, and if He didn't, then it's nothing for you to do but enjoy the few minutes you got left the best way you can—by killing somebody or burning down his house or doing some other meanness to him. No pleasure but meanness," he said and his voice had become almost a snarl.

"Maybe He didn't raise the dead," the old lady mumbled, not knowing what she was saying and feeling so dizzy that she sank down in the ditch with her legs twisted under her.

"I wasn't there so I can't say He didn't," The Misfit said. "I wisht I had of been there," he said, hitting the ground with his fist. "It ain't right I wasn't there because if I had of been there I would of known. Listen lady," he said in a high voice, "if I had of been there I would of known and I wouldn't be like I am now." His voice seemed about to crack and the grandmother's head cleared for an instant. She saw the man's face twisted close to her own as if he were going to cry and she murmured, "Why you're one of my babies. You're one of my own children!" She reached out and touched him on the shoulder. The Misfit sprang back as if a snake had bitten him and shot her three times through the chest. Then he put his gun down on the ground and took off his glasses and began to clean them.

Hiram and Bobby Lee returned from the woods and stood over the ditch, looking down at the grandmother who half sat and half lay in a puddle of blood with her legs crossed under her like a child's and her face smiling up at the cloudless sky.

Without his glasses, The Misfit's eyes were red-rimmed and pale and defenseless-looking. "Take her off and thow her where you thown the others," he said, picking up the cat that was rubbing itself against his leg.

"She was a talker, wasn't she?" Bobby Lee said, sliding down the ditch with a yodel.

"She would of been a good woman," The Misfit said, "if it had been somebody there to shoot her every minute of her life."

"Some fun!" Bobby Lee said.

"Shut up, Bobby Lee," The Misfit said. "It's no real pleasure in life."

DONALD BARTHELME (1931–1989)

The Balloon

The balloon, beginning at a point on Fourteenth Street, the exact location of which I cannot reveal, expanded northward all one night, while people were sleeping, until it reached the Park. There, I stopped it; at dawn the northernmost edges lay over the Plaza; the free-hanging motion was frivolous and gentle. But experiencing a faint irritation at stopping, even to protect the trees, and seeing no reason the balloon should not be allowed to expand upward, over the parts of the city it was already covering, into the "air space" to be found there, I asked the engineers to see to it. This expansion took place throughout the morning, soft imperceptible sighing of gas through the valves. The balloon then covered forty-five blocks north-south and an irregular area east-west, as many as six crosstown blocks on either side of the Avenue in some places. That was the situation, then.

But it is wrong to speak of "situations," implying sets of circumstances leading to some resolution, some escape of tension; there were no situations, simply the balloon hanging there—muted heavy grays and browns for the most part, contrasting with walnut and soft yellows. A deliberate lack of finish, enhanced by skillful installation, gave the surface a rough, forgotten quality; sliding weights on the inside, carefully adjusted, anchored the great, vari-shaped mass at a number of points. Now we have had a flood of original ideas in all media, works of singular beauty as well as significant milestones in the history of inflation, but at that moment there was only *this balloon,* concrete particular, hanging there.

There were reactions. Some people found the balloon "interesting." As a response this seemed inadequate to the immensity of the balloon, the suddenness of its appearance over the city; on the other hand, in the absence of hysteria or other societally-induced anxiety, it must be judged a calm, "mature" one. There was a certain amount of initial argumentation about the "meaning" of the balloon; this subsided, because we have learned not to insist on meanings, and they are rarely even looked for now, except in cases involving the simplest, safest phenomena. It was agreed that since the meaning of the balloon could never be known absolutely, extended discussion was pointless, or at least less purposeful than the activities of those who, for example, hung green and blue paper lanterns from the warm gray underside, in certain streets, or seized the occasion to write messages on the surface, announcing their availability for the performance of unnatural acts, or the availability of acquaintances.

Daring children jumped, especially at those points where the balloon hovered close to a building, so that the gap between balloon and building was a matter of a few inches, or points where the balloon actually made contact, exerting an ever-so-slight pressure against the side of a building, so that balloon and building seemed a unity. The upper surface was so structured that a "landscape" was presented, small valleys as well as slight knolls, or mounds; once atop the balloon, a stroll was possible, or even a trip, from one place to another. There was pleasure in being able to run down an incline, then up the opposing slope, both gently graded, or in making a leap from one side to the other. Bouncing was possible, because of the pneumaticity of the surface, and even falling, if that was your wish. That all these varied motions, as well as others, were within one's possibilities, in experiencing the "up" side of the balloon, was extremely exciting for children, accustomed to the city's flat, hard skin. But the purpose of the balloon was not to amuse children.

Too, the number of people, children and adults, who took advantage of the opportunities described was not so large as it might have been: a certain timidity, lack of trust in the balloon, was seen. There was, furthermore, some hostility. Because we had hidden the pumps, which fed helium to the interior, and because the surface was so vast that the authorities could not determine the point of entry—that is, the point at which the gas was injected—a degree of frustration was evidenced by those city officers into whose province such manifestations normally fell. The apparent purposelessness of the balloon was vexing (as was the fact that it was "there" at all). Had we painted, in great letters, "LABORATORY TESTS PROVE" OR "18% MORE EFFECTIVE" on the sides of the balloon, this difficulty would have been circumvented. But I could not bear to do so. On the whole, these officers were remarkably tolerant, considering the dimensions of the anomaly, this tolerance being the result of, first, secret tests conducted by night that convinced them that little or nothing could be done in the way of removing or destroying the balloon, and, secondly, a public warmth that arose (not uncolored by touches of the aforementioned hostility) toward the balloon, from ordinary citizens.

As a single balloon must stand for a lifetime of thinking about balloons, so each citizen expressed, in the attitude he chose, a complex of attitudes. One man might consider that the balloon had to do with the notion *sullied*, as in the sentence *The big balloon sullied the otherwise clear and radiant Manhattan sky.* That is, the balloon was, in this man's view, an imposture, something inferior to the sky that had formerly been there, something interposed between the people and their "sky." But in fact it was January, the sky was dark and ugly; it was not a sky you could look up into, lying on your back in the street, with pleasure, unless pleasure, for you, proceeded from having been threatened, from having been misused. And the underside of the balloon was a pleasure to look up into, we had seen to that, muted grays and browns for the most part, contrasted with walnut and soft, forgotten yellows. And so, while this man was thinking *sullied,* still there was an admixture of pleasurable cognition in his thinking, struggling with the original perception.

Another man, on the other hand, might view the balloon as if it were part of a system of unanticipated rewards, as when one's employer walks in and says, "Here, Henry, take this package of money I have wrapped for you, because we have been doing so well in the business here, and I admire the way you bruise the tulips, without which bruising your department would not be a success, or at least not the success that it is." For this man the balloon might be a brilliantly heroic "muscle and pluck" experience, even if an experience poorly understood.

Another man might say, "Without the example of ———, it is doubtful that ——— would exist today in its present form," and find many to agree with him, or to argue with him. Ideas of "bloat" and "float" were introduced, as well as concepts of dream and responsibility. Others engaged in remarkably detailed fantasies having to do with a wish either to lose themselves in the balloon, or to engorge it. The private character of these wishes, of their origins, deeply buried and unknown, was such that they were not much spoken of; yet there is evidence that they were widespread. It was also argued that what was important was what you felt when you stood under the balloon; some people claimed that they felt sheltered, warmed, as never before, while enemies of the balloon felt, or reported feeling, constrained, a "heavy" feeling.

Critical opinion was divided:

   "monstrous pourings"

                              "harp"

XXXXXXX "certain contrasts with darker portions"

          "inner joy"

      "large, square corners"

   "conservative eclecticism that has so far governed
      modern balloon design"

::::::: "abnormal vigor"

"warm, soft, lazy passages"

"Has unity been sacrificed for a sprawling quality?"

"Quelle catastrophe!"

"munching"

People began, in a curious way, to locate themselves in relation to aspects of the balloon: "I'll be at that place where it dips down into Forty-seventh Street almost to the sidewalk, near the Alamo Chile House," or, "Why don't we go stand on top, and take the air, and maybe walk about a bit, where it forms a tight, curving line with the façade of the Gallery of Modern Art—" Marginal intersections offered entrances within a given time duration, as well as "warm, soft, lazy passages" in which . . . But it is wrong to speak of "marginal intersections," each intersection was crucial, none could be ignored (as if, walking there, you might not find someone capable of turning your attention, in a flash, from old exercises to new exercises, risks and escalations). Each intersection was crucial, meeting of balloon and building, meeting of balloon and man, meeting of balloon and balloon.

It was suggested that what was admired about the balloon was finally this: that it was not limited, or defined. Sometimes a bulge, blister, or sub-section would carry all the way east to the river on its own initiative, in the manner of an army's movements on a map, as seen in a headquarters remote from the fighting. Then that part would be, as it were, thrown back again, or would withdraw into new dispositions; the next morning, that part would have made another sortie, or disappeared altogether. This ability of the balloon to shift its shape, to change, was very pleasing, especially to people whose lives were rather rigidly patterned, persons to whom change, although desired, was not available. The balloon, for the twenty-two days of its existence, offered the possibility, in its randomness, of mislocation of the self, in contradistinction to the grid of precise, rectangular pathways under our feet. The amount of specialized training currently needed, and the consequent desirability of long-term commitments, has been occasioned by the steadily growing importance of complex machinery, in virtually all kinds of operations; as this tendency increases, more and more people will turn, in bewildered inadequacy, to solutions for which the balloon may stand as a prototype, or "rough draft."

I met you under the balloon, on the occasion of your return from Norway; you asked if it was mine; I said it was. The balloon, I said, is a spontaneous autobiographical disclosure, having to do with the unease I felt at your absence, and with sexual deprivation, but now that your visit to Bergen has been terminated, it is no longer necessary or appropriate. Removal of the balloon was easy; trailer trucks carried away the depleted fabric, which is now stored in West Virginia, awaiting some other time of unhappiness, sometime, perhaps, when we are angry with one another.

URSULA K. LE GUIN (1929–)

The Author of the Acacia Seeds

And Other Extracts from the *Journal of the Association of*
Therolinguistics

Ms. Found in an Anthill

The messages were found written in touch-gland exudation on deger-
minated acacia seeds laid in rows at the end of a narrow, erratic tunnel
leading off from one of the deeper levels of the colony. It was the orderly
arrangement of the seeds that first drew the investigator's attention.

The messages are fragmentary, and the translation approximate and
highly interpretative; but the text seems worthy of interest if only for its
striking lack of resemblance to any other Ant texts known to us.

Seeds 1–13

[I will] not touch feelers. [I will] not stroke. [I will] spend on dry seeds [my]
soul's sweetness. It may be found when [I am] dead. Touch this dry wood!
[I] call! [I am] here!

Alternatively, this passage may be read:

[Do] not touch feelers. [Do] not stroke. Spend on dry seeds [your] soul's
sweetness. [Others] may find it when [you are] dead. Touch this dry wood!
Call: [I am] here!

No known dialect of Ant employs any verbal person except the third person
singular and plural and the first person plural. In this text, only the root
forms of the verbs are used; so there is no way to decide whether the passage
was intended to be an autobiography or a manifesto.

Seeds 14–22

Long are the tunnels. Longer is the untunneled. No tunnel reaches the end
of the untunneled. The untunneled goes on farther than we can go in ten
days [*i.e.*, forever]. Praise!

The mark translated "Praise!" is half of the customary salutation "Praise the
Queen!" or "Long live the Queen!" or "Huzza for the Queen!"—but the
word/mark signifying "Queen" has been omitted.

Seeds 23–29

As the ant among foreign-enemy ants is killed, so the ant without ants dies,
but being without ants is as sweet as honeydew.

An ant intruding in a colony not its own is usually killed. Isolated from other
ants, it invariably dies within a day or so. The difficulty in this passage is the

word/mark "without ants," which we take to mean "alone"—a concept for which no word/mark exists in Ant.

Seeds 30–31

Eat the eggs! Up with the Queen!

There has already been considerable dispute over the interpretation of the phrase on Seed 31. It is an important question, since all the preceding seeds can be fully understood only in the light cast by this ultimate exhortation. Dr. Rosbone ingeniously argues that the author, a wingless neuter-female worker, yearns hopelessly to be a winged male, and to found a new colony, flying upward in the nuptial flight with a new Queen. Though the text certainly permits such a reading, our conviction is that nothing in the text *supports* it—least of all the text of the immediately preceding seed, No. 30: "Eat the eggs!" This reading, though shocking, is beyond disputation.

We venture to suggest that the confusion over Seed 31 may result from an ethnocentric interpretation of the word "up." To us, "up" is a "good" direction. Not so, or not necessarily so, to an ant. "Up" is where the food comes from, to be sure; but "down" is where security, peace, and home are to be found. "Up" is the scorching sun; the freezing night; no shelter in the beloved tunnels; exile; death. Therefore we suggest that this strange author, in the solitude of her lonely tunnel, sought with what means she had to express the ultimate blasphemy conceivable to an ant, and that the correct reading of Seeds 30–31, in human terms, is:

Eat the eggs! Down with the Queen!

The desiccated body of a small worker was found beside Seed 31 when the manuscript was discovered. The head had been severed from the thorax, probably by the jaws of a soldier of the colony. The seeds, carefully arranged in a pattern resembling a musical stave, had not been disturbed. (Ants of the soldier caste are illiterate; thus the soldier was presumably not interested in the collection of useless seeds from which the edible germs had been removed.) No living ants were left in the colony, which was destroyed in a war with a neighboring anthill at some time subsequent to the death of the Author of the Acacia Seeds.

G. D'Arbay, T. R. Bardol

Announcement of an Expedition

The extreme difficulty of reading Penguin has been very much lessened by the use of the underwater motion-picture camera. On film it is at least possible to repeat, and to slow down, the fluid sequences of the script, to the point where, by constant repetition and patient study, many elements of this most elegant and lively literature may be grasped, though the nuances, and perhaps the essence, must forever elude us.

It was Professor Duby who, by pointing out the remote affiliation of the script with Low Greylag, made possible the first tentative glossary of Penguin. The analogies with Dolphin which had been employed up to that time never proved very useful, and were often quite misleading.

Indeed it seemed strange that a script written almost entirely in wings, neck, and air should prove the key to the poetry of short-necked, flipper-winged water-writers. But we should not have found it so strange if we had kept in mind the fact that penguins are, despite all evidence to the contrary, birds.

Because their script resembles Dolphin in *form*, we should never have assumed that it must resemble Dolphin in *content*. And indeed it does not. There is, of course, the same extraordinary wit, the flashes of crazy humor, the inventiveness, and the inimitable grace. In all the thousands of literatures of the Fish stock, only a few show any humor at all, and that usually of a rather simple, primitive sort; and the superb gracefulness of Shark or Tarpon is utterly different from the joyous vigor of all Cetacean[1] scripts. The joy, the vigor, and the humor are all shared by Penguin authors; and, indeed, by many of the finer Seal *auteurs*.[2] The temperature of the blood is a bond. But the construction of the brain, and of the womb, makes a barrier! Dolphins do not lay eggs. A world of difference lies in that simple fact.

Only when Professor Duby reminded us that penguins are birds, that they do not swim but *fly in water*, only then could the therolinguist begin to approach the sea literature of the penguin with understanding; only then could the miles of recordings already on film be restudied and, finally, appreciated.

But the difficulty of translation is still with us.

A satisfying degree of promise has already been made in Adélie. The difficulties of recording a group kinetic performance in a stormy ocean as thick as pea soup with plankton at a temperature of 31° Fahrenheit are considerable; but the perseverance of the Ross Ice Barrier Literary Circle has been fully rewarded with such passages as "Under the Iceberg," from the *Autumn Song*—a passage now world famous in the rendition by Anna Serebryakova of the Leningrad Ballet. No verbal rendering can approach the felicity of Miss Serebryakova's version. For, quite simply, there is no way to reproduce in writing the all-important *multiplicity* of the original text, so beautifully rendered by the full chorus of the Leningrad Ballet company.

Indeed, what we call "translations" from the Adélie—or from any group kinetic text—are, to put it bluntly, mere notes—libretto without the opera. The ballet version is the true translation. Nothing in words can be complete.

I therefore suggest, though the suggestion may well be greeted with frowns of anger or with hoots of laughter, that *for the therolinguist*—as opposed to the artist and the amateur—the kinetic sea writings of Penguin are

---

[1] whale
[2] authors

the *least* promising field of study: and, further, that Adélie, for all its charm and relative simplicity, is a less promising field of study than is Emperor.

Emperor!—I anticipate my colleagues' response to this suggestion. Emperor! The most difficult, the most remote, of all the dialects of Penguin! The language of which Professor Duby himself remarked, "The literature of the emperor penguin is as forbidding, as inaccessible, as the frozen heart of Antarctica itself. Its beauties may be unearthly, but they are not for us."

Maybe. I do not underestimate the difficulties: not least of which is the imperial temperament, so much more reserved and aloof than that of any other penguin. But, paradoxically, it is just in this reserve that I place my hope. The emperor is not a solitary, but a social bird; and while on land for the breeding season dwells in colonies, as does the adélie; but these colonies are very much smaller and very much quieter than those of the adélie. The bonds between the members of an emperor colony are rather personal than social. The emperor is an individualist. Therefore I think it almost certain that the literature of the emperor will prove to be composed by single authors, instead of chorally; and therefore it will be translatable into human speech. It will be a kinetic literature, but how different from the spatially extensive, rapid, multiplex choruses of sea writing! Close analysis, and genuine transcription, will at last be possible.

What! say my critics—Should we pack up and go to Cape Crozier, to the dark, to the blizzards, to the −60° cold, in the mere hope of recording the problematic poetry of a few strange birds who sit there, in the mid-winter dark, in the blizzards, in the −60° cold, on the eternal ice, with an egg on their feet?

My reply is, Yes. For, like Professor Duby, my instinct tells me that the beauty of that poetry is as unearthly as anything we shall ever find on earth.

To those of my colleagues in whom the spirit of scientific curiosity and aesthetic risk is strong, I say, Imagine it: the ice, the scouring snow, the darkness, the ceaseless whine and scream of wind. In that black desolation a little band of poets crouches. They are starving; they will not eat for weeks. On the feet of each one, under the warm belly feathers, rests one large egg, thus preserved from the mortal touch of the ice. The poets cannot hear each other; they cannot see each other. They can only feel the other's *warmth*. That is their poetry, that is their art. Like all kinetic literatures, it is silent; unlike other kinetic literatures, it is all but immobile, ineffably subtle. The ruffling of a feather; the shifting of a wing; the touch, the slight, faint, warm touch of the one beside you. In unutterable, miserable, black solitude, the affirmation. In absence, presence. In death, life.

I have obtained a sizable grant from UNESCO[3] and have stocked an expedition. There are still four places open. We leave for Antarctica on Thursday. If anyone wants to come along, welcome!

D. Petri

---

[3] United Nations Educational, Scientific, and Cultural Organization

Editorial by the President of the Therolinguistics Association

What is Language?

This question, central to the science of therolinguistics, has been answered—heuristically—by the very existence of the science. Language is communication. That is the axiom on which all our theory and research rest, and from which all our discoveries derive; and the success of the discoveries testifies to the validity of the axiom. But to the related, yet not identical question, What is Art? we have not yet given a satisfactory answer.

Tolstoy,[4] in the book whose title is that very question, answered it firmly and clearly: Art, too, is communication. This answer has, I believe, been accepted without examination or criticism by therolinguistics. For example: Why do therolinguists study only animals?

Why, because plants do not communicate.

Plants do not communicate; that is a fact. Therefore plants have no language; very well; that follows from our basic axiom. Therefore, also, plants have no art. But stay! That does *not* follow from the basic axiom, but only from the unexamined Tolstoyan corollary.

What if art is not communicative?

Or, what if some art is communicative, and some art is not?

Ourselves animals, active, predators, we look (naturally enough) for an active, predatory, communicative art; and when we find it, we recognise it. The development of this power of recognition and the skills of appreciation is a recent and glorious achievement.

But I submit that, for all the tremendous advances made by therolinguistics during the last decades, we are only at the beginning of our age of discovery. We must not become slaves to our own axioms. We have not yet lifted our eyes to the vaster horizons before us. We have not faced the almost terrifying challenge of the Plant.

If a non-communicative, vegetative art exists, we must rethink the very elements of our science, and learn a whole new set of techniques.

For it is simply not possible to bring the critical and technical skills appropriate to the study of Weasel murder mysteries, or Batrachian erotica, or the tunnel sagas of the earthworm, to bear on the art of the redwood or the zucchini.

This is proved conclusively by the failure—a noble failure—of the efforts of Dr. Srivas, in Calcutta, using time-lapse photography, to produce a lexicon of Sunflower. His attempt was daring, but doomed to failure. For his approach was kinetic—a method appropriate to the *communicative* arts of the tortoise, the oyster, and the sloth. He saw the extreme slowness of the kinesis of plants, and only that, as the problem to be solved.

But the problem was far greater. The art he sought, if it exists, is a non-communicative art: and probably a non-kinetic one. It is possible that Time, the essential element, matrix, and measure of all known animal art, does not

---

[4] Leo Tolstoy (1828–1910), *What Is Art?* (1898)

enter into vegetable art at all. The plants may use the meter of eternity. We do not know.

We do not know. All we can guess is that the putative Art of the Plant is *entirely different* from the Art of the Animal. What it is, we cannot say; we have not yet discovered it. Yet I predict with some certainty that it exists, and that when it is found it will prove to be, not an action, but a reaction: not a communication, but a reception. It will be exactly the opposite of the art we know and recognise. It will be the first *passive* art known to us.

Can we in fact know it? Can we ever understand it?

It will be immensely difficult. That is clear. But we should not despair. Remember that so late as the mid-twentieth century, most scientists, and many artists, did not believe that even Dolphin would ever be comprehensible to the human brain—or worth comprehending! Let another century pass, and we may seem equally laughable. "Do you realise," the phytolinguist will say to the aesthetic critic, "that they couldn't even read Eggplant?" And they will smile at our ignorance, as they pick up their rucksacks and hike on up to read the newly deciphered lyrics of the lichen on the north face of Pike's Peak.

And with them, or after them, may there not come that even bolder adventurer—the first geolinguist, who, ignoring the delicate, transient lyrics of the lichen, will read beneath it the still less communicative, still more passive, wholly atemporal, cold, volcanic poetry of the rocks: each one a word spoken, how long ago, by the earth itself, in the immense solitude, the immenser community, of space.

READING AND WRITING
ABOUT POETRY

1 *Reading and Writing About Poetry*

Poetry may well be the oldest of all literary forms. Certainly, a great deal of the oldest literature of which we have written records is in verse. Yet today poetry is often regarded as the most sophisticated or difficult of literary forms. What has happened to cause the change? Why should something that seems so difficult to us today have seemed so natural to our ancestors? There are two answers to these questions. The first deals with music; the second with memory.

Poetry is musical, or at least rhythmic, speech. It is also usually a harmonious speech, employing words whose sounds echo each other or blend well. It may even be set to music, to be chanted or sung rather than simply spoken.

Because of its musical nature, poetry is easily remembered. Everyone knows how much easier it is to memorize the words to a song than to memorize even a few paragraphs from a newspaper or textbook. Poetry can thus serve as an aid to memory. If you must remember something, and have no written notes to help you, you can make a song of what you need to remember, and your chances of keeping it in your head will improve.

In almost any society, the desire to keep records, remember events, or tell stories precedes the invention of writing. Poetry, being pleasant and memorable, is then the natural first form for histories and tales. Once the art of writing develops, however, poetry is no longer essential. But it is still pleasing and has by now a tradition of use behind it. Prose takes over for record keeping and for transmitting technical information, but poetry keeps its hold on certain important affairs. Songs are still written to celebrate victories and loves, to mourn deaths, and to worship.

The printing of books, which gave so many people access to written words, has been one factor in the promotion of prose in our society. The invention of radio and television—whose announcers universally speak in the blandest, least musical cadences possible—has been another factor. After the age of nursery rhymes, most of us live in a world where the cadences of poetry are no longer part of our everyday life. Moreover, we live in a society where so many written and spoken words bombard us that we learn to skim through them quickly for whatever information they carry. We take no time to look for the beauty of words or for rhythm—neither of which is very likely to be there anyway.

Poetry, however, cannot be read rapidly. Newspapers can be, and, in fact, are meant to be. Fiction can be. And, again, some of it is meant for the quick, careless reader, though most good fiction improves with slow, thoughtful reading. Drama, in general, must be read more slowly, if we are to catch the sound of the individual speeches. But poetry must be read most slowly of all. It requires not only that we read it silently at the same pace that we would read it aloud, but also that we pause after we read it, to think about it for a few moments at least, to savor the mood the poem has created before we go on to something else.

It is no wonder, then, that poetry sometimes seems strange or difficult. Almost every other influence in our environment is telling us, "Hurry up! Grab the central fact or idea I'm selling and run!" Poetry is saying, "Slow down! Enjoy the music; let yourself become part of the emotion. I have many suggestions to make. Take time to let them unfold for you." In today's rush of prepackaged ideas, the stubborn individualism and refusal to be hurried that poetry represents are indeed unusual.

But anything that lets us think for ourselves, that offers us a chance to find our own feelings, ideas, and emotions, is worth pursuing. And poetry certainly encourages this kind of thinking and reflection. Moreover, once we agree to slow down enough to savor a poem completely, we discover that poetry is very similar to the literature we've been enjoying all along. Like fiction and drama, poetry tells us of people, of what it means to them and to us to be human. And, like the other forms of literature, it relays this information through the sound of human voices.

So closely related are poetry, fiction, and drama, in fact, that it is sometimes hard to tell which is which. Some poetic dramas seem better suited for reading than for performance. Should they be classed as poetry or as plays? Similarly, there are narratives that tell a complete story in verse. Should they be considered fiction as well as poetry? Or shall we simply ignore the classifications and enjoy each work for what we like best in it, whether that be a supposedly "poetic" quality, such as rhythm, or a supposedly "fictional" or "dramatic" one, such as plot, characterization, or dramatic irony?

We must, then, read poetry with the same close attention we give to all our readings in this course. Poetry, too, demands these basic questions:

1. Who is speaking?
2. What kind of person is he or she? In what mood? Thinking what thoughts? Feeling what emotions?
3. Of whom or what is he or she speaking?
4. How is this person or object being described?
5. What attitudes are being projected?
6. Are we led to share the attitudes and emotions in sympathy, or to rebel against them with feelings of anger or irony?

But, since poetry is both the most structured and the most subjective of literary forms, we may also ask questions about its forms and its sounds, to learn how they contribute to the poem's effect on us. In doing this, we may get some sense of what qualities we want to consider poetic.

Because poetry is a genre of great variety, it cannot easily be defined. Only by reading and writing about many poems can we enhance our knowledge and enjoyment of poetry.

Writing for Discovery and Understanding

1. *Write about your experience of reading a poem.* The place to start with poetry is your initial response. To call a response "initial" may be a misnomer, for you may have to read the poem several times, silently and aloud, to begin to appreciate it. As a prewriting activity, describe the mood a poem creates, the emotions it evokes, and the rhythms of the language it uses. You're writing for discovery, so allow yourself to free associate. Does the poem remind you of personal experiences, of other poems, of songs you've heard?

2. *Write about the occasion for a poem.* Many poems are "occasional"; that is, they celebrate or commemorate an event. Poets such as Robert Frost and James Dickey wrote poems for the inaugurations of Presidents John Kennedy and Jimmy Carter, respectively. As your instructor describes the circumstances surrounding a poem, or as you discover background information on various poems through library research, write about the poem in that context. How does the poet respond to his or her occasion for writing? How does the poem strive for an effect that is suited to the occasion?

3. *What does a poem say about itself?* Sometimes such statements are obvious and at other times quite subtle. In the largest sense, we may consider that the poems of an accomplished poet represent what he or she believes this art form should be. As you read, consider how the poem represents the poet's idea of poetry. This is a question that you can continue asking as you read

more than one poem by a single poet and as you read poems in relation to one another. (For example, the anonymous Middle English lyric "Sumer Is Icumen In" and Ezra Pound's "Ancient Music" [p. 524] represent distinct ideas about poetry that are cast in relief by Pound's parody of the first poem in his own.)

4. *Write an explication for a poem.* The term *explication* is from the French verb *expliquer,* to explain or interpret. Explication is a tool of literary critics, sometimes done for its own sake and sometimes done to place a critic's understanding of a poem in the context of an idea or theme that may connect several poems or poets. An explication is a line by line "reading" of the poem. For each line or passage, a prose passage is written to describe how the "reader" understands the poem. (The words *reading* and *reader* are in quotation marks because in this context they refer to writing as a kind of reading.) This type of writing is distinct from the thesis-oriented papers you often write, for it may not be held together by a governing idea of your own. Rather it is held together by the poem itself. Explication is a way to "get inside" a poem by writing about it. It is an excellent way to write about a poem in your journal in order to explain it to yourself, and it makes a fine point of reference for further writing and study.

Let us begin by reading some traditional ballads. Ballads are tales told in song. Traditional ballads (or folk ballads) are songs that have been passed from one singer to another, not by having been written down but by having been sung, heard, and resung.* Ballads are thus very like folk tales in their mode of creation and in their sense of the audience. So we may expect that the voices within the ballads will be like the voices of those archetypal story-tellers we first met when reading fiction. And yet ballads are sung. Their creators are singers, not speakers. How, then, will these tales sung in verse differ from tales told in prose? How will their stories be told? What will we hear that we have not heard before?

---

* This oral tradition accounts for the number of variations ballads possess. A singer may repeat a ballad just as he or she first heard it; or he or she may change the ballad slightly, either on purpose or accidentally. A third singer then learns this new version, and either preserves or changes it. Thus a ballad of any great age may exist in many versions, each being sung by a different group of singers.

ANONYMOUS

Get Up and Bar the Door

It fell about the Martinmas[1] time,
　And a gay time it was then,
When our good wife got puddings[2] to make,
　And she's boild them in the pan.

5　The wind sae cauld blew south and north,
　And blew into the floor;
Quoth our goodman to our goodwife,
　"Gae out and bar the door."

"My hands is in my hussyfskap,[3]
10　Goodman, as ye may see;
An it shoud nae be barrd this hundred year,
　It's no be barrd for me."

They made a paction tween them twa,
　They made it firm and sure,
15　That the first word whaeer shoud speak,
　Shoud rise and bar the door.

Then by there came two gentlemen,
　At twelve oclock at night,
And they could neither see house nor hall,
20　Nor coal nor candle-light.

"Now whether is this a rich man's house,
　Or whether is it a poor?"
But neer a word wad ane o them speak,
　For barring of the door.

25　And first they ate the white puddings,
　And then they ate the black;
Tho muckle[4] thought the goodwife to hersel,
　Yet neer a word she spake.

Then said the one unto the other,
30　"Here, man, tak ye my knife;

---

[1] November 11.
[2] Sausages.
[3] Household chores.
[4] Much.

Do ye tak aff the auld man's beard,
      And I'll kiss the goodwife."

"But there's nae water in the house,
      And what shall we do than?"
35 "What ails ye at the pudding-broo,
      That boils into the pan?"

O up then started our goodman,
      An angry man was he:
"Will ye kiss my wife before my een,
40   And scad me wi pudding-bree?"

Then up and started our goodwife,
      Gied three skips on the floor:
"Goodman, you've spoken the foremost word,
      Get up and bar the door."

Lord Randal

"O where ha you been, Lord Randal, my son?
And where ha you been, my handsome young man?"
"I ha been at the greenwood; mother, mak my bed soon,
For I'm wearied wi hunting, and fain wad lie down."

5 "An wha met ye there, Lord Randal, my son?
An wha met you there, my handsome young man?"
"O I met wi my true-love; mother, mak my bed soon,
For I'm wearied wi hunting, and fain wad lie down."

"And what did she give you, Lord Randal, my son?
10 And what did she give you, my handsome young man?"
"Eels fried in a pan; mother, mak my bed soon,
For I'm wearied wi huntin, and fain wad lie down."

"And wha gat your leavins, Lord Randal, my son?
And wha gat your leavins, my handsome young man?"
15 "My hawks and my hounds; mother, mak my bed soon,
For I'm wearied wi hunting, and fain wad lie down."

"And what becam of them, Lord Randal, my son?
And what becam of them, my handsome young man?"
"They stretched their legs out and died; mother, mak my bed soon,
20 For I'm wearied wi huntin, and fain wad lie down."

"O I fear you are poisoned, Lord Randal, my son!
I fear you are poisoned, my handsome young man!"
"O yes, I am poisoned: mother, mak my bed soon,
For I'm sick at the heart, and I fain wad lie down."

25 "What d'ye leave to your mother, Lord Randal, my son?
What d'ye leave to your mother, my handsome young man?"
"Four and twenty milk kye;[1] mother, mak my bed soon,
For I'm sick at the heart, and I fain wad lie down."

"What d'ye leave to your sister, Lord Randal, my son?
30 What d'ye leave to your sister, my handsome young man?"
"My gold and my silver; mother, mak my bed soon,
For I'm sick at the heart, an I fain wad lie down."

"What d'ye leave to your brother, Lord Randal, my son?
What d'ye leave to your brother, my handsome young man?"
35 "My houses and my lands; mother, mak my bed soon,
For I'm sick at the heart, and I fain wad lie down."

"What d'ye leave to your true-love, Lord Randal, my son?
What d'ye leave to your true-love, my handsome young man?"
"I leave her hell and fire; mother, mak my bed soon,
40 For I'm sick at the heart, and I fain wad lie down."

Sir Patrick Spens

The king sits in Dumferling town,
    Drinking the blude-reid wine:
"O whar will I get guid sailor,
    To sail this ship of mine?"

5 Up and spak an eldern knicht,
    Sat at the king's richt knee:
"Sir Patrick Spens is the best sailor
    That sails upon the sea."

The king has written a braid letter
10   And signed it wi' his hand,
And sent it to Sir Patrick Spens,
    Was walking on the sand.

---

[1] Kine = cows.

The first line that Sir Patrick read,
    A loud lauch[1] lauched he;
15 The next line that Sir Patrick read,
    The tear blinded his ee.[2]

"O wha is this has done this deed,
    This ill deed done to me,
To send me out this time o' the year,
20   To sail upon the sea?

"Mak haste, mak haste, my mirry men all,
    Our guid ship sails the morn."
"O say na sae, my master dear,
    For I fear a deadly storm.

25 "Late, late yestre'en I saw the new moon
    Wi' the auld moon in hir arm,
And I fear, I fear, my dear master,
    That we will come to harm."

O our Scots nobles were richt laith[3]
30   To weet[4] their cork-heeled shoon,[5]
But lang or[6] a' the play were played
    Their hats they swam aboon.[7]

O lang, lang may their ladies sit,
    Wi' their fans into their hand,
35 Or ere they see Sir Patrick Spens
    Come sailing to the land.

O lang, lang may the ladies stand
    Wi' their gold kems[8] in their hair,
Waiting for their ain dear lords,
40   For they'll see them na mair.

---

[1] Laugh.
[2] Eye.
[3] Loath.
[4] Wet.
[5] Shoes.
[6] Before.
[7] Above.
[8] Combs.

Half o'er, half o'er to Aberdour[9]
    It's fifty fadom[10] deep,
And there lies guid Sir Patrick Spens
    Wi' the Scots lords at his feet.

The Cherry-Tree Carol

Joseph was an old man,
    and an old man was he,
When he wedded Mary,
    in the land of Galilee.

5 Joseph and Mary walked
    through an orchard good,
Where was cherries and berries,
    so red as any blood.

Joseph and Mary walked
10   through an orchard green,
Where was berries and cherries,
    as thick as might be seen.

O then bespoke Mary,
    so meek and so mild:
15 "Pluck me one cherry, Joseph,
    for I am with child."

O then bespoke Joseph:
    with words most unkind:
"Let him pluck thee a cherry
20   that brought thee with child."

O then bespoke the babe,
    within his mother's womb:
"Bow down then the tallest tree,
    for my mother to have some."

25 Then bowed down the highest tree
    unto his mother's hand;
Then she cried, "See, Joseph,
    I have cherries at command."

---

[9] Halfway back to Aberdour, on the Firth of Forth.
[10] Fathoms.

O then bespoke Joseph:
30   "I have done Mary wrong;
    But cheer up, my dearest,
      and be not cast down."

Then Mary plucked a cherry,
    as red as the blood,
35 Then Mary went home
    with her heavy load.

Then Mary took her babe,
    and sat him on her knee,
Saying, "My dear son, tell me
40   what this world will be."

"O I shall be as dead, mother,
    as the stones in the wall;
O the stones in the streets, mother,
    shall mourn for me all.

45 "Upon Easter-day, mother,
    my uprising shall be;
O the sun and the moon, mother,
    shall both rise with me."

DUDLEY RANDALL (1914–   )

Ballad of Birmingham

(*On the bombing of a church in Birmingham,
Alabama, 1963*)

"Mother dear, may I go downtown
Instead of out to play,
And march the streets of Birmingham
In a Freedom March today?"

5 "No, baby, no, you may not go,
For the dogs are fierce and wild,
And clubs and hoses, guns and jails
Aren't good for a little child."

"But, mother, I won't be alone,
10 Other children will go with me,
And march the streets of Birmingham
To make our country free."

"No, baby, no, you may not go,
For I fear those guns will fire.
15 But you may go to church instead
And sing in the children's choir."

She has combed and brushed her night-dark hair.
And bathed rose petal sweet,
And drawn white gloves on her small brown hands,
20 And white shoes on her feet.

The mother smiled to know her child
Was in the sacred place,
But that smile was the last smile
To come upon her face.

25 For when she heard the explosion,
Her eyes grew wet and wild.
She raced through the streets of Birmingham
Calling for her child.

She clawed through bits of glass and brick,
30 Then lifted out a shoe.
"O, here's the shoe my baby wore,
But, baby, where are you?"

QUESTIONS FOR THINKING AND WRITING

1. Although "Ballad of Birmingham" was written by a twentieth-century poet,
   both its form and its content qualify it as a true ballad in the folk tradition.
   Discuss the various elements in the poem that make this so. What special
   power or perspective does Randall give to his telling of this historical incident
   by putting it in ballad form?
2. Read one of the ballads aloud slowly. As you read, try to catch the rhythms
   and feelings of the ballad in your voice. Now do a freewriting in which you
   describe this experience. What did you discover about the ballad as you read
   it? List some of the characteristics of the ballad that distinguish it from other
   poems and songs familiar to you.
3. *Writing project:* There is a story in each ballad. How would that story be told if
   it were written as a short story? Create such a story, adding details and
   dialogue as needed. Your story will be more than a plot synopsis of the tale
   told in the ballad. Just as novels and stories are rendered as separate works
   when they become movies and television programs, your story should stand
   on its own and tell its own tale, based on the concept and narrative of the
   ballad.

ELEMENTS OF POETRY

2 *Repetition and Rhythm*

Two elements prominent in ballads are **repetition** and **rhythm.** Sometimes single words or phrases are repeated for emphasis, as in "Lord Randal": "O where ha you been. . . . And where ha you been." Sometimes one or more lines appear in every verse as a refrain: "Mother, mak my bed soon,/For I'm wearied wi hunting, and fain wad lie down." In each case, the repetition emphasizes both the content and the rhythm of the ballad, calling our attention to the meter (that is, to the rhythmic pattern of each line) or to the grouping of lines into stanzas.

Of the three ballads printed in the previous chapter, "Lord Randal" is easily the most repetitive. In fact, it is built on a technique known as **incremental repetition.** At least half of each line is repeated from stanza to stanza, and the pattern of question and answer never varies. Yet the changes that occur reveal and develop the dying lord's story.

Repetition is important not only in ballads, but in lyric poetry in general. It is most pronounced in songs, as in the next example. But it appears frequently (and often quite subtly) in spoken lyrics as well. Let us look at some poems in which repetition plays an important role, and let us see what effects are being gained by it.

WILLIAM SHAKESPEARE (1564–1616)

It Was a Lover and His Lass

It was a lover and his lass,
　With a hey, and a ho, and hey nonino,
That o'er the green corn-field did pass
　In the spring time, the only pretty ring time,
5　When birds do sing, hey ding a ding, ding:
Sweet lovers love the spring.

Between the acres of the rye,
　With a hey, and a ho, and a hey nonino,
These pretty country folk would lie,
10　In the spring time, the only pretty ring time,
When birds do sing, hey ding a ding, ding:
Sweet lovers love the spring.

This carol they began that hour,
　With a hey, and a ho, and a hey nonino,
15　How that a life was but a flower
　In the spring time, the only pretty ring time,
When birds do sing, hey ding a ding, ding:
Sweet lovers love the spring.

And therefore take the present time,
20　With a hey, and a ho, and a hey nonino,
For love is crownèd with the prime
　In the spring time, the only pretty ring time,
When birds do sing, hey ding a ding, ding:
Sweet lovers love the spring.

QUESTIONS FOR THINKING AND WRITING

1. How would you characterize this song? What is its mood?
2. How does the refrain help set the mood of the song?
3. What other repetitions of sounds do you find in the poem? What do they contribute? (Note: Two important categories here are **rhyme**—the use of words that end with the same sound, like *rye* and *lie*—and **alliteration,** the use of words that begin with the same sound, like *lover* and *lass; hey, ho,* and *hey.*)
4. Discuss the progression of thought and feeling from the first stanza to the final one. What sense of completeness does the progression impart to Shakespeare's song?

THOMAS HARDY (1840–1928)

The Ruined Maid

"O 'Melia, my dear, this does everything crown!
Who could have supposed I should meet you in Town?
And whence such fair garments, such prosperi-ty?"—
"O didn't you know I'd been ruined?" said she.

5   —"You left us in tatters, without shoes or socks,
Tired of digging potatoes, and spudding up docks;[1]
And now you've gay bracelets and bright feathers three!"—
"Yes: that's how we dress when we're ruined," said she.

—"At home in the barton[2] you said 'thee' and 'thou,'
10 And 'thik oon,' and 'theäs oon,' and 't'other'; but now
Your talking quite fits 'ee for high compa-ny!"—
"Some polish is gained with one's ruin," said she.

—"Your hands were like paws then, your face blue and bleak
But now I'm bewitched by your delicate cheek,
15 And your little gloves fit as on any la-dy!"—
"We never do work when we're ruined," said she.

—"You used to call home-life a hag-ridden dream,
And you'd sigh, and you'd sock; but at present you seem
To know not of megrims[3] or melancho-ly!"—
20 "True. One's pretty lively when ruined," said she.

—"I wish I had feathers, a fine sweeping gown,
And a delicate face, and could strut about Town!"—
"My dear—a raw country girl, such as you be,
Cannot quite expect that. You ain't ruined," said she.

QUESTIONS FOR THINKING AND WRITING

1. How does Hardy use question and answer to characterize the two women?
2. What balance exists here between the two sides of the dialogue? What is the effect of the repetitions in the final line of each stanza?
3. What sort of tone or consciousness would you expect to find in a poem about a "ruined maid" that is absent from this poem? What effect does this have on the tone of the poem and on the characterization of the speakers? On the poet's apparent attitude toward them?

---

[1] Digging up weeds.
[2] Farmyard.
[3] Low spirits.

WILLIAM BLAKE (1757–1827)

From **Songs of Innocence**

The Lamb

Little Lamb, who made thee?
Dost thou know who made thee?
Gave thee life & bid thee feed,
By the stream & o'er the mead;
5 Gave thee clothing of delight,
Softest clothing wooly bright;
Gave thee such a tender voice,
Making all the vales rejoice!
Little Lamb who made thee?
10 Dost thou know who made thee?

Little Lamb I'll tell thee,
Little Lamb I'll tell thee!
He is callèd by thy name,
For he calls himself a Lamb:
15 He is meek & he is mild,
He became a little child:
I a child & thou a lamb,
We are callèd by his name.
Little Lamb God bless thee.
20 Little Lamb God bless thee.

From **Songs of Experience**

The Tyger

Tyger! Tyger! burning bright
In the forests of the night,
What immortal hand or eye
Could frame thy fearful symmetry?

5 In what distant deeps or skies
Burnt the fire of thine eyes?
On what wings dare he aspire?
What the hand, dare seize the fire?

And what shoulder, & what art,
10 Could twist the sinews of thy heart?
And when thy heart began to beat,
What dread hand? & what dread feet?

What the hammer? what the chain?
In what furnace was thy brain?
15 What the anvil? what dread grasp
Dare its deadly terrors clasp?

When the stars threw down their spears,
And water'd heaven with their tears,
Did he smile his work to see?
20 Did he who made the Lamb make thee?

Tyger! Tyger! burning bright
In the forests of the night,
What immortal hand or eye
Dare frame thy fearful symmetry?

QUESTIONS FOR THINKING AND WRITING

If you were to write an essay on "The Lamb" and "The Tyger," you might start with the following question:

1. Both "The Lamb" and "The Tyger" are essentially religious poems. Yet they seem to describe two different aspects of religious feeling. How would you characterize each aspect? How does the first fit the conception of "innocence," the second of "experience"? How are the animals, and the feelings they represent, characterized within the poem?

To develop the answer, you could then look at the following aspects of each poem:

2. "The Lamb" and "The Tyger" have almost the same rhythm, being based on a seven-syllable line with the odd-numbered syllables accented: Ty-ger! Ty-ger! burn-ing bright. But "The Lamb" varies this meter in places, while "The Tyger" holds to it firmly throughout. Look at the rhythm and repetitions carefully in each poem, and then explain how they reinforce each other. Why is the effect so different for each poem?
3. "The Lamb" and "The Tyger" both make use of repeated questions. How does their use in "The Lamb" differ from their use in "The Tyger"? How do these differences help create the contrasting tones of the two poems?
4. What images are connected with the lamb? With the tiger? How are they related? How contrasted?
5. What attitude does the speaker seem to have toward each animal? With what evidence would you support your answer to this question?

The next two poems show what can happen to the ballad form in the hands of highly sophisticated poets who are concerned less with relating incidents than with conveying emotion and demonstrating the various effects that can be gained by a concentration on the sounds and rhythms of words. We may note that these poems provide freer and more self-consciously artistic variations on balladic themes than do any we have previously read. In contrast to folk ballads or to modern ballads that adhere closely to the folk tradition, such as Randall's "Ballad of Birmingham," these freer adaptations of the ballad form are known as **literary ballads.** We will read one nineteenth-century and one twentieth-century example.

EDGAR ALLAN POE (1809–1849)

Annabel Lee

It was many and many a year ago,
      In a kingdom by the sea,
That a maiden there lived whom you may know
      By the name of Annabel Lee;—
5 And this maiden she lived with no other thought
      Than to love and be loved by me.

She was a child and *I* was a child,
      In this kingdom by the sea,
But we loved with a love that was more than love—
10   I and my Annabel Lee—
With a love that the wingèd seraphs of Heaven
      Coveted her and me.

And this was the reason that, long ago,
      In this kingdom by the sea,
15 A wind blew out of a cloud by night
      Chilling my Annabel Lee;
So that her highborn kinsmen came
      And bore her away from me,
To shut her up in a sepulchre
20   In this kingdom by the sea.

The angels, not half so happy in Heaven,
      Went envying her and me—
Yes!—that was the reason (as all men know,
      In this kingdom by the sea)
25 That the wind came out of the cloud chilling
      And killing my Annabel Lee.

But our love it was stronger by far than the love
      Of those who were older than we—
      Of many far wiser than we—

30 And neither the angels in Heaven above,
　　Nor the demons down under the sea,
　Can ever dissever my soul from the soul
　　Of the beautiful Annabel Lee: —

　For the moon never beams without bringing me dreams
35　　Of the beautiful Annabel Lee;
　And the stars never rise but I see the bright eyes
　　Of the beautiful Annabel Lee;
　And so, all the night-tide, I lie down by the side
　Of my darling, my darling, my life and my bride,
40　　In her sepulchre there by the sea—
　　In her tomb by the side of the sea.

QUESTIONS FOR THINKING AND WRITING

1. What elements in "Annabel Lee" come from the ballad tradition? What elements have been added or altered? In developing your answer, consider the basic use of rhythm and rhyme, repetition, refrain, alliteration, vocabulary, and so on.
2. Consider the story told by the poem, and the emotions it evokes. Is the story one that fits well into the ballad form? Again, what elements harmonize well with the ballad tradition? Which suggest a more sophisticated speaker and audience?

E. E. CUMMINGS (1894–1963)

All in green went my love riding

All in green went my love riding
on a great horse of gold
into the silver dawn.

four lean hounds crouched low and smiling
5 the merry deer ran before.

Fleeter be they than dappled dreams
the swift sweet deer
the red rare deer.

Four red roebuck[1] at a white water
10 the cruel bugle sang before.

---

[1] Male roe deer.

Horn at hip went my love riding
riding the echo down
into the silver dawn.

four lean hounds crouched low and smiling
15 the level meadows ran before.

Softer be they than slippered sleep
the lean lithe deer
the fleet flown deer.

Four fleet does at a gold valley
20 the famished arrow sang before.

Bow at belt went my love riding
riding the mountain down
into the silver dawn.

four lean hounds crouched low and smiling
25 the sheer peaks ran before.

Paler be they than daunting death
the sleek slim deer
the tall tense deer.

Four tall stags at a green mountain
30 the lucky hunter sang before.

All in green went my love riding
on a great horse of gold
into the silver dawn.

four lean hounds crouched low and smiling
35 my heart fell dead before.

QUESTIONS FOR THINKING AND WRITING

1. Incremental repetition is used in this modern poem for an almost balladlike effect. But how would you describe the way stanzas are linked in this poem?
2. What effects would you say the poem achieves? How would you distinguish between its effects and those of traditional ballads?

3 Compression and Verse Forms

To write a short story based on the tale told in "Lord Randal" or "Get Up and Bar the Door" would require at least one thousand words. (That would be roughly the length of "If Not Higher"—quite a short story, as stories go.) These two ballads, however, have less than five hundred words each, including refrains and repetitions. And even though the ballads are much shorter than a very short story, they seem long and loosely constructed when they are compared with such tightly written lyrics as "The Tyger."

Verse, then, is a highly compressed form. Eliminating inessentials—the name of Lord Randal's sweetheart, the reason she killed him—it takes us directly to the heart of a situation, to the one or two moments most highly charged with emotion. In the case of "Lord Randal," this technique reduces the ballad to a single moment, that in which mother and son discover that the son has been poisoned. In the case of "Get Up and Bar the Door," it produces a ballad centering on two episodes: the one that begins the quarrel and the one that ends it.

Time becomes flexible in these ballads, as one memorable moment is juxtaposed with the next, ignoring all that may have gone between: "Then by there came two gentlemen,/At twelve oclock at night." We can imagine that the lateness of the hour would have made the silent house seem even stranger than it was to the "gentlemen," and we may also suspect that quite a few hours must have passed since the feuding couple made their pact. But all the singer gives us is the crucial hour— "twelve"—and the number of intruders. The time between incidents is not important. The conflict between the couple is.

Similarly, "The Cherry-Tree Carol" moves with almost no consciousness of elapsed time from the wedding of Joseph and Mary to the scene in the orchard to a final scene between Mary and her infant son. In each case, a simple "then" defines the sequence, whether the incidents follow each other instantly, as in "then bespoke the babe," "then bowed down the highest tree," and "O then bespoke Joseph," or whether a gap of several months is indicated: "Then Mary took her babe." The passage of time, which affects everyone, is of no concern to the singer. The unique situation of parents confronted with their child's divinity engrosses all the attention, linking together the unusual circumstances of Joseph's marriage, the miracle in the orchard, and Christ's prophecy of his death and resurrection. "The Cherry-Tree Carol" assumes that its hearers are all familiar with the story of Christ's birth and death; it therefore feels free to concentrate on those aspects of the legend that bear on its central theme, leaving us to place them in chronological time if we wish.

Every literary form is somewhat selective in its choice of times and episodes, and in the amount of attention it gives to each. "If Not Higher," for example, tells its tale of a conflict between two types of religion by focusing on two men and spending half of its narration following the two through a single hour of a morning. Similarly, *Oedipus Rex*'s tale of the fall of a king focuses on the last day of his reign, a day of crisis and steadily mounting emotion. But neither drama nor fiction can match the intense selectivity, the rigorous paring-down, of poetry.

Poetic form demands **compression**. A line of eight or ten syllables, a stanza of two, four, or six lines will not allow any wasted words. The poet must pare away all the needless background and inessential details in order to fit the essential ones into those brief stanzas.

Yet this strictness of form also helps the hearer to accept the compression it produces. We would not accept so few details as "Lord Randal" gives us in a prose account of his death. Nor could the information given in "The Lamb" or "The Tyger" stand alone as prose. Ballad and lyric alike need the cadence of their verse—the rhyme, the rhythm, the rounded-off pattern formed by the stanzas—to give our ear and mind the sense of completeness and satisfaction that allows us to enjoy the brief, tightly focused statements their poetry makes.

Compression, then, is another technique that allows the material presented and the form of its presentation to reinforce each other, providing for the reader not only a satisfying unity, but also one that seems notably poetic. Let us now examine that technique in action by looking at a few types of poetry that have compression as their most notable feature, beginning with the oldest of these forms, the **epigram.**

Epigrams may be serious or humorous, flattering or insulting. But they are usually descriptive of a person, animal, or object; and they are invariably brief. Probably the most popular type today is the **satiric epigram,** a form that can be described as a description with a sting. Here is an example:

COUNTEE CULLEN (1903–1946)

For a Lady I Know

She even thinks that up in heaven
Her class lies late and snores,
While poor black cherubs rise at seven
To do celestial chores.

QUESTIONS FOR THINKING AND WRITING

1. What single fact do the four lines of this poem tell us about the "Lady" who is their subject?
2. What further facts do they suggest about her?
3. How do words like *her class* and *poor black cherubs* characterize the lady and the attitudes that the poet suggests she holds?
4. What do words like *snores* and *celestial chores* do for the poem? What do they suggest about the poet's attitude?

Not all brief poems with a punch are epigrams, however. The following poem has a sting of its own and is as highly compressed in technique as any poem you will see. Yet its structure is not that of the epigram. How would you define it?

GWENDOLYN BROOKS (1917–   )

We Real Cool

The Pool Players.
Seven at the Golden Shovel.

We real cool. We
Left school. We

5 Lurk late. We
Strike straight. We

Sing sin. We
Thin gin. We

Jazz June. We
10 Die soon.

QUESTIONS FOR THINKING AND WRITING

1. What does the subtitle tell us about the speakers of the poem?
2. How do the speakers characterize themselves?
3. Discuss the use of repetition in the poem.
4. Note also the breaks in the pattern. Why has Brooks placed the word *We* at the end of each line rather than letting it come at the beginning as it does in the first line? Is the word *We* stressed more heavily, less heavily, or just as heavily at the end of the line as it would be at the beginning? What happens to the verbs? Does placing them at the beginning of the line give them any extra stress? What happens to the length of the last line? What effect does it produce?
5. What does Brooks seem to be saying in this poem about the "Seven" or about people like them? How does the form of her poem express or emphasize her feelings?

In contrast with these two very brief poems, here is a slightly longer poem. Like the other two, it is thought-provoking. But while Cullen's and Brooks's speakers merely make their statements, leaving us to gather the implications for ourselves, the next speaker argues with us quite directly.

WILLIAM WORDSWORTH (1770–1850)

The World Is Too Much with Us

The world is too much with us; late and soon,
Getting and spending, we lay waste our powers:
Little we see in Nature that is ours;
We have given our hearts away, a sordid boon!
5 This Sea that bares her bosom to the moon;
The winds that will be howling at all hours,
And are up-gathered now like sleeping flowers;
For this, for everything, we are out of tune;
It moves us not.—Great God! I'd rather be
10 A Pagan suckled in a creed outworn;
So might I, standing on this pleasant lea,

Have glimpses that would make me less forlorn;
Have sight of Proteus rising from the sea;
Or hear old Triton blow his wreathèd horn.[1]

QUESTIONS FOR THINKING AND WRITING

1. What is the argument of this poem?
2. How does Wordsworth's invocation of Triton and Proteus fit in with the argument of the poem?
3. What words or images in the poem do you find most striking? How do they support the poem's argument?
4. Note the poem's movement from "us" and "we" in the first lines to "I" at the end. At what line does the change take place? How is it marked or signaled? What changes of tone of voice and of mood go with it? What change of imagery?
5. What qualities in the poem make it suitable as a study in compression? Alternatively, if you disagree with this classification, why do you challenge the poem's placement in this chapter?

Another extremely brief form, which was introduced to English and American poetry in the twentieth century, is the **imagist** poem. Imagist poetry grew out of an interest in Oriental poetry, especially in the brief, seventeen-syllable form known as **haiku**. (The poems by Pound that follow are sometimes called haiku.) As the word *imagist* implies, this poetry focuses on a single sensory image—a sight, sound, or feeling—and presents it in as brief and vivid a form as the writer can manage. Read the following four poems, and then ask what image each poem starts from and what further images it uses to reinforce the first one. How are the images combined? How would you contrast the form and effect of these poems with the form and effect of the epigrams you have just read, or with the effect and form of Blake's lyrics?

EZRA POUND (1885–1972)

In a Station of the Metro

The apparition of these faces in the crowd;
Petals on a wet, black bough.

---

1 In Greek mythology Proteus was a prophetic sea god who, when seized, changed shape to try to escape prophesying. Triton, the son of the sea god Poseidon, played a trumpet made of a conch shell.

AMY LOWELL (1874–1925)

Wind and Silver

Greatly shining,
The Autumn moon floats in the thin sky;
And the fish-ponds shake their backs and flash their
    dragon scales
As she passes over them.

DENISE LEVERTOV (1923–   )

Six Variations (part iii)

Shlup, shlup, the dog
as it laps up
water
makes intelligent
5 music, resting
now and then to take breath in irregular
measure.

H. D. (HILDA DOOLITTLE) (1886–1961)

Heat

O wind, rend open the heat,
cut apart the heat,
rend it to tatters.

Fruit cannot drop
5 through this thick air—
fruit cannot fall into heat
that presses up and blunts
the points of pears
and rounds the grapes.

10 Cut the heat—
plough through it,
turning it on either side
of your path.

Here is one more poem by Pound, who was one of the founders of imagist poetry. What does this poem do with imagist techniques? How does it differ from the preceding poems?

EZRA POUND (1885–1972)

L'Art 1910

Green arsenic smeared on an egg-white cloth,
Crushed strawberries! Come, let us feast our eyes.

A slightly longer descriptive poem is William Carlos Williams's "The Dance," in which the crowding of as many words and images as possible into eight lines is in contrast with the spareness of imagist poetry. The form seems almost too limited for the magnitude of the sounds and motions "The Dance" attempts to contain.

WILLIAM CARLOS WILLIAMS (1883–1963)

The Dance

In Breughel's[1] great picture, The Kermess,[2]
the dancers go round, they go round and
around, the squeal and the blare and the
tweedle of bagpipes, a bugle and fiddles
5   tipping their bellies (round as the thick-
sided glasses whose wash they impound)
their hips and their bellies off balance
to turn them. Kicking and rolling about
the Fair Grounds, swinging their butts, those
10 shanks must be sound to bear up under such
rollicking measures, prance as they dance
in Breughel's picture, The Kermess.

QUESTIONS FOR THINKING AND WRITING

1. Although you might expect a poem describing a painting to concentrate on color or form, Williams's poem concentrates at least as heavily on motion and sound. What words or phrases describe the sounds of the scene? Which describe shapes or forms? Which describe motion? What sorts of music and dancers does Williams seem to be portraying with these terms?

2. How do the poem's rhythm and shape support the sense of sound and motion? Note particularly the large number of heavily stressed monosyllables. What effect do they provide? How have sentence structure and grammar been reshaped to contribute to the sensation of noise and speed?

---

[1] Peter Breughel, or Brueghel (1525?–1569), a Flemish painter.
[2] A kermess is a carnival or fair.

3. Note the plays on words within the poem: "bellies" for both fiddles and dancers, legs called "sound" in a poem much concerned with musical sounds. How does such wordplay help unify the scene? Note also the use of repetition: how does it help shape the poem?
4. If you are able to find a print of *The Kermess,* decide how well you think Williams has caught the spirit of the painting. What aspects of the poem stand out for you as being particularly apt?

Finally, we should look at some poems by Emily Dickinson. No study of compression in poetry would be complete without a consideration of the work of this American poet, who was far ahead of her time in the concentration and spareness of her verse. Description and argument blend in Dickinson's poetry into a remarkable unity of vision and idea. Notice, in the following two poems, how images of light and motion bridge the gap between the physical and spiritual worlds and between our own physical and spiritual responses to these worlds.

EMILY DICKINSON (1830–1886)

There's a Certain Slant of Light (#258)

There's a certain Slant of light,
Winter Afternoons—
That oppresses, like the Heft
Of Cathedral Tunes—

5 Heavenly Hurt, it gives us—
We can find no scar,
But internal difference,
Where the Meanings, are—

None may teach it—Any—
10 'Tis the Seal Despair—
An imperial affliction
Sent us of the Air—

When it comes, the Landscape listens—
Shadows—hold their breath—
15 When it goes, 'tis like the Distance
On the look of Death—

Tell All the Truth but Tell It Slant (#1129)

Tell all the Truth but tell it slant—
Success in Circuit lies

Too bright for our infirm Delight
The Truth's superb surprise
5 As Lightning to the Children eased
With explanation kind
The Truth must dazzle gradually
Or every man be blind—

QUESTIONS FOR THINKING AND WRITING

1. Select two to four lines from one of the poems and copy it into your reading journal or onto separate paper. Now do a freewriting on what it means to you.
2. Both poems use images of light. Write a paragraph for each poem on the effect and meaning of light images. Now write a couple of paragraphs that compare and contrast the use of light imagery in the two poems. [*Hint:* This prewriting exercise may lead to an excellent full-length essay.]
3. Dickinson's poetry is highly compressed. Copy two or three lines that reveal that compression. Write two or three paragraphs explaining how Dickinson creates this effect. What is compressed? What is the nature of the effect she achieves?

4 *Word Choice: Meanings and Suggestions*

Common Phrases and New Meanings

Our study of ballads gave us insight into the use of repetition and selectivity in poetry, and thus into poetry's balance of narrative and rhythmic patterns. We saw that poetry is based on the combination of satisfying sounds and sharply focused content. And we saw how the pattern of sounds and words created by the skillful use of rhythm, repetition, and word-sound can be used to heighten the effect of compression or to set a mood.

But ballads could not tell us a great deal about word choice in poetry. For ballads, like other oral poetry, tend to rely on a shared vocabulary of predictable phrases and stock epithets. Hearing ballads, we recognize in them traditional terms, pairings, and comparisons: "my true-love," "my hawks and my hounds," "the sun and the moon," "as red as the blood," and "as dead as the stones." We are not meant to linger on any of them, or on any particular line. Rather, we let each recognized phrase add its bit to mood or situation, while we reserve our main attention for the pattern made by the story as it unfolds.

In written poetry, on the other hand, word choice is all-important. The play on words by which Shakespeare blends spring, songs, and rings to create an atmosphere (p. 439); the indelicate verb *snores* with which Cullen mocks his "lady's" pretensions to gentility (p. 448); and even the archaic spelling "tyger," which gives Blake's beast its first hint of strangeness and mystery, all testify to the power of the well-chosen word. The words themselves are not unusual ones; but they surprise us when they appear, nonetheless. They call on us to pay attention and reward us for our attention by bringing their overtones of meaning and suggestion into the poem, enriching our enjoyment and understanding.

The language of poetry, then, is not necessarily composed of strange, unusual, or uniquely "poetic" words. More often, poetry gains its effects through unexpected juxtapositions of common words, bringing new meaning into the ordinary. Look, for instance, at this poem by Emily Dickinson, and consider how the poet gives significance to the simplest language.

The Bustle in a House (#1078)

The Bustle in a House
The Morning after Death
Is solemnest of industries
Enacted upon Earth—

5 The Sweeping up the Heart
And putting Love away
We shall not want to use again
Until Eternity.

The language of the first stanza is almost like prose. A few extra words, and it would be a simple prose statement: The bustle that takes place in a house, the day after someone who lived there has died, represents one of the most solemn tasks on earth. (The word *industries* may seem a bit strange in this context. At the time this poem was written, however, it was used to denote any sort of labor, just as the word *industrious* does today.)

In the second stanza, however, we notice a change. Here the poet is amplifying her first statement. She is explaining that the "bustle" is caused by the housecleaning that takes place between a death and the funeral, and that it is "solemn" because the workers must reconcile themselves to the loss of a loved one. In fact, the workers are coming to grips with their emotions even as they do the chores.

She does not, however, resort to wordy explanations. Rather, she combines housework and emotions in a tightly compressed pair of images. The verbs of the second stanza speak of housecleaning matters; the nouns, of love. It is not dust that is swept up, but "the heart"; not blankets to be put away, but "love." The combination conveys the sense of loss. "The sweeping up the heart," in particular, suggests that the heart is broken, is in pieces; and the thought of a broken heart, in turn, suggests grief.

But the poet also says that the grief and loss are not permanent. "Love" is not thrown away, but rather "put away" to be used again on a future occasion. "Until eternity": the phrase suggests a fearfully long wait, but insists, nonetheless, that the waiting will end. "Eternity" thus balances "earth," tempering the present sense of loss with faith in restoration. And in that balance the poem ends and rests.

Here is another poem by Dickinson that is notable for its unusual use of words. How would you analyze it?

EMILY DICKINSON (1830–1886)

Because I Could Not Stop for Death (#712)

Because I could not stop for Death—
He kindly stopped for me—
The Carriage held but just Ourselves—
And Immortality.

5 We slowly drove—He knew no haste
And I had put away
My labor and my leisure too,
For His Civility—

We passed the School, where Children strove
10 At Recess—in the Ring—
We passed the Fields of Gazing Grain—
We passed the Setting Sun—

Or rather—He passed Us—
The Dews drew quivering and chill—
15 For only Gossamer, my Gown—
My Tippet[1]—only Tulle[2]—

We paused before a House that seemed
A Swelling of the Ground—
The Roof was scarcely visible—
20 The Cornice—in the Ground—

---

[1] A shoulder cape.
[2] A stiff, sheer fabric.

Since then—'tis Centuries—and yet
Feels shorter than the Day
I first surmised the Horses' Heads
Were toward Eternity—

Suggestion and Interpretation

The language of Blake's "The Tyger" is stranger and more complex than Dickinson's. The description of the tiger as "Burning bright/In the forests of the night" links notions of burning passion, glowing cat-eyes, dark trees, and forests of stars to create, from words that literally are near nonsense, a beast half earthly and half unearthly, combining in his "fearful symmetry" brutal ferocity and supernatural beauty.

"The Tyger" again brings us to realize that word choice in poetry often means choosing words that can carry many meanings at once and then combining those words for the greatest power of suggestion. Blake's tiger is more than mere animal. The striking images and the strong sense of awe that pervade the poem insist that the tiger stands for something special in its questioner's eyes. But they will not tell us specifically what that something is. In this the language of the poem is poetic—it moves always toward greater suggestiveness, never toward a narrowing of meaning. As a result, the tiger symbolizes many things for many people, with all readers bringing their own experiences to this "Song of Experience" and coming away with their own visions of what the tiger can mean for them.

Sound, sense, and suggestion all blend in poetry. Words gain new relevance, new connections. They carry several meanings, suggest several more, and join with other words to suggest yet further meanings. Word choice, the craft of selecting and joining words to enrich their power to communicate, is one of the basic skills of the poet's craft.

Since the rhythms of the following two poems are smoother than those of "The Bustle in the House," and their rhymes are more satisfyingly matched, they have a more traditional sound. Yet their use of language resembles that in Dickinson's poem in that their words and syntax, basically simple and straightforward, are highlighted by a few unexpected words or images. Discuss what you think the highlights in these poems are, and how you think they function.

WILLIAM WORDSWORTH (1770–1850)

She Dwelt Among the Untrodden Ways

She dwelt among the untrodden ways
    Beside the springs of Dove.

A Maid whom there were none to praise
  And very few to love;

5 A violet by a mossy stone
  Half hidden from the eye!
—Fair as a star, when only one
  Is shining in the sky.

She lived unknown, and few could know
10 When Lucy ceased to be;
  But she is in her grave, and, oh,
  The difference to me!

ROBERT HERRICK (1591–1674)

Upon Julia's Clothes

Whenas in silks my Julia goes,
Then, then, methinks, how sweetly flows
The liquefaction of her clothes.

Next, when I cast mine eyes and see
5 The brave vibration each way free,
O how that glittering taketh me!

Again, the following poem presents a straightforward statement. But here the language is slightly richer, the play on words is more pronounced, and the words take on more resonance of meaning. Discuss the poem and its language. How does the choice of words give the poem more impact than its main statement, "Many friends of mine have died," would have?

A. E. HOUSMAN (1859–1936)

With Rue My Heart Is Laden

With rue my heart is laden
  For golden friends I had,
For many a rose-lipt maiden
  And many a lightfoot lad.

5 By brooks too broad for leaping
  The lightfoot boys are laid;
The rose-lipt girls are sleeping
  In fields where roses fade.

QUESTIONS FOR THINKING AND WRITING

1. What repetitions do you find in the poem? How does the second stanza develop the images begun in the first stanza?
2. How does the word *golden* in line 2 fit into the mood and imagery?
3. Note the heavy use of "r" and "l" sounds. What effect does the alliteration of these sounds produce? What other examples of alliteration can you find in the poem? How would you summarize your view of Housman's choice of words for sound and sense?

The next poem uses a number of straightforward statements to create a debate on the importance of love. Note how the longer lines and more formal construction of this poem set off the total simplicity of its language. But note, too, the movement from the detachment and objectivity of the opening to the restrained intensity of the final line.

EDNA ST. VINCENT MILLAY (1892–1950)

Love Is Not All: It Is Not Meat nor Drink

Love is not all: it is not meat nor drink
Nor slumber nor a roof against the rain;
Nor yet a floating spar to men that sink
And rise and sink and rise and sink again;
5 Love can not fill the thickened lung with breath,
Nor clean the blood, nor set the fractured bone;
Yet many a man is making friends with death
Even as I speak, for lack of love alone.
It well may be that in a difficult hour,
10 Pinned down by pain and moaning for release,
Or nagged by want past resolution's power,
I might be driven to sell your love for peace,
Or trade the memory of this night for food.
It well may be. I do not think I would.

QUESTIONS FOR THINKING AND WRITING

1. How does the argument in this poem progress?
   a. What is being said in the lines 1–4? In lines 5–6?
   b. What shift occurs in lines 7–8?
   c. What shift occurs in lines 9–13? What is being discussed now?
   d. What happens in line 14?
2. List the verbs in the poem. What progressions, repetitions, and changes do you find in the verbs that support and emphasize the movement of the debate?
3. What words suggest time? Where are they located in the poem? What is their function? Note especially the phrase, "Even as I speak," in line 8. How is that pivotal, in terms of the poem's structure, its sense of time and person?

4. How many sentences does the poem contain? How long (in terms of lines of verse) is each one?
5. How many words does the poem contain? How many of them are monosyllables? Do you notice any lines that consist wholly of monosyllables?
6. Putting all the above facts together—and adding any others you think important—what effect would you say Millay was trying to produce? How successful do you think she was?

The next two poems are written in **free verse,** a verse form invented in the early twentieth century. Free verse is marked by uneven line lengths and often by the absence of rhyme, as well. Note how these poems mix repetition and compression to create their very different effects.

CARL SANDBURG (1878–1967)

Cool Tombs

When Abraham Lincoln was shoveled into the tombs, he forgot the
    copperheads and the assassin . . . in the dust, in the cool tombs.
And Ulysses Grant lost all thought of con men and Wall Street, cash
    and collateral turned ashes . . . in the dust, in the cool tombs.
5 Pocahontas' body, lovely as a poplar, sweet as a red haw in November
    or a pawpaw in May, did she wonder? does she remember? . . . in
    the dust, in the cool tombs?
Take any streetful of people buying clothes and groceries, cheering a
    hero or throwing confetti and blowing tin horns . . . tell me if the
10   lovers are losers . . . tell me if any get more than the lovers . . . in
    the dust . . . in the cool tombs.

QUESTIONS FOR THINKING AND WRITING

1. What images are associated with each person? Why have they been chosen? What do they suggest?
2. Is there a message to the poem? If so, what is it? How does the poem travel from its opening statements to its final suggestions?
3. How would you describe the sound of this poem? The rhythm? How do sound and rhythm fit the meaning of the poem? How do they create its mood?

EZRA POUND (1885–1972)

These Fought in Any Case[1]

These fought in any case,
and some believing,
        pro domo,[2] in any case . . .

---

[1] Section IV from "E. P. Ode pour L'Election de Son Sépulcre" ("E. P. Ode on the Selection of His Tomb").
[2] "For homeland."

Some quick to arm,
5 some for adventure,
some from fear of weakness,
some from fear of censure,
some for love of slaughter, in imagination,
learning later . . .
10 some in fear, learning love of slaughter;

Died some, pro patria,
                non "dulce" non "et decor"[3] . . .
walked eye-deep in hell
believing in old men's lies, then unbelieving
15 came home, home to a lie,
home to many deceits,
home to old lies and new infamy;
usury age-old and age-thick
and liars in public places.

20 Daring as never before, wastage as never before.
Young blood and high blood,
fair cheeks, and fine bodies;

fortitude as never before

frankness as never before,
25 disillusions as never told in the old days,
hysterias, trench confessions,
laughter out of dead bellies.

QUESTIONS FOR THINKING AND WRITING

1. How would you describe the tone of voice in this poem? What do the repetitions contribute to it? The word choice? (Be sure you give examples to prove your assertions.)
2. What attitude does the poem suggest towards the soldiers of which it speaks? Is the attitude simple or complex? How is it suggested?
3. What of the poem's attitude to war in general?
4. An **ode** is a poem of irregular form. How does Pound use irregularity of form to reinforce the suggestions his poem makes?
5. Although "Cool Tombs" and "These Fought in Any Case" are both written in free verse and make heavy use of repetition, the **tone** and **pace** of the two poems are completely different. Why?

---

[3] An ironic allusion to the famous line of Horace: "Dulce et decorum est pro patria mori" ("It is sweet and fitting to die for one's country").

The words in this next poem deserve special notice. Their under-lying tone and syntax are more casual and friendly than any we have met so far. And yet Cummings has taken enormous liberties with words and syntax alike, even to the point of inventing new words and positioning each word individually on the page. To what new responses does the resulting poem seem to invite you?

E. E. CUMMINGS (1894–1963)

in Just-

in Just-
spring   when the world is mud-
luscious the little
lame balloonman

5 whistles   far   and wee

and eddieandbill come
running from marbles and
piracies and it's
spring

10 when the world is puddle-wonderful

the queer
old balloonman whistles
far   and   wee
and bettyandisbel come dancing

15 from hop-scotch and jump-rope and

it's
spring
and
    the
20   goat-footed

balloonMan   whistles
far
and
wee

QUESTIONS FOR THINKING AND WRITING

1. In analyzing this poem, we may begin with its wordplay. How do compound words such as *mud-luscious* and *puddle-wonderful* affect the sound and meaning of the lines in which they occur? How many meanings does the word *wee* have, and what is the effect of using it? The balloon-man is described through incremental repetition, beginning as "lame" and ending as "goat-footed." Why goat-footed?
2. We may then note two unusual rhythmic devices: the breaking of lines in the middle of words or phrases, and the spacing out or running together of words. And we may ask how these affect the sound and mood of the poem, and our sense of the scene it describes.
3. Then we may put this play with words and rhythms together with the poem's use of names and detail, and ask how Cummings creates and enhances his description. What does the intent of the poem seem to be? What message does it seem to carry? How do the sound and word choices create the tone and the message?

THE SPEAKER IN THE POEM

5

The Speaker's Voice

We have said that ballads, being traditional, oral poetry, rely on common words and images rather than on the unique images of written poetry. We may now make one final distinction by remarking that this stylization of ballads leaves these songs lacking uniquely memorable voices. A deserted lover in one ballad, for instance, sounds much like a deserted lover in any other ballad. They will speak at least some of the same words in the same tones and rhythms. This is not the case in written poetry, where we would take the appearance of a lover who sounds like any other lover as the sign of a second-rate poem. If we read twenty lyrics about love—or even twenty lyrics about lost love—we expect to hear twenty different voices.

This reflection brings us to one of the basic paradoxes of poetry. Because of its use of rhythm and sound patterns, the language of poetry may be the farthest of all literary languages from everyday speech. Yet the voices within poems are the most intimate of literary voices, speaking to us most vividly and directly and conveying to us most openly the speakers' deepest and most immediate emotions. No other form of literature demands so much care and craft in its writing as poetry; yet no other form can seem to present the spontaneous flow of emotion as convincingly as poetry can.

Because poetry can so thoroughly convince us that in responding to it we are sharing a genuine, strongly felt emotion, it can attract our strongest response. Subjectively, this is good; it represents poetry doing what it should do. Objectively, however, poetry's seeming frankness raises the critical danger that we may mistake the voice within the poem for the voice of the poet. The further danger then arises that we may generalize from a single poem, slipping from the critically acceptable statement, "Blake's 'Tyger' presents the tiger as a beautiful but terrifying creature" to the unacceptable, "As 'The Tyger' shows, Blake was afraid of tigers."

We cannot fall into this error so easily in drama or fiction, where the number of characters and the abundance of circumstantial detail continually warn us of the distance between author and work. Poetry, however, often has but one voice in a poem. The voice often speaks in the first person: "Oh, how that glittering taketh me!" And the intensity of emotion that is felt only in the climatic scenes of fiction and drama may illuminate an entire lyric. This combination of single voice, first person, and unflagging intensity of emotion often obliterates the distance between the poet and speaker. If the speaker then gives us the slightest hint that he or she may represent the poet, we become all too willing to make the identification.

But we must not make the identification so simply. We can speak of a poet's voice—can compare Blake's voice to Dickinson's, for example. But when we do this we must compare all the voices from at least a dozen of Blake's poems to all the voices from an equal number of Dickinson's. We can then speak either of a range of voices that seems typical of each poet or of some specific characteristics that remain constant through all their individual voices. Moreover, we may equally well make comparisons between voices belonging to a single poet—comparing the voices of Blake's early poems to those of his later poems, for instance—which we could not do if the voice in each poem were the poet's only voice.

To further emphasize this distance between speaker and poet, we may look again at poems such as "We Real Cool" and "Sir Patrick Spens." They seem to speak to us as directly and to be as immediately felt as any other poems, but we know no author for "Sir Patrick Spens" and are sure that Gwendolyn Brooks is not seven adolescents in a pool hall.

The poem is the poet's vision, nothing more. Its speakers may be inside the action (as in "Upon Julia's Clothes") or outside it (as in "The Cherry-Tree Carol"). They may have elements of the poet's own situation or emotions in them, or they may not. But they are speakers and not writers; they are the poet's creations and not the poet's self.

For discussing speakers who do seem to mirror their poets, we have the useful critical term **persona**. The speakers of "The Lamb" and "The Tyger," of "There's a Certain Slant of Light," and of "Upon Julia's Clothes" may be called their poets' personae. Personae represent one aspect of their poet's personality or experience, isolated from the rest of the poet's life, dramatized, and re-created through art. Poets—like all human beings—are complex and changeable. Personae are simpler: fixed, changeless, and slightly exaggerated. Unlike their makers, who must respond to the many demands of the everyday world in which they live, personae exist only within their poems and respond only to the thoughts and sensations that gave the poems birth.

Here, for the further study of speakers in poetry, are four groups of poems. The first three groups employ speakers who might well be spoken of as personae; the fourth has speakers who cannot. Be aware, as you read these poems, of sound and language and total effect. But pay most attention to the characterization of the speakers and to the varying voices with which they speak.

THEODORE ROETHKE (1908–1963)

My Papa's Waltz

The whiskey on your breath
Could make a small boy dizzy;
But I hung on like death:
Such waltzing was not easy.

5 We romped until the pans
Slid from the kitchen shelf;
My mother's countenance
Could not unfrown itself.

The hand that held my wrist
10 Was battered on one knuckle;
At every step you missed
My right ear scraped a buckle.

You beat time on my head
With a palm caked hard by dirt,
15 Then waltzed me off to bed
Still clinging to your shirt.

I Knew a Woman

I knew a woman, lovely in her bones,
When small birds sighed, she would sigh back at them;
Ah, when she moved, she moved more ways than one:
The shapes a bright container can contain!
5 Of her choice virtues only gods should speak,

Or English poets who grew up on Greek
(I'd have them sing in chorus, cheek to cheek).

How well her wishes went! She stroked my chin,
She taught me Turn, and Counter-turn, and Stand;[1]
10 She taught me Touch, that undulant white skin;
I nibbled meekly from her proffered hand;
She was the sickle; I, poor I, the rake,
Coming behind her for her pretty sake
(But what prodigious mowing we did make).

15 Love likes a gander, and adores a goose:
Her full lips pursed, the errant note to seize;
She played it quick, she played it light and loose;
My eyes, they dazzled at her flowing knees;
Her several parts could keep a pure repose,
20 Or one hip quiver with a mobile nose
(She moved in circles, and those circles moved).

Let seed be grass, and grass turn into hay:
I'm martyr to a motion not my own;
What's freedom for? To know eternity.
25 I swear she cast a shadow white as stone.
But who would count eternity in days?
These old bones live to learn her wanton ways:
(I measure time by how a body sways).

QUESTIONS FOR THINKING AND WRITING

1. What is the subject of each of these poems? What is the emotional state of the speaker?
2. How does the language of the two poems compare? What sort of images does each use? How does the language match the subject and mood in each?
3. How would you characterize the speaker of each poem? What would you have to say to move from a characterization of the speakers to a characterization of the poet?

ROBERT FROST (1908–1963)

Two Tramps in Mud Time

Out of the mud two strangers came
And caught me splitting wood in the yard.

---

1 Terms for the three parts of a Pindaric ode.

And one of them put me off my aim
By hailing cheerily "Hit them hard!"
5 I knew pretty well why he dropped behind
And let the other go on a way.
I knew pretty well what he had in mind:
He wanted to take my job for pay.

Good blocks of oak it was I split,
10 As large around as the chopping block;
And every piece I squarely hit
Fell splinterless as a cloven rock.
The blows that a life of self-control
Spares to strike for the common good,
15 That day, giving a loose to my soul,
I spent on the unimportant wood.

The sun was warm but the wind was chill.
You know how it is with an April day
When the sun is out and the wind is still,
20 You're one month on in the middle of May.
But if you so much as dare to speak,
A cloud comes over the sunlit arch,
A wind comes off a frozen peak,
And you're two months back in the middle of March.

25 A bluebird comes tenderly up to alight
And turns to the wind to unruffle a plume,
His song so pitched as not to excite
A single flower as yet to bloom.
It is snowing a flake: and he half knew
30 Winter was only playing possum.
Except in color he isn't blue,
But he wouldn't advise a thing to blossom.

The water for which we may have to look
In summertime with a witching wand,
35 In every wheelrut's now a brook,
In every print of a hoof a pond.
Be glad of water, but don't forget
The lurking frost in the earth beneath
That will steal forth after the sun is set
40 And show on the water its crystal teeth.

The time when most I loved my task
These two must make me love it more

By coming with what they came to ask.
You'd think I never had felt before
45 The weight of an ax-head poised aloft,
The grip on earth of outspread feet,
The life of muscles rocking soft
And smooth and moist in vernal heat.

Out of the woods two hulking tramps
50 (From sleeping God knows where last night,
But not long since in the lumber camps).
They thought all chopping was theirs of right.
Men of the woods and lumberjacks,
They judged me by their appropriate tool.
55 Except as a fellow handled an ax
They had no way of knowing a fool.

Nothing on either side was said.
They knew they had but to stay their stay
And all their logic would fill my head:
60 As that I had no right to play
With what was another man's work for gain.
My right might be love but theirs was need.
And where the two exist in twain
Theirs was the better right—agreed.

65 But yield who will to their separation,
My object in living is to unite
My avocation and my vocation
As my two eyes make one in sight.
Only where love and need are one,
70 And the work is play for mortal stakes,
Is the deed ever really done
For Heaven and the future's sakes.

Provide, Provide

The witch that came (the withered hag)
To wash the steps with pail and rag
Was once the beauty Abishag,

The picture pride of Hollywood.
5 Too many fall from great and good
For you to doubt the likelihood.

Die early and avoid the fate.
Or if predestined to die late,
Make up your mind to die in state.

10 Make the whole stock exchange your own!
If need be occupy a throne,
Where nobody can call *you* crone.

Some have relied on what they knew,
Others on being simply true.
15 What worked for them might work for you.

No memory of having starred
Atones for later disregard
Or keeps the end from being hard.

Better to go down dignified
20 With boughten friendship at your side
Than none at all. Provide, provide!

QUESTIONS FOR THINKING AND WRITING

Each of these two poems starts with an incident and ends with a moral drawn from the incident.

1. To what extent do incident and moral affect the speaker in each poem? To what extent does he seem to hope they'll affect his audience?
2. How much of each poem does Frost spend describing the incident that supposedly triggered the poem? How much on generalizations and lessons? What is the effect of this balance on your sense of each poem?
3. How would you describe the speaker's tone (or tones) of voice in each poem?
4. What uses of language do you find notable in each poem?
5. How would you describe the overall tone and philosophy of each poem? Do both seem capable of forming parts of one person's philosophy? What effect does their diversity have on your sense of Frost as a poet?

ANONYMOUS—MIDDLE ENGLISH LYRIC

Western Wind

Western wind, when will thou blow,
    The small rain down can rain?
Christ, if my love were in my arms
    And I in my bed again.

SIR THOMAS WYATT (1503–1542)

To a Lady to Answer Directly
with Yea or Nay

Madame, withouten many words,
Once I am sure you will or no;
And if you will, then leave your boords[1]
And use your wit, and shew[2] it so,
5 For with a beck[3] you shall me call.
And if of one that burns alway
Ye have pity or ruth[4] at all,
Answer him fair[5] with yea or nay.
If it be yea, I shall be fain;[6]
10 If it be nay, friends as before.
You shall another man obtain,
And I mine own, and yours no more.

SIR JOHN SUCKLING (1609–1642)

The Constant Lover

Out upon it! I have loved
   Three whole days together;
And am like to love three more,
   If it prove fair weather!

5 Time shall moult away his wings,
   Ere he shall discover
In the whole wide world again
   Such a constant lover.

But the spite on't is, no praise
10   Is due at all to me:
Love with me had made no stays,
   Had it any been but she.

---

[1] Jokes.
[2] Show.
[3] Gesture.
[4] Compassion.
[5] Clearly, honestly.
[6] Glad, delighted.

Had it any been but she,
   And that very face,
15 There had been at least ere this
   A dozen dozen in her place!

QUESTIONS FOR THINKING AND WRITING

These three poems are spoken by three different lovers. How would you compare and contrast them?

1. To whom does each speak?
2. In what situation does each find himself? What is his reaction to the situation? What emotions and/or thoughts does he express?
3. How do the form and language of each poem, together with the emotion and situation represented, create your picture of each of these lovers?

THOMAS HARDY (1840–1928)

The Man He Killed

"Had he and I but met
   By some old ancient inn,
We should have sat us down to wet
   Right many a nipperkin![1]

5   "But ranged as infantry,
   And staring face to face,
I shot at him as he at me,
   And killed him in his place.

"I shot him dead because—
10   Because he was my foe,
Just so: my foe of course he was;
   That's clear enough; although

"He thought he'd 'list, perhaps,
   Off-hand like—just as I—
15 Was out of work—had sold his traps—
   No other reason why.

"Yes; quaint and curious war is!
   You shoot a fellow down

---

[1] About a half-pint.

You'd treat if met where any bar is,
20   Or help to half-a-crown."

WILLIAM BUTLER YEATS (1865–1939)

An Irish Airman Foresees His Death[1]

I know that I shall meet my fate
Somewhere among the clouds above;
Those that I fight I do not hate,
Those that I guard I do not love;
5 My country is Kiltartan Cross,[2]
My countrymen Kiltartan's poor,
No likely end could bring them loss
Or leave them happier than before.
Nor law, nor duty bade me fight,
10 Nor public men, nor cheering crowds,
A lonely impulse of delight
Drove to this tumult in the clouds;
I balanced all, brought all to mind,
The years to come seemed waste of breath,
15 A waste of breath the years behind
In balance with this life, this death.

QUESTIONS FOR THINKING AND WRITING

1. What theme is common to these two poems?
2. How would you compare the two speakers?
3. How would you characterize the tone of each poem? The language? (Note
   the use of repetition. What effect does it produce in Hardy's poem? In
   Yeats's? How does it help characterize each speaker?)
4. How does the difference in character and mood of the two speakers contribute
   to the difference in overall effect of the two poems? (What reaction does each
   poet seem to want from you? What message—if any—does his poem seem
   to carry?)

The final poem in this chapter represents a form known as **dramatic
monologue.** After you have read the poem, answer the following questions:

---

[1] Major Robert Gregory, son of Yeats's friend and patroness Lady Augusta
Gregory, was killed in action in 1918.
[2] Kiltartan is an Irish village near Coole Park, the estate of the Gregorys.

1. Who is the speaker?
2. To whom is he speaking? On what occasion?
3. What does the speaker tell you about his own character? How does he do so?
4. What do you think happened to the "last duchess"?
5. If you were the person being addressed, how would you feel at the end of the monologue?

ROBERT BROWNING (1812–1889)

My Last Duchess

Ferrara

That's my last duchess painted on the wall,
Looking as if she were alive. I call
That piece a wonder, now: Frà Pandolf's[1] hands
Worked busily a day, and there she stands.
5 Will't please you sit and look at her? I said
"Frà Pandolf" by design, for never read
Strangers like you that pictured countenance,
The depth and passion of its earnest glance,
But to myself they turned (since none puts by
10 The curtain I have drawn for you, but I)
And seemed as they would ask me, if they durst,
How such a glance came there; so, not the first
Are you to turn and ask thus. Sir, 'twas not
Her husband's presence only, called that spot
15 Of joy into the Duchess' cheek: perhaps
Frà Pandolf chanced to say "Her mantle laps
"Over my lady's wrist too much," or "Paint
"Must never hope to reproduce the faint
"Half-flush that dies along her throat": such stuff
20 Was courtesy, she thought, and cause enough
For calling up that spot of joy. She had
A heart—how shall I say?—too soon made glad,
Too easily impressed; she liked whate'er
She looked on, and her looks went everywhere.
25 Sir, 'twas all one! My favor at her breast,
The dropping of the daylight in the West,

---

[1] A fictitious artist, as is Claus of Innsbruck in the last line.

The bough of cherries some officious fool
Broke in the orchard for her, the white mule
She rode with round the terrace—all and each
30 Would draw from her alike the approving speech,
Or blush, at least. She thanked men—good! but thanked
Somehow—I know not how—as if she ranked
My gift of a nine-hundred-years-old name
With anybody's gift. Who'd stoop to blame
35 This sort of trifling? Even had you skill
In speech—which I have not—to make your will
Quite clear to such an one, and say, "Just this
"Or that in you disgusts me; here you miss,
"Or there exceed the mark"—and if she let
40 Herself be lessoned so, nor plainly set
Her wits to yours, forsooth, and made excuse,
—E'en then would be some stooping; and I choose
Never to stoop. Oh sir, she smiled, no doubt,
Whene'er I passed her; but who passed without
45 Much the same smile? This grew; I gave commands;
Then all smiles stopped together. There she stands
As if alive. Will 't please you rise? We'll meet
The company below, then. I repeat,
The Count your master's known munificence
50 Is ample warrant that no just pretense
Of mine for dowry will be disallowed;
Though his fair daughter's self, as I avowed
At starting, is my object. Nay, we'll go
Together down, sir. Notice Neptune, though,
55 Taming a sea-horse, thought a rarity,
Which Claus of Innsbruck cast in bronze for me!

6

The Speaker's Vision

Like other writers, poets find their visions in three basic sources: the world around them, their own experiences, and their inner vision of what is or might be. The speakers of their poems, who are charged with communicating these visions, may therefore be observers, recording scenes and experiences for our mutual pleasure and insight; or they may be visionaries, recasting real or imagined scenes to produce a new vision for our sharing.

We can see the distinction clearly enough in poems we have already read. For instance, we have already seen two types of reporters at work. The speakers in "Get Up and Bar the Door" and "The Cherry-Tree Carol" are most obviously reporters; they simply tell us what occurred and let us draw our own conclusions about it. The speakers of "We Real Cool" and "For a Lady I Know" are also reporters but are less obviously so, because we sense that the poets are not as objective as their speakers. The speakers provide no interpretation and show no emotion. But the poets' attitudes come through, nonetheless. Indeed, much of the effectiveness of these poems comes from the disparity between the speakers' objectivity and the poets' concern, a disparity felt by the reader as irony. But that is a subject we will speak of more thoroughly in the next chapter.

We can also recall poems in which the speaker was primarily a visionary. Dickinson's poems come to mind here, and Blake's. "The Lamb" and "The Tyger" are far more concerned with the religious visions the animals arouse in Blake's speakers than they are with the animals themselves; and "Tell All the Truth" is pure vision, having no objective scene or experience whatever as its starting point. Another visionary is the speaker of Pound's "These Fought in Any Case," who draws on visions of so many real or imagined soldiers that we soon lose all sense of individuals in the more compelling vision of the war itself.

These, then, are poems that mark the two extremes of the speaker's stance: the objective extreme and the visionary extreme. Between them come those poems (probably typical of the majority of poems) in which the speaker is reporter and interpreter both. These poems balance what is seen and what is felt, allowing neither to overwhelm the other. Their speakers report on what is happening while explaining or suggesting its implications. Thus, "There's a Certain Slant of Light" conveys its atmospheric sensation most vividly by interpreting its spiritual overtones. And poems such as "in Just-," and "I Knew a Woman" blend recollection and response so perfectly that it's hard to say where one stops and the other begins. Through the speaker's emotional response, the vision is made real for us; reporter, responder, and interpreter are one.

The poems we shall look at in this chapter blend objective and visionary stances, observation and interpretation. Take careful note of the speaker's character and stance within each poem. Before you answer any of the questions, make sure you know what sort of person is speaking, to what the speaker is responding, and how much of the speaker's response is to things outside himself or herself and how much to inner visions or emotions.

The common factor in the first two poems is memory. Read each poem, and then discuss:

1. The details by which the memories are presented.
2. The comparisons and contrasts created between the memories and the speaker's present circumstances or emotional state.
3. Any sense of movement through time the poem may create, and the way in which it creates it.
4. What we are told in the poem's conclusion, and what sense of the speaker's feelings or attitudes the conclusion gives us.

D. H. LAWRENCE (1885–1930)

Piano

Softly, in the dusk, a woman is singing to me;
Taking me back down the vista of years, till I see
A child sitting under the piano, in the boom of the tingling strings
And pressing the small, poised feet of a mother who smiles as she
  sings.

5 In spite of myself, the insidious mastery of song
Betrays me back, till the heart of me weeps to belong
To the old Sunday evenings at home, with winter outside
And hymns in the cozy parlor, the tinkling piano our guide.

So now it is vain for the singer to burst into clamor
10 With the great black piano appassionato. The glamour
Of childish days is upon me, my manhood is cast
Down in the flood of remembrance, I weep like a child for the past.

ROBERT FROST (1874–1963)

Birches

When I see birches bend to left and right
Across the lines of straighter darker trees,
I like to think some boy's been swinging them.
But swinging doesn't bend them down to stay
5 As ice-storms do. Often you must have seen them
Loaded with ice a sunny winter morning
After a rain. They click upon themselves
As the breeze rises, and turn many-colored
As the stir cracks and crazes their enamel.
10 Soon the sun's warmth makes them shed crystal shells
Shattering and avalanching on the snowcrust—
Such heaps of broken glass to sweep away
You'd think the inner dome of heaven had fallen.
They are dragged to the withered bracken by the load,
15 And they seem not to break; though once they are bowed
So low for long, they never right themselves:
You may see their trunks arching in the woods
Years afterwards, trailing their leaves on the ground
Like girls on hands and knees that throw their hair
20 Before them over their heads to dry in the sun.
But I was going to say when Truth broke in
With all her matter of fact about the ice-storm,
I should prefer to have some boy bend them
As he went out and in to fetch the cows—
25 Some boy too far from town to learn baseball,
Whose only play was what he found himself,
Summer or winter, and could play alone.
One by one he subdued his father's trees
By riding them down over and over again
30 Until he took the stiffness out of them,

And not one but hung limp, not one was left
For him to conquer. He learned all there was
To learn about not launching out too soon
And so not carrying the tree away
35 Clear to the ground. He always kept his poise
To the top branches, climbing carefully
With the same pains you use to fill a cup
Up to the brim, and even above the brim.
Then he flung outward, feet first, with a swish,
40 Kicking his way down through the air to the ground.
So was I once myself a swinger of birches.
And so I dream of going back to be.
It's when I'm weary of considerations,
And life is too much like a pathless wood
45 Where your face burns and tickles with the cobwebs
Broken across it, and one eye is weeping
From a twig's having lashed across it open.
I'd like to get away from earth awhile
And then come back to it and begin over.
50 May no fate willfully misunderstand me
And half grant what I wish and snatch me away
Not to return. Earth's the right place for love:
I don't know where it's likely to go better.
I'd like to go by climbing a birch tree,
55 And climb black branches up a snow-white trunk
Toward heaven, till the tree could bear no more,
But dipped its top and set me down again.
That would be good both going and coming back.
One could do worse than be a swinger of birches.

The next three poems all concern ongoing relationships between the speakers and the natural and social worlds around them. In each case, the speaker's reaction to the "natural" world is linked with and contrasted to a more problematical relationship with the "social" world and with the speaker's place—as poet, lover, family member, citizen—within that world. Notice, in each of these three poems, how the two relationships illuminate each other, and how they ultimately fuse to create the vision presented by the poem.

SIR PHILIP SIDNEY (1554–1586)

From **Astrophil and Stella**

Sonnet 31

With how sad steps, O moon, thou climb'st the skies!
    How silently, and with how wan a face!
    What! may it be that even in heavenly place
    That busy archer his sharp arrows tries?
5 Sure, if that long-with-love-acquainted eyes
    Can judge of love, thou feel'st a lover's case;
    I read it in thy looks—thy languished grace
    To me, that feel the like, thy state descries.
    Then, even of fellowship, O moon, tell me,
10   Is constant love deemed there but want of wit?
    Are beauties there as proud as here they be?
Do they above love to be loved, and yet
    Those lovers scorn whom that love doth possess?
    Do they call virtue there ungratefulness?

QUESTIONS FOR THINKING AND WRITING

1. The technique of having the speaker seem to address someone or something within a poem is called **apostrophe**. What use is Sidney making of apostrophe in this poem?
2. What features of the moon's appearance does the speaker note? What interpretation does he put on them? Why?
3. Who is "that busy archer"? What overtones does his mention lend to the poem?
4. Why does the speaker claim "fellowship" with the moon? What do his questions to her tell you of his own state?
5. How would you describe the tone of the poem? How seriously does the speaker seem to take his interpretation of the moon's condition? What seems to be his attitude toward his own state?

JOHN KEATS (1795–1821)

When I Have Fears

When I have fears that I may cease to be
    Before my pen has gleaned my teeming brain,
Before high-piled books, in charactery,[1]

---

[1] Characters, writing.

Hold like rich garners the full ripened grain;
5 When I behold, upon the night's starred face,
    Huge cloudy symbols of a high romance,
And think that I may never live to trace
    Their shadows, with the magic hand of chance;
And when I feel, fair creature of an hour,
10   That I shall never look upon thee more,
Never have relish in the faery power
    Of unreflecting love;—then on the shore
Of the wide world I stand alone, and think
Till love and fame to nothingness do sink.

QUESTIONS FOR THINKING AND WRITING

1. Since the whole poem is one sentence, its syntax gets a bit complicated. Let's start, therefore, by examining it clause by clause, beginning with the three "when" clauses that make up the first eleven-and-a-half lines of the poem: What are the first four lines concerned with? The second four? The third? How are the three tied together? (Who is the "fair creature of an hour"? Why might the speaker call her so at this point in the poem?)
2. What overtones do words like *rich, romance, magic* and *faery* give to the poem? What contrast do they suggest between the poet's wishes and his sense of reality?
3. Then look at the final clause of the sentence—the last two-and-a-half lines. What action does it show the speaker taking? How explicit are his feelings made? What are you left to fill in?

NIKKI GIOVANNI (1943–   )

The Beep Beep Poem

I should write a poem
but there's almost nothing
that hasn't been said
and said and said
5 beautifully, ugly, blandly
excitingly
    stay in school
    make love not war
    death to all tyrants
10   where have all the flowers gone
and don't they understand at kent state
the troopers will shoot . . . again

i could write a poem
because i love walking
15 in the rain
and the solace of my naked
body in a tub of warm water
cleanliness may not be next
to godliness but it sure feels
20 good

i wrote a poem
for my father but it was so constant
i burned it up
he hates change
25 and i'm baffled by sameness

i composed a ditty
about encore american and worldwide news
but the editorial board
said no one would understand it
30 as if people have to be tricked
into sensitivity
though of course they do

i love to drive my car
hours on end
35 along back country roads
i love to stop for cider and apples and acorn squash
three for a dollar
i love my CB when the truckers talk
and the hum of the diesel in my ear
40 i love the aloneness of the road
when I ascend descending curves
the power within my toe delights me
and i fling my spirit down the highway
i love the way i feel
45 when i pass the moon and i holler to the stars
i'm coming through

Beep Beep

QUESTIONS FOR THINKING AND WRITING

1. The earlier poems in this chapter were each tightly focussed on a single
   memory or emotion. "The Beep Beep Poem" is much looser in construction,

each stanza presenting a separate topic. When interpreting this poem, therefore, it may be useful to go through the following sequence of steps:
   a. Look at each stanza separately. Consider: the topic of each stanza; the speaker's tone of voice and attitude; and any notable uses of language (wordplay, repetition, imagery, etc.) within the stanza.
   b. Then consider the progression from stanza to stanza throughout the poem. (Note, for example, the opening verbs of each stanza. What progression do they suggest? How is that progression carried out?)
   c. Finally, put together your answers to items (a) and (b), along with any overall impressions you may want to add to them, to describe your interpretation of the poem.
2. There is a certain paradox in the fact that all poems that touch on their speakers' frustration as poets unable to write as freely or as well as they would like to are, nonetheless, completed and successful poems—and thus are signs that their poets have, at least for the moment, triumphed in some way over their frustration, even while acknowledging it.
   In how many ways does "The Beep Beep Poem" suggest frustration? Triumph? How do the two blend to create the "vision" of the poem?

So far, the poems in this chapter have all had realistic settings; that is, they have all been based on scenes, incidents, or persons that have or could have occurred in the poet's own life. Poetry is not limited to the real world, however, for either its settings or its characters. The next poem portrays a wholly imaginary landscape, speaker, and incident. Its emotions and resonances, however, are as fully "human" as those of any poem we have read so far. Read the poem, and then consider how Browning uses imagination and fantasy to illuminate a human dilemma.

ROBERT BROWNING (1812–1889)

Childe Roland to the Dark Tower Came[1]

1

My first thought was, he lied in every word,
   That hoary cripple, with malicious eye
   Askance to watch the working of his lie
On mine, and mouth scarce able to afford
5 Suppression of the glee, that pursed and scored
   Its edge, at one more victim gained thereby.

---

[1] In Shakespeare's *King Lear,* II. iv, Edgar, Gloucester's son, disguised as a madman, meets Lear in the midst of a storm; at the end of the scene, Edgar sings: "Child Rowland to the dark tower came;/His word was still, 'Fie, foh, and fum,/I smell the blood of a British man.' " (*Childe:* medieval title applied to a youth awaiting knighthood.)

2

What else should he be set for, with his staff?
  What, save to waylay with his lies, ensnare
  All travelers who might find him posted there,
10 And ask the road? I guessed what skull-like laugh
  Would break, what crutch 'gin write my epitaph
    For pastime in the dusty thoroughfare,

3

If at his counsel I should turn aside
  Into that ominous tract which, all agree,
15   Hides the Dark Tower. Yet acquiescingly
  I did turn as he pointed: neither pride
  Nor hope rekindling at the end descried,
    So much as gladness that some end might be.

4

For, what with my whole world-wide wandering,
20   What with my search drawn out through years, my hope
    Dwindled into a ghost not fit to cope
  With that obstreperous joy success would bring,—
  I hardly tried now to rebuke the spring
    My heart made, finding failure in its scope.

5

25 As when a sick man very near to death
    Seems dead indeed, and feels begin and end
    The tears, and takes the farewell of each friend,
  And hears one bid the other go, draw breath
  Freelier outside, ("since all is o'er," he saith,
30   "And the blow fallen no grieving can amend;")

6

While some discuss if near the other graves
    Be room enough for this, and when a day
    Suits best for carrying the corpse away,
  With care about the banners, scarves and staves:
35 And still the man hears all, and only craves
    He may not shame such tender love and stay.

7

Thus, I had so long suffered in this quest,
   Heard failure prophesied so oft, been writ
   So many times among "The Band"—to wit,
40 The knights who to the Dark Tower's search addressed
   Their steps—that just to fail as they, seemed best,
   And all the doubt was now—should I be fit?

8

So, quiet as despair, I turned from him,
   That hateful cripple, out of his highway
45   Into the path he pointed. All the day
Had been a dreary one at best, and dim
Was settling to its close, yet shot one grim
   Red leer to see the plain catch its estray.[2]

9

For mark! no sooner was I fairly found
50   Pledged to the plain, after a pace or two,
   Than, pausing to throw backward a last view
O'er the safe road, 'twas gone; gray plain all round:
Nothing but plain to the horizon's bound.
   I might go on; naught else remained to do.

10

55 So, on I went. I think I never saw
   Such starved ignoble nature; nothing throve:
   For flowers—as well expect a cedar grove!
But cockle, spurge,[3] according to their law
Might propagate their kind, with none to awe,
60   You'd think: a burr had been a treasure trove.

11

No! penury, inertness and grimace,
   In some strange sort, were the land's portion. "See
   Or shut your eyes," said Nature peevishly,
"It nothing skills:[4] I cannot help my case:

---

[2] A stray or unclaimed domestic animal.
[3] Cockle here is a weed that grows in wheatfields; spurge, a plant with minute flowers.
[4] Avails.

65 'Tis the Last Judgment's fire must cure this place,
Calcine[5] its clods and set my prisoners free."

12

If there pushed any ragged thistle-stalk
Above its mates, the head was chopped; the bents[6]
Were jealous else. What made those holes and rents
70 In the dock's[7] harsh swarth[8] leaves, bruised as to balk
All hope of greenness? 'tis a brute must walk
Pashing[9] their life out, with a brute's intents.

13

As for the grass, it grew as scant as hair
In leprosy; thin dry blades pricked the mud
75 Which underneath looked kneaded up with blood.
One stiff blind horse, his every bone a-stare,
Stood stupefied, however he came there:
Thrust out past service from the devil's stud!

14

Alive? he might be dead for aught I know,
80 With that red gaunt and colloped[10] neck a-strain,
And shut eyes underneath the rusty mane;
Seldom went such grotesqueness with such woe;
I never saw a brute I hated so;
He must be wicked to deserve such pain.

15

85 I shut my eyes and turned them on my heart.
As a man calls for wine before he fights,
I asked one draught of earlier, happier sights,
Ere fitly I could hope to play my part.
Think first, fight afterwards—the soldier's art:
90 One taste of the old time sets all to rights.

---

[5] Burn to powder.
[6] Reeds, rushes.
[7] Coarse weedy plant.
[8] Dark.
[9] Crushing.
[10] Chafed, ridged.

16

Not it! I fancied Cuthbert's reddening face
  Beneath its garniture of curly gold,
  Dear fellow, till I almost felt him fold
An arm in mine to fix me to the place,
95 That way he used. Alas, one night's disgrace!
  Out went my heart's new fire and left it cold.

17

Giles then, the soul of honor—there he stands
  Frank as ten years ago when knighted first.
  What honest man should dare (he said) he durst.
100 Good—but the scene shifts—faugh! what hangman hands
Pin to his breast a parchment? His own bands
  Read it. Poor traitor, spit upon and curst!

18

Better this present than a past like that;
  Back therefore to my darkening path again!
105   No sound, no sight as far as eye could strain.
Will the night send a howlet[11] or a bat?
I asked: when something on the dismal flat
  Came to arrest my thoughts and change their train.

19

A sudden little river crossed my path
110   As unexpected as a serpent comes.
  No sluggish tide congenial to the glooms;
This, as it frothed by, might have been a bath
For the fiend's glowing hoof—to see the wrath
  Of its black eddy bespate[12] with flakes and spumes.

20

115 So petty yet so spiteful! All along,
  Low scrubby alders kneeled down over it;
  Drenched willows flung them headlong in a fit
Of mute despair, a suicidal throng:

---

[11] Owl.
[12] Spattered.

The river which had done them all the wrong,
120   Whate'er that was, rolled by, deterred no whit.

21

Which, while I forded,—good saints, how I feared
    To set my foot upon a dead man's cheek,
    Each step, or feel the spear I thrust to seek
For hollows, tangled in his hair or beard!
125 —It may have been a water-rat I speared,
    But, ugh! it sounded like a baby's shriek.

22

Glad was I when I reached the other bank.
    Now for a better country. Vain presage!
    Who were the strugglers, what war did they wage,
130 Whose savage trample thus could pad the dank
Soil to a plash?[13] Toads in a poisoned tank,
    Or wild cats in a red-hot iron cage—

23

The fight must so have seemed in that fell cirque.[14]
    What penned them there, with all the plain to choose?
135   No footprint leading to that horrid mews.[15]
None out of it. Mad brewage set to work
Their brains, no doubt, like galley-slaves the Turk
    Pits for his pastime, Christians against Jews.

24

And more than that—a furlong on—why, there!
140   What bad use was that engine[16] for, that wheel,
    Or brake,[17] not wheel—that harrow fit to reel
Men's bodies out like silk? with all the air
Of Tophet's[18] tool, on earth left unaware,
    Or brought to sharpen its rusty teeth of steel.

---

[13] Puddle.
[14] Rounded hollow encircled by heights.
[15] Stabling area.
[16] Mechanical contrivance.
[17] Here in the sense of a tool for breaking up flax or hemp, to separate the fiber.
[18] Hell's.

25

145 Then came a bit of stubbed ground, once a wood,
       Next a marsh, it would seem, and now mere earth
       Desperate and done with; (so a fool finds mirth,
     Makes a thing and then mars it, till his mood
     Changes and off he goes!) within a rood[19]—
150   Bog, clay and rubble, sand and stark black dearth.

26

     Now blotches rankling,[20] colored gay and grim,
       Now patches where some leanness of the soil's
       Broke into moss or substances like boils;
     Then came some palsied oak, a cleft in him
155 Like a distorted mouth that splits its rim
       Gaping at death, and dies while it recoils.

27

     And just as far as ever from the end!
       Nought in the distance but the evening, nought
       To point my footstep further! At the thought,
160 A great black bird, Apollyon's[21] bosom-friend,
       Sailed past, nor beat his wide wing dragon-penned[22]
         That brushed my cap—perchance the guide I sought.

28

     For, looking up, aware I somehow grew,
       'Spite of the dusk, the plain had given place
165   All round to mountains—with such name to grace
     Mere ugly heights and heaps now stolen in view.
     How thus they had surprised me,—solve it, you!
       How to get from them was no clearer case.

29

     Yet half I seemed to recognize some trick
170   Of mischief happened to me, God knows when—

---

[19] Linear measure, varying locally from six to eight yards.
[20] Festering.
[21] ". . . The angel of the bottomless pit, whose name in the Hebrew tongue is Abaddon, but in the Greek tongue . . . Apollyon." Revelation ix.11.
[22] With pinions like a dragon's.

In a bad dream perhaps. Here ended, then,
  Progress this way. When, in the very nick
  Of giving up, one time more, came a click
    As when a trap shuts—you're inside the den!

30

175 Burningly it came on me all at once,
    This was the place! those two hills on the right,
    Crouched like two bulls locked horn in horn in fight;
  While to the left, a tall scalped mountain . . . Dunce,
  Dotard, a-dozing at the very nonce,[23]
180   After a life spent training for the sight!

31

What in the midst lay but the Tower itself?
    The round squat turret, blind as the fool's heart,
    Built of brown stone, without a counterpart
  In the whole world. The tempest's mocking elf
185 Points to the shipman thus the unseen shelf
    He strikes on, only when the timbers start.

32

Not see? because of night perhaps?—why, day
    Came back again for that! before it left,
    The dying sunset kindled through a cleft:
190 The hills, like giants at a hunting, lay,
    Chin upon hand, to see the game at bay,—
      "Now stab and end the creature—to the heft!"[24]

33

Not hear? when noise was everywhere! it tolled
    Increasing like a bell. Names in my ears
195   Of all the lost adventurers my peers,—
  How such a one was strong, and such was bold,
  And such was fortunate, yet each of old
    Lost, lost! one moment knelled the woe of years.

---

[23] Moment.
[24] Handle of dagger or knife.

34

There they stood, ranged along the hillsides, met
200   To view the last of me, a living frame
   For one more picture! in a sheet of flame
I saw them and I knew them all. And yet
Dauntless the slug-horn[25] to my lips I set,
   And blew. *"Childe Roland to the Dark Tower came."*

---

[25] Rough trumpet made from the horn of an ox or cow.

7

Beyond the Speaker:
The Double Vision of Irony

Irony exists whenever we say one thing and mean the opposite. "An exam? What fun!" is an ironic statement. More generally, irony exists whenever we feel a disparity between what someone says or thinks and what we know to be the truth. Irony can be intentional or unintentional, depending on whether the speaker means the statement to be ironic or not. A student who says, "A test today? What fun!" is almost certainly indulging in deliberate irony: he or she neither thinks of the test as fun nor expects others to think of it in that manner.

Suppose, however, that we are fellow students; suppose that you know (but I don't) that an English test has been scheduled for today; and suppose that I now say something like, "Boy, am I tired! I think I'll sleep through English class today!" This is unintentional irony. I am seriously planning to sleep. You know, however, that I will *not* be sleeping through English class. Instead, I will be cudgeling my tired brain, trying to pass an unexpected exam. In this case, it is your perception (as audience) that creates the irony. You know (as I, the innocent speaker, cannot know) how far from reality my words and expectations are.

The emotions of irony arise from our perceptions of a conflict between intent or ideal and reality. The technique of irony consists of creating a parallel disparity in words, by creating an opposition between the apparent meaning of the words and their ironic significance. Always there is some hint of pain in irony, some overtone of pity or anger. And always the emotion is a shared one: shared between reader and speaker if the irony is intentional, shared between reader and writer if it is not.

In responding to irony, then, we are aligning ourselves with someone whose perceptions we share, having been invited—as one right-thinking person by another—to share both the ironist's view of the subject and the emotions of scorn or pity or rage that go with it. Always, therefore, there will be some hint of argument (implicit or explicit) in an ironic poem. And always, the use of irony will produce some distancing of effect, as we stand back and judge the presented disparity.

Beyond these basic facts, however, we will see that irony is a technique that allows many variations of meaning, tone, and effect. As with most definitions, when we have defined a poem as ironic, we have only begun to talk about its construction, its meaning, and its power to touch us.

When you have read the poems that follow, review them in order to write about the following questions:

1. What disparity is being highlighted?
2. What ideals or beliefs that you hold are being appealed to? Is the appeal explicit or implicit?
3. Is the speaker conscious or unconscious of the irony of his or her speech?
4. If there is more than one voice in the poem, how are they contrasted? What part does the contrast play in your sense of the poem's irony?
5. What range of feelings does the poem suggest?

Then discuss each poem more fully, making whatever points you think are most helpful in deciding what role the irony plays in your appreciation of the poem as a whole.

ADRIENNE RICH (1929–   )

Aunt Jennifer's Tigers

Aunt Jennifer's tigers prance across a screen,
Bright topaz denizens of a world of green.
They do not fear the men beneath the tree;
They pace in sleek chivalric certainty.

5 Aunt Jennifer's fingers fluttering through her wool
Find even the ivory needle hard to pull.
The massive weight of Uncle's wedding band
Sits heavily upon Aunt Jennifer's hand.

When Aunt is dead, her terrified hands will lie
10 Still ringed with ordeals she was mastered by.
The tigers in the panel that she made
Will go on prancing, proud and unafraid.

ARTHUR HUGH CLOUGH (1819–1861)

The Latest Decalogue

Thou shalt have one God only; who
Would be at the expense of two?
No graven images may be
Worshiped, except the currency:
5 Swear not at all; for for thy curse
Thine enemy is none the worse:
At church on Sunday to attend
Will serve to keep the world thy friend:
Honour thy parents; that is, all
10 From whom advancement may befall:
Thou shalt not kill; but need'st not strive
Officiously to keep alive:
Do not adultery commit;
Advantage rarely comes of it:
15 Thou shalt not steal; an empty feat,
When it's so lucrative to cheat:
Bear not false witness; let the lie
Have time on its own wings to fly:
Thou shalt not covet; but tradition
20 Approves all forms of competition.

The sum of all is, thou shalt love,
If any body, God above:
At any rate shall never labour
More than thyself to love thy neighbour.

A. E. HOUSMAN (1859–1936)

From **A Shropshire Lad**

When I Was One-and-Twenty

When I was one-and-twenty
    I heard a wise man say,
"Give crowns and pounds and guineas
    But not your heart away;

5 Give pearls away and rubies
    But keep your fancy free."
But I was one-and-twenty,
    No use to talk to me.

When I was one-and-twenty
10   I heard him say again,

"The heart out of the bosom
  Was never given in vain;

'Tis paid with sighs a plenty
  And sold for endless rue."
15 And I am two-and-twenty,
  And oh, 'tis true, 'tis true.

WILLIAM BUTLER YEATS (1865–1939)

The Folly of Being Comforted

One that is ever kind said yesterday:
"Your well-belovèd's hair has threads of gray,
And little shadows come about her eyes;
Time can but make it easier to be wise
5 Though now it seem impossible, and so
All that you need is patience."
                                    Heart cries, "No,
I have not a crumb of comfort, not a grain.
Time can but make her beauty over again:
Because of that great nobleness of hers
10 The fire that stirs about her, when she stirs,
Burns but more clearly. O she had not these ways
When all the wild summer was in her gaze."

O heart! O heart! if she'd but turn her head,
You'd know the folly of being comforted.

PERCY BYSSHE SHELLEY (1792–1822)

Ozymandias

I met a traveler from an antique land
Who said: Two vast and trunkless legs of stone
Stand in the desert . . . Near them, on the sand,
Half sunk, a shattered visage lies, whose frown,
5 And wrinkled lip, and sneer of cold command,
Tell that its sculptor well those passions read
Which yet survive, stamped on these lifeless things,
The hand that mocked them, and the heart that fed:
And on the pedestal these words appear:
10 "My name is Ozymandias, king of kings:
Look on my works, ye Mighty, and despair!"
Nothing beside remains. Round the decay
Of that colossal wreck, boundless and bare
The lone and level sands stretch far away.

W. H. AUDEN (1907–1973)

The Unknown Citizen

(To JS/07/M/378
This Marble Monument
Is Erected by the State)

He was found by the Bureau of Statistics to be
One against whom there was no official complaint,
And all the reports on his conduct agree
That, in the modern sense of an old-fashioned word, he was
    a saint,
5 For in everything he did he served the Greater Community.
Except for the War till the day he retired
He worked in a factory and never got fired,
But satisfied his employers, Fudge Motors Inc.
Yet he wasn't a scab or odd in his views,
10 For his Union reports that he paid his dues,
(Our report on his Union shows it was sound)
And our Social Psychology workers found
That he was popular with his mates and liked a drink.
The Press are convinced that he bought a paper every day
15 And that his reactions to advertisements were normal in every
    way.
Policies taken out in his name prove that he was fully insured,
And his Health-card shows he was once in hospital but left it
    cured.
Both Producers Research and High-Grade Living declare
He was fully sensible to the advantages of the Instalment Plan
20 And had everything necessary to the Modern Man,
A phonograph, a radio, a car, and a frigidaire.
Our researchers into Public Opinion are content
That he held the proper opinions for the time of year;
When there was peace, he was for peace; when there was war, he
    went.
25 He was married and added five children to the population,
Which our Eugenist says was the right number for a parent of his
    generation,
And our teachers report that he never interfered with their
    education.
Was he free? Was he happy? The question is absurd:
Had anything been wrong, we should certainly have heard.

IMAGERY

8 *Similes, Metaphors, and Personification*

The three basic elements of any poem are the vision it embodies, the speaker who gives voice to the vision, and the language that creates voice and vision alike. (By stretching the terminology a bit, we could call them the three V's: voice, vision, and vocabulary.) In the preceding chapters, we examined the ways in which the language of a poem—its vocabulary, its connotations, its sounds—created and characterized the poem's speaker. Now it is time to look at the ways in which the language creates the vision.

Vision in literature always implies a shared vision. Originating in the writer's mind, the vision is first translated into words and then re-created in our minds, to be felt by us as it was felt by its writer. When we come to the end of a poem, therefore, the feeling we experience is likely to be a blend of recognition and surprise. We will have seen something familiar—perhaps even something of ourselves—as we have never seen it before.

There are two ways in which poets can go about creating this feeling. The first is to word their vision so precisely that we feel we are seeing things with a new closeness and clearness. This is the method chosen by Levertov in "Six Variations (part iii)" and Lawrence in "Piano."

The second method relies on figures of speech or on unexpected comparisons to lead us into making connections we may not have made before. This is Pound's method in "In a Station of the Metro," where human "faces in the crowd" are seen as "petals on a wet black bough," beauty and impersonality mingling. It is Dickinson's method, too, when she describes her "certain slant of light" as being one that "oppresses, like the weight/Of cathedral tunes."

This trick of mingling appeals to different senses in a single image—of describing a sound in terms of color, or a sight in terms of sound or feel —is called **synaesthesia**. Rather than trying to define a type of light in terms of its appearance, Dickinson compares it to a sound. But she speaks of both in terms of weight that presses down physically or spiritually. The word *cathedral*, meanwhile, not only defines the solemn, religious music that parallels the "slant of light," but also prepares us for the image of "heavenly hurt" introduced in the next line. Thus the poem weaves its pattern of imagery.

We have, then, already met poems that make use of both the literal and the figurative styles of imagery. To make sure the contrast is clear, however, let's look at two poems on one subject and see how the language works in each.

WALT WHITMAN (1819–1892)

The Dalliance of the Eagles

Skirting the river road, (my forenoon walk, my rest,)
Skyward in air a sudden muffled sound, the dalliance of the eagles,
The rushing amorous contact high in space together,
The clinching interlocking claws, a living, fierce, gyrating wheel,
5 Four beating wings, two beaks, a swirling mass tight grappling,
In tumbling turning clustering loops, straight downward falling,
Till o'er the river pois'd, the twain yet one, a moment's lull,
A motionless still balance in the air, then parting, talons loosing,
Upward again on slow-firm pinions slanting, their separate diverse
flight,
10 She hers, he his, pursuing.

ALFRED, LORD TENNYSON (1809–1892)

The Eagle

He clasps the crag with crooked hands;
Close to the sun in lonely lands,
Ringed with the azure world, he stands.

The wrinkled sea beneath him crawls;
5 He watches from his mountain walls,
And like a thunderbolt he falls.

Obviously, these are very dissimilar poems. One, talking of a single eagle that remains unmoving throughout most of the poem, creates an atmosphere of space and solitude. The other, speaking of two eagles, seems a constant rush of motion. In part, it is the sound of the words the poets have chosen that creates these different atmospheres. Tennyson's words, lines, and sentences are all short, and the stop at the end of each line is strongly marked. Whitman uses longer lines, with less pronounced breaks between them; and his sentences are so involved and complex that they keep the reader's mind and voice in almost constant motion as dizzying as that of the eagles themselves. Yet the basic difference in the way these eagles are shown to us lies not in their motion or motionlessness, but rather in the imagery in which they are described.

If we go through each poem, noting carefully each descriptive term used, we will discover a marked contrast. Whitman relies heavily on adjectives, particularly on participles (adjectives formed from verbs). *Clinching, interlocking, living, gyrating, beating, swirling, grappling, tumbling, turning, clustering, falling*—from these comes the poem's sense of action, as well as much of its power of description. The poet's stance is primarily that of the observer. Taking a walk, he has been startled first by the "sudden muffled sound" and then by the sight of the eagles; and he describes sight and sound alike as carefully and vividly as he can:

> The clinching interlocking claws, a living, fierce, gyrating
>   wheel,
> Four beating wings, two beaks, a swirling mass tight
>   grappling,
> In tumbling turning clustering loops, straight downward
>   falling.

Tennyson's fragment, too, is pure description. But its phrasing and its imagery come as much from the poet's imagination as from his powers of observation. Where Whitman uses no words that could not, in sober prose, be applied to an eagle, Tennyson uses almost none that could. His eagle is presented largely in terms that compare it to other things: an old man, grown crooked with age; an explorer in "lonely lands"; a thunderbolt. By calling our attention to these other things, he draws on our feelings about them (respect, for instance, or awe) and uses those feelings to influence our feelings about the eagle itself. Thus, instead of a bird's "clinching . . . claws," Tennyson's eagle has "crooked hands." He "stands"—which, to some readers, may sound more human than birdlike— and "watches," as men and birds both do. Later, he "falls"—an ambiguous verb. The landscape in which he is pictured is similarly humanized. The lands are "lonely," the sea is "wrinkled" and "crawls." There is exaggeration (or **hyperbole**) as well. The eagle's perch is "close to the sun"; the sky against which he is seen is an entire "azure world"; the eagle falls "like a thunderbolt." High and remote, yet somehow in his very remoteness human, Tennyson's eagle presents a striking image of a being in lofty isolation.

By linking disparate things, by forcing us to think of one thing in terms of another, poets make us see those things in new ways, creating new images, calling forth unexpected emotions, fostering new insights. With homely and familiar images, they bring strange things closer to us, while with exotic images they cast new light on everyday things. Abstract ideas are given vivid life by concrete images, while more abstract imagery suggests new significance for particular items or experiences. Poets can speak of their subjects in the most precise, closely fitting words they can find; or they can seek out unexpected startling terms that will call our own imaginations and creative impulses into play. Since it is so largely this choice of how language will be handled in any given poem that determines our sense of that poem, our first or final reaction to it—the totally different feelings that Whitman's torrent of precisely denotative adjectives and Tennyson's careful balance of connotations of humanity, space, and isolation provoke—it will be worth our while to examine some of the techniques that poets use in the creation of imagery. Let us look, therefore, at some of the commoner forms of imagery found in poetry. Since comparisons are often the result of figurative speech, we will start with figures that are forms of comparison: the explicit comparisons, the simile and the metaphor; and the implicit ones, implied metaphor and personification.

Simile

A **simile** is a comparison and is always stated as such. You will always find *like, as, so,* or some such word of comparison within it. Usually, the things it compares resemble each other in only one or two ways, differing in all other respects. An eagle and a thunderbolt are not really much alike; yet the fact that both go from the sky to the ground can allow Tennyson to declare that "like a thunderbolt he falls." In the differences between the two lies the simile's power. The fact that a thunderbolt is so much swifter, so much more powerful and dangerous than the eagle, lends a sense of speed and power and danger to the eagle's fall. A simile may be as brief as the traditional "red as blood," or it may be considerably more complicated, as in this example from "Tell All the Truth":

> As Lightning to the Children eased
> With explanation kind
> The Truth must dazzle gradually
> Or every man be blind—

Notice the use of similes in the following poem.

LANGSTON HUGHES (1902–1967)

Harlem

What happens to a dream deferred?

Does it dry up
like a raisin in the sun?
Or fester like a sore—
5 And then run?
Does it stink like rotten meat?
Or crust and sugar over—
like a syrupy sweet?

Maybe it just sags
10 like a heavy load.

Or does it explode?

QUESTIONS FOR THINKING AND WRITING

1. What relationship do the various similes have to each other and to the subject of the poem, as defined by the title and first line?
2. What has been done with the last simile? Why?

Metaphor and Implied Metaphor

Like similes, **metaphors** are direct comparisons of one object with another. In metaphors, however, the fusion between the two objects is more complete, for metaphor uses no "as" or "like" to separate the two things being compared. Instead, a metaphor simply declares that *A* "is" *B;* one element of the comparison becomes, for the moment at least, the other.

Some metaphors go even farther and omit the "is." They simply talk about *A* as if it were *B,* using terms appropriate to *B.* They may not even name *B* at all but rather let us guess what it is from the words being used. In this case, the metaphor becomes an **implied metaphor.**

Since a simile merely says that *A* is "like" *B,* it needs to find only one point or moment of similarity between two otherwise dissimilar objects in order to achieve its effect. (For example, the cherry that is "red as the blood" resembles blood in no other way.) Metaphors, in contrast, tend to make more detailed claims for closer likenesses between the subjects of their comparisons. Notice, for instance, how many points of similarity are suggested by the metaphors in the next two poems. Ask yourself, in each case, what points of comparison the metaphor makes openly or explicitly and what further points of comparison it suggests to you.

JOHN KEATS (1795–1821)

On First Looking into Chapman's Homer

Much have I travelled in the realms of gold,
　And many goodly states and kingdoms seen;
　Round many western islands have I been
Which bards in fealty to Apollo hold.
5 Oft of one wide expanse had I been told
　That deep-browed Homer ruled as his demesne;
　Yet did I never breathe its pure serene
Till I heard Chapman speak out loud and bold:
Then felt I like some watcher of the skies
10　When a new planet swims into his ken;
　Or like stout Cortez when with eagle eyes
He stared at the Pacific—and all his men
Looked at each other with a wild surmise—
　Silent, upon a peak in Darien.

QUESTIONS FOR THINKING AND WRITING

1. The vocabulary in the first eight lines of this poem is taken mostly from the Middle Ages and its system of feudalism: *realms* for *kingdoms,* for example; *bards* for *poets; fealty* for the system under which a nobleman would rule part of a country, being himself ruled by a king or a greater nobleman; and *demesne* for the nobleman's domain, the part of the country he ruled. (*Oft* for *often, serene* for *air,* and *ken* for *knowledge* are also old words that are no longer in daily use.) Apollo, on the other hand, comes from classical mythology, and is the god of poets. (He's also the god of the sun, but that doesn't particularly enter into this poem.) Homer is an ancient Greek poet and Chapman a sixteenth-century English poet who translated Homer's *Iliad* into English verse. The question therefore arises: why should Keats use the language of the Middle Ages and the metaphor of traveling to talk about his joy in reading poetry and the great delight he felt when his discovery of Chapman's translation let him feel that he was really hearing Homer for the first time?
2. When Keats does discover Chapman's translation, two new similes occur to him that support the traveler metaphor. What is the first (ll. 9–10)? What sort of progression has been made: how does the new identity the poet feels resemble his earlier identity as traveler? How is it different? What sort of feelings go with each identity? (Note the phrase "a new planet"; why *new?*)
3. In lines 11–14, the second simile is set out. Whom does Keats feel like now? What kinds of feelings go with this third identity? How do they form a climax for the poem? (It was really Balboa, and not Cortez, who was the first European to see the Pacific Ocean. Does this make any difference to your enjoyment of the poem?)

CARL SANDBURG (1878–1967)

Fog

The fog comes
on little cat feet.
It sits looking
over harbor and city
5 on silent haunches
and then moves on.

Personification

Implied metaphors, being more compact and requiring the reader to share in their creation slightly more than regular metaphors do, are frequent in poetry. But one type appears so frequently that it has a name of its own. This is **personification,** the trick of talking about some non-human thing as if it were human. We saw personification used in Blake's "When the stars threw down their spears" and in the "crooked hands" of Tennyson's "Eagle."

The poems in the rest of this chapter are notable for their figures of speech. They can thus serve both as exercises in identifying metaphors, similes, and implied metaphors, and as poems illustrating how these figures of speech can help create tone and meaning in poetry. Read each of the poems through at least once. Then go through the poem and note the figures of speech you find in it. Identify each one: is it a simile, a metaphor, an implied metaphor, a personification? Decide what elements make up the comparison: what is being compared to what? And jot down your ideas on why the poet might have wanted his or her readers to think about that comparison.

When you have done this, read the poem through once more. Then look again at the figures of speech you have found. Decide how each relates to the subject of the poem, and how each contributes to your sense of the speaker's feelings toward that subject. Decide, too, how many subjects of comparison there are. Is each subject compared to one other thing, or is one subject compared to several things?

If one subject is compared to one other thing, is that comparison developed at any length? If it is, what does its development lend your sense of the poem and its progression?

If one subject is compared to more than one other thing, or if several subjects of comparison exist, how are the different images fitted together? Are unrelated images juxtaposed for you to fit into some total picture; or does the speaker suggest some relationship of similarity or contrast between them? How does the pattern thus created of related or juxtaposed images help create your sense of the speaker's vision, of the poem's meaning or movement?

Finally, read the poem through once again to see whether you are satisfied with the conclusions you have come to, or whether you think there are other things that should be said about the poem or its imagery.

This may sound like a very complicated procedure. But the method of reading through, looking closely, and reading through again allows you to give attention to details of technique without losing your grip on the poem as a whole. When dealing with relatively simple poems, it's a handy practice. When dealing with more complex poetry, it's essential.

ROBERT BURNS (1759–1796)

A Red, Red Rose

O my luve's like a red, red rose,
  That's newly sprung in June;
O my luve's like the melodie
  That's sweetly played in tune.

5 As fair art thou, my bonnie lass,
    So deep in luve am I;
  And I will luve thee still, my dear,
    Till a' the seas gang[1] dry.

  Till a' the seas gang dry, my dear,
10   And the rocks melt wi' the sun:
  O I will love thee still, my dear,
    While the sands o' life shall run.

  And fare thee weel, my only luve,
    And fare thee weel awhile!
15 And I will come again, my luve,
    Though it were ten thousand mile.

EMILY DICKINSON (1830–1886)

I Like to See It Lap the Miles (#585)

I like to see it lap the Miles—
And lick the Valleys up—
And stop to feed itself at Tanks—
And then—prodigious step

---

[1] Go.

5 Around a Pile of Mountains—
And supercilious peer
In Shanties—by the sides of Roads—
And then a Quarry pare

To fit its sides
10 And crawl between
Complaining all the while
In horrid—hooting stanza—
Then chase itself down Hill—

And neigh like Boanerges[1]—
15 Then—prompter than a Star
Stop—docile and omnipotent
At its own stable door—

NIKKI GIOVANNI (1943–   )

Woman

she wanted to be a blade
of grass amid the fields
but he wouldn't agree
to be the dandelion

5 she wanted to be a robin singing
through the leaves
but he refused to be
her tree

she spun herself into a web
10 and   looking for a place to rest
turned to him
but he stood straight
declining to be her corner

she tried to be a book
15 but he wouldn't read

she turned herself into a bulb
but he wouldn't let her grow

---

[1] Jesus' name for his apostles John and James; also used to refer to a loud-voiced preacher or speaker.

she decided to become
a woman
20 and though he still refused
to be a man
she decided it was all
right

SEAMUS HEANEY (1939–   )

Docker

There, in the corner, staring at his drink.
The cap juts like a gantry's crossbeam,
Cowling plated forehead and sledgehead jaw.
Speech is clamped in the lips' vice.

5 That fist would drop a hammer on a Catholic—
Oh yes, that kind of thing could start again;
The only Roman collar he tolerates
Smiles all round his sleek pint of porter.[1]

Mosaic imperatives bang home like rivets;
10 God is a foreman with certain definite views
Who orders life in shifts of work and leisure.
A factory horn will blare the Resurrection.

He sits, strong and blunt as a Celtic cross,
Clearly used to silence and an armchair:
15 Tonight the wife and children will be quiet
At slammed door and smoker's cough in the hall.

WILLIAM WORDSWORTH (1770–1850)

Composed upon Westminster Bridge, September 3, 1802

Earth has not anything to show more fair:
Dull would he be of soul who could pass by
A sight so touching in its majesty;
This City now doth, like a garment, wear
5 The beauty of the morning; silent, bare,
Ships, towers, domes, theaters, and temples lie
Open unto the fields, and to the sky;
All bright and glittering in the smokeless air.
Never did sun more beautifully steep

---

[1] Short for porter's beer—a dark beer resembling light stout.

10 In his first splendor, valley, rock, or hill;
   Ne'er saw I, never felt, a calm so deep!
   The river glideth at his own sweet will:
   Dear God! the very houses seem asleep;
   And all that mighty heart is lying still!

SYLVIA PLATH (1932–1963)

Morning Song

Love set you going like a fat gold watch.
The midwife slapped your footsoles, and your bald cry
Took its place among the elements.

Our voices echo, magnifying your arrival. New statue.
5 In a drafty museum, your nakedness
Shadows our safety. We stand round blankly as walls.

I'm no more your mother
Than the cloud that distils a mirror to reflect its own slow
Effacement at the wind's hand.

10 All night your moth-breath
Flickers among the flat pink roses. I wake to listen:
A far sea moves in my ear.

One cry, and I stumble from bed, cow-heavy and floral
In my Victorian nightgown.
15 Your mouth opens clean as a cat's. The window square

Whitens and swallows its dull stars. And now you try
Your handful of notes;
The clear vowels rise like balloons.

Most metaphors and similes have a certain timelessness to them. Wordsworth's vision of London asleep and Hughes's picture of energy turning angry in Harlem are both visions of something real and, therefore, enduring. In the following poem, however, the metaphorical vision is transitory and illusory. Nonetheless, it illuminates the speaker's view of the world. Note the movement of the imagery from metaphorical to literal within the poem. Consider how it expresses and develops the statement made by the poem's title. (Note particularly the "difficult balance" in the last line. What meanings does that phrase have here at the end of the poem?) Then discuss how the metaphor's statement and development create both the specific picture of the waking man and the wider vision that fills the speaker's mind.

RICHARD WILBUR (1921–   )

Love Calls Us to the Things of This World

The eyes open to a cry of pulleys,
And spirited from sleep, the astounded soul
Hangs for a moment bodiless and simple
As false dawn.
5   Outside the open window
The morning air is all awash with angels.

Some are in bed-sheets, some are in blouses,
Some are in smocks: but truly there they are.
Now they are rising together in calm swells
10 Of halcyon feeling, filling whatever they wear
With the deep joy of their impersonal breathing;

Now they are flying in place, conveying
The terrible speed of their omnipresence, moving
And staying like white water; and now of a sudden
15 They swoon down into so rapt a quiet
That nobody seems to be there.
                   The soul shrinks

From all that it is about to remember,
From the punctual rape of every blessèd day,
20 And cries,
          "Oh, let there be nothing on earth but laundry,
Nothing but rosy hands in the rising steam
And clear dances done in the sight of heaven."

Yet, as the sun acknowledges
25 With a warm look the world's hunks and colors,
The soul descends once more in bitter love
To accept the waking body, saying now
In a changed voice as the man yawns and rises,

"Bring them down from their ruddy gallows;
30 Let there be clean linen for the backs of thieves;
Let lovers go fresh and sweet to be undone,
And the heaviest nuns walk in a pure floating
Of dark habits,
            keeping their difficult balance."

9

Symbol and Allegory

Similes and metaphors make their comparisons quickly and explicitly. They occupy a line or two; and then they are set, ready for further development, but equally ready to be superseded by another simile or metaphor. How the poet uses them, or how many are used within a poem, is up to the poet. The range of possibilities is wide.

Symbol and allegory, however, tend to dominate the poems in which they are used. Moreover, they usually stand alone: one symbol or allegory is usually the most any given poem can support.

Similes and metaphors are used to make us look more attentively at the poem's subject: at the beauty of an evening or early morning scene, at laundry on a clothesline, at a newborn child. They appeal directly to our senses: "cow-heavy," "clean as a cat's," "the clear vowels rise like balloons." Often, they illuminate some larger question: "What happens to a dream deferred?" What are some of the feelings a new mother might have toward her child and her own motherhood? But they illuminate the larger question by keeping our attention on the things they describe: the rotten meat and the early-morning cries.

Symbols and allegories, on the other hand, urge us to look beyond the literal significance of the poem's statements or action. "Birches," for instance, goes beyond a simple description of trees to express a freedom of spirit that the birch trees symbolize for the speaker. "The Tyger" does not call our attention to tigers so much as to the awesome qualities suggested by the tiger's fierce beauty and to the godlike powers involved in the beast's creation. If we wish, in fact, "The Tyger" can take us even further, to the question of the existence of evil, as symbolized by the tiger's murderous nature. How far we wish to pursue the questionings begun by the poem is up to us.

When we meet with imagery that seems to be calling to us to look beyond the immediate event and its emotional ramifications, we may suspect we are dealing with symbol or allegory. But how are we to distinguish which we are dealing with?

An **allegory** always tells of an action. The events of that action should make sense literally but make more profound sense through a second, allegorical, interpretation. Usually that second interpretation will have a spiritual or a psychological significance; for allegories are particularly good at using physical actions to describe the workings of the human mind and spirit. "Young Goodman Brown," we recall, was an allegory of this type. On the literal level, it described a young man's encounter with witchcraft (or his dream of witchcraft). On the allegorical level, it described the process by which a person (who can be anyone, male or female) loses faith in human goodness.

In allegory, then, we are given a story that presents a one-to-one correspondence between some physical action (most often an encounter of some kind) and some second action (usually psychological or spiritual), with each step in the literal tale corresponding to a parallel step on the allegorical level. **Symbolism** may likewise present us with a tale or an action. But it may equally well present us with a description of some unchanging being or object. And it is more likely to suggest several possible interpretations than it is to insist on a single one.

In "Ozymandias," for instance, the whole tale of the power and fall of the king is symbolic. But the most striking symbol within it is the broken statue with its vainly boastful inscription. (For many of us, it's the sight of that statue that leaps to mind when anyone says "Ozymandias." The full tale tends to come as an afterthought.)

And how do we explain the tale's symbolism? Does the king's fall symbolize the fall of the proud (which would give the poem a moral interpretation), the fall of tyranny (which would give it a political one), or merely the inevitable destruction by time of human lives and civilizations? May we not, in fact, read overtones of all three types of meaning into the traveler's tale? Certainly the tyrant, with his "sneer of cold command," seems unpleasant enough for us to rejoice in his overthrow. But the sculptor, he with "the hand that mocked" the sneer, is dead as well; and even his longer-enduring work is half destroyed. How do we feel about that? The picture the sonnet paints is straightforward enough; its tone and message are somewhat more complicated.

Some symbols are conventional; and these will suggest a single interpretation. "The Lamb," relying on the traditional association of the lamb as Christ, is an example of conventional symbolism in poetry. Alternatively, the poet may invent a symbol and provide its interpretation as well. In general, however, symbols in poetry ask the reader to interpret them. The interaction between poet and reader thus admits the greatest possible freedom of suggestion and response.

As you read the following poems, decide whether you think them better interpreted symbolically or allegorically. How would you discuss the poem's language, imagery, and progression to support your interpretation?

GEORGE HERBERT (1593–1633)

Love (III)

Love bade me welcome; yet my soul drew back,
    Guilty of dust and sin.
But quick-eyed Love, observing me grow slack
    From my first entrance in,
5 Drew nearer to me, sweetly questioning
    If I lacked anything.

"A guest," I answered, "worthy to be here."
    Love said, "You shall be he."
"I, the unkind, ungrateful? Ah my dear,
10   I cannot look on Thee."
Love took my hand, and smiling, did reply,
    "Who made the eyes but I?"

"Truth, Lord, but I have marred them; let my shame
    Go where it doth deserve."
15 "And know you not," says Love, "who bore the blame?"
    "My dear, then I will serve."
"You must sit down," says Love, "and taste my meat."
    So I did sit and eat.

WILLIAM BLAKE (1757–1827)

From Songs of Experience

The Sick Rose

O Rose, thou art sick.
The invisible worm
That flies in the night
In the howling storm

5 Has found out thy bed
  Of crimson joy,
  And his dark secret love
  Does thy life destroy.

RALPH WALDO EMERSON (1803–1882)

Days

Daughters of Time, the hypocritic Days,
Muffled and dumb like barefoot dervishes,
And marching single in an endless file,
Bring diadems and fagots in their hands.
5 To each they offer gifts after his will,
Bread, kingdoms, stars, and sky that holds them all.
I, in my pleached garden, watched the pomp,
Forgot my morning wishes, hastily
Took a few herbs and apples, and the Day
10 Turned and departed silent. I, too late,
Under her solemn fillet saw the scorn.

AMY LOWELL (1874–1925)

Patterns

I walk down the garden paths,
And all the daffodils
Are blowing, and the bright blue squills.
I walk down the patterned garden paths
5 In my stiff, brocaded gown.
With my powdered hair and jewelled fan,
I too am a rare
Pattern. As I wander down
The garden paths.

10 My dress is richly figured,
And the train
Makes a pink and silver stain
On the gravel, and the thrift
Of the borders.
15 Just a plate of current fashion,
Tripping by in high-heeled, ribboned shoes.

Not a softness anywhere about me,
Only whalebone and brocade.
And I sink on a seat in the shade
20 Of a lime tree. For my passion
Wars against the stiff brocade.
The daffodils and squills
Flutter in the breeze
As they please.
25 And I weep;
For the lime-tree is in blossom
And one small flower has dropped upon my bosom.

And the plashing of waterdrops
In the marble fountain
30 Comes down the garden paths.
The dripping never stops.
Underneath my stiffened gown
Is the softness of a woman bathing in a marble basin,
A basin in the midst of hedges grown
35 So thick, she cannot see her lover hiding,
But she guesses he is near,
And the sliding of the water
Seems the stroking of a dear
Hand upon her.
40 What is Summer in a fine brocaded gown!
I should like to see it lying in a heap upon the ground.
All the pink and silver crumpled up on the ground.

I would be the pink and silver as I ran along the paths,
And he would stumble after,
45 Bewildered by my laughter.
I should see the sun flashing from his sword-hilt and the
    buckles on his shoes.
I would choose
To lead him in a maze along the patterned paths,
A bright and laughing maze for my heavy-booted lover.
50 Till he caught me in the shade,
And the buttons of his waistcoat bruised my body as he
    clasped me,
Aching, melting, unafraid.
With the shadows of the leaves and the sundrops,
And the plopping of the waterdrops,
55 All about us in the open afternoon—
I am very like to swoon

With the weight of this brocade,
For the sun sifts through the shade.

Underneath the fallen blossom
60 In my bosom,
Is a letter I have hid.
It was brought to me this morning by a rider from the
Duke.
'Madam, we regret to inform you that Lord Hartwell
Died in action Thursday se'nnight.'
65 As I read it in the white, morning sunlight,
The letters squirmed like snakes.
'Any answer, Madam,' said my footman.
'No,' I told him.
'See that the messenger takes some refreshment.
70 No, no answer.'
And I walked into the garden,
Up and down the patterned paths,
In my stiff, correct brocade.
The blue and yellow flowers stood up proudly in the sun,
75 Each one.
I stood upright too,
Held rigid to the pattern
By the stiffness of my gown.
Up and down I walked,
80 Up and down.

In a month he would have been my husband.
In a month, here, underneath this lime,
We would have broke the pattern;
He for me, and I for him,
85 He as Colonel, I as Lady,
On this shady seat.
He had a whim
That sunlight carried blessing.
And I answered, 'It shall be as you have said.'
90 Now he is dead.

In Summer and in Winter I shall walk
Up and down
The patterned garden paths
In my stiff, brocaded gown.
95 The squills and daffodils

Will give place to pillared roses, and to asters, and to snow.
I shall go
Up and down,
In my gown.
100 Gorgeously arrayed,
Boned and stayed.
And the softness of my body will be guarded from embrace
By each button, hook, and lace.
For the man who should loose me is dead,
105 Fighting with the Duke in Flanders,
In a pattern called a war.
Christ! What are patterns for?

ALLEN GINSBERG (1926–   )

In back of the real

railroad yard in San Jose
    I wandered desolate
in front of a tank factory
    and sat on a bench
5 near the switchman's shack.

    A flower lay on the hay on
        the asphalt highway
    —the dread hay flower
        I thought—It had a
10 brittle black stem and
        corolla of yellowish dirty
    spikes like Jesus' inchlong
        crown, and a soiled
    dry center cotton tuft
15   like a used shaving brush
    that's been lying under
        the garage for a year.

    Yellow, yellow flower, and
        flower of industry,
20 tough spikey ugly flower,
        flower nonetheless,
    with the form of the great yellow
        Rose in your brain!
    This is the flower of the World.

JOHN KEATS (1795–1821)

Ode on a Grecian Urn

I

Thou still unravished bride of quietness,
   Thou foster-child of silence and slow time,
Sylvan historian, who canst thus express
   A flowery tale more sweetly than our rhyme:
5 What leaf-fringed legend haunts about thy shape
     Of deities or mortals, or of both,
       In Tempe or the dales of Arcady?[1]
     What men or gods are these? What maidens loath?
What mad pursuit? What struggle to escape?
10   What pipes and timbrels? What wild ecstasy?

2

Heard melodies are sweet, but those unheard
   Are sweeter; therefore, ye soft pipes, play on;
Not to the sensual ear, but, more endeared,
   Pipe to the spirit ditties of no tone:
15 Fair youth, beneath the trees, thou canst not leave
     Thy song, nor ever can those trees be bare;
       Bold Lover, never, never canst thou kiss,
     Though winning near the goal—yet, do not grieve;
       She cannot fade, though thou hast not thy bliss,
20   Forever wilt thou love, and she be fair!

3

Ah, happy, happy boughs! that cannot shed
   Your leaves, nor ever bid the Spring adieu;
And, happy melodist, unwearièd,
   Forever piping songs forever new;
25 More happy love! more happy, happy love!
     Forever warm and still to be enjoyed,
       Forever panting, and forever young;
All breathing human passion far above,
     That leaves a heart high-sorrowful and cloyed,
30   A burning forehead, and a parching tongue.

---

[1] The vale of Tempe and Arcady (Arcadia) in Greece are symbolic of pastoral beauty.

4

Who are these coming to the sacrifice?
  To what green altar, O mysterious priest,
Lead'st thou that heifer lowing at the skies,
  And all her silken flanks with garlands dressed?
35 What little town by river or sea shore,
  Or mountain-built with peaceful citadel,
    Is emptied of this folk, this pious morn?
And, little town, thy streets for evermore
  Will silent be; and not a soul to tell
40   Why thou art desolate, can e'er return.

5

O Attic[2] shape! Fair attitude! with brede[3]
  Of marble men and maidens overwrought,
With forest branches and the trodden weed;
  Thou, silent form, dost tease us out of thought
45 As doth eternity: Cold Pastoral!
  When old age shall this generation waste,
    Thou shalt remain, in midst of other woe
Than ours, a friend to man, to whom thou say'st,
  "Beauty is truth, truth beauty,—that is all
50   Ye know on earth, and all ye need to know."

WILLIAM BUTLER YEATS (1865–1939)

The Circus Animals' Desertion

1

I sought a theme and sought for it in vain,
I sought it daily for six weeks or so.
Maybe at last, being but a broken man,
I must be satisfied with my heart, although
5 Winter and summer till old age began
My circus animals were all on show,
Those stilted boys, that burnished chariot,
Lion and woman and the Lord knows what.

---

[2] Grecian, especially Athenian.
[3] Embroidery.

2

What can I but enumerate old themes?
10 First that sea-rider Oisin[1] led by the nose
    Through three enchanted islands, allegorical dreams,
    Vain gaiety, vain battle, vain repose,
    Themes of the embittered heart, or so it seems,
    That might adorn old songs or courtly shows;
15 But what cared I that set him on to ride,
    I, starved for the bosom of his faery bride?

And then a counter-truth filled out its play,
The Countess Cathleen[2] was the name I gave it;
She, pity-crazed, had given her soul away,
20 But masterful Heaven had intervened to save it.
    I thought my dear must her own soul destroy,
    So did fanaticism and hate enslave it,
    And this brought forth a dream and soon enough
    This dream itself had all my thought and love.

25 And when the Fool and Blind Man stole the bread
    Cuchulain[3] fought the ungovernable sea;
    Heart-mysteries there, and yet when all is said
    It was the dream itself enchanted me:
    Character isolated by a deed
30 To engross the present and dominate memory.
    Players and painted stage took all my love,
    And not those things that they were emblems of.

3

Those masterful images because complete
Grew in pure mind, but out of what began?

---

[1] In Irish legend, Oisin was a bard who married a fairy and travelled throughout fairyland with her. *The Wanderings of Oisin and Other Poems*, published in 1889, was Yeats' first volume of verse.

[2] Yeats' first published play, written in 1891 and inspired in part by Yeats' love for Maud Gonne and his concern over the intensity of her involvement in political activism. Cathleen, a figure from Irish folk tale, sold her soul to the devil to save the lives and souls of her tenants during a famine.

[3] Various poems throughout Yeats' career mention Cuchulain, a legendary Irish king who became for Yeats a symbol of Ireland's heroic past. "Cuchulain's Fight with the Sea" appeared in 1893. ("The Circus Animals' Desertion" itself was written in the 1930's.)

35 A mound of refuse or the sweeping of a street,
  Old kettles, old bottles, and a broken can,
  Old iron, old bones, old rags, that raving slut
  Who keeps the till. Now that my ladder's gone,
  I must lie down where all the ladders start,
40 In the foul rag-and-bone shop of the heart.

ROBERT HAYDEN (1913–1980)

Those Winter Sundays

Sundays too my father got up early
and put his clothes on in the blueblack cold,
then with cracked hands that ached
from labor in the weekday weather made
5 banked fires blaze. No one ever thanked him.

I'd wake and hear the cold splintering, breaking.
When the rooms were warm, he'd call,
and slowly I would rise and dress,
fearing the chronic angers of that house,

10 Speaking indifferently to him,
  who had driven out the cold
  and polished my good shoes as well.
  What did I know, what did I know
  of love's austere and lonely offices?

10 *Conceits and Allusions*

Metaphors and similes, because of their instant appeal, are usually the first types of figurative speech to catch our attention. Symbols and allegories, which develop as their poems progress, require more preparation from us if we are to enjoy them fully. They offer themselves only to those who are willing not only to read closely and well, but also to go beyond the poem's literal meaning into a realm of wider suggestion. Conceits and allusions may be brief or extensive in scope; but they are the most demanding figures of all, requiring extreme alertness and some outside knowledge in order to be unraveled.

Conceits

A **conceit** could be defined as an outrageous metaphor, but a more traditional definition is a comparison between two highly dissimilar objects. Conceits are often developed at some length, revealing and weighing point after point of comparison or contrast between their two objects. In love poetry, they often grow out of Renaissance traditions that depict the man as a warrior and the woman as a walled town; he attacks, she defends herself or surrenders. Or the man might be a hunter and the woman a wild animal. Or she might be the warrior, wounding him with sharp looks or sharper words. Or, if she were kinder, she might be a treasure mine or a goddess of love. (The list could go on and on.) Some

Renaissance poets take the conceits seriously; others play with them, making use of the surprise that can come from turning an expected cliché upside down.

With the metaphysical poets of the seventeenth century, the unexpected becomes a key ingredient in the conceit. The metaphysical poets used conceits not only in love poetry, but in religious poetry as well, thereby creating for both types of poetry conceits of unparalleled complexity and ingenuity. Physics, astronomy, navigation—any science, any intellectual endeavor—might yield a conceit that viewed the soul's progress and passions as parallels to the workings of the universe it inhabited. The resulting poetry tends to be remarkably tough intellectually (you read this poetry *very* slowly the first few times), but also remarkably free, self-assured, and optimistic in its visions.

Here is an example of conceits in metaphysical poetry. Note that there are two main clusters of imagery in the poem. The first turns on maps and voyages, the second on the image of Christ as "the second Adam." And note also that the two are connected by the concept of the soul's journey to salvation as an annihilation of time and space and by the physical image of the sick man, flat on his back in bed and sweating heavily with fever.

JOHN DONNE (1572–1631)

Hymn to God My God, in My Sickness

Since I am coming to that holy room,
    Where, with thy choir of Saints for evermore,
I shall be made thy music; as I come
    I tune the instrument here at the door,
5   And what I must do then, think now before.

Whilst my physicians by their love are grown
    Cosmographers, and I their map, who lie
Flat on this bed, that by them may be shown
    That this is my Southwest discovery
10   *Per fretum febris*,[1] by these straits to die,

I joy, that in these straits, I see my west;[2]
    For, though their currents yield return to none,
What shall my west hurt me? As west and east
    In all flat maps (and I am one) are one,
15   So death doth touch the Resurrection.

---

[1] Through the straits of fever.
[2] My death.

Is the Pacific Sea my home? Or are
   The eastern riches? Is Jerusalem?
Anyan,[3] and Magellan, and Gibraltàr,
   All straits, and none but straits, are ways to them,
20   Whether where Japhet dwelt, or Cham, or Shem.[4]

We think that Paradise and Calvary,
   Christ's Cross, and Adam's tree, stood in one place;
Look Lord, and find both Adams met in me;
   As the first Adam's sweat surrounds my face,
25   May the last Adam's blood my soul embrace.

So, in his purple wrapped receive me, Lord,
   By these his thorns give me his other crown;
And as to others' souls I preached thy word,
   Be this my text, my sermon to mine own,
30   Therefore that he may raise, the Lord throws down.

Allusions

Conceits ask that we bring some knowledge to our reading if we are to understand their implications. For example, we must understand the distortions of space involved in making a flat map represent a round world if we are to understand Donne's hymn. An **allusion** likewise asks us to bring some knowledge to our reading. For an allusion may be defined as a reference to some work of art or literature, or to some well-known person, event, or story. If we do not catch the reference, then we will miss the point of the allusion.

Here is a frequently anthologized Middle English poem that celebrates spring. Following that poem is a "celebration" of winter by a twentieth-century poet who, knowing of the earlier poem's popularity, felt free to burlesque it. Note that Pound's poem can stand on its own, and that it makes no direct reference to the lyric to which it alludes. But note also how much more effective its irascible tone becomes when set off in its reader's mind against the cheerfulness of its medieval model.

---

[3] Modern Annam, then thought of as a strait between Asia and America.
[4] Sons of Noah, said to have settled Europe, Asia, and Africa after the flood.

ANONYMOUS—MIDDLE ENGLISH LYRIC

Sumer Is Icumen In [1]

Sumer is icumen in,
  Lhude sing cuccu!
Groweth sed and bloweth med
And springth the wude nu.
5   Sing cuccu!

Awe bleteth after lomb,
  Lhouth after calve cu,
Bulluc sterteth, bucke verteth;
  Murie sing cuccu!
10   Cuccu! cuccu!
Wel sings thu cuccu.
Ne swik thu naver nu!

Sing cuccu nu, Sing cuccu!
Sing cuccu, Sing cuccu nu!

EZRA POUND (1885–1972)

Ancient Music

Winter is icumen in,
Lhude sing Goddamm,
Raineth drop and staineth slop,
And how the wind doth ramm!
5   Sing : Goddamm.
Skiddeth bus and sloppeth us,
An ague hath my ham.
Freezeth river, turneth liver,
          Damn you, sing : Goddamm.

---

[1] *Translation:*

Spring has come in,
  Loudly sing cuckoo!
Grows seed and blooms mead
  And springs the wood now.
    Sing cuckoo!

Ewe bleats after lamb,
  Lows after calf the cow,

Bullock starts, buck farts;
  Merrily sing cuckoo!
    Cuckoo! cuckoo!
Well sing thou cuckoo.
Cease thou never now!

Sing cuckoo now etc.

10 Goddamm, Goddamm, 'tis why I am, Goddamm,
     So 'gainst the winter's balm.
Sing goddamm, damm, sing Goddamm,
Sing goddamm, sing goddam, DAMM.

Discuss how the speakers of the following three poems use conceits or allusions to praise the women they love and to enlarge on the benefits of love. (You will want to concentrate on the poems' imagery; but note also the use of apostrophe, or direct address, and the different tones and logical progressions within each poem. Use the questions that follow each poem to help you.)

EDMUND SPENSER (1552?–1599)

From **Amoretti**

Sonnet 15

Ye tradefull Merchants, that with weary toyle,
Do seeke most pretious things to make your gain,
And both the Indias of their treasure spoile,
What needeth you to seeke so farre in vaine?
5 For loe, my Love doth in her selfe containe
All this worlds riches that may farre be found:
If saphyres, loe her eies be saphyres plaine;
If rubies, loe hir lips be rubies sound;
If pearles, hir teeth be pearles both pure and round;
10 If yvorie, her forhead yvory weene;
If gold, her locks are finest gold on ground;
If silver, her faire hands are silver sheene:
    But that which fairest is but few behold:—
    Her mind, adornd with vertues manifold.

QUESTIONS FOR THINKING AND WRITING

1. To whom is the poet speaking in the opening four lines (and, by implication, in the rest of the poem as well)? Why should he select this audience? How do the merchants differ from the poet? What do the words *weary* and *in vain* suggest about them or their activities?

2. What similarities do you find among the successive metaphors that occupy lines 7–12?

3. How does the conclusion continue the theme of treasure? How does it alter it? (Note especially the phrase "adorned with virtues manifold.") What new questions does the conclusion raise about the usefulness of the merchants' search for precious things?

WILLIAM SHAKESPEARE (1564–1616)

Sonnet 18

Shall I compare thee to a summer's day?
Thou art more lovely and more temperate:
Rough winds do shake the darling buds of May,
And summer's lease hath all too short a date:
5 Sometime too hot the eye of heaven shines,
And often is his gold complexion dimmed;
And every fair from fair sometime declines,
By chance or nature's changing course untrimmed:
But thy eternal summer shall not fade
10 Nor lose possession of that fair thou ow'st,[1]
Nor shall Death brag thou wand'rest in his shade,
When in eternal lines to time thou grow'st.
   So long as men can breathe or eyes can see,
   So long lives this, and this gives life to thee.

QUESTIONS FOR THINKING AND WRITING

This sonnet, too, starts with a question relating to physical qualities—beauty and temperature—and ends up dealing with intangible ones. By what contrasts and what train of logic does it achieve this progression? (Note in particular the "summer's day" of line 1, "the eye of heaven" in line 5, and "eternal summer" in line 9. These phrases mark the starting points of three stages in the argument, with the last two lines marking the final stage. And be warned that "fair" has three meanings. It's a noun meaning "a lovely thing," an adjective meaning "lovely", and a noun meaning "beauty.")

JOHN DONNE (1572–1631)

The Sun Rising

   Busy old fool, unruly sun,
     Why dost thou thus
Through windows and through curtains call on us?
Must to thy motions lovers' seasons run?
5   Saucy, pedantic wretch, go chide
     Late schoolboys and sour 'prentices,
  Go tell court huntsmen that the king will ride,
  Call country ants to harvest offices.
  Love, all alike, no season knows nor clime,
10 Nor hours, days, months, which are the rags of time.

---

[1] Ownest.

Thy beams, so reverend and strong
   Why shouldst thou think?
I could eclipse and cloud them with a wink,
But that I would not lose her sight so long.
15   If her eyes have not blinded thine,
     Look, and tomorrow late tell me
    Whether both th' Indias of spice and mine
    Be where thou left'st them, or lie here with me;
Ask for those kings whom thou saw'st yesterday,
20 And thou shalt hear: All here in one bed lay.

She's all states, and all princes I;
   Nothing else is.
Princes do but play us; compared to this,
All honor's mimic, all wealth alchemy.
25   Thou, sun, art half as happy as we,
     In that the world's contracted thus;
    Thine age asks ease, and since thy duties be
To warm the world, that's done in warming us.
Shine here to us, and thou art everywhere;
30 This bed thy center is, these walls thy sphere.

QUESTIONS FOR THINKING AND WRITING

1. This poem falls into the category of **aubades,** or "dawn songs." What dramatic value does this placement in time give it?
2. Note that here again earthly riches are first equated with the woman's beauty and then devalued by it, and that time is forced to yield to timelessness. How does Donne's treatment of these conceits differ from those of Shakespeare and Spenser?
3. In general, how would you compare this love poem with those two earlier ones?

The next three poems are spoken by discontented lovers. What could you say about the ways in which they use conceits or allusions to describe their predicaments or to convince themselves or their hearers that some change should be made?

SIR PHILIP SIDNEY (1554–1586)

From **Astrophil and Stella**

Leave Me, O Love

Leave me, O Love, which reachest but to dust,
And thou, my mind, aspire to higher things.

Grow rich in that which never taketh rust.
Whatever fades but fading pleasure brings.

5 Draw in thy beams and humble all thy might
To that sweet yoke where lasting freedoms be,
Which breaks the clouds and opens forth the light
That doth both shine and give us sight to see.

O take fast hold; let that light be thy guide
10 In this small course which birth draws out to death,
And think how evil becometh him to slide
Who seeketh heaven and comes of heavenly breath.
Then farewell, world! Thy uttermost I see!
Eternal Love, maintain thy life in me.

ANDREW MARVELL (1621–1678)

To His Coy Mistress

Had we but world enough, and time,
This coyness, lady, were no crime.
We would sit down, and think which way
To walk, and pass our long love's day.
5 Thou by the Indian Ganges' side
Shouldst rubies find; I by the tide
Of Humber would complain. I would
Love you ten years before the Flood,
And you should, if you please, refuse
10 Till the conversion of the Jews.
My vegetable love should grow
Vaster than empires, and more slow;
An hundred years should go to praise
Thine eyes and on thy forehead gaze,
15 Two hundred to adore each breast,
But thirty thousand to the rest:
An age at least to every part,
And the last age should show your heart.
For, lady, you deserve this state,
20 Nor would I love at lower rate.
    But at my back I always hear
Time's wingèd chariot hurrying near;
And yonder all before us lie
Deserts of vast eternity.
25 Thy beauty shall no more be found,
Nor in thy marble vault shall sound

My echoing song; then worms shall try
That long preserved virginity,
And your quaint honor turn to dust,
30 And into ashes all my lust.
The grave's a fine and private place,
But none, I think, do there embrace.
  Now, therefore, while the youthful hue
Sits on thy skin like morning dew,
35 And while thy willing soul transpires
At every pore with instant fires,
Now let us sport us while we may,
And now, like amorous birds of prey,
Rather at once our time devour
40 Than languish in his slow-chapped power.
Let us roll all our strength and all
Our sweetness up into one ball,
And tear our pleasures with rough strife
Thorough the iron gates of life.
45 Thus, though we cannot make our sun
Stand still, yet we will make him run.

ROBERT GRAVES (1895–1985)

Down, Wanton, Down!

Down, wanton, down! Have you no shame
That at the whisper of Love's name,
Or Beauty's, presto! up you raise
Your angry head and stand at gaze?

5 Poor bombard-captain, sworn to reach
The ravelin and effect a breach—
Indifferent what you storm or why,
So be that in the breach you die!

Love may be blind, but Love at least
10 Knows what is man and what mere beast;
Or Beauty wayward, but requires
More delicacy from her squires.

Tell me, my witless, whose one boast
Could be your staunchness at the post,
15 When were you made a man of parts
To think fine and profess the arts?

Will many-gifted Beauty come
Bowing to your bald rule of thumb,
Or Love swear loyalty to your crown?
20 Be gone, have done! Down, wanton, down!

Although it is the work of a twentieth-century poet, "Down, Wanton, Down!" contains conceits that are very much in the fashion of the seventeenth century. Graves chooses one central comparison and then elaborates it and varies it throughout the poem. (The theme of love and the use of the word *wanton* to describe an overeager lover are also well within the seventeenth-century tradition.) In the next poem, the twentieth-century poet Marianne Moore adapts the use of conceits to her own equally playful and thoughtful but more kaleidoscopic style. What theme do the conceits in "The Mind Is an Enchanting Thing" combine to create? How do they do so? How are such disparate images fitted together?

MARIANNE MOORE (1887–1972)

The Mind Is an Enchanting Thing

is an enchanted thing
    ˘ like the glaze on a
katydid-wing
        subdivided by sun
5   till the nettings are legion.
Like Gieseking[1] playing Scarlatti;[2]

like the apteryx-awl [3]
    as a beak, or the
kiwi's rain-shawl
10   of haired feathers, the mind
        feeling its way as though blind,
walks along with its eyes on the ground.

It has memory's ear
    that can hear without

---

[1] Walter Gieseking (1895–1956), eminent German pianist.
[2] Domenico Scarlatti (1685–1757), Italian composer of brilliant keyboard sonatas.
[3] A flightless bird with a long, slender beak resembling the shape of an awl.

15 having to hear.
              Like the gyroscope's fall,
              truly unequivocal
because trued by regnant certainty,

      it is a power of
20   strong enchantment. It
      is like the dove-
              neck animated by
                      sun; it is memory's eye;
      it's conscientious inconsistency.

25 It tears off the veil; tears
              the temptation, the
      mist the heart wears,
                      from its eyes,—if the heart
                      has a face; it takes apart
30 dejection. It's fire in the dove-neck's

      iridescence; in the
              inconsistencies
      of Scarlatti.
                      Unconfusion submits
35 its confusion to proof; it's
      not a Herod's oath[4] that cannot change.

---

[4] See Matthew 2 : 1–16.

11
Patterns of Imagery

So far, we have spoken of different figures of speech in isolation. In practice, however, the various figures are almost always found in combination with each other. "Days," for instance, is an allegory. But the various gifts the Days carry are symbolic; and the phrase "morning wishes" is metaphorical. Moreover, just as form and meaning reinforce each other, so a poem's figures of speech reinforce each other to create the poem's overall patterns of meaning and imagery. When we discuss a poem, we may start by discussing some particularly striking aspect; and that may mean a particular use of imagery. But eventually we will want to talk of the complete poem; and that will mean talking of the patterns it contains.

The poems in the last chapter were heavily patterned. The Renaissance poems tended to be static, stating a position and then elaborating on it. The metaphysical poems showed more movement, following the speaker's mind through the ramifications of an idea or situation. The poems in this chapter will also display carefully worked-out patterns of imagery. And, as most of them are somewhat longer poems, the patterns will be even more complex. But these poems will also show a freer and more passionate movement, for they come either from the Romantic poetry of the nineteenth century or from twentieth-century poetry that was influenced by that movement. In the more melodious rhythms and harmonies of these poems, we find a vivid sense of immediacy, of unfolding memories or emotions, of minds and spirits caught up in vision and experience. Flowing sound and richly suggestive imagery create the sense of intense experience that was a trademark of the Romantic movement and that still provides some overtones of meaning to the common use of the word *romantic*.

As you read the following poems, be prepared for shifts of emotion as much as for shifts of thought. Note how these more modern poets create scenes, moods, and speakers through sound and imagery.

PERCY BYSSHE SHELLEY (1792–1822)

Ode to the West Wind

I

O wild West Wind, thou breath of Autumn's being,
Thou, from whose unseen presence the leaves dead
Are driven, like ghosts from an enchanter fleeing,

Yellow, and black, and pale, and hectic red,
5 Pestilence-stricken multitudes: O thou,
Who chariotest to their dark wintry bed

The wingèd seeds, where they lie cold and low,
Each like a corpse within its grave, until
Thine azure sister of the Spring shall blow

10 Her clarion o'er the dreaming earth, and fill
(Driving sweet buds like flocks to feed in air)
With living hues and odors plain and hill:

Wild Spirit, which art moving everywhere;
Destroyer and preserver; hear, oh, hear!

2

15 Thou on whose stream, mid the steep sky's commotion,
Loose clouds like earth's decaying leaves are shed,
Shook from the tangled boughs of Heaven and Ocean,

Angels of rain and lightning: there are spread
On the blue surface of thine aery surge,
20 Like the bright hair uplifted from the head

Of some fierce Maenad,[1] even from the dim verge
Of the horizon to the zenith's height,
The locks of the approaching storm. Thou dirge

Of the dying year, to which this closing night
25 Will be the dome of a vast sepulcher,
    Vaulted with all thy congregated might

Of vapors, from whose solid atmosphere
Black rain, and fire, and hail will burst: oh, hear!

3

Thou who didst waken from his summer dreams
30 The blue Mediterranean, where he lay,
    Lulled by the coil of his crystàlline streams,

Beside a pumice isle in Baiae's[2] bay,
And saw in sleep old palaces and towers
Quivering within the wave's intenser day,

35 All overgrown with azure moss and flowers
   So sweet, the sense faints picturing them! Thou
   For whose path the Atlantic's level powers

Cleave themselves into chasms, while far below
The sea-blooms and the oozy woods which wear
40 The sapless foliage of the ocean, know

Thy voice, and suddenly grow gray with fear,
And tremble and despoil themselves: oh, hear!

4

If I were a dead leaf thou mightest bear;
If I were a swift cloud to fly with thee;
45 A wave to pant beneath thy power, and share

The impulse of thy strength, only less free
Than thou, O uncontrollable! If even
I were as in my boyhood, and could be

The comrade of thy wanderings over Heaven,
50 As then, when to outstrip thy skiey speed
   Scarce seemed a vision; I would ne'er have striven

---

[1] A female attendant of Dionysus.
[2] Ancient Roman resort whose submerged ruins can be seen north of Naples.

As thus with thee in prayer in my sore need.
Oh, lift me as a wave, a leaf, a cloud!
I fall upon the thorns of life! I bleed!

55 A heavy weight of hours has chained and bowed
One too like thee: tameless, and swift, and proud.

5

Make me thy lyre, even as the forest is:
What if my leaves are falling like its own!
The tumult of thy mighty harmonies

60 Will take from both a deep, autumnal tone,
Sweet though in sadness. Be thou, Spirit fierce,
My spirit! Be thou me, impetuous one!

Drive my dead thoughts over the universe
Like withered leaves to quicken a new birth!
65 And, by the incantation of this verse,

Scatter, as from an unextinguished hearth
Ashes and sparks, my words among mankind!
Be through my lips to unawakened earth

The trumpet of a prophecy! O Wind,
70 If Winter comes, can Spring be far behind?

JOHN KEATS (1795–1821)

Ode to a Nightingale

I

My heart aches, and a drowsy numbness pains
   My sense, as though of hemlock I had drunk,
Or emptied some dull opiate to the drains
   One minute past, and Lethe-wards[1] had sunk:
5 'Tis not through envy of thy happy lot,
   But being too happy in thine happiness—
      That thou, light-wingèd Dryad of the trees,
         In some melodious plot
   Of beechen green, and shadows numberless,
10   Singest of summer in full-throated ease.

---

[1] Towards the river Lethe, in the underworld.

2

O, for a draught of vintage! that hath been
  Cooled a long age in the deep-delvèd earth,
Tasting of Flora[2] and the country green,
  Dance, and Provençal song, and sunburnt mirth!
15 O for a beaker full of the warm South,
    Full of the true, the blushful Hippocrene,[3]
      With beaded bubbles winking at the brim,
        And purple-stainèd mouth;
    That I might drink, and leave the world unseen,
20   And with thee fade away into the forest dim:

3

Fade far away, dissolve, and quite forget
  What thou among the leaves hast never known,
The weariness, the fever, and the fret
  Here, where men sit and hear each other groan;
25 Where palsy shakes a few, sad, last gray hairs,
    Where youth grows pale, and spectre-thin, and dies,
      Where but to think is to be full of sorrow
        And leaden-eyed despairs,
    Where Beauty cannot keep her lustrous eyes,
30   Or new Love pine at them beyond tomorrow.

4

Away! away! for I will fly to thee,
  Not charioted by Bacchus and his pards,[4]
But on the viewless wings of Poesy,
  Though the dull brain perplexes and retards:
35 Already with thee! tender is the night,
    And haply the Queen-Moon is on her throne,
      Clustered around by all her starry Fays;
        But here there is no light,
    Save what from heaven is with the breezes blown
40   Through verdurous glooms and winding mossy ways.

5

I cannot see what flowers are at my feet,
  Nor what soft incense hangs upon the boughs,

---

[2] Goddess of flowers.
[3] Fountain of the Muses on Mt. Helicon.
[4] Leopards drawing the chariot of Bacchus, god of wine.

But, in embalmèd darkness, guess each sweet
Wherewith the seasonable month endows
45 The grass, the thicket, and the fruit-tree wild;
White hawthorn, and the pastoral eglantine;
Fast fading violets covered up in leaves;
And mid-May's eldest child,
The coming musk-rose, full of dewy wine,
50 The murmurous haunt of flies on summer eves.

6

Darkling[5] I listen; and for many a time
I have been half in love with easeful Death,
Called him soft names in many a musèd rhyme,
To take into the air my quiet breath;
55 Now more than ever seems it rich to die,
To cease upon the midnight with no pain,
While thou art pouring forth thy soul abroad
In such an ecstasy!
Still wouldst thou sing, and I have ears in vain—
60 To thy high requiem become a sod.

7

Thou wast not born for death, immortal Bird!
No hungry generations tread thee down;
The voice I hear this passing night was heard
In ancient days by emperor and clown:
65 Perhaps the selfsame song that found a path
Through the sad heart of Ruth, when, sick for home,
She stood in tears amid the alien corn:
The same that oft-times hath
Charmed magic casements, opening on the foam
70 Of perilous seas, in faery lands forlorn.

8

Forlorn! the very word is like a bell
To toll me back from thee to my sole self!
Adieu! the fancy cannot cheat so well
As she is famed to do, deceiving elf.

---

[5] In the darkness.

75 Adieu! adieu! thy plaintive anthem fades
      Past the near meadows, over the still stream,
         Up the hill side; and now 'tis buried deep
            In the next valley-glades:
         Was it a vision, or a waking dream?
         Fled is that music:—Do I wake or sleep?

MATTHEW ARNOLD (1822–1888)

Dover Beach

The sea is calm tonight.
The tide is full, the moon lies fair
Upon the straits;—on the French coast the light
Gleams and is gone; the cliffs of England stand,
5 Glimmering and vast, out in the tranquil bay.
Come to the window, sweet is the night-air!
Only, from the long line of spray
Where the sea meets the moon-blanched land,
Listen! you hear the grating roar
10 Of pebbles which the waves draw back, and fling,
At their return, up the high strand,
Begin, and cease, and then again begin,
With tremulous cadence slow, and bring
The eternal note of sadness in.

15 Sophocles long ago
Heard it on the Aegean, and it brought
Into his mind the turbid ebb and flow
Of human misery; we
Find also in the sound a thought,
20 Hearing it by this distant northern sea.

The Sea of Faith
Was once, too, at the full, and round earth's shore
Lay like the folds of a bright girdle furled.
But now I only hear
25 Its melancholy, long, withdrawing roar,
Retreating, to the breath
Of the night-wind, down the vast edges drear
And naked shingles of the world.

Ah, love, let us be true
30 To one another! for the world, which seems

To lie before us like a land of dreams,
So various, so beautiful, so new,
Hath really neither joy, nor love, nor light,
Nor certitude, nor peace, nor help for pain;
35 And we are here as on a darkling plain
Swept with confused alarms of struggle and flight,
Where ignorant armies clash by night.

WILLIAM BUTLER YEATS (1865–1939)

Sailing to Byzantium

I

That is no country for old men. The young
In one another's arms, birds in the trees
—Those dying generations—at their song,
The salmon-falls, the mackerel-crowded seas,
5 Fish, flesh, or fowl, commend all summer long
Whatever is begotten, born, and dies.
Caught in that sensual music all neglect
Monuments of unageing intellect.

2

An aged man is but a paltry thing,
10 A tattered coat upon a stick, unless
Soul clap its hands and sing, and louder sing
For every tatter in its mortal dress,
Nor is there singing school but studying
Monuments of its own magnificence;
15 And therefore I have sailed the seas and come
To the holy city of Byzantium.

3

O sages standing in God's holy fire
As in the gold mosaic of a wall,
Come from the holy fire, perne in a gyre,
20 And be the singing-masters of my soul.
Consume my heart away; sick with desire
And fastened to a dying animal
It knows not what it is; and gather me
Into the artifice of eternity.

4

25 Once out of nature I shall never take
    My bodily form from any natural thing,
    But such a form as Grecian goldsmiths make
    Of hammered gold and gold enamelling
    To keep a drowsy Emperor awake;
30 Or set upon a golden bough to sing
    To lords and ladies of Byzantium
    Of what is past, or passing, or to come.

DYLAN THOMAS (1914–1953)

Fern Hill

Now as I was young and easy under the apple boughs
About the lilting house and happy as the grass was green,
   The night above the dingle starry,
    Time let me hail and climb
5   Golden in the heydays of his eyes,
And honored among wagons I was prince of the apple towns
And once below a time I lordly had the trees and leaves
    Trail with daisies and barley
   Down the rivers of the windfall light.

10 And as I was green and carefree, famous among the barns
About the happy yard and singing as the farm was home,
   In the sun that is young once only,
    Time let me play and be
   Golden in the mercy of his means,
15 And green and golden I was huntsman and herdsman, the calves
Sang to my horn, the foxes on the hills barked clear and cold,
    And the sabbath rang slowly
   In the pebbles of the holy streams.

All the sun long it was running, it was lovely, the hay
20 Fields high as the house, the tunes from the chimneys, it was air
   And playing, lovely and watery
    And fire green as grass.
   And nightly under the simple stars
As I rode to sleep the owls were bearing the farm away,
25 All the moon long I heard, blessed among stables, the night-jars
    Flying with the ricks, and the horses
    Flashing into the dark.

And then to awake, and the farm, like a wanderer white
With the dew, come back, the cock on his shoulder: it was all
30   Shining, it was Adam and maiden,
          The sky gathered again
       And the sun grew round that very day.
So it must have been after the birth of the simple light
In the first, spinning place, the spellbound horses walking warm
35   Out of the whinnying green stable
          On to the fields of praise.

And honored among foxes and pheasants by the gay house
Under the new made clouds and happy as the heart was long,
       In the sun born over and over,
40   I ran my heedless ways,
       My wishes raced through the house high hay
And nothing I cared, at my sky blue trades, that time allows
In all his tuneful turning so few and such morning songs
       Before the children green and golden
45   Follow him out of grace,

Nothing I cared, in the lamb white days, that time would take me
Up to the swallow thronged loft by the shadow of my hand,
       In the moon that is always rising,
          Nor that riding to sleep
50   I should hear him fly with the high fields
And wake to the farm forever fled from the childless land.
Oh as I was young and easy in the mercy of his means,
       Time held me green and dying
       Though I sang in my chains like the sea.

SOUND

Meter and Its Variations

Sound in poetry is a function of two elements: the rhythm of a poem's lines, and the sounds of its words. Throughout our study of poetry, we have been aware of the important part sound and rhythm play in establishing our sense of a poem. But we have been more concerned with recognizing how the sounds of a given poem reinforce its ideas or emotions than with classifying the sounds themselves; and so we have not paused to build up a vocabulary of technical terms for meter and versification. Now it is time to learn that vocabulary, so that we may supplement our discussions of character and language in poetry with more detailed comments on the techniques of sound that reinforce them. Since rhythm is perhaps the most basic element of sound in a poem, and meter the most basic element of rhythm, we will start with meter.

Meter is the term used to describe the underlying rhythm of a poem, based on the number and the placement of stressed syllables in each line. In most poetry, these **stresses** will fall into a pattern and the pattern will have a particular name: **iambic pentameter,** for instance, to name one of the most common. When we learn to **scan** a poem, therefore, to find out the rhythm or meter in which it is written, these stresses and their patterns are what we will be looking at.

What do we mean by a **stress** or a **stressed syllable?** We mean that the word or syllable involved is one to which our voice will give greater emphasis than to its neighbors. Every word of more than one syllable in English has one accented, or stressed, syllable and one or more unaccented or unstressed ones. Thus, in the word *human* we stress the first syllable: *hú - man;* while in the word *humane* we stress the second: *hu - máne.* When we speak a sentence, these natural accents, or stresses, will be heard. Usually they will be joined by a second type of stress, one used for emphasis. If I say, "Is she coming?," for instance, and leave the strongest stress on the first syllable of *coming* ("Is she *coming?*"), there will be nothing startling in the sentence. If, however, I move the accent to the word *is* ("*Is* she coming?"), I sound doubtful or surprised that she'd come; while if I accent the word *she* (" Is *she* coming?") the stressed word suggests that "she" is the last person I would have expected (or perhaps wanted) to come. The emphasis may fall in an expected or an unexpected place. But it is sure to fall somewhere, for English is a heavily accented language; it sounds neither normal nor natural without the contrast of its stressed and unstressed syllables.

The number of stresses in a line of poetry, therefore, is the number of syllables on which our voice naturally tends to put a stronger emphasis. The emphasis must be natural; it must come either from the sound of the words themselves or from the meaning and emphasis of the lines. Thus, we must be able to find the meter by reading naturally; we should not distort either the sense or the natural rhythm of the lines to make them fit some preconceived meter.

So basic is this matter of stresses, in fact, that line lengths receive their names according to the number of stressed syllables they contain. One simply counts up the stressed syllables, translates the resulting number into Greek, and adds the word *meter* to finish out the term, as follows:

1. **Dimeter:** two stresses per line

   Díe soón

2. **Trimeter:** three stresses

   Dóst thou knów who máde thee?

3. **Tetrameter:** four stresses

   Tell all the trúth but téll it slánt

4. **Pentameter:** five stresses:

   Leáve me, O Lóve, which reáches bút to dúst

5. **Hexameter:** six stresses (also known as an **alexandrine**)

   Which, like a wóunded snake, drágs its slow length alóng

By counting the number of stresses per line, we thus discover the skeleton of a poem's rhythm. The question then becomes how those stresses are linked. In **accentual poetry,** they are linked by **alliteration** or **assonance.** There will be (usually) four stressed syllables per line; and two or three of them will start with the same sound or contain the same vowel. Here is an example, from a poem you will meet again at the chapter's end:

> Bitter breást-cares have Í abíded,
> Knówn on my kéel many a cáre's hold,
> And díre seá-surge, and there I oft spent
> Narrow nightwatch nigh the ship's héad
> While she tossed close to cliffs. Coldly afflicted,
> My feet were by frost benumbed.

The first line is marked by the alliteration of *bitter* and *breast* and the assonance of *I* and *abided.* The second is similarly linked by the alliteration of the *k* sound in *keel* and *care* and the assonance of the *o* sound in *known* and *hold.* But the other lines are all marked by the alliteration of one sound each: *s* in the third line, *n* in the fourth, *c* in the fifth, and *f* in the sixth. This is the patterning of Old English poetry, a patterning used for several hundred years before the Norman Conquest brought French influences and rhymed verse to England. Since that time, accentual poetry has been relatively rare. One nineteenth-century poet, Gerard Manley Hopkins, however, worked out an accentual style of his own, which he called **sprung rhythm.** His style reflects the Old English influence in its irregular placement of stresses and its marked use of alliteration and assonance.

Most English and American verse is **accentual syllabic.** This means that its rhythm depends not only on the number of stressed syllables, but also on the total number of syllables per line, and on the placement of the stresses within that totality. Tetrameter lines, for instance, vary in length from the four stressed syllables of "We real cool. We," to the eight syllables, half of them stressed, of "Tell all the truth but tell it slant," to the eleven or twelve syllables (every third syllable stressed) of "You left us in tatters, without shoes or socks,/Tired of digging potatoes and spudding up docks."

To define its various combinations of stressed and unstressed syllables, therefore, accentual-syllabic meters divide each line of poetry into **feet,** a **foot** consisting of one stressed syllable with its attendant unstressed syllables. Each type of foot—that is, each pattern of syllables—is given a name. An unstressed syllable followed by a stressed one, for instance (*the wórd*) is an **iamb;** two unstressed syllables followed by a stressed one (*that she heárd*) make an **anapest.** The meter of the poem thus consists of the *name of the foot* most frequently found in the poem joined to the basic *line length.* "There's a certain slant of light" thus becomes **iambic trimeter,** despite the fact that not all its feet are iambs and not all its lines have three feet.

With this background in mind, let us chart the types of feet most commonly found in English poetry. One of the most common **duple meters** is the **iambic,** which has two syllables, the second stressed.

Tell áll | the trúth | but téll | it slánt

The **trochaic** has two syllables, the first stressed.

Dóst thou | knów who | máde thee?

One of the two most common **triple meters** is the **anapestic:** with three syllables, the last stressed.

And thére | was my Ró- | land to béar | the whole weíght

The **dactylic** has three syllables, the first stressed.

Táking me | báck down the | vísta of | yéars, till I | sée

One should also know the **spondee,** a two-syllable foot with both syllables accented. The spondee is used only to lend particular emphasis or variety to poetry written in other meters; there is no "spondaic meter." The **amphibrach** is a three-syllable foot with the accent on the middle syllable. Unlike the spondee, the amphibrach can be used as a sustained meter; but it's not an easy meter to work with and isn't often used for an entire poem. The **monosyllabic foot** has one syllable, accented; Gwendolyn Brooks's "We Real Cool" is an example of this foot in action. The **paeon** is a four-syllable foot. It may be called first paeon, second paeon, third paeon, or fourth paeon, depending on whether the accented syllable comes first, second, third, or fourth. There may also be a secondary accent within the foot. Traditional ballads are often written in paeonic meters.

Meter, then, will create the basic rhythm of a poem, setting up a pattern to be repeated or varied with each line. Seldom does the pattern remain perfectly regular, for to hold too closely to a meter in spoken verse is to risk monotony and boredom.

How does a poet avoid monotony? By shifting stresses, so that a poem written in iambic meter will have some feet that are trochees and some that are spondees. By adding syllables, so that an iambic line will contain an occasional dactyl or anapest. By dropping syllables, substituting a pause for the expected sound, or laying greater stress on the remaining syllables, as when a spondee is substituted for an anapest.

More importantly, poets vary their meters by making the sense of the poem, and the cadence of the speaker's voice, move in counterpoint to the rhythm.

> The sea is calm tonight.
> The tide is full, the moon lies fair
> Upon the straits;—on the French coast the light
> Gleams and is gone; the cliffs of England stand,
> Glimmering and vast, out in the tranquil bay.

The first statement fits the first line perfectly. But the next overlaps the second line, so that your voice cannot stop on "fair" but must continue with "Upon the straits." A pause, then, and the thought continues through that line and half of the next; then pauses more briefly, finishes the line with a slight pause, and comes to rest at the end of the fifth line. Because your voice stops at the end of them, the first and fifth lines are called **end-stopped lines.** Because the movement of thought and phrase forces your voice to continue past their ends, the second, third, and fourth lines are called **run-on lines.** Both end-stopped and run-on lines may contain internal pauses. We find one such pause after "full" in the second line, one after "straits" in the third," one after "gone" in the fourth, and one after "vast" in the fifth. These pauses are called **cesuras;** and their use and placement are vital in breaking the rhythms of poetry to create the sound of a speaking voice.

In contrast to "Dover Beach" (which you might want to reread in its entirety, to notice how flexible the lines are throughout), recall Blake's poems "The Lamb" and "The Tyger." Notice that many of their lines are end-stopped and that the regularity of the rhythm, with its procession of end-stopped lines and repeated questions, gives these poems almost the sound of incantations, sounds far removed from the wistful accents of Arnold's speaker. But notice, too, that even here, although each phrase is strongly separated from its fellows and heavily accented, the length of the phrases still varies, and cesuras and occasional run-on lines are still found:

> What the hammer? what the chain?
> In what furnace was thy brain?
> What the anvil? what dread grasp
> Dare its deadly terrors clasp?

We may notice, too, that Blake restricts himself to seven-syllable lines in "The Tyger," and to a patterned alternation between trimeter and tetrameter lines in "The Lamb," while Arnold varies his line lengths in "Dover Beach," the lines growing longer as the speaker warms to his topic. And, finally, we notice that all the lines quoted from Blake and Arnold end with stressed syllables. Your voice rises slightly to the stress at the end of these lines, and they are therefore said to have a **rising rhythm.** In contrast, lines that end on unstressed syllables—"O wild West Wind, thou breath of Autumn's being"—are said to have a **falling rhythm.** It's a small thing, but it can create subtle variations in tone.

These, then, are the basic meters of accentual-syllabic verse and the most common devices used to lend them variety. You will no doubt find many other devices at work as you continue your study of poetry. And you will also find that in much modern verse, such as that of Whitman and Cummings, the rules of accentual-syllabic verse have been replaced by the uncharted techniques and devices of **free verse.** Pauses and phrasings in free verse tend to be visual devices as well as rhythmic ones; line lengths and stress placement vary at the poet's will. Sounds are still being shaped with care, but the writers of free verse are being equally careful to avoid setting up rules to which critics can then bind them. In free verse, as in all verse, ultimately the total effect is the sole criterion.

Here are a modern translation of an Old English poem and a brief example of Hopkins's sprung rhythm. How would you compare and contrast the two types of verse?

ANONYMOUS (Eighth Century)

The Seafarer (modern version by Ezra Pound)

May I for my own self song's truth reckon,
Journey's jargon, how I in harsh days
Hardship endured oft.
Bitter breast-cares have I abided,
5 Known on my keel many a care's hold,
And dire sea-surge, and there I oft spent
Narrow nightwatch nigh the ship's head
While she tossed close to cliffs. Coldly afflicted,
My feet were by frost benumbed.
10 Chill its chains are; chafing signs
Hew my heart round and hunger begot.
Mere-weary mood. Lest man know not
That he on dry land loveliest liveth,
List how I, care-wretched, on ice-cold sea,
15 Weathered the winter, wretched outcast
Deprived of my kinsmen;
Hung with hard ice-flakes, where hail-scur flew,
There I heard naught save the harsh sea
And ice-cold wave, at whiles the swan cries,
20 Did for my games the gannet's clamor,
Sea-fowls' loudness was for me laughter,
The mews' singing all my mead-drink.
Storms, on the stone-cliffs beaten, fell on the stern
In icy feathers; full oft the eagle screamed
25 With spray on his pinion.
                                    Not any protector
May make merry man faring needy.
This he little believes, who aye in winsome life
Abides 'mid burghers some heavy business,
Wealthy and wine-flushed, how I weary oft

30 Must bide above brine.
   Neareth nightshade, snoweth from north,
   Frost froze the land, hail fell on earth then,
   Corn of the coldest. Nathless there knocketh now
   The heart's thought that I on high streams
35 The salt-wavy tumult traverse alone.
   Moaneth alway my mind's lust
   That I fare forth, that I afar hence
   Seek out a foreign fastness.
   For this there's no mood-lofty man over earth's midst,
40 Not though he be given his good, but will have in his youth greed;
   Nor his deed to the daring, nor his king to the faithful
   But shall have his sorrow for sea-fare
   Whatever his lord will.
   He hath not heart for harping, nor in ring-having
45 Nor winsomeness to wife, nor world's delight
   Nor any whit else save the wave's slash,
   Yet longing comes upon him to fare forth on the water.
   Bosque taketh blossom, cometh beauty of berries,
   Fields to fairness, land fares brisker,
50 All this admonisheth man eager of mood,
   The heart turns to travel so that he then thinks
   On flood-ways to be far departing.
   Cuckoo calleth with gloomy crying,
   He singeth summerward, bodeth sorrow,
55 The bitter heart's blood. Burgher knows not—
   He the prosperous man—what some perform
   Where wandering them widest draweth.
   So that but now my heart burst from my breastlock,
   My mood 'mid the mere-flood,
60 Over the whale's acre, would wander wide.
   On earth's shelter cometh oft to me,
   Eager and ready, the crying lone-flyer,
   Whets for the whale-path the heart irresistibly,
   O'er tracks of ocean; seeing that anyhow
65 My lord deems to me this dead life
   On loan and on land, I believe not
   That any earth-weal eternal standeth
   Save there be somewhat calamitous
   That, ere a man's tide go, turn it to twain.
70 Disease or oldness or sword-hate
   Beats out the breath from doom-gripped body.
   And for this, every earl whatever, for those speaking after—
   Laud of the living, boasteth some last word,

That he will work ere he pass onward,
75 Frame on the fair earth 'gainst foes his malice,
Daring ado, . . .
So that all men shall honor him after
And his laud beyond them remain 'mid the English,
Aye, for ever a lasting life's-blast,
80 Delight 'mid the doughty.
                      Days little durable,
And all arrogance of earthen riches,
There come now no kings nor Caesars
Nor gold-giving lords like those gone.
Howe'er in mirth most magnified,
85 Whoe'er lived in life most lordliest,
Drear all this excellence, delights undurable!
Waneth the watch, but the world holdeth.
Tomb hideth trouble. The blade is layed low.
Earthly glory ageth and seareth.
90 No man at all going the earth's gait,
But age fares against him, his face paleth,
Grey-haired he groaneth, knows gone companions,
Lordly men, are to earth o'ergiven,
Nor may he then the flesh-cover, whose life ceaseth,
95 Nor eat the sweet nor feel the sorry,
Nor stir hand nor think in mid heart,
And though he strew the grave with gold,
His born brothers, their buried bodies
Be an unlikely treasure hoard.

QUESTIONS FOR THINKING AND WRITING

Notice the movement of the speaker's mood and thought. How does he characterize himself? What response does he seek from his audience?

GERARD MANLEY HOPKINS (1844–1889)

Pied Beauty

Glory be to God for dappled things—
     For skies of couple-colour as a brindled cow;
         For rose-moles all in stipple upon trout that swim;
Fresh-firecoal chestnut-falls; finches wings;
5   Landscape plotted and pieced—fold, fallow, and plough;
       And áll trádes, their gear and tackle and trim.

All things, counter, original, spare, strange;
  Whatever is fickle, freckled (who knows how?)
   With swift, slow; sweet, sour; adazzle, dim;
10 He fathers-forth whose beauty is past change:
       Praise him.

QUESTIONS FOR THINKING AND WRITING

1. How do the examples of dappled things given in lines 2–4 differ from those in lines 5 and 6? How do those in the first stanza (lines 2–6) differ from those in the second stanza (lines 7–9)? What has Hopkins expanded the notion of "dappled things" to include?
2. What holds all these examples and images together? Is there any unity to them; anything single or unchanging behind them? If so, what is it? How and where in the poem is it expressed? How important is it to the speaker's vision of "pied beauty"?

Now read these two examples of accentual-syllable verse. Note the metrical techniques that make the first sound like a song. The second is like the voice of a man arguing with himself.

ALFRED, LORD TENNYSON (1809–1892)

The Splendor Falls on Castle Walls

  The splendor falls on castle walls
    And snowy summits old in story:
  The long light shakes across the lakes,
    And the wild cataract leaps in glory.
5 Blow, bugle, blow, set the wild echoes flying,
Blow, bugle; answer, echoes, dying, dying, dying.

  O hark, O hear! how thin and clear,
    And thinner, clearer, farther going!
  O sweet and far from cliff and scar
10   The horns of Elfland faintly blowing!
Blow, let us hear the purple glens replying:
Blow, bugle; answer, echoes, dying, dying, dying.

    O love, they die in yon rich sky,
      They faint on hill or field or river;
15   Our echoes roll from soul to soul,
      And grow for ever and for ever.
Blow, bugle, blow, set the wild echoes flying,
And answer, echoes, answer, dying, dying, dying.

QUESTIONS FOR THINKING AND WRITING

1. What is the meter of the main part of the poem? What is the meter of the refrain? What has been achieved by combining the two?
2. What does Tennyson mean by the phrase "our echoes" (line 15)? How do these echoes differ from the other "echoes" of which the poem speaks?
3. Fairyland and fairy things are usually pictured in literature as being immortal and unchanging, in contrast to human affairs, which are transitory. Why does Tennyson reverse that contrast in this poem?
4. How do sound and imagery combine in this poem to reinforce the speaker's message?

GEORGE HERBERT (1593–1633)

The Collar[1]

I struck the board[2] and cried, "No more!
　　　I will abroad!
What, shall I ever sigh and pine?
My lines and life are free: free as the road,
5　　Loose as the wind, as large as store.
　　　　Shall I be still in suit?[3]
Have I no harvest but a thorn
To let me blood, and not restore
What I have lost with cordial[4] fruit?
10　　　　Sure there was wine
Before my sighs did dry it; there was corn
　　　Before my tears did drown it.
　　Is the year only lost to me?
　　　Have I no bays[5] to crown it,
15　No flowers, no garlands gay? all blasted?
　　　　All wasted?
　Not so, my heart; but there is fruit,
　　　And thou hast hands.
　Recover all thy sigh-blown age
20　On double pleasures. Leave thy cold dispute
Of what is fit and not. Forsake thy cage,
　　　　Thy rope of sands,

---

[1] The iron band encircling the neck of a prisoner or slave; also perhaps a pun on "choler" as "rebellious anger."
[2] Dining table.
[3] Always petitioning.
[4] Restorative.
[5] Laurels.

Which petty thoughts have made and made to thee
  Good cable, to enforce and draw,
25   And be thy law,
While thou didst wink and wouldst not see.
         Away! take heed!
         I will abroad!
Call in thy death's-head there! Tie up thy fears!
30   He that forbears
    To suit and serve his need,
         Deserves his load."
But as I raved, and grew more fierce and wild
         At every word,
35 Methought I heard one calling, "Child!"
         And I replied, "My Lord."

QUESTIONS FOR THINKING AND WRITING

Discuss how the movement of sound in "The Collar" helps create the sound
of the speaker arguing with himself. (Note the addition of a second voice near
the end of the poem. How do the speech of this second voice and the speaker's
response to it bring the poem to its resolution?)

Finally, here are two examples of iambic pentameter by two masters
of that meter. Note that even the use of the identical meter does not
give these poems identical sounds. The rhythm of Shakespeare's sonnet,
for all its basic regularity, is flexible and almost conversational; the
rhythm of Milton's poem is as firm and regular as the marble tomb he
uses as his poem's chief conceit. Read the two poems and then answer
the following questions:

1. How does each poet handle his meter? How are phrasing and sentence structure fitted to the pentameter? How is the progression of
   the speaker's thought emphasized?
2. How does each poem's rhythm enhance or emphasize its imagery?
   Give examples.

WILLIAM SHAKESPEARE (1564–1616)

Sonnet 29

When, in disgrace with Fortune and men's eyes,
I all alone beweep my outcast state,
And trouble deaf heaven with my bootless cries,

And look upon myself and curse my fate,
5 Wishing me like to one more rich in hope,
Featured like him, like him with friends possessed,
Desiring this man's art, and that man's scope,
With what I most enjoy contented least;
Yet in these thoughts myself almost depising,
10 Haply I think on thee, and then my state,
Like to the lark at break of day arising
From sullen earth, sings hymns at heaven's gate;
   For thy sweet love remembered such wealth brings
   That then I scorn to change my state with kings.

JOHN MILTON (1608–1674)

On Shakespeare

What needs my Shakespeare for his honored bones
The labor of an age in pilèd stones?
Or that his hallowed reliques should be hid
Under a star-ypointing[1] pyramid?
5 Dear son of memory, great heir of fame,
What need'st thou such weak witness of thy name?
Thou in our wonder and astonishment
Has built thyself a livelong monument.
For whilst, to the shame of slow-endeavoring art,
10 Thy easy numbers flow, and that each heart
Hath from the leaves of thy unvalued[2] book
Those Delphic[3] lines with deep impression took,
Then thou, our fancy of itself bereaving,
Dost make us marble with too much conceiving,[4]
15 And so sepùlchred in such pomp dost lie
That kings for such a tomb would wish to die.

QUESTIONS FOR THINKING AND WRITING

Look back at the poems you have read in this book. Select several that you especially like. Analyze the meter in each, and consider the techniques by which it is varied. Then discuss how these metrical techniques enhance your enjoyment of each poem.

---

[1] Milton added the "y" for the sake of rhythm.
[2] Invaluable.
[3] Inspired—as by the oracle at Delphi.
[4] Thinking.

13 *Rhyme Schemes and Verse Forms*

Although rhyme is not found in all poetry written in English, it has been so important in the history of English and American verse that we often first divide poetry into two categories—rhymed and unrhymed—and then divide further from there. Accepting that categorization for the moment, we will note that unrhymed poems tend to fall into one of three major divisions: accentual verse, which has existed from Old English times and which we met in "The Seafarer" and "Pied Beauty"; blank verse (unrhymed iambic pentameter), a sixteenth-century invention of which Hamlet's soliloquies are classic examples; or free verse, sometimes called by the French name **vers libre,** a modern (and not always unrhymed) form that we met in the works of such diverse poets as Whitman, Cummings, Pound, and Levertov.

Rhymed Verse

Rhymed verse is harder to classify. There are so many ways of combining rhymed lines! Still, one can distinguish between those forms of rhymed verse that have a fixed total length (such as the **limerick,** with five lines; the **sonnet,** with fourteen; and the **villanelle,** with nineteen) and those that do not. Rhymed verse with no fixed length is usually composed of **stanzas.** Each stanza usually has a fixed length; but the number of stanzas, and hence the length of the poem as a whole, remain variable.

Underlying both types of rhymed verse, however, stand the basic combinations of rhyme. These embrace two-, three-, and four-line patterns, called the couplet, triplet, terza rima, and the quatrain. The **couplet** has two consecutive lines that rhyme:

> So long as men can breathe or eyes can see,
> So long lives this, and this gives life to thee.

The **tercet** or **triplet** has three lines that rhyme:

> He clasps the crag with crooked hands;
> Close to the sun in lonely lands,
> Ringed with the azure world, he stands.

The **terza rima** also has three lines, but only the first and last rhyme. When terza rima stanzas are linked together, the middle line of one stanza rhymes with the first and third lines of the stanza that follows.

> O wild West Wind, thou breath of Autumn's being,
> Thou, from whose unseen presence the leaves dead
> Are driven, like ghosts from an enchanter fleeing,
>
> Yellow, and black, and pale, and hectic red,
> Pestilence-stricken multitudes: O thou
> Who chariotest to their dark wintry bed

The **quatrain** has four lines joined by any one of the following rhyme schemes:

1. Second and fourth lines rhyming (*abcb*):

> When I was one-and-twenty
>   I heard a wise man say,
> "Give crowns and pounds and guineas
>   But not your heart away;

2. First and third, second and fourth lines rhyming (*abab*):

> She even thinks that up in heaven
> Her class lies late and snores,
> While poor black cherubs rise at seven
> To do celestial chores.

3. First and fourth, second and third lines rhyming (*abba*):

> Earth hath not anything to show more fair!
> Dull would he be of soul who could pass by
> A sight so touching in its majesty.
> The city now doth, like a garment, wear

4. First and second, third and fourth lines rhyming (*aabb*):

"O 'Melia, my dear, this does everything crown!
Who could have supposed I should meet you in Town?
And whence such fair garments, such prosperi-ty?"—
"O didn't you know I'd been ruined?" said she.

Any of these patterns can stand alone as a stanza. Or, patterns may be
added to or combined to produce more complicated stanzas, such as the
rime royale in which the following poem is written. Notice, in this poem, not
only the stanzaic pattern, but also the change of tone and of tense in each
stanza. What progression of argument and emotion occurs in this poem?
What is its effect?

SIR THOMAS WYATT (1503–1542)

They Flee from Me

They flee from me that sometime did me seek
With naked foot stalking in my chamber.
I have seen them gentle, tame, and meek
That now are wild and do not remember
5 That sometime they put themselves in danger
To take bread at my hand; and now they range
Busily seeking with a continual change.

Thankèd be Fortune, it hath been otherwise
Twenty times better; but once in special,
10 In thin array after a pleasant guise,
When her loose gown from her shoulders did fall,
And she me caught in her arms long and small;
And therewithall sweetly did me kiss,
And softly said, "Dear heart, how like you this?"

15 It was no dream; I lay broad waking.
But all is turned thorough my gentleness
Into a strange fashion of forsaking;
And I have leave to go of her goodness,
And she also to use newfangleness.
20 But since that I so kindely am served,
I fain would know what she hath deserved.

Limericks and Villanelles

Let us now look at two rhymed forms of fixed length: the limerick and the villanelle. (We will consider a third fixed-length form, the sonnet, in the next chapter.)

Limericks have five lines. The rhyme scheme is *aabba*, with all *a* lines having three feet, and all *b* lines two feet. The meter is usually anapestic.

Limericks are humorous verse, frequently employing puns, off-color humor, or deliberately tortured rhymes or rhythms. As one anonymous writer and critic remarks,

> The limerick packs laughs anatomical,
> Into space that is quite economical.
> But the good ones I've seen
> So seldom are clean,
> And the clean ones so seldom are comical.

More serious, but equally tightly controlled in form, is the **villanelle**. Entire lines, as well as rhyme sounds, are repeated in the villanelle to make up its prescribed pattern. Here is one of the finest twentieth-century villanelles. Analyze its form and discuss what the poet has done with it.

DYLAN THOMAS (1914–1953)

Do Not Go Gentle into That Good Night

Do not go gentle into that good night,
Old age should burn and rave at close of day;
Rage, rage against the dying of the light.

Though wise men at their end know dark is right,
5 Because their words had forked no lightning they
Do not go gentle into that good night.

Good men, the last wave by, crying how bright
Their frail deeds might have danced in a green bay,
Rage, rage against the dying of the light.

10 Wild men who caught and sang the sun in flight,
And learn, too late, they grieved it on its way,
Do not go gentle into that good night.

Grave men, near death, who see with blinding sight
Blind eyes could blaze like meteors and be gay,
15 Rage, rage against the dying of the light.

And you, my father, there on the sad height,
Curse, bless, me now with your fierce tears, I pray.
Do not go gentle into that good night.
Rage, rage against the dying of the light.

Ballades, Ballads, and Odes

Three forms without fixed length are the **ballade, ballad,** and **ode.**

The **ballade** was popular during the Middle Ages. It uses seven- or eight-line stanzas, usually in groups of three. Each stanza ends with the same line, the **refrain.** The ballade itself ends with a shorter stanza, the **envoy** or **envoi.** The envoy is addressed directly to the person for whom the ballade is being written. It, too, ends with the refrain.

Here is a nineteenth-century translation of a medieval French ballade. Note how the envoy provides both a personal note and a conclusion to a catalog that might otherwise have no logical ending.

DANTE GABRIEL ROSSETTI (1828–1882)

The Ballad of Dead Ladies[1]

François Villon, 1450

Tell me now in what hidden way is
  Lady Flora[2] the lovely Roman?
Where's Hipparchia,[3] and where is Thaïs,[4]
  Neither of them the fairer woman?
5 Where is Echo, beheld of no man,
Only heard on river and mere,—
  She whose beauty was more than human? . . .
But where are the snows of yester-year?

Where's Héloïse, the learned nun,
10 For whose sake Abeillard, I ween,

---

[1] This is a translation of the "Ballade des Dames de Temps Jadis" by François Villon (b. 1431).
[2] A famous Roman courtesan.
[3] A Greek courtesan.
[4] An Athenian courtesan.

Lost manhood and put priesthood on?[5]
(From Love he won such dule and teen!)
And where, I pray you, is the Queen[6]
Who willed that Buridan should steer
15   Sewed in a sack's mouth down the Seine? . . .
But where are the snows of yester-year?

White Queen Blanche, like a queen of lilies,[7]
With a voice like any mermaiden,—
Bertha Broadfoot, Beatrice, Alice,[8]
20   And Ermengarde the lady of Maine,[9]—
And that good Joan[10] whom Englishmen
At Rouen doomed and burned her there,—
Mother of God, where are they then? . . .
But where are the snows of yester-year?

25 Nay, never ask this week, fair lord,
Where they are gone, nor yet this year,
Except with this for an overword,—
But where are the snows of yester-year?

In contrast to the tightly defined ballade, the term **ballad** (without the final **e**) may be used for any poem that is, or can be, sung, and that has regular stanzas. Usually, the poems we refer to as ballads have four-line stanzas. Frequently, like the ballade, they make use of repeated lines or refrains. Note, in this next poem, how thoroughly and skillfully William Morris uses the battle cry he has chosen for his refrain, hammering it home at the end of each short stanza until it almost takes on the sound of the speaker's own pulse pounding in his temples.

---

[5] Héloïse, the beautiful niece of a church official, fell in love with her teacher, the famous philosopher Abelard (1079–1142). They eloped, and the uncle was so incensed that he caused Abelard to be set upon and emasculated. As a result Abelard became a monk and Héloïse a nun, and the reward of their love was sorrow and pain.

[6] Queen Margaret of Burgundy who used to have her lovers, among whom was the scholar Buridan, sewn in sacks and thrown into the Seine.

[7] Perhaps Blanche of Castile, or perhaps a figment of Villon's imagination.

[8] Bertha Broadfoot, in epic accounts is the mother of Charlemagne. The identity of Beatrice and Alice is uncertain.

[9] The countess of Anjou in France.

[10] Joan of Arc.

WILLIAM MORRIS (1834–1896)

The Gillyflower of Gold

A golden gillyflower today
I wore upon my helm alway,
And won the prize of this tourney.
   Hah! hah! la belle jaune giroflée.[1]

5 However well Sir Giles might sit,
His sun was weak to wither it;
Lord Miles's blood was dew on it.
   Hah! hah! la belle jaune giroflée.

Although my spear in splinters flew,
10 From John's steel-coat, my eye was true;
I wheeled about, and cried for you,
   Hah! hah! la belle jaune giroflée.

Yea, do not doubt my heart was good,
Though my sword flew like rotten wood,
15 To shout, although I scarcely stood,
   Hah! hah! la belle jaune giroflée.

My hand was steady too, to take,
My ax from round my neck, and break
John's steel-coat up for my love's sake.
20   *Hah! hah! la belle jaune giroflée—*

When I stood in my tent again,
Arming afresh, I felt a pain
Take hold of me, I was so fain—
   Hah! hah! la belle jaune giroflée—

25 To hear *Honneur aux fils des preux!*[2]
Right in my ears again, and shew
The gillyflower blossomed new.
   Hah! hah! la belle jaune giroflée.

The Sieur Guillaume against me came,
30 His tabard[3] bore three points of flame

---

[1] The beautiful yellow gillyflower.
[2] Honor to the sons of valiant knights!
[3] A kind of cloak or mantle worn by knights.

From a red heart; with little blame[4]—
    Hah! hah! la belle jaune giroflée—

Our tough spears crackled up like straw;
He was the first to turn and draw
35 His sword, that had nor speck nor flaw;
    Hah! hah! la belle jaune giroflée.

But I felt weaker than a maid,
And my brain, dizzied and afraid,
Within my helm a fierce tune played,
40   *Hah! hah! la belle jaune giroflée,*

Until I thought of your dear head,
Bowed to the gillyflower bed,
The yellow flowers stained with red;
    Hah! hah! la belle jaune giroflée.

45 Crash! how the swords met—*giroflée!*
The fierce tune in my helm would play,
La belle! la belle! jaune giroflée!
    Hah! hah! la belle jaune giroflée.

Once more the great swords met again;
50 *"La belle! la belle!"* but who fell then?
Le Sieur Guillaume, who struck down ten;
    Hah! hah! la belle jaune giroflée.

And as with mazed and unarmed face
Toward my own crown and the Queen's place,
55 They led me at a gentle pace—
    Hah! hah! la belle jaune giroflée—

I almost saw your quiet head
Bowed o'er the gillyflower bed,
The yellow flowers stained with red.
60   *Hah! hah! la belle jaune giroflée.*

---

[4] Damage.

Among the rhymed poetic forms, the **ode** is unique in leaving both the rhyme scheme and the length of each individual line to the poet's discretion. The one constant feature of odes in English poetry, in fact, is their elevated tone. In Keats's "Ode on a Grecian Urn" and "Ode to a Nightingale," and in Shelley's "Ode to the West Wind," we saw three different stanzaic patterns. Look back at these odes now (on pages 517, 535, and 533) and define their patterns. Note, too, that in each case the stanzaic form is constant throughout the ode. For this reason, these are sometimes called **Horatian odes.**

To conclude this chapter, we will read one further ode, this one of the type called the **irregular ode.** This particular ode, written by the early Romantic poet William Wordsworth, makes skillful use of rhyme and rhythm both. Yet, for all its careful contrivance, it maintains a remarkable freshness of tone, in keeping with its subject of early joys and maturer delights. Because it is an irregular ode, the stanzas in this poem vary among themselves, changing shape to follow the motions of the poet's mind. The basic meter remains iambic throughout, but line lengths and rhyme schemes shift constantly. The result is an unusual blend of patterning and fluidity that sometimes mutes its tone to a thoughtful expression of philosophy and sometimes rises to a hymn of joyful praise.

The ode deals with the relations between the human soul, nature, and immortality. In it, Wordsworth suggests not only that we know immortality after death, but that we know it before birth as well: "trailing clouds of glory do we come, / From God, who is our home." The ode thus celebrates the heavenlike joy the young child sees in the natural world; and it laments the dulling of that joy that occurs when the child, responding to the novelty of his mundane existence, turns his mind more fully upon earthly things. Yet the final tone is not sorrow but a greater joy, as Wordsworth passes beyond mourning this early loss into celebrating the fully human joys and loves that are the gift of the mature soul.

As you read the ode, pay careful attention to the way Wordsworth develops this train of thought, and notice how the sound and shape of the stanzas convey the changing emotions the speaker feels.

WILLIAM WORDSWORTH (1770–1850)

Ode

Intimations of Immortality from Recollections
of Early Childhood

The Child is father of the Man;
And I could wish my days to be
Bound each to each by natural piety.

1

There was a time when meadow, grove, and stream,
The earth, and every common sight,
    To me did seem
    Apparelled in celestial light,
5 The glory and the freshness of a dream.
It is not now as it hath been of yore;—
    Turn wheresoe'er I may,
      By night or day,
The things which I have seen I now can see no more.

2

10   The Rainbow comes and goes,
    And lovely is the Rose,
    The Moon doth with delight
Look round her when the heavens are bare;
    Waters on a starry night
15   Are beautiful and fair;
    The sunshine is a glorious birth;
    But yet I know, where'er I go,
That there hath past away a glory from the earth.

3

Now, while the birds thus sing a joyous song,
20   And while the young lambs bound
      As to the tabor's sound,
To me alone there came a thought of grief:
A timely utterance gave that thought relief,
      And I again am strong:
25 The cataracts blow their trumpets from the steep;
No more shall grief of mine the season wrong;
I hear the Echoes through the mountains throng,
The Winds come to me from the fields of sleep,
      And all the earth is gay;
30   Land and sea
    Give themselves up to jollity,
      And with the heart of May
    Doth every Beast keep holiday;—
      Thou Child of Joy,
35 Shout round me, let me hear thy shouts, thou happy Shepherd-boy!

4

Ye blessèd Creatures, I have heard the call
  Ye to each other make; I see
The heavens laugh with you in your jubilee;
  My heart is at your festival,
40   My head hath its coronal,
The fulness of your bliss, I feel—I feel it all.
     Oh evil day! if I were sullen
     While Earth herself is adorning,
       This sweet May-morning,
45   And the Children are culling
       On every side,
     In a thousand valleys far and wide,
     Fresh flowers; while the sun shines warm,
And the Babe leaps up on his Mother's arm:—
50   I hear, I hear, with joy I hear!
     —But there's a Tree, of many, one,
A single Field which I have looked upon,
Both of them speak of something that is gone:
     The Pansy at my feet
55   Doth the same tale repeat:
Whither is fled the visionary gleam?
Where is it now, the glory and the dream?

5

Our birth is but a sleep and a forgetting:
The Soul that rises with us, our life's Star,
60   Hath had elsewhere its setting,
      And cometh from afar:
     Not in entire forgetfulness,
     And not in utter nakedness,
But trailing clouds of glory do we come
65   From God, who is our home:
Heaven lies about us in our infancy!
Shades of the prison-house begin to close
     Upon the growing Boy,
      But He
70 Beholds the light, and whence it flows,
     He sees it in his joy;
The Youth, who daily farther from the east
     Must travel, still is Nature's Priest,
     And by the vision splendid

75   Is on his way attended;
At length the Man perceives it die away,
And fade into the light of common day.

6

Earth fills her lap with pleasures of her own;
Yearnings she hath in her own natural kind,
80 And, even with something of a Mother's mind,
    And no unworthy aim,
    The homely Nurse doth all she can
To make her Foster-child, her Inmate Man,
    Forget the glories he hath known,
85 And that imperial palace whence he came.

7

Behold the Child among his new-born blisses,
A six years' Darling of a pigmy size!
See, where 'mid work of his own hand he lies,
Fretted by sallies of his mother's kisses,
90 With light upon him from his father's eyes!
See, at his feet, some little plan or chart,
Some fragment from his dream of human life,
Shaped by himself with newly-learnèd art;
    A wedding or a festival,
95   A mourning or a funeral;
      And this hath now his heart,
    And unto this he frames his song:
      Then will he fit his tongue
To dialogues of business, love, or strife;
100   But it will not be long
    Ere this be thrown aside,
    And with new joy and pride
The little Actor cons another part;
Filling from time to time his "humorous stage"
105 With all the Persons, down to palsied Age,
That Life brings with her in her equipage;
    As if his whole vocation
    Were endless imitation.

8

Thou, whose exterior semblance doth belie
110   Thy Soul's immensity;

Thou best Philosopher, who yet dost keep
Thy heritage, thou Eye among the blind,
That, deaf and silent, read'st the eternal deep,
Haunted for ever by the eternal mind,—
115   Mighty Prophet! Seer blest!
        On whom those truths do rest,
Which we are toiling all our lives to find,
In darkness lost, the darkness of the grave;
Thou, over whom thy Immortality
120 Broods like the Day, a Master o'er a Slave,
A Presence which is not to be put by;
Thou little Child, yet glorious in the might
Of heaven-born freedom on thy being's height,
Why with such earnest pains dost thou provoke
125 The years to bring the inevitable yoke,
Thus blindly with thy blessedness at strife?
Full soon thy Soul shall have her earthly freight,
And custom lie upon thee with a weight,
Heavy as frost, and deep almost as life!

                9

130   O joy! that in our embers
        Is something that doth live,
        That nature yet remembers
        What was so fugitive!
The thought of our past years in me doth breed
135 Perpetual benediction: not indeed
For that which is most worthy to be blest;
Delight and liberty, the simple creed
Of Childhood, whether busy or at rest,
With new-fledged hope still fluttering in his breast:—
140   Not for these I raise
        The song of thanks and praise;
        But for those obstinate questionings
        Of sense and outward things,
        Falling from us, vanishings;
145   Blank misgivings of a Creature
Moving about in worlds not realised,
High instincts before which our mortal Nature
Did tremble like a guilty Thing surprised:
        But for those first affections,
150   Those shadowy recollections,
        Which, be they what they may,
Are yet the fountain-light of all our day,

Are yet a master-light of all our seeing;
　　Uphold us, cherish, and have power to make
155 Our noisy years seem moments in the being
Of the eternal Silence: truths that wake,
　　　　To perish never:
Which neither listlessness, nor mad endeavor,
　　　　Nor Man nor Boy,
160 Nor all that is at enmity with joy,
Can utterly abolish or destroy!
　　　Hence in a season of calm weather
　　　　Though inland far we be,
Our Souls have sight of that immortal sea
165　　　Which brought us hither,
　　　Can in a moment travel thither,
And see the Children sport upon the shore,
And hear the mighty waters rolling evermore.

10

Then sing, ye Birds, sing, sing a joyous song!
170　　　And let the young Lambs bound
　　　　As to the tabor's sound!
We in thought will join your throng,
　　　Ye that pipe and ye that play,
　　　Ye that through your hearts to-day
175　　　Feel the gladness of the May!
What though the radiance which was once so bright
Be now for ever taken from my sight,
　　　Though nothing can bring back the hour
Of splendor in the grass, of glory in the flower;
180　　　We will grieve not, rather find
　　　　Strength in what remains behind;
　　　　In the primal sympathy
　　　　Which having been must ever be;
　　　　In the soothing thoughts that spring
185　　　Out of human suffering;
　　　In the faith that looks through death,
In years that bring the philosophic mind.

11

And O, ye Fountains, Meadows, Hills, and Groves,
Forebode not any severing of our loves!
190 Yet in my heart of hearts I feel your might;

I only have relinquished one delight
To live beneath your more habitual sway.
I love the Brooks which down their channels fret,
Even more than when I tripped lightly as they;
195 The innocent brightness of a new-born Day
       Is lovely yet;
The Clouds that gather round the setting sun
Do take a sober coloring from an eye
That hath kept watch o'er man's mortality;
200 Another race hath been, and other palms are won.
Thanks to the human heart by which we live,
Thanks to its tenderness, its joys, and fears,
To me the meanest flower that blows can give
Thoughts that do often lie too deep for tears.

14 *The Sonnet*

Without a doubt, the most popular of the defined forms in English and American poetry is the **sonnet.** Sonnets are always fourteen lines long. Traditionally, they are divided into two main forms. The **Petrarchan sonnet** consists of an octet, rhymed *abba abba*, and a sestet, rhymed either *cdcdcd* or *cdecde;* and the **Shakespearean sonnet,** with three quatrains, usually rhymes *abab cdcd efef*, and a couplet at the end, *gg*. Less standard rhyme forms do, of course, exist. Notice, for example, the rhyme scheme in Cummings's "the Cambridge ladies who live in furnished souls," at the end of this chapter.

Of the two traditional forms, the Shakespearean usually seems the more emphatic. Because no sound needs to be used more than twice, it is also slightly easier to write. It was the favored form during the Renaissance. The Petrarchan sonnet, on the other hand, tends to have a somewhat smoother flow and often seems more graceful. It was therefore preferred by the Romantic poets of the nineteenth century.

The sonnet came into English as a love poem: we have read love sonnets by Shakespeare, Sidney, and Spenser. But the sonnet has proved capable of handling almost any subject and of expressing many moods and tones. Look back, for example, at "Ozymandias" (p. 496) and "Composed upon Westminster Bridge" (p. 507). And look, too, at the following examples of what can be done with the sonnet form.

WILLIAM SHAKESPEARE (1564–1616)

Sonnet 116

Let me not to the marriage of true minds
Admit impediments. Love is not love
Which alters when it alteration finds,
Or bends with the remover to remove.
5 O no! it is an ever-fixèd mark
That looks on tempests and is never shaken;
It is the star to every wand'ring bark,
Whose worth's unknown, although his height be taken.
Love's not Time's fool, though rosy lips and cheeks
10 Within his bending sickle's compass come.
Love alters not with his brief hours and weeks,
But bears it out even to the edge of doom.
   If this be error, and upon me proved,
   I never writ, nor no man ever loved.

JOHN DONNE (1572–1631)

Sonnet 10

Death, be not proud, though some have callèd thee
Mighty and dreadful, for thou art not so;
For those whom thou think'st thou dost overthrow
Die not, poor Death, nor yet canst thou kill me.
5 From rest and sleep, which but thy pictures be,
Much pleasure; then from thee much more must flow;
And soonest our best men with thee do go,
Rest of their bones and souls' delivery.
Thou'rt slave to fate, chance, kings, and desperate men,
10 And dost with poison, war, and sickness dwell;
And poppy or charms can make us sleep as well
And better than thy stroke. Why swell'st thou then?
One short sleep past, we wake eternally,
And Death shall be no more: Death, thou shalt die.

JOHN MILTON (1608–1674)

On His Blindness

When I consider how my light is spent,
Ere half my days, in this dark world and wide,
And that one talent which is death to hide

Lodged with me useless, though my soul more bent
5 To serve therewith my Maker, and present
My true account, lest he returning chide,
"Doth God exact day labor, light denied?"
I fondly ask; but Patience, to prevent
That murmur, soon replies: "God doth not need
10 Either man's work or his own gifts; who best
Bear his mild yoke, they serve him best. His state
Is kingly: thousands at his bidding speed
And post o'er land and ocean without rest.
They also serve who only stand and wait."

GERARD MANLEY HOPKINS (1844–1899)

(Carrion Comfort[1])

Not, I'll not, carrion comfort, Despair, not feast on thee;
Not untwist—slack they may be—these last strands of man
In me ór, most weary, cry *I can no more*. I can;
Can something, hope, wish day come, not choose not to be.

5 But ah, but O thou terrible, why wouldst thou rude on me
Thy wring-world right foot rock? lay a lionlimb against me? scan
With darksome devouring eyes my bruisèd bones? and fan,
O in turns of tempest, me heaped there; me frantic to avoid thee and
flee?

Why? That my chaff might fly; my grain lie, sheer and clear.
10 Nay in all that toil, that coil, since (seems) I kissed the rod,
Hand rather, my heart lo! lapped strength, stole joy, would laugh,
chéer.
Cheer whom though? the hero whose heaven-handling flung me, fóot
tród
Me? or me that fought him? O which one? is it each one? That
night, that year
Of now done darkness I wretch lay wrestling with (my God!) my
God.

---

[1] The title was added by Robert Bridges.

ROBERT FROST (1874–1963)

Design

I found a dimpled spider, fat and white,
On a white heal-all, holding up a moth
Like a white piece of rigid satin cloth—
Assorted characters of death and blight
5 Mixed ready to begin the morning right,
Like the ingredients of a witches' broth—
A snow-drop spider, a flower like a froth,
And dead wings carried like a paper kite.

What had that flower to do with being white,
10 The wayside blue and innocent heal-all?
What brought the kindred spider to that height,
Then steered the white moth thither in the night?
What but design of darkness to appall?—
If design govern in a thing so small.

EDNA ST. VINCENT MILLAY (1892–1950)

What Lips My Lips Have Kissed, and Where, and Why

What lips my lips have kissed, and where, and why,
I have forgotten, and what arms have lain
Under my head till morning; but the rain
Is full of ghosts tonight, that tap and sigh
5 Upon the glass and listen for reply,
And in my heart there stirs a quiet pain
For unremembered lads that not again
Will turn to me at midnight with a cry.
Thus in the winter stands the lonely tree,
10 Nor knows what birds have vanished one by one,
Yet knows its boughs more silent than before:
I cannot say what loves have come and gone, ʹ
I only know that summer sang in me
A little while, that in me sings no more.

WILFRED OWEN (1893–1918)

Anthem for Doomed Youth

What passing-bells for these who die as cattle?
   Only the monstrous anger of the guns.
   Only the stuttering rifles' rapid rattle
Can patter out their hasty orisons.
5 No mockeries now for them; no prayers nor bells,
   Nor any voice of mourning save the choirs—
The shrill, demented choirs of wailing shells;
   And bugles calling for them from sad shires.

What candles may be held to speed them all?
10   Not in the hands of boys, but in their eyes
Shall shine the holy glimmers of good-byes.
   The pallor of girls' brows shall be their pall;
Their flowers the tenderness of patient minds,
And each slow dusk a drawing-down of blinds.

E. E. CUMMINGS (1894–1963)

**the Cambridge ladies who live in
furnished souls**

the Cambridge ladies who live in furnished souls
are unbeautiful and have comfortable minds
(also, with the church's protestant blessings,
daughters, unscented shapeless spirited)
5 they believe in Christ and Longfellow, both dead,
are invariably interested in so many things—
at the present writing one still finds
delighted fingers knitting for the is it Poles?
perhaps. While permanent faces coyly bandy
10 scandal of Mrs. N and Professor D
. . . . the Cambridge ladies do not care, above
Cambridge if sometimes in its box of
sky lavender and cornerless, the
moon rattles like a fragment of angry candy

AN ANTHOLOGY OF POEMS

CHRISTOPHER MARLOWE (1564–1593)

The Passionate Shepherd to His Love

Come live with me, and be my love,
And we will all the pleasures prove
That hills and valleys, dales and fields,
Woods, or steepy mountain yields.

5 And we will sit upon the rocks,
Seeing the shepherds feed their flocks,
By shallow rivers, to whose falls
Melodious birds sings madrigals.

And I will make thee beds of roses
10 And a thousand fragrant posies.
A cap of flowers, and a kirtle
Embroidered all with leaves of myrtle;

A gown made of the finest wool,
Which from our pretty lambs we pull,
15 Fair linèd slippers, for the cold,
With buckles of the purest gold;

A belt of straw and ivy-buds
With coral clasps and amber studs.
And if these pleasures may thee move,
20 Come live with me, and be my love.

The shepherds' swains shall dance and sing
For thy delight each May morning.
If these delights thy mind may move,
Then live with me, and be my love.

SIR WALTER RALEGH (1552?–1618)

The Nymph's Reply to the Shepherd

If all the world and love were young,
And truth in every shepherd's tongue,
These pretty pleasures might me move
To live with thee and be thy love.

5 Time drives the flocks from field to fold
When rivers rage and rocks grow cold,
And Philomel becometh dumb;
The rest complains of cares to come.

The flowers do fade, and wanton fields
10 To wayward winter reckoning yields;
A honey tongue, a heart of gall,
Is fancy's spring, but sorrow's fall.

Thy gowns, thy shoes, thy beds of roses,
Thy cap, thy kirtle, and thy posies
15 Soon break, soon wither, soon forgotten—
In folly ripe, in reason rotten.

Thy belt of straw and ivy buds,
Thy coral clasps and amber studs,
All these in me no means can move
20 To come to thee and be thy love.

But could youth last and love still breed,
Had joys no date nor age no need,
Then these delights my mind might move
To live with thee and be thy love.

WILLIAM SHAKESPEARE (1564–1616)

Sonnet 55

Not marble nor the gilded monuments
Of princes shall outlive this powerful rime;
But you shall shine more bright in these contents
Than unswept stone, besmeared with sluttish time.
5 When wasteful war shall statues overturn,
And broils root out the work of masonry,

Nor Mars his sword nor war's quick fire shall burn
The living record of your memory.
'Gainst death and all oblivious enmity
10 Shall you pace forth; your praise shall still find room
Even in the eyes of all posterity
That wear this world out to the ending doom.
   So, till the Judgment that yourself arise,
   You live in this, and dwell in lovers' eyes.

JOHN DONNE (1572–1631)

Sonnet 7

At the round earth's imagined corners, blow
Your trumpets, angels, and arise, arise
From death, you numberless infinities
Of souls, and to your scattered bodies go;
5 All whom the flood did, and fire shall o'erthrow;
All whom war, dearth, age, agues, tyrannies,
Despair, law, chance, hath slain, and you whose eyes
Shall behold God, and never taste death's woe.
But let them sleep, Lord, and me mourn a space,
10 For if above all these my sins abound,
'Tis late to ask abundance of thy grace
When we are there; here on this lowly ground
Teach me how to repent; for that's as good
As if thou hadst sealed my pardon with thy blood.

ROBERT HERRICK (1591–1674)

The Night-Piece, to Julia

Her eyes the glowworm lend thee;
The shooting stars attend thee;
   And the elves also,
   Whose little eyes glow
5 Like the sparks of fire, befriend thee.

No will-o'-the-wisp mislight thee;
Nor snake or slowworm bite thee;
   But on, on thy way,
   Not making a stay,
10 Since ghost there's none to affright thee.

Let not the dark thee cumber;
What though the moon does slumber?
   The stars of the night
   Will lend thee their light,
15 Like tapers clear without number.

Then, Julia, let me woo thee,
Thus, thus to come unto me;
   And when I shall meet
   Thy silvery feet,
20 My soul I'll pour into thee.

ALEXANDER POPE (1688–1744)

Ode on Solitude

Happy the man whose wish and care
   A few paternal acres bound,
Content to breathe his native air,
         In his own ground.

5 Whose herds with milk, whose fields with bread,
   Whose flocks supply him with attire,
Whose trees in summer yield him shade,
         In winter fire.

Blest, who can unconcernedly find
10   Hours, days, and years slide soft away,
In health of body, peace of mind,
         Quiet by day,

Sound sleep by night; study and ease,
   Together mixed; sweet recreation;
15 And innocence, which most does please
         With meditation.

Thus let me live, unseen, unknown;
   Thus unlamented let me die;
Steal from the world, and not a stone
20   Tell where I lie.

WILLIAM BLAKE (1757–1827)

London

I wander thro' each charter'd street,
Near where the charter'd Thames does flow,
And mark in every face I meet
Marks of weakness, marks of woe.

5 In every cry of every Man,
In every Infant's cry of fear,
In every voice, in every ban,
The mind-forg'd manacles I hear.

How the Chimney-sweeper's cry
10 Every blackning Church appalls;
And the hapless Soldier's sigh
Runs in blood down Palace walls.

But most thro' midnight streets I hear
How the youthful Harlot's curse
15 Blasts the new-born Infant's tear,
And blights with plagues the Marriage hearse.

SAMUEL TAYLOR COLERIDGE (1772–1834)

Kubla Khan

In Xanadu did Kubla Kahn
A stately pleasure-dome decree:
Where Alph, the sacred river, ran
Through caverns measureless to man
5   Down to a sunless sea.
So twice five miles of fertile ground
With walls and towers were girdled round:
And there were gardens bright with sinuous rills,
Where blossomed many an incense-bearing tree;
10 And here were forests ancient as the hills,
Enfolding sunny spots of greenery.

But oh! that deep romantic chasm which slanted
Down the green hill athwart a cedarn cover!
A savage place! as holy and enchanted
15 As e'er beneath a waning moon was haunted
By woman wailing for her demon-lover!

And from this chasm, with ceaseless turmoil seething,
As if this earth in thick pants were breathing,
A mighty fountain momently was forced:
20 Amid whose swift half-intermitted burst
Huge fragments vaulted like rebounding hail,
Or chaffy grain beneath the thresher's flail:
And 'mid these dancing rocks at once and ever
It flung up momently the sacred river.
25 Five miles meandering with a mazy motion
Through wood and dale the sacred river ran,
Then reached the caverns measureless to man,

And sank in tumult to a lifeless ocean:
And 'mid this tumult Kubla heard from far
30 Ancestral voices prophesying war!

The shadow of the dome of pleasure
Floated midway on the waves;
Where was heard the mingled measure
From the fountain and the caves.

35 It was a miracle of rare device,
A sunny pleasure-dome with caves of ice!

A damsel with a dulcimer
In a vision once I saw:
It was an Abyssinian maid,
40   And on her dulcimer she played,
Singing of Mount Abora.
Could I revive within me
Her symphony and song,
To such a deep delight 'twould win me,

45 That with music loud and long,
I would build that dome in air,
That sunny dome! those caves of ice!
And all who heard should see them there,
And all should cry, Beware! Beware!
50 His flashing eyes, his floating hair!
Weave a circle round him thrice,
And close your eyes with holy dread,
For he on honey-dew hath fed,
And drunk the milk of Paradise.

ALFRED, LORD TENNYSON (1809–1892)

Ulysses

It little profits that an idle king,
By this still hearth, among these barren crags,
Matched with an aged wife, I mete and dole
Unequal laws unto a savage race,
5 That hoard, and sleep, and feed, and know not me.
I cannot rest from travel; I will drink
Life to the lees. All times I have enjoyed
Greatly, have suffered greatly, both with those
That loved me, and alone; on shore, and when
10 Through scudding drifts the rainy Hyades[1]
Vexed the dim sea: I am become a name;
For always roaming with a hungry heart
Much have I seen and known—cities of men
And manners, climates, councils, governments,
15 Myself not least, but honored of them all;
And drunk delight of battle with my peers,
Far on the ringing plains of windy Troy.
I am a part of all that I have met;
Yet all experience is an arch wherethrough
20 Gleams that untraveled world whose margin fades
For ever and for ever when I move.
How dull it is to pause, to make an end,
To rust unburnished, not to shine in use!
As though to breathe were life! Life piled on life
25 Were all too little, and of one to me
Little remains; but every hour is saved
From that eternal silence, something more,
A bringer of new things; and vile it were
For some three suns to store and hoard myself,
30 And this gray spirit yearning in desire
To follow knowledge like a sinking star,
Beyond the utmost bound of human thought.

This is my son, mine own Telemachus,
To whom I leave the scepter and the isle—
35 Well-loved of me, discerning to fulfil
This labor, by slow prudence to make mild
A rugged people, and through soft degrees

---

[1] A group of stars in the constellation Taurus, whose rise with the sun heralded the spring rains.

Subdue them to the useful and the good.
Most blameless is he, centered in the sphere
40 Of common duties, decent not to fail
In offices of tenderness, and pay
Meet adoration to my household gods,
When I am gone. He works his work, I mine.

There lies the port; the vessel puffs her sail;
45 There gloom the dark, broad seas. My mariners,
Souls that have toiled, and wrought, and thought with me—
That ever with a frolic welcome took
The thunder and the sunshine, and opposed
Free hearts, free foreheads—you and I are old;
50 Old age hath yet his honor and his toil.
Death closes all; but something ere the end,
Some work of noble note, may yet be done,
Not unbecoming men that strove with Gods.
The lights begin to twinkle from the rocks:
55 The long day wanes: the slow moon climbs: the deep
Moans round with many voices. Come, my friends,
'Tis not too late to seek a newer world.
Push off, and sitting well in order smite
The sounding furrows; for my purpose holds
60 To sail beyond the sunset, and the baths
Of all the western stars, until I die.
It may be that the gulfs will wash us down;
It may be we shall touch the Happy Isles,
And see the great Achilles, whom we knew.
65 Though much is taken, much abides; and though
We are not now that strength which in old days
Moved earth and heaven, that which we are, we are;
One equal temper of heroic hearts,
Made weak by time and fate, but strong in will
70 To strive, to seek, to find, and not to yield.

ROBERT BROWNING (1812–1889)

The Bishop Orders His Tomb at Saint Praxed's Church

Rome, 15—

Vanity, saith the preacher, vanity!
Draw round my bed: is Anselm keeping back?

Nephews[1]—sons mine . . . ah God, I know not! Well—
She, men would have to be your mother once,
5 Old Gandolf envied me, so fair she was!
What's done is done, and she is dead beside,
Dead long ago, and I am Bishop since,
And as she died so must we die ourselves,
And thence ye may perceive the world's a dream.
10 Life, how and what is it? As here I lie
In this state-chamber, dying by degrees,
Hours and long hours in the dead night, I ask
"Do I live, am I dead?" Peace, peace seems all.
Saint Praxed's ever was the church for peace;
15 And so, about this tomb of mine. I fought
With tooth and nail to save my niche, ye know:
—Old Gandolf cozened me, despite my care;
Shrewd was that snatch from out the corner South
He graced his carrion with, God curse the same!
20 Yet still my niche is not so cramped but thence
One sees the pulpit o' the epistle side,[2]
And somewhat of the choir, those silent seats,
And up into the aery dome where live
The angels, and a sunbeam's sure to lurk:
25 And I shall fill my slab of basalt there,
And 'neath my tabernacle take my rest,
With those nine columns round me, two and two,
The odd one at my feet where Anselm stands:
Peach-blossom marble all, the rare, the ripe
30 As fresh-poured red wine of a mighty pulse.
—Old Gandolf with his paltry onion-stone,
Put me where I may look at him! True peach,
Rosy and flawless: how I earned the prize!
Draw close: that conflagration of my church
35 —What then? So much was saved if aught were missed!
My sons, ye would not be my death? Go dig
The white-grape vineyard where the oil-press stood,
Drop water gently till the surface sink,
And if ye find . . . Ah God, I know not, I! . . .
40 Bedded in store of rotten fig-leaves soft,
And corded up in a tight olive-frail,
Some lump, ah God, of *lapis lazuli,*

---

[1] Euphemism for illegitimate sons.
[2] The right-hand side, as one faces the altar.

Big as a Jew's head cut off at the nape,
Blue as a vein o'er the Madonna's breast . . .
45 Sons, all have I bequeathed you, villas, all,
That brave Frascati villa with its bath,
So, let the blue lump poise between my knees,
Like God the Father's globe on both his hands
Ye worship in the Jesu Church so gay,
50 For Gandolf shall not choose but see and burst!
Swift as a weaver's shuttle fleet our years:
Man goeth to the grave, and where is he?
Did I say basalt for my slab, sons? Black—
'Twas ever antique-black I meant! How else
55 Shall ye contrast my frieze to come beneath?
The bas-relief in bronze ye promised me,
Those Pans and Nymphs ye wot of, and perchance
Some tripod,³ thyrsus,⁴ with a vase or so,
The Saviour at his sermon on the mount,
60 Saint Praxed in a glory, and one Pan
Ready to twitch the Nymph's last garment off,
And Moses with the tables . . . but I know
Ye mark me not! What do they whisper thee,
Child of my bowels, Anselm? Ah, ye hope
65 To revel down my villas while I gasp
Bricked o'er with beggar's moldy travertine
Which Gandolf from his tomb-top chuckles at!
Nay, boys, ye love me—all of jasper, then!
'Tis jasper ye stand pledged to, lest I grieve
70 My bath must needs be left behind, alas!
One block, pure green as a pistachio nut,
There's plenty jasper somewhere in the world—
And have I not Saint Praxed's ear to pray
Horses for ye, and brown Greek manuscripts,
75 And mistresses with great smooth marbly limbs?
—That's if ye carve my epitaph aright,
Choice Latin, picked phrase, Tully's⁵ every word,
No gaudy ware like Gandolf's second line—
Tully, my masters? Ulpian⁶ serves his need!
80 And then how I shall lie through centuries,
And hear the blessed mutter of the mass,
And see God made and eaten all day long,

---

³ Three-legged stool used by the oracle at Delphi.
⁴ Staff carried by Dionysus and his followers.
⁵ Marcus Tullius Cicero, master of Latin prose style.
⁶ Domitius Ulpianus, third century Roman jurist, noted for **bad prose**.

And feel the steady candle-flame, and taste
Good strong thick stupefying incense-smoke!
85 For as I lie here, hours of the dead night,
Dying in state and by such slow degrees,
I fold my arms as if they clasped a crook,
And stretch my feet forth straight as stone can point,
And let the bedclothes, for a mortcloth, drop
90 Into great laps and folds of sculptor's-work:
And as yon tapers dwindle, and strange thoughts
Grow, with a certain humming in my ears,
About the life before I lived this life,
And this life too, popes, cardinals, and priests,
95 Saint Praxed at his sermon on the mount,[7]
Your tall pale mother with her talking eyes,
And new-found agate urns as fresh as day,
And marble's language, Latin pure, discreet
—Aha, ELUCESCEBAT[8] quoth our friend?
100 No Tully, said I, Ulpian at the best!
Evil and brief hath been my pilgrimage.
All *lapis*, all, sons! Else I give the Pope
My villas! Will ye ever eat my heart?
Ever your eyes were as a lizard's quick,
105 They glitter like your mother's for my soul,
Or ye would heighten my impoverished frieze,
Piece out its starved design, and fill my vase
With grapes, and add a vizor and a Term,[9]
And to the tripod you would tie a lynx
110 That in his struggle throws the thyrsus down,
To comfort me on my entablature
Whereon I am to lie till I must ask
"Do I live, am I dead?" There, leave me, there!
For ye have stabbed me with ingratitude
115 To death—ye wish it—God, ye wish it! Stone—
Gritstone, a-crumble! Clammy squares which sweat
As if the corpse they keep were oozing through—
And no more *lapis* to delight the world!
Well go! I bless ye. Fewer tapers there,
120 But in a row: and, going, turn your backs
—Aye, like departing altar-ministrants,
And leave me in my church, the church for peace,

---

[7] The bishop's failing mind attributes the Sermon on the Mount to Saint Praxed (a woman) instead of Christ.
[8] "He was illustrious," an example of Ulpian Latin.
[9] A mask and bust on a pedestal.

That I may watch at leisure if he leers—
Old Gandolf, at me, from his onion-stone,
125 As still he envied me, so fair she was!

ROBERT BROWNING (1812–1889)

Home-Thoughts, from Abroad

I

Oh, to be in England
Now that April's there,
And whoever wakes in England
Sees, some morning, unaware,
5 That the lowest boughs and the brushwood sheaf
Round the elm-tree bole are in tiny leaf,
While the chaffinch sings on the orchard bough
In England—now!

2

And after April, when May follows,
10 And the whitethroat builds, and all the swallows!
Hark, where my blossomed pear-tree in the hedge
Leans to the field and scatters on the clover
Blossoms and dewdrops—at the bent spray's edge—
That's the wise thrush; he sings each song twice over,
15 Lest you should think he never could recapture
The first fine careless rapture!
And though the fields look rough with hoary dew,
All will be gay when noontide wakes anew
The buttercups, the little children's dower
20 —Far brighter than this gaudy melon-flower!

WALT WHITMAN (1819–1892)

Out of the Cradle Endlessly Rocking

Out of the cradle endlessly rocking,
Out of the mocking-bird's throat, the musical shuttle,
Out of the Ninth-month midnight,
Over the sterile sands and the fields beyond, where the child leaving
 his bed wander'd alone, bareheaded, barefoot,

5 Down from the shower'd halo,
 Up from the mystic play of shadows twining and twisting as if they
    were alive,
 Out from the patches of briers and blackberries,
 From the memories of the bird that chanted to me,
 From your memories sad brother, from the fitful risings and fallings
    I heard,
10 From under that yellow half-moon late-risen and swollen as if with
    tears,
 From those beginning notes of yearning and love there in the mist,
 From the thousand responses of my heart never to cease,
 From the myriad thence-arous'd words,
 From the word stronger and more delicious than any,
15 From such as now they start the scene revisiting,
 As a flock, twittering, rising, or overhead passing,
 Borne hither, ere all eludes me, hurriedly,
 A man, yet by these tears a little boy again,
 Throwing myself on the sand, confronting the waves,
20 I, chanter of pains and joys, uniter of here and hereafter,
 Taking all hints to use them, but swiftly leaping beyond them,
 A reminiscence sing.

 Once Paumanok,[1]
 When the lilac-scent was in the air and Fifth-month grass was grow-
    ing,
25 Up this seashore in some briers,
 Two feather'd guests from Alabama, two together,
 And their nest, and four light-green eggs spotted with brown,
 And every day the he-bird to and fro near at hand,
 And every day the she-bird crouch'd on her nest, silent, with bright
    eyes,
30 And every day I, a curious boy, never too close, never disturbing
    them,
 Cautiously peering, absorbing, translating.

 Shine! shine! shine!
 Pour down your warmth, great sun!
 While we bask, we two together.

35 *Two together!*
 Winds blow south, or winds blow north,

---

[1] The Indian name for Long Island.

Day come white, or night come black,
Home, or rivers and mountains from home,
Singing all time, minding no time,
40 *While we two keep together.*

Till of a sudden,
May-be kill'd unknown to her mate,
One forenoon, the she-bird crouch'd not on the nest,
Nor return'd that afternoon, nor the next,
45 Nor ever appear'd again.

And thenceforward all summer in the sound of the sea,
And at night under the full of the moon in calmer weather,
Over the hoarse surging of the sea,
Or flitting from brier to brier by day,
50 I saw, I heard at intervals the remaining one, the he-bird,
The solitary guest from Alabama.

Blow! blow! blow!
Blow up sea-winds along Paumanok's shore;
I wait and I wait till you blow my mate to me.

55 Yes, when the stars glisten'd,
All night long on the prong of a moss-scallop'd stake,
Down almost amid the slapping waves,
Sat the lone singer wonderful causing tears.

He call'd on his mate,
60 He pour'd forth the meanings which I of all men know.

Yes my brother I know,
The rest might not, but I have treasur'd every note,
For more than once dimly down to the beach gliding,
Silent, avoiding the moonbeams, blending myself with the shadows,
65 Recalling now the obscure shapes, the echoes, the sounds and sights
        after their sorts,
The white arms out in the breakers tirelessly tossing,
I, with bare feet, a child, the wind wafting my hair,
Listen'd long and long.

Listen'd to keep, to sing, now translating the notes,
70 Following you my brother.

Soothe! soothe! soothe!
Close on its wave soothes the wave behind,

And again another behind embracing and lapping, every one close,
But my love soothes not me, not me.

75 *Low hangs the moon, it rose late,*
It is lagging—O I think it is heavy with love, with love.

O madly the sea pushes upon the land,
With love, with love.

O night! do I not see my love fluttering out among the breakers?
80 *What is that little black thing I see there in the white?*

Loud! loud! loud!
Loud I call to you, my love!
High and clear I shoot my voice over the waves,
Surely you must know who is here, is here,
85 *You must know who I am, my love.*

Low-hanging moon!
What is that dusky spot in your brown yellow?
O it is the shape, the shape of my mate!
O moon do not keep her from me any longer.

90 *Land! land! O land!*
Whichever way I turn, O I think you could give me my mate back
again if you only would,
For I am almost sure I see her dimly whichever way I look.

O rising stars!
Perhaps the one I want so much will rise, will rise with some of you.

95 *O throat! O trembling throat!*
Sound clearer through the atmosphere!
Pierce the woods, the earth,
Somewhere listening to catch you must be the one I want.

Shake out carols!
100 *Solitary here, the night's carols!*
Carols of lonesome love! death's carols!
Carols under that lagging, yellow, waning moon!
O under that moon where she droops almost down into the sea!
O reckless despairing carols.

105 *But soft! sink low!*
Soft! let me just murmur,

And do you wait a moment you husky-nois'd sea,
For somewhere I believe I heard my mate responding to me,
So faint, I must be still, be still to listen,
110 *But not altogether still, for then she might not come immediately*
to me.

Hither my love!
Here I am! here!
With this just-sustain'd note I announce myself to you,
This gentle call is for you my love, for you.

115 *Do not be decoy'd elsewhere,*
That is the whistle of the wind, it is not my voice,
That is the fluttering, the fluttering of the spray,
Those are the shadows of leaves.

O darkness! O in vain!
120 *O I am very sick and sorrowful.*

O brown halo in the sky near the moon, drooping upon the sea!
O troubled reflection in the sea!
O throat! O throbbing heart!
And I singing uselessly, uselessly all the night.

125 *O past! O happy life! O songs of joy!*
In the air, in the woods, over fields,
Loved! loved! loved! loved! loved!
But my mate no more, no more with me!
We two together no more.

130 The aria sinking,
All else continuing, the stars shining,
The winds blowing, the notes of the bird continuous echoing,
With angry moans the fierce old mother incessantly moaning,
On the sands of Paumanok's shore gray and rustling,
135 The yellow half-moon enlarged, sagging down, drooping, the face of
the sea almost touching,
The boy ecstatic, with his bare feet the waves, with his hair the
atmosphere dallying,
The love in the heart long pent, now loose, now at last tumultuously
bursting,
The aria's meaning, the ears, the soul, swiftly depositing,
The strange tears down the cheeks coursing,
140 The colloquy there, the trio, each uttering,

The undertone, the savage old mother incessantly crying,
To the boy's soul's questions sullenly timing, some drown'd secret
   hissing,
To the outsetting bard.

Demon or bird! (said the boy's soul,)
145 Is it indeed toward your mate you sing? or is it really to me?
For I, that was a child, my tongue's use sleeping, now I have heard
   you,
Now in a moment I know what I am for, I awake,
And already a thousand singers, a thousand songs, clearer, louder
   and more sorrowful than yours,
A thousand warbling echoes have started to life within me, never
   to die.

150 O you singer solitary, singing by yourself, projecting me,
O solitary me listening, never more shall I cease perpetuating you,
Never more shall I escape, never more the reverberations,
Never more the cries of unsatisfied love be absent from me,
Never again leave me to be the peaceful child I was before what
   there in the night,
155 By the sea under the yellow and sagging moon,
The messenger there arous'd, the fire, the sweet hell within,
The unknown want, the destiny of me.

O give me the clew! (it lurks in the night here somewhere,)
O if I am to have so much, let me have more!

160 A word then, (for I will conquer it,)
The word final, superior to all,
Subtle, sent up—what is it?—I listen;
Are you whispering it, and have been all the time, you sea-waves?
Is that it from your liquid rims and wet sands?

165 Whereto answering, the sea,
Delaying not, hurrying not,
Whisper'd me through the night, and very plainly before daybreak,
Lisp'd to me the low and delicious word death,
And again death, death, death, death,
170 Hissing melodious, neither like the bird nor like my arous'd child's
   heart,
But edging near as privately for me rustling at my feet,
Creeping thence steadily up to my ears and laving me softly all over,
Death, death, death, death, death.

Which I do not forget,
175 But fuse the song of my dusky demon and brother,
That he sang to me in the moonlight on Paumanok's gray beach,
With the thousand responsive songs at random,
My own songs awaked from that hour,
And with them the key, the word up from the waves,
180 The word of the sweetest song and all songs,
That strong and delicious word which, creeping to my feet,
(Or like some old crone rocking the cradle, swathed in sweet gar-
ments, bending aside,)
The sea whisper'd me.

EMILY DICKINSON (1830–1886)

The Poets Light but Lamps (#883)

The Poets light but Lamps—
Themselves—go out—
The Wicks they stimulate—
If vital Light

5 Inhere as do the Suns—
Each Age a Lens
Disseminating their
Circumference—

A. E. HOUSMAN (1859–1936)

"Terence, This Is Stupid Stuff . . ."

"Terence, this is stupid stuff:
You eat your victuals fast enough;
There can't be much amiss, 'tis clear,
To see the rate you drink your beer.
5 But oh, good Lord, the verse you make,
It gives a chap the belly-ache.
The cow, the old cow, she is dead;
It sleeps well, the hornèd head:
We poor lads, 'tis our turn now
10 To hear such tunes as killed the cow.
Pretty friendship 'tis to rhyme
Your friends to death before their time
Moping melancholy mad:
Come, pipe a tune to dance to, lad."

15   Why, if 'tis dancing you would be,
       There's brisker pipes than poetry.
       Say, for what were hop-yards meant,
       Or why was Burton built on Trent?[1]
       Oh many a peer of England brews
20   Livelier liquor than the Muse,
       And malt does more than Milton can
       To justify God's ways to man.
       Ale, man, ale's the stuff to drink
       For fellows whom it hurts to think:
25   Look into the pewter pot
       To see the world as the world's not.
       And faith, 'tis pleasant till 'tis past:
       The mischief is that 'twill not last.
       Oh I have been to Ludlow fair
30   And left my necktie God knows where,
       And carried half-way home, or near,
       Pints and quarts of Ludlow beer:
       Then the world seemed none so bad,
       And I myself a sterling lad;
35   And down in lovely muck I've lain,
       Happy till I woke again.
       Then I saw the morning sky:
       Heigho, the tale was all a lie;
       The world, it was the old world yet,
40   I was I, my things were wet,
       And nothing now remained to do
       But begin the game anew.

       Therefore, since the world has still
       Much good, but much less good than ill,
45   And while the sun and moon endure
       Luck's a chance, but trouble's sure,
       I'd face it as a wise man would,
       And train for ill and not for good.
       'Tis true, the stuff I bring for sale
50   Is not so brisk a brew as ale:
       Out of a stem that scored the hand
       I wrung it in a weary land.
       But take it: if the smack is sour,
       The better for the embittered hour;

---

[1] A town noted for its breweries.

55 It should do good to heart and head
     When your soul is in my soul's stead;
     And I will friend you, if I may,
     In the dark and cloudy day.

        There was a king reigned in the East:
60 There, when kings will sit to feast,
     They get their fill before they think
     With poisoned meat and poisoned drink.
     He gathered all that springs to birth
     From the many-venomed earth;
65 First a little, thence to more,
     He sampled all her killing store;
     And easy, smiling, seasoned sound,
     Sate the king when healths went round.
     They put arsenic in his meat
70 And stared aghast to watch him eat;
     They poured strychnine in his cup
     And shook to see him drink it up:
     They shook, they stared as white's their shirt:
     Them it was their poison hurt.
75 —I tell the tale that I heard told.
     Mithridates,[2] he died old.

A. E. HOUSMAN (1859–1936)

To an Athlete Dying Young

The time you won your town the race
We chaired you through the market-place;
Man and boy stood cheering by,
And home we brought you shoulder-high.

5 To-day, the road all runners come,
    Shoulder-high we bring you home,
    And set you at your threshold down,
    Townsman of a stiller town.

    Smart lad, to slip betimes away
10 From fields where glory does not stay
    And early though the laurel grows
    It withers quicker than the rose.

---

[2] King of Pontus in the first century B.C., who made himself immune to certain
poisons by taking them frequently in small doses.

Eyes the shady night has shut
Cannot see the record cut,
15 And silence sounds no worse than cheers
After earth has stopped the ears:

Now you will not swell the rout
Of lads that wore their honors out,
Runners whom renown outran
20 And the name died before the man.

So set, before its echoes fade,
The fleet foot on the sill of shade,
And hold to the low lintel up
The still-defended challenge-cup.

25 And round that early-laurelled head
Will flock to gaze the strengthless dead,
And find unwithered on its curls
The garland briefer than a girl's.

EDWIN ARLINGTON ROBINSON (1869–1935)

Mr. Flood's Party

Old Eben Flood, climbing alone one night
Over the hill between the town below
And the forsaken upland hermitage
That held as much as he should ever know
5 On earth again of home, paused warily.
The road was his with not a native near;
And Eben, having leisure, said aloud,
For no man else in Tilbury Town to hear:

"Well, Mr. Flood, we have the harvest moon
10 Again, and we may not have many more;
The bird is on the wing, the poet says,[1]
And you and I have said it here before.
Drink to the bird." He raised up to the light
The jug that he had gone so far to fill,
15 And answered huskily: "Well, Mr. Flood,
Since you propose it, I believe I will."

---

[1] A reference to stanza 7 of *The Rubáiyát of Omar Khayyám.*

Alone, as if enduring to the end
A valiant armor of scarred hopes outworn,
He stood there in the middle of the road
20 Like Roland's ghost winding a silent horn.[2]
Below him, in the town among the trees,
Where friends of other days had honored him,
A phantom salutation of the dead
Rang thinly till old Eben's eyes were dim.

25 Then, as a mother lays her sleeping child
Down tenderly, fearing it may awake,
He set the jug down slowly at his feet
With trembling care, knowing that most things break;
And only when assured that on firm earth
30 It stood, as the uncertain lives of men
Assuredly did not, he paced away,
And with his hand extended paused again:

"Well, Mr. Flood, we have not met like this
In a long time; and many a change has come
35 To both of us, I fear, since last it was
We had a drop together. Welcome home!"
Convivially returning with himself,
Again he raised the jug up to the light;
And with an acquiescent quaver said:
40 "Well, Mr. Flood, if you insist, I might.

"Only a very little, Mr. Flood—
For auld lang syne. No more, sir; that will do."
So, for the time, apparently it did,
And Eben evidently thought so too;
45 For soon amid the silver loneliness
Of night he lifted up his voice and sang,
Secure, with only two moons listening,
Until the whole harmonious landscape rang—

"For auld lang syne." The weary throat gave out,
50 The last word wavered; and the song being done,
He raised again the jug regretfully

---

[2] In the medieval *Song of Roland,* the hero refuses to blow his horn for help at
the Battle of Roncevaux and loses his life.

And shook his head, and was again alone.
There was not much that was ahead of him,
And there was nothing in the town below—
55 Where strangers would have shut the many doors
That many friends had opened long ago.

JAMES WELDON JOHNSON (1871–1938)

O Black and Unknown Bards

O black and unknown bards of long ago,
How came your lips to touch the sacred fire?
How, in your darkness, did you come to know
The power and beauty of the minstrel's lyre?
5 Who first from midst his bonds lifted his eyes?
Who first from out the still watch, lone and long,
Feeling the ancient faith of prophets rise
Within his dark-kept soul, burst into song?

Heart of what slave poured out such melody
10 As "Steal away to Jesus"? On its strains
His spirit must have nightly floated free,
Though still about his hands he felt his chains.
Who heard great "Jordan roll"? Whose starward eye
Saw chariot "swing low"? And who was he
15 That breathed that comforting, melodic sigh,
"Nobody knows de trouble I see"?

What merely living clod, what captive thing,
Could up toward God through all its darkness grope,
And find within its deadened heart to sing
20 These songs of sorrow, love and faith, and hope?
How did it catch that subtle undertone,
That note in music heard not with the ears?
How sound the elusive reed so seldom blown,
Which stirs the soul or melts the heart to tears?

25 Not that great German master[1] in his dream
Of harmonies that thundered amongst the stars
At the creation, ever heard a theme
Nobler than "Go down, Moses." Mark its bars,

---

[1] Beethoven.

How like a mighty trumpet-call they stir
30 The blood. Such are the notes that men have sung
Going to valorous deeds; such tones there were
That helped make history when Time was young.

There is a wide, wide wonder in it all,
That from degraded rest and servile toil
35 The fiery spirit of the seer should call
These simple children of the sun and soil.

O black slave singers, gone, forgot, unfamed,
You—you alone, of all the long, long line
Of those who've sung untaught, unknown, unnamed,
40 Have stretched out upward, seeking the divine.

You sang not deeds of heroes or of kings;
No chant of bloody war, no exulting paean
Of arms-won triumphs; but your humble strings
You touched in chord with music empyrean.
45 You sang far better than you knew; the songs
That for your listeners' hungry hearts sufficed
Still live—but more than this to you belongs:
You sang a race from wood and stone to Christ.

ROBERT FROST (1874–1963)

"Out, Out—" [1]

The buzz-saw snarled and rattled in the yard
And made dust and dropped stove-length sticks of wood,
Sweet-scented stuff when the breeze drew across it.
And from there those that lifted eyes could count
5 Five mountain ranges one behind the other
Under the sunset far into Vermont.
And the saw snarled and rattled, snarled and rattled,
As it ran light, or had to bear a load.
And nothing happened: day was all but done.
10 Call it a day, I wish they might have said
To please the boy by giving him the half hour
That a boy counts so much when saved from work.
His sister stood beside them in her apron

---

[1] An allusion to *Macbeth*, Act 5, Scene 5.

To tell them "Supper." At the word, the saw,
15 As if to prove saws knew what supper meant,
Leaped out at the boy's hand, or seemed to leap—
He must have given the hand. However it was,
Neither refused the meeting. But the hand!
The boy's first outcry was a rueful laugh,
20 As he swung toward them holding up the hand
Half in appeal, but half as if to keep
The life from spilling. Then the boy saw all—
Since he was old enough to know, big boy
Doing a man's work, though a child at heart—
25 He saw all spoiled. "Don't let him cut my hand off—
The doctor, when he comes. Don't let him, sister!"

So. But the hand was gone already.
The doctor put him in the dark of ether.
He lay and puffed his lips out with his breath.
30 And then—the watcher at his pulse took fright.
No one believed. They listened at his heart.
Little—less—nothing!—and that ended it.
No more to build on there. And they, since they
Were not the one dead, turned to their affairs.

WALLACE STEVENS (1879–1955)

Thirteen Ways of Looking at a Blackbird

I

Among twenty snowy mountains,
The only moving thing
Was the eye of the blackbird.

II

I was of three minds,
5 Like a tree
In which there are three blackbirds.

III

The blackbird whirled in the autumn winds.
It was a small part of the pantomime.

IV

A man and a woman
10 Are one.
A man and a woman and a blackbird
Are one.

V

I do not know which to prefer,
The beauty of inflections,
15 Or the beauty of innuendoes,
The blackbird whistling
Or just after.

VI

Icicles filled the long window
With barbaric glass.
20 The shadow of the blackbird
Crossed it, to and fro.
The mood
Traced in the shadow
An indecipherable cause.

VII

25 O thin men of Haddam,[1]
Why do you imagine golden birds?
Do you not see how the blackbird
Walks around the feet
Of the women about you?

VIII

30 I know noble accents
And lucid, inescapable rhythms;
But I know, too,
That the blackbird is involved
In what I know.

IX

35 When the blackbird flew out of sight
It marked the edge
Of one of many circles.

---

[1] A town in Connecticut; Stevens liked its name.

X

At the sight of blackbirds
Flying in a green light,
40 Even the bawds of euphony
Would cry out sharply.

XI

He rode over Connecticut
In a glass coach.
Once, a fear pierced him,
45 In that he mistook
The shadow of his equipage
For blackbirds.

XII

The river is moving.
The blackbird must be flying.

XIII

50 It was evening all afternoon.
It was snowing
And it was going to snow.
The blackbird sat
In the cedar-limbs.

ROBINSON JEFFERS (1887–1962)

Love the Wild Swan

"I hate my verses, every line, every word.
Oh pale and brittle pencils ever to try
One grass-blade's curve, or the throat of one bird
That clings to twig, ruffled against white sky.
5 Oh cracked and twilight mirrors ever to catch
One color, one glinting flash, of the splendor of things.
Unlucky hunter, Oh bullets of wax,
The lion beauty, the wild-swan wings, the storm of the wings."
—This wild swan of a world is no hunter's game.
10 Better bullets than yours would miss the white breast,
Better mirrors than yours would crack in the flame.
Does it matter whether you hate your . . . self? At least
Love your eyes that can see, your mind that can
Hear the music, the thunder of the wings. Love the wild swan.

MARIANNE MOORE (1887–1972)

Poetry

I, too, dislike it: there are things that are important beyond all this
        fiddle.
   Reading it, however, with a perfect contempt for it, one discovers
        in
   it after all, a place for the genuine.
        Hands that can grasp, eyes
5   that can dilate, hair that can rise
           if it must, there things are important not because a

high-sounding interpretation can be put upon them but because they
        are
useful. When they become so derivative as to become unintelligble,
   the same thing may be said for all of us, that we
10   do not admire what
        we cannot understand: the bat
           holding on upside down or in quest of something to

eat, elephants pushing, a wild horse taking a roll, a tireless wolf
        under
   a tree, the immovable critic twitching his skin like a horse that
        feels a flea, the base-
15   ball fan, the statistician—
        nor is it valid
           to discriminate against "business documents and

school-books";[1] all these phenomena are important. One must make
        a distinction
however: when dragged into prominence by half poets, the result
        is not poetry,
20   nor till the poets among us can be
        "literalists of
        the imagination" [2]—above
           insolence and triviality and can present

for inspection, "imaginary gardens with real toads in them," shall we
        have
25   it. In the meantime, if you demand on the one hand,

---

[1] Moore's note cites the Diary of Tolstoy: "poetry is everything with the exception
of business documents and school books."
[2] From Yeats, *Ideas of Good and Evil.*

the raw material of poetry in
  all its rawness and
    that which is on the other hand
      genuine, you are interested in poetry.

JOHN CROWE RANSOM (1888–1974)

Bells for John Whiteside's Daughter

There was such speed in her little body,
And such lightness in her footfall,
It is no wonder her brown study
Astonishes us all.

5 Her wars were bruited in our high window.
We looked among orchard trees and beyond
Where she took arms against her shadow,
Or harried unto the pond

The lazy geese, like a snow cloud
10 Dripping their snow on the green grass,
Tricking and stopping, sleepy and proud,
Who cried in goose, Alas,

For the tireless heart within the little
Lady with rod that made them rise
15 From their noon apple-dreams and scuttle
Goose-fashion under the skies!

But now go the bells, and we are ready,
In one house we are sternly stopped
To say we are vexed at her brown study,
20 Lying so primly propped.

T. S. ELIOT (1888–1965)

The Love Song of J. Alfred Prufrock

S'io credesse che mia risposta fosse
A persona che mai tornasse al mondo,
Questa fiamma staria senza piu scosse.
Ma perciocche giammai di questo fondo

Non torno vivo alcun, s'i'odo il vero,
Senza tema d'infamia ti rispondo.[1]

Let us go then, you and I,
When the evening is spread out against the sky
Like a patient etherized upon a table;
Let us go, through certain half-deserted streets,
5 The muttering retreats
Of restless nights in one-night cheap hotels
And sawdust restaurants with oyster-shells:
Streets that follow like a tedious argument
Of insidious intent
10 To lead you to an overwhelming question . . .

Oh, do not ask, "What is it?"
Let us go and make our visit.

In the room the women come and go
Talking of Michelangelo.

15 The yellow fog that rubs its back upon the window-panes
The yellow smoke that rubs its muzzle on the window-panes
Licked its tongue into the corners of the evening,
Lingered upon the pools that stand in drains,
Let fall upon its back the soot that falls from chimneys,
20 Slipped by the terrace, made a sudden leap,
And seeing that it was a soft October night,
Curled once about the house, and fell asleep.

And indeed there will be time
For the yellow smoke that slides along the street,
25 Rubbing its back upon the window-panes;
There will be time, there will be time
To prepare a face to meet the faces that you meet;
There will be time to murder and create,
And time for all the works and days of hands
30 That lift and drop a question on your plate;
Time for you and time for me,

---

[1] "If I thought that my response were given to one who would ever return to the world, this flame would move no more. But since never from this depth has man returned alive, if what I hear is true, without fear of infamy I answer thee." In Dante's *Inferno* these words are addressed to the poet by the spirit of Guido da Montefeltro.

And time yet for a hundred indecisions,
And for a hundred visions and revisions,
Before the taking of a toast and tea.

35 In the room the women come and go
Talking of Michelangelo.

And indeed there will be time
To wonder, "Do I dare?" and, "Do I dare?"
Time to turn back and descend the stair,
40 With a bald spot in the middle of my hair—
[They will say: "How his hair is growing thin!"]
My morning coat, my collar mounting firmly to the chin,
My necktie rich and modest, but asserted by a simple pin—
[They will say: "But how his arms and legs are thin!"]
45 Do I dare
Disturb the universe?
In a minute there is time
For decisions and revisions which a minute will reverse.

For I have known them all already, known them all:
50 Have known the evenings, mornings, afternoons,
I have measured out my life with coffee spoons;
I know the voices dying with a dying fall
Beneath the music from a farther room.
    So how should I presume?

55 And I have known the eyes already, known them all—
The eyes that fix you in a formulated phrase,
And when I am formulated, sprawling on a pin,
When I am pinned and wriggling on the wall,
Then how should I begin
60 To spit out all the butt-ends of my days and ways?
    And how should I presume?

And I have known the arms already, known them all—
Arms that are braceleted and white and bare
[But in the lamplight, downed with light brown hair!]
65 Is it perfume from a dress
That makes me so digress?
Arms that lie along a table, or wrap about a shawl.
    And should I then presume?
    And how should I begin?

                    .   .   .   .   .

70 Shall I say, I have gone at dusk through narrow streets
And watched the smoke that rises from the pipes
Of lonely men in shirt-sleeves, leaning out of windows? . . .

I should have been a pair of ragged claws
Scuttling across the floors of silent seas.

. . . . .

75 And the afternoon, the evening, sleeps so peacefully!
Smoothed by long fingers,
Asleep . . . tired . . . or it malingers,
Stretched on the floor, here beside you and me.
Should I, after tea and cakes and ices,
80 Have the strength to force the moment to its crisis?
But though I have wept and fasted, wept and prayed,
Though I have seen my head [grown slightly bald] brought in upon a
platter,
I am no prophet—and here's no great matter;
I have seen the moment of my greatness flicker,
85 And I have seen the eternal Footman hold my coat, and snicker,
And in short, I was afraid.

And would it have been worth it, after all,
After the cups, the marmalade, the tea,
Among the porcelain, among some talk of you and me,
90 Would it have been worth while,
To have bitten off the matter with a smile,
To have squeezed the universe into a ball
To roll it toward some overwhelming question,

To say: "I am Lazarus, come from the dead,
95 Come back to tell you all, I shall tell you all"—
If one, settling a pillow by her head,
Should say: "That is not what I meant at all.
That is not it, at all."

And would it have been worth it, after all,
100 Would it have been worth while,
After the sunsets and the dooryards and the sprinkled streets,
After the novels, after the teacups, after the skirts that trail along the
floor—
And this, and so much more?—
It is impossible to say just what I mean!
105 But as if a magic lantern threw the nerves in patterns on a screen:
Would it have been worth while
If one, settling a pillow or throwing off a shawl,
And turning toward the window, should say:

"That is not it at all,
110   That is not what I meant, at all."

. . . . .

No! I am not Prince Hamlet, nor was meant to be;
Am an attendant lord, one that will do
To swell a progress, start a scene or two,
Advise the prince; no doubt, an easy tool,
115 Deferential, glad to be of use,
Politic, cautious, and meticulous;
Full of high sentence, but a bit obtuse;
At times, indeed, almost ridiculous—
Almost, at times, the Fool.

120 I grow old . . . I grow old . . .
I shall wear the bottoms of my trousers rolled.

Shall I part my hair behind? Do I dare to eat a peach?
I shall wear white flannel trousers, and walk upon the beach.
I have heard the mermaids singing, each to each.

125 I do not think that they will sing to me.

I have seen them riding seaward on the waves
Combing the white hair of the waves blown back
When the wind blows the water white and black.

We have lingered in the chambers of the sea
130 By sea-girls wreathed with seaweed red and brown
Till human voices wake us, and we drown.

ARCHIBALD MacLEISH   (1892–1982)

Ars Poetica

A poem should be palpable and mute
As a globed fruit,

Dumb
As old medallions to the thumb,

5 Silent as the sleeve-worn stone
Of casement ledges where the moss has grown—

A poem should be wordless
As the flight of birds.

A poem should be motionless in time
10 As the moon climbs,

Leaving, as the moon releases
Twig by twig the night-entangled trees,

Leaving, as the moon behind the winter leaves
Memory by memory the mind—

15 A poem should be motionless in time
As the moon climbs.

A poem should be equal to:
Not true.

For all the history of grief
20 An empty doorway and a maple leaf.

For love
The leaning grasses and two lights above the sea—

A poem should not mean
But be.

DOROTHY PARKER (1893–1967)

Résumé

Razors pain you;
Rivers are damp;
Acids stain you;
And drugs cause cramp.
5 Guns aren't lawful;
Nooses give;
Gas smells awful;
You might as well live.

E. E. CUMMINGS (1894–1963)

"next to of course god america i

"next to of course god america i
love you land of the pilgrims' and so forth oh
say can you see by the dawn's early my

country 'tis of centuries come and go
5 and are no more what of it we should worry
in every language even deafanddumb
thy sons acclaim your glorious name by gorry
by jingo by gee by gosh by gum
why talk of beauty what could be more beaut-
10 iful than these heroic happy dead
who rushed like lions to the roaring slaughter
they did not stop to think they died instead
then shall the voice of liberty be mute?"

He spoke. And drank rapidly a glass of water

W. H. AUDEN (1907–1973)

Musée des Beaux Arts[1]

About suffering they were never wrong,
The Old Masters: how well they understood
Its human position; how it takes place
While someone else is eating or opening a window or just walking
    dully along;
5 How, when the aged are reverently, passionately waiting
For the miraculous birth, there always must be
Children who did not specially want it to happen, skating
On a pond at the edge of the wood:
They never forgot
10 That even the dreadful martyrdom must run its course
Anyhow in a corner, some untidy spot
Where the dogs go on with their doggy life and the torturer's horse
Scratches its innocent behind on a tree.

In Brueghel's *Icarus*,[2] for instance: how everything turns away
15 Quite leisurely from the disaster; the plowman may
Have heard the splash, the forsaken cry,
But for him it was not an important failure; the sun shone
As it had to on the white legs disappearing into the green
Water; and the expensive delicate ship that must have seen

---

[1] The Museum of Fine Arts in Brussels, where Brueghel's *Landscape with the Fall of Icarus* hangs.
[2] In Greek mythology Icarus falls into the sea and drowns when he flies too close to the sun on his wings of wax. In Brueghel's painting Icarus is an insignificant part of the picture.

20 Something amazing, a boy falling out of the sky,
Had somewhere to get to and sailed calmly on.

DYLAN THOMAS (1914–1953)

In My Craft or Sullen Art

In my craft or sullen art
Exercised in the still night
When only the moon rages
And the lovers lie abed
5 With all their griefs in their arms,
I labor by singing light
Not for ambition or bread
Or the strut and trade of charms
On the ivory stages
10 But for the common wages
Of their most secret heart.

Not for the proud man apart
From the raging moon I write
On these spindrift pages
15 Nor for the towering dead
With their nightingales and psalms
But for the lovers, their arms
Round the griefs of the ages,
Who pay no praise or wages
20 Nor heed my craft or art.

GWENDOLYN BROOKS (1917–   )

The Bean Eaters

They eat beans mostly, this old yellow pair .
Dinner is a casual affair.
Plain chipware on a plain and creaking wood,
Tin flatware.

5 Two who are Mostly Good.
Two who have lived their day,
But keep on putting on their clothes
And putting things away.

And remembering . . .
10 Remembering, with twinklings and twinges,
   As they lean over the beans in their rented back room that is full of
      beads and receipts and dolls and clothes, tobacco crumbs, vases
      and fringes.

ROBERT LOWELL (1917–1977)

For the Union Dead

"Relinquunt Omnia Servare Rem Publican."[1]

The old South Boston Aquarium stands
in a Sahara of snow now. Its broken windows are boarded.
The bronze weathervane cod has lost half its scales.
The airy tanks are dry.

5 Once my nose crawled like a snail on the glass;
my hand tingled
to burst the bubbles
drifting from the noses of the cowed, compliant fish.

My hand draws back. I often sigh still
10 for the dark downward and vegetating kingdom
of the fish and reptile. One morning last March,
I pressed against the new barbed and galvanized

fence on the Boston Common. Behind their cage,
yellow dinosaur steamshovels were grunting
15 as they cropped up tons of mush and grass
to gouge their underworld garage.

Parking spaces luxuriate like civic
sandpiles in the heart of Boston.
A girdle of orange, Puritan-pumpkin colored girders
20 braces the tingling Statehouse,

shaking over the excavations, as it faces Colonel Shaw
and his bell-cheeked Negro infantry
on St. Gaudens' shaking Civil War relief,
propped by a plank splint against the garage's earthquake.

---

1 "They gave up all to serve the republic."

25 Two months after marching through Boston,
    half the regiment was dead;
    at the dedication,
    William James could almost hear the bronze Negroes breathe.

    Their monument sticks like a fishbone
30 in the city's throat.
    Its Colonel is as lean
    as a compass-needle.

    He has an angry wrenlike vigilance,
    a greyhound's gentle tautness;
35 he seems to wince at pleasure,
    and suffocate for privacy.

    He is out of bounds now. He rejoices in man's lovely,
    peculiar power to choose life and die—
    when he leads his black soldiers to death,
40 he cannot bend his back.

    On a thousand small town New England greens,
    the old white churches hold their air
    of sparse, sincere rebellion; frayed flags
    quilt the graveyards of the Grand Army of the Republic.

45 The stone statues of the abstract Union Soldier
    grow slimmer and younger each year—
    wasp-waisted, they doze over muskets
    and muse through their sideburns . . .

    Shaw's father wanted no monument
50 except the ditch,
    where his son's body was thrown
    and lost with his "niggers."

    The ditch is nearer.
    There are no statues for the last war here;
55 on Boylston Street, a commercial photograph
    shows Hiroshima boiling

    over a Mosler Safe, the "Rock of Ages"
    that survived the blast. Space is nearer.
    When I crouch to my television set,
60 the drained faces of Negro school-children rise like balloons.

Colonel Shaw
is riding on his bubble,
he waits
for the blessèd break.

65 The Aquarium is gone. Everywhere,
giant finned cars nose forward like fish;
a savage servility
slides by on grease.

LAWRENCE FERLINGHETTI (1919–   )

The pennycandystore beyond the El

The pennycandystore beyond the El
is where I first
                    fell in love
                            with unreality
5 Jellybeans glowed in the semi-gloom
of that september afternoon
A cat upon the counter moved among
                            the licorice sticks
                    and tootsie rolls
10   and Oh Boy Gum

Outside the leaves were falling as they died

A wind had blown away the sun
A girl ran in
Her hair was rainy
15 Her breasts were breathless in the little room

Outside the leaves were falling
                    and they cried
                            Too soon! too soon!

RICHARD WILBUR (1921–   )

Place Pigalle

Now homing tradesmen scatter through the streets
Toward suppers, thinking on improved conditions,
While evening, with a million simple fissions,
Takes up its warehouse watches, storefront beats,
5 By nursery windows its assigned positions.

Now at the corners of the Place Pigalle
Bright bars explode against the dark's embraces;
The soldiers come, the boys with ancient faces.
Seeking their ancient friends, who stroll and loll
10 Amid the glares and glass: electric graces.

The puppies are asleep, and snore the hounds;
But here wry hares, the soldier and the whore,
Mark off their refuge with a gaudy door,
Brazen at bay, and boldly out of bounds:
15 The puppies dream, the hounds superbly snore.

Ionized innocence: this pair reclines,
She on the table, he in a tilting chair,
With Arden ease; her eyes as pale as air
Travel his priestgoat face; his hand's thick tines
20 Touch the gold whorls of her Corinthian hair.

"Girl, if I love thee not, then let me die;
Do I not scorn to change my state with kings?
Your muchtouched flesh, incalculable, which wrings
Me so, now shall I gently seize in my
25 Desperate soldier's hands which kill all things."

ALLEN GINSBERG (1926–   )

A Supermarket in California

What thoughts I have of you tonight, Walt Whitman, for I
walked down the sidestreets under the trees with a headache self-
conscious looking at the full moon.

In my hungry fatigue, and shopping for images, I went into the
neon fruit supermarket, dreaming of your enumerations!

What peaches and what penumbras! Whole families shopping at
night! Aisles full of husbands! Wives in the avocados, babies in the
tomatoes!—and you, Garcia Lorca,[1] what were you doing down by
the watermelons?

I saw you, Walt Whitman, childless, lonely old grubber, poking
among the meats in the refrigerator and eyeing the grocery boys.

---

[1] Federico García Lorca (1899–1936), Spanish poet and playwright. He was murdered at the start of the Spanish Civil War; his works were suppressed by the
Franco government.

5   I heard you asking questions of each: Who killed the pork chops? What price bananas? Are you my Angel?

I wandered in and out of the brilliant stacks of cans following you, and followed in my imagination by the store detective.

We strode down the open corridors together in our solitary fancy tasting artichokes, possessing every frozen delicacy, and never passing the cashier.

Where are we going, Walt Whitman? The doors close in an hour. Which way does your beard point tonight?

(I touch your book and dream of our odyssey in the supermarket and feel absurd.)

10   Will we walk all night through solitary streets? The trees add shade to shade, lights out in the houses, we'll both be lonely.

Will we stroll dreaming of the lost America of love past blue automobiles in driveways, home to our silent cottage?

Ah, dear father, graybeard, lonely old courage-teacher, what America did you have when Charon quit poling his ferry and you got out on a smoking bank and stood watching the boat disappear on the black waters of Lethe?[2]

ANNE SEXTON (1928–1974)

Her Kind

I have gone out, a possessed witch,
haunting the black air, braver at night;
dreaming evil, I have done my hitch
over the plain houses, light by light:
5 lonely thing, twelve-fingered, out of mind.
A woman like that is not a woman, quite.
I have been her kind.

I have found the warm caves in the woods,
filled them with skillets, carvings, shelves,
10 closets, silks, innumerable goods;
fixed the suppers for the worms and the elves:
whining, rearranging the disaligned.
A woman like that is misunderstood.
I have been her kind.

---

[2] Charon, in Greek myth, ferried the shades of the dead to Hades across Lethe, River of Forgetfulness.

15 I have ridden in your cart, driver,
    waved my nude arms at villages going by,
    learning the last bright routes, survivor
    where your flames still bite my thigh
    and my ribs crack where your wheels wind.
20 A woman like that is not ashamed to die.
    I have been her kind.

TED HUGHES (1930–   )

Pike

Pike, three inches long, perfect
Pike in all parts, green tigering the gold.
Killers from the egg: the malevolent aged grin.
They dance on the surface among the flies.

 5 Or move, stunned by their own grandeur,
    Over a bed of emerald, silhouette
    Of submarine delicacy and horror.
    A hundred feet long in their world.

    In ponds, under the heat-struck lily pads—
10 Gloom of their stillness:
    Logged on last year's black leaves, watching upwards.
    Or hung in an amber cavern of weeds

    The jaw's hooked clamp and fangs
    Not to be changed at this date;
15 A life subdued to its instrument;
    The gills kneading quietly, and the pectorals.

    Three we kept behind glass,
    Jungled in weed: three inches, four,
    And four and a half: fed fry to them—
20 Suddenly there were two. Finally one

    With a sag belly and the grin it was born with.
    And indeed they spare nobody.
    Two, six pounds each, over two feet long,
    High and dry and dead in the willow-herb—

25 One jammed past its gills down the other's gullet:
    The outside eye stared: as a vice locks—
    The same iron in this eye
    Though its film shrank in death.

A pond I fished, fifty yards across,
30 Whose lilies and muscular tench
Had outlasted every visible stone
Of the monastery that planted them—

Stilled legendary depth:
It was as deep as England. It held
35 Pike too immense to stir, so immense and old
That past nightfall I dared not cast

But silently cast and fished
With the hair frozen on my head
For what might move, for what eye might move.
40 The still splashes on the dark pond,

Owls hushing the floating woods
Frail on my ear against the dream
Darkness beneath night's darkness had freed,
That rose slowly towards me, watching.

SYLVIA PLATH (1932–1963)

Metaphors

I'm a riddle in nine syllables,
An elephant, a ponderous house,
A melon strolling on two tendrils.
O red fruit, ivory, fine timbers!
5 This loaf's big with its yeasty rising.
Money's new-minted in this fat purse.
I'm a means, a stage, a cow in calf.
I've eaten a bag of green apples,
Boarded the train there's no getting off.

AMIRI BARAKA (LeROI JONES) (1934–   )

W.W.

Back home the black women are all beautiful,
and the white ones fall back, cutoff from 1000
years stacked booty, and Charles of the Ritz
where jooshladies turn into billy burke in blueglass
5 kicks. With wings, and jingly bew-teeful things.
The black women in Newark are fine. Even with all that grease

in their heads. I mean even the ones where the wigs
slide around, and they coming at you 75 degrees off course.
I could talk to them. Bring them around. To something.
10 Some kind of quick course, on the sidewalk, like Hey baby
why don't you take that thing off yo' haid. You look like
Miss Muffet in a runaway ugly machine. I mean. Like that.

READING AND WRITING ABOUT DRAMA

1 Reading and Writing About Drama

Analyzing Greek drama around 330 B.C., the philosopher Aristotle found each play to be composed of six parts: plot, character, thought, diction, spectacle, and music. Of these, he considered the plot—the putting together of diverse happenings to create a complete and unified action—to be the most important. Without plot, he says, there can be no play; for the chief purpose of drama is the acting-out of an action.

Characters come next in importance for Aristotle. Thought—by which he seems to mean not only the ideas expressed by the various speakers, but also their use of speech to sway the emotions of the audience—comes third. Diction, the choice of words, is fourth. Music and scenery, being pleasant and often impressive, but not essential, come last.

With the exception of music and spectacle, which apply only to plays in performance, Aristotle's categories are essentially the same categories we've been using in discussing fiction. The further we read in Aristotle, the more similarities we find: Aristotle warns would-be authors that their plots, to be complete, must have a natural beginning, middle, and end; that they must provide scope for their heroes to pass from happiness to unhappiness, or from unhappiness to happiness; and that they must be unified, containing nothing that could be taken away without leaving the drama incomplete.

In addition, Aristotle points out that the most important moments in the plot are those concerned with **reversals** and **recognition**. A reversal occurs when an action that is expected to have one result produces the opposite result instead. A recognition occurs when a character suddenly "recognizes" some fact or person, thus moving from a state of ignorance to a state of knowledge. In the best plays, the two events are joined and form the turning point of the play: the hero suddenly learns something of great personal importance, either by being informed of some facts by another character or by coming to a realization or insight himself. In either case, the result of the hero's enlightenment is a reversal, changing the course of the play's action and of the hero's life (from happiness to unhappiness or vice versa).

In discussing characterization Aristotle reminds us that all characters must be people basically like ourselves, though some may be better and some worse. And again, he insists that consistency and probability are the two most important standards of judgment. The writer must make sure that the characters' actions are consistent with their natures, and that their natures remain consistent throughout the drama.

If we have not already discussed all of these ideas, at least we have no difficulty in applying them to the fiction we've read. To discuss consistency of character, for instance, we could look at any number of characters—at the narrator of "Bartleby the Scrivener," for example, with his deep and basically kindly desire for tranquility in human relations and his persistent and misplaced faith in money as a means of attaining that tranquility. These are consistently drawn characters. Given their natures and situations created by their authors, they have no chance of escaping their fate.*

The basic elements of drama, then, are the same as those of fiction. It is the method of presentation that differs.

Fiction is the telling of tales. Its roots go back to the archetypal figure of the storyteller, rehearsing old legends and inventing new marvels for the listeners who surround him. The importance of voice in fiction, therefore, can hardly be overemphasized. One use of voice is evident in the many tales in which the narrative voice is that of the storyteller: tales such as those by Faulkner and O'Connor. Another use can be seen in works such as Barthelme's that begin in a storytelling voice but then move beyond that voice to more direct (if occasionally less coherent) appeals to the reader, asking the reader to join the narrator in considering what speech, writing, or storytelling implies.

---

* Two other Aristotelian concepts are illustrated here as well. One is the movement from happiness to unhappiness: both characters are happier when their tales begin than when they end. The second concept is that of inevitability.

As fiction has become a more silent experience, writers seem to have attached increasing importance to the question of what voice would speak through their works. Listening to stories is still enjoyable. Any good story can be read aloud and be enjoyed the better for it. But our society seems to feel that listening to tales is a pleasure most proper for children and for those who cannot read to themselves. For most of us, therefore, fiction is something read silently and alone. It involves one book, one writer, one reader. We discuss stories in company, but we tend to read them in solitude.

Drama—in performance, at least—is wholly different. It is not written for one voice, but for many. It depends not on storytellers but on actors, men and women who impersonate their tale's characters not only in voice, but also in motion, gesture, and appearance, making them live for our eyes as well as our ears. Moreover, it is written for many viewers, for only in the midst of an audience can we appreciate fully the magic of drama. Laughing alone at a joke in print is enjoyable; being one laughing person among a hundred people can be hilarious.

Actors know this well. They know how fully they must bring their characters alive for their audience. They know, too, how dependent they are on the audience's response if they are to perform well. Many actors have declared that the best performances are those during which the emotions portrayed on stage are caught and sent back by the audience until audience and actors alike are caught up in the atmosphere they have created between them, and the illusion of the play becomes more real than the realities of the world outside. Similarly, many have said that acting in films, where no audience is present to reflect the emotional impact of the scene, is a more difficult and less enjoyable form of acting than acting on the stage. Playgoers and filmgoers, in their turn, agree that the experience of attending a live performance has an electric quality not to be found in viewing a film.

The fervor with which most of us discuss a really good play or film we've just seen, as opposed to the milder delight with which we discuss a really good book, testifies to the power of drama to move and delight us. A knowledge of the origins of drama, about which we shall speak in the next chapter, may help explain the intensity of our response. Within this course, however, we are readers rather than viewers of drama. And so the very power of drama in performance is likely to raise questions for us. "Here we are," we say, "with no stage, no actors—nothing but a playscript in front of us. What can we expect from this experience?"

Reading drama is certainly different from reading fiction. Drama gives us no narrator to describe scenes and characters, to comment on the significance of the action, to tie scenes together, or to provide a unifying viewpoint. Instead, drama gives us several characters, distinguished in the text only by their names, talking mostly to each other instead of to us, intent on their own affairs, entering and leaving the scene in bewildering succession.

If we were watching a play, we would recognize the characters by their appearance, mannerisms, and voices. Knowing the characters, we would then find it easy to follow the action. When we read a play, however, we must do without these visual clues. Or, rather, we must supply them for ourselves. We must use the text as the play's director would, judging from its words and from the actions they describe how the play would look and sound on stage.

Reading plays, in fact, gives our imagination free rein. How would I stage this scene? What sort of actor would I want for this role? What kind of stage setting would I use? Or, what kind of camera work would I use in a film? Which would be my long shots, which my close-ups? What emotions would my filming be trying to capture?

Most of all, perhaps, you will think of the various characters as they are revealed in the text. What characteristics will each one exhibit? How will they carry themselves on stage? What tones of voice will they use in their speeches? How will they act toward each other?* The more clearly you can visualize the play's action and characters, the more readily the text will come alive for you.

Don't be afraid to experiment in your thinking. Actors, directors, and scene designers all allow themselves some freedom of interpretation when they put on a play. You can read for days about famous actors who have played Hamlet, each applying a very personal interpretation to emphasize one aspect or another of the prince's complex personality. Why should not we, as readers, enjoy the same freedom to visualize the play, inter-preting and fitting together its parts to develop our vision of its conflicts and its meanings?

Writing for Discovery and Understanding

The term *playwright* suggests that one who writes plays is a craftsman, like a shipwright or wheelwright. Dramatists *construct* their plays, working with certain materials and expectations, trying to anticipate the needs of their audiences. Unlike other kinds of writing, dramas are fully realized when they are performed before an audience. Seldom do fiction writers or poets get to watch their work take shape before an actual audience. From Sopho-cles and Aeschylus to Sam Shepard and Alice Walker, however, dramatists participate in preparing the play for its performance and then can sit in the audience (or in the wings or the lobby) when the play goes on.

The elements of the dramatist's craft offer many possibilities for writing about plays. Here are some suggestions.

---

* A handy device for keeping track of a play's characters, in fact, is to "cast" the play for yourself with actors you'd enjoy watching in it. Then you can follow those actors through each scene, imagining how they would interpret the roles.

1. *Write about character and characterization.* At the heart of the playwright's art is the ability to create people who are believable. As a prewriting activity, write character descriptions for several of the characters in the play. Include such items as what they say about themselves, what they say about one another, what the playwright may say about them in stage directions and descriptions.

Consider, too, what type of characters they are. Hamlet and Antigonê, for example, are *heroic* figures, while Willie Loman, the main character in *Death of a Salesman,* is often considered as a model of the modern *anti-hero.* In your description of such figures, describe the attributes that make them what they are. Some characters are more fully realized than others. Hamlet, Antigonê, Nora, and Willie Loman, to name a few, are *rounded* characters, meaning they have depth—there are many sides to their personalities. Other figures in the plays may be *stock* or *flat* characters (for example, the gravediggers in *Hamlet*). For such characters, the dramatist relies on stereotypes and doesn't reveal much about their backgrounds. Each type of character has a function in the play. Select characters from the play to describe in terms of the overall contribution they make to the story.

Another technique is to consider the *dynamics* among various characters. For example, describing Hamlet's relationship to his mother or to his step-father will reveal a great deal about all of these characters and about the play as a whole. As you examine various combinations, consider that some characters act as *foils* to others; that is, certain qualities in one character will reveal certain qualities in another. In *Antigonê,* for instance, Ismenê is a foil to Antigonê; in *Hamlet,* Laertes is a foil to Hamlet. Write about how one character helps to reveal another character. Such prewritings, whether in a journal or simply on scrap paper, are highly productive and may lead to interesting possibilities for essays.

2. *Write about the structure of the play.* This is a subject about which you know quite a bit, even though you may not have thought about it as such. When you attend a play or watch a movie, you have certain expectations about such matters as plot and conflict. Usually, during the early scenes, the characters and action are revealed. The sense that all of this revelation may be leading somewhere is called *rising action.* When the plot and the conflicts are at their highest pitch, the play has reached its *climax,* and the action that follows is known as *falling action.* Of course, playwrights handle this general pattern in many ways and with many effects. There may be, as is the case in *Antigonê* and *Hamlet,* several points of climax even as the action continues to rise. As a prewriting activity, analyze how this pattern evolves in the plays you read. Examine how the playwright accomplishes each of the elements in the pattern, what new turns in the plot may take place, how the dynamics between two characters may move things along.

Drama is predicated upon tension and conflict. A story in which everyone agrees with everyone else has little interest. As you read, consider where the key tensions are in the play. Who is at odds with whom, and why? A prewrit-

ing that examines, for example, the reasons for Antigonê's conflict with
Kreon may lead to an excellent essay on the theme of individual versus
states' rights in *Antigonê*.

3. *Write about a play's settings.* Setting is an element of the drama that may
be important for reasons that range from the simple curiosity audiences
may have about remote and exotic settings to the profound influence that a
culture exerts over its people. A play's setting helps explain who the characters are and why their conflicts have arisen. It also creates the atmosphere of
the play, its tone or ambience. To prewrite effectively about setting, you
should begin with a particular scene in a play. Where does it take place (a
kitchen, a sentinel's outpost, a chapel), and how is that setting related to the
scene it contains? A successful essay on setting might explore, for example, a
pattern within a play (domestic setting in *The Glass Menagerie*) or how in-
congruous settings make revelations about characters (Hamlet, the Prince of
Denmark, at a gravesite while the workmen dig).

Consider, too, how the dialogue creates the setting. In most plays, the
setting is revealed through the speech of the characters rather than by the
brief stage directions of the playwright. Study the dialogue for such descriptions. Consider how different characters may view the same setting. (In the
first act of *Hamlet*, for example, compare Hamlet's view of the outpost with
that of the guards.) Effective dialogue will allow an audience to imagine a
setting even in the absence of any stage scenery. As you read, look for
occasions when the playwright uses dialogue for this purpose. Copy such
passages into your reading journal and then analyze how the speech accomplishes its purpose. Like a scenic designer, you may find it helpful to sketch
the scene into your notes and then compare how you imagined it with other
students in your class.

4. *Write about the theme of the play.* By *theme* we mean the subject or idea that
the central conflicts in the play may evoke. For example, we can say that
The Glass Menagerie is about a mother trying to find a husband for her
daughter, but that statement has more to do with plot than theme. One of
the important ideas behind this play about a woman looking for a husband is
that in the 1940's (when this play was written) a woman's sense of worth and
identity was linked to her marital status, and as the play reveals, this was a
fragile link indeed. When we speak of theme, then, we are speaking about
such ideas. Some of the prewriting activities we have suggested above may
lead you to think about a play's theme, and it may be helpful to start with
character or setting in order to discover the themes—there are usually more
than one—in a play. When you have done some prewriting on other topics,
look over your work and begin a fifteen-minute freewriting on the theme(s)
of the play. Some idea or discovery you make in the course of such a
freewriting may lead to a second freewriting and possibly to a meaningful
topic for an essay.

5. *Attend a play.* Seeing a play performed will help you to understand a
variety of techniques in the dramatist's art that may seem confusing on

paper. For example, it sometimes takes a while for a reader's eye to adjust to reading dialogue because at every few lines the reading is disrupted by the speakers' names and the stage directions, while in a performance no such disruptions take place. It is also true that performances vary in quality and in intent. One director will see one thing in a script, while another sees something entirely different. Thus performances have a subjective quality of their own.

If you have the opportunity to see a performance of a play you are studying (or even another drama by one of these authors), doing so will enrich your reading and understanding of this genre. Write a review of the performance, just as a theatre critic would, evaluating the actors' performances, the settings, the quality of the direction, and the interpretation offered by the director. Such writing will further help you to imagine readings and interpretations you don't get to see. It might be fun, for example, to describe how several different performers might do the same role.

2 *Greek Tragedy*

Western drama is often said to have originated in ancient Greece. Certainly its two most outstanding forms, tragedy and comedy, began there.

About the beginnings of this drama, little is known, for few records have survived. We do know, however, that it began at festivals honoring Dionysus, or Bacchus, a god who was supposed to have taught men to cultivate grapes and make wine. Song and dance were the means by which this god was worshipped. At early festivals, choruses of fifty men dressed in tattered garments with wine-smeared faces or disguised as Dionysus' mythical companions, the satyrs, sang hymns praising the god's deeds while they half-danced, half-mimed his exploits. Eventually one man stepped out of the chorus and engaged his fellows in dialogue. Later still, the soloist began impersonating the god, thus dramatizing the events of which he was singing.

Sometime during this process, the content of the songs also shifted. Some still pertained to Dionysus, but some dealt with other, human, heroes. Although worshippers were reportedly shocked at the first introduction of the new tales, asking, "What has this to do with Dionysus?", the novelty soon became the rule. By 530 B.C., the performances were being called tragedies and were competing in Athens for an annual prize.

In the next hundred years, tragedy reached what Aristotle considered its full form. A second actor was added, and then a third. Episodes of dialogue among the actors, with the chorus occasionally joining in, became as important as the choric songs and dances with which they alternated. Painted backdrops, stage machinery, and special effects were introduced.

For all its developments, however, Greek drama remained a religious event. Plays were performed only at Dionysus' festivals; actors were considered his servants. Performances took place three times a year: twice at Athens, once at various rural festivals. The older of the Athenian festivals, the *Lenaea,* became the festival for comedy; but the *City Dionysia,* which drew visitors from all over Greece, was the festival for tragedy.

For this festival, three playwrights were chosen by Athenian authorities. Each was given a chorus and actors, who were paid and costumed by some rich citizen as a public service; each was allotted one day of the festival on which to perform. The performance would consist of three tragedies (sometimes on the same subject, sometimes not), followed by a satyr play, an obscene or satiric parody of some legendary event. At the end of the three days of playing, a jury of ten citizens, chosen by lot, judged the plays and awarded the prizes.* Any Athenian was welcome to attend these plays, which were held in a natural amphitheater that seated some 30,000 people. Since the theater was reported to be crowded at every performance, we may assume that virtually everybody who could attend, did.

All in all, drama in ancient Athens seems to have been regarded almost as a public possession. Looked on with a mixture of religious devotion, civic pride, and open enjoyment, it maintained a great and general popularity that seems to have declined only with the decline of Athens itself. And still the plays remained influential, both in themselves and in the theory of drama that Aristotle's comments on them provided. First the Romans copied them. Then, some 1500 years later, Renaissance playwrights took ideas from both Greek and Roman drama. We will discuss that development in the next chapter.

---

* Sophocles, the author of *Antigonê,* held the all-time record of eighteen first prizes and is said never to have won less than second prize.

SOPHOCLES (496–406 B.C.)

Antigonê

An English version by Dudley Fitts and Robert Fitzgerald

CHARACTERS

ANTIGONÊ
ISMENÊ
EURYDICÊ
KREON
HAIMON
TEIRESIAS
A SENTRY
A MESSENGER
CHORUS

SCENE. *Before the palace of* KREON, *King of Thebes. A central double door, and two lateral doors. A platform extends the length of the façade, and from this platform three steps lead down into the "orchestra," or chorus-ground.*

TIME. *Dawn of the day after the repulse of the Argive army from the assault on Thebes.*

PROLOGUE

(ANTIGONÊ *and* ISMENÊ *enter from the central door of the palace.*)

ANTIGONÊ Ismenê, dear sister,
You would think that we had already suffered enough
5 For the curse on Oedipus.
I cannot imagine any grief
That you and I have not gone through. And now—
Have they told you of the new decree of our King Kreon?
ISMENÊ I have heard nothing: I know
10 That two sisters lost two brothers, a double death
In a single hour; and I know that the Argive army
Fled in the night; but beyond this, nothing.

ANTIGONÊ   I thought so. And that is why I wanted you
To come out here with me. There is something we must do.
ISMENÊ   Why do you speak so strangely?
ANTIGONÊ   Listen, Ismenê:
5   Kreon buried our brother Eteoclês
With military honors, gave him a soldier's funeral,
And it was right that he should; but Polyneicês,
Who fought as bravely and died as miserably,—
They say that Kreon has sworn
10   No one shall bury him, no one mourn for him,
But his body must lie in the fields, a sweet treasure
For carrion birds to find as they search for food.
That is what they say, and our good Kreon is coming here
To announce it publicly; and the penalty—
15   Stoning to death in the public square!

There it is,
And now you can prove what you are:
A true sister, or a traitor to your family.
ISMENÊ   Antigonê, you are mad! What could I possibly do?
20   ANTIGONÊ   You must decide whether you will help me or not.
ISMENÊ   I do not understand you. Help you in what?
ANTIGONÊ   Ismenê, I am going to bury him. Will you come?
ISMENÊ   Bury him! You have just said the new law forbids it.
ANTIGONÊ   He is my brother. And he is your brother, too.
25   ISMENÊ   But think of the danger! Think what Kreon will do!
ANTIGONÊ   Kreon is not strong enough to stand in my way.
ISMENÊ   Ah sister!
Oedipus died, everyone hating him
For what his own search brought to light, his eyes
30   Ripped out by his own hand; and Iokastê died,
His mother and wife at once: she twisted the cords
That strangled her life; and our two brothers died,
Each killed by the other's sword. And we are left:
But oh, Antigonê,
35   Think how much more terrible than these
Our own death would be if we should go against Kreon
And do what he has forbidden! We are only women,
We cannot fight with men, Antigonê!
The law is strong, we must give in to the law
40   In this thing, and in worse. I beg the Dead
To forgive me, but I am helpless: I must yield
To those in authority. And I think it is dangerous business
To be always meddling.
ANTIGONÊ   If that is what you think,
45   I should not want you, even if you asked to come.

You have made your choice, you can be what you want to be.
But I will bury him; and if I must die,
I say that this crime is holy: I shall lie down
With him in death, and I shall be as dear
5 To him as he to me.
                                    It is the dead,
Not the living, who make the longest demands:
We die for ever . . .
                                    You may do as you like,
10 Since apparently the laws of the gods mean nothing to you.
ISMENÊ   They mean a great deal to me; but I have no strength
To break laws that were made for the public good.
ANTIGONÊ   That must be your excuse, I suppose. But as for me,
I will bury the brother I love.
15 ISMENÊ   Antigonê,
I am so afraid for you!
ANTIGONÊ   You need not be:
You have yourself to consider, after all.
ISMENÊ   But no one must hear of this, you must tell no one!
20 I will keep it a secret, I promise!
ANTIGONÊ   O tell it! Tell everyone!
Think how they'll hate you when it all comes out
If they learn that you knew about it all the time!
ISMENÊ   So fiery! You should be cold with fear.
25 ANTIGONÊ   Perhaps. But I am doing only what I must.
ISMENÊ   But can you do it? I say that you cannot.
ANTIGONÊ   Very well: when my strength gives out,
I shall do no more.
ISMENÊ   Impossible things should not be tried at all.
30 ANTIGONÊ   Go away, Ismenê:
I shall be hating you soon, and the dead will too,
For your words are hateful. Leave me my foolish plan:
I am not afraid of the danger; if it means death,
It will not be the worst of deaths—death without honor.
35 ISMENÊ   Go then, if you feel that you must.
You are unwise,
But a loyal friend indeed to those who love you.

(*Exit into the palace.* ANTIGONÊ *goes off, left. Enter the* CHORUS.)

PÁRODOS

40 **Strophe 1**

CHORUS   Now the long blade of the sun, lying
Level east to west, touches with glory

Thebes of the Seven Gates. Open, unlidded
Eye of golden day! O marching light
Across the eddy and rush of Dircê's stream,[1]
Striking the white shields of the enemy
5   Thrown headlong backward from the blaze of morning!
CHORAGOS[2]   Polyneicês their commander
Roused them with windy phrases,
He the wild eagle screaming
Insults above our land,
10   His wings their shields of snow,
His crest their marshalled helms.

Antistrophe 1

CHORUS   Against our seven gates in a yawning ring
The famished spears came onward in the night;
15   But before his jaws were sated with our blood,
Or pinefire took the garland of our towers,
He was thrown back; and as he turned, great Thebes—
No tender victim for his noisy power—
Rose like a dragon behind him, shouting war.
20   CHORAGOS   For God hates utterly
The bray of bragging tongues;
And when he beheld their smiling,
Their swagger of golden helms,
The frown of his thunder blasted
25   Their first man from our walls.

Strophe 2

CHORUS   We heard his shout of triumph high in the air
Turn to a scream; far out in a flaming arc
He fell with his windy torch, and the earth struck him.
30   And others storming in fury no less than his
Found shock of death in the dusty joy of battle.
CHORAGOS   Seven captains at seven gates
Yielded their clanging arms to the god
That bends the battle-line and breaks it.
35   These two only, brothers in blood,
Face to face in matchless rage,
Mirroring each the other's death,
Clashed in long combat.

---

1 *Dircês stream* a stream to the west of Thebes
2 *Choragos* the leader of the Chorus

Antistrophe 2

CHORUS   But now in the beautiful morning of victory
Let Thebes of the many chariots sing for joy!
With hearts for dancing we'll take leave of war:
5   Our temples shall be sweet with hymns of praise,
And the long nights shall echo with our chorus.

SCENE I

CHORAGOS   But now at last our new King is coming:
Kreon of Thebes, Menoikeus' son.
10   In this auspicious dawn of his rein
What are the new complexities
That shifting Fate has woven for him?
What is his counsel? Why has he summoned
The old men to hear him?

15   (*Enter* KREON *from the palace, center. He addresses the* CHORUS *from the top step.*)

KREON   Gentlemen: I have the honor to inform you that our Ship of State, which recent storms have threatened to destroy, has come safely to harbor at last, guided by the merciful wisdom of Heaven.
20   I have summoned you here this morning because I know that I can depend upon you: your devotion to King Laïos was absolute; you never hesitated in your duty to our late ruler Oedipus; and when Oedipus died, your loyalty was transferred to his children. Unfortunately, as you know, his two sons, the princes Eteoclês
25   and Polyneicês, have killed each other in battle; and I, as the next in blood, have succeeded to the full power of the throne.

I am aware, of course, that no Ruler can expect complete loyalty from his subjects until he has been tested in office. Nevertheless, I say to you at the very outset that I have nothing but
30   contempt for the kind of Governor who is afraid, for whatever reason, to follow the course that he knows is best for the State; and as for the man who sets private friendship above the public welfare,—I have no use for him, either. I call God to witness that if I saw my country headed for ruin, I should not be afraid
35   to speak out plainly; and I need hardly remind you that I would never have any dealings with an enemy of the people. No one values friendship more highly than I; but we must remember that friends made at the risk of wrecking our Ship are not real friends at all.
40   These are my principles, at any rate, and that is why I have made the following decision concerning the sons of Oedipus:

Eteoclês, who died as a man should die, fighting for his country, is to be buried with full military honors, with all the ceremony that is usual when the greatest heroes die; but his brother Polyneicês, who broke his exile to come back with fire and sword against his native city and the shrines of his fathers' gods, whose one idea was to spill the blood of his blood and sell his own people into slavery—Polyneicês, I say, is to have no burial: no man is to touch him or say the least prayer for him; he shall lie on the plain, unburied; and the birds and the scavenging dogs can do with him whatever they like.

This is my command, and you can see the wisdom behind it. As long as I am King, no traitor is going to be honored with the loyal man. But whoever shows by word and deed that he is on the side of the State,—he shall have my respect while he is living and my reverence when he is dead.

CHORAGOS If that is your will, Kreon son of Menoikeus,
You have the right to enforce it: we are yours.

KREON That is my will. Take care that you do your part.

CHORAGOS We are old men: let the younger ones carry it out.

KREON I do not mean that: the sentries have been appointed.

CHORAGOS Then what is it that you would have us do?

KREON You will give no support to whoever breaks this law.

CHORAGOS Only a crazy man is in love with death!

KREON And death it is; yet money talks, and the wisest
Have sometimes been known to count a few coins too many.

(Enter SENTRY *from left.)*

SENTRY I'll not say that I'm out of breath from running, King,
because every time I stopped to think about what I have to tell
you, I felt like going back. And all the time a voice kept saying,
"You fool, don't you know you're walking straight into trouble?";
and then another voice: "Yes, but if you let somebody else get
the news to Kreon first, it will be even worse than that for you!"
But good sense won out, at least I hope it was good sense, and
here I am with a story that makes no sense at all; but I'll tell it
anyhow, because, as they say, what's going to happen's going to
happen and—

KREON Come to the point. What have you to say?

SENTRY I did not do it. I did not see who did it. You must not
punish me for what someone else has done.

KREON A comprehensive defense! More effective, perhaps,
If I knew its purpose. Come: what is it?

SENTRY A dreadful thing . . . I don't know how to put it—

KREON Out with it!

SENTRY   Well, then;
  The dead man—
     Polyneicês—

 (Pause. The SENTRY *is overcome, fumbles for words.* KREON *waits*
5 *impassively.)*

        out there—
           someone,—

 New dust on the slimy flesh!

 (Pause. No sign from KREON.*)*

10 Someone has given it burial that way, and
 Gone . . .

 (Long pause. KREON *finally speaks with deadly control.)*

KREON And the man who dared do this?
SENTRY   I swear I
15 Do not know! You must believe me!
          Listen:
 The ground was dry, not a sign of digging, no,
 Not a wheeltrack in the dust, no trace of anyone.
 It was when they relieved us this morning: and one of them,
20 The corporal, pointed to it.
         There it was,
 The strangest—
    Look:
 The body, just mounded over with light dust: you see?
25 Not buried really, but as if they'd covered it
 Just enough for the ghost's peace. And no sign
 Of dogs or any wild animal that had been there.

 And then what a scene there was! Every man of us
 Accusing the other: we all proved the other man did it,
30 We all had proof that we could not have done it.
 We were ready to take hot iron in our hands,
 Walk through fire, swear by all the gods,
 It was not I!
 I do not know who it was, but it was not I!

35 *(*KREON's *rage has been mounting steadily, but the* SENTRY *is too intent
 upon his story to notice it.)*

 And then, when this came to nothing, someone said
 A thing that silenced us and made us stare
 Down at the ground: you had to be told the news,
40 And one of us had to do it! We threw the dice,

And the bad luck fell to me. So here I am,
No happier to be here than you are to have me:
Nobody likes the man who brings bad news.

CHORAGOS   I have been wondering, King: can it be that the gods
5   have done this?

KREON   (*furiously*)   Stop!
Must you doddering wrecks
Go out of your heads entirely? "The gods"!
Intolerable!
10   The gods favor this corpse? Why? How had he served them?
Tried to loot their temples, burn their images,
Yes, and the whole State, and its laws with it!
Is it your senile opinion that the gods love to honor bad men?
A pious thought!—
15   No, from the very beginning
There have been those who have whispered together,
Stiff-necked anarchists, putting their heads together,
Scheming against me in alleys. These are the men,
And they have bribed my own guard to do this thing.
20   (*Sententiously.*)   Money!
There's nothing in the world so demoralizing as money.
Down go your cities,
Homes gone, men gone, honest hearts corrupted,
Crookedness of all kinds, and all for money!
25   (*To* SENTRY.)   But you—!
I swear by God and by the throne of God,
The man who has done this thing shall pay for it!
Find that man, bring him here to me, or your death
Will be the least of your problems: I'll string you up
30   Alive, and there will be certain ways to make you
Discover your employer before you die;
And the process may teach you a lesson you seem to have
        missed:
The dearest profit is sometimes all too dear:
35   That depends on the source. Do you understand me?
A fortune won is often misfortune.

SENTRY   King, may I speak?

KREON   Your very voice distresses me.

SENTRY   Are you sure that it is my voice, and not your conscience?

40   KREON   By God, he wants to analyze me now!

SENTRY   It is not what I say, but what has been done, that hurts
you.

KREON   You talk too much.

SENTRY   Maybe; but I've done nothing.

45   KREON   Sold your soul for some silver: that's all you've done.

SENTRY   How dreadful it is when the right judge judges wrong!
KREON   Your figures of speech
     May entertain you now; but unless you bring me the man,
     You will get little profit from them in the end.

5   (*Exit* KREON *into the palace.*)

SENTRY   "Bring me the man"—!
     I'd like nothing better than bringing him the man!
     But bring him or not, you have seen the last of me here.
     At any rate, I am safe!

10   (*Exit* SENTRY.)

ODE I

Strophe 1

CHORUS   Numberless are the world's wonders, but none
     More wonderful than man; the stormgray sea
15   Yields to his prows, the huge crests bear him high;
     Earth, holy and inexhaustible, is graven
     With shining furrows where his plows have gone
     Year after year, the timeless labor of stallions.

Antistrophe 1

20   The lightboned birds and beasts that cling to cover,
     The lithe fish lighting their reaches of dim water,
     All are taken, tamed in the net of his mind;
     The lion on the hill, the wild horse windy-maned,
     Resign to him; and his blunt yoke has broken
25   The sultry shoulders of the mountain bull.

Strophe 2

     Words also, and thought as rapid as air,
     He fashions to his good use; statecraft is his,
     And his the skill that deflects the arrows of snow,
30   The spears of winter rain: from every wind
     He has made himself secure—from all but one:
     In the late wind of death he cannot stand.

Antistrophe 2

     O clear intelligence, force beyond all measure!
35   O fate of man, working both good and evil!
     When the laws are kept, how proudly his city stands!
     When the laws are broken, what of his city then?
     Never may the anárchic man find rest at my hearth,
     Never be it said that my thoughts are his thoughts.

SCENE II

(*Reenter* SENTRY *leading* ANTIGONÊ.)

CHORAGOS   What does this mean? Surely this captive woman
Is the Princess, Antigonê. Why should she be taken?

5   SENTRY   Here is the one who did it! We caught her
In the very act of burying him.—Where is Kreon?

CHORAGOS   Just coming from the house.

(*Enter* KREON, *center.*)

KREON   What has happened?
10   Why have you come back so soon?

SENTRY (*expansively*)   O King,
A man should never be too sure of anything:
I would have sworn
That you'd not see me here again: your anger
15   Frightened me so, and the things you threatened me with;
But how could I tell then
That I'd be able to solve the case so soon?
No dice-throwing this time: I was only too glad to come!
Here is this woman. She is the guilty one:
20   We found her trying to bury him.
Take her, then; question her; judge her as you will.
I am through with the whole thing now, and glad of it.

KREON   But this is Antigonê! Why have you brought her here?

SENTRY   She was burying him, I tell you!

25   KREON (*severely*)   Is this the truth?

SENTRY   I saw her with my own eyes. Can I say more?

KREON   The details: come, tell me quickly!

SENTRY   It was like this:
After those terrible threats of yours, King,
30   We went back and brushed the dust away from the body.
The flesh was soft by now, and stinking,
So we sat on a hill to windward and kept guard.
No napping this time! We kept each other awake.
But nothing happened until the white round sun
35   Whirled in the center of the round sky over us:
Then, suddenly,
A storm of dust roared up from the earth, and the sky
Went out, the plain vanished with all its trees
In the stinging dark. We closed our eyes and endured it.
4c   The whirlwind lasted a long time, but it passed;
And then we looked, and there was Antigonê!
I have seen
A mother bird come back to a stripped nest, heard

Her crying bitterly a broken note or two
For the young ones stolen. Just so, when this girl
Found the bare corpse, and all her love's work wasted,
She wept, and cried on heaven to damn the hands
5   That had done this thing.
                              And then she brought more dust
And sprinkled wine three times for her brother's ghost.

We ran and took her at once. She was not afraid,
Not even when we charged her with what she had done.
10 She denied nothing.
                          And this was a comfort to me,
And some uneasiness: for it is a good thing
To escape from death, but it is no great pleasure
To bring death to a friend.
15   Yet I always say
There is nothing so comfortable as your own safe skin!
KREON *(slowly, dangerously)*   And you, Antigonê,
You with your head hanging,—do you confess this thing?
ANTIGONÊ   I do. I deny nothing.
20 KREON *(to* SENTRY)   You may go.

   (Exit SENTRY.)

   (To ANTIGONÊ.) Tell me, tell me briefly:
Had you heard my proclamation touching this matter?
ANTIGONÊ   It was public. Could I help hearing it?
25 KREON   And yet you dared defy the law.
ANTIGONÊ   I dared.
It was not God's proclamation. That final Justice
That rules the world below makes no such laws.

Your edict, King, was strong,
30 But all your strength is weakness itself against
The immortal unrecorded laws of God.
They are not merely now: they were, and shall be,
Operative for ever, beyond man utterly.

I knew I must die, even without your decree:
35 I am only mortal. And if I must die
Now, before it is my time to die,
Surely this is no hardship: can anyone
Living, as I live, with evil all about me,
Think Death less than a friend? This death of mine
40 Is of no importance; but if I had left my brother
Lying in death unburied, I should have suffered.

Now I do not.
You smile at me. Ah Kreon,

Think me a fool, if you like; but it may well be
That a fool convicts me of folly.

5 CHORAGOS   Like father, like daughter: both headstrong,
    deaf to reason!
She has never learned to yield:
KREON   She has much to learn.
The inflexible heart breaks first, the toughest iron
10 Cracks first, and the wildest horses bend their necks
At the pull of the smallest curb.
Pride? In a slave?

This girl is guilty of a double insolence,
Breaking the given laws and boasting of it.
15 Who is the man here,
She or I, if this crime goes unpunished?
Sister's child, or more than sister's child,
Or closer yet in blood—she and her sister
Win bitter death for this!
20 (*To* SERVANTS.)   Go, some of you,
Arrest Ismenê. I accuse her equally.
Bring her: you will find her sniffling in the house there.

Her mind's a traitor: crimes kept in the dark
Cry for light, and the guardian brain shudders;
25 But how much worse than this
Is brazen boasting of barefaced anarchy!
ANTIGONÊ   Kreon, what more do you want than my death?
KREON   Nothing.
That gives me everything.
30 ANTIGONÊ   Then I beg you: kill me.
This talking is a great weariness: your words
Are distasteful to me, and I am sure that mine
Seem so to you. And yet they should not seem so:
I should have praise and honor for what I have done.
35 All these men here would praise me
Were their lips not frozen shut with fear of you.
(*Bitterly.*) Ah the good fortune of kings,
Licensed to say and do whatever they please!
KREON   You are alone here in that opinion.
40 ANTIGONÊ   No, they are with me. But they keep their tongues
    in leash.
KREON   Maybe. But you are guilty, and they are not.
ANTIGONÊ   There is no guilt in reverence for the dead.
KREON   But Eteoclês—was he not your brother too?

ANTIGONÊ   My brother too.

KREON   And you insult his memory?

ANTIGONÊ *(softly)*   The dead man would not say that I insult it.

KREON   He would: for you honor a traitor as much as him.

5   ANTIGONÊ   His own brother, traitor or not, and equal in blood.

KREON   He made war on his country. Eteoclês defended it.

ANTIGONÊ   Nevertheless, there are honors due all the dead.

KREON   But not the same for the wicked as for the just.

ANTIGONÊ   Ah Kreon, Kreon,

10   Which of us can say what the gods hold wicked?

KREON   An enemy is an enemy, even dead.

ANTIGONÊ   It is my nature to join in love, not hate.

KREON *(finally losing patience)*   Go join them then; if you must have your love,

15   Find it in hell!

CHORAGOS   But see, Ismenê comes:

(Enter ISMENÊ, *guarded.)*

Those tears are sisterly, the cloud
That shadows her eyes rains down gentle sorrow.

20   KREON   You too, Ismenê,
Snake in my ordered house, sucking my blood
Stealthily—and all the time I never knew
That these two sisters were aiming at my throne!

                                                                    Ismenê

25   Do you confess your share in this crime, or deny it?
Answer me.

ISMENÊ   Yes, if she will let me say so. I am guilty.

ANTIGONÊ *(coldly)*   No, Ismenê. You have no right to say so.
You would not help me, and I will not have you help me.

30   ISMENÊ   But now I know what you meant; and I am here
To join you, to take my share of punishment.

ANTIGONÊ   The dead man and the gods who rule the dead
Know whose act this was. Words are not friends.

ISMENÊ   Do you refuse me, Antigonê? I want to die with you:

35   I too have a duty that I must discharge to the dead.

ANTIGONÊ   You shall not lessen my death by sharing it.

ISMENÊ   What do I care for life when you are dead?

ANTIGONÊ   Ask Kreon. You're always hanging on his opinions.

ISMENÊ   You are laughing at me. Why, Antigonê?

40   ANTIGONÊ   It's a joyless laughter, Ismenê.

ISMENÊ   But can I do nothing?

ANTIGONÊ   Yes. Save yourself. I shall not envy you.
There are those who will praise you; I shall have honor, too.

ISMENÊ   But we are equally guilty!

ANTIGONÊ   No more, Ismenê.
You are alive, but I belong to Death.

KREON (*to the* CHORUS)   Gentlemen, I beg you to observe these
    girls:

5   One has just now lost her mind; the other,
It seems, has never had a mind at all.

ISMENÊ   Grief teaches the steadiest minds to waver, King.

KREON   Yours certainly did, when you assumed guilt with the guilty!

ISMENÊ   But how could I go on living without her?

10 KREON   You are.
She is already dead.

ISMENÊ   But your own son's bride!

KREON   There are places enough for him to push his plow.
I want no wicked women for my sons!

15 ISMENÊ   O dearest Haimon, how your father wrongs you!

KREON   I've had enough of your childish talk of marriage!

CHORAGOS   Do you really intend to steal this girl from your son?

KREON   No; Death will do that for me.

CHORAGOS   Then she must die?

20 KREON (*ironically*)   You dazzle me.
                           —But enough of this talk!
(*To* GUARDS.) You, there, take them away and guard them well:
For they are but women, and even brave men run
When they see Death coming.

25 (*Exeunt* ISMENÊ, ANTIGONÊ, *and* GUARDS.)

ODE II

Strophe 1

CHORUS   Fortunate is the man who has never tasted God's
    vengeance!

30 Where once the anger of heaven has struck, that house is
    shaken
For ever: damnation rises behind each child
Like a wave cresting out of the black northeast,
When the long darkness under sea roars up

35 And bursts drumming death upon the windwhipped sand.

Antistrophe 1

I have seen this gathering sorrow from time long past
Loom upon Oedipus' children: generation from generation
Takes the compulsive rage of the enemy god.

40 So lately this last flower of Oedipus' line

Drank the sunlight; but now a passionate word
And a handful of dust have closed up all its beauty.

Strophe 2

What mortal arrogance
5   Transcends the wrath of Zeus?
Sleep cannot lull him nor the effortless long months
Of the timeless gods: but he is young for ever,
And his house is the shining day of high Olympos.
All that is and shall be,
10   And all the past, is his.
No pride on earth is free of the curse of heaven.

Antistrophe 2

The straying dreams of men
May bring them ghosts of joy:
15   But as they drowse, the waking embers burn them;
Or they walk with fixed eyes, as blind men walk.
But the ancient wisdom speaks for our own time:
Fate works most for woe
With Folly's fairest show.
20   Man's little pleasure is the spring of sorrow.

SCENE III

CHORAGOS   But here is Haimon, King, the last of all your sons.
Is it grief for Antigonê that brings him here,
And bitterness at being robbed of his bride?

25   (*Enter* HAIMON.)

KREON   We shall soon see, and no need of diviners.
                         —Son,
You have heard my final judgment on that girl:
Have you come here hating me, or have you come
30   With deference and with love, whatever I do?
HAIMON   I am your son, father. You are my guide.
You make things clear for me, and I obey you.
No marriage means more to me than your continuing
wisdom.
35   KREON   Good. That is the way to behave: subordinate
Everything else, my son, to your father's will.
This is what a man prays for, that he may get
Sons attentive and dutiful in his house,
Each one hating his father's enemies,
40   Honoring his father's friends. But if his sons

Fail him, if they turn out unprofitably,
What has he fathered but trouble for himself
And amusement for the malicious?

                                    So you are right

5   Not to lose your head over this woman.
Your pleasure with her would soon grow cold, Haimon,
And then you'd have a hellcat in bed and elsewhere.
Let her find her husband in Hell!
Of all the people in this city, only she

10   Has had contempt for my law and broken it.

Do you want me to show myself weak before the people?
Or to break my sworn word? No, and I will not.
The woman dies.
I suppose she'll plead "family ties." Well, let her.

15   If I permit my own family to rebel,
How shall I earn the world's obedience?
Show me the man who keeps his house in hand,
He's fit for public authority.

                              I'll have no dealings

20   With lawbreakers, critics of the government:
Whoever is chosen to govern should be obeyed—
Must be obeyed, in all things, great and small,
Just and unjust! O Haimon,
The man who knows how to obey, and that man only,

25   Knows how to give commands when the time comes.
You can depend on him, no matter how fast
The spears come: he's a good soldier, he'll stick it out.

Anarchy, anarchy! Show me a greater evil!
This is why cities tumble and the great houses rain down,

30   This is what scatters armies!
No, no: good lives are made so by discipline.
We keep the laws then, and the lawmakers,
And no woman shall seduce us. If we must lose,
Let's lose to a man, at least! Is a woman stronger than we?

35   CHORAGOS   Unless time has rusted my wits,
What you say, King, is said with point and dignity.
HAIMON (*boyishly earnest*)   Father:
Reason is God's crowning gift to man, and you are right
To warn me against losing mine. I cannot say—

40   I hope that I shall never want to say!—that you
Have reasoned badly. Yet there are other men
Who can reason, too; and their opinions might be helpful.
You are not in a position to know everything

That people say or do, or what they feel:
Your temper terrifies—everyone
Will tell you only what you like to hear.
But I, at any rate, can listen; and I have heard them
5   Muttering and whispering in the dark about this girl.
They say no woman has ever, so unreasonably,
Died so shameful a death for a generous act:
"She covered her brother's body. Is this indecent?
She kept him from dogs and vultures. Is this a crime?
10   Death?—She should have all the honor that we can give her!"

This is the way they talk out there in the city.

You must believe me:
Nothing is closer to me than your happiness.
What could be closer? Must not any son
15   Value his father's fortune as his father does his?
I beg you, do not be unchangeable:
Do not believe that you alone can be right.
The man who thinks that,
The man who maintains that only he has the power
20   To reason correctly, the gift to speak, the soul—
A man like that, when you know him, turns out empty.

It is not reason never to yield to reason!

In flood time you can see how some trees bend,
And because they bend, even their twigs are safe,
25   While stubborn trees are torn up, roots and all.
And the same thing happens in sailing:
Make your sheet fast, never slacken,—and over you go,
Head over heels and under: and there's your voyage.
Forget you are angry! Let yourself be moved!
30   I know I am young; but please let me say this:
The ideal condition
Would be, I admit, that men should be right by instinct;
But since we are all too likely to go astray,
The reasonable thing is to learn from those who can teach.
35   CHORAGOS   You will do well to listen to him, King,
If what he says is sensible. And you, Haimon,
Must listen to your father.—Both speak well.
KREON   You consider it right for a man of my years
and experience
40   To go to school to a boy?

HAIMON   It is not right
If I am wrong. But if I am young, and right,
What does my age matter?
   KREON   You think it right to stand up for an anarchist?
5   HAIMON   Not at all. I pay no respect to criminals.
   KREON   Then she is not a criminal?
   HAIMON   The City would deny it, to a man.
   KREON   And the City proposes to teach me how to rule?
   HAIMON   Ah. Who is it that's talking like a boy now?
10 KREON   My voice is the one voice giving orders in this City!
   HAIMON   It is no City if it takes orders from one voice.
   KREON   The State is the King!
   HAIMON   Yes, if the State is a desert.

   Pause.

15 KREON   This boy, it seems, has sold out to a woman.
   HAIMON   If you are a woman: my concern is only for you.
   KREON   So? Your "concern"! In a public brawl with your
father!
   HAIMON   How about you, in a public brawl with justice?
20 KREON   With justice, when all that I do is within my rights?
   HAIMON   You have no right to trample on God's right.
   KREON (*completely out of control*)   Fool, adolescent fool! Taken
in by a woman!
   HAIMON   You'll never see me taken in by anything vile.
25 KREON   Every word you say is for her!
   HAIMON (*quietly, darkly*)   And for you.
And for me. And for the gods under the earth.
   KREON   You'll never marry her while she lives.
   HAIMON   Then she must die.—But her death will cause another.
30 KREON   Another?
Have you lost your senses? Is this an open threat?
   HAIMON   There is no threat in speaking to emptiness.
   KREON   I swear you'll regret this superior tone of yours!
You are the empty one!
35 HAIMON   If you were not my father,
I'd say you were perverse.
   KREON   You girlstruck fool, don't play at words with me!
   HAIMON   I am sorry. You prefer silence.
   KREON   Now, by God—!
40 I swear, by all the gods in heaven above us,
You'll watch it, I swear you shall!
(*To the* SERVANTS.)   Bring her out!
Bring the woman out! Let her die before his eyes!
Here, this instant, with her bridegroom beside her!

HAIMON   Not here, no; she will not die here, King.
And you will never see my face again.
Go on raving as long as you've a friend to endure you.

(*Exit* HAIMON.)

5 CHORAGOS   Gone, gone.
Kreon, a young man in a rage is dangerous!
KREON   Let him do, or dream to do, more than a man can.
He shall not save these girls from death.
CHORAGOS   These girls?
10 You have sentenced them both?
KREON   No, you are right.
I will not kill the one whose hands are clean.
CHORAGOS   But Antigonê?
KREON (*somberly*)   I will carry her far away
15 Out there in the wilderness, and lock her
Living in a vault of stone. She shall have food,
As the custom is, to absolve the State of her death.
And there let her pray to the gods of hell:
They are her only gods:
20 Perhaps they will show her an escape from death,
Or she may learn,
though late,
That piety shown the dead is pity in vain.

(*Exit* KREON.)

25 ODE III

Strophe

CHORUS   Love, unconquerable
Waster of rich men, keeper
Of warm lights and all-night vigil
30 In the soft face of a girl:
Sea-wanderer, forest-visitor!
Even the pure Immortals cannot escape you,
And mortal man, in his one day's dusk,
Trembles before your glory.

35 **Antistrophe**

Surely you swerve upon ruin
The just man's consenting heart,
As here you have made bright anger
Strike between father and son—

And none has conquered but Love!
A girl's glance working the will of heaven:
Pleasure to her alone who mocks us,
Merciless Aphroditê.[1]

5 SCENE IV

CHORAGOS (*as* ANTIGONÊ *enters guarded*)   But I can no longer
    stand in awe of this,
Nor, seeing what I see, keep back my tears.
Here is Antigonê, passing to that chamber
10   Where all find sleep at last.

Strophe 1

ANTIGONÊ   Look upon me, friends, and pity me
    Turning back at the night's edge to say
    Good-by to the sun that shines for me no longer;
15   Now sleepy Death
    Summons me down to Acheron,[2] that cold shore:
    There is no bridesong there, nor any music.
CHORUS   Yet not unpraised, not without a kind of honor,
    You walk at last into the underworld;
20   Untouched by sickness, broken by no sword.
    What woman has ever found your way to death?

Antistrophe 1

ANTIGONÊ   How often I have heard the story
    of Niobê,[3]
25   Tantalos' wretched daughter, how the stone
    Clung fast about her, ivy-close: and they say
    The rain falls endlessly
    And sifting soft snow; her tears are never done.
    I feel the loneliness of her death in mine.
30   CHORUS   But she was born of heaven, and you
    Are woman, woman-born. If her death is yours,
    A mortal woman's, is this not for you
    Glory in our world and in the world beyond?

---

[1] *Aphroditê* goddess of love
[2] *Acheron* a river in the underworld
[3] *Niobê* Niobê, the daughter of Tantalos, was turned into a stone on Mount
   Sipylus while bemoaning the destruction of her many children by Leto, the
   mother of Apollo.

Strophe 2

ANTIGONÊ   You laugh at me. Ah, friends, friends,
Can you not wait until I am dead? O Thebes,
O men many-charioted, in love with Fortune,
5   Dear springs of Dircê, sacred Theban grove,
Be witnesses for me, denied all pity,
Unjustly judged! and think a word of love
For her whose path turns
Under dark earth, where there are no more tears.
10   CHORUS   You have passed beyond human daring and come at last
Into a place of stone where Justice sits.
I cannot tell
What shape of your father's guilt appears in this.

Antistrophe 2

15   ANTIGONÊ   You have touched it at last:
       that bridal bed
Unspeakable, horror of son and mother mingling:
Their crime, infection of all our family!
O Oedipus, father and brother!
20   Your marriage strikes from the grave to murder mine.
I have been a stranger here in my own land:
All my life
The blasphemy of my birth has followed me.
CHORUS   Reverence is a virtue, but strength
25   Lives in established law: that must prevail.
You have made your choice,
Your death is the doing of your conscious hand.

Epode

ANTIGONÊ   Then let me go, since all your words are bitter,
30   And the very light of the sun is cold to me.
Lead me to my vigil, where I must have
Neither love nor lamentation; no song, but silence.

(KREON *interrupts impatiently.*)

KREON   If dirges and planned lamentations could put off death,
35   Men would be singing for ever.
(*To the* SERVANTS)   Take her, go!
You know your orders: take her to the vault
And leave her alone there. And if she lives or dies,
That's her affair, not ours: our hands are clean.

40   ANTIGONÊ   O tomb, vaulted bride-bed in eternal rock,
Soon I shall be with my own again

Where Persephonê[1] welcomes the thin ghosts
　underground:
And I shall see my father again, and you, mother,
And dearest Polyneicês—

5
　　　　　　　　　　　　　dearest indeed
To me, since it was my hand
That washed him clean and poured the ritual wine:
And my reward is death before my time!

And yet, as men's hearts know, I have done no wrong,
10　I have not sinned before God. Or if I have,
I shall know the truth in death. But if the guilt
Lies upon Kreon who judged me, then, I pray,
May his punishment equal my own.

CHORAGOS　　　　　　　　　　　O passionate heart,
15　Unyielding, tormented still by the same winds!
KREON　Her guards shall have good cause to regret their delaying.
ANTIGONÊ　Ah! That voice is like the voice of death!
KREON　I can give you no reason to think you are mistaken.
ANTIGONÊ　Thebes, and you my fathers' gods,
20　And rulers of Thebes, you see me now, the last
Unhappy daughter of a line of kings,
Your kings, led away to death. You will remember
What things I suffer, and at what men's hands,
Because I would not transgress the laws of heaven.
25　(*To the* GUARDS, *simply.*) Come: let us wait no longer.

(*Exit* ANTIGONÊ, *left, guarded.*)

ODE IV

Strophe 1

CHORUS　All Danaê's[2] beauty was locked away
30　In a brazen cell where the sunlight could not come:
A small room still as any grave, enclosed her.
Yet she was a princess too,
And Zeus in a rain of gold poured love upon her.
O child, child,
35　No power in wealth or war

---

[1] *Persephonê* queen of the underworld
[2] *Danaê* the mother of Perseus by Zeus, who visited her during her imprisonment in the form of a golden rain

Or tough sea-blackened ships
Can prevail against untiring Destiny!

Antistrophe 1

And Dryas' son[1] also, that furious king,

5   Bore the god's prisoning anger for his pride:
Sealed up by Dionysos in deaf stone,
His madness died among echoes.
So at the last he learned what dreadful power
His tongue had mocked:

10   For he had profaned the revels,
And fired the wrath of the nine
Implacable Sisters[2] that love the sound of the flute.

Strophe 2

And old men tell a half-remembered tale

15   Of horror where a dark ledge splits the sea
And a double surf beats on the gráy shóres:
How a king's new woman,[3] sick
With hatred for the queen he had imprisoned,
Ripped out his two sons' eyes with her bloody hands

20   While grinning Arês[4] watched the shuttle plunge
Four times: four blind wounds crying for revenge.

Antistrophe 2

Crying, tears and blood mingled.—Piteously born,
Those sons whose mother was of heavenly birth!

25   Her father was the god of the North Wind
And she was cradled by gales,
She raced with young colts on the glittering hills
And walked untrammeled in the open light:
But in her marriage deathless Fate found means

30   To build a tomb like yours for all her joy.

SCENE V

(*Enter blind* TEIRESIAS, *led by a boy. The opening speeches of* TEIRE-
SIAS *should be in singsong contrast to the realistic lines of* KREON.)

TEIRESIAS   This is the way the blind man comes, Princes, Princes,

35   Lock-step, two heads lit by the eyes of one.

---

1 *Dryas' son* Lycurgus, king of Thrace
2 *Sisters* the Muses
3 *king's new woman* Eidothea, King Phineus' second wife, blinded her step-
sons.
4 *Arês* god of war

KREON   What new thing have you to tell us, old Teiresias?

TEIRESIAS   I have much to tell you: listen to the prophet, Kreon.

KREON   I am not aware that I have ever failed to listen.

TEIRESIAS   Then you have done wisely, King, and ruled well.

5   KREON   I admit my debt to you. But what have you to say?

TEIRESIAS   This, Kreon: you stand once more on the edge of fate.

KREON   What do you mean? Your words are a kind of dread.

TEIRESIAS   Listen, Kreon:

I was sitting in my chair of augury, at the place

10   Where the birds gather about me. They were all a-chatter,

As is their habit, when suddenly I heard

A strange note in their jangling, a scream, a

Whirring fury; I knew that they were fighting,

Tearing each other, dying

15   In a whirlwind of wings clashing. And I was afraid.

I began the rites of burnt-offering at the altar,

But Hephaistos[1] failed me: instead of bright flame,

There was only the sputtering slime of the fat thigh-flesh

Melting: the entrails dissolved in gray smoke,

20   The bare bone burst from the welter. And no blaze!

This was a sign from heaven. My boy described it,

Seeing for me as I see for others.

I tell you, Kreon, you yourself have brought

This new calamity upon us. Our hearths and altars

25   Are stained with the corruption of dogs and carrion birds

That glut themselves on the corpse of Oedipus' son.

The gods are deaf when we pray to them, their fire

Recoils from our offering, their birds of omen

Have no cry of comfort, for they are gorged

30   With the thick blood of the dead.

O my son,

These are no trifles! Think: all men make mistakes,

But a good man yields when he knows his course is wrong,

And repairs the evil. The only crime is pride.

35   Give in to the dead man, then: do not fight with a corpse—

What glory is it to kill a man who is dead?

Think, I beg you:

---

[1] *Hephaistos* god of fire

It is for your own good that I speak as I do.
You should be able to yield for your own good.

KREON   It seems that prophets have made me their especial
    province.
5 All my life long
I have been a kind of butt for the dull arrows
Of doddering fortune-tellers!
                No, Teiresias:
If your birds—if the great eagles of God himself
10 Should carry him stinking bit by bit to heaven,
I would not yield. I am not afraid of pollution:
No man can defile the gods.
                  Do what you will,
Go into business, make money, speculate
15 In India gold or that synthetic gold from Sardis,
Get rich otherwise than by my consent to bury him.
Teiresias, it is a sorry thing when a wise man
Sells his wisdom, lets out his words for hire!

TEIRESIAS   Ah Kreon! Is there no man left in the world—
20 KREON   To do what?—Come, let's have the aphorism!
TEIRESIAS   No man who knows that wisdom outweighs any wealth?
KREON   As surely as bribes are baser than any baseness.
TEIRESIAS   You are sick, Kreon! You are deathly sick!
KREON   As you say: it is not my place to challenge a prophet.
25 TEIRESIAS   Yet you have said my prophecy is for sale.
KREON   The generation of prophets has always loved gold.
TEIRESIAS   The generation of kings has always loved brass.
KREON   You forget yourself! You are speaking to your King.
TEIRESIAS   I know it. You are a king because of me.
30 KREON   You have a certain skill; but you have sold out.
TEIRESIAS   King, you will drive me to words that—
KREON   Say them, say them!
Only remember: I will not pay you for them.
TEIRESIAS   No, you will find them too costly,
35 KREON   No doubt. Speak:
Whatever you say, you will not change my will.
TEIRESIAS   Then take this, and take it to heart!
The time is not far off when you shall pay back
Corpse for corpse, flesh of your own flesh.
40 You have thrust the child of this world into living night,
You have kept from the gods below the child that is theirs:
The one in a grave before her death, the other,
Dead, denied the grave. This is your crime:
And the Furies and the dark gods of Hell
45 Are swift with terrible punishment for you.

Do you want to buy me now, Kreon?

Not many days,
And your house will be full of men and women weeping,
And curses will be hurled at you from far
5   Cities grieving for sons unburied, left to rot
Before the walls of Thebes.

These are my arrows, Kreon: they are all for you.

(*To* Boy.) But come, child: lead me home.
Let him waste his fine anger upon younger men.
10   Maybe he will learn at last
To control a wiser tongue in a better head.

(*Exit* Teiresias.)

CHORAGOS   The old man has gone, King, but his words
Remain to plague us. I am old, too,
15   But I cannot remember that he was ever false.
KREON   That is true. . . . It troubles me.
Oh it is hard to give in! but it is worse
To risk everything for stubborn pride.
CHORAGOS   Kreon: take my advice.
20   KREON   What shall I do?
CHORAGOS   Go quickly: free Antigonê from her vault
And build a tomb for the body of Polyneicês.
KREON   You would have me do this!
CHORAGOS   Kreon, yes!
25   And it must be done at once: God moves
Swiftly to cancel the folly of stubborn men.
KREON   It is hard to deny the heart! But I
Will do it: I will not fight with destiny.
CHORAGOS   You must go yourself, you cannot leave it to others.
30   KREON   I will go.
—Bring axes, servants:
Come with me to the tomb. I buried her, I
Will set her free.
Oh quickly!
35   My mind misgives—
The laws of the gods are mighty, and a man must serve them
To the last day of his life!

(*Exit* Kreon.)

PAEAN [1]

Strophe 1

CHORAGOS   God of many names

CHORUS   O Iacchos[2]

5   son

of Kadmeian Sémelê[3]

O born of the Thunder!

Guardian of the West

Regent

10   of Eleusis' plain

O Prince of maenad Thebes

and the Dragon Field by rippling Ismenós: [4]

Antistrophe 1

CHORAGOS   God of many names

15   CHORUS   the flame of torches

flares on our hills

the nymphs of Iacchos

dance at the spring of Castalia: [5]

from the vine-close mountain

20   come ah come in ivy:

Evohé evohé! sings through the streets of Thebes

Strophe 2

CHORAGOS   God of many names

CHORUS   Iacchos of Thebes

25   heavenly Child

of Sémelê bride of the Thunderer!

The shadow of plague is upon us:

come

with clement feet

30   oh come from Parnasos

down the long slopes

across the lamenting water

Antistrophe 2

CHORAGOS   Iô Fire! Chorister of the throbbing stars!

35   O purest among the voices of the night!

Thou son of God, blaze for us!

---

1 *Paean* a hymn of praise

2 *Iacchos* another name for Dionysos (Bacchus)

3 *Sémelê* the daughter of Kadmos, the founder of Thebes

4 *Ismenós* a river east of Thebes. The ancestors of the Theban nobility sprang from dragon's teeth sown by the Ismenós.

5 *Castalia* a spring on Mount Parnasos

CHORUS   Come with choric rapture of circling Maenads[1]
Who cry *Iô Iacche!*
            God of many names!

EXODOS

5   (*Enter* MESSENGER *from left.*)

MESSENGER   Men of the line of Kadmos, you who live
Near Amphion's citadel,[2]
                    I cannot say
Of any condition of human life "This is fixed,
10   This is clearly good, or bad." Fate raises up,
And Fate casts down the happy and unhappy alike:
No man can foretell his Fate.
                    Take the case of Kreon:
Kreon was happy once, as I count happiness:
15   Victorious in battle, sole governor of the land,
Fortunate father of children nobly born.
And now it has all gone from him! Who can say
That a man is still alive when his life's joy fails?
He is a walking dead man. Grant him rich,
20   Let him live like a king in his great house:
If his pleasure is gone, I would not give
So much as the shadow of smoke for all he owns.
CHORAGOS   Your words hint at sorrow: what is your news for us?
MESSENGER   They are dead. The living are guilty of their death.
25   CHORAGOS   Who is guilty? Who is dead? Speak!
MESSENGER   Haimon.
Haimon is dead; and the hand that killed him
Is his own hand.
CHORAGOS   His father's? or his own?
30   MESSENGER   His own, driven mad by the murder his father had
    done.
CHORAGOS   Teiresias, Teiresias, how clearly you saw it all!
MESSENGER   This is my news: you must draw what conclusions
    you can from it.
35   CHORAGOS   But look: Eurydicê, our Queen:
Has she overheard us?

(*Enter* EURYDICÊ *from the palace, center.*)

---

[1] *Maenads* the worshippers of Dionysos
[2] *Amphion's citadel* Amphion used the music of his magic lyre to lure stones
to form a wall around Thebes.

EURYDICÊ   I have heard something, friends:
As I was unlocking the gate of Pallas' [1] shrine,
For I needed her help today, I heard a voice
Telling of some new sorrow. And I fainted
5 There at the temple all my maidens about me.
But speak again: whatever it is, I can bear it:
Grief and I are no strangers.

MESSENGER   Dearest Lady,
I will tell you plainly all that I have seen.
10 I shall not try to comfort you: what is the use,
Since comfort could lie only in what is not true?
The truth is always best.

                        I went with Kreon
To the outer plain where Polyneicês was lying,
15 No friend to pity him, his body shredded by dogs.
We made our prayers in that place to Hecatê
And Pluto,[2] that they would be merciful. And we bathed
The corpse with holy water, and we brought
Fresh-broken branches to burn what was left of it,
20 And upon the urn we heaped up a towering barrow
Of the earth of his own land.

                        When we were done, we ran
To the vault where Antigonê lay on her couch of stone.
One of the servants had gone ahead,
25 And while he was yet far off he heard a voice
Grieving within the chamber, and he came back
And told Kreon. And as the King went closer,
The air was full of wailing, the words lost,
And he begged us to make all haste. "Am I a prophet?"
30 He said, weeping, "And must I walk this road,
The saddest of all that I have gone before?
My son's voice calls me on. Oh quickly, quickly!
Look through the crevice there, and tell me
If it is Haimon, or some deception of the gods!"

35 We obeyed; and in the cavern's farthest corner
We saw her lying:
She had made a noose of her fine linen veil
And hanged herself. Haimon lay beside her,
His arms about her waist, lamenting her,

---

1 *Pallas* Pallas Athena, the goddess of wisdom
2 *Hecatê . . . Pluto* the ruling deities of the underworld

His love lost under ground, crying out
That his father had stolen her away from him.

When Kreon saw him the tears rushed to his eyes
And he called to him: "What have you done, child?
5   Speak to me.
What are you thinking that makes your eyes so strange?
O my son, my son, I come to you on my knees!"
But Haimon spat in his face. He said not a word,
Staring—
10   And suddenly drew his sword
And lunged. Kreon shrank back, the blade missed; and the
    boy,
Desperate against himself, drove it half its length
Into his own side, and fell. And as he died
15 He gathered Antigonê close in his arms again,
Choking, his blood bright red on her white cheek.
And now he lies dead with the dead, and she is his
At last, his bride in the house of the dead.

(*Exit* Eurydicê *into the palace.*)

20 CHORAGOS   She has left us without a word. What can this mean?
MESSENGER   It troubles me, too; yet she knows what is best,
Her grief is too great for public lamentation,
And doubtless she has gone to her chamber to weep
For her dead son, leading her maidens in his dirge.

25   (*Pause.*)

CHORAGOS   It may be so: but I fear this deep silence.
MESSENGER   I will see what she is doing. I will go in.

(*Exit* Messenger *into the palace. Enter* Kreon *with attendants, bearing* Haimon's *body.*)

30 CHORAGOS   But here is the king himself: oh look at him,
Bearing his own damnation in his arms.
KREON   Nothing you say can touch me any more.
My own blind heart has brought me
From darkness to final darkness. Here you see
35 The father murdering, the murdered son—
And all my civic wisdom!

Haimon my son, so young, so young to die,
I was the fool, not you; and you died for me.
CHORAGOS   That is the truth; but you were late in learning it.

KREON   This truth is hard to bear. Surely a god
Has crushed me beneath the hugest weight of heaven,
And driven me headlong a barbaric way
To trample out the thing I held most dear.

5   The pains that men will take to come to pain!

(*Enter* MESSENGER *from the palace.*)

MESSENGER   The burden you carry in your hands is heavy,
But it is not all: you will find more in your house.
KREON   What burden worse than this shall I find there?
10   MESSENGER   The Queen is dead.
KREON   O port of death, deaf world,
Is there no pity for me? And you, Angel of evil,
I was dead, and your words are death again.
Is it true, boy? Can it be true?
15   Is my wife dead? Has death bred death?
MESSENGER   You can see for yourself.

(*The doors are opened and the body of* EURYDICÊ *is disclosed within.*)

KREON   Oh pity!
All true, all true, and more than I can bear!
20   O my wife, my son!
MESSENGER   She stood before the altar, and her heart
Welcomed the knife her own hand guided,
And a great cry burst from her lips for Megareus[1] dead,
And for Haimon dead, her sons; and her last breath
25   Was a curse for their father, the murderer of her sons.
And she fell, and the dark flowed in through her closing eyes.
KREON   O God, I am sick with fear.
Are there no swords here? Has no one a blow for me?
MESSENGER   Her curse is upon you for the deaths of both.
30   KREON   It is right that it should be. I alone am guilty.
I know it, and I say it. Lead me in,
Quickly, friends.
I have neither life nor substance. Lead me in.
CHORAGOS   You are right, if there can be right in so much wrong.
35   The briefest way is best in a world of sorrow.
KREON   Let it come,
Let death come quickly, and be kind to me.
I would not ever see the sun again.
CHORAGOS   All that will come when it will; but we, meanwhile,

---

1 *Megareus* Megareus, brother of Haimon, had died in the assault on Thebes.

Have much to do. Leave the future to itself.
KREON   All my heart was in that prayer!
CHORAGOS   Then do not pray any more: the sky is deaf.
KREON   Lead me away. I have been rash and foolish.
5   I have killed my son and my wife.
I look for comfort; my comfort lies here dead.
Whatever my hands have touched has come to nothing.
Fate has brought all my pride to a thought of dust.

(*As* KREON *is being led into the house, the* CHORAGOS *advances and*
10   *speaks directly to the audience.*)

CHORAGOS   There is no happiness where there is no wisdom;
No wisdom but in submission to the gods.
Big words are always punished,
And proud men in old age learn to be wise.

QUESTIONS FOR THINKING AND WRITING

1. One might argue that in *Antigonê* each of the major characters undergoes his or her own moment of "recognition" and subsequent reversal of fortune. For instance, one can say that the play opens on Antigonê's recognition of Kreon's edict—both because she has just learned of the edict and because she here expresses her realization of how she must react to it and of what retaliation her reaction is likely to draw.
   a. Arguing along these lines, identify the scenes, events, and speeches that mark Kreon's recognition. What reversal would you say follows from it?
   b. Would you also want to argue for recognitions for Haimon, Eurydicê, and Ismenê? If so, where would you place them, and what reversals would you say follow them?
   c. Write an essay that (1) discusses each of these recognitions and their significance to the characters involved, and (2) demonstrates how the placement and cumulative effect of these several recognitions and reversals give the play its shape and dramatic impact. (Remember that you must define the structure and movement of the play as you see it, to ensure that you and your reader are working from the same basic understanding.)
2. How would you balance the claims of "thought" and "character" as the more important element in *Antigonê*? (In other words, is it the questions argued or the character and fate of the debaters that you feel provide the strongest source of the play's appeal?) Would either element alone suffice? Why or why not?
3. Antigonê and Kreon are, of course, the major antagonists in *Antigonê*. But each has another opponent as well. Ismenê argues against Antigonê's actions, and Haimon argues against Kreon. What do the presence and actions of these two characters add to the play?

3 Hamlet *and Elizabethan Tragedy*

Origins of English Drama

English drama can be traced back to two origins, one in tenth-century England and one in ancient Greece. The two beginnings differed greatly in style and content but did have one important thing in common: both formed parts of religious rituals.

Medieval Drama

Drama in medieval Europe seems to have begun as part of the Easter services. At some appropriate point during the Mass or the matins service, one or two men would unobtrusively position themselves near the altar or near some representation of a tomb. There, they would be approached by three other men, whose heads were covered to look like women and who moved slowly, as if seeking something. Singing in the Latin of the church service, the "angel" at the tomb would question the "women," "Whom seek you in the tomb, O followers of Christ?" The women would then sing the answer of the three Mary's, "Jesus of Nazareth, who was crucified, O heavenly one." The angel then would sing again, "He is not here; he is risen, just as he foretold. Go, announce that he is risen from the tomb."

The dramatization might stop there, or it might continue with the showing of the empty tomb to the women, their song of joy, and the spreading of the good news to the disciples. In either case, the culmination of the drama would mark a return to the service itself with the singing of the Mass's *Ressurexi* ("I have risen") or the matins' final *Te deum, laudamus* ("We praise thee, Lord").

One medieval manuscript in particular emphasizes the closeness of the connection. It describes the singers of the *Te Deum* as rejoicing with the three women at Christ's triumph over death and commands that all the church bells be rung together as soon as the hymn of praise has begun. Drama and service thus celebrate the same event. The joy expressed by the women at the news of the resurrection is the same joy felt by the worshippers in the congregation.

Latin drama continued to develop within the church services. Manuscripts still survive, not only of Easter and Christmas plays but of plays dealing with prophets and saints as well. They show the plays growing longer and more elaborate than the early one just described, but they still emphasize the close ties between the plays and the services at which they are performed. Thus, one Christmas pageant of the shepherds calls for many boys dressed as angels to sit in the roof of the church and sing in loud voices the angels' song, "Glory to God." But it also directs that, at the end of the pageant, the shepherds must return into the choir and there act as choir leaders for the Mass that follows.

By the fourteenth century, however, drama had also moved outside the church. There it was spoken almost wholly in the vernacular, though some bits of Latin, and a good deal of singing, remained. The plays were acted by laymen (including some professional actors) rather than by clerics, and they were developing modes of performance that might encompass up to three days of playing and involve most of the citizens of the towns where they were performed.

These were the Corpus Christi plays, also known as the "cycle plays" or the "mystery plays." Performed in celebration of Corpus Christi day, they comprised a series of pageants beginning with the creation of the world, proceeding through the history of the Old and New Testaments, and ending with the Last Judgment. Each pageant was performed on its own movable stage—its "pageant wagon." Mounted on four or six wheels, two stories high, the wagons provided facilities for some surprisingly complex stage effects and allowed each pageant to be presented several times at several different locations. One after another, the pageants would move through a town, usually stopping at three or four prearranged places to repeat their performances, so that everyone in town might see all of the twenty to fifty plays that made up the cycle.

The presentation of these cycles was undertaken by the towns themselves, with the town authorities ordering the performances. But the individual pageants were produced by the local trade and craft guilds. Ordinarily each guild would present one pageant, but sometimes several small guilds would team up to perform a single pageant or share the cost of a wagon that each could use. It is easy to imagine the competition this could produce, with each guild trying to outdo the next. But the plays were still religious in subject and import. They often spoke directly to the audience and always emphasized how the events they depicted pertained to each viewer's salvation.

Early English Dramatic Forms

As we suggested in the last chapter, Greek drama carefully labeled and segregated its forms. Tragedy dealt with noble persons and heroic actions. Comedy dealt with everyday affairs.

Medieval drama did not so carefully distinguish its forms. It had one central sacrificial subject: the death of Christ for the salvation of mankind. This sacrifice was always treated seriously; neither Christ nor Mary were ever burlesqued. But the world that Christ entered at his birth was the world of thin clothes and bad weather, of thieves and tricksters and con men, with the Devil himself, the arch-trickster, as Christ's opponent. It was, in short, the world of comedy. A drama that dealt with the history of man's fall and salvation would thus have to be both comic and tragic. There would be no way of separating the two.

Nor would medieval writers have wanted to separate them. Medieval art always seems to have preferred inclusiveness to exclusiveness. The great Gothic cathedrals themselves, with their profusion of sculpture and stained glass, would give their most prominent and most beautiful art to scenes of Christ, the Virgin, and the saints. But less prominent carvings would be likely to show small boys stealing apples, or people quarreling; while, in other places, comically or frighteningly grotesque demons would round out the portrayals.

A Corpus Christi cycle, therefore, would contain both serious and humorous elements. Some plays would be wholly serious; others would mix the serious with the comic. "The Sacrifice of Isaac," for instance, was always serious. The dilemma of the father, the emotions of the son as he realized what was happening, combined to produce plays that could virtually be described as tragedies with happy endings. "Noah's Flood," on the other hand, was usually given a comic treatment. (What would you do if your husband suddenly started building a giant boat in your front yard?) In some of the plays, Noah's wife thinks her husband has gone crazy. In others, she joins in the building until it is time to get on board, then rebels against leaving the world she knows and loves. In either case, a physical fight ensues before Noah can get her on board, and Noah's prophecies of doom are mixed with his complaints about marriage. Crucifixion plays, meanwhile, generally mixed the solemnity of the highest sacrifice with a certain amount of low comedy centering on the executioners. There was no thought of separating the two. Both were parts of the same event.

In this way, seeking to mirror life and to emphasize its mixture of noble and ignoble, sacred and mundane, the medieval drama provided Elizabethan playwrights a heritage of flexible, all-inclusive drama, capable at its best of seeing both sides of a subject at once, always insistent that both must be recognized. By mixing this heritage with the more single-minded Greek tragic tradition, Elizabethan dramatists produced a tragic form of their own as rich and compelling as any that has existed.

In this chapter, we shall study one of the most highly praised and frequently acted Elizabethan tragedies—William Shakespeare's *Hamlet*.

Hamlet

Hamlet, as we suggested earlier, is a play derived from both Greek and medieval drama. From Greek tragedy, it has taken the tragic hero— dominant, strong-willed, determined to accomplish his desires. From Greek tragedy also it has taken a certain elevation of tone and insistence on the dignity of human beings. From medieval drama, it has taken the medieval desire for inclusiveness and the medieval love of significant detail. *Hamlet* is a long play, with many characters, a complex plot, and a generous amount of comedy.

Let us look at each of these elements in turn. Regarding characters, we notice that Hamlet sees himself reflected in two other characters: first in Fortinbras, another son of a warrior king whose father has died and whose uncle has seized the throne, leaving him practically powerless; and later in Laertes, another son determined to avenge himself on his father's murderer. The deeds of Laertes and Fortinbras contrast with and comment on the actions of Hamlet himself, thus enriching our view of Hamlet and his dilemma. At the same time, the actions of the three men intertwine to create three of the play's major themes: fathers and sons, honor, and thought versus action.

Regarding plot, we can be sure that the affairs of three families will create a more complex plot than the affairs of one family. Thus critics sometimes speak of the Fortinbras "overplot" (which is mostly concerned with war and kingship) and the Laertes "underplot" (concerned with private family relationships), while discussing how these two "subplots" complement the "main plot" (which deals with Hamlet's familial and princely concerns). But the English inclusiveness goes even beyond this, adding also a love story between Hamlet and Laertes' sister, Ophelia, a study of true versus false friendship in the persons of Horatio and Rosencrantz and Guildenstern, and a few comments on the contemporary theater by a troupe of strolling players. There are also glimpses of three purely comic characters: two gravediggers and one intolerably affected courtier. Again, all these themes and characters are interwoven to illuminate Hamlet's character and dilemma. (The gravediggers, for instance, who seem at first wildly irrelevant, ultimately serve to bring Hamlet to a new understanding of mortality, an understanding that is crucial to his ability to face his own death.)

In *Hamlet* comedy is not separate from tragedy. Rather, it is used as a means to create a fuller awareness of tragedy. Hamlet himself is a master of comic wordplay. His first speech turns on a pun; and puns and bitter quips mark his speech to Claudius and his courtiers throughout the play. Many of these quips are spoken under the guise of pretended madness; and here the audience shares secrets with Hamlet. We know he is not really mad. But those on stage think he is. (The exception is Claudius, who suspects that Hamlet is not mad but who cannot reveal Hamlet's sanity without revealing his own crimes.) Pretending madness, therefore, Hamlet makes speeches that sound like nonsense to the courtiers but that we recognize as referring to his father's murder and his recognition of treachery in those around him. We are thus let into Hamlet's secrets and feelings as no single character in the play is let into them. Hamlet's use of jesting speech thus becomes not merely a weapon in his fight against Claudius, but also a means of winning the sympathetic partnership of the audience. In comic speech and tragic soliloquy alike, Hamlet reveals himself to us. By the play's end, we know Hamlet as we know few other stage characters.

Adding to our sense of knowledge is the fact that Hamlet is a complex and changing character. The essentially fixed character is typical of Greek drama, which seems to have been more interested in the clash of character against character (or of character against fate) than it was in the changes within or the development of a single character. It is far less typical of Elizabethan tragedy.

This emphasis on Hamlet's developing character is an indication of the influence of medieval Christian drama, with its concern for salvation and the dangers and triumphs of the soul. English drama was secular drama by Shakespeare's time, being performed regularly by professional troupes for paying audiences. Concern for the soul, however, remained one of its major concerns. When Elizabethan dramatists wrote tragedies, therefore, they tended to make the hero's inner concerns—his passions, his temptations, his spiritual triumphs or defeats—the central focus of their plays. Even the ghost in *Hamlet,* coming to call for revenge, warns Hamlet to "taint not thy mind, nor let thy soul contrive/Against thy mother aught." Hamlet must avenge his father and free Denmark from the polluting rule of Claudius; but he must do so in a manner that will imperil neither his own nor his mother's salvation.

When the play opens, Hamlet is a bitter man. So far from being at peace with himself or his surroundings is he that he seems to have little chance of fulfilling the ghost's demands. So close does he come to flinging away his own soul in pursuit of Claudius, in fact, that some critics have refused to believe that Hamlet's speeches in Act III, Scene 3, mean what they say. In fact, they mean exactly what they say. Hamlet in this scene is on the brink of disaster.

In the next scene, the "closet scene," the unexpected happens. Hamlet is caught in the wrong, realizes it, and begins the painful process of returning from his bitterness and hatreds to a reconciliation with himself, his mother, and humanity in general. Throughout the rest of the play, we watch Hamlet's speeches on human nature become gentler, his attitude more compassionate; we hear a new acceptance of his fate, a new trust in providence, revealed. By the play's end, when Hamlet gets his one chance at Claudius, he is fully ready for the task and its consequences. And so the play ends in mingled triumph and loss: a loss to Denmark and to us in the death of Hamlet, a joy that Hamlet has nobly achieved his purpose.

One final word must be said about the language of *Hamlet,* which is like the language of no other play we will read in this book. Seeking some meter in English that would match the beauty and dignity of the meters in which classical tragedy had been written, the sixteenth century dramatists had created **blank verse.** Blank verse does not rhyme. It usually has ten syllables to a line (though lines may be shorter or longer by a few syllables), and the second, fourth, sixth, eighth, and tenth syllables are generally accented more strongly than the rest. This meter was easily spoken. It was dignified and flexible. And it could slip neatly into prose (for comic scenes) or into rhymed couplets to mark a scene's end.

Blank verse was fairly new when Shakespeare began writing. In some of his early plays, it still sounds stiff and awkward. By the time he wrote *Hamlet,* however, Shakespeare was entering into a mastery of blank verse that no one has ever surpassed. The rhythms and imagery of Hamlet's language warn us of every change in his moods, from pretended madness to honest friendship to bitter passion. By the modulation of Hamlet's language, as well as by his actions, Shakespeare shows us the battle within Hamlet's soul.

If you can see *Hamlet*—live or on film—or if you can hear recordings of it, do so. If not, read as much of it aloud as you can. For readers unfamiliar with Shakespearean language, *Hamlet* is not an easy play to read. Nearly every word of it counts; so every word must be attended to. But the play is well worth the effort it takes, for it is truly one of the finest plays of all time.

WILLIAM SHAKESPEARE   (1564–1616)

Hamlet

CHARACTERS

CLAUDIUS, *King of Denmark*
HAMLET, *son to the late, and nephew to the present, King*
POLONIUS, *Lord Chamberlain*
HORATIO, *friend to Hamlet*
LAERTES, *son to Polonius*
VOLTEMAND ⎤
CORNELIUS ⎥
ROSENCRANTZ ⎥   *courtiers*
GUILDENSTERN ⎥
OSRIC ⎥
A GENTLEMAN ⎦
A PRIEST
MARCELLUS ⎤   *officers*
BERNARDO ⎦
FRANCISCO, *a soldier*
REYNALDO, *servant to Polonius*
PLAYERS
TWO CLOWNS, *gravediggers*
FORTINBRAS, *Prince of Norway*
A NORWEGIAN CAPTAIN
ENGLISH AMBASSADORS
GERTRUDE, *Queen of Denmark, mother to Hamlet*
OPHELIA, *daughter to Polonius*
GHOST OF HAMLET'S FATHER
LORDS, LADIES, OFFICERS, SOLDIERS, SAILORS, MESSENGERS,
   ATTENDANTS

ACT I

Scene I

Elsinore Castle: a sentry-post

(*Enter* BERNARDO *and* FRANCISCO, *two sentinels*)

5 BERNARDO Who's there?

FRANCISCO Nay, answer me. Stand and unfold yourself.

BERNARDO Long live the king!

FRANCISCO Bernardo?

BERNARDO He.

10 FRANCISCO You come most carefully upon your hour.

BERNARDO 'Tis now struck twelve. Get thee to bed, Francisco.

FRANCISCO For this relief much thanks. 'Tis bitter cold,
And I am sick at heart.

BERNARDO Have you had quiet guard?

15 FRANCISCO   Not a mouse stirring.

BERNARDO Well, good night.
If you do meet Horatio and Marcellus,
The rivals[1] of my watch, bid them make haste.

(*Enter* HORATIO *and* MARCELLUS)

20 FRANCISCO I think I hear them. Stand, ho! Who is there?

HORATIO Friends to this ground.

MARCELLUS   And liegemen to the Dane.[2]

FRANCISCO Give you good night.

MARCELLUS   O, farewell, honest soldier.

25 Who hath relieved you?

FRANCISCO   Bernardo hath my place.
Give you good night.

(*Exit* FRANCISCO)

MARCELLUS   Holla, Bernardo!

30 BERNARDO   Say—
What, is Horatio there?

HORATIO   A piece of him.

BERNARDO Welcome, Horatio. Welcome, good Marcellus.

HORATIO What, has this thing appeared again to-night?

35 BERNARDO I have seen nothing.

MARCELLUS Horatio says 'tis but our fantasy,
And will not let belief take hold of him

---

[1] *rivals* sharers   [2] *Dane* King of Denmark

Touching this dreaded sight twice seen of us.
Therefore I have entreated him along
With us to watch the minutes of this night,
That, if again this apparition come,
5   He may approve[3] our eyes and speak to it.
HORATIO   Tush, tush, 'twill not appear.
BERNARDO   Sit down awhile,
And let us once again assail your ears,
That are so fortified against our story,
10   What we two nights have seen.
HORATIO   Well, sit we down,
And let us hear Bernardo speak of this.
BERNARDO   Last night of all,
When yond same star that's westward from the pole[4]
15   Had made his course t' illume that part of heaven
Where now it burns, Marcellus and myself,
The bell then beating one—

   (*Enter* GHOST)

MARCELLUS   Peace, break thee off. Look where it comes again.
20   BERNARDO   In the same figure like the king that's dead.
MARCELLUS   Thou art a scholar; speak to it, Horatio.
BERNARDO   Looks 'a not like the king? Mark it, Horatio.
HORATIO   Most like. It harrows me with fear and wonder.
BERNARDO   It would be spoke to.
25   MARCELLUS   Speak to it, Horatio.
HORATIO   What art thou that usurp'st this time of night
Together with that fair and warlike form
In which the majesty of buried Denmark[5]
Did sometimes[6] march? By heaven I charge thee, speak.
30   MARCELLUS   It is offended.
BERNARDO   See, it stalks away.
HORATIO   Stay. Speak, speak. I charge thee, speak.

   (*Exit* GHOST)

MARCELLUS   'Tis gone and will not answer.
35   BERNARDO   How now, Horatio? You tremble and look pale.
Is not this something more than fantasy?
What think you on't?
HORATIO   Before my God, I might not this believe

---

[3] *approve* confirm   [4] *pole* polestar   [5] *buried Denmark* the buried King of
Denmark   [6] *sometimes* formerly

Without the sensible and true avouch
Of mine own eyes.

MARCELLUS   Is it not like the king?

HORATIO   As thou art to thyself.

5   Such was the very armor he had on
When he th' ambitious Norway[7] combated.
So frowned he once when, in an angry parle,[8]
He smote the sledded Polacks on the ice.
'Tis strange.

10 MARCELLUS   Thus twice before, and jump[9] at this dead hour,
With martial stalk hath he gone by our watch.

HORATIO   In what particular thought to work I know not;
But, in the gross and scope[10] of my opinion,
This bodes some strange eruption to our state.

15 MARCELLUS   Good now, sit down, and tell me he that knows,
Why this same strict and most observant watch
So nightly toils the subject[11] of the land,
And why such daily cast of brazen cannon
And foreign mart[12] for implements of war,

20 Why such impress[13] of shipwrights, whose sore task
Does not divide the Sunday from the week.
What might be toward [14] that this sweaty haste
Doth make the night joint-laborer with the day?
Who is't that can inform me?

25 HORATIO   That can I.
At least the whisper goes so. Our last king,
Whose image even but now appeared to us,
Was as you know by Fortinbras of Norway,
Thereto pricked on by a most emulate[15] pride,

30 Dared to the combat; in which our valiant Hamlet
(For so this side of our known world esteemed him)
Did slay this Fortinbras; who, by a sealed compact
Well ratified by law and heraldry,[16]
Did forfeit, with his life, all those his lands

35 Which he stood seized [17] of to the conqueror;
Against the which a moiety competent[18]
Was gagèd [19] by our king, which had returned
To the inheritance of Fortinbras

---

[7] *Norway* King of Norway   [8] *parle* parley   [9] *jump* just, exactly   [10] *gross and scope* gross scope, general view   [11] *toils* makes toil; *subject* subjects   [12] *mart* trading   [13] *impress* conscription   [14] *toward* in preparation   [15] *emulate* jealously rivalling   [16] *law and heraldry* law of heralds regulating combat   [17] *seized* possessed   [18] *moiety competent* sufficient portion   [19] *gagèd* engaged, staked

Had he been vanquisher, as, by the same comart[20]
And carriage[21] of the article designed,
His fell to Hamlet. Now, sir, young Fortinbras,
Of unimprovèd [22] mettle hot and full,

5   Hath in the skirts of Norway here and there
Sharked [23] up a list of lawless resolutes[24]
For food and diet to some enterprise
That hath a stomach[25] in't; which is no other,
As it doth well appear unto our state,

10   But to recover of us by strong hand
And terms compulsatory those foresaid lands
So by his father lost; and this, I take it,
Is the main motive of our preparations,
The source of this our watch, and the chief head [26]

15   Of this posthaste and romage[27] in the land.

BERNARDO   I think it be no other but e'en so.
Well may it sort[28] that this portentous figure
Comes armèd through our watch so like the king
That was and is the question of these wars.

20   HORATIO   A mote[29] it is to trouble the mind's eye.
In the most high and palmy state of Rome,
A little ere the mightiest Julius fell,
The graves stood tenantless and the sheeted [30] dead
Did squeak and gibber in the Roman streets;

25   As stars with trains of fire and dews of blood,
Disasters[31] in the sun; and the moist star[32]
Upon whose influence Neptune's empire stands
Was sick almost to doomsday with eclipse.
And even the like precurse[33] of feared events,

30   As harbingers[34] preceding still [35] the fates
And prologue to the omen[36] coming on,
Have heaven and earth together demonstrated
Unto our climatures[37] and countrymen.

(*Enter* GHOST)

35   But soft, behold, lo where it comes again!

---

20 *comart* joint bargain   21 *carriage* purport   22 *unimprovèd* unused
23 *Sharked* snatched indiscriminately as the shark takes prey   24 *resolutes*
desperadoes   25 *stomach* show of venturesomeness   26 *head* fountainhead,
source   27 *romage* intense activity   28 *sort* suit   29 *mote* speck of dust
30 *sheeted* in shrouds   31 *Disasters* ominous signs   32 *moist star* moon   33 *precurse* foreshadowing   34 *harbingers* forerunners   35 *still* constantly   36 *omen*
calamity   37 *climatures* regions

I'll cross it,[38] though it blast me.—Stay, illusion.

(*He spreads his arms*)

If thou hast any sound or use of voice,
Speak to me.
5   If there be any good thing to be done
That may to thee do ease and grace to me,
Speak to me.
If thou art privy to thy country's fate,
Which happily[39] foreknowing may avoid,
10 O, speak!
Or if thou hast uphoarded in thy life
Extorted treasure in the womb of earth,
For which, they say, you spirits oft walk in death,

(*The cock crows*)

15 Speak of it. Stay and speak. Stop it, Marcellus.
MARCELLUS   Shall I strike at it with my partisan? [40]
HORATIO   Do, if it will not stand.
BERNARDO   'Tis here.
HORATIO   'Tis here.

20 (*Exit* GHOST)

MARCELLUS   'Tis gone.
We do it wrong, being so majestical,
To offer it the show of violence,
For it is as the air invulnerable,
25 And our vain blows malicious mockery.
BERNARDO   It was about to speak when the cock crew.
HORATIO   And then it started, like a guilty thing
Upon a fearful summons. I have heard
The cock, that is the trumpet to the morn,
30 Doth with his lofty and shrill-sounding throat
Awake the god of day, and at his warning,
Whether in sea or fire, in earth or air,
Th' extravagant[41] and erring[42] spirit hies
To his confine; and of the truth herein
35 This present object made probation.[43]

---

[38] *cross it* cross its path   [39] *happily* haply, perchance   [40] *partisan* pike   [41] *extravagant* wandering beyond bounds   [42] *erring* wandering   [43] *probation* proof

MARCELLUS   It faded on the crowing of the cock.
    Some say that ever 'gainst[44] that season comes
    Wherein our Saviour's birth is celebrated,
    This bird of dawning singeth all night long,
5   And then, they say, no spirit dare stir abroad,
    The nights are wholesome, then no planets strike,[45]
    No fairy takes,[46] nor witch hath power to charm.
    So hallowed and so gracious is that time.
HORATIO   So have I heard and do in part believe it.
10 But look, the morn in russet mantle clad
    Walks o'er the dew of yon high eastward hill.
    Break we our watch up, and by my advice
    Let us impart what we have seen to-night
    Unto young Hamlet, for upon my life
15 This spirit, dumb to us, will speak to him.
    Do you consent we shall acquaint him with it,
    As needful in our loves, fitting our duty?
MARCELLUS   Let's do't, I pray, and I this morning know
    Where we shall find him most conveniently.

20 (*Exeunt*)

Act I, Scene II

Elsinore Castle: a room of state

Flourish. Enter CLAUDIUS, *King of Denmark,* GERTRUDE *the Queen,* COUN-
CILLORS, POLONIUS *and his son* LAERTES, HAMLET, *cum aliis*[1] [*including*
25 VOLTEMAND *and* CORNELIUS]

KING   Though yet of Hamlet our dear brother's death
    The memory be green, and that it us befitted
    To bear our hearts in grief, and our whole kingdom
    To be contracted in one brow of woe,
30 Yet so far hath discretion fought with nature
    That we with wisest sorrow think on him
    Together with remembrance of ourselves.
    Therefore our sometime sister, now our queen,
    Th' imperial jointress[2] to this warlike state,
35 Have we, as 'twere with a defeated joy,
    With an auspicious and a dropping eye,

---

44 *'gainst* just before   45 *strike* work evil by influence   46 *takes* bewitches
1 *cum aliis* with others   2 *jointress* a woman who has a jointure, or joint ten-
ancy of an estate

With mirth in funeral and with dirge in marriage,
In equal scale weighing delight and dole,
Taken to wife. Nor have we herein barred ³
Your better wisdoms, which have freely gone
5　With this affair along. For all, our thanks.
Now follows, that you know, young Fortinbras,
Holding a weak supposal of our worth,
Or thinking by our late dear brother's death
Our state to be disjoint and out of frame,
10　Colleaguèd ⁴ with this dream of his advantage,
He hath not failed to pester us with message
Importing the surrender of those lands
Lost by his father, with all bands of law,
To our most valiant brother. So much for him.
15　Now for ourself and for this time of meeting.
Thus much the business is: we have here writ
To Norway, uncle of young Fortinbras—
Who, impotent and bedrid, scarcely hears
Of this his nephew's purpose—to suppress
20　His further gait⁵ herein, in that the levies,
The lists, and full proportions⁶ are all made
Out of his subject; and we here dispatch
You, good Cornelius, and you, Voltemand,
For bearers of this greeting to old Norway,
25　Giving to you no further personal power
To business with the king, more than the scope
Of these delated ⁷ articles allow.
Farewell, and let your haste commend your duty.
　CORNELIUS, VOLTEMAND　In that, and all things, will we show our
30　　duty.
　KING　We doubt it nothing. Heartily farewell.

　(*Exeunt* VOLTEMAND *and* CORNELIUS)

And now, Laertes, what's the news with you?
You told us of some suit. What is't, Laertes?
35　You cannot speak of reason to the Dane⁸
And lose your voice.⁹ What wouldst thou beg, Laertes,
That shall not be my offer, not thy asking?
The head is not more native¹⁰ to the heart,

---

³ *barred* excluded　⁴ *Colleaguèd* united　⁵ *gait* going　⁶ *proportions* amounts
of forces and supplies　⁷ *delated* detailed　⁸ *Dane* King of Denmark　⁹ *lose
your voice* speak in vain　¹⁰ *native* joined by nature

The hand more instrumental [11] to the mouth,
Than is the throne of Denmark to thy father.
What wouldst thou have, Laertes?

LAERTES   My dread lord,
5   Your leave and favor to return to France,
From whence though willingly I came to Denmark
To show my duty in your coronation,
Yet now I must confess, that duty done,
My thoughts and wishes bend again toward France
10   And bow them to your gracious leave and pardon.

KING   Have you your father's leave? What says Polonius?

POLONIUS   He hath, my lord, wrung from me my slow leave
By laborsome petition, and at last
Upon his will I sealed my hard consent.
15   I do beseech you give him leave to go.

KING   Take thy fair hour, Laertes. Time be thine,
And thy best graces spend it at thy will.
But now, my cousin[12] Hamlet, and my son—

HAMLET (*aside*)   A little more than kin,[13] and less than kind! [14]
20   KING   How is it that the clouds still hang on you?

HAMLET   Not so, my lord. I am too much in the sun.[15]

QUEEN   Good Hamlet, cast thy nighted color off,
And let thine eye look like a friend on Denmark.
Do not for ever with thy vailèd [16] lids
25   Seek for thy noble father in the dust.
Thou know'st 'tis common. All that lives must die,
Passing through nature to eternity.

HAMLET   Ay, madam, it is common.

QUEEN   If it be,
30   Why seems it so particular with thee?

HAMLET   Seems, madam? Nay, it is. I know not "seems."
'Tis not alone my inky cloak, good mother,
Nor customary suits of solemn black,
Nor windy suspiration of forced breath,
35   No, nor the fruitful [17] river in the eye,
Nor the dejected havior of the visage,
Together with all forms, moods, shapes of grief,

---

[11] *instrumental* serviceable   [12] *cousin* kinsman more distant than parent, child, brother, or sister   [13] *kin* related as nephew   [14] *kind* kindly in feeling, as by kind, or nature, a son would be to his father   [15] *sun* sunshine of the king's undesired favor (with the punning additional meaning of "place of a son")   [16] *vailèd* downcast   [17] *fruitful* copious

That can denote me truly. These indeed seem,
For they are actions that a man might play,
But I have that within which passeth show—
These but the trappings and the suits of woe.

5   KING   'Tis sweet and commendable in your nature, Hamlet,
To give these mourning duties to your father,
But you must know your father lost a father,
That father lost, lost his, and the survivor bound
In filial obligation for some term

10   To do obsequious[18] sorrow. But to persever[19]
In obstinate condolement is a course
Of impious stubbornness. 'Tis unmanly grief.
It shows a will most incorrect to heaven,
A heart unfortified, a mind impatient,

15   An understanding simple and unschooled.
For what we know must be and is as common
As any the most vulgar thing to sense,
Why should we in our peevish opposition
Take it to heart? Fie, 'tis a fault to heaven,

20   A fault against the dead, a fault to nature,
To reason most absurd, whose common theme
Is death of fathers, and who still hath cried,
From the first corse till he that died to-day,
"This must be so." We pray you throw to earth

25   This unprevailing woe, and think of us
As a father, for let the world take note
You are the most immediate to our throne,
And with no less nobility of love
Than that which dearest father bears his son

30   Do I impart toward you. For your intent
In going back to school in Wittenberg,
It is most retrograde[20] to our desire,
And we beseech you, bend you to remain
Here in the cheer and comfort of our eye,

35   Our chiefest courtier, cousin, and our son.
    QUEEN   Let not thy mother lose her prayers, Hamlet.
I pray thee stay with us, go not to Wittenberg.
    HAMLET   I shall in all my best obey you, madam.
    KING   Why, 'tis a loving and a fair reply.

40   Be as ourself in Denmark. Madam, come.

---

[18] *obsequious* proper to obsequies or funerals   [19] *persever* persevere (accented on the second syllable, as always in Shakespeare)   [20] *retrograde* contrary

This gentle and unforced accord of Hamlet
Sits smiling to my heart, in grace whereof
No jocund health that Denmark drinks to-day
But the great cannon to the clouds shall tell,
5   And the king's rouse[21] the heaven shall bruit[22] again,
Respeaking earthly thunder. Come away.

(*Flourish. Exeunt all but* HAMLET)

HAMLET   O that this too too sullied flesh would melt,
Thaw, and resolve itself into a dew,
10   Or that the Everlasting had not fixed
His canon[23] gainst self-slaughter. O God, God,
How weary, stale, flat, and unprofitable
Seem to me all the uses of this world!
Fie on't, ah, fie, 'tis an unweeded garden
15   That grows to seed. Things rank and gross in nature
Possess it merely.[24] That it should come to this,
But two months dead, nay, not so much, not two,
So excellent a king, that was to this
Hyperion[25] to a satyr, so loving to my mother
20   That he might not beteem[26] the winds of heaven
Visit her face too roughly. Heaven and earth,
Must I remember? Why, she would hang on him
As if increase of appetite had grown
By what it fed on, and yet within a month—
25   Let me not think on't; frailty, thy name is woman—
A little month, or ere those shoes were old
With which she followed my poor father's body
Like Niobe,[27] all tears, why she, even she—
O God, a beast that wants discourse[28] of reason
30   Would have mourned longer—married with my uncle,
My father's brother, but no more like my father
Than I to Hercules. Within a month,
Ere yet the salt of most unrighteous tears
Had left the flushing in her gallèd [29] eyes,
35   She married. O, most wicked speed, to post
With such dexterity to incestuous sheets!

---

[21] *rouse* toast drunk in wine   [22] *bruit* echo   [23] *canon* law   [24] *merely* completely   [25] *Hyperion* the sun god   [26] *beteem* allow   [27] *Niobe* the proud mother who boasted of having more children than Leto and was punished when they were slain by Apollo and Artemis, children of Leto; the grieving Niobe was changed by Zeus into a stone, which continually dropped tears   [28] *discourse* logical power or process   [29] *gallèd* irritated

It is not nor it cannot come to good.
But break my heart, for I must hold my tongue.

(*Enter* HORATIO, MARCELLUS, *and* BERNARDO)

HORATIO   Hail to your lordship!
5 HAMLET   I am glad to see you well.
Horatio—or I do forget myself.
HORATIO   The same, my lord, and your poor servant ever.
HAMLET   Sir, my good friend, I'll change[30] that name with you.
And what make[31] you from Wittenberg, Horatio?
10 Marcellus?
MARCELLUS   My good lord!
HAMLET   I am very glad to see you. (*to* BERNARDO) Good even, sir.
But what, in faith, make you from Wittenberg?
HORATIO   A truant disposition, good my lord.
15 HAMLET   I would not hear your enemy say so,
Nor shall you do my ear that violence
To make it truster of your own report
Against yourself. I know you are no truant.
But what is your affair in Elsinore?
20 We'll teach you to drink deep ere you depart.
HORATIO   My lord, I came to see your father's funeral.
HAMLET   I prithee do not mock me, fellow student.
I think it was to see my mother's wedding.
HORATIO   Indeed, my lord, it followed hard upon.
25 HAMLET   Thrift, thrift, Horatio. The funeral baked meats
Did coldly furnish forth the marriage tables.
Would I had met my dearest[32] foe in heaven
Or ever I had seen that day, Horatio!
My father—methinks I see my father.
30 HORATIO   Where, my lord?
HAMLET   In my mind's eye, Horatio.
HORATIO   I saw him once. 'A was a goodly king.
HAMLET   'A was a man, take him for all in all,
I shall not look upon his like again.
35 HORATIO   My lord, I think I saw him yesternight.
HAMLET   Saw? who?
HORATIO   My lord, the king your father.
HAMLET   The king my father?
HORATIO   Season your admiration[33] for a while

---

[30] *change* exchange   [31] *make* do   [32] *dearest* direst, bitterest   [33] *Season your admiration* control your wonder

With an attent ear till I may deliver
Upon the witness of these gentlemen
This marvel to you.

HAMLET   For God's love let me hear!

5   HORATIO   Two nights together had these gentlemen,
Marcellus and Bernardo, on their watch
In the dead waste and middle of the night
Been thus encountered. A figure like your father,
Armèd at point[34] exactly, cap-a-pe,[35]

10   Appears before them and with solemn march
Goes slow and stately by them. Thrice he walked
By their oppressed and fear-surprisèd eyes
Within his truncheon's[36] length, whilst they, distilled
Almost to jelly with the act of fear,

15   Stand dumb and speak not to him. This to me
In dreadful secrecy impart they did,
And I with them the third night kept the watch,
Where, as they had delivered, both in time,
Form of the thing, each word made true and good,

20   The apparition comes. I knew your father.
These hands are not more like.

HAMLET   But where was this?

MARCELLUS   My lord, upon the platform where we watched.

HAMLET   Did you not speak to it?

25   HORATIO   My lord, I did,
But answer made it none. Yet once methought
It lifted up it[37] head and did address
Itself to motion like as it would speak.
But even then the morning cock crew loud,

30   And at the sound it shrunk in haste away
And vanished from our sight.

HAMLET   'Tis very strange.

HORATIO   As I do live, my honored lord, 'tis true,
And we did think it writ down in our duty

35   To let you know of it.

HAMLET   Indeed, indeed, sirs, but this troubles me.
Hold you the watch to-night?

ALL   We do, my lord.

HAMLET   Armed, say you?

40   ALL   Armed, my lord.

---

[34] *at point* completely   [35] *cap-a pe* from head to foot   [36] *truncheon* military
commander's baton   [37] *it* its

	HAMLET	From top to toe?
	ALL	My lord, from head to foot.
	HAMLET	Then saw you not his face?
	HORATIO	O, yes, my lord. He wore his beaver[38] up.
5	HAMLET	What, looked he frowningly?
	HORATIO	A countenance more in sorrow than in anger.
	HAMLET	Pale or red?
	HORATIO	Nay, very pale.
	HAMLET	And fixed his eyes upon you?
10	HORATIO	Most constantly.
	HAMLET	I would I had been there.
	HORATIO	It would have much amazed you.
	HAMLET	Very like, very like. Stayed it long?
	HORATIO	While one with moderate haste might tell [39] a hundred.
15	BOTH	Longer, longer.
	HORATIO	Not when I saw't.
	HAMLET	His beard was grizzled,[40] no?
	HORATIO	It was as I have seen it in his life,

A sable silvered.[41]

20 HAMLET   I will watch to-night.
Perchance 'twill walk again.

HORATIO   I warr'nt it will.

HAMLET   If it assume my noble father's person,
I'll speak to it though hell itself should gape

25 And bid me hold my peace. I pray you all,
If you have hitherto concealed this sight,
Let it be tenable[42] in your silence still,
And whatsomever else shall hap to-night,
Give it an understanding but no tongue.

30 I will requite your loves. So fare you well.
Upon the platform, 'twixt eleven and twelve
I'll visit you.

ALL   Our duty to your honor.

HAMLET   Your loves, as mine to you. Farewell.

35   (*Exeunt all but* HAMLET)

My father's spirit—in arms? All is not well.
I doubt[43] some foul play. Would the night were come!

---

38 *beaver* visor or movable faceguard of the helmet   39 *tell* count   40 *grizzled* grey   41 *sable silvered* black mixed with white   42 *tenable* held firmly   43 *doubt* suspect, fear

Till then sit still, my soul. Foul deeds will rise,
Though all the earth o'erwhelm them, to men's eyes.

(*Exit*)

Act I, Scene III

5   *Elsinore Castle: the chambers of* POLONIUS

(*Enter* LAERTES *and* OPHELIA, *his sister*)

LAERTES   My necessaries are embarked. Farewell.
And, sister, as the winds give benefit
And convoy[1] is assistant, do not sleep,
10   But let me hear from you.
OPHELIA   Do you doubt that?
LAERTES   For Hamlet, and the trifling of his favor,
Hold it a fashion and a toy in blood,
A violet in the youth of primy[2] nature,
15   Forward, not permanent, sweet, not lasting,
The perfume and suppliance[3] of a minute,
No more.
OPHELIA   No more but so?
LAERTES   Think it no more.
20   For nature crescent[4] does not grow alone
In thews and bulk, but as this temple[5] waxes
The inward service of the mind and soul
Grows wide withal. Perhaps he loves you now,
And now no soil nor cautel [6] doth besmirch
25   The virtue of his will,[7] but you must fear,
His greatness weighed,[8] his will is not his own.
(For he himself is subject to his birth.)
He may not, as unvalued persons do,
Carve for himself, for on his choice depends
30   The safety and health of this whole state,
And therefore must his choice be circumscribed
Unto the voice and yielding[9] of that body
Whereof he is the head. Then if he says he loves you,
It fits your wisdom so far to believe it
35   As he in his particular act and place

---

[1] *convoy* means of transport   [2] *primy* of the springtime   [3] *perfume and suppliance* filling sweetness   [4] *crescent* growing   [5] *this temple* the body   [6] *cautel* deceit   [7] *will* desire   [8] *greatness weighed* high position considered   [9] *yielding* assent

May give his saying deed, which is no further
Than the main voice of Denmark goes withal.
Then weigh what loss your honor may sustain
If with too credent[10] ear you list his songs,
5   Or lose your heart, or your chaste treasure open
To his unmastered importunity.
Fear it, Ophelia, fear it, my dear sister,
And keep you in the rear of your affection,[11]
Out of the shot and danger of desire.
10   The chariest maid is prodigal enough
If she unmask her beauty to the moon.
Virtue itself scapes not calumnious strokes.
The canker[12] galls[13] the infants of the spring
Too oft before their buttons[14] be disclosed,
15   And in the morn and liquid dew of youth
Contagious blastments[15] are most imminent.
Be wary then; best safety lies in fear.
Youth to itself rebels, though none else near.
OPHELIA   I shall the effect of this good lesson keep
20   As watchman to my heart, but, good my brother,
Do not as some ungracious pastors do,
Show me the steep and thorny way to heaven,
Whiles like a puffed and reckless libertine
Himself the primrose path of dalliance treads
25   And recks[16] not his own rede.[17]

(*Enter* POLONIUS)

LAERTES   O, fear me not.
I stay too long. But here my father comes.
A double blessing is a double grace;
30   Occasion smiles upon a second leave.
POLONIUS   Yet here, Laertes? Aboard, aboard, for shame!
The wind sits in the shoulder of your sail,
And you are stayed for. There—my blessing with thee,
And these few precepts in thy memory
35   Look thou character.[18] Give thy thoughts no tongue,
Nor any unproportioned[19] thought his act.

---

[10] *credent* credulous   [11] *affection* feelings, which rashly lead forward into dangers   [12] *canker* rose worm   [13] *galls* injures   [14] *buttons* buds   [15] *blastments* blights   [16] *recks* regards   [17] *rede* counsel   [18] *character* inscribe   [19] *unproportioned* unadjusted to what is right

Be thou familiar, but by no means vulgar.
Those friends thou hast, and their adoption tried,
Grapple them unto thy soul with hoops of steel,
But do not dull thy palm with entertainment
5   Of each new-hatched, unfledged courage.[20] Beware
Of entrance to a quarrel; but being in,
Bear't that th' opposèd may beware of thee.
Give every man thine ear, but few thy voice;
Take each man's censure,[21] but reserve thy judgment.
10   Costly thy habit as thy purse can buy,
But not expressed in fancy; rich, not gaudy,
For the apparel oft proclaims the man,
And they in France of the best rank and station
Are of a most select and generous chief [22] in that.
15   Neither a borrower nor a lender be,
For loan oft loses both itself and friend,
And borrowing dulleth edge of husbandry.[23]
This above all, to thine own self be true,
And it must follow as the night the day
20   Thou canst not then be false to any man.
Farewell. My blessing season[24] this in thee!
LAERTES   Most humbly do I take my leave, my lord.
POLONIUS   The time invites you. Go, your servants tend.[25]
LAERTES   Farewell, Ophelia, and remember well
25   What I have said to you.
OPHELIA   'Tis in my memory locked,
And you yourself shall keep the key of it.
LAERTES   Farewell.

(*Exit* LAERTES)

30   POLONIUS   What is't, Ophelia, he hath said to you?
OPHELIA   So please you, something touching the Lord Hamlet.
POLONIUS   Marry,[26] well bethought.
'Tis told me he hath very oft of late
Given private time to you, and you yourself
35   Have of your audience been most free and bounteous.
If it be so—as so 'tis put on me,
And that in way of caution—I must tell you

---

[20] *courage* man of spirit, young blood [21] *censure* judgment [22] *chief* eminence [23] *husbandry* thriftiness [24] *season* ripen and make fruitful [25] *tend* wait [26] *Marry* by Mary

You do not understand yourself so clearly
As it behooves my daughter and your honor.
What is between you? Give me up the truth.

OPHELIA   He hath, my lord, of late made many tenders[27]
5   Of his affection to me.

POLONIUS   Affection? Pooh! You speak like a green girl,
Unsifted [28] in such perilous circumstance.
Do you believe his tenders, as you call them?

OPHELIA   I do not know, my lord, what I should think.

10 POLONIUS   Marry, I will teach you. Think yourself a baby
That you have ta'en these tenders[29] for true pay
Which are not sterling. Tender yourself more dearly,
Or (not to crack the wind of [30] the poor phrase,
Running it thus) you'll tender me a fool.

15 OPHELIA   My lord, he hath importuned me with love
In honorable fashion.

POLONIUS   Ay, fashion you may call it. Go to, go to.[31]

OPHELIA   And hath given countenance to his speech, my lord,
With almost all the holy vows of heaven.

20 POLONIUS   Ay, springes[32] to catch woodcocks.[33] I do know,
When the blood burns, how prodigal the soul
Lends the tongue vows. These blazes, daughter,
Giving more light than heat, extinct in both
Even in their promise, as it is a-making,
25 You must not take for fire. From this time
Be something scanter of your maiden presence.
Set your entreatments[34] at a higher rate
Than a command to parley.[35] For Lord Hamlet,
Believe so much in him that he is young,
30 And with a larger tether may he walk
Than may be given you. In few, Ophelia,
Do not believe his vows, for they are brokers,[36]
Not of that dye which their investments[37] show,

---

27 *tenders* offers   28 *Unsifted* untested   29 *tenders . . . Tender . . . tender* offers . . . hold in regard . . . present (a word play going through three meanings,
the last use of the word yielding further complexity with its valid implications
that she will show herself to him as a fool, will show him to the world as a
fool, and may go so far as to present him with a baby, which would be a fool
because "fool" was an Elizabethan term of endearment especially applicable
to an infant as a "little innocent")   30 *crack . . . of* make wheeze like a horse
driven too hard   31 *Go to* go away, go on (expressing impatience)   32 *springes*
snares   33 *woodcocks* birds believed foolish   34 *entreatments* military negotia-
tions for surrender   35 *parley* confer with a besieger   36 *brokers* middlemen,
panders   37 *investments* clothes

But mere implorators of unholy suits,
Breathing like sanctified and pious bawds,
The better to beguile. This is for all:
I would not, in plain terms, from this time forth
5   Have you so slander[38] any moment[39] leisure
As to give words or talk with the Lord Hamlet.
Look to't, I charge you. Come your ways.

OPHELIA   I shall obey, my lord.

(*Exeunt*)

10 ## Act I, Scene IV

The sentry-post

(*Enter* HAMLET, HORATIO, *and* MARCELLUS)

HAMLET   The air bites shrewdly[1]; it is very cold.
HORATIO   It is a nipping and an eager[2] air.
15 HAMLET   What hour now?
HORATIO   I think it lacks of twelve.
MARCELLUS   No, it is struck.
HORATIO   Indeed? I heard it not. It then draws near the season
Wherein the spirit held his wont to walk.

20 (*A flourish of trumpets, and two pieces goes off*)

What does this mean, my lord?
HAMLET   The king doth wake to-night and takes his rouse,[3]
Keeps wassail, and the swaggering upspring[4] reels,
And as he drains his draughts of Rhenish[5] down
25 The kettledrum and trumpet thus bray out
The triumph[6] of his pledge.
HORATIO   Is it a custom?
HAMLET   Ay, marry, is't,
But to my mind, though I am native here
30 And to the manner born, it is a custom
More honored in the breach than the observance.[7]
This heavy-headed revel east and west
Makes us traduced and taxed of [8] other nations.
They clepe[9] us drunkards and with swinish phrase

---

38 *slander* use disgracefully   39 *moment* momentary
1 *shrewdly* wickedly   2 *eager* sharp   3 *rouse* carousal   4 *upspring* a German
dance   5 *Rhenish* Rhine wine   6 *triumph* achievement, feat (in downing a
cup of wine at one draught)   7 *More . . . observance* better broken than observed   8 *taxed of* censured by   9 *clepe* call

Soil our addition,[10] and indeed it takes
From our achievements, though performed at height,
The pith and marrow of our attribute.[11]
So oft it chances in particular men
5   That (for some vicious mole[12] of nature in them,
As in their birth, wherein they are not guilty,
Since nature cannot choose his[13] origin)
By the o'ergrowth of some complexion,[14]
Oft breaking down the pales[15] and forts of reason,
10   Or by some habit that too much o'erleavens[16]
The form of plausive[17] manners—that (these men
Carrying, I say, the stamp of one defect,
Being nature's livery,[18] or fortune's star)[19]
Their virtues else, be they as pure as grace,
15   As infinite as man may undergo,
Shall in the general censure take corruption
From that particular fault. The dram of evil
Doth all the noble substance of a doubt,
To his own scandal.

20   (*Enter* GHOST)

HORATIO   Look, my lord, it comes.
HAMLET   Angels and ministers of grace defend us!
Be thou a spirit of health[20] or goblin[21] damned,
Bring with thee airs from heaven or blasts from hell,
25   Be thy intents wicked or charitable,
Thou com'st in such a questionable shape
That I will speak to thee. I'll call thee Hamlet,
King, father, royal Dane. O, answer me!
Let me not burst in ignorance, but tell
30   Why thy canonized [22] bones, hearsèd in death,
Have burst their cerements,[23] why the sepulchre
Wherein we saw thee quietly interred
Hath oped his ponderous and marble jaws
To cast thee up again. What may this mean

---

10 *addition* reputation, title added as a distinction   11 *attribute* reputation, what is attributed   12 *mole* blemish, flaw   13 *his* its   14 *complexion* part of the make-up, combination of humors   15 *pales* barriers, fences   16 *o'erleavens* works change throughout, as yeast ferments dough   17 *plausive* pleasing   18 *livery* characteristic equipment or provision   19 *star* make-up as formed by stellar influence   20 *of health* sound, good   21 *goblin* fiend   22 *canonized* buried with the established rites of the Church   23 *cerements* waxed grave-cloths

That thou, dead corse, again in complete steel,
Revisits thus the glimpses of the moon,
Making night hideous, and we fools of nature[24]
So horridly to shake our disposition
5   With thoughts beyond the reaches of our souls?
Say, why is this? wherefore? what should we do?

(GHOST *beckons*)

HORATIO   It beckons you to go away with it,
As if it some impartment did desire
10   To you alone.
MARCELLUS   Look with what courteous action
It waves you to a more removèd ground.
But do not go with it.
HORATIO   No, by no means.
15   HAMLET   It will not speak. Then will I follow it.
HORATIO   Do not, my lord.
HAMLET   Why, what should be the fear?
I do not set my life at a pin's fee,
And for my soul, what can it do to that,
20   Being a thing immortal as itself?
It waves me forth again. I'll follow it.
HORATIO   What if it tempt you toward the flood, my lord,
Or to the dreadful summit of the cliff
That beetles[25] o'er his base into the sea,
25   And there assume some other horrible form,
Which might deprive[26] your sovereignty of reason[27]
And draw you into madness? Think of it.
The very place puts toys[28] of desperation,
Without more motive, into every brain
30   That looks so many fathoms to the sea
And hears it roar beneath.
HAMLET   It waves me still.
Go on. I'll follow thee.
MARCELLUS   You shall not go, my lord.
35   HAMLET   Hold off your hands.
HORATIO   Be ruled. You shall not go.
HAMLET   My fate cries out
And makes each petty artere[29] in this body

---

[24] *fools of nature* men made conscious of natural limitations by a supernatural manifestation   [25] *beetles* juts out   [26] *deprive* take away   [27] *sovereignty of reason* state of being ruled by reason   [28] *toys* fancies   [29] *artere* artery

As hardy as the Nemean lion's [30] nerve.[31]
Still am I called. Unhand me, gentlemen.
By heaven, I'll make a ghost of him that lets[32] me!
I say, away! Go on. I'll follow thee.

5   (*Exit* GHOST, *and* HAMLET)

HORATIO   He waxes desperate with imagination.
MARCELLUS   Let's follow. 'Tis not fit thus to obey him.
HORATIO   Have after. To what issue will this come?
MARCELLUS   Something is rotten in the state of Denmark.
10   HORATIO   Heaven will direct it.
MARCELLUS   Nay, let's follow him.

   (*Exeunt*)

Act I, Scene V

Another part of the fortifications

15   (*Enter* GHOST *and* HAMLET)

HAMLET   Whither wilt thou lead me? Speak. I'll go no further.
GHOST   Mark me.
HAMLET   I will.
GHOST   My hour is almost come,
20   When I to sulph'rous and tormenting flames[1]
Must render up myself.
HAMLET   Alas, poor ghost!
GHOST   Pity me not, but lend thy serious hearing
To what I shall unfold.
25   HAMLET   Speak. I am bound to hear.
GHOST   So art thou to revenge, when thou shalt hear.
HAMLET   What?
GHOST   I am thy father's spirit,
Doomed for a certain term to walk the night,
30   And for the day confined to fast[2] in fires,
Till the foul crimes done in my days of nature
Are burnt and purged away. But that I am forbid
To tell the secrets of my prison house,
I could a tale unfold whose lightest word
35   Would harrow up thy soul, freeze thy young blood,

---

[30] *Nemean lion* a lion slain by Hercules in the performance of one of his twelve labors   [31] *nerve* sinew   [32] *lets* hinders
[1] *flames* sufferings in purgatory (not hell)   [2] *fast* do penance

Make thy two eyes like stars start from their spheres,[3]
Thy knotted and combinèd locks to part,
And each particular hair to stand an[4] end
Like quills upon the fretful porpentine.[5]

5   But this eternal blazon[6] must not be
To ears of flesh and blood. List, list, O, list!
If thou didst ever thy dear father love—

HAMLET   O God!

GHOST   Revenge his foul and most unnatural murder.

10   HAMLET   Murder?

GHOST   Murder most foul, as in the best it is,
But this most foul, strange, and unnatural.

HAMLET   Haste me to know't, that I, with wings as swift
As meditation[7] or the thoughts of love,

15   May sweep to my revenge.

GHOST   I find thee apt,
And duller shouldst thou be than the fat weed
That roots itself in ease on Lethe[8] wharf,
Wouldst thou not stir in this. Now, Hamlet, hear.

20   'Tis given out that, sleeping in my orchard,
A serpent stung me. So the whole ear of Denmark
Is by a forgèd process[9] of my death
Rankly abused. But know, thou noble youth,
The serpent that did sting thy father's life

25   Now wears his crown.

HAMLET   O my prophetic soul!
My uncle?

GHOST   Ay, that incestuous, that adulterate[10] beast,
With witchcraft of his wit, with traitorous gifts—

30   O wicked wit and gifts, that have the power
So to seduce!—won to this shameful lust
The will of my most seeming-virtuous queen.
O Hamlet, what a falling-off was there,
From me, whose love was of that dignity

35   That it went hand in hand even with the vow
I made to her in marriage, and to decline

---

[3] *spheres* transparent revolving shells in each of which, according to the Ptolemaic astronomy, a planet or other heavenly body was placed   [4] *an* on   [5] *porpentine* porcupine [6] *eternal blazon* revelation of eternity [7] *meditation* thought [8] *Lethe* the river in Hades which brings forgetfulness of past life to a spirit who drinks of it [9] *forgèd process* falsified official report [10] *adulterate* adulterous

Upon a wretch whose natural gifts were poor
To those of mine!
But virtue, as it never will be moved,
Though lewdness court it in a shape of heaven,[11]
5   So lust, though to a radiant angel linked,
Will sate itself in a celestial bed
And prey on garbage.
But soft, methinks I scent the morning air.
Brief let me be. Sleeping within my orchard,
1C   My custom always of the afternoon,
Upon my secure[12] hour thy uncle stole
With juice of cursed hebona[13] in a vial,
And in the porches of my ears did pour
The leperous distilment, whose effect
15   Holds such an enmity with blood of man
That swift as quicksilver it courses through
The natural gates and alleys of the body,
And with a sudden vigor it doth posset[14]
And curd, like eager[15] droppings into milk,
20   The thin and wholesome blood. So did it mine,
And a most instant tetter[16] barked [17] about
Most lazar-like[18] with vile and loathsome crust
All my smooth body.
Thus was I sleeping by a brother's hand
25   Of life, of crown, of queen at once dispatched,
Cut off even in the blossoms of my sin,
Unhouseled,[19] disappointed,[20] unaneled,[21]
No reck'ning made, but sent to my account
With all my imperfections on my head.
30   O, horrible! O, horrible! most horrible!
If thou hast nature in thee, bear it not.
Let not the royal bed of Denmark be
A couch for luxury[22] and damnèd incest.
But howsomever thou pursues this act,
35   Taint not thy mind, nor let thy soul contrive
Against thy mother aught. Leave her to heaven
And to those thorns that in her bosom lodge

---

[11] *shape of heaven* angelic disguise   [12] *secure* carefree, unsuspecting   [13] *hebona* some poisonous plant   [14] *posset* curdle   [15] *eager* sour   [16] *tetter* eruption   [17] *barked* covered as with a bark   [18] *lazar-like* leper-like   [19] *Unhouseled* without the Sacrament   [20] *disappointed* unprepared spiritually   [21] *unaneled* without extreme unction   [22] *luxury* lust

To prick and sting her. Fare thee well at once.
The glowworm shows the matin[23] to be near
And gins to pale his uneffectual fire.
Adieu, adieu, adieu. Remember me.

5   (*Exit*)

HAMLET   O all you host of heaven! O earth! What else?
And shall I couple hell? O fie! Hold, hold, my heart,
And you, my sinews, grow not instant old,
But bear me stiffly up. Remember thee?
10   Ay, thou poor ghost, while memory holds a seat
In this distracted globe.[24] Remember thee?
Yea, from the table[25] of my memory
I'll wipe away all trivial fond records,
All saws[26] of books, all forms,[27] all pressures[28] past
15   That youth and observation copied there,
And thy commandment all alone shall live
Within the book and volume of my brain,
Unmixed with baser matter. Yes, by heaven!
O most pernicious woman!
20   O villain, villain, smiling, damnèd villain!
My tables—meet it is I set it down
That one may smile, and smile, and be a villain.
At least I am sure it may be so in Denmark.

(*Writes*)

25   So, uncle, there you are. Now to my word:
It is "Adieu, adieu, remember me."
I have sworn't.

(*Enter* HORATIO *and* MARCELLUS)

HORATIO   My lord, my lord!
30   MARCELLUS   Lord Hamlet!
HORATIO   Heavens secure him!
HAMLET   So be it!
MARCELLUS   Illo, ho, ho,[29] my lord!
HAMLET   Hillo, ho, ho, boy! Come, bird, come.
35   MARCELLUS   How is't, my noble lord?
HORATIO   What news, my lord?

---

[23] *matin* morning   [24] *globe* head   [25] *table* writing tablet, record book
[26] *saws* wise sayings   [27] *forms* mental images, concepts   [28] *pressures* impressions   [29] *Illo, ho, ho* cry of the falconer to summon his hawk

HAMLET   O, wonderful!

HORATIO   Good my lord, tell it.

HAMLET   No, you will reveal it.

HORATIO   Not I, my lord, by heaven.

5   MARCELLUS   Nor I, my lord.

HAMLET   How say you then? Would heart of man once think it?
But you'll be secret?

BOTH   Ay, by heaven, my lord.

HAMLET   There's never a villain dwelling in all Denmark

10   But he's an arrant knave.

HORATIO   There needs no ghost, my lord, come from the grave
To tell us this.

HAMLET   Why, right, you are in the right,
And so, without more circumstance[30] at all,

15   I hold it fit that we shake hands and part:
You, as your business and desires shall point you,
For every man hath business and desire
Such as it is, and for my own poor part,
Look you, I'll go pray.

20   HORATIO   These are but wild and whirling words, my lord.

HAMLET   I am sorry they offend you, heartily;
Yes, faith, heartily.

HORATIO   There's no offense, my lord.

HAMLET   Yes, by Saint Patrick, but there is, Horatio,

25   And much offense too. Touching this vision here,
It is an honest[31] ghost, that let me tell you.
For your desire to know what is between us,
O'ermaster't as you may. And now, good friends,
As you are friends, scholars, and soldiers,

30   Give me one poor request.

HORATIO   What is't, my lord? We will.

HAMLET   Never make known what you have seen to-night.

BOTH   My lord, we will not.

HAMLET   Nay, but swear't.

35   HORATIO   In faith,
My lord, not I.

MARCELLUS   Nor I, my lord—in faith.

HAMLET   Upon my sword.[32]

MARCELLUS   We have sworn, my lord, already.

---

[30] *circumstance* ceremony   [31] *honest* genuine (not a disguised demon)
[32] *sword* i.e. upon the cross formed by the sword hilt

HAMLET   Indeed, upon my sword, indeed.

(GHOST *cries under the stage*)

GHOST   Swear.
HAMLET   Ha, ha, boy, say'st thou so? Art thou there, truepenny? [33]
5   Come on. You hear this fellow in the cellarage.
Consent to swear.
HORATIO   Propose the oath, my lord.
HAMLET   Never to speak of this that you have seen,
Swear by my sword.
10 GHOST (*beneath*)   Swear.
HAMLET   Hic et ubique? [34] Then we'll shift our ground.
Come hither, gentlemen,
And lay your hands again upon my sword.
Swear by my sword
15   Never to speak of this that you have heard.
GHOST (*beneath*)   Swear by his sword.
HAMLET   Well said, old mole! Canst work i' th' earth so fast?
A worthy pioner! [35] Once more remove, good friends.
HORATIO   O day and night, but this is wondrous strange!
20 HAMLET   And therefore as a stranger give it welcome.
There are more things in heaven and earth, Horatio,
Than are dreamt of in your philosophy.[36]
But come:
Here as before, never, so help you mercy,
25   How strange or odd some'er I bear myself
(As I perchance hereafter shall think meet
To put an antic[37] disposition on),
That you, at such times seeing me, never shall,
With arms encumb'red [38] thus, or this head-shake,
30   Or by pronouncing of some doubtful phrase,
As "Well, well, we know," or "We could, an if [39] we would,"
Or "If we list to speak," or "There be, an if they might,"
Or such ambiguous giving out, to note
That you know aught of me—this do swear,
35   So grace and mercy at your most need help you.
GHOST (*beneath*)   Swear.

(*They swear*)

---

[33] *truepenny* honest old fellow   [34] *Hic et ubique* here and everywhere   [35] *pioner* pioneer, miner   [36] *your philosophy* this philosophy one hears about
[37] *antic* grotesque, mad   [38] *encumb'red* folded   [39] *an if* if

HAMLET Rest, rest, perturbèd spirit! So, gentlemen,
With all my love I do commend [40] me to you,
And what so poor a man as Hamlet is
May do t' express his love and friending to you,
5 God willing, shall not lack. Let us go in together,
And still [41] your fingers on your lips, I pray.
The time is out of joint. O cursèd spite
That ever I was born to set it right!
Nay, come, let's go together.

10 (*Exeunt*)

ACT II

Scene I

The chambers of POLONIUS

(*Enter old* POLONIUS, *with his man* [REYNALDO])

15 POLONIUS Give him this money and these notes, Reynaldo.
REYNALDO I will, my lord.
POLONIUS You shall do marvellous wisely, good Reynaldo,
Before you visit him, to make inquire
Of his behavior.
20 REYNALDO   My lord, I did intend it.
POLONIUS Marry, well said, very well said. Look you, sir,
Enquire me first what Danskers[1] are in Paris,
And how, and who, what means,[2] and where they keep,[3]
What company, at what expense; and finding
25 By this encompassment[4] and drift of question
That they do know my son, come you more nearer
Than your particular demands[5] will touch it.
Take you as 'twere some distant knowledge of him,
As thus, "I know his father and his friends,
30 And in part him"—do you mark this, Reynaldo?
REYNALDO Ay, very well, my lord.
POLONIUS "And in part him, but," you may say, "not well,
But if't be he I mean, he's very wild
Addicted so and so." And there put on him
35 What forgeries[6] you please; marry, none so rank

---

[40] *commend* entrust   [41] *still* always
[1] *Danskers* Danes   [2] *what means* what their wealth   [3] *keep* dwell   [4] *encompassment* circling about   [5] *particular demands* definite questions   [6] *forgeries* invented wrongdoings

As may dishonor him—take heed of that—
But, sir, such wanton, wild, and usual slips
As are companions noted and most known
To youth and liberty.

5   REYNALDO   As gaming, my lord.

POLONIUS   Ay, or drinking, fencing, swearing, quarrelling,
Drabbing.[7] You may go so far.

REYNALDO   My lord, that would dishonor him.

POLONIUS   Faith, no, as you may season[8] it in the charge.

10   You must not put another scandal on him,
That he is open to incontinency.[9]
That's not my meaning. But breathe his faults so quaintly[10]
That they may seem the taints of liberty,
The flash and outbreak of a fiery mind,

15   A savageness in unreclaimèd [11] blood,
Of general assault.[12]

REYNALDO   But, my good lord—

POLONIUS   Wherefore should you do this?

REYNALDO   Ay, my lord,

20   I would know that.

POLONIUS   Marry, sir, here's my drift,
And I believe it is a fetch of warrant.[13]
You laying these slight sullies on my son
As 'twere a thing a little soiled i' th' working,

25   Mark you,
Your party in converse, him you would sound,
Having ever[14] seen in the prenominate[15] crimes
The youth you breathe of guilty, be assured
He closes with you[16] in this consequence:[17]

30   "Good sir," or so, or "friend," or "gentleman"—
According to the phrase or the addition[18]
Of man and country—

REYNALDO   Very good, my lord.

POLONIUS   And then, sir, does 'a this—'a does—

35   What was I about to say? By the mass, I was about to say something! Where did I leave?

---

[7] *Drabbing* whoring   [8] *season* soften   [9] *incontinency* extreme sensuality
[10] *quaintly* expertly, gracefully   [11] *unreclaimèd* untamed   [12] *Of general assault* assailing all young men   [13] *fetch of warrant* allowable trick   [14] *Having ever* if he has ever   [15] *prenominate* aforementioned   [16] *closes with you* follows your lead to a conclusion   [17] *consequence* following way   [18] *addition* title

REYNALDO At "closes in the consequence," at "friend or so," and "gentleman."

POLONIUS At "closes in the consequence"—Ay, marry!
He closes thus: "I know the gentleman;
5 I saw him yesterday, or t' other day,
Or then, or then, with such or such, and, as you say,
There was 'a gaming, there o'ertook[19] in's rouse,[20]
There falling[21] out at tennis"; or perchance,
"I saw him enter such a house of sale,"
10 Videlicet,[22] a brothel, or so forth.
See you now—
Your bait of falsehood takes this carp of truth,
And thus do we of wisdom and of reach,[23]
With windlasses[24] and with assays of bias,[25]
15 By indirections find directions[26] out.
So, by my former lecture and advice,
Shall you my son. You have me, have you not?

REYNALDO My lord, I have.

POLONIUS   God bye ye,[27] fare ye well.

20 REYNALDO Good my lord.

POLONIUS Observe his inclination in yourself.

REYNALDO I shall, my lord.

POLONIUS And let him ply his music.

REYNALDO   Well, my lord.

25 POLONIUS Farewell.

(*Exit* REYNALDO)

(*Enter* OPHELIA)

                          How now, Ophelia, what's the matter?

OPHELIA O my lord, my lord, I have been so affrighted!

30 POLONIUS With what, i' th' name of God?

OPHELIA My lord, as I was sewing in my closet,[28]
Lord Hamlet, with his doublet[29] all unbraced,[30]
No hat upon his head, his stockings fouled,
Ungartered, and down-gyvèd [31] to his ankle,
35 Pale as his shirt, his knees knocking each other,

---

[19] *o'ertook* overcome with drunkenness [20] *rouse* carousal [21] *falling out* quarrelling [22] *Videlicet* namely [23] *reach* far-reaching comprehension [24] *windlasses* roundabout courses [25] *assays of bias* devious attacks [26] *directions* ways of procedure [27] *God bye ye* God be with you, good-bye [28] *closet* private living-room [29] *doublet* jacket [30] *unbraced* unlaced [31] *down-gyvèd* fallen down like gyves or fetters on a prisoner's legs

And with a look so piteous in purport
As if he had been loosèd out of hell
To speak of horrors—he comes before me.
POLONIUS   Mad for thy love?
5   OPHELIA   My lord, I do not know,
But truly I do fear it.
POLONIUS   What said he?
OPHELIA   He took me by the wrist and held me hard.
Then goes he to the length of all his arm,
10   And with his other hand thus o'er his brow
He falls to such perusal of my face
As 'a would draw it. Long stayed he so.
At last, a little shaking of mine arm
And thrice his head thus waving up and down,
15   He raised a sigh so piteous and profound
As it did seem to shatter all his bulk
And end his being. That done, he lets me go,
And with his head over his shoulder turned
He seemed to find his way without his eyes,
20   For out o' doors he went without their helps
And to the last bended their light on me.
POLONIUS   Come, go with me. I will go seek the king.
This is the very ecstasy[32] of love,
Whose violent property[33] fordoes[34] itself
25   And leads the will to desperate undertakings
As oft as any passion under heaven
That does afflict our natures. I am sorry.
What, have you given him any hard words of late?
OPHELIA   No, my good lord; but as you did command
30   I did repel his letters and denied
His access to me.
POLONIUS   That hath made him mad.
I am sorry that with better heed and judgment
I had not quoted[35] him. I feared he did but trifle
35   And meant to wrack thee; but beshrew[36] my jealousy.
By heaven, it is as proper to our age
To cast beyond ourselves[37] in our opinions
As it is common for the younger sort
To lack discretion. Come, go we to the king.

---

[32] *ecstasy* madness   [33] *property* quality   [34] *fordoes* destroys   [35] *quoted* observed   [36] *beshrew* curse   [37] *cast beyond ourselves* find by calculation more significance in something than we ought to

This must be known, which, being kept close,[38] might move[39]
More grief to hide than hate to utter love.[40]
Come.

(*Exeunt*)

5 **Act II, Scene II**

A chamber in the castle

(*Flourish. Enter* KING *and* QUEEN, ROSENCRANTZ, *and* GUILDENSTERN [*with others*])

KING Welcome, dear Rosencrantz and Guildenstern.
10   Moreover that[1] we much did long to see you,
      The need we have to use you did provoke
      Our hasty sending. Something have you heard
      Of Hamlet's transformation—so call it,
      Sith[2] nor th' exterior nor the inward man
15   Resembles that it was. What it should be,
      More than his father's death, that thus hath put him
      So much from th' understanding of himself,
      I cannot dream of. I entreat you both
      That, being of so young days brought up with him,
20   And sith so neighbored to his youth and havior,[3]
      That you vouchsafe your rest here in our court
      Some little time, so by your companies
      To draw him on to pleasures, and to gather
      So much as from occasion you may glean,
25   Whether aught to us unknown afflicts him thus,
      That opened [4] lies within our remedy.
QUEEN Good gentlemen, he hath much talked of you,
      And sure I am two men there are not living
      To whom he more adheres.[5] If it will please you
30   To show us so much gentry[6] and good will
      As to expend your time with us awhile
      For the supply and profit of our hope,
      Your visitation shall receive such thanks
      As fits a king's remembrance.

---

[38] *close* secret   [39] *move* cause   [40] *to hide ... love* by such hiding of love than there would be hate moved by a revelation of it (a violently condensed putting of the case which is a triumph of special statement for Polonius)   [1] *Moreover that* besides the fact that   [2] *Sith* since   [3] *youth and havior* youthful ways of life   [4] *opened* revealed   [5] *more adheres* is more attached   [6] *gentry* courtesy

ROSENCRANTZ   Both your majesties
       Might, by the sovereign power you have of us,
       Put your dread pleasures more into command
       Than to entreaty.
5   GUILDENSTERN   But we both obey,
       And here give up ourselves in the full bent[7]
       To lay our service freely at your feet,
       To be commanded.
     KING   Thanks, Rosencrantz and gentle Guildenstern.
10   QUEEN   Thanks, Guildenstern and gentle Rosencrantz.
       And I beseech you instantly to visit
       My too much changèd son.—Go, some of you,
       And bring these gentlemen where Hamlet is.
     GUILDENSTERN   Heavens make our presence and our practices
15   Pleasant and helpful to him!
     QUEEN   Ay, amen!

       (*Exeunt* ROSENCRANTZ *and* GUILDENSTERN [*with some* ATTENDANTS])

       (*Enter* POLONIUS)

     POLONIUS   Th' ambassadors from Norway, my good lord,
20   Are joyfully returned.
     KING   Thou still [8] hast been the father of good news.
     POLONIUS   Have I, my lord? Assure you, my good liege,
       I hold my duty as I hold my soul,
       Both to my God and to my gracious king,
25   And I do think—or else this brain of mine
       Hunts not the trail of policy so sure
       As it hath used to do—that I have found
       The very cause of Hamlet's lunacy.
     KING   O, speak of that! That do I long to hear.
30   POLONIUS   Give first admittance to th' ambassadors.
       My news shall be the fruit[9] to that great feast.
     KING   Thyself do grace[10] to them and bring them in.

       (*Exit* POLONIUS)

       He tells me, my dear Gertrude, he hath found
35   The head and source of all your son's distemper.
     QUEEN   I doubt[11] it is no other but the main,
       His father's death and our o'erhasty marriage.

---

[7] *in the full bent* at the limit of bending (of a bow), to full capacity   [8] *still*
always   [9] *fruit* dessert   [10] *grace* honor   [11] *doubt* suspect

KING   Well, we shall sift him.

(*Enter* AMBASSADORS [VOLTEMAND *and* CORNELIUS, *with* POLONIUS])

Welcome, my good friends.
Say, Voltemand, what from our brother Norway?
5 VOLTEMAND   Most fair return of greetings and desires.
Upon our first,[12] he sent out to suppress
His nephew's levies, which to him appeared
To be a preparation 'gainst the Polack,
But better looked into, he truly found
10 It was against your highness, whereat grieved,
That so his sickness, age, and impotence
Was falsely borne in hand,[13] sends out arrests
On Fortinbras; which he in brief obeys,
Receives rebuke from Norway, and in fine[14]
15 Makes vow before his uncle never more
To give th' assay[15] of arms against your majesty.
Whereon old Norway, overcome with joy,
Gives him threescore thousand crowns in annual fee
And his commission to employ those soldiers,
20 So levied as before, against the Polack,
With an entreaty, herein further shown,

(*Gives a paper*)

That it might please you to give quiet pass
Through your dominions for this enterprise,
25 On such regards[16] of safety and allowance
As therein are set down.
KING   It likes us well;
And at our more considered time[17] we'll read,
Answer, and think upon this business.
30 Meantime we thank you for your well-took labor.
Go to your rest; at night we'll feast together.
Most welcome home!

(*Exeunt* AMBASSADORS)

POLONIUS   This business is well ended.
35 My liege and madam, to expostulate[18]
What majesty should be, what duty is,

---

[12] *our first* our first words about the matter   [13] *borne in hand* deceived   [14] *in fine* in the end   [15] *assay* trial   [16] *regards* terms   [17] *considered time* convenient time for consideration   [18] *expostulate* discuss

Why day is day, night night, and time is time,
Were nothing but to waste night, day, and time.
Therefore, since brevity is the soul of wit,[19]
And tediousness the limbs and outward flourishes,
5   I will be brief. Your noble son is mad.
Mad call I it, for, to define true madness,
What is't but to be nothing else but mad?
But let that go.
QUEEN   More matter, with less art.
10   POLONIUS   Madam, I swear I use no art at all.
That he is mad, 'tis true: 'tis true 'tis pity,
And pity 'tis 'tis true—a foolish figure.[20]
But farewell it, for I will use no art.
Mad let us grant him then, and now remains
15   That we find out the cause of this effect—
Or rather say, the cause of this defect,
For this effect defective comes by cause.
Thus it remains, and the remainder thus.
Perpend.[21]
20   I have a daughter (have while she is mine),
Who in her duty and obedience, mark,
Hath given me this. Now gather, and surmise.

(Reads the letter)

"To the celestial, and my soul's idol, the most beautified
25   Ophelia,"—
That's an ill phrase, a vile phrase; "beautified" is a vile phrase.
 But you shall hear. Thus:

(Reads)

"In her excellent white bosom, these, &c."
30   QUEEN   Came this from Hamlet to her?
POLONIUS   Good madam, stay awhile. I will be faithful.

(Reads)

"Doubt thou the stars are fire;
 Doubt that the sun doth move;
35   Doubt[22] truth to be a liar;
 But never doubt I love.
O dear Ophelia, I am ill at these numbers.[23] I have not art to

---

[19] *wit* understanding   [20] *figure* figure in rhetoric   [21] *Perpend* ponder
[22] *Doubt* suspect   [23] *numbers* verses

reckon my groans, but that I love thee best, O most best, believe it.
Adieu.
>   Thine evermore, most dear lady,
>   whilst this machine²⁴ is to²⁵ him, Hamlet."

5   This in obedience hath my daughter shown me,
    And more above²⁶ hath his solicitings,
    As they fell out by time, by means, and place,
    All given to mine ear.
    KING   But how hath she
10 Received his love?
    POLONIUS   What do you think of me?
    KING As of a man faithful and honorable.
    POLONIUS I would fain prove so. But what might you think,
    When I had seen this hot love on the wing
15 (As I perceived it, I must tell you that,
    Before my daughter told me), what might you,
    Or my dear majesty your queen here, think,
    If I had played the desk or table book,²⁷
    Or given my heart a winking,²⁸ mute and dumb,
20 Or looked upon this love with idle sight?
    What might you think? No, I went round ²⁹ to work
    And my young mistress thus I did bespeak:
    "Lord Hamlet is a prince, out of thy star.³⁰
    This must not be." And then I prescripts³¹ gave her,
25 That she should lock herself from his resort,
    Admit no messengers, receive no tokens.
    Which done, she took the fruits of my advice,
    And he, repellèd, a short tale to make,
    Fell into a sadness, then into a fast,
30 Thence to a watch,³² thence into a weakness,
    Thence to a lightness,³³ and, by this declension,
    Into the madness wherein now he raves,
    And all we mourn for.
    KING   Do you think 'tis this?
35 QUEEN It may be, very like.
    POLONIUS Hath there been such a time—I would fain know that—

---

²⁴ *machine* body   ²⁵ *to* attached to   ²⁶ *above* besides   ²⁷ *desk or table book*
i.e. silent receiver   ²⁸ *winking* closing of the eyes   ²⁹ *round* roundly, plainly
³⁰ *star* condition determined by stellar influence   ³¹ *prescripts* instructions
³² *watch* sleepless state   ³³ *lightness* lightheadedness

That I have positively said " 'Tis so,"
When it proved otherwise?

KING   Not that I know.

POLONIUS (*pointing to his head and shoulder*)

5   Take this from this, if this be otherwise.
If circumstances lead me, I will find
Where truth is hid, though it were hid indeed
Within the center.[34]

KING   How may we try it further?

10 POLONIUS   You know sometimes he walks four hours together
Here in the lobby.

QUEEN   So he does indeed.

POLONIUS   At such a time I'll loose my daughter to him.
Be you and I behind an arras[35] then.

15   Mark the encounter. If he love her not,
And be not from his reason fallen thereon,[36]
Let me be no assistant for a state
But keep a farm and carters.

KING   We will try it.

20   (*Enter* HAMLET [*reading on a book*])

QUEEN   But look where sadly the poor wretch comes reading.

POLONIUS   Away, I do beseech you both, away.

(*Exit* KING *and* QUEEN [*with* ATTENDANTS])

I'll board [37] him presently.[38] O, give me leave.

25   How does my good Lord Hamlet?

HAMLET   Well, God-a-mercy.[39]

POLONIUS   Do you know me, my lord?

HAMLET   Excellent well. You are a fishmonger.[40]

POLONIUS   Not I, my lord.

30 HAMLET   Then I would you were so honest a man.

POLONIUS   Honest, my lord?

HAMLET   Ay, sir. To be honest, as this world goes, is to be one man
picked out of ten thousand.

POLONIUS   That's very true, my lord.

---

[34] *center* center of the earth and also of the Ptolemaic universe   [35] *arras*
hanging tapestry   [36] *thereon* on that account   [37] *board* accost   [38] *presently*
at once   [39] *God-a-mercy* thank you (literally, "God have mercy!")   [40] *fishmonger* seller of harlots, procurer (a cant term used here with a glance at
the fishing Polonius is doing when he offers Ophelia as bait)

HAMLET   For if the sun breed maggots in a dead dog, being a good
kissing carrion[41]—Have you a daughter?

POLONIUS   I have, my lord.

HAMLET   Let her not walk i' th' sun. Conception is a blessing, but
5   as your daughter may conceive, friend, look to't.

POLONIUS (*aside*)   How say you by that? Still harping on my daughter. Yet he knew me not at first. 'A said I was a fishmonger. 'A is
far gone, far gone. And truly in my youth I suffered much extremity for love, very near this. I'll speak to him again.—What do
10   you read, my lord?

HAMLET   Words, words, words.

POLONIUS   What is the matter, my lord?

HAMLET   Between who? [42]

POLONIUS   I mean the matter that you read, my lord.

15   HAMLET   Slanders, sir, for the satirical rogue says here that old men
have grey beards, that their faces are wrinkled, their eyes purging
thick amber and plum-tree gum, and that they have a plentiful
lack of wit, together with most weak hams. All which, sir, though
I most powerfully and potently believe, yet I hold it not honesty
20   to have it thus set down, for you yourself, sir, should be old as I
am if, like a crab, you could go backward.

POLONIUS (*aside*)   Though this be madness, yet there is method in't.
—Will you walk out of the air, my lord?

HAMLET   Into my grave?

25   POLONIUS   Indeed, that's out of the air. (*aside*) How pregnant[43]
sometimes his replies are! a happiness[44] that often madness hits
on, which reason and sanity could not so prosperously be delivered
of. I will leave him and suddenly contrive the means of meeting
between him and my daughter.—My honorable lord, I will most
30   humbly take my leave of you.

HAMLET   You cannot, sir, take from me anything that I will more
willingly part withal [45]—except my life, except my life, except my
life.

(*Enter* GUILDENSTERN *and* ROSENCRANTZ)

35   POLONIUS   Fare you well, my lord.

HAMLET   These tedious old fools!

POLONIUS   You go to seek the Lord Hamlet. There he is.

---

[41] *good kissing carrion* good bit of flesh for kissing   [42] *Between who* matter
for a quarrel between what persons (Hamlet's willful misunderstanding)
[43] *pregnant* full of meaning   [44] *happiness* aptness of expression   [45] *withal*
with

ROSENCRANTZ (*to* POLONIUS)   God save you, sir!

(*Exit* POLONIUS)

GUILDENSTERN   My honored lord!

ROSENCRANTZ   My most dear lord!

5 HAMLET   My excellent good friends! How dost thou, Guildenstern? Ah, Rosencrantz! Good lads, how do ye both?

ROSENCRANTZ   As the indifferent[46] children of the earth.

GUILDENSTERN   Happy in that we are not over-happy. On Fortune's cap we are not the very button.

10 HAMLET   Nor the soles of her shoe?

ROSENCRANTZ   Neither, my lord.

HAMLET   Then you live about her waist, or in the middle of her favors?

GUILDENSTERN   Faith, her privates[47] we.

15 HAMLET   In the secret parts of Fortune? O, most true! she is a strumpet. What news?

ROSENCRANTZ   None, my lord, but that the world's grown honest.

HAMLET   Then is doomsday near. But your news is not true. (Let me question more in particular.) What have you, my good friends,

20 deserved at the hands of Fortune that she sends you to prison hither?

GUILDENSTERN   Prison, my lord?

HAMLET   Denmark 's a prison.

ROSENCRANTZ   Then is the world one.

25 HAMLET   A goodly one; in which there are many confines,[48] wards,[49] and dungeons, Denmark being one o' th' worst.

ROSENCRANTZ   We think not so, my lord.

HAMLET   Why, then 'tis none to you, for there is nothing either good or bad but thinking makes it so. To me it is a prison.

30 ROSENCRANTZ   Why, then your ambition makes it one. 'Tis too narrow for your mind.

HAMLET   O God, I could be hounded in a nutshell and count myself a king of infinite space, were it not that I have bad dreams.

GUILDENSTERN   Which dreams indeed are ambition, for the very

35 substance of the ambitious is merely the shadow of a dream.

HAMLET   A dream itself is but a shadow.

ROSENCRANTZ   Truly, and I hold ambition of so airy and light a quality that it is but a shadow's shadow.

---

[46] *indifferent* average   [47] *privates* ordinary men in private, not public, life (with obvious play upon the sexual term "private parts")   [48] *confines* places of imprisonment   [49] *wards* cells

HAMLET   Then are our beggars bodies,[50] and our monarchs and outstretched [51] heroes the beggars' shadows. Shall we to th' court?
for, by my fay,[52] I cannot reason.

BOTH   We'll wait upon[53] you.

5   HAMLET   No such matter. I will not sort you with the rest of my
servants, for, to speak to you like an honest man, I am most dreadfully attended. But in the beaten way of friendship, what make[54]
you at Elsinore?

ROSENCRANTZ   To visit you, my lord; no other occasion.

10   HAMLET   Beggar that I am, I am even poor in thanks, but I thank
you; and sure, dear friends, my thanks are too dear a halfpenny.[55]
Were you not sent for? Is it your own inclining? Is it a free visitation? Come, come, deal justly with me. Come, come. Nay, speak.

GUILDENSTERN   What should we say, my lord?

15   HAMLET   Why, anything—but to th' purpose. You were sent for,
and there is a kind of confession in your looks, which your modes-
ties have not craft enough to color. I know the good king and
queen have sent for you.

ROSENCRANTZ   To what end, my lord?

20   HAMLET   That you must teach me. But let me conjure you by the
rights of our fellowship, by the consonancy[56] of our youth, by the
obligation of our ever-preserved love, and by what more dear a
better proposer[57] can charge you withal,[58] be even[59] and direct
with me whether you were sent for or no.

25   ROSENCRANTZ   (*aside to* GUILDENSTERN)   What say you?

HAMLET   (*aside*)   Nay then, I have an eye of you.—If you love me,
hold not off.

GUILDENSTERN   My lord, we were sent for.

HAMLET   I will tell you why. So shall my anticipation prevent[60]
30   your discovery,[61] and your secrecy to the king and queen moult no
feather.[62] I have of late—but wherefore I know not—lost all my
mirth, forgone all custom of exercises; and indeed, it goes so heavily with my disposition that this goodly frame the earth seems to
me a sterile promontory; this most excellent canopy, the air, look
35   you, this brave o'erhanging firmament,[63] this majestical roof

---

[50] *bodies* solid substances, not shadows (because beggars lack ambition)
[51] *outstretched* elongated as shadows (with a corollary implication of far-
reaching with respect to the ambitions that make both heroes and monarchs
into shadows)   [52] *fay* faith   [53] *wait upon* attend   [54] *make* do   [55] *a halfpenny* at a halfpenny   [56] *consonancy* accord (in sameness of age)   [57] *proposer* propounder   [58] *withal* with   [59] *even* straight   [60] *prevent* forestall
[61] *discovery* disclosure   [62] *moult no feather* be left whole   [63] *firmament* sky

fretted [64] with golden fire—why, it appeareth nothing to me but a foul and pestilent congregation of vapors. What a piece of work is a man, how noble in reason, how infinite in faculties; in form and moving how express[65] and admirable, in action how like an
5   angel, in apprehension how like a god: the beauty of the world, the paragon of animals! And yet to me what is this quintessence[66] of dust? Man delights not me—nor woman neither, though by your smiling you seem to say so.

ROSENCRANTZ   My lord, there was no such stuff in my thoughts.
10   HAMLET   Why did ye laugh then, when I said "Man delights not me"?

ROSENCRANTZ   To think, my lord, if you delight not in man, what lenten[67] entertainment the players shall receive from you. We coted [68] them on the way, and hither are they coming to offer you
15   service.

HAMLET   He that plays the king shall be welcome—his majesty shall have tribute of me—, the adventurous knight shall use his foil and target,[69] the lover shall not sigh gratis, the humorous man[70] shall end his part in peace, the clown shall make those laugh whose
20   lungs are tickle o' th' sere,[71] and the lady shall say her mind freely, or the blank verse shall halt[72] for't. What players are they?

ROSENCRANTZ   Even those you were wont to take such delight in, the tragedians of the city.

HAMLET   How chances it they travel? Their residence,[73] both in
25   reputation and profit, was better both ways.

ROSENCRANTZ   I think their inhibition[74] comes by the means of the late innovation.[75]

HAMLET   Do they hold the same estimation they did when I was in the city? Are they so followed?

30   ROSENCRANTZ   No indeed, are they not.

HAMLET   How comes it? Do they grow rusty?

ROSENCRANTZ   Nay, their endeavor keeps in the wonted pace, but there is, sir, an eyrie[76] of children, little eyases,[77] that cry out on

---

[64] *fretted* decorated with fretwork   [65] *express* well framed   [66] *quintessence* fifth or last and finest essence (an alchemical term)   [67] *lenten* scanty   [68] *coted* overtook   [69] *foil and target* sword and shield   [70] *humorous man* eccentric character dominated by one of the humours   [71] *tickle o' th' sere* hair-triggered for the discharge of laughter ("sere": part of a gunlock)   [72] *halt* go lame   [73] *residence* residing at the capital   [74] *inhibition* impediment to acting in residence (formal prohibition?)   [75] *innovation* new fashion of having companies of boy actors play on the "private" stage (?), political upheaval (?)   [76] *eyrie* nest   [77] *eyases* nestling hawks

the top of question[78] and are most tyranically clapped for't. These are now the fashion, and so berattle[79] the common stages[80] (so they call them) that many wearing rapiers are afraid of goose-quills[81] and dare scarce come thither.

5   HAMLET   What, are they children? Who maintains 'em? How are they escoted? [82] Will they pursue the quality[83] no longer than they can sing? [84] Will they not say afterwards, if they should grow themselves to common players (as it is most like, if their means are no better), their writers do them wrong to make them exclaim

10   against their own succession?

ROSENCRANTZ   Faith, there has been much to do on both sides, and the nation holds it no sin to tarre[85] them to controversy. There was, for a while, no money bid for argument[86] unless the poet and the player went to cuffs in the question.

15   HAMLET   Is't possible?

GUILDENSTERN   O, there has been much throwing about of brains.

HAMLET   Do the boys carry it away?

ROSENCRANTZ   Ay, that they do, my lord—Hercules and his load [87] too.

20   HAMLET   It is not very strange, for my uncle is King of Denmark, and those that would make mows[88] at him while my father lived give twenty, forty, fifty, a hundred ducats apiece for his picture in little. 'Sblood,[89] there is something in this more than natural, if philosophy could find it out.

25   *A flourish*

GUILDENSTERN   There are the players.

HAMLET   Gentlemen, you are welcome to Elsinore. Your hands, come then. Th' appurtenance of welcome is fashion and cere-mony. Let me comply with you in this garb,[90] lest my extent[91] to

30   the players (which I tell you must show fairly outwards) should more appear like entertainment than yours. You are welcome. But my uncle-father and aunt-mother are deceived.

---

[78] *on the top of question* above others on matter of dispute   [79] *berattle* be-rate   [80] *common stages* "public" theatres of the "common" players, who were organized in companies mainly composed of adult actors (allusion being made to the "War of the Theatres" in Shakespeare's London)   [81] *goosequills* pens (of satirists who made out that the London public stage showed low taste)   [82] *escoted* supported   [83] *quality* profession of acting   [84] *sing* i.e. with unchanged voices   [85] *tarre* incite   [86] *argument* matter of a play   [87] *load* i.e. the whole word (with a topical reference to the sign of the Globe Theatre, a representation of Hercules bearing the world on his shoulders)   [88] *mows* grimaces   [89] *'Sblood* by God's blood   [90] *garb* fashion   [91] *extent* showing of welcome

GUILDENSTERN   In what, my dear lord?

HAMLET   I am but mad north-north-west. When the wind is souther-
ly I know a hawk from a handsaw.[92]

(*Enter* POLONIUS)

5 POLONIUS   Well be with you, gentlemen.

HAMLET   Hark you, Guildenstern—and you too—at each ear a
hearer. That great baby you see there is not yet out of his swad-
dling clouts.[93]

ROSENCRANTZ   Happily[94] he is the second time come to them, for
10 they say an old man is twice a child.

HAMLET   I will prophesy he comes to tell me of the players. Mark
it.—You say right, sir; a Monday morning, 'twas then indeed.

POLONIUS   My lord, I have news to tell you.

HAMLET   My lord, I have news to tell you. When Roscius[95] was an
15 actor in Rome—

POLONIUS   The actors are come hither, my lord.

HAMLET   Buzz, buzz.

POLONIUS   Upon my honor—

HAMLET   Then came each actor on his ass—

20 POLONIUS   The best actors in the world, either for tragedy, comedy,
history, pastoral, pastoral-comical, historical-pastoral, tragical-
historical, tragical-comical-historical-pastoral; scene individable,[96]
or poem unlimited.[97] Seneca[98] cannot be too heavy, nor Plautus[99]
too light. For the law of writ[100] and the liberty,[101] these are the
25 only men.

HAMLET   O Jephthah,[102] judge of Israel, what a treasure hadst
thou!

POLONIUS   What treasure had he, my lord?

HAMLET   Why,
30   "One fair daughter, and no more,
            The which he lovèd passing[103] well."

---

[92] *hawk* mattock or pickaxe (also called "hack"; here used apparently with
a play on "hawk": a bird); *handsaw* carpenter's tool (apparently with a play
on some corrupt form of "hernshaw"; heron, a bird often hunted with the
hawk)   [93] *clouts* clothes   [94] *Happily* haply, perhaps   [95] *Roscius* the greatest
of Roman comic actors   [96] *scene individable* drama observing the unities
[97] *poem unlimited* drama not observing the unities   [98] *Seneca* Roman writer
of tragedies   [99] *Plautus* Roman writer of comedies   [100] *law of writ* orthodoxy determined by critical rules of the drama   [101] *liberty* freedom from
such orthodoxy   [102] *Jephthah* the compelled sacrificer of a dearly beloved
daughter (Judges xi)   [103] *passing* surpassingly (verses are from a ballad on
Jephthah)

POLONIUS (*aside*)   Still on my daughter.

HAMLET   Am I not i' th' right, old Jephthah?

POLONIUS   If you call me Jephthah, my lord, I have a daughter that I love passing well.

5   HAMLET   Nay, that follows not.

POLONIUS   What follows then, my lord?

HAMLET   Why,

"As by lot, God wot,"

and then, you know,

10   "It came to pass, as most like it was."

The first row[104] of the pious chanson[105] will show you more, for look where my abridgment[106] comes.

(*Enter the* PLAYERS)

You are welcome, masters, welcome, all.—I am glad to see thee
15   well.—Welcome, good friends.—O, old friend, why, thy face is valanced [107] since I saw thee last. Com'st thou to beard me in Denmark?—What, my young lady[108] and mistress? By'r Lady, your ladyship is nearer to heaven than when I saw you last by the altitude of a chopine.[109] Pray God your voice, like a piece of un-
20   current[110] gold, be not cracked within the ring.[111]—Masters, you are all welcome. We'll e'en to't like French falconers, fly at any-thing we see. We'll have a speech straight. Come, give us a taste of your quality. Come, a passionate speech.

PLAYER   What speech, my good lord?

25   HAMLET   I heard thee speak me a speech once, but it was never acted, or if it was, not above once, for the play, I remember, pleased not the million; 'twas caviary[112] to the general,[113] but it was (as I received it, and others, whose judgments in such matters cried in the top of [114] mine) an excellent play, well digested in the
30   scenes, set down with as much modesty as cunning. I remember one said there were no sallets[115] in the lines to make the matter savory, nor no matter in the phrase that might indict the author of affectation, but called it an honest method, as wholesome as sweet, and by very much more handsome than fine. One speech

---

104 *row* stanza   105 *chanson* song   106 *my abridgment* that which shortens my talk   107 *valanced* fringed (with a beard)   108 *young lady* boy who plays women's parts   109 *chopine* women's thick-soled shoe   110 *uncurrent* not le-gal tender   111 *within the ring* from the edge through the line circling the design on the coin (with a play on "ring": a sound)   112 *caviary* caviare   113 *general* multitude   114 *in the top of* more authoritatively than   115 *sallets* salads, highly seasoned passages

in't I chiefly loved. 'Twas Aeneas' tale to Dido, and thereabout of
it especially where he speaks of Priam's[116] slaughter. If it live in
your memory, begin at this line—let me see, let me see:
"The rugged Pyrrhus, like th' Hyrcanian beast[117]—"

5   'Tis not so; it begins with Pyrrhus:
"The rugged Pyrrhus, he whose sable[118] arms,
Black as his purpose, did the night resemble
When he lay couchèd in the ominous[119] horse,[120]
Hath now this dread and black complexion smeared

10   With heraldry more dismal.[121] Head to foot
Now is he total gules,[122] horridly tricked [123]
With blood of fathers, mothers, daughters, sons,
Baked and impasted with the parching[124] streets,
That lend a tyrannous and a damnèd light

15   To their lord's murder. Roasted in wrath and fire,
And thus o'ersizèd [125] with coagulate[126] gore,
With eyes like carbuncles, the hellish Pyrrhus
Old grandsire Priam seeks."
So, proceed you.

20   POLONIUS   Fore God, my lord, well spoken, with good accent and
good discretion.

PLAYER   "Anon he finds him,
Striking too short at Greeks. His antique sword,
Rebellious to his arms, lies where it falls,

25   Repugnant to command. Unequal matched,
Pyrrhus at Priam drives, in rage strikes wide,
But with the whiff and wind of his fell [127] sword
Th' unnervèd father falls. Then senseless[128] Ilium,
Seeming to feel this blow, with flaming top

30   Stoops to his[129] base, and with a hideous crash
Takes prisoner Pyrrhus' ear. For lo! his sword,
Which was declining on the milky head
Of reverend Priam, seemed i' th' air to stick.
So as a painted [130] tyrant Pyrrhus stood,

---

116 *Priam's slaughter* i.e. at the fall of Troy (Aeneid II, 506 ff.)   117 *Hyrcanian beast* tiger   118 *sable* black   119 *ominous* fateful   120 *horse* the wooden
horse by which the Greeks gained entrance to Troy   121 *dismal* ill-omened
122 *gules* red (heraldic term)   123 *tricked* decorated in color (heraldic term)
124 *parching* i.e. because Troy was burning   125 *o'ersizèd* covered as with
size, a glutinous material used for filling pores of plaster, etc.   126 *coagulate*
clotted   127 *fell* cruel   128 *senseless* without feeling   129 *his* its   130 *painted*
pictured

And like a neutral to his will and matter[131]
Did nothing.
But as we often see, against[132] some storm,
A silence in the heavens, the rack[133] stand still,
5 The bold winds speechless, and the orb below
As hush as death, anon the dreadful thunder
Doth rend the region,[134] so after Pyrrhus' pause,
Arousèd vengeance sets him new awork,
And never did the Cyclops' [135] hammers fall
10 On Mars' armor, forged for proof eterne,[136]
With less remorse than Pyrrhus' bleeding sword
Now falls on Priam.
Out, out, thou strumpet Fortune! All you gods,
In general synod take away her power,
15 Break all the spokes and fellies[137] from her wheel,
And bowl the round nave[138] down the hill of heaven,
As low as to the fiends."
POLONIUS   This is too long.
HAMLET   It shall to the barber's, with your beard.—Prithee say on.
20 He's for a jig[139] or a tale of bawdry, or he sleeps. Say on; come to
Hecuba.
PLAYER   "But who (ah woe!) had seen the mobled [140] queen—"
HAMLET   "The mobled queen"?
POLONIUS   That's good. "Mobled queen" is good.
25 PLAYER   "Run barefoot up and down, threat'ning the flames
With bisson rheum;[141] a clout[142] upon that head
Where late the diadem stood, and for a robe,
About her lank and all o'erteemèd [143] loins,
A blanket in the alarm of fear caught up—
30 Who this had seen, with tongue in venom steeped
'Gainst Fortune's state[144] would treason have pronounced.
But if the gods themselves did see her then,
When she saw Pyrrhus make malicious sport
In mincing with his sword her husband's limbs,
35 The instant burst of clamor that she made

---

131 *will and matter* purpose and its realization (between which he stands motionless)   132 *against* just before   133 *rack* clouds   134 *region* sky   135 *Cyclops* giant workmen who made armor in the smithy of Vulcan   136 *proof eterne* eternal protection   137 *fellies* segments of the rim   138 *nave* hub   139 *jig* short comic piece with singing and dancing often presented after a play   140 *mobled* muffled   141 *bisson rheum* blinding tears   142 *clout* cloth   143 *o'erteemèd* overproductive of children   144 *state* government of worldly events

(Unless things mortal move them not at all)
Would have made milch[145] the burning eyes[146] of heaven
And passion in the gods."
POLONIUS   Look, whe'r[147] he has not turned his color, and has tears
5   in's eyes. Prithee no more.
HAMLET   'Tis well. I'll have thee speak out the rest of this soon.—
Good my lord, will you see the players well bestowed?[148] Do you
hear? Let them be well used, for they are the abstract and brief
chronicles of the time. After your death you were better have a
10   bad epitaph than their ill report while you live.
POLONIUS   My lord, I will use them according to their desert.
HAMLET   God's bodkin,[149] man, much better! Use every man after
his desert, and who shall scape whipping? Use them after your
own honor and dignity. The less they deserve, the more merit is
15   in your bounty. Take them in.
POLONIUS   Come, sirs.
HAMLET   Follow him, friends. We'll hear a play tomorrow. (*aside
to* PLAYER) Dost thou hear me, old friend? Can you play "The
Murder of Gonzago"?
20   PLAYER   Ay, my lord.
HAMLET   We'll ha't to-morrow night. You could for a need study a
speech of some dozen or sixteen lines which I would set down and
insert in't, could you not?
PLAYER   Ay, my lord.
25   HAMLET   Very well. Follow that lord, and look you mock him not.
—My good friends, I'll leave you till night. You are welcome to
Elsinore.

(*Exeunt* POLONIUS *and* PLAYERS)

ROSENCRANTZ   Good my lord.

30   (*Exeunt* ROSENCRANTZ *and* GUILDENSTERN)

HAMLET   Ay, so, God bye to you.—Now I am alone.
O, what a rogue and peasant slave am I!
Is it not monstrous that this player here,
But in a fiction, in a dream of passion,
35   Could force his soul so to his own conceit[150]
That from her working all his visage wanned,
Tears in his eyes, distraction in his aspect.

---

145 *milch* tearful (milk-giving)   146 *eyes* i.e. stars   147 *whe'r* whether   148 *bestowed* lodged   149 *God's bodkin* by God's little body   150 *conceit* conception, idea

A broken voice, and his whole function[151] suiting
With forms to his conceit? And all for nothing,
For Hecuba!
What's Hecuba to him, or he to Hecuba,

5   That he should weep for her? What would he do
Had he the motive and the cue for passion
That I have? He would drown the stage with tears
And cleave the general ear with horrid speech,
Make mad the guilty and appal the free,

10   Confound the ignorant, and amaze indeed
The very faculties of eyes and ears.
Yet I,
A dull and muddy-mettled [152] rascal, peak[153]
Like John-a-dreams,[154] unpregnant[155] of my cause,

15   And can say nothing. No, not for a king,
Upon whose property and most dear life
A damned defeat was made. Am I a coward?
Who calls me villain? breaks my pate across?
Plucks off my beard and blows it in my face?

20   Tweaks me by the nose? gives me the lie i' th' throat
As deep as to the lungs? Who does me this?
Ha, 'swounds,[156] I should take it, for it cannot be
But I am pigeon-livered [157] and lack gall
To make oppression bitter, or ere this

25   I should ha' fatted all the region kites[158]
With this slave's offal.[159] Bloody, bawdy villain!
Remorseless, treacherous, lecherous, kindless[160] villain!
O, vengeance!
Why, what an ass am I! This is most brave,

30   That I, the son of a dear father murdered,
Prompted to my revenge by heaven and hell,
Must like a whore unpack my heart with words
And fall a-cursing like a very drab,
A stallion! [161] Fie upon't, foh! About, my brains.

35   Hum—
I have heard that guilty creatures sitting at a play
Have by the very cunning of the scene

---

[151] *function* action of bodily powers   [152] *muddy-mettled* dull-spirited
[153] *peak* mope   [154] *John-a-dreams* a sleepy dawdler   [155] *unpregnant* barren
of realization   [156] *'swounds* by God's wounds   [157] *pigeon-livered* of dove-like
gentleness   [158] *region kites* kites of the air   [159] *offal* guts   [160] *kindless* unnatural   [161] *stallion* prostitute (male or female)

Been struck so to the soul that presently[162]
They have proclaimed their malefactions.
For murder, though it have no tongue, will speak
With most miraculous organ. I'll have these players
5 Play something like the murder of my father
Before mine uncle. I'll observe his looks.
I'll tent[163] him to the quick. If 'a do blench,[164]
I know my course. The spirit that I have seen
May be a devil, and the devil hath power
10 T' assume a pleasing shape, yea, and perhaps
Out of my weakness and my melancholy,
As he is very potent with such spirits,
Abuses[165] me to damn me. I'll have grounds
More relative[166] than this. The play 's the thing
15 Wherein I'll catch the conscience of the king.

(*Exit*)

ACT III

Scene I

A chamber in the castle

20 (*Enter* KING, QUEEN, POLONIUS, OPHELIA, ROSENCRANTZ, GUILDEN-
STERN, LORDS)

KING And can you by no drift of conference[1]
Get from him why he puts on this confusion,
Grating so harshly all his days of quiet
25 With turbulent and dangerous lunacy?
ROSENCRANTZ He does confess he feels himself distracted,
But from what cause 'a will by no means speak.
GUILDENSTERN Nor do we find him forward to be sounded,
But with a crafty madness keeps aloof
30 When we would bring him on to some confession
Of his true state.
QUEEN   Did he receive you well?
ROSENCRANTZ Most like a gentleman.
GUILDENSTERN But with much forcing of his disposition.
35 ROSENCRANTZ Niggard of question, but of our demands
Most free in his reply.

---

162 *presently* immediately   163 *tent* probe   164 *blench* flinch   165 *Abuses* de-
ludes   166 *relative* pertinent
1 *drift of conference* direction of conversation

QUEEN   Did you assay[2] him
  To any pastime?
ROSENCRANTZ   Madam, it so fell out that certain players
  We o'erraught[3] on the way. Of these we told him,
5   And there did seem in him a kind of joy
  To hear of it. They are here about the court,
  And, as I think, they have already order
  This night to play before him.
POLONIUS   'Tis most true,
10   And he beseeched me to entreat your majesties
  To hear and see the matter.
KING   With all my heart, and it doth much content me
  To hear him so inclined.
  Good gentlemen, give him a further edge[4]
15   And drive his purpose into these delights.
ROSENCRANTZ   We shall, my lord.

  (*Exeunt* ROSENCRANTZ *and* GUILDENSTERN)

KING   Sweet Gertrude, leave us too,
  For we have closely[5] sent for Hamlet hither,
20   That he, as 'twere by accident, may here
  Affront[6] Ophelia.
  Her father and myself (lawful espials[7])
  Will so bestow ourselves that, seeing unseen,
  We may of their encounter frankly judge
25   And gather by him, as he is behaved,
  If't be th' affliction of his love or no
  That thus he suffers for.
QUEEN   I shall obey you.—
  And for your part, Ophelia, I do wish
30   That your good beauties be the happy cause
  Of Hamlet's wildness. So shall I hope your virtues
  Will bring him to his wonted way again,
  To both your honors.
OPHELIA   Madam, I wish it may.

35   (*Exit* QUEEN)

POLONIUS   Ophelia, walk you here.—Gracious, so please you,
  We will bestow ourselves.—

---

[2] *assay* try to win   [3] *o'erraught* overtook   [4] *edge* keenness of desire   [5] *closely* privately   [6] *Affront* come face to face with   [7] *espials* spies

(*To* OPHELIA)

                        Read on this book,
That show of such an exercise[8] may color[9]
Your loneliness. We are oft to blame in this,
5   'Tis too much proved, that with devotion's visage
And pious action we do sugar o'er
The devil himself.
  KING (*aside*)   O, 'tis too true.
How smart a lash that speech doth give my conscience!
10   The harlot's cheek, beautied with plast'ring art,
Is not more ugly to[10] the thing that helps it
Than is my deed to my most painted word.
O heavy burthen!
  POLONIUS   I hear him coming. Let's withdraw, my lord.

15   (*Exeunt* KING *and* POLONIUS)

    (*Enter* HAMLET)

  HAMLET   To be, or not to be—that is the question:
Whether 'tis nobler in the mind to suffer
The slings and arrows of outrageous fortune
20   Or to take arms against a sea of troubles
And by opposing end them. To die, to sleep—
No more—and by a sleep to say we end
The heartache, and the thousand natural shocks
That flesh is heir to. 'Tis a consummation
25   Devoutly to be wished. To die, to sleep—
To sleep—perchance to dream: ay, there's the rub,[11]
For in that sleep of death what dreams may come
When we have shuffled off [12] this mortal coil,[13]
Must give us pause. There's the respect[14]
30   That makes calamity of so long life.[15]
For who would bear the whips and scorns of time,
Th' oppressor's wrong, the proud man's contumely
The pangs of despised love, the law's delay,
The insolence of office, and the spurns
35   That patient merit of th' unworthy takes,
When he himself might his quietus[16] make

---

[8] *exercise* religious exercise (the book being obviously one of devotion) [9] *color* give an appearance of naturalness to [10] *to* compared to [11] *rub* obstacle (literally, obstruction encountered by a bowler's ball) [12] *shuffled off* cast off as an encumbrance [13] *coil* to-do, turmoil [14] *respect* consideration [15] *of so long life* so long-lived [16] *quietus* settlement (literally, release from debt)

With a bare bodkin? [17] Who would fardels[18] bear,
To grunt and sweat under a weary life,
But that the dread of something after death,
The undiscovered country, from whose bourn[19]
5   No traveller returns, puzzles the will,
And makes us rather bear those ills we have
Than fly to others that we know not of?
Thus conscience does make cowards of us all,
And thus the native hue of resolution
10   Is sicklied o'er with the pale cast of thought,
And enterprises of great pitch[20] and moment
With this regard [21] their currents turn awry
And lose the name of action.—Soft you now,
The fair Ophelia!—Nymph, in thy orisons[22]
15   Be all my sins remembered.

OPHELIA   Good my lord,
How does your honor for this many a day?

HAMLET   I humbly thank you, well, well, well.

OPHELIA   My lord, I have remembrances of yours
20   That I have longèd long to re-deliver.
I pray you, now receive them.

HAMLET   No, not I,
I never gave you aught.

OPHELIA   My honored lord, you know right well you did,
25   And with them words of so sweet breath composed
As made the things more rich. Their perfume lost,
Take these again, for to the noble mind
Rich gifts wax poor when givers prove unkind.
There, my lord.

30   HAMLET   Ha, ha! Are you honest? [23]

OPHELIA   My lord?

HAMLET   Are you fair?

OPHELIA   What means your lordship?

HAMLET   That if you be honest and fair, your honesty should admit
35   no discourse to your beauty.

OPHELIA   Could beauty, my lord, have better commerce[24] than
with honesty?

HAMLET   Ay, truly; for the power of beauty will sooner transform

---

[17] *bodkin* dagger   [18] *fardels* burdens   [19] *bourn* confine, region   [20] *pitch* height (of a soaring falcon's flight)   [21] *regard* consideration   [22] *orisons* prayers (because of the book of devotion she reads)   [23] *honest* chaste   [24] *commerce* intercourse

honesty from what it is to a bawd than the force of honesty can translate beauty into his likeness. This was sometime a paradox,[25] but now the time gives it proof. I did love you once.

OPHELIA   Indeed, my lord, you made me believe so.

5   HAMLET   You should not have believed me, for virtue cannot so inoculate[26] our old stock but we shall relish[27] of it. I loved you not.

OPHELIA   I was the more deceived.

HAMLET   Get thee to a nunnery. Why wouldst thou be a breeder
10   of sinners? I am myself indifferent honest,[28] but yet I could accuse me of such things that it were better my mother had not borne me: I am very proud, revengeful, ambitious, with more offenses at my beck than I have thoughts to put them in, imagination to give them shape, or time to act them in. What should
15   such fellows as I do crawling between earth and heaven? We are arrant knaves all; believe none of us. Go thy ways to a nunnery. Where's your father?

OPHELIA   At home, my lord.

HAMLET   Let the doors be shut upon him, that he may play the
20   fool nowhere but in's own house. Farewell.

OPHELIA   O, help him, you sweet heavens!

HAMLET   If thou dost marry, I'll give thee this plague for thy dowry: be thou as chaste as ice, as pure as snow, thou shalt not escape calumny. Get thee to a nunnery. Go, farewell. Or if thou
25   wilt needs marry, marry a fool, for wise men know well enough what monsters[29] you make of them. To a nunnery, go, and quickly too. Farewell.

OPHELIA   O heavenly powers, restore him!

HAMLET   I have heard of your paintings too, well enough. God
30   hath given you one face, and you make yourselves another. You jig, you amble, and you lisp; you nickname God's creatures and make your wantonness[30] your ignorance.[31] Go to, I'll no more on't; it hath made me mad. I say we will have no more marriage. Those that are married already—all but one—shall live. The rest
35   shall keep as they are. To a nunnery, go.

(*Exit*)

OPHELIA   O, what a noble mind is here o'erthrown!

---

[25] *paradox* idea contrary to common opinion   [26] *inoculate* graft   [27] *relish* have a flavor (because of original sin)   [28] *indifferent honest* moderately respectable   [29] *monsters* i.e. unnatural combinations of wisdom and uxorious folly   [30] *wantonness* affectation   [31] *your ignorance* a matter for which you offer the excuse that you don't know any better

The courtier's, soldier's, scholar's, eye, tongue, sword,
Th' expectancy and rose[32] of the fair state,
The glass[33] of fashion and the mould of form,
Th' observed of all observers, quite, quite down!
5   And I, of ladies most deject and wretched,
That sucked the honey of his music vows,
Now see that noble and most sovereign reason
Like sweet bells jangled, out of time and harsh,
That unmatched form and feature of blown youth
10 Blasted with ecstasy.[34] O, woe is me
T' have seen what I have seen, see what I see!

(*Enter* KING *and* POLONIUS)

KING   Love? his affections[35] do not that way tend,
Nor what he spake, though it lacked form a little,
15 Was not like madness. There's something in his soul
O'er which his melancholy sits on brood,
And I do doubt[36] the hatch and the disclose
Will be some danger; which for to prevent,
I have in quick determination
20 Thus set it down: he shall with speed to England
For the demand of our neglected tribute.
Haply the seas, and countries different,
With variable objects, shall expel
This something-settled [37] matter in his heart,
25 Whereon his brains still beating puts him thus
From fashion of himself. What think you on't?
POLONIUS   It shall do well. But yet do I believe
The origin and commencement of his grief
Sprung from neglected love.—How now, Ophelia?
30 You need not tell us what Lord Hamlet said.
We heard it all.—My lord, do as you please,
But if you hold it fit, after the play
Let his queen mother all alone entreat him
To show his grief. Let her be round [38] with him,
35 And I'll be placed, so please you, in the ear
Of all their conference. If she find him not,
To England send him, or confine him where
Your wisdom best shall think.

---

[32] *expectancy and rose* fair hope   [33] *glass* mirror   [34] *ecstasy* madness   [35] *affections* emotions   [36] *doubt* fear   [37] *something-settled* somewhat settled
[38] *round* plain-spoken

KING   It shall be so.
Madness in great ones must not unwatched go.

(*Exeunt*)

Act III, Scene II

5   *The hall of the castle*

(*Enter* HAMLET *and three of the* PLAYERS)

HAMLET   Speak the speech, I pray you, as I pronounced it to you,
trippingly[1] on the tongue. But if you mouth it, as many of our
players do, I had as lief the town crier spoke my lines. Nor do
10   not saw the air too much with your hand, thus, but use all gently,
for in the very torrent, tempest, and (as I may say) whirlwind of
your passion, you must acquire and beget a temperance that may
give it smoothness. O, it offends me to the soul to hear a robustious[2] periwig-pated [3] fellow tear a passion to tatters, to very rags,
15   to split the ears of the groundlings,[4] who for the most part are
capable of nothing but inexplicable dumb shows[5] and noise. I
would have such a fellow whipped for o'erdoing Termagant.[6] It
out-herods Herod.[7] Pray you avoid it.
PLAYER   I warrant your honor.
20   HAMLET   Be not too tame neither, but let your own discretion be
your tutor. Suit the action to the word, the word to the action,
with this special observance, that you o'erstep not the modesty of
nature. For anything so overdone is from[8] the purpose of playing,
whose end, both at the first and now, was and is, to hold, as
25   'twere, the mirror up to nature, to show virtue her own feature,
scorn her own image, and the very age and body of the time his
form and pressure.[9] Now this overdone, or come tardy off,[10]
though it make the unskillful laugh, cannot but make the judi-
cious grieve, the censure of the which one[11] must in your allow-
30   ance o'erweigh a whole theatre of others. O, there be players that
I have seen play, and heard others praise, and that highly (not to

---

[1] *trippingly* easily   [2] *robustious* boisterous   [3] *periwig-pated* wig-wearing (after the custom of actors)   [4] *groundlings* spectators who paid least and stood on
the ground in the pit or yard of the theatre   [5] *dumb shows* brief actions
without words, forecasting dramatic matter to follow (the play presented
later in this scene giving an old-fashioned example)   [6] *Termagant* a Saracen
"god" in medieval romance and drama   [7] *Herod* the raging tyrant of old
Biblical plays   [8] *from* apart from   [9] *pressure* impressed or printed character
[10] *come tardy off* brought off slowly and badly   [11] *the censure of the which
one* the judgment of even one of whom

speak it profanely), that neither having th' accent of Christians, nor the gait of Christian, pagan, nor man, have so strutted and bellowed that I have thought some of Nature's journeymen[12] had made men, and not made them well, they imitated humanity so

5　abominably.

PLAYER　I hope we have reformed that indifferently[13] with us, sir.

HAMLET　O, reform it altogether! And let those that play your clowns speak no more than is set down for them, for there be of them[14] that will themselves laugh, to set on some quantity of

10　barren spectators to laugh too, though in the mean time some necessary question of the play be then to be considered. That's villainous and shows a most pitiful ambition in the fool that uses it. Go make you ready.

(*Exeunt* PLAYERS)

15　(*Enter* POLONIUS, GUILDENSTERN, *and* ROSENCRANTZ)

How now, my lord? Will the king hear this piece of work?

POLONIUS　And the queen too, and that presently.[15]

HAMLET　Bid the players make haste.

(*Exit* POLONIUS)

20　Will you two help to hasten them?

ROSENCRANTZ　Ay, my lord.

(*Exeunt they two*)

HAMLET　What, ho, Horatio!

(*Enter* HORATIO)

25　HORATIO　Here, sweet lord, at your service.

HAMLET　Horatio, thou art e'en as just a man
As e'er my conversation coped withal.[16]

HORATIO　O, my dear lord—

HAMLET　　　　　　　　Nay, do not think I flatter.

30　For what advancement may I hope from thee,
That no revenue hast but thy good spirits
To feed and clothe thee? Why should the poor be flattered?
No, let the candied tongue lick absurd pomp,
And crook the pregnant[17] hinges of the knee

---

12 *journeymen* workmen not yet masters of their trade　13 *indifferently* fairly well　14 *of them* some of them　15 *presently* at once　16 *conversation coped withal* intercourse with men encountered　17 *pregnant* quick to move

Where thrift[18] may follow fawning. Dost thou hear?
Since my dear soul was mistress of her choice
And could of men distinguish her election,
S' hath sealed [19] thee for herself, for thou hast been
5   As one in suff'ring all that suffers nothing,
A man that Fortune's buffets and rewards
Hast ta'en with equal thanks; and blest are those
Whose blood [20] and judgment are so well commeddled [21]
That they are not a pipe for Fortune's finger
10 To sound what stop she please. Give me that man
That is not passion's slave, and I will wear him
In my heart's core, ay, in my heart of heart,
As I do thee. Something too much of this—
There is a play to-night before the king.
15 One scene of it comes near the circumstance
Which I have told thee, of my father's death.
I prithee, when thou seest that act afoot,
Even with the very comment of thy soul [22]
Observe my uncle. If his occulted [23] guilt
20 Do not itself unkennel in one speech,
It is a damnèd ghost[24] that we have seen,
And my imaginations are as foul
As Vulcan's stithy.[25] Give him heedful note,
For I mine eyes will rivet to his face,
25 And after we will both our judgments join
In censure of [26] his seeming.
HORATIO   Well, my lord.
If 'a steal aught the while this play is playing,
And scape detecting, I will pay the theft.

30 (*Enter* TRUMPETS *and* KETTLEDRUMS, KING, QUEEN, POLONIUS, OPHE-
LIA, [ROSENCRANTZ, GUILDENSTERN, *and other* LORDS *attendant*])

HAMLET   They are coming to the play. I must be idle.[27]
Get you a place.
KING   How fares our cousin[28] Hamlet?
35 HAMLET   Excellent, i' faith, of the chameleon's dish.[29] I eat the air,
promise-crammed. You cannot feed capons so.

---

[18] *thrift* profit   [19] *sealed* marked   [20] *blood* passion   [21] *commeddled* mixed
together   [22] *the very ... soul* thy deepest sagacity   [23] *occulted* hidden
[24] *damnèd ghost* evil spirit, devil   [25] *stithy* smithy   [26] *censure of* sentence
upon   [27] *be idle* be foolish, act the madman   [28] *cousin* nephew   [29] *chameleon's dish* i.e. air (which was believed the chameleon's food; Hamlet willfully takes *fares* in the sense of "feeds")

KING   I have nothing with this answer, Hamlet. These words are
not mine.[30]

HAMLET   No, nor mine now. (*to Polonius*) My lord, you played
once i' th' university, you say?

5   POLONIUS   That did I, my lord, and was accounted a good actor.

HAMLET   What did you enact?

POLONIUS   I did enact Julius Caesar. I was killed i' th' Capitol;
Brutus killed me.

HAMLET   It was a brute part of him to kill so capital a calf there.
10   Be the players ready?

ROSENCRANTZ   Ay, my lord. They stay upon your patience.[31]

QUEEN   Come hither, my dear Hamlet, sit by me.

HAMLET   No, good mother. Here's metal more attractive.

POLONIUS (*to the King*)   O ho! do you mark that?

15   HAMLET   Lady, shall I lie in your lap?

He lies at OPHELIA'S *feet*

OPHELIA   No, my lord.

HAMLET   I mean, my head upon your lap?

OPHELIA   Ay, my lord.

20   HAMLET   Do you think I meant country matters?[32]

OPHELIA   I think nothing, my lord.

HAMLET   That's a fair thought to lie between maids' legs.

OPHELIA   What is, my lord?

HAMLET   Nothing.

25   OPHELIA   You are merry, my lord.

HAMLET   Who, I?

OPHELIA   Ay, my lord.

HAMLET   O God, your only jig-maker![33] What should a man do
but be merry? For look you how cheerfully my mother looks, and
30   my father died within's two hours.

OPHELIA   Nay, 'tis twice two months, my lord.

HAMLET   So long? Nay then, let the devil wear black, for I'll have
a suit of sables.[34] O heavens! die two months ago, and not forgotten yet? Then there's hope a great man's memory may out-
35   live his life half a year. But, by'r Lady, 'a must build churches
then, or else shall 'a suffer not thinking on, with the hobby-

---

[30] *not mine* not for me as the asker of my question   [31] *stay upon your patience* await your indulgence   [32] *country matters* rustic goings-on, barnyard
mating (with a play upon a sexual term)   [33] *jig-maker* writer of jigs
[34] *sables* black furs (luxurious garb, not for mourning)

horse,[35] whose epitaph is "For O, tor O, the hobby-horse is forgot!"

The trumpets sound. Dumb show follows:
Enter a KING *and a* QUEEN [*very lovingly*], *the* QUEEN *embracing him, and*
5   *he her.* [*She kneels; and makes show of protestation unto him.*] *He takes her up, and declines his head upon her neck. He lies him down upon a bank of flowers. She, seeing him asleep, leaves him. Anon come in another man: takes off his crown, kisses it, pours poison in the sleeper's ears, and leaves him. The* QUEEN *returns, finds the* KING *dead, makes passionate*
10   *action. The poisoner, with some three or four, come in again, seem to condole with her. The dead body is carried away. The poisoner woos the* QUEEN *with gifts; she seems harsh awhile, but in the end accepts love.*

(*Exeunt*)

OPHELIA   What means this, my lord?
15   HAMLET   Marry, this is miching mallecho;[36] it means mischief.
OPHELIA   Belike this show imports the argument of the play.

(*Enter* PROLOGUE)

HAMLET   We shall know by this fellow. The players cannot keep counsel; they'll tell all.
20   OPHELIA   Will 'a tell us what this show meant?
HAMLET   Ay, or any show that you'll show him. Be not you ashamed to show, he'll not shame to tell you what it means.
OPHELIA   You are naught, you are naught.[37] I'll mark the play.
PROLOGUE   For us and for our tragedy,
25   Here stooping to your clemency,
                   We beg your hearing patiently.

(*Exit*)

HAMLET   Is this a prologue, or the posy[38] of a ring? [39]
OPHELIA   'Tis brief, my lord.
30   HAMLET   As woman's love.

(*Enter* [*two* PLAYERS *as*] KING *and* QUEEN)

[P.] KING   Full thirty times hath Phoebus' cart[40] gone round
Neptune's salt wash and Tellus' [41] orbèd ground,
And thirty dozen moons with borrowed [42] sheen

---

[35] *hobby-horse* traditional figure strapped round the waist of a performer in May games and morris dances   [36] *miching mallecho* sneaking iniquity
[37] *naught* indecent   [38] *posy* brief motto in rhyme ("poesy")   [39] *ring* finger ring   [40] *Phoebus' cart* the sun's chariot   [41] *Tellus* Roman goddess of the earth   [42] *borrowed* i.e. taken from the sun

About the world have times twelve thirties been,
Since love our hearts, and Hymen[43] did our hands,
Unite commutual [44] in most sacred bands.

[P.] QUEEN   So many journeys may the sun and moon
5   Make us again count o'er ere love be done!
But woe is me, you are so sick of late,
So far from cheer and from your former state,
That I distrust you.[45] Yet, though I distrust,
Discomfort you, my lord, it nothing must.
10   For women fear too much, even as they love,
And women's fear and love hold quantity,[46]
In neither aught, or in extremity.
Now what my love is, proof hath made you know,
And as my love is sized, my fear is so.
15   Where love is great, the littlest doubts are fear;
Where little fears grow great, great love grows there.

[P.] KING   Faith, I must leave thee, love, and shortly too;
My operant powers[47] their functions leave to do.
And thou shalt live in this fair world behind,
20   Honored, beloved, and haply one as kind
For husband shalt thou—

[P.] QUEEN   O, confound the rest!
Such love must needs be treason in my breast.
In second husband let me be accurst!
25   None wed the second but who killed the first.

HAMLET *(aside)*   That's wormwood.[48]

[P.] QUEEN   The instances[49] that second marriage move
Are base respects of thrift, but none of love.
A second time I kill my husband dead
30   When second husband kisses me in bed.

[P.] KING   I do believe you think what now you speak,
‧ But what we do determine oft we break.
Purpose is but the slave to[50] memory,
Of violent birth, but poor validity,[51]
35   Which now like fruit unripe sticks on the tree,
But fall unshaken when they mellow be.
Most necessary 'tis that we forget
To pay ourselves what to ourselves is debt.

---

[43] *Hymen* Greek god of marriage   [44] *commutual* mutually   [45] *distrust you*
fear for you   [46] *quantity* proportion   [47] *operant powers* active bodily forces
[48] *wormwood* a bitter herb   [49] *instances* motives   [50] *slave to* i.e. dependent
upon for life   [51] *validity* strength

What to ourselves in passion we propose,
The passion ending, doth the purpose lose.
The violence of either grief or joy
Their own enactures[52] with themselves destroy.
5   Where joy most revels, grief doth most lament;
Grief joys, joy grieves, on slender accident.
This world is not for aye, nor 'tis not strange
That even our loves should with our fortunes change,
For 'tis a question left us yet to prove,
10   Whether love lead fortune, or else fortune love.
The great man down, you mark his favorite flies,
The poor advanced makes friends of enemies;
And hitherto doth love on fortune tend,
For who not needs shall never lack a friend,
15   And who in want a hollow friend doth try,
Directly seasons him[53] his enemy.
But, orderly to end where I begun,
Our wills and fates do so contrary run
That our devices still [54] are overthrown;
20   Our thoughts are ours, their ends none of our own.
So think thou wilt no second husband wed,
But die thy thoughts when thy first lord is dead.
[P.] QUEEN   Nor earth to me give food, nor heaven light,
Sport and repose lock from me day and night,
25   To desperation turn my trust and hope,
An anchor's[55] cheer in prison be my scope,
Each opposite that blanks[56] the face of joy
Meet what I would have well, and it destroy,
Both here and hence[57] pursue me lasting strife,
30   If, once a widow, ever I be wife!
HAMLET   If she should break it now!
[P.] KING   'Tis deeply sworn. Sweet, leave me here awhile.
My spirits grow dull, and fain I would beguile
The tedious day with sleep.
35   [P.] QUEEN   Sleep rock thy brain,

(*He sleeps*)

And never come mischance between us twain!

(*Exit*)

---

[52] *enactures* fulfillments   [53] *seasons him* ripens him into   [54] *still* always
[55] *anchor's* hermit's   [56] *blanks* blanches, makes pale   [57] *hence* in the next world.

HAMLET   Madam, how like you this play?

QUEEN   The lady doth protest too much, methinks.

HAMLET   O, but she'll keep her word.

KING   Have you heard the argument? [58] Is there no offense in't?

5 HAMLET   No, no, they do but jest, poison in jest; no offense i' th' world.

KING   What do you call the play?

HAMLET   "The Mousetrap." Marry, how? Tropically.[59] This play is the image of a murder done in Vienna. Gonzago is the duke's
10 name; his wife, Baptista. You shall see anon. 'Tis a knavish piece of work, but what o' that? Your majesty, and we that have free[60] souls, it touches us not. Let the galled [61] jade[62] winch;[63] our withers[64] are unwrung.

(*Enter* LUCIANUS)

15 This is one Lucianus, nephew to the king.

OPHELIA   You are as good as a chorus,[65] my lord.

HAMLET   I could interpret between you and your love, if I could see the puppets[66] dallying.

OPHELIA   You are keen, my lord, you are keen.

20 HAMLET   It would cost you a groaning to take off my edge.

OPHELIA   Still better, and worse.

HAMLET   So you must take your husbands.—Begin, murderer. Leave thy damnable faces and begin. Come, the croaking raven doth bellow for revenge.

25 LUCIANUS   Thoughts black, hands apt, drugs fit, and time agreeing, Confederate season,[67] else no creature seeing,
Thou mixture rank, of midnight weeds collected,
With Hecate's[68] ban[69] thrice blasted, thrice infected,
Thy natural magic and dire property
30 On wholesome life usurps immediately.

(*Pours the poison in his ears*)

HAMLET   'A poisons him i' th' garden for his estate. His name's Gonzago. The story is extant, and written in very choice Italian. You shall see anon how the murderer gets the love of Gonzago's
35 wife.

---

[58] *argument* plot summary   [59] *Tropically* in the way of a trope or figure (with a play on "trapically")   [60] *free* guiltless   [61] *galled* sore-backed   [62] *jade* horse   [63] *winch* wince   [64] *withers* shoulders   [65] *chorus* one in a play who explains the action   [66] *puppets* i.e. you and your lover as in a puppet show   [67] *Confederate season* the occasion being my ally   [68] *Hecate* goddess of witchcraft and black magic   [69] *ban* curse

OPHELIA   The king rises.
HAMLET   What, frighted with false fire? [70]
QUEEN   How fares my lord?
POLONIUS   Give o'er the play.
5   KING   Give me some light. Away!
POLONIUS   Lights, lights, lights!

(*Exeunt all but* HAMLET *and* HORATIO)

HAMLET   Why, let the strucken deer go weep,
             The hart ungallèd play.
10   For some must watch, while some must sleep;
             Thus runs the world away.
Would not this, sir, and a forest of feathers[71]—if the rest of my
fortunes turn Turk[72] with me—with two Provincial roses[73] on my
razed [74] shoes, get me a fellowship in a cry[75] of players, sir?
15   HORATIO   Half a share.
HAMLET   A whole one, I.
             For thou dost know, O Damon dear,
                This realm dismantled was
             Of Jove himself; and now reigns here
20   A very, very—peacock.
HORATIO   You might have rhymed.
HAMLET   O good Horatio, I'll take the ghost's word for a thousand
pound. Didst perceive?
HORATIO   Very well, my lord.
25   HAMLET   Upon the talk of the poisoning?
HORATIO   I did very well note him.
HAMLET   Aha! Come, some music! Come, the recorders! [76]
             For if the king like not the comedy,
             Why then, belike he likes it not, perdy.[77]
30   Come, some music!

(*Enter* ROSENCRANTZ *and* GUILDENSTERN)

GUILDENSTERN   Good my lord, vouchsafe me a word with you.
HAMLET   Sir, a whole history.
GUILDENSTERN   The king, sir—
35   HAMLET   Ay, sir, what of him?

---

[70] *false fire* a firing of a gun charged with powder but no shot, a blank-discharge   [71] *feathers* plumes for actors' costumes   [72] *turn Turk* turn renegade, like a Christian turning Mohammedan   [73] *Provincial roses* ribbon rosettes   [74] *razed* decorated with cut patterns   [75] *cry* pack   [76] *recorders* musical instruments of the flute class   [77] *perdy* by God (*"par dieu"*)

GUILDENSTERN   Is in his retirement marvellous distempered.[78]

HAMLET   With drink, sir?

GUILDENSTERN   No, my lord, with choler.[79]

HAMLET   Your wisdom should show itself more richer to signify this
5   to the doctor, for for me to put him to his purgation would perhaps plunge him into more choler.

GUILDENSTERN   Good my lord, put your discourse into some
frame,[80] and start not so wildly from my affair.

HAMLET   I am tame, sir; pronounce.

1c GUILDENSTERN   The queen, your mother, in most great affliction of
spirit hath sent me to you.

HAMLET   You are welcome.

GUILDENSTERN   Nay, good my lord, this courtesy is not of the right
breed. If it shall please you to make me a wholesome answer, I
15   will do your mother's commandment. If not, your pardon and my
return shall be the end of my business.

HAMLET   Sir, I cannot.

ROSENCRANTZ   What, my lord?

HAMLET   Make you a wholesome answer; my wit's diseased. But,
20   sir, such answer as I can make, you shall command, or rather, as
you say, my mother. Therefore no more, but to the matter. My
mother, you say—

ROSENCRANTZ   Then thus she says: your behavior hath struck her
into amazement and admiration.[81]

25 HAMLET   O wonderful son, that can so stonish a mother! But is
there no sequel at the heels of this mother's admiration? Impart.

ROSENCRANTZ   She desires to speak with you in her closet[82] ere you
go to bed.

HAMLET   We shall obey, were she ten times our mother. Have you
30   any further trade with us?

ROSENCRANTZ   My lord, you once did love me.

HAMLET   And do still, by these pickers and stealers.[83]

ROSENCRANTZ   Good my lord, what is your cause of distemper?
You do surely bar the door upon your own liberty, if you deny
35   your griefs to your friend.

HAMLET   Sir, I lack advancement.

ROSENCRANTZ   How can that be, when you have the voice of the
king himself for your succession in Denmark?

---

[78] *distempered* out of temper, vexed (twisted by Hamlet into "deranged")
[79] *choler* anger (twisted by Hamlet into "biliousness")   [80] *frame* logical order
[81] *admiration* wonder   [82] *closet* private room   [83] *pickers and stealers* i.e.
hands

HAMLET   Ay, sir, but "while the grass grows" [84] the proverb is
something musty.

(*Enter the* PLAYER *with recorders*)

O, the recorders. Let me see one. To withdraw[85] with you—why
5   do you go about to recover the wind [86] of me, as if you would
drive me into a toil? [87]

GUILDENSTERN   O my lord, if my duty be too bold, my love is too
unmannerly.[88]

HAMLET   I do not well understand that. Will you play upon this
10   pipe?

GUILDENSTERN   My lord, I cannot.

HAMLET   I pray you.

GUILDENSTERN   Believe me, I cannot.

HAMLET   I do beseech you.

15   GUILDENSTERN   I know no touch of it, my lord.

HAMLET   It is as easy as lying. Govern these ventages[89] with your
fingers and thumb, give it breath with your mouth, and it will
discourse most eloquent music. Look you, these are the stops.

GUILDENSTERN   But these cannot I command to any utt'rance of
20   harmony. I have not the skill.

HAMLET   Why, look you now, how unworthy a thing you make of
me! You would play upon me, you would seem to know my stops,
you would pluck out the heart of my mystery, you would sound
me from my lowest note to the top of my compass; and there is
25   much music, excellent voice, in this little organ, yet cannot you
make it speak. 'Sblood, do you think I am easier to be played on
than a pipe? Call me what instrument you will, though you can
fret[90] me, you cannot play upon me.

(*Enter* POLONIUS)

30   God bless you, sir!

POLONIUS   My lord, the queen would speak with you, and presently.[91]

HAMLET   Do you see yonder cloud that's almost in shape of a
camel?

35   POLONIUS   By th' mass and 'tis, like a camel indeed.

---

[84] *while the grass grows* (a proverb, ending: "the horse starves")   [85] *withdraw* step aside   [86] *recover the wind* come up to windward like a hunter
[87] *toil* snare   [88] *is too unmannerly* leads me beyond the restraint of good
manners   [89] *ventages* holes, vents   [90] *fret* irritate (with a play on the fret-
fingering of certain stringed musical instruments)   [91] *presently* at once

HAMLET   Methinks it is like a weasel.

POLONIUS   It is backed like a weasel.

HAMLET   Or like a whale.

POLONIUS   Very like a whale.

5   HAMLET   Then I will come to my mother by and by.[92]   (*aside*)
They fool me to the top of my bent.—I will come by and by.

POLONIUS   I will say so.

(*Exit*)

HAMLET   "By and by" is easily said. Leave me, friends.

10   (*Exeunt all but* HAMLET)

'Tis now the very witching time of night,
When churchyards yawn, and hell itself breathes out
Contagion to this world. Now could I drink hot blood
And do such bitter business as the day
15   Would quake to look on. Soft, now to my mother.
O heart, lose not thy nature; let not ever
The soul of Nero[93] enter this firm bosom.
Let me be cruel, not unnatural;
I will speak daggers to her, but use none.
20   My tongue and soul in this be hypocrites:
How in my words somever she be shent,[94]
To give them seals[95] never, my soul, consent!

(*Exit*)

Act III, Scene III

25   *A chamber in the castle*

(*Enter* KING, ROSENCRANTZ, *and* GUILDENSTERN)

KING   I like him not, nor stands it safe with us
To let his madness range. Therefore prepare you.
I your commission will forthwith dispatch,
30   And he to England shall along with you.
The terms[1] of our estate[2] may not endure
Hazard so near's as doth hourly grow
Out of his brows.[3]

---

[92] *by and by* immediately   [93] *Nero* murderer of his mother   [94] *shent* reproved
[95] *seals* authentications in actions
[1] *terms* circumstances   [2] *estate* royal position   [3] *brows* effronteries (apparently with an implication of knitted brows)

GUILDENSTERN   We will ourselves provide.
Most holy and religious fear it is
To keep those many many bodies safe
That live and feed upon your majesty.

5   ROSENCRANTZ   The single and peculiar[4] life is bound
With all the strength and armor of the mind
To keep itself from noyance,[5] but much more
That spirit upon whose weal depends and rests
The lives of many. The cess[6] of majesty

10   Dies not alone, but like a gulf [7]doth draw
What's near it with it; or 'tis a massy wheel
Fixed on the summit of the highest mount,
To whose huge spokes ten thousand lesser things
Are mortised and adjoined, which when it falls,

15   Each small annexment, petty consequence,
Attends[8] the boist'rous ruin. Never alone
Did the king sigh, but with a general groan.

KING   Arm[9] you, I pray you, to this speedy voyage,
For we will fetters put upon this fear,

20   Which now goes too free-footed.

ROSENCRANTZ   We will haste us.

(*Exeunt* GENTLEMEN)

(*Enter* POLONIUS)

POLONIUS   My lord, he's going to his mother's closet.

25   Behind the arras I'll convey myself
To hear the process.[10] I'll warrant she'll tax him home,[11]
And, as you said, and wisely was it said,
'Tis meet that some more audience than a mother,
Since nature makes them partial, should o'erhear

30   The speech, of vantage.[12] Fare you well, my liege.
I'll call upon you ere you go to bed
And tell you what I know.

KING   Thanks, dear my lord.

(*Exit* POLONIUS)

35   O, my offense is rank, it smells to heaven;
It hath the primal eldest curse[13] upon't,

---

[4] *peculiar* individual   [5] *noyance* harm   [6] *cess* cessation, decease   [7] *gulf*
whirlpool   [8] *Attends* joins in (like a royal attendant)   [9] *Arm* prepare
[10] *process* proceedings   [11] *tax him home* thrust home in reprimanding him
[13] *of vantage* from an advantageous position   [13] *primal eldest curse* that of
Cain, who also murdered a brother

A brother's murder. Pray can I not,
Though inclination be as sharp as will.
My stronger guilt defeats my strong intent,
And like a man to double business bound
5   I stand in pause where I shall first begin,
And both neglect. What if this cursèd hand
Were thicker than itself with brother's blood,
Is there not rain enough in the sweet heavens
To wash it white as snow? Whereto serves mercy
10   But to confront the visage of offense? [14]
And what's in prayer but this twofold force,
To be forestallèd ere we come to fall,
Or pardoned being down? Then I'll look up.
My fault is past. But, O, what form of prayer
15   Can serve my turn? "Forgive me my foul murder"?
That cannot be, since I am still possessed
Of those effects[15] for which I did the murder,
My crown, mine own ambition, and my queen.
May one be pardoned and retain th' offense?
20   In the corrupted currents of this world
Offense's gilded [16] hand may shove by justice,
And oft 'tis seen the wicked prize itself
Buys out the law. But 'tis not so above.
There is no shuffling;[17] there the action[18] lies
25   In his true nature, and we ourselves compelled,
Even to the teeth and forehead [19] of our faults,
To give in evidence. What then? What rests?
Try what repentance can. What can it not?
Yet what can it when one cannot repent?
30   O wretched state! O bosom black as death!
O limèd [20] soul, that struggling to be free
Art more engaged! [21] Help, angels! Make assay.[22]
Bow, stubborn knees, and, heart with strings of steel,
Be soft as sinews of the new-born babe.
35   All may be well.

He kneels

(*Enter* HAMLET)

---

[14] *offense* sin   [15] *effects* things acquired   [16] *gilded* gold-laden   [17] *shuffling* sharp practice, double-dealing   [18] *action* legal proceeding (in heaven's court)   [19] *teeth and forehead* face-to-face recognition   [20] *limèd* caught in birdlime, a gluey material spread as a bird-snare   [21] *engaged* embedded   [22] *assay* an attempt

HAMLET   Now might I do it pat,[23] now 'a is a-praying,
And now I'll do't. And so 'a goes to heaven,
And so am I revenged. That would be scanned.
A villain kills my father, and for that
5   I, his sole son, do this same villain send
To heaven.
Why, this is hire and salary, not revenge.
'A took my father grossly,[24] full of bread,[25]
With all his crimes broad blown,[26] as flush[27] as May;
10   And how his audit[28] stands, who knows save heaven?
But in our circumstance and course of thought,
'Tis heavy with him; and am I then revenged,
To take him in the purging of his soul,
When he is fit and seasoned for his passage?
15   No.
Up, sword, and know thou a more horrid hent.[29]
When he is drunk asleep, or in his rage,
Or in th' incestuous pleasure of his bed,
At game a-swearing, or about some act
20   That has no relish[30] of salvation in't—
Then trip him, that his heels may kick at heaven,
And that his soul may be as damned and black
As hell, whereto it goes. My mother stays.
This physic but prolongs thy sickly days.

25   (*Exit*)

KING (*rises*)   My words fly up, my thoughts remain below.
Words without thoughts never to heaven go.

(*Exit*)

Act III, Scene IV

30   *The private chamber of the* QUEEN

(*Enter* [QUEEN] GERTRUDE *and* POLONIUS)

POLONIUS   'A will come straight. Look you lay[1] home to him.
Tell him his pranks have been too broad [2] to bear with,
And that your grace hath screened and stood between

---

[23] *pat* opportunely [24] *grossly* in a state of gross unpreparedness [25] *bread*
i.e. worldly sense gratification [26] *broad blown* fully blossomed [27] *flush* vigorous [28] *audit* account [29] *more horrid hent* grasping by me on a more
horrid occasion [30] *relish* flavor
[1] *lay* thrust [2] *broad* unrestrained

Much heat and him. I'll silence me even here.
Pray you be round [3] with him.
[HAMLET (*within*)   Mother, mother, mother!]
QUEEN   I'll warrant you; fear me not. Withdraw; I hear him
5   coming.

   (POLONIUS *hides behind the arras*)

   (*Enter* HAMLET)

HAMLET   Now, mother, what's the matter?
QUEEN   Hamlet, thou hast thy father much offended.
10   HAMLET   Mother, you have my father much offended.
QUEEN   Come, come, you answer with an idle[4] tongue.
HAMLET   Go, go, you question with a wicked tongue.
QUEEN   Why, how now, Hamlet?
HAMLET   What's the matter now?
15   QUEEN   Have you forgot me?
HAMLET   No, by the rood,[5] not so!
   You are the queen, your husband's brother's wife,
   And (would it were not so) you are my mother.
QUEEN   Nay, then I'll set those to you that can speak.
20   HAMLET   Come, come, and sit you down. You shall not budge.
   You go not till I set you up a glass
   Where you may see the inmost part of you.
QUEEN   What wilt thou do? Thou wilt not murder me?
   Help, ho!
25   POLONIUS (*behind*)   What, ho! help!
HAMLET (*draws*)   How now? a rat? Dead for a ducat, dead!

   (*Makes a pass through the arras and kills* POLONIUS)

POLONIUS (*behind*)   O, I am slain!
QUEEN   O me, what hast thou done?
30   HAMLET   Nay, I know not. Is it the king?
QUEEN   O, what a rash and bloody deed is this!
HAMLET   A bloody deed—almost as bad, good mother,
   As kill a king, and marry with his brother.
QUEEN   As kill a king?
35   HAMLET   Ay, lady, it was my word.

   (*Lifts up the arras and sees* POLONIUS)

   Thou wretched, rash, intruding fool, farewell!

---

[3] *round* plain-spoken   [4] *idle* foolish   [5] *rood* cross

I took thee for thy better. Take thy fortune.
Thou find'st to be too busy is some danger.—
Leave wringing of your hands. Peace, sit you down
And let me wring your heart, for so I shall
5   If it be made of penetrable stuff,
If damnèd custom[6] have not brazed [7] it so
That it is proof [8] and bulwark against sense.[9]
QUEEN   What have I done that thou dar'st wag thy tongue
In noise so rude against me?
10   HAMLET   Such an act
That blurs the grace and blush of modesty,
Calls virtue hypocrite, takes off the rose
From the fair forehead of an innocent love,
And sets a blister[10] there, makes marriage vows
15   As false as dicers' oaths. O, such a deed
As from the body of contraction[11] plucks
The very soul, and sweet religion[12] makes
A rhapsody of words! Heaven's face does glow,
And this solidity and compound mass,[13]
20   With heated visage, as against[14] the doom,[15]
Is thought-sick at the act.
QUEEN   Ay me, what act,
That roars so loud and thunders in the index? [16]
HAMLET   Look here upon this picture, and on this,
25   The counterfeit presentment[17] of two brothers.
See what a grace was seated on this brow:
Hyperion's[18] curls, the front[19] of Jove himself,
An eye like Mars, to threaten and command,
A station[20] like the herald Mercury
30   New lighted on a heaven-kissing hill—
A combination and a form indeed
Where every god did seem to set his seal
To give the world assurance of a man.
This was your husband. Look you now what follows.
35   Here is your husband, like a mildewed ear
Blasting his wholesome brother. Have you eyes?

---

[6] *custom* habit   [7] *brazed* hardened like brass   [8] *proof* armor   [9] *sense* feeling   [10] *blister* brand (of degradation)   [11] *contraction* the marriage contract   [12] *religion* i.e. sacred marriage vows   [13] *compound mass* the earth as compounded of the four elements   [14] *against* in expectation of   [15] *doom* Day of Judgment   [16] *index* table of contents preceding the body of a book   [17] *counterfeit presentment* portrayed representation   [18] *Hyperion* the sun god   [19] *front* forehead   [20] *station* attitude in standing

Could you on this fair mountain leave to feed,
And batten[21] on this moor? Ha! have you eyes?
You cannot call it love, for at your age
The heyday[22] in the blood is tame, it's humble,
5   And waits upon[23] the judgment, and what judgment
Would step from this to this? Sense[24] sure you have,
Else could you not have motion,[25] but sure that sense
Is apoplexed,[26] for madness would not err,
Nor sense to ecstasy[27] was ne'er so thralled
10   But it reserved some quantity of choice
To serve in such a difference. What devil was't
That thus hath cozened [28] you at hoodman-blind? [29]
Eyes without feeling, feeling without sight,
Ears without hands or eyes, smelling sans[30] all,
15   Or but a sickly part of one true sense
Could not so mope.[31]
O shame, where is thy blush? Rebellious hell,
If thou canst mutine[32] in a matron's bones,
To flaming youth let virtue be as wax
20   And melt in her own fire. Proclaim no shame
When the compulsive[33] ardor gives the charge,[34]
Since frost itself as actively doth burn,
And reason panders will.[35]
QUEEN   O Hamlet, speak no more.
25   Thou turn'st mine eyes into my very soul,
And there I see such black and grainèd [36] spots
As will not leave their tinct.[37]
HAMLET   Nay, but to live
In the rank sweat of an enseamèd [38] bed,
30   Stewed in corruption, honeying and making love
Over the nasty sty—
QUEEN   O, speak to me no more.
These words like daggers enter in mine ears.
No more, sweet Hamlet.
35   HAMLET   A murderer and a villain,
A slave that is not twentieth part the tithe[39]

---

21 *batten* feed greedily   22 *heyday* excitement of passion   23 *waits upon* yields
to   24 *Sense* feeling   25 *motion* desire, impulse   26 *apoplexed* paralyzed
27 *ecstasy* madness   28 *cozened* cheated   29 *hoodman-blind* blindman's buff
30 *sans* without   31 *mope* be stupid   32 *mutine* mutiny   33 *compulsive* compelling   34 *gives the charge* delivers the attack   35 *panders will* acts as procurer for desire   36 *grainèd* dyed in grain   37 *tinct* color   38 *enseamèd*
grease-laden 39 *tithe* tenth part

Of your precedent lord, a vice[40] of kings,
A cutpurse[41] of the empire and the rule,
That from a shelf the precious diadem stole
And put it in his pocket—

5   QUEEN   No more.

    (*Enter* [*the*] GHOST [*in his nightgown*[42]])

HAMLET   A king of shreds and patches—
Save me and hover o'er me with your wings,
You heavenly guards? What would your gracious figure?

10   QUEEN   Alas, he's mad.

HAMLET   Do you not come your tardy son to chide,
That, lapsed in time and passion,[43] lets go by
Th' important acting of your dread command?
O, say!

15   GHOST   Do not forget. This visitation
Is but to whet thy almost blunted purpose.
But look, amazement on thy mother sits.
O, step between her and her fighting soul!
Conceit[44] in weakest bodies strongest works.

20   Speak to her, Hamlet.

HAMLET   How is it with you, lady?

QUEEN   Alas, how is't with you,
That you do bend your eye on vacancy,
And with th' incorporal [45] air do hold discourse?

25   Forth at your eyes your spirits wildly peep,
And as the sleeping soldiers in th' alarm
Your bedded hairs like life in excrements[46]
Start up and stand an[47] end. O gentle son,
Upon the heat and flame of thy distemper[48]

30   Sprinkle cool patience. Whereon do you look?

HAMLET   On him, on him! Look you, how pale he glares!
His form and cause conjoined, preaching to stones,
Would make them capable.[49]—Do not look upon me,
Lest with his piteous action you convert

35   My stern effects.[50] Then what I have to do
Will want true color—tears perchance for blood.

---

[40] *vice* clownish rogue (like the Vice of the morality plays)   [41] *cutpurse* skulking thief   [42] *nightgown* dressing gown   [43] *lapsed . . . passion* having let the moment slip and passion cool   [44] *Conceit* imagination   [45] *incorporal* bodiless   [46] *excrements* outgrowths   [47] *an* on   [48] *distemper* mental disorder   [49] *capable* susceptible   [50] *effects* manifestations of emotion and purpose

QUEEN   To whom do you speak this?
HAMLET   Do you see nothing there?
QUEEN   Nothing at all; yet all that is I see.
HAMLET   Nor did you nothing hear?
5 QUEEN   No, nothing but ourselves.
HAMLET   Why, look you there! Look how it steals away!
My father, in his habit as he lived!
Look where he goes even now out at the portal!

(*Exit* GHOST)

1c QUEEN   This is the very coinage of your brain.
This bodiless creation ecstasy[51]
Is very cunning in.
HAMLET   Ecstasy?
My pulse as yours doth temperately keep time
15 And makes as healthful music. It is not madness
That I have uttered. Bring me to the test,
And I the matter will reword, which madness
Would gambol [52] from. Mother, for love of grace,
Lay not that flattering unction[53] to your soul,
2c That not your trespass but my madness speaks.
It will but skin and film the ulcerous place
Whiles rank corruption, mining[54] all within,
Infects unseen. Confess yourself to heaven,
Repent what's past, avoid what is to come,
25 And do not spread the compost[55] on the weeds
To make them ranker. Forgive me this my virtue.
For in the fatness[56] of these pursy[57] times
Virtue itself of vice must pardon beg,
Yea, curb[58] and woo for leave to do him good.
30 QUEEN   O Hamlet, thou hast cleft my heart in twain.
HAMLET   O, throw away the worser part of it,
And live the purer with the other half.
Good night—but go not to my uncle's bed.
Assume a virtue, if you have it not.
35 That monster custom, who all sense doth eat,
Of habits devil, is angel yet in this,
That to the use of actions fair and good

---

[51] *ecstasy* madness [52] *gambol* shy (like a startled horse) [53] *unction* ointment [54] *mining* undermining [55] *compost* fertilizing mixture [56] *fatness*
gross slackness [57] *pursy* corpulent [58] *curb* bow to

He likewise gives a frock or livery[59]
That aptly is put on. Refrain to-night,
And that shall lend a kind of easiness
To the next abstinence; the next more easy;
5 For use[60] almost can change the stamp[61] of nature,
And either [. . .] [62] the devil, or throw him out
With wondrous potency. Once more, good night,
And when you are desirous to be blest,
I'll blessing beg of you.—For this same lord,
10 I do repent; but heaven hath pleased it so,
To punish me with this, and this with me,
That I must be their scourge and minister.
I will bestow[63] him and will answer well
The death I gave him. So again, good night.
15 I must be cruel only to be kind.
Thus bad begins, and worse remains behind.[64]
One word more, good lady.
    QUEEN   What shall I do?
    HAMLET   Not this, by no means, that I bid you do:
20 Let the bloat[65] king tempt you again to bed,
Pinch wanton on your cheek, call you his mouse,
And let him, for a pair of reechy[66] kisses,
Or paddling in your neck with his damned fingers,
Make you to ravel all this matter out,[67]
25 That I essentially am not in madness,
But mad in craft. 'Twere good you let him know,
For who that's but a queen, fair, sober, wise,
Would from a paddock,[68] from a bat, a gib,[69]
Such dear concernings[70] hide? Who would do so?
30 No, in despite of sense and secrecy,
Unpeg the basket on the house's top,
Let the birds fly, and like the famous ape,[71]
To try conclusions,[72] in the basket creep
And break your own neck down.
35 QUEEN   Be thou assured, if words be made of breath,
And breath of life, I have no life to breathe

---

[59] *livery* characteristic dress (accompanying the suggestion of "garb" in *habits*) [60] *use* habit [61] *stamp* impression, form [62] A word is apparently omitted here [63] *bestow* stow, hide [64] *behind* to come [65] *bloat* bloated with sense gratification [66] *reechy* filthy [67] *ravel . . . out* disentangle [68] *paddock* toad [69] *gib* tomcat [70] *dear concernings* matters of great personal significance [71] *famous ape* (one in a story now unknown) [72] *conclusions* experiments

What thou hast said to me.

HAMLET   I must to England; you know that?

QUEEN   Alack,
I had forgot. 'Tis so concluded on.

5   HAMLET   There's letters sealed, and my two schoolfellows,
Whom I will trust as I will adders fanged,
They bear the mandate;[73] they must sweep my way
And marshal me to knavery. Let it work.
For 'tis the sport to have the enginer[74]

10   Hoist[75] with his own petar,[76] and 't shall go hard
But I will delve one yard below their mines
And blow them at the moon. O, 'tis most sweet
When in one line two crafts directly meet.
This man shall set me packing.[77]

15   I'll lug the guts into the neighbor room.
Mother, good night. Indeed, this counsellor
Is now most still, most secret, and most grave,
Who was in life a foolish prating knave.
Come, sir, to draw toward an end with you.

20   Good night, mother.

(*Exit the* QUEEN. *Then exit* HAMLET, *tugging in* POLONIUS)

ACT IV

Scene I

A chamber in the castle

25   (*Enter* KING *and* QUEEN, *with* ROSENCRANTZ *and* GUILDENSTERN)

KING   There's matter in these sighs. These profound heaves
You must translate; 'tis fit we understand them.
Where is your son?

QUEEN   Bestow this place on us a little while.

30   (*Exeunt* ROSENCRANTZ *and* GUILDENSTERN)

Ah, mine own lord, what have I seen to-night!

KING   What, Gertrude? How does Hamlet?

---

[73] *mandate* order   [74] *enginer* engineer, constructor of military engines or
works   [75] *Hoist* blown up   [76] *petar* petard, bomb or mine   [77] *packing* travelling in a hurry (with a play upon his "packing" or shouldering of Polonius'
body and also upon his "packing" in the sense of "plotting" or "contriving")

QUEEN   Mad as the sea and wind when both contend
Which is the mightier. In his lawless fit,
Behind the arras hearing something stir,
Whips out his rapier, cries, "A rat, a rat!"
5   And in this brainish apprehension[1] kills
The unseen good old man.
KING   O heavy deed!
It had been so with us, had we been there.
His liberty is full of threats to all,
10   To you yourself, to us, to every one.
Alas, how shall this bloody deed be answered?
It will be laid to us, whose providence[2]
Should have kept short, restrained, and out of haunt[3]
This mad young man. But so much was our love
15   We would not understand what was most fit,
But, like the owner of a foul disease,
To keep it from divulging,[4] let it feed
Even on the pith of life. Where is he gone?
QUEEN   To draw apart the body he hath killed;
20   O'er whom his very madness, like some ore[5]
Among a mineral [6] of metals base,
Shows itself pure. 'A weeps for what is done.
KING   O Gertrude, come away!
The sun no sooner shall the mountains touch
25   But we will ship him hence, and this vile deed
We must with all our majesty and skill
Both countenance and excuse. Ho, Guildenstern!

(*Enter* ROSENCRANTZ *and* GUILDENSTERN)

Friends both, go join you with some further aid.
30   Hamlet in madness hath Polonius slain,
And from his mother's closet hath he dragged him.
Go seek him out; speak fair, and bring the body
Into the chapel. I pray you haste in this.

(*Exeunt* ROSENCRANTZ *and* GUILDENSTERN)

35   Come, Gertrude, we'll call up our wisest friends
And let them know both what we mean to do
And what's untimely done [. . .] [7]

---

[1] *brainish   apprehension* headstrong conception   [2] *providence* foresight
[3] *haunt* association with others   [4] *divulging* becoming known   [5] *ore* vein of
gold   [6] *mineral* mine   [7] Incomplete line; Capell suggests "So, haply, slander"

Whose whisper o'er the world's diameter,
As level [8] as the cannon to his blank[9]
Transports his poisoned shot, may miss our name
And hit the woundless air. O, come away!

5   My soul is full of discord and dismay.

(*Exeunt*)

Act IV, Scene II

A passage in the castle

(*Enter* HAMLET)

10   HAMLET   Safely stowed.

GENTLEMEN (*within*)   Hamlet! Lord Hamlet!

HAMLET   But soft, what noise? Who calls on Hamlet? O, here they
come.

(*Enter* ROSENCRANTZ, GUILDENSTERN, *and others*)

15   ROSENCRANTZ   What have you done, my lord, with the dead body?

HAMLET   Compounded it with dust, whereto 'tis kin.

ROSENCRANTZ   Tell us where 'tis, that we may take it thence
And bear it to the chapel.

HAMLET   Do not believe it.

20   ROSENCRANTZ   Believe what?

HAMLET   That I can keep your counsel and not mine own. Besides,
to be demanded of a sponge, what replication[1] should be made
by the son of a king?

ROSENCRANTZ   Take you me for a sponge, my lord?

25   HAMLET   Ay, sir, that soaks up the king's countenance,[2] his rewards, his authorities. But such officers do the king best service in
the end. He keeps them, like an ape, in the corner of his jaw, first
mouthed, to be last swallowed. When he needs what you have
gleaned, it is but squeezing you and, sponge, you shall be dry

30   again.

ROSENCRANTZ   I understand you not, my lord.

HAMLET   I am glad of it. A knavish speech sleeps in[3] a foolish ear.

ROSENCRANTZ   My lord, you must tell us where the body is and go
with us to the king.

35   HAMLET   The body is with the king, but the king is not with the
body. The king is a thing—

---

[8] *As level* with as direct aim   [9] *blank* mark, central white spot on a target
[1] *replication* reply   [2] *countenance* favor   [3] *sleeps in* means nothing to

GUILDENSTERN   A thing, my lord?
HAMLET   Of nothing.[4] Bring me to him. Hide fox, and all after.[5]

(*Exeunt*)

Act IV, Scene III

5   *A chamber in the castle*

(*Enter* KING, *and two or three*)

KING   I have sent to seek him and to find the body.
How dangerous is it that this man goes loose!
Yet must not we put the strong law on him;
10   He's loved of the distracted [1] multitude,
Who like not in their judgment, but their eyes,
And where 'tis so, th' offender's scourge[2] is weighed,
But never the offense. To bear all smooth and even,
This sudden sending him away must seem
15   Deliberate pause.[3] Diseases desperate grown
By desperate appliance are relieved,
Or not at all.

(*Enter* ROSENCRANTZ, GUILDENSTERN, *and all the rest*)

How now? What hath befallen?
20   ROSENCRANTZ   Where the dead body is bestowed, my lord,
We cannot get from him.
KING   But where is he?
ROSENCRANTZ   Without, my lord; guarded, to know your pleasure.
KING   Bring him before us.
25   ROSENCRANTZ   Ho! Bring in the lord.

(*They enter* [*with* HAMLET])

KING   Now, Hamlet, where's Polonius?
HAMLET   At supper.
KING   At supper? Where?
30   HAMLET   Not where he eats, but where 'a is eaten. A certain convocation of politic worms[4] are e'en at him. Your worm is your

---

[4] *Of nothing* (cf. Prayer Book, Psalm cxliv, 4, "Man is like a thing of naught: his time passeth away like a shadow")   [5] *Hide ... after* (apparently well-known words from some game of hide-and-seek)
[1] *distracted* confused   [2] *scourge* punishment   [3] *Deliberate pause* something done with much deliberation   [4] *politic worms* political and craftily scheming worms (such as Polonius might well attract)

only emperor for diet.[5] We fat all creatures else to fat us, and we fat ourselves for maggots. Your fat king and your lean beggar is but variable service[6]—two dishes, but to one table. That's the end.

KING   Alas, alas!

5   HAMLET   A man may fish with the worm that hath eat of a king, and eat of the fish that hath fed of that worm.

KING   What dost thou mean by this?

HAMLET   Nothing but to show you how a king may go a progress[7] through the guts of a beggar.

10   KING   Where is Polonius?

HAMLET   In heaven. Send thither to see. If your messenger find him not there, seek him i' th' other place yourself. But if indeed you find him not within this month, you shall nose him as you go up the stairs into the lobby.

15   KING (*to* ATTENDANTS)   Go seek him there.

HAMLET   'A will stay till you come.

(*Exeunt* ATTENDANTS)

KING   Hamlet, this deed, for thine especial safety,
Which we do tender[8] as we dearly[9] grieve
20   For that which thou hast done, must send thee hence
With fiery quickness. Therefore prepare thyself.
The bark is ready and the wind at help,
Th' associates tend,[10] and everything is bent[11]
For England.

25   HAMLET   For England?

KING   Ay, Hamlet.

HAMLET   Good.

KING   So is it, if thou knew'st our purposes.

HAMLET   I see a cherub[12] that sees them. But come, for England!
30   Farewell, dear mother.

KING   Thy loving father, Hamlet.

HAMLET   My mother—father and mother is man and wife, man and wife is one flesh, and so, my mother. Come, for England!

(*Exit*)

---

[5] *diet* food and drink (perhaps with a play upon a famous "convocation," the Diet of Worms opened by the Emperor Charles V on January 28, 1521, before which Luther appeared)   [6] *variable service* different servings of one food   [7] *progress* royal journey of state   [8] *tender* hold dear   [9] *dearly* intensely   [10] *tend* wait   [11] *bent* set in readiness (like a bent bow)   [12] *cherub* one of the cherubim (angels with a distinctive quality of knowledge)

KING   Follow him at foot;[13] tempt him with speed aboard.
Delay it not; I'll have him hence to-night.
Away! for everything is sealed and done
That else leans on[14] th' affair. Pray you make haste.

5   (*Exeunt all but the* KING)

And, England,[15] if my love thou hold'st at aught—
As my great power thereof may give thee sense,
Since yet thy cicatrice looks raw and red
After the Danish sword, and thy free awe[16]
10   Pays homage to us—thou mayst not coldly set[17]
Our sovereign process,[18] which imports at full
By letters congruing[19] to that effect
The present[20] death of Hamlet. Do it, England,
For like the hectic[21] in my blood he rages,
15   And thou must cure me. Till I know 'tis done,
Howe'er my haps,[22] my joys were ne'er begun.

(*Exit*)

Act IV, Scene IV

A coastal highway

20   (*Enter* FORTINBRAS *with his* ARMY *over the stage*)

FORTINBRAS   Go, captain, from me greet the Danish king.
Tell him that by his license Fortinbras
Craves the conveyance[1] of a promised march
Over his kingdom. You know the rendezvous.
25   If that his majesty would aught with us,
We shall express our duty in his eye;[2]
And let him know so.
CAPTAIN   I will do't, my lord.
FORTINBRAS   Go softly[3] on.

30   (*Exeunt all but the* CAPTAIN)

(*Enter* HAMLET, ROSENCRANTZ, GUILDENSTERN, *and others*)

HAMLET   Good sir, whose powers[4] are these?

---

[13] *at foot* at heel, close   [14] *leans on* is connected with   [15] *England* King of
England   [16] *free awe* voluntary show of respect   [17] *set* esteem   [18] *process*
formal command   [19] *congruing* agreeing   [20] *present* instant   [21] *hectic* a
continuous fever   [22] *haps* fortunes
[1] *conveyance* escort   [2] *eye* presence   [3] *softly* slowly   [4] *powers* forces

	CAPTAIN	They are of Norway, sir.
	HAMLET	How purposed, sir, I pray you?
	CAPTAIN	Against some part of Poland.
	HAMLET	Who commands them, sir?
5	CAPTAIN	The nephew to old Norway, Fortinbras.
	HAMLET	Goes it against the main⁵ of Poland, sir,

HAMLET Goes it against the main[5] of Poland, sir,
Or for some frontier?
CAPTAIN Truly to speak, and with no addition,[6]
We go to gain a little patch of ground
10 That hath in it no profit but the name.
To pay[7] five ducats, five, I would not farm it,
Nor will it yield to Norway or the Pole
A ranker[8] rate, should it be sold in fee.[9]
HAMLET Why, then the Polack never will defend it.
15 CAPTAIN Yes, it is already garrisoned.
HAMLET Two thousand souls and twenty thousand ducats
Will not debate the question of this straw.
This is th' imposthume[10] of much wealth and peace,
That inward breaks, and shows no cause without
20 Why the man dies. I humbly thank you, sir.
CAPTAIN God bye you, sir.

(*Exit*)

ROSENCRANTZ Will't please you go, my lord?
HAMLET I'll be with you straight. Go a little before.

25 (*Exeunt all but* HAMLET)

How all occasions do inform[11] against me
And spur my dull revenge! What is a man,
If his chief good and market of [12] his time
Be but to sleep and feed? A beast, no more.
30 Sure he that made us with such large discourse,[13]
Looking before and after, gave us not
That capability and godlike reason
To fust[14] in us unused. Now, whether it be
Bestial oblivion,[15] or some craven scruple
35 Of thinking too precisely on th' event—[16]

---

⁵ *main* main body   ⁶ *addition* exaggeration   ⁷ *To pay* i.e. for a yearly rental of   ⁸ *ranker* more abundant   ⁹ *in fee* outright   ¹⁰ *imposthume* abscess   ¹¹ *inform* take shape   ¹² *market of* compensation for   ¹³ *discourse* power of thought   ¹⁴ *fust* grow mouldy   ¹⁵ *oblivion* forgetfulness   ¹⁶ *event* outcome

A thought which, quartered, hath but one part wisdom
And ever three parts coward—I do not know
Why yet I live to say, "This thing 's to do,"
Sith I have cause, and will, and strength, and means
5   To do 't. Examples gross[17] as earth exhort me.
Witness this army of such mass and charge,[18]
Led by a delicate and tender prince,
Whose spirit, with divine ambition puffed,
Makes mouths[19] at the invisible event,
10   Exposing what is mortal and unsure
To all that fortune, death, and danger dare,
Even for an eggshell. Rightly to be great
Is not to stir without great argument,
But greatly to find quarrel in a straw[20]
15   When honor 's at the stake. How stand I then,
That have a father killed, a mother stained,
Excitements of my reason and my blood,
And let all sleep, while to my shame I see
The imminent death of twenty thousand men
20   That for a fantasy[21] and trick[22] of fame
Go to their graves like beds, fight for a plot
Whereon the numbers cannot try the cause,[23]
Which is not tomb enough and continent[24]
To hide the slain? O, from this time forth,
25   My thoughts be bloody, or be nothing worth!

(*Exit*)

Act IV, Scene V

A chamber in the castle

(*Enter* HORATIO, [QUEEN] GERTRUDE, *and a* GENTLEMAN)

30   QUEEN   I will not speak with her.
GENTLEMAN   She is importunate, indeed distract.[1]
Her mood will needs be pitied.
QUEEN   What would she have?
GENTLEMAN   She speaks much of her father, says she hears

---

17 *gross* large and evident   18 *charge* expense   19 *Makes mouths* makes faces
scornfully   20 *greatly . . . straw* to recognize the great argument even in some
small matter   21 *fantasy* fanciful image   22 *trick* toy   23 *try the cause* find
space in which to settle the issue by battle   24 *continent* receptacle
1 *distract* insane

There's tricks² i' th' world, and hems, and beats her heart,
Spurns enviously³ at straws,⁴ speaks things in doubt
That carry but half sense. Her speech is nothing,
Yet the unshapèd use⁵ of it doth move
5   The hearers to collection;⁶ they aim⁷ at it,
And botch⁸ the words up fit to their own thoughts,
Which, as her winks and nods and gestures yield them,
Indeed would make one think there might be thought,
Though nothing sure, yet much unhappily.
10 HORATIO   'Twere good she were spoken with, for she may strew
Dangerous conjectures in ill-breeding minds.
QUEEN   Let her come in.

  (*Exit* GENTLEMAN)

  (*Aside*)

15 To my sick soul (as sin's true nature is)
Each toy⁹ seems prologue to some great amiss.¹⁰
So full of artless¹¹ jealousy¹² is guilt
It spills¹³ itself in fearing to be spilt.

  (*Enter* OPHELIA [*distracted*])

20 OPHELIA   Where is the beauteous majesty of Denmark?
QUEEN   How now, Ophelia?
OPHELIA (*She sings.*)
       How should I your true-love know
          From another one?
25   By his cockle hat¹⁴ and staff
          And his sandal shoon.¹⁵
QUEEN   Alas, sweet lady, what imports this song?
OPHELIA   Say you? Nay, pray you mark.

Song

30   He is dead and gone, lady,
          He is dead and gone;
       At his head a grass-green turf,
          At his heels a stone.
       O, ho!

---

² *tricks* deceits ³ *Spurns enviously* kicks spitefully, takes offense ⁴ *straws*
trifles ⁵ *unshapèd use* disordered manner ⁶ *collection* attempts at shaping
meaning ⁷ *aim* guess ⁸ *botch* patch ⁹ *toy* trifle ¹⁰ *amiss* calamity ¹¹ *art-
less* unskillfully managed ¹² *jealousy* suspicion ¹³ *spills* destroys ¹⁴ *cockle
hat* hat bearing a cockle shell, worn by a pilgrim who had been to the shrine
of St James of Compostela ¹⁵ *shoon* shoes

QUEEN   Nay, but Ophelia—
OPHELIA   Pray you mark.
(*Sings*) White his shroud as the mountain snow—

(*Enter* KING)

5 QUEEN   Alas, look here, my lord.
OPHELIA

Song

     Larded [16] all with sweet flowers;
   Which bewept to the grave did not go
10   With true-love showers.
KING   How do you, pretty lady?
OPHELIA   Well, God dild [17] you! They say the owl [18] was a baker's
daughter. Lord, we know what we are, but know not what we
may be. God be at your table!
15 KING   Conceit[19] upon her father.
OPHELIA   Pray let's have no words of this, but when they ask you
what it means, say you this:

Song

   To-morrow is Saint Valentine's day.
20   All in the morning betime,[20]
And I a maid at your window,
   To be your Valentine.
Then up he rose and donned his clo'es
   And dupped [21] the chamber door,
25 Let in the maid, that out a maid
   Never departed more.
KING   Pretty Ophelia!
OPHELIA   Indeed, la, without an oath, I'll make an end on't:
(*Sings*)   By Gis[22] and by Saint Charity,
30   Alack, and fie for shame!
Young men will do't if they come to't.
   By Cock,[23] they are to blame.
Quoth she, "Before you tumbled me,
   You promised me to wed."

---

[16] *Larded* garnished   [17] *dild* yield, repay   [18] *the owl* an owl into which, according to a folk-tale, a baker's daughter was transformed because of her failure to show whole-hearted generosity when Christ asked for bread in the
baker's shop   [19] *Conceit* thought   [20] *betime* early   [21] *dupped* opened   [22] *Gis*
Jesus   [23] *Cock* God (with a perversion of the name not uncommon in oaths)

He answers:
>"So would I 'a' done, by yonder sun,
>   And thou hadst not come to my bed."

KING   How long hath she been thus?

5   OPHELIA   I hope all will be well. We must be patient, but I cannot choose but weep to think they would lay him i' th' cold ground. My brother shall know of it; and so I thank you for your good counsel. Come, my coach! Good night, ladies, good night. Sweet ladies, good night, good night.

10   (*Exit*)

KING   Follow her close; give her good watch, I pray you.

(*Exit* HORATIO)

O, this is the poison of deep grief; it springs
All from her father's death—and now behold!
15   O Gertrude, Gertrude,
When sorrows come, they come not single spies,
But in battalions: first, her father slain;
Next, your son gone, and he most violent author
Of his own just remove; the people muddied,[24]
20   Thick and unwholesome in their thoughts and whispers
For good Polonius' death, and we have done but greenly[25]
In hugger-mugger[26] to inter him; poor Ophelia
Divided from herself and her fair judgment,
Without the which we are pictures or mere beasts;
25   Last, and as much containing as all these,
Her brother is in secret come from France,
Feeds on his wonder, keeps himself in clouds,[27]
And wants[28] not buzzers[29] to infect his ear
With pestilent speeches of his father's death,
30   Wherein necessity, of matter beggared,[30]
Will nothing stick[31] our person to arraign[32]
In ear and ear. O my dear Gertrude, this,
Like to a murd'ring piece,[33] in many places
Gives me superfluous death.

35   *A noise within*

---

[24] *muddied* stirred up and confused   [25] *greenly* foolishly   [26] *hugger-mugger* secrecy and disorder   [27] *clouds* obscurity   [28] *wants* lacks   [29] *buzzers* whispering tale-bearers   [30] *of matter beggared* unprovided with facts   [31] *nothing stick* in no way hesitate   [32] *arraign* accuse   [33] *murd'ring piece* cannon loaded with shot meant to scatter

(*Enter a* MESSENGER)

QUEEN   Alack, what noise is this?
KING   Attend, where are my Switzers? [34] Let them guard the door.
    What is the matter?
5 MESSENGER   Save yourself, my lord.
    The ocean, overpeering of [35] his list,[36]
    Eats not the flats with more impiteous[37] haste
    Than young Laertes, in a riotous head,[38]
    O'erbears your officers. The rabble call him lord,
10   And, as the world were now but to begin,
    Antiquity forgot, custom not known,
    The ratifiers and props of every word,[39]
    They cry, "Choose we! Laertes shall be king!"
    Caps, hands, and tongues applaud it to the clouds,
15   "Laertes shall be king! Laertes king!"

A noise within

QUEEN   How cheerfully on the false trail they cry!
    O, this is counter,[40] you false Danish dogs!
KING   The doors are broke.

20   (*Enter* LAERTES *with others*)

LAERTES   Where is this king?—Sirs, stand you all without.
ALL   No, let's come in.
LAERTES   I pray you give me leave.
ALL   We will, we will.
25 LAERTES   I thank you. Keep the door.

    (*Exeunt his* FOLLOWERS)

                              O thou vile king,
    Give me my father.
QUEEN   Calmly, good Laertes.
30 LAERTES   That drop of blood that's calm proclaims me bastard,
    Cries cuckold to my father, brands the harlot
    Even here between the chaste unsmirchèd brows
    Of my true mother.
KING   What is the cause, Laertes,
35   That thy rebellion looks so giant-like?
    Let him go, Gertrude. Do not fear[41] our person.

---

[34] *Switzers* hired Swiss guards [35] *overpeering of* rising to look over and pass
beyond [36] *list* boundary [37] *impiteous* pitiless [38] *head* armed force [39] *word*
promise [40] *counter* hunting backward on the trail [41] *fear* fear for

There's such divinity doth hedge a king
That treason can but peep to[42] what it would,
Acts little of his will. Tell me, Laertes,
Why thou art thus incensed. Let him go, Gertrude.
5   Speak, man.

LAERTES   Where is my father?

KING   Dead.

QUEEN   But not by him.

KING   Let him demand his fill.

10 LAERTES   How came he dead? I'll not be juggled with.
To hell allegiance, vows to the blackest devil,
Conscience and grace to the profoundest pit!
I dare damnation. To this point I stand,
That both the worlds[43] I give to negligence,[44]
15   Let come what comes, only I'll be revenged
Most throughly[45] for my father.

KING   Who shall stay you?

LAERTES   My will, not all the world's.
And for my means, I'll husband them so well
20   They shall go far with little.

KING   Good Laertes,
If you desire to know the certainty
Of your dear father, is't writ in your revenge
That swoopstake[46] you will draw both friend and foe,
25   Winner and loser?

LAERTES   None but his enemies.

KING   Will you know them then?

LAERTES   To his good friends thus wide I'll ope my arms
And like the kind life-rend'ring[47] pelican
30   Repast them with my blood.

KING   Why, now you speak
Like a good child and a true gentleman.
That I am guiltless of your father's death,
And am most sensibly[48] in grief for it,
35   It shall as level[49] to your judgment 'pear
As day does to your eye.
     A noise within: "Let her come in!"

---

[42] *peep to* i.e. through the barrier   [43] *both the worlds* whatever may result in this world or the next   [44] *give to negligence* disregard   [45] *throughly* thoroughly   [46] *swoopstake* sweepstake, taking all stakes on the gambling table   [47] *life-rend'ring* life-yielding (because the mother pelican supposedly took blood from her breast with her bill to feed her young)   [48] *sensibly* feelingly   [49] *level* plain

LAERTES   How now? What noise is that?

(*Enter* OPHELIA)

O heat, dry up my brains; tears seven times salt
Burn out the sense and virtue of mine eye!
5   By heaven, thy madness shall be paid by weight
Till our scale turn the beam.[50] O rose of May,
Dear maid, kind sister, sweet Ophelia!
O heavens, is't possible a young maid's wits
Should be as mortal as an old man's life?
10   Nature is fine[51] in love, and where 'tis fine,
It sends some precious instance[52] of itself
After the thing it loves.

OPHELIA

Song

15   They bore him barefaced on the bier
             Hey non nony, nony, hey nony
         And in his grave rained many a tear—
Fare you well, my dove!

LAERTES   Hadst thou thy wits, and didst persuade revenge,
20   It could not move thus.

OPHELIA   You must sing "A-down a-down, and you call him
a-down-a." O, how the wheel [53] becomes it! It is the false steward, that stole his master's daughter.

LAERTES   This nothing 's more than matter.[54]

25   OPHELIA   There's rosemary, that's for remembrance. Pray you, love,
remember. And there is pansies, that's for thoughts.

LAERTES   A document[55] in madness, thoughts and remembrance
fitted.

OPHELIA   There's fennel [56] for you, and columbines.[57] There's rue[58]
30   for you, and here's some for me. We may call it herb of grace o'
Sundays. O, you must wear your rue with a difference. There's
a daisy.[59] I would give you some violets,[60] but they withered all
when my father died. They say 'a made a good end.
(*Sings*)   For bonny sweet Robin is all my joy.

35   LAERTES   Thought and affliction, passion, hell itself,
She turns to favor[61] and to prettiness.

---

[50] *beam* bar of a balance   [51] *fine* refined to purity   [52] *instance* token   [53] *wheel*
burden, refrain   [54] *more than matter* more meaningful than sane speech
[55] *document* lesson   [56] *fennel* symbol of flattery   [57] *columbines* symbol of
thanklessness   [58] *rue* symbol of repentance   [59] *daisy* symbol of dissembling
[60] *violets* symbol of faithfulness   [61] *favor* charm

OPHELIA

Song

        And will 'a not come again?
        And will 'a not come again?
5   No, no, he is dead;
          Go to thy deathbed;
        He never will come again.
        His beard was as white as snow,
        All flaxen was his poll.[62]
10   He is gone, he is gone,
          And we cast away moan.
        God 'a' mercy on his soul!
    And of [63] all Christian souls, I pray God. God bye you.

    (*Exit*)

15 LAERTES   Do you see this, O God?
    KING   Laertes, I must commune with your grief,
    Or you deny me right. Go but apart,
    Make choice of whom your wisest friends you will,
    And they shall hear and judge 'twixt you and me.
20   If by direct or by collateral [64] hand
    They find us touched,[65] we will our kingdom give,
    Our crown, our life, and all that we call ours,
    To you in satisfaction; but if not,
    Be you content to lend your patience to us,
25   And we shall jointly labor with your soul
    To give it due content.
    LAERTES   Let this be so.
    His means of death, his obscure funeral—
    No trophy,[66] sword, nor hatchment[67] o'er his bones,
30   No noble rite nor formal ostentation[68]—
    Cry to be heard, as 'twere from heaven to earth,
    That[69] I must call't in question.
    KING   So you shall;
    And where th' offense is, let the great axe fall.
35   I pray you go with me.

    (*Exeunt*)

---

[62] *poll* head   [63] *of* on   [64] *collateral* indirect   [65] *touched* i.e. with the crime
[66] *trophy* memorial   [67] *hatchment* coat of arms   [68] *ostentation* ceremony
[69] *That* so that

Act IV, Scene VI

A chamber in the castle

(*Enter* HORATIO *and others*)

HORATIO   What are they that would speak with me?
5   GENTLEMAN   Seafaring men, sir. They say they have letters for you.
HORATIO   Let them come in.

(*Exit* ATTENDANT)

I do not know from what part of the world
I should be greeted, if not from Lord Hamlet.

10   (*Enter* SAILORS)

SAILOR   God bless you, sir.
HORATIO   Let him bless thee too.
SAILOR   'A shall, sir, an't please him. There's a letter for you, sir—
it came from th' ambassador that was bound for England—if
15   your name be Horatio, as I am let to know it is.
HORATIO   (*reads the letter*)   "Horatio, when thou shalt have overlooked [1] this, give these fellows some means[2] to the king. They
have letters for him. Ere we were two days old at sea, a pirate of
very warlike appointment[3] gave us chase. Finding ourselves too
20   slow of sail, we put on a compelled valor, and in the grapple I
boarded them. On the instant they got clear of our ship; so I
alone became their prisoner. They have dealt with me like thieves
of mercy,[4] but they knew what they did: I am to do a good turn
for them. Let the king have the letters I have sent, and repair
25   thou to me with as much speed as thou wouldest fly death. I have
words to speak in thine ear will make thee dumb; yet are they
much too light for the bore[5] of the matter. These good fellows
will bring thee where I am. Rosencrantz and Guildenstern hold
their course for England. Of them I have much to tell thee.
30   Farewell.
                                        He that thou knowest thine, Hamlet."
Come, I will give you way for these your letters,
And do't the speedier that you may direct me
To him from whom you brought them.

35   (*Exeunt*)

---

[1] *overlooked* surveyed, scanned   [2] *means* i.e. of access   [3] *appointment* equipment   [4] *thieves of mercy* merciful thieves   [5] *bore* caliber (as of a gun)

Act IV, Scene VII

A chamber in the castle

(*Enter* KING *and* LAERTES)

KING   Now must your conscience my acquittance seal,
5   And you must put me in your heart for friend,
Sith you have heard, and with a knowing ear,
That he which hath your noble father slain
Pursued my life.

LAERTES   It well appears. But tell me
10   Why you proceeded not against these feats[1]
So crimeful and so capital [2] in nature,
As by your safety, wisdom, all things else,
You mainly[3] were stirred up.

KING   O, for two special reasons,
15   Which may to you perhaps seem much unsinewed,
But yet to me they're strong. The queen his mother
Lives almost by his looks, and for myself—
My virtue or my plague, be it either which—
She is so conjunctive[4] to my life and soul
20   That, as the star moves not but in his sphere,
I could not but by her. The other motive
Why to a public count[5] I might not go
Is the great love the general gender[6] bear him,
Who, dipping all his faults in their affection,
25   Would, like the spring that turneth wood to stone,
Convert his gyves[7] to graces; so that my arrows,
Too slightly timbered for so loud a wind,
Would have reverted to my bow again,
And not where I had aimed them.

30 LAERTES   And so have I a noble father lost,
A sister driven into desp'rate terms,[8]
Whose worth, if praises may go back again,[9]
Stood challenger on mount[10] of all the age
For her perfections. But my revenge will come.

35 KING   Break not your sleeps for that. You must not think
That we are made of stuff so flat and dull
That we can let our beard be shook with danger,

---

[1] *feats* deeds   [2] *capital* punishable by death   [3] *mainly* powerfully   [4] *conjunctive* closely united   [5] *count* trial, accounting   [6] *general gender* common people   [7] *gyves* fetters   [8] *terms* circumstances   [9] *back again* i.e. to her better circumstances   [10] *on mount* on a height

And think it pastime. You shortly shall hear more.
I loved your father, and we love ourself,
And that, I hope, will teach you to imagine—

(*Enter a* MESSENGER *with letters*)

5   How now? What news?
MESSENGER   Letters, my lord, from Hamlet:
These to your majesty, this to the queen.
KING   From Hamlet? Who brought them?
MESSENGER   Sailors, my lord, they say; I saw them not.
10   They were given me by Claudio; he received them
Of him that brought them.
KING   Laertes, you shall hear them.—
Leave us.

(*Exit* MESSENGER)

15   (*Reads*)   "High and mighty, you shall know I am set naked [11]
on your kingdom. To-morrow shall I beg leave to see your kingly
eyes; when I shall (first asking your pardon thereunto) recount
the occasion of my sudden and more strange return.   Hamlet."
What should this mean? Are all the rest come back?
20   Or is it some abuse,[12] and no such thing?
LAERTES   Know you the hand?
KING   'Tis Hamlet's character.[13] "Naked"!
And in a postscript here, he says "alone."
Can you devise[14] me?
25   LAERTES   I am lost in it, my lord. But let him come.
It warms the very sickness in my heart
That I shall live and tell him to his teeth,
"Thus diddest thou."
KING   If it be so, Laertes,
30   (As how should it be so? how otherwise?)
Will you be ruled by me?
LAERTES   Ay, my lord,
So you will not o'errule me to a peace.
KING   To thine own peace. If he be now returned,
35   As checking at[15] his voyage, and that he means
No more to undertake it, I will work him

---

[11] *naked* destitute   [12] *abuse* imposture   [13] *character* handwriting   [14] *devise*
explain to   [15] *checking at* turning aside from (like a falcon turning from its
quarry for other prey)

To an exploit now ripe in my device,
Under the which he shall not choose but fall;
And for his death no wind of blame shall breathe,
But even his mother shall uncharge the practice[16]
5   And call it accident.

LAERTES   My lord, I will be ruled;
The rather if you could devise it so
That I might be the organ.[17]

KING   It falls right.
10   You have been talked of since your travel much,
And that in Hamlet's hearing, for a quality
Wherein they say you shine. Your sum of parts
Did not together pluck such envy from him
As did that one, and that, in my regard,
15   Of the unworthiest siege.[18]

LAERTES   What part is that, my lord?

KING   A very riband [19] in the cap of youth,
Yet needful too, for youth no less becomes
The light and careless livery[20] that it wears
20   Than settled age his sables[21] and his weeds,[22]
Importing health[23] and graveness. Two months since
Here was a gentleman of Normandy.
I have seen myself, and served against, the French,
And they can well [24] on horseback, but this gallant
25   Had witchcraft in't. He grew unto his seat,
And to such wondrous doing brought his horse
As had he been incorpsed [25] and demi-natured [26]
With the brave beast. So far he topped [27] my thought[28]
That I, in forgery[29] of shapes and tricks,
30   Come short of what he did.

LAERTES   A Norman was't?

KING   A Norman.

LAERTES   Upon my life, Lamord.

KING   The very same.

35   LAERTES   I know him well. He is the brooch[30] indeed

---

[16] *uncharge the practice* acquit the stratagem of being a plot [17] *organ* instrument [18] *siege* seat, rank [19] *riband* decoration [20] *livery* distinctive attire [21] *sables* dignified robes richly furred with sable [22] *weeds* distinctive garments [23] *health* welfare, prosperity [24] *can well* can perform well [25] *incorpsed* made one body [26] *demi-natured* made sharer of nature half and half (as man shares with horse in the centaur) [27] *topped* excelled [28] *thought* imagination of possibilities [29] *forgery* invention [30] *brooch* ornament

And gem of all the nation.

KING   He made confession[31] of you,
And gave you such a masterly report
For art and exercise in your defense,
5   And for your rapier most especial,
That he cried out 'twould be a sight indeed
If one could match you. The scrimers[32] of their nation
He swore had neither motion, guard, nor eye,
If you opposed them. Sir, this report of his
10   Did Hamlet so envenom with his envy
That he could nothing do but wish and beg
Your sudden coming o'er to play with you.
Now, out of this—

LAERTES   What out of this, my lord?

15   KING   Laertes, was your father dear to you?
Or are you like the painting of a sorrow,
A face without a heart?

LAERTES   Why ask you this?

KING   Not that I think you did not love your father,
20   But that I know love is begun by time,
And that I see, in passages of proof,[33]
Time qualifies[34] the spark and fire of it.
There lives within the very flame of love
A kind of wick or snuff [35] that will abate it,
25   And nothing is at a like goodness still,[36]
For goodness, growing to a plurisy,[37]
Dies in his own too-much. That we would do
We should do when we would, for this "would" changes,
And hath abatements and delays as many
30   As there are tongues, are hands, are accidents,
And then this "should" is like a spendthrift sigh,
That hurts[38] by easing. But to the quick[39] o' th' ulcer—
Hamlet comes back; what would you undertake
To show yourself your father's son in deed
35   More than in words?

LAERTES   To cut his throat i' th' church!

---

[31] *made confession* admitted the rival accomplishments   [32] *scrimers* fencers
[33] *passages of proof* incidents of experience   [34] *qualifies* weakens   [35] *snuff*
unconsumed portion of the burned wick   [36] *still* always   [37] *plurisy* excess
[38] *hurts* i.e. shortens life by drawing blood from the heart (as was believed)
[39] *quick* sensitive flesh

KING   No place indeed should murder sanctuarize;[40]
Revenge should have no bounds. But, good Laertes,
Will you do this? Keep close within your chamber.
Hamlet returned shall know you are come home.
5   We'll put on[41] those shall praise your excellence
And set a double varnish on the fame
The Frenchman gave you, bring you in fine[42] together
And wager on your heads. He, being remiss,[43]
Most generous, and free from all contriving,
10   Will not peruse[44] the foils, so that with ease,
Or with a little shuffling, you may choose
A sword unbated,[45] and, in a pass of practice,[46]
Requite him for your father.
LAERTES   I will do't,
15   And for that purpose I'll anoint my sword.
I bought an unction[47] of a mountebank,[48]
So mortal that, but dip a knife in it,
Where it draws blood no cataplasm[49] so rare,
Collected from all simples[50] that have virtue
20   Under the moon, can save the thing from death
That is but scratched withal.[51] I'll touch my point
With this contagion, that, if I gall[52] him slightly,
It may be death.
KING   Let's further think of this,
25   Weigh what convenience both of time and means
May fit us to our shape.[53] If this should fail,
And that our drift[54] look[55] through our bad performance,
'Twere better not assayed. Therefore this project
Should have a back or second, that might hold
30   If this did blast in proof.[56] Soft, let me see.
We'll make a solemn wager on your cunnings—
I ha't!
When in your motion you are hot and dry—
As make your bouts more violent to that end—
35   And that he calls for drink, I'll have preferred[57] him
A chalice for the nonce,[58] whereon but sipping,

---

40 *sanctuarize* protect from punishment, give sanctuary to   41 *put on* instigate
42 *in fine* finally   43 *remiss* negligent   44 *peruse* scan   45 *unbated* not blunted
46 *pass of practice* thrust made effective by trickery   47 *unction* ointment
48 *mountebank* quack-doctor   49 *cataplasm* poultice   50 *simples* herbs   51 *withal*
with it   52 *gall* scratch   53 *shape* plan   54 *drift* intention   55 *look* show
56 *blast in proof* burst during trial (like a faulty cannon)   57 *preferred* offered
58 *nonce* occasion

If he by chance escape your venomed stuck,[59]
Our purpose may hold there.—But stay, what noise?

(*Enter* QUEEN)

QUEEN   One woe doth tread upon another's heel,
5   So fast they follow. Your sister 's drowned, Laertes.
LAERTES   Drowned! O, where?
QUEEN   There is a willow grows askant[60] the brook,
That shows his hoar[61] leaves in the glassy stream.
Therewith fantastic garlands did she make
10   Of crowflowers, nettles, daisies, and long purples,
That liberal [62] shepherds give a grosser name,
But our cold maids do dead men's fingers call them.
There on the pendent boughs her crownet[63] weeds
Clamb'ring to hang, an envious sliver broke,
15   When down her weedy trophies and herself
Fell in the weeping brook. Her clothes spread wide,
And mermaid-like awhile they bore her up,
Which time she chanted snatches of old lauds,[64]
As one incapable of [65] her own distress,
20   Or like a creature native and indued [66]
Unto that element. But long it could not be
Till that her garments, heavy with their drink,
Pulled the poor wretch from her melodious lay
To muddy death.
25 LAERTES   Alas, then she is drowned?
QUEEN   Drowned, drowned.
LAERTES   Too much of water hast thou, poor Ophelia,
And therefore I forbid my tears; but yet
It is our trick;[67] nature her custom holds,
30   Let shame say what it will. When these are gone,
The woman[68] will be out. Adieu, my lord.
I have a speech o' fire, that fain would blaze
But that this folly drowns it.

(*Exit*)

35 KING   Let's follow, Gertrude.
How much I had to do to calm his rage!

---

[59] *stuck* thrust [60] *askant* alongside [61] *hoar* grey [62] *liberal* free-spoken, licentious [63] *crownet* coronet [64] *lauds* hymns [65] *incapable of* insensible to [66] *indued* endowed [67] *trick* way (i.e. to shed tears when sorrowful) [68] *woman* unmanly part of nature.

Now fear I this will give it start again;
Therefore let's follow.

(*Exeunt*)

ACT V

5 **Scene I**

A churchyard

(*Enter two* CLOWNS[1])

CLOWN   Is she to be buried in Christian burial [2] when she willfully seeks her own salvation?

10 OTHER   I tell thee she is. Therefore make her grave straight.[3] The crowner[4] hath sate on her, and finds it Christian burial.

CLOWN   How can that be, unless she drowned herself in her own defense?

OTHER   Why, 'tis found so.

15 CLOWN   It must be *se offendendo*;[5] it cannot be else. For here lies the point: if I drown myself wittingly, it argues an act, and an act hath three branches—it is to act, to do, and to perform. Argal,[6] she drowned herself wittingly.

OTHER   Nay, but hear you, Goodman Delver.[7]

20 CLOWN   Give me leave. Here lies the water—good. Here stands the man—good. If the man go to this water and drown himself, it is, will he nill he,[8] he goes, mark you that. But if the water come to him and drown him, he drowns not himself. Argal, he that is not guilty of his own death shortens not his own life.

25 OTHER   But is this law?

CLOWN   Ay marry, is't—crowner's quest[9] law.

OTHER   Will you ha' the truth on't? If this had not been a gentle-woman, she should have been buried out o' Christian burial.

CLOWN   Why, there thou say'st.[10] And the more pity that great folk

30 should have count'nance[11] in this world to drown or hang themselves more than their even-Christen.[12] Come, my spade. There

---

[1] *Clowns* rustics   [2] *in Christian burial* in consecrated ground with the prescribed service of the Church (a burial denied to suicides)   [3] *straight* straightway, at once   [4] *crowner* coroner   [5] *se offendendo* a clownish transformation of *"se defendendo,"* "in self-defense"   [6] *Argal* for *"ergo,"* "therefore"   [7] *Delver* Digger   [8] *will he nill he* willy-nilly   [9] *quest* inquest   [10] *thou say'st* you have it right   [11] *count'nance* privilege   [12] *even-Christen* fellow Christian

is no ancient gentlemen but gard'ners, ditchers, and grave-makers. They hold up Adam's profession.

OTHER   Was he a gentleman?

CLOWN   'A was the first that ever bore arms.

5   OTHER   Why, he had none.[13]

CLOWN   What, art a heathen? How dost thou understand the Scripture? The Scripture says Adam digged. Could he dig without arms? I'll put another question to thee. If thou answerest me not to the purpose, confess thyself—

10   OTHER   Go to.

CLOWN   What is he that builds stronger than either the mason, the shipwright, or the carpenter?

OTHER   The gallows-maker, for that frame outlives a thousand tenants.

15   CLOWN   I like thy wit well, in good faith. The gallows does well. But how does it well? It does well to those that do ill. Now thou dost ill to say the gallows is built stronger than the church. Argal, the gallows may do well to thee. To't again, come.

OTHER   Who builds stronger than a mason, a shipwright, or a car-

20   penter?

CLOWN   Ay, tell me that, and unyoke.[14]

OTHER   Marry, now I can tell.

CLOWN   To't.

OTHER   Mass,[15] I cannot tell.

25   CLOWN   Cudgel thy brains no more about it, for your dull ass will not mend his pace with beating. And when you are asked this question next, say "a grave-maker." The houses he makes last till doomsday. Go, get thee in, and fetch me a stoup[16] of liquor.

(*Exit* OTHER CLOWN)

30   (*Enter* HAMLET *and* HORATIO [*as* CLOWN *digs and sings*])

Song

In youth when I did love, did love,
    Methought it was very sweet
    To contract—O—the time for—a—my behove,[17]
35   O, methought there—a—was nothing—a—meet.

HAMLET   Has this fellow no feeling of his business, that 'a sings at grave-making?

---

[13] *had none* i.e. had no gentleman's coat of arms   [14] *unyoke* i.e. unharness your powers of thought after a good day's work   [15] *Mass* by the Mass   [16] *stoup* large mug   [17] *behove* behoof, benefit

HORATIO   Custom hath made it in him a property[18] of easiness.[19]

HAMLET   'Tis e'en so. The hand of little employment hath the daintier sense.[20]

CLOWN

5   **Song**

> But age with his stealing steps
>   Hath clawed me in his clutch,
> And hath shipped me intil [21] the land,
>   As if I had never been such.

10   (*Throws up a skull*)

HAMLET   That skull had a tongue in it, and could sing once. How the knave jowls[22] it to the ground, as if 'twere Cain's jawbone, that did the first murder! This might be the pate of a politician,[23] which this ass now o'erreaches;[24] one that would circumvent

15   God, might it not?

HORATIO   It might, my lord.

HAMLET   Or of a courtier, which could say "Good morrow, sweet lord! How dost thou, sweet lord?" This might be my Lord Such-a-one, that praised my Lord Such-a-one's horse when 'a meant to

20   beg it, might it not?

HORATIO   Ay, my lord.

HAMLET   Why, e'en so, and now my Lady Worm's, chapless,[25] and knocked about the mazzard [26] with a sexton's spade. Here's fine revolution, an we had the trick to see't. Did these bones cost no

25   more the breeding but to play at loggets[27] with 'em? Mine ache to think on't.

CLOWN

Song

> A pickaxe and a spade, a spade,
>   For and [28] a shrouding sheet;
30 > O, a pit of clay for to be made
>   For such a guest is meet.

(*Throws up another skull*)

---

[18] *property* peculiarity   [19] *easiness* easy acceptability   [20] *daintier sense* more delicate feeling (because the hand is less calloused)   [21] *intil* into   [22] *jowls* hurls   [23] *politician* crafty schemer   [24] *o'erreaches* gets the better of (with a play upon the literal meaning)   [25] *chapless* lacking the lower chap or jaw   [26] *mazzard* head   [27] *loggets* small pieces of wood thrown in a game   [28] *For and* and

HAMLET   There's another. Why may not that be the skull of a lawyer? Where be his quiddities[29] now, his quillities,[30] his cases, his
tenures,[31] and his tricks? Why does he suffer this mad knave now
to knock him about the sconce[32] with a dirty shovel, and will not
5   tell him of his action of battery? Hum! This fellow might be in's
time a great buyer of land, with his statutes, his recognizances,[33]
his fines,[34] his double vouchers,[35] his recoveries. Is this the fine[36]
of his fines, and the recovery of his recoveries, to have his fine
pate full of fine dirt? Will his vouchers vouch him no more of his
10   purchases, and double ones too, than the length and breadth of
a pair of indentures? [37] The very conveyances[38] of his lands will
scarcely lie in this box, and must th' inheritor himself have no
more, ha?

HORATIO   Not a jot more, my lord.

15   HAMLET   Is not parchment made of sheepskins?

HORATIO   Ay, my lord, and of calveskins too.

HAMLET   They are sheep and calves which seek out assurance in
that. I will speak to this fellow. Whose grave 's this, sirrah?

CLOWN   Mine, sir.

20   *(Sings)*   O, a pit of clay for to be made
For such a guest is meet.

HAMLET   I think it be thine indeed, for thou liest in't.

CLOWN   You lie out on't, sir, and therefore 'tis not yours. For my
part, I do not lie in't, yet it is mine.

25   HAMLET   Thou dost lie in't, to be in't and say it is thine. 'Tis for
the dead, not for the quick;[39] therefore thou liest.

CLOWN   'Tis a quick lie, sir; 'twill away again from me to you.

HAMLET   What man dost thou dig it for?

CLOWN   For no man, sir.

30   HAMLET   What woman then?

CLOWN   For none neither.

HAMLET   Who is to be buried in't?

CLOWN   One that was a woman, sir; but, rest her soul, she's dead.

HAMLET   How absolute[40] the knave is! We must speak by the

---

[29] *quiddities* subtleties (from scholastic *"quidditas,"* meaning the distinctive
nature of anything)   [30] *quillities* nice distinctions   [31] *tenures* holdings of
property   [32] *sconce* head   [33] *statutes, recognizances* legal documents or bonds
acknowledging debt   [34] *fines, recoveries* modes of converting estate tail into
fee simple   [35] *vouchers* persons vouched or called on to warrant a title
[36] *fine* end (introducing a word play involving four meanings of "fine")
[37] *pair of indentures* deed or legal agreement in duplicate   [38] *conveyances*
deeds   [39] *quick* living   [40] *absolute* positive

card,[41] or equivocation[42] will undo us. By the Lord, Horatio, this three years I have taken note of it, the age is grown so picked [43] that the toe of the peasant comes so near the heel of the courtier he galls[44] his kibe.[45]—How long hast thou been a grave-maker?

5 CLOWN Of all the days i' th' year, I came to't that day that our last king Hamlet overcame Fortinbras.

HAMLET How long is that since?

CLOWN Cannot you tell that? Every fool can tell that. It was the very day that young Hamlet was born—he that is mad, and sent

10 into England.

HAMLET Ay, marry, why was he sent into England?

CLOWN Why, because 'a was mad. 'A shall recover his wits there; or, if 'a do not, 'tis no great matter there.

HAMLET Why?

15 CLOWN 'Twill not be seen in him there. There the men are as mad as he.

HAMLET How came he mad?

CLOWN Very strangely, they say.

HAMLET How strangely?

20 CLOWN Faith, e'en with losing his wits.

HAMLET Upon what ground?

CLOWN Why, here in Denmark. I have been sexton here, man and boy, thirty years.

HAMLET How long will a man lie i' th' earth ere he rot?

25 CLOWN Faith, if 'a be not rotten before 'a die (as we have many pocky[46] corses now-a-days that will scarce hold the laying in), 'a will last you some eight year or nine year. A tanner will last you nine year.

HAMLET Why he more than another?

30 CLOWN Why, sir, his hide is so tanned with his trade that 'a will keep out water a great while, and your water is a sore decayer of your whoreson dead body. Here's a skull now hath lien you i' th' earth three-and-twenty years.

HAMLET Whose was it?

35 CLOWN A whoreson mad fellow's it was. Whose do you think it was?

HAMLET Nay, I know not.

---

[41] *by the card* by the card on which the points of the mariner's compass are marked, absolutely to the point [42] *equivocation* ambiguity [43] *picked* refined, spruce [44] *galls* chafes [45] *kibe* chilblain [46] *pocky* rotten (literally, corrupted by pox, or syphilis)

CLOWN   A pestilence on him for a mad rogue! 'A poured a flagon
of Rhenish[47] on my head once. This same skull, sir, was—sir—
Yorick's skull, the king's jester.

HAMLET   This?

5   CLOWN   E'en that.

HAMLET   Let me see. (*Takes the skull.*) Alas, poor Yorick! I knew
him, Horatio, a fellow of infinite jest, of most excellent fancy. He
hath borne me on his back a thousand times. And now how ab-
horred in my imagination it is! My gorge rises at it. Here hung
10   those lips that I have kissed I know not how oft. Where be your
gibes now? Your gambols, your songs, your flashes of merriment
that were wont to set the table on a roar? Not one now to mock
your own grinning? Quite chapfall'n? [48] Now get you to my lady's
chamber, and tell her, let her paint an inch thick, to this favor[49]
15   she must come. Make her laugh at that. Prithee, Horatio, tell me
one thing.

HORATIO   What's that, my lord?

HAMLET   Dost thou think Alexander looked o' this fashion i' th'
earth?

20   HORATIO   E'en so.

HAMLET   And smelt so? Pah!

(*Puts down the skull*)

HORATIO   E'en so, my lord.

HAMLET   To what base uses we may return, Horatio! Why may
25   not imagination trace the noble dust of Alexander till 'a find it
stopping a bunghole?

HORATIO   'Twere to consider too curiously,[50] to consider so.

HAMLET   No, faith, not a jot, but to follow him thither with modesty[51] enough, and likelihood to lead it; as thus: Alexander died,
30   Alexander was buried, Alexander returneth to dust; the dust is
earth; of earth we make loam; and why of that loam whereto he
was converted might they not stop a beer barrel?
Imperious[52] Caesar, dead and turned to clay,
Might stop a hole to keep the wind away.
35   O, that that earth which kept the world in awe
Should patch a wall t' expel the winter's flaw! [53]

---

[47] *Rhenish* Rhine wine   [48] *chapfall'n* lacking the lower chap, or jaw (with a
play on the sense "down in the mouth," "dejected")   [49] *favor* countenance,
aspect   [50] *curiously* minutely   [51] *modesty* moderation   [52] *Imperious* imperial
[53] *flaw* gust of wind

But soft, but soft awhile! Here comes the king—

(*Enter* KING, QUEEN, LAERTES, *and the* CORSE [*with* LORDS *attendant and a* DOCTOR OF DIVINITY *as* PRIEST])

The queen, the courtiers. Who is this they follow?
5   And with such maimèd rites? This doth betoken
The corse they follow did with desp'rate hand
Fordo⁵⁴ it⁵⁵ own life. 'Twas of some estate.⁵⁶
Couch⁵⁷ we awhile, and mark.

(*Retires with* HORATIO)

10 LAERTES What ceremony else?
    HAMLET   That is Laertes,
    A very noble youth. Mark.
    LAERTES What ceremony else?
    DOCTOR Her obsequies have been as far enlarged
15 As we have warranty. Her death was doubtful,
    And, but that great command o'ersways the order,
    She should in ground unsanctified have lodged
    Till the last trumpet. For charitable prayers,
    Shards,⁵⁸ flints, and pebbles should be thrown on her.
20 Yet here she is allowed her virgin crants,⁵⁹
    Her maiden strewments,⁶⁰ and the bringing home⁶¹
    Of bell and burial.
    LAERTES Must there no more be done?
    DOCTOR   No more be done.
25 We should profane the service of the dead
    To sing a requiem and such rest to her
    As to peace-parted souls.
    LAERTES   Lay her i' th' earth,
    And from her fair and unpolluted flesh
30 May violets spring! I tell thee, churlish priest,
    A minist'ring angel shall my sister be
    When thou liest howling.
    HAMLET   What, the fair Ophelia?
    QUEEN Sweets to the sweet! Farewell.

35   (*Scatters flowers*)

    I hoped thou shouldst have been my Hamlet's wife.

---

⁵⁴ *Fordo* destroy   ⁵⁵ *it* its   ⁵⁶ *estate* rank   ⁵⁷ *Couch* hide   ⁵⁸ *Shards* broken pieces of pottery   ⁵⁹ *crants* garland   ⁶⁰ *strewments* strewings of the grave with flowers   ⁶¹ *bringing home* laying to rest

I thought thy bride-bed to have decked, sweet maid,
And not have strewed thy grave.

LAERTES   O, treble woe
Fall ten times treble on that cursèd head
5   Whose wicked deed thy most ingenious[62] sense
Deprived thee of! Hold off the earth awhile,
Till I have caught her once more in mine arms.

(Leaps in the grave)

Now pile your dust upon the quick and dead
10   Till of this flat a mountain you have made
T' o'ertop old Pelion[63] or the skyish head
Of blue Olympus.

HAMLET *(coming forward)*   What is he whose grief
Bears such an emphasis? whose phrase of sorrow
15   Conjures[64] the wand'ring stars,[65] and makes them stand
Like wonder-wounded hearers? This is I,
Hamlet the Dane.

(Leaps in after LAERTES*)*

LAERTES   The devil take thy soul!

20   *(Grapples with him)*

HAMLET   Thou pray'st not well.
I prithee take thy fingers from my throat,
For, though I am not splenitive[66] and rash,
Yet have I in me something dangerous,
25   Which let thy wisdom fear. Hold off thy hand.
KING   Pluck them asunder.
QUEEN   Hamlet, Hamlet!
ALL   Gentlemen!
HORATIO   Good my lord, be quiet.

30   *(*ATTENDANTS *part them, and they come out of the grave)*

HAMLET   Why, I will fight with him upon this theme
Until my eyelids will no longer wag.
QUEEN   O my son, what theme?

---

[62] *most ingenious* of quickest apprehension   [63] *Pelion* a mountain in Thessaly,
like Olympus and also Ossa (the allusion being to the war in which the Titans
fought the gods and attempted to heap Ossa and Olympus on Pelion, or
Pelion and Ossa on Olympus, in order to scale heaven)   [64] *Conjures* charms,
puts a spell upon   [65] *wand'ring stars* planets   [66] *splenitive* of fiery temper
(the spleen being considered the seat of anger)

HAMLET   I loved Ophelia. Forty thousand brothers
   Could not with all their quantity of love
   Make up my sum. What wilt thou do for her?
KING   O, he is mad, Laertes.
5   QUEEN   For love of God, forbear him.
HAMLET   'Swounds, show me what thou't do.
   Woo't [67] weep? woo't fight? woo't fast? woo't tear thyself?
   Woo't drink up esill? [68] eat a crocodile?
   I'll do't. Dost thou come here to whine?
10   To outface me with leaping in her grave?
   Be buried quick[69] with her, and so will I.
   And if thou prate of mountains, let them throw
   Millions of acres on us, till our ground,
   Singeing his pate against the burning zone,
15   Make Ossa like a wart! Nay, an thou'lt mouth,
   I'll rant as well as thou.
QUEEN   This is mere[70] madness;
   And thus a while the fit will work on him.
   Anon, as patient as the female dove
20   When that her golden couplets[71] are disclosed,[72]
   His silence will sit drooping.
HAMLET   Hear you, sir.
   What is the reason that you use me thus?
   I loved you ever. But it is no matter.
25   Let Hercules himself do what he may,
   The cat will mew, and dog will have his day.
KING   I pray thee, good Horatio, wait upon him.

(*Exit* HAMLET *and* HORATIO)

(*To* LAERTES)

30   Strengthen your patience in[73] our last night's speech.
   We'll put the matter to the present push.[74]
   Good Gertrude, set some watch over your son.—
   This grave shall have a living monument.
   An hour of quiet shortly shall we see;
35   Till then in patience our proceeding be.

(*Exeunt*)

---

[67] *Woo't* wilt (thou)   [68] *esill* vinegar   [69] *quick* alive   [70] *mere* absolute
[71] *couplets* pair of fledglings   [72] *disclosed* hatched   [73] *in* by calling to mind
[74] *present push* immediate trial

Act V, Scene II

The hall of the castle

(*Enter* HAMLET *and* HORATIO)

HAMLET   So much for this, sir; now shall you see the other.
5   You do remember all the circumstance?

HORATIO   Remember it, my lord!

HAMLET   Sir, in my heart there was a kind of fighting
That would not let me sleep. Methought I lay
Worse than the mutines[1] in the bilboes.[2] Rashly,
10   And praised be rashness for it—let us know,
Our indiscretion sometime serves us well
When our deep plots do pall,[3] and that should learn us
There's a divinity that shapes our ends,
Rough-hew[4] them how we will—

15   HORATIO   That is most certain.

HAMLET   Up from my cabin,
My sea-gown scarfed about me, in the dark
Groped I to find out them, had my desire,
Fingered [5] their packet, and in fine[6] withdrew
20   To mine own room again, making so bold,
My fears forgetting manners, to unseal
Their grand commission; where I found, Horatio—
Ah, royal knavery!—an exact command,
Larded [7] with many several sorts of reasons,
25   Importing[8] Denmark's health, and England's too,
With, ho! such bugs[9] and goblins in my life,[10]
That on the supervise,[11] no leisure bated,[12]
No, not to stay the grinding of the axe,
My head should be struck off.

30   HORATIO   Is't possible?

HAMLET   Here's the commission; read it at more leisure.
But wilt thou hear me how I did proceed?

HORATIO   I beseech you.

HAMLET   Being thus benetted round with villainies,
35   Or[13] I could make a prologue to my brains,
They had begun the play. I sat me down,

---

[1] *mutines* mutineers   [2] *bilboes* fetters   [3] *pall* fail   [4] *Rough-hew* shape roughly in trial form   [5] *Fingered* filched   [6] *in fine* finally   [7] *Larded* enriched   [8] *Importing* relating to   [9] *bugs* bugbears   [10] *in my life* to be encountered as dangers if I should be allowed to live   [11] *supervise* perusal   [12] *bated* deducted, allowed   [13] *Or* ere

Devised a new commission, wrote it fair.
I once did hold it, as our statists[14] do,
A baseness to write fair,[15] and labored much
How to forget that learning, but, sir, now
5   It did me yeoman's service.[16] Wilt thou know
Th' effect[17] of what I wrote?

HORATIO   Ay, good my lord.

HAMLET   An earnest conjuration from the king,
As England was his faithful tributary,
10   As love between them like the palm might flourish,
As peace should still her wheaten garland [18] wear
And stand a comma[19] 'tween their amities,
And many such-like as's of great charge,[20]
That on the view and knowing of these contents,
15   Without debatement further, more or less,
He should the bearers put to sudden death,
Not shriving time[21] allowed.

HORATIO   How was this sealed?

HAMLET   Why, even in that was heaven ordinant.[22]
20   I had my father's signet in my purse,
Which was the model [23] of that Danish seal,
Folded the writ up in the form of th' other,
Subscribed it, gave't th' impression,[24] placed it safely,
The changeling never known. Now, the next day
25   Was our sea-fight, and what to this was sequent[25]
Thou know'st already.

HORATIO   So Guildenstern and Rosencrantz go to't.

HAMLET   Why, man, they did make love to this employment.
They are not near my conscience; their defeat
30   Does by their own insinuation[26] grow.
'Tis dangerous when the baser nature comes
Between the pass[27] and fell [28] incensèd points
Of mighty opposites.

---

[14] *statists* statesmen   [15] *fair* with professional clarity (like a clerk or a scrivener, not like a gentleman)   [16] *yeoman's service* stout service such as yeomen footsoldiers gave as archers   [17] *effect* purport   [18] *wheaten garland* adornment of fruitful agriculture   [19] *comma* connective (because it indicates continuity of thought in a sentence)   [20] *charge* burden (with a double meaning to fit a play that makes *as's* into "asses"   [21] *shriving time* time for confession and absolution   [22] *ordinant* controlling   [23] *model* counterpart   [24] *impression* i.e. of the signet   [25] *sequent* subsequent   [26] *insinuation* intrusion   [27] *pass* thrust   [28] *fell* fierce

HORATIO   Why, what a king is this!

HAMLET   Does it not, think thee, stand [29] me now upon—
He that hath killed my king, and whored my mother,
Popped in between th' election[30] and my hopes,
5   Thrown out his angle[31] for my proper[32] life,
And with such coz'nage[33]—is't not perfect conscience
To quit[34] him with this arm? And is't not to be damned
To let this canker[35] of our nature come
In further evil?

10   HORATIO   It must be shortly known to him from England
What is the issue of the business there.

HAMLET   It will be short; the interim is mine,
And a man's life 's no more than to say "one."
But I am very sorry, good Horatio,
15   That to Laertes I forgot myself,
For by the image of my cause I see
The portraiture of his. I'll court his favors.
But sure the bravery[36] of his grief did put me
Into a tow'ring passion.

20   HORATIO   Peace, who comes here?

(*Enter* OSRIC, *a courtier*)

OSRIC   Your lordship is right welcome back to Denmark.

HAMLET   I humbly thank you, sir. (*aside to* HORATIO) Dost know
this waterfly?

25   HORATIO (*aside to* HAMLET)   No, my good lord.

HAMLET (*aside to* HORATIO)   Thy state is the more gracious, for
'tis a vice to know him. He hath much land, and fertile. Let a
beast be lord of beasts, and his crib shall stand at the king's
mess.[37] 'Tis a chough,[38] but, as I say, spacious in the possession
30   of dirt.

OSRIC   Sweet lord, if your lordship were at leisure, I should impart
a thing to you from his majesty.

HAMLET   I will receive it, sir, with all diligence of spirit. Put your
bonnet to his right use. 'Tis for the head.

35   OSRIC   I thank your lordship, it is very hot.

HAMLET   No, believe me, 'tis very cold; the wind is northerly.

OSRIC   It is indifferent[39] cold, my lord, indeed.

---

[29] *stand* rest incumbent   [30] *election* i.e. to the kingship (the Danish kingship
being elective)   [31] *angle* fishing line   [32] *proper* own   [33] *coz'nage* cozenage,
trickery   [34] *quit* repay   [35] *canker* cancer, ulcer   [36] *bravery* ostentatious display   [37] *mess* table   [38] *chough* jackdaw, chatterer   [39] *indifferent* somewhat

HAMLET   But yet methinks it is very sultry and hot for my complexion.[40]

OSRIC   Exceedingly, my lord; it is very sultry, as 'twere—I cannot tell how. But, my lord, his majesty bade me signify to you that 'a has laid a great wager on your head. Sir, this is the matter—

HAMLET   I beseech you remember.[41]

(HAMLET *moves him to put on his hat*)

OSRIC   Nay, good my lord; for mine ease,[42] in good faith. Sir, here is newly come to court Laertes—believe me, an absolute gentleman, full of most excellent differences,[43] of very soft society[44] and great showing.[45] Indeed, to speak feelingly[46] of him, he is the card [47] or calendar[48] of gentry,[49] for you shall find in him the continent[50] of what part a gentleman would see.

HAMLET   Sir, his definement[51] suffers no perdition[52] in you, though, I know, to divide him inventorially would dozy[53] th' arithmetic of memory, and yet but yaw[54] neither[55] in respect of [56] his quick sail. But, in the verity of extolment, I take him to be a soul of great article,[57] and his infusion[58] of such dearth[59] and rareness as, to make true diction of him, his semblable[60] is his mirror, and who else would trace[61] him, his umbrage,[62] nothing more.

OSRIC   Your lordship speaks most infallibly of him.

HAMLET   The concernancy,[63] sir? Why do we wrap the gentleman in our more rawer[64] breath?

OSRIC   Sir?

HORATIO   Is't not possible to understand in another tongue? You will to't,[65] sir, really.

HAMLET   What imports the nomination[66] of this gentleman?

OSRIC   Of Laertes?

---

[40] *complexion* temperament   [41] *remember* i.e. remember you have done all that courtesy demands   [42] *for mine ease* i.e. I keep my hat off just for comfort (a conventional polite phrase)   [43] *differences* differentiating characteristics, special qualities   [44] *soft society* gentle manners   [45] *great showing* noble appearance   [46] *feelingly* appropriately   [47] *card* map   [48] *calendar* guide   [49] *gentry* gentlemanliness   [50] *continent* all-containing embodiment (with an implication of geographical continent to go with *card*)   [51] *definement* definition   [52] *perdition* loss   [53] *dozy* dizzy, stagger   [54] *yaw* hold to a course unsteadily like a ship that steers wild   [55] *neither* for all that   [56] *in respect of* in comparison with   [57] *article* scope, importance   [58] *infusion* essence   [59] *dearth* scarcity   [60] *semblable* likeness (i.e. only true likeness)   [61] *trace* follow   [62] *umbrage* shadow   [63] *concernancy* relevance   [64] *rawer breath* cruder speech   [65] *to't* i.e. get to an understanding   [66] *nomination* mention

HORATIO (*aside to* HAMLET)   His purse is empty already. All's golden words are spent.

HAMLET   Of him, sir.

OSRIC   I know you are not ignorant—

5   HAMLET   I would you did, sir; yet, in faith, if you did, it would not much approve me.[67] Well, sir?

OSRIC   You are not ignorant of what excellence Laertes is—

HAMLET   I dare not confess that, lest I should compare[68] with him in excellence; but to know a man well were to know himself.

10   OSRIC   I mean, sir, for his weapon; but in the imputation laid on him by them, in his meed [69] he's unfellowed.

HAMLET   What's his weapon?

OSRIC   Rapier and dagger.

HAMLET   That's two of his weapons—but well.

15   OSRIC   The king, sir, hath wagered with him six Barbary horses, against the which he has impawned,[70] as I take it, six French rapiers and poniards, with their assigns,[71] as girdle, hangers,[72] and so. Three of the carriages, in faith, are very dear to fancy,[73] very responsive[74] to the hilts, most delicate carriages, and of very

20   liberal conceit.[75]

HAMLET   What call you the carriages?

HORATIO (*aside to* HAMLET)   I knew you must be edified by the margent[76] ere you had done.

OSRIC   The carriages, sir, are the hangers.

25   HAMLET   The phrase would be more germane to the matter if we could carry a cannon by our sides. I would it might be hangers till then. But on! Six Barbary horses against six French swords, their assigns, and three liberal-conceited carriages—that's the French bet against the Danish. Why is this all impawned, as you

30   call it?

OSRIC   The king, sir, hath laid, sir, that in a dozen passes between yourself and him he shall not exceed you three hits; he hath laid on twelve for nine, and it would come to immediate trial if your lordship would vouchsafe the answer.

35   HAMLET   How if I answer no?

OSRIC   I mean, my lord, the opposition of your person in trial.

---

[67] *approve me* be to my credit   [68] *compare* compete   [69] *meed* worth   [70] *impawned* staked   [71] *assigns* appurtenances   [72] *hangers* straps by which the sword hangs from the belt   [73] *dear to fancy* finely designed   [74] *responsive* corresponding closely   [75] *liberal conceit* tasteful design, refined conception   [76] *margent* margin (i.e. explanatory notes there printed)

HAMLET   Sir, I will walk here in the hall. If it please his majesty,
it is the breathing time[77] of day with me. Let the foils be brought,
the gentleman willing, and the king hold his purpose, I will win
for him an[78] I can; if not, I will gain nothing but my shame and
5   the odd hits.

OSRIC   Shall I redeliver you e'en so?

HAMLET   To this effect, sir, after what flourish your nature will.

OSRIC   I commend my duty to your lordship.

HAMLET   Your, yours. (*Exit* OSRIC) He does well to commend it
10   himself; there are no tongues else for's turn.

HORATIO   This lapwing[79] runs away with the shell on his head.

HAMLET   'A did comply,[80] sir, with his dug[81] before 'a sucked it.
Thus has he, and many more of the same bevy[82] that I know the
drossy[83] age dotes on, only got the tune of the time and, out of
15   an habit of encounter, a kind of yeasty collection, which carries
them through and through the most fanned and winnowed [84]
opinions; and do but blow them to their trial, the bubbles are
out.

(*Enter a* LORD)

20   LORD   My lord, his majesty commended him to you by young Osric,
who brings back to him that you attend him in the hall. He sends
to know if your pleasure hold to play with Laertes, or that you
will take longer time.

HAMLET   I am constant to my purposes; they follow the king's
25   pleasure. If his fitness speaks, mine is ready; now or whensoever,
provided I be so able as now.

LORD   The king and queen and all are coming down.

HAMLET   In happy time.[85]

LORD   The queen desires you to use some gentle entertainment[86] to
30   Laertes before you fall to play.

HAMLET   She well instructs me.

(*Exit* LORD)

HORATIO   You will lose this wager, my lord.

HAMLET   I do not think so. Since he went into France I have been
35   in continual practice. I shall win at the odds. But thou wouldst
not think how ill all's here about my heart. But it is no matter.

---

[77] *breathing time* exercise hour   [78] *an* if   [79] *lapwing* a bird reputed to be so
precocious as to run as soon as hatched   [80] *comply* observe formalities of
courtesy   [81] *dug* mother's nipple   [82] *bevy* company   [83] *drossy* frivolous
[84] *fanned and winnowed* select and refined   [85] *In happy time* I am happy (a
polite response)   [86] *entertainment* words of reception or greeting

HORATIO Nay, good my lord—

HAMLET It is but foolery, but it is such a kind of gaingiving[87] as would perhaps trouble a woman.

HORATIO If your mind dislike anything, obey it. I will forestall
5   their repair hither and say you are not fit.

HAMLET Not a whit, we defy augury. There is special providence in the fall of a sparrow. If it be now, 'tis not to come; if it be not to come, it will be now; if it be not now, yet it will come. The readiness is all.[88] Since no man of aught he leaves knows,
10   what is't to leave betimes? Let be.

A table prepared. Enter TRUMPETS, DRUMS, *and* OFFICERS *with cushions;* KING, QUEEN, OSRIC, *and all the* STATE, *with foils, daggers, and stoups of wine borne in; and* LAERTES

KING Come, Hamlet, come, and take this hand from me.

15   (*The* KING *puts* LAERTES' *hand into* HAMLET's)

HAMLET Give me your pardon, sir. I have done you wrong,
    But pardon't, as you are a gentleman.
    This presence[89] knows, and you must needs have heard,
    How I am punished with a sore distraction.
20   What I have done
    That might your nature, honor, and exception[90]
    Roughly awake, I here proclaim was madness.
    Was't Hamlet wronged Laertes? Never Hamlet.
    If Hamlet from himself be ta'en away,
25   And when he's not himself does wrong Laertes,
    Then Hamlet does it not, Hamlet denies it.
    Who does it then? His madness. If't be so,
    Hamlet is of the faction[91] that is wronged;
    His madness is poor Hamlet's enemy.
30   Sir, in this audience,
    Let my disclaiming from a purposed evil
    Free me so far in your most generous thoughts
    That I have shot my arrow o'er the house
    And hurt my brother.

35 LAERTES   I am satisfied in nature,[92]
    Whose motive in this case should stir me most
    To my revenge. But in my terms of honor[93]

---

[87] *gaingiving* misgiving   [88] *all* all that matters   [89] *presence* assembly   [90] *exception* disapproval   [91] *faction* body of persons taking a side in a contention   [92] *nature* natural feeling as a person   [93] *terms of honor* position as a man of honor

I stand aloof, and will no reconcilement
Till by some elder masters of known honor
I have a voice[94] and precedent of peace
To keep my name ungored.[95] But till that time
5 I do receive your offered love like love,
And will not wrong it.
HAMLET   I embrace it freely,
And will this brother's wager frankly play.
Give us the foils. Come on.
10 LAERTES   Come, one for me.
HAMLET   I'll be your foil,[96] Laertes. In mine ignorance
Your skill shall, like a star i' th' darkest night,
Stick fiery off [97] indeed.
LAERTES   You mock me, sir.
15 HAMLET   No, by this hand.
KING   Give them the foils, young Osric. Cousin Hamlet,
You know the wager?
HAMLET   Very well, my lord.
Your grace has laid the odds o' the' weaker side.
20 KING   I do not fear it, I have seen you both;
But since he is bettered, we have therefore odds.
LAERTES   This is too heavy; let me see another.
HAMLET   This likes me well. These foils have all a length?

Prepare to play

25 OSRIC   Ay, my good lord.
KING   Set me the stoups of wine upon that table.
If Hamlet give the first or second hit,
Or quit[98] in answer of the third exchange,
Let all the battlements their ordnance fire.
30 The king shall drink to Hamlet's better breath,
And in the cup an union[99] shall he throw
Richer than that which four successive kings
In Denmark's crown have worn. Give me the cups,
And let the kettle[100] to the trumpet speak,
35 The trumpet to the cannoneer without,
The cannons to the heavens, the heaven to earth,

---

[94] *voice* authoritative statement   [95] *ungored* uninjured   [96] *foil* setting that displays a jewel advantageously (with a play upon the meaning "weapon")   [97] *Stick fiery off* show in brilliant relief   [98] *quit* repay by a hit   [99] *union* pearl   [100] *kettle* kettledrum

"Now the king drinks to Hamlet." Come, begin.

Trumpets the while

And you, the judges, bear a wary eye.
HAMLET   Come on, sir.

5   LAERTES   Come, my lord.

They play

HAMLET   One.
LAERTES   No.
HAMLET   Judgment?
10   OSRIC   A hit, a very palpable hit.

DRUM, TRUMPETS, *and* SHOT. *Flourish; a piece goes off*

LAERTES   Well, again.
KING   Stay, give me drink. Hamlet, this pearl is thine.
Here's to thy health. Give him the cup.
15   HAMLET   I'll play this bout first; set it by awhile.
Come. (*They play*) Another hit. What say you?
LAERTES   A touch, a touch; I do confess't.
KING   Our son shall win.
QUEEN   He's fat,[101] and scant of breath.
20   Here, Hamlet, take my napkin,[102] rub thy brows.
The queen carouses[103] to thy fortune, Hamlet.
HAMLET   Good madam!
KING   Gertrude, do not drink.
QUEEN   I will, my lord; I pray you pardon me.

25   *Drinks*

KING (*aside*)   It is the poisoned cup; it is too late.
HAMLET   I dare not drink yet, madam—by and by.
QUEEN   Come, let me wipe thy face.
LAERTES   My lord, I'll hit him now.
30   KING   I do not think't.
LAERTES (*aside*)   And yet it is almost against my conscience.
HAMLET   Come for the third, Laertes. You but dally.
I pray you pass with your best violence;
I am afeard you make a wanton[104] of me.

---

[101] *fat* not physically fit, out of training   [102] *napkin* handkerchief   [103] *carouses* drinks a toast   [104] *wanton* pampered child

LAERTES   Say you so? Come on.

They play

OSRIC   Nothing neither way.
LAERTES   Have at you now!

5   *In scuffling they change rapiers, and both are wounded with the poisoned
weapon*

KING   Part them. They are incensed.
HAMLET   Nay, come—again!

The QUEEN *falls*

10   OSRIC   Look to the queen there, ho!
HORATIO   They bleed on both sides. How is it, my lord?
OSRIC   How is't, Laertes?
LAERTES   Why, as a woodcock[105] to mine own springe,[106] Osric.
I am justly killed with mine own treachery.
15   HAMLET   How does the queen?
KING   She sounds[107] to see them bleed.
QUEEN   No, no, the drink, the drink! O my dear Hamlet!
The drink, the drink! I am poisoned.

Dies

20   HAMLET   O villainy! Ho! let the door be locked.
Treachery! Seek it out.

LAERTES *falls*

LAERTES   It is here, Hamlet. Hamlet, thou art slain;
No med'cine in the world can do thee good.
25   In thee there is not half an hour's life.
The treacherous instrument is in thy hand,
Unbated [108] and envenomed. The foul practice[109]
Hath turned itself on me. Lo, here I lie,
Never to rise again. Thy mother 's poisoned.
30   I can no more. The king, the king 's to blame.
HAMLET   The point envenomed too?
Then venom, to thy work.

Hurts the KING

ALL   Treason! treason!

---

[105] *woodcock* a bird reputed to be stupid and easily trapped   [106] *springe* trap
[107] *sounds* swoons   [108] *Unbated* unblunted   [109] *practice* stratagem

KING   O, yet defend me, friends. I am but hurt.

HAMLET   Here, thou incestuous, murd'rous, damnèd Dane,
Drink off this potion. Is thy union here?
Follow my mother.

5   KING *dies*

LAERTES   He is justly served.
It is a poison tempered [110] by himself.
Exchange forgiveness with me, noble Hamlet.
Mine and my father's death come not upon thee,
10   Nor thine on me!

Dies

HAMLET   Heaven make thee free of it! I follow thee.
I am dead, Horatio. Wretched queen, adieu!
You that look pale and tremble at this chance,
15   That are but mutes[111] or audience to this act,
Had I but time—as this fell sergeant,[112] Death,
Is strict in his arrest—O, I could tell you—
But let it be. Horatio, I am dead;
Thou livest; report me and my cause aright
20   To the unsatisfied.

HORATIO   Never believe it.
I am more an antique Roman than a Dane.
Here's yet some liquor left.

HAMLET   As th' art a man,
25   Give me the cup. Let go. By heaven, I'll ha't!
O God, Horatio, what a wounded name,
Things standing thus unknown, shall live behind me!
If thou didst ever hold me in thy heart,
Absent thee from felicity awhile,
30   And in this harsh world draw thy breath in pain,
To tell my story.

A march afar off

What warlike noise is this?

OSRIC   Young Fortinbras, with conquest come from Poland,
35   To the ambassadors of England gives
This warlike volley.

HAMLET   O, I die, Horatio!

---

[110] *tempered* mixed   [111] *mutes* actors in a play who speak no lines   [112] *sergeant* sheriff's officer

The potent poison quite o'ercrows[113] my spirit.
I cannot live to hear the news from England,
But I do prophesy th' election[114] lights
On Fortinbras. He has my dying voice.[115]
5   So tell him, with th' occurrents,[116] more and less,
Which have solicited [117]—the rest is silence.

Dies

HORATIO   Now cracks a noble heart. Good night, sweet prince,
And flights of angels sing thee to thy rest!

10   *March within*

Why does the drum come hither?

(*Enter* FORTINBRAS, *with the* AMBASSADORS [*and with his train of* DRUM, COLORS, *and* ATTENDANTS])

FORTINBRAS   Where is this sight?
15   HORATIO   What is it you would see?
If aught of woe or wonder, cease your search.
FORTINBRAS   This quarry[118] cries on[119] havoc.[120] O proud Death,
What feast is toward [121] in thine eternal cell
That thou so many princes at a shot
20   So bloodily hast struck?
AMBASSADOR   The sight is dismal;
And our affairs from England come too late.
The ears are senseless that should give us hearing
To tell him his commandment is fulfilled,
25   That Rosencrantz and Guildenstern are dead.
Where should we have our thanks?
HORATIO   Not from his mouth,
Had it th' ability of life to thank you.
He never gave commandment for their death.
30   But since, so jump[122] upon this bloody question,
You from the Polack wars, and you from England,
Are here arrived, give order that these bodies
High on a stage[123] be placèd to the view,

---

[113] *o'ercrows* triumphs over (like a victor in a cockfight)   [114] *election* i.e. to the throne   [115] *voice* vote   [116] *occurrents* occurrences   [117] *solicited* incited, provoked   [118] *quarry* pile of dead (literally, of dead deer gathered after the hunt)   [119] *cries on* proclaims loudly   [120] *havoc* indiscriminate killing and destruction such as would follow the order "havoc," or "pillage," given to an army   [121] *toward* forthcoming   [122] *jump* precisely   [123] *stage* platform

And let me speak to th' yet unknowing world
How these things came about. So shall you hear
Of carnal, bloody, and unnatural acts,
Of accidental judgments,[124] casual [125] slaughters,

5   Of deaths put on[126] by cunning and forced cause,
And, in this upshot, purposes mistook
Fall'n on th' inventors' heads. All this can I
Truly deliver.

FORTINBRAS   Let us haste to hear it,

10   And call the noblest to the audience.
For me, with sorrow I embrace my fortune.
I have some rights of memory[127] in this kingdom,
Which now to claim my vantage[128] doth invite me.

HORATIO   Of that I shall have also cause to speak,

15   And from his mouth whose voice will draw on more.[129]
But let this same be presently[130] performed,
Even while men's minds are wild, lest more mischance
On[131] plots and errors happen.

FORTINBRAS   Let four captains

20   Bear Hamlet like a soldier to the stage,
For he was likely, had he been put on,[132]
To have proved most royal; and for his passage[133]
The soldiers' music and the rites of war
Speak loudly for him.

25   Take up the bodies. Such a sight as this
Becomes the field, but here shows much amiss.
Go, bid the soldiers shoot.

(*Exeunt [marching; after the which a peal of ordinance are shot off]*))

QUESTIONS FOR THINKING AND WRITING

1. Madness is a theme in *Hamlet*. In an essay of five or more pages, compare
   Hamlet's apparent madness with Ophelia's. Begin with a freewriting that
   considers each character individually. Next go through the play and find
   passages in which other characters refer to the psychological state of these
   characters. It may help to chart your comparison as we suggested in the
   earlier section on Mary Freeman's "A Far-Away Melody."

---

[124] *judgments* retributions   [125] *casual* not humanly planned (reinforcing *accidental*)   [126] *put on* instigated   [127] *of memory* traditional and kept in mind
[128] *vantage* advantageous opportunity   [129] *more* i.e. more voices, or votes,
for the kingship   [130] *presently* immediately   [131] *On* on the basis of   [132] *put
on* set to perform in office   [133] *passage* death

2. It has often been said that the play would end in Act II if Hamlet acted immediately to revenge his father's death. Write an extended summary of the various points at which Hamlet seems indecisive about what he should do. Follow this with a freewriting on why he delays to act. Despite the many writings that have been done on this subject, the question of Hamlet's delay remains wide open. Perhaps your freewriting will lead to an essay that offers a theory of your own.

3. In many ways this play concerns itself with acting and drama. This theme is most evident in the scenes involving the traveling company of actors, yet all of the major characters and some minor ones put on masks and create characters for themselves. In a freewriting of ten to fifteen minutes describe how one character dramatizes him or herself. Then pick another character and do the same. When you have completed these prewriting exercises, develop a full-length essay on this topic.

4. The climax of *Hamlet* extends over several scenes. Write a brief narrative summary in which you describe how the climax unfolds and which scenes it includes. Now describe the changes in Hamlet that become evident during this point in the play. Copy out passages (including numbers for act, scene, and lines) that reveal these changes.

5. The climax of the play is a turning point. The fate of the characters and of the nation itself changes from its apparent course at the outset of the play. Develop an essay in which you describe what has changed and why.

4 Realistic Drama

Our study of *Hamlet* brought us from the early Greek drama to the first great age of professional drama in England. In this chapter we move on to another period of notable theatrical growth and development throughout Europe and America—the late nineteenth and early twentieth centuries— the age of **realism.** From this period, we present two full-length plays— Ibsen's *A Doll's House* and Wilde's *The Importance of Being Earnest*.

Realism of the nineteenth century was an international style, here repre- sented by Norwegian and English playwrights, but practiced by writers in the United States, Europe, and Russia. A close look at the scene descriptions that open each play tells us that realism was a style of production as well as a literary style. Note how carefully these sets are put together to imitate actual rooms, such as those the characters, if they were real, would inhabit.

Look, for instance, at the opening of *A Doll's House* on page 793. Not only does Ibsen carefully list the placement of the four doors and the furniture used in the action; he even details the "copperplate etchings on the walls" and the "deluxe editions" that are to fill the "small bookcase."

Note, too, that Ibsen speaks of the "rear wall," "left wall," and "right wall" of the room. To most of us, this seems quite natural. Of course a room has four walls. Of course three of them are shown onstage and the fourth is imagined to be at the front of the stage. Of course characters enter and exit through doors in these walls; how else does one enter or leave a room? In fact, however, this form of stage setting, known as the "box set," was a new form of stage setting. The box set was far more realistic than the older "wings"; but it was more cumbersome as well, requiring long intermissions between acts to allow for scene changes. Thus, it may have helped to promote the popularity, not only of realistic drama, but also of the one-act play, which is often set in one scene and thus requires no change of scenery.

Realism in production, then, meant sets and costumes as like those of everyday life as possible. In playwriting, it meant plots, characters, and language drawn from everyday life, as well. (Comedy, as usual, retained the right of exaggeration in all these areas.)

In addition, realism implied a new approach to drama. The realistic play hoped to make two impacts on its audience. First, of course, it sought to make the audience sympathize with the plight of its characters. But it also strove to raise in the minds of its audience questions as to the rightness of some aspect of social order, and the desire to change what the dramatist perceived as evil or wrong.

From these goals came a new form of play known as the **realistic drama:** a serious play, usually on a domestic or semi-domestic theme, featuring middle-class (or sometimes lower-class) characters, a contemporary setting, and a plot that questions some aspect or dictate of society.

Take, for example, *A Doll's House* by Henrik Ibsen, a Norwegian playwright who was one of the earliest and most admired of the realists. We see in *A Doll's House,* one of Ibsen's most popular plays, the mixture of elements described above. The scene is unrelievedly domestic. Money and marriage (normally the concerns of comedy) are both major concerns in this play. Yet the movement within the play is more like that of tragedy, being, in general, "from happiness to unhappiness." Comedy usually ends in the making of a marriage. *A Doll's House* details the breakup of one. In line with the domesticity of the scene, we notice a new concern with detail: the clothes Nora wears, the ornaments she puts on her Christmas tree, the macaroons she eats or does not eat all reflect her struggle for self-identity. We see, too, her concern with upbringing: what effect has Nora's father had on her? What effect is she having on her own children? Finally, we observe how the domestic nature of the realistic drama heightens the disparity between what the play's main characters perceive and feel and what is perceived of them by those around them. The onlookers in *Antigonê* recognize the magnitude of the struggles they are watching. The onlookers in *A Doll's House* see only a peaceful, prosperous, well-ordered household.

Today, *A Doll's House* is most frequently read as a complaint against the undervaluation and suppression of women. But strong arguments can be made for the theory that Ibsen is showing men and women as equal victims of society's insistence on "respectability." Notice, as you read this play, how the characters are grouped in this regard, how each sins and is sinned against. Consider, too, the ending, which is of a type impossible for both tragedy and comedy. What effect does it have on your response to the play?

Comedy and Realism

Comedy was a favorite form in the nineteenth century, both before and during the age of realism. For one thing, nineteenth-century theater was very strongly oriented toward the middle class; and comedy has always been very much at home in dealing with middle-class characters and dilemmas. For another thing, comedy deals with people as social beings; and so, too, did the nineteenth century most often consider them.

Comedy, indeed, has always been a preeminently social form of drama. Tragedy looks at its heroes when they are becoming involved in dilemmas that will separate them from their fellows or from the normal concerns of society. Thus, Hamlet accepts death as the price of freeing Denmark from Claudius. Comedy, in contrast, studies people within society. Its concerns are most often those of everyday life; its problems are the problems involved in dealing with the people and customs of contemporary society. If the typical end of tragedy is death, with its total separation from the affairs of the world, the typical ending of comedy is marriage, with its commitment to worldly affairs. No matter how hard comic characters may struggle to escape the bonds of society—no matter what unusual methods they may use to outwit other characters or to solve some particular conflict between society's dictates and their own desires—at the play's end they return to the very society they've been fighting. The conflict has been solved, the goal or the marriage won; and society promises to go on exactly as it did before.

Seldom is this game of struggle and surrender more clearly played out than in Oscar Wilde's *The Importance of Being Earnest*. The lovers in this comedy belong to Society with a capital S—a carefully defined world admitting only those who can claim proper birth, breeding, and behavior. Lady Bracknell epitomizes the protocols of this world and seeks to govern (that is, to manipulate the lovers) in its name. The young men, Jack and Algernon, try to manipulate the rules of social behavior, escaping their responsibilities whenever possible; the young women, Cecily and Gwendolyn, manipulate social rules and individuals alike in order to attain their desires. And the entire comedy of maneuver and counter-maneuver is accompanied by Algernon's relentless commentary on social pretense and psychological realities.

HENRIK IBSEN (1828–1906)

A Doll's House

A new translation by Otto Reinert

CHARACTERS

TORVALD HELMER, *a lawyer*
NORA, *his wife*
DR. RANK
MRS. LINDE
KROGSTAD
THE HELMERS' THREE SMALL CHILDREN
ANNE-MARIE, *the children's nurse*
A HOUSEMAID
A PORTER

SCENE. *The Helmers' living room.*

ACT I

A pleasant, tastefully but not expensively furnished, living room. A door on the rear wall, right, leads to the front hall, another door, left, to HELMER'S *study. Between the two doors a piano. A third door in the middle of the left wall; further front a window. Near the window a round table and a small couch. Towards the rear of the right wall a fourth door; further front a tile stove with a rocking chair and a couple of armchairs in front of it. Between the stove and the door a small table. Copperplate etchings on the walls. A whatnot with porcelain figurines and other small objects. A small bookcase with de luxe editions. A rug on the floor; fire in the stove. Winter day.*

The doorbell rings, then the sound of the front door opening. NORA, *dressed for outdoors, enters, humming cheerfully. She carries several packages, which she puts down on the table, right. She leaves the door to the front hall open; there a* PORTER *is seen holding a Christmas tree and a basket. He gives them to the* MAID *who has let them in.*

NORA Be sure to hide the Christmas tree, Helene. The children mustn't see it before tonight when we've trimmed it. (*Opens her purse; to the* PORTER.) How much?

PORTER   Fifty ore.

NORA   Here's a crown. No, keep the change. (*The* PORTER *thanks her, leaves.* NORA *closes the door. She keeps laughing quietly to herself as she takes off her coat, etc. She takes a bag of macaroons from her pocket and eats a couple. She walks cautiously over to the door to the study and listens.*) Yes, he's home. (*Resumes her humming, walks over to the table, right.*)

HELMER   (*in his study*)   Is that my little lark twittering out there?

NORA   (*opening some packages*)   That's right.

HELMER   My squirrel bustling about?

NORA   Yes.

HELMER   When did squirrel come home?

NORA   Just now. (*Puts the bag of macaroons back in her pocket, wipes her mouth.*) Come out here, Torvald. I want to show you what I've bought.

HELMER   I'm busy! (*After a little while he opens the door and looks in, pen in hand.*) Bought, eh? All that? So little wastrel has been throwing money around again?

NORA   Oh but Torvald, this Christmas we can be a little extravagant, can't we? It's the first Christmas we don't have to scrimp.

HELMER   I don't know about that. We certainly don't have money to waste.

NORA   Yes, Torvald, we do. A little, anyway. Just a tiny little bit? Now that you're going to get that big salary and make lots and lots of money.

HELMER   Starting at New Year's, yes. But payday isn't till the end of the quarter.

NORA   That doesn't matter. We can always borrow.

HELMER   Nora! (*Goes over to her and playfully pulls her ear.*) There you go being irresponsible again. Suppose I borrowed a thousand crowns today and you spent it all for Christmas and on New Year's Eve a tile hit me in the head and laid me out cold.

NORA   (*putting her hand over his mouth*)   I won't have you say such horrid things.

HELMER   But suppose it happened. Then what?

NORA   If it did, I wouldn't care whether we owed money or not.

HELMER   But what about the people I had borrowed from?

NORA   Who cares about them! They are strangers.

HELMER   Nora, Nora, you *are* a woman! No, really! You know how I feel about that. No debts! A home in debt isn't a free home, and if it isn't free it isn't beautiful. We've managed nicely so far, you and I, and that's the way we'll go on. It won't be for much longer.

NORA (*walks over toward the stove*)   All right, Torvald. Whatever you say.

HELMER (*follows her*)   Come, come, my little songbird mustn't droop her wings. What's this? Can't have a pouty squirrel in the house, you know. (*Takes out his wallet.*) Nora, what do you think I have here?

NORA (*turns around quickly*)   Money!

HELMER   Here. (*Gives her some bills.*) Don't you think I know Christmas is expensive?

NORA (*counting*)   Ten—twenty—thirty—forty. Thank you, thank you, Torvald. This helps a lot.

HELMER   I certainly hope so.

NORA   It does, it does. But I want to show you what I got. It was cheap, too. Look. New clothes for Ivar. And a sword. And a horse and trumpet for Bob. And a doll and a little bed for Emmy. It isn't any good, but it wouldn't last, anyway. And here's some dress material and scarves for the maids. I feel bad about old Anne-Marie, though. She really should be getting much more.

HELMER   And what's in here?

NORA (*cries*)   Not till tonight!

HELMER   I see. But now what does my little prodigal have in mind for herself?

NORA   Oh, nothing. I really don't care.

HELMER   Of course you do. Tell me what you'd like. Within reason.

NORA   Oh, I don't know. Really, I don't. The only thing—

HELMER   Well?

NORA (*fiddling with his buttons, without looking at him*)   If you really want to give me something, you might—you could—

HELMER   All right, let's have it.

NORA (*quickly*)   Some money, Torvald. Just as much as you think you can spare. Then I'll buy myself something one of these days.

HELMER   No, really Nora—

NORA   Oh yes, please, Torvald. Please? I'll wrap the money in pretty gold paper and hang it on the tree. Won't that be nice?

HELMER   What's the name for little birds that are always spending money?

NORA   Wastrels, I know. But please let's do it my way, Torvald. Then I'll have time to decide what I need most. Now that's sensible, isn't it?

HELMER (*smiling*)   Oh, very sensible. That is, if you really bought yourself something you could use. But it all disappears in the household expenses or you buy things you don't need. And then you come back to me for more.

NORA   Oh, but Torvald—

HELMER   That's the truth, dear little Nora, and you know it. (*Puts his arm around her.*) My wastrel is a little sweetheart, but she *does* go through an awful lot of money awfully fast. You've no idea how expensive it is for a man to keep a wastrel.

NORA   That's not fair, Torvald. I really save all I can.

HELMER (*laughs*)   Oh, I believe that. All you can. Meaning, exactly nothing!

NORA (*hums, smiles mysteriously*)   You don't know all the things we songbirds and squirrels need money for, Torvald.

HELMER   You know, you're funny. Just like your father. You're always looking for ways to get money, but as soon as you do it runs through your fingers and you can never say what you spent it for. Well, I guess I'll just have to take you the way you are. It's in your blood. Yes, that sort of thing is hereditary, Nora.

NORA   In that case, I wish I had inherited many of Daddy's qualities.

HELMER   And I don't want you any different from just what you are—my own sweet little songbird. Hey!—I think I just noticed something. Aren't you looking—what's the word?—a little—sly—?

NORA   I am?

HELMER   You definitely are. Look at me.

NORA (*looks at him*)   Well?

HELMER (*wagging a finger*)   Little sweet-tooth hasn't by any chance been on a rampage today, has she?

NORA   Of course not. Whatever makes you think that?

HELMER   A little detour by the pastryshop maybe?

NORA   No, I assure you, Torvald—

HELMER   Nibbled a little jam?

NORA   Certainly not!

HELMER   Munched a macaroon or two?

NORA   No, really, Torvald, I honestly—

HELMER   All right. Of course I was only joking.

NORA (*walks toward the table, right*)   You know I wouldn't do anything to displease you.

HELMER   I know. And I have your promise. (*Over to her.*) All right, keep your little Christmas secrets to yourself, Nora darling. They'll all come out tonight, I suppose, when we light the tree.

NORA   Did you remember to invite Rank?

HELMER   No, but there's no need to. He knows he'll have dinner with us. Anyway, I'll see him later this morning. I'll ask him then. I did order some good wine. Oh Nora, you've no idea how much I'm looking forward to tonight!

NORA   Me, too. And the children Torvald! They'll have such a good time!

HELMER   You know, it *is* nice to have a good, safe job and a comfortable income. Feels good just thinking about it. Don't you agree?

NORA   Oh, it's wonderful!

HELMER   Remember last Christmas? For three whole weeks you shut yourself up every evening till long after midnight making ornaments for the Christmas tree and I don't know what else. Some big surprise for all of us, anyway. I'll be damned if I've ever been so bored in my whole life!

NORA   I wasn't bored at all!

HELMER   (*smiling*)   But you've got to admit you didn't have much to show for it in the end.

NORA   Oh, don't tease me again about that! Could I help it that the cat got in and tore up everything?

HELMER   Of course you couldn't, my poor little Nora. You just wanted to please the rest of us, and that's the important thing. But I *am* glad the hard times are behind us. Aren't you?

NORA   Oh yes. I think it's just wonderful.

HELMER   This year, I won't be bored and lonely. And you won't have to strain your dear eyes and your delicate little hands—

NORA   (*claps her hands*)   No I won't, will I Torvald? Oh, how wonderful, how lovely, to hear you say that! (*Puts her arm under his.*) Let me tell you how I think we should arrange things, Torvald. Soon as Christmas is over—(*The doorbell rings.*) Someone's at the door. (*Straightens things up a bit.*) A caller, I suppose. Bother!

HELMER   Remember, I'm not home for visitors.

THE MAID   (*in the door to the front hall*)   Ma'am, there's a lady here—

NORA   All right. Ask her to come in.

THE MAID   (*to* HELMER)   And the Doctor just arrived.

HELMER   Is he in the study?

THE MAID   Yes, sir.

(HELMER *exits into his study.* THE MAID *shows* MRS. LINDE *in and closes the door behind her as she leaves.* MRS. LINDE *is in travel dress.*)

MRS. LINDE   (*timid and a little hesitant*)   Good morning, Nora.

NORA   (*uncertainly*)   Good morning.

MRS. LINDE   I don't believe you know who I am.

NORA   No—I'm not sure—Though I know I should—Of course! Kristine! It's you!

MRS. LINDE   Yes, it's me.

NORA   And I didn't even recognize you! I had no idea (*In a lower voice.*) You've changed, Kristine.

MRS. LINDE I'm sure I have. It's been nine or ten long years.

NORA Has it really been that long? Yes, you're right. I've been so happy these last eight years. And now you're here. Such a long trip in the middle of winter. How brave!

MRS. LINDE I got in on the steamer this morning.

NORA To have some fun over the holidays, of course. That's lovely. For we are going to have fun. But take off your coat! You aren't cold, are you? (*Helps her.*) There, now! Let's sit down here by the fire and just relax and talk. No, you sit there. I want the rocking chair. (*Takes her hands.*) And now you've got your old face back. It was just for a minute, right at first—Though you are a little more pale, Kristine. And maybe a little thinner.

MRS. LINDE And much, much older, Nora.

NORA Maybe a little older. Just a teeny-weeny bit, not much. (*Interrupts herself, serious.*) Oh, but how thoughtless of me, chatting away like this! Sweet, good Kristine, can you forgive me?

MRS. LINDE Forgive you what, Nora?

NORA (*in a low voice*) You poor dear, you lost your husband, didn't you?

MRS. LINDE Three years ago, yes.

NORA I know. I saw it in the paper. Oh please believe me, Kristine. I really meant to write you, but I never got around to it. Something was always coming up.

MRS. LINDE Of course, Nora. I understand.

NORA No, that wasn't very nice of me. You poor thing, all you must have been through. And he didn't leave you much, either, did he?

MRS. LINDE No.

NORA And no children?

MRS. LINDE No.

NORA Nothing at all, in other words?

MRS. LINDE Not so much as a sense of loss—a grief to live on—

NORA (*incredulous*) But Kristine, how can that *be*?

MRS. LINDE (*with a sad smile, strokes* NORA's *hair*) That's the way it sometimes is, Nora.

NORA All alone. How awful for you. I have three darling children. You can't see them right now, though; they're out with their nurse. But now you must tell me everything—

MRS. LINDE No, no; I'd rather listen to you.

NORA No, you begin. Today I won't be selfish. Today I'll think only of you. Except there's one thing I've just got to tell you first. Something marvelous that's happened to us just these last few days. You haven't heard, have you?

MRS. LINDE No; tell me.

NORA   Just think. My husband's been made manager of the Mutual Bank.

MRS. LINDE   Your husband—! Oh, I'm so glad!

NORA   Yes, isn't that great? You see, private law practice is so uncertain, especially when you won't have anything to do with cases that aren't—you know—quite nice. And of course Torvald won't do that and I quite agree with him. Oh, you've no idea how delighted we are! He takes over at New Year's, and he'll be getting a big salary and all sorts of extras. From now on we'll be able to live in quite a different way—exactly as we like. Oh, Kristine! I feel so carefree and happy! It's lovely to have lots and lots of money and not have to worry about a thing! Don't you agree?

MRS. LINDE   It would be nice to have enough at any rate.

NORA   No, I don't mean just enough. I mean lots and lots!

MRS. LINDE   (*smiles*) Nora, Nora, when are you going to be sensible? In school you spent a great deal of money.

NORA   (*quietly laughing*) Yes, and Torvald says I still do. (*Raises her finger at* MRS. LINDE.) But "Nora, Nora" isn't so crazy as you all think. Believe me, we've had nothing to be extravagant with. We've both had to work.

MRS. LINDE   You too?

NORA   Yes. Oh, it's been little things, mostly—sewing, crocheting, embroidery—that sort of thing. (*Casually.*) And other things too. You know, of course, that Torvald left government service when we got married? There was no chance of promotion in his department, and of course he had to make more money than he had been making. So for the first few years he worked altogether too hard. He had to take jobs on the side and work night and day. It turned out to be too much for him. He became seriously ill. The doctors told him he needed to go south.

MRS. LINDE   That's right; you spent a year in Italy, didn't you?

NORA   Yes, we did. But you won't believe how hard it was to get away. Ivar had just been born. But of course we had to go. Oh, it was a wonderful trip. And it saved Torvald's life. But it took a lot of money, Kristine.

MRS. LINDE   I'm sure it did.

NORA   Twelve hundred specie dollars. Four thousand eight hundred crowns. That's a lot of money.

MRS. LINDE   Yes. So it's lucky you have it when something like that happens.

NORA   Well, actually we got the money from Daddy.

MRS. LINDE   I see. That was about the time your father died, I believe.

NORA   Yes, just about then. And I couldn't even go and take care of him. I was expecting little Ivar any day. And I had poor Torvald to look after, desperately sick and all. My dear, good Daddy! I never saw him again, Kristine. That's the saddest thing that's happened to me since I got married.

MRS. LINDE   I know you were very fond of him. But then you went to Italy?

NORA   Yes, for now we had the money, and the doctors urged us to go. So we left about a month later.

MRS. LINDE   And when you came back your husband was well again?

NORA   Healthy as a horse!

MRS. LINDE   But—the doctor?

NORA   What do you mean?

MRS. LINDE   I thought the maid said it was the doctor, that gentleman who came the same time I did.

NORA   Oh, that's Dr. Rank. He doesn't come as a doctor. He's our closest friend. He looks in at least once every day. No, Torvald hasn't been sick once since then. And the children are strong and healthy, too, and so am I. (*Jumps up and claps her hands.*) Oh God, Kristine! Isn't it wonderful to be alive and happy! Isn't it just lovely!—But now I'm being mean again, talking only about myself and my things. (*Sits down on a footstool close to* MRS. LINDE *and puts her arm on her lap.*) Please don't be angry with me! Tell me, is it really true that you didn't care for your husband? Then why did you marry him?

MRS. LINDE   Mother was still alive then, but she was bedridden and helpless. And I had my two younger brothers to look after. I didn't think I had the right to turn him down.

NORA   No, I suppose not. So he had money then?

MRS. LINDE   He was quite well off, I think. But it was an uncertain business, Nora. When he died, the whole thing collapsed and there was nothing left.

NORA   And then—?

MRS. LINDE   Well, I had to manage as best I could. With a little store and a little school and anything else I could think of. The last three years have been one long work day for me, Nora, without any rest. But now it's over. My poor mother doesn't need me any more. She's passed away. And the boys are on their own too. They've both got jobs and support themselves.

NORA   What a relief for you—

MRS. LINDE   No, not relief. Just a great emptiness. Nobody to live for any more. (*Gets up restlessly.*) That's why I couldn't stand it any longer in that little hole. Here in town it has to be easier to find something to keep me busy and occupy my thoughts. With a little luck I should be able to find a permanent job, something in an office—

NORA Oh but Kristine, that's exhausting work, and you look worn out already. It would be much better for you to go to a resort.

MRS. LINDE *(walks over to the window)* I don't have a Daddy who can give me the money, Nora.

NORA *(getting up)* Oh, don't be angry with me.

MRS. LINDE *(over to her)* Dear Nora, don't *you* be angry with *me*. That's the worst thing about my kind of situation: you become so bitter. You've nobody to work for, and yet you have to look out for yourself, somehow. You've got to keep on living, and so you become selfish. Do you know—when you told me about your husband's new position I was delighted not so much for your sake as for my own.

NORA Why was that? Oh, I see. You think maybe Torvald can give you a job?

MRS. LINDE That's what I had in mind.

NORA And he will too, Kristine. Just leave it to me. I'll be ever so subtle about it. I'll think of something nice to tell him, something he'll like. Oh I so much want to help you.

MRS. LINDE That's very good of you, Nora—making an effort like that for me. Especially since you've known so little trouble and hardship in your own life.

NORA I—?—have known so little—?

MRS. LINDE *(smiling)* Oh well, a little sewing or whatever it was. You're still a child, Nora.

NORA *(with a toss of her head, walks away)* You shouldn't sound so superior.

MRS. LINDE I shouldn't?

NORA You're just like all the others. None of you think I'm good for anything really serious.

MRS. LINDE Well, now—

NORA That I've never been through anything difficult.

MRS. LINDE But Nora! You just told me all your troubles!

NORA That's nothing! *(Lowers her voice.)* I haven't told you about *it*.

MRS. LINDE It? What's that? What do you mean?

NORA You patronize me, Kristine, and that's not fair. You're proud that you worked so long and so hard for your mother.

MRS. LINDE I don't think I patronize anyone. But it *is* true that I'm both proud and happy that I could make mother's last years comparatively easy.

NORA And you're proud of all you did for your brothers.

MRS. LINDE   I think I have the right to be.

NORA   And so do I. But now I want to tell you something, Kristine. I have something to be proud and happy about too.

MRS. LINDE   I don't doubt that for a moment. But what exactly do you mean?

NORA   Not so loud! Torvald mustn't hear—not for anything in the world. Nobody must know about this, Kristine. Nobody but you.

MRS. LINDE   But what is it?

NORA   Come here. (*Pulls her down on the couch beside her.*) You see, I *do* have something to be proud and happy about. I've saved Torvald's life.

MRS. LINDE   Saved—? How do you mean—"saved"?

NORA   I told you about our trip to Italy. Torvald would have died if he hadn't gone.

MRS. LINDE   I understand that. And so your father gave you the money you needed.

NORA   (*smiles*)   Yes, that's what Torvald and all the others think. But—

MRS. LINDE   But what?

NORA   Daddy didn't give us a penny. *I* raised that money.

MRS. LINDE   *You* did? That whole big amount?

NORA   Twelve hundred specie dollars. Four thousand eight hundred crowns. *Now* what do you say?

MRS. LINDE   But Nora, how could you? Did you win in the state lottery?

NORA   (*contemptuously*)   State lottery! (*Snorts.*) What is so great about that?

MRS. LINDE   Where did it come from then?

NORA   (*humming and smiling, enjoying her secret*)   Hmmm. Tra-la-la-la-la!

MRS. LINDE   You certainly couldn't have borrowed it.

NORA   Oh? And why not?

MRS. LINDE   A wife can't borrow money without her husband's consent.

NORA   (*with a toss of her head*)   Oh, I don't know—take a wife with a little bit of a head for business—a wife who knows how to manage things—

MRS. LINDE   But Nora, I don't understand at all—

NORA   You don't have to. I didn't say I borrowed the money, did I? I could have gotten it some other way. (*Leans back.*) An admirer may have given it to me. When you're as tolerably good-looking as I am—

MRS. LINDE   Oh, you're crazy.

NORA   I think you're dying from curiosity, Kristine.

MRS. LINDE   I'm beginning to think you've done something very foolish, Nora.

NORA *(sits up)*   Is it foolish to save your husband's life?

MRS. LINDE   I say it's foolish to act behind his back.

NORA   But don't you see: he couldn't be told! You're missing the whole point, Kristine. We couldn't even let him know how seriously ill he was. The doctors came to *me* and told me his life was in danger, that nothing could save him but a stay in the south. Don't you think I tried to work on him? I told him how lovely it would be if I could go abroad like other young wives. I cried and begged. I said he'd better remember what condition I was in, that he had to be nice to me and do what I wanted. I even hinted he could borrow the money. But that almost made him angry with me. He told me I was being irresponsible and that it was his duty as my husband not to give in to my moods and whims—I think that's what he called it. All right, I said to myself, you've got to be saved somehow, and so I found a way—

MRS. LINDE   And your husband never learned from your father that the money didn't come from him?

NORA   Never. Daddy died that same week. I thought of telling him all about it and ask him not to say anything. But since he was so sick—It turned out I didn't have to—

MRS. LINDE   And you've never told your husband?

NORA   Of course not! Good heavens, how could I? He, with his strict principles! Besides, you know how men are. Torvald would find it embarrassing and humiliating to learn that he owed me anything. It would upset our whole relationship. Our happy, beautiful home would no longer be what it is.

MRS. LINDE   Aren't you ever going to tell him?

NORA *(reflectively, half smiling)*   Yes—one day, maybe. Many, many years from now, when I'm no longer young and pretty. Don't laugh! I mean when Torvald no longer feels about me the way he does now, when he no longer thinks it's fun when I dance for him and put on costumes and recite for him. Then it will be good to have something in reserve—*(Interrupts herself.)* Oh, I'm just being silly! That day will never come.—Well, now, Kristine, what do you think of my great secret? Don't you think I'm good for something too?—By the way, you wouldn't believe all the worry I've had because of it. It's been very hard to meet my obligations on schedule. You see, in business there's something called quarterly interest and something called installments on the principal, and those are terribly hard to come up with. I've had to save a little here and a little there, whenever I could. I couldn't use much of the housekeeping money, for Torvald has to eat well.

And I couldn't use what I got for clothes for the children. They have to look nice, and I didn't think it would be right to spend less than I got—the sweet little things!

MRS. LINDE   Poor Nora! So you had to take it from your own allowance!

NORA   Yes, of course. After all, it was my affair. Every time Torvald gave me money for a new dress and things like that, I never used more than half of it. I always bought the cheapest, simplest things for myself. Thank God, everything looks good on me, so Torvald never noticed. But it was hard many times, Kristine, for it's fun to have pretty clothes. Don't you think?

MRS. LINDE   Certainly.

NORA   Anyway, I had other ways of making money too. Last winter I was lucky enough to get some copying work. So I locked the door and sat up writing every night till quite late. God! I often got so tired—! But it was great fun, too, working and making money. It was almost like being a man.

MRS. LINDE   But how much have you been able to pay off this way?

NORA   I couldn't tell you exactly. You see, it's very difficult to keep track of business like that. All I know is I have been paying off as much as I've been able to scrape together. Many times I just didn't know what to do. (*Smiles.*) Then I used to imagine a rich old gentleman had fallen in love with me—

MRS. LINDE   What! What old gentleman?

NORA   Phooey! And now he was dead and they were reading his will, and there it said in big letters, "All my money is to be paid in cash immediately to the charming Mrs. Nora Helmer."

MRS. LINDE   But dearest Nora—who *was* this old gentleman?

NORA   For heaven's sake, Kristine, don't you see? There *was* no old gentleman. He was just somebody I made up when I couldn't think of any way to raise the money. But never mind him. The old bore can be anyone he likes to for all I care. I have no use for him or his last will, for now I don't have a single worry in the world. (*Jumps up.*) Dear God, what a lovely thought this is! To be able to play and have fun with the children, to have everything nice and pretty in the house, just the way Torvald likes it! Not a care! And soon spring will be here, and the air will be blue and high. Maybe we can travel again. Maybe I'll see the ocean again! Oh, yes, yes!—it's wonderful to be alive and happy!

The doorbell rings.

MRS. LINDE   (*getting up*) There's the doorbell. Maybe I better be going.

NORA   No, please stay. I'm sure it's just someone for Torvald—

THE MAID (*in the hall door*) Excuse me, ma'am. There's a gentleman here who'd like to see Mr. Helmer.

NORA You mean the bank manager.

THE MAID Sorry, ma'am; the bank manager. But I didn't know—since the Doctor is with him—

NORA Who is the gentleman?

KROGSTAD (*appearing in the door*) It's just me, Mrs. Helmer.

MRS. LINDE *starts, looks, turns away toward the window.*

NORA (*takes a step toward him, tense, in a low voice*) You? What do you want? What do you want with my husband?

KROGSTAD Bank business—in a way. I have a small job in the Mutual, and I understand your husband is going to be our new boss—

NORA So it's just—

KROGSTAD Just routine business, ma'am. Nothing else.

NORA All right. In that case, why don't you go through the door to the office.

Dismisses him casually as she closes the door. Walks over to the stove and tends the fire.

MRS. LINDE Nora—who was that man?

NORA His name's Krogstad. He's a lawyer.

MRS. LINDE So it *was* him.

NORA Do you know him?

MRS. LINDE I used to—many years ago. For a while he clerked in our part of the country.

NORA Right. He did.

MRS. LINDE He has changed a great deal.

NORA I believe he had a very unhappy marriage.

MRS. LINDE And now he's a widower, isn't he?

NORA With many children. There now; it's burning nicely again. (*Closes the stove and moves the rocking chair a little to the side.*)

MRS. LINDE They say he's into all sorts of business.

NORA Really? Maybe so. I wouldn't know. But let's not think about business. It's such a bore.

DR. RANK (*appears in the door to* HELMER'*s study.*) No. I don't want to be in the way. I'd rather talk to your wife a bit. (*Closes the door and notices* MRS. LINDE.) Oh, I beg your pardon. I believe I'm in the way here too.

NORA No, not at all. (*Introduces them.*) Dr. Rank. Mrs. Linde.

RANK Aha. A name often heard in this house. I believe I passed you on the stairs coming up.

MRS. LINDE Yes. I'm afraid I climb stairs very slowly. They aren't good for me.

RANK   I see. A slight case of inner decay, perhaps?

MRS. LINDE   Overwork, rather.

RANK   Oh, is that all? And now you've come to town to relax at all the parties?

MRS. LINDE   I have come to look for a job.

RANK   A proven cure for overwork, I take it?

MRS. LINDE   One has to live, Doctor.

RANK   Yes, that seems to be the common opinion.

NORA   Come on, Dr. Rank—you want to live just as much as the rest of us.

RANK   Of course I do. Miserable as I am, I prefer to go on being tortured as long as possible. All my patients feel the same way. And that's true of the moral invalids too. Helmer is talking with a specimen right this minute.

MRS. LINDE *(in a low voice)*   Ah!

NORA   What do you mean?

RANK   Oh, this lawyer, Krogstad. You don't know him. The roots of his character are decayed. But even he began by saying something about having *to live*—as if it were a matter of the highest importance.

NORA   Oh? What did he want with Torvald?

RANK   I don't really know. All I heard was something about the bank.

NORA   I didn't know that Krog—that this Krogstad had anything to do with the Mutual Bank.

RANK   Yes, he seems to have some kind of job there. *(To* MRS. LINDE.*)* I don't know if you are familiar in your part of the country with the kind of person who is always running around trying to sniff out cases of moral decrepitude and as soon as he finds one puts the individual under observation in some excellent position or other. All the healthy ones are left out in the cold.

MRS. LINDE   I should think it's the sick who need looking after the most.

RANK *(shrugs his shoulders)*   There we are. That's the attitude that turns society into a hospital.

(NORA, *absorbed in her own thoughts, suddenly starts giggling and clapping her hands.*)

RANK   What's so funny about that? Do you even know what society is?

NORA   What do I care about your stupid society! I laughed at something entirely different—something terribly amusing. Tell me, Dr. Rank—all the employees in the Mutual Bank, from now on they'll all be dependent on Torvald, right?

RANK   Is that what you find so enormously amusing?

NORA   (*smiles and hums*)   That's my business, that's my business!
(*Walks around.*) Yes, I do think it's fun that we—that Torvald
is going to have so much influence on so many people's lives.
(*Brings out the bag of macaroons.*) Have a macaroon, Dr. Rank.

RANK   Well, well—macaroons. I thought they were banned around
here.

NORA   Yes, but these were some that Kristine gave me.

MRS. LINDE   What! I?

NORA   That's all right. Don't look so scared. You couldn't know that
Torvald won't let me have them. He's afraid they'll ruin my teeth.
But who cares! Just once in a while—! Right, Dr. Rank? Have
one! (*Puts a macaroon into his mouth.*) You too, Kristine. And
one for me. A very small one. Or at most two. (*Walks around
again.*) Yes, I really feel very, very happy. Now there's just one
thing I'm dying to do.

RANK   Oh, And what's that?

NORA   Something I'm dying to say so Torvald could hear.

RANK   And why can't you?

NORA   I don't dare to, for it's not nice.

MRS. LINDE   Not nice?

RANK   In that case, I guess you'd better not. But surely to the two
of us—? What is it you'd like to say for Helmer to hear?

NORA   I want to say, "Goddammit!"

RANK   Are you out of your mind!

MRS. LINDE   For heaven's sake, Nora!

RANK   Say it. Here he comes.

NORA   (*hiding the macaroons*).   Shhh!

(HELMER *enters from his study, carrying his hat and overcoat.*)

NORA   (*going to him*)   Well, dear, did you get rid of him?

HELMER   Yes, he just left.

NORA   Torvald, I want you to meet Kristine. She's just come to
town.

HELMER   Kristine—? I'm sorry; I don't think—

NORA   Mrs. Linde, Torvald dear. Mrs. Kristine Linde.

HELMER   Ah, yes. A childhood friend of my wife's, I suppose.

MRS. LINDE   Yes, we've known each other for a long time.

NORA   Just think; she has come all this way just to see you.

HELMER   I'm not sure I understand—

MRS. LINDE   Well, not really—

NORA   You see, Kristine is an absolutely fantastic secretary, and she
would so much like to work for a competent executive and learn
more than she knows already—

HELMER   Very sensible, I'm sure, Mrs. Linde.

NORA   So when she heard about your appointment—there was a wire—she came here as fast as she could. How about it, Torvald? Couldn't you do something for Kristine? For my sake. Please?

HELMER   Quite possibly. I take it you're a widow, Mrs. Linde?

MRS. LINDE   Yes.

HELMER   And you've had office experience?

MRS. LINDE   Some—yes.

HELMER   In that case I think it's quite likely that I'll be able to find you a position.

NORA   (*claps her hands*)   I knew it! I knew it!

HELMER   You've arrived at a most opportune time, Mrs. Linde.

MRS. LINDE   Oh, how can I ever thank you—

HELMER   Not at all, not at all. (*Puts his coat on.*) But today you'll have to excuse me—

RANK   Wait a minute; I'll come with you. (*Gets his fur coat from the front hall, warms it by the stove.*)

NORA   Don't be long, Torvald.

HELMER   An hour or so; no more.

NORA   Are you leaving, too, Kristine?

MRS. LINDE   (*putting on her things*)   Yes, I'd better go and find a place to stay.

HELMER   Good. Then we'll be going the same way.

NORA   (*helping her*)   I'm sorry this place is so small, but I don't think we very well could—

MRS. LINDE   Of course! Don't be silly, Nora. Goodbye, and thank you for everything.

NORA   Goodbye. We'll see you soon. You'll be back this evening, of course. And you too, Dr. Rank; right? If you feel well enough? Of course you will. Just wrap yourself up.

(*General small talk as all exit into the hall. Children's voices are heard on the stairs.*)

NORA   There they are! There they are! (*She runs and opens the door. The nurse ANNE-MARIE enters with the children.*)

NORA   Come in! Come in! (*Bends over and kisses them.*) Oh, you sweet, sweet darlings! Look at them, Kristine! Aren't they beautiful?

RANK   No standing around in the draft!

HELMER   Come along, Mrs. Linde. This place isn't fit for anyone but mothers right now.

(*DR. RANK, HELMER, and MRS. LINDE go down the stairs. The NURSE enters the living room with the children. NORA follows, closing the door behind her.*)

NORA   My, how nice you all look! Such red cheeks! Like apples and roses. (*The children all talk at the same time.*) You've had so much fun? I bet you have. Oh, isn't that nice! You pulled both Emmy and Bob on your sleigh? Both at the same time? That's very good, Ivar. Oh, let me hold her for a minute, Anne-Marie. My sweet little doll baby! (*Takes the smallest of the children from the* NURSE *and dances with her.*) Yes, yes, of course; Mama'll dance with you too, Bob. What? You threw snowballs? Oh, I wish I'd been there! No, no; *I* want to take their clothes off, Anne-Marie. Please let me; I think it's so much fun. You go on in. You look frozen. There's hot coffee on the stove.

(*The* NURSE *exits into the room to the left.* NORA *takes the children's wraps off and throws them all around. They all keep telling her things at the same time.*)

NORA   Oh, really? A big dog ran after you? But it didn't bite you. Of course not. Dogs don't bite sweet little doll babies. Don't peek at the packages, Ivar! What's in them? Wouldn't you like to know! No, no; that's something terrible! Play? You want to play? What do you want to play? Okay, let's play hide-and-seek. Bob hides first. You want *me* to? All right. I'll go first.

(*Laughing and shouting,* NORA *and the children play in the living room and in the adjacent room, right. Finally,* NORA *hides herself under the table; the children rush in, look for her, can't find her. They hear her low giggle, run to the table, lift the rug that covers it, see her. General hilarity. She crawls out, pretends to scare them. New delight. In the meantime there has been a knock on the door between the living room and the front hall, but nobody has noticed. Now the door is opened half-way;* KROGSTAD *appears. He waits a little. The play goes on.*)

KROGSTAD   Pardon me, Mrs. Helmer—
NORA   (*with a muted cry turns around, jumps up*)   Ah! What do you want?
KROGSTAD   I'm sorry. The front door was open. Somebody must have forgotten to close it—
NORA   (*standing up*)   My husband isn't here, Mr. Krogstad.
KROGSTAD   I know.
NORA   So what do you want?
KROGSTAD   I'd like a word with you.
NORA   With—? (*To the children.*) Go in to Anne-Marie. What? No, the strange man won't do anything bad to Mama. When he's gone we'll play some more.

(*She takes the children into the room to the left and closes the door.*)

NORA   (*tense, troubled*)   You want to speak with me?
KROGSTAD   Yes I do.

NORA Today—? It isn't the first of the month yet.

KROGSTAD No, it's Christmas Eve. It's up to you what kind of holiday you'll have.

NORA What do you want? I can't possibly—

KROGSTAD Let's not talk about that just yet. There's something else. You do have a few minutes, don't you?

NORA Yes. Yes, of course. That is,—

KROGSTAD Good. I was sitting in Olsen's restaurant when I saw your husband go by.

NORA Yes—?

KROGSTAD —with a lady.

NORA What of it?

KROGSTAD May I be so free as to ask: wasn't that lady Mrs. Linde?

NORA Yes.

KROGSTAD Just arrived in town?

NORA Yes, today.

KROGSTAD She's a good friend of yours, I understand?

NORA Yes, she is. But I fail to see—

KROGSTAD I used to know her myself.

NORA I know that.

KROGSTAD So you know about that. I thought as much. In that case, let me ask you a simple question. Is Mrs. Linde going to be employed in the bank?

NORA What makes you think you have the right to cross-examine me like this, Mr. Krogstad—you, one of my husband's employees? But since you ask, I'll tell you. Yes, Mrs. Linde is going to be working in the bank. And it was I who recommended her, Mr. Krogstad. Now you know.

KROGSTAD So I was right.

NORA (*walks up and down*) After all, one does have a little influence, you know. Just because you're a woman, it doesn't mean that—Really, Mr. Krogstad, people in a subordinate position should be careful not to offend someone who—oh well—

KROGSTAD —has influence?

NORA Exactly.

KROGSTAD (*changing his tone*) Mrs. Helmer, I must ask you to be good enough to use your influence on my behalf.

NORA What do you mean?

KROGSTAD I want you to make sure that I am going to keep my subordinate position in the bank.

NORA I don't understand. Who is going to take your position away from you?

KROGSTAD There's no point in playing ignorant with me, Mrs. Helmer. I can very well appreciate that your friend would find it unpleasant to run into me. So now I know who I can thank for my dismissal.

NORA   But I assure you—

KROGSTAD   Never mind. Just want to say you still have time. I advise you to use your influence to prevent it.

NORA   But Mr. Krogstad, I don't have any influence—none at all.

KROGSTAD   No? I thought you just said—

NORA   Of course I didn't mean it that way. I! Whatever makes you think that I have any influence of that kind on my husband?

KROGSTAD   I went to law school with your husband. I have no reason to think that the bank manager is less susceptible than other husbands.

NORA   If you're going to insult my husband, I'll ask you to leave.

KROGSTAD   You're brave, Mrs. Helmer.

NORA   I'm not afraid of you any more. After New Year's I'll be out of this thing with you.

KROGSTAD   (*more controlled*)   Listen, Mrs. Helmer. If necessary I'll fight as for my life to keep my little job in the bank.

NORA   So it seems.

KROGSTAD   It isn't just the money; that's really the smallest part of it. There is something else—Well, I guess I might as well tell you. It's like this. I'm sure you know, like everybody else, that some years ago I committed—an impropriety.

NORA   I believe I've heard it mentioned.

KROGSTAD   The case never came to court, but from that moment all doors were closed to me. So I took up the kind of business you know about. I had to do something, and I think I can say about myself that I have not been among the worst. But now I want to get out of all that. My sons are growing up. For their sake I must get back as much of my good name as I can. This job in the bank was like the first rung on the ladder. And now your husband wants to kick me down and leave me back in the mud again.

NORA   But I swear to you, Mr. Krogstad; it's not at all in my power to help you.

KROGSTAD   That's because you don't want to. But I have the means to force you.

NORA   You don't mean you're going to tell my husband I owe you money?

KROGSTAD   And if I did?

NORA   That would be a mean thing to do. (*Almost crying.*) That secret, which is my joy and my pride—for him to learn about it in such a coarse and ugly manner—to learn it from *you*—! It would be terribly unpleasant for me.

KROGSTAD   Just unpleasant?

NORA (*heatedly*)   But go ahead! Do it! It will be worse for you than for me. When my husband realizes what a bad person you are, you'll be sure to lose your job.

KROGSTAD   I asked you if it was just domestic unpleasantness you were afraid of?

NORA   When my husband finds out, of course he'll pay off the loan, and then we won't have anything more to do with you.

KROGSTAD (*stepping closer*)   Listen, Mrs. Helmer—either you have a very bad memory, or you don't know much about business. I think I had better straighten you out on a few things.

NORA   What do you mean?

KROGSTAD   When your husband was ill, you came to me to borrow twelve hundred dollars.

NORA   I knew nobody else.

KROGSTAD   I promised to get you the money—

NORA   And you did.

KROGSTAD   I promised to get you the money on certain conditions. At the time you were so anxious about your husband's health and so set on getting him away that I doubt very much that you paid much attention to the details of our transaction. That's why I remind you of them now. Anyway, I promised to get you the money if you would sign an I.O.U., which I drafted.

NORA   And which I signed.

KROGSTAD   Good. But below your signature I added a few lines, making your father security for the loan. Your father was supposed to put his signature to those lines.

NORA   Supposed to—? He did.

KROGSTAD   I had left the date blank. That is, your father was to date his own signature. You recall that, don't you, Mrs. Helmer?

NORA   I guess so—

KROGSTAD   I gave the note to you. You were to mail it to your father. Am I correct?

NORA   Yes.

KROGSTAD   And of course you did so right away, for no more than five or six days later you brought the paper back to me, signed by your father. Then I paid you the money.

NORA   Well? And haven't I been keeping up with the payments?

KROGSTAD   Fairly well, yes. But to get back to what we were talking about—those were difficult days for you, weren't they, Mrs. Helmer?

NORA   Yes, they were.

KROGSTAD   Your father was quite ill, I believe.

NORA   He was dying.

KROGSTAD   And died shortly afterwards?

NORA   That's right.

KROGSTAD   Tell me, Mrs. Helmer; do you happen to remember the date of your father's death? I mean the exact day of the month?

NORA   Daddy died on September 29.

KROGSTAD   Quite correct. I have ascertained that fact. That's why there is something peculiar about this (*takes out a piece of paper*), which I can't account for.

NORA   Peculiar? How? I don't understand—

KROGSTAD   It seems very peculiar, Mrs. Helmer, that your father signed this promissory note three days after his death.

NORA   How so? I don't see what—

KROGSTAD   Your father died on September 29. Now look. He has dated his signature October 2. Isn't that odd?

(NORA *remains silent.*)

KROGSTAD   Can you explain it?

(NORA *is still silent.*)

KROGSTAD   I also find it striking that the date and the month and the year are not in your father's handwriting but in a hand I think I recognize. Well, that might be explained. Your father may have forgotten to date his signature and somebody else may have done it here, guessing at the date before he had learned of your father's death. That's all right. It's only the signature itself that matters. And that is genuine, isn't it, Mrs. Helmer? Your father *did* put his name to this note?

NORA   (*after a brief silence tosses her head back and looks defiantly at him*) No, he didn't. *I* wrote Daddy's name.

KROGSTAD   Mrs. Helmer—do you realize what a dangerous admission you just made?

NORA   Why? You'll get your money soon.

KROGSTAD   Let me ask you something. Why didn't you mail this note to your father?

NORA   Because it was impossible. Daddy was sick—you know that. If I had asked him to sign it, I would have had to tell him what the money was for. But I couldn't tell him, as sick as he was, that my husband's life was in danger. That was impossible. Surely you can see that.

KROGSTAD   Then it would have been better for you if you had given up your trip abroad.

NORA   No, that was impossible! That trip was to save my husband's life. I couldn't give it up.

KROGSTAD   But didn't you realize that what you did amounted to fraud against me?

NORA   I couldn't let that make any difference. I didn't care about you at all. I hated the way you made all those difficulties for me, even though you knew the danger my husband was in. I thought you were cold and unfeeling.

KROGSTAD   Mrs. Helmer, obviously you have no clear idea of what you have done. Let me tell you that what I did that time was no more and no worse. And it ruined my name and reputation.

NORA   You! Are you trying to tell me that you did something brave once in order to save your wife's life?

KROGSTAD   The law doesn't ask about motives.

NORA   Then it's a bad law.

KROGSTAD   Bad or not—if I produce this note in court you'll be judged according to the law.

NORA   I refuse to believe you. A daughter shouldn't have the right to spare her dying old father worry and anxiety? A wife shouldn't have the right to save her husband's life? I don't know the laws very well, but I'm sure that somewhere they make allowance for cases like that. And you, a lawyer, don't know that? I think you must be a bad lawyer, Mr. Krogstad.

KROGSTAD   That may be. But business—the kind of business you and I have with one another—don't you think I know something about that? Very well. Do what you like. But let me tell you this: if I'm going to be kicked out again, you'll keep me company. (*He bows and exits through the front hall.*)

NORA   (*pauses thoughtfully; then, with a defiant toss of her head*) Oh, nonsense! Trying to scare me like that! I'm not all that silly. (*Starts picking up the children's clothes; soon stops.*) But—? No! That's impossible! I did it for love!

THE CHILDREN   (*in the door to the left*)   Mama, the strange man just left. We saw him.

NORA   Yes, yes; I know. But don't tell anybody about the strange man. Do you hear? Not even Daddy.

THE CHILDREN   We won't. But now you'll play with us again, won't you, Mama?

NORA   No, not right now.

THE CHILDREN   But Mama—you promised.

NORA   I know, but I can't just now. Go to your own room. I've so much to do. Be nice now, my little darlings. Do as I say. (*She nudges them gently into the other room and closes the door. She sits down on the couch, picks up a piece of embroidery, makes a few stitches, then stops.*) No! (*Throws the embroidery down, goes to the hall door and calls out.*) Helene! Bring the Christmas tree

in here, please! (*Goes to the table, left, opens the drawer, halts.*)
No—that's impossible!

THE MAID (*with the Christmas tree*)   Where do you want it, ma'am?

NORA   There. The middle of the floor.

THE MAID   You want anything else?

NORA   No, thanks. I have everything I need. (THE MAID *goes out.*
NORA *starts trimming the tree.*) I want candles—and flowers—
That awful man! Oh, nonsense! There's nothing wrong. This will
be a lovely tree. I'll do everything you want me to, Torvald. I'll
sing for you—dance for you—

(*Helmer, a bundle of papers under his arm, enters from outside.*)

NORA   Ah—you're back already?

HELMER   Yes. Has anybody been here?

NORA   Here? No.

HELMER   That's funny. I saw Krogstad leaving just now.

NORA   Oh? Oh yes, that's right. Krogstad was here for just a
moment.

HELMER   I can tell from your face that he came to ask you to put
in a word for him.

NORA   Yes.

HELMER   And it was supposed to be your own idea, wasn't it? You
were not to tell me he'd been here. He asked you that too, didn't
he?

NORA   Yes, Torvald, but—

HELMER   Nora, Nora, how could you! Talk to a man like that and
make him promises! And lying to me about it afterwards—!

NORA   Lying—?

HELMER   Didn't you say nobody had been here? (*Shakes his finger
at her.*) My little songbird must never do that again. Songbirds
are supposed to have clean beaks to chirp with—no false notes.
(*Puts his arms around her waist.*) Isn't that so? Of course it is.
(*Lets her go.*) And that's enough about that. (*Sits down in front
of the fireplace.*) Ah, it's nice and warm in here. (*Begins to leaf
through his papers.*)

NORA (*busy with the tree; after a brief pause*)   Torvald.

HELMER   Yes.

NORA   I'm looking forward so much to the Stenborgs' costume party
day after tomorrow.

HELMER   And I can't wait to find out what you're going to surprise
me with.

NORA   Oh, that silly idea!

HELMER   Oh?

NORA   I can't think of anything. It all seems so foolish and pointless.

HELMER   Ah, my little Nora admits that?

NORA   (*behind his chair, her arms on the back of the chair*)   Are you very busy, Torvald?

HELMER   Well—

NORA   What are all those papers?

HELMER   Bank business.

NORA   Already?

HELMER   I've asked the board to give me the authority to make certain changes in organization and personnel. That's what I'll be doing over the holidays. I want it all settled before New Year's.

NORA   So that's why this poor Krogstad—

HELMER   Hm.

NORA   (*leisurely playing with the hair on his neck*)   If you weren't so busy, Torvald, I'd ask you for a great big favor.

HELMER   Let's hear it, anyway.

NORA   I don't know anyone with better taste than you, and I want so much to look nice at the party. Couldn't you sort of take charge of me, Torvald, and decide what I'll wear—Help me with my costume?

HELMER   Aha! Little Lady Obstinate is looking for someone to rescue her?

NORA   Yes, Torvald. I won't get anywhere without your help.

HELMER   All right. I'll think about it. We'll come up with something.

NORA   Oh, you *are* nice! (*Goes back to the Christmas tree. A pause.*) Those red flowers look so pretty.—Tell me, was it really all that bad what this Krogstad fellow did?

HELMER   He forged signatures. Do you have any idea what that means?

NORA   Couldn't it have been because he felt he had to?

HELMER   Yes, or like so many others he may simply have been thoughtless. I'm not so heartless as to condemn a man absolutely because of a single imprudent act.

NORA   Of course not, Torvald!

HELMER   People like him can redeem themselves morally by openly confessing their crime and taking their punishment.

NORA   Punishment—?

HELMER   But that was not the way Krogstad chose. He got out of it with tricks and evasions. That's what has corrupted him.

NORA   So you think that if—?

HELMER   Can't you imagine how a guilty person like that has to lie and fake and dissemble wherever he goes—putting on a mask before everybody he's close to, even his own wife and children. It's this thing with the children that's the worst part of it, Nora.

NORA   Why is that?

HELMER   Because when a man lives inside such a circle of stinking lies he brings infection into his own home and contaminates his whole family. With every breath of air his children inhale the germs of something ugly.

NORA   (*moving closer behind him*)   Are you so sure of that?

HELMER   Of course I am. I have seen enough examples of that in my work. Nearly all young criminals have had mothers who lied.

NORA   Why mothers—particularly?

HELMER   Most often mothers. But of course fathers tend to have the same influence. Every lawyer knows that. And yet, for years this Krogstad has been poisoning his own children in an atmosphere of lies and deceit. That's why I call him a lost soul morally. (*Reaches out for her hands.*) And that's why my sweet little Nora must promise me never to take his side again. Let's shake on that.—What? What's this? Give me your hand. There! Now that's settled. I assure you, I would find it impossible to work in the same room with that man. I feel literally sick when I'm around people like that.

NORA   (*withdraws her hand and goes to the other side of the Christmas tree*)   It's so hot in here. And I have so much to do.

HELMER   (*gets up and collects his papers*)   Yes, and I really should try to get some of this reading done before dinner. I must think about your costume too. And maybe just possibly I'll have something to wrap in gilt paper and hang on the Christmas tree. (*Puts his hand on her head.*) Oh my adorable little songbird! (*Enters his study and closes the door.*)

NORA   (*after a pause, in a low voice*)   It's all a lot of nonsense. It's not that way at all. It's impossible. It has to be impossible.

THE NURSE   (*in the door, left*)   The little ones are asking ever so nicely if they can't come in and be with their mama.

NORA   No, no no! Don't let them in here! You stay with them, Anne-Marie.

THE NURSE   If you say so, ma'am. (*Closes the door.*)

NORA   (*pale with terror*)   Corrupt my little children—! Poison my home—? (*Brief pause; she lifts her head.*) That's not true. Never. Never in a million years.

ACT II

The same room. The Christmas tree is in the corner by the piano, stripped, shabby-looking, with burnt-down candles. NORA's outside clothes are on the couch. NORA is alone. She walks around restlessly. She stops by the couch and picks up her coat.

NORA (*drops the coat again*)   There's somebody now! (*Goes to the door, listens.*) No. Nobody. Of course not—not on Christmas. And not tomorrow either.[1]—But perhaps—(*Opens the door and looks.*) No, nothing in the mailbox. All empty. (*Comes forward.*) How silly I am! Of course he isn't serious. Nothing like that could happen. After all, I have three small children.

(*The* NURSE *enters from the room, left, carrying a big carton.*)

THE NURSE   Well, at last I found it—the box with your costume.

NORA   Thanks. Just put it on the table.

NURSE (*does so*)   But it's all a big mess, I'm afraid.

NORA   Oh, I wish I could tear the whole thing to little pieces!

NURSE   Heavens! It's not as bad as all that. It can be fixed all right. All it takes is a little patience.

NORA   I'll go over and get Mrs. Linde to help me.

NURSE   Going out again? In this awful weather? You'll catch a cold.

NORA   That might not be such a bad thing. How are the children?

NURSE   The poor little dears are playing with their presents, but—

NORA   Do they keep asking for me?

NURSE   Well, you know, they're used to being with their mamma.

NORA   I know. But Anne-Marie, from now on I can't be with them as much as before.

NURSE   Oh well. Little children get used to everything.

NORA   You think so? Do you think they'll forget their mamma if I were gone altogether?

NURSE   Goodness me—gone altogether?

NORA   Listen, Anne-Marie—something I've wondered about. How could you bring yourself to leave your child with strangers?

NURSE   But I had to, if I were to nurse you.

NORA   Yes, but how could you *want* to?

NURSE   When I could get such a nice place? When something like that happens to a poor young girl, she'd better be grateful for whatever she gets. For *he* didn't do a thing for me—the louse!

NORA   But your daughter has forgotten all about you, hasn't she?

NURSE   Oh no! Not at all! She wrote to me both when she was confirmed and when she got married.

NORA (*putting her arms around her neck*)   You dear old thing— you were a good mother to me when I was little.

NURSE   Poor little Nora had no one else, you know.

NORA   And if my little ones didn't, I know you'd—oh, I'm be-

---

1 In Norway both December 25 and 26 are legal holidays.

ing silly! (*Opens the carton.*) Go in to them, please. I really should—. Tomorrow you'll see how pretty I'll be.

NURSE   I know. There won't be anybody at that party half as pretty as you, ma'am. (*Goes out, left.*)

NORA   (*begins to take clothes out of the carton; in a moment she throws it all down*)   If only I dared to go out. If only I knew nobody would come. That nothing would happen while I was gone.—How silly! Nobody'll come. Just don't think about it. Brush the muff. Beautiful gloves. Beautiful gloves. Forget it. Forget it. One, two, three, four, five, six—(*Cries out.*) There they are! (*Moves toward the door, stops irresolutely.*)

(MRS. LINDE *enters from the hall. She has already taken off her coat.*)

NORA   Oh, it's you, Kristine. There's no one else out there, is there? I'm so glad you're here.

MRS. LINDE   They told me you'd asked for me.

NORA   I just happened to walk by. I need your help with something—badly. Let's sit here on the couch. Look. Torvald and I are going to a costume party tomorrow night—at Consul Stenborg's upstairs—and Torvald wants me to go as a Neapolitan fisher girl and dance the tarantella. I learned it when we were on Capri.

MRS. LINDE   Well, well! So you'll be putting on a whole show?

NORA   Yes. Torvald thinks I should. Look, here's the costume. Torvald had it made for me while we were there. But it's all so torn and everything. I just don't know—

MRS. LINDE   Oh, that can be fixed. It's not that much. The trimmings have come loose in a few places. Do you have needle and thread? Ah, here we are. All set.

NORA   I really appreciate it, Kristine.

MRS. LINDE   (*sewing*).   So you'll be in disguise tomorrow night, eh? You know—I may come by for just a moment, just to look at you. —Oh dear. I haven't even thanked you for the nice evening last night.

NORA   (*gets up, moves around*).   Oh, I don't know. I don't think last night was as nice as it usually is.—You should have come to town a little earlier, Kristine.—Yes, Torvald knows how to make it nice and pretty around here.

MRS. LINDE   You too, I should think. After all, you're your father's daughter. By the way, is Dr. Rank always as depressed as he was last night?

NORA   No, last night was unusual. He's a very sick man, you know —very sick. Poor Rank, his spine is rotting away. Tuberculosis, I think. You see, his father was a nasty old man with mistresses and all that sort of thing. Rank has been sickly ever since he was a little boy.

MRS. LINDE (*dropping her sewing to her lap*)   But dearest, Nora, where have you learned about things like that?

NORA (*still walking about*)   Oh, you know—with three children you sometimes get to talk with—other wives. Some of them know quite a bit about medicine. So you pick up a few things.

MRS. LINDE (*resumes her sewing; after a brief pause*)   Does Dr. Rank come here every day?

NORA   Every single day. He's Torvald's oldest and best friend, after all. And my friend too, for that matter. He's part of the family, almost.

MRS. LINDE   But tell me, is he quite sincere? I mean, isn't he the kind of man who likes to say nice things to people?

NORA   No, not at all. Rather the opposite, in fact. What makes you say that?

MRS. LINDE   When you introduced us yesterday, he told me he'd often heard my name mentioned in this house. But later on it was quite obvious that your husband really had no idea who I was. So how could Dr. Rank—?

NORA   You're right, Kristine, but I can explain that. You see, Torvald loves me so very much that he wants me all to himself. That's what he says. When we were first married he got almost jealous when I as much as mentioned anybody from back home that I was fond of. So of course I soon stopped doing that. But with Dr. Rank I often talk about home. You see, he likes to listen to me.

MRS. LINDE   Look here, Nora. In many ways you're still a child. After all, I'm quite a bit older than you and have had more experience. I want to give you a piece of advice. I think you should get out of this thing with Dr. Rank.

NORA   Get out of what thing?

MRS. LINDE   Several things in fact, if you want my opinion. Yesterday you said something about a rich admirer who was going to give you money—

NORA   One who doesn't exist, unfortunately. What of it?

MRS. LINDE   Does Dr. Rank have money?

NORA   Yes, he does.

MRS. LINDE   And no dependents?

NORA   No. But—?

MRS. LINDE   And he comes here every day?

NORA   Yes, I told you that already.

MRS. LINDE   But how can that sensitive man be so tactless?

NORA   I haven't the slightest idea what you're talking about.

MRS. LINDE   Don't play games with me, Nora. Don't you think I know who you borrowed the twelve hundred dollars from?

NORA   Are you out of your mind! The very idea—! A friend of both of us who sees us every day—! What a dreadfully uncomfortable position that would be!

MRS. LINDE   So it really isn't Dr. Rank?

NORA   Most certainly not! I would never have dreamed of asking him—not for a moment. Anyway, he didn't have any money then. He inherited it afterwards.

MRS. LINDE   Well, I still think it may have been lucky for you, Nora dear.

NORA   The idea! It would never have occurred to me to ask Dr. Rank—. Though I'm sure that if I *did* ask him—

MRS. LINDE   But of course you wouldn't.

NORA   Of course not. I can't imagine that that would ever be necessary. But I am quite sure that if I told Dr. Rank—

MRS. LINDE   Behind your husband's back?

NORA   I must get out of—this other thing. That's also behind his back. I *must* get out of it.

MRS. LINDE   That's what I told you yesterday. But—

NORA   (*walking up and down*)   A man manages these things so much better than a woman—

MRS. LINDE   One's husband, yes.

NORA   Silly, silly! (*Stops.*) When you've paid off all you owe, you get your I.O.U. back; right?

MRS. LINDE   Yes, of course.

NORA   And you can tear it into a hundred thousand little pieces and burn it—that dirty, filthy, paper!

MRS. LINDE   (*looks hard at her, puts down her sewing, rises slowly*) Nora—you're hiding something from me.

NORA   Can you tell?

MRS. LINDE   Something's happened to you, Nora, since yesterday morning. What is it?

NORA   (*going to her*)   Kristine! (*Listens.*) Shhh. Torvald just came back. Listen. Why don't you go in to the children for a while. Torvald can't stand having sewing around. Get Anne-Marie to help you.

MRS. LINDE   (*gathers some of the sewing things together*)   All right, but I'm not leaving here till you and I have talked.

(*She goes out left, as* HELMER *enters from the front hall.*)

NORA   (*towards him*)   I have been waiting and waiting for you, Torvald.

HELMER   Was that the dressmaker?

NORA   No, it was Kristine. She's helping me with my costume. Oh Torvald, just wait till you see how nice I'll look!

HELMER   I told you. Pretty good idea I had, wasn't it?

NORA   Lovely! And wasn't it nice of me to go along with it?

HELMER   (*his hands under her chin*)   Nice? To do what your husband tells you? All right, you little rascal; I know you didn't mean it that way. But don't let me interrupt you. I suppose you want to try it on.

NORA   And you'll be working?

HELMER   Yes. (*Shows her a pile of papers.*) Look. I've been down to the bank. (*Is about to enter his study.*)

NORA   Torvald.

HELMER   (*halts*)   Yes?

NORA   What if your little squirrel asked you ever so nicely—

HELMER   For what?

NORA   Would you do it?

HELMER   Depends on what it is.

NORA   Squirrel would run around and do all sorts of fun tricks if you'd be nice and agreeable.

HELMER   All right. What is it?

NORA   Lark would chirp and twitter in all the rooms, up and down—

HELMER   So what? Lark does that anyway.

NORA   I'll be your elfmaid and dance for you in the moonlight, Torvald.

HELMER   Nora, don't tell me it's the same thing you mentioned this morning?

NORA   (*closer to him*)   Yes, Torvald. I beg you!

HELMER   You really have the nerve to bring that up again?

NORA   Yes. You've just got to do as I say. You *must* let Krogstad keep his job.

HELMER   My dear Nora. It's his job I intend to give to Mrs. Linde.

NORA   I know. And that's ever so nice of you. But can't you just fire somebody else?

HELMER   This is incredible! You just don't give up do you? Because you make some foolish promise, *I* am supposed to—!

NORA   That's not the reason, Torvald. It's for your own sake. That man writes for the worst newspapers. You've said so yourself. There's no telling what he may do to you. I'm scared to death of him.

HELMER   Ah, I understand. You're afraid because of what happened before.

NORA   What do you mean?

HELMER   You're thinking of your father, of course.

NORA Yes. Yes, you're right. Remember the awful things they wrote about Daddy in the newspapers. I really think they might have forced him to resign if the ministry hadn't sent you to look into the charges and if you hadn't been so helpful and understanding.

HELMER My dear little Nora, there is a world of difference between your father and me. Your father's official conduct was not above reproach. Mine is, and I intend for it to remain that way as long as I hold my position.

NORA Oh, but you don't know what vicious people like that may think of. Oh, Torvald! Now all of us could be so happy together here in our own home, peaceful and carefree. Such a good life, Torvald, for you and me and the children! That's why I implore you—

HELMER And it's exactly because you plead for him that you make it impossible for me to keep him. It's already common knowledge in the bank that I intend to let Krogstad go. If it gets out that the new manager has changed his mind because of his wife—

NORA Yes? What then?

HELMER No, of course, that wouldn't matter at all as long as little Mrs. Pighead here got her way! Do you want me to make myself look ridiculous before my whole staff—make people think I can be swayed by just anybody—by outsiders? Believe me, I would soon enough find out what the consequences would be! Besides, there's another thing that makes it absolutely impossible for Krogstad to stay on in the bank now that I'm in charge.

NORA What's that?

HELMER I suppose in a pinch I could overlook his moral shortcomings—

NORA Yes, you could; couldn't you, Torvald?

HELMER And I understand he's quite a good worker, too. But we've known each other for a long time. It's one of those imprudent relationships you get into when you're young that embarrass you for the rest of your life. I guess I might as well be frank with you: he and I are on a first name basis. And that tactless fellow never hides the fact even when other people are around. Rather, he seems to think it entitles him to be familiar with me. Every chance he gets he comes out with his damn "Torvald, Torvald." I'm telling you, I find it most awkward. He would make my position in the bank intolerable.

NORA You don't really mean any of this, Torvald.

HELMER Oh? I don't? And why not?

NORA No, for it's all so petty.

HELMER What! Petty? You think I'm being petty!

NORA   No, I *don't* think you are petty, Torvald dear. That's exactly why I—

HELMER   Never mind. You think my reasons are petty, so it follows that I must be petty too. Petty! Indeed! By God, I'll put an end to this right now! (*Opens the door to the front hall and calls out.*) Helene!

NORA   What are you doing?

HELMER   (*searching among his papers*)   Making a decision. (THE MAID *enters.*) Here. Take this letter. Go out with it right away. Find somebody to deliver it. But quick. The address is on the envelope. Wait. Here's money.

THE MAID   Very good sir. (*She takes the letter and goes out.*)

HELMER   (*collecting his papers*)   There now, little Mrs. Obstinate!

NORA   (*breathless*)   Torvald—what was that letter?

HELMER   Krogstad's dismissal.

NORA   Call it back, Torvald! There's still time! Oh Torvald, please —call it back! For my sake, for your own sake, for the sake of the children! Listen to me, Torvald! Do it! You don't know what you're doing to all of us!

HELMER   Too late.

NORA   Yes. Too late.

HELMER   Dear Nora, I forgive you this fear you're in, although it really is an insult to me. Yes, it is! It's an insult to think that I am scared of a shabby scrivener's revenge. But I forgive you, for it's such a beautiful proof how much you love me. (*Takes her in his arms.*) And that's the way it should be, my sweet darling. Whatever happens, you'll see that when things get really rough I have both strength and courage. You'll find out that I am man enough to shoulder the whole burden.

NORA   (*terrified*)   What do you mean by that?

HELMER   All of it, I tell you—

NORA   (*composed*)   You'll never have to do that.

HELMER   Good. Then we'll share the burden, Nora—like husband and wife, the way it ought to be. (*Caresses her.*) Now are you satisfied? There, there, there. Not that look in your eyes—like a frightened dove. It's all your own foolish imagination.—Why don't you practice the tarantella—and your tambourine, too. I'll be in the inner office and close both doors, so I won't hear you. You can make as much noise as you like. (*Turning in the doorway.*) And when Rank comes, tell him where to find me. (*He nods to her, enters his study carrying his papers, and closes the door.*)

NORA   (*transfixed by terror, whispers*)   He would do it. He'll do it. He'll do it in spite of the whole world.—No, this mustn't happen.

Anything rather than that! There must be a way—! (*The doorbell rings.*) Dr. Rank! Anything rather than that! Anything—
anything at all!

(*She passes her hand over her face, pulls herself together, and opens
the door to the hall. DR. RANK is out there, hanging up his coat. Darkness begins to fall during the following scene.*)

NORA Hello there, Dr. Rank. I recognized your ringing. Don't go
in to Torvald yet. I think he's busy.

RANK And you?

NORA (*as he enters and she closes the door behind him*) You
know I always have time for you.

RANK Thanks. I'll make use of that as long as I can.

NORA What do you mean by that—As long as you can?

RANK Does that frighten you?

NORA Well, it's a funny expression. As if something was going to
happen.

RANK Something is going to happen that I've long been expecting.
But I admit I hadn't thought it would come quite so soon.

NORA (*seizes his arm*) What is it you've found out? Dr. Rank—
tell me!

RANK (*sits down by the stove*) I'm going downhill fast. There's
nothing to do about that.

NORA (*with audible relief*) So it's you—

RANK Who else? No point in lying to myself. I'm in worse shape
than any of my other patients, Mrs. Helmer. These last few days
I've been making up my inner status. Bankrupt. Chances are that
within a month I'll be rotting up in the cemetery.

NORA Shame on you! Talking that horrid way!

RANK The thing itself is horrid—damn horrid. The worst of it,
though, is all that other horror that comes first. There is only
one more test I need to make. After that I'll have a pretty good
idea when I'll start coming apart. There is something I want to
say to you. Helmer's refined nature can't stand anything hideous.
I don't want him in my sick room.

NORA Oh, but Dr. Rank—

RANK I don't want him there. Under no circumstances. I'll close
my door to him. As soon as I have full certainty that the worst
is about to begin I'll give you my card with a black cross on it.
Then you'll know the last horror of destruction has started.

NORA Today you're really quite impossible. And I had hoped you'd
be in a particularly good mood.

RANK With death on my hands? Paying for someone else's sins?
Is there justice in that? And yet there isn't a single family that

isn't ruled by the same law of ruthless retribution, in one way or another.

NORA (*puts her hands over her ears*) Poppycock! Be fun! Be fun!

RANK Well, yes. You may just as well laugh at the whole thing. My poor, innocent spine is suffering from my father's frolics as a young lieutenant.

NORA (*over by the table, left*) Right. He was addicted to asparagus and goose liver paté, wasn't he?

RANK And truffles.

NORA Of course. Truffles. And oysters too, I think.

RANK And oysters. Obviously.

NORA And all the port and champagne that go with it. It's really too bad that goodies like that ruin your backbone.

RANK Particularly an unfortunate backbone that never enjoyed any of it.

NORA Ah yes, that's the saddest part of it all.

RANK (*looks searchingly at her*) Hm—

NORA (*after a brief pause*) Why did you smile just then?

RANK No, it was you that laughed.

NORA No, it was you that smiled, Dr. Rank!

RANK (*gets up*) You're more of a mischief-maker than I thought.

NORA I feel in the mood for mischief today.

RANK So it seems.

NORA (*with both her hands on his shoulders*) Dear, dear Dr. Rank, don't you go and die and leave Torvald and me.

RANK Oh, you won't miss me for very long. Those who go away are soon forgotten.

NORA (*with an anxious look*) Do you believe that?

RANK You'll make new friends, and then—

NORA Who'll make new friends?

RANK Both you and Helmer, once I'm gone. You yourself seem to have made a good start already. What was this Mrs. Linde doing here last night?

NORA Aha—Don't tell me you're jealous of poor Kristine?

RANK Yes, I am. She'll be my successor in this house. As soon as I have made my excuses, that woman is likely to—

NORA Shh—not so loud. She's in there.

RANK Today too? There you are!

NORA She's mending my costume. My God, you really *are* unreasonable. (*Sits down on the couch*). Now be nice, Dr. Rank. Tomorrow you'll see how beautifully I'll dance, and then you are to pretend I'm dancing just for you—and for Torvald too, of course. (*Takes several items out of the carton.*) Sit down, Dr. Rank; I want to show you something.

RANK (*sitting down*)   What?

NORA Look.

RANK Silk stockings.

NORA Flesh-colored. Aren't they lovely? Now it's getting dark in here, but tomorrow—No, no. You only get to see the foot. Oh well, you might as well see all of it.

RANK Hmm.

NORA Why do you look so critical? Don't you think they'll fit?

RANK That's something I can't possibly have a reasoned opinion about.

NORA (*looks at him for a moment*)   Shame on you. (*Slaps his ear lightly with the stocking.*) That's what you get. (*Puts the things back in the carton.*)

RANK And what other treasures are you going to show me?

NORA Nothing at all, because you're naughty. (*She hums a little and rummages in the carton.*)

RANK (*after a brief silence*)   When I sit here like this, talking confidently with you, I can't imagine—I can't possibly imagine what would have become of me if I hadn't had you and Helmer.

NORA (*smiles*)   Well, yes—I do believe you like being with us.

RANK (*in a lower voice, lost in thought*)   And then to have to go away from it all—

NORA Nonsense. You are not going anywhere.

RANK (*as before*)   —and not to leave behind as much as a poor little token of gratitude, hardly a brief memory of someone missed, nothing but a vacant place that anyone can fill.

NORA And what if I were to ask you—? No—

RANK Ask me what?

NORA For a great proof of your friendship—

RANK Yes, yes—?

NORA No, I mean— for an enormous favor—

RANK Would you really for once make me as happy as all that?

NORA But you don't even know what it is.

RANK Well, then; tell me.

NORA Oh, but I can't, Dr. Rank. It's altogether too much to ask— It's advice and help and a favor—

RANK So much the better. I can't even begin to guess what it is you have in mind. So for heaven's sake tell me! Don't you trust me?

NORA Yes, I trust you more than anyone else I know. You are my best and most faithful friend. I know that. So I will tell you. All right, Dr. Rank. There is something you can help me prevent. You know how much Torvald loves me—beyond all words. Never for a moment would he hesitate to give his life for me.

RANK (*leaning over to her*) Nora—do you really think he's the only one—?

NORA (*with a slight start*)   Who—?

RANK   —would gladly give his life for you.

NORA (*heavily*)   I see.

RANK   I have sworn an oath to myself to tell you before I go. I'll never find a better occasion.—All right, Nora; now you know. And now you also know that you can confide in me more than in anyone else.

NORA (*gets up; in a calm, steady voice*)   Let me get by.

RANK (*makes room for her but remains seated*)   Nora—

NORA (*in the door to the front hall*)   Helene, bring the lamp in here, please. (*Walks over to the stove.*) Oh, dear Dr. Rank. That really wasn't very nice of you.

RANK (*gets up*)   That I have loved you as much as anybody—was that not nice?

NORA   No; not that. But that you told me. There was no need for that.

RANK   What do you mean? Have you known—?

(THE MAID *enters with the lamp, puts it on the table, and goes out.*)

RANK   Nora—Mrs. Helmer—I'm asking you: did you know?

NORA   Oh, how can I tell what I knew and didn't know! I really can't say—But that you could be so awkward, Dr. Rank! Just when everything was so comfortable.

RANK   Well, anyway, now you know that I'm at your service with my life and soul. And now you must speak.

NORA (*looks at him*)   After what just happened?

RANK   I beg of you—let me know what it is.

NORA   There is nothing I can tell you now.

RANK   Yes, yes. You mustn't punish me this way. Please let me do for you whatever anyone *can* do.

NORA   Now there is nothing you can do. Besides, I don't think I really need any help, anyway. It's probably just my imagination. Of course that's all it is. I'm sure of it! (*Sits down in the rocking chair, looks at him, smiles.*) Well, well, well, Dr. Rank! What a fine gentleman you turned out to be! Aren't you ashamed of yourself, now that we have light?

RANK   No, not really. But perhaps I ought to leave—and not come back?

NORA   Don't be silly; of course not! You'll come here exactly as you have been doing. You know perfectly well that Torvald can't do without you.

RANK   Yes, but what about you?

NORA Oh, I always think it's perfectly delightful when you come.

RANK That's the very thing that misled me. You are a riddle to me. It has often seemed to me that you'd just as soon be with me as with Helmer.

NORA Well, you see, there are people you love, and then there are other people you'd almost rather be with.

RANK Yes, there is something in that.

NORA When I lived at home with Daddy, of course I loved him most. But I always thought it was so much fun to sneak off down to the maids' room, for they never gave me good advice and they always talked about such fun things.

RANK Aha! So it's *their* place I have taken.

NORA (*jumps up and goes over to him*) Oh dear, kind Dr. Rank, you know very well I didn't mean it that way. Can't you see that with Torvald it is the way it used to be with Daddy?

(THE MAID *enters from the front hall.*)

THE MAID Ma'am! (*Whispers to her and gives her a caller's card.*)

NORA (*glances at the card*) Ah! (*Puts it in her pocket*).

RANK Anything wrong?

NORA No, no; not at all. It's nothing—just my new costume—

RANK But your costume is lying right there!

NORA Oh yes, that one. But this is another one. I ordered it. Torvald mustn't know—

RANK Aha. So that's the great secret.

NORA That's it. Why don't you go in to him, please. He's in the inner office. And keep him there for a while—

RANK Don't worry. He won't get away. (*Enters* HELMER's *study.*)

NORA (*to* THE MAID) You say he's waiting in the kitchen?

THE MAID Yes. He came up the back stairs.

NORA But didn't you tell him there was somebody with me?

THE MAID Yes, but he wouldn't listen.

NORA He won't leave?

THE MAID No, not till he's had a word with you, ma'am.

NORA All right. But try not to make any noise. And, Helene— don't tell anyone he's here. It's supposed to be a surprise for my husband.

THE MAID I understand, ma'am—(*She leaves.*)

NORA The terrible is happening. It's happening, after all. No, no, no. It can't happen. It won't happen. (*She bolts the study door.*)

(THE MAID *opens the front hall door for* KROGSTAD *and closes the door behind him. He wears a fur coat for traveling, boots, and a fur hat.*)

NORA (*toward him*) Keep your voice down. My husband's home.

KROGSTAD That's all right.

NORA What do you want?

KROGSTAD To find out something.

NORA Be quick, then. What is it?

KROGSTAD I expect you know I've been fired.

NORA I couldn't prevent it, Mr. Krogstad. I fought for you as long and as hard as I could but it didn't do any good.

KROGSTAD Your husband doesn't love you any more than that? He knows what I can do to you, and yet he runs the risk—

NORA Surely you didn't think I'd tell him?

KROGSTAD No, I really didn't. It wouldn't be like Torvald Helmer to show that kind of guts—

NORA Mr. Krogstad, I insist that you show respect for my husband.

KROGSTAD By all means. All due respect. But since you're so anxious to keep this a secret, may I assume that you are a little better informed than yesterday about exactly what you have done?

NORA Better than *you* could ever teach me.

KROGSTAD Of course. Such a bad lawyer as I am—

NORA What do you want of me?

KROGSTAD I just wanted to find out how you are, Mrs. Helmer. I've been thinking about you all day. You see, even a bill collector, a pen pusher, a—anyway, someone like me—even he has a little of what they call a heart.

NORA Then show it. Think of my little children.

KROGSTAD Have you and your husband thought of mine? Never mind. All I want to tell you is that you don't need to take this business too seriously. I have no intention of bringing charges right away.

NORA Oh no, you wouldn't; would you? I knew you wouldn't.

KROGSTAD The whole thing can be settled quite amiably. Nobody else needs to know anything. It will be between the three of us.

NORA My husband must never find out about this.

KROGSTAD How are you going to prevent that? Maybe you can pay me the balance on the loan?

NORA No, not right now.

KROGSTAD Or do you have a way of raising the money one of these next few days?

NORA None I intend to make use of.

KROGSTAD It wouldn't do you any good, anyway. Even if you had the cash in your hand right this minute, I wouldn't give you your note back. It wouldn't make any difference *how* much money you offered me.

NORA Then you'll have to tell me what you plan to use the note *for*.

KROGSTAD   Just keep it; that's all. Have it on hand, so to speak. I won't say a word to anybody else. So if you've been thinking about doing something desperate—

NORA   I have.

KROGSTAD   —like leaving house and home—

NORA   I have!

KROGSTAD   —or even something worse—

NORA   How did you know?

KROGSTAD   —then: don't.

NORA   How did you know I was thinking of *that*?

KROGSTAD   Most of us do, right at first. I did, too, but when it came down to it I didn't have the courage—

NORA   (*tonelessly*)   Nor do I.

KROGSTAD   (*relieved*)   See what I mean? I thought so. You don't either.

NORA   I don't. I don't.

KROGSTAD   Besides, it would be very silly of you. Once that first domestic blowup is behind you—. Here in my pocket is a letter for your husband.

NORA   Telling him everything?

KROGSTAD   As delicately as possible.

NORA   (*quickly*)   He mustn't get that letter. Tear it up. I'll get you the money somehow.

KROGSTAD   Excuse me, Mrs. Helmer, I thought I just told you—

NORA   I'm not talking about the money I owe you. Just let me know how much money you want from my husband, and I'll get it for you.

KROGSTAD   I want no money from your husband.

NORA   Then, what *do* you want?

KROGSTAD   I'll tell you, Mrs. Helmer. I want to rehabilitate myself; I want to get up in the world; and your husband is going to help me. For a year and a half I haven't done anything disreputable. All that time I have been struggling with the most miserable circumstances. I was content to work my way up step by step. Now I've been kicked out, and I'm no longer satisfied just getting my old job back. I want more than that; I want to get to the top. I'm being quite serious. I want the bank to take me back but in a higher position. I want your husband to create a new job for me—

NORA   He'll never do that!

KROGSTAD   He will. I know him. He won't dare not to. And once I'm back inside and he and I are working together, you'll see! Within a year I'll be the manager's right hand. It will be Nils

Krogstad and not Torvald Helmer who'll be running the Mutual Bank!

NORA   You'll never see that happen!

KROGSTAD   Are you thinking of—?

NORA   Now I *do* have the courage.

KROGSTAD   You can't scare me. A fine, spoiled lady like you—

NORA   You'll see, you'll see!

KROGSTAD   Under the ice, perhaps? Down into that cold, black water? Then spring comes, and you float up again—hideous, can't be identified, hair all gone—

NORA   You don't frighten me.

KROGSTAD   Nor you me. One doesn't do that sort of thing, Mrs. Helmer. Besides, what good would it do? He'd still be in my power.

NORA   Afterwards? When I'm no longer—?

KROGSTAD   Aren't you forgetting that your reputation would be in my hands?

(NORA *stares at him, speechless.*)

KROGSTAD   All right; now I've told you what to expect. So don't do anything foolish. When Helmer gets my letter I expect to hear from him. And don't you forget that it's your husband himself who forces me to use such means again. That I'll never forgive him. Goodbye, Mrs. Helmer. (*Goes out through the hall.*)

NORA (*at the door, opens it a little, listens*)   He's going. And no letter. Of course not! That would be impossible. (*Opens the door more.*) What's he doing? He's still there. Doesn't go down. Having second thoughts—? Will he—?

(*The sound of a letter dropping into the mailbox. Then* KROGSTAD'S *steps are heard going down the stairs, gradually dying away.*)

NORA (*with a muted cry runs forward to the table by the couch; brief pause*)   In the mailbox. (*Tiptoes back to the door to the front hall.*) There it is. Torvald, Torvald—now we're lost!

MRS. LINDE (*enters from the left, carrying* NORA'*s Capri costume*)   There now. I think it's all fixed. Why don't we try it on you—

NORA (*in a low, hoarse voice*)   Kristine, come here.

MRS. LINDE   What's wrong with you? You look quite beside yourself.

NORA   Come over here. Do you see that letter? There, look—through the glass in the mailbox.

MRS. LINDE   Yes, yes; I see it.

NORA   That letter is from Krogstad.

MRS. LINDE   Nora—it was Krogstad who lent you the money!

NORA   Yes, and now Torvald will find out about it.

MRS. LINDE Oh believe me, Nora. That's the best thing for both of you.

NORA There's more to it than you know. I forged a signature—

MRS. LINDE Oh my God—!

NORA I just want to tell you this, Kristine, that you must be my witness.

MRS. LINDE Witness? How? Witness to what?

NORA If I lose my mind—and that could very well happen—

MRS. LINDE Nora!

NORA —or if something were to happen to me—something that made it impossible for me to be here—

MRS. LINDE Nora, Nora! You're not yourself!

NORA —and if someone were to take all the blame, assume the whole responsibility—Do you understand—?

MRS. LINDE Yes, yes; but how can you think—!

NORA Then you are to witness that that's not so, Kristine. I am not beside myself. I am perfectly rational, and what I'm telling you is that nobody else has known about this. I've done it all by myself, the whole thing. Just remember that.

MRS. LINDE I will. But I don't understand any of it.

NORA Oh, how could you! For it's the wonderful that's about to happen.

MRS. LINDE The wonderful?

NORA Yes, the wonderful. But it's so terrible, Kristine. It mustn't happen for anything in the whole world!

MRS. LINDE I'm going over to talk to Krogstad right now.

NORA No, don't. Don't go to him. He'll do something bad to you.

MRS. LINDE There was a time when he would have done anything for me.

NORA He!

MRS. LINDE Where does he live?

NORA Oh, I don't know—Yes, wait a minute—(*Reaches into her pocket.*) here's his card.—But the letter, the letter—!

HELMER (*in his study, knocks on the door*) Nora!

NORA (*cries out in fear*) Oh, what is it? What do you want?

HELMER That's all right. Nothing to be scared about. We're not coming in. For one thing, you've bolted the door, you know. Are you modeling your costume?

NORA Yes, yes; I am. I'm going to be so pretty, Torvald.

MRS. LINDE (*having looked at the card*) He lives just around the corner.

NORA Yes, but it's no use. Nothing can save us now. The letter is in the mailbox.

MRS. LINDE And your husband has the key?

NORA   Yes. He always keeps it with him.

MRS. LINDE   Krogstad must ask for his letter back, unread. He's got to think up some pretext or other—

NORA   But this is just the time of day when Torvald—

MRS. LINDE   Delay him. Go in to him. I'll be back as soon as I can. (*She hurries out through the hall door.*)

NORA   (*walks over to* HELMER's *door, opens it, and peeks in*)   Torvald.

HELMER   (*still offstage*)   Well, well! So now one's allowed in one's own living room again. Come on, Rank. Now we'll see—(*In the doorway.*) But what's this?

NORA   What, Torvald dear?

HELMER   Rank prepared me for a splendid metamorphosis.

RANK   (*in the doorway*)   That's how I understood it. Evidently I was mistaken.

NORA   Nobody gets to admire me in my costume before tomorrow.

HELMER   But, dearest Nora—you look all done in. Have you been practicing too hard?

NORA   No, I haven't practiced at all.

HELMER   But you'll have to, you know.

NORA   I know it, Torvald. I simply must. But I can't do a thing unless you help me. I have forgotten everything.

HELMER   Oh it will all come back. We'll work on it.

NORA   Oh yes, please, Torvald. You just have to help me. Promise? I am so nervous. That big party—. You mustn't do anything else tonight. Not a bit of business. Don't even touch a pen. Will you promise, Torvald?

HELMER   I promise. Tonight I'll be entirely at your service—you helpless little thing.—Just a moment, though. First I want to— (*Goes to the door to the front hall.*)

NORA   What are you doing out there?

HELMER   Just looking to see if there's any mail.

NORA   No, no! Don't, Torvald!

HELMER   Why not?

NORA   Torvald, I beg you. There is no mail.

HELMER   Let me just look, anyway. (*Is about to go out.*)

(NORA *by the piano, plays the first bars of the tarantella dance.*)

HELMER   (*halts at the door*)   Aha!

NORA   I won't be able to dance tomorrow if I don't get to practice with you.

HELMER   (*goes to her*)   Are you really all that scared, Nora dear?

NORA   Yes, so terribly scared. Let's try it right now. There's still time before we eat. Oh please, sit down and play for me, Torvald. Teach me, coach me, the way you always do.

HELMER   Of course I will, my darling, if that's what you want. (*Sits down at the piano.*)

(NORA *takes the tambourine out of the carton, as well as a long, many-colored shawl. She quickly drapes the shawl around herself, then leaps into the middle of the floor.*)

NORA   Play for me! I want to dance!

(HELMER *plays and* NORA *dances.* DR. RANK *stands by the piano behind* HELMER *and watches.*)

HELMER (*playing*)   Slow down, slow down!
NORA   Can't!
HELMER   Not so violent, Nora!
NORA   It has to be this way.
HELMER (*stops playing*)   No, no. This won't do at all.
NORA (*laughing, swinging her tambourine*)   What did I tell you?
RANK   Why don't you let me play?
HELMER (*getting up*)   Good idea. Then I can direct her better.

(RANK *sits down at the piano and starts playing.* NORA *dances more and more wildly.* HELMER *stands over by the stove, repeatedly correcting her. She doesn't seem to hear. Her hair comes loose and falls down over her shoulders. She doesn't notice but keeps on dancing.* MRS. LINDE *enters.*)

MRS. LINDE (*stops by the door, dumbfounded*)   Ah—!
NORA (*dancing*)   We're having such fun, Kristine!
HELMER   My dearest Nora, you're dancing as if it were a matter of life and death!
NORA   It is! It is!
HELMER   Rank, stop. This is sheer madness. Stop, I say!

(RANK *stops playing;* NORA *suddenly stops dancing.*)

HELMER (*goes over to her*)   If I hadn't seen it I wouldn't have believed it. You've forgotten every single thing I ever taught you.
NORA (*tosses away the tambourine*)   See? I told you.
HELMER   Well! You certainly need coaching.
NORA   Didn't I tell you I did? Now you've seen for yourself. I'll need your help till the very minute we're leaving for the party. Will you promise, Torvald?
HELMER   You can count on it.
NORA   You're not to think of anything except me—not tonight and

not tomorrow. You're not to read any letters—not to look in the mailbox—

HELMER   Ah, I see. You're still afraid of that man.

NORA   Yes—yes, that too.

HELMER   Nora, I can tell from looking at you. There's a letter from him out there.

NORA   I don't know. I think so. But you're not to read it now. I don't want anything ugly to come between us before it's all over.

RANK   (*to* HELMER *in a low voice*)   Better not argue with her.

HELMER   (*throws his arm around her*)   The child shall have her way. But tomorrow night, when you've done your dance—

NORA   Then you'll be free.

THE MAID   (*in the door, right*)   Dinner can be served any time, ma'am.

NORA   We want champagne, Helene.

THE MAID   Very good, ma'am. (*Goes out.*)

HELMER   Aha! Having a party, eh?

NORA   Champagne from now till sunrise! (*Calls out.*) And some macaroons, Helene. Lots!—just this once.

HELMER   (*taking her hands*)   There, there—I don't like this wild—frenzy—Be my own sweet little lark again, the way you always are.

NORA   Oh, I will. But you go on in. You too, Dr. Rank. Kristine, please help me put up my hair.

RANK   (*in a low voice to* HELMER *as they go out*)   You don't think she is—you know—expecting—?

HELMER   Oh no. Nothing like that. It's just this childish fear I was telling you about. (*They go out, right.*)

NORA   Well?

MRS. LINDE   Left town.

NORA   I saw it in your face.

MRS. LINDE   He'll be back tomorrow night. I left him a note.

NORA   You shouldn't have. I don't want you to try to stop anything. You see, it's a kind of ecstasy, too, this waiting for the wonderful.

MRS. LINDE   But what is it you're waiting *for*?

NORA   You wouldn't understand. Why don't you go in to the others. I'll be there in a minute.

(MRS. LINDE *enters the dining room, right.*)

NORA   (*stands still for a little while, as if collecting herself; she looks at her watch*)   Five o'clock. Seven hours till midnight. Twenty-four more hours till next midnight. Then the tarantella is over. Twenty-four plus seven—thirty-one more hours to live.

HELMER   (*in the door, right*)   What's happening to my little lark?

NORA   (*to him, with open arms*)   Here's your lark!

ACT III

The same room. The table by the couch and the chairs around it have been moved to the middle of the floor. A lighted lamp is on the table. The door to the front hall is open. Dance music is heard from upstairs.

   MRS. LINDE *is seated by the table, idly leafing through the pages of a book. She tries to read but seems unable to concentrate. Once or twice she turns her head in the direction of the door, anxiously listening.*)

MRS. LINDE *(looks at her watch)*   Not yet. It's almost too late. If only he hasn't—*(Listens again.)* Ah! There he is. *(She goes to the hall and opens the front door carefully. Quiet footsteps on the stairs. She whispers.)*   Come in. There's nobody here.

KROGSTAD *(in the door)*   I found your note when I got home. What's this all about?

MRS. LINDE I've got to talk to you.

KROGSTAD Oh? And it has to be here?

MRS. LINDE It couldn't be at my place. My room doesn't have a separate entrance. Come in. We're quite alone. The maid is asleep and the Helmers are at a party upstairs.

KROGSTAD *(entering)*   Really? The Helmers are dancing tonight, are they?

MRS. LINDE And why not?

KROGSTAD You're right. Why not, indeed.

MRS. LINDE All right, Krogstad. Let's talk, you and I.

KROGSTAD I didn't know we had anything to talk about.

MRS. LINDE We have much to talk about.

KROGSTAD I didn't think so.

MRS. LINDE No, because you've never really understood me.

KROGSTAD What was there to understand? What happened was perfectly commonplace. A heartless woman jilts a man when she gets a more attractive offer.

MRS. LINDE Do you think I'm all that heartless? And do you think it was easy for me to break with you?

KROGSTAD No?

MRS. LINDE You really thought it was?

KROGSTAD If it wasn't, why did you write the way you did that time?

MRS. LINDE What else could I do? If I had to make a break, I also had the duty to destroy whatever feelings you had for me.

KROGSTAD *(clenching his hands)*   So that's the way it was. And you did—*that*—just for money!

MRS. LINDE Don't forget I had a helpless mother and two small brothers. We couldn't wait for you, Krogstad. You know yourself how uncertain your prospects were then.

KROGSTAD   All right. But you still didn't have the right to throw me over for somebody else.

MRS. LINDE   I don't know. I have asked myself that question many times. Did I have that right?

KROGSTAD (*in a lower voice*)   When I lost you I lost my footing. Look at me now. A shipwrecked man on a raft.

MRS. LINDE   Rescue may be near.

KROGSTAD   It *was* near. Then you came between.

MRS. LINDE   I didn't know that, Krogstad. Only today did I find out it's your job I'm taking over in the bank.

KROGSTAD   I believe you when you say so. But now that you *do* know, aren't you going to step aside?

MRS. LINDE   No, for it wouldn't do you any good.

KROGSTAD   Whether it would or not—*I* would do it.

MRS. LINDE   I have learned common sense. Life and hard necessity have taught me that.

KROGSTAD   And life has taught me not to believe in pretty speeches.

MRS. LINDE   Then life has taught you a very sensible thing. But you do believe in actions, don't you?

KROGSTAD   How do you mean?

MRS. LINDE   You referred to yourself just now as a shipwrecked man.

KROGSTAD   It seems to me I had every reason to do so.

MRS. LINDE   And I am a shipwrecked woman. No one to grieve for, no one to care for.

KROGSTAD   You made your choice.

MRS. LINDE   I had no other choice that time.

KROGSTAD   Let's say you didn't. What then?

MRS. LINDE   Krogstad, how would it be if we two shipwrecked people got together?

KROGSTAD   What's this!

MRS. LINDE   Two on one wreck are better off than each on his own.

KROGSTAD   Kristine!

MRS. LINDE   Why do you think I came to town?

KROGSTAD   Surely not because of me?

MRS. LINDE   If I'm going to live at all I must work. All my life, for as long as I can remember, I have worked. That's been my one and only pleasure. But now that I'm all alone in the world I feel nothing but this terrible emptiness and desolation. There is no joy in working just for yourself. Krogstad—give me someone and something to work for.

KROGSTAD   I don't believe this. Only hysterical females go in for that kind of high-minded self-sacrifice.

MRS. LINDE   Did you ever know me to be hysterical?

KROGSTAD   You really could do this? Listen—do you know about my past? All of it?

MRS. LINDE   Yes, I do.

KROGSTAD   Do you also know what people think of me around here?

MRS. LINDE   A little while ago you sounded as if you thought that together with me you might have become a different person.

KROGSTAD   I'm sure of it.

MRS. LINDE   Couldn't that still be?

KROGSTAD   Kristine—do you know what you are doing? Yes, I see you do. And you think you have the courage—?

MRS. LINDE   I need someone to be a mother to, and your children need a mother. You and I need one another. Nils, I believe in you—in the real you. Together with you I dare to do anything.

KROGSTAD   (*seizes her hands*)   Thanks, thanks, Kristine—Now I know I'll raise myself in the eyes of others—Ah, but I forget—!

MRS. LINDE   (*listening*)   Shh!—there's the tarantella. You must go; hurry!

KROGSTAD   Why? What is it?

MRS. LINDE   Do you hear what they're playing up there? When that dance is over they'll be down.

KROGSTAD   All right. I'm leaving. The whole thing is pointless, any-way. Of course you don't know what I'm doing to the Helmers.

MRS. LINDE   Yes, Krogstad; I do know.

KROGSTAD   Still, you're brave enough—?

MRS. LINDE   I very well understand to what extremes despair can drive a man like you.

KROGSTAD   If only it could be undone!

MRS. LINDE   It could, for your letter is still out there in the mailbox.

KROGSTAD   Are you sure?

MRS. LINDE   Quite sure. But—

KROGSTAD   (*looks searchingly at her*)   Maybe I'm beginning to un-derstand. You want to save your friend at any cost. Be honest with me. That's it, isn't it?

MRS. LINDE   Krogstad, you may sell yourself once for somebody else's sake, but you don't do it twice.

KROGSTAD   I'll demand my letter back.

MRS. LINDE   No, no.

KROGSTAD   Yes, of course. I'll wait here till Helmer comes down. Then I'll ask him for my letter. I'll tell him it's just about my dismissal—that he shouldn't read it.

MRS. LINDE   No, Krogstad. You are not to ask for that letter back.

KROGSTAD   But tell me—wasn't that the real reason you wanted to meet me here?

MRS. LINDE   At first it was, because I was so frightened. But that was yesterday. Since then I have seen the most incredible things going on in this house. Helmer must learn the whole truth. This miserable secret must come out in the open; those two must come to a full understanding. They simply can't continue with all this concealment and evasion.

KROGSTAD   All right; if you want to take that chance. But there is one thing I *can* do, and I'll do that right now.

MRS. LINDE   (*listening*)   But hurry! Go! The dance is over. We aren't safe another minute.

KROGSTAD   I'll be waiting for you downstairs.

MRS. LINDE   Yes, do. You must see me home.

KROGSTAD   I've never been so happy in my whole life. (*He leaves through the front door. The door between the living room and the front hall remains open.*)

MRS. LINDE   (*straightens up the room a little and gets her things ready*)   What a change! Oh yes!—what a change! People to work for—to live for—a home to bring happiness to. I can't wait to get to work—! If only they'd come soon—(*Listens.*) Ah, there they are. Get my coat on—(*Puts on her coat and hat.*)

(HELMER's and NORA's voices are heard outside. A key is turned in the lock, and HELMER almost forces NORA into the hall. She is dressed in her Italian costume, with a big black shawl over her shoulders. He is in evening dress under an open black cloak.)

NORA   (*in the door, still resisting*)   No, no, no! I don't want to! I want to go back upstairs. I don't want to leave so early.

HELMER   But dearest Nora—

NORA   Oh please, Torvald—please! I'm asking you as nicely as I can—just another hour!

HELMER   Not another minute, sweet. You know we agreed. There now. Get inside. You'll catch a cold out here. (*She still resists, but he guides her gently into the room.*)

MRS. LINDE   Good evening.

NORA   Kristine!

HELMER   Ah, Mrs. Linde. Still here?

MRS. LINDE   I know. I really should apologize, but I so much wanted to see Nora in her costume.

NORA   You've been waiting up for me?

MRS. LINDE   Yes, unfortunately I didn't get here in time. You were already upstairs, but I just didn't feel like leaving till I had seen you.

HELMER   (*removing NORA's shawl*)   Yes, do take a good look at her, Mrs. Linde. I think I may say she's worth looking at. Isn't she lovely?

MRS. LINDE   She certainly is—

HELMER   Isn't she a miracle of loveliness, though? That was the general opinion at the party, too. But dreadfully obstinate—that she is, the sweet little thing. What can we do about that? Will you believe it—I practically had to use force to get her away.

NORA   Oh Torvald, you're going to be sorry you didn't give me even half an hour more.

HELMER   See what I mean, Mrs. Linde? She dances the tarantella —she is a tremendous success—quite deservedly so, though perhaps her performance was a little too natural—I mean, more than could be reconciled with the rules of art. But all right! The point is: she's a success, a tremendous success. So should I let her stay after that? Weaken the effect? Of course not. So I take my lovely little Capri girl—I might say, my capricious little Capri girl— under my arm—a quick turn around the room—a graceful bow in all directions, and—as they say in the novels—the beautiful apparition is gone. A finale should always be done for effect, Mrs. Linde, but there doesn't seem to be any way of getting that into Nora's head. Poooh—! It's hot in here. (*Throws his cloak down on a chair and opens the door to his room.*) Why, it's dark in here! Of course. Excuse me—(*Goes inside and lights a couple of candles.*)

NORA   (*in a hurried, breathless whisper*)   Well?

MRS. LINDE   (*in a low voice*)   I have talked to him.

NORA   And—?

MRS. LINDE   Nora—you've got to tell your husband everything.

NORA   (*no expression in her voice*)   I knew it.

MRS. LINDE   You have nothing to fear from Krogstad. But you must speak.

NORA   I'll say nothing.

MRS. LINDE   Then the letter will.

NORA   Thank you, Kristine. Now I know what I have to do. Shh!

HELMER   (*returning*)   Well, Mrs. Linde, have you looked your fill?

MRS. LINDE   Yes. And now I'll say goodnight.

HELMER   So soon? Is that your knitting?

MRS. LINDE   (*takes it*)   Yes, thank you. I almost forgot.

HELMER   So you knit, do you?

MRS. LINDE   Oh yes.

HELMER   You know—you ought to take up embroidery instead.

MRS. LINDE   Oh? Why?

HELMER   Because it's so much more beautiful. Look. You hold the embroidery so—in your left hand. Then with your right you move the needle—like this—in an easy, elongated arc—you see?

MRS. LINDE   Maybe you're right—

HELMER   Knitting, on the other hand, can never be anything but ugly. Look here: arms pressed close to the sides—the needles going up and down—there's something Chinese about it somehow—. That really was an excellent champagne they served us tonight.

MRS. LINDE   Well, goodnight! Nora. And don't be obstinate any more.

HELMER   Well said, Mrs. Linde!

MRS. LINDE   Goodnight, sir.

HELMER   (*sees her to the front door*)   Goodnight, goodnight. I hope you'll get home all right? I'd be very glad to—but of course you don't have far to walk, do you? Goodnight, goodnight. (*She leaves. He closes the door behind her and returns to the living room.*) There! At last we got rid of her. She really is an incredible bore, that woman.

NORA   Aren't you very tired, Torvald?

HELMER   No, not in the least.

NORA   Not sleepy either?

HELMER   Not at all. Quite the opposite. I feel enormously—animated. How about you? Yes, you do look tired and sleepy.

NORA   Yes, I am very tired. Soon I'll be asleep.

HELMER   What did I tell you? I was right, wasn't I? Good thing I didn't let you stay any longer.

NORA   Everything you do is right.

HELMER   (*kissing her forehead*)   Now my little lark is talking like a human being. But did you notice what splended spirits Rank was in tonight?

NORA   Was he? I didn't notice. I didn't get to talk with him.

HELMER   Nor did I—hardly. But I haven't seen him in such a good mood for a long time. (*Looks at her, comes closer to her.*) Ah! It does feel good to be back in our own home again, to be quite alone with you—my young, lovely, ravishing woman!

NORA   Don't look at me like that, Torvald!

HELMER   Am I not to look at my most precious possession? All that loveliness that is mine, nobody's but mine, all of it mine.

NORA   (*walks to the other side of the table*)   I won't have you talk to me like that tonight.

HELMER   (*follows her*)   The Tarantella is still in your blood. I can tell. That only makes you all the more alluring. Listen! The guests are beginning to leave. (*Softly.*) Nora—soon the whole house will be quiet.

NORA   Yes, I hope so.

HELMER   Yes, don't you, my darling? Do you know—when I'm at a party with you, like tonight—do you know why I hardly ever talk to you, why I keep away from you, only look at you once in a while—a few stolen glances—do you know why I do that? It's because I pretend that you are my secret love, my young, secret bride-to-be, and nobody has the slightest suspicion that there is anything between us.

NORA   Yes, I know. All your thoughts are with me.

HELMER   Then when we're leaving and I lay your shawl around your delicate young shoulders—around that wonderful curve of your neck—then I imagine you're my young bride, that we're coming away from the wedding, that I am taking you to my home for the first time—that I am alone with you for the first time— quite alone with you, you young, trembling beauty! I have desired you all evening—there hasn't been a longing in me that hasn't been for you. When you were dancing the tarantella, chasing, inviting—my blood was on fire; I couldn't stand it any longer— that's why I brought you down so early—

NORA   Leave me now, Torvald. Please! I don't want all this.

HELMER   What do you mean? You're only playing your little teasing bird game with me; aren't you, Nora? Don't want to? I'm your husband, aren't I?

(There is a knock on the front door.)

NORA *(with a start)*   Did you hear that—?

HELMER *(on his way to the hall)*   Who is it?

RANK *(outside)*   It's me. May I come in for a moment?

HELMER *(in a low voice, annoyed)*   Oh, what does he want now? *(Aloud.)* Just a minute. *(Opens the door.)* Well! How good of you not to pass by our door.

RANK   I thought I heard your voice, so I felt like saying hello. *(Looks around.)* Ah yes—this dear, familiar room. What a cozy, comfortable place you have here, you two.

HELMER   Looked to me as if you were quite comfortable upstairs too.

RANK   I certainly was. Why not? Why not enjoy all you can in this world? As much as you can for as long as you can, anyway. Excellent wine.

HELMER   The champagne, particularly.

RANK   You noticed that too? Incredible how much I managed to put away.

NORA   Torvald drank a lot of champagne tonight, too.

RANK   Did he?

NORA   Yes, he did, and then he's always so much fun afterwards.

RANK   Well, why not have some fun in the evening after a well spent day?

HELMER   Well spent? I'm afraid I can't claim that.

RANK (*slapping him lightly on the shoulder*)   But you see, I can!

NORA   Dr. Rank, I believe you must have been conducting a scientific test today.

RANK   Exactly.

HELMER   What do you know—little Nora talking about scientific tests!

NORA   May I congratulate you on the result?

RANK   You may indeed.

NORA   It was a good one?

RANK   The best possible for both doctor and patient—certainty.

NORA (*a quick query*)   Certainty?

RANK   Absolute certainty. So why shouldn't I have myself an enjoyable evening afterwards?

NORA   I quite agree with you, Dr. Rank. You should.

HELMER   And so do I. If only you don't pay for it tomorrow.

RANK   Oh well—you get nothing for nothing in this world.

NORA   Dr. Rank—you are fond of costume parties, aren't you?

RANK   Yes, particularly when there is a reasonable number of amusing disguises.

NORA   Listen—what are the two of us going to be the next time?

HELMER   You frivolous little thing! Already thinking about the next party!

RANK   You and I? That's easy. You'll be Fortune's Child.

HELMER   Yes, but what is a fitting costume for that?

RANK   Let your wife appear just the way she always is.

HELMER   Beautiful. Very good indeed. But how about yourself? Don't you know what you'll go as?

RANK   Yes, my friend. I know precisely what I'll be.

HELMER   Yes?

RANK   At the next masquerade I'll be invisible.

HELMER   That's a funny idea.

RANK   There's a certain black hat—you've heard about the hat that makes you invisible, haven't you? You put that on, and nobody can see you.

HELMER (*suppressing a smile*)   I guess that's right.

RANK   But I'm forgetting what I came for. Helmer, give me a cigar —one of your dark Havanas.

HELMER   With the greatest pleasure. (*Offers him his case.*)

RANK (*takes one and cuts off the tip*)   Thanks.

NORA (*striking a match*)   Let me give you a light.

RANK   Thanks. (*She holds the match; he lights his cigar.*) And now goodbye!

HELMER   Goodbye, goodbye, my friend.

NORA   Sleep well, Dr. Rank.

RANK   I thank you.

NORA   Wish me the same.

RANK   You? Well, if you really want me to—. Sleep well. And thanks for the light. (*He nods to both of them and goes out.*)

HELMER   (*in a low voice*)   He had had quite a bit to drink.

NORA   (*absently*)   Maybe so.

(HELMER *takes out his keys and goes out into the hall.*)

NORA   Torvald—what are you doing out there?

HELMER   Emptying the mailbox. It is quite full. There wouldn't be room for the newspapers in the morning—

NORA   Are you going to work tonight?

HELMER   You know very well I won't.—Say! What's this? Some-body's been at the lock.

NORA   The lock—?

HELMER   Yes. Why, I wonder. I hate to think that any of the maids—. Here's a broken hairpin. It's one of yours. Nora.

NORA   (*quickly*)   Then it must be one of the children.

HELMER   You better make damn sure they stop that. Hm, hm.—There! I got it open, finally. (*Gathers up the mail, calls out to the kitchen.*) Helene?—Oh Helene—turn out the light here in the hall, will you? (*He comes back into the living room and closes the door.*) Look how it's been piling up. (*Shows her the bundle of letters. Starts leafing through it.*) What's this?

NORA   (*by the window*)   The letter! Oh no, no, Torvald!

HELMER   Two calling cards—from Rank.

NORA   From Dr. Rank?

HELMER   (*looking at them*)   "Doctor medicinae Rank." They were on top. He must have put them there when he left just now.

NORA   Anything written on them?

HELMER   A black cross above the name. What a macabre idea. Like announcing his own death.

NORA   That's what it is.

HELMER   Hm? You know about this? Has he said anything to you?

NORA   That card means he has said goodbye to us. He'll lock him-self up to die.

HELMER   My poor friend. I knew of course he wouldn't be with me very long. But so soon—. And hiding himself away like a wounded animal—

NORA   When it has to be, it's better it happens without words. Don't you think so, Torvald?

HELMER   (*walking up and down*)   He'd grown so close to us. I find it hard to think of him as gone. With his suffering and lone-liness he was like a clouded background for our happy sunshine.

Well, it may be better this way. For him, at any rate. (*Stops.*)
And perhaps for us, too, Nora. For now we have nobody but each
other. (*Embraces her.*) Oh you—my beloved wife! I feel I just
can't hold you close enough. Do you know, Nora—many times I
have wished some great danger threatened you, so I could risk
my life and blood and everything—everything, for your sake.

NORA (*frees herself and says in a strong and firm voice*)   I think
you should go and read your letters now, Torvald.

HELMER   No, no—not tonight. I want to be with you, my darling.

NORA   With the thought of your dying friend—?

HELMER   You are right. This has shaken both of us. Something
not beautiful has come between us. Thoughts of death and dissolution. We must try to get over it—out of it. Till then—we'll
each go to our own room.

NORA (*her arms around his neck*)   Torvald—goodnight! Goodnight!

HELMER (*kisses her forehead*)   Goodnight, my little songbird.
Sleep well, Nora. Now I'll read my letters. (*He goes into his
room, carrying the mail. Closes the door.*)

NORA (*her eyes desperate, her hands groping, finds Helmer's black
cloak and throws it around her; she whispers, quickly, brokenly,
hoarsely*)   Never see him again. Never. Never. Never. (*Puts her
shawl over her head.*) And never see the children again, either.
Never; never.—The black, icy water—fathomless—this—! If only
it was all over.—Now he has it. Now he's reading it. No, no;
not yet. Torvald—goodbye—you—the children—

(*She is about to hurry through the hall, when* HELMER *flings open the
door to his room and stands there with an open letter in his hand.*)

HELMER   Nora!

NORA (*cries out*)   Ah—!

HELMER   What is it? You know what's in this letter?

NORA   Yes, I do! Let me go! Let me out!

HELMER (*holds her back*).   Where do you think you're going?

NORA (*trying to tear herself loose from him*)   I won't let you save
me, Torvald!

HELMER (*tumbles back*).   True! Is it true what he writes? Oh my
God! No, no—this can't possibly be true.

NORA   It is true. I have loved you more than anything else in the
whole world.

HELMER   Oh, don't give me any silly excuses.

NORA (*taking a step towards him*)   Torvald—!

HELMER   You wretch! What have you done!

NORA   Let me go. You are not to sacrifice yourself for me. You are not to take the blame.

HELMER   No more playacting. (*Locks the door to the front hall.*) You'll stay here and answer me. Do you understand what you have done? Answer me! Do you understand?

NORA   (*gazes steadily at him with an increasingly frozen expression*) Yes. Now I'm beginning to understand.

HELMER   (*walking up and down*)   What a dreadful awakening. All these years—all these eight years—she, my pride and my joy—a hypocrite, a liar—oh worse! worse!—a criminal! Oh, the bottomless ugliness in all this! Damn! Damn! Damn!

(NORA, *silent, keeps gazing at him.*)

HELMER   (*stops in front of her*)   I ought to have guessed that something like this would happen. I should have expected it. All your father's loose principles—Silence! You have inherited every one of your father's loose principles. No religion, no morals, no sense of duty—. Now I am being punished for my leniency with him. I did it for your sake, and this is how you pay me back.

NORA   Yes. This is how.

HELMER   You have ruined all my happiness. My whole future— that's what you have destroyed. Oh, it's terrible to think about. I am at the mercy of an unscrupulous man. He can do with me whatever he likes, demand anything of me, command me and dispose of me just as he pleases—I dare not say a word! To go down so miserably, to be destroyed—all because of an irresponsible woman!

NORA   When I am gone from the world, you'll be free.

HELMER   No noble gestures, please. Your father was always full of such phrases too. What good would it do me if you were gone from the world, as you put it? Not the slightest good at all. He could still make the whole thing public, and if he did, people would be likely to think I had been your accomplice. They might even think it was my idea—that it was I who urged you to do it! And for all this I have you to thank—you, whom I've borne on my hands through all the years of our marriage. *Now* do you understand what you've done to me?

NORA   (*with cold calm*)   Yes.

HELMER   I just can't get it into my head that this is happening; it's all so incredible. But we have to come to terms with it somehow. Take your shawl off. Take it off, I say! I have to satisfy him one way or another. The whole affair must be kept quiet at whatever cost.—And as far as you and I are concerned, nothing must seem to have changed. I'm talking about appearances, of course. You'll go on living here; that goes without saying. But I won't let you bring up the children; I dare not trust you with them. —Oh! Having to say this to one I have loved so much, and whom I still—! But all that is past. It's not a question of happiness any more but of hanging on to what can be salvaged—pieces, appearances—(*The doorbell rings.*)

HELMER (*jumps*) What's that? So late. Is the worst—? Has he—! Hide, Nora! Say you're sick.

NORA *doesn't move.* HELMER *opens the door to the hall.*

THE MAID (*half dressed, out in the hall*) A letter for your wife, sir.

HELMER Give it to me. (*Takes the letter and closes the door.*) Yes, it's from him. But I won't let you have it. I'll read it myself.

NORA Yes—you read it.

HELMER (*by the lamp*) I hardly dare. Perhaps we're lost, both you and I. No; I've got to know. (*Tears the letter open, glances through it, looks at an enclosure; a cry of joy.*) Nora!

(NORA *looks at him with a question in her eyes.*)

HELMER Nora!—No, I must read it again.—Yes, yes; it is so! I'm saved! Nora, I'm saved!

NORA And I?

HELMER You too, of course; we're both saved, both you and I. Look! He's returning your note. He writes that he's sorry, he regrets, a happy turn in his life—oh, it doesn't matter what he writes. We're saved, Nora! Nobody can do anything to you now. Oh Nora, Nora—. No, I want to get rid of this disgusting thing first. Let me see—(*Looks at the signature.*) No, I don't want to see it. I don't want it to be more than a bad dream, the whole thing. (*Tears up the note and both letters, throws the pieces in the stove, and watches them burn.*) There! Now it's gone.—He wrote that ever since Christmas Eve—. Good God, Nora, these must have been three terrible days for you.

NORA I have fought a hard fight these last three days.

HELMER And been in agony and seen no other way out than—. No, we won't think of all that ugliness. We'll just rejoice and tell ourselves it's over, it's all over! Oh, listen to me, Nora. You don't seem to understand. It's over. What *is* it? Why do you look like that—that frozen expression on your face? Oh my poor little Nora, don't you think I know what it is? You can't make yourself believe that I have forgiven you. But I have, Nora; I swear to you, I have forgiven you for everything. Of course I know that what you did was for love of me.

NORA   That is true.

HELMER   You have loved me the way a wife ought to love her husband. You just didn't have the wisdom to judge the means. But do you think I love you any less because you don't know how to act on your own? Of course not. Just lean on me. I'll advise you; I'll guide you. I wouldn't be a man if I didn't find you twice as attractive because of your womanly helplessness. You mustn't pay any attention to the hard words I said to you right at first. It was just that first shock when I thought everything was collapsing all around me. I have forgiven you, Nora. I swear to you—I really have forgiven you.

NORA   I thank you for your forgiveness. (*She goes out through the door, right.*)

HELMER   No, stay—(*Looks into the room she entered.*) What are you doing in there?

NORA (*within*)   Getting out of my costume.

HELMER (*by the open door*)   Good, good. Try to calm down and compose yourself, my poor little frightened songbird. Rest safely; I have broad wings to cover you with. (*Walks around near the door.*) What a nice and cozy home we have, Nora. Here's shelter for you. Here I'll keep you safe like a hunted dove I have rescued from the hawk's talons. Believe me: I'll know how to quiet your beating heart. It will happen by and by, Nora; you'll see. Why, tomorrow you'll look at all this in quite a different light. And soon everything will be just the way it was before. I won't need to keep reassuring you that I have forgiven you; you'll feel it yourself. Did you really think I could have abandoned you, or even reproached you? Oh, you don't know a real man's heart, Nora. There is something unspeakably sweet and satisfactory for a man to know deep in himself that he has forgiven his wife—forgiven her in all the fullness of his honest heart. You see, that way she becomes his very own all over again—in a double sense, you might say. He has, so to speak, given her a second birth; it is as if she had become his wife and his child, both. From now on that's what you'll be to me, you lost and helpless creature. Don't worry about a thing, Nora. Only be frank with me, and I'll be your will and your conscience.—What's this? You're not in bed? You've changed your dress—!

NORA (*in an everyday dress*)   Yes, Torvald. I have changed my dress.

HELMER   But why—now—this late—?

NORA   I'm not going to sleep tonight.

HELMER   But my dear Nora—

NORA (*looks at her watch*)   It isn't all that late. Sit down here with me, Torvald. You and I have much to talk about. (*Sits down at the table.*)

HELMER   Nora—what is this all about? That rigid face—

NORA   Sit down. This will take a while. I have much to say to you.

HELMER   (*sits down, facing her across the table*)   You worry me, Nora. I don't understand you.

NORA   No, that's just it. You don't understand me. And I have never understood you—not till tonight. No, don't interrupt me. Just listen to what I have to say.—This is a settling of accounts, Torvald.

HELMER   What do you mean by that?

NORA   (*after a brief silence*)   Doesn't one thing strike you, now that we are sitting together like this?

HELMER   What would that be?

NORA   We have been married for eight years. Doesn't it occur to you that this is the first time that you and I, husband and wife, are having a serious talk?

HELMER   Well—serious—. What do you mean by that?

NORA   For eight whole years—longer, in fact—ever since we first met, we have never talked seriously to each other about a single serious thing.

HELMER   You mean I should forever have been telling you about worries you couldn't have helped me with anyway?

NORA   I am not talking about worries. I'm saying we have never tried seriously to get to the bottom of anything together.

HELMER   But dearest Nora, I hardly think that would have been something *you*—

NORA   That's the whole point. You have never understood me. Great wrong has been done to me, Torvald. First by Daddy and then by you.

HELMER   What! By us two? We who have loved you more deeply than anyone else?

NORA   (*shakes her head*)   You never loved me—neither Daddy nor you. You only thought it was fun to be in love with me.

HELMER   But, Nora—what an expression to use!

NORA   That's the way it has been, Torvald. When I was home with Daddy, he told me all his opinions, and so they became my opinions too. If I disagreed with him I kept it to myself, for he wouldn't have liked that. He called me his little doll baby, and he played with me the way I played with my dolls. Then I came to your house—

HELMER   What a way to talk about our marriage!

NORA   (*imperturbably*)   I mean that I passed from Daddy's hands into yours. You arranged everything according to your taste, and so I came to share it—or I pretended to; I'm not sure which. I think it was a little of both, now one and now the other. When I look back on it now, it seems to me I've been living here like a pauper—just a hand-to-mouth kind of existence. I have earned my keep by doing tricks for you, Torvald. But that's the way you wanted it. You have great sins against me to answer for, Daddy and you. It's your fault that nothing has become of me.

HELMER   Nora, you're being both unreasonable and ungrateful. Haven't you been happy here?

NORA   No, never. I thought I was, but I wasn't.

HELMER   Not—not happy!

NORA   No; just having fun. And you have always been very good to me. But our home has never been more than a playroom. I have been your doll wife here, just the way I used to be Daddy's doll child. And the children have been my dolls. I thought it was fun when you played with me, just as they thought it was fun when I played with them. That's been our marriage, Torvald.

HELMER   There is something in what you are saying—exaggerated and hysterical though it is. But from now on things will be different. Playtime is over; it's time for growing up.

NORA   Whose growing up—mine or the children's?

HELMER   Both yours and the children's, Nora darling.

NORA   Oh Torvald, you're not the man to bring me up to be the right kind of wife for you.

HELMER   How can you say that?

NORA   And I—? What qualifications do I have for bringing up the children?

HELMER   Nora!

NORA   You said so yourself a minute ago—that you didn't dare to trust me with them.

HELMER   In the first flush of anger, yes. Surely, you're not going to count that.

NORA   But you were quite right. I am *not* qualified. Something else has to come first. Somehow I have to grow up myself. And you are not the man to help me do that. That's a job I have to do by myself. And that's why I'm leaving you.

HELMER   (*jumps up*)   What did you say!

NORA   I have to be by myself if I am to find out about myself and about all the other things too. So I can't stay here with you any longer.

HELMER   Nora, Nora!

NORA   I'm leaving now. I'm sure Kristine will put me up for tonight.

HELMER   You're out of your mind! I won't let you! I forbid you!

NORA   You can't forbid me anything any more; it won't do any good. I'm taking my own things with me. I won't accept anything from you, either now or later.

HELMER   But this is madness!

NORA   Tomorrow I'm going home—I mean back to my old home town. It will be easier for me to find some kind of job there.

HELMER   Oh, you blind, inexperienced creature—!

NORA   I must see to it that I get experience, Torvald.

HELMER   Leaving your home, your husband, your children! Not a thought of what people will say!

NORA   I can't worry about that. All I know is that I have to leave.

HELMER   Oh, this is shocking! Betraying your most sacred duties like this!

NORA   And what do you consider my most sacred duties?

HELMER   Do I need to tell you that? They are your duties to your husband and your children.

NORA   I have other duties equally sacred.

HELMER   You do not. What duties would they be?

NORA   My duties to myself.

HELMER   You are a wife and a mother before you are anything else.

NORA   I don't believe that any more. I believe I am first of all a human being, just as much as you—or at any rate that I must try to become one. Oh, I know very well that most people agree with you, Torvald, and that it says something like that in all the books. But what people say and what the books say is no longer enough for me. I have to think about these things myself and see if I can't find the answers.

HELMER   You mean to tell me you don't know what your proper place in your own home is? Don't you have a reliable guide in such matters? Don't you have religion?

NORA   Oh but Torvald—I don't really know what religion is.

HELMER   What are you saying!

NORA   All I know is what the Reverend Hansen told me when he prepared me for confirmation. He said that religion was *this* and it was *that*. When I get by myself, away from here, I'll have to look into that, too. I have to decide if what the Reverend Hansen said was right, or anyway if it is right for *me*.

HELMER   Oh, this is unheard of in a young woman! If religion can't guide you, let me appeal to your conscience. For surely you have moral feelings? Or—answer me—maybe you don't?

NORA   Well, you see, Torvald, I don't really know what to say. I just don't know. I am confused about these things. All I know is that my ideas are quite different from yours. I have just found out that the laws are different from what I thought they were, but in no way can I get it into my head that those laws are right. A woman shouldn't have the right to spare her dying old father or save her husband's life! I just can't believe that.

HELMER   You speak like a child. You don't understand the society you live in.

NORA   No, I don't. But I want to find out about it. I have to make up my mind who is right, society or I.

HELMER   You are sick, Nora; you have a fever. I really don't think you are in your right mind.

NORA   I have never felt so clearheaded and sure of myself as I do tonight.

HELMER   And clearheaded and sure of yourself you're leaving your husband and children?

NORA   Yes.

HELMER   Then there is only one possible explanation.

NORA   What?

HELMER   You don't love me any more.

NORA   No, that's just it.

HELMER   Nora! Can you say that?

NORA   I am sorry, Torvald, for you have always been so good to me. But I can't help it. I don't love you any more.

HELMER   (*with forced composure*)   And this too is a clear and sure conviction?

NORA   Completely clear and sure. That's why I don't want to stay here any more.

HELMER   And are you ready to explain to me how I came to forfeit your love?

NORA   Certainly I am. It was tonight, when the wonderful didn't happen. That was when I realized you were not the man I thought you were.

HELMER   You have to explain. I don't understand.

NORA   I have waited patiently for eight years, for I wasn't such a fool that I thought the wonderful is something that happens any old day. Then this—thing—came crashing in on me, and then there wasn't a doubt in my mind that now—now comes the wonderful. When Krogstad's letter was in that mailbox, never for a moment did it even occur to me that you would submit to his conditions. I was so absolutely certain that you would say to him: make the whole thing public—tell everybody. And when that had happened—

HELMER   Yes, then what? When I had surrendered my wife to shame and disgrace—!

NORA   When that had happened, I was absolutely certain that you would stand up and take the blame and say, "I'm the guilty one."

HELMER   Nora!

NORA   You mean I never would have accepted such a sacrifice from you? Of course not. But what would my protests have counted against yours. *That* was the wonderful I was hoping for in terror. And to prevent that I was going to kill myself.

HELMER   I'd gladly work nights and days for you, Nora—endure sorrow and want for your sake. But nobody sacrifices his *honor* for his love.

NORA   A hundred thousand women have done so.

HELMER   Oh, you think and talk like a silly child.

NORA   All right. But you don't think and talk like the man I can live with. When you had gotten over your fright—not because of what threatened *me* but because of the risk to *you*—and the whole danger was past, then you acted as if nothing at all had happened. Once again I was your little songbird, your doll, just as before, only now you had to handle her even more carefully, because she was so frail and weak. (*Rises.*) Torvald—that moment I realized that I had been living here for eight years with a stranger and had borne him three children—Oh, I can't stand thinking about it! I feel like tearing myself to pieces!

HELMER   (*heavily*)   I see it, I see it. An abyss has opened up between us.—Oh but Nora—surely it can be filled?

NORA   The way I am now I am no wife for you.

HELMER   I have it in me to change.

NORA   Perhaps—if your doll is taken from you.

HELMER   To part—to part from you! No, no, Nora! I can't grasp that thought!

NORA   (*goes out, right*)   All the more reason why it has to be. (*She returns with her outdoor clothes and a small bag, which she sets down on the chair by the table.*)

HELMER   Nora, Nora! Not now! Wait till tomorrow.

NORA   (*putting on her coat*)   I can't spend the night in a stranger's rooms.

HELMER   But couldn't we live here together like brother and sister—?

NORA   (*tying on her hat*)   You know very well that wouldn't last long—. (*Wraps her shawl around her.*) Goodbye, Torvald. I don't want to see the children. I know I leave them in better hands than mine. The way I am now I can't be anything to them.

HELMER   But some day, Nora—some day—?

NORA   How can I tell? I have no idea what's going to become of me.

HELMER   But you're still my wife, both as you are now and as you will be.

NORA Listen, Torvald—when a wife leaves her husband's house, the way I am doing now, I have heard he has no more legal responsibilities for her. At any rate, I now release you from all responsibility. You are not to feel yourself obliged to me for anything, and I have no obligations to you. There has to be full freedom on both sides. Here is your ring back. Now give me mine.

HELMER Even this?

NORA Even this.

HELMER Here it is.

NORA There. So now it's over. I'm putting the keys here. The maids know everything about the house—better than I. Tomorrow, after I'm gone, Kristine will come over and pack my things from home. I want them sent after me.

HELMER Over! It's all over! Nora, will you never think of me?

NORA I'm sure I'll often think of you and the children and this house.

HELMER May I write to you, Nora?

NORA No—never. I won't have that.

HELMER But send you things—? You must let me.

NORA Nothing, nothing.

HELMER —help you, when you need help—?

NORA I told you, no; I won't have it. I'll accept nothing from strangers.

HELMER Nora—can I never again be more to you than a stranger?

NORA (*picks up her bag*) Oh Torvald—then the most wonderful of all would have to happen—

HELMER Tell me what that would be—!

NORA For that to happen, both you and I would have to change so that—Oh Torvald, I no longer believe in the wonderful.

HELMER But I *will* believe. Tell me! Change, so that—?

NORA So that our living together would become a true marriage. Goodbye. (*She goes out through the hall.*)

HELMER (*sinks down on a chair near the door and covers his face with his hands*) Nora! Nora! (*Looks around him and gets up.*) All empty. She's gone. (*With sudden hope.*) The most wonderful—?!

(*From downstairs comes the sound of a heavy door slamming shut.*)

QUESTIONS FOR THINKING AND WRITING

1. The action of *A Doll's House* centers on the development and the alterations of the relationships among Nora, Helmer, Krogstad, and Mrs. Linde. How does Ibsen portray these characters? How do their relationships illuminate their personalities and their actions? How do they emphasize the themes and social comments of the play?

2. Both Nora and Antigonê are women who place moral principles above legal values. What happens to each character in consequence, in terms of her play's plot? Other characters' reactions to her action? Her view of their reaction, and of herself?

3. Discuss the play's ending. Do you find it successful? What is its effect? What do you think is "the most wonderful of all"?

OSCAR WILDE (1854–1900)

The Importance of Being Earnest

CHARACTERS

John Worthing, J.P.
Algernon Moncrieff
Rev. Canon Chasuble, D.D.
Merriman, *butler*
Lane, *manservant*
Lady Bracknell
Hon. Gwendolen Fairfax
Cecily Cardew
Miss Prism, *governess*

THE SCENES OF THE PLAY

act   i.   *Algernon Moncrieff's Flat in Half-Moon Street, W.*
act   ii.   *The Garden at the Manor House, Woolton.*
act   iii.   *Drawing-Room of the Manor House, Woolton.*

Time—*The Present.*
Place—*London.*

ACT I

Scene.   *Morning-room in* Algernon's *flat in Half-Moon Street. The room is luxuriously and artistically furnished. The sound of a piano is heard in the adjoining room.*

(Lane *is arranging afternoon tea on the table, and after the music has ceased,* Algernon *enters.*)

algernon   Did you hear what I was playing, Lane?
lane   I didn't think it polite to listen, sir.
algernon   I'm sorry for that, for your sake. I don't play accurately— any one can play accurately—but I play with wonderful expression. As far as the piano is concerned, sentiment is my forte. I keep science for Life.
lane   Yes, sir.

ALGERNON   And, speaking of the science of Life, have you got the cucumber sandwiches cut for Lady Bracknell?

LANE   Yes, sir. (*Hands them on a salver.*)

ALGERNON (*inspects them, takes two, and sits down on the sofa*)   Oh! . . . by the way, Lane, I see from your book that on Thursday night, when Lord Shoreman and Mr. Worthing were dining with me, eight bottles of champagne are entered as having been consumed.

LANE   Yes, sir; eight bottles and a pint.

ALGERNON   Why is it that at a bachelor's establishment the servants invariably drink the champagne? I ask merely for information.

LANE   I attribute it to the superior quality of the wine, sir. I have often observed that in married households the champagne is rarely of a first-rate brand.

ALGERNON   Good Heavens! Is marriage so demoralizing as that?

LANE   I believe it *is* a very pleasant state, sir. I have had very little experience of it myself up to the present. I have only been married once. That was in consequence of a misunderstanding between myself and a young woman.

ALGERNON (*languidly*)   I don't know that I am much interested in your family life, Lane.

LANE   No, sir; it is not a very interesting subject. I never think of it myself.

ALGERNON   Very natural, I am sure. That will do, Lane, thank you.

LANE   Thank you, sir. (LANE *goes out.*)

ALGERNON   Lane's views on marriage seem somewhat lax. Really, if the lower orders don't set us a good example, what on earth is the use of them? They seem, as a class, to have absolutely no sense of moral responsibility.

Enter LANE.

LANE   Mr. Ernest Worthing.

Enter JACK. LANE *goes out.*

ALGERNON   How are you, my dear Ernest? What brings you up to town?

JACK   Oh, pleasure, pleasure! What else should bring one anywhere? Eating as usual, I see, Algy!

ALGERNON (*stiffly*)   I believe it is customary in good society to take some slight refreshment at five o'clock. Where have you been since last Thursday?

JACK (*sitting down on the sofa*)   In the country.

ALGERNON   What on earth do you do there?

JACK (*pulling off his gloves*)   When one is in town one amuses oneself. When one is in the country one amuses other people. It is excessively boring.

ALGERNON   And who are the people you amuse?

JACK (*airily*)   Oh, neighbors, neighbors.

ALGERNON   Got nice neighbors in your part of Shropshire?

JACK   Perfectly horrid! Never speak to one of them.

ALGERNON   How immensely you must amuse them! (*Goes over and takes sandwich.*) By the way, Shropshire is your county, is it not?

JACK   Eh? Shropshire? Yes, of course. Hallo! Why all these cups? Why cucumber sandwiches? Why such reckless extravagance in one so young? Who is coming to tea?

ALGERNON   Oh! merely Aunt Augusta and Gwendolen.

JACK   How perfectly delightful!

ALGERNON   Yes, that is all very well; but I am afraid Aunt Augusta won't quite approve of your being here.

JACK   May I ask why?

ALGERNON   My dear fellow, the way you flirt with Gwendolen is perfectly disgraceful. It is almost as bad as the way Gwendolen flirts with you.

JACK   I am in love with Gwendolen. I have come up to town expressly to propose to her.

ALGERNON   I thought you had come up for pleasure? . . . I call that business.

JACK   How utterly unromantic you are!

ALGERNON   I really don't see anything romantic in proposing. It is very romantic to be in love. But there is nothing romantic about a definite proposal. Why, one may be accepted. One usually is, I believe. Then the excitement is all over. The very essence of romance is uncertainty. If ever I get married, I'll certainly try to forget the fact.

JACK   I have no doubt about that, dear Algy. The Divorce Court was specially invented for people whose memories are so curiously constituted.

ALGERNON   Oh! there is no use speculating on that subject. Divorces are made in Heaven—(JACK *puts out his hand to take a sandwich.* ALGERNON *at once interferes.*) Please don't touch the cucumber sandwiches. They are ordered specially for Aunt Augusta. (*Takes one and eats it.*)

JACK   Well, you have been eating them all the time.

ALGERNON   That is quite a different matter. She is my aunt. (*Takes plate from below.*) Have some bread and butter. The bread and butter is for Gwendolen. Gwendolen is devoted to bread and butter.

JACK (*advancing to table and helping himself*)   And very good bread and butter it is, too.

ALGERNON   Well, my dear fellow, you need not eat as if you were going to eat it all. You behave as if you were married to her already. You are not married to her already, and I don't think you ever will be.

JACK   Why on earth do you say that?

ALGERNON   Well, in the first place girls never marry the men they flirt with. Girls don't think it right.

JACK   Oh, that is nonsense!

ALGERNON   It isn't. It is a great truth. It accounts for the extraordinary number of bachelors that one sees all over the place. In the second place, I don't give my consent.

JACK   Your consent!

ALGERNON   My dear fellow, Gwendolen is my first cousin. And before I allow you to marry her, you will have to clear up the whole question of Cecily. (*Rings bell.*)

JACK   Cecily! What on earth do you mean? What do you mean, Algy, by Cecily? I don't know any one of the name of Cecily.

Enter LANE.

ALGERNON   Bring me that cigarette case Mr. Worthing left in the smoking-room the last time he dined here.

LANE   Yes, sir. (LANE *goes out.*)

JACK   Do you mean to say you have had my cigarette case all this time? I wish to goodness you had let me know. I have been writing frantic letters to Scotland Yard about it. I was very nearly offering a large reward.

ALGERNON   Well, I wish you would offer one. I happen to be more than usually hard up.

JACK   There is no good offering a large reward now that the thing is found.

Enter LANE *with the cigarette case on a salver.* ALGERNON *takes it at once.* LANE *goes out.*

ALGERNON   I think that is rather mean of you, Ernest, I must say. (*Opens case and examines it.*) However, it makes no matter, for, now that I look at the inscription, I find that the thing isn't yours after all.

JACK   Of course it's mine. (*Moving to him.*) You have seen me with it a hundred times, and you have no right whatsoever to read what is written inside. It is a very ungentlemanly thing to read a private cigarette case.

ALGERNON   Oh! it is absurd to have a hard-and-fast rule about what one should read and what one shouldn't. More than half of modern culture depends on what one shouldn't read.

JACK   I am quite aware of the fact, and I don't propose to discuss modern culture. It isn't the sort of thing one should talk of in private. I simply want my cigarette case back.

ALGERNON   Yes; but this isn't your cigarette case. This cigarette case is a present from some one of the name of Cecily, and you said you didn't know any one of that name.

JACK   Well, if you want to know, Cecily happens to be my aunt.

ALGERNON   Your aunt!

JACK   Yes. Charming old lady she is, too. Lives at Tunbridge Wells. Just give it back to me, Algy.

ALGERNON (*retreating to back of sofa*)   But why does she call herself little
Cecily if she is your aunt and lives at Tunbridge Wells? (*Reading.*)
"From little Cecily with her fondest love."

JACK (*moving to sofa and kneeling upon it*)   My dear fellow, what on earth
is there in that? Some aunts are tall, some aunts are not tall. That is a
matter that surely an aunt may be allowed to decide for herself. You
seem to think that every aunt should be exactly like your aunt! That is
absurd! For Heaven's sake give me back my cigarette case. (*Follows*
ALGERNON *round the room.*)

ALGERNON   Yes. But why does your aunt call you her uncle? "From
little Cecily, with her fondest love to her dear Uncle Jack." There is
no objection, I admit, to an aunt being a small aunt, but why an aunt,
no matter what her size may be, should call her own nephew her
uncle, I can't quite make out. Besides, your name isn't Jack at all; it is
Ernest.

JACK   It isn't Ernest; it's Jack.

ALGERNON   You have always told me it was Ernest. I have introduced
you to every one as Ernest. You answer to the name of Ernest. You
look as if your name was Ernest. You are the most earnest looking
person I ever saw in my life. It is perfectly absurd your saying that
your name isn't Ernest. It's on your cards. Here is one of them.
(*Taking it from case.*) "Mr. Ernest Worthing, B 4, The Albany." I'll
keep this as a proof your name is Ernest if ever you attempt to deny
it to me, or to Gwendolen, or to any one else. (*Puts the card in his
pocket.*)

JACK   Well, my name is Ernest in town and Jack in the country, and the
cigarette case was given to me in the country.

ALGERNON   Yes, but that does not account for the fact that your small
Aunt Cecily, who lives at Tunbridge Wells, calls you her dear uncle.
Come, old boy, you had much better have the thing out at once.

JACK   My dear Algy, you talk exactly as if you were a dentist. It is very
vulgar to talk like a dentist when one isn't a dentist. It produces a false
impression.

ALGERNON   Well, that is exactly what dentists always do. Now, go on!
Tell me the whole thing, I may mention that I have always suspected
you of being a confirmed and secret Bunburyist; and I am quite sure
of it now.

JACK   Bunburyist? What on earth do you mean by a Bunburyist?

ALGERNON   I'll reveal to you the meaning of that incomparable expression as soon as you are kind enough to inform me why you are Ernest
in town and Jack in the country.

JACK   Well, produce my cigarette case first.

ALGERNON   Here it is. (*Hands cigarette case.*) Now produce your explanation, and pray make it improbable. (*Sits on sofa.*)

JACK   My dear fellow, there is nothing improbable about my explanation at all. In fact it's perfectly ordinary. Old Mr. Thomas Cardew,

who adopted me when I was a little boy, made me in his will guardian to his grand-daughter, Miss Cecily Cardew. Cecily, who addresses me as her uncle from motives of respect that you could not possibly appreciate, lives at my place in the country under the charge of her admirable governess, Miss Prism.

ALGERNON   Where is that place in the country, by the way?

JACK   That is nothing to you, dear boy. You are not going to be invited. . . . I may tell you candidly that the place is not in Shropshire.

ALGERNON   I suspected that, my dear fellow! I have Bunburyed all over Shropshire on two separate occasions. Now, go on. Why are you Ernest in town and Jack in the country?

JACK   My dear Algy, I don't know whether you will be able to understand my real motives. You are hardly serious enough. When one is placed in the position of guardian, one has to adopt a very high moral tone on all subjects. It's one's duty to do so. And as a high moral tone can hardly be said to conduce very much to either one's health or one's happiness, in order to get up to town I have always pretended to have a younger brother of the name of Ernest, who lives in the Albany, and gets into the most dreadful scrapes. That, my dear Algy, is the whole truth pure and simple.

ALGERNON   The truth is rarely pure and never simple. Modern life would be very tedious if it were either, and modern literature a complete impossibility!

JACK   That wouldn't be at all a bad thing.

ALGERNON   Literary criticism is not your forte, my dear fellow. Don't try it. You should leave that to people who haven't been at a University. They do it so well in the daily papers. What you really are is a Bunburyist. I was quite right in saying you were a Bunburyist. You are one of the most advanced Bunburyists I know.

JACK   What on earth do you mean?

ALGERNON   You have invented a very useful younger brother called Ernest, in order that you may be able to come up to town as often as you like. I have invented an invaluable permanent invalid called Bunbury, in order that I may be able to go down into the country whenever I choose. Bunbury is perfectly invaluable. If it wasn't for Bunbury's extraordinary bad health, for instance, I wouldn't be able to dine with you at Willis's to-night, for I have been really engaged to Aunt Augusta for more than a week.

JACK   I haven't asked you to dine with me anywhere tonight.

ALGERNON   I know. You are absolutely careless about sending out invitations. It is very foolish of you. Nothing annoys people so much as not receiving invitations.

JACK   You had much better dine with your Aunt Augusta.

ALGERNON   I haven't the smallest intention of doing anything of the kind. To begin with, I dined there on Monday, and once a week is quite enough to dine with one's own relatives. In the second place, whenever I do dine there I am always treated as a member of the family, and sent down with either no woman at all, or two. In the third place, I know perfectly well whom she will place me next to, tonight. She will place me next Mary Farquhar, who always flirts with her own husband across the dinner-table. That is not very pleasant. Indeed, it is not even decent . . . and that sort of thing is enormously on the increase. The amount of women in London who flirt with their own husbands is perfectly scandalous. It looks so bad. It is simply washing one's clean linen in public. Besides, now that I know you to be a confirmed Bunburyist I naturally want to talk to you about Bunburying. I want to tell you the rules.

JACK   I'm not a Bunburyist at all. If Gwendolen accepts me, I am going to kill my brother, indeed I think I'll kill him in any case. Cecily is a little too much interested in him. It is rather a bore. So I am going to get rid of Ernest. And I strongly advise you to do the same with Mr. —— with your invalid friend who has the absurd name.

ALGERNON   Nothing will induce me to part with Bunbury, and if you ever get married, which seems to me extremely problematic, you will be very glad to know Bunbury. A man who marries without knowing Bunbury has a very tedious time of it.

JACK   That is nonsense. If I marry a charming girl like Gwendolen, and she is the only girl I ever saw in my life that I would marry, I certainly won't want to know Bunbury.

ALGERNON   Then your wife will. You don't seem to realize, that in married life three is company and two is none.

JACK (*sententiously*)   That, my dear young friend, is the theory that the corrupt French Drama has been propounding for the last fifty years.

ALGERNON   Yes; and that the happy English home has proved in half the time.

JACK   For heaven's sake, don't try to be cynical. It's perfectly easy to be cynical.

ALGERNON   My dear fellow, it isn't easy to be anything now-a-days. There's such a lot of beastly competition about. (*The sound of an electric bell is heard.*) Ah! that must be Aunt Augusta. Only relatives, or creditors, ever ring in that Wagnerian manner. Now, if I get her out of the way for ten minutes, so that you can have an opportunity for proposing to Gwendolen, may I dine with you to-night at Willis's?

JACK   I suppose so, if you want to.

ALGERNON   Yes, but you must be serious about it. I have people who are not serious about meals. It is so shallow of them.

Enter LANE.

LANE   Lady Bracknell and Miss Fairfax. (ALGERNON *goes forward to meet them. Enter* LADY BRACKNELL *and* GWENDOLEN.)

LADY BRACKNELL Good afternoon, dear Algernon, I hope you are behaving very well.

ALGERNON I'm feeling very well, Aunt Augusta.

LADY BRACKNELL That's not quite the same thing. In fact the two things rarely go together. (*Sees* JACK *and bows to him with icy coldness.*)

ALGERNON (*to* GWENDOLEN) Dear me, you are smart!

GWENDOLEN I am always smart! Aren't I, Mr. Worthing?

JACK You're quite perfect, Miss Fairfax.

GWENDOLEN Oh! I hope I am not that. It would leave no room for developments, and I intend to develop in many directions. (GWENDOLEN *and* JACK *sit down together in the corner.*)

LADY BRACKNELL I'm sorry if we are a little late, Algernon, but I was obliged to call on dear Lady Harbury. Hadn't been there since her poor husband's death. I never saw a woman so altered; she looks quite twenty years younger. And now I'll have a cup of tea, and one of those nice cucumber sandwiches you promised me.

ALGERNON Certainly, Aunt Augusta. (*Goes over to tea-table.*)

LADY BRACKNELL Won't you come and sit here, Gwendolen?

GWENDOLEN Thanks, mamma, I'm quite comfortable where I am.

ALGERNON (*picking up empty plate in horror*) Good heavens! Lane! Why are there no cucumber sandwiches? I ordered them specially.

LANE (*gravely*) There were no cucumbers in the market this morning, sir. I went down twice.

ALGERNON No cucumbers!

LANE No, sir. Not even for ready money.

ALGERNON That will do, Lane, thank you.

LANE Thank you, sir. (*Goes out.*)

ALGERNON I am greatly distressed, Aunt Augusta, about there being no cucumbers, not even for ready money.

LADY BRACKNELL It really makes no matter, Algernon. I had some crumpets with Lady Harbury, who seems to me to be living entirely for pleasure now.

ALGERNON I hear her hair has turned quite gold from grief.

LADY BRACKNELL It certainly has changed its color. From what cause I, of course, cannot say. (ALGERNON *crosses and hands tea.*) Thank you. I've quite a treat for you to-night, Algernon. I am going to send you down with Mary Farquhar. She is such a nice woman, and so attentive to her husband. It's delightful to watch them.

ALGERNON I am afraid, Aunt Augusta, I shall have to give up the pleasure of dining with you to-night after all.

LADY BRACKNELL (*frowning*) I hope not, Algernon. It would put my table completely out. Your uncle would have to dine upstairs. Fortunately he is accustomed to that.

ALGERNON It is a great bore, and, I need hardly say, a terrible disappointment to me, but the fact is I have just had a telegram to say that my poor friend Bunbury is very ill again. (*Exchanges glances with* JACK.) They seem to think I should be with him.

LADY BRACKNELL   It is very strange. This Mr. Bunbury seems to suffer from curiously bad health.

ALGERNON   Yes; poor Bunbury is a dreadful invalid.

LADY BRACKNELL   Well, I must say, Algernon, that I think it is high time that Mr. Bunbury made up his mind whether he was going to live or to die. This shilly-shallying with the question is absurd. Nor do I in any way approve of the modern sympathy with invalids. I consider it morbid. Illness of any kind is hardly a thing to be encouraged in others. Health is the primary duty of life. I am always telling that to your poor uncle, but he never seems to take much notice . . . as far as any improvement in his ailments goes. I should be much obliged if you would ask Mr. Bunbury, from me, to be kind enough not to have a relapse on Saturday, for I rely on you to arrange my music for me. It is my last reception and one wants something that will encourage conversation, particularly at the end of the season when every one has practically said whatever they had to say, which, in most cases, was probably not much.

ALGERNON   I'll speak to Bunbury, Aunt Augusta, if he is still conscious, and I think I can promise you he'll be all right by Saturday. Of course the music is a great difficulty. You see, if one plays good music, people don't listen, and if one plays bad music, people don't talk. But I'll run over the program I've drawn out, if you will kindly come into the next room for a moment.

LADY BRACKNELL   Thank you, Algernon. It is very thoughtful of you. (*Rising, and following* ALGERNON.) I'm sure the program will be delightful, after a few expurgations. French songs I cannot possibly allow. People always seem to think that they are improper, and either look shocked, which is vulgar, or laugh, which is worse. But German sounds a thoroughly respectable language, and indeed, I believe is so. Gwendolen, you will accompany me.

GWENDOLEN   Certainly, mamma. (LADY BRACKNELL *and* ALGERNON *go into the music-room;* GWENDOLEN *remains behind.*)

JACK   Charming day it has been, Miss Fairfax.

GWENDOLEN   Pray don't talk to me about the weather, Mr. Worthing. Whenever people talk to me about the weather, I always feel quite certain that they mean something else. And that makes me so nervous.

JACK   I do mean something else.

GWENDOLEN   I thought so. In fact, I am never wrong.

JACK   And I would like to be allowed to take advantage of Lady Bracknell's temporary absence . . .

GWENDOLEN   I would certainly advise you to do so. Mamma has a way of coming back suddenly into a room that I have often had to speak to her about.

JACK (*nervously*)   Miss Fairfax, ever since I met you I have admired you more than any girl . . . I have ever met since . . . I met you.

GWENDOLEN   Yes, I am quite aware of the fact. And I often wish that in public, at any rate, you had been more demonstrative. For me you have always had an irresistible fascination. Even before I met you I was far from indifferent to you. (JACK *looks at her in amazement.*) We live, as I hope you know, Mr. Worthing, in an age of ideals. The fact is constantly mentioned in the more expensive monthly magazines, and has reached the provincial pulpits I am told: and my ideal has always been to love some one of the name of Ernest. There is something in that name that inspires absolute confidence. The moment Algernon first mentioned to me that he had a friend called Ernest, I knew I was destined to love you.

JACK   You really love me, Gwendolen?

GWENDOLEN   Passionately!

JACK   Darling! You don't know how happy you've made me.

GWENDOLEN   My own Ernest!

JACK   But you don't really mean to say that you couldn't love me if my name wasn't Ernest?

GWENDOLEN   But your name is Ernest.

JACK   Yes, I know it is. But supposing it was something else? Do you mean to say you couldn't love me then?

GWENDOLEN (*glibly*)   Ah! that is clearly a metaphysical speculation, and like most metaphysical speculations has very little reference at all to the actual facts of real life, as we know them.

JACK   Personally, darling, to speak quite candidly, I don't much care about the name of Ernest . . . I don't think that name suits me at all.

GWENDOLEN   It suits you perfectly. It is a divine name. It has a music of its own. It produces vibrations.

JACK   Well, really, Gwendolen, I must say that I think there are lots of other much nicer names. I think, Jack, for instance, a charming name.

GWENDOLEN   Jack? . . . No, there is very little music in the name Jack, if any at all, indeed. It does not thrill. It produces absolutely no vibrations. . . . I have known several Jacks, and they all, without exception, were more than usually plain. Besides, Jack is a notorious domesticity for John! And I pity any woman who is married to a man called John. She would probably never be allowed to know the entrancing pleasure of a single moment's solitude. The only really safe name is Ernest.

JACK   Gwendolen, I must get christened at once—I mean we must get married at once. There is no time to be lost.

GWENDOLEN   Married, Mr. Worthing?

JACK (*astounded*)   Well . . . surely. You know that I love you, and you led me to believe, Miss Fairfax, that you were not absolutely indifferent to me.

GWENDOLEN   I adore you. But you haven't proposed to me yet. Nothing has been said at all about marriage. The subject has not even been touched on.

JACK   Well . . . may I propose to you now?

GWENDOLEN   I think it would be an admirable opportunity. And to spare you any possible disappointment, Mr. Worthing, I think it only fair to tell you quite frankly beforehand that I am fully determined to accept you.

JACK   Gwendolen!

GWENDOLEN   Yes, Mr. Worthing, what have you got to say to me?

JACK   You know what I have got to say to you.

GWENDOLEN   Yes, but you don't say it.

JACK   Gwendolen, will you marry me? (*Goes on his knees.*)

GWENDOLEN   Of course I will, darling. How long you have been about it! I am afraid you have had very little experience in how to propose.

JACK   My own one, I have never loved any one in the world but you.

GWENDOLEN   Yes, but men often propose for practice. I know my brother Gerald does. All my girl-friends tell me so. What wonderfully blue eyes you have, Ernest! They are quite, quite blue. I hope you will always look at me just like that, especially when there are other people present.

Enter LADY BRACKNELL.

LADY BRACKNELL   Mr. Worthing! Rise, sir, from this semi-recumbent posture. It is most indecorous.

GWENDOLEN   Mamma! (*He tries to rise; she restrains him.*) I must beg you to retire. This is no place for you. Besides, Mr. Worthing has not quite finished yet.

LADY BRACKNELL   Finished what, may I ask?

GWENDOLEN   I am engaged to Mr. Worthing, mamma. (*They rise together.*)

LADY BRACKNELL   Pardon me, you are not engaged to any one. When you do become engaged to some one, I, or your father, should his health permit him, will inform you of the fact. An engagement should come on a young girl as a surprise, pleasant or unpleasant, as the case may be. It is hardly a matter that she could be allowed to arrange for herself. . . . And now I have a few questions to put to you, Mr. Worthing. While I am making these inquiries, you, Gwendolen, will wait for me below in the carriage.

GWENDOLEN (*reproachfully*)   Mamma!

LADY BRACKNELL   In the carriage, Gwendolen! (GWENDOLEN *goes to the door. She and* JACK *blow kisses to each other behind* LADY BRACKNELL'S *back.* LADY BRACKNELL *looks vaguely about as if she could not understand what the noise was. Finally turns round.*) Gwendolen, the carriage!

GWENDOLEN   Yes, mamma. (*Goes out, looking back at* JACK.)

LADY BRACKNELL (*sitting down*)   You can take a seat, Mr. Worthing. (*Looks in her pocket for note-book and pencil.*)

JACK   Thank you, Lady Bracknell, I prefer standing.

LADY BRACKNELL (*pencil and note-book in hand*)   I feel bound to tell you that you are not down on my list of eligible young men, although I have the same list as the dear Duchess of Bolton has. We work together, in fact. However, I am quite ready to enter your name, should your answers be what a really affectionate mother requires. Do you smoke?

JACK   Well, yes, I must admit I smoke.

LADY BRACKNELL   I am glad to hear it. A man should always have an occupation of some kind. There are far too many idle men in London as it is. How old are you?

JACK   Twenty-nine.

LADY BRACKNELL   A very good age to be married at. I have always been of the opinion that a man who desires to get married should know either everything or nothing. Which do you know?

JACK (*after some hesitation*)   I know nothing, Lady Bracknell.

LADY BRACKNELL   I am pleased to hear it. I do not approve of anything that tampers with natural ignorance. Ignorance is like a delicate exotic fruit; touch it and the bloom is gone. The whole theory of modern education is radically unsound. Fortunately in England, at any rate, education produces no effect whatsoever. If it did, it would prove a serious danger to the upper classes, and probably lead to acts of violence in Grosvenor Square. What is your income?

JACK   Between seven and eight thousand a year.

LADY BRACKNELL (*makes a note in her book*)   In land, or in investments?

JACK   In investments, chiefly.

LADY BRACKNELL   That is satisfactory. What between the duties expected of one during one's life-time, and the duties exacted from one after one's death, land has ceased to be either a profit or a pleasure. It gives one position, and prevents one from keeping it up. That's all that can be said about land.

JACK   I have a country house with some land, of course, attached to it, about fifteen hundred acres, I believe; but I don't depend on that for my real income. In fact, as far as I can make out, the poachers are the only people who make anything out of it.

LADY BRACKNELL   A country house! How many bedrooms? Well, that point can be cleared up afterwards. You have a town house, I hope? A girl with a simple, unspoiled nature, like Gwendolen, could hardly be expected to reside in the country.

JACK   Well, I own a house in Belgrave Square, but it is let by the year to Lady Bloxham. Of course, I can get it back whenever I like, at six months' notice.

LADY BRACKNELL   Lady Bloxham? I don't know her.

JACK   Oh, she goes about very little. She is a lady considerably advanced in years.

LADY BRACKNELL   Ah, now-a-days that is no guarantee of respectability of character. What number in Belgrave Square?

JACK   149.

LADY BRACKNELL (*shaking her head*)   The unfashionable side. I thought there was something. However, that could easily be altered.

JACK   Do you mean the fashion, or the side?

LADY BRACKNELL (*sternly*)   Both, if necessary, I presume. What are your politics?

JACK   Well, I am afraid I really have none. I am a Liberal Unionist.

LADY BRACKNELL   Oh, they count as Tories. They dine with us. Or come in the evening, at any rate. Now to minor matters. Are your parents living?

JACK   I have lost both my parents.

LADY BRACKNELL   Both? . . . That seems like carelessness. Who was your father? He was evidently a man of some wealth. Was he born in what the Radical papers call the purple of commerce, or did he rise from the ranks of the aristocracy?

JACK   I am afraid I really don't know. The fact is, Lady Bracknell, I said I had lost my parents. It would be nearer the truth to say that my parents seem to have lost me . . . I don't actually know who I am by birth. I was . . . well, I was found.

LADY BRACKNELL   Found!

JACK   The late Mr. Thomas Cardew, an old gentleman of a very charitable and kindly disposition, found me, and gave me the name of Worthing, because he happened to have a first-class ticket for Worthing in his pocket at the time. Worthing is a place in Sussex. It is a seaside resort.

LADY BRACKNELL   Where did the charitable gentleman who had a first-class ticket for this seaside resort find you?

JACK (*gravely*)   In a hand-bag.

LADY BRACKNELL   A hand-bag?

JACK (*very seriously*)   Yes, Lady Bracknell. I was in a hand-bag—a somewhat large, black leather hand-bag, with handles to it—an ordinary hand-bag in fact.

LADY BRACKNELL   In what locality did this Mr. James, or Thomas, Cardew come across this ordinary hand-bag?

JACK   In the cloak-room at Victoria Station. It was given to him in mistake for his own.

LADY BRACKNELL   The cloak-room at Victoria Station?

JACK   Yes. The Brighton line.

LADY BRACKNELL   The line is immaterial. Mr. Worthing, I confess I feel somewhat bewildered by what you have just told me. To be born, or at any rate bred, in a handbag, whether it had handles or not, seems to me to display a contempt for the ordinary decencies of family life that remind one of the worst excesses of the French Revolution. And I presume you know what that unfortunate movement led to? As for the particular locality in which the hand-bag was found, a cloak-room at a railway station might serve to conceal a social indiscretion—has probably, indeed, been used for that purpose before now—but it could hardly be regarded as an assured basis for a recognized position in good society.

JACK   May I ask you then what you would advise me to do? I need hardly say I would do anything in the world to ensure Gwendolen's happiness.

LADY BRACKNELL   I would strongly advise you, Mr. Worthing, to try and acquire some relations as soon as possible, and to make a definite effort to produce at any rate one parent, of either sex, before the season is quite over.

JACK   Well, I don't see how I could possibly manage to do that. I can produce the hand-bag at any moment. It is in my dressing-room at home. I really think that should satisfy you, Lady Bracknell.

LADY BRACKNELL   Me, sir! What has it to do with me? You can hardly imagine that I and Lord Bracknell would dream of allowing our only daughter—a girl brought up with the utmost care—to marry into a cloak-room, and form an alliance with a parcel? Good morning, Mr. Worthing! (LADY BRACKNELL *sweeps out in majestic indignation.*)

JACK   Good morning! (ALGERNON, *from the other room, strikes up the Wedding March.* JACK *looks perfectly furious, and goes to the door.*) For goodness' sake don't play that ghastly tune, Algy! How idiotic you are! (*The music stops, and* ALGERNON *enters cheerily.*)

ALGERNON   Didn't it go off all right, old boy? You don't mean to say Gwendolen refused you? I know it is a way she has. She is always refusing people. I think it is most ill-natured of her.

JACK   Oh, Gwendolen is as right as a trivet. As far as she is concerned, we are engaged. Her mother is perfectly unbearable. Never met such a Gorgon . . . I don't really know what a Gorgon is like, but I am quite sure that Lady Bracknell is one. In any case, she is a monster, without being a myth, which is rather unfair. . . . I beg your pardon, Algy, I suppose I shouldn't talk about your own aunt in that way before you.

ALGERNON   My dear boy, I love hearing my relations abused. It is the only thing that makes me put up with them at all. Relations are simply a tedious pack of people, who haven't got the remotest knowledge of how to live, nor the smallest instinct about when to die.

JACK   Oh, that is nonsense!

ALGERNON   It isn't!

JACK   Well, I won't argue about the matter. You always want to argue about things.

ALGERNON   That is exactly what things were originally made for.

JACK   Upon my word, if I thought that, I'd shoot myself . . . (*A pause.*) You don't think there is any chance of Gwendolen becoming like her mother in about a hundred and fifty years, do you, Algy?

ALGERNON   All women become like their mothers. That is their tragedy. No man does. That's his.

JACK   Is that clever?

ALGERNON   It is perfectly phrased! and quite as true as any observation in civilized life should be.

JACK   I am sick to death of cleverness. Everybody is clever now-a-days. You can't go anywhere without meeting clever people. The thing has become an absolute public nuisance. I wish to goodness we had a few fools left.

ALGERNON   We have.

JACK   I should extremely like to meet them. What do they talk about?

ALGERNON   The fools? Oh! about the clever people, of course.

JACK   What fools!

ALGERNON   By the way, did you tell Gwendolen the truth about your being Ernest in town, and Jack in the country?

JACK (*in a very patronizing manner*)   My dear fellow, the truth isn't quite the sort of thing one tells to a nice, sweet, refined girl. What extraordinary ideas you have about the way to behave to a woman!

ALGERNON   The only way to behave to a woman is to make love to her, if she is pretty, and to some one else if she is plain.

JACK   Oh, that is nonsense.

ALGERNON   What about your brother? What about the profligate Ernest?

JACK   Oh, before the end of the week I shall have got rid of him. I'll say he died in Paris of apoplexy. Lots of people die of apoplexy, quite suddenly, don't they?

ALGERNON   Yes, but it's hereditary, my dear fellow. It's a sort of thing that runs in families. You had much better say a severe chill.

JACK   You are sure a severe chill isn't hereditary, or anything of that kind?

ALGERNON   Of course it isn't!

JACK   Very well, then. My poor brother Ernest is carried off suddenly in Paris, by a severe chill. That gets rid of him.

ALGERNON   But I thought you said that . . . Miss Cardew was a little too much interested in your poor brother Ernest? Won't she feel his loss a good deal?

JACK   Oh, that is all right. Cecily is not a silly, romantic girl, I am glad to say. She has got a capital appetite, goes for long walks, and pays no attention at all to her lessons.

ALGERNON   I would rather like to see Cecily.

JACK   I will take very good care you never do. She is excessively pretty, and she is only just eighteen.

ALGERNON   Have you told Gwendolen yet that you have an excessively pretty ward who is only just eighteen?

JACK   Oh, one doesn't blurt these things out to people. Cecily and Gwendolen are perfectly certain to be extremely great friends. I'll bet you anything you like that half an hour after they have met, they will be calling each other sister.

ALGERNON   Women only do that when they have called each other a lot of other things first. Now, my dear boy, if we want to get a good table at Willis's, we really must go and dress. Do you know it is nearly seven?

JACK   (*irritably*)   Oh! it always is nearly seven.

ALGERNON   Well, I'm hungry.

JACK   I never knew you when you weren't. . . .

ALGERNON   What shall we do after dinner? Go to a theater?

JACK   Oh, no! I loathe listening.

ALGERNON   Well, let us go to the Club?

JACK   Oh, no! I hate talking.

ALGERNON   Well, we might trot round to the Empire at ten?

JACK   Oh, no! I can't bear looking at things. It is so silly.

ALGERNON   Well, what shall we do?

JACK   Nothing!

ALGERNON   It is awfully hard work doing nothing. However, I don't mind hard work where there is no definite object of any kind.

> *Enter* LANE.

LANE   Miss Fairfax.

> *Enter* GWENDOLEN. LANE *goes out.*

ALGERNON   Gwendolen, upon my word!

GWENDOLEN   Algy, kindly turn your back. I have something very particular to say to Mr. Worthing.

ALGERNON   Really, Gwendolen, I don't think I can allow this at all.

GWENDOLEN   Algy, you always adopt a strictly immoral attitude towards life. You are not quite old enough to do that. (ALGERNON *retires to the fireplace.*)

JACK   My own darling!

GWENDOLEN   Ernest, we may never be married. From the expression on mamma's face I fear we never shall. Few parents now-a-days pay any regard to what their children say to them. The old-fashioned respect for the young is fast dying out. Whatever influence I ever had over mamma, I lost at the age of three. But although she may prevent us from becoming man and wife, and I may marry some one else, and marry often, nothing that she can possibly do can alter my eternal devotion to you.

JACK   Dear Gwendolen.

GWENDOLEN   The story of your romantic origin, as related to me by mamma, with unpleasing comments, has naturally stirred the deeper fibers of my nature. Your Christian name has an irresistible fascination. The simplicity of your character makes you exquisitely incomprehensible to me. Your town address at the Albany I have. What is your address in the country?

JACK   The Manor House, Woolton, Hertfordshire. (ALGERNON, *who has been carefully listening, smiles to himself, and writes the address on his shirt-cuff. Then picks up the Railway Guide.*)

GWENDOLEN   There is a good postal service, I suppose? It may be necessary to do something desperate. That, of course, will require serious consideration. I will communicate with you daily.

JACK   My own one!

GWENDOLEN   How long do you remain in town?

JACK   Till Monday.

GWENDOLEN   Good! Algy, you may turn round now.

ALGERNON   Thanks, I've turned round already.

GWENDOLEN   You may also ring the bell.

JACK   You will let me see you to your carriage, my own darling?

GWENDOLEN   Certainly.

JACK (*to LANE, who now enters*)   I will see Miss Fairfax out.

LANE   Yes, sir. (JACK *and* GWENDOLEN *go off.* LANE *presents several letters on a salver to* ALGERNON. *It is to be surmised that they are bills, as* ALGERNON, *after looking at the envelopes, tears them up.*)

ALGERNON   A glass of sherry, Lane.

LANE   Yes, sir.

ALGERNON   To-morrow, Lane. I'm going Bunburying.

LANE   Yes, sir.

ALGERNON   I shall probably not be back till Monday. You can put up my dress clothes, my smoking jacket, and all the Bunbury suits . . .

LANE   Yes, sir. (*Handing sherry.*)

ALGERNON   I hope to-morrow will be a fine day, Lane.

LANE   It never is, sir.

ALGERNON   Lane, you're a perfect pessimist.

LANE   I do my best to give satisfaction, sir.

> *Enter* JACK. LANE *goes off.*

JACK   There's a sensible, intellectual girl! the only girl I ever cared for in my life. (ALGERNON *is laughing immoderately.*) What on earth are you so amused at?

ALGERNON   Oh, I'm a little anxious about poor Bunbury, that's all.

JACK   If you don't take care, your friend Bunbury will get you into a serious scrape some day.

ALGERNON   I love scrapes. They are the only things that are never serious.

JACK   Oh, that's nonsense, Algy. You never talk anything but nonsense.

ALGERNON   Nobody ever does. (JACK *looks indignantly at him, and leaves the room.* ALGERNON *lights a cigarette, reads his shirt-cuff and smiles.*)

Curtain

ACT II

SCENE   *Garden at the Manor House. A flight of gray stone steps leads up to the house. The garden, an old-fashioned one, full of roses. Time of year, July. Basket chairs, and a table covered with books, are set under a large yew tree.*

(MISS PRISM *discovered seated at the table.* CECILY *is at the back watering flowers.*)

MISS PRISM (*calling*)   Cecily, Cecily! Surely such a utilitarian occupation as the watering of flowers is rather Moulton's duty than yours? Especially at a moment when intellectual pleasures await you. Your German grammar is on the table. Pray open it at page fifteen. We will repeat yesterday's lesson.

CECILY (*coming over very slowly*)   But I don't like German. It isn't at all a becoming language. I know perfectly well that I look quite plain after my German lesson.

MISS PRISM   Child, you know how anxious your guardian is that you should improve yourself in every way. He laid particular stress on your German, as he was leaving for town yesterday. Indeed, he always lays stress on your German when he is leaving for town.

CECILY   Dear Uncle Jack is so very serious! Sometimes he is so serious that I think he cannot be quite well.

MISS PRISM (*drawing herself up*)   Your guardian enjoys the best of health, and his gravity of demeanor is especially to be commended in one so comparatively young as he is. I know no one who has a higher sense of duty and responsibility.

CECILY   I suppose that is why he often looks a little bored when we three are together.

MISS PRISM   Cecily! I am surprised at you. Mr. Worthing has many troubles in his life. Idle merriment and triviality would be out of place in his conversation. You must remember his constant anxiety about that unfortunate young man, his brother.

CECILY   I wish Uncle Jack would allow that unfortunate young man, his brother, to come down here sometimes. We might have a good influence over him, Miss Prism. I am sure you certainly would. You know German, and geology, and things of that kind influence a man very much. (CECILY *begins to write in her diary.*)

MISS PRISM (*shaking her head*)   I do not think that even I could produce any effect on a character that, according to his own brother's admission, is irretrievably weak and vacillating. Indeed, I am not sure that I would desire to reclaim him. I am not in favor of this modern mania for turning bad people into good people at a moment's notice. As a man sows so let him reap. You must put away your diary, Cecily. I really don't see why you should keep a diary at all.

CECILY   I keep a diary in order to enter the wonderful secrets of my life. If I didn't write them down I should probably forget all about them.

MISS PRISM   Memory, my dear Cecily, is the diary that we all carry about with us.

CECILY   Yes, but it usually chronicles the things that have never happened, and couldn't possibly have happened. I believe that Memory is responsible for nearly all the three-volume novels that Mudie sends us.

MISS PRISM   Do not speak slightingly of the three-volume novel, Cecily. I wrote one myself in earlier days.

CECILY   Did you really, Miss Prism? How wonderfully clever you are! I hope it did not end happily? I don't like novels that end happily. They depress me so much.

MISS PRISM   The good ended happily, and the bad unhappily. That is what Fiction means.

CECILY   I suppose so. But it seems very unfair. And was your novel ever published?

MISS PRISM   Alas! no. The manuscript unfortunately was abandoned. I use the word in the sense of lost or mislaid. To your work, child, these speculations are profitless.

CECILY (*smiling*)   But I see dear Dr. Chasuble coming up through the garden.

MISS PRISM (*rising and advancing*)   Dr. Chasuble! This is indeed a pleasure.

Enter CANON CHASUBLE.

CHASUBLE   And how are we this morning? Miss Prism, you are, I trust, well?

CECILY   Miss Prism has just been complaining of a slight headache. I think it would do her so much good to have a short stroll with you in the park, Dr. Chasuble.

MISS PRISM   Cecily, I have not mentioned anything about a headache.

CECILY   No, dear Miss Prism, I know that, but I felt instinctively that you had a headache. Indeed I was thinking about that, and not about my German lesson, when the Rector came in.

CHASUBLE   I hope, Cecily, you are not inattentive.

CECILY   Oh, I am afraid I am.

CHASUBLE   That is strange. Were I fortunate enough to be Miss Prism's pupil, I would hang upon her lips. (MISS PRISM *glares.*) I spoke metaphorically.—My metaphor was drawn from bees. Ahem! Mr. Worthing, I suppose, has not returned from town yet?

MISS PRISM We do not expect him till Monday afternoon.

CHASUBLE Ah, yes, he usually likes to spend his Sunday in London. He is not one of those whose sole aim is enjoyment, as, by all accounts, that unfortunate young man, his brother, seems to be. But I must not disturb Egeria and her pupil any longer.

MISS PRISM Egeria? My name is Laetitia, Doctor.

CHASUBLE (*bowing*) A classical allusion merely, drawn from the Pagan authors. I shall see you both no doubt at Evensong.

MISS PRISM I think, dear Doctor, I will have a stroll with you. I find I have a headache after all, and a walk might do it good.

CHASUBLE With pleasure, Miss Prism, with pleasure. We might go as far as the schools and back.

MISS PRISM That would be delightful. Cecily, you will read your Political Economy in my absence. The chapter on the Fall of the Rupee you may omit. It is somewhat too sensational. Even these metallic problems have their melodramatic side. (*Goes down the garden with* DR. CHASUBLE.)

CECILY (*picks up books and throws them back on table*) Horrid Political Economy! Horrid Geography! Horrid, horrid German!

Enter MERRIMAN *with a card on a salver.*

MERRIMAN Mr. Ernest Worthing has just driven over from the station. He has brought his luggage with him.

CECILY (*takes the card and reads it*) "Mr. Ernest Worthing, B4, The Albany, W." Uncle Jack's brother! Did you tell him Mr. Worthing was in town?

MERRIMAN Yes, Miss. He seemed very much disappointed. I mentioned that you and Miss Prism were in the garden. He said he was anxious to speak to you privately for a moment.

CECILY Ask Mr. Ernest Worthing to come here. I suppose you had better talk to the housekeeper about a room for him.

MERRIMAN Yes, Miss. (MERRIMAN *goes off.*)

CECILY I have never met any really wicked person before. I feel rather frightened. I am so afraid he will look just like every one else.

Enter ALGERNON, *very gay and debonair.*

He does!

ALGERNON (*raising his hat*) You are my little cousin Cecily, I'm sure.

CECILY You are under some strange mistake. I am not little. In fact, I am more than usually tall for my age. (ALGERNON *is rather taken aback.*) But I am your cousin Cecily. You, I see from your card, are Uncle Jack's brother, my cousin Ernest, my wicked cousin Ernest.

ALGERNON Oh! I am not really wicked at all, cousin Cecily. You mustn't think that I am wicked.

CECILY If you are not, then you have certainly been deceiving us all in a very inexcusable manner. I hope you have not been leading a double life, pretending to be wicked and being really good all the time. That would be hypocrisy.

ALGERNON (*looks at her in amazement*)   Oh! of course I have been rather reckless.

CECILY   I am glad to hear it.

ALGERNON   In fact, now you mention the subject, I have been very bad in my own small way.

CECILY   I don't think you should be so proud of that, though I am sure it must have been very pleasant.

ALGERNON   It is much pleasanter being here with you.

CECILY   I can't understand how you are here at all. Uncle Jack won't be back till Monday afternoon.

ALGERNON   That is a great disappointment. I am obliged to go up by the first train on Monday morning. I have a business appointment that I am anxious . . . to miss.

CECILY   Couldn't you miss it anywhere but in London?

ALGERNON   No; the appointment is in London.

CECILY   Well, I know, of course, how important it is not to keep a business engagement, if one wants to retain any sense of the beauty of life, but still I think you had better wait till Uncle Jack arrives. I know he wants to speak to you about your emigrating.

ALGERNON   About my what?

CECILY   Your emigrating. He has gone up to buy your outfit.

ALGERNON   I certainly wouldn't let Jack buy my outfit. He has no taste in neckties at all.

CECILY   I don't think you will require neckties. Uncle Jack is sending you to Australia.

ALGERNON   Australia! I'd sooner die.

CECILY   Well, he said at dinner on Wednesday night, that you would have to choose between this world, the next world, and Australia.

ALGERNON   Oh, well! The accounts I have received of Australia and the next world, are not particularly encouraging. This world is good enough for me, cousin Cecily.

CECILY   Yes, but are you good enough for it?

ALGERNON   I'm afraid I'm not that. That is why I want you to reform me. You might make that your mission, if you don't mind, cousin Cecily.

CECILY   I'm afraid I've not time, this afternoon.

ALGERNON   Well, would you mind my reforming myself this afternoon?

CECILY   That is rather Quixotic of you. But I think you should try.

ALGERNON   I will. I feel better already.

CECILY   You are looking a little worse.

ALGERNON   That is because I am hungry.

CECILY   How thoughtless of me. I should have remembered that when one is going to lead an entirely new life, one requires regular and wholesome meals. Won't you come in?

ALGERNON   Thank you. Might I have a button-hole first? I never have any appetite unless I have a button-hole first.

CECILY   A Maréchal Niel? (*Picks up scissors.*)

ALGERNON   No, I'd sooner have a pink rose.

CECILY   Why? (*Cuts a flower.*)

ALGERNON   Because you are like a pink rose, cousin Cecily.

CECILY   I don't think it can be right for you to talk to me like that. Miss Prism never says such things to me.

ALGERNON   Then Miss Prism is a short-sighted old lady. (CECILY *puts the rose in his button-hole.*) You are the prettiest girl I ever saw.

CECILY   Miss Prism says that all good looks are a snare.

ALGERNON   They are a snare that every sensible man would like to be caught in.

CECILY   Oh! I don't think I would care to catch a sensible man. I shouldn't know what to talk to him about. (*They pass into the house.* MISS PRISM *and* DR. CHASUBLE *return.*)

MISS PRISM   You are too much alone, dear Dr. Chasuble. You should get married. A misanthrope I can understand—a womanthrope, never!

CHASUBLE (*with a scholar's shudder*)   Believe me, I do not deserve so neologistic a phrase. The precept as well as the practice of the Primitive Church was distinctly against matrimony.

MISS PRISM (*sententiously*)   That is obviously the reason why the Primitive Church has not lasted up to the present day. And you do not seem to realize, dear Doctor, that by persistently remaining single, a man converts himself into a permanent public temptation. Men should be careful; this very celibacy leads weaker vessels astray.

CHASUBLE   But is a man not equally attractive when married?

MISS PRISM   No married man is ever attractive except to his wife.

CHASUBLE   And often, I've been told, not even to her.

MISS PRISM   That depends on the intellectual sympathies of the woman. Maturity can always be depended on. Ripeness can be trusted. Young women are green. (DR. CHASUBLE *starts.*) I spoke horticulturally. My metaphor was drawn from fruits. But where is Cecily?

CHASUBLE   Perhaps she followed us to the schools.

> *Enter* JACK *slowly from the back of the garden. He is dressed in the deepest mourning, with crape hatband and black gloves.*

MISS PRISM   Mr. Worthing!

CHASUBLE   Mr. Worthing?

MISS PRISM   This is indeed a surprise. We did not look for you till Monday afternoon.

JACK (*shakes* MISS PRISM'S *hand in a tragic manner*)   I have returned sooner than I expected. Dr. Chasuble, I hope you are well?

CHASUBLE   Dear Mr. Worthing, I trust this garb of woe does not betoken some terrible calamity?

JACK   My brother.

MISS PRISM   More shameful debts and extravagance?

CHASUBLE   Still leading his life of pleasure?

JACK (*shaking his head*)   Dead!

CHASUBLE   Your brother Ernest dead?

JACK   Quite dead.

MISS PRISM   What a lesson for him! I trust he will profit by it.

CHASUBLE   Mr. Worthing, I offer you my sincere condolence. You have at least the consolation of knowing that you were always the most generous and forgiving of brothers.

JACK   Poor Ernest! He had many faults, but it is a sad, sad blow.

CHASUBLE   Very sad indeed. Were you with him at the end?

JACK   No. He died abroad; in Paris, in fact. I had a telegram last night from the manager of the Grand Hotel.

CHASUBLE   Was the cause of death mentioned?

JACK   A severe chill, it seems.

MISS PRISM   As a man sows, so shall he reap.

CHASUBLE (*raising his hand*)   Charity, dear Miss Prism, charity! None of us are perfect. I myself am peculiarly susceptible to draughts. Will the interment take place here?

JACK   No. He seems to have expressed a desire to be buried in Paris.

CHASUBLE   In Paris! (*Shakes his head.*) I fear that hardly points to any very serious state of mind at the last. You would no doubt wish me to make some slight allusion to this tragic domestic affliction next Sunday. (JACK *presses his hand convulsively.*) My sermon on the meaning of the manna in the wilderness can be adapted to almost any occasion, joyful, or, as in the present case, distressing. (*All sigh.*) I have preached it at harvest celebrations, christenings, confirmations, on days of humiliation and festal days. The last time I delivered it was in the Cathedral, as a charity sermon on behalf of the Society for the Prevention of Discontentment among the Upper Orders. The Bishop, who was present, was much struck by some of the analogies I drew.

JACK   Ah, that reminds me, you mentioned christenings I think, Dr. Chasuble? I suppose you know how to christen all right? (DR. CHASUBLE *looks astounded.*) I mean, of course, you are continually christening, aren't you?

MISS PRISM   It is, I regret to say, one of the Rector's most constant duties in this parish. I have often spoken to the poorer classes on the subject. But they don't seem to know what thrift is.

CHASUBLE   But is there any particular infant in whom you are interested, Mr. Worthing? Your brother was, I believe, unmarried, was he not?

JACK   Oh, yes.

MISS PRISM   (*bitterly*)   People who live entirely for pleasure usually are.

JACK   But it is not for any child, dear Doctor. I am very fond of children. No! the fact is, I would like to be christened myself, this afternoon, if you have nothing better to do.

CHASUBLE   But surely, Mr. Worthing, you have been christened already?

JACK   I don't remember anything about it.

CHASUBLE   But have you any grave doubts on the subject?

JACK   I certainly intend to have. Of course, I don't know if the thing would bother you in any way, or if you think I am a little too old now.

CHASUBLE   Not at all. The sprinkling, and, indeed, the immersion of adults is a perfectly canonical practice.

JACK   Immersion!

CHASUBLE   You need have no apprehensions. Sprinkling is all that is necessary, or indeed I think advisable. Our weather is so changeable. At what hour would you wish the ceremony performed?

JACK   Oh, I might trot around about five if that would suit you.

CHASUBLE   Perfectly, perfectly! In fact I have two similar ceremonies to perform at that time. A case of twins that occurred recently in one of the outlying cottages on your own estate. Poor Jenkins the carter, a most hard-working man.

JACK   Oh! I don't see much fun in being christened along with other babies. It would be childish. Would half-past five do?

CHASUBLE   Admirably! Admirably! (*Takes out watch.*) And now, dear Mr. Worthing, I will not intrude any longer into a house of sorrow. I would merely beg you not to be too much bowed down by grief. What seem to us bitter trials at the moment are often blessings in disguise.

MISS PRISM   This seems to me a blessing of an extremely obvious kind.

Enter CECILY *from the house.*

CECILY   Uncle Jack! Oh, I am pleased to see you back. But what horrid clothes you have on! Do go and change them.

MISS PRISM   Cecily!

CHASUBLE   My child! my child! (CECILY *goes towards* JACK; *he kisses her brow in a melancholy manner.*)

CECILY   What is the matter, Uncle Jack? Do look happy! You look as if you had a toothache and I have such a surprise for you. Who do you think is in the dining-room? Your brother!

JACK   Who?

CECILY Your brother Ernest. He arrived about half an hour ago.

JACK What nonsense! I haven't got a brother.

CECILY Oh, don't say that. However badly he may have behaved to you in the past he is still your brother. You couldn't be so heartless as to disown him. I'll tell him to come out. And you will shake hands with him, won't you, Uncle Jack? (*Runs back into the house.*)

CHASUBLE These are very joyful tidings.

MISS PRISM After we had all been resigned to his loss, his sudden return seems to me peculiarly distressing.

JACK My brother is in the dining-room? I don't know what it all means. I think it is perfectly absurd.

Enter ALGERNON *and* CECILY *hand in hand. They come slowly up to* JACK.

JACK Good heavens! (*Motions* ALGERNON *away.*)

ALGERNON Brother John, I have come down from town to tell you that I am very sorry for all the trouble I have given you, and that I intend to lead a better life in the future. (JACK *glares at him and does not take his hand.*)

CECILY Uncle Jack, you are not going to refuse your own brother's hand?

JACK Nothing will induce me to take his hand. I think his coming down here disgraceful. He knows perfectly well why.

CECILY Uncle Jack, do be nice. There is some good in every one. Ernest has just been telling me about his poor invalid friend, Mr. Bunbury, whom he goes to visit so often. And surely there must be much good in one who is kind to an invalid, and leaves the pleasures of London to sit by a bed of pain.

JACK Oh, he has been talking about Bunbury, has he?

CECILY Yes, he has told me all about poor Mr. Bunbury, and his terrible state of health.

JACK Bunbury! Well, I won't have him talk to you about Bunbury or about anything else. It is enough to drive one perfectly frantic.

ALGERNON Of course I admit that the faults were all on my side. But I must say that I think that Brother John's coldness to me is peculiarly painful. I expected a more enthusiastic welcome, especially considering it is the first time I have come here.

CECILY Uncle Jack, if you don't shake hands with Ernest I will never forgive you.

JACK Never forgive me?

CECILY Never, never, never!

JACK Well, this is the last time I shall ever do it. (*Shakes hands with* ALGERNON *and glares.*)

CHASUBLE It's pleasant, is it not, to see so perfect a reconciliation? I think we might leave the two brothers together.

MISS PRISM Cecily, you will come with us.

CECILY   Certainly, Miss Prism. My little task of reconciliation is over.

CHASUBLE   You have done a beautiful action to-day, dear child.

MISS PRISM   We must not be premature in our judgments.

CECILY   I feel very happy. (*They all go off.*)

JACK   You young scoundrel, Algy, you must get out of this place as soon as possible. I don't allow any Bunburying here.

   Enter MERRIMAN.

MERRIMAN   I have put Mr. Ernest's things in the room next to yours, sir. I suppose that is all right?

JACK   What?

MERRIMAN   Mr. Ernest's luggage, sir. I have unpacked it and put it in the room next to your own.

JACK   His luggage?

MERRIMAN   Yes, sir. Three portmanteaus, a dressing-case, two hat-boxes, and a large luncheon-basket.

ALGERNON   I am afraid I can't stay more than a week this time.

JACK   Merriman, order the dog-cart at once. Mr. Ernest has been suddenly called back to town.

MERRIMAN   Yes, sir. (*Goes back into the house.*)

ALGERNON   What a fearful liar you are, Jack. I have not been called back to town at all.

JACK   Yes, you have.

ALGERNON   I haven't heard any one call me.

JACK   Your duty as a gentleman calls you back.

ALGERNON   My duty as a gentleman has never interfered with my pleasures in the smallest degree.

JACK   I can quite understand that.

ALGERNON   Well, Cecily is a darling.

JACK   You are not to talk of Miss Cardew like that. I don't like it.

ALGERNON   Well, I don't like your clothes. You look perfectly ridiculous in them. Why on earth don't you go up and change? It is perfectly childish to be in deep mourning for a man who is actually staying for a whole week with you in your house as a guest. I call it grotesque.

JACK   You are certainly not staying with me for a whole week as a guest or anything else. You have got to leave . . . by the four-five train.

ALGERNON   I certainly won't leave you so long as you are in mourning. It would be most unfriendly. If I were in mourning you would stay with me, I suppose. I should think it very unkind if you didn't.

JACK   Well, will you go if I change my clothes?

ALGERNON   Yes, if you are not too long. I never saw anybody take so long to dress, and with such little result.

JACK   Well, at any rate, that is better than being always over-dressed as you are.

ALGERNON   If I am occasionally a little over-dressed, I make up for it by being always immensely over-educated.

JACK   Your vanity is ridiculous, your conduct an outrage, and your presence in my garden utterly absurd. However, you have got to catch the four-five, and I hope you will have a pleasant journey back to town. This Bunburying, as you call it, has not been a great success for you. (*Goes into the house.*)

ALGERNON   I think it has been a great success. I'm in love with Cecily, and that is everything. (*Enter* CECILY *at the back of the garden. She picks up the can and begins to water the flowers.*) But I must see her before I go, and make arrangements for another Bunbury. Ah, there she is.

CECILY   Oh, I merely came back to water the roses. I thought you were with Uncle Jack.

ALGERNON   He's gone to order the dog-cart for me.

CECILY   Oh, is he going to take you for a nice drive?

ALGERNON   He's going to send me away.

CECILY   Then have we got to part?

ALGERNON   I am afraid so. It's a very painful parting.

CECILY   It is always painful to part from people whom one has known for a very brief space of time. The absence of old friends one can endure with equanimity. But even a momentary separation from any one to whom one has just been introduced is almost unbearable.

ALGERNON   Thank you.

   Enter MERRIMAN.

MERRIMAN   The dog-cart is at the door, sir. (ALGERNON *looks appealingly at* CECILY.)

CECILY   It can wait, Merriman . . . for . . . five minutes.

MERRIMAN   Yes, miss.

   Exit MERRIMAN.

ALGERNON   I hope, Cecily, I shall not offend you if I state quite frankly and openly that you seem to me to be in every way the visible personification of absolute perfection.

CECILY   I think your frankness does you great credit, Ernest. If you will allow me I will copy your remarks into my diary. (*Goes over to table and begins writing in diary.*)

ALGERNON   Do you really keep a diary? I'd give anything to look at it. May I?

CECILY   Oh, no. (*Puts her hand over it.*) You see it is simply a very young girl's record of her own thoughts and impressions, and consequently meant for publication. When it appears in volume form I hope you will order a copy. But pray, Ernest, don't stop. I delight in taking down from dictation. I have reached "absolute perfection." You can go on. I am quite ready for more.

ALGERNON (*somewhat taken aback*)   Ahem! Ahem!

CECILY   Oh, don't cough, Ernest. When one is dictating one should speak fluently and not cough. Besides, I don't know how to spell a cough. (*Writes as* ALGERNON *speaks.*)

ALGERNON (*speaking very rapidly*)   Cecily, ever since I first looked upon your wonderful and incomparable beauty, I have dared to love you wildly, passionately, devotedly, hopelessly.

CECILY   I don't think that you should tell me that you love me wildly, passionately, devotedly, hopelessly. Hopelessly doesn't seem to make much sense, does it?

ALGERNON   Cecily!

   Enter MERRIMAN.

MERRIMAN   The dog-cart is waiting, sir.

ALGERNON   Tell it to come round next week, at the same hour.

MERRIMAN (*looks at* CECILY, *who makes no sign*)   Yes, sir.

   MERRIMAN *retires.*

CECILY   Uncle Jack would be very much annoyed if he knew you were staying on till next week, at the same hour.

ALGERNON   Oh, I don't care about Jack. I don't care for anybody in the whole world but you. I love you, Cecily. You will marry me, won't you?

CECILY   You silly you! Of course. Why, we have been engaged for the last three months.

ALGERNON   For the last three months?

CECILY   Yes, it will be exactly three months on Thursday.

ALGERNON   But how did we become engaged?

CECILY   Well, ever since dear Uncle Jack first confessed to us that he had a younger brother who was very wicked and bad, you of course have formed the chief topic of conversation between myself and Miss Prism. And of course a man who is much talked about is always very attractive. One feels there must be something in him after all. I daresay it was foolish of me, but I fell in love with you, Ernest.

ALGERNON   Darling! And when was the engagement actually settled?

CECILY   On the 4th of February last. Worn out by your entire ignorance of my existence, I determined to end the matter one way or the other, and after a long struggle with myself I accepted you under this dear old tree here. The next day I bought this little ring in your name, and this is the little bangle with the true lovers' knot I promised you always to wear.

ALGERNON   Did I give you this? It's very pretty, isn't it?

CECILY   Yes, you've wonderfully good taste, Ernest. It's the excuse I've always given for your leading such a bad life. And this is the box in which I keep all your dear letters. (*Kneels at table, opens box, and produces letters tied up with blue ribbon.*)

ALGERNON   My letters! but my own sweet Cecily, I have never written
you any letters.

CECILY   You need hardly remind me of that, Ernest. I remember only
too well that I was forced to write your letters for you. I wrote always
three times a week, and sometimes oftener.

ALGERNON   Oh, do let me read them, Cecily?

CECILY   Oh, I couldn't possibly. They would make you far too con-
ceited. (*Replaces box.*) The three you wrote me after I had broken off
the engagement are so beautiful, and so badly spelled, that even now
I can hardly read them without crying a little.

ALGERNON   But was our engagement ever broken off?

CECILY   Of course it was. On the 22nd of last March. You can see the
entry if you like. (*Shows diary.*) "To-day I broke off my engagement
with Ernest. I feel it is better to do so. The weather still continues
charming."

ALGERNON   But why on earth did you break it off? What had I done? I
had done nothing at all. Cecily, I am very much hurt indeed to hear
you broke it off. Particularly when the weather was so charming.

CECILY   It would hardly have been a really serious engagement if it
hadn't been broken off at least once. But I forgave you before the
week was out.

ALGERNON (*crossing to her, and kneeling*)   What a perfect angel you are,
Cecily.

CECILY   You dear romantic boy. (*He kisses her, she puts her fingers through
his hair.*) I hope your hair curls naturally, does it?

ALGERNON   Yes, darling, with a little help from others.

CECILY   I am so glad.

ALGERNON   You'll never break off our engagement again, Cecily?

CECILY   I don't think I could break it off now that I have actually met
you. Besides, of course, there is the question of your name.

ALGERNON   Yes, of course. (*Nervously.*)

CECILY   You must not laugh at me, darling, but it had always been a
girlish dream of mine to love some one whose name was Ernest.
(ALGERNON *rises,* CECILY *also.*) There is something in that name that
seems to inspire absolute confidence. I pity any poor married woman
whose husband is not called Ernest.

ALGERNON   But, my dear child, do you mean to say you could not love
me if I had some other name?

CECILY   But what name?

ALGERNON   Oh, any name you like—Algernon, for instance. . . .

CECILY   But I don't like the name of Algernon.

ALGERNON   Well, my own dear, sweet, loving little darling, I really can't
see why you should object to the name of Algernon. It is not at all a
bad name. In fact, it is rather an aristocratic name. Half of the chaps
who get into the Bankruptcy Court are called Algernon. But seri-

ously, Cecily . . . (*moving to her*) . . . if my name was Algy, couldn't you love me?

CECILY (*rising*)   I might respect you, Ernest, I might admire your character, but I fear that I should not be able to give you my undivided attention.

ALGERNON   Ahem! Cecily! (*Picking up hat.*) Your Rector here is, I suppose, thoroughly experienced in the practice of all the rites and ceremonials of the church?

CECILY   Oh, yes. Dr. Chasuble is a most learned man. He has never written a single book, so you can imagine how much he knows.

ALGERNON   I must see him at once on a most important christening—I mean on most important business.

CECILY   Oh!

ALGERNON   I sha'n't be away more than half an hour.

CECILY   Considering that we have been engaged since February the 14th, and that I only met you to-day for the first time, I think it is rather hard that you should leave me for so long a period as half an hour. Couldn't you make it twenty minutes?

ALGERNON   I'll be back in no time. (*Kisses her and rushes down the garden.*)

CECILY   What an impetuous boy he is. I like his hair so much. I must enter his proposal in my diary.

Enter MERRIMAN.

MERRIMAN   A Miss Fairfax has just called to see Mr. Worthing. On very important business, Miss Fairfax states.

CECILY   Isn't Mr. Worthing in his library?

MERRIMAN   Mr. Worthing went over in the direction of the Rectory some time ago.

CECILY   Pray ask the lady to come out here; Mr. Worthing is sure to be back soon. And you can bring tea.

MERRIMAN   Yes, miss. (*Goes out.*)

CECILY   Miss Fairfax! I suppose one of the many good elderly women who are associated with Uncle Jack in some of his philanthropic work in London. I don't quite like women who are interested in philanthropic work. I think it is so forward of them.

Enter MERRIMAN.

MERRIMAN   Miss Fairfax.

Enter GWENDOLEN. *Exit* MERRIMAN.

CECILY (*advancing to meet her*)   Pray let me introduce myself to you. My name is Cecily Cardew.

GWENDOLEN   Cecily Cardew? (*Moving to her and shaking hands.*) What a very sweet name! Something tells me that we are going to be great friends. I like you already more than I can say. My first impressions of people are never wrong.

CECILY   How nice of you to like me so much after we have known each
other such a comparatively short time. Pray sit down.

GWENDOLEN (*still standing up*)   I may call you Cecily, may I not?

CECILY   With pleasure!

GWENDOLEN   And you will always call me Gwendolen, won't you?

CECILY   If you wish.

GWENDOLEN   Then that is all quite settled, is it not?

CECILY   I hope so. (*A pause; they both sit down together.*)

GWENDOLEN   Perhaps this might be a favorable opportunity for my
mentioning who I am. My father is Lord Bracknell. You have never
heard of papa, I suppose?

CECILY   I don't think so.

GWENDOLEN   Outside the family circle, papa, I am glad to say, is entirely unknown. I think that is quite as it should be. The home seems
to me to be the proper sphere for the man. And certainly once a man
begins to neglect his domestic duties he becomes painfully effemi-
nate, does he not? And I don't like that. It makes men so very attractive. Cecily, mamma, whose views on education are remarkably strict,
has brought me up to be extremely short-sighted; it is part of her
system; so do you mind my looking at you through my glasses?

CECILY   Oh, not at all, Gwendolen. I am very fond of being looked at.

GWENDOLEN (*after examining* CECILY *carefully through a lorgnette*)   You
are here on a short visit, I suppose.

CECILY   Oh, no, I live here.

GWENDOLEN (*severely*)   Really? Your mother, no doubt, or some female
relative of advanced years, resides here also?

CECILY   Oh, no. I have no mother, nor, in fact, any relations.

GWENDOLEN   Indeed?

CECILY   My dear guardian, with the assistance of Miss Prism, has the
arduous task of looking after me.

GWENDOLEN   Your guardian?

CECILY   Yes, I am Mr. Worthing's ward.

GWENDOLEN   Oh! It is strange he never mentioned to me that he had a
ward. How secretive of him! He grows more interesting hourly. I am
not sure, however, that the news inspires me with feelings of unmixed delight. (*Rising and going to her.*) I am very fond of you, Cecily; I
have liked you ever since I met you. But I am bound to state that now
that I know that you are Mr. Worthing's ward, I cannot help expressing a wish you were—well, just a little older than you seem to be—
and not quite so very alluring in appearance. In fact, if I may speak
candidly—

CECILY   Pray do! I think that whenever one has anything unpleasant to
say, one should always be quite candid.

GWENDOLEN   Well, to speak with perfect candor, Cecily, I wish that you
were fully forty-two, and more than usually plain for your age. Ernest
has a strong upright nature. He is the very soul of truth and honor.

Disloyalty would be as impossible to him as deception. But even men of the noblest possible moral character are extremely susceptible to the influence of the physical charms of others. Modern, no less than Ancient History, supplies us with many most painful examples of what I refer to. If it were not so, indeed, History would be quite unreadable.

CECILY   I beg your pardon, Gwendolen, did you say Ernest?

GWENDOLEN   Yes.

CECILY   Oh, but it is not Mr. Ernest Worthing who is my guardian. It is his brother—his elder brother.

GWENDOLEN (*sitting down again*)   Ernest never mentioned to me that he had a brother.

CECILY   I am sorry to say they have not been on good terms for a long time.

GWENDOLEN   Ah! that accounts for it. And now that I think of it I have never heard any man mention his brother. The subject seems distasteful to most men. Cecily, you have lifted a load from my mind. I was growing almost anxious. It would have been terrible if any cloud had come across a friendship like ours, would it not? Of course you are quite, quite sure that it is not Mr. Ernest Worthing who is your guardian?

CECILY   Quite sure. (*A pause.*) In fact, I am going to be his.

GWENDOLEN (*enquiringly*)   I beg your pardon?

CECILY (*rather shy and confidingly*)   Dearest Gwendolen, there is no reason why I should make a secret of it to you. Our little county newspaper is sure to chronicle the fact next week. Mr. Ernest Worthing and I are engaged to be married.

GWENDOLEN (*quite politely, rising*)   My darling Cecily, I think there must be some slight error. Mr. Ernest Worthing is engaged to me. The announcement will appear in the *Morning Post* on Saturday at the latest.

CECILY (*very politely, rising*)   I am afraid you must be under some misconception. Ernest proposed to me exactly ten minutes ago. (*Shows diary.*)

GWENDOLEN (*examines diary through her lorgnette carefully*)   It is certainly very curious, for he asked me to be his wife yesterday afternoon at 5:30. If you would care to verify the incident, pray do so. (*Produces diary of her own.*) I never travel without my diary. One should always have something sensational to read in the train. I am so sorry, dear Cecily, if it is any disappointment to you, but I'm afraid *I* have the prior claim.

CECILY   It would distress me more than I can tell you, dear Gwendolen, if it caused you any mental or physical anguish, but I feel bound to point out that since Ernest proposed to you he clearly has changed his mind.

GWENDOLEN (*meditatively*)   If the poor fellow has been entrapped into any foolish promise I shall consider it my duty to rescue him at once, and with a firm hand.

CECILY (*thoughtfully and sadly*)   Whatever unfortunate entanglement my dear boy may have got into, I will never reproach him with it after we are married.

GWENDOLEN   Do you allude to me, Miss Cardew, as an entanglement? You are presumptuous. On an occasion of this kind it becomes more than a moral duty to speak one's mind. It becomes a pleasure.

CECILY   Do you suggest, Miss Fairfax, that I entrapped Ernest into an engagement? How dare you? This is no time for wearing the shallow mask of manners. When I see a spade I call it a spade.

GWENDOLEN (*satirically*)   I am glad to say that I have never seen a spade. It is obvious that our social spheres have been widely different.

Enter MERRIMAN, *followed by the footman. He carries a salver, table-cloth, and plate-stand.* CECILY *is about to retort. The presence of the servants exercises a restraining influence, under which both girls chafe.*

MERRIMAN   Shall I lay tea here as usual, miss?

CECILY (*sternly, in a calm voice*)   Yes, as usual. (MERRIMAN *begins to clear and lay cloth. A long pause.* CECILY *and* GWENDOLEN *glare at each other.*)

GWENDOLEN   Are there many interesting walks in the vicinity, Miss Cardew?

CECILY   Oh, yes, a great many. From the top of one of the hills quite close one can see five counties.

GWENDOLEN   Five counties! I don't think I should like that. I hate crowds.

CECILY (*sweetly*)   I suppose that is why you live in town? (GWENDOLYN *bites her lip, and beats her foot nervously with her parasol.*)

GWENDOLEN (*looking round*)   Quite a well-kept garden this is, Miss Cardew.

CECILY   So glad you like it, Miss Fairfax.

GWENDOLEN   I had no idea there were any flowers in the country.

CECILY   Oh, flowers are as common here, Miss Fairfax, as people are in London.

GWENDOLEN   Personally I cannot understand how anybody manages to exist in the country, if anybody who is anybody does. The country always bores me to death.

CECILY   Ah! This is what the newspapers call agricultural depression, is it not? I believe the aristocracy are suffering very much from it just at present. It is almost an epidemic amongst them, I have been told. May I offer you some tea, Miss Fairfax?

GWENDOLEN (*with elaborate politeness*)   Thank you. (*Aside.*) Detestable girl! But I require tea!

CECILY (*sweetly*)   Sugar?

GWENDOLEN (*superciliously*)   No, thank you. Sugar is not fashionable any more. (CECILY *looks angrily at her, takes up the tongs and puts four lumps of sugar into the cup.*)

CECILY (*severely*)   Cake or bread and butter?

GWENDOLEN (*in a bored manner*)   Bread and butter, please. Cake is rarely seen at the best houses now-a-days.

CECILY (*cuts a very large slice of cake, and puts it on the tray*).   Hand that to Miss Fairfax. (MERRIMAN *does so, and goes out with footman.* GWENDOLEN *drinks the tea and makes a grimace. Puts down cup at once, reaches out her hand to the bread and butter, looks at it, and finds it is cake. Rises in indignation.*)

GWENDOLEN   You have filled my tea with lumps of sugar, and though I asked most distinctly for bread and butter, you have given me cake. I am known for the gentleness of my disposition, and the extraordinary sweetness of my nature, but I warn you, Miss Cardew, you may go too far.

CECILY (*rising*)   To save my poor, innocent, trusting boy from the machinations of any other girl there are no lengths to which I would not go.

GWENDOLEN   From the moment I saw you I distrusted you. I felt that you were false and deceitful. I am never deceived in such matters. My first impressions of people are invariably right.

CECILY   It seems to me, Miss Fairfax, that I am trespassing on your valuable time. No doubt you have many other calls of a similar character to make in the neighborhood.

> *Enter* JACK.

GWENDOLEN (*catching sight of him*)   Ernest! My own Ernest!

JACK   Gwendolen! Darling! (*Offers to kiss her.*)

GWENDOLEN (*drawing back*)   A moment! May I ask if you are engaged to be married to this young lady? (*Points to* CECILY.)

JACK (*laughing*)   To dear little Cecily! Of course not! What could have put such an idea into your pretty little head?

GWENDOLEN   Thank you. You may. (*Offers her cheek.*)

CECILY (*very sweetly*)   I knew there must be some misunderstanding, Miss Fairfax. The gentleman whose arm is at present around your waist is my dear guardian, Mr. John Worthing.

GWENDOLEN   I beg your pardon?

CECILY   This is Uncle Jack.

GWENDOLEN (*receding*)   Jack! Oh!

> *Enter* ALGERNON.

CECILY   Here is Ernest.

ALGERNON (*goes straight over to* CECILY *without noticing any one else*)   My own love! (*Offers to kiss her.*)

CECILY (*drawing back*) A moment, Ernest! May I ask you—are you engaged to be married to this young lady?

ALGERNON (*looking round*) To what young lady? Good heavens! Gwendolen!

CECILY Yes, to good heavens, Gwendolen, I mean to Gwendolen.

ALGERNON (*laughing*) Of course not! What could have put such an idea into your pretty little head?

CECILY Thank you. (*Presenting her cheek to be kissed.*) You may. (ALGERNON *kisses her.*)

GWENDOLEN I felt there was some slight error, Miss Cardew. The gentleman who is now embracing you is my cousin, Mr. Algernon Moncrieff.

CECILY (*breaking away from* ALGERNON) Algernon Moncrieff! Oh! (*The two girls move towards each other and put their arms round each other's waists as if for protection.*)

CECILY Are you called Algernon?

ALGERNON I cannot deny it.

CECILY Oh!

GWENDOLEN Is your name really John?

JACK (*standing rather proudly*) I could deny it if I liked. I could deny anything if I liked. But my name certainly is John. It has been John for years.

CECILY (*to* GWENDOLEN) A gross deception has been practiced on both of us.

GWENDOLEN My poor wounded Cecily!

CECILY My sweet, wronged Gwendolen!

GWENDOLEN (*slowly and seriously*) You will call me sister, will you not? (*They embrace.* JACK *and* ALGERNON *groan and walk up and down.*)

CECILY (*rather brightly*) There is just one question I would like to be allowed to ask my guardian.

GWENDOLEN An admirable idea! Mr. Worthing, there is just one question I would like to be permitted to put to you. Where is your brother Ernest? We are both engaged to be married to your brother Ernest, so it is a matter of some importance to us to know where your brother Ernest is at present.

JACK (*slowly and hesitatingly*) Gwendolen—Cecily—it is very painful for me to be forced to speak the truth. It is the first time in my life that I have ever been reduced to such a painful position, and I am really quite inexperienced in doing anything of the kind. However I will tell you quite frankly that I have no brother Ernest. I have no brother at all. I never had a brother in my life, and I certainly have not the smallest intention of ever having one in the future.

CECILY (*surprised*) No brother at all?

JACK (*cheerily*) None!

GWENDOLEN (*severely*) Had you never a brother of any kind?

JACK (*pleasantly*)   Never. Not even of any kind.

GWENDOLEN   I am afraid it is quite clear, Cecily, that neither of us is engaged to be married to any one.

CECILY   It is not a very pleasant position for a young girl suddenly to find herself in. Is it?

GWENDOLEN   Let us go into the house. They will hardly venture to come after us there.

CECILY   No, men are so cowardly, aren't they? (*They retire into the house with scornful looks.*)

JACK   This ghastly state of things is what you call Bunburying, I suppose?

ALGERNON   Yes, and a perfectly wonderful Bunbury it is. The most wonderful Bunbury I have ever had in my life.

JACK   Well, you've no right whatsoever to Bunbury here.

ALGERNON   That is absurd. One has a right to Bunbury anywhere one chooses. Every serious Bunburyist knows that.

JACK   Serious Bunburyist! Good heavens!

ALGERNON   Well, one must be serious about something, if one wants to have any amusement in life. I happen to be serious about Bunburying. What on earth you are serious about I haven't got the remotest idea. About everything, I should fancy. You have such an absolutely trivial nature.

JACK   Well, the only small satisfaction I have in the whole of this wretched business is that your friend Bunbury is quite exploded. You won't be able to run down to the country quite so often as you used to do, dear Algy. And a very good thing, too.

ALGERNON   Your brother is a little off color, isn't he, dear Jack? You won't be able to disappear to London quite so frequently as your wicked custom was. And not a bad thing, either.

JACK   As for your conduct towards Miss Cardew, I must say that your taking in a sweet, simple, innocent girl like that is quite inexcusable. To say nothing of the fact that she is my ward.

ALGERNON   I can see no possible defense at all for your deceiving a brilliant, clever, thoroughly experienced young lady like Miss Fairfax. To say nothing of the fact that she is my cousin.

JACK   I wanted to be engaged to Gwendolen, that is all. I love her.

ALGERNON   Well, I simply wanted to be engaged to Cecily. I adore her.

JACK   There is certainly no chance of your marrying Miss Cardew.

ALGERNON   I don't think there is much likelihood, Jack, of you and Miss Fairfax being united.

JACK   Well, that is no business of yours.

ALGERNON   If it was my business, I wouldn't talk about it. (*Begins to eat muffins.*) It is very vulgar to talk about one's business. Only people like stock-brokers do that, and then merely at dinner parties.

JACK   How you can sit there, calmly eating muffins, when we are in this horrible trouble, I can't make out. You seem to me to be perfectly heartless.

ALGERNON   Well, I can't eat muffins in an agitated manner. The butter would probably get on my cuffs. One should always eat muffins quite calmly. It is the only way to eat them.

JACK   I say it's perfectly heartless your eating muffins at all, under the circumstances.

ALGERNON   When I am in trouble, eating is the only thing that consoles me. Indeed, when I am in really great trouble, as any one who knows me intimately will tell you, I refuse everything except food and drink. At the present moment I am eating muffins because I am unhappy. Besides, I am particularly fond of muffins. (*Rising.*)

JACK (*rising*)   Well, that is no reason why you should eat them all in that greedy way. (*Takes muffins from* ALGERNON.)

ALGERNON (*offering tea-cake*)   I wish you would have tea-cake instead. I don't like tea-cake.

JACK   Good heavens! I suppose a man may eat his own muffins in his own garden.

ALGERNON   But you have just said it was perfectly heartless to eat muffins.

JACK   I said it was perfectly heartless of you, under the circumstances. That is a very different thing.

ALGERNON   That may be. But the muffins are the same. (*He seizes the muffin-dish from* JACK.)

JACK   Algy, I wish to goodness you would go.

ALGERNON   You can't possibly ask me to go without having some dinner. It's absurd. I never go without my dinner. No one ever does, except vegetarians, and people like that. Besides I have just made arrangements with Dr. Chasuble to be christened at a quarter to six under the name of Ernest.

JACK   My dear fellow, the sooner you give up that nonsense the better. I made arrangements this morning with Dr. Chasuble to be christened myself at 5:30, and I naturally will take the name of Ernest. Gwendolen would wish it. We can't both be christened Ernest. It's absurd. Besides, I have a perfect right to be christened if I like. There is no evidence at all that I ever have been christened by anybody. I should think it extremely probable I never was, and so does Dr. Chasuble. It is entirely different in your case. You have been christened already.

ALGERNON   Yes, but I have not been christened for years.

JACK   Yes, but you have been christened. That is the important thing.

ALGERNON   Quite so. So I know my constitution can stand it. If you are not quite sure about your ever having been christened, I must say I think it rather dangerous your venturing on it now. It might make you very unwell. You can hardly have forgotten that some one very closely connected with you was very nearly carried off this week in Paris by a severe chill.

JACK   Yes, but you said yourself that a severe chill was not hereditary.

ALGERNON   It usedn't to be, I know—but I daresay it is now. Science is always making wonderful improvements in things.

JACK (*picking up the muffin-dish*)   Oh, that is nonsense, you are always talking nonsense.

ALGERNON   Jack, you are at the muffins again! I wish you wouldn't. There are only two left. (*Takes them.*) I told you I was particularly fond of muffins.

JACK   But I hate tea-cake.

ALGERNON   Why on earth then do you allow tea-cake to be served up for your guests? What ideas you have of hospitality!

JACK   Algernon! I have already told you to go. I don't want you here. Why don't you go?

ALGERNON   I haven't quite finished my tea yet, and there is still one muffin left. (JACK *groans, and sinks into a chair.* ALGERNON *still continues eating.*)

Curtain

ACT III

SCENE   *Morning-room at the Manor House.* GWENDOLEN *and* CECILY *are at the window, looking out into the garden.*

GWENDOLEN   The fact that they did not follow us at once into the house, as any one else would have done, seems to me to show that they have some sense of shame left.

CECILY   They have been eating muffins. That looks like repentance.

GWENDOLEN (*after a pause*)   They don't seem to notice us at all. Couldn't you cough?

GWENDOLEN   They're looking at us. What effrontery!

CECILY   They're approaching. That's very forward of them.

GWENDOLEN   Let us preserve a dignified silence.

CECILY   Certainly. It's the only thing to do now.

Enter JACK, *followed by* ALGERNON. *They whistle some dreadful popular air from a British opera.*

GWENDOLEN   This dignified silence seems to produce an unpleasant effect.

CECILY   A most distasteful one.

GWENDOLEN   But we will not be the first to speak.

CECILY   Certainly not.

GWENDOLEN   Mr. Worthing, I have something very particular to ask you. Much depends on your reply.

CECILY   Gwendolen, your common sense is invaluable. Mr. Moncrieff, kindly answer me the following question. Why did you pretend to be my guardian's brother?

ALGERNON   In order that I might have an opportunity of meeting you.

CECILY (*to* GWENDOLEN)   That certainly seems a satisfactory explanation, does it not?

GWENDOLEN   Yes, dear, if you can believe him.

CECILY   I don't. But that does not affect the wonderful beauty of his answer.

GWENDOLEN   True. In matters of grave importance, style, not sincerity, is the vital thing. Mr. Worthing, what explanation can you offer to me for pretending to have a brother? Was it in order that you might have an opportunity of coming up to town to see me as often as possible?

JACK   Can you doubt it, Miss Fairfax?

GWENDOLEN   I have the gravest doubts upon the subject. But I intend to crush them. This is not the moment for German skepticism. (*Moving to* CECILY.) Their explanations appear to be quite satisfactory, especially Mr. Worthing's. That seems to me to have the stamp of truth upon it.

CECILY   I am more than content with what Mr. Moncrieff said. His voice alone inspires one with absolute credulity.

GWENDOLEN   Then you think we should forgive them?

CECILY   Yes. I mean no.

GWENDOLEN   True! I had forgotten. There are principles at stake that one cannot surrender. Which of us should tell them? The task is not a pleasant one.

CECILY   Could we not both speak at the same time?

GWENDOLEN   An excellent idea! I nearly always speak at the same time as other people. Will you take the time from me?

CECILY   Certainly. (GWENDOLEN *beats time with uplifted finger.*)

GWENDOLEN *and* CECILY (*speaking together*)   Your Christian names are still an insuperable barrier. That is all!

JACK and ALGERNON (*speaking together*)   Our Christian names! Is that all? But we are going to be christened this afternoon.

GWENDOLEN (*to* JACK)   For my sake you are prepared to do this terrible thing?

JACK   I am.

CECILY (*to* ALGERNON)   To please me you are ready to face this fearful ordeal?

ALGERNON   I am!

GWENDOLEN   How absurd to talk of the equality of the sexes! Where questions of self-sacrifice are concerned, men are infinitely beyond us.

JACK   We are. (*Clasps hands with* ALGERNON.)

CECILY   They have moments of physical courage of which we women know absolutely nothing.

GWENDOLEN (*to* JACK)   Darling!

ALGERNON (*to* CECILY) Darling! (*They fall into each other's arms.*)

Enter MERRIMAN. *When he enters he coughs loudly, seeing the situation.*

MERRIMAN Ahem! Ahem! Lady Bracknell!

JACK Good heavens!

Enter LADY BRACKNELL. *The couples separate in alarm. Exit* MERRIMAN.

LADY BRACKNELL Gwendolen! What does this mean?

GWENDOLEN Merely that I am engaged to be married to Mr. Worthing, mamma.

LADY BRACKNELL Come here. Sit down. Sit down immediately. Hesitation of any kind is a sign of mental decay in the young, of physical weakness in the old. (*Turns to* JACK.) Apprised, sir, of my daughter's sudden flight by her trusty maid, whose confidence I purchased by means of a small coin, I followed her at once by a luggage train. Her unhappy father is, I am glad to say, under the impression that she is attending a more than usually lengthy lecture by the University Extension Scheme on the Influence of a Permanent Income on Thought. I do not propose to undeceive him. Indeed I have never undeceived him on any question. I would consider it wrong. But of course you will clearly understand that all communication between yourself and my daughter must cease immediately from this moment. On this point, as indeed on all points, I am firm.

JACK I am engaged to be married to Gwendolen, Lady Bracknell!

LADY BRACKNELL You are nothing of the kind, sir. And now, as regards Algernon! . . . Algernon!

ALGERNON Yes, Aunt Augusta.

LADY BRACKNELL May I ask if it is in this house that your invalid friend Mr. Bunbury resides?

ALGERNON (*stammering*) Oh, no! Bunbury doesn't live here. Bunbury is somewhere else at present. In fact, Bunbury is dead.

LADY BRACKNELL Dead! When did Mr. Bunbury die? His death must have been extremely sudden.

ALGERNON (*airily*) Oh, I killed Bunbury this afternoon. I mean poor Bunbury died this afternoon.

LADY BRACKNELL What did he die of?

ALGERNON Bunbury? Oh, he was quite exploded.

LADY BRACKNELL Exploded! Was he the victim of a revolutionary outrage? I was not aware that Mr. Bunbury was interested in social legislation. If so, he is well punished for his morbidity.

ALGERNON My dear Aunt Augusta, I mean he was found out! The doctors found out that Bunbury could not live, that is what I mean—so Bunbury died.

LADY BRACKNELL He seems to have had great confidence in the opinion of his physicians. I am glad, however, that he made up his mind at the last to some definite course of action, and acted under proper medical advice. And now that we have finally got rid of this Mr. Bunbury, may I ask, Mr. Worthing, who is that young person whose hand my nephew Algernon is now holding in what seems to me a peculiarly unnecessary manner?

JACK   That lady is Miss Cecily Cardew, my ward. (LADY BRACKNELL *bows coldly to* CECILY.)

ALGERNON   I am engaged to be married to Cecily, Aunt Augusta.

LADY BRACKNELL   I beg your pardon?

CECILY   Mr. Moncrieff and I are engaged to be married, Lady Bracknell.

LADY BRACKNELL (*with a shiver, crossing to the sofa and sitting down*)   I do not know whether there is anything peculiarly exciting in the air of this particular part of Hertfordshire, but the number of engagements that go on seems to me considerably above the proper average that statistics have laid down for our guidance. I think some preliminary enquiry on my part would not be out of place. Mr. Worthing, is Miss Cardew at all connected with any of the larger railway stations in London? I merely desire information. Until yesterday I had no idea that there were any families or persons whose origin was a Terminus. (JACK *looks perfectly furious, but restrains himself.*)

JACK (*in a clear, cold voice*)   Miss Cardew is the granddaughter of the late Mr. Thomas Cardew of 149, Belgrave Square, S.W.; Gervase Park, Dorking, Surrey; and the Sporran, Fifeshire, N.B.

LADY BRACKNELL   That sounds not unsatisfactory. Three addresses always inspire confidence, even in tradesmen. But what proof have I of their authenticity?

JACK   I have carefully preserved the Court Guides of the period. They are open to your inspection, Lady Bracknell.

LADY BRACKNELL (*grimly*)   I have known strange errors in that publication.

JACK   Miss Cardew's family solicitors are Messrs. Markby, Markby, and Markby.

LADY BRACKNELL   Markby, Markby, and Markby? A firm of the very highest position in their profession. Indeed I am told that one of the Mr. Markbys is occasionally to be seen at dinner parties. So far I am satisfied.

JACK (*very irritably*)   How extremely kind of you, Lady Bracknell! I have also in my possession, you will pleased to hear, certificates of Miss Cardew's birth, baptism, whooping cough, registration, vaccination, confirmation, and the measles; both the German and the English variety.

LADY BRACKNELL   Ah! A life crowded with incident, I see; though perhaps somewhat too exciting for a young girl. I am not myself in favor of premature experiences. (*Rises, looks at her watch.*) Gwendolen! the time approaches for our departure. We have not a moment to lose. As a matter of form, Mr. Worthing, I had better ask you if Miss Cardew has any little fortune?

JACK   Oh, about a hundred and thirty thousand pounds in the Funds. That is all. Goodby, Lady Bracknell. So pleased to have seen you.

LADY BRACKNELL (*sitting down again*)   A moment, Mr. Worthing. A hundred and thirty thousand pounds! And in the Funds! Miss Cardew seems to me a most attractive young lady, now that I look at her. Few girls of the present day have any really solid qualities, any of the qualities that last, and improve with time. We live, I regret to say, in an age of surfaces. (*To* CECILY.) Come over here, dear. (CECILY *goes across.*) Pretty child! your dress is sadly simple, and your hair seems almost as Nature might have left it. But we can soon alter all that. A thoroughly experienced French maid produces a really marvelous result in a very brief space of time. I remember recommending one to young Lady Lancing, and after three months her own husband did not know her.

JACK (*aside*)   And after six months nobody knew her.

LADY BRACKNELL (*glares at* JACK *for a few moments, then bends, with a practiced smile, to* CECILY)   Kindly turn round, sweet child. (CECILY *turns completely round.*) No, the side view is what I want. (CECILY *presents her profile.*) Yes, quite as I expected. There are distinct social possibilities in your profile. The two weak points in our age are its want of principle and its want of profile. The chin a little higher, dear. Style largely depends on the way the chin is worn. They are worn very high, just at present. Algernon!

ALGERNON   Yes, Aunt Augusta!

LADY BRACKNELL   There are distinct social possibilities in Miss Cardew's profile.

ALGERNON   Cecily is the sweetest, dearest, prettiest girl in the whole world. And I don't care twopence about social possibilities.

LADY BRACKNELL   Never speak disrespectfully of society, Algernon. Only people who can't get into it do that. (*To* CECILY.) Dear child, of course you know that Algernon has nothing but his debts to depend upon. But I do not approve of mercenary marriages. When I married Lord Bracknell I had no fortune of any kind. But I never dreamed for a moment of allowing that to stand in my way. Well, I suppose I must give my consent.

ALGERNON   Thank you, Aunt Augusta.

LADY BRACKNELL   Cecily, you may kiss me!

CECILY (*kisses her*)   Thank you, Lady Bracknell.

LADY BRACKNELL   You may address me as Aunt Augusta for the future.

CECILY   Thank you, Aunt Augusta.

LADY BRACKNELL   The marriage, I think, had better take place quite soon.

ALGERNON   Thank you, Aunt Augusta.

CECILY   Thank you, Aunt Augusta.

LADY BRACKNELL   To speak frankly, I am not in favor of long engagements. They give people the opportunity of finding out each other's character before marriage, which I think is never advisable.

JACK   I beg your pardon for interrupting you, Lady Bracknell, but this engagement is quite out of the question. I am Miss Cardew's guardian, and she cannot marry without my consent until she comes of age. That consent I absolutely decline to give.

LADY BRACKNELL   Upon what grounds, may I ask? Algernon is an extremely, I may almost say an ostentatiously, eligible young man. He has nothing, but he looks everything. What more can one desire?

JACK   It pains me very much to have to speak frankly to you, Lady Bracknell, about your nephew, but the fact is that I do not approve at all of his moral character. I suspect him of being untruthful. (ALGERNON *and* CECILY *look at him in indignant amazement.*)

LADY BRACKNELL   Untruthful! My nephew Algernon? Impossible! He is an Oxonian.

JACK   I fear there can be no possible doubt about the matter. This afternoon, during my temporary absence in London on an important question of romance, he obtained admission to my house by means of the false pretense of being my brother. Under an assumed name he drank, I've just been informed by my butler, an entire pint bottle of my Perrier-Jouet, Brut, '89; a wine I was specially reserving for myself. Continuing his disgraceful deception, he succeeded in the course of the afternoon in alienating the affections of my only ward. He subsequently stayed to tea, and devoured every single muffin. And what makes his conduct all the more heartless is, that he was perfectly well aware from the first that I have no brother, that I never had a brother, and that I don't intend to have a brother, not even of any kind. I distinctly told him so myself yesterday afternoon.

LADY BRACKNELL   Ahem! Mr. Worthing, after careful consideration I have decided entirely to overlook my nephew's conduct to you.

JACK   That is very generous of you, Lady Bracknell. My own decision, however, is unalterable. I decline to give my consent.

LADY BRACKNELL (*to* CECILY)   Come here, sweet child. (CECILY *goes over.*) How old are you, dear?

CECILY   Well, I am really only eighteen, but I always admit to twenty when I go to evening parties.

LADY BRACKNELL   You are perfectly right in making some slight alteration. Indeed, no woman should ever be quite accurate about her age. It looks so calculating. . . . (*In meditative manner.*) Eighteen, but admitting to twenty at evening parties. Well, it will not be very long before you are of age and free from the restraints of tutelage. So I don't think your guardian's consent is, after all, a matter of any importance.

JACK   Pray excuse me, Lady Bracknell, for interrupting you again, but it is only fair to tell you that according to the terms of her grandfather's will Miss Cardew does not come legally of age till she is thirty-five.

LADY BRACKNELL   That does not seem to me to be a grave objection. Thirty-five is a very attractive age. London society is full of women of the very highest birth who have, of their own free choice, remained thirty-five for years. Lady Dumbleton is an instance in point. To my own knowledge she has been thirty-five ever since she arrived at the age of forty, which was many years ago now. I see no reason why our dear Cecily should not be even still more attractive at the age you mention than she is at present. There will be a large accumulation of property.

CECILY   Algy, could you wait for me till I was thirty-five?

ALGERNON   Of course I could, Cecily. You know I could.

CECILY   Yes, I felt it instinctively, but I couldn't wait all that time. I hate waiting even five minutes for anybody. It always makes me rather cross. I am not punctual myself, I know, but I do like punctuality in others, and waiting, even to be married, is quite out of the question.

ALGERNON   Then what is to be done, Cecily?

CECILY   I don't know, Mr. Moncrieff.

LADY BRACKNELL   My dear Mr. Worthing, as Miss Cardew states positively that she cannot wait till she is thirty-five—a remark which I am bound to say seems to me to show a somewhat impatient nature—I would beg of you to reconsider your decision.

JACK   But, my dear Lady Bracknell, the matter is entirely in your own hands. The moment you consent to my marriage with Gwendolen, I will most gladly allow your nephew to form an alliance with my ward.

LADY BRACKNELL   (*rising and drawing herself up*) You must be quite aware that what you propose is out of the question.

JACK   Then a passionate celibacy is all that any of us can look forward to.

LADY BRACKNELL   That is not the destiny I propose for Gwendolen. Algernon, of course, can choose for himself. (*Pulls out her watch.*) Come, dear (GWENDOLEN *rises*), we have already missed five, if not six, trains. To miss any more might expose us to comment on the platform.

Enter DR. CHASUBLE.

CHASUBLE   Everything is quite ready for the christenings.

LADY BRACKNELL   The christenings, sir! Is not that somewhat premature?

CHASUBLE (*looking rather puzzled, and pointing to* JACK *and* ALGERNON) Both these gentlemen have expressed a desire for immediate baptism.

LADY BRACKNELL   At their age? The idea is grotesque and irreligious! Algernon, I forbid you to be baptized. I will not hear of such excesses. Lord Bracknell would be highly displeased if he learned that that was the way in which you wasted your time and money.

CHASUBLE   Am I to understand then that there are to be no christenings at all this afternoon?

JACK   I don't think that, as things are now, it would be of much practical value to either of us, Dr. Chasuble.

CHASUBLE   I am grieved to hear such sentiments from you, Mr. Worthing. They savor of the heretical views of the Anabaptists, views that I have completely refuted in four of my unpublished sermons. However, as your present mood seems to be one peculiarly secular, I will return to the church at once. Indeed, I have just been informed by the pewopener that for the last hour and a half Miss Prism has been waiting for me in the vestry.

LADY BRACKNELL (*starting*)   Miss Prism! Did I hear you mention a Miss Prism?

CHASUBLE   Yes, Lady Bracknell. I am on my way to join her.

LADY BRACKNELL   Pray allow me to detain you for a moment. This matter may prove to be one of vital importance to Lord Bracknell and myself. Is this Miss Prism a female of repellent aspect, remotely connected with education?

CHASUBLE (*somewhat indignantly*)   She is the most cultivated of ladies, and the very picture of respectability.

LADY BRACKNELL   It is obviously the same person. May I ask what position she holds in your household?

CHASUBLE (*severely*)   I am a celibate, madam.

JACK (*interposing*)   Miss Prism, Lady Bracknell, has been for the last three years Miss Cardew's esteemed governess and valued companion.

LADY BRACKNELL   In spite of what I hear of her, I must see her at once. Let her be sent for.

CHASUBLE (*looking off*)   She approaches; she is nigh.

   Enter MISS PRISM *hurriedly.*

MISS PRISM   I was told you expected me in the vestry, dear Canon. I have been waiting for you there for an hour and three-quarters. (*Catches sight of* LADY BRACKNELL, *who has fixed her with a stony glare.* MISS PRISM *grows pale and quails. She looks anxiously round as if desirous to escape.*)

LADY BRACKNELL (*in a severe, judicial voice*) Prism! (MISS PRISM *bows her head in shame.*) Come here, Prism! (MISS PRISM *approaches in a humble manner.*) Prism! Where is that baby? (*General consternation. The Canon starts back in horror.* ALGERNON *and* JACK *pretend to be anxious to shield* CECILY *and* GWENDOLEN *from hearing the details of a terrible public scandal.*) Twenty-eight years ago, Prism, you left Lord Bracknell's house, Number 104, Upper Grosvenor Street, in charge of a perambulator that contained a baby, of the male sex. You never returned. A few weeks later, through the elaborate investigations of the Metropolitan police, the perambulator was discovered at midnight, standing by itself in a remote corner of Bayswater. It contained the manuscript of a three-volume novel of more than usually revolting sentimentality. (MISS PRISM *starts in involuntary indignation.*) But the baby was not there! (*Every one looks at* MISS PRISM.) Prism, where is that baby? (*A pause.*)

MISS PRISM Lady Bracknell, I admit with shame that I do not know. I only wish I did. The plain facts of the case are these. On the morning of the day you mention, a day that is forever branded on my memory, I prepared as usual to take the baby out in its perambulator. I had also with me a somewhat old but capacious hand-bag in which I had intended to place the manuscript of a work of fiction that I had written during my few unoccupied hours. In a moment of mental abstraction, for which I never can forgive myself, I deposited the manuscript in the bassinet, and placed the baby in the hand-bag.

JACK (*who has been listening attentively*) But where did you deposit the hand-bag?

MISS PRISM Do not ask me, Mr. Worthing.

JACK Miss Prism, this is a matter of no small importance to me. I insist on knowing where you deposited the hand-bag that contained that infant.

MISS PRISM I left it in the cloak-room of one of the larger railway stations in London.

JACK What railway station?

MISS PRISM (*quite crushed*) Victoria. The Brighton line. (*Sinks into a chair.*)

JACK I must retire to my room for a moment. Gwendolen, wait here for me.

GWENDOLEN If you are not too long, I will wait here for you all my life.

Exit JACK *in great excitement.*

CHASUBLE What do you think this means, Lady Bracknell?

LADY BRACKNELL I dare not even suspect, Dr. Chasuble. I need hardly tell you that in families of high position strange coincidences are not supposed to occur. They are hardly considered the thing. (*Noises heard overhead as if some one was throwing trunks about. Everybody looks up.*)

CECILY   Uncle Jack seems strangely agitated.

CHASUBLE   Your guardian has a very emotional nature.

LADY BRACKNELL   This noise is extremely unpleasant. It sounds as if he was having an argument. I dislike arguments of any kind. They are always vulgar, and often convincing.

CHASUBLE (*looking up*)   It has stopped now. (*The noise is redoubled.*)

LADY BRACKNELL   I wish he would arrive at some conclusion.

GWENDOLEN   This suspense is terrible. I hope it will last.

Enter JACK *with a hand-bag of black leather in his hand.*

JACK (*rushing over to* MISS PRISM)   Is this the hand-bag, Miss Prism? Examine it carefully before you speak. The happiness of more than one life depends on your answer.

MISS PRISM (*calmly*)   It seems to be mine. Yes, here is the injury it received through the upsetting of a Gower Street omnibus in younger and happier days. Here is the stain on the lining caused by the explosion of a temperance beverage, an incident that occurred at Leamington. And here, on the lock, are my initials. I had forgotten that in an extravagant mood I had had them placed there. The bag is undoubtedly mine. I am delighted to have it so unexpectedly restored to me. It has been a great inconvenience being without it all these years.

JACK (*in a pathetic voice*)   Miss Prism, more is restored to you than this hand-bag. I was the baby you placed in it.

MISS PRISM (*amazed*)   You?

JACK (*embracing her*)   Yes . . . mother!

MISS PRISM (*recoiling in indignant astonishment*)   Mr. Worthing! I am unmarried!

JACK   Unmarried! I do not deny that is a serious blow. But after all, who has the right to cast a stone against one who has suffered? Cannot repentance wipe out an act of folly? Why should there be one law for men and another for women? Mother, I forgive you. (*Tries to embrace her again.*)

MISS PRISM (*still more indignant*)   Mr. Worthing, there is some error. (*Pointing to* LADY BRACKNELL.) There is the lady who can tell you who you really are.

JACK (*after a pause*)   Lady Bracknell, I hate to seem inquisitive, but would you kindly inform me who I am?

LADY BRACKNELL   I am afraid that the news I have to give you will not altogether please you. You are the son of my poor sister, Mrs. Moncrieff, and consequently Algernon's elder brother.

JACK   Algy's elder brother! Then I have a brother after all. I knew I had a brother! I always said I had a brother! Cecily,—how could you have ever doubted that I had a brother? (*Seizes hold of* ALGERNON.) Dr. Chasuble, my unfortunate brother. Miss Prism, my unfortunate brother. Gwendolen, my unfortunate brother. Algy, you young scoundrel, you will have to treat me with more respect in the future. You have never behaved to me like a brother in all your life.

ALGERNON   Well, not till to-day, old boy, I admit. I did my best, however, though I was out of practice. (*Shakes hands.*)

GWENDOLEN (*to* JACK)   My own! but what own are you? What is your Christian name, now that you have become some one else?

JACK   Good heavens! . . . I had quite forgotten that point. Your decision on the subject of my name is irrevocable, I suppose?

GWENDOLEN   I never change, except in my affections.

CECILY   What a noble nature you have, Gwendolen!

JACK   Then the question had better be cleared up at once. Aunt Augusta, a moment. At the time when Miss Prism left me in the handbag, had I been christened already?

LADY BRACKNELL   Every luxury that money could buy, including christening, had been lavished on you by your fond and doting parents.

JACK   Then I was christened! That is settled. Now, what name was I given? Let me know the worst.

LADY BRACKNELL   Being the eldest son you were naturally christened after your father.

JACK (*irritably*)   Yes, but what was my father's Christian name?

LADY BRACKNELL (*meditatively*)   I cannot at the present moment recall what the General's Christian name was. But I have no doubt he had one. He was eccentric, I admit. But only in later years. And that was the result of the Indian climate, and marriage, and indigestion, and other things of that kind.

JACK   Algy! Can't you recollect what our father's Christian name was?

ALGERNON   My dear boy, we were never even on speaking terms. He died before I was a year old.

JACK   His name would appear in the Army Lists of the period, I suppose, Aunt Augusta?

LADY BRACKNELL   The General was essentially a man of peace, except in his domestic life. But I have no doubt his name would appear in any military directory.

JACK   The Army Lists of the last forty years are here. These delightful records should have been my constant study. (*Rushes to bookcase and tears the books out.*) M. Generals . . . Mallam, Maxbohm, Magley, what ghastly names they have—Markby, Migsby, Mobbs, Moncrieff! Lieutenant 1840, Captain, Lieutenant-Colonel, Colonel, General 1869, Christian names, Ernest John. (*Puts book very quietly down and speaks quite calmly.*) I always told you, Gwendolen, my name was Ernest, didn't I? Well, it is Ernest after all. I mean it naturally is Ernest.

LADY BRACKNELL   Yes, I remember that the General was called Ernest. I knew I had some particular reason for disliking the name.

GWENDOLEN   Ernest! My own Ernest! I felt from the first that you could have no other name!

JACK   Gwendolen, it is a terrible thing for a man to find out suddenly that all his life he has been speaking nothing but the truth. Can you forgive me?

GWENDOLEN   I can. For I feel that you are sure to change.

JACK   My own one!

CHASUBLE (*to* MISS PRISM)   Laetitia! (*Embraces her.*)

MISS PRISM (*enthusiastically*)   Frederick! At last!

ALGERNON   Cecily! (*Embraces her.*) At last!

JACK   Gwendolen! (*Embraces her.*) At last!

LADY BRACKNELL   My nephew, you seem to be displaying signs of triviality.

JACK   On the contrary, Aunt Augusta, I've now realized for the first time in my life the vital Importance of Being Earnest.

Tableau

Curtain

QUESTIONS FOR THINKING AND WRITING

1. This comedy has been called one of the wittiest plays in the English language. What might you say about the play, or what lines from it might you quote, in support of this statement?
2. Compare and contrast the town and country milieus depicted in *The Importance of Being Earnest*. Why might Wilde have used both in the play?
3. It's hard not to notice the amount of eating and drinking that occurs in this play. Discuss how Wilde uses this to support particular themes and characterizations.
4. Do you think a production of *The Importance of Being Earnest* would be a success at your school? Why or why not?

5 Contemporary Drama

Our final reading in the drama section, Tennessee Williams's *The Glass Menagerie* (premiered 1944, published 1945), brings our study up to the middle of the twentieth century. When reading works in the order in which they were written or published, the student may sense that there is a sort of historical "progress" in literature. This may tempt the student to believe in what one teacher has called (with irony in his voice) "the Detroit theory of literature"—that is, the idea that each successive work of literature improves upon the last one, as though writers were like factory workers at an assembly line. Yet as T. S. Eliot reminds us in "Tradition and the Individual Talent" (see pp. 91–97), "No poet, no artist of any art, has his complete meaning alone." And Tennessee Williams's production notes for *The Glass Menagerie* give us a clear indication of how he saw the relationship between his work and the drama that came before him. In particular, he describes how his play departs from the drama of realism "with its genuine frigidaire and authentic ice-cubes." Photographic representation, according to Williams, does not necessarily offer the truth about reality. Literary realism is not the same as philosophical reality.

Williams calls his play a "memory play"; its story emanates from the memory of the narrator, Tom Wingfield, and memory itself becomes one of the major themes of the play. It is not surprising that Williams would find the conventions of realistic theater unsatisfactory in developing this theme. Instead, he turns to techniques that enhance the atmosphere: the screen device, the music, the lighting. As you read the play, consider all of the ways in which the atmosphere is created and how the effects contribute to the idea of memory. Consider, too, how memory creates delusions, and how these in turn create realities—a frightening paradox, but certainly realized in the character of Amanda Wingfield, Tom's mother. Her selective and creative recollections of her own past as a southern belle predominate the present life of the Wingfields in a tenement in St. Louis, Missouri.

Williams's play is a product of the twentieth century, and his work occupies an important place in the American theater, alongside that of Arthur Miller and Clifford Odets. These and other modern dramatists have all shifted their focus away from heroes and heroines of high political and social stature (Kreon, Antigonê, and Hamlet, for example) toward characters who have no power to alter society. Instead, these people are at society's mercy. Even their own sense of worth is formed less from self-knowledge than from the dictates of their society. Amanda is nearly tragic in the way she illustrates this concept, but Laura retreats into her world of dreams, indicating an alternative for someone who is not ruled by the vision of others.

Twentieth-century drama blends realism and fantasy, striving for a truth-fulness deeper than realism alone can convey. Contemporary writing has discovered a common ground between fantasy and psychological truth. Like any other art form, drama is at its best when it is not static. Its enduring appeal lies in our sense of anticipation, our curiosity about what comes next.

TENNESSEE WILLIAMS (1911–1983)

The Glass Menagerie

The Author's Production Notes

Being a "memory play," *The Glass Menagerie* can be presented with unusual freedom of convention. Because of its considerable delicate or tenuous material, atmospheric touches and subtleties of direction play a particularly important part. Expressionism and all other unconventional techniques in drama have only one valid aim, and that is a closer approach to truth. When a play employs unconventional techniques, it is not, or certainly shouldn't be, trying to escape its responsibility of dealing with reality, or interpreting experience, but is actually or should be attempting to find a closer approach, a more penetrating and vivid expression of things as they are. The straight realistic play with its genuine frigidaire and authentic ice-cubes, its characters that speak exactly as its audience speaks, corresponds to the academic landscape and has the same virtue of photographic likeness. Everyone should know nowadays the unimportance of the photographic in art: that truth, life, or reality is an organic thing which the poetic imagination can represent or suggest, in essence, only through transformation, through changing into other forms than those which were merely present in appearance.

These remarks are not meant as a preface only to this particular play. They have to do with a conception of a new, plastic theatre which must take the place of the exhausted theatre of realistic conventions if the theatre is to resume vitality as a part of our culture.

The Screen Device

There is *only one important difference between the original and acting version of the play* and that is the *omission* in the latter of the device which I tentatively included in my *original* script. This device was the use of a screen on which were projected magic-lantern slides bearing images or titles. I do not regret the omission of this device from the present Broadway production. The extraordinary power of Miss Taylor's performance made it suitable to have the utmost simplicity in the physical production. But I think it may be interesting to some readers to see how this device was conceived. So I am putting it into the published manuscript. These images and legends, projected from behind, were cast on a section of wall between the front-room and dining-room areas, which should be indistinguishable from the rest when not in use.

The purpose of this will probably be apparent. It is to give accent to certain values in each scene. Each scene contains a particular point (or several) which is structurally the most important. In an episodic play, such as this, the basic structure or narrative line may be obscured from the audience; the effect may seem fragmentary rather than architectural. This may not be the fault of the play so much as a lack of attention in the audience. The legend or image upon the screen will strengthen the effect of what is merely allusion in the writing and allow the primary point to be made more simply and lightly than if the entire responsibility were on the spoken lines. Aside from this structural value, I think the screen will have a definite emotional appeal, less definable but just as important. An imaginative producer or director may invent many other uses for this device than those indicated in the present script. In fact the possibilities of the device seem much larger to me than the instance of this play can possibly utilize.

THE MUSIC

Another extra-literary accent in this play is provided by the use of music. A single recurring tune, "The Glass Menagerie," is used to give emotional emphasis to suitable passages. This tune is like circus music, not when you are on the grounds or in the immediate vicinity of the parade, but when you are at some distance and very likely thinking of something else. It seems under those circumstances to continue almost interminably and it weaves in and out of your preoccupied consciousness; then it is the lightest, most delicate music in the world and perhaps the saddest. It expresses the surface vivacity of life with the underlying strain of immutable and inexpressible sorrow. When you look at a piece of delicately spun glass you think of two things: how beautiful it is and how easily it can be broken. Both of those ideas should be woven into the recurring tune, which dips in and out of the play as if it were carried on a wind that changes. It serves as a thread of connection and allusion between the narrator with his separate point in time and space and the subject of his story. Between each episode it returns as reference to the emotion, nostalgia, which is the first condition of the play. It is primarily Laura's music and therefore comes out most clearly when the play focuses upon her and the lovely fragility of glass which is her image.

THE LIGHTING

The lighting in the play is not realistic. In keeping with the atmosphere of memory, the stage is dim. Shafts of light are focused on selected areas or actors, sometimes a contradistinction to what is the apparent content. For instance, in the quarrel scene between Tom and Amanda, in which Laura has an active part, the clearest pool of light is on her figure. This is also true of the supper scene, when her silent figure on the sofa should remain the visual center. The light upon Laura should be distinct from the others, having a peculiar pristine clarity such as light used in early religious portraits of female saints or madonnas. A certain correspondence to light in religious paintings, such as El Greco's, where the figures are radiant in atmosphere that is relatively dusky, could be effectively used throughout the play. (It will also permit a more effective use of the screen.) A free, imaginative use of light can be of enormous value in giving a mobile, plastic quality to plays of a more or less static nature.

CHARACTERS

AMANDA WINGFIELD, *the mother.*
A little woman of great but confused vitality clinging frantically to another time and place. Her characterization must be carefully created, not copied from type. She is not paranoiac, but her life is paranoia. There is much to admire in AMANDA, *and as much to love and pity as there is to laugh at. Certainly she has endurance and a kind of heroism, and though her foolishness makes her unwittingly cruel at times, there is tenderness in her slight person.*

LAURA WINGFIELD, *her daughter.*
AMANDA, *having failed to establish contact with reality, continues to live vitally in her illusions, but* LAURA's *situation is even graver. A childhood illness has left her crippled, one leg slightly shorter than the other, and held in a brace. This defect need not be more than suggested on the stage. Stemming from this,* LAURA's *separation increases till she is like a piece of her own glass collection, too exquisitely fragile to move from the shelf.*

TOM WINGFIELD, *her son, and the narrator of the play.*
A poet with a job in a warehouse. His nature is not remorseless, but to escape from a trap he has to act without pity.

JIM O'CONNOR, *the gentleman caller.*
A nice, ordinary, young man.

SCENE: *An alley in St. Louis.*
PART I: *Preparation for a Gentleman Caller.*
PART II: *The Gentleman Calls.*
TIME: *Now and the Past.*

SCENE I

The Wingfield apartment is in the rear of the building, one of those vast hive-like conglomerations of cellular living-units that flower as warty growths in overcrowded urban centers of lower middle-class population and are symptomatic of the impulse of this largest and fundamentally enslaved section of American society to avoid fluidity and differentiation and to exist and function as one interfused mass of automatism.
   The apartment faces an alley and is entered by a fire-escape, a structure whose name is a touch of accidental poetic truth, for all of these huge buildings are always burning with the slow and implacable fires of human desperation. The fire-escape is included in the set—that is, the landing of it and steps descending from it.
   The scene is memory and is therefore nonrealistic. Memory takes a lot of poetic

license. It omits some details; others are exaggerated, according to the emotional value of the articles it touches, for memory is seated predominantly in the heart. The interior is therefore rather dim and poetic.

At the rise of the curtain, the audience is faced with the dark, grim rear wall of the Wingfield tenement. This building, which runs parallel to the footlights, is flanked on both sides by dark, narrow alleys which run into murky canyons of tangled clothes-lines, garbage cans and the sinister lattice-work of neighboring fire-escapes. It is up and down these side alleys that exterior entrances and exits are made, during the play. At the end of TOM's *opening commentary, the dark tenement wall slowly reveals (by means of a transparency) the interior of the ground floor Wingfield apartment.*

Downstage is the living room, which also serves as a sleeping room for LAURA, *the sofa unfolding to make her bed. Upstage, center, and divided by a wide arch or second proscenium with transparent faded portieres (or second curtain), is the dining room. In an old-fashioned what-not in the living room are seen scores of transparent glass animals. A blown-up photograph of the father hangs on the wall of the living room, facing the audience, to the left of the archway. It is the face of a very handsome young man in a doughboy's First World War cap. He is gallantly smiling, ineluctably smiling, as if to say, "I will be smiling forever."*

The audience hears and sees the opening scene in the dining room through both the transparent fourth wall of the building and the transparent gauze portieres of the dining-room arch. It is during this revealing scene that the fourth wall slowly ascends, out of sight. This transparent exterior wall is not brought down again until the very end of the play, during TOM's *final speech.*

The narrator is an undisguised convention of the play. He takes whatever license with dramatic convention as is convenient to his purposes.

TOM enters dressed as a merchant sailor from alley, stage left, and strolls across the front of the stage to the fire-escape. There he stops and lights a cigarette. He addresses the audience.

TOM   Yes, I have tricks in my pocket, I have things up my sleeve. But I am the opposite of a stage magician. He gives you illusion that has the appearance of truth. I give you truth in the pleasant disguise of illusion. To begin with, I turn back time. I reverse it to that quaint period, the thirties, when the huge middle class of America was matriculating in a school for the blind. Their eyes had failed them, or they had failed their eyes, and so they were having their fingers pressed forcibly down on the fiery Braille alphabet of a dissolving economy. In Spain there was revolution. Here there was only shouting and confusion. In Spain there was Guernica. Here there were disturbances of labor, sometimes pretty violent, in otherwise peaceful cities such as Chicago, Cleveland, Saint Louis. . . . This is the social background of the play.

(MUSIC.)

The play is memory. Being a memory play, it is dimly lighted, it is sentimental, it is not realistic. In memory everything seems to happen to music. That explains the fiddle in the wings. I am the narrator of the play, and also a character in it. The other characters are my mother, Amanda, my sister, Laura, and a gentleman caller who appears in the final scenes. He is the most realistic character in the play, being an emissary from a world of reality that we were somehow set apart from. But since I have a poet's weakness for symbols, I am using this character also as a symbol; he is the long delayed but always expected something that we live for. There is a fifth character in the play who doesn't appear except in this larger-than-life photograph over the mantel. This is our father who left us a long time ago. He was a telephone man who fell in love with long distances; he gave up his job with the telephone company and skipped the light fantastic out of town. . . . The last we heard of him was a picture post-card from Mazatlan, on the Pacific coast of Mexico, containing a message of two words—"Hello—Goodbye!" and an address. I think the rest of the play will explain itself. . . .

AMANDA's *voice becomes audible through the portieres.*

(LEGEND ON SCREEN: "OÙ SONT LES NEIGES.")

He divides the portieres and enters the upstage area.
    AMANDA *and* LAURA *are seated at a drop-leaf table. Eating is indicated by gestures without food or utensils.* AMANDA *faces the audience.* TOM *and* LAURA *are seated in profile.*
    The interior has lit up softly and through the scrim we see AMANDA *and* LAURA *seated at the table in the upstage area.*

AMANDA (*calling*) Tom?
TOM Yes, Mother.
AMANDA We can't say grace until you come to the table!
TOM Coming, Mother. (*He bows slightly and withdraws, reappearing a few moments later in his place at the table*).
AMANDA (*to her son*) Honey, don't *push* with your *fingers.* If you have to push with something, the thing to push with is a crust of bread. And chew—chew! Animals have sections in their stomachs which enable them to digest food without mastication, but human beings are supposed to chew their food before they swallow it down. Eat food leisurely, son, and really enjoy it. A well-cooked meal has lots of delicate flavors that have to be held in the mouth for appreciation. So chew your food and give your salivary glands a chance to function!

TOM *deliberately lays his imaginary fork down and pushes his chair back from the table.*

TOM I haven't enjoyed one bite of this dinner because of your constant directions on how to eat it. It's you that makes me rush through meals with your hawk-like attention to every bite I take. Sickening— spoils my appetite—all this discussion of animals' secretion—salivary glands—mastication!
AMANDA (*lightly*) Temperament like a Metropolitan star! (*He rises and crosses downstage.*) You're not excused from the table.
TOM I am getting a cigarette.

AMANDA   You smoke too much.

LAURA *rises.*

LAURA   I'll bring in the blanc mange.

He remains standing with his cigarette by the portieres during the following.

AMANDA (*rising*)   No, sister, no, sister—you be the lady this time and I'll be the darky.

LAURA   I'm already up.

AMANDA   Resume your seat, little sister—I want you to stay fresh and pretty—for gentlemen callers!

LAURA   I'm not expecting any gentlemen callers.

AMANDA (*crossing out to kitchenette. Airily*)   Sometimes they come when they are least expected! Why, I remember one Sunday afternoon in Blue Mountain—(*Enters kitchenette.*)

TOM   I know what's coming!

LAURA   Yes. But let her tell it.

TOM   Again?

LAURA   She loves to tell it.

AMANDA *returns with bowl of dessert.*

AMANDA   One Sunday afternoon in Blue Mountain—your mother received—*seventeen!*—gentlemen callers! Why, sometimes there weren't chairs enough to accommodate them all. We had to send the nigger over to bring in folding chairs from the parish house.

TOM   (*remaining at portieres*)   How did you entertain those gentlemen callers?

AMANDA   I understood the art of conversation!

TOM   I bet you could talk.

AMANDA   Girls in those days *knew* how to talk, I can tell you.

TOM   Yes?

(IMAGE: AMANDA AS A GIRL ON A PORCH GREETING CALLERS.)

AMANDA   They knew how to entertain their gentlemen callers. It wasn't enough for a girl to be possessed of a pretty face and a graceful figure—although I wasn't slighted in either respect. She also needed to have a nimble wit and a tongue to meet all occasions.

TOM   What did you talk about?

AMANDA   Things of importance going on in the world! Never anything coarse or common or vulgar. (*She addresses* TOM *as though he were seated in the vacant chair at the table though he remains by portieres. He plays this scene as though he held the book.*) My callers were gentlemen—all! Among my callers were some of the most prominent young planters of the Mississippi Delta—planters and sons of planters!

TOM *motions for music and a spot of light on* AMANDA.
Her eyes lift, her face glows, her voice becomes rich and elegiac.

(SCREEN LEGEND: "OÙ SONT LES NEIGES.")

There was young Champ Laughlin who later became vice-president of the Delta Planters Bank. Hadley Stevenson who was drowned in Moon Lake and left his widow one hundred and fifty thousand in Government bonds. There were the Cutrere brothers, Wesley and Bates. Bates was one of my bright particular beaux! He got in a quarrel with that wild Wainright boy. They shot it out on the floor of Moon Lake Casino. Bates was shot through the stomach. Died in the ambulance on his way to Memphis. His widow was also well-provided for, came into eight or ten thousand acres, that's all. She married him on the rebound—never loved her—carried my picture on him the night he died! And there was that boy that every girl in the Delta had set her cap for! That beautiful, brilliant young Fitzhugh boy from Green County!

TOM   What did he leave his widow?

AMANDA   He never married! Gracious, you talk as though all of my old admirers had turned up their toes to the daisies!

TOM   Isn't this the first you mentioned that still survives?

AMANDA   That Fitzhugh boy went North and made a fortune—came to be known as the Wolf of Wall Street! He had the Midas touch, whatever he touched turned to gold! And I could have been Mrs. Duncan J. Fitzhugh, mind you! But—I picked your *father!*

LAURA (*rising*)   Mother, let me clear the table.

AMANDA   No, dear, you go in front and study your typewriter chart. Or practice your shorthand a little. Stay fresh and pretty—It's almost time for our gentlemen callers to start arriving. (*She flounces girlishly toward the kitchenette.*) How many do you suppose we're going to entertain this afternoon?

TOM *throws down the paper and jumps up with a groan.*

LAURA (*alone in the dining room*)   I don't believe we're going to receive any, Mother.

AMANDA (*reappearing, airily*)   What? No one—not one? You must be joking! (LAURA *nervously echoes her laugh. She slips in a fugitive manner through the half-open portieres and draws them gently behind her. A shaft of very clear light is thrown on her face against the faded tapestry of the curtains.* MUSIC: "THE GLASS MENAGERIE" UNDER FAINTLY. *Lightly.*) Not one gentleman caller? It can't be true! There must be a flood, there must have been a tornado!

LAURA   It isn't a flood, it's not a tornado, Mother. I'm just not popular like you were in Blue Mountain. . . . (TOM *utters another groan.* LAURA *glances at him with a faint, apologetic smile. Her voice catching a little.*) Mother's afraid I'm going to be an old maid.

(THE SCENE DIMS OUT WITH "GLASS MENAGERIE" MUSIC.)

SCENE II

"Laura, Haven't You Ever Liked Some Boy?"

> On the dark stage the screen is lighted with the image of blue roses.
> Gradually LAURA's figure becomes apparent and the screen goes out.
> The music subsides.
> LAURA is seated in the delicate ivory chair at the small clawfoot table.
> She wears a dress of soft violet material for a kimono—her hair tied back from her forehead with a ribbon.
> She is washing and polishing her collection of glass.
> AMANDA appears on the fire-escape steps. At the sound of her ascent, LAURA catches her breath, thrusts the bowl of ornaments away and seats herself stiffly before the diagram of the typewriter keyboard as though it held her spellbound. Something has happened to AMANDA. It is written in her face as she climbs to the landing: a look that is grim and hopeless and a little absurd.
> She has on one of those cheap or imitation velvety-looking cloth coats with imitation fur collar. Her hat is five or six years old, one of those dreadful cloche hats that were worn in the late twenties and she is clasping an enormous black patent-leather pocket-book with nickel clasp and initials. This is her full-dress outfit, the one she usually wears to the D.A.R.
> Before entering she looks through the door.
> She purses her lips, opens her eyes wide, rolls them upward, and shakes her head.
> Then she slowly lets herself in the door. Seeing her mother's expression LAURA touches her lips with a nervous gesture.

LAURA   Hello, Mother, I was—(*She makes a nervous gesture toward the chart on the wall.* AMANDA *leans against the shut door and stares at* LAURA *with a martyred look.*)

AMANDA   Deception? Deception? (*She slowly removes her hat and gloves, continuing the swift suffering stare. She lets the hat and gloves fall on the floor—a bit of acting.*)

LAURA (*shakily*)   How was the D.A.R. meeting? (AMANDA *slowly opens her purse and removes a dainty white handkerchief which she shakes out delicately and delicately touches to her lips and nostrils.*) Didn't you go to the D.A.R. meeting, Mother?

AMANDA (*faintly, almost inaudibly*)   —No.—No. (*Then more forcibly.*) I did not have the strength—to go to the D.A.R. In fact, I did not have the courage! I wanted to find a hole in the ground and hide myself in it forever! (*She crosses slowly to the wall and removes the diagram of the typewriter keyboard. She holds it in front of her for a second, staring at it sweetly and sorrowfully—then bites her lips and tears it in two pieces.*)

LAURA (*faintly*)   Why did you do that, Mother? (AMANDA *repeats the same procedure with the chart of the Gregg Alphabet.*) Why are you—

AMANDA   Why? Why? How old are you, Laura?

LAURA   Mother, you know my age.

AMANDA   I thought that you were an adult; it seems that I was mistaken. (*She crosses slowly to the sofa and sinks down and stares at* LAURA.)

LAURA   Please don't stare at me, Mother.

AMANDA *closes her eyes and lowers her head. Count ten.*

AMANDA   What are we going to do, what is going to become of us, what is the future?

Count ten.

LAURA   Has something happened, Mother? (AMANDA *draws a long breath and takes out the handkerchief again. Dabbing process.*) Mother, has—something happened?

AMANDA   I'll be all right in a minute. I'm just bewildered—(*Count five.*)—by life. . . .

LAURA   Mother, I wish that you would tell me what's happened.

AMANDA   As you know, I was supposed to be inducted into my office at the D.A.R. this afternoon. (IMAGE: A SWARM OF TYPEWRITERS.) But I stopped off at Rubicam's Business College to speak to your teachers about your having a cold and ask them what progress they thought you were making down there.

LAURA   Oh. . . .

AMANDA   I went to the typing instructor and introduced myself as your mother. She didn't know who you were. Wingfield, she said. We don't have any such student enrolled at the school! I assured her she did, that you had been going to classes since early in January. "I wonder," she said, "if you could be talking about that terribly shy little girl who dropped out of school after only a few days' attendance?" "No," I said, "Laura, my daughter, has been going to school every day for the past six weeks!" "Excuse me," she said. She took the attendance book out and there was your name, unmistakably printed, and all the dates you were absent until they decided that you had dropped out of school. I still said, "No, there must have been some mistake! There must have been some mix-up in the records!" And she said, "No—I remember her perfectly now. Her hand shook so that she couldn't hit the right keys! The first time we gave a speed-test, she broke down completely—was sick at the stomach and almost had to be carried into the wash-room! After that morning she never showed up any more. We phoned the house but never got any answer—while I was working at Famous and Barr, I suppose, demonstrating those—Oh!" I felt so weak I could barely keep on my feet! I had to sit down while they got me a glass of water! Fifty dollars' tuition, all of our plans— my hopes and ambitions for you—just gone up the spout, just gone up the spout like that. (LAURA *draws a long breath and gets awkwardly to her feet. She crosses to the victrola and winds it up.*) What are you doing?

LAURA   Oh! (*She releases the handle and returns to her seat.*)

AMANDA   Laura, where have you been going when you've gone out pretending that you were going to business college?

LAURA   I've just been going out walking.

AMANDA   That's not true.

LAURA   It is. I just went walking.

AMANDA   Walking? Walking? In winter? Deliberately courting pneumonia in that light coat? Where did you walk to, Laura?

LAURA   All sorts of places—mostly in the park.

AMANDA   Even after you'd started catching that cold?

LAURA   It was the lesser of two evils, Mother. (IMAGE: WINTER SCENE IN PARK.) I couldn't go back up. I—threw up—on the floor!

AMANDA   From half past seven till after five every day you mean to tell me you walked around in the park, because you wanted to make me think that you were still going to Rubicam's Business College?

LAURA   It wasn't as bad as it sounds. I went inside places to get warmed up.

AMANDA   Inside where?

LAURA   I went in the art museum and the bird-houses at the Zoo. I visited the penguins every day! Sometimes I did without lunch and went to the movies. Lately I've been spending most of my afternoons in the Jewel-box, that big glass house where they raise the tropical flowers.

AMANDA   You did all this to deceive me, just for the deception? (LAURA *looks down.*) Why?

LAURA   Mother, when you're disappointed, you get that awful suffering look on your face, like the picture of Jesus' mother in the museum!

AMANDA   Hush!

LAURA   I couldn't face it.

Pause. A whisper of strings.

(LEGEND: "THE CRUST OF HUMILITY.")

AMANDA (*hopelessly fingering the huge pocketbook*)   So what are we going to do the rest of our lives? Stay home and watch the parades go by? Amuse ourselves with the glass menagerie, darling? Eternally play those worn-out phonograph records your father left as a painful reminder of him? We won't have a business career—we've given that up because it gave us nervous indigestion! (*Laughs wearily.*) What is there left but dependency all our lives? I know so well what becomes of unmarried women who aren't prepared to occupy a position. I've seen such pitiful cases in the South—barely tolerated spinsters living upon the grudging patronage of sister's husband or brother's wife!— stuck away in some little mouse-trap of a room—encouraged by one in-law to visit another—little birdlike women without any nest— eating the crust of humility all their life! Is that the future that we've mapped out for ourselves? I swear it's the only alternative I can think of! It isn't a very pleasant alternative, is it? Of course—some girls *do* marry. (LAURA *twists her hands nervously.*) Haven't you ever liked some boy?

LAURA   Yes. I liked one once. (*Rises.*) I came across his picture a while ago.

AMANDA (*with some interest*)   He gave you his picture?

LAURA   No, it's in the year-book.

AMANDA (*disappointed*)   Oh—a high-school boy.

(SCREEN IMAGE: JIM AS A HIGH-SCHOOL HERO BEARING A SILVER CUP.)

LAURA   Yes. His name was Jim. (LAURA *lifts the heavy annual from the claw-foot table.*) Here he is in *The Pirates of Penzance.*

AMANDA (*absently*)   The what?

LAURA   The operetta the senior class put on. He had a wonderful voice and we sat across the aisle from each other Mondays, Wednesdays and Fridays in the Aud. Here he is with the silver cup for debating! See his grin?

AMANDA (*absently*)   He must have had a jolly disposition.

LAURA   He used to call me—Blue Roses.

(IMAGE: BLUE ROSES.)

AMANDA   Why did he call you such a name as that?

LAURA   When I had that attack of pleurosis—he asked me what was the matter when I came back. I said pleurosis—he thought that I said Blue Roses! So that's what he always called me after that. Whenever he saw me, he'd holler, "Hello, Blue Roses!" I didn't care for the girl that he went out with. Emily Meisenbach. Emily was the best-dressed girl at Soldan. She never struck me, though, as being sincere . . . It says in the Personal Section—they're engaged. That's—six years ago! They must be married by now.

AMANDA   Girls that aren't cut out for business careers usually wind up married to some nice man. (*Gets up with a spark of revival.*) Sister, that's what you'll do!

LAURA *utters a startled, doubtful laugh. She reaches quickly for a piece of glass.*

LAURA   But, Mother—

AMANDA   Yes? (*Crossing to photograph.*)

LAURA (*in a tone of frightened apology*)   I'm—crippled!

(IMAGE: SCREEN.)

AMANDA   Nonsense! Laura, I've told you never, never to use that word. Why, you're not crippled, you just have a little defect—hardly noticeable, even! When people have some slight disadvantage like that, they cultivate other things to make up for it—develop charm—and vivacity—and—*charm!* That's all you have to do! (*She turns again to the photograph.*) One thing your father had *plenty of*—was *charm!*

TOM *motions to the fiddle in the wings.*

(THE SCENE FADES OUT WITH MUSIC.)

SCENE III

(LEGEND ON SCREEN: "AFTER THE FIASCO—")

TOM *speaks from the fire-escape landing.*

TOM   After the fiasco at Rubicam's Business College, the idea of getting a gentleman caller for Laura began to play a more important part in Mother's calculations. It became an obsession. Like some archetype of the universal unconscious, the image of the gentleman caller haunted our small apartment. . . . (IMAGE: YOUNG MAN AT DOOR WITH FLOWERS.) An evening at home rarely passed without some allusion to this image, this spectre, this hope. . . . Even when he wasn't mentioned, his presence hung in Mother's preoccupied look and in my sister's frightened, apologetic manner—hung like a sentence passed upon the Wingfields! Mother was a woman of action as well as words. She began to take logical steps in the planned direction. Late that winter and in the early spring—realizing that extra money would be needed to properly feather the nest and plume the bird—she conducted a vigorous campaign on the telephone, roping in subscribers to one of those magazines for matrons called *The Home-maker's Companion,* the type of journal that features the serialized sublimations of ladies of letters who think in terms of delicate cup-like breasts, slim, tapering waists, rich, creamy thighs, eyes like wood-smoke in autumn, fingers that soothe and caress like strains of music, bodies as powerful as Etruscan sculpture.

(SCREEN IMAGE: GLAMOR MAGAZINE COVER.)

AMANDA *enters with phone on long extension cord. She is spotted in the dim stage.*

AMANDA   Ida Scott? This is Amanda Wingfield! We *missed* you at the D.A.R. last Monday! I said to myself: She's probably suffering with that sinus condition! How is that sinus condition? Horrors! Heaven have mercy!—You're a Christian martyr, yes, that's what you are, a Christian martyr! Well, I just now happened to notice that your subscription to the *Companion's* about to expire! Yes, it expires with the next issue, honey!—just when that wonderful new serial by Bessie Mae Hopper is getting off to such an exciting start. Oh, honey, it's something that you can't miss! You remember how *Gone With the Wind* took everybody by storm? You simply couldn't go out if you hadn't read it. All everybody *talked* was Scarlett O'Hara. Well, this is a book that critics already compare to *Gone With the Wind.* It's the *Gone With the Wind* of the post–World War generation!—What?— Burning?—Oh, honey, don't let them burn, go take a look in the oven and I'll hold the wire! Heavens—I think she's hung up!

(DIM OUT.)

(LEGEND ON SCREEN: "YOU THINK I'M IN LOVE WITH CONTINENTAL SHOE-MAKERS?")

Before the stage is lighted, the violent voices of TOM *and* AMANDA *are heard.*

They are quarreling behind the portieres. In front of them stands LAURA *with clenched hands and panicky expression.*

A clear pool of light on her figure throughout this scene.

TOM   What in Christ's name am I—

AMANDA (*shrilly*) Don't you use that—

TOM   Supposed to do!

AMANDA Expression! Not in my—

TOM   Ohhh!

AMANDA Presence! Have you gone out of your senses?

TOM   I have, that's true, *driven* out!

AMANDA What is the matter with you, you—big—big—IDIOT!

TOM   Look—I've got *no thing*, no single thing—

AMANDA Lower your voice!

TOM   In my life here that I can call my OWN! Everything is—

AMANDA Stop that shouting!

TOM   Yesterday you confiscated my books! You had the nerve to—

AMANDA I took that horrible novel back to the library—yes! That hideous book by that insane Mr. Lawrence. (TOM *laughs wildly.*) I cannot control the output of diseased minds or people who cater to them— (TOM *laughs still more wildly.*) BUT I WON'T ALLOW SUCH FILTH BROUGHT INTO MY HOUSE! No, no, no, no, no!

TOM   House, house! Who pays rent on it, who makes a slave of himself to—

AMANDA (*fairly screeching*) Don't you DARE to—

TOM   No, no, *I* mustn't say things! *I've* got to just—

AMANDA Let me tell you—

TOM   I don't want to hear any more! (*He tears the portieres open. The upstage area is lit with a turgid smoky red glow.*)

AMANDA'*s hair is in metal curlers and she wears a very old bathrobe much too large for her slight figure, a relic of the faithless Mr. Wingfield.*

An upright typewriter and a wild disarray of manuscripts is on the dropleaf table. The quarrel was probably precipitated by AMANDA'*s interruption of his creative labor. A chair lying overthrown on the floor.*

Their gesticulating shadows are cast on the ceiling by the fiery glow.

AMANDA You *will* hear more, you—

TOM   No, I won't hear more, I'm going out!

AMANDA You come right back in—

TOM   Out, out, out! Because I'm—

AMANDA Come back here, Tom Wingfield! I'm not through talking to you!

TOM   Oh, go—

LAURA (*desperately*) —Tom!

AMANDA You're going to listen, and no more insolence from you! I'm at the end of my patience! (*He comes back toward her.*)

TOM   What do you think I'm at? Aren't I supposed to have any patience to reach the end of, Mother? I know, I know. It seems unimportant to you, what I'm *doing*—what I *want* to do—having a little
difference between them! You don't think that—
AMANDA   I think you've been doing things that you're ashamed of.
That's why you act like this. I don't believe that you go every night to
the movies. Nobody goes to the movies night after night. Nobody in
their right minds goes to the movies as often as you pretend to.
People don't go to the movies at nearly midnight, and movies don't let
out at two A.M. Come in stumbling. Muttering to yourself like a ma-
niac! You get three hours sleep and then go to work. Oh, I can
picture the way you're doing down there. Moping, doping, because
you're in no condition.
TOM   (*wildly*)   No, I'm in no condition!
AMANDA   What right have you got to jeopardize your job? Jeopardize
the security of us all? How do you think we'd manage if you were—
TOM   Listen! You think I'm crazy *about* the *warehouse?* (*He bends fiercely
toward her slight figure.*) You think I'm in love with the Continental
Shoemakers? You think I want to spend fifty-five *years* down there in
that—*celotex interior!* with—*fluorescent—tubes!* Look! I'd rather somebody picked up a crowbar and battered out my brains—than go back
mornings! I *go!* Every time you come in yelling that God damn *"Rise
and Shine!" "Rise and Shine!"* I say to myself "How *lucky dead* people
are!" But I get up. I *go!* For sixty-five dollars a month I give up all
that I dream of doing and being *ever!* And you say self—*self's* all I
ever think of. Why, listen, if self is what I thought of, Mother, I'd be
where he is—GONE! (*Pointing to father's picture.*) As far as the system of
transportation reaches! (*He starts past her. She grabs his arm.*) Don't grab
me, Mother!
AMANDA   Where are you going?
TOM   I'm going to the *movies!*
AMANDA   I don't believe that lie!
TOM   (*crouching toward her, overtowering her tiny figure. She backs away,
gasping*)   I'm going to opium dens! Yes, opium dens, dens of vice
and criminals' hang-outs, Mother. I've joined the Hogan gang, I'm a
hired assassin, I carry a tommy-gun in a violin case! I run a string of
cat-houses in the Valley! They call me Killer, Killer Wingfield, I'm
leading a double-life, a simple, honest warehouse worker by day, by
night, a dynamic *czar* of the *underworld, Mother.* I go to gambling
casinos, I spin away fortunes on the roulette table! I wear a patch over
one eye and a false mustache, sometimes I put on green whiskers. On
those occasions they call me—*El Diablo!* Oh, I could tell you things to
make you sleepless! My enemies plan to dynamite this place. They're
going to blow us all sky-high some night! I'll be glad, very happy, and
so will you! You'll go up, up on a broomstick, over Blue Mountain
with seventeen gentlemen callers! You ugly—babbling old—*witch.* . . .

(He goes through a series of violent, clumsy movements, seizing his overcoat, lunging to the door, pulling it fiercely open. The women watch him, aghast. His arm catches in the sleeve of the coat as he struggles to pull it on. For a moment he is pinioned by the bulky garment. With an outraged groan he tears the coat off again, splitting the shoulders of it, and hurls it across the room. It strikes against the shelf of LAURA's *glass collection, there is a tinkle of shattering glass.* LAURA *cries out as if wounded.)*

(MUSIC LEGEND: "THE GLASS MENAGERIE.")

LAURA *(shrilly)*   My glass!—menagerie. . . . *(She covers her face and turns away.)*

But AMANDA *is still stunned and stupefied by the "ugly witch" so that she barely notices this occurrence. Now she recovers her speech.*

AMANDA *(in an awful voice)*   I won't speak to you—until you apologize! *(She crosses through portieres and draws them together behind her.* TOM *is left with* LAURA. LAURA *clings weakly to the mantel with her face averted.* TOM *stares at her stupidly for a moment. Then he crosses to shelf. Drops awkwardly to his knees to collect the fallen glass, glancing at* LAURA *as if he would speak but couldn't.)*

"The Glass Menagerie" steals in as

(THE SCENE DIMS OUT.)

SCENE IV

The interior is dark. Faint light in the alley.

A deep-voiced bell in a church is tolling the hour of five as the scene commences.

TOM *appears at the top of the alley. After each solemn boom of the bell in the tower, he shakes a little noise-maker or rattle as if to express the tiny spasm of man in contrast to the sustained power and dignity of the Almighty. This and the unsteadiness of his advance make it evident that he has been drinking.*

As he climbs the few steps to the fire-escape landing light steals up inside. LAURA *appears in night-dress, observing* TOM's *empty bed in the front room.*

TOM *fishes in his pockets for the door-key, removing a motley assortment of articles in the search, including a perfect shower of movie-ticket stubs and an empty bottle. At last he finds the key, but just as he is about to insert it, it slips from his fingers. He strikes a match and crouches below the door.*

TOM *(bitterly)*   One crack—and it falls through!

LAURA *opens the door.*

LAURA   Tom! Tom, what are you doing?

TOM   Looking for a door-key.

LAURA   Where have you been all this time?

TOM   I have been to the movies.

LAURA   All this time at the movies?

TOM   There was a very long program. There was a Garbo picture and a

Mickey Mouse and a travelogue and a newsreel and a preview of coming attractions. And there was an organ solo and a collection for the milk-fund—simultaneously—which ended up in a terrible fight between a fat lady and an usher!

LAURA (*innocently*)   Did you have to stay through everything?

TOM   Of course! And, oh, I forgot! There was a big stage show! The headliner on this stage show was Malvolio the Magician. He performed wonderful tricks, many of them, such as pouring water back and forth between pitchers. First it turned to wine and then it turned to beer and then it turned to whiskey. I know it was whiskey it finally turned into because he needed somebody to come up out of the audience to help him, and I came up—both shows! It was Kentucky Straight Bourbon. A very generous fellow, he gave souvenirs. (*He pulls from his back pocket a shimmering rainbow-colored scarf.*) He gave me this. This is his magic scarf. You can have it, Laura. You wave it over a canary cage and you get a bowl of gold-fish. You wave it over the gold-fish bowl and they fly away canaries. . . . But the wonderfullest trick of all was the coffin trick. We nailed him into a coffin and he got out of the coffin without removing one nail. (*He has come inside.*) There is a trick that would come in handy for me—get me out of this 2 by 4 situation! (*Flops onto bed and starts removing shoes.*)

LAURA   Tom—Shhh!

TOM   What you shushing me for?

LAURA   You'll wake up Mother.

TOM   Goody, goody! Pay 'er back for all those "Rise an' Shines." (*Lies down, groaning.*) You know it don't take much intelligence to get yourself into a nailed-up coffin, Laura. But who in hell ever got himself out of one without removing one nail?

As if in answer, the father's grinning photograph lights up.

(SCENE DIMS OUT.)

Immediately following: The church bell is heard striking six. At the sixth stroke the alarm goes off in AMANDA's *room, and after a few moments we hear her calling: "Rise and Shine! Rise and Shine! Laura, go tell your brother to rise and shine!"*

TOM (*Sitting up slowly*)   I'll rise—but I won't shine.

The light increases.

AMANDA   Laura, tell your brother his coffee is ready.

LAURA *slips into front room.*

LAURA   Tom! it's nearly seven. Don't make Mother nervous. (*He stares at her stupidly. Beseechingly.*) Tom, speak to Mother this morning. Make up with her, apologize, speak to her!

TOM   She won't to me. It's her that started not speaking.

LAURA   If you just say you're sorry she'll start speaking.

TOM   Her not speaking—is that such a tragedy?

LAURA   Please—please!

AMANDA (*calling from kitchenette*)   Laura, are you going to do what I asked you to do, or do I have to get dressed and go out myself?

LAURA   Going, going—soon as I get on my coat! (*She pulls on a shapeless felt hat with nervous, jerky movement, pleadingly glancing at* TOM. *Rushes awkwardly for coat. The coat is one of* AMANDA's, *inaccurately made-over, the sleeves too short for* LAURA.) Butter and what else?

AMANDA (*entering upstage*)   Just butter. Tell them to charge it.

LAURA   Mother, they make such faces when I do that.

AMANDA   Sticks and stones may break my bones, but the expression on Mr. Garfinkel's face won't harm us! Tell your brother his coffee is getting cold.

LAURA (*at door*)   Do what I asked you, will you, will you, Tom?

He looks sullenly away.

AMANDA   Laura, go now or just don't go at all!

LAURA (*rushing out*)   Going—going! (*A second later she cries out.* TOM *springs up and crosses to the door.* AMANDA *rushes anxiously in.* TOM *opens the door.*)

TOM   Laura?

LAURA   I'm all right. I slipped, but I'm all right.

AMANDA (*peering anxiously after her*)   If anyone breaks a leg on those fire-escape steps, the landlord ought to be sued for every cent he possesses! (*She shuts door. Remembers she isn't speaking and returns to other room.*)

As TOM *enters listlessly for his coffee, she turns her back to him and stands rigidly facing the window on the gloomy gray vault of the areaway. Its light on her face with its aged but childish features is cruelly sharp, satirical as a Daumier print.*

(MUSIC UNDER: "AVE MARIA.")

TOM *glances sheepishly but sullenly at her averted figure and slumps at the table. The coffee is scalding hot; he sips it and gasps and spits it back in the cup. At his gasp,* AMANDA *catches her breath and half turns. Then catches herself and turns back to window.*

TOM *blows on his coffee, glancing sidewise at his mother. She clears her throat.* TOM *clears his. He starts to rise. Sinks back down again, scratches his head, clears his throat again.* AMANDA *coughs.* TOM *raises his cup in both hands to blow on it, his eyes staring over the rim of it at his mother for several moments. Then he slowly sets the cup down and awkwardly and hesitantly rises from the chair.*

TOM (*hoarsely*)   Mother. I—I apologize. Mother. (AMANDA *draws a quick, shuddering breath. Her face works grotesquely. She breaks into childlike tears.*) I'm sorry for what I said, for everything that I said, I didn't mean it.

AMANDA (*sobbingly*)   My devotion has made me a witch and so I make myself hateful to my children!

TOM   No, you *don't.*

AMANDA   I worry so much, don't sleep, it makes me nervous!

TOM (*gently*) I understand that.

AMANDA I've had to put up a solitary battle all these years. But you're my right-hand bower! Don't fall down, don't fail!

TOM (*gently*) I try, Mother.

AMANDA (*with great enthusiasm*) Try and you will SUCCEED! (*The notion makes her breathless.*) Why, you—you're just *full* of natural endowments! Both of my children—they're *unusual* children! Don't you think I know it? I'm so—*proud!* Happy and—feel I've—so much to be thankful for but—Promise me one thing, son!

TOM What, Mother?

AMANDA Promise, son, you'll—never be a drunkard!

TOM (*turns to her grinning*) I will never be a drunkard, Mother.

AMANDA That's what frightened me so, that you'd be drinking! Eat a bowl of Purina!

TOM Just coffee, Mother.

AMANDA Shredded wheat biscuit?

TOM No. No, Mother, just coffee.

AMANDA You can't put in a day's work on an empty stomach. You've got ten minutes—don't gulp! Drinking too-hot liquids makes cancer of the stomach. . . . Put cream in.

TOM No, thank you.

AMANDA To cool it.

TOM No! No, thank you, I want it black.

AMANDA I know, but it's not good for you. We have to do all that we can to build ourselves up. In these trying times we live in, all that we have to cling to is—each other. . . . That's why it's so important to—Tom, I—I sent out your sister so I could discuss something with you. If you hadn't spoken I would have spoken to you. (*Sits down.*)

TOM (*gently*) What is it, Mother, that you want to discuss?

AMANDA Laura!

Tom *puts his cup down slowly.*

(LEGEND ON SCREEN: "LAURA.")

(MUSIC: "THE GLASS MENAGERIE.")

TOM —Oh.—Laura . . .

AMANDA (*touching his sleeve*) You know how Laura is. So quiet but—still water runs deep! She notices things and I think she—broods about them. (TOM *looks up.*) A few days ago I came in and she was crying.

TOM What about?

AMANDA You.

TOM Me?

AMANDA She has an idea that you're not happy here.

TOM What gave her that idea?

AMANDA What gives her any idea? However, you do act strangely. I— I'm not criticizing, understand *that!* I know your ambitions do not lie in the warehouse, that like everybody in the whole wide world—you've had to—make sacrifices, but—Tom—Tom—life's not easy, it calls for—Spartan endurance! There's so many things in my heart that I cannot describe to you! I've never told you but I—*loved* your father. . . .

TOM (*gently*) I know that, Mother.

AMANDA And you—when I see you taking after his ways! Staying out late—and—well, you *had* been drinking the night you were in that—terrifying condition! Laura says that you hate the apartment and that you go out nights to get away from it! Is that true, Tom?

TOM No. You say there's so much in your heart that you can't describe to me. That's true of me, too. There's so much in my heart that I can't describe to *you!* So let's respect each other's—

AMANDA But, why—*why*, Tom—are you always so *restless*? Where do you go to, nights?

TOM I—go to the movies.

AMANDA Why do you go to the movies so much, Tom?

TOM I go to the movies because—I like adventure. Adventure is something I don't have much of at work, so I go to the movies.

AMANDA But, Tom, you go to the movies *entirely* too *much!*

TOM I like a lot of adventure.

AMANDA *looks baffled, then hurt. As the familiar inquisition resumes, he becomes hard and impatient again.* AMANDA *slips back into her querulous attitude toward him.*

(IMAGE ON SCREEN: SAILING VESSEL WITH JOLLY ROGER.)

AMANDA Most young men find adventure in their careers.

TOM Then most young men are not employed in a warehouse.

AMANDA The world is full of young men employed in warehouses and offices and factories.

TOM Do all of them find adventure in their careers?

AMANDA They do or they do without it! Not everybody has a craze for adventure.

TOM Man is by instinct a lover, a hunter, a fighter, and none of those instincts are given much play at the warehouse!

AMANDA Man is by instinct! Don't quote instinct to me! Instinct is something that people have got away from! It belongs to animals! Christian adults don't want it!

TOM What do Christian adults want, then, Mother?

AMANDA Superior things! Things of the mind and the spirit! Only animals have to satisfy instincts! Surely your aims are somewhat higher than theirs! Than monkeys—pigs—

TOM I reckon they're not.

AMANDA You're joking. However, that isn't what I wanted to discuss.

TOM (*rising*) I haven't much time.

AMANDA (*pushing his shoulders*) Sit down.

TOM   You want me to punch in red at the warehouse, Mother?

AMANDA   You have five minutes. I want to talk about Laura.

(LEGEND: "PLANS AND PROVISIONS.")

TOM   All right! What about Laura?

AMANDA   We have to be making plans and provisions for her. She's older than you, two years, and nothing has happened. She just drifts along doing nothing. It frightens me terribly how she just drifts along.

TOM   I guess she's the type that people call home girls.

AMANDA   There's no such type, and if there is, it's a pity! That is unless the home is hers, with a husband!

TOM   What?

AMANDA   Oh, I can see the handwriting on the wall as plain as I see the nose in front of my face! It's terrifying! More and more you remind me of your father! He was out all hours without explanation—Then *left! Goodbye!* And me with a bag to hold. I saw that letter you got from the Merchant Marine. I know what you're dreaming of. I'm not standing here blindfolded. Very well, then. Then *do* it! But not till there's somebody to take your place.

TOM   What do you mean?

AMANDA   I mean that as soon as Laura has got somebody to take care of her, married, a home of her own, independent—why, then you'll be free to go wherever you please, on land, on sea, whichever way the wind blows! But until that time you've got to look out for your sister. I don't say me because I'm old and don't matter! I say for your sister because she's young and dependent. I put her in business college—a dismal failure! Frightened her so it made her sick to her stomach. I took her over to the Young People's League at the church. Another fiasco. She spoke to nobody, nobody spoke to her. Now all she does is fool with those pieces of glass and play those worn-out records. What kind of a life is that for a girl to lead?

TOM   What can I do about it?

AMANDA   Overcome selfishness! Self, self, self is all that you ever think of! (TOM *springs up and crosses to get his coat. It is ugly and bulky. He pulls on a cap with earmuffs.*) Where is your muffler? Put your wool muffler on! (*He snatches it angrily from the closet and tosses it around his neck and pulls both ends tight.*) Tom! I haven't said what I had in mind to ask you.

TOM   I'm too late to—

AMANDA (*catching his arm—very importunately. Then shyly*).   Down at the warehouse, aren't there some—nice young men?

TOM   No!

AMANDA   There *must* be—*some* . . .

TOM   Mother—

Gesture.

AMANDA   Find out one that's clean-living—doesn't drink and—ask him out for sister!

TOM   What?

AMANDA   For *sister!* To *meet!* Get *acquainted!*

TOM (*stamping to door*)   Oh, my go-osh!

AMANDA   Will you? (*He opens door. Imploringly.*) Will you? (*He starts down.*) Will you? *Will* you, dear?

TOM (*calling back*)   YES!

AMANDA *closes the door hesitantly and with a troubled but faintly hopeful expression.*

(SCREEN IMAGE: GLAMOR MAGAZINE COVER.)

Spot AMANDA *at phone.*

AMANDA   Ella Cartwright? This is Amanda Wingfield! How are you, honey? How is that kidney condition? (*Count five.*) Horrors! (*Count five.*) You're a Christian martyr, yes, honey, that's what you are, a Christian martyr! Well, I just happened to notice in my little red book that your subscription to the *Companion* has just run out! I knew that you wouldn't want to miss out on the wonderful serial starting in this new issue. It's by Bessie Mae Hopper, the first thing she's written since *Honeymoon for Three.* Wasn't that a strange and interesting story? Well, this one is even lovelier, I believe. It has a sophisticated society background. It's all about the horsey set on Long Island!

(FADE OUT.)

SCENE V

(LEGEND ON SCREEN: "ANNUNCIATION.")

Fade with music.

It is early dusk of a spring evening. Supper has just been finished in the Wingfield apartment. AMANDA *and* LAURA *in light colored dresses are removing dishes from the table, in the upstage area, which is shadowy, their movements formalized almost as a dance or ritual, their moving forms as pale and silent as moths.*

Tom, in white shirt and trousers, rises from the table and crosses toward the fire-escape.

AMANDA (*as he passes her*)   Son, will you do me a favor?

TOM   What?

AMANDA   Comb your hair! You look so pretty when your hair is combed! (TOM *slouches on sofa with evening paper. Enormous caption "Franco Triumphs."*) There is only one respect in which I would like you to emulate your father.

TOM   What respect is that?

AMANDA   The care he always took of his appearance. He never allowed himself to look untidy. (*He throws down the paper and crosses to fire-escape.*) Where are you going?

TOM I'm going out to smoke.

AMANDA You smoke too much. A pack a day at fifteen cents a pack. How much would that amount to in a month? Thirty times fifteen is how much, Tom? Figure it out and you will be astounded at what you could save. Enough to give you a night-school course in accounting at Washington U! Just think what a wonderful thing that would be for you, son!

TOM *is unmoved by the thought.*

TOM I'd rather smoke. (*He steps out on landing, letting the screen door slam.*)

AMANDA (*sharply*) I know! That's the tragedy of it. . . . (*Alone, she turns to look at her husband's picture.*)

(DANCE MUSIC: "ALL THE WORLD IS WAITING FOR THE SUNRISE!")

TOM (*to the audience*) Across the alley from us was the Paradise Dance Hall. On evenings in spring the windows and doors were open and the music came outdoors. Sometimes the lights were turned out except for a large glass sphere that hung from the ceiling. It would turn slowly about and filter the dusk with delicate rainbow colors. Then the orchestra played a waltz or a tango, something that had a slow and sensuous rhythm. Couples would come outside, to the relative privacy of the alley. You could see them kissing behind ash-pits and telephone poles. This was the compensation for lives that passed like mine, without any change or adventure. Adventure and change were imminent in this year. They were waiting around the corner for all these kids. Suspended in the mist over Berchtesgaden, caught in the folds of Chamberlain's umbrella—In Spain there was Guernica! But here there was only hot swing music and liquor, dance halls, bars, and movies, and sex that hung in the gloom like a chandelier and flooded the world with brief, deceptive rainbows. . . . All the world was waiting for bombardments!

AMANDA *turns from the picture and comes outside.*

AMANDA (*sighing*) A fire-escape landing's a poor excuse for a porch. (*She spreads a newspaper on a step and sits down, gracefully and demurely as if she were settling into a swing on a Mississippi veranda.*) What are you looking at?

TOM The moon.

AMANDA Is there a moon this evening?

TOM It's rising over Garfinkel's Delicatessen.

AMANDA So it is! A little silver slipper of a moon. Have you made a wish on it yet?

TOM Um-hum.

AMANDA What did you wish for?

TOM That's a secret.

AMANDA   A secret, huh? Well, I won't tell mine either. I will be just as mysterious as you.

TOM   I bet I can guess what yours is.

AMANDA   Is my head so transparent?

TOM   You're not a sphinx.

AMANDA   No, I don't have secrets. I'll tell you what I wished for on the moon. Success and happiness for my precious children! I wish for that whenever there's a moon, and when there isn't a moon, I wish for it, too.

TOM   I thought perhaps you wished for a gentleman caller.

AMANDA   Why do you say that?

TOM   Don't you remember asking me to fetch one?

AMANDA   I remember suggesting that it would be nice for your sister if you brought home some nice young man from the warehouse. I think I've made that suggestion more than once.

TOM   Yes, you have made it repeatedly.

AMANDA   Well?

TOM   We are going to have one.

AMANDA   *What?*

TOM   A gentleman caller!

(THE ANNUNCIATION IS CELEBRATED WITH MUSIC.)

AMANDA *rises.*

(IMAGE ON SCREEN: CALLER WITH BOUQUET.)

AMANDA   You mean you have asked some nice young man to come over?

TOM   Yep. I've asked him to dinner.

AMANDA   You really did?

TOM   I did!

AMANDA   You did, and did he—*accept?*

TOM   He did!

AMANDA   Well, well—well, well! That's—lovely!

TOM   I thought that you would be pleased.

AMANDA   It's definite, then?

TOM   Very definite.

AMANDA   Soon?

TOM   Very soon.

AMANDA   For heaven's sake, stop putting on and tell me some things, will you?

TOM   What things do you want me to tell you?

AMANDA   *Naturally* I would like to know when he's *coming!*

TOM   He's coming tomorrow.

AMANDA   *Tomorrow?*

TOM   Yep. Tomorrow.

AMANDA   But, Tom!

TOM   Yes, Mother?

AMANDA   Tomorrow gives me no time!

TOM   Time for what?

AMANDA   Preparations! Why didn't you phone me at once, as soon as you asked him, the minute that he accepted? Then, don't you see, I could have been getting ready!

TOM   You don't have to make any fuss.

AMANDA   Oh, Tom, Tom, Tom, of course I have to make a fuss! I want things nice, not sloppy! Not thrown together. I'll certainly have to do some fast thinking, won't I?

TOM   I don't see why you have to think at all.

AMANDA   You just don't know. We can't have a gentleman caller in a pig-sty! All my wedding silver has to be polished, the monogrammed table linen ought to be laundered! The windows have to be washed and fresh curtains put up. And how about clothes? We have to *wear* something, don't we?

TOM   Mother, this boy is no one to make a fuss over!

AMANDA   Do you realize he's the first young man we've introduced to your sister? It's terrible, dreadful, disgraceful that poor little sister has never received a single gentleman caller! Tom, come inside! (*She opens the screen door.*)

TOM   What for?

AMANDA   I want to ask you some things.

TOM   If you're going to make such a fuss, I'll call it off, I'll tell him not to come.

AMANDA   You certainly won't do anything of the kind. Nothing offends people worse than broken engagements. It simply means I'll have to work like a Turk! We won't be brilliant, but we'll pass inspection. Come on inside. (TOM *follows, groaning.*) Sit down.

TOM   Any particular place you would like me to sit?

AMANDA   Thank heavens I've got that new sofa! I'm also making payments on a floor lamp I'll have sent out! And put the chintz covers on, they'll brighten things up! Of course I'd hoped to have these walls re-papered. . . . What is the young man's name?

TOM   His name is O'Connor.

AMANDA   That, of course, means fish—tomorrow is Friday! I'll have that salmon loaf—with Durkee's dressing! What does he do? He works at the warehouse?

TOM   Of course! How else would I—

AMANDA   Tom, he—doesn't drink?

TOM   Why do you ask me that?

AMANDA   Your father *did!*

TOM   Don't get started on that!

AMANDA   He *does* drink, then?

TOM   Not that I know of!

AMANDA   Make sure, be certain! The last thing I want for my daughter's a boy who drinks!

TOM   Aren't you being a little premature? Mr. O'Connor has not yet appeared on the scene!

AMANDA   But will tomorrow. To meet your sister, and what do I know about his character? Nothing! Old maids are better off than wives of drunkards!

TOM   Oh, my God!

AMANDA   Be still!

TOM (*leaning forward to whisper*)   Lots of fellows meet girls whom they don't marry!

AMANDA   Oh, talk sensibly, Tom—and don't be sarcastic! (*She has gotten a hairbrush.*)

TOM   What are you doing?

AMANDA   I'm brushing that cow-lick down! What is this young man's position at the warehouse?

TOM (*submitting grimly to the brush and the interrogation*)   This young man's position is that of a shipping clerk, Mother.

AMANDA   Sounds to me like a fairly responsible job, the sort of a job *you* would be in if you just had more *get-up*. What is his salary? Have you got any idea?

TOM   I would judge it to be approximately eighty-five dollars a month.

AMANDA   Well—not princely, but—

TOM   Twenty more than I make.

AMANDA   Yes, how well I know! But for a family man, eighty-five dollars a month is not much more than you can just get by on. . . .

TOM   Yes, but Mr. O'Connor is not a family man.

AMANDA   He might be, mightn't he? Some time in the future?

TOM   I see. Plans and provisions.

AMANDA   You are the only young man that I know of who ignores the fact that the future becomes the present, the present the past, and the past turns into everlasting regret if you don't plan for it!

TOM   I will think that over and see what I can make of it.

AMANDA   Don't be supercilious with your mother! Tell me some more about this—what do you call him?

TOM   James D. O'Connor. The D. is for Delaney.

AMANDA   Irish on *both* sides! *Gracious!* And doesn't drink?

TOM   Shall I call him up and ask him right this minute?

AMANDA   The only way to find out about those things is to make discreet inquiries at the proper moment. When I was a girl in Blue Mountain and it was suspected that a young man drank, the girl whose attentions he had been receiving, if any girl *was*, would sometimes speak to the minister of his church, or rather her father would if her father was living, and sort of feel him out on the young man's character. That is the way such things are discreetly handled to keep a young woman from making a tragic mistake!

TOM   Then how did you happen to make a tragic mistake?

AMANDA   That innocent look of your father's had everyone fooled! He *smiled*—the world was *enchanted!* No girl can do worse than put herself at the mercy of a handsome appearance! I hope that Mr. O'Connor is not too good-looking.

TOM   No, he's not too good-looking. He's covered with freckles and hasn't too much of a nose.

AMANDA   He's not right-down homely, though?

TOM   Not right-down homely. Just medium homely. I'd say.

AMANDA   Character's what to look for in a man.

TOM   That's what I've always said, Mother.

AMANDA   You've never said anything of the kind and I suspect you would never give it a thought.

TOM   Don't be suspicious of me.

AMANDA   At least I hope he's the type that's up and coming.

TOM   I think he really goes in for self-improvement.

AMANDA   What reason have you to think so?

TOM   He goes to night school.

AMANDA (*beaming*)   Splendid! What does he do, I mean study?

TOM   Radio engineering and public speaking!

AMANDA   Then he has visions of being advanced in the world! Any young man who studies public speaking is aiming to have an executive job some day! And radio engineering? A thing for the future! Both of these facts are very illuminating. Those are the sort of things that a mother should know concerning any young man who comes to call on her daughter. Seriously or—not.

TOM   One little warning. He doesn't know about Laura. I didn't let on that we had dark ulterior motives. I just said, why don't you come have dinner with us? He said okay and that was the whole conversation.

AMANDA   I bet it was! You're eloquent as an oyster. However, he'll know about Laura when he gets here. When he sees how lovely and sweet and pretty she is, he'll thank his lucky stars he was asked to dinner.

TOM   Mother, you mustn't expect too much of Laura.

AMANDA   What do you mean?

TOM   Laura seems all those things to you and me because she's ours and we love her. We don't even notice she's crippled any more.

AMANDA   Don't say crippled! You know that I never allow that word to be used!

TOM   But face facts, Mother. She is and—that's not all—

AMANDA   What do you mean "not all"?

TOM   Laura is very different from other girls.

AMANDA   I think the difference is all to her advantage.

TOM   Not quite all—in the eyes of others—strangers—she's terribly shy and lives in a world of her own and those things make her seem a little peculiar to people outside the house.

AMANDA   Don't say peculiar.

TOM   Face the facts. She is.

(THE DANCE-HALL MUSIC CHANGES TO A TANGO THAT HAS A MINOR AND SOMEWHAT OMINOUS TONE.)

AMANDA   In what way is she peculiar—may I ask?

TOM (*gently*)   She lives in a world of her own—a world of—little glass ornaments, Mother.... (*Gets up.* AMANDA *remains holding brush, looking at him, troubled.*) She plays old phonograph records and—that's about all—(*He glances at himself in the mirror and crosses to door.*)

AMANDA (*sharply*)   Where are you going?

TOM   I'm going to the movies. (*Out screen door.*)

AMANDA   Not to the movies, every night to the movies! (*Follows quickly to screen door.*) I don't believe you always go to the movies! (*He is gone.* AMANDA *looks worriedly after him for a moment. Then vitality and optimism return and she turns from the door. Crossing to portieres.*) Laura! Laura! (LAURA *answers from kitchenette.*)

LAURA   Yes, Mother.

AMANDA   Let those dishes go and come in front! (LAURA *appears with dish towel. Gaily.*) Laura, come here and make a wish on the moon!

LAURA (*entering*)   Moon—moon?

AMANDA   A little silver slipper of a moon. Look over your left shoulder, Laura, and make a wish! (LAURA *looks faintly puzzled as if called out of sleep.* AMANDA *seizes her shoulders and turns her at an angle by the door.*) No! Now, darling, *wish!*

LAURA   What shall I wish for, Mother?

AMANDA (*her voice trembling and her eyes suddenly filling with tears*)   Happiness! Good Fortune!

The violin rises and the stage dims out.

SCENE VI

(IMAGE: HIGH SCHOOL HERO.)

TOM   And so the following evening I brought Jim home to dinner. I had known Jim slightly in high school. In high school Jim was a hero. He had tremendous Irish good nature and vitality with the scrubbed and polished look of white chinaware. He seemed to move in a continual spotlight. He was a star in basketball, captain of the debating club, president of the senior class and the glee club and he sang the male lead in the annual light operas. He was always running or bounding, never just walking. He seemed always at the point of defeating the law of gravity. He was shooting with such velocity through his adolescence that you would logically expect him to arrive at nothing short of the White House by the time he was thirty. But Jim apparently ran into more interference after his graduation from Soldan. His speed had definitely slowed. Six years after he left high school he was holding a job that wasn't much better than mine.

(IMAGE: CLERK.)

He was the only one at the warehouse with whom I was on friendly terms. I was valuable to him as someone who could remember his former glory, who had seen him win basketball games and the silver cup in debating. He knew of my secret practice of retiring to a cabinet of the washroom to work on poems when business was slack in the warehouse. He called me Shakespeare. And while the other boys in the warehouse regarded me with suspicious hostility, Jim took a humorous attitude toward me. Gradually his attitude affected the others, their hostility wore off and they also began to smile at me as people smile at an oddly fashioned dog who trots across their path at some distance.

I knew that Jim and Laura had known each other at Soldan, and I had heard Laura speak admiringly of his voice. I didn't know if Jim remembered her or not. In high school Laura had been as unobtrusive as Jim had been astonishing. If he did remember Laura, it was not as my sister, for when I asked him to dinner, he grinned and said, "You know, Shakespeare, I never thought of you as having folks!"

He was about to discover that I did. . . .

(LIGHT UP STAGE.)

(LEGEND ON SCREEN: "THE ACCENT OF A COMING FOOT.")

Friday evening. It is about five o'clock of a late spring evening which comes "scattering poems in the sky."

A delicate lemony light is in the Wingfield apartment.

AMANDA has worked like a Turk in preparation for the gentleman caller. The results are astonishing. The new floor lamp with its rose-silk shade is in place, a colored paper lantern conceals the broken light fixture in the ceiling, new billowing white curtains are at the windows, chintz covers are on chairs and sofa, a pair of new sofa pillows make their initial appearance.

Open boxes and tissue paper are scattered on the floor.

LAURA stands in the middle with lifted arms while AMANDA crouches before her, adjusting the hem of the new dress, devout and ritualistic. The dress is colored and designed by memory. The arrangement of LAURA's hair is changed; it is softer and more becoming. A fragile, unearthly prettiness has come out in LAURA: she is like a piece of translucent glass touched by light, given a momentary radiance, not actual, not lasting.

AMANDA (*impatiently*) Why are you trembling?

LAURA Mother, you've made me so nervous!

AMANDA How have I made you nervous?

LAURA By all this fuss! You make it seem so important!

AMANDA I don't understand you, Laura. You couldn't be satisfied with just sitting home, and yet whenever I try to arrange something for you, you seem to resist it. (*She gets up.*) Now take a look at yourself. No, wait! Wait just a moment—I have an idea!

LAURA What is it now?

AMANDA *produces two powder puffs which she wraps in handkerchiefs and stuffs in*
LAURA's *bosom.*

LAURA   Mother, what are you doing?

AMANDA   They call them "Gay Deceivers"!

LAURA   I won't wear them!

AMANDA   You will!

LAURA   Why should I?

AMANDA   Because, to be painfully honest, your chest is flat.

LAURA   You make it seem like we were setting a trap.

AMANDA   All pretty girls are a trap, a pretty trap, and men expect them
to be. (LEGEND: "A PRETTY TRAP.") Now look at yourself, young lady.
This is the prettiest you will ever be! I've got to fix myself now! You're
going to be surprised by your mother's appearance! (*She crosses
through portieres, humming gaily.*)

LAURA *moves slowly to the long mirror and stares solemnly at herself.*
*A wind blows the white curtains inward in a slow, graceful motion and with a
faint, sorrowful sighing.*

AMANDA (*off stage*)   It isn't dark enough yet. (*She turns slowly before the
mirror with a troubled look.*)

(LEGEND ON SCREEN: "THIS IS MY SISTER: CELEBRATE HER WITH STRINGS!"
MUSIC.)

AMANDA (*laughing, off*)   I'm going to show you something. I'm going to
make a spectacular appearance!

LAURA   What is it, Mother?

AMANDA   Possess your soul in patience—you will see! Something I've
resurrected from that old trunk! Styles haven't changed so terribly
much after all. . . . (*She parts the portieres.*) Now just look at your
mother! (*She wears a girlish frock of yellowed voile with a blue silk sash. She
carries a bunch of jonquils—the legend of her youth is nearly revived. Fe-
verishly.*)This is the dress in which I led the cotillion. Won the cake-
walk twice at Sunset Hill, wore one spring to the Governor's ball in
Jackson! See how I sashayed around the ballroom, Laura? (*She raises
her skirt and does a mincing step around the room.*) I wore it on Sundays
for my gentlemen callers! I had it on the day I met your father—I
had malaria fever all that spring. The change of climate from East
Tennessee to the Delta—weakened resistance—I had a little temperature all the time—not enough to be serious—just enough to make
me restless and giddy! Invitations poured in—parties all over the
Delta!—"Stay in bed," said Mother, "you have fever!"—but I just
wouldn't.—I took quinine but kept on going, going!—Evenings,
dances!—Afternoons, long, long rides! Picnics—lovely!—So
lovely, that country in May.—All lacy with dogwood, literally flooded
with jonquils!—That was the spring I had the craze for jonquils.
Jonquils became an absolute obsession. Mother said, "Honey, there's

no more room for jonquils." And still I kept bringing in more jonquils. Whenever, wherever I saw them, I'd say, "Stop! Stop! I see jonquils!" I made the young men help me gather the jonquils! It was a joke, Amanda and her jonquils! Finally there were no more vases to hold them, every available space was filled with jonquils. No vases to hold them? All right, I'll hold them myself! And then I—(*She stops in front of the picture.* MUSIC.) met your father! Malaria fever and jonquils and then—this—boy. . . . (*She switches on the rose-colored lamp.*) I hope they get here before it starts to rain. (*She crosses upstage and places the jonquils in bowl on table.*) I gave your brother a little extra change so he and Mr. O'Connor could take the service car home.

LAURA (*with altered look*)   What did you say his name was?

AMANDA   O'Connor.

LAURA   What is his first name?

AMANDA   I don't remember. Oh, yes, I do. It was—Jim!

LAURA *sways slightly and catches hold of a chair.*

(LEGEND ON SCREEN: "NOT JIM!")

LAURA (*faintly*)   Not—Jim!

AMANDA   Yes, that was it, it was Jim! I've never known a Jim that wasn't nice!

(MUSIC: OMINOUS.)

LAURA   Are you sure his name is Jim O'Connor?

AMANDA   Yes. Why?

LAURA   Is he the one that Tom used to know in high school?

AMANDA   He didn't say so. I think he just got to know him at the warehouse.

LAURA   There was a Jim O'Connor we both knew in high school—(*Then, with effort.*) If that is the one that Tom is bringing to dinner—you'll have to excuse me, I won't come to the table.

AMANDA   What sort of nonsense is this?

LAURA   You asked me once if I'd ever liked a boy. Don't you remember I showed you this boy's picture?

AMANDA   You mean the boy you showed me in the year book?

LAURA   Yes, that boy.

AMANDA   Laura, Laura, were you in love with that boy?

LAURA   I don't know, Mother. All I know is I couldn't sit at the table if it was him!

AMANDA   It won't be him! It isn't the least bit likely. But whether it is or not, you will come to the table. You will not be excused.

LAURA   I'll have to be, Mother.

AMANDA   I don't intend to humor your silliness, Laura. I've had too much from you and your brother, both! So just sit down and compose yourself till they come. Tom has forgotten his key so you'll have to let them in, when they arrive.

LAURA (*panicky*)   Oh, Mother—*you* answer the door!
AMANDA (*lightly*)   I'll be in the kitchen—busy!
LAURA   Oh, Mother, please answer the door, don't make me do it!
AMANDA (*crossing into kitchenette*)   I've got to fix the dressing for the
salmon. Fuss, fuss—silliness!—over a gentleman caller!

Door swings shut. LAURA *is left alone.*

(LEGEND: "TERROR!")

*She utters a low moan and turns off the lamp—sits stiffly on the edge of the sofa,
knotting her fingers together.*

(LEGEND ON SCREEN: "THE OPENING OF A DOOR!")

TOM *and* JIM *appear on the fire-escape steps and climb to landing. Hearing their
approach,* LAURA *rises with a panicky gesture. She retreats to the portieres.
The doorbell.* LAURA *catches her breath and touches her throat. Low drums.*

AMANDA (*calling*)   Laura, sweetheart! The door!

LAURA *stares at it without moving.*

JIM   I think we just beat the rain.
TOM   Uh-huh. (*He rings again, nervously.* JIM *whistles and fishes for a cigarette.*)
AMANDA (*very, very gaily*)   Laura, that is your brother and Mr. O'Connor! Will you let them in, darling?

LAURA *crosses toward kitchenette door.*

LAURA (*breathlessly*)   Mother—you go to the door!

AMANDA *steps out of kitchenette and stares furiously at* LAURA. *She points imperi-
ously at the door.*

LAURA   Please, please!
AMANDA (*in a fierce whisper*)   What is the matter with you, you silly
thing?
LAURA (*desperately*)   Please, you answer it, *please!*
AMANDA   I told you I wasn't going to humor you, Laura. Why have you
chosen this moment to lose your mind?
LAURA   Please, please, please, you go!
AMANDA   You'll have to go to the door because I can't!
LAURA (*despairingly*)   I can't either!
AMANDA   Why?
LAURA   I'm *sick!*
AMANDA   I'm sick, too—of your nonsense! Why can't you and your
brother be normal people? Fantastic whims and behavior! (TOM *gives
a long ring.*) Preposterous goings on! Can you give me one reason—
(*Calls out lyrically*). COMING! JUST ONE SECOND!—why should you be
afraid to open a door? Now you answer it, Laura!

LAURA   Oh, oh, oh . . . (*She returns through the portieres. Darts to the victrola and winds it frantically and turns it on.*)

AMANDA   Laura Wingfield, you march right to that door!

LAURA   Yes—yes, Mother!

A faraway, scratchy rendition of "Dardanella" softens the air and gives her strength to move through it. She slips to the door and draws it cautiously open.
   TOM *enters with the caller,* JIM O'CONNOR.

TOM   Laura, this is Jim. Jim, this is my sister, Laura.

JIM (*stepping inside*)   I didn't know that Shakespeare had a sister!

LAURA (*retreating stiff and trembling from the door*)   How—how do you do?

JIM (*heartily extending his hand*)   Okay!

LAURA *touches it hesitantly with hers.*

JIM   Your hand's *cold*, Laura!

LAURA   Yes, well—I've been playing the victrola. . . .

JIM   Must have been playing classical music on it! You ought to play a little hot swing music to warm you up!

LAURA   Excuse me—I haven't finished playing the victrola. . . .

She turns awkwardly and hurries into the front room. She pauses a second by the victrola. Then catches her breath and darts through the portieres like a frightened deer.

JIM (*grinning*)   What was the matter?

TOM   Oh—with Laura? Laura is—terribly shy.

JIM   Shy, huh? It's unusual to meet a shy girl nowadays. I don't believe you ever mentioned you had a sister.

TOM   Well, now you know. I have one. Here is the *Post Dispatch*. You want a piece of it?

JIM   Uh-huh.

TOM   What piece? The comics?

JIM   Sports! (*Glances at it.*) Ole Dizzy Dean is on his bad behavior.

TOM (*disinterest*)   Yeah? (*Lights cigarette and crosses back to fire-escape door.*)

JIM   Where are *you* going?

TOM   I'm going out on the terrace.

JIM (*goes after him*)   You know, Shakespeare—I'm going to sell you a bill of goods!

TOM   What goods?

JIM   A course I'm taking.

TOM   Huh?

JIM   In public speaking! You and me, we're not the warehouse type.

TOM   Thanks—that's good news. But what has public speaking got to do with it?

JIM   It fits you for—executive positions!

TOM   Awww.

JIM   I tell you it's done a helluva lot for me.

(IMAGE: EXECUTIVE AT DESK.)

TOM   In what respect?

JIM   In every! Ask yourself what is the difference between you an' me and men in the office down front? Brains?—No!—Ability?—No! Then what? Just one little thing—

TOM   What is that one little thing?

JIM   Primarily it amounts to—social poise! Being able to square up to people and hold your own on any social level!

AMANDA (*off stage*)   Tom?

TOM   Yes, Mother?

AMANDA   Is that you and Mr. O'Connor?

TOM   Yes, Mother.

AMANDA   Well, you just make yourselves comfortable in there.

TOM   Yes, Mother.

AMANDA   Ask Mr. O'Connor if he would like to wash his hands.

JIM   Aw—no—no—thank you—I took care of that at the warehouse. Tom—

TOM   Yes?

JIM   Mr. Mendoza was speaking to me about you.

TOM   Favorably?

JIM   What do you think?

TOM   Well—

JIM   You're going to be out of a job if you don't wake up.

TOM   I am waking up—

JIM   You show no signs.

TOM   The signs are interior.

(IMAGE ON SCREEN: THE SAILING VESSEL WITH JOLLY ROGER AGAIN.)

TOM   I'm planning to change. (*He leans over the rail speaking with quiet exhilaration. The incandescent marquees and signs of the first-run movie houses light his face from across the alley. He looks like a voyager.*) I'm right at the point of committing myself to a future that doesn't include the warehouse and Mr. Mendoza or even a night-school course in public speaking.

JIM   What are you gassing about?

TOM   I'm tired of the movies.

JIM   Movies!

TOM   Yes, movies! Look at them—(*A wave toward the marvels of Grand Avenue.*) All of those glamorous people—having adventures— hogging it all, gobbling the whole thing up! You know what happens? People go to the *movies* instead of *moving!* Hollywood characters are supposed to have all the adventures for everybody in America, while everybody in America sits in a dark room and watches them have them! Yes, until there's a war. That's when adventure becomes available to the masses! *Everyone's* dish, not only Gable's! Then the people in the dark room come out of the dark room to have some adventures themselves—Goody, goody!—It's our turn now, to go to the South

Sea Island—to make a safari—to be exotic, far-off!—But I'm not patient. I don't want to wait till then. I'm tired of the *movies* and I am *about* to *move!*

JIM (*incredulously*) Move?

TOM Yes.

JIM When?

TOM Soon!

JIM Where? Where?

(THEME THREE MUSIC SEEMS TO ANSWER THE QUESTION, WHILE TOM THINKS IT OVER. HE SEARCHES AMONG HIS POCKETS.)

TOM I'm starting to boil inside. I know I seem dreamy, but inside— well, I'm boiling! Whenever I pick up a shoe, I shudder a little thinking how short life is and what I am doing!—Whatever that means. I know it doesn't mean shoes—except as something to wear on a traveler's feet! (*Finds paper.*) Look—

JIM What?

TOM I'm a member.

JIM (*reading*) The Union of Merchant Seamen.

TOM I paid my dues this month, instead of the light bill.

JIM You will regret it when they turn the lights off.

TOM I won't be here.

JIM How about your mother?

TOM I'm like my father. The bastard son of a bastard! See how he grins? And he's been absent going on sixteen years!

JIM You're just talking, you drip. How does your mother feel about it?

TOM Shhh!—Here comes Mother! Mother is not acquainted with my plans!

AMANDA (*enters portieres*) Where are you all?

TOM On the terrace, Mother.

They start inside. She advances to them. TOM *is distinctly shocked at her appearance. Even* JIM *blinks a little. He is making his first contact with girlish Southern vivacity and in spite of the night-school course in public speaking is somewhat thrown off the beam by the unexpected outlay of social charm.*

Certain responses are attempted by JIM *but are swept aside by* AMANDA's *gay laughter and chatter.* TOM *is embarrassed but after the first shock* JIM *reacts very warmly. Grins and chuckles, is altogether won over.*

(IMAGE: AMANDA AS A GIRL.)

AMANDA (*coyly smiling, shaking her girlish ringlets*). Well, well, well, so this is Mr. O'Connor. Introductions entirely unnecessary. I've heard so much about you from my boy. I finally said to him, Tom—good gracious!—why don't you bring this paragon to supper? I'd like to meet this nice young man at the warehouse!—Instead of just hearing him sing your praises so much! I don't know why my son is so standoffish—that's not Southern behavior! Let's sit down and—I think we could stand a little more air in here! Tom, leave the door open. I felt a nice fresh breeze a moment ago. Where has it gone? Mmm, so warm already! And not quite summer, even. We're going to burn up when summer really gets started. However, we're having—we're having a very light supper. I think light things are better fo' this time of year. The same as light clothes are. Light clothes an' light food are what warm weather calls fo'. You know our blood gets so thick during th' winter—it takes a while fo' us to *adjust* ou'selves!—when the season changes . . . It's come so quick this year. I wasn't prepared. All of a sudden—heavens! Already summer!—I ran to the trunk an' pulled out this light dress—Terribly old! Historical almost! But feels so good—so good an' co-ol, y'know. . . .

TOM   Mother—

AMANDA   Yes, honey?

TOM   How about—supper?

AMANDA   Honey, you go ask Sister if supper is ready! You know that Sister is in full charge of supper! Tell her you hungry boys are waiting for it. (*To* JIM.) Have you met Laura?

JIM   She—

AMANDA   Let you in? Oh, good, you've met already! It's rare for a girl as sweet an' pretty as Laura to be domestic! But Laura is, thank heavens, not only pretty but also very domestic. I'm not at all. I never was a bit. I never could make a thing but angel-food cake. Well, in the South we had so many servants. Gone, gone, gone. All vestige of gracious living! Gone completely! I wasn't prepared for what the future brought me. All of my gentlemen callers were sons of planters and so of course I assumed that I would be married to one and raise my family on a large piece of land with plenty of servants. But man proposes—and woman accepts the proposal!—To vary that old, old saying a little bit—I married no planter! I married a man who worked for the telephone company!—That gallantly smiling gentleman over there! (*Points to the picture.*) A telephone man who—fell in love with long-distance!—Now he travels and I don't even know where!—But what am I going on for about my—tribulations? Tell me yours—I hope you don't have any! Tom?

TOM (*returning*)   Yes, Mother?

AMANDA   Is supper nearly ready?

TOM   It looks to me like supper is on the table.

AMANDA   Let me look—(*She rises prettily and looks through portieres.*) Oh, lovely!—But where is Sister?

TOM   Laura is not feeling well and she says that she thinks she'd better not come to the table.

AMANDA   What?—Nonsense!—Laura? Oh, Laura!

LAURA (*off stage, faintly*)   Yes, Mother.

AMANDA   You really must come to the table. We won't be seated until you come to the table! Come in, Mr. O'Connor. You sit over there and I'll—Laura? Laura Wingfield! You're keeping us waiting, honey! We can't say grace until you come to the table!

The back door is pushed weakly open and LAURA *comes in. She is obviously quite faint, her lips trembling, her eyes wide and staring. She moves unsteadily toward the table.*

(LEGEND: "TERROR!")

Outside a summer storm is coming abruptly. The white curtains billow inward at the windows and there is a sorrowful murmur and deep blue dusk.
LAURA *suddenly stumbles—she catches at a chair with a faint moan.*

TOM   Laura!

AMANDA   Laura! (*There is a clap of thunder.*) (LEGEND: "AH!") (*Despairingly.*) Why, Laura, you *are* sick, darling! Tom, help your sister into the living room, dear! Sit in the living room, Laura—rest on the sofa. Well! (*To the gentleman caller.*) Standing over the hot stove made her ill!—I told her that it was just too warm this evening, but—(TOM *comes back in.* LAURA *is on the sofa.*) Is Laura all right now?

TOM   Yes.

AMANDA   What *is* that? Rain? A nice cool rain has come up! (*She gives the gentleman caller a frightened look.*) I think we may—have grace— now . . . (TOM *looks at her stupidly*). Tom, honey—you say grace!

TOM   Oh . . . "For these and all thy mercies—" (*They bow their heads,* AMANDA *stealing a nervous glance at* JIM. *In the living room* LAURA, *stretched on the sofa, clenches her hand to her lips, to hold back a shuddering sob.*) God's Holy Name be praised—

(THE SCENE DIMS OUT.)

SCENE VII

(LEGEND: "A SOUVENIR.")

Half an hour later. Dinner is just being finished in the upstage area which is concealed by the drawn portieres.
As the curtain rises LAURA *is still huddled upon the sofa, her feet drawn under her, her head resting on a pale blue pillow, her eyes wide and mysteriously watchful. The new floor lamp with its shade of rose-colored silk gives a soft, becoming light to her face, bringing out the fragile, unearthly prettiness which usually escapes attention. There is a steady murmur of rain, but it is slackening and stops soon after the scene begins; the air outside becomes pale and luminous as the moon breaks out.*
A moment after the curtain rises, the lights in both rooms flicker and go out.

JIM   Hey, there, Mr. Light Bulb!

AMANDA *laughs nervously.*

(LEGEND: "SUSPENSION OF A PUBLIC SERVICE.")

AMANDA   Where was Moses when the lights went out? Ha-ha. Do you know the answer to that one, Mr. O'Connor?

JIM   No, Ma'am, what's the answer?

AMANDA   In the dark! (JIM *laughs appreciably.*) Everybody sit still. I'll light the candles. Isn't it lucky we have them on the table? Where's a match? Which of you gentlemen can provide a match?

JIM   Here.

AMANDA   Thank you, sir.

JIM   Not at all, Ma'am!

AMANDA   I guess the fuse has burnt out. Mr. O'Connor, can you tell a burnt-out fuse? I know I can't and Tom is a total loss when it comes to mechanics. (SOUND: GETTING UP: VOICES RECEDE A LITTLE TO KITCH-ENETTE.) Oh, be careful you don't bump into something. We don't want our gentleman caller to break his neck. Now wouldn't that be a fine howdy-do?

JIM   Ha-ha! Where is the fuse-box?

AMANDA   Right here next to the stove. Can you see anything?

JIM   Just a minute.

AMANDA   Isn't electricity a mysterious thing? Wasn't it Benjamin Franklin who tied a key to a kite? We live in such a mysterious universe, don't we? Some people say that science clears up all the mysteries for us. In my opinion it only creates more! Have you found it yet?

JIM   No, Ma'am. All these fuses look okay to me.

AMANDA   Tom!

TOM   Yes, Mother?

AMANDA   That light bill I gave you several days ago. The one I told you we got the notices about?

TOM   Oh.—Yeah.

(LEGEND: "HA!")

AMANDA   You didn't neglect to pay it by any chance?

TOM   Why, I—

AMANDA   Didn't! I might have known it!

JIM   Shakespeare probably wrote a poem on that light bill, Mrs. Wing-field.

AMANDA   I might have known better than to trust him with it! There's such a high price for negligence in this world!

JIM   Maybe the poem will win a ten-dollar prize.

AMANDA   We'll just have to spend the remainder of the evening in the nineteenth century, before Mr. Edison made the Mazda lamp!

JIM   Candlelight is my favorite kind of light.

AMANDA   That shows you're romantic! But that's no excuse for Tom. Well, we got through dinner. Very considerate of them to let us get through dinner before they plunged us into everlasting darkness, wasn't it, Mr. O'Connor?

JIM   Ha-ha!

AMANDA   Tom, as a penalty for your carelessness you can help me with the dishes.

JIM   Let me give you a hand.

AMANDA   Indeed you will not!

JIM   I ought to be good for something.

AMANDA   Good for something? (*Her tone is rhapsodic.*) *You?* Why, Mr. O'Connor, nobody, *nobody's* given me this much entertainment in years—as you have!

JIM   Aw, now, Mrs. Wingfield!

AMANDA   I'm not exaggerating, not one bit! But Sister is all by her lonesome. You go keep her company in the parlor! I'll give you this lovely old candelabrum that used to be on the altar at the church of the Heavenly Rest. It was melted a little out of shape when the church burnt down. Lightning struck it one spring. Gypsy Jones was holding a revival at the time and he intimated that the church was destroyed because the Episcopalians gave card parties.

JIM   Ha-ha.

AMANDA   And how about coaxing Sister to drink a little wine? I think it would be good for her! Can you carry both at once?

JIM   Sure. I'm Superman!

AMANDA   Now, Thomas, get into this apron!

The door of kitchenette swings closed on AMANDA's *gay laughter; the flickering light approaches the portieres.*

LAURA *sits up nervously as he enters. Her speech at first is low and breathless from the almost intolerable strain of being alone with a stranger.*

(THE LEGEND: "I DON'T SUPPOSE YOU REMEMBER ME AT ALL!")

In her first speeches in this scene, before JIM's *warmth overcomes her paralyzing shyness,* LAURA's *voice is thin and breathless as though she has just run up a steep flight of stairs.*

JIM's *attitude is gently humorous. In playing this scene it should be stressed that while the incident is apparently unimportant, it is to* LAURA *the climax of her secret life.*

JIM   Hello, there, Laura.

LAURA (*faintly*)   Hello (*She clears her throat.*)

JIM   How are you feeling now? Better?

LAURA   Yes. Yes, thank you.

JIM   This is for you. A little dandelion wine. (*He extends it toward her with extravagant gallantry.*)

LAURA   Thank you.

JIM   Drink it—but don't get drunk! (*He laughs heartily.* LAURA *takes the glass uncertainly; laughs shyly.*) Where shall I set the candles?

LAURA   Oh—oh, anywhere . . .

JIM   How about here on the floor? Any objections?

LAURA   No.

JIM   I'll spread a newspaper under to catch the drippings. I like to sit on the floor. Mind if I do?

LAURA   Oh, no.

JIM   Give me a pillow?

LAURA   What?

JIM   A pillow!

LAURA   Oh . . . (*Hands him one quickly.*)

JIM   How about you? Don't you like to sit on the floor?

LAURA   Oh—yes.

JIM   Why don't you, then?

LAURA   I—will.

JIM   Take a pillow! (LAURA *does. Sits on the other side of the candelabrum.* JIM *crosses his legs and smiles engagingly at her.*) I can't hardly see you sitting way over there.

LAURA   I can—see you.

JIM   I know, but that's not fair. I'm in the limelight. (LAURA *moves her pillow closer.*) Good! Now I can see you! Comfortable?

LAURA   Yes.

JIM   So am I. Comfortable as a cow. Will you have some gum?

LAURA   No, thank you.

JIM   I think that I will indulge, with your permission. (*Musingly unwraps it and holds it up.*) Think of the fortune made by the guy that invented the first piece of chewing gum. Amazing, huh? The Wrigley Building is one of the sights of Chicago.—I saw it summer before last when I went up to the Century of Progress. Did you take in the Century of Progress?

LAURA   No, I didn't.

JIM   Well, it was quite a wonderful exposition. What impressed me most was the Hall of Science. Gives you an idea of what the future will be in America, even more wonderful than the present time is! (*Pause. Smiling at her.*) Your brother tells me you're shy. Is that right, Laura?

LAURA   I—don't know.

JIM   I judge you to be an old-fashioned type of girl. Well, I think that's a pretty good type to be. Hope you don't think I'm being too personal—do you?

LAURA (*hastily, out of embarrassment*)   I believe I *will* take a piece of gum, if you—don't mind. (*Clearing her throat.*) Mr. O'Connor, have you—kept up with your singing?

JIM   Singing? Me?

LAURA   Yes. I remember what a beautiful voice you had.

JIM   When did you hear me sing?

(VOICE OFF STAGE IN THE PAUSE.)

VOICE   (*off stage*)

> O blow, ye winds, heigh-ho,
> A-roving I will go!
> I'm off to my love
> With a boxing glove—
> Ten thousand miles away!

JIM   You say you've heard me sing?

LAURA   Oh, yes! Yes, very often . . . I—don't suppose you remember me—at all?

JIM (*smiling doubtfully*)   You know I have an idea I've seen you before. I had that idea soon as you opened the door. It seemed almost like I was about to remember your name. But the name that I started to call you—wasn't a name! And so I stopped myself before I said it.

LAURA   Wasn't it—Blue Roses?

JIM (*springs up, grinning*)   Blue Roses! My gosh, yes—Blue Roses! That's what I had on my tongue when you opened the door! Isn't it funny what tricks your memory plays? I didn't connect you with the high school somehow or other. But that's where it was; it was high school. I didn't even know you were Shakespeare's sister! Gosh, I'm sorry.

LAURA   I didn't expect you to. You—barely knew me!

JIM   But we did have a speaking acquaintance, huh?

LAURA   Yes, we—spoke to each other.

JIM   When did you recognize me?

LAURA   Oh, right away!

JIM   Soon as I came in the door?

LAURA   When I heard your name I thought it was probably you. I knew that Tom used to know you a little in high school. So when you came in the door—Well, then I was—sure.

JIM   Why didn't you *say* something, then?

LAURA (*breathlessly*)   I didn't know what to say, I was—too surprised!

JIM   For goodness' sakes! You know, this sure is funny!

LAURA   Yes! Yes, isn't it, though . . .

JIM   Didn't we have a class in something together?

LAURA   Yes, we did.

JIM   What class was that?

LAURA   It was—singing—Chorus!

JIM   Aw!

LAURA   I sat across the aisle from you in the Aud.

JIM   Aw.

LAURA   Mondays, Wednesdays and Fridays.

JIM   Now I remember—you always came in late.

LAURA   Yes, it was so hard for me, getting upstairs. I had that brace on my leg—it clumped so loud!

JIM   I never heard any clumping.

LAURA (*wincing at the recollection*)   To me it sounded like—thunder!

JIM   Well, well, well. I never even noticed.

LAURA   And everybody was seated before I came in. I had to walk in front of all those people. My seat was in the back row. I had to go clumping all the way up the aisle with everyone watching!

JIM   You shouldn't have been self-conscious.

LAURA   I know, but I was. It was always such a relief when the singing started.

JIM   Aw, yes. I've placed you now! I used to call you Blue Roses. How was it that I got started calling you that?

LAURA   I was out of school a little while with pleurosis. When I came back you asked me what was the matter. I said I had pleurosis—you thought I said Blue Roses. That's what you always called me after that!

JIM   I hope you didn't mind.

LAURA   Oh, no—I liked it. You see, I wasn't acquainted with many—people. . . .

JIM   As I remember you sort of stuck by yourself.

LAURA   I—I—never had much luck at—making friends.

JIM   I don't see why you wouldn't.

LAURA   Well, I—started out badly.

JIM   You mean being—

LAURA   Yes, it sort of—stood between me—

JIM   You shouldn't have let it!

LAURA   I know, but it did, and—

JIM   You were shy with people!

LAURA   I tried not to be but never could—

JIM   Overcome it?

LAURA   No, I—I never could!

JIM   I guess being shy is something you have to work out of kind of gradually.

LAURA (*sorrowfully*)   Yes—I guess it—

JIM   Takes time!

LAURA   Yes—

JIM   People are not so dreadful when you know them. That's what you have to remember! And everybody has problems, not just you, but practically everybody has got some problems. You think of yourself as having the only problems, as being the only one who is disappointed. But just look around you and you will see lots of people as disappointed as you are. For instance, I hoped when I was going to high school that I would be further along at this time, six years later, than I am now—You remember that wonderful write-up I had in *The Torch?*

LAURA   Yes! (*She rises and crosses to table.*)

JIM   It said I was bound to succeed in anything I went into! (LAURA *returns with the annual.*) Holy Jeez! *The Torch!* (*He accepts it reverently. They smile across it with mutual wonder.* LAURA *crouches beside him and they begin to turn through it.* LAURA's *shyness is dissolving in his warmth.*)

LAURA   Here you are in *Pirates of Penzance!*

JIM (*wistfully*)   I sang the baritone lead in that operetta.

LAURA (*rapidly*)   So—*beautifully!*

JIM (*protesting*)   Aw—

LAURA　Yes, yes—beautifully—beautifully!

JIM　You heard me?

LAURA　All three times!

JIM　No!

LAURA　Yes!

JIM　All three performances?

LAURA (*looking down*)　Yes.

JIM　Why?

LAURA　I—wanted to ask you to—autograph my program.

JIM　Why didn't you ask me to?

LAURA　You were always surrounded by your own friends so much that I never had a chance to.

JIM　You should have just—

LAURA　Well, I—thought you might think I was—

JIM　Thought I might think you was—what?

LAURA　Oh—

JIM (*with reflective relish*)　I was beleaguered by females in those days.

LAURA　You were terribly popular!

JIM　Yeah—

LAURA　You had such a—friendly way—

JIM　I was spoiled in high school.

LAURA　Everybody—liked you!

JIM　Including you?

LAURA　I—yes, I—I did, too—(*She gently closes the book in her lap.*)

JIM　Well, well, well!—Give me that program, Laura. (*She hands it to him. He signs it with a flourish.*) There you are—better late than never!

LAURA　Oh, I—what a—surprise!

JIM　My signature isn't worth very much right now. But some day—maybe—it will increase in value! Being disappointed is one thing and being discouraged is something else. I am disappointed but I am not discouraged. I'm twenty-three years old. How old are you?

LAURA　I'll be twenty-four in June.

JIM　That's not old age!

LAURA　No, but—

JIM　You finished high school?

LAURA (*with difficulty*)　I didn't go back.

JIM　You mean you dropped out?

LAURA　I made bad grades in my final examinations. (*She rises and replaces the book and the program. Her voice strained.*) How is—Emily Meisenbach getting along?

JIM　Oh, that kraut-head!

LAURA　Why do you call her that?

JIM　That's what she was.

LAURA　You're not still—going with her?

JIM　I never see her.

LAURA　It said in the Personal Section that you were—engaged!

JIM   I know, but I wasn't impressed by that—propaganda!

LAURA   It wasn't—the truth?

JIM   Only in Emily's optimistic opinion!

LAURA   Oh—

(LEGEND: "WHAT HAVE YOU DONE SINCE HIGH SCHOOL?")

JIM *lights a cigarette and leans indolently back on his elbows smiling at* LAURA *with a warmth and charm which lights her inwardly with altar candles. She remains by the table and turns in her hands a piece of glass to cover her tumult.*

JIM (*after several reflective puffs on a cigarette*)   What have you done since high school? (*She seems not to hear him.*) Huh? (LAURA *looks up.*) I said what have you done since high school, Laura?

LAURA   Nothing much.

JIM   You must have been doing something these six long years.

LAURA   Yes.

JIM   Well, then, such as what?

LAURA   I took a business course at business college—

JIM   How did that work out?

LAURA   Well, not very—well—I had to drop out, it gave me—indigestion—

JIM *laughs gently.*

JIM   What are you doing now?

LAURA   I don't do anything—much. Oh, please don't think I sit around doing nothing! My glass collection takes up a good deal of my time. Glass is something you have to take good care of.

JIM   What did you say—about glass?

LAURA   Collection I said—I have one—(*She clears her throat and turns away again, acutely shy.*)

JIM (*abruptly*)   You know what I judge to be the trouble with you? Inferiority complex! Know what that is? That's what they call it when someone low-rates himself! I understand it because I had it, too. Although my case was not so aggravated as yours seems to be. I had it until I took up public speaking, developed my voice, and learned that I had an aptitude for science. Before that time I never thought of myself as being outstanding in any way whatsoever! Now I've never made a regular study of it, but I have a friend who says I can analyze people better than doctors that make a profession of it. I don't claim that to be necessarily true, but I can sure guess a person's psychology, Laura! (*Takes out his gum.*) Excuse me, Laura. I always take it out when the flavor is gone. I'll use this scrap of paper to wrap it in. I know how it is to get it stuck on a shoe. Yep—that's what I judge to be your principal trouble. A lack of confidence in yourself as a person. You don't have the proper amount of faith in yourself. I'm basing that fact on a number of your remarks and also on certain observations I've made. For instance that clumping you thought was so awful in high school. You said that you even dreaded to walk into class. You see what you did? You dropped out of school, you gave up an education because of a clump, which as far as I know was practically non-existent! A little physical defect is what you have. Hardly noticeable even! Magnified thousands of times by imagination. You know what my strong advice to you is? Think of yourself as *superior* in some way!

LAURA   In what way would I think?

JIM   Why, man alive, Laura! Just look about you a little. What do you see? A world full of common people! All of 'em born and all of 'em going to die! Which of them has one-tenth of your good points! Or mine! Or anyone else's, as far as that goes—Gosh! Everybody excels in some one thing. Some in many! (*Unconsciously glances at himself in the mirror.*) All you've got to do is discover in *what!* Take me, for instance. (*He adjusts his tie at the mirror.*) My interest happens to lie in electro-dynamics. I'm taking a course in radio engineering at night school, Laura, on top of a fairly responsible job at the warehouse. I'm taking that course and studying public speaking.

LAURA   Ohhhh.

JIM   Because I believe in the future of television! (*Turning back to her.*) I wish to be ready to go up right along with it. Therefore I'm planning to get in on the ground floor. In fact, I've already made the right connections and all that remains is for the industry itself to get under way! Full steam—(*His eyes are starry.*) *Knowledge*—Zzzzzp! *Money*—Zzzzzp!—*Power!* That's the cycle democracy is built on! (*His attitude is convincingly dynamic.* LAURA *stares at him, even her shyness eclipsed in her absolute wonder. He suddenly grins.*) I guess you think I think a lot of myself!

LAURA   No—o-o-o, I—

JIM   Now how about you? Isn't there something you take more interest in than anything else?

LAURA   Well, I do—as I said—have my—glass collection—

A peal of girlish laughter from the kitchen.

JIM   I'm not right sure I know what you're talking about. What kind of glass is it?

LAURA   Little articles of it, they're ornaments mostly! Most of them are little animals made out of glass, the tiniest little animals in the world. Mother calls them a glass menagerie! Here's an example of one, if you'd like to see it! This one is one of the oldest. It's nearly thirteen. (*He stretches out his hand.*) (MUSIC: "THE GLASS MENAGERIE.") Oh, be careful—if you breathe, it breaks!

JIM   I'd better not take it. I'm pretty clumsy with things.

LAURA   Go on, I trust you with him! (*Places it in his palm.*) There now—you're holding him gently! Hold him over the light, he loves the light! You see how the light shines through him?

JIM   It sure does shine!

LAURA   I shouldn't be partial, but he is my favorite one.

JIM   What kind of a thing is this one supposed to be?

LAURA   Haven't you noticed the single horn on his forehead?

JIM   A unicorn, huh?

LAURA   Mmm-hmmm!

JIM   Unicorns, aren't they extinct in the modern world?

LAURA   I know!

JIM   Poor little fellow, he must feel sort of lonesome.

LAURA (*smiling*)   Well, if he does he doesn't complain about it. He stays on a shelf with some horses that don't have horns and all of them seem to get along nicely together.

JIM   How do you know?

LAURA (*lightly*)   I haven't heard any arguments among them!

JIM (*grinning*)   No arguments, huh? Well, that's a pretty good sign! Where shall I set him?

LAURA   Put him on the table. They all like a change of scenery once in a while!

JIM (*stretching*)   Well, well, well, well—Look how big my shadow is when I stretch!

LAURA   Oh, oh, yes—it stretches across the ceiling!

JIM (*crossing to door*)   I think it's stopped raining. (*Opens fire-escape door.*) Where does the music come from?

LAURA   From the Paradise Dance Hall across the alley.

JIM   How about cutting the rug a little, Miss Wingfield?

LAURA   Oh, I—

JIM   Or is your program filled up? Let me have a look at it. (*Grasps imaginary card.*) Why, every dance is taken! I'll just have to scratch some out. (WALTZ MUSIC: "LA GOLONDRINA.") Ahhh, a waltz! (*He executes some sweeping turns by himself, then holds his arms toward* LAURA.)

LAURA (*breathlessly*)   I—can't dance!

JIM   There you go, that inferiority stuff!

LAURA   I've never danced in my life!

JIM   Come on, try!

LAURA   Oh, but I'd step on you!

JIM   I'm not made out of glass.

LAURA   How—how—how do we start?

JIM   Just leave it to me. You hold your arms out a little.

LAURA   Like this?

JIM   A little bit higher. Right. Now don't tighten up, that's the main thing about it—relax.

LAURA (*laughing breathlessly*)   It's hard not to.

JIM   Okay.

LAURA   I'm afraid you can't budge me.

JIM   What do you bet I can't? (*He swings her into motion.*)

LAURA   Goodness, yes, you can!

JIM   Let yourself go, now, Laura, just let yourself go.

LAURA I'm—

JIM Come on!

LAURA Trying!

JIM Not so stiff—Easy does it!

LAURA I know but I'm—

JIM Loosen th' backbone! There now, that's a lot better.

LAURA Am I?

JIM Lots, lots better! (*He moves her about the room in a clumsy waltz.*)

LAURA Oh, my!

JIM Ha-ha!

LAURA Goodness, yes you can!

JIM Ha-ha-ha! (*They suddenly bump into the table.* JIM *stops.*) What did we hit on?

LAURA Table.

JIM Did something fall off it? I think—

LAURA Yes.

JIM I hope that it wasn't the little glass horse with the horn!

LAURA Yes.

JIM Aw, aw, aw. Is it broken?

LAURA Now it is just like all the other horses.

JIM It's lost its—

LAURA Horn! It doesn't matter. Maybe it's a blessing in disguise.

JIM You'll never forgive me. I bet that that was your favorite piece of glass.

LAURA I don't have favorites much. It's no tragedy, Freckles. Glass breaks so easily. No matter how careful you are. The traffic jars the shelves and things fall off them.

JIM Still I'm awfully sorry that I was the cause.

LAURA (*smiling*) I'll just imagine he had an operation. The horn was removed to make him feel less—freakish! (*They both laugh.*) Now he will feel more at home with the other horses, the ones that don't have horns . . .

JIM Ha-ha, that's very funny! (*Suddenly serious.*) I'm glad to see that you have a sense of humor. You know—you're—well—very different! Surprisingly different from anyone else I know! (*His voice becomes soft and hesitant with a genuine feeling.*) Do you mind me telling you that? (LAURA *is abashed beyond speech.*) You make me feel sort of—I don't know how to put it! I'm usually pretty good at expressing things, but—This is something that I don't know how to say! (LAURA *touches her throat and clears it—turns the broken unicorn in her hands.*) (*Even softer.*) Has anyone ever told you that you were pretty? (PAUSE: MUSIC.) (LAURA *looks up slowly, with wonder, and shakes her head.*) Well, you are! In a very different way from anyone else. And all the nicer because of the difference, too. (*His voice becomes low and husky.* LAURA *turns away, nearly faint with the novelty of her emotions.*) I wish that you were my sister. I'd teach you to have some confidence in yourself. The different people are not like other people, but being different is nothing to be ashamed of. Because other people are not such wonderful people. They're one hundred times one thousand. You're one times one! They walk all over the earth. You just stay here. They're common as—weeds, but—you—well, you're—*Blue Roses!*

(IMAGE ON SCREEN: BLUE ROSES)

(MUSIC CHANGES.)

LAURA   But blue is wrong for—roses . . .

JIM   It's right for you—You're—pretty!

LAURA   In what respect am I pretty?

JIM   In all respects—believe me! Your eyes—your hair—are pretty! Your hands are pretty! (*He catches hold of her hand.*) You think I'm making this up because I'm invited to dinner and have to be nice. Oh, I could do that! I could put on an act for you, Laura, and say lots of things without being very sincere. But this time I am. I'm talking to you sincerely. I happened to notice you had this inferiority complex that keeps you from feeling comfortable with people. Somebody needs to build your confidence up and make you proud instead of shy and turning away and—blushing—Somebody ought to—Ought to—*kiss* you, Laura! (*His hand slips slowly up her arm to her shoulder.*) (MUSIC SWELLS TUMULTUOUSLY.) (*He suddenly turns her about and kisses her on the lips. When he releases her* LAURA *sinks on the sofa with a bright, dazed look.* JIM *backs away and fishes in his pocket for a cigarette.*) (LEGEND ON SCREEN: "SOUVENIR.") Stumble-john! (*He lights the cigarette, avoiding her look. There is a peal of girlish laughter from* AMANDA *in the kitchen.* LAURA *slowly raises and opens her hand. It still contains the little broken glass animal. She looks at it with a tender, bewildered expression.*) Stumble-john! I shouldn't have done that—That was way off the beam. You don't smoke, do you? (*She looks up, smiling, not hearing the question. He sits beside her a little gingerly. She looks at him speechlessly—waiting. He coughs decorously and moves a little farther aside as he considers the situation and senses her feelings, dimly, with perturbation. Gently.*) Would you—care for a—mint? (*She doesn't seem to hear him but her look grows brighter even.*) Peppermint—Life Saver? My pocket's a regular drug store— wherever I go . . . (*He pops a mint in his mouth. Then gulps and decides to make a clean breast of it. He speaks slowly and gingerly.*) Laura, you know, if I had a sister like you, I'd do the same thing as Tom. I'd bring out fellows—introduce her to them. The right type of boys of a type to —appreciate her. Only—well—he made a mistake about me. Maybe I've got no call to be saying this. That may not have been the idea in having me over. But what if it was? There's nothing wrong about that. The only trouble is that in my case—I'm not in a situation to— do the right thing. I can't take down your number and say I'll phone. I can't call up next week and—ask for a date. I thought I had better explain the situation in case you misunderstood it and—hurt your feelings. . . . (*Pause. Slowly, very slowly,* LAURA's *look changes, her eyes returning slowly from his to the ornament in her palm.*)

AMANDA *utters another gay laugh in the kitchen.*

LAURA (*faintly*)   You—won't—call again?

JIM   No, Laura, I can't. (*He rises from the sofa.*) As I was just explaining, I've—got strings on me, Laura, I've—been going steady! I go out all the time with a girl named Betty. She's a home-girl like you, and Catholic, and Irish, and in a great many ways we—get along fine. I met her last summer on a moonlight boat trip up the river to Alton, on the *Majestic*. Well—right away from the start it was—love! (LEGEND: LOVE!) (LAURA *sways slightly forward and grips the arm of the sofa. He fails to notice, now enrapt in his own comfortable being.*) Being in love has made a new man of me! (*Leaning stiffly forward, clutching the arm of the sofa,* LAURA *struggles visibly with her storm. But* JIM *is oblivious, she is a long way off.*) The power of love is really pretty tremendous! Love is something that—changes the whole world, Laura! (*The storm abates a little and* LAURA *leans back. He notices her again.*) It happened that Betty's aunt took sick, she got a wire and had to go to Centralia. So Tom—when he asked me to dinner—I naturally just accepted the invitation, not knowing that you—that he—that I—(*He stops awkwardly.*) Huh—I'm a stumble-john! (*He flops back on the sofa. The holy candles in the altar of* LAURA's *face have been snuffed out! There is a look of almost infinite desolation.* JIM *glances at her uneasily.*) I wish that you would—say something. (*She bites her lip which was trembling and then bravely smiles. She opens her hand again on the broken glass ornament. Then she gently takes his hand and raises it level with her own. She carefully places the unicorn in the palm of his hand, then pushes his fingers closed upon it.*) What are you—doing that for? You want me to have him?—Laura? (*She nods.*) What for?

LAURA   A—souvenir . . .

She rises unsteadily and crouches beside the victrola to wind it up.

(LEGEND ON SCREEN: "THINGS HAVE A WAY OF TURNING OUT SO BADLY.")

(OR IMAGE: "GENTLEMAN CALLER WAVING GOODBYE!—GAILY.")

At this moment AMANDA *rushes brightly back in the front room. She bears a pitcher of fruit punch in an old-fashioned cut-glass pitcher and a plate of macaroons. The plate has a gold border and poppies painted on it.*

AMANDA   Well, well, well! Isn't the air delightful after the shower? I've made you children a little liquid refreshment. (*Turns gaily to the gentleman caller.*) Jim, do you know that song about lemonade?

> "Lemonade, lemonade
> Made in the shade and stirred with a spade—
> Good enough for any old maid!"

JIM (*uneasily*)   Ha-ha! No—I never heard it.

AMANDA   Why, Laura! You look so serious!

JIM   We were having a serious conversation.

AMANDA   Good! Now you're better acquainted!

JIM (*uncertainly*)   Ha-ha! Yes.

AMANDA   You modern young people are much more serious-minded than my generation. I was so gay as a girl!

JIM   You haven't changed, Mrs. Wingfield.

AMANDA   Tonight I'm rejuvenated! The gaiety of the occasion, Mr. O'Connor! (*She tosses her head with a peal of laughter. Spills lemonade.*) Oooo! I'm baptizing myself!

JIM   Here—let me—

AMANDA (*setting the pitcher down*)   There now. I discovered we had some maraschino cherries. I dumped them in, juice and all!

JIM   You shouldn't have gone to that trouble, Mrs. Wingfield.

AMANDA   Trouble, trouble? Why it was loads of fun! Didn't you hear me cutting up in the kitchen? I bet your ears were burning! I told Tom how outdone with him I was for keeping you to himself so long a time! He should have brought you over much, much sooner! Well, now that you've found your way, I want you to be a very frequent caller! Not just occasional but all the time. Oh, we're going to have a lot of gay times together! I see them coming! Mmm, just breathe that air! So fresh, and the moon's so pretty! I'll skip back out—I know where my place is when young folks are having a—serious conversation!

JIM   Oh, don't go out, Mrs. Wingfield. The fact of the matter is I've got to be going.

AMANDA   Going, now? You're joking! Why, it's only the shank of the evening, Mr. O'Connor!

JIM   Well, you know how it is.

AMANDA   You mean you're a young workingman and have to keep workingmen's hours. We'll let you off early tonight. But only on the condition that next time you stay later. What's the best night for you? Isn't Saturday night the best night for you workingmen?

JIM   I have a couple of time-clocks to punch, Mrs. Wingfield. One at morning, another one at night!

AMANDA   My, but you *are* ambitious! You work at night, too?

JIM   No, Ma'am, not work but—Betty! (*He crosses deliberately to pick up his hat. The band at the Paradise Dance Hall goes into a tender waltz.*)

AMANDA   Betty? Betty? Who's—Betty! (*There is an ominous cracking sound in the sky.*)

JIM   Oh, just a girl. The girl I go steady with! (*He smiles charmingly. The sky falls.*)

(LEGEND: "THE SKY FALLS.")

AMANDA (*a long-drawn exhalation*)   Ohhhh . . . Is it a serious romance, Mr. O'Connor?

JIM   We're going to be married the second Sunday in June.

AMANDA   Ohhhh—how nice! Tom didn't mention that you were engaged to be married.

JIM   The cat's not out of the bag at the warehouse yet. You know how they are. They call you Romeo and stuff like that. (*He stops at the oval mirror to put on his hat. He carefully shapes the brim and the crown to give a discreetly dashing effect.*) It's been a wonderful evening, Mrs. Wingfield. I guess this is what they mean by Southern hospitality.

AMANDA   It really wasn't anything at all.

JIM   I hope it don't seem like I'm rushing off. But I promised Betty I'd pick her up at the Wabash depot, an' by the time I get my jalopy down there her train'll be in. Some women are pretty upset if you keep 'em waiting.

AMANDA   Yes, I know—The tyranny of women! (*Extends her hand.*) Goodbye, Mr. O'Connor. I wish you luck—and happiness—and success! All three of them, and so does Laura! Don't you, Laura?

LAURA   Yes!

JIM (*taking her hand*)   Good-bye, Laura. I'm certainly going to treasure that souvenir. And don't you forget the good advice I gave you. (*Raises his voice to a cheery shout.*) So long, Shakespeare! Thanks again, ladies—Good night!

He grins and ducks jauntily out.
    Still bravely grimacing, AMANDA *closes the door on the gentleman caller. Then she turns back to the room with a puzzled expression. She and* LAURA *don't dare to face each other.* LAURA *crouches beside the victrola to wind it.*

AMANDA (*faintly*)   Things have a way of turning out so badly. I don't believe that I would play the victrola. Well, well—well—Our gentleman caller was engaged to be married! Tom!

TOM (*from back*)   Yes, Mother?

AMANDA   Come in here a minute. I want to tell you something awfully funny.

TOM (*enters with a macaroon and a glass of the lemonade*)   Has the gentleman caller gotten away already?

AMANDA   The gentleman caller has made an early departure. What a wonderful joke you played on us!

TOM   How do you mean?

AMANDA   You didn't mention that he was engaged to be married.

TOM   Jim? Engaged?

AMANDA   That's what he just informed us.

TOM   I'll be jiggered! I didn't know about that.

AMANDA   That seems very peculiar.

TOM   What's peculiar about it?

AMANDA   Didn't you call him your best friend down at the warehouse?

TOM   He is, but how did I know?

AMANDA   It seems extremely peculiar that you wouldn't know your best friend was going to be married!

TOM   The warehouse is where I work, not where I know things about people!

AMANDA   You don't know things anywhere! You live in a dream; you manufacture illusions! (*He crosses to door.*) Where are you going?

TOM   I'm going to the movies.

AMANDA   That's right, now that you've had us make such fools of ourselves. The effort, the preparations, all the expense! The new floor lamp, the rug, the clothes for Laura! All for what? To entertain some other girl's fiancé! Go to the movies, go! Don't think about us, a mother deserted, an unmarried sister who's crippled and has no job! Don't let anything interfere with your selfish pleasure! Just go, go, go—to the movies!

TOM   All right, I will! The more you shout about my selfishness to me the quicker I'll go, and I won't go to the movies!

AMANDA   Go, then! Then go to the moon—you selfish dreamer!

TOM *smashes his glass on the floor. He plunges out on the fire-escape, slamming the door,* LAURA *screams—cut off by the door.*
     Dance-hall music up. TOM *goes to the rail and grips it desperately, lifting his face in the chill white moonlight penetrating the narrow abyss of the alley.*

(LEGEND ON SCREEN: "AND SO GOOD-BYE . . .")

TOM'S *closing speech is timed with the interior pantomime. The interior scene is played as though viewed through soundproof glass.* AMANDA *appears to be making a comforting speech to* LAURA *who is huddled upon the sofa. Now that we cannot hear the mother's speech, her silliness is gone and she has dignity and tragic beauty.* LAURA'S *dark hair hides her face until at the end of the speech she lifts it to smile at her mother.* AMANDA'S *gestures are slow and graceful, almost dancelike, as she comforts the daughter. At the end of her speech she glances a moment at the father's picture—then withdraws through the portieres. At close of* TOM'S *speech,* LAURA *blows out the candles, ending the play.*

TOM   I didn't go to the moon, I went much further—for time is the longest distance between two places—Not long after that I was fired for writing a poem on the lid of a shoe-box. I left Saint Louis. I descended the steps of this fire-escape for a last time and followed, from then on, in my father's footsteps, attempting to find in motion what was lost in space—I traveled around a great deal. The cities swept about me like dead leaves, leaves that were brightly colored but torn away from the branches. I would have stopped, but I was pursued by something. It always came upon me unawares, taking me altogether by surprise. Perhaps it was a familiar bit of music. Perhaps it was only a piece of transparent glass—Perhaps I am walking along a street at night, in some strange city, before I have found companions. I pass the lighted window of a shop where perfume is sold. The window is filled with pieces of colored glass, tiny transparent bottles in delicate colors, like bits of a shattered rainbow. Then all at once my sister touches my shoulder. I turn around and look into her eyes

. . . Oh, Laura, Laura, I tried to leave you behind me, but I am more faithful than I intended to be! I reach for a cigarette, I cross the street, I run into the movies or a bar, I buy a drink, I speak to the nearest stranger—anything that can blow your candles out! (LAURA *bends over the candles.*)—for nowadays the world is lit by lightning! Blow out your candles, Laura—and so good-bye. . . .

She blows the candles out.

(THE SCENE DISSOLVES.)

QUESTIONS FOR THINKING AND WRITING

1. Consider Tom's role in the play. He is both an observer and a participant. How does this dual role contribute to the total effect of the play? Do a fifteen-minute freewriting in which you explore this question.

2. Tennessee Williams's production notes are an especially rich addition to the experience of this play. How do they contribute? As an exercise, write a set of production notes of your own. You might explore options for casting the roles or describe how you imagined the setting while you read the play.

3. Williams's character description of Amanda suggests that she is multidimensional. He notes that she has "endurance and a kind of heroism." What evidence does the play offer of her endurance and heroism? After freewriting briefly, consider how you might develop this topic into an essay. Try the same technique in applying the author's character descriptions to the way other characters are represented in the play.

4. Amanda's description of herself as a young girl is all that we know of her past. In this sense she creates one of the key elements of her own character. But keep in mind that Amanda's youth is probably as much fiction as fact. Imagine the next generation. What would Laura's story be? Quite different, no doubt. Write a narrative from Laura's point of view, when she is Amanda's age. What has become of her? How will she remember Tom, her mother, and the day the gentleman caller came?

5. Consider the way Amanda's sense of social propriety plays against the economic condition of the family. There is more than a hint in the play that the present condition has determined the values of the characters. Write an essay in which you examine this issue as it affects each of the main characters.

Appendix: Documenting the Research Paper

You will undoubtedly be required at some time to write a research paper, in which you develop your readings fully and, where necessary, quote other readers, critics, and authorities. We suggest you set out your research paper according to the following guidelines, which are in accord with the MLA documentation system (1984 version).

Jennifer J. Even

Professor McCormick

76-242

28 April 1986

"Unending Dream of Commentary":

How Critics Engage with Doris Lessing's

Summer Before the Dark

As the reader drowns under the ever ac-
cumulating flood of criticism, he is justified in asking, why is there criticism
rather than silent admiration? What in-
eluctable necessity in literature makes it
generate unending oceans of commentary,
wave after wave covering the primary tex-
tual rocks, hiding them, washing them, un-
covering them again, but leaving them,
after all, just as they were?

J. Hillis Miller

Criticism, according to J. Hillis Miller, is
"an ever-renewed, ever-unsuccessful attempt
to 'get it right,' to name things by their
right names" (331). I would like to add to

Figure 11   Sample First Page of the Research Paper

Miller's definition that criticism is a particular reading of the text based on the
critic's literary, social, and cultural repertoire, a reading that is often viewed as
unacceptable only because the critic's repertoire differs from the reader's. In this paper
I would like first of all to explain briefly
the notion of repertoire, and second to examine several critical readings of Doris
Lessing's <u>Summer Before the Dark</u> to illustrate how these critics often assume the
universality of their particular repertoires
and thus seem to come up with "wrong" interpretations in the eyes of readers with different repertoires. Then perhaps finally I can
attempt to deal with Hillis Miller's question, <u>Why is there criticism?</u>

A person's repertoire is a subset of assumptions from the ideology that surrounds him or
her--cultural, social, literary assumptions.
One's literary repertoire contains strategies
for reading a piece of discourse--traditional
strategies, with expectations of full plot
development, unity of details, and resolution
revolving around the author's intended meaning; and what we may call Hillis Miller<u>ish</u>
strategies, deconstructionist assumptions

Figure 11   Continued

Document Sources Fully and Accurately

Although you need not acknowledge a source for generally known information such as the dates during which William Wordsworth lived or the nation-
ality of Nathaniel Hawthorne, you must identify the exact source and

location of each statement, fact, or idea you borrow from another person or work. There are many different ways to acknowledge sources, but one of the simplest and most efficient is the MLA system, which requires only a brief parenthetical reference in the text of the paper, keyed to a complete bibliographical entry in the list of works cited at the end of the essay. For most parenthetical references, you will need to cite only the author's last name and the number of the page from which the statement or idea was taken; if you mention the author's name in the text of your paper, the page number alone is sufficient. This format also allows you to include within the parentheses additional information, such as title or volume number, if it is needed for clarity. Documentation for some of the most common types of sources is discussed in the sections below.

References to Single-Volume Books

In research papers, articles and single-volume books are the two types of works you are most likely to refer to. When citing them, either mention the author's name in the text and note the appropriate page number in parentheses immediately after the citation, or acknowledge both name and page number in the parenthetical reference, leaving a space between the two. If punctuation is needed, insert the mark outside the final parenthesis.

Author's name cited in the text

> Terry Eagleton has argued that Literary and Cultural Studies should "look to the various sign-systems and signifying practices in our society, all the way from *Moby-Dick* to the Muppet Show" (207).

Note that the period ending the sentence occurs *after* the parenthetical reference, not before.

Author's name cited in parentheses

> Literary and Cultural Studies should "look at the various sign-systems and signifying practices in our society, all the way from *Moby-Dick* to the Muppet Show" (Eagleton 207).

Corresponding bibliographic entry

> Eagleton, Terry. *Literary Theory: An Introduction.* Oxford: Basil Blackwell, 1983.

If the work you are citing has two or three authors, cite all their last names in parentheses, following the conventions for spacing and punctuation noted above. If there are more than three authors, use the last name of the author listed first on the title page, plus the abbreviation et al.

Sample parenthetical references

> (Dollimore and Sinfield 153)

> (Barker et al. 111)

> (McCormick, Waller, and Flower 65)

Corresponding bibliographic entries

> Dollimore, Jonathan, and Alan Sinfield. *Political Shakespeare: New Essays in Cultural Materialism.* Manchester: Manchester UP, 1985.

> McCormick, Kathleen, Gary Waller, and Linda Flower. *Reading Texts.* Lexington: Heath, 1987.

> Barker, Francis, et al. *Confronting the Crisis: War, Politics and Culture in the Eighties.* Colchester: U of Essex, 1984.

References to Articles

In text, references to articles are handled in exactly the same way as references to single-volume books. The bibliographic citations, however, are somewhat different in that you don't cite a publisher, but must cite the volume in which the article appeared. Scholarly journals generally appear four to six times annually, and each year of the journal has a volume number (that is, Volume 12 for all of 1986). Each individual issue within a given year is also numbered or labeled with a month or a season (that is, Volume 12, Number 3; or Volume 12, Spring 1986).

Journals with Continuous Pagination

If the journal you are citing paginates its issues for a given year continuously (for example, Volume 12, Number 3, begins with page 467, where the previous issue left off), you need not cite the issue number, month, or season in your bibliographic entry.

Bibliographic entry for article in journal with continuous pagination

> Booth, Wayne C. "Pluralism in the Classroom." *Critical Inquiry* 12 (1986): 468–79.

Journals That Page Each Issue Separately

If the journal issues for a given year are not paginated continuously (that is, issue number 3 of Volume 12 begins with page 1), then you must cite the issue number, month, or season as well as the volume number in your bibliographic entry.

*Bibliographic entry for article in journal that pages each
issue separately or that uses only issue numbers*

> Fish, Stanley, "Why No One's Afraid of Wolfgang Iser." *Diacritics* 11 (Spring 1981): 2–13.

> Lyon, George Ella. "Contemporary Appalachian Poetry: Sources and Directions." *Kentucky Review* 2.2 (1981): 3–22.

References to Works in an Anthology

When referring to a work in an anthology, either cite the author's name in the text and indicate in parentheses the page number in the anthology where the source is located, or acknowledge both name and page reference parenthetically. Only in the full citation in your bibliography do you give the name of the editor of the anthology.

Author's name cited in text

> One of the most widely recognized facts about James Joyce, in Lionel Trilling's view, "is his ambivalence toward Ireland, of which the hatred was as relentless as the love was unfailing" (153).

Author's name cited in parentheses

> One of the most widely recognized facts about James Joyce "is his ambivalence toward Ireland, of which the hatred was as relentless as the love was unfailing" (Trilling 153).

Corresponding bibliographic entry

> Trilling, Lionel. "James Joyce in His Letters." In *Joyce: A Collection of Critical Essays*. Ed. William M. Chace. Englewood Cliffs: Prentice, 1974.

References to More Than One Work by an Author

When you paraphrase or quote from more than one work by an author, give the title as well as the name of the author and the page reference so that the reader will know which work is being cited. If you mention the author's name in the text, you need not duplicate it in the parenthetical reference. Just cite the title (or a shortened version of it), skip a space, and insert the page number, as in the second example below. If you do not mention the author's name in the text, cite it first in the parenthetical reference, put a comma after it, skip a space, and insert the title. Then skip a space again and insert the page number (see the third example below).

Title cited in text

> Siegfried J. Schmidt argues in his article "On Writing Histories of Literature" that the seventies "will go down in the history [of literary studies] as a period concerned with the writing of new histories of literature" (279).

Title cited in parentheses

> Siegfried J. Schmidt argues that the seventies "will go down in the history [of literary studies] as a period concerned with the writing of new histories of literature" ("Histories" 279).

> In the words of a major critic of the field, the seventies "will go down in the history [of literary studies] as a period concerned with the writing of new histories of literature" (Schmidt, "Histories" 279).

Corresponding entries in the list of works cited

> Schmidt, Siegfried J. *Foundations for the Empirical Study of Literature.* Trans. Robert de Beaugrande. Hamburg: Buske, 1982.
> ———. "On Writing Histories of Literature. Some Remarks from a Constructivist Point of View." *Poetics* 14 (1985): 279–301.

References to Works of Unknown Authorship

If you borrow information or ideas from an article or book in which the name of the author is not given, cite the title instead, either in the text of the paper or in parentheses, and include the page reference.

Title cited in the text

> According to an article entitled "Sidney at Kalamazoo" in the *Sidney Newsletter,* planning is now under way for next year's Kalamazoo sessions (43).

Title cited in parentheses

> Planning is now under way for next year's Kalamazoo sessions ("Sidney at Kalamazoo" 43).

Corresponding bibliographic entry

> "Sidney at Kalamazoo." *Sidney Newsletter* 2.2 (1981): 27.

References to Multivolume Works

When you borrow from one volume of a multivolume work, cite the volume of your source in parentheses as an arabic number *without* the abbreviation Vol., and put a colon after it. Then skip a space and insert the page reference.

Sample references

> Frazer points out that scapegoat rituals have been common throughout history, not only in primitive societies but also "among the civilized nations of Europe" (9: 47).

> Scapegoat rituals have been common throughout history, not only in primitive societies but also "among the civilized nations of Europe" (Frazer 9: 47).

Corresponding bibliographic entry

> Frazer, Sir James G. *The Golden Bough: A Study of Magic and Religion*. 3rd ed. 12 vols. New York: Macmillan, 1935.

References to Information Gathered from Interviews

When citing an oral source, either mention the informant's name when you introduce the quotation or paraphrase or give the name in a parenthetical reference.

Informant's name cited in text

> When asked about her response, Debra Bernstein, one of our students, said that "it grew out of my belief that all contemporary fiction should be disruptive."

Informant's name cited in parentheses

> When asked about her response, one of our students said that "it grew out of my belief that all contemporary fiction should be disruptive" (Bernstein).

Corresponding bibliographic entry

> Bernstein, Debra. Personal interview, July 4, 1987.

References to Literary Works

When citing works of literature, observe the following guidelines for each genre.

Novels and Other Prose Works Subdivided into Chapters or Sections

Begin the parenthetical reference with the author's last name and the page number (the author's name may be omitted if it is mentioned in the text of the paper or if the authorship is evident from the context) and insert a semicolon. Then skip a space and give the number of the chapter (with the abbreviation Ch.) as well as the number of any other subdivisions.

Sample reference

> At the beginning of *The Great Gatsby*, Nick Carraway characterizes himself as someone who has "a sense of the fundamental decencies" (Fitzgerald 1; Ch. 1)—a trait that he displays throughout the novel.

Corresponding bibliographic entry

> Fitzgerald, F. Scott. *The Great Gatsby*. New York: Scribner's, 1925.

Poems

When quoting or paraphrasing a poem that is divided into sections, cite the number of the book, part, or canto plus the line number(s). There is no need for abbreviations such as bk. (book) or l. (line), but the first time you cite the work write out the word line or lines so that the reader will not mistake the line numbers for page references. If the poem you are citing has no subdivisions, line numbers alone are usually sufficient to identify the source—provided that the author and title are identified in the text of the paper.

Sample reference to a poem with subdivisions

> One of Byron's satiric techniques is to juxtapose the comical with the serious, as in this passage from *Don Juan:*
>
>> But I am apt to grow too metaphysical:
>> "The time is out of joint,"—and so am I;
>> I quite forget this poem's merely quizzical,
>> And deviate from matters rather dry.
>>   (9: lines 321–24)

Note: If you omit the word *lines,* put a period after the number of the section (in this case Canto 9) and, without spacing, insert the line number(s): (9.321–324).

Sample reference to a poem without subdivisions

> One of the questions that might be answered in any analysis of Jeffers's "Hurt Hawks" is whether the author's viewpoint is reflected in the narrator's statement "I'd sooner, except the penalties, kill a man than a hawk" (line 18).

Corresponding bibliographic entries

> Byron, George Gordon, Lord. *Don Juan.* In *Lord Byron: Don Juan and Other Satirical Poems.* Ed. Louis Bredvold, New York: Odyssey, 1935.
>
> Jeffers, Robinson. "Hurt Hawks." *Selected Poems.* New York: Random, 1928.

Plays

When citing a play, give the act and scene number without abbreviations, plus the line numbers if the work is in verse.

Sample reference

> Shakespeare repeatedly describes Denmark in images of unnaturalness, as in Horatio's comparison of Denmark with Rome just before Caesar's murder, when "The graves stood tenantless and sheeted dead/Did squeak and gibber in the Roman streets" (I.i.115–6).

Note: Upper-case Roman numerals are traditionally used for act numbers and lower-case Roman numerals for scene numbers.

Corresponding bibliographic entry

Shakespeare, William. *Hamlet.* In *Shakespeare: Twenty-Three Plays and the Sonnets.* Ed. Thomas Parrot. Rev. ed. New York: Scribner's, 1953.

Bibliography

In preparing the bibliography (or list of Works Cited) for your research paper, arrange all the works cited alphabetically.

Works Cited

Barker, Frances, et al. *Confronting the Crisis: War, Politics, and Culture in the Eighties.* Colchester: U of Essex, 1984.

Byron, George Gordon, Lord. *Don Juan.* In *Lord Byron: Don Juan and Other Satirical Poems.* Ed. Louis Bredvold. New York: Odyssey, 1935.

Dollimore, Jonathan, and Alan Sinfield. *Shakespeare: New Essays in Cultural Materialism.* Manchester: Manchester UP, 1985.

Eagleton, Terry. *Theory: An Introduction.* Oxford: Basil Blackwell, 1983.

Fitzgerald, F. Scott. *The Great Gatsby.* New York: Scribner's, 1925.

Frazer, Sir James G. *The Golden Bough: A Study of Magic and Religion.* 3rd ed. 12 vols. New York: Macmillan, 1935.

Jeffers, Robinson. *Selected Poems.* New York: Random, 1928.

Lessing, Doris. *Summer Before the Dark.* New York: Knopf, 1973.

McCormick, Kathleen A., Gary F. Waller, and Linda Flower. *Reading Texts.* Lexington: Heath, 1987.

Miller, Hillis. "Stevens' Rock and Criticism as Cure, II." *Georgia Review* 30.2 (1976), 330–48.

Schmidt, Siegfried J. *For the Empirical Study of Literature.* Trans. Robert de Beaugrande. Hamburg: Buske, 1982.

———. "On Writing Histories of Literature: Some Remarks from a Constructivist Point of View." *Poetics* 14 (1985): 279–301.

Shakespeare, William. *Shakespeare: Twenty-Three Plays and the Sonnets.* Ed. Thomas Parrot. Rev. ed. New York: Scribner's, 1953.

"Sidney at Kalamazoo." *Sidney Newsletter* 4.3 (1982): 43.

Trilling, Lionel. "James Joyce in His Letters." In *Joyce: A Collection of Critical Essays.* Ed. William M. Chace. Englewood Cliffs: Prentice, 1974. 143–165.

Index of Terms

Index of Authors and Titles

Index of First Lines